Read this book online today:

With SAP PRESS BooksOnline we offer you online access to knowledge from the leading SAP experts. Whether you use it as a beneficial supplement or as an alternative to the printed book, with SAP PRESS BooksOnline you can:

- Access your book anywhere, at any time. All you need is an Internet connection.
- Perform full text searches on your book and on the entire SAP PRESS library.
- Build your own personalized SAP library.

The SAP PRESS customer advantage:

Register this book today at *www.sap-press.com* and obtain exclusive free trial access to its online version. If you like it (and we think you will), you can choose to purchase permanent, unrestricted access to the online edition at a very special price!

Here's how to get started:

1. Visit *www.sap-press.com.*
2. Click on the link for SAP PRESS BooksOnline and login (or create an account).
3. Enter your free trial license key, shown below in the corner of the page.
4. Try out your online book with full, unrestricted access for a limited time!

Your personal free trial **license key** for this online book is: gq4r-p9jx-8ukw-bcsm

SAP® A[illegible] Practical Guide

SAP PRESS is a joint initiative of SAP and Galileo Press. The know-how offered by SAP specialists combined with the expertise of the Galileo Press publishing house offers the reader expert books in the field. SAP PRESS features first-hand information and expert advice, and provides useful skills for professional decision-making.

SAP PRESS offers a variety of books on technical and business related topics for the SAP user. For further information, please visit our website: *www.sap-press.com*.

Frank Föse, Sigrid Hagemann, Liane Will
SAP NetWeaver AS ABAP System Administration
2008, app. 650 pp.
978-1-59229-174-8

Thomas Schneider
SAP Performance Optimization Guide
2010, app. 800 pp.
978-1-59229-368-1

Bögelsack, Gradl, Mayer, Krcmar
SAP MaxDB Administration
2009, app. 350 pp.
978-1-59229-299-8

Faustmann, Höding, Klein, Zimmermann
SAP Database Administration with Oracle
2008, app. 800 pp.
978-1-59229-120-5

Sebastian Schreckenbach

SAP® Administration—Practical Guide

Bonn • Boston

Galileo Press is named after the Italian physicist, mathematician and philosopher Galileo Galilei (1564–1642). He is known as one of the founders of modern science and an advocate of our contemporary, heliocentric worldview. His words *Eppur si muove* (And yet it moves) have become legendary. The Galileo Press logo depicts Jupiter orbited by the four Galilean moons, which were discovered by Galileo in 1610.

Editor Patricia Kremer
English Edition Editor Kelly Grace Harris
Translation Lemoine International, Inc., Salt Lake City, UT
Copyeditor Julie McNamee
Cover Design Daniel Kratzke and Graham Geary
Photo Credit iStockphoto.com/zentilia, kinugraphick, dlewis33
Layout Design Vera Brauner
Production Graham Geary
Typesetting Publishers' Design and Production Services, Inc.
Printed and bound in Canada

ISBN 978-1-59229-383-4

1st edition 2011
1st German edition published 2010 by Galileo Press, Bonn, Germany

Library of Congress Cataloging-in-Publication Data
Schreckenbach, Sebastian.
[Praxishandbuch SAP Administration. English]
SAP administration : practical guide / Sebastian Schreckenbach.—1st ed.
p. cm.
Includes bibliographical references and index.
ISBN-13: 978-1-59229-383-4
ISBN-10: 1-59229-383-2
1. SAP NetWeaver. 2. Computer networks—Management. 3. Database management. 4. Industrial management—Data processing. I. Title.
TK5105.8885.S24S37 2011
004.6—dc22
2011004329

Contents at a Glance

Dear Reader,

Welcome to your practical guide to SAP administration! This book will teach you about both commonly-performed and special system administrator tasks, aiding you with concrete and detailed instructions that use step-by-step instructions and hundreds of screenshots. With the help of the information presented in these pages, you are well on your way to becoming an expert on the topic of SAP administration.

It wasn't long after Sebastian finished his work on the German version of *SAP Administration—Practical Guide* that we at SAP PRESS were already hounding him for an English translation. Fortunately, we were lucky to have an extremely dedicated author who was willing to put in the time. I wasn't easy on him, but he always came through—and thanks to his great work, I'm confident you'll be thrilled with the content and presentation of the information in his book.

We appreciate your business, and welcome your feedback. Your comments and suggestions are the most useful tools to help us improve our books for you, the reader. We encourage you to visit our website at *www.sap-press.com* and share your feedback about this work.

Thank you for purchasing a book from SAP PRESS!

Kelly Grace Harris
Editor, SAP PRESS

Galileo Press
Boston, MA

kelly.harris@galileo-press.com
www.sap-press.com

Contents

Introduction

This book introduces you to the tasks associated with the role of an SAP system administrator. An SAP system administrator ensures that the Basis components of every SAP system and their functions are working correctly during live operation. If this is not the case, specialized SAP components, such as Financials, Materials Management, and Sales and Distribution, will not be able to run smoothly.

The software components within SAP Basis include the SAP NetWeaver Application Server (formerly known as the SAP Web Application Server, component SAP_BASIS) and the cross-application component SAP_ABA. These software components supply the basic functions, transactions and programs that every SAP system needs.

This book includes many real-world examples, step-by-step guides, and checklists to provide an overview of the wide range of tasks involved in SAP administration and to familiarize you with the most important tools available to administrators.

Who Is This Book For?

This book is aimed, in particular, at the following groups of readers:

- Newcomers to SAP administration
- System administrators in SMEs and large enterprises
- Administrators who are in a position to focus on a SAP system and are only involved to a limited extent in the administration of the operating system and database
- Junior consultants

Large sections of this book may offer information that is too basic for senior consultants, experienced system administrators, and database administrators (DBAs), who would need to consult more specialized literature to answer specific questions. However, this book may prove useful as a reference material.

Content and Structure

An SAP administrator is responsible for a wide range of tasks, and so this book is also designed to cover a broad range of topics. Each chapter provides essential information about the most commonly-used and most significant elements that are fundamental to the day-to-day operation of SAP systems.

The book's broad focus means that it is not possible to enter into the finer details of each individual topic; thus, wherever the discussion is cut short in this book, you will find references to additional sources of information, such as specialist literature, help pages, and SAP Notes.

The key tasks of administrators and the tools and transactions they can use are explained in detail using many screenshots and step-by-step guides based on real-world examples. The content of the book is structured as follows.

Chapter 1, Fundamentals of SAP System Administration, provides basic information about system administration. This is followed in **Chapter 2**, SAP System Administration, by a detailed discussion of the key tasks and transactions associated with SAP administration, such as starting and stopping the server and controlling the most important functions. Monitoring of SAP systems is examined in **Chapter 3**, System Monitoring. **Chapter 4**, System Administration with SAP Solution Manager, explains how the SAP Solution Manager can be used as part of system administration.

Chapter 5, Scheduled Tasks, consists mainly of checklists that can be used for tasks that must be carried out on a regular basis and can be scheduled in advance. You will find general information about how to perform data backups in SAP systems in **Chapter 6**, Backup and Restore, while **Chapter 7**, Disaster Recovery, explains how to restore a system in the event of a disaster.

Chapter 8, Database Administration, and **Chapter 9**, Operating System Administration, briefly discuss the essential transactions used for the administration of databases and operating systems. **Chapter 10**, Security Administration, describes how to increase and monitor the security level in SAP systems. **Chapter 11**, Performance, then provides an introduction to the analysis and handling of performance issues.

Next, **Chapter 12**, SAP GUI, is devoted to the SAP Graphical User Interface, which enables you to use an SAP system from a PC. **Chapter 13**, User Administration, and **Chapter 14**, Authorization Management, cover such topics as the creation of user master data records and the assignment of authorizations.

Chapter 15, Background Processing, describes how to schedule and manage batch jobs in SAP systems. This is followed in **Chapter 16**, Output Management, by a discussion of how data can be output (primarily by using printing).

Chapter 17, Change and Transport Management, includes a description of the SAP transport system and how you can use it to distribute changes to the SAP systems in your system landscape. The following chapter, **Chapter 18**, System Maintenance, provides instructions on importing support packages. Finally, **Chapter 19**, Diagnostics and Troubleshooting, provides information about how to use the SAP Support Portal and import SAP Notes.

The **appendices** list useful, security-related transactions (Appendix A and B) as well as important tables (Appendix C) and provide recommendations on the design of specific forms (Appendix D). All sources and publications referred to in this book are listed in the bibliography in Appendix E.

The Basis Layer of SAP Components

The various SAP components that belong to the application layer, such as Customer Relationship Management (CRM), Advanced Planning & Optimization (APO), and SAP NetWeaver Business Warehouse (BW), are all based on a shared Basis layer. The tasks and tools associated with system administration are always the same for this Basis layer. In other words, capabilities and expertise in the area of system administration can be transferred between SAP components because administration of the Basis layer always remains the same. However, some administration tasks may also be component-specific and therefore fall outside of the scope of this book.

The administration of the Java stack in SAP systems is also omitted. The Java stack is used for web applications such as the SAP NetWeaver Portal, for example. However, this book is limited to the administration of the ABAP layer of SAP systems.

Version and Visual Differences

Most of the screenshots in this book originate in systems with SAP NetWeaver version 7.01. The transaction screens in earlier or later releases may differ from those shown here. For this reason, the screen in your system may not look the same as the screen shown in the screenshot. In addition to possible release-specific differences, your system's support package level is also relevant. However, the differences, if any, will be minute.

Other factors influencing the appearance of the transaction screens include the version used and the activated design of the SAP GUI. The screenshots included in this book were created with the SAP Signature Design of SAP GUI 7.10.

Prerequisites

This book assumes that you already have a certain level of knowledge and that specific system prerequisites are in place. Details of the required knowledge and system configuration are set out next.

Requirements for Users

We assume that you possess a basic level of knowledge of the SAP components, the operating system, and the database.

You should also be able to perform the following tasks:

- **SAP component level**
  - Log on to the SAP system.
  - Use menus and transaction codes for navigation in the SAP system.
- **Operating system level**
  - Be familiar with the file and directory structure.
  - Use the command line for navigation and to run programs.
  - Set up a printer.
  - Perform a backup using the standard tools of the operating system or third-party tools.
  - Use the operating system's basic security functions.
  - Copy and move data.
  - Start up and shut down the operating system and server correctly.
- **Database level**
  - Stop and start the database correctly.
  - Use the tools provided in the database system.
  - Create a database backup copy.

You should have access to the SAP system, the database, and the operating system, and be familiar with basic navigation in each. In addition, you should have sufficient authorization to execute the tasks described.

Requirements for the System

The SAP system must be fully installed, and its infrastructure must be set up and in full working order. Installation and related one-off tasks are not described in this book.

You can use the following checklist to determine whether your system has been set up in accordance with the prerequisites for this book. If you can log on to your SAP system, you know that most of these tasks have already been completed.

- **SAP level**
  - Has the SAP system been installed in accordance with SAP recommendations?
  - Are the profile files available?
  - Is the Transport Management System (TMS) configured?
  - Is the SAP router configured?
  - Is the ABAP Workbench configured?
  - Were any security functions configured for logon (for example, default passwords changed)?
  - Is the online documentation installed?
- **Database level**
  - Is the database configured?
  - Does the database have a working connection to the SAP system?
- **Operating system level**
  - Are all drives configured (for example, *sapmnt*)?
- **Software**
  - Is a backup program installed?
  - Is a hardware monitor installed?
  - Is a system monitor installed?
  - Is a UPS control installed?

- **Hardware**
  - Is the hardware of the application and database server working?
  - Have the backup devices been installed and tested?
- **Infrastructure**
  - Is the network configured?
  - Is an uninterrupted power supply (UPS) installed?
  - Is a server monitor or system monitor available?
- **Desktop**
  - Is the SAP GUI installed on the desktop PC?
  - Can users log on to the SAP system from their desktops?

Check whether these prerequisites are in place. If in doubt, ask for assistance from a colleague from operating system, database or network administration, or from an external consultant.

How to Use This Book

Important points to note and additional information are provided throughout this book in info boxes. These boxes can be divided into various categories depending on their focus, and these categories are indicated using various icons:

[!] **Note:** Please take particular care when performing this task or executing this step. An explanation of why particular care is needed in these cases is also provided.

[+] **Tip:** This icon identifies useful hints and shortcuts, which are intended to make your job easier.

[Ex] **Example:** Useful real-world examples are indicated by this symbol.

[⚙] **Tech talk:** Information indicated by this icon will help you understand the topic at a deeper level. This information is not essential to performing the task.

I hope that this book will help you to fulfill your tasks in relation to SAP administration, and I wish you every success and happy reading! Any feedback would be gratefully appreciated.

Sebastian Schreckenbach

This chapter deals with the essential tasks of a system administrator. It also explains the terms that occur most frequently in connection with SAP system administration.

1 Fundamentals of SAP System Administration

Depending on the size of the enterprise and the available resources, either a single individual or several specialists in one or more departments are responsible for the administration of an SAP system.

The allocation of tasks, positions, and roles for system administrators depends on the following factors:

- Size of the enterprise
- Available resources (size of the SAP Basis group)
- Available infrastructure support for:
  - Desktop support
  - Databases
  - Networks
  - Implementations

This means that, depending on the circumstances, the system administrator may be responsible for performing only a few or, alternatively, a large number of the tasks described below, all of which are related directly or indirectly to the SAP system.

1.1 Tasks of a System Administrator

The tasks of an SAP system administrator can be divided into a number of different areas. Each area is represented by a specific role, which is, in turn, assigned to one or more individuals.

System administrators may be assigned the following roles that relate directly to the SAP system:

- **System administrator**
  Keeps the system in good working order and monitors and manages system performance and system logons.
- **User administrator**
  Creates and manages user accounts.
- **Authorization administrator**
  Creates and manages SAP roles and profiles.
- **Security administrator**
  Guarantees the security of the SAP system and monitors breaches of security.
- **Transport administrator**
  Copies changes between systems and manages change requests.
- **Background job administrator**
  Schedules, monitors, and manages background jobs.
- **Data backup administrator**
  Schedules, performs, and monitors backup jobs in the SAP database and in all required files at system level.
- **Disaster recovery manager**
  Creates, tests, and executes the plan for an SAP system restore following a disaster.
- **Programmer**
  Imports SAP Notes and, if necessary, makes changes to the ABAP Dictionary.

Additional tasks arise in relation to an SAP system, which play a key role in influencing system operation. These tasks are related more or less indirectly to the SAP system and mainly have to do with the underlying infrastructure:

- **Database administrator**
  Manages database-specific tasks and keeps the database in good working order.
- **Operating system administrator**
  Manages access to the operating system and performs operating system-specific tasks

- **Network administrator**
  Manages network access and guarantees network support and maintenance.
- **Server administrator**
  Manages servers.
- **Desktop support specialist**
  Provides support for users' desktop PCs.
- **Print operator**
  Manages network and desktop printers.
- **Facility manager**
  Manages the technical/physical infrastructure (for example, power supply, air conditioning, etc.).

From an organizational perspective, these roles must be assigned to one or more individuals to distribute the tasks that need to be performed and guarantee system operation.

Another important aspect is the definition of substitute rules to ensure that tasks will be taken care of by another person if the administrator is on vacation or ill. Checklists, sets of instructions, and documentation relating to key tasks must be created because not all employees will possess all of the information required. This approach improves availability and the transfer of knowledge within the enterprise.

1.2 Guiding Principles for System Administrators

In your role as SAP system administrator, you should follow some basic guiding principles.

Protect the System

Everything you do as system administrator should serve a single purpose: to secure and protect system integrity. If the integrity of the system—and, in particular, the data it contains—cannot be guaranteed, the wrong decisions may be taken on the basis of incorrect information. Your enterprise may suffer serious losses if the system cannot be restored following a system failure.

It is your responsibility to guarantee system operation and system availability for employees, customers, suppliers, etc. You need to minimize the risk of downtime and minimize the length of periods of downtime because every minute that the system cannot be used may have a negative economic impact on your own enterprise and any enterprises associated with it.

Given these considerations, it is essential that the system administrator takes positive, responsible action. After all, the system administrator has responsibility for the enterprise's data backbone and, as such, must proceed with particular caution because any mistake may cost the enterprise dearly.

Another important task of a system administrator is to protect the system from attack. Such attacks may be external (hackers) or internal (for example, unauthorized access by "curious" employees).

Don't Be Afraid to Ask for Help

Some SAP components are so large and complex that it's impossible for a single person to know all there is to know about them. Without the requisite knowledge, tasks are difficult to perform, and errors are almost inevitable In some cases, these errors can't be undone. Often, asking for help is the only way to avoid errors and bridge knowledge gaps. There are no stupid questions!

Help can come from many different sources: SAP Notes, various web sites and newsgroups, or consultants. More information is provided in the following guiding principles.

Make Contact with Other Customers and with Consultants

To broaden your knowledge base, you can establish contact with the Basis team and system administrators in other enterprises. Other SAP customers may have solutions to the problems you encounter based on their own experience in the same area. If a colleague can answer your question, you can save yourself a consultant's fee.

Good networking opportunities are provided by training courses, professional organizations, SAP events (such as the TechEd and SAPPHIRE conferences organized by SAP), and user groups (such as the Americas' SAP Users' Group, ASUG, and the SAP Community Network (former SAP Developer Network, SDN)).

Use the KISS Principle (Keep It Short and Simple)

This principle is very important. If you follow it, you won't make tasks more complicated than they already are. Large or complex tasks become easier to handle if you can break them down into smaller, manageable units.

Sometimes a technically simple solution is best. Depending on the situation, a solution that appears to be rather primitive may actually work better than a highly sophisticated solution and also reduce your costs.

Document Every Step

Make sure to document all processes, procedures, hardware changes, configuration changes, checks, problems, errors, and so on. If you're ever in doubt as to how much detail you should include in your documentation, it's best to write everything down.

Over time, you may forget important details of a process or a problem. If this occurs, you can rest assured that you can access your detailed documentation of the procedures to refresh your memory. Detailed documentation can also help others to perform your tasks when you're not there. Because high staff turnover is the norm in today's world, detailed documentation also facilitates the training of new employees.

The documentation must grow and develop in tandem with the system. Make sure that older documents are updated on an ongoing basis. Any change to the system must also be reflected in the documentation. Inaccuracies in the documentation may result in costly errors. Your documentation should be comprehensive, clearly structured, and easily understood. Where relevant, use graphics, flow charts, and screenshots to illustrate content and provide additional information.

Make sure that the documentation is stored in an easily accessible location. Keep a log book for each server, where you can note any changes made.

Document Your Work Promptly and Thoroughly [!]

It's easy to forget about documentation in the "hot" phase of a project or in the event of an emergency. You should record everything done in the system—ideally while it is being done. Never put the task of documentation on the back burner, or you may never get around to doing it.

Use Checklists

Checklists allow you to standardize processes and minimize the risk of overlooking important steps. By using a checklist, you are also forced to document events (such as runtimes) that may prove to be significant at a later stage.

Checklists are particularly useful in the case of complex or important tasks. Serious errors may occur if one step is omitted or not executed correctly (for example, you may be unable to restore the database).

You'll find a checklist helpful the first time you perform a task or for any tasks that you only need to perform occasionally. Some pre-prepared checklists are provided in various parts of this book. You can use these as a starting point for creating lists that meet you own requirements. These checklists serve as documentation of your work and ensure that your steps can be retraced later.

Perform Planned Maintenance

By scheduling regular, preventive maintenance measures, you can prevent minor nuisances from spiraling into major issues. In this way, potential problems are eliminated before they can impact negatively on the system and on business processes.

[Ex]

Losses Are Often Due to Neglected Maintenance Tasks

The database stops when the available memory for the log file drops to zero. This can shut down the entire SAP system. The system can then only be restarted when a sufficient amount of memory has been freed up. The resulting delays may hinder business processes, such as shipping.

Troubleshooting should therefore form part of your routine tasks and should be done at a time when the disruption to users can be kept to a minimum. You should keep an eye on the various logs and event monitors and be on the lookout for potential sources of problems. In addition, you should check the integrity and consistency of the database on a regular basis.

Remember, however, that physical maintenance is also required. Check whether the hardware is located in a clean and cool environment. If necessary, perform hardware updates, for example, to provide additional disk storage space. And, finally, check that you have a fully functional, uninterrupted power supply.

Only Change What Needs to Be Changed

In today's high-tech world, we may feel compelled to constantly equip ourselves with the latest and best hardware and software. However, it's not always advisable to give in to this temptation. If your system is running without any problems, then you should leave it alone.

Don't perform upgrades simply because you can. Upgrading with new software or hardware may introduce new elements and therefore new risks to a previously stable system. In addition, upgrades are frequently costly, in terms of time, resources, money, or potential system downtime.

You should only make changes to the system environment if this is necessitated by the business structures or by legal requirements. Of course, if hardware or software is no longer supported by the manufacturer, this is also a good reason to perform an upgrade.

If you're planning to change your system environment, you should first make sure that the system can be reset to its original status before the change. Conduct regression tests with the operational functions team and users to ensure that the changes do not impact other parts of the system.

We recommend planning and testing a change using the following sequence of system steps:

1. Test system
2. Development system
3. Quality assurance system
4. Production system

Even if your enterprise does not have all of these systems in place, you should still follow this sequence as a general guide.

Don't Change the System during Critical Phases

We strongly recommend that you never make any changes to the system during critical phases. A critical phase refers to a time during which a system failure could result in serious operational problems and business losses.

[Ex]

Critical Phases

At the *end of the month*, a system administrator changes the printer in the shipping department but forgets to adjust the printer settings in the SAP system. As a result, the SAP system is unable to send any print jobs to this new printer. This means that users cannot print any shipping documents, so the enterprise is unable to ship any products, which has consequences on the enterprise's revenue for the month.

Other examples of critical phases include the following:

- The start of the month, when the accounting department prepares the month-end closing for the previous month
- The final month of the year (calendar year or fiscal year), when the posting and shipping activities of the sales and distribution department and the shipping department are intensified to maximize revenue for the current year
- The start of the year, when the accounting department is performing the year-end closing for the previous year and preparing for the financial audit
- Key project phases, such as training, testing, or the go-live phase of a new SAP component

You should always inform users about any system events that may potentially disrupt their use of the system. Your scheduling must take account of the fact that various user groups, such as accounting users and order entry users, have certain periods of relatively low activity during the year. Schedule potentially disruptive system events during quiet phases when the effects of any problems on users are minimized. Organize the times at which urgent and less important maintenance tasks are to be performed and decide how users are to be informed. Define contact persons for system administration and SAP users, and coordinate the maintenance plan with all involved.

Minimize Single Points of Failure

With a single point of failure, the failure of a single component, task, or activity causes the failure of the entire system or leads to a critical event. Any risk of a single point of failure therefore simultaneously increases the risk of a system failure or critical event.

[Ex]

Single Point of Failure

Some examples of single-point-of-failure scenarios are provided here:

- You only have a single tape drive. The tape drive fails. You can no longer save your database.
- You depend on the mains power supply because you have no uninterrupted power source. In the event of a power outage, the server crashes and may damage the database.
- You are the only person capable of performing a specific task. If you go on a vacation or are ill, this task can't be performed until you return to work.

To avoid such single points of failure, proceed as follows:

- Configure your system with an integrated system backup.
- Ensure redundancy, for example, with a redundant power supply system.
- Keep replacement parts on hand.
- Ensure that you have enough human resources, and distribute knowledge.
- Have consultants on call.
- Consider cross-training.
- Consider outsourcing.

Prevent Direct Database Access

Direct database access means that a user can query or change the database directly without authorization in the SAP system. If a user has direct access to the database, there is a risk that the database may suffer damage. Direct access also interferes with the synchronization of the database with the SAP-internal buffers.

SAP applications usually write their data to several tables in the database when a specific transaction or document is saved, for example. If a user writes data to the database tables directly, the database may be damaged if a single table is omitted because there is then a mismatch between the tables. With direct database access, a user may also accidentally change or delete the database instead of reading data from it.

Outlaw All Non-SAP Activities on the SAP Server

The servers on which your SAP instances are running should only ever be used for this purpose. If other services also run on these servers, they may make the server run more slowly and also increase the risk of unintentional data changes or deletions.

[!]

Preventing Access to the Server

Do not allow users to access the SAP server directly by Telnet or external access. This is necessary to protect confidential or sensitive information. Don't use the SAP application server as a complete file server. In this way, you can ensure that no data can be deleted or changed by mistake. Don't run any programs on the servers of the SAP components that are not directly related to the application. As a result, system resources remain open for SAP tasks.

1.3 Definitions

This book uses some terms with a very specific meaning. These terms are defined next for the purpose of clarification.

Database Server

This server contains the SAP components and the database. The system clock of the database server sets the time for the SAP application.

Application Server

This server contains the SAP applications. In systems with two layers, this server forms part of the database server. Application servers can be set up for online users, for background processing, or for both.

Instance

An instance refers to an installation of the SAP application on a server. We can distinguish between a central instance and dialog instances. The *central instance*, which contains the database, exists only once in a system environment. The *dialog instances* are the application servers. Any system environment may have several dialog instances. More than one instance may be installed on a physical server.

System

The system is the complete SAP installation for a system ID (SID), for example, NSP. A system logically consists of the SAP central instances and the dialog instances for the SID. Physically, it comprises the database server and the application servers for this SID.

SAP Configuration with Three Layers

Table 1.1 shows an SAP configuration with three layers.

Layer	Physical Device	SAP Instance	What Runs on This Layer?
Display	Several desktop PCs	None	SAP GUI
Application	Several application servers	Dialog	SAP
Database	A single database server	Central	Database: SQL Server, DB2, Oracle

Table 1.1 Configuration with Three Layers

In a two-layer configuration, the application layer and database layer are run in combination on a single server.

Client

A client is an area containing independent application data within an SAP system. You log on to the SAP system in a specific client. Several clients may exist in parallel in a single SAP system, with each client representing a self-contained unit in terms of master data and application data. This delineation is often used to map organizational structures, for example, scenarios where an SAP system is shared by several enterprises, each of which has its own client. The clients in a system share various cross-client system resources, such as the SAP instances, the database, and the ABAP Dictionary.

1.4 Summary

This chapter has familiarized you with the essential areas of responsibility of an SAP system administrator. Based on this knowledge, you can decide how to distribute the tasks in your administration group from an organizational perspective.

In addition, we set out some basic principles to guide administrators in their tasks. These should be followed as part of routine system operation to maximize system availability and minimize the risk of downtime.

The terms and definitions provided here should also assist you in your understanding of the rest of the book.

Your main role as SAP system administrator is to manage the day-to-day operation of the SAP system. This chapter describes the tasks, tools, and transactions that you need to know for system administration.

2 SAP System Administration

On a day-to-day basis, most of your time as an SAP administrator will be taken up with general system administration. The system must be configured in a way that ensures stable operation with the available resources and avoids system downtimes.

As administrator, you are also required to eliminate errors that inevitably occur during operation. You must investigate these errors, determine their cause, and find an appropriate solution.

In addition, critical situations will regularly occur that do not originate in the SAP system directly but are, instead, caused by a problem at the database or operating system level. In cases like these, you are expected to quickly and accurately assess system status and to use the information obtained to make the right decision concerning how to proceed.

This chapter introduces you to the essential tasks and SAP tools in the system administration environment that you need to use for routine system operation.[1]

2.1 Starting and Stopping the SAP System

Today's SAP systems comprise three layers: the operating system layer, database layer, and application layer.

1 For more information about the administration of SAP systems, see *SAP NetWeaver AS ABAP System Administration* (SAP PRESS, 2008).

The individual layers build on one another in this sequence. As a result, the individual components must be started in exactly the same sequence because each layer can only run if the underlying layer is active.

The operating system layer provides a basis for the database and application layers, and it runs on a server. The database and SAP system are installed on this server, or, if necessary, the database and application can also be operated on two separate servers. The server and operating system must be running for you to start the database and application. The operating system manages the hardware resources of the physical server, and makes it available to the running applications. This book does not cover the individual steps involved in the startup and shutdown of a server or of the installed operating system.

All SAP system data are stored in the database. This includes the application data (such as POs, invoices, and so on) generated by daily transactions, as well as the system settings (*Customizing*) and the source code of programs, functions modules, and so on. The database must be active if you want to start an SAP application because this is the only way to ensure that the application can access the data. Chapter 8 describes how to start and stop the database.

You can only start the SAP application itself if the operating system and database are already running. While it is running, the application accesses the information stored in the database.

To stop an SAP system, it is necessary to repeat the same steps in exactly the reverse order. You stop the SAP system before stopping the database. The operating system and the physical server can then be shut down.

[!]

Steps to Follow When Stopping the System

If you stop the database without stopping the SAP system first, the application can't save buffered data that hasn't yet been stored. In this case, data loss is inevitable. The same applies if you shut down the operating system or physical server without closing the SAP system and database properly. The application and database buffers cannot be emptied, and the buffered data cannot be saved.

2.1.1 Starting the SAP System

Follow these steps to start the SAP system:

1. Start the server and the operating system. Check the operating system log to determine whether the start has been successful.
2. Start the database (see Chapter 8). Check the database log to determine whether the start has been successful.

[+]

Starting the Database

This step is optional because the database is started first automatically by the start script when you start the SAP system. However, if you start the database manually, you can check the database log before starting the SAP system.

3. Start the SAP system. If you have a Microsoft Windows operating system, use the *SAP Management Console*. In the taskbar, choose START • PROGRAMS • SAP MANAGEMENT CONSOLE.

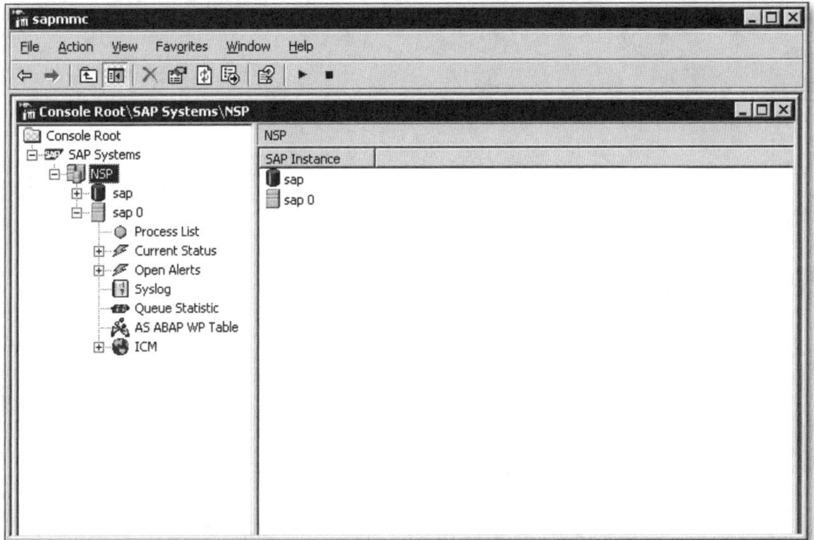

[+]

Starting Without the SAP Management Console

The SAP Management Console is only installed at the Microsoft operating system level. If you use a different operating system, open a shell and use the startsap console command to start the SAP system. This also works with the Microsoft command prompt.

4. Right-click on the system ID of the system you want to start (for example, NSP).

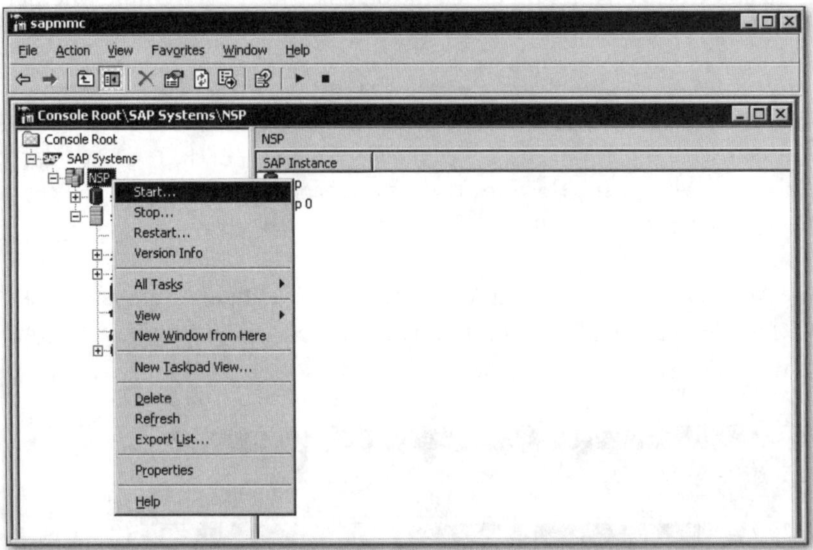

5. Enter a start timeout in the dialog box that opens. If you're only running a single instance, simply click OK to confirm.

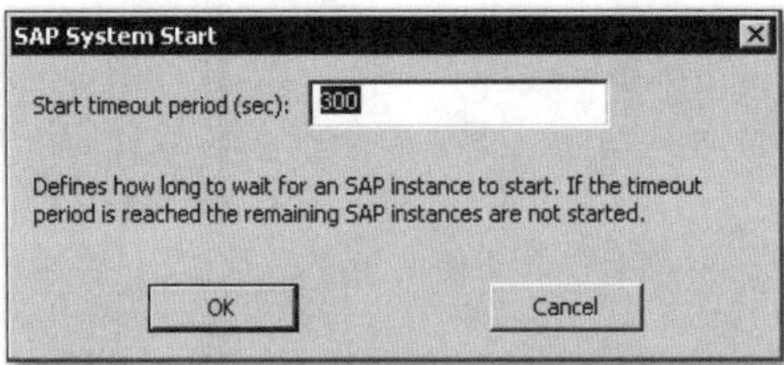

[+]

Start Timeout

A start timeout is only relevant if you're running other system instances alongside the central instance. The central instance must be running before you can start the other instances.

Entering a start timeout value indicates how many seconds the system should wait before starting the other instances. The value is based on the length of time it takes to start your central instance, based on past experience.

6. Another dialog box opens, in which you must enter your password to gain authentication as an administrator. Only administrators are authorized to start and stop an SAP system.

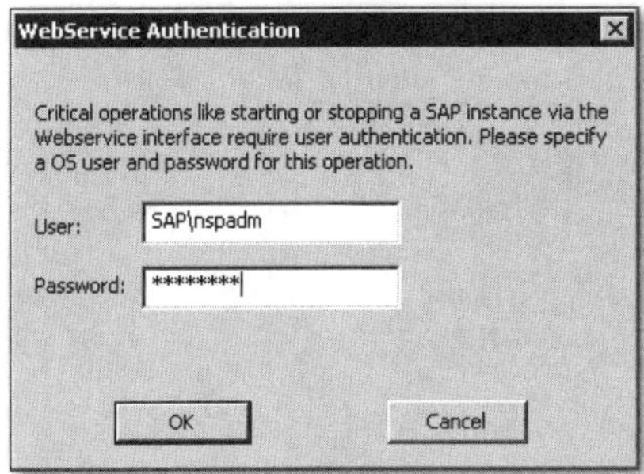

7. If the database has not already been started, it is started now automatically, followed by the SAP system. In the SAP Management Console, the status is initially yellow, which changes to green after a successful start.

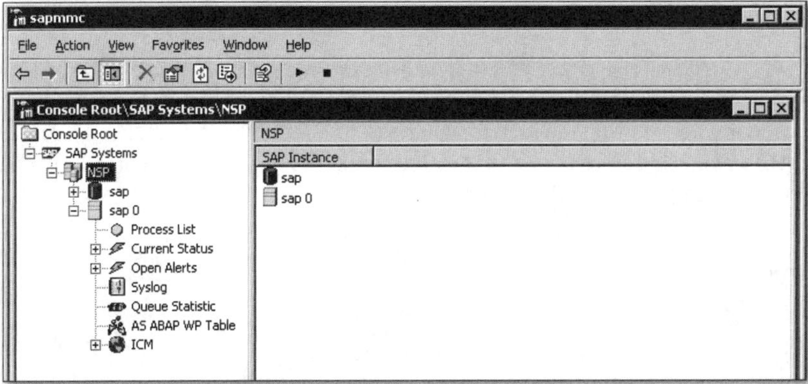

Patience Is a Virtue [+]

It may take several minutes to start an SAP instance. Patience really is an essential characteristic of good system administrators. You need to wait and remain calm if it takes longer than expected.

A red traffic-light icon will alert you to the occurrence of errors. As long as you don't see any red traffic lights, simply give the system the time it needs.

8. The system has started. To check whether the SAP system is running, log on to the system with the SAP GUI. You know that the system has been started correctly if the logon screen appears.

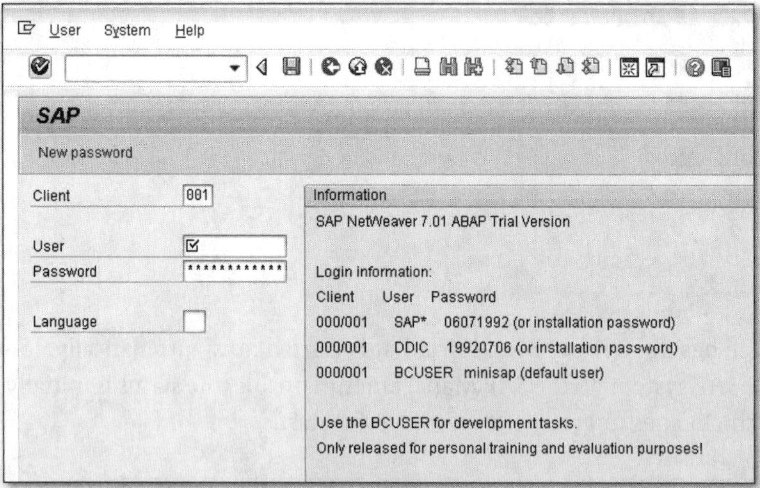

[⚙]

Checking the Start Logs

If problems occur when starting the system, you need to check the start logs. You'll find these logs at the operating system level in the directory */usr/sap/<SID>/<Instance>/work*. Check for error messages in the following files:

- *sapstart.log*
- *sapstartsrv.log*
- *dev_disp*
- *dev_ms*
- *dev_w0*

Eliminate the error, and restart the system.

9. Log on, and check the *system log* (Transaction SM21—see Section 2.4.1, System Log) to determine whether any errors occurred at startup.

[+]

Checking the System Log After Startup

You should wait for a minute or so after starting the SAP system. This makes it easier to read the system log. Several log entries may still be in the process of being written to the log during the start phase. If you wait, you won't need to refresh the system log view several times to display all of these.

2.1.2 Stopping the SAP System

There are several reasons why you may need to stop or restart the SAP system:

- An unplanned hardware or software failure
- Planned hardware or software maintenance
- Changes to profile parameters that cannot be switched dynamically
- A planned complete backup of the server

If you need to stop the SAP system, it is essential that you do so in consultation with your end users. Stopping the system at your own discretion and without any prior warning is very likely to infuriate users because all unsaved data are lost.

Preparing for a System Stop

Before you stop the system, you must perform checks and take precautions to ensure that system activities have ceased at the time of the system stop.

[!]

Checking System Activities Before Stopping the System

For certain activities, such as large posting jobs, you may find that some transactions have already been posted, while others have not. A subsequent restore may be problematic in such cases.

Follow these steps before a system shutdown:

- Coordinate the system shutdown with all departments affected. If a group of users has already scheduled an activity for the period during which you want to shut the system down, and the activity is dependent on a live SAP system, you may have to postpone your system stop and give a higher priority to the needs of these users.

- Create a system message (Transaction SM02) to inform all users of the planned system stop.
- Before you stop the system, make sure that no users are still logged on or active in the system (Transaction SM04 or AL08—see Chapter 13).
- In Transaction SM37 (see Chapter 16), check whether any jobs are active or have been scheduled for the time during which the system stop is to take place. Reschedule all jobs, or cancel the jobs that are due to either run or be started during the planned system stop.
- Check whether any active processes are still running (Transaction SM50 or SM51—see Section 2.4.3).
- Use Transaction SMGW to search for any active RFC connections, which may indicate interfaces that are currently running.

Use the checklist shown in Table 2.1 as preparation for stopping the system.

Task	Date	Initials
The following tasks must be completed in sufficient time before the SAP system is stopped:		
Coordinate the system stop with all departments affected (for example, accounting, shipping, distribution, and so on).		
Create a system message to inform all users of the planned system stop (SM02).		
Send an additional email notification to all users affected.		
Reschedule jobs or cancel the jobs that are either due to run or be started during the planned system stop (SM37).		
The following additional tasks must also be completed shortly before the SAP system is stopped:		
Make sure that no active users are still logged on to the system (SM04 and AL08).		
Make sure that no active background jobs are running (SM37).		
Make sure that no active processes are running (SM50 and SM51).		

Table 2.1 Checklist for Preparing for a System Stop

Task	Date	Initials
Check for active external interfaces (SMGW).		
How to stop the SAP system:		
Stop the application server instances.		
Stop the central instance.		
Stop the database (optional).		

Table 2.1 Checklist for Preparing for a System Stop (Cont.)

In the event of an emergency, or if the system stop has priority over all other requirements (for example, if you have a file system overflow, log storage overflow, device failure, and so on), the system must be stopped immediately. In such cases, end users are forced by circumstances to adapt. However, you should still try to work through the checklist.

Stopping the SAP System

You should not stop the SAP system until you've completed all necessary checks and are certain that all system activities have ceased.

To stop the SAP system, follow these steps:

1. First, stop the SAP system. If you have a Microsoft Windows operating system, use the *SAP Management Console*. In the taskbar, choose START • PROGRAMS • SAP MANAGEMENT CONSOLE.

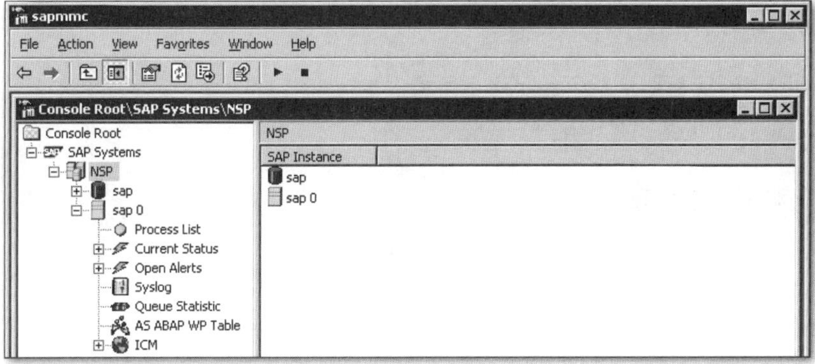

2. You can choose to stop the SAP system only or to stop both the SAP system and the database. To stop the SAP system only, right-click on the name of the instance you want to stop (for example, SAP 0), and choose STOP.

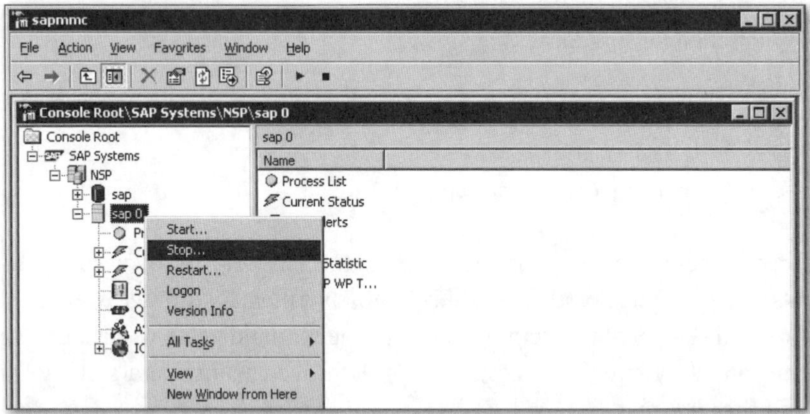

[+]

Stopping the Database

In contrast to the start process, the database can be stopped separately. This might be to your advantage, because it's not always essential to stop the database in addition to the SAP system (for example, when changing profile parameters). It is must faster to restart the SAP system alone than to restart both the system and the database.

3. To stop the database as well as the SAP system, right-click on the system ID (for example, NSP), and choose STOP.

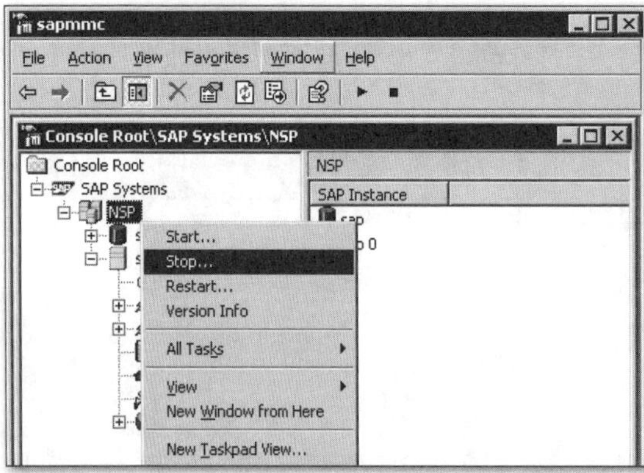

[+]

Stopping Without the SAP Management Console

If you don't use a Microsoft operating system and therefore have no access to the SAP Management Console, you must stop the SAP system using the console. Open a shell or the command prompt, and enter the stopsap r3 console command. To stop the SAP system and the database, execute the stopsap or stopsap all command.

4. Select the shutdown type in the dialog box that opens.
   - HARD (SIGINT): The SAP system is shut down immediately.
   - SOFT WITH TIMEOUT (SIGQUIT/SIGINT): The system first attempts a *soft shutdown*. If the specified period elapses without a successful shutdown of the SAP system, a *hard shutdown* is executed instead.
   - SOFT WITHOUT TIMEOUT (SIGQUIT): When the system is shutting down, a *core dump* is generated first. In other words, the current status of the application is written to a log file, which can be used for subsequent troubleshooting.

   Choose OK to continue.

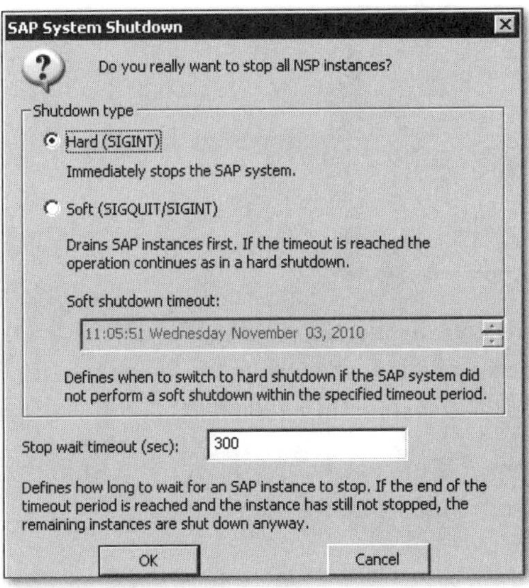

5. A dialog box opens, in which you are required to enter your password to gain authentication as an administrator. The SAP system may only be shut down by administrators.

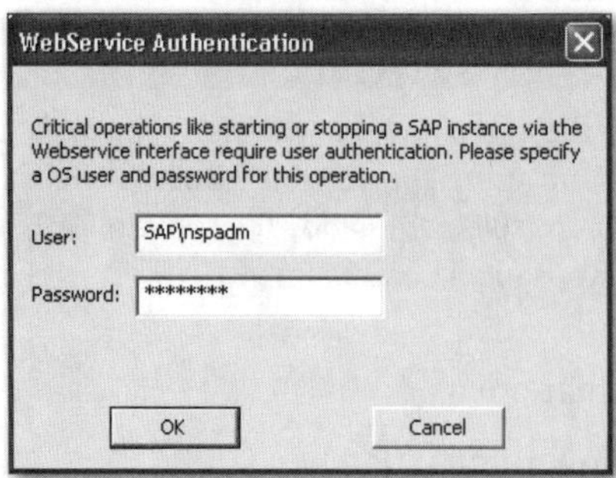

6. Next, the database is stopped, followed by the SAP system or, alternatively, only the SAP system is stopped, depending on which selection you have made. The status changes from green to gray in the SAP Management Console.

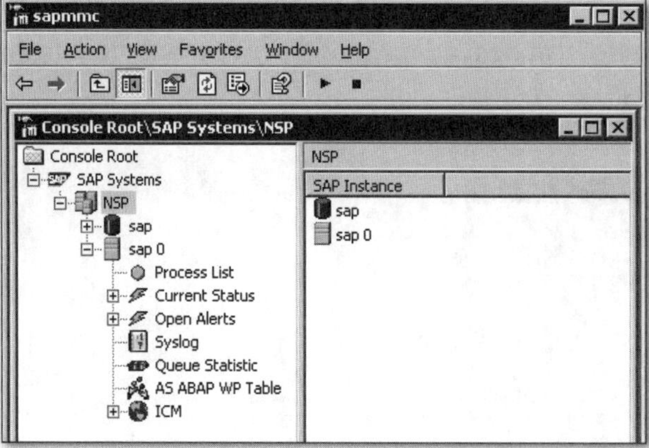

You have now stopped the SAP system or both the database and SAP system. If you have stopped the SAP system only in order to allow changes to profile parameters to become effective, you can now restart the system immediately.

If you have stopped both the SAP system and the database, you can now stop the operating system if necessary and shut down the phyical server.

2.2 Instances and Operation Modes

Servers at the SAP application level are referred to as *instance servers* or *application servers* in the SAP system architecture. The SAP application (application server) and the database usually share a server. More powerful system landscapes have an SAP system and a database running on two separate servers. The next step up from this configuration is to create instance clusters, in other words, to set up various SAP instances, which can run on different servers. This enhances the capabilities of the system at the application level. However, the individual instances all still access the same database.

Each instance provides a configurable number of *work processes*. These processes are responsible for the actual processing of the tasks that are transferred to the system. These may include executing a transaction in a user dialog or processing a background job, for example. Work processes are divided into various types based on the tasks for which they are reserved:

- Dialog work processes—execute ABAP dialog programs
- Batch work processes—execute background jobs
- Update work processes—control asynchronous database changes
- Enqueue work processes—execute lock operations
- Spool work processes—process print data

As an SAP administrator, you must consider, on the one hand, whether your SAP system should comprise one or more instances. On the other, you can also determine the number and distribution of the work process types of the instances. For example, you could have one instance for dialog logons, and a second instance for background processing only.

The total number of work processes in an instance is relatively static because it can only be changed by restarting the application server. However, you can use *operation modes* to influence the type distribution of the work processes dynamically (in other words, during live operation). As a rule, work processes are switched in synchronization with different times of the day. For example, more dialog processes can be made available during daytime hours to handle the higher number of users logging on. At night, when only a small number of users at most are using the system, and the focus is on the processing of scheduled background jobs, the dialog processes can be switched to batch processes. This ensures that more processes are available for background processing.

Operation modes therefore allow you to adjust the SAP system configuration in accordance with your enterprise's requirements. However, the total number of work processes remains unchanged. In small installations where at most a handful of batch jobs are processed at night, you may be able to dispense with the additional process of configuring and managing operation modes. Fewer operation modes mean less administrative work to maintain the system. However, after the system has been configured correctly, the subsequent administrative effort required is low.

Creating Instance Definitions

To use operation modes, you must create the instances of your system as instance definitions by following these steps:

1. Enter Transaction "RZ04" in the command window, and press the Enter key (or select the menu option Tools • CCMS • Configuration • RZ04—Operation modes/Instances).
2. Click on Instances/Operation modes.

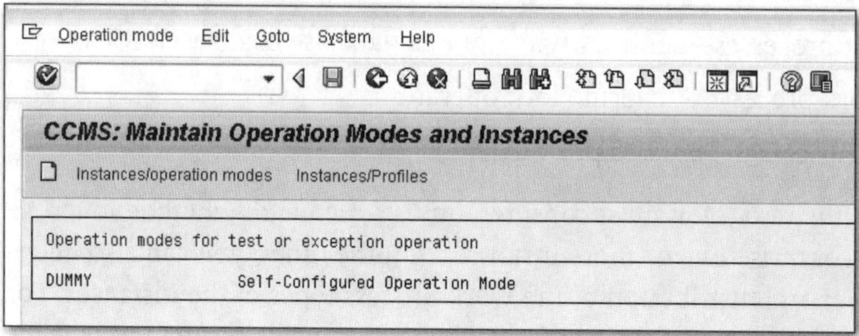

3. Choose the Create new instance icon (☐).

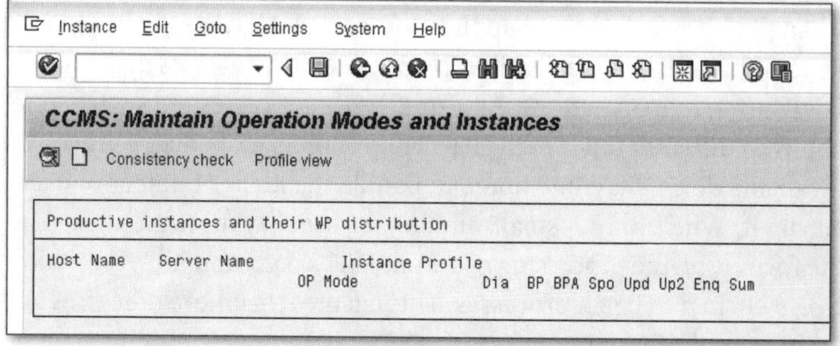

4. The instance data must be maintained on the next screen:
   - Enter the name of the server under Host name.
   - Enter the system number in the SAP System Number field.

- Define the instance's start profile under START PROFILE.
- Enter the name of the instance profile under INSTANCE PROFILE.
- When you have finished, choose SAVE ( ).

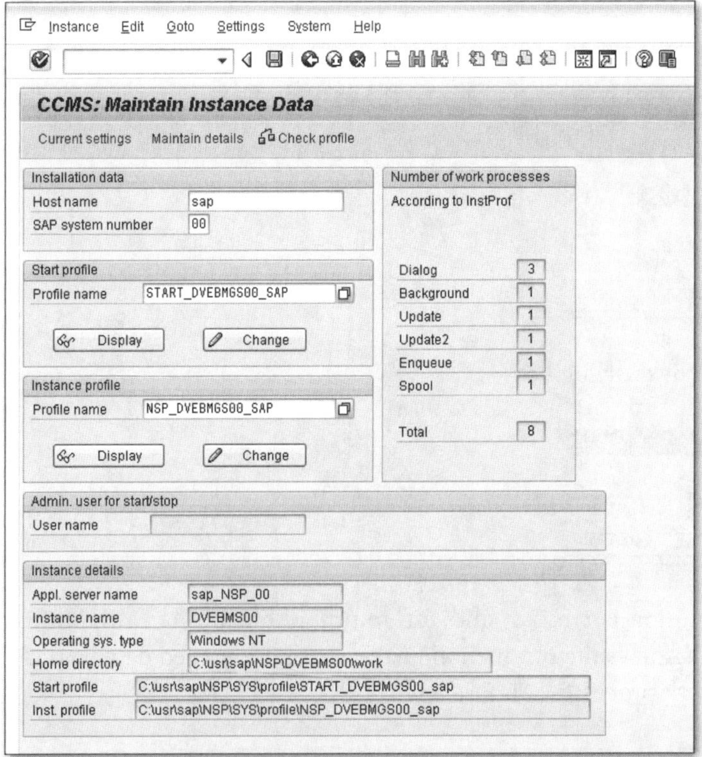

Creating an Instance for the First Time [+]

If no instances have been created and you want to create the current instance as an instance definition, fill in the HOST NAME, number, and click on the CURRENT SETTINGS button. The system automatically determines the data required from the current instance configuration.

5. A dialog box appears, in which you must specify how the work process types are to be distributed. Because these settings are to be defined later by operation modes, enter the placeholder "*" in the OPERATION MODE field, and leave the other settings unchanged. Choose SAVE ( ).

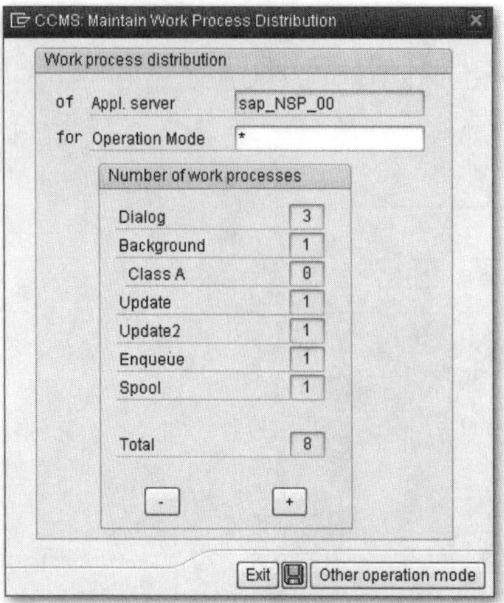

6. Choose No in the next dialog box.

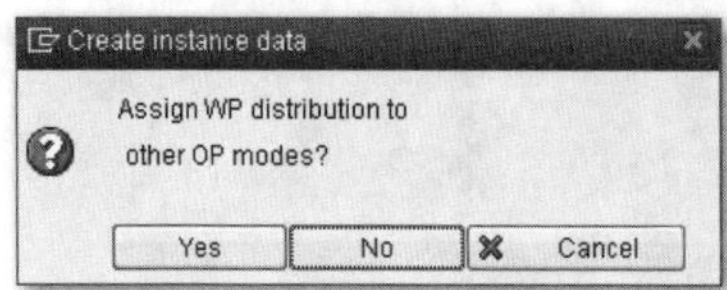

7. The instance definition is created, and you return automatically to the initial screen. The table displays the production instances, their detailed data, and the distribution of work processes. Choose Save (💾).

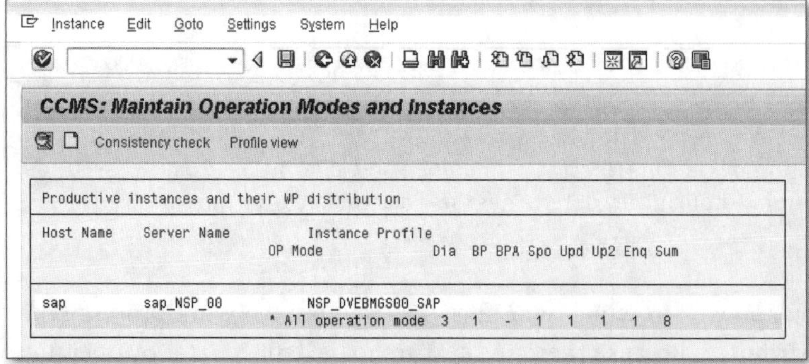

[!]

Creating Additional Instance Definitions

At this point, you can add more application servers as instance definitions. However, the corresponding instances must already be installed and running on a separate server.

Defining Operation Modes

Next, create the operation modes you want your system to have:

1. Enter Transaction "RZ04" in the command field, and press the Enter key (or select the menu option Tools • CCMS • Configuration • RZ04—Operation Modes/Instances).
2. Choose Create operation mode (□).

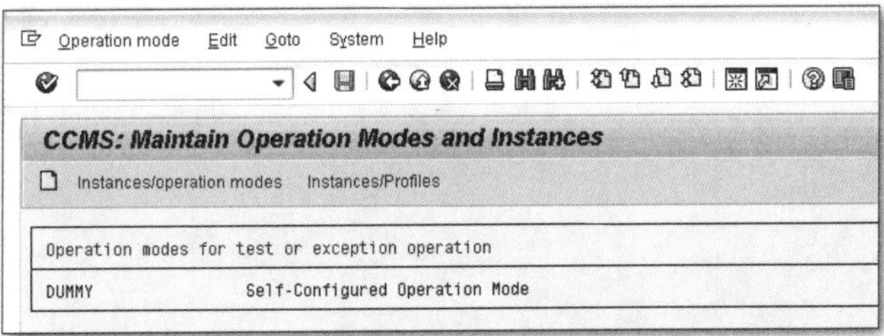

3. On the next screen, enter a name (for example, Daytime) in the Operation mode field, and, in the Short description field, enter a description that is as meaningful as possible. Choose Save (💾).

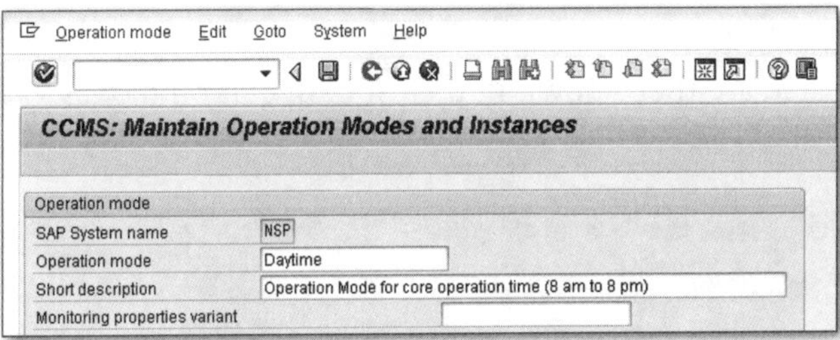

4. You return automatically to the initial screen of the existing operation modes, where the operation mode you just created is now displayed in the list of production operation modes. Choose Create operation mode (□) to create another operation mode.

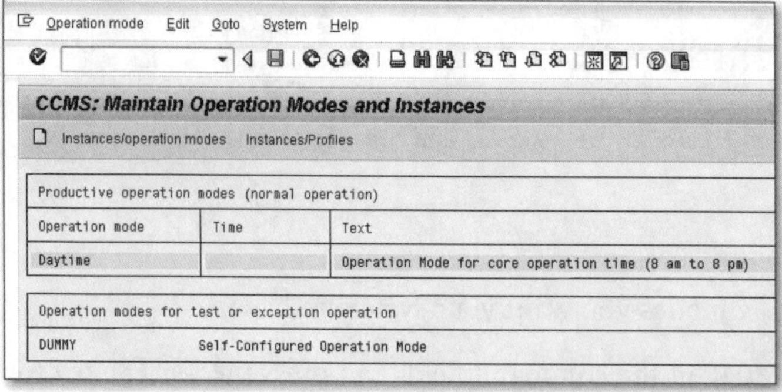

[+]

Distinguishing Between Different Operation Modes

Production operation modes refer to normal SAP operation, *while test* or *special operation modes* are used, for example, for development or test systems, or for specific tasks (such as system maintenance or year-end closing activities).

5. Assign a name (for example, nighttime) and a short description to the operation mode, and click on SAVE ( ).

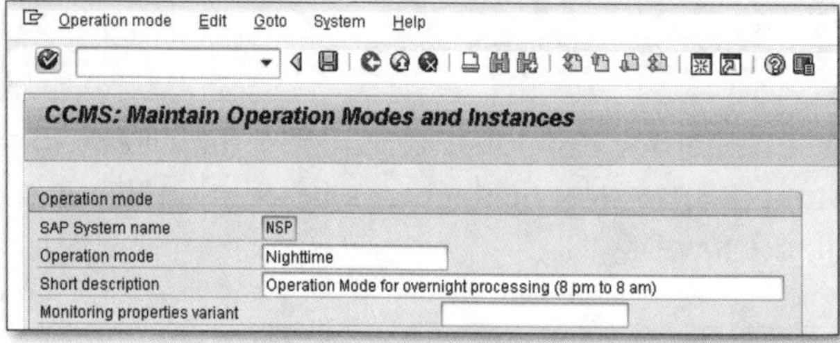

6. Both definitions you created are then shown in the list of operation modes.

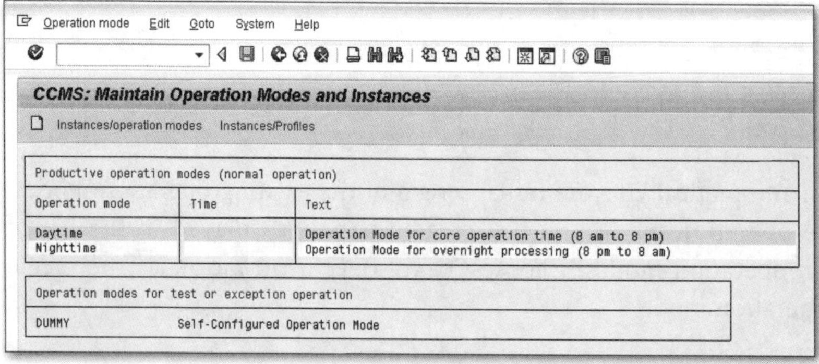

[+]

Useful Operation Modes

The operation modes that will prove useful for your enterprise will be determined by the question of whether or not your system is used differently at different times. In an enterprise with a single location, for example, it may make sense to define one operation mode for daytime operation and one for nighttime operation, with these two modes differing largely in terms of the distribution of dialog and background processes.

However, if you need to ensure smooth operation in dialog mode 24/7 (for example, because various locations in time zones that are very far apart need access to the system), the distribution described here would not make much sense. In a case like this, you would need to base your operation modes on the working hours and needs of all locations, for example.

Assigning Operation Modes and Defining Work Process Distribution

After you've created the operation modes, you can assign these to the instance definitions:

1. To do this, enter Transaction "RZ04" in the command field, and press the Enter key (or select the menu option TOOLS • CCMS • CONFIGURATION • RZ04—OPERATION MODES/INSTANCES).
2. Click on INSTANCES/OPERATION MODES.

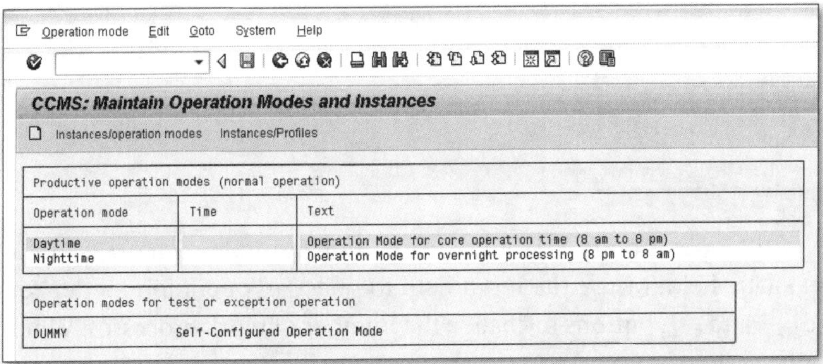

3. On the following screen, position the cursor on the first operation mode row (entry "*"), and click on CHOOSE.

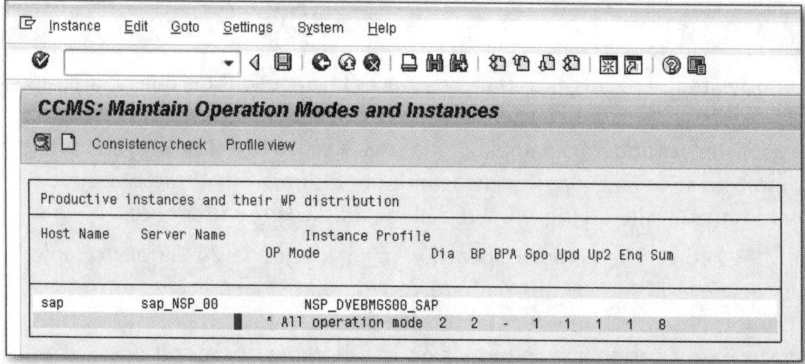

4. In the dialog box that opens, choose the OTHER OPERATION MODE button.

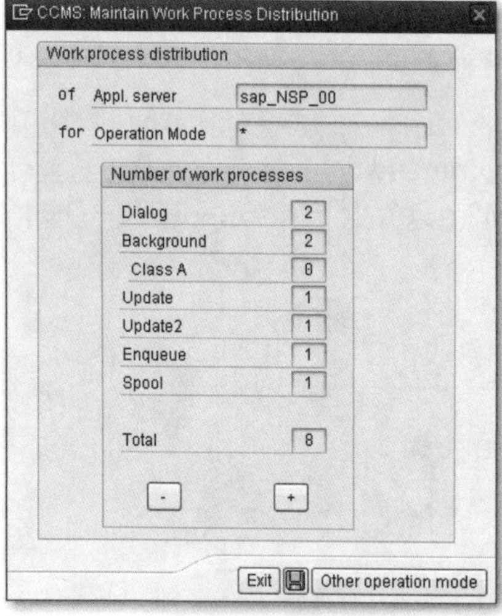

5. Enter one of the operation modes you created (for example, DAYTIME) in the OPERATION MODE field, or use the input help to select an operation mode. You can use the [-] and [+] buttons to change the number of work processes. When you've finished, choose SAVE.

[+]

Changing the Number of Work Processes

The number of dialog work processes is always determined by the other work process types. In other words, you can't configure the dialog processes using the plus and minus buttons. You can, for example, reduce the number of batch processes so that the number of dialog processes increases.

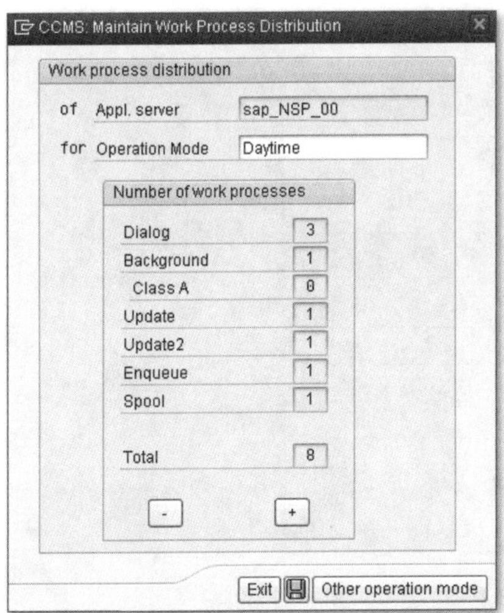

6. Repeat steps 3 and 4, and select the next operation mode (for example, NIGHTTIME). Configure the work process distribution, and click on SAVE ( ).

[!]

Minimum Number of Dialog Work Processes

Note that an instance must have at least two dialog work processes. The system will not allow you to configure fewer dialog processes for any operation mode.

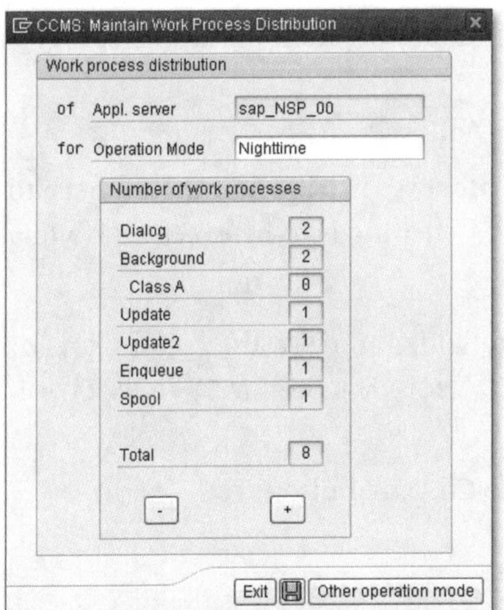

7. In the table view, position your cursor on the "*" entry, which is not needed, and select the menu option INSTANCE • DELETE ENTRY to delete it.

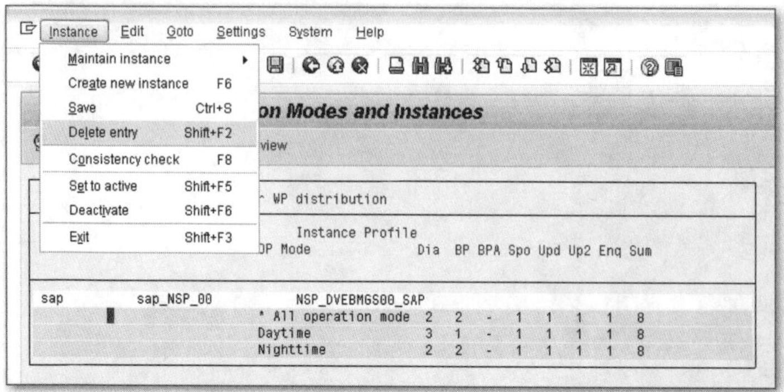

8. Choose YES to confirm the dialog box, and then choose SAVE (💾).

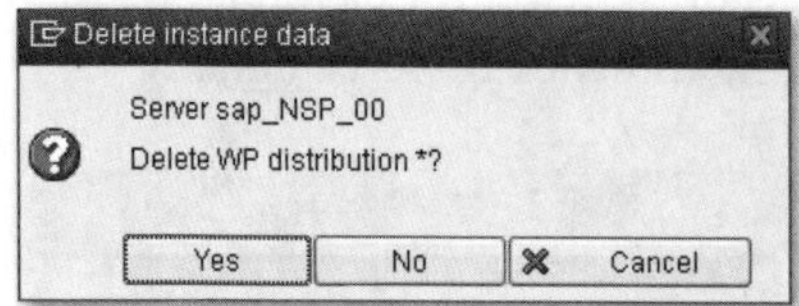

By following these steps, you have assigned the relevant operation modes to the instance, and defined how the work processes are to be distributed for each operation mode. Next, you need to configure time-dependent operation mode switching.

Configuring a Time Allocation for Operation Modes

The operation modes and associated work process distribution are subject to time-dependent switching. To define how this switching is to be executed, follow these steps:

1. Enter Transaction "SM63" in the command field, and press the [Enter] key (or select the menu option TOOLS • CCMS • CONFIGURATION • SM63—OPERATION MODE CALENDAR).
2. Select NORMAL OPERATION, and click on the CHANGE button.

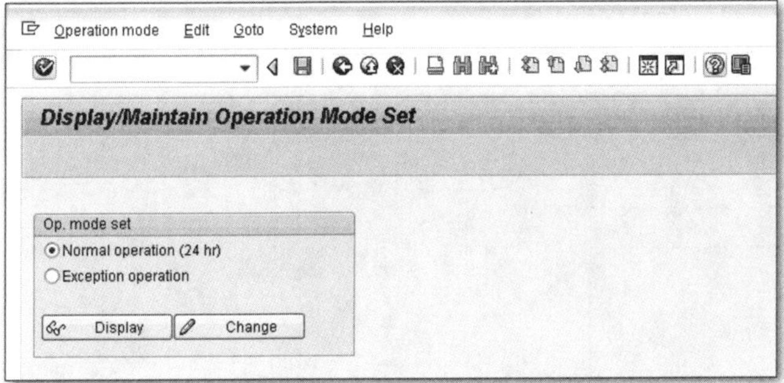

3. On the next screen, you define the time interval for which the operation mode is to be valid. Position your cursor at the start of the period (for example, 08.00—09.00, if daytime operations are to start at 8.00 a.m.). Select the menu option OPERATION MODE • SELECT INTERVAL, or press the [F2] key.

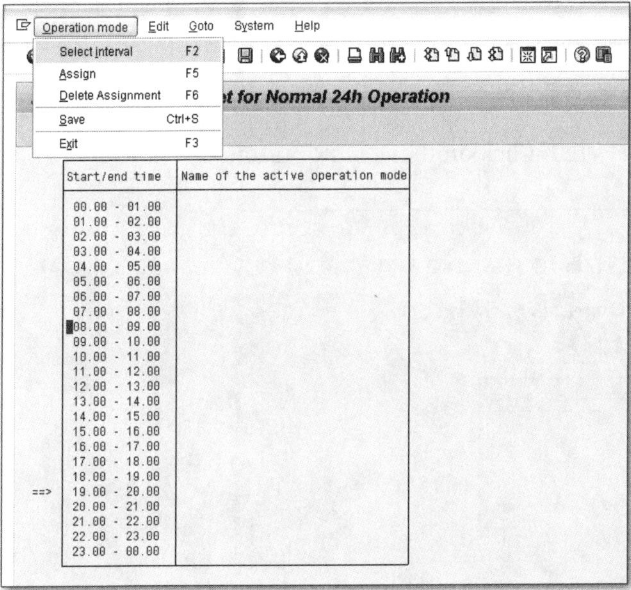

4. Then position your cursor at the end of the interval (for example, 19.00 – 20.00, if daytime operations are to end at 20.00). Once again, select the menu option OPERATION MODE • SELECT INTERVAL, or press the [F2] key.

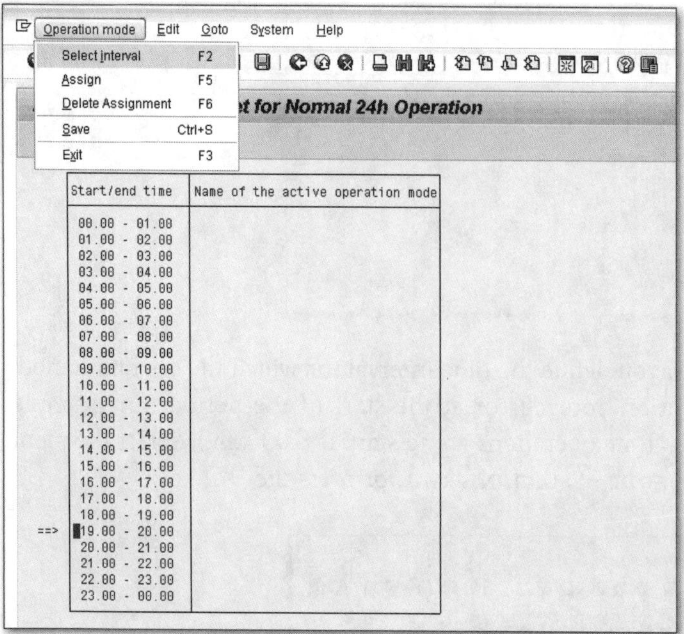

5. The interval has been selected. Click on the Assign button.

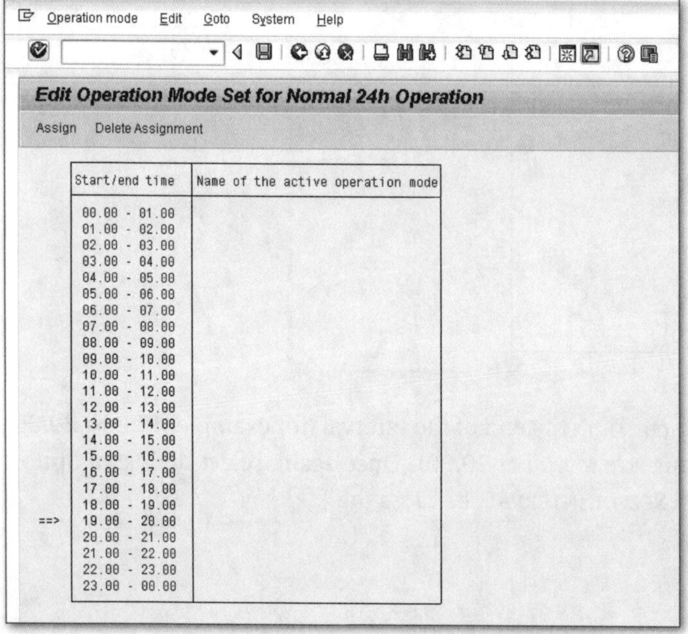

6. In the dialog box, use the input help to select the relevant operation mode, and click on CONTINUE (✔).

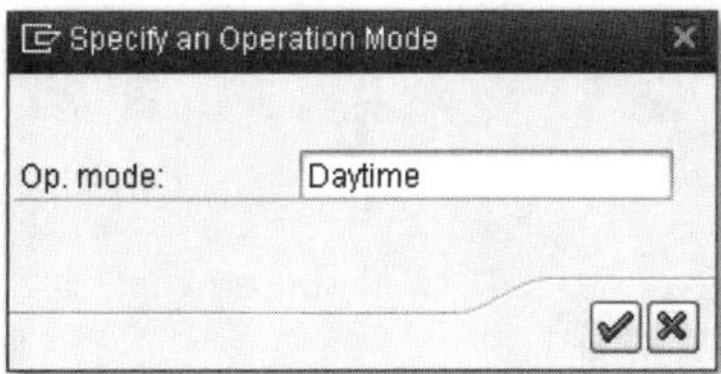

7. The assignment is shown in the table.

   Repeat steps 3 to 6 to assign an operation mode to the other times.

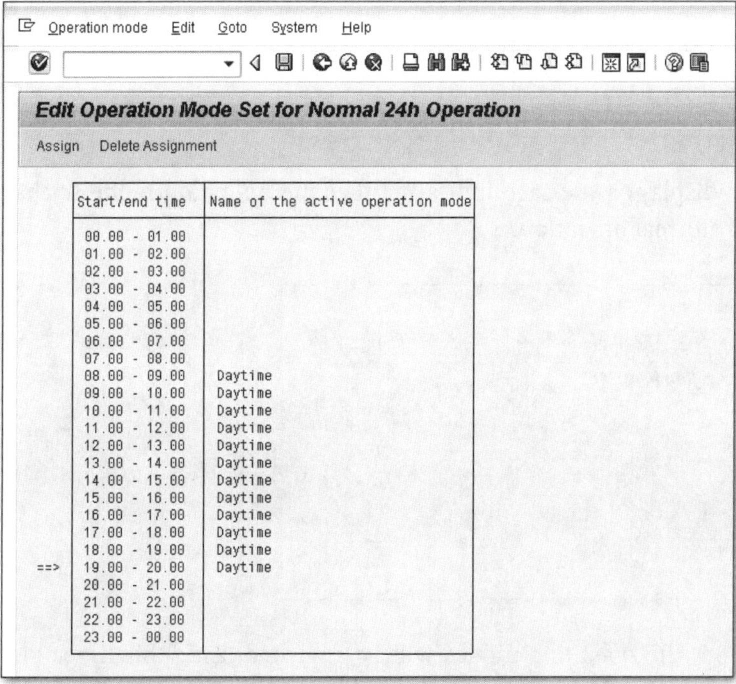

Start/end time	Name of the active operation mode
00.00 - 01.00	
01.00 - 02.00	
02.00 - 03.00	
03.00 - 04.00	
04.00 - 05.00	
05.00 - 06.00	
06.00 - 07.00	
07.00 - 08.00	
08.00 - 09.00	Daytime
09.00 - 10.00	Daytime
10.00 - 11.00	Daytime
11.00 - 12.00	Daytime
12.00 - 13.00	Daytime
13.00 - 14.00	Daytime
14.00 - 15.00	Daytime
15.00 - 16.00	Daytime
16.00 - 17.00	Daytime
17.00 - 18.00	Daytime
18.00 - 19.00	Daytime
19.00 - 20.00	Daytime
20.00 - 21.00	
21.00 - 22.00	
22.00 - 23.00	
23.00 - 00.00	

8. When you've finished, choose SAVE (💾).

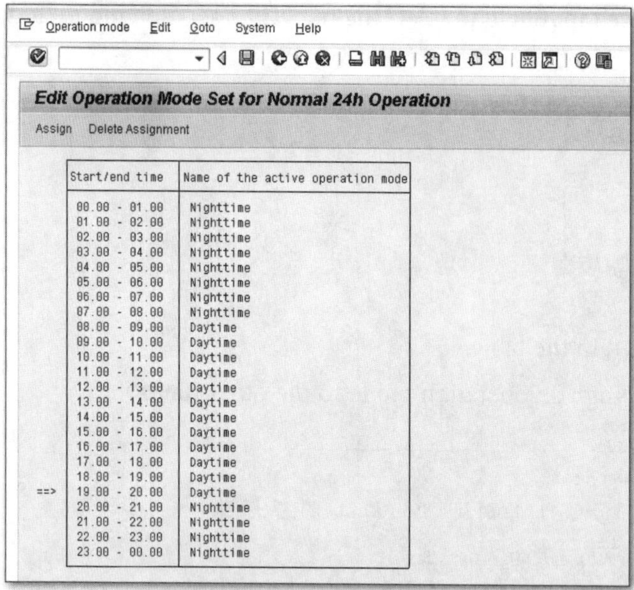

9. The status bar displays a message indicating that the operation mode set has been saved for normal operation.

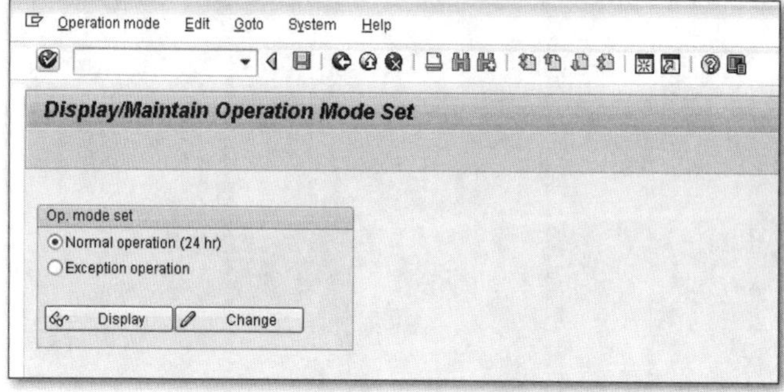

From this point on, the operation modes will be switched using this timetable. A log entry is generated in the system log (Transaction SM21) when a switch has been made. Both the old and new process types are recorded for each work process that is switched.

However, the type of a work process can't be switched until the process becomes available. In other words, a delay may be experienced while the work process is still occupied. For example, if all background processes to be switched are still executing jobs, the processes are switched one by one, as soon as the corresponding jobs have been completed. Processing is not interrupted, and normal system operation proceeds without disruption during switching.

Manual Switching of Operation Modes

Operation modes can also be switched manually if necessary. This function is required if, for example, you want to switch to a special operation mode, use a new operation mode immediately, or nighttime operations need to be brought forward for an important reason.

To switch operation modes manually, follow these steps:

1. Enter Transaction "RZ03" in the command field, and press the [Enter] key (or select the menu option TOOLS • CCMS • CONTROL/MONITORING • RZ03—CONTROL PANEL).
2. Position the cursor on the application server whose operation mode you want to select. Click on CHOOSE OPERATION MODE.

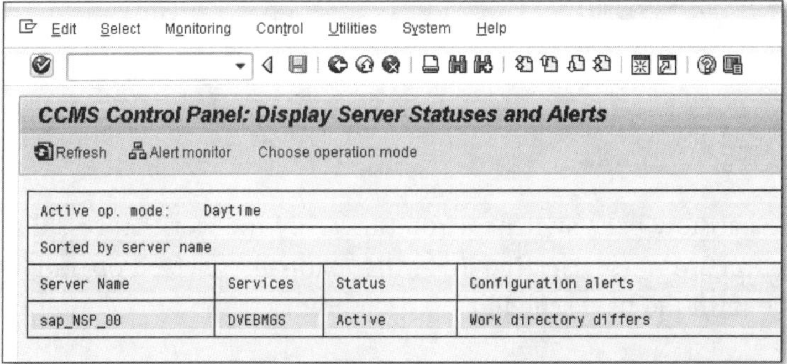

3. Place the cursor on the operation mode to which you want to switch, and click on CHOOSE.

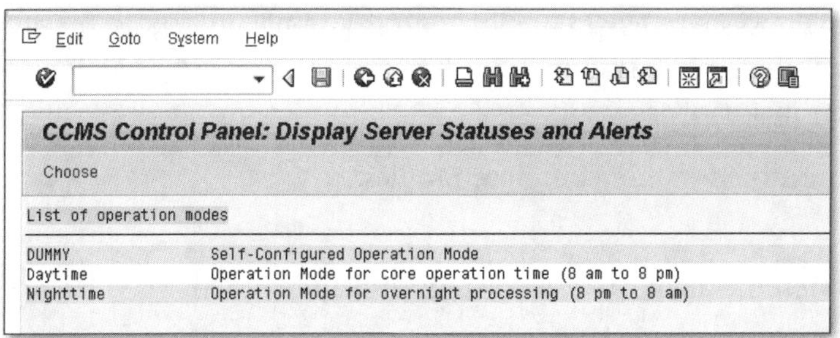

4. The view switches back to the screen showing the server statuses and alerts. Your selected operation mode is now displayed as the active operation mode. Position the cursor on the relevant server, and select the menu option CONTROL • SWITCH OPERATION MODE • SELECTED SERVERS.

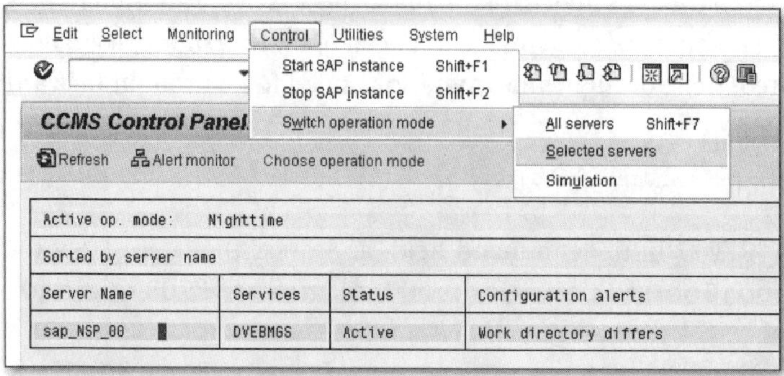

5. Choose YES to confirm the dialog box that opens.

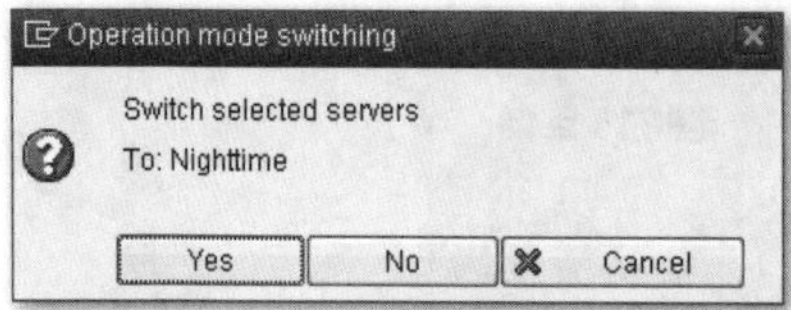

The operation mode has now been switched. You can verify the work process distribution in Transaction SM50 (see Section 2.3). The manually selected operation mode remains active until the next scheduled switch point.

2.3 Maintaining Profile Parameters

Profile parameters are used in the SAP system to control basic technical settings that are required to start the system. For example, you can use parameters to specify the number of work processes a system should have or the required minimum number of characters in a user password.

Profile parameters are stored in three different profiles:

- **Start profile**
  This profile defines the name of the system and which SAP services are started.

- **Default profile**
  This profile contains all parameters that must be identical for all instances of the system.
- **Instance profile**
  This profile determines the detailed configuration of a specific instance. This makes it possible to have different configurations for individual application servers (or instances) that are intended for different tasks.

The profiles are loaded in the sequence given in the preceding list at startup.

File Directory at the Operating System Level [⚙]

The profiles are saved as files at the operating system level. They are located in the directory */usr/sap/<System-ID>/SYS/profiles*.

These profiles may only be changed in Transaction RZ10 (System Profiles), and must not be changed at operating system level. You should only edit the files directly as an emergency measure if the system cannot be started after a change.

Changes to profile parameters are critical for system operation, and must only be carried out by administrators. If a parameter is set incorrectly, it may no longer be possible to start the SAP system. Only change a value for a specific purpose, and be very sure of what you want to change and why.

Saving the Profile Files [!]

Before you change system profiles, make sure that you have a current backup copy of the system profile files. This backup copy may be your only hope if a profile change means you can no longer start the SAP system.

Follow these steps to maintain profile parameters:

1. Enter Transaction "RZ10" in the command field, and press the `Enter` key (or select the menu option TOOLS • CCMS • CONFIGURATION • RZ10—SYSTEM PROFILE).
2. Enter the relevant system profile in the PROFILE field, or use the input help to select it.
3. Three options are already available in the EDIT PROFILES area:
   - ADMINISTRATIVE DATA: This option is not a maintenance option. Instead, it is used to change the file name if you need to change the profile.

- BASIC MAINTENANCE: In this mode, you can define buffers, work processes, and directories in the system profiles. You can also specify which SAP components are to be started in start profiles (for example, message server, application server, SNA gateway). This type of maintenance protects most profile parameters from being changed by potentially incorrect settings.
- EXTENDED MAINTENANCE: This mode enables full access to all profile parameters.

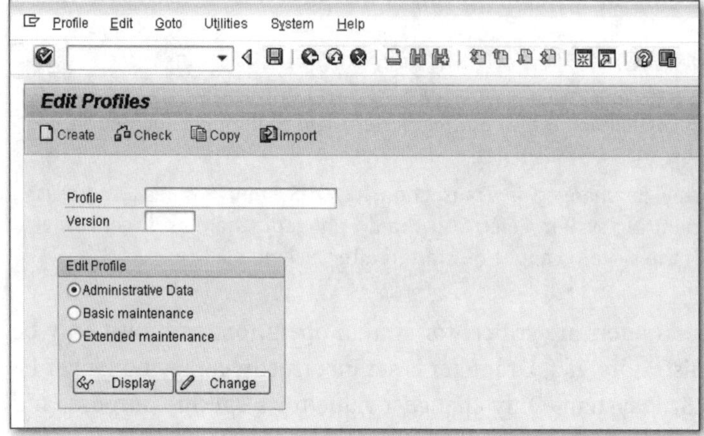

Select the EXTENDED MAINTENANCE option, and click on CHANGE.

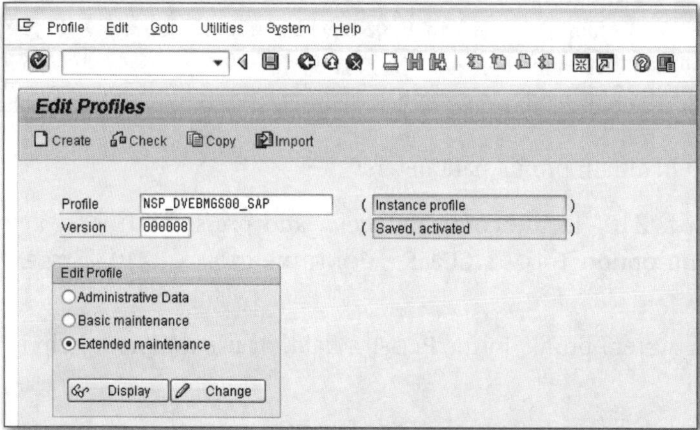

4. Position the cursor on the row below the new row you want to be inserted with the profile parameter. Click the CREATE PARAMETER button (□) to create the parameter.

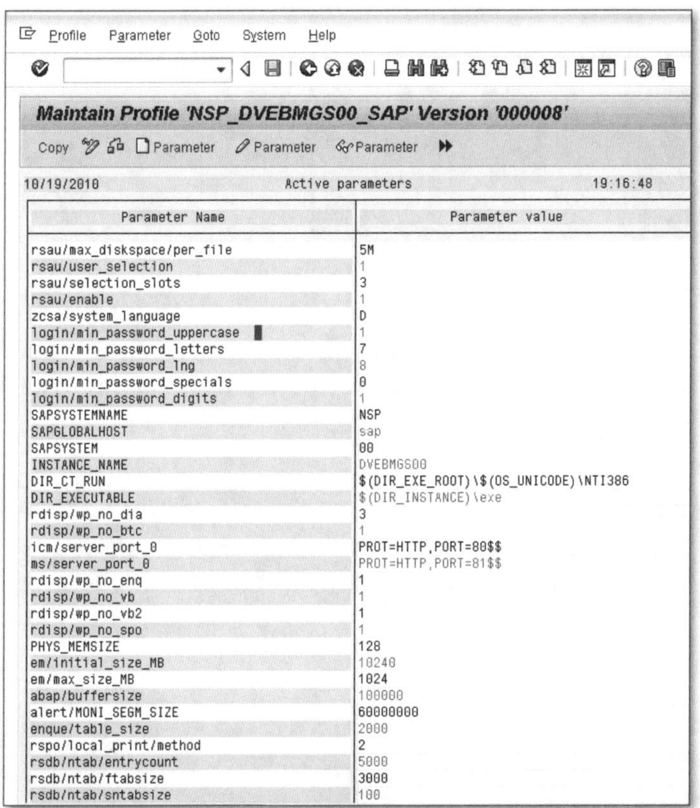

Adding New Parameters [+]

The location in which you insert the new profile parameter has no effect on the process. However, for the sake of clarity, we recommend grouping or sorting the parameters (for example, by keeping all logon parameters together).

It is difficult to move profile parameters after they have been entered. You should therefore give careful consideration to where you insert the parameters.

5. Enter the name of the new parameter in the PARAMETER NAME field, and press the Enter key.

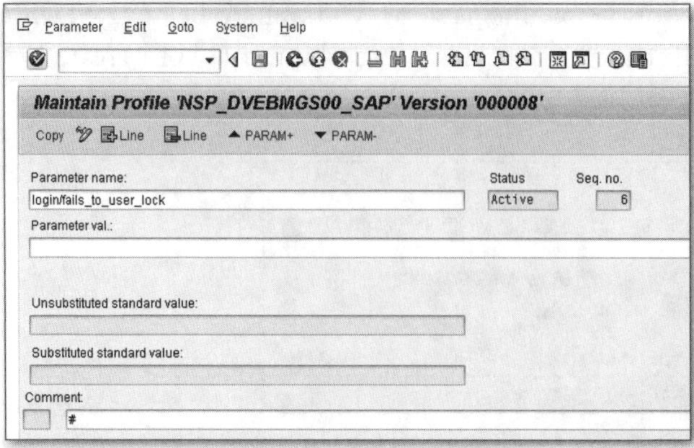

6. The SAP default value of the parameters is displayed under UNSUBSTITUTED DEFAULT VALUE. Enter the desired value in the PARAMETER VALUE field. Under COMMENT, enter the reason for the change for documentation purposes. When you've finished, click on COPY.

[+]

Displaying Profile Parameters in Transaction RZ11

Use Transaction RZ11 (Maintain Profile Parameters) to display the profile parameters that are available in the system. You can display detailed parameter documentation in this transaction.

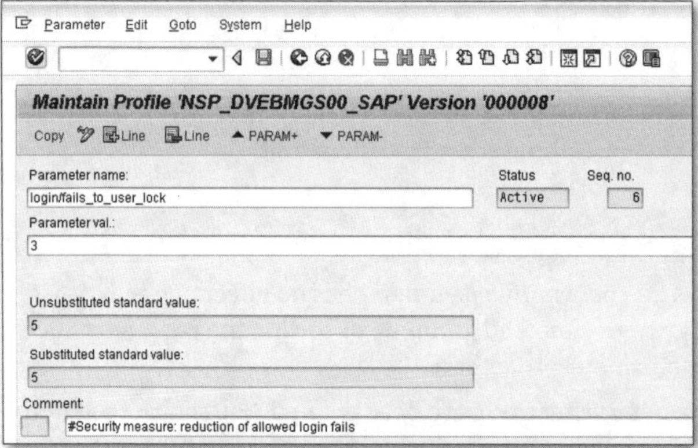

7. The system enters your user ID and the current date in the comment field. This feature allows you to keep track of which persons have made profile changes at which times. A message is also displayed to confirm that the changes have been applied. Choose BACK (◎).

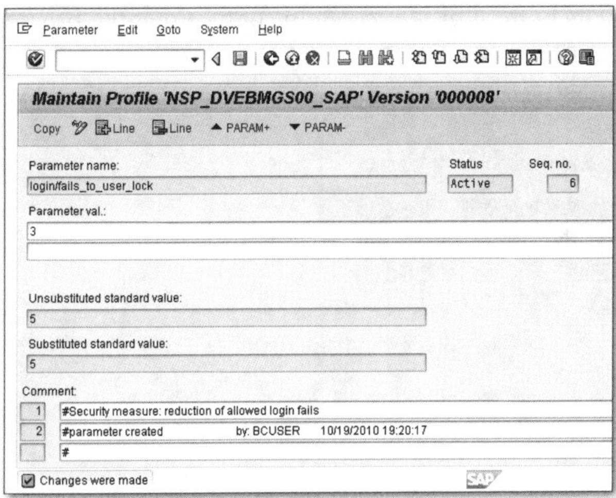

8. You are then returned automatically to the list of profile parameters. The new parameter has been added to the list. Click on Copy.

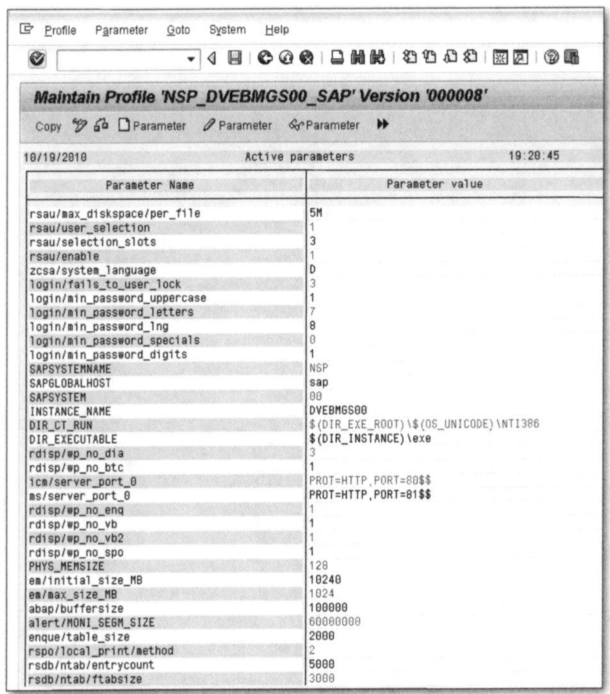

9. A message is displayed at the bottom of the screen to confirm that the profile has been changed. Click on BACK (⟲).

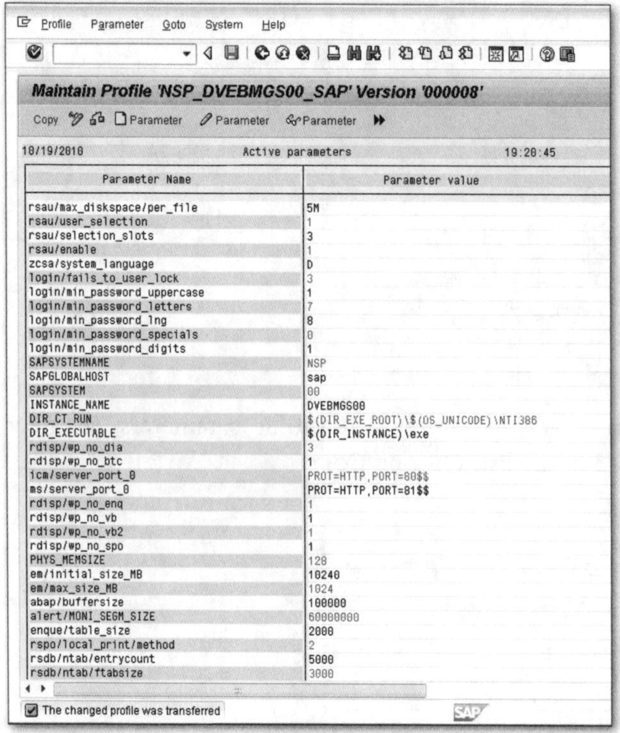

10. On the EDIT PROFILES screen, click on SAVE (💾).

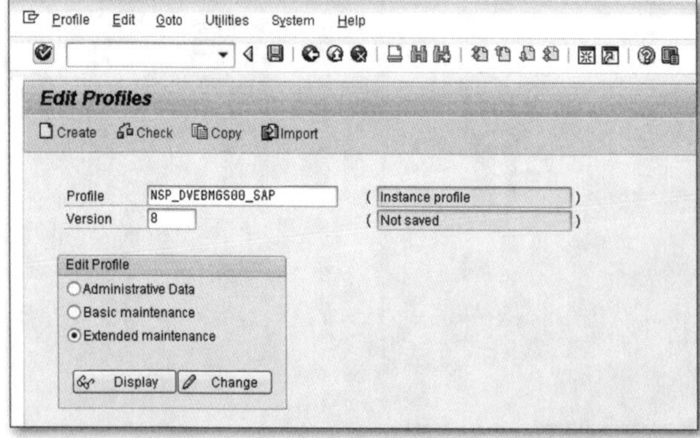

11. Choose YES to confirm activation of the profile.

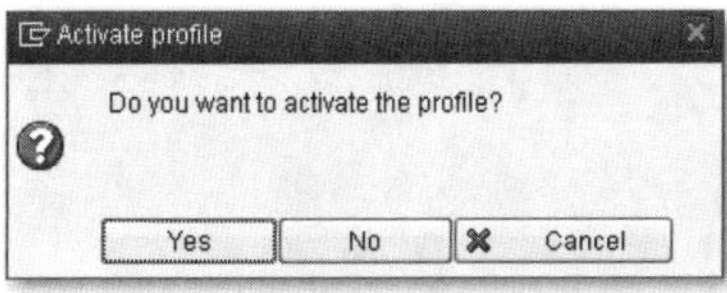

12. Click on CONTINUE (✔).

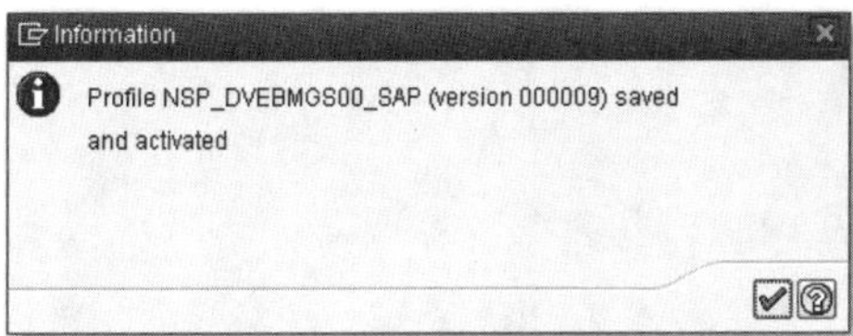

13. Choose CONTINUE (✔).

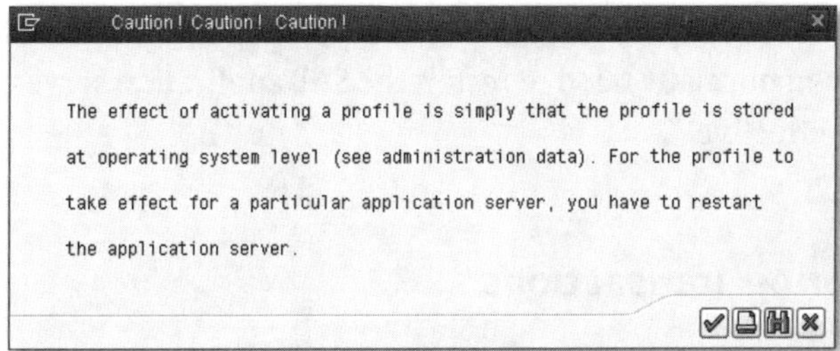

14. The following screen only appears if you've configured operation modes. If it is displayed, click on YES, and examine the check log closely. Then choose BACK (⊙).

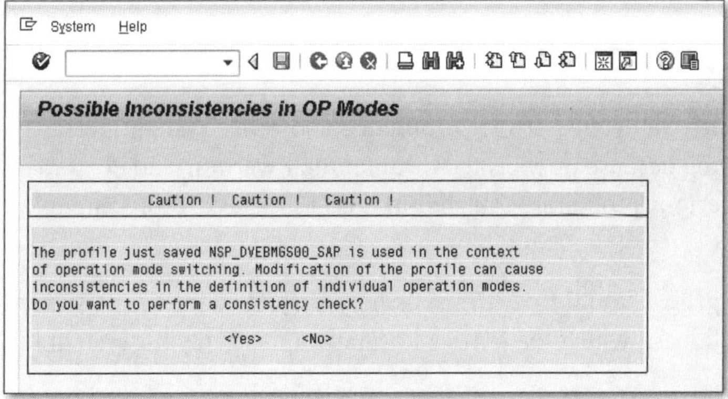

15. The EDIT PROFILES initial screen is displayed. Note that the version number of the profile has now changed.

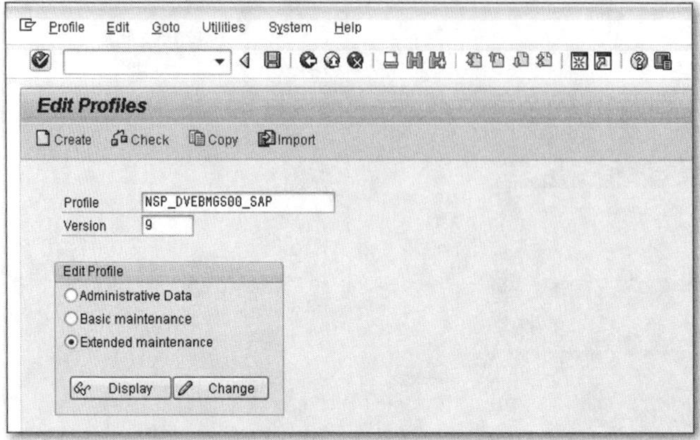

Your change to the parameter file has been saved at the operating system level. When maintaining profiles, you normally need to restart the SAP application server for your changes to become effective.

2.4 Specific Monitoring Transactions

The SAP system provides a range of transactions that you can use to monitor general or very specific system statuses or problems. This section explains how to use the most widely used tools. Additional transactions may be relevant, depending on the type and scope of your SAP system. However, those described here are very important in all systems.

2.4.1 System Log

The system log records all events, errors, problems, and other system messages. This is an important log because unexpected or unfamiliar warning and error messages may indicate serious problems. You should therefore check your system log several times a day.

As your experience grows, you'll find it increasingly easy to monitor the system log. Over time, you'll learn which log entries normally appear in your system log and which are unusual and need to be investigated. To check the system log, follow these steps:

1. Enter Transaction "SM21" in the command field, and press the [Enter] key (or select the menu option: Tools • Administration • Monitor • SM21—System Log).
2. In the From date/time field, enter the start of the period you want to examine.

   You can restrict your selection further if required, for example, to a specific user or transaction.

   Using the Problem classes radio buttons, you can specify whether all messages are to be listed or critical events only. Click on the Reread System Log button.

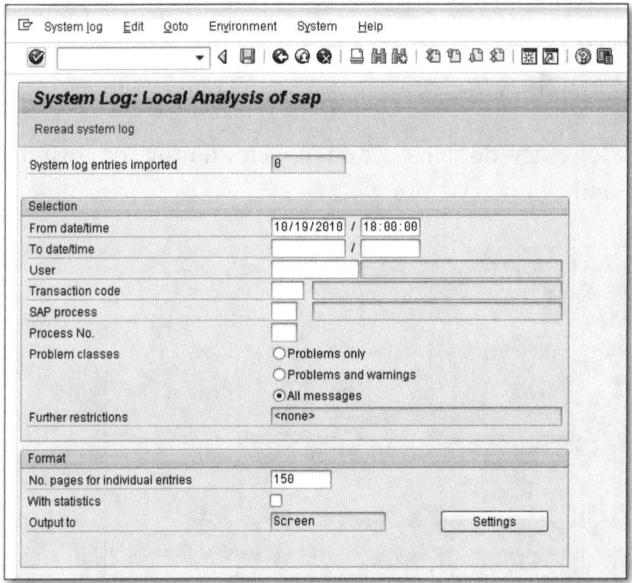

3. A chronological list of logged system events appears. Check the entries for errors or warnings, using the colored icons in the Priority column as a guide.

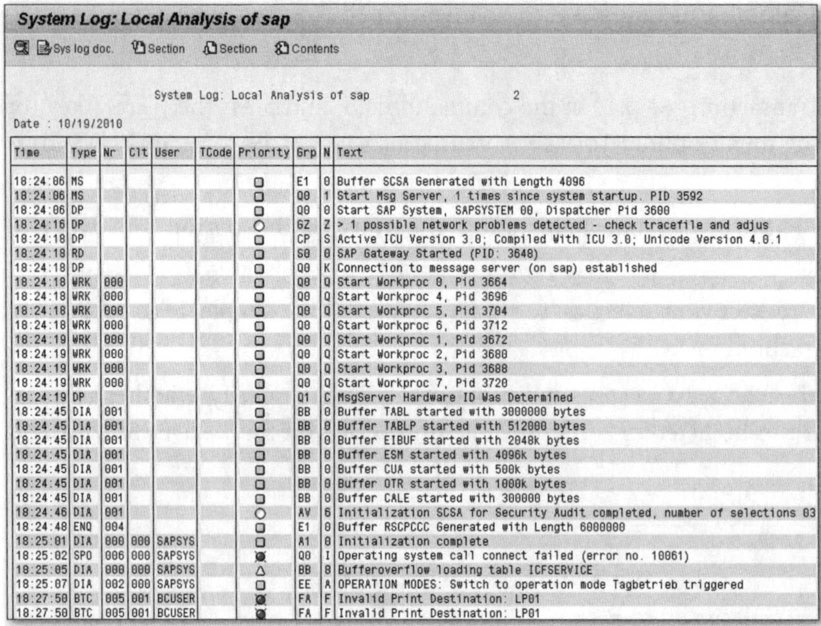

System Log: Local Analysis of sap

Sys log doc. Section Section Contents

System Log: Local Analysis of sap 2

Date : 10/19/2010

Time	Type	Nr	Clt	User	TCode	Priority	Grp	N	Text
18:24:06	MS						E1	0	Buffer SCSA Generated with Length 4096
18:24:06	MS						Q0	1	Start Msg Server, 1 times since system startup. PID 3592
18:24:06	DP						Q0	0	Start SAP System, SAPSYSTEM 00, Dispatcher Pid 3600
18:24:16	DP						GZ	Z	> 1 possible network problems detected - check tracefile and adjus
18:24:18	DP						CP	S	Active ICU Version 3.0; Compiled With ICU 3.0; Unicode Version 4.0.1
18:24:18	RD						S0	0	SAP Gateway Started (PID: 3648)
18:24:18	DP						Q0	K	Connection to message server (on sap) established
18:24:18	WRK	000					Q0	Q	Start Workproc 0, Pid 3664
18:24:18	WRK	000					Q0	Q	Start Workproc 4, Pid 3696
18:24:18	WRK	000					Q0	Q	Start Workproc 5, Pid 3704
18:24:18	WRK	000					Q0	Q	Start Workproc 6, Pid 3712
18:24:19	WRK	000					Q0	Q	Start Workproc 1, Pid 3672
18:24:19	WRK	000					Q0	Q	Start Workproc 2, Pid 3680
18:24:19	WRK	000					Q0	Q	Start Workproc 3, Pid 3688
18:24:19	WRK	000					Q0	Q	Start Workproc 7, Pid 3720
18:24:19	DP						Q1	C	MsgServer Hardware ID Was Determined
18:24:45	DIA	001					BB	0	Buffer TABL started with 3000000 bytes
18:24:45	DIA	001					BB	0	Buffer TABLP started with 512000 bytes
18:24:45	DIA	001					BB	0	Buffer EIBUF started with 2048k bytes
18:24:45	DIA	001					BB	0	Buffer ESM started with 4096k bytes
18:24:45	DIA	001					BB	0	Buffer CUA started with 500k bytes
18:24:45	DIA	001					BB	0	Buffer OTR started with 1000k bytes
18:24:45	DIA	001					BB	0	Buffer CALE started with 300000 bytes
18:24:46	DIA	001					AV	6	Initialization SCSA for Security Audit completed, number of selections 03
18:24:48	ENQ	004					E1	0	Buffer RSCPCCC Generated with Length 6000000
18:25:01	DIA	000	000	SAPSYS			A1	0	Initialization complete
18:25:02	SPO	006	000	SAPSYS			Q0	I	Operating system call connect failed (error no. 10061)
18:25:05	DIA	000	000	SAPSYS			BB	8	Bufferoverflow loading table ICFSERVICE
18:25:07	DIA	002	000	SAPSYS			EE	A	OPERATION MODES: Switch to operation mode Tagbetrieb triggered
18:27:50	BTC	005	001	BCUSER			FA	F	Invalid Print Destination: LP01
18:27:50	BTC	005	001	BCUSER			FA	F	Invalid Print Destination: LP01

4. To display the details of a log entry, double-click on the relevant row, or position your cursor on the row, and choose DETAILS (icon).

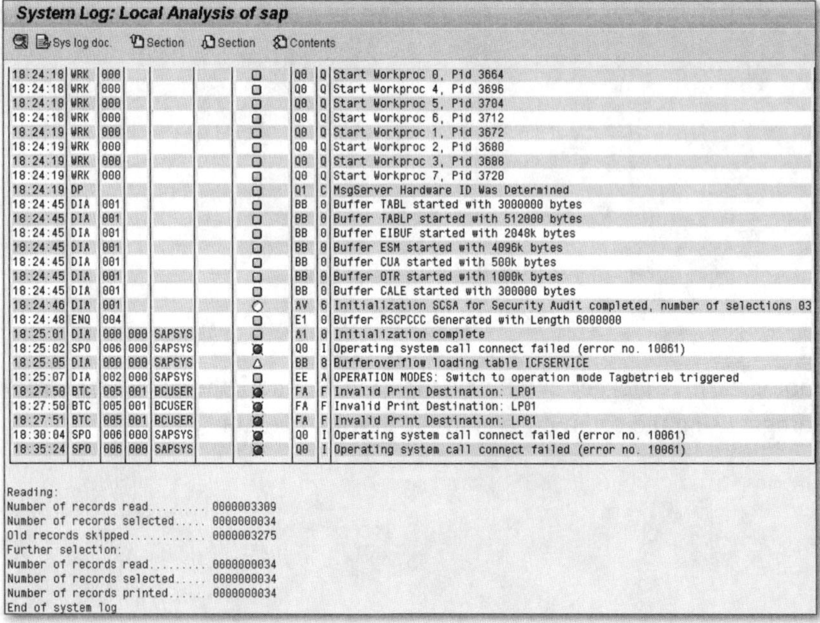

System Log: Local Analysis of sap

Sys log doc. Section Section Contents

Time	Type	Nr	Clt	User	TCode	Priority	Grp	N	Text
18:24:18	WRK	000					Q0	Q	Start Workproc 0, Pid 3664
18:24:18	WRK	000					Q0	Q	Start Workproc 4, Pid 3696
18:24:18	WRK	000					Q0	Q	Start Workproc 5, Pid 3704
18:24:18	WRK	000					Q0	Q	Start Workproc 6, Pid 3712
18:24:19	WRK	000					Q0	Q	Start Workproc 1, Pid 3672
18:24:19	WRK	000					Q0	Q	Start Workproc 2, Pid 3680
18:24:19	WRK	000					Q0	Q	Start Workproc 3, Pid 3688
18:24:19	WRK	000					Q0	Q	Start Workproc 7, Pid 3720
18:24:19	DP						Q1	C	MsgServer Hardware ID Was Determined
18:24:45	DIA	001					BB	0	Buffer TABL started with 3000000 bytes
18:24:45	DIA	001					BB	0	Buffer TABLP started with 512000 bytes
18:24:45	DIA	001					BB	0	Buffer EIBUF started with 2048k bytes
18:24:45	DIA	001					BB	0	Buffer ESM started with 4096k bytes
18:24:45	DIA	001					BB	0	Buffer CUA started with 500k bytes
18:24:45	DIA	001					BB	0	Buffer OTR started with 1000k bytes
18:24:45	DIA	001					BB	0	Buffer CALE started with 300000 bytes
18:24:46	DIA	001					AV	6	Initialization SCSA for Security Audit completed, number of selections 03
18:24:48	ENQ	004					E1	0	Buffer RSCPCCC Generated with Length 6000000
18:25:01	DIA	000	000	SAPSYS			A1	0	Initialization complete
18:25:02	SPO	006	000	SAPSYS			Q0	I	Operating system call connect failed (error no. 10061)
18:25:05	DIA	000	000	SAPSYS			BB	8	Bufferoverflow loading table ICFSERVICE
18:25:07	DIA	002	000	SAPSYS			EE	A	OPERATION MODES: Switch to operation mode Tagbetrieb triggered
18:27:50	BTC	005	001	BCUSER			FA	F	Invalid Print Destination: LP01
18:27:50	BTC	005	001	BCUSER			FA	F	Invalid Print Destination: LP01
18:27:51	BTC	005	001	BCUSER			FA	F	Invalid Print Destination: LP01
18:30:04	SPO	006	000	SAPSYS			Q0	I	Operating system call connect failed (error no. 10061)
18:35:24	SPO	006	000	SAPSYS			Q0	I	Operating system call connect failed (error no. 10061)

Reading:
Number of records read......... 0000003309
Number of records selected..... 0000000034
Old records skipped............ 0000003275
Further selection:
Number of records read......... 0000000034
Number of records selected..... 0000000034
Number of records printed...... 0000000034
End of system log

5. Check for indications of the cause of the error or the solution to the problem in the detailed information for the log entry. Click on BACK (⊕) to return to the system log.

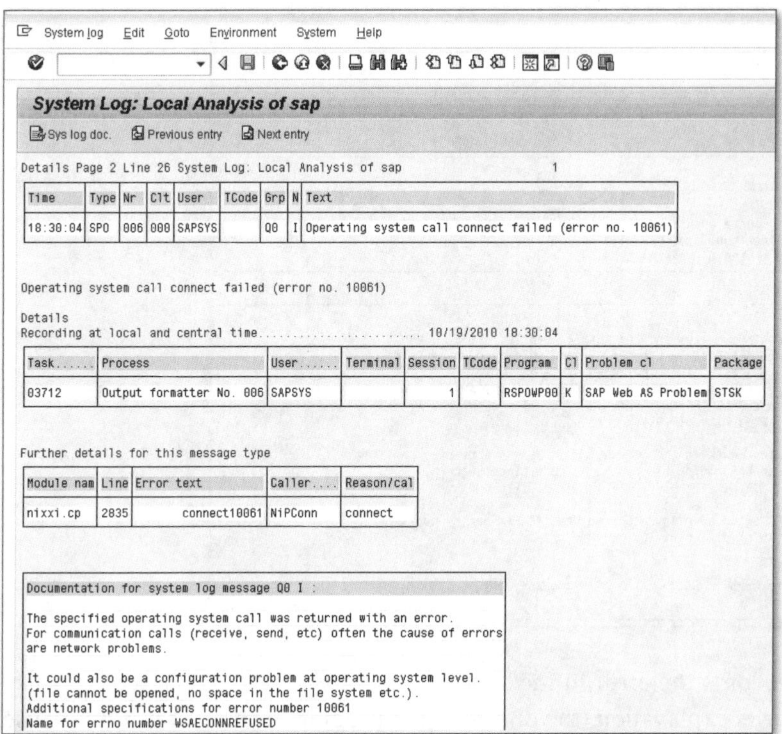
System log Edit Goto Environment System Help

System Log: Local Analysis of sap

Sys log doc. Previous entry Next entry

Details Page 2 Line 26 System Log: Local Analysis of sap 1

Time	Type	Nr	Clt	User	TCode	Grp	N	Text
18:30:04	SPO	006	000	SAPSYS		Q0	I	Operating system call connect failed (error no. 10061)

Operating system call connect failed (error no. 10061)

Details
Recording at local and central time........................ 10/19/2010 18:30:04

Task......	Process	User......	Terminal	Session	TCode	Program	Cl	Problem cl	Package
03712	Output formatter No. 006	SAPSYS		1		RSPOWP00	K	SAP Web AS Problem	STSK

Further details for this message type

Module nam	Line	Error text	Caller....	Reason/cal
nixxi.cp	2835	connect10061	NiPConn	connect

Documentation for system log message Q0 I :

The specified operating system call was returned with an error.
For communication calls (receive, send, etc) often the cause of errors are network problems.

It could also be a configuration problem at operating system level.
(file cannot be opened, no space in the file system etc.).
Additional specifications for error number 10061
Name for errno number WSAECONNREFUSED

You can use the system log to gain a quick overview of recent events at a superficial level and to track error messages. When checking the log, focus on errors (red/pink) and warnings (yellow), as well as any unusual entries. Learning to filter the relevant entries is largely a matter of experience.

2.4.2 ABAP Dump Analysis

An *ABAP dump* (also known as a *short dump*) is a runtime error, which is always generated whenever a report or transaction is terminated due to a serious error. If a short dump occurs in dialog mode, an error message is displayed for the user.

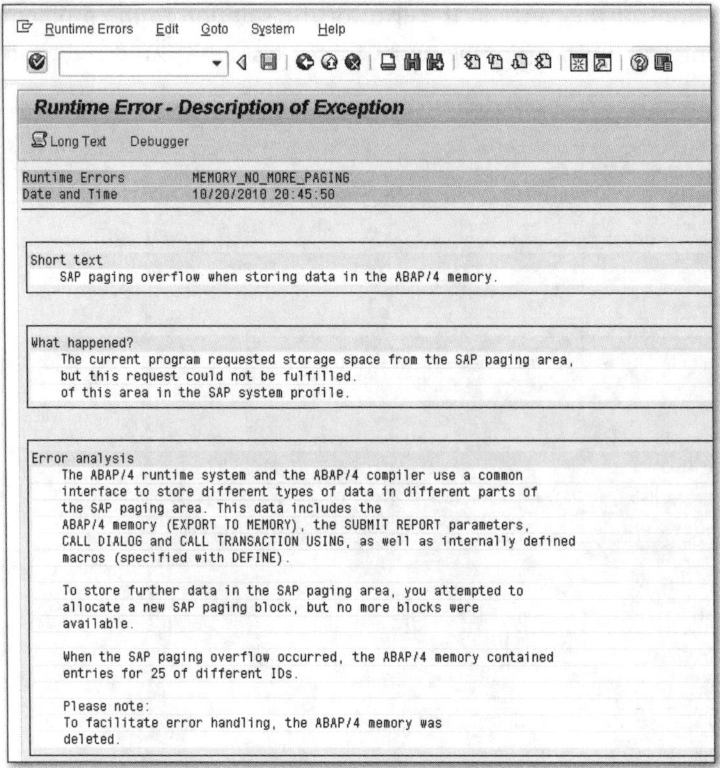

The system records the error in the system log (Transaction SM21), where it also generates a brief explanation (the dump) of the program termination. You can use Transaction ST22 (Dump Analysis) to analyze ABAP dumps in detail and draw conclusions regarding the cause of the error and a possible solution.

1. Enter Transaction "ST22" in the command field, and press the Enter key (or select the menu option: TOOLS • ADMINISTRATION • MONITOR • ST22—DUMP ANALYSIS).
2. You can select the dumps to be displayed in one of the following ways:
   - For a simple selection, select one of the buttons TODAY or YESTERDAY in the STANDARD screen area.
   - To restrict the selection using precise criteria, enter the relevant parameters in the OWN SELECTION area, and click on START.

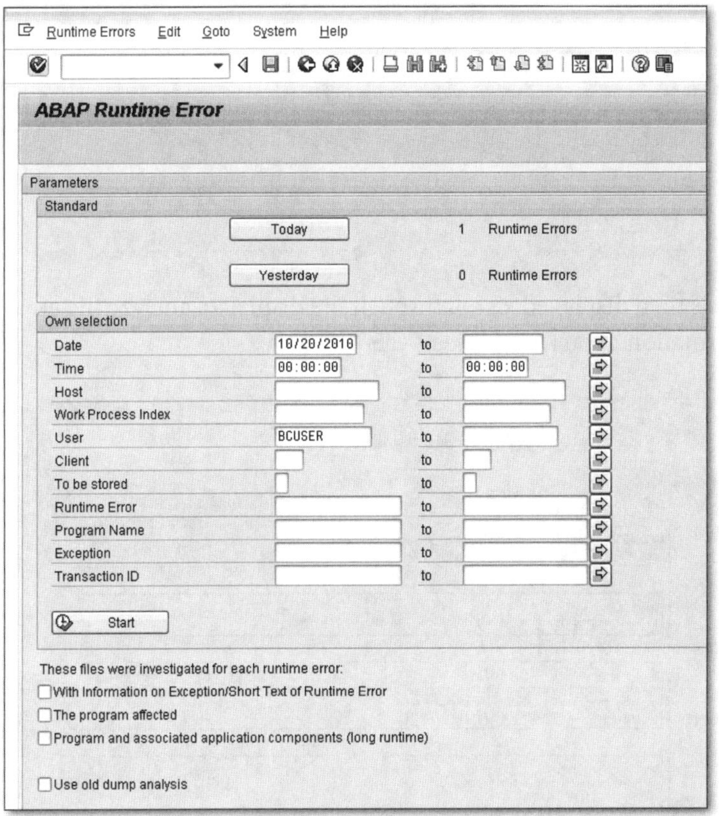

Initial Screen for Runtime Error Analysis [!]

The number of runtime errors displayed on the initial screen of Transaction ST22 when you click the TODAY or YESTERDAY buttons provides a rough indication of system status. If a large number of short dumps have been recorded, there may be a general problem with the system, which is affecting a large number of users. In this case, a quick response is essential. If the number of short dumps is small, the system obviously has a more or less stable status.

Check the recorded ABAP runtime errors at regular intervals several times a day.

3. A list of the runtime errors that have occurred is displayed. Double-click on a dump to analyze it.

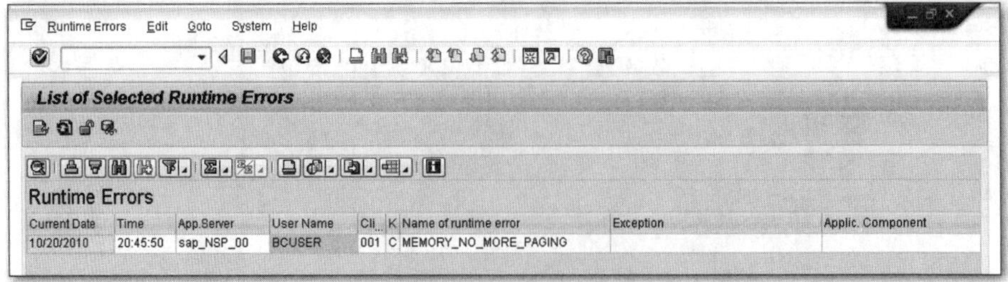

4. The short dump is then displayed. Scroll through the display to analyze the error and obtain information about the cause of the problem.

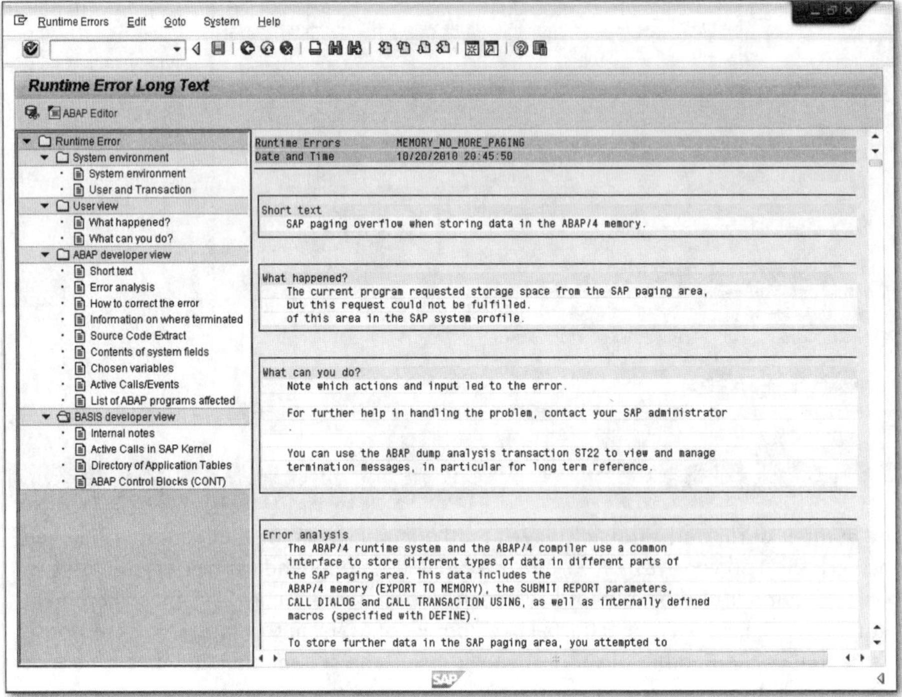

5. If you come to a dead end in your analysis and need to ask SAP Support for assistance, it's useful to save the short dump as a file and attach it to a problem notification, for example. To do this, select the menu option SYSTEM • LIST • SAVE • LOCAL FILE in the long text of the runtime error, and save the short dump to your PC.

[+]

Scope of Runtime Errors

The term *short dump* doesn't reflect the length of the explanation of the runtime error that is provided. ABAP short dumps may, in fact, run to several dozen pages. The reason for this is that, when a runtime error occurs, the log records very detailed information about the system status and the cause of the error. It is recommended that you save important dumps locally, and only print out the section of the long text that you actually need.

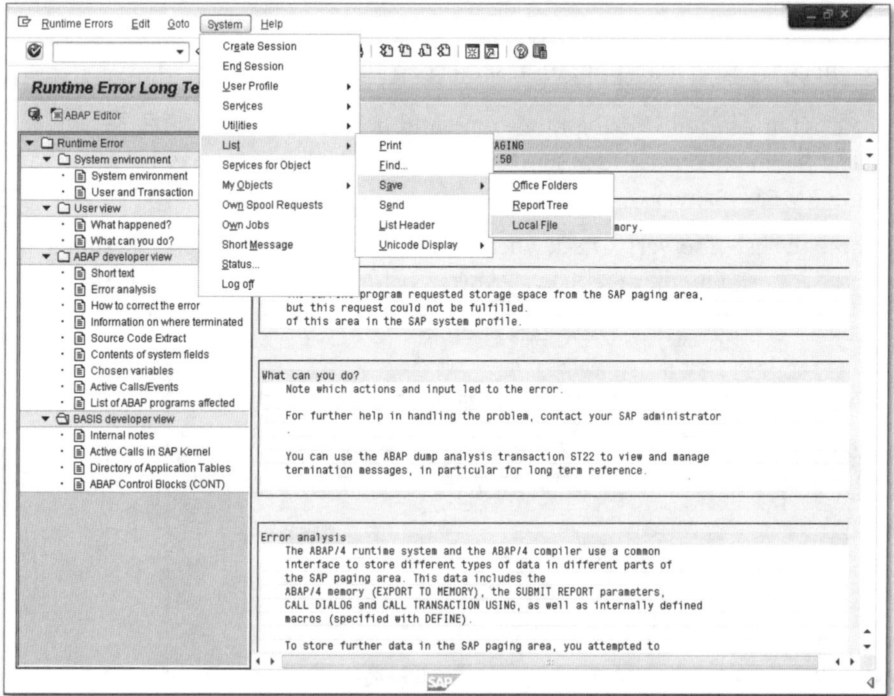

2.4.3 Checking the Application Servers and Work Processes

During system operation, you can use Transactions SM50 and SM51 to monitor the application servers and work processes in your SAP system. This monitoring function is important for the following reasons:

- When a dialog application server is inactive, users who normally log on to this server are unable to log on.

- When the batch application server is inactive, batch jobs that have been scheduled for this server cannot be executed.
- When all work processes are occupied, no further tasks can be processed. This situation may arise if too many users are logged on, too many background jobs are running in parallel, or if a posting problem occurs.

In the event of problems like these, you can use Transactions SM50 and SM51 to determine whether an application server is inactive or whether all work processes are occupied.

First, check whether the application servers are active:

1. Enter Transaction "SM51" in the command field, and press the [Enter] key (or select the menu option TOOLS • ADMINISTRATION • MONITOR • SYSTEM MONITORING • SM51—SERVERS).
2. Check the list of servers. Check whether the list contains all servers that should be active. Check whether the SERVER STATUS column contains the entry ACTIVE.

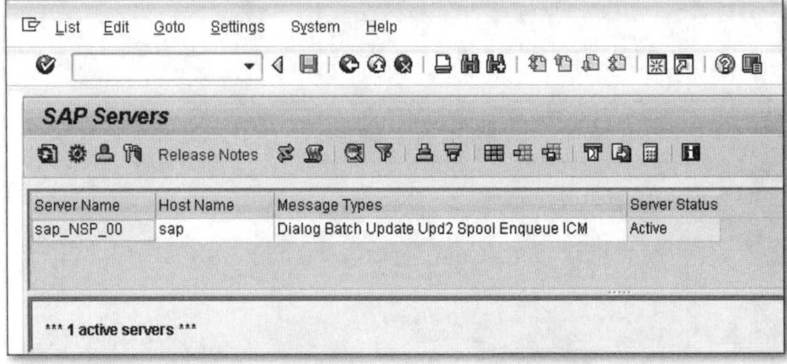

If all applications are displayed as active, you can begin checking the work processes:

1. Enter Transaction "SM50" in the command field, and press the [Enter] key (or select the menu option TOOLS • ADMINISTRATION • MONITOR • SYSTEM MONITORING • SM50—PROCESS OVERVIEW).
2. Check the statuses of the individual work processes. Processes that have the status WAITING are available, while processes with the status RUNNING are currently

occupied by the system. The ACTION column provides details about the processes that are currently running.

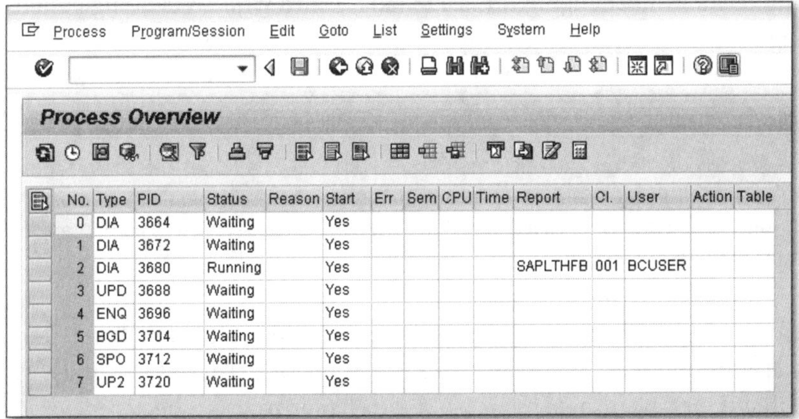

No.	Type	PID	Status	Reason	Start	Err	Sem	CPU	Time	Report	Cl.	User	Action	Table
0	DIA	3664	Waiting		Yes									
1	DIA	3672	Waiting		Yes									
2	DIA	3680	Running		Yes					SAPLTHFB	001	BCUSER		
3	UPD	3688	Waiting		Yes									
4	ENQ	3696	Waiting		Yes									
5	BGD	3704	Waiting		Yes									
6	SPO	3712	Waiting		Yes									
7	UP2	3720	Waiting		Yes									

Checking Processes [+]

When checking the process overview, focus on the following information provided:

- Dialog work processes (DIA) with high TIME values may point to a problem or to a step in a background process that is taking a long time to execute and that start a dialog process.
- If STOPPED is shown in the STATUS column for a work process, this may also indicate a problem because this process may have failed or been interrupted.

In certain cases, you may need to cancel processes manually to eliminate a blockage in the system.

Cancelling Processes Manually [+]

If necessary, you can select the menu option PROCESS • CANCEL WITH/WITHOUT CORE to make system resources available.

This procedure is described in connection with performance problems in Chapter 11.

The application server overview and process overview provide you with a quick initial impression of the system status. Using this approach, you may be able to detect, even at this early stage, any indications of system instability or insufficient hardware resources.

2.4.4 Lock Entries

A data record is locked by the system while it is being edited by a user. This lock prevents other users from changing this same data record while it is being edited. The following example illustrates the importance of this function.

Example: The Advantage of Using Locks

You're in the process of changing a customer's postal address, while, at the same time, another user is changing the telephone number for this same customer. You save your change first, followed by the other user. The other user's change overwrites your change and, as a result, your entry is lost.

Sometimes, an old lock still exists in the system, for example, after a system failure or after a user abruptly loses a connection to the network. These locks must be removed so that the relevant data record and the change to it can be accessed.

Check the log entries regularly, paying particular attention to older lock entries (entries that are more than a day old). However, a user may inform you of a lock, and you may discover that the user responsible for triggering the lock is no longer logged on to the system.

1. Enter Transaction "SM12" in the command field, and press the [Enter] key (or select the menu option: Tools • Administration • Monitor • SM12—Lock Entries).
2. If you only want to analyze lock entries in general, clear all fields. To restrict the selection, enter the relevant parameters in the fields provided. Click the List button.

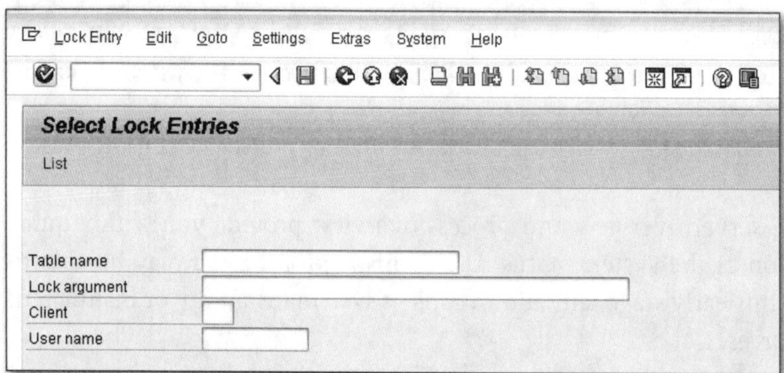

3. Check the lock entries. Pay particular attention to any locks from the previous day that appear in the Time column. A lock dating from the previous day suggests that the user may have lost his connection to the network and the SAP system.

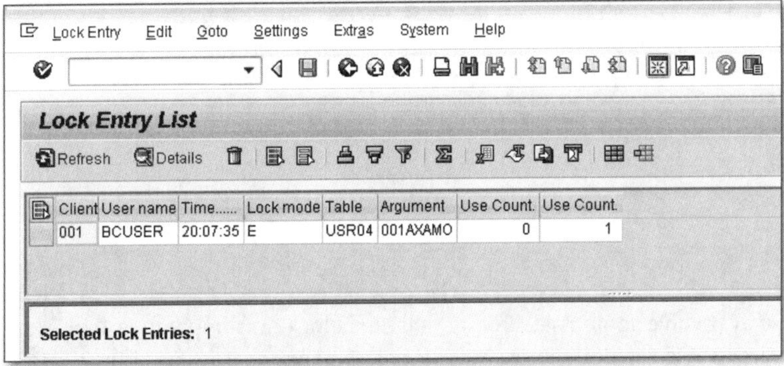

4. Double-click on a lock entry, or choose Details. Details of the selected lock are displayed. Choose Continue (✔) to return to the list view.

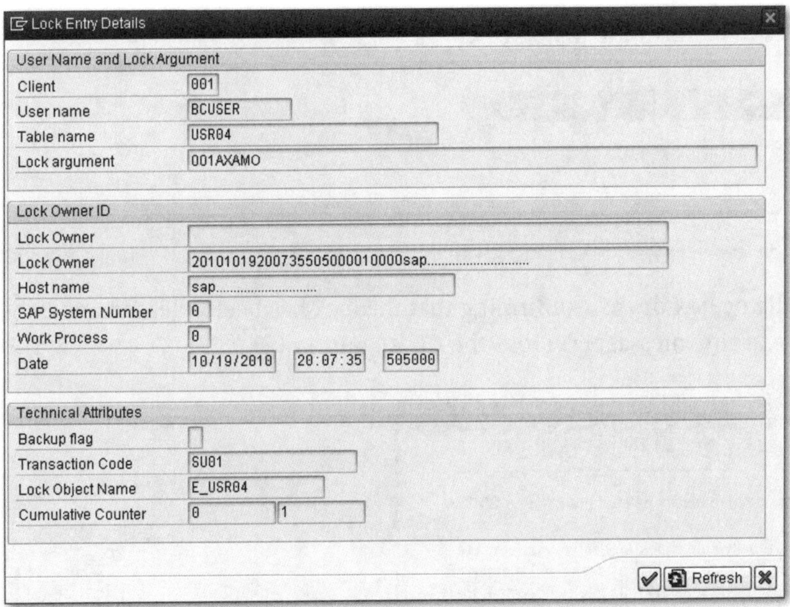

5. To release a lock, select it in the list display, and click on Delete (🗑).

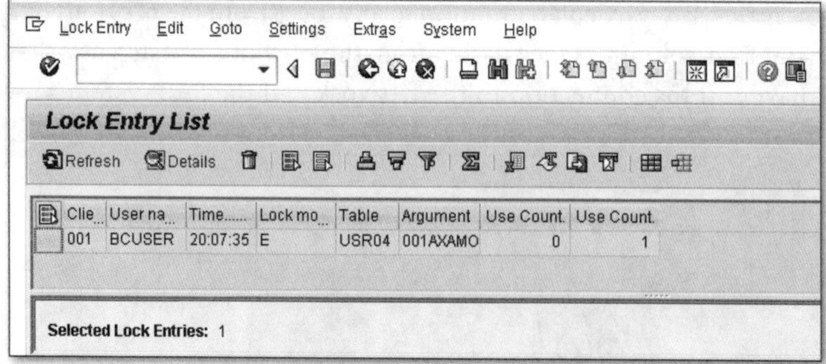

[!]

Deleting Locks

Deleting a lock may involve some risks. Before deleting a lock, it is imperative that you check whether the lock is currently in use. If you delete a lock that is currently in use, you risk damaging the database.

No further steps should be executed until you're certain that the user ID specified in the lock entry is no longer active in the system.

6. Choose YES to confirm the dialog box.

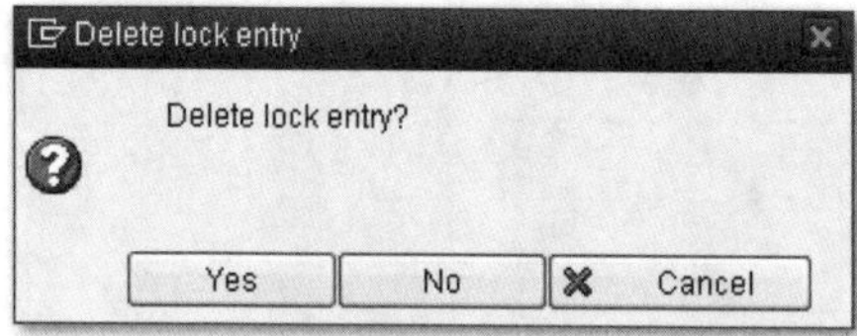

7. Another dialog box opens, confirming that the lock has been released and containing a warning message. Choose the CLOSE button (☒).

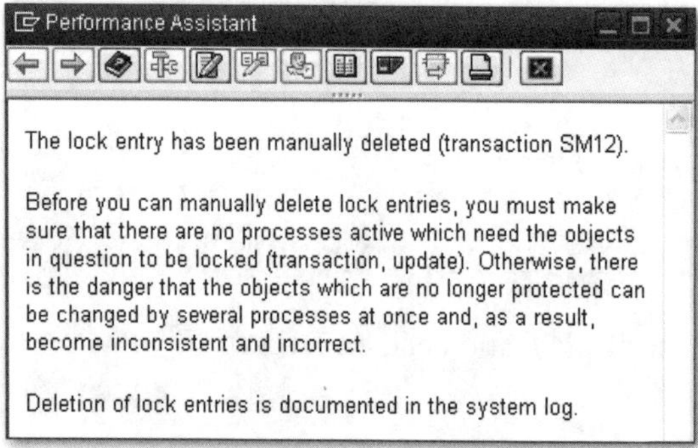

Deleting a lock is critical, so it should not be done lightly or without due consideration. Before you delete a lock, you should clarify and answer the following questions (see Table 2.2).

Task	Transaction Code for This Task
Is the relevant user logged on to a server?	Transaction SM04 (User List) or AL08 (User List—All Instances) If the user is not logged on to the system but is displayed in Transaction SM04 or AL08, delete the user session (see Chapter 13). In some cases, this step is sufficient to remove the lock.
Are any processes running under the user ID?	Transaction SM50 (Process Overview) Even if the user is not logged on to the system, processes may still be active under the user ID. Wait until there are no longer any active processes under the user ID or, in case of an emergency, cancel the process.
Are any background jobs running under the user ID?	Transaction SM37 (Job Monitor) Check whether any background job is active for the relevant user ID. Wait until the job is finished or, in case of an emergency, cancel it.
Are update records currently being processed for this user ID?	Transaction SM13 (Update Requests) The data records will remain locked until the update has been completed in the database. Wait until all update requests have been processed. In some cases, there may be a problem, which you must eliminate first.

Table 2.2 Things to Check Before Deleting a Lock

[!]

Take Care When Deleting Locks

Check the user ID again before deleting the lock. You may damage the database by deleting the wrong lock. Delete locks in sequence.

Never use the DELETE ALL option. This option deletes all locks, not just those you have selected.

2.4.5 Canceled Update Requests

The SAP system sends update requests to the database so that data changes are saved there permanently. In certain cases, an update request may fail, and the update may be canceled.

[Ex]

Example: The Update Concept

The following example explains the update concept:

- An accountant hands a file to a clerical assistant. This is the equivalent of saving a transaction in the system.
- The clerical assistant issues the accountant with an acknowledgement of receipt. This equates to the creation of an SAP document number.
- On the way to the filing cabinet, the clerical assistant stumbles and is injured. As a result, the file is not filed in the filing cabinet. We can compare this incident with an update error.
- The result: The file is *not* in the filing cabinet, even though the accountant has received an acknowledgement. The same thing happens in an SAP update environment. The document is not in the SAP system, even though the user has been given a document number for it.

When users receive a document number, they assume that the corresponding entry has been successfully entered in the system. However, if the update record is canceled, the entry doesn't exist in the system, even though the user has a document number for it.

You should therefore check the system for canceled update records several times a day. In global systems, you should adjust the times at which you search for canceled update records in accordance with the various time zones. Employees located within the relevant time zone should also be involved in this check.

[⚙]

Asynchronous Updates

To enhance performance, changes to the database are made in asynchronous mode. In this mode, the user continues working while the system takes charge of the update process, and then waits until the database change has been completed.

In synchronous mode, users must wait until the database has been successfully changed before continuing with their work.

The more time that elapses between the cancellation of the update and your detection of it, the more difficult it is for users to remember exactly what they were doing when the update record was canceled. If you act quickly, you can also reduce the frequency with which update records are canceled.

1. Enter Transaction "SM13" in the command field, and press the [Enter] key (or select the menu option: Tools • Administration • Monitor • SM13—Update).

2. Complete the selection fields:
   - Enter the placeholder "*" in the CLIENT field.
   - Enter the placeholder "*" in the USER field.
   - Under STATUS, select the entry ALL.
   - Leave the FROM DATE field blank, or enter a date in the distant past.
   - When you've finished, choose EXECUTE (⊕).

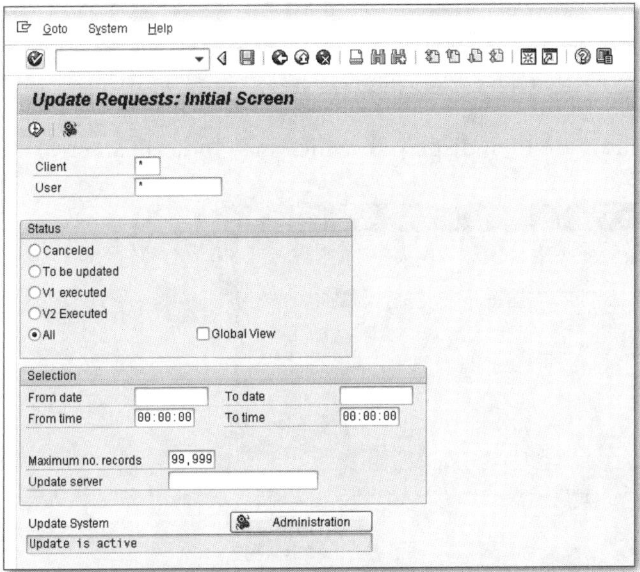

3. Search the STATUS column for entries with the status ERROR. This status indicates a terminated update record. If you find no canceled update records, your task ends here. You can double-click on an entry to display its details.

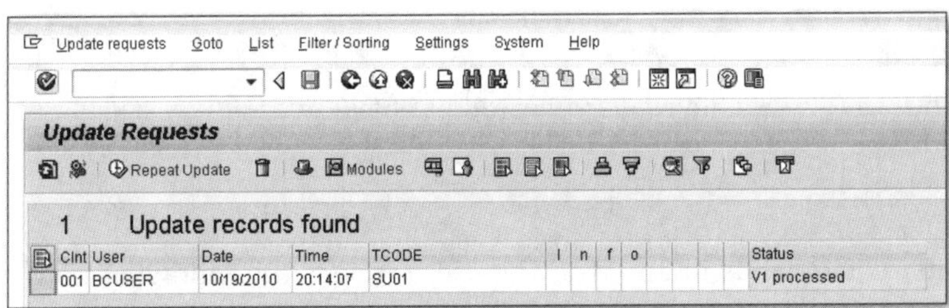

4. The UPDATE MODULES screen provides details of the user, transaction, and function that is to be updated. Click on the ERROR INFORMATION BUTTON ( ).

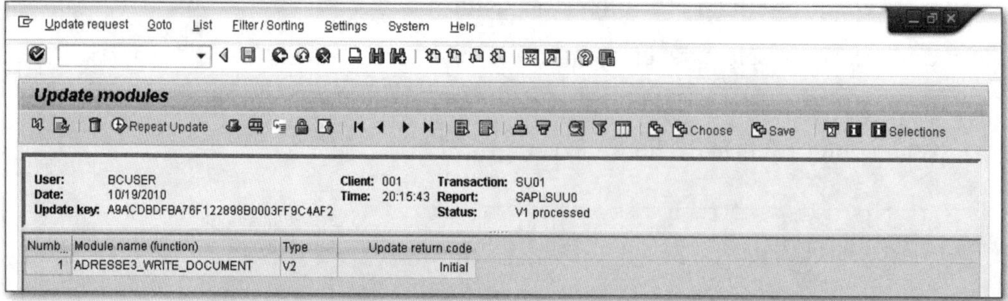

5. Details of the update status are then displayed, which may indicate an error.

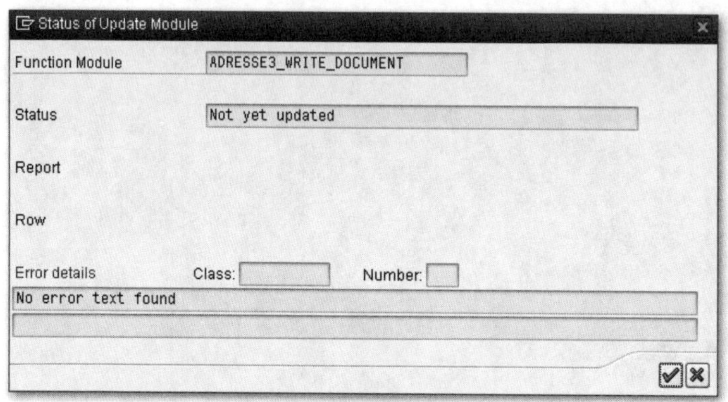

If you detect the occurrence of update errors, you must then notify the affected users. These users should search for missing entries and re-enter the data records that have not been updated.

[!]

Reposting Canceled Update Records

Don't try to update a canceled update record again! In certain cases, this may damage the database. Instead, you should always ask the users to execute the failed transaction again.

When an update request ends in an error, the user receives the following notification: EXPRESS DOCUMENT RECEIVED. SAP uses express messages to notify users immediately of canceled update records. It is therefore easiest for the user to repair the damage as soon as the problem occurs. The user should stop working immediately and ask for help with pinpointing the problem. Users should be made aware of this procedure as part of training.

[⚙]

Administration of the Update System

In certain, exceptional cases, it is recommended that you deactivate the update system. For example, it may not be possible to save data following a serious database error. As a result, the update requests that cannot be executed begin to accumulate.

In *Update Program Administration* (Transaction SM14), you can deactivate updates in the SAP system as a whole. If you do this, update requests are no longer sent to the database, and the error can be eliminated without any further interruptions.

While the update system is deactivated, the following information is displayed to users in the status bar: UPDATE DELAYED. PLEASE WAIT. The work process stops and remains blocked until the update function is reactivated. Data can be sent to the database after the update system has been reactivated.

2.5 System Messages

A system message is a dialog box that is displayed for all users. System messages are useful for making information available to all users (for example, if you need to carry out unplanned system maintenance). After a new message is created, this dialog box is displayed at each logon and each time a user executes an action (for example, pressing a button). To create a system message, follow these steps:

1. Enter Transaction "SM02" in the command field, and press the [Enter] key (or select the option TOOLS • ADMINISTRATION • ADMINISTRATION • SM02—SYSTEM MESSAGES in the SAP standard menu).
2. On the SYSTEM MESSAGES screen, click on the CREATE button (🗋).

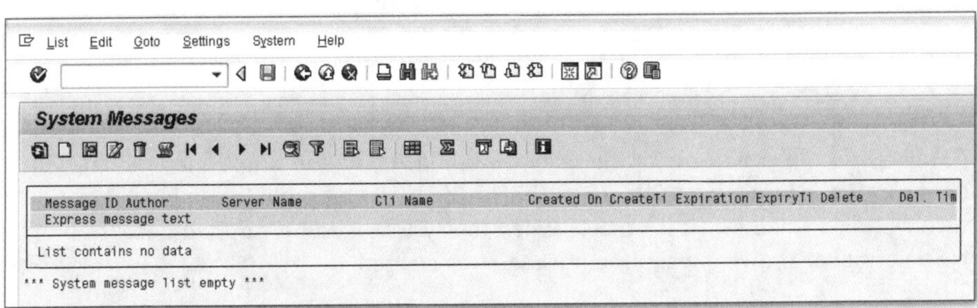

3. The CREATE SYSTEM MESSAGES dialog box opens.
   - Enter the text of your message under SYSTEM MESSAGE TEXT.
   - If you only want the message to apply to a specific application server (for example, because you only need to shut down one server), you can specify this server in the SERVER field.
   - If the message is only relevant for users of a specific client (for example, because postings are locked in that client due to the year-end closing), you can specify this client in the CLIENT field.
   - The LANG. (language) field allows you to restrict your message to a single logon language. In international enterprises, you can define a translated system message for each logon language.
   - In the EXPIRES ON field, enter the date and time as of which you no longer want the message to be displayed.
   - In the DELETE ON field, enter the date and time at which you want the message to be permanently deleted.
   - Choose SAVE (✔).

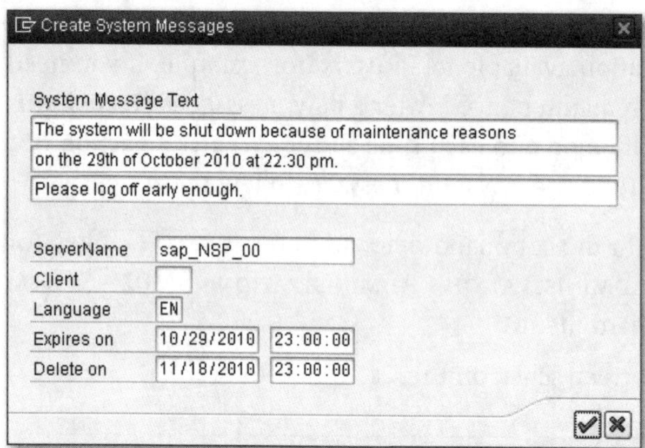

[+] **Specifying Exact Times in System Messages**

Always enter the exact time of the system stop, including the time zone and date (for example, Wednesday, June 9th, 2010, 22:30 CEST). If you provide vague information such as "in 15 minutes," it isn't clear when the system is to be stopped because users have no way of knowing when the message was created.

4. A message in the status bar indicates that the system message has been saved.

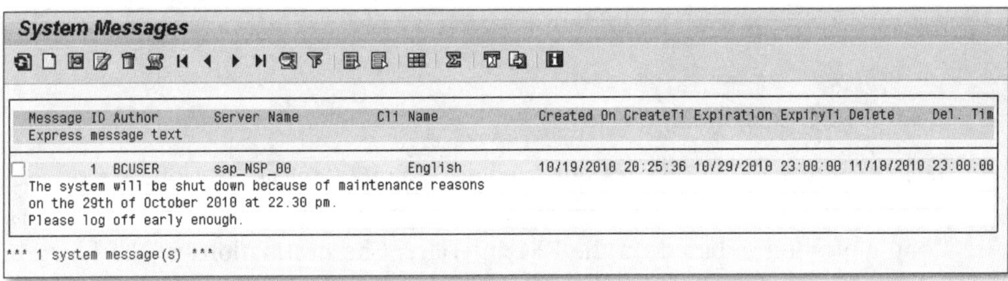

5. The message will then be displayed in a dialog box whenever a user logs on to the SAP system or whenever a user who is already logged on executes an action.

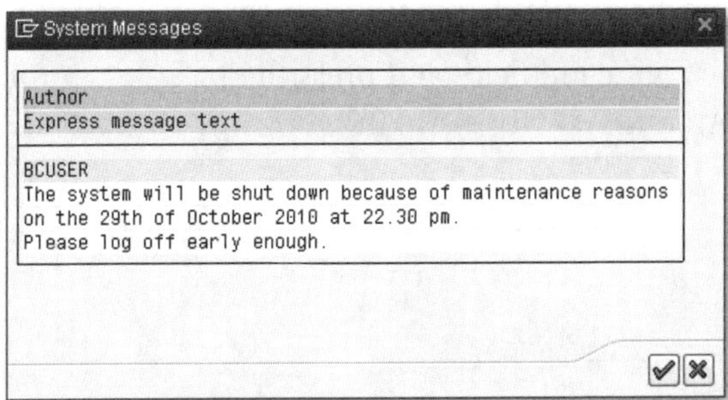

Using System Messages [+]

Use system messages with caution. Users may feel that automatically displayed dialog boxes interfere with their work.

Note also that, whenever you make a change to a system message, it will be displayed again for all users.

2.6 Connections

The SAP system offers a range of interfaces with other systems. Various standard logs can be used for communication purposes. You, as the SAP administrator, are responsible for configuring and monitoring these connections, and for correcting any errors that occur.

This section describes the various forms that communication with external systems may take and presents the tools that can be used for monitoring and administering these connections.

2.6.1 RFC Destinations

Remote Function Calls (RFCs) can be used, for example, to call ABAP function modules in remote SAP systems, which then trigger a transaction in those systems. Communication is based on the RFC interface. The destinations of the function call (for example, a server, system, client, and so on) are defined in *RFC destinations* (or *RFC connections*).

It is essential for you to know how to create and maintain these destinations because RFC connections need to be used relatively frequently in the ABAP environment.

1. Enter Transaction "SM59" in the command field, and press the Enter key (or select the menu option TOOLS • ADMINISTRATION • ADMINISTRATION • NETWORK • SM59—RFC DESTINATIONS).
2. On the CONFIGURATION OF RFC CONNECTIONS screen, select the ABAP CONNECTIONS folder under RFC CONNECTIONS.

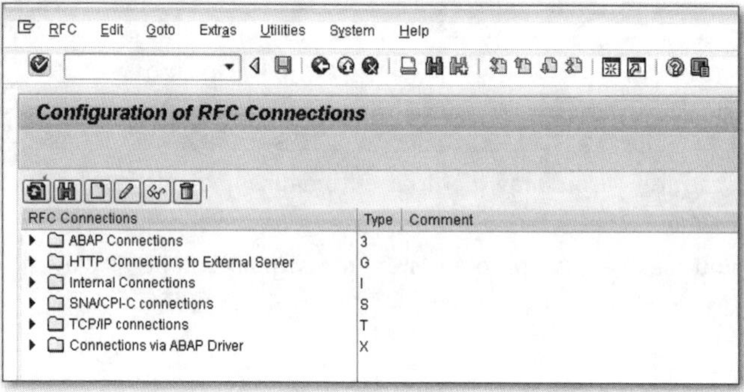

3. The existing RFC connections are displayed. Double-click on any destination you want to display. To set up a new connection, choose CREATE (🗋).

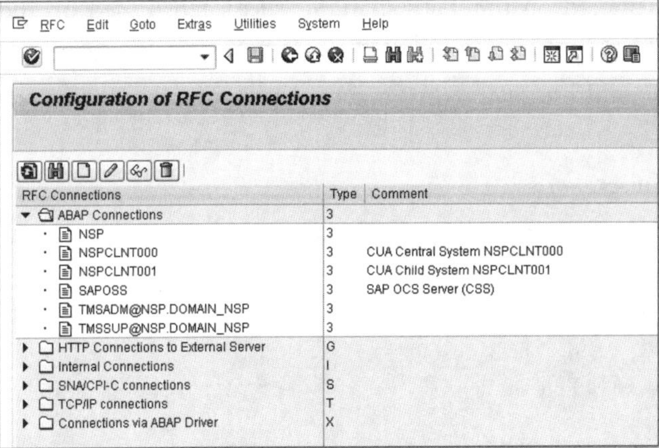

4. Enter the following details:
   - Enter a name under RFC DESTINATION.
   - Select a CONNECTION TYPE, for example, type "3" for a new ABAP connection.
   - Enter explanatory texts in the DESCRIPTION fields.
   - Press the Enter key.

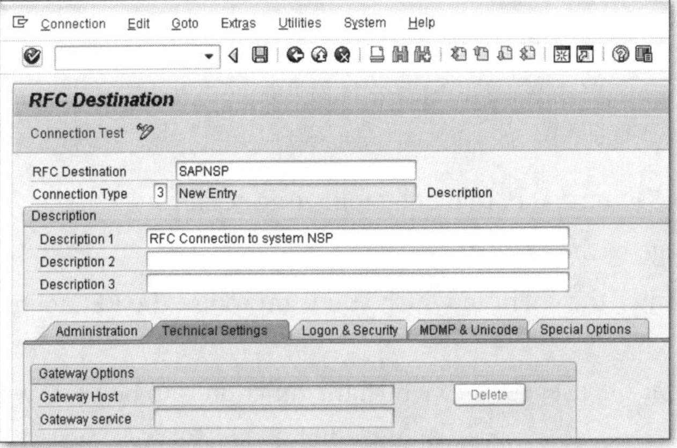

5. New input fields are provided on the TECHNICAL SETTINGS tab, based on the connection type you selected. Enter the following data here:
   - Enter the name or IP address of the SAP server that is to be called in the TARGET HOST field.
   - Enter the system number.

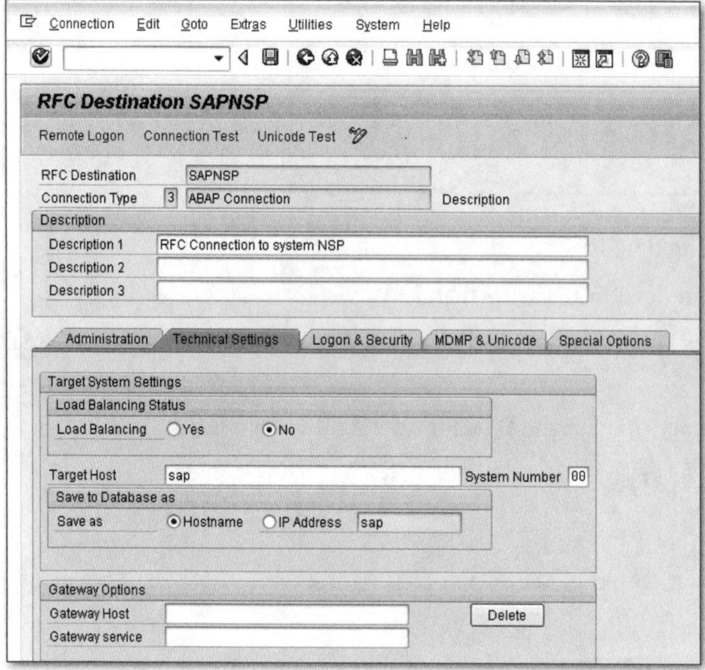

6. Switch to the LOGON & SECURITY tab. Make the following settings:
   - Enter a logon language in the LANGUAGE field.
   - In the CLIENT field, enter the client in which you want to use the RFC logon function.
   - In the USER field, enter the user ID with which the function is to be executed in the target system.
   - Enter the password of the user in the target system.

Press the Enter key.

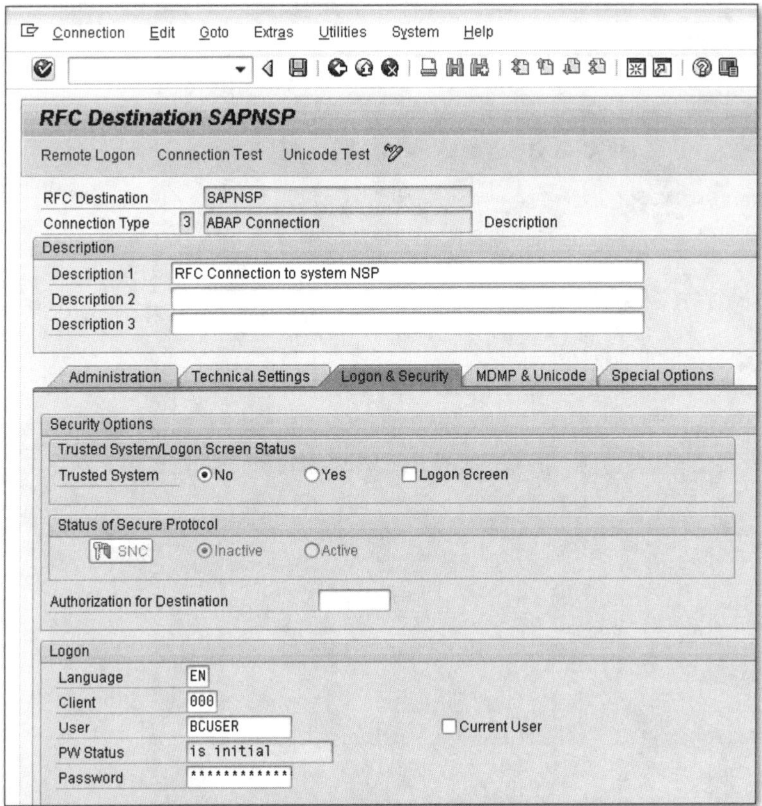

7. Choose CONTINUE to confirm the dialog box (✔).

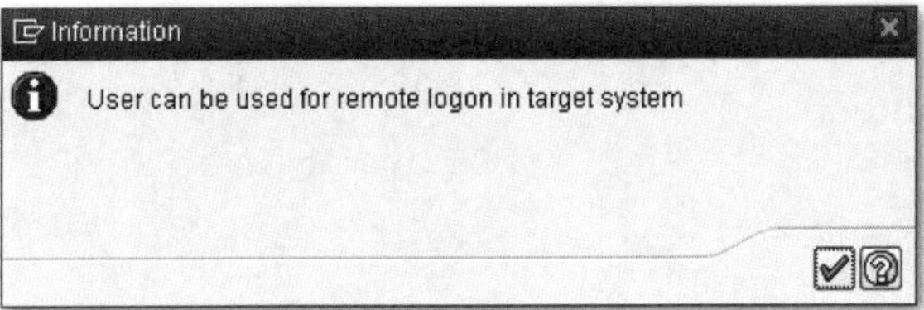

8. The RFC Destination SAPNSP view is displayed again. Here you can see that your entries have been copied into the Logon field group.

   Choose Save (💾).

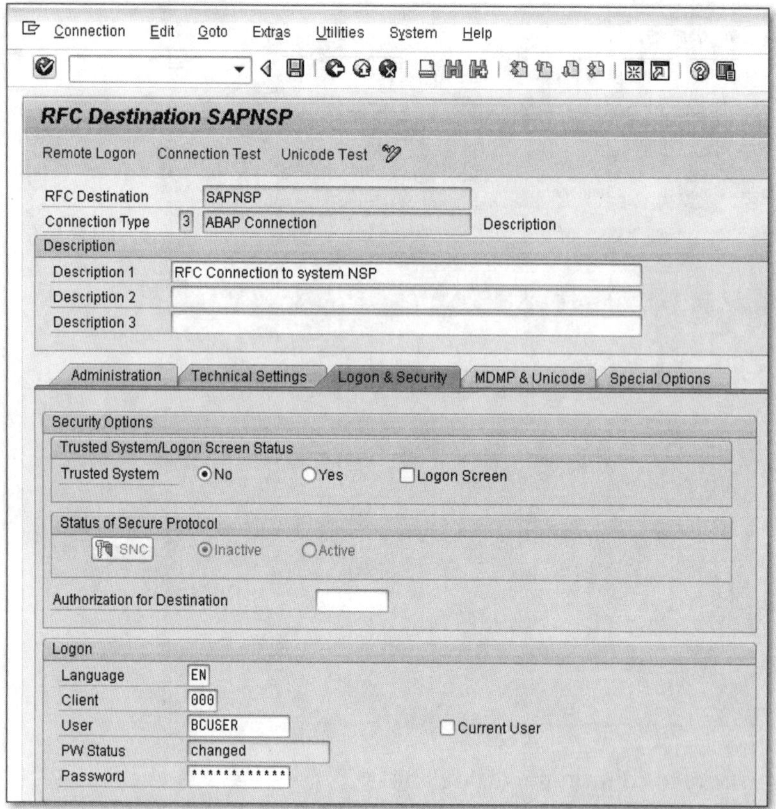

9. A message in the status bar confirms that your RFC connection has been saved. Click the Connection test button.

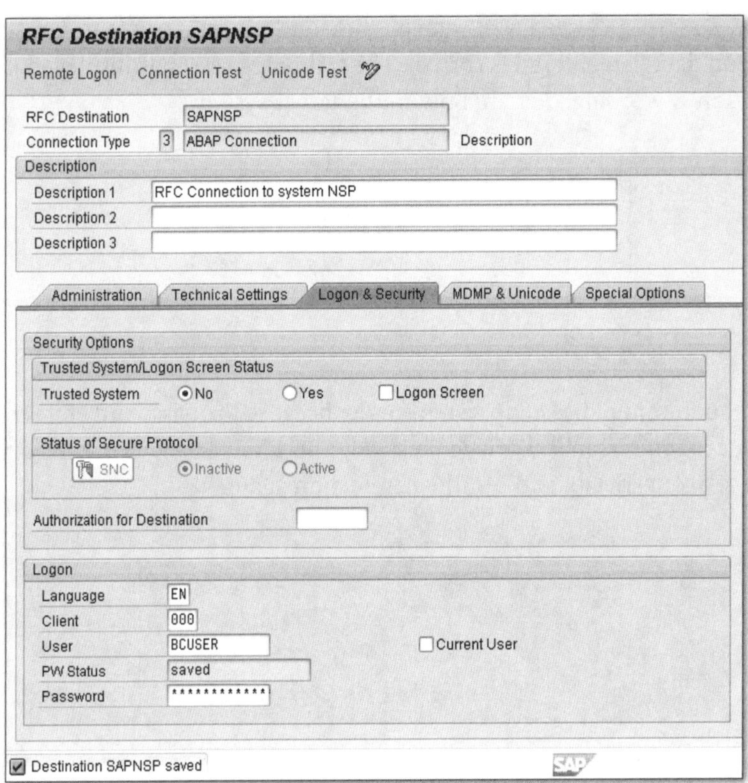

10. The system now attempts to reach the remote server in the network using the ping command. If this test is successful, a connection can be set up at TCP/IP level. Choose Back ().

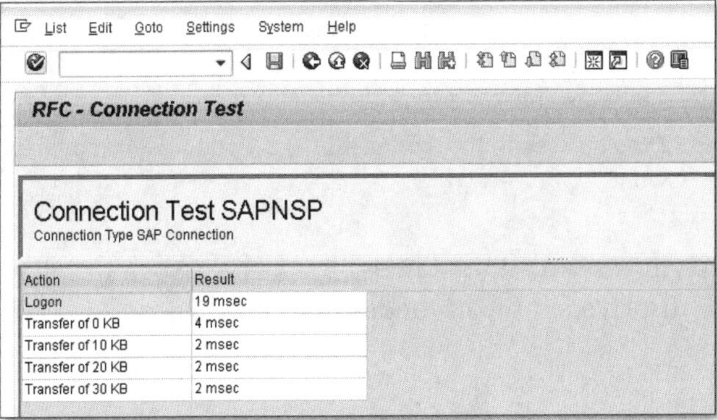

11. On the RFC DESTINATION SAPNSP screen, click on REMOTE LOGON to verify that the logon data you entered is correct. The following screen is displayed if the connection is working. You are now in the target system.

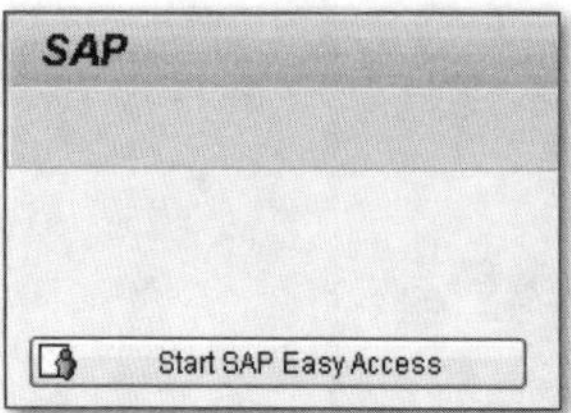

12. If the connection cannot be set up, for example, because the password entered is incorrect, a logon screen is displayed instead. Check the data you entered on the LOGON & SECURITY tab, and test the connection again.

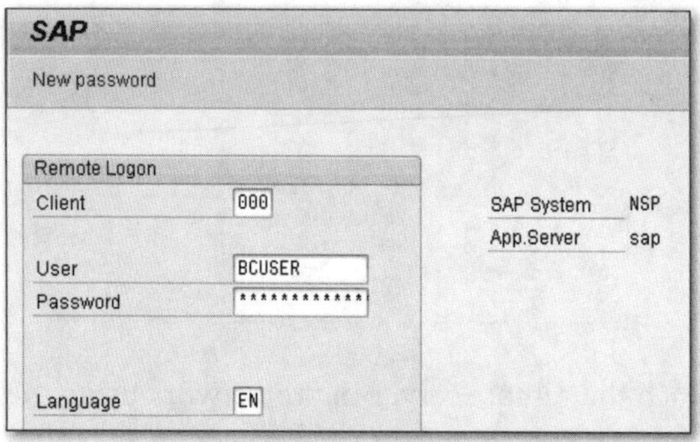

[!]

Testing RFC Connections via Remote Logon

If nothing happens when a remote logon is attempted, this means that the connection is working and that the logon was successful. This may happen, for example, if you entered a user of the "Communication" type for the RFC logon.

You only need to check the data you entered for the connection if a logon screen appears, prompting you to enter a password.

13. The RFC connection has now been set up. Choose BACK (⊙) to exit the view. The new connection is displayed in the list of destinations.

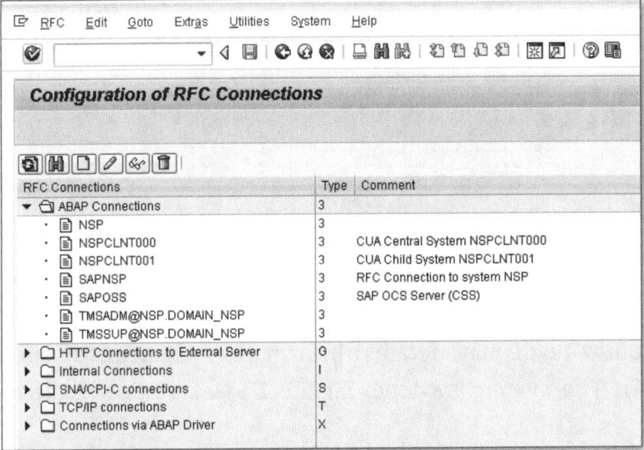

RFC connections not only allow you to call ABAP function modules in other SAP systems but also to start programs in non-SAP systems. These connections have many and varied applications.

[+]

Testing RFC Connections

If errors occur with RFC connections, perform a connection test as described earlier before attempting a remote logon. In most cases, the server you are calling can't be reached due to problems with the network or because incorrect logon data was entered for the connection. For example, an RFC connection can't be set up if the user entered is locked in the target system, has been deleted, or has changed his password.

2.6.2 SAP Gateway Monitor

The SAP Gateway is used to create connections between external systems and programs that use the TCP/IP protocol. In the SAP environment, this category includes all RFC connections, for example. The Gateway Monitor (Transaction SMGW) is used for monitoring, analysis, and administration of the SAP Gateway. To use the monitor, follow these steps:

1. Enter Transaction "SMGW" in the command field, and press the Enter key (or select the menu option Tools • Administration • Monitor • System Monitoring • SMGW—Gateway Monitor).
2. All existing inbound and outbound RFC connections are initially displayed. Click on Refresh (icon) to refresh the display.

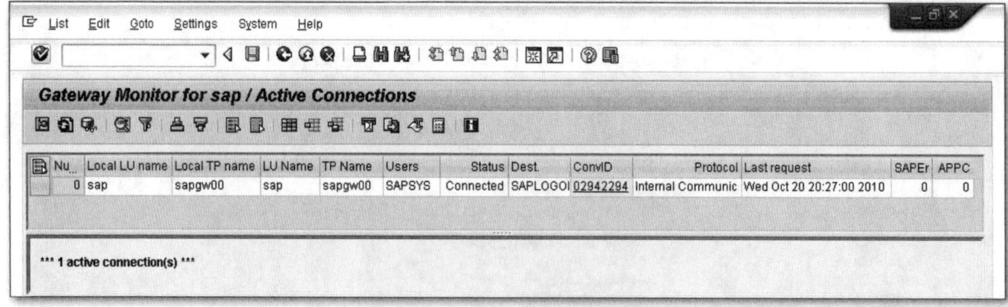

3. Double-click on a list entry to display detailed information about it, or click on CHOOSE DETAIL ( ). The system switches to the DETAILED CONNECTION INFORMATION view.

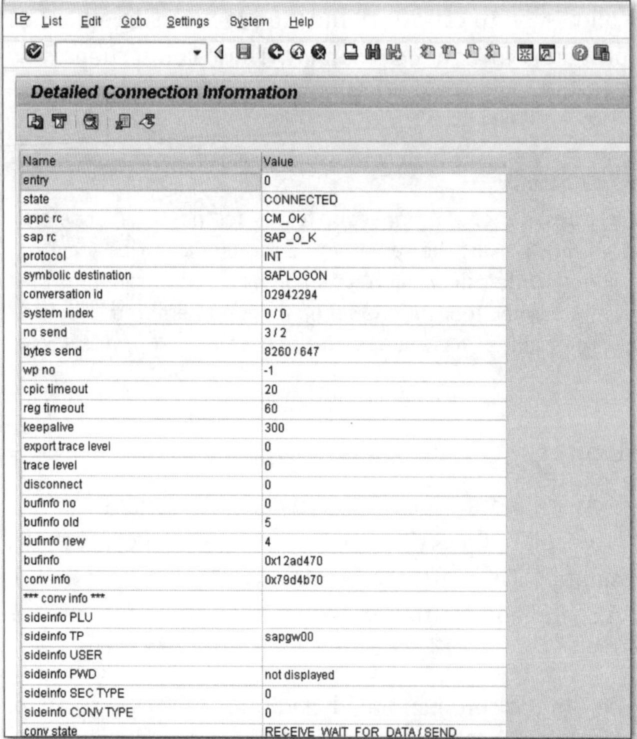

On this screen, you can see, for example, the IP addresses that are connected by the new connection (HOSTADDR LIST ENTRY). You can also identify the connection partner for any suspicious-looking RFC connections.

2.6.3 SAPconnect

SAPconnect is an RFC interface used for external communication (or *information broadcasting*). For example, you can use SAPconnect to send and receive emails via the SMTP protocol. The following communication types are provided by SAPconnect:

- Fax
- Internet (SMTP)
- X.400
- SAP to SAP
- Paging (SMS)
- Printer

You use Transaction SCOT (SAPconnect) for SAPconnect administration. Here you can configure and monitor the communication services.

1. Enter Transaction "SCOT" in the command field, and press the Enter key (or select the menu option TOOLS • BUSINESS COMMUNICATION • COMMUNICATION • SCOT—SAPCONNECT).
2. The available communication types are listed under a server node identified by the system ID. The SMTP plugin is usually preconfigured and is displayed under the INT NODE. To configure the SMTP service, for example, position the cursor on the relevant entry and choose CHANGE (✎).

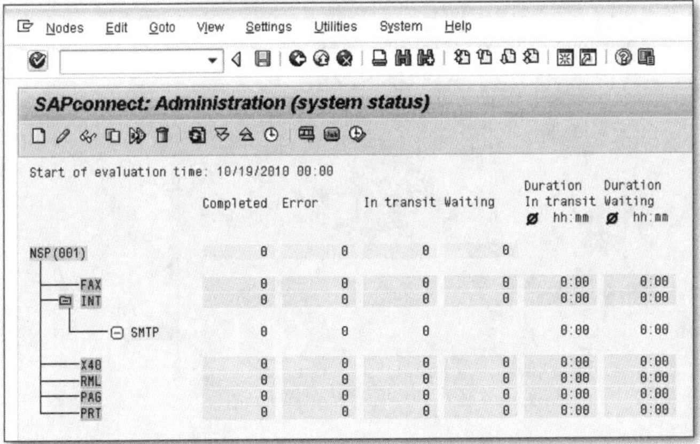

3. Maintain the settings for the SMTP service. Under SMTP CONNECTION, enter the SMTP server and the corresponding port. Choose CONTINUE (✔) to save your entries.

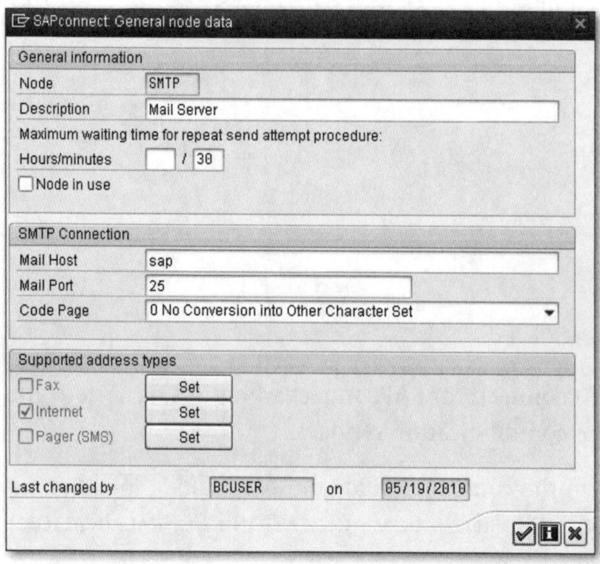

4. If you want emails to be sent via the SMTP server, you need to run a corresponding *send job*, which transfers the communication items. Click the SEND JOBS button (Job).

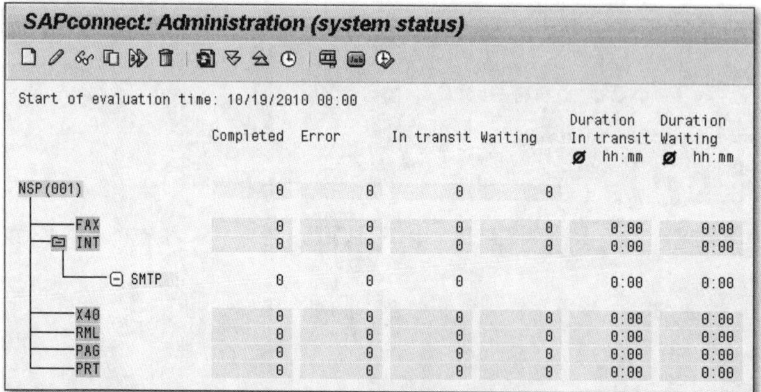

5. A dialog box then displays all planned or active send jobs. To define a new send job, click on SCHEDULE JOB (), and select the relevant communication type (for example, JOB FOR INT).

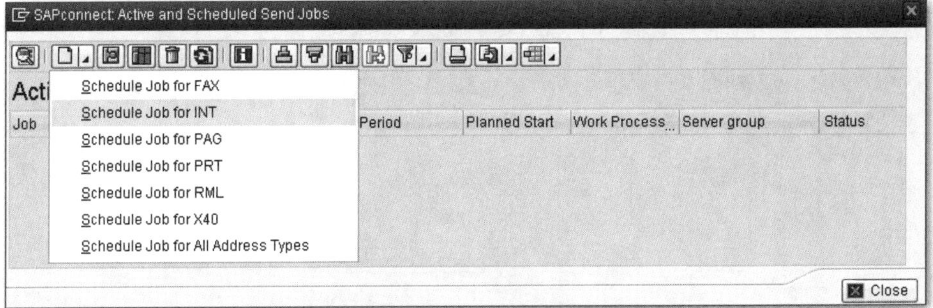

6. Make the following settings on the next screen:
   - Enter a name for the job (try to make it as meaningful as possible) in the JOB field.
   - Enter an execution interval for the job in the PERIOD field.
   - Enter a time for the first job run in the PLANNED START field.
   - In the BACKGROUND USER field, enter the SAP user ID with which the job is to be scheduled.

   Choose CONTINUE to accept the settings.

Send Job: Select Variant

Job Z_SMTP
Variant SAP&CONNECTINT

Variant Values
AddrType INT Internet mail address
No. Work Processes 1
Server group
Details

Job Values
Start Immed.
Period 5 min.
Planned Start 21:00:00
Background User BCUSER

Continue

7. The data you enter here is copied to the DEFINE JOB view (for more information, see Chapter 15). To schedule the job, click on SAVE (💾).

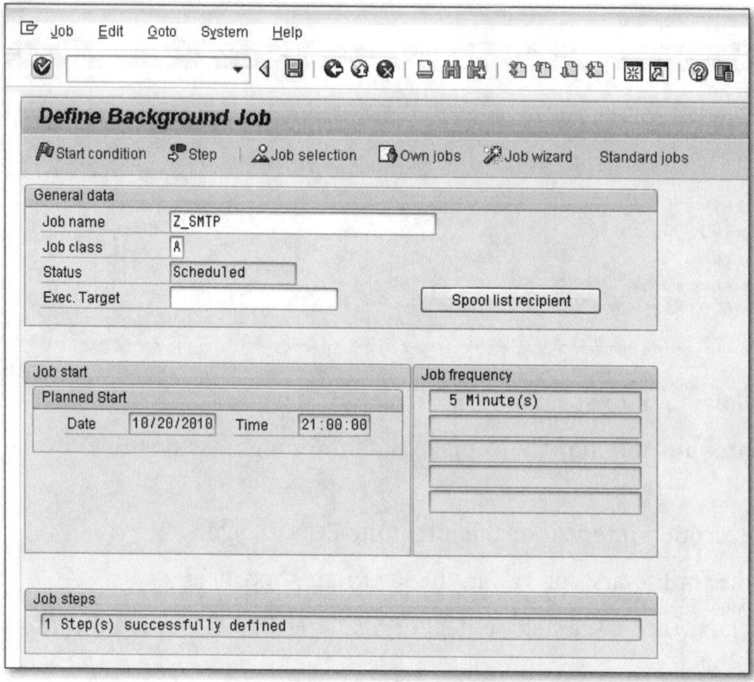

8. The display switches back to the ACTIVE AND SCHEDULED SEND JOBS window. The new job you have just defined is now included in the list. The SCHEDULED icon (🕒) in the STATUS column indicates that the send job has been scheduled. Choose the CLOSE button to exit the view.

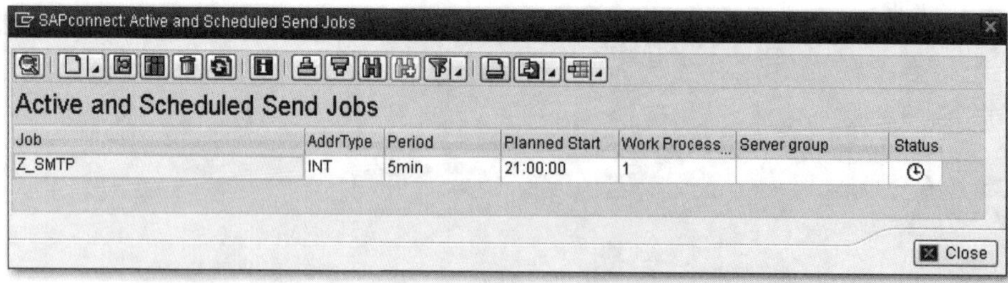

After you set up the communication type and schedule the send job, the emails created in the system (for example, *SAP Business Workplace* (Transaction SBWP)) are sent at the correct time. You can follow the same steps for sending faxes and SMS messages, for example.

[!]

Activating the SMTP Service

Note that the SAPconnect service must be activated in Transaction SICF (see Section 2.6.2) for your configuration to work.

2.6.4 Message Server Monitor

The message server is a system process of the central instance, which manages the communication between the individual instances of an SAP system. If load distribution is configured in your system, the message server also selects the application server to which the user logs on, for example.

If problems occur, use the Message Server Monitor (Transaction SMMS) to monitor the message server. The Message Server Monitor also provides access to the administration functions of the message server.

To check the status of the message server, follow these steps:

1. Enter Transaction "SMMS" in the command field, and press the [Enter] key (or select the menu option TOOLS • ADMINISTRATION • MONITOR • SYSTEM MONITORING • SMMS—MESSAGE SERVER MONITOR).
2. The message server data are displayed. The SERVER STATUS column indicates whether the server is active. The SAP SERVICES column, meanwhile, specifies the services that are available on the individual application servers.

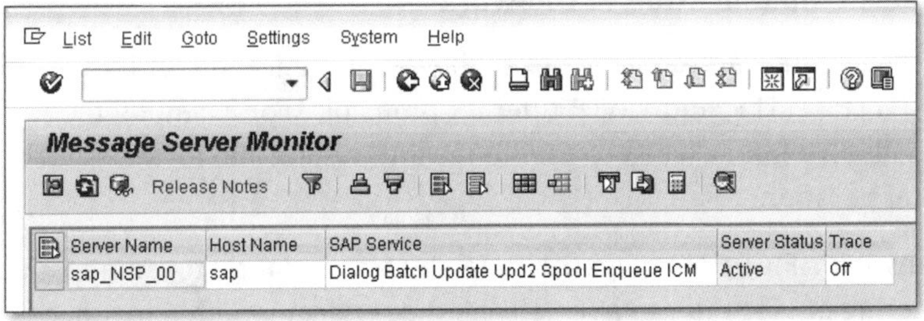

3. To restart the message server following an error, select the menu option GOTO • EXPERT FUNCTIONS • SERVER ADMINISTRATION • SHUT DOWN SERVER (HARD)/(SOFT).

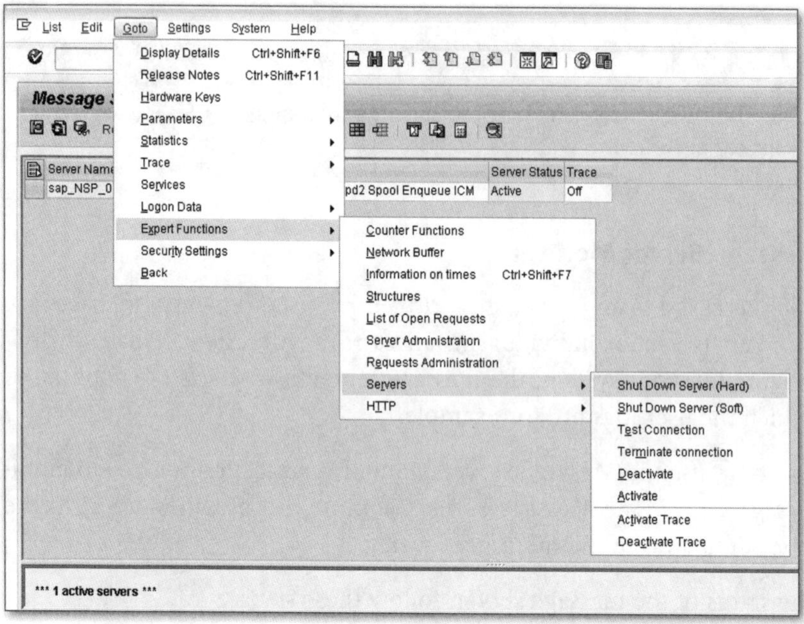

If there is an error on the message server, communication between the instances may be threatened in certain cases. In other words, it may no longer be possible to reach certain application servers. The other advanced functions of the Message Server Monitor (follow the menu path in step 3 shown previously) allow you to bring about this status deliberately, and to analyze and eliminate errors.

2.6.5 Internet Communication Framework

The *Internet Communication Framework* (ICF) enables communication with the SAP system via the HTTP, HTTPS, and SMTP Internet protocols. For example, the ICF receives HTTP calls sent from a web browser to the SAP system and forwards these to the relevant application.

You can use Transaction SICF (HTTP Service Hierarchy Maintenance) for administration and monitoring of ICF. You can also activate the services required for specific applications on this screen.

1. Enter Transaction "SICF" in the command field, and press the Enter key (or select the menu option: TOOLS • SYSTEM ADMINISTRATION • ADMINISTRATION • NETWORK • SICF—HTTP SERVICE HIERARCHY MAINTENANCE).
2. SERVICE is always preconfigured as the HIERARCHY TYPE to be maintained. Choose the EXECUTE BUTTON (⊕).

Maintain Services

Filter for Calling ICF Hierarchy

Hierarchy Type	SERVICE
Virtual Host	
Service Path	
Service Name	
PA_RFSRV	
Description	
Language	English

Filter for Detail Information

Created By			
Created On		to	
Last Changed By			
Changed On		to	

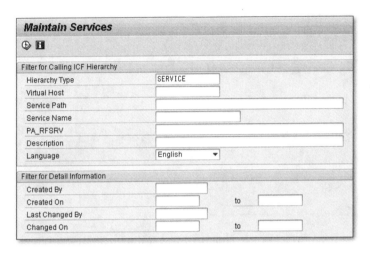

3. You can activate or deactivate services on the next screen. You can use the field in the FILTER DETAILS area to restrict your search for a service based on specific criteria. Alternatively, expand the tree structure below VIRTUAL HOSTS/SERVICES.

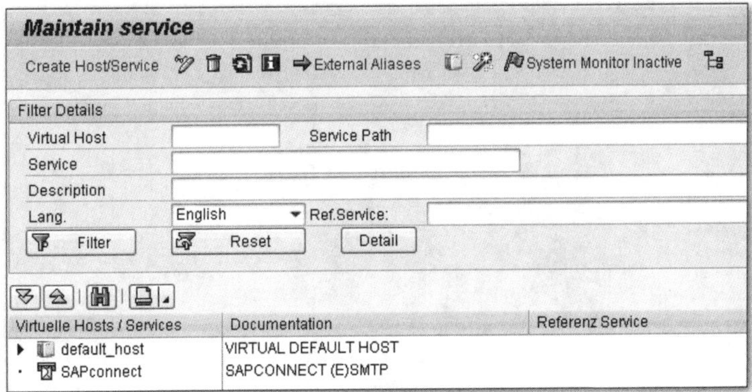

4. For example, expand the path DEFAULT_HOST • SAP • PUBLIC • BC • WEBDYNPRO. Inactive services are displayed in gray font, while active services are indicated by black font.

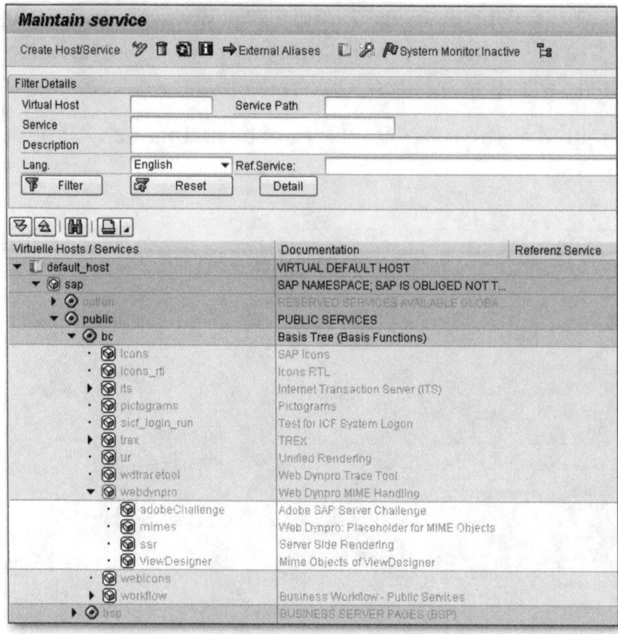

5. Right-click on the service you want to activate (for example, web dynpro), and select the ACTIVATE SERVICE entry.

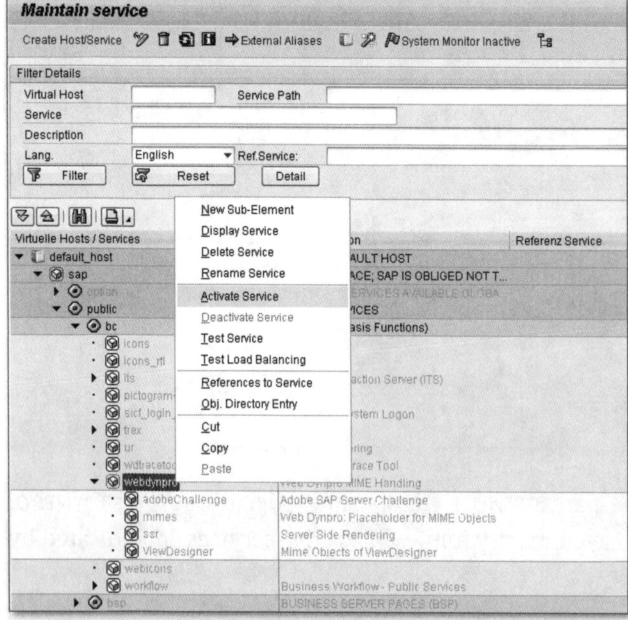

6. Choose Yes to confirm activation. If you want to activate all lower-level services within a tree, choose Yes (icon).

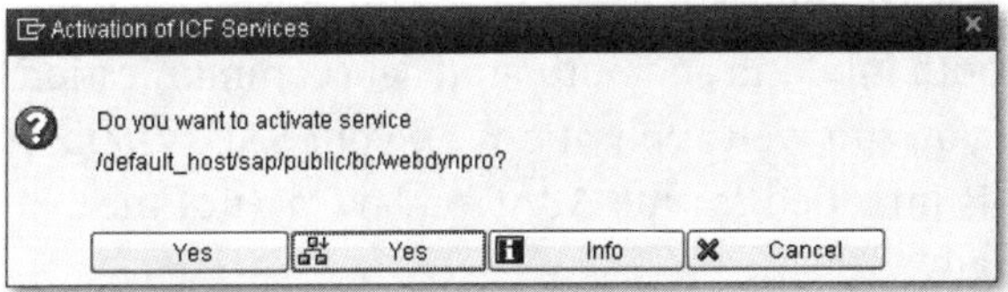

7. Click on the Refresh button (icon) to refresh the display. There services have been activated and are now shown in black font.

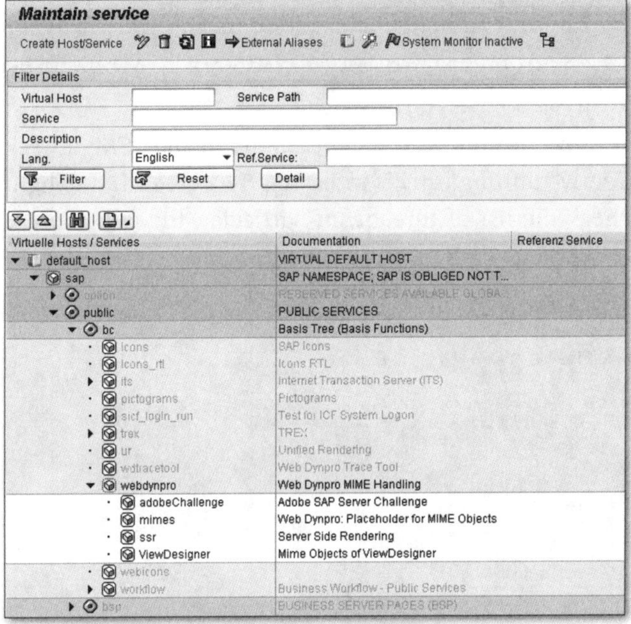

[+]

Which Services to Activate

If you aren't sure which services to activate, seek the assistance of a programmer or consultant. In most cases, the services that need to be activated are specified in an error message when a user calls the relevant function.

In addition to the administration of services, Transaction SICF also offers other monitoring and administration functions for the ICF. These functions are available in the Edit menu.

2.6.6 ICM Monitor

The *Internet Communication Manager* (ICM) is responsible for any communication between the SAP system and external applications that uses the protocols HTTP, HTTPS or SMTP. This applies to both inbound and outbound data communication. The ICM is particularly useful if you run web applications on your SAP system. It decides whether a browser call is intended for the ABAP or Java part of the SAP system and forwards it accordingly.

If problems arise with web applications, you need to check whether the ICM is running and if any errors have occurred. You can use the ICM Monitor (Transaction SMICM) for this purpose:

1. Enter Transaction "SMICM" in the command field, and press the [Enter] key (or select the menu option TOOLS • ADMINISTRATION • MONITOR • SYSTEM MONITORING • SMICM—ICM MONITOR).
2. The initial screen of the ICM Monitor shows the status of the ICM. Check whether the ICM is currently running (this is indicated by a green traffic-light icon). You should also check the list of threads, in particular, the entry in the STATUS column. Click on REFRESH (icon) to refresh the display.

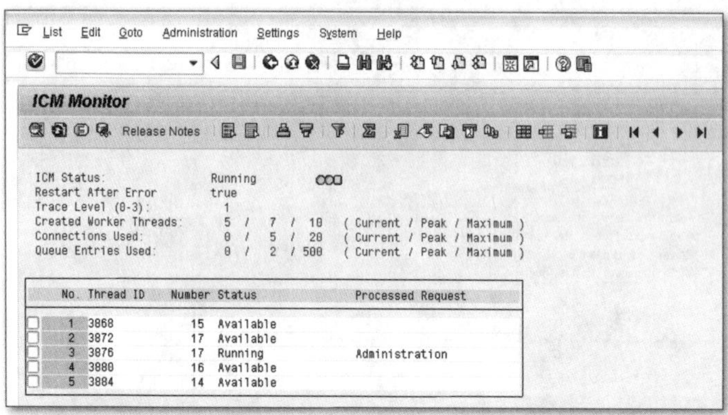

ICM Threads

The work processes of the ICM, called *threads* or *worker threads*, are responsible for accepting external requests and sending responses.

3. You may need to restart the ICM if an error occurs. To do this, select the menu option ADMINISTRATION • ICM • EXIT SOFT • LOCAL.

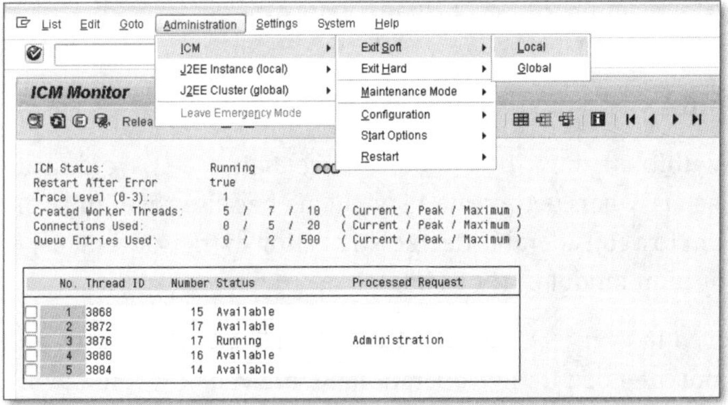

"Exit Soft" or "Hard Exit" [+]

Sometimes, you need to restart the ICM to eliminate an error. You can perform a *soft* or *hard* restart in this case. With a soft shutdown, the ICM stops accepting requests but tries to complete any tasks that are still open. With a hard shutdown, the ICM shuts down immediately, without taking account of any open connections.

2.7 Client Administration

A *client* is, by definition, an organizationally and technically self-contained unit within an SAP system. While all clients in the system access the same repository objects (programs, tables, and so on; in other words, cross-client data), the Customizing settings and system master data are largely client-specific.

As a result, clients are often used to keep data separate to comply with commercial or corporate law requirements. For example, several enterprises may each operate their own client in a shared SAP system. In this case, the use of clients ensures a very clear separation between the data belonging to individual enterprises (which isn't the case if you use company codes, for example).

Client administration, which involves the following tasks, is one of your responsibilities as system administrator:

- Creating, changing, and deleting clients
- Copying clients within a system
- Copying clients across systems

This section describes the main functions of client administration.

2.7.1 Creating Clients

A client is identified within a system by a unique three-digit code. Avoid using letters or special characters when you create new clients because this limits the functionality of the client to a considerable degree (in relation to transport management and certain application modules, for example).

Three clients are reserved in every SAP standard system delivered: 000, 001, and 066. These clients are not intended for live operation. Before you fill a system with Customizing settings or data, create a new client (usually client 100).

A new client is normally created using the following two steps:

1. Create a new entry in the client table.
2. Execute a client copy.

You therefore begin by maintaining the client table:

1. Enter Transaction "SCC4" in the command field, and press the Enter key (or select the menu option TOOLS • ADMINISTRATION • ADMINISTRATION • CLIENT ADMINISTRATION • SCC4—CLIENT MAINTENANCE).
2. The client table is then displayed. Click on DISPLAY <-> CHANGE ().

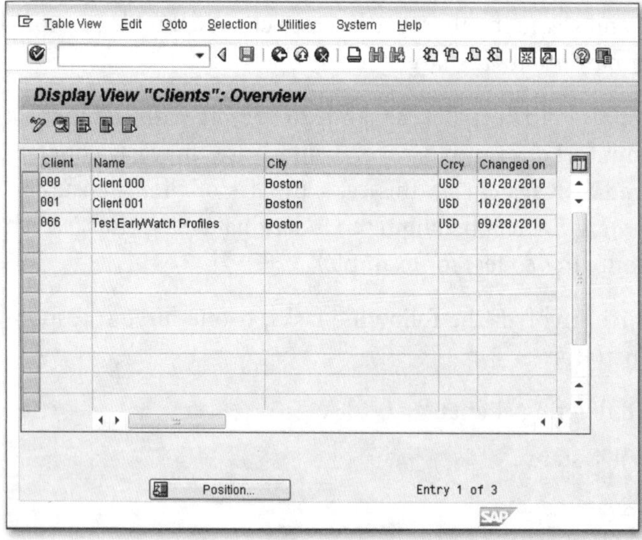

3. In the dialog box that opens, click on CONTINUE (✔).

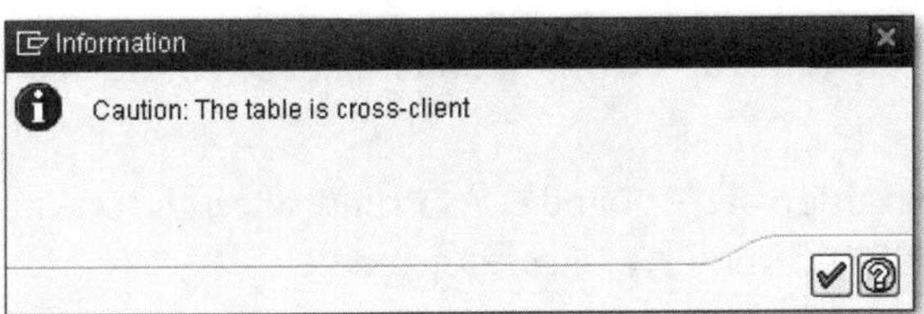

4. Click the NEW ENTRIES button.

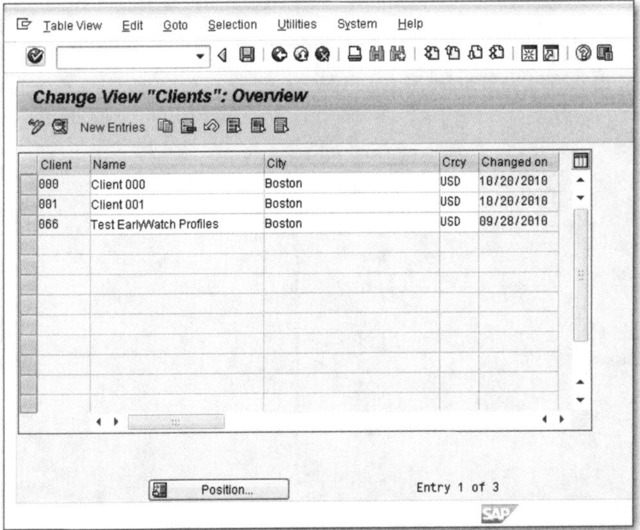

5. Complete the fields in the detailed view for new clients as follows:

- Under CLIENT, enter a client number (for example, 100), and a name (for example, Customizing client).
- Enter the location name under CITY (for example, New York).
- Under STD CURRENCY, enter a default currency for the client (for example, USD).
- In the CLIENT ROLE field, select an entry from the drop-down list (for example, Customizing).
- Enter the relevant option under CHANGES AND TRANSPORTS FOR CLIENT-SPECIFIC OBJECTS (see Chapter 10).

- Select the relevant option from the drop-down list under CROSS-CLIENT OBJECT CHANGES.
- Select the relevant option from the drop-down list under PROTECTION: CLIENT COPIER AND COMPARISON TOOL.
- If you want to enable the execution of CATT and eCATT runs, select the ECATT AND CATT OPTION UNDER CATT AND ECATT RESTRICTIONS.

Finally, click on SAVE.

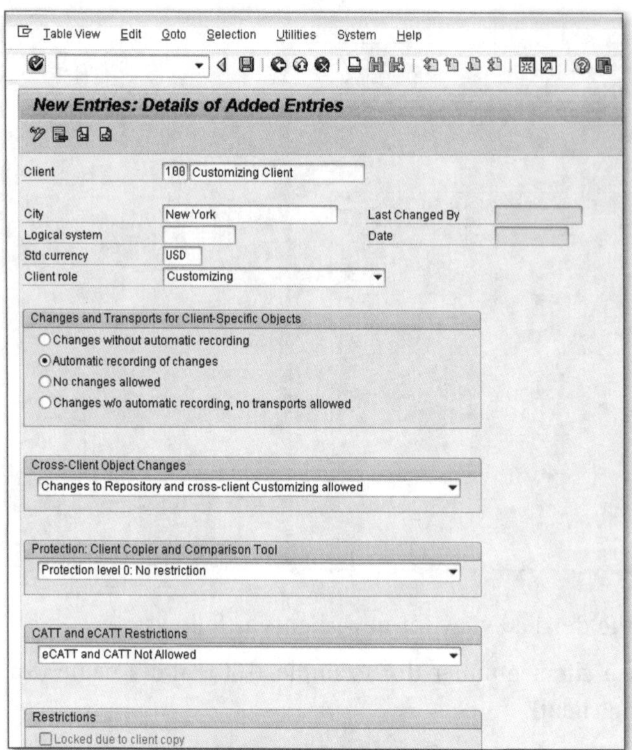

6. A message appears in the status bar to confirm that the client has been created. Click on BACK.

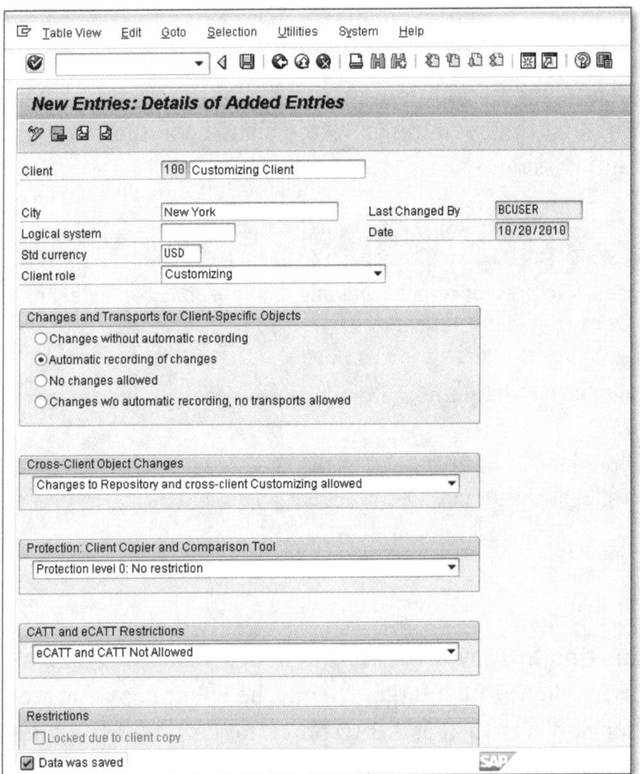

7. The client you just created is now also listed in the table.

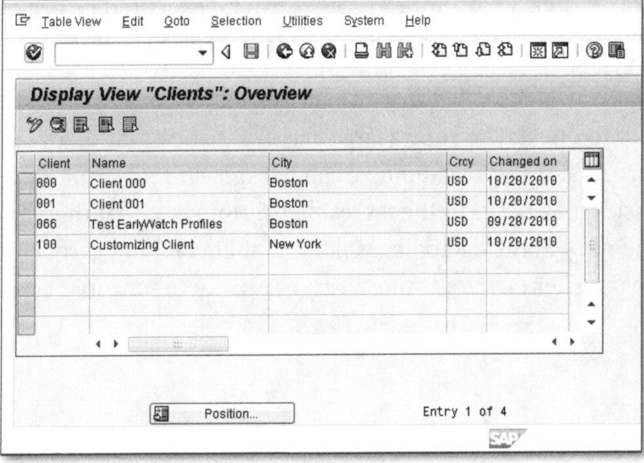

The client is now ready to be used as the target client in a client copy. The new client contains no Customizing, master, or application data. You therefore need to fill the client with data using a client copy. In addition, the new client does not contain any user master records. The first time you log on to the client, you therefore use the user SAP* and the default password "pass".

[!]

The SAP* User in New Clients

The user *SAP** and default password *pass* represent generally recognized logon data, and this user account also has unrestricted authorizations. You should therefore create an actual SAP* user and change the password as soon as possible.

Access by this user is only possible if the login/no_automatic_user_sapstar profile parameter has the value "0".

As soon as you've created your new client and finished the client copy, check whether the passwords for all system IDs are secure in the new client.

2.7.2 Copying Clients

You use the client copy function to copy or transport client-specific Customizing settings or data from a source client into a target client. The client copy function doesn't copy any cross-client objects such as ABAP programs or table structures. You can use copy profiles to determine the scope of the data copy, which means that you don't need to copy all of the data in a client.

The target client may be in the same or another system. A copy within the same system is known as a *local client copy*. Cross-system copies can be executed either as a *remote copy* (using an RFC connection) or as a *client transport* using the TMS.

It may take several hours to copy a client because the datasets may be very large in some cases. You may need up to one day to copy a large client. For the duration of the copy, all users should be locked and the scheduling of all background jobs canceled; otherwise, data inconsistencies may occur in the target client. Note also that the new client requires additional memory in the database. Make sure that you have sufficient memory in reserve because the client copy is otherwise very likely to terminate.

[+]

Information About Client Copies

For more information about tools you can use for client copies, refer to SAP Notes 24853 and 552711.

Local Client Copy

You perform a client copy to copy a client within the same system. This is the fastest way to copy a client.

1. To log on to your newly created client, use the SAP* user ID and the password "pass".

[!]

Log On to the Correct Client

It is essential to ensure that you are logged on to the correct target client. Otherwise, you may unintentionally destroy another client.

2. Enter Transaction "SCCL" in the command field, and press the Enter key (or select the menu option Tools • Administration • Administration • Client Administration • Client Copy • SCCL—Local Copy).
3. On the Client Copy - Copy a client screen, open the input help () for the Selected profile field.

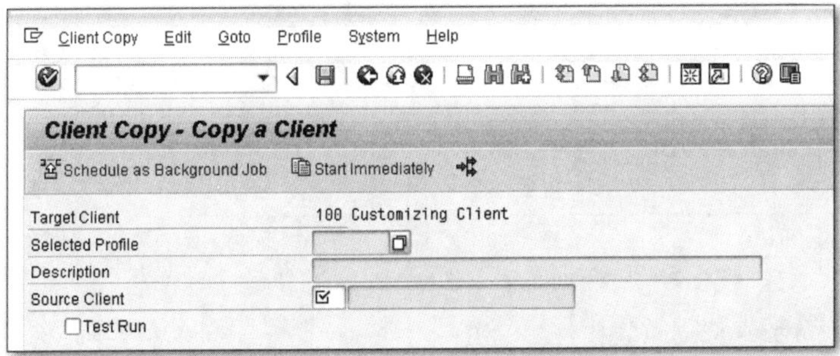

4. Select a copy profile (for example, SAP_ALL). The profile determines the type and scope of the data to be copied (see the Description column). Click on Choose.

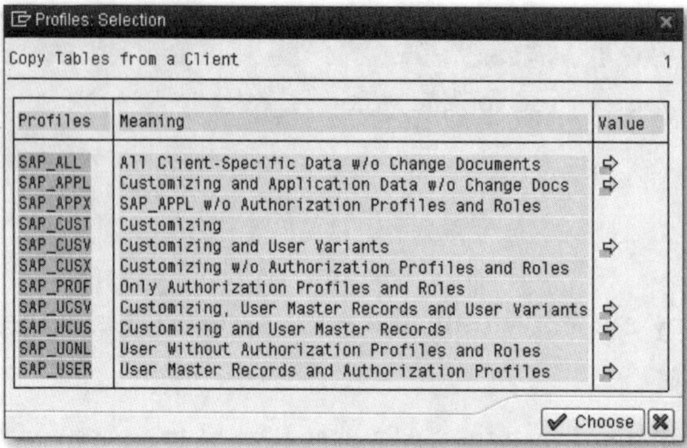

5. Enter the number of the source client (for example, "001") in the SOURCE CLIENT field. You may also need to enter a value in the SOURCE CLIENT USER MASTERS field, depending on the copy profile selected. You can specify two different source clients for the data. Click the SCHEDULE AS BACKGROUND JOB BUTTON.

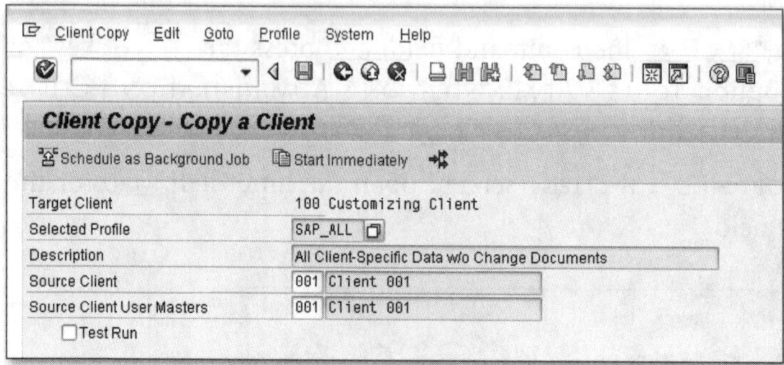

6. Click the SCHEDULE JOB button.

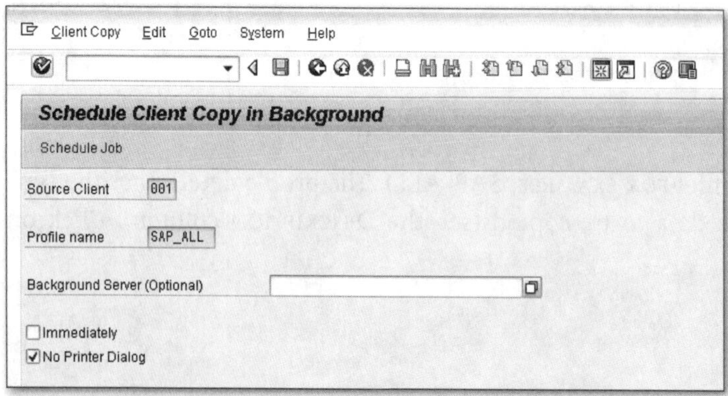

7. Enter a start time for the job. The job is scheduled the same way as any other background process (see Chapter 15). Choose SAVE (💾).

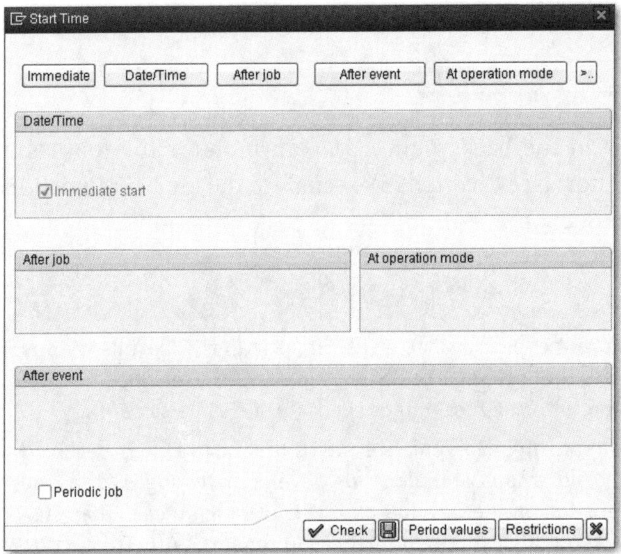

8. The copy options are then displayed. The activated contents result from the copy profile selected in step 4. Check the settings, and click on CONTINUE.

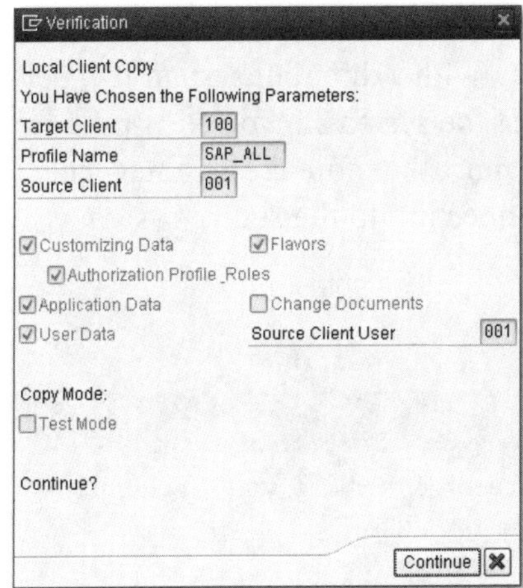

9. Scheduling of the copy job is confirmed in a dialog box, which you can close by choosing CONTINUE (✔).

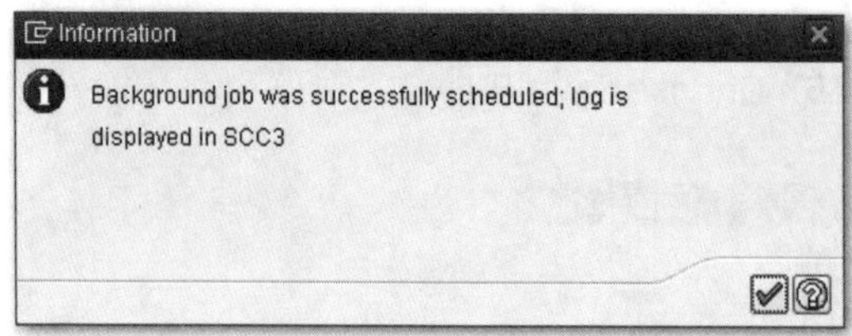

The client copy is executed in the background. You can monitor the job using Transaction SM37 (Job Monitor) (see Chapter 15) or analyze the log in Transaction SCC3 (Client Copy Log) (see Section 2.7.4).

[+]

Local Client Copies Using Transport Requests

A special variant of the local client copy is available with Transaction SCC1 (Client Copy by Transport Request): With this variant, only the objects included in a specific transport request are copied from a client into the local target client (in the same system).

This function is useful, for example, in development systems that have a client reserved exclusively for development, and a separate client for developer testing. Often, the creation of test cases is not possible in the development client, which means that Customizing settings must be tested with data in another environment. With Transaction SCC1, it isn't necessary to transfer every transport request to the test system; an initial test can be performed in the development system.

Remote Copy

If you want to copy a client into another system (with a different system ID), perform a remote client copy. The RFC interface of the systems involved is used for the remote copy. To prepare for the copy, you must therefore create a new client and use Transaction SM59 to set up an RFC connection to the source system (see Section 2.6.1). To do this, follow these steps:

1. Log on to the target system and client.

[!]

Log On to the Correct Client

Make sure you are logged on to the correct target client. Otherwise, you may unintentionally destroy another client.

2. Enter Transaction "SCC9" in the command field, and press the [Enter] key (or select the menu option TOOLS • ADMINISTRATION • ADMINISTRATION • CLIENT ADMINISTRATION • CLIENT COPY • SCC9—REMOTE COPY).

   On the CLIENT COPY - COPY A CLIENT SCREEN, open the input help (□) for the SELECTED PROFILE field.

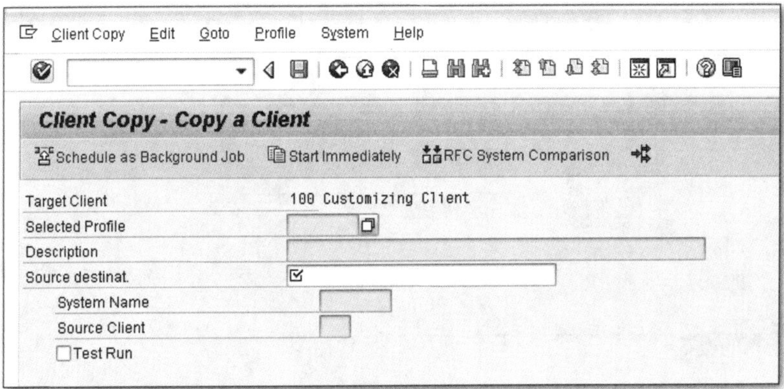

3. Select a copy profile (FOR EXAMPLE, SAP_ALL). The profile determines the type and scope of the data to be copied. Click on CHOOSE.

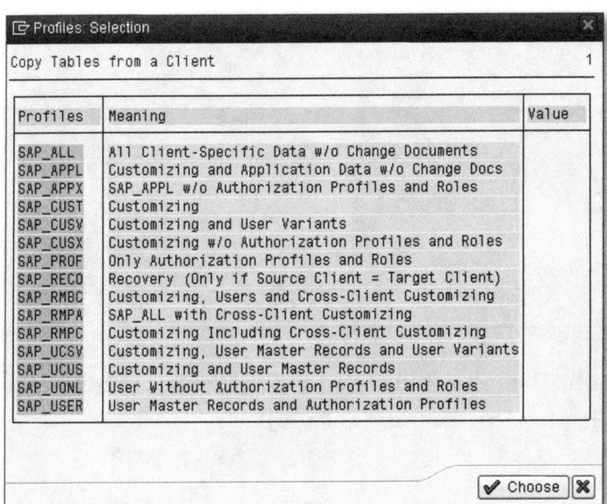

4. Enter the RFC connection to the source system in the SOURCE DESTINATION field. The SYSTEM NAME and SOURCE CLIENT fields are filled automatically using the settings of the RFC connection. Click the SCHEDULE AS BACKGROUND JOB BUTTON.

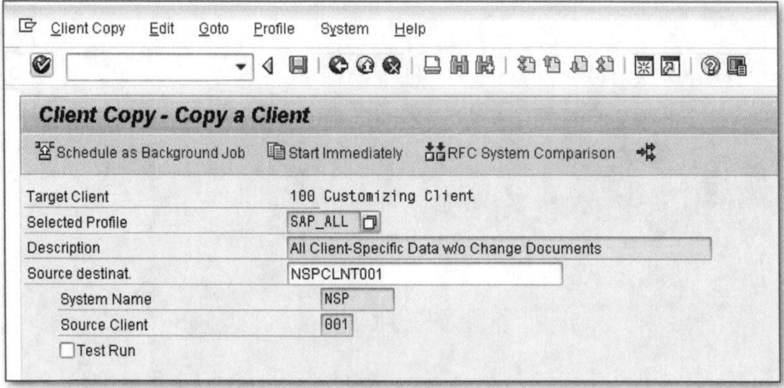

5. Click the SCHEDULE JOB button.

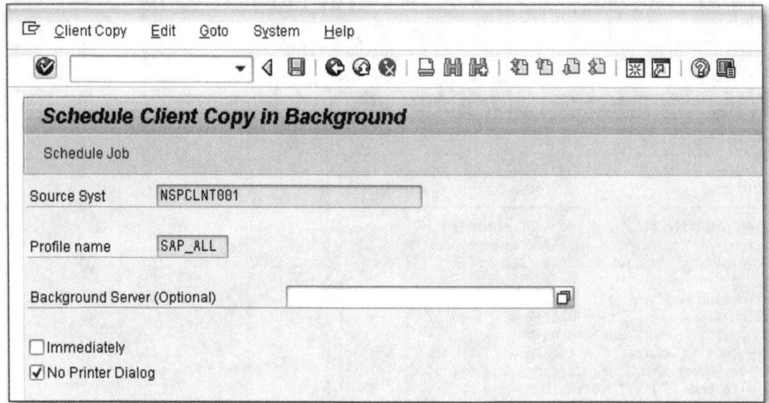

6. Enter a start time for the job. The job is scheduled the same way as any other background process (see Chapter 15). Choose SAVE (💾).

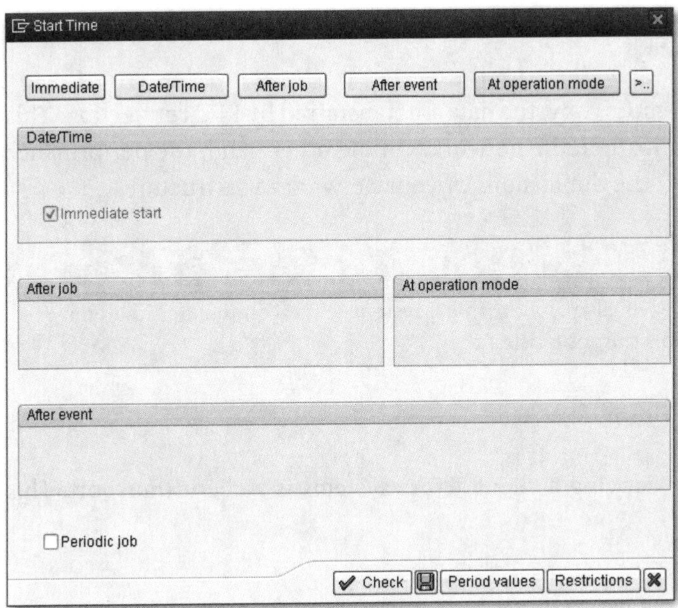

7. The copy options are then displayed.

   Check the settings, and click on CONTINUE.

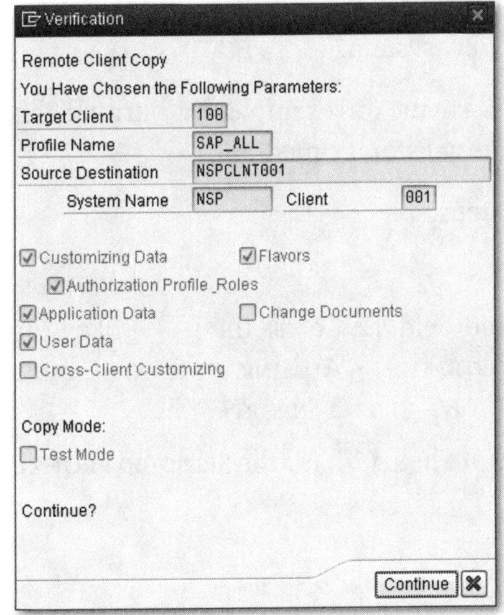

Scheduling of the copy job is confirmed in a dialog box, which you can close by choosing CONTINUE (✔).

When you perform a remote copy, the data are transferred by RFC connection. This places a corresponding load on the network. On the other hand, the performance of the copy depends on the dimensions of your network infrastructure.

[+]

Client Copies within a System

Although a remote copy will also work within a system, it is recommended that you use a local client copy for this purpose instead.

Client Transport

The second option for copying a client across systems is a client transport. This comprises three steps:

1. Client export
2. Client import
3. Import postprocessing

The client export generates transport files, which are then imported into another system using the TMS (see Chapter 17). After the import, a postprocessing job must also be run to adapt the copied data to the new system.

The client export also allows you to save a client, for example, by burning the generated files to a CD or using another external storage medium.

To perform the client export, follow these steps:

1. Log on to the source client.
2. Enter Transaction "SCC8" in the command field, and press the Enter key (or select the menu option TOOLS • ADMINISTRATION • ADMINISTRATION • CLIENT ADMINISTRATION • CLIENT TRANSPORT • SCC8—CLIENT EXPORT).
3. On the CLIENT EXPORT screen, open the input help (□) for the SELECTED PROFILE field.

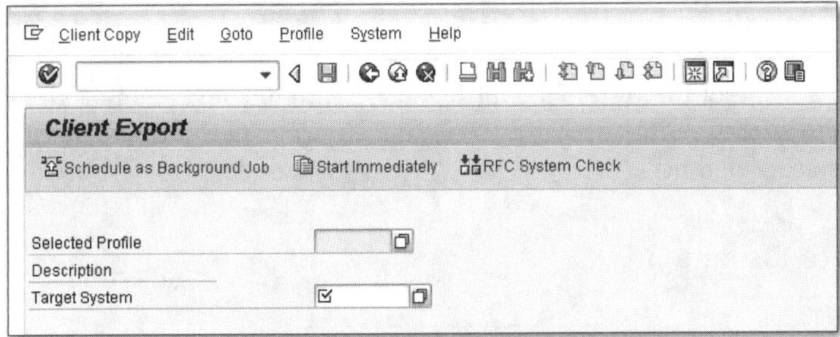

4. Select a copy profile (for example, SAP_ALL). The profile determines the type and scope of the data to be copied. Click on CHOOSE.

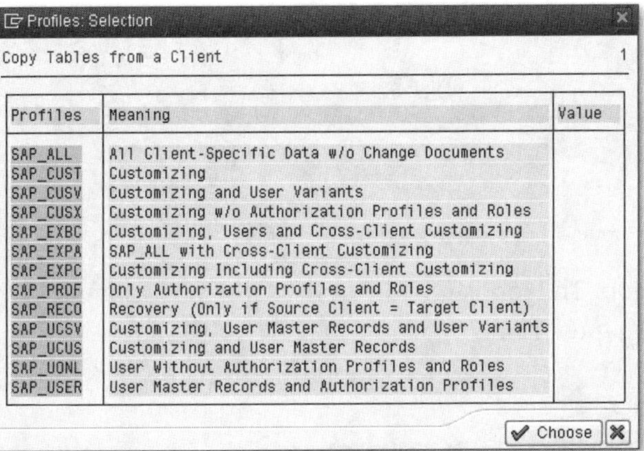

5. Enter the system into which you want the export file to be imported later in the TARGET SYSTEM field. You may only select selected that are part of the transport landscape. Click the SCHEDULE AS BACKGROUND JOB button.

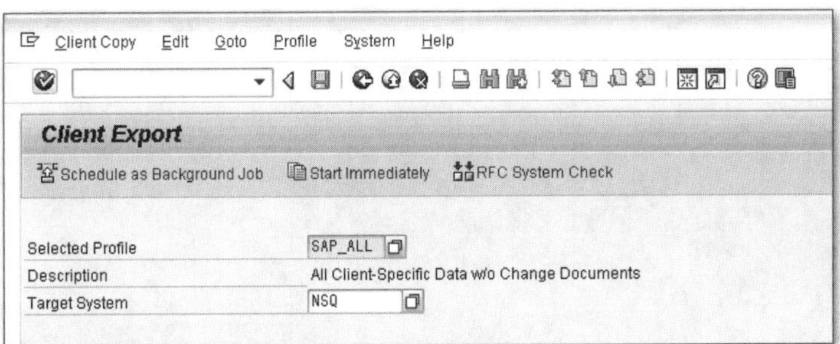

[+]

Selecting the Target System

You can also enter the name of the system in which you are currently logged on as the target system. You can subsequently import the relevant transport files into a system other than the system specified here.

6. Click the SCHEDULE JOB button.

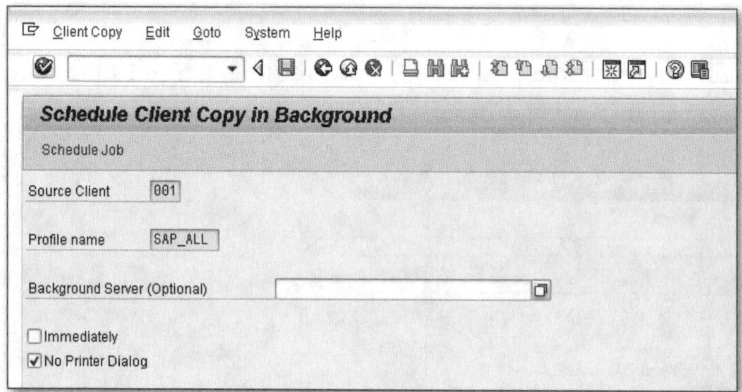

7. Enter a start time for the job. The job is scheduled the same way as any other background process (see Chapter 15).

   Choose SAVE (💾).

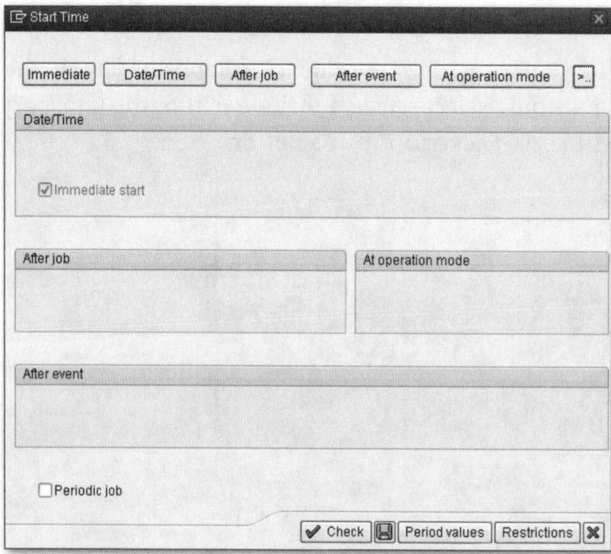

8. The copy options are then displayed. Check the settings, and click on CONTINUE.

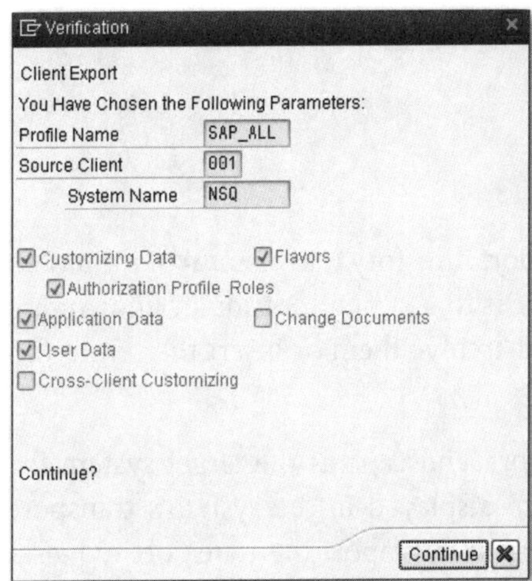

9. The transport request files created by the export are displayed in a dialog box. Take note of the file names, and choose CONTINUE (✔).

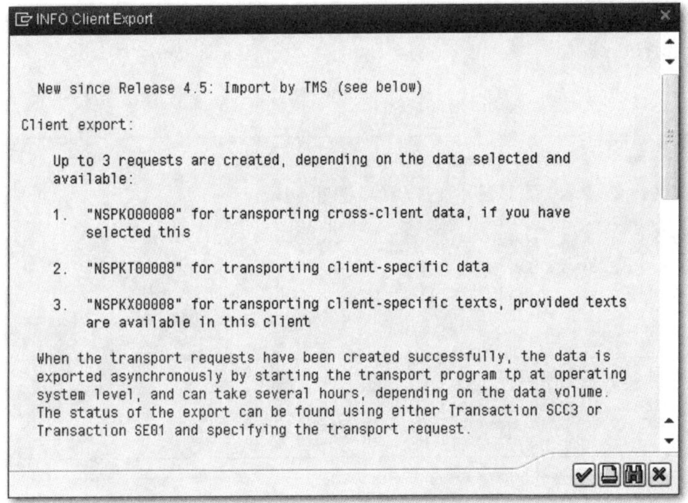

Scheduling of the copy job is confirmed in a dialog box, which you can close by choosing CONTINUE (✔).

Three files are generated by the client export:

- **<SID>KO<number>:** Cross-client data
- **<SID>KT<number>:** Client-specific data
- **<SID>KX<number>:** Texts and forms

These files are saved to your system's transport directory (*<drive>:\usr\sap\trans* or */usr/sap/trans*). To save the client or transfer it to a system outside of your transport landscape, you can copy these files and archive them or insert them into the transport directory of the remote system.

If you specify a system within your transport landscape as the target system for the client export, the transport requests are displayed in the system's transport queue after the export is completed. You can then import the transport requests as described in Chapter 17. To do this, select the requests, and click on IMPORT REQUESTS ().

[!]

Log On to the Correct Client

Make sure you are logged on to the correct target client. Otherwise, you may unintentionally destroy another client.

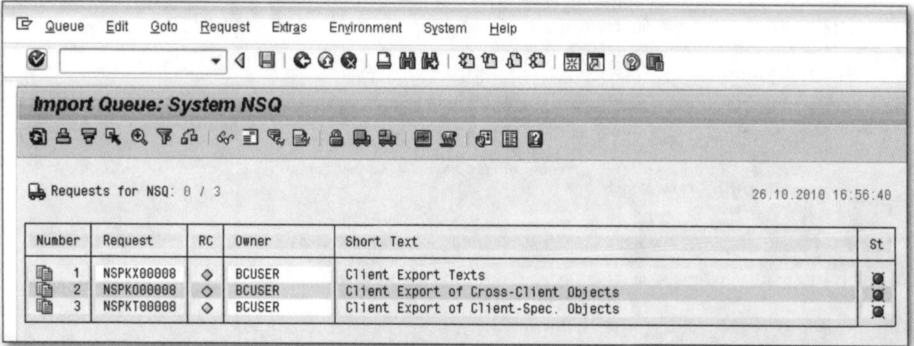

Now you only need to specify the target client, before starting the transport with the START IMPORT button.

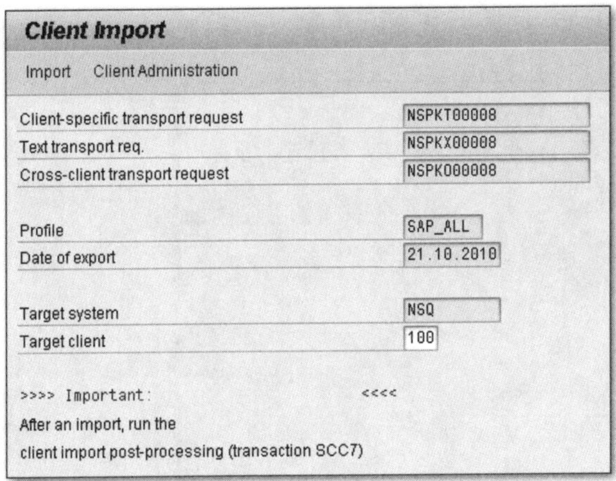

The client data are then imported into the new client via the transport system. Wait until the import is completed, and then execute import postprocessing:

1. Log on to the target system and client.
2. Enter Transaction "SCC7" in the command field, and press the [Enter] key (or select the menu option Tools • Administration • Administration • Client Administration • Client Transport • SCC7—Import Editing).
3. Click the Schedule as background job button.

[+]

Selecting the Target System

You can also enter the name of the system in which you are currently logged on as the target system. You can subsequently import the relevant transport files into a system other than the system specified here.

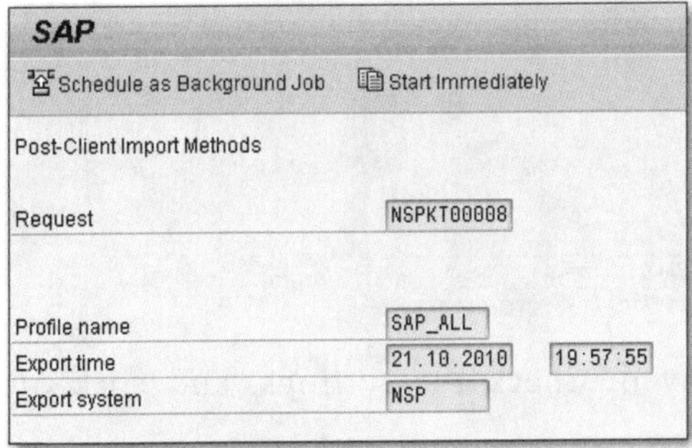

4. Click the Schedule Job button.

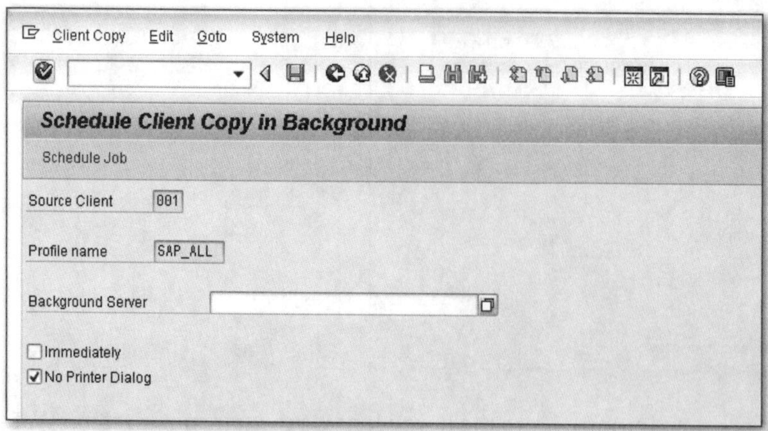

5. Enter a start time for the job. The job is scheduled the same way as any other background process (see Chapter 15). Choose the Save button (💾).

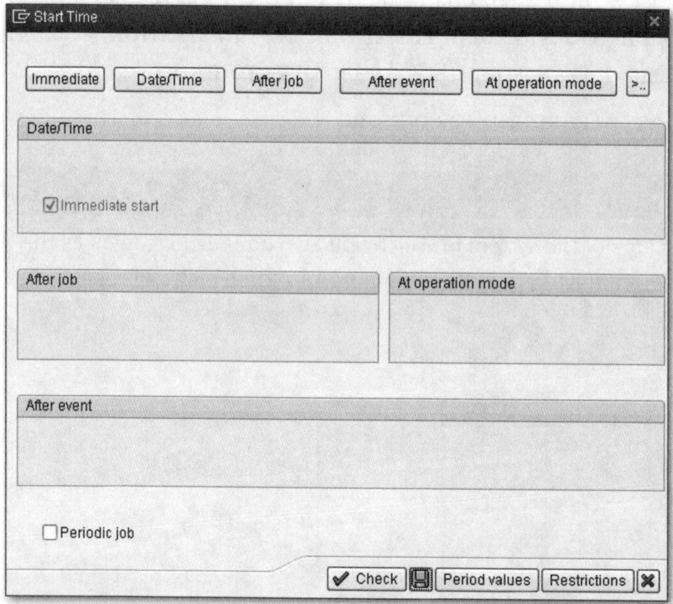

6. The copy options are then displayed. Check the settings, and click on Continue.

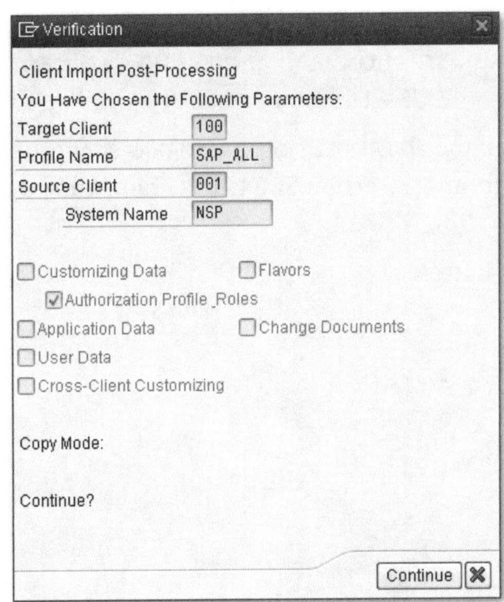
Verification
Client Import Post-Processing
You Have Chosen the Following Parameters:

Target Client	100
Profile Name	SAP_ALL
Source Client	001
System Name	NSP

- [ ] Customizing Data
- [ ] Flavors
- [x] Authorization Profile _Roles
- [ ] Application Data
- [ ] Change Documents
- [ ] User Data
- [ ] Cross-Client Customizing

Copy Mode:

Continue?

Continue

Scheduling of the copy job is confirmed in a dialog box, which you can close by choosing CONTINUE (✔).

The client transport essentially produces the same result as a remote client copy. However, whereas the remote copy is significantly faster because it allows for a "live" data copy, the client export option offers the advantage of being network-independent. In addition, the transport requests generated during the export can be used more than once, for example, for several remote systems, or as backup files.

2.7.3 Deleting Clients

You can delete clients in Transaction SCC5 (Delete Client). If you choose to do so, all client-specific data are deleted from the database. To delete a client, it's not enough to merely remove the corresponding entry from the client table (Transaction SCC4). To delete a client, you should follow these steps:

1. Log on to the client you want to delete.

[!]

Log On to the Correct Client

Make sure you are logged on to the correct target client. Otherwise, you may unintentionally destroy another client.

2. Enter Transaction "SCC5" in the command field, and press the Enter key (or select the menu option Tools • Administration • Administration • Client Administration • Special Functions • SCC5—Delete Client).
3. On the Delete Client screen, activate the Delete entry from T000 checkbox if you want to delete the table entry from Transaction SCC4 at the same time as your deletion of the client.

   Click on the Delete in Background button.

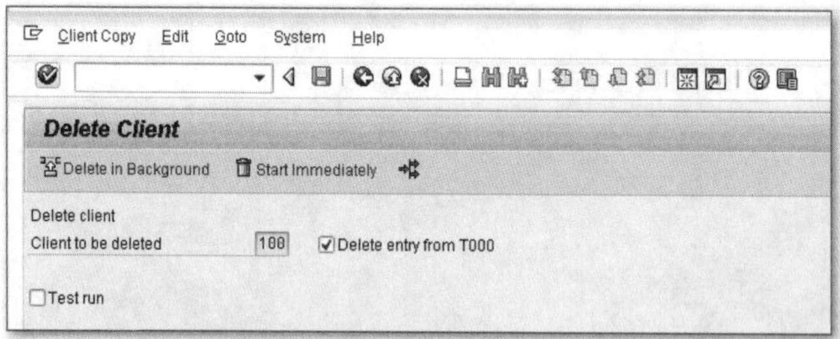

4. Click the Schedule Job button.

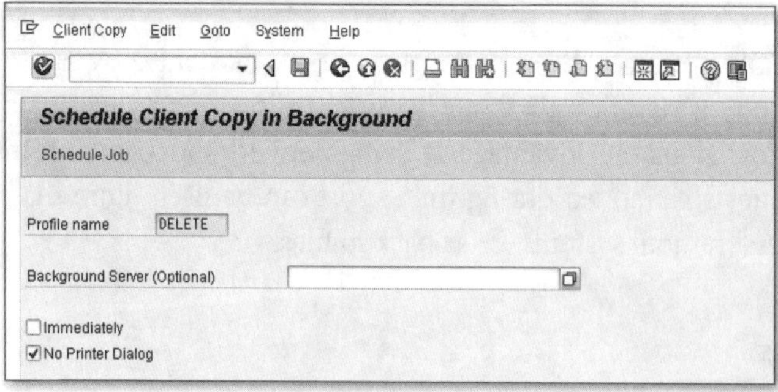

5. Enter a start time for the job. The job is scheduled the same way as any other background process (see Chapter 15).

   Choose the Save button (💾).

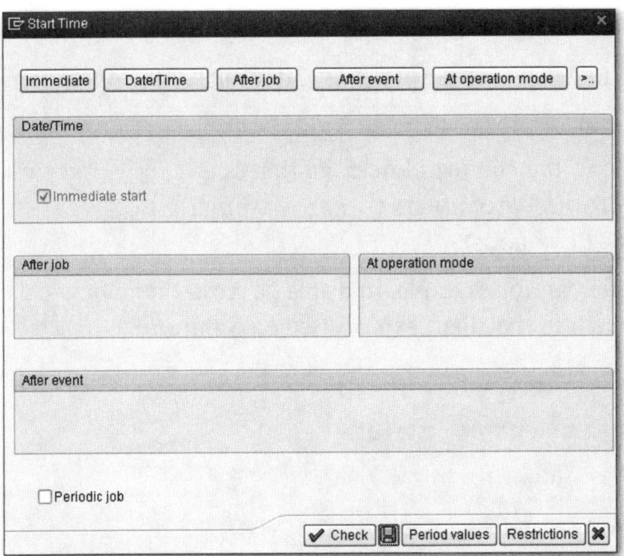

6. The copy options are then displayed. Check the settings, and click on CONTINUE.

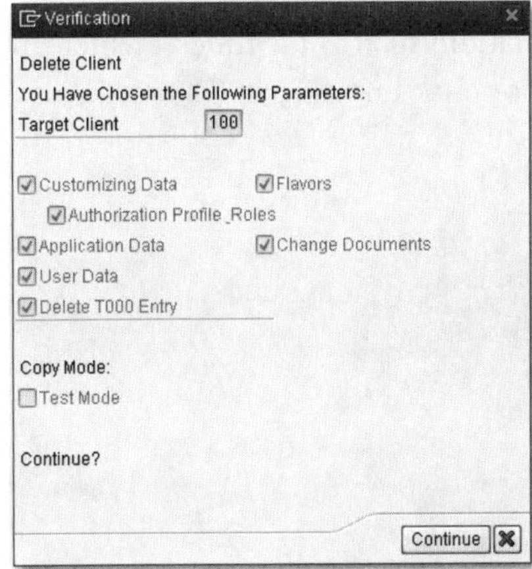

Scheduling of the copy job is confirmed in a dialog box, which you can close by choosing CONTINUE (✔).

Following deletion, all client data are permanently lost. You should therefore only execute this action if you're certain that you no longer need the client. If necessary, create a backup copy of the client beforehand using a client export, or create a full backup of the entire database.

2.7.4 Checking the Client Copy Log

You can check the client log to determine the progress and results of the operations just described:

1. Enter Transaction "SCC3" in the command field, and press the [Enter] key (or select the menu option Tools • Administration • Administration • Client Administration • SCC3—Copy Logs).
2. Use the buttons in the title bar, for example, to display a cross-client view (All Clients button) or to switch to the client exports (Exports button).

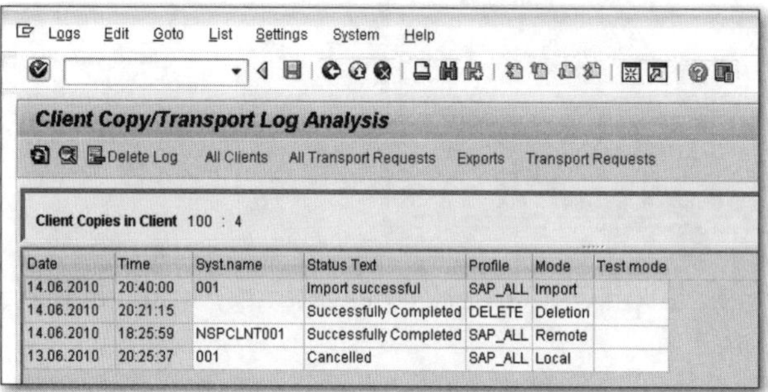

3. The detailed view provides additional information, such as the time at which an error occurred. Double-click on a log entry, or click on Choose () to display the details.

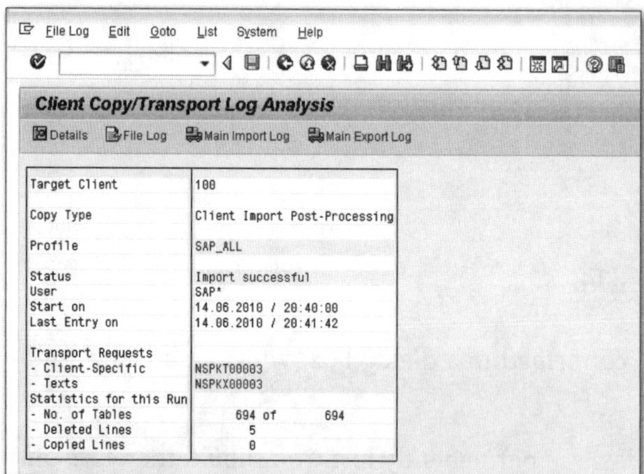

The display works in all clients, which means you don't need to be logged on to the correct client. If an operation has not yet been completed, it is displayed with the status EXECUTING. Choose the REFRESH button (🔄) to refresh the display.

2.8 System Copy

There are several reasons for executing a system copy:

- Transferring data from the production system into a test or QA system to make a large dataset available for testing.
- Preparing for an upgrade. The upgrade test system should be an exact replica of the production system so that the upgrade can be tested in as realistic a manner as possible.
- Synchronizing the configuration in the test and development system with the production system. The configuration in various systems may diverge over time so that they no longer correspond to the production system. This makes Customizing, programming, and testing more difficult.

Synchronizing the production system and the quality system is the most common reason for creating a system copy. Following the copy process, the test system contains the current data from the production system. This enables meaningful testing and should reduce the time and effort required to create test cases.

Note that large volumes of data are involved in the creation of a system copy. A production system may be several hundred gigabytes or terabytes in size, and a system copy requires just as much storage space as the original system. However, this argument against their use has faded in recent years given the current costs of hard disk space.

Another point to consider is that data from the production system is actual data. This involves a risk from the point of view of data security because this data may be of a confidential and sensitive nature. The development and test systems should therefore meet security standards that are at least as high as those that apply to the production system. Test data, in contrast, is usually invented data, so the issue of data security is of much less concern in this case.

There are two ways to perform a system copy:

- A database copy of the production system
- A client copy of the production client

A database copy is usually performed with the tools available in the database management system. If in doubt, consult your database administrator. The steps involved in a client copy are described in Section 2.7.2.

The benefits and drawbacks of the two variants are briefly outlined next.

2.8.1 Database Copy of the Production System

You can reproduce the complete production database using a database copy.

- **Benefits**
  The benefits of using a database copy are as follows:
  - The updated system is an exact copy of the production system.
  - Client-specific changes are also recorded and copied to the target system.
  - The copy can then be made using standard backup tapes to avoid impacting the production system. The creation of the copy simultaneously tests the backup and restore process.
- **Drawbacks**
  The drawbacks of using a database copy are as follows:
  - The version history of the current system is lost. This loss is usually acceptable for the test system, but, in most cases, it's unacceptable for the development system.
  - The target database must be the same size as the source database.
  - The target system has to be reconfigured after the copy.
  - The client structure in the target system is lost because it's overwritten with the client structure from the source system. If the source system has a single client, and the target system has three, only a single client will remain in the target system after the database copy is created. The other two clients are lost if they haven't been backed up using a client export prior to the copy.

Copying the database alone is not particularly time-consuming, provided that the relevant infrastructure is available in the data center. Most of the work involves reconfiguring the target system in this case. This complex process comprises many steps and cannot be described here. If necessary, consult with an internal or external expert in relation to this option.

2.8.2 Client Copy with Data

In a client copy, the active client is copied from the source system (instead of the complete database, as in a database copy, for example).

- **Benefits**
  The benefits of using a client copy with data are as follows:
  - In contrast to a database copy, you don't need to reconfigure the target system.
  - The client structure of the target system isn't overwritten.
- **Drawbacks**
  The drawbacks of using a client copy with data are as follows:
  - Users can't work in the source or target system during the execution of a client copy. This constitutes a disadvantage for many enterprises because the time required to complete the client copy may cause the limits of acceptable downtime to be exceeded. If the source client is very large, it may take days to create the client copy.
  - Client-specific objects (such as programs, table structures, and so on) that were changed and are not identical in both systems are not copied.

While a client copy is an alternative to a database copy, you must ensure that it is appropriate for your enterprise.

2.8.3 Client Copy without Data

With this option, you can create a basic client copy, including Customizing settings, for example. No master data, transaction data, or, in most cases, user data are copied. The required (test) data are then loaded into the new client. The following tools are used for this purpose:

- CATT or eCATT
- Data Transfer Workbench (Transaction LSMW, Legacy System Migration Workbench)
- Application Link Enabling (ALE)

This option offers the following benefits, in addition to those listed earlier for the client copy option:

- You can control which data are loaded into the new clients.
- Data can be created to test specific objects.
- You don't need to access production data to test specific objects.
- Production data may not include data that are suitable for the testing of specific objects. Test data must then be created in any case.

The disadvantages of this option are the same as those specified for the creation of a client copy of the production system with data.

2.9 Summary

This chapter described the main tasks involved in system maintenance. You now know how to start and stop the SAP system. You also understand the significance of instances, operation modes, and work processes. You know how to maintain profile parameters to adapt the system configuration to the needs of your enterprise.

This chapter also introduced you to transactions that you can use to monitor the main areas of an SAP system. You can use these transactions to find out very quickly if any problems have occurred in your system.

In addition, this chapter discussed the administration of connections from, to, and between SAP systems, as well as client administration.

System administrators must be able to get a quick overview of the system status and be notified immediately of critical situations. This chapter presents the CCMS Alert Monitor, the essential tool for live system monitoring.

3 System Monitoring

Chapter 2 described how to manually monitor your system and check its status. In some systems, however, it may require a lot of time and effort to call the relevant transactions individually and to investigate warning and error messages.

For this reason, SAP offers tools to help you set up automatic system monitoring to continuously collect data about your system. If you don't have much time, you can use these tools to gain a quick overview of the system status. They also notify you automatically if the system status becomes critical. One of these tools is the CCMS Alert Monitor, which is described in this chapter. Another tool for monitoring SAP systems is the EarlyWatch Alert, which is described in Chapter 4, Section 4.4.3.

The following section provides essential information about the system monitoring techniques that are possible with the CCMS Alert Monitor. For more information about setting up a monitoring concept, and implementing this concept with SAP Solution Manager, refer, for example, to *Conception and Installation of System Monitoring Using the SAP Solution Manager* (SAP PRESS, 2009).

3.1 The CCMS Alert Monitor

The *CCMS Alert Monitor* (Computing Center Management System Alert Monitor) enables real-time, live monitoring of SAP systems. You can use Transaction RZ20 to monitor the servers in your system environment. You can use the tool to monitor individual systems or several systems from a central system.

The CCMS Alert Monitor has a hierarchical tree structure:

- At the highest level, the Monitor consists of several *monitor sets*.
- These, in turn, comprise several *monitors*.
- Monitors represent a grouping of *monitoring tree elements* (MTEs).
- The level below MTEs comprises *monitor objects*, which are the components of the system that are to be monitored.
- Each monitor has one or more *monitor attributes*, such as a value or a status.
- Threshold values are defined for each monitor attribute. As soon as a value exceeds or falls short of a threshold value, an *alert* is triggered. These alert messages usually indicate a serious problem that should be eliminated quickly. If a problem of this kind is not eliminated, an emergency situation may arise.

The CCMS Alert Monitor comes with a range of standard monitor sets for general system monitoring tasks. However, you can also define your own monitor sets, consisting exclusively of the monitor objects that you actually need. The advantage of doing so is that you can then obtain an ever faster overview of the system components that are important to you, as well as their statuses.

This chapter begins by describing the basic functions of the CCMS Alert Monitor, using the SAP standard monitor sets as examples. We will then explain how to create your own monitor sets.

[⚙]

Customizing the CCMS Alert Monitor

This book doesn't include a discussion of the technical settings of the CCMS Alert Monitor, which are defined in Transaction RZ21. Very detailed information about the configuration of this tool is provided in the SAP Help Portal (*http://help.sap.com*) under *Alert Monitor*.

This chapter assumes that your monitoring system landscape has already been preconfigured and is fully functional.

3.2 System Monitoring with the Standard CCMS Alert Monitor

Follow these steps to display alerts with the CCMS Alert Monitor:

1. Enter Transaction "RZ20" in the command field, and press the Enter key (or select the menu option Tools • CCMS • Control/Monitoring • RZ20—CCMS Monitor Sets).

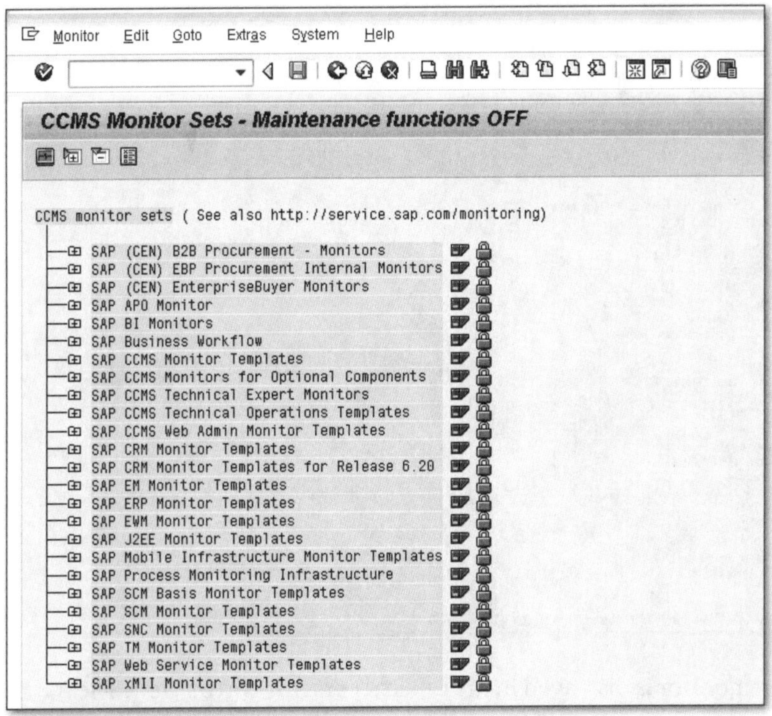

2. The screen displays all monitor sets provided in the SAP standard system. You can expand a monitor set (for example, CCMS Monitor Templates) to view the monitors it contains.

[+]

CCMS Monitor Sets in the SAP Standard System

The SAP standard sets are indicated by the Monitor set delivered by SAP icon (). These monitor templates can't be changed (as indicated by the not modifiable icon (). Only user-defined monitor sets can be adjusted.

3. To start a monitor (for example, Entire System), double-click on it, or position your cursor on the relevant row, and choose Load Monitor () on the top left of the screen.

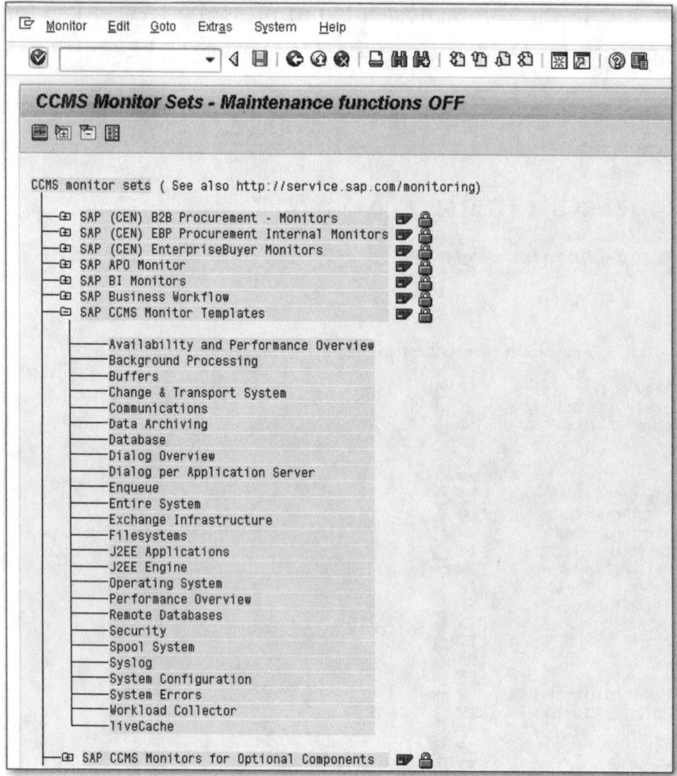

4. The selected monitor is displayed in the CURRENT SYSTEM STATUS view. The monitor objects belonging to the monitor are arranged in a tree structure. The color coding used in the monitor indicates immediately whether any alerts exist:
   - **Green:** No alerts exist.
   - **Yellow:** Less serious alerts exist (warnings).
   - **Red:** Serious alerts exist (errors).

   Expand the tree structure to display the individual monitor objects.

[+]

CCMS Alert Monitor Views

The CCMS Alert Monitor offers two different views: one view of the current system status (in which the current alert situation is displayed), and one view of alerts that are currently open (displaying alerts that have been generated but have not yet been confirmed).

You should eliminate the problems shown in the view showing the current system status before turning your attention to the open alerts.

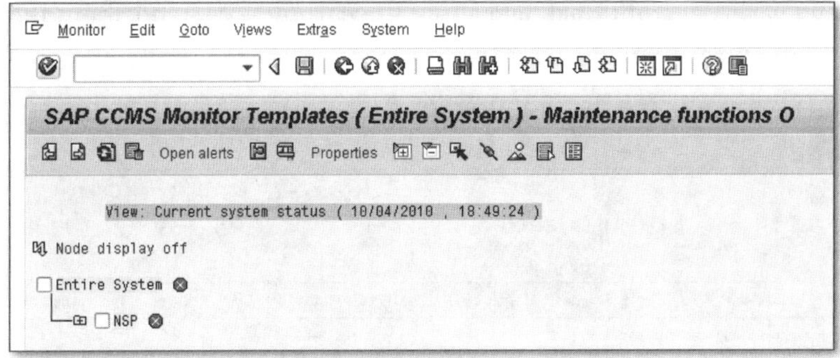

5. The lowest level in the tree structure shows the monitor objects, that is, the components or aspects of the system that are being monitored (for example, available memory on the C:\ drive). Each monitor object has a monitor attribute (such as available memory in MB). To display detailed information, position the cursor on a monitor object, and choose DISPLAY DETAILS ( ).

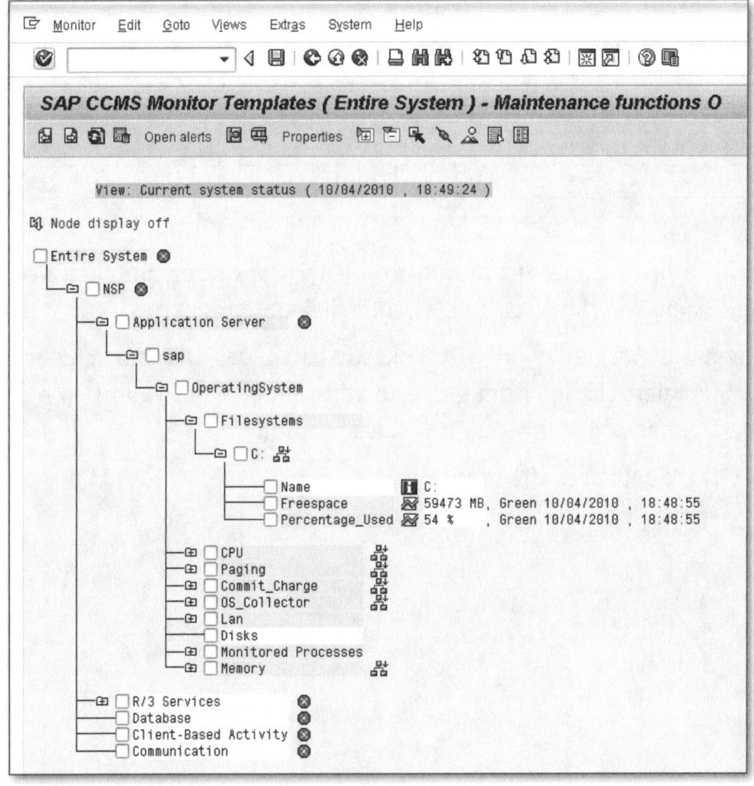

6. The detailed view shows additional data about the current status and about the progression of the measurements over time.

   Choose BACK (🡄 to return to the monitor view).

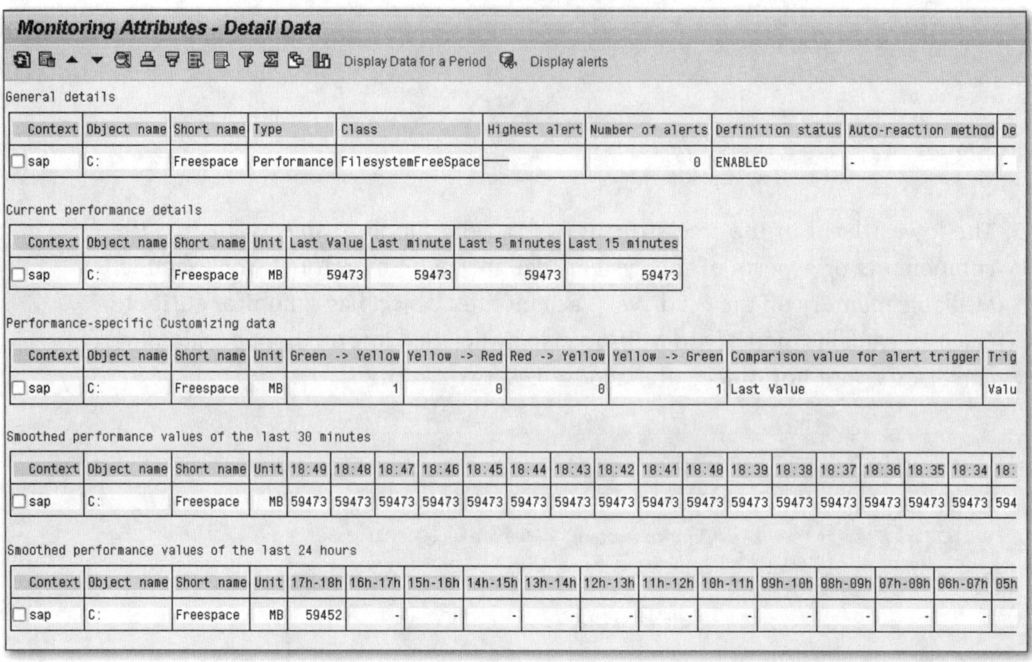

Monitoring Attributes - Detail Data

Display Data for a Period   Display alerts

General details

Context	Object name	Short name	Type	Class	Highest alert	Number of alerts	Definition status	Auto-reaction method	De
sap	C:	Freespace	Performance	FilesystemFreeSpace	—	0	ENABLED	-	-

Current performance details

Context	Object name	Short name	Unit	Last Value	Last minute	Last 5 minutes	Last 15 minutes
sap	C:	Freespace	MB	59473	59473	59473	59473

Performance-specific Customizing data

Context	Object name	Short name	Unit	Green -> Yellow	Yellow -> Red	Red -> Yellow	Yellow -> Green	Comparison value for alert trigger	Trig
sap	C:	Freespace	MB	1	0	0	1	Last Value	Valu

Smoothed performance values of the last 30 minutes

Context	Object name	Short name	Unit	18:49	18:48	18:47	18:46	18:45	18:44	18:43	18:42	18:41	18:40	18:39	18:38	18:37	18:36	18:35	18:34	18:
sap	C:	Freespace	MB	59473	59473	59473	59473	59473	59473	59473	59473	59473	59473	59473	59473	59473	59473	59473	59473	594

Smoothed performance values of the last 24 hours

Context	Object name	Short name	Unit	17h-18h	16h-17h	15h-16h	14h-15h	13h-14h	12h-13h	11h-12h	10h-11h	09h-10h	08h-09h	07h-08h	06h-07h	05h
sap	C:	Freespace	MB	59452	-	-	-	-	-	-	-	-	-	-	-	

7. To display the threshold values of a monitoring object, position your cursor on the object in the monitor view (see step 6), and click on PROPERTIES.

   On the PERFORMANCEATTRIBUTE tab, the THRESHOLD VALUES area indicates the values at which an alert change from green to yellow, and from yellow to red, as well as the values at which these alert levels are reset.

   Choose BACK (🡄) to return to the monitor.

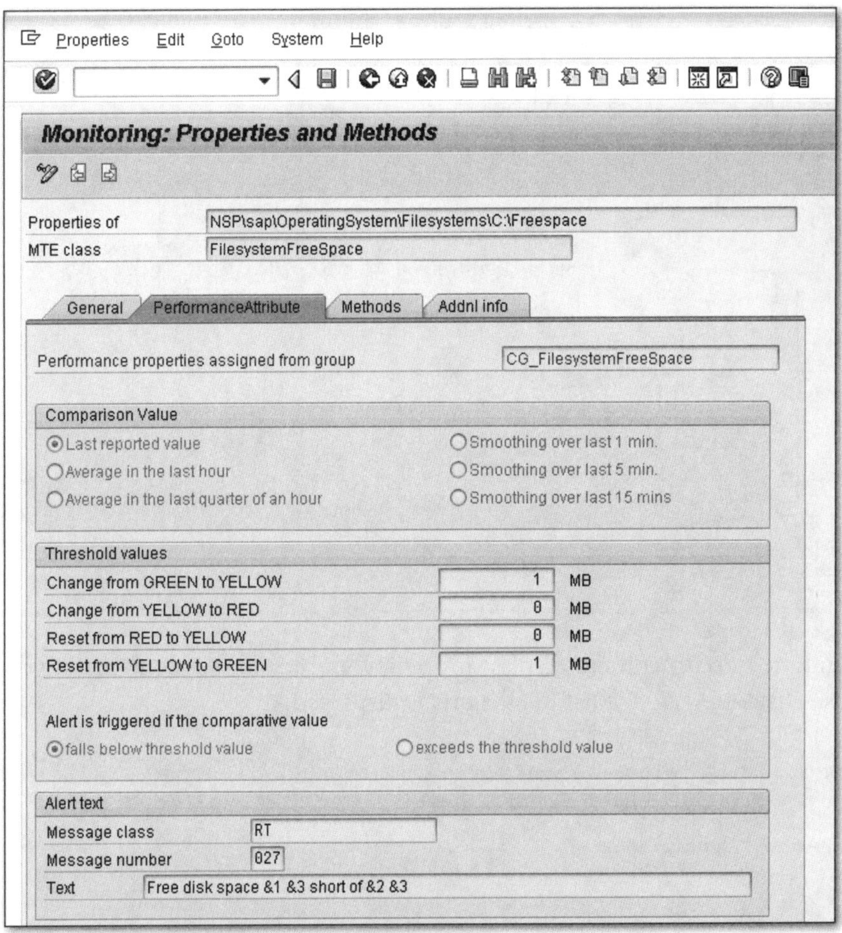

You now know how to display alerts with the CCMS Alert Monitor. You should always start by checking whether the current view contains any alerts. These must be investigated as high-priority issues to prevent or resolve serious problems in the system.

Next, check whether any older open alerts also exist using the following steps:

1. Click on OPEN ALERTS in the monitor to switch to the view of open alerts.

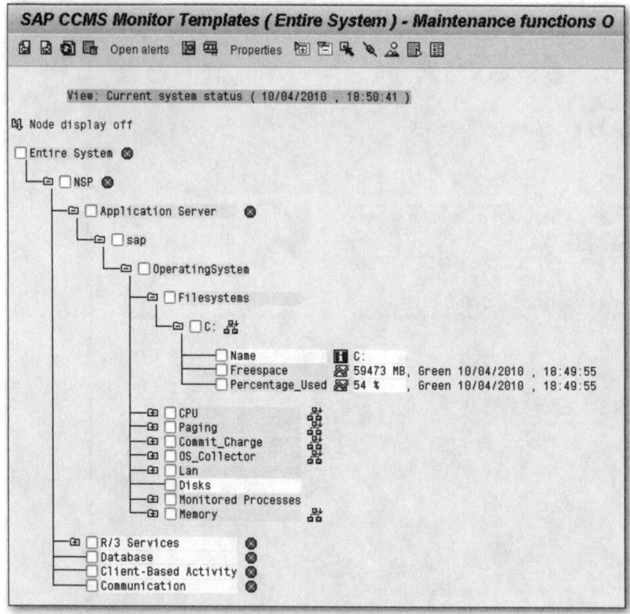

2. Expand the tree structure to display any yellow or red alerts it contains. If you choose DISPLAY ALERTS, a list of all alerts is displayed.

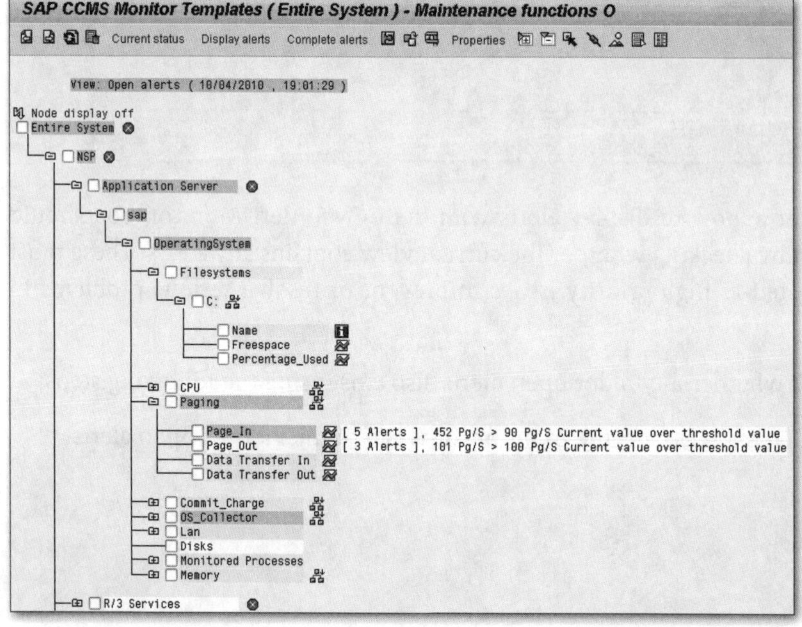

3. All alerts that have occurred are shown here. The alerts are listed according to their priority (red alerts before yellow). From here, you can also navigate to the details or properties of a monitor, for example, in order to show the history of the alert's occurrence and the threshold values.

   Choose DISPLAY DETAILS (icon).

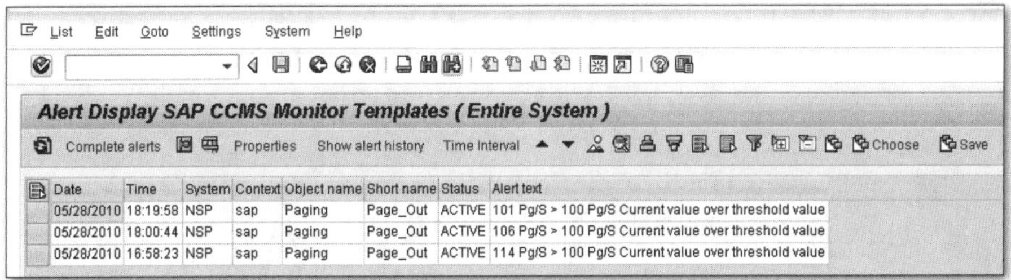

Date	Time	System	Context	Object name	Short name	Status	Alert text
05/28/2010	18:19:58	NSP	sap	Paging	Page_Out	ACTIVE	101 Pg/S > 100 Pg/S Current value over threshold value
05/28/2010	18:00:44	NSP	sap	Paging	Page_Out	ACTIVE	106 Pg/S > 100 Pg/S Current value over threshold value
05/28/2010	16:58:23	NSP	sap	Paging	Page_Out	ACTIVE	114 Pg/S > 100 Pg/S Current value over threshold value

4. To view a graphical representation of the alert history, select the values from the past 30 minutes, and click on DISPLAY PERFORMANCE VALUES GRAPHICALLY (icon).

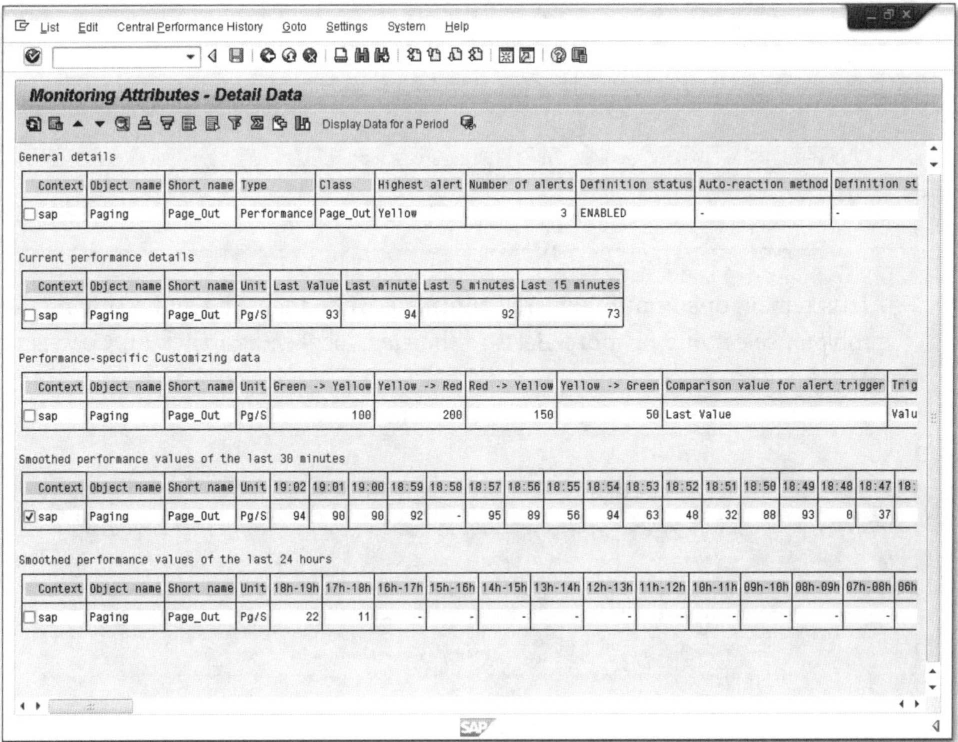

General details

Context	Object name	Short name	Type	Class	Highest alert	Number of alerts	Definition status	Auto-reaction method	Definition st
sap	Paging	Page_Out	Performance	Page_Out	Yellow	3	ENABLED	-	-

Current performance details

Context	Object name	Short name	Unit	Last Value	Last minute	Last 5 minutes	Last 15 minutes
sap	Paging	Page_Out	Pg/S	93	94	92	73

Performance-specific Customizing data

Context	Object name	Short name	Unit	Green -> Yellow	Yellow -> Red	Red -> Yellow	Yellow -> Green	Comparison value for alert trigger	Trig
sap	Paging	Page_Out	Pg/S	100	200	150	50	Last Value	Valu

Smoothed performance values of the last 30 minutes

Context	Object name	Short name	Unit	19:02	19:01	19:00	18:59	18:58	18:57	18:56	18:55	18:54	18:53	18:52	18:51	18:50	18:49	18:48	18:47	18:
sap	Paging	Page_Out	Pg/S	94	90	90	92	-	95	89	56	94	63	48	32	88	93	0	37	

Smoothed performance values of the last 24 hours

Context	Object name	Short name	Unit	18h-19h	17h-18h	16h-17h	15h-16h	14h-15h	13h-14h	12h-13h	11h-12h	10h-11h	09h-10h	08h-09h	07h-08h	06h
sap	Paging	Page_Out	Pg/S	22	11	-	-	-	-	-	-	-	-	-	-	

5. The graphical display indicates how the values have changed over the past half-hour.

   Choose BACK (⊕) to return to the previous screen.

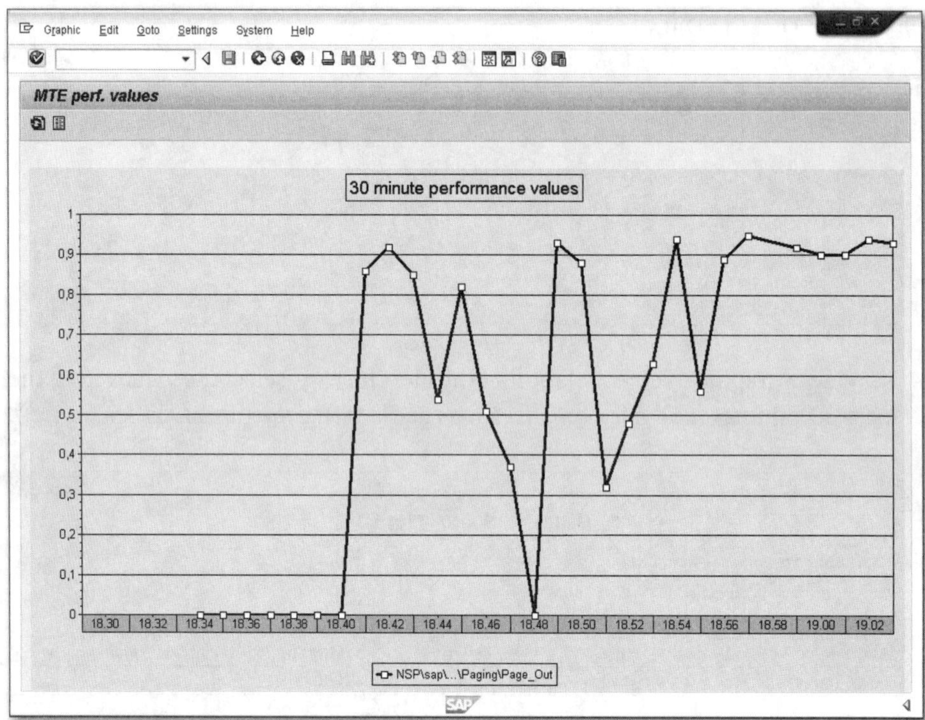

6. Alerts remain open until they are confirmed. After analyzing and resolving the problem, select one or more alerts in the alert display, and click on COMPLETE ALERTS.

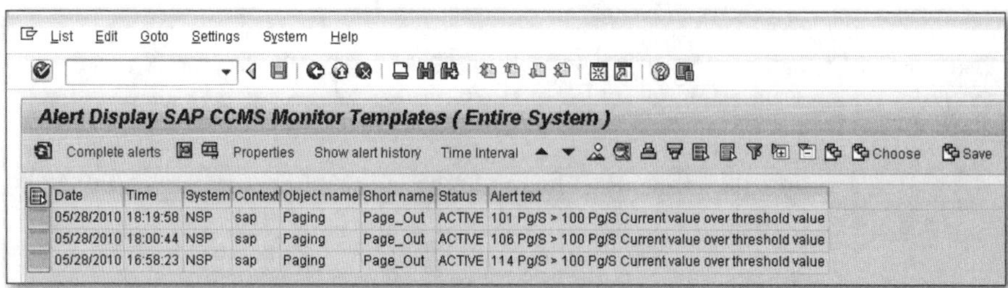

7. A message in the status bar confirms that the alerts have been completed. Choose BACK (⊕) to return to the monitor view.

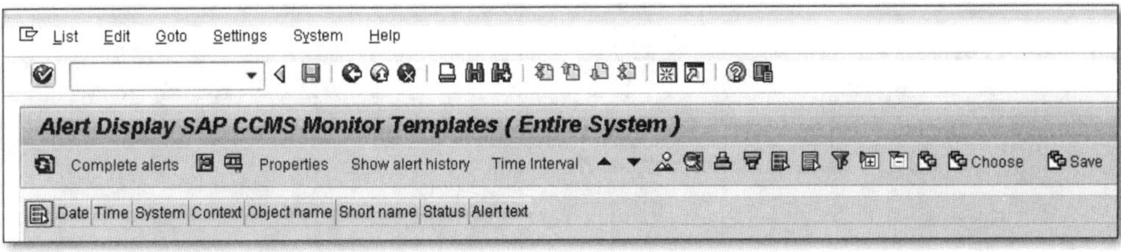

8. If you have set all alerts to COMPLETED, the monitor display appears as a green tree structure. It now contains no more open alerts:

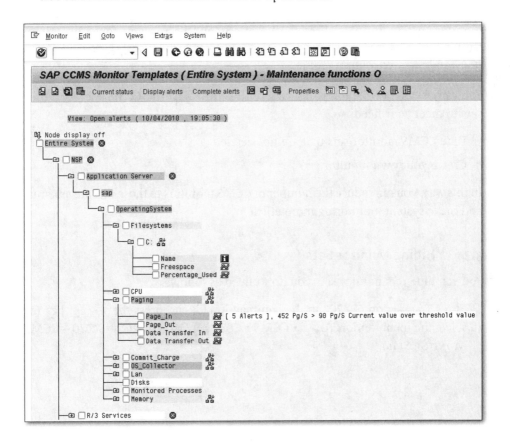

Monitor Edit Goto Views Extras System Help

SAP CCMS Monitor Templates (Entire System) - Maintenance functions O

Current status Display alerts Complete alerts Properties

View: Open alerts (10/04/2010 , 19:05:30)

Node display off
Entire System
NSP
Application Server
sap
OperatingSystem
Filesystems
C:
Name
Freespace
Percentage_Used
CPU
Paging
Page_In [5 Alerts], 452 Pg/S > 90 Pg/S Current value over threshold value
Page_Out
Data Transfer In
Data Transfer Out
Commit_Charge
OS_Collector
Lan
Disks
Monitored Processes
Memory
R/3 Services

By completing alerts, you also delete them from the OPEN ALERTS view. The list of open alerts will fill up again as soon as the system detects any new threshold violations.

[!] **Completing Alerts**

You still need to resolve the issue highlighted by the alert. Confirming an alert merely indicates that you have taken note of it.

3.3 Adapting the CCMS Monitor Sets

The CCMS monitors provided in the standard SAP delivery offer very extensive monitoring options. Not all of these options will be relevant for your system landscape. Moreover, the extensive nature of the monitors hampers fast access to the really important information.

You can use one of the following two options to adjust the CCMS Alert Monitor sets to meet your needs:

- Hide CCMS monitor sets that are not needed
- Create your own monitor sets

In this way, you can reduce the number of CCMS monitors to those that are essential and make system monitoring more efficient.

3.3.1 Hiding Monitor Sets

You can hide the monitor sets you don't need as follows:

1. Enter Transaction "RZ20" in the command field, and press the Enter key (or select the menu option TOOLS • CCMS • CONTROL/MONITORING • RZ20—CCMS MONITOR SETS).

2. On the CCMS Monitor Sets—Maintenance Functions Off screen, select the menu option Extras • Activate Maintenance function.

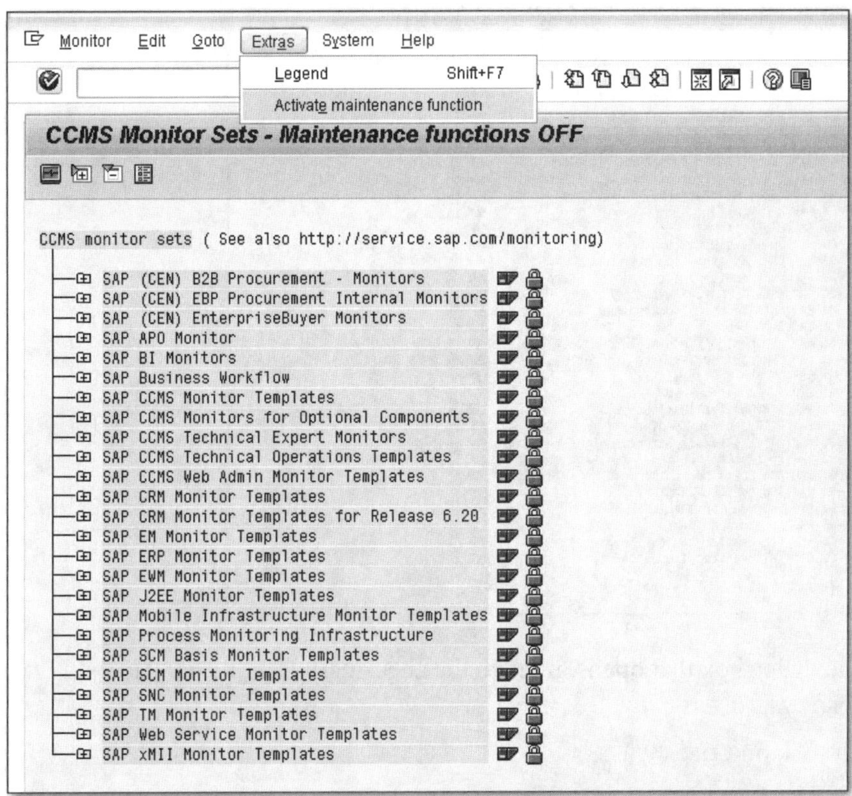

3. The screen title then changes to CCMS Monitor Sets—Maintenance Functions ON. The tree structure of the monitor sets is divided into the two root nodes My favorites and All.

   To hide a CCMS monitor set, position your cursor on the relevant set (for example, SAP J2EE Monitor Templates if you only want to monitor ABAP systems), and choose Change (✎).

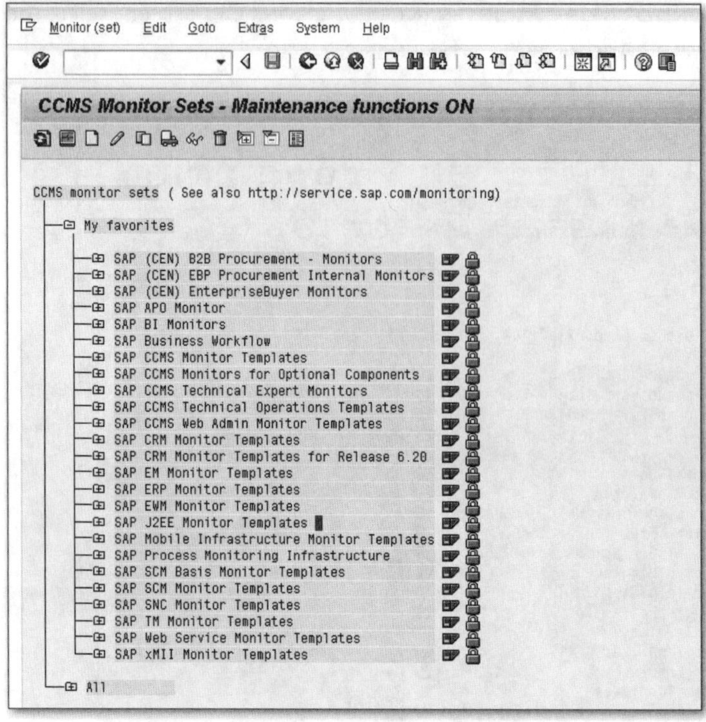

4. In the dialog box that opens, remove the checkmark from the PUBLIC field (VISIBLE FOR ALL USERS).

   Then click on COPY (✓).

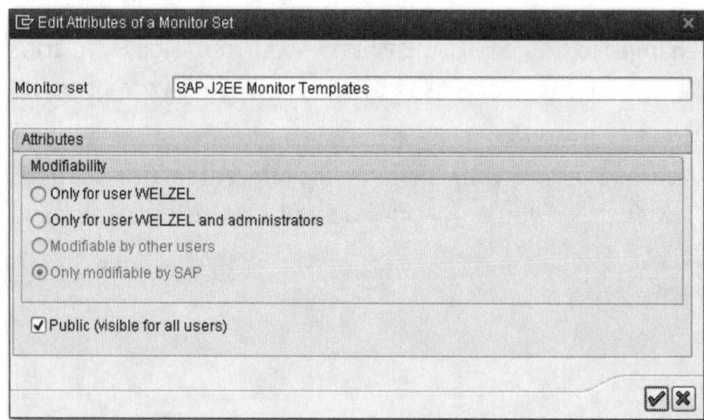

5. A message in the status bar confirms that your changes have been saved. The monitor set has been deleted from the My favorites node. Repeat these steps for all monitors that are not required.

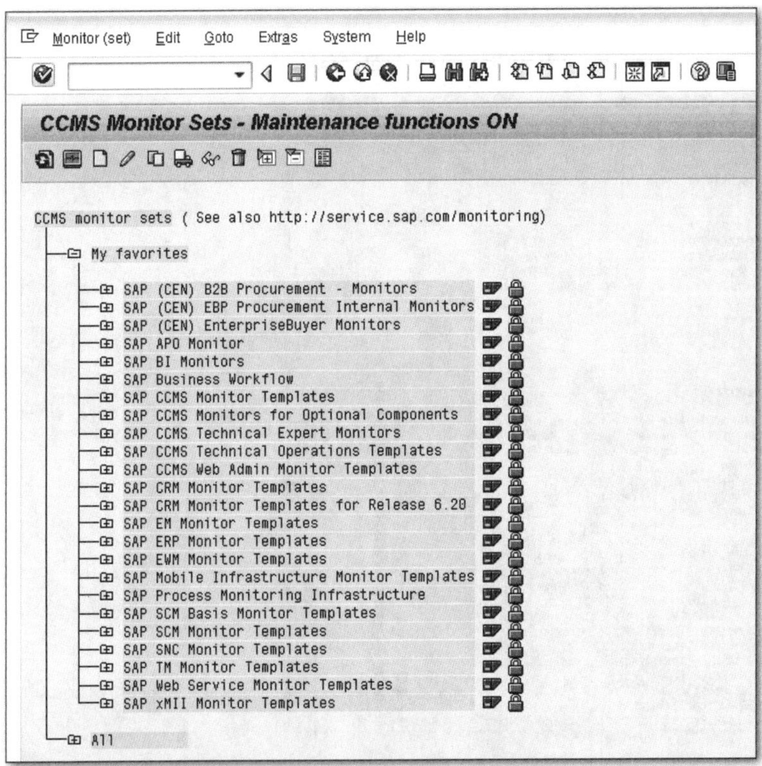

6. To check your change, select the menu option Extras • Deactivate Maintenance function. When you do so, the monitor set is no longer shown on the initial screen of Transaction RZ20.

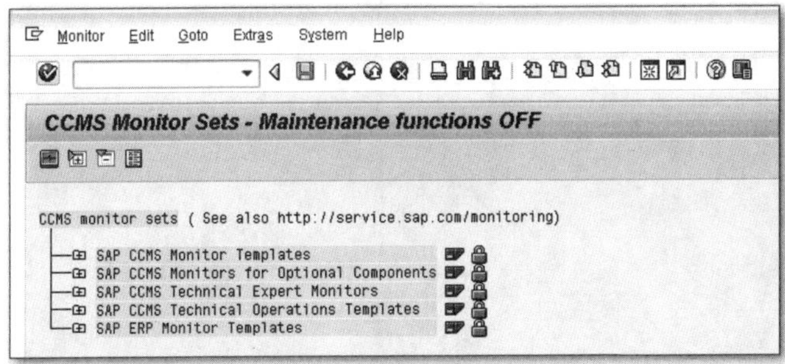

7. If you want to show the hidden CCMS monitor set again, activate the maintenance functions, and find the monitor set under ALL • SAP in the tree structure. Position your cursor on the monitor set you want to show, and choose CHANGE (✎).

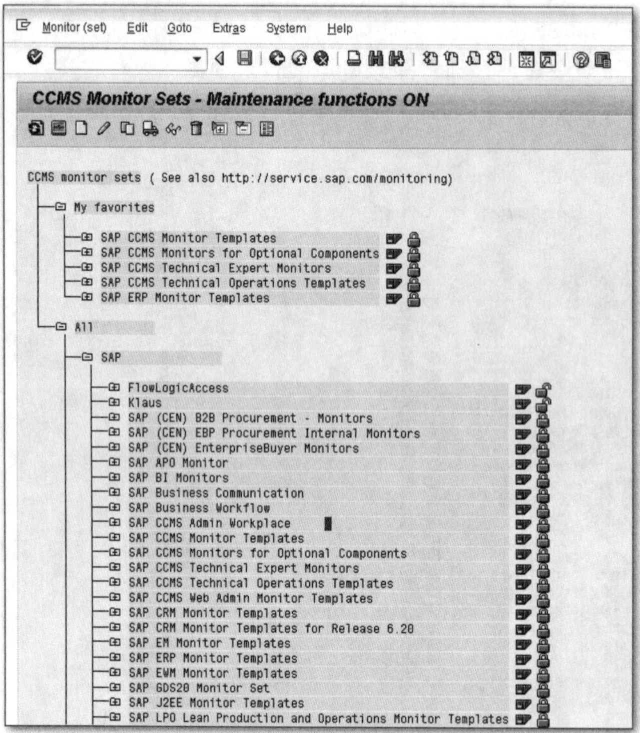

8. Activate the PUBLIC field (VISIBLE FOR ALL USERS) in the dialog box, and choose COPY (✔).

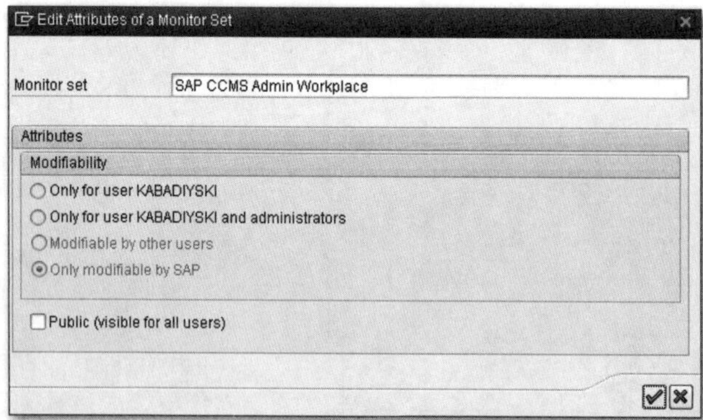

9. Saving is confirmed, and the monitor is displayed under the My FAVORITES node.

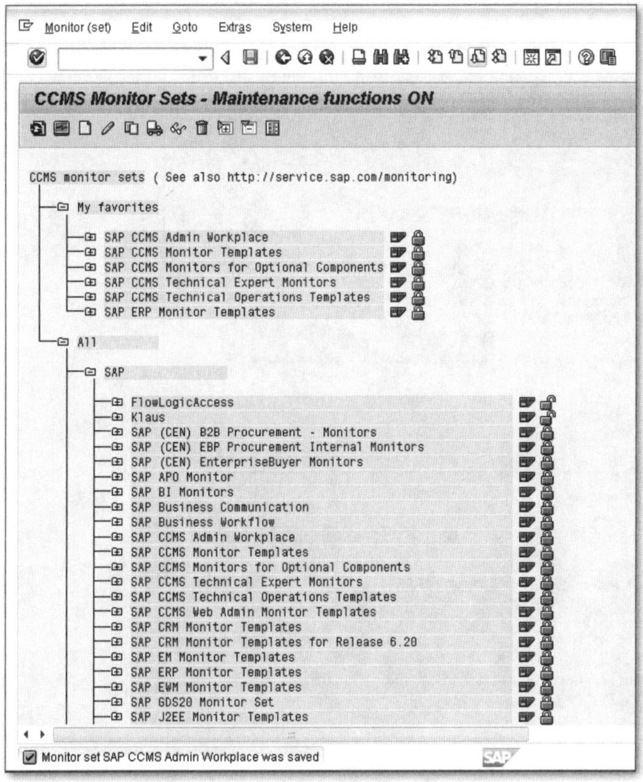

By hiding unnecessary CCMS monitor sets, you've taken a first step toward making monitoring more manageable. This may be sufficient for your routine monitoring tasks. If not, you can make further adjustments.

3.3.2 Defining a New Monitor Set

If the standard monitor sets don't meet your requirements, you can create or build your own monitor sets:

1. Enter Transaction "RZ20" in the command field, and press the Enter key (or select the menu option TOOLS • CCMS • CONTROL/MONITORING • RZ20—CCMS MONITOR SETS).

2. Select the menu option EXTRAS • ACTIVATE MAINTENANCE FUNCTION to activate the maintenance functions.

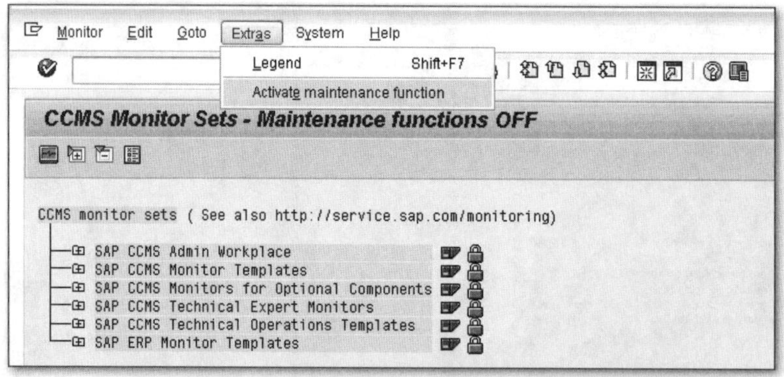

3. Choose CREATE (□).

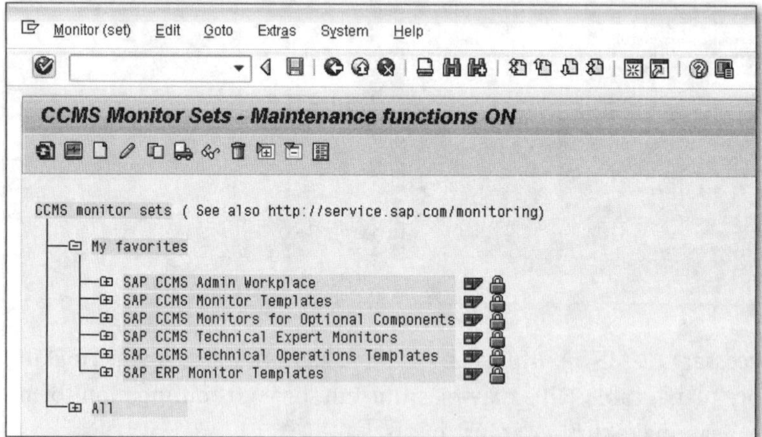

Copying Monitor Sets

An alternative option to creating a new monitor set is to copy an existing one. This is useful if, for example, you want to copy most of one of the standard monitor sets but eliminate a small number of monitors that are not required. In this case, click the COPY button (⧉).

4. In the dialog box that opens, select the NEW MONITOR SET option, and click on CONTINUE (✔).

5. Enter the following details on the next screen:
   - Enter a name for the set in the MONITOR SET field.
   - Under MODIFIABILITY, specify which users are permitted to modify the set.
   - If you want the monitor set to be displayed on the initial screen of Transaction RZ20, activate the PUBLIC field.

   Then choose CONTINUE (✔).

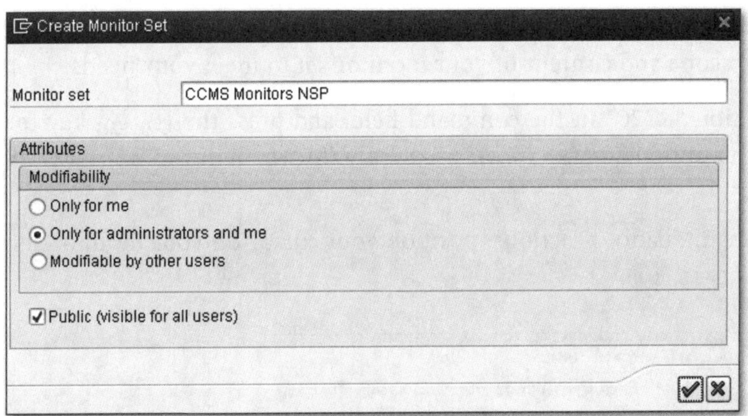

6. The new monitor set is now shown under MY FAVORITES. The PUBLIC MONITOR SET icon (👥) indicates entries that you have created yourself. The MODIFIABLE icon (🔓) signals that the set can be edited.

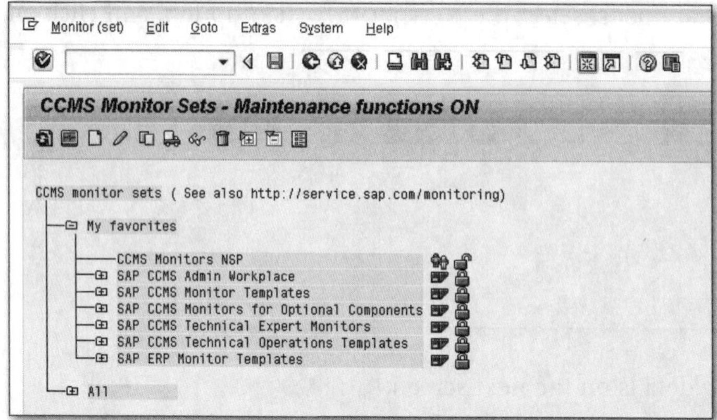

Your CCMS monitor set has now been created. The next step involves making changes to the monitors contained in the set. You can add new monitors and remove any that you don't need.

3.3.3 Adding a Monitor to a Monitor Set

You can add monitors to CCMS monitor sets you created yourself. This option allows you to adapt the scope and content of your monitor set to meet your needs.

1. Enter Transaction "RZ20" in the command field, and press the Enter key (or select the menu option TOOLS • CCMS • CONTROL/MONITORING • RZ20—CCMS MONITOR SETS).
2. Activate the maintenance functions, position your cursor on your monitor set, and choose CREATE (🗋).

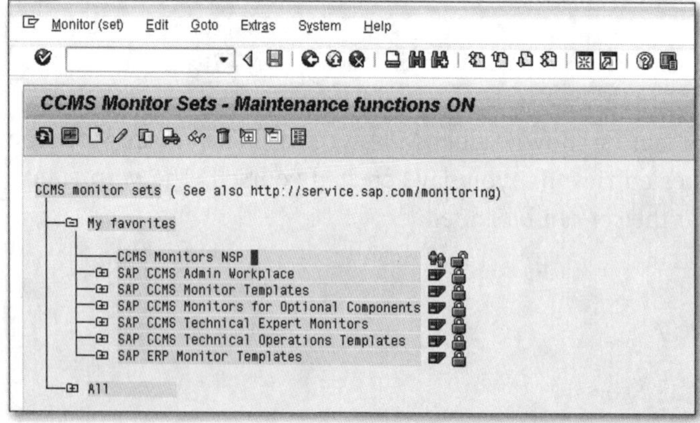

3. The monitor objects you added are displayed in a tree structure. Expand the monitor tree, and select the node you want to add to your monitor set (for example, BACKGROUND). When you have selected all of the monitor objects you want to add, click on SAVE (💾).

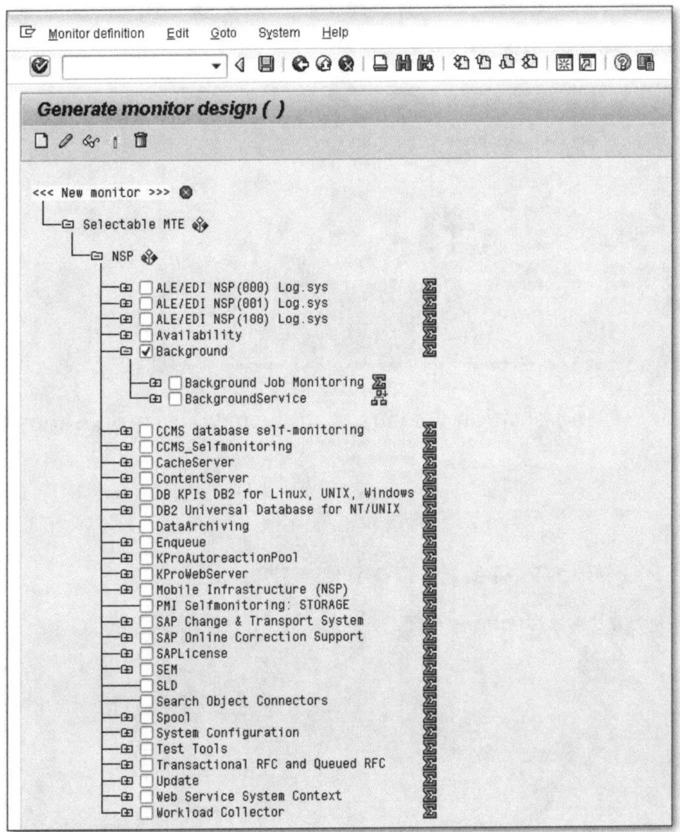

4. In the dialog box that opens, enter a meaningful name for your new monitor in the MONITOR field. Choose CONTINUE (✔) to save the monitor definition.

5. A message in the status bar confirms that your monitor definition has been saved. You can now deactivate the maintenance functions again.

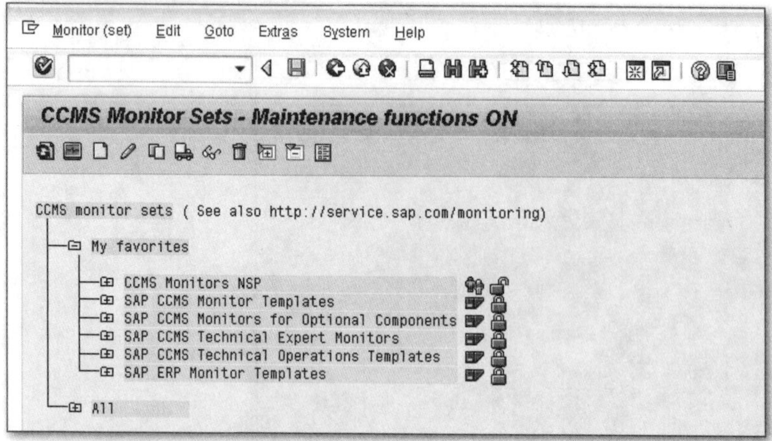

6. Expand your monitor set, and position the cursor on the new monitor. Choose LOAD MONITOR (icon).

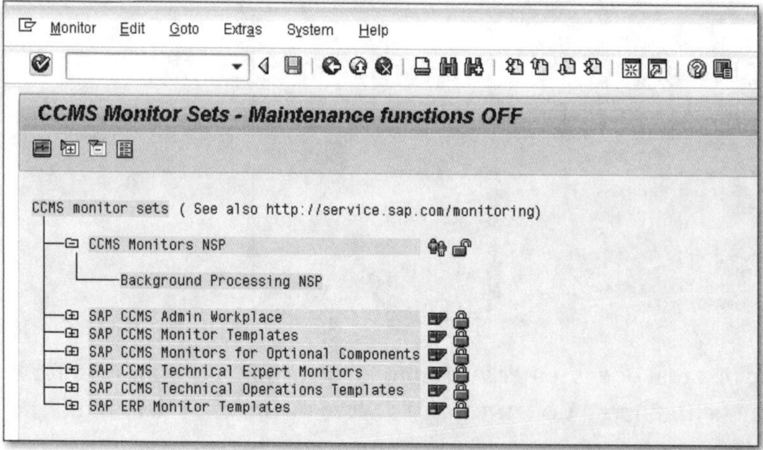

7. Expand the monitor tree. This new monitor only displays the nodes you selected. In the example provided here, the monitor is used for monitoring background processing by the system.

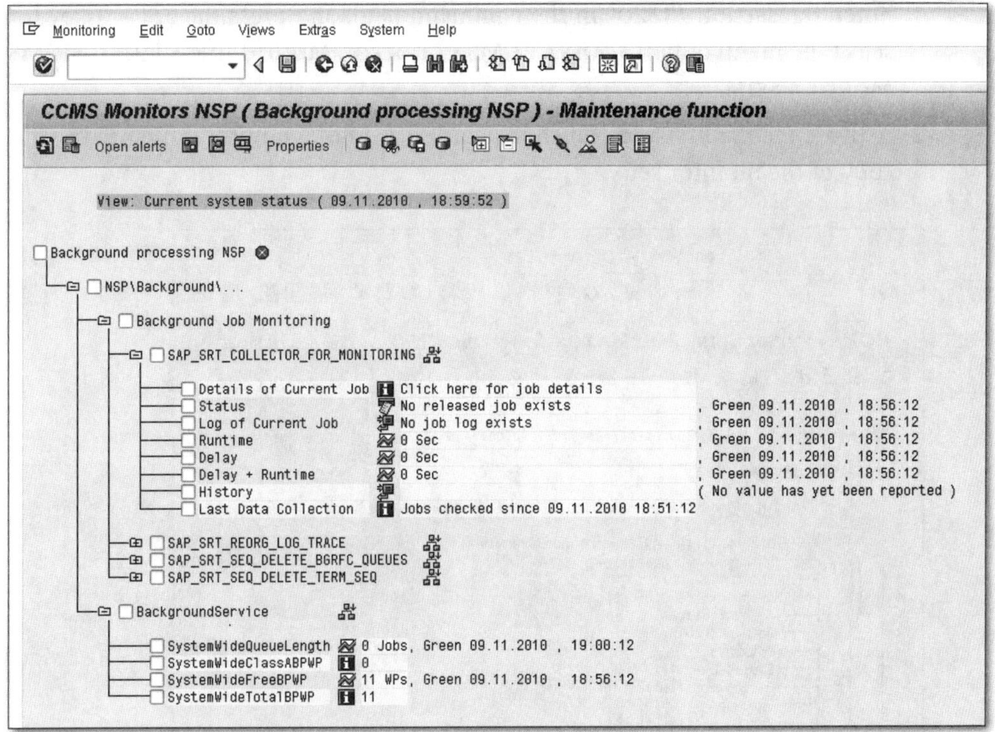

It may be useful to build your own user-defined monitors if you use CCMS Alert Monitoring on a frequent basis and want to be able to view the most important alerts at a glance. This allows you to monitor critical areas of SAP systems with greater efficiency.

Even if you monitor several systems, having your own monitor sets is still useful. You can, for example, check certain aspects of all monitored systems (for example, background processing) and create a new monitor for this purpose.

3.3.4 Deleting a Monitor from a Monitor Set

SAP standard monitors provide a sound starting point for creating customer-specific monitor sets. After copying these standard monitor sets, you can eliminate any monitors you don't need from your copy. This allows you to create your own custom monitoring solution.

1. Enter Transaction "RZ20" in the command field, and press the Enter key (or select the menu option TOOLS • CCMS • CONTROL/MONITORING • RZ20—CCMS MONITOR SETS).
2. Activate the maintenance functions, and expand the monitor structure in your copy of the monitor set.

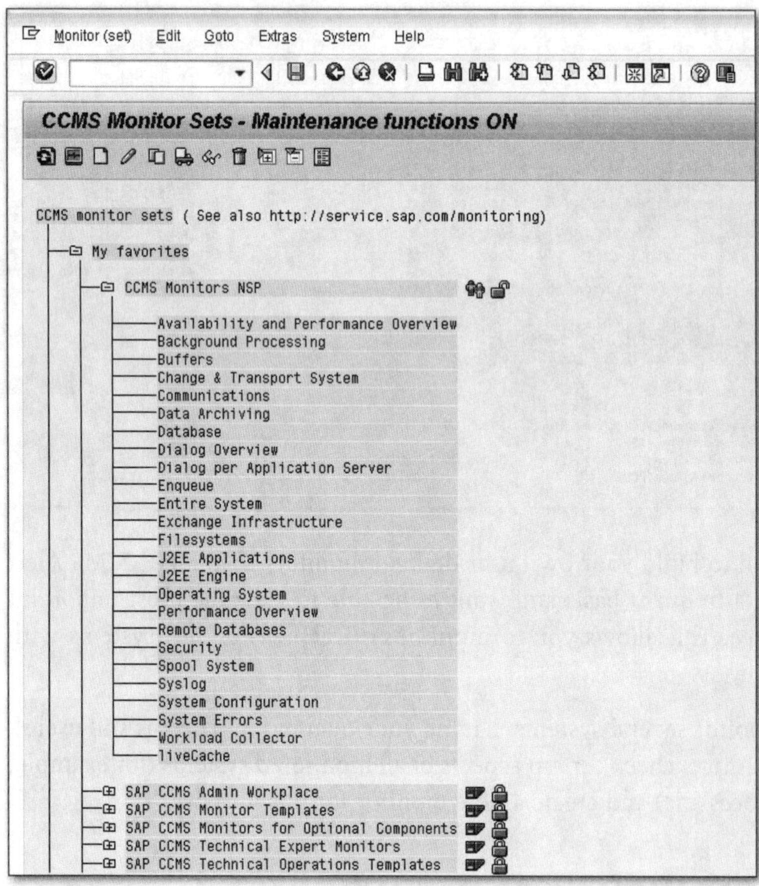

3. Position the cursor on the monitor you want to delete (for example, J2EE ENGINE), and choose DELETE (🗑).

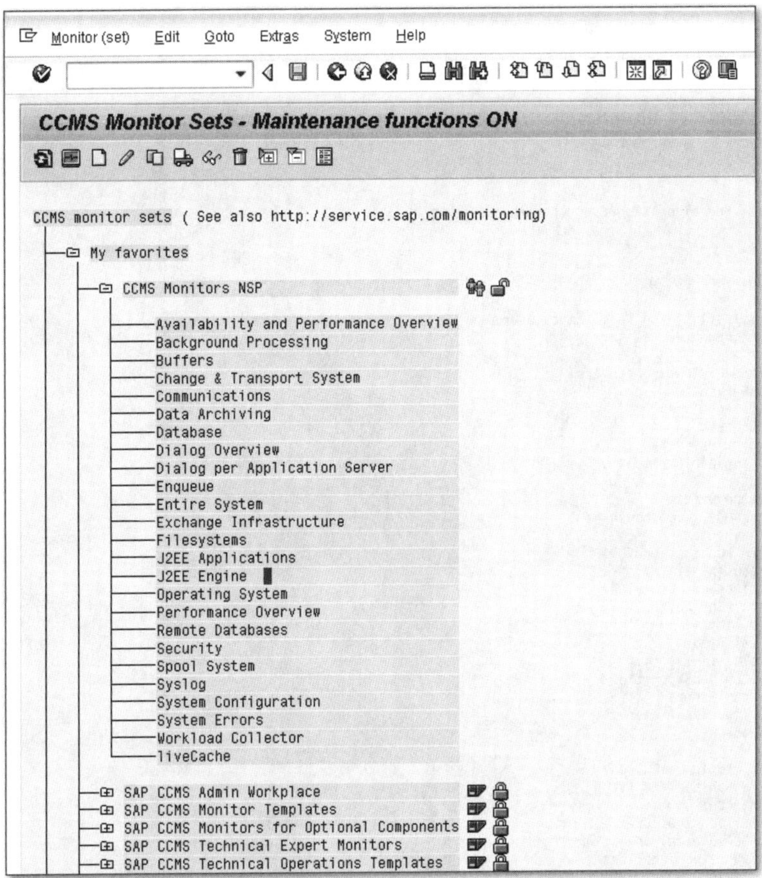

4. Choose YES to confirm deletion in the dialog box.

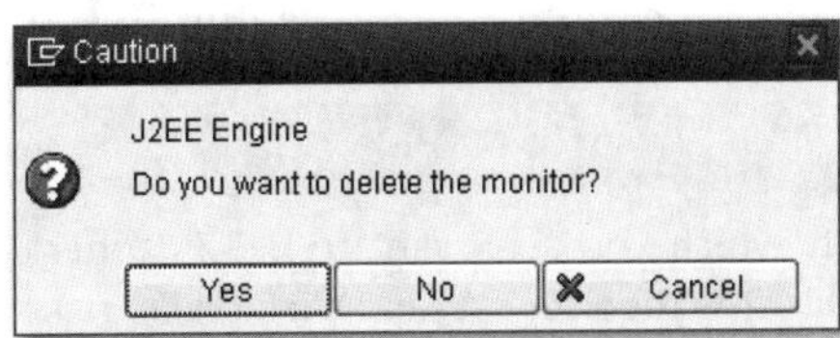

5. A message appears in the status bar to confirm that the monitor has been deleted.

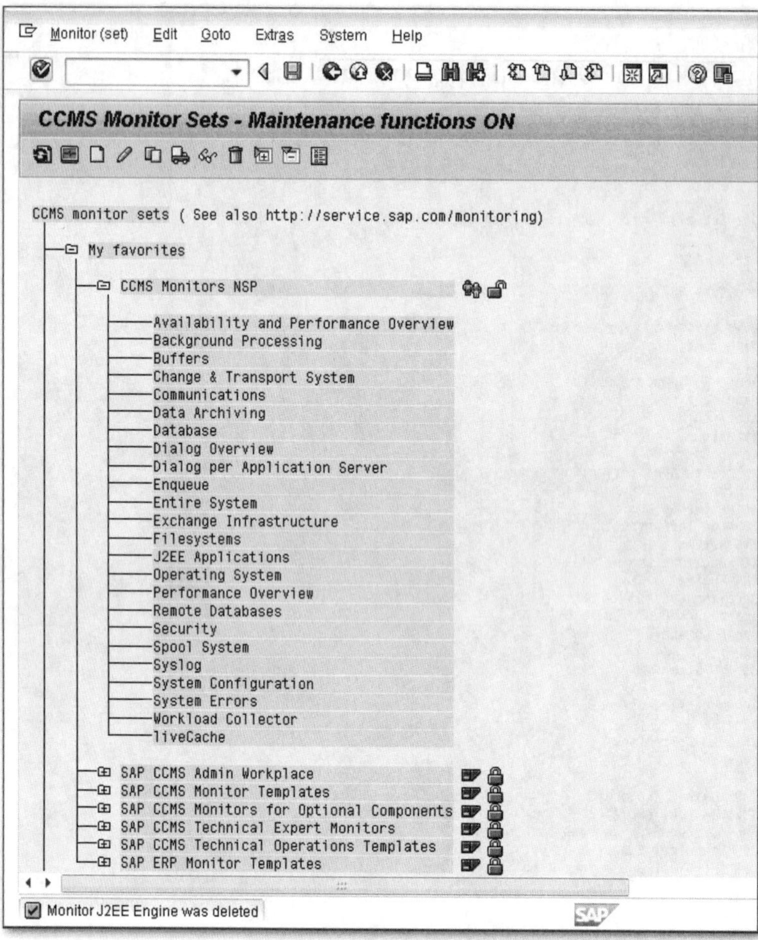

6. Repeat these steps until you are only left with the monitors you require.

Transporting Monitor Sets

If you've created your own CCMS monitor set, which you also want to use in other systems, you can use the transport function: Select the monitor set, and click on TRANSPORT MONITOR SET (). You can then use a transport request to import the monitor set into other systems.

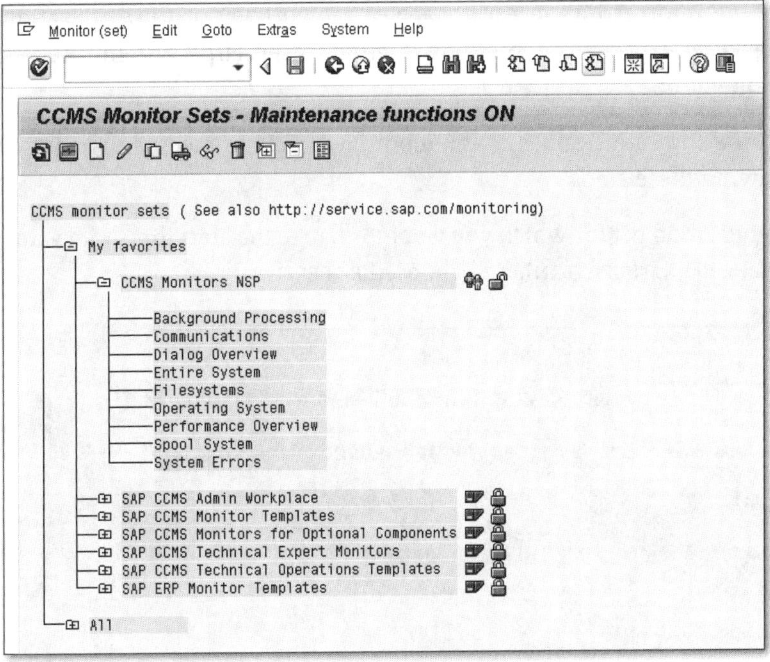

3.3.5 Changing Alert Threshold Values

An alert threshold value is a value at which an alert indicator changes color. The color changes from green to yellow, and from yellow to red, depending on the severity of the problem to which you are being alerted. The indicator then switches back from red to yellow, and yellow to green, when the system returns to an uncritical status.

Because every SAP installation is unique, various threshold values may be useful. You may want to change the threshold values in the example scenarios described here:

- A large amount of paging (or, more accurately, swapping, that is, the removal of data from the main memory [RAM] to the virtual memory on the hard disk) is problematic in the production system but is not critical in the development system.
- The database file is the only file on a drive, and it takes up all of that drive. A file system full alert is therefore superfluous because the configuration of the database allows it to occupy the entire drive.

- You need to be informed at an early stage of a high level of CPU utilization because, based on experience, you know that you need large system reserves during live operation.

You can adjust the threshold values of the monitor objects to meet your requirements by following these steps:

1. Select the monitor object for which you want to change the alert threshold value (for example, CPU_UTILIZATION), and choose PROPERTIES.

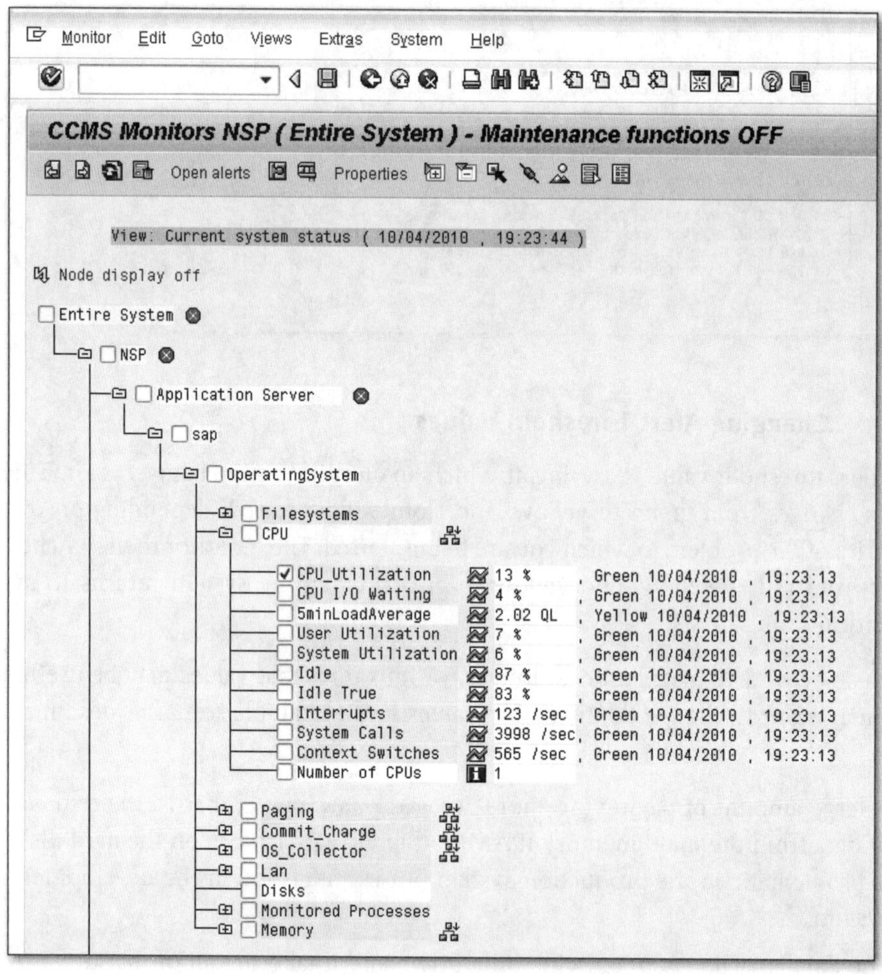

2. Click on DISPLAY <-> CHANGE (icon) to switch to change mode.

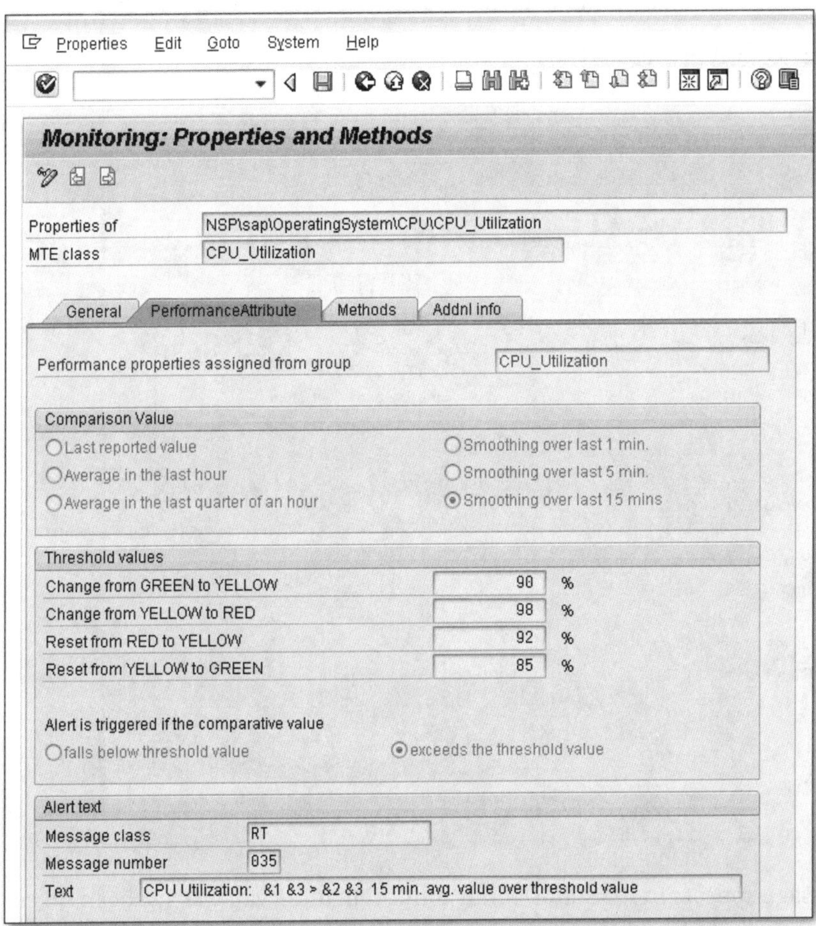

3. Under THRESHOLD VALUES, enter the values that meet your requirements. Choose SAVE (icon).

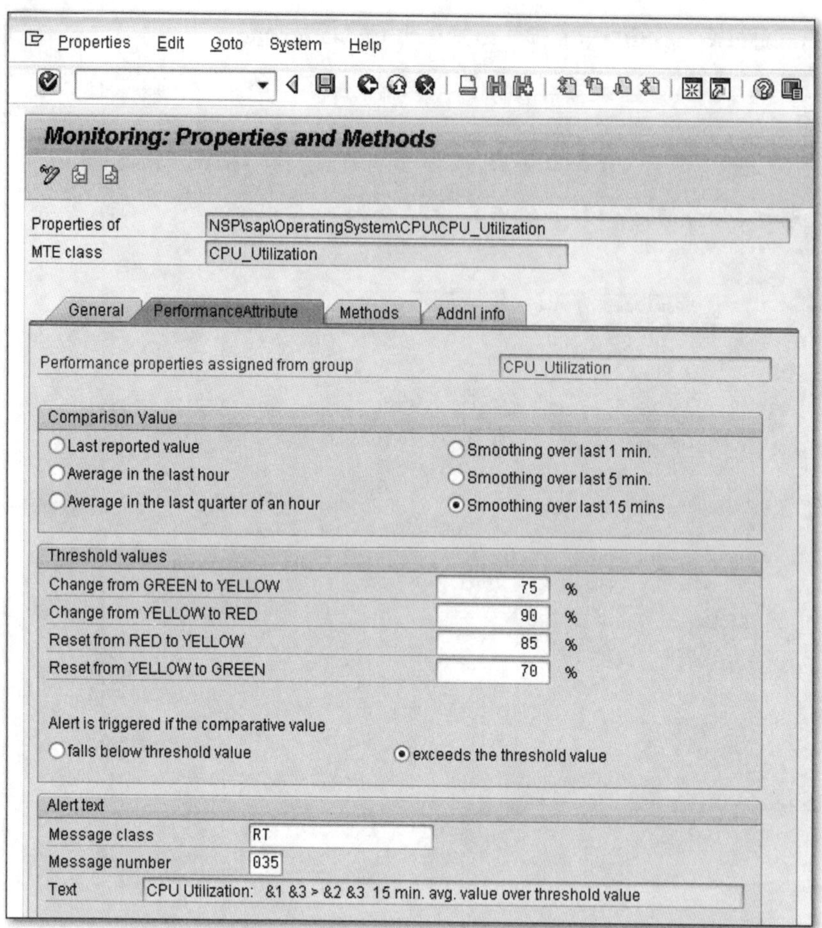

4. A message appears in the status bar to confirm that the values have been saved. Choose Back (◉) to return to the monitor.

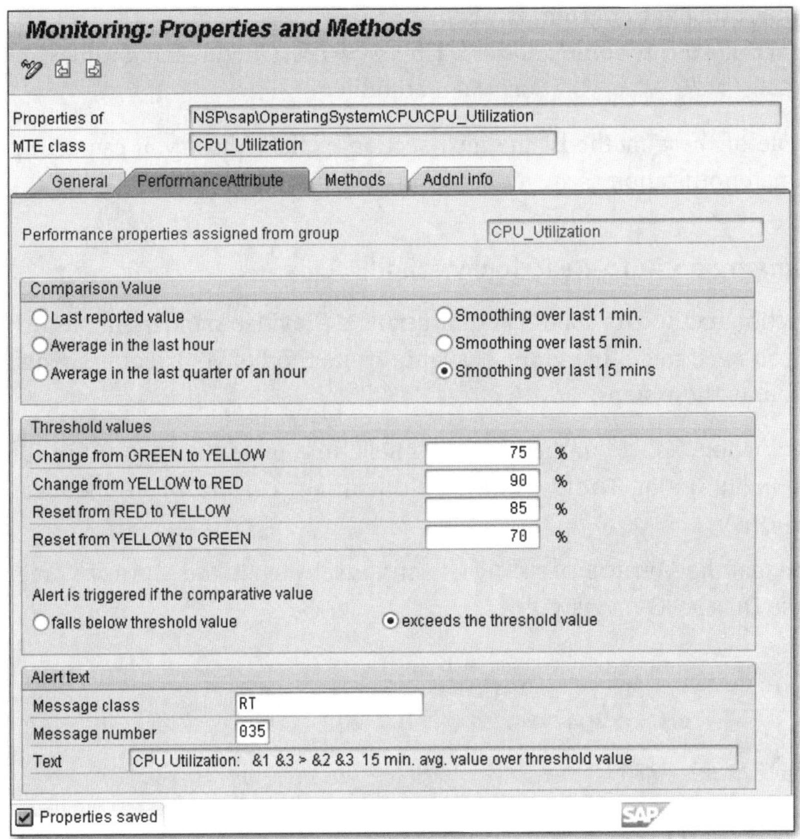

From now on, the alerts of the monitor object will be switched as soon as the relevant values exceed or fall short of the threshold values you defined.

3.4 Auto-Reaction Methods

Auto-reaction methods are key components of the CCMS Alert Monitor. You can use these methods to determine how the system responds in the event of an alert. Possible auto-reaction methods include the following:

- **Automatic alert notification**
  You can ensure that the system automatically sends you a notification, for example, by email or text message whenever an alert occurs (`CCMS_OnAlert_Email` method).

- **Execute operating system commands**
  The system can execute commands or scripts when certain threshold values are reached (CCMS_AUTO_REACT_OP_COMMAND method).

As an example of these methods, the next section explains how you can set up automatic email notification as an auto-reaction to an alert.

3.4.1 Changing an Auto-Reaction Method

The auto-reaction method for sending notifications is provided standard in the SAP system. All you need to do, therefore, is adapt this method to your requirements. To do this, follow these steps:

1. Enter Transaction "RZ21" in the command field, and press the Enter key (or select the menu option TOOLS • CCMS • CONFIGURATION • RZ21—ATTRIBUTES AND METHODS).
2. Make sure that the METHOD DEFINITIONS entry is selected in the METHODS area, and choose DISPLAY OVERVIEW.

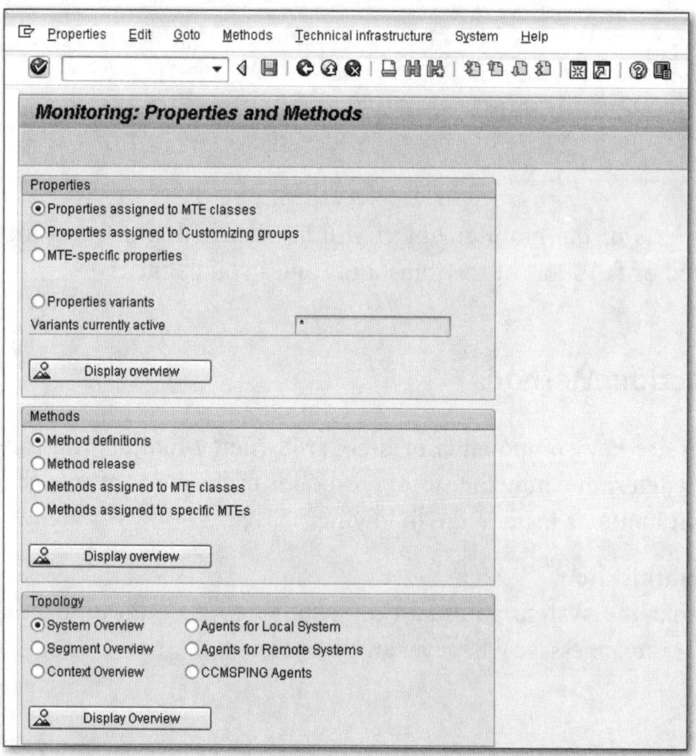

3. Scroll in the list until you find the CCMS_ONALERT_EMAIL method, and then select it. Choose COPY (📋).

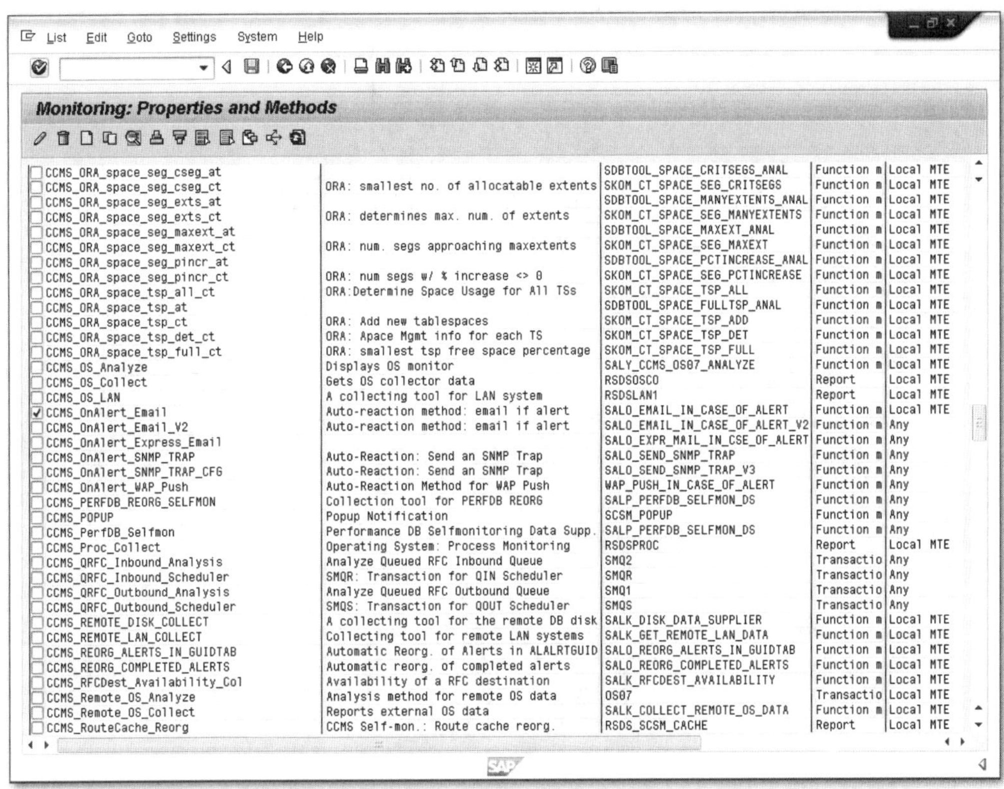

Copying Auto-Reaction Methods [+]

Avoid changing the SAP standard auto-reaction methods. Instead, make a copy of these methods, and then modify your copies. This approach means that you'll always have access to the unaltered original method definitions should you need them again. You may need to make several copies of an auto-reaction method in certain cases, for example, to send notification to a different set of recipients, depending on the alert.

4. In the dialog box displayed, give the auto-reaction method a new name (for example, Z_CCMS_ONALERT_EMAIL_01), and click CONTINUE (✔) to confirm.

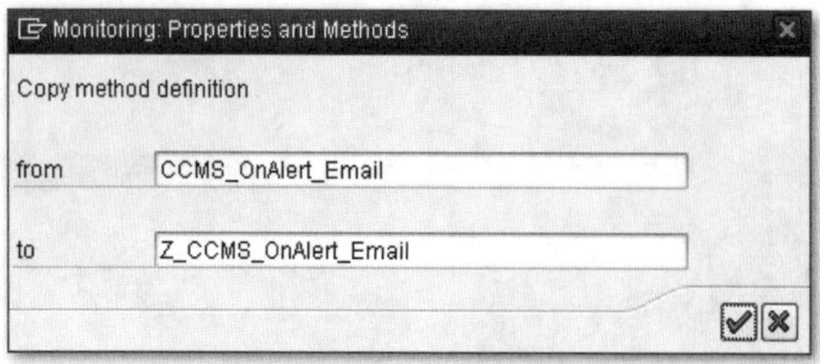

5. Your copy of the auto-reaction method is displayed. Click on Display <-> Change (✎) to switch to change mode.

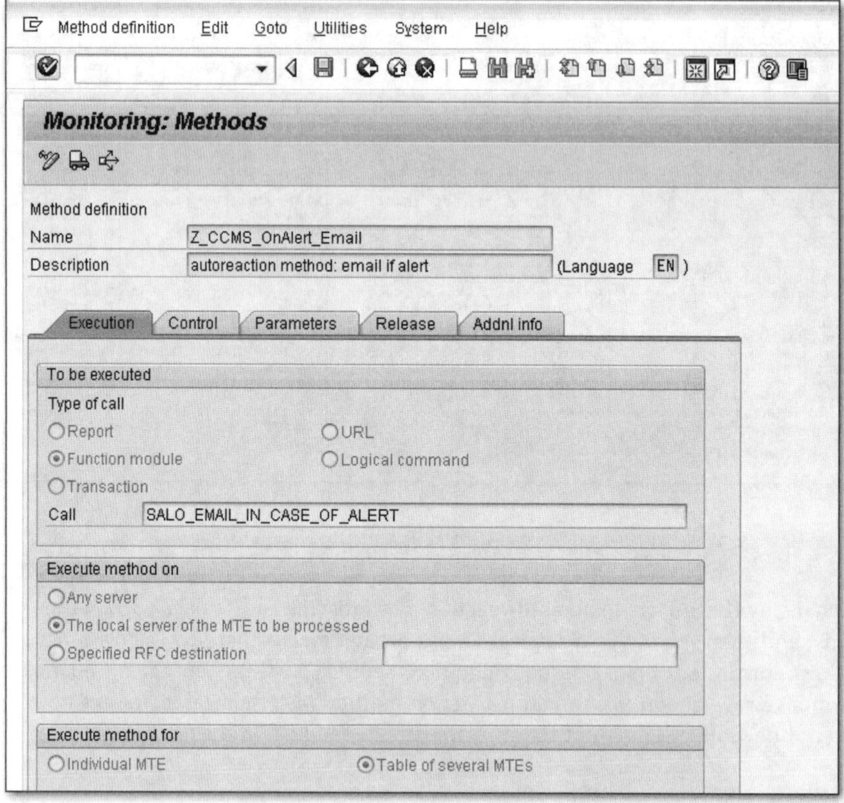

6. Choose the Parameters tab.

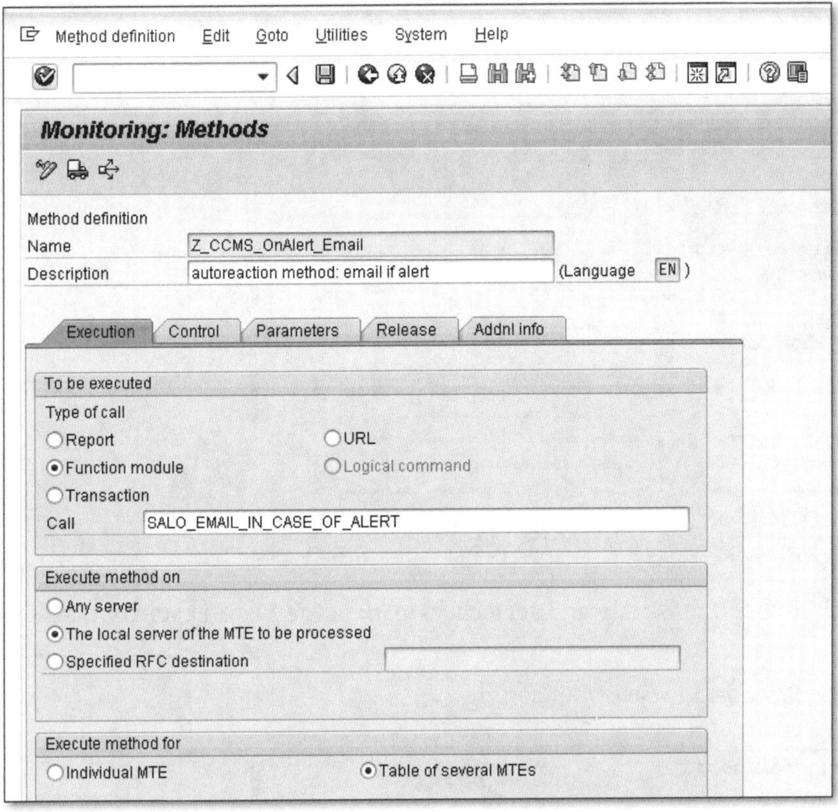

7. Make the following settings:

   - As a parameter value for the `SENDER` parameter, enter the SAP user you want to be used as the sender of the notification.
   - For the `RECIPIENT` parameter, enter the user you want to receive the notification (for example, an email address).
   - Use the `RECIPIENT-TYPEID` parameter to define the address type of the address you entered as a `RECIPIENT` (for example, U for an Internet address).

Email Distribution Lists [!]

You can also use distribution lists when defining the recipients of a notification. Distribution lists are created in the SAP Business Workplace (Transaction SBWP). Note that distribution lists must be created and maintained in client 000 because the CCMS agent communicates exclusively with this client.

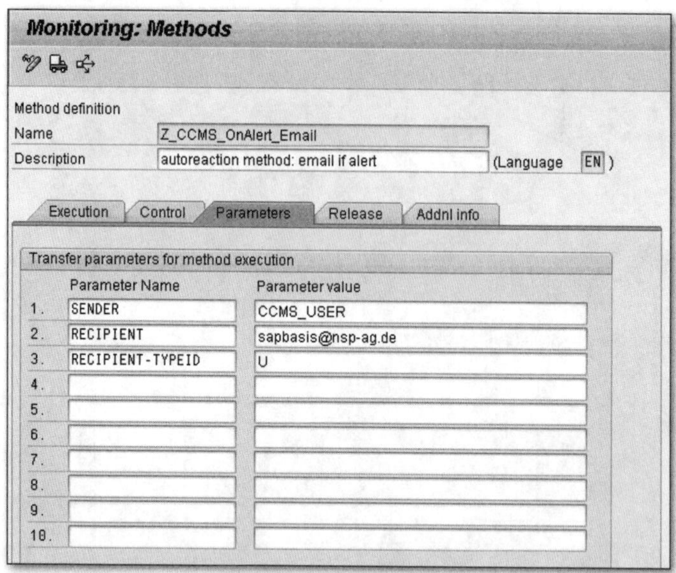

8. Switch to the RELEASE tab, and set a checkmark in the AUTO-REACTION METHOD field.

   Choose SAVE (💾) to save your settings.

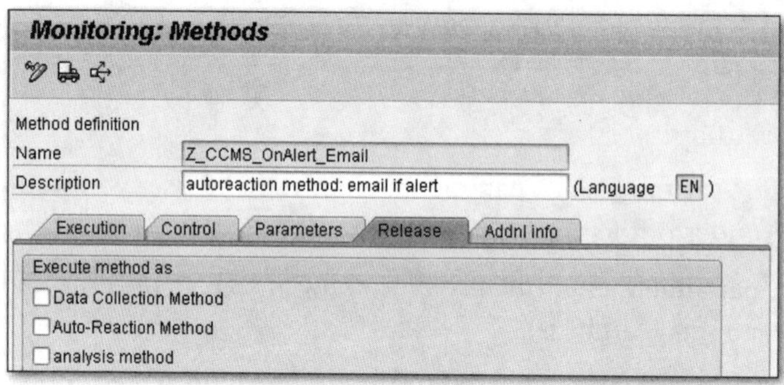

9. A message in the status bar confirms that the method definition has been saved and released. Choose BACK (⮐) to exit Transaction RZ21.

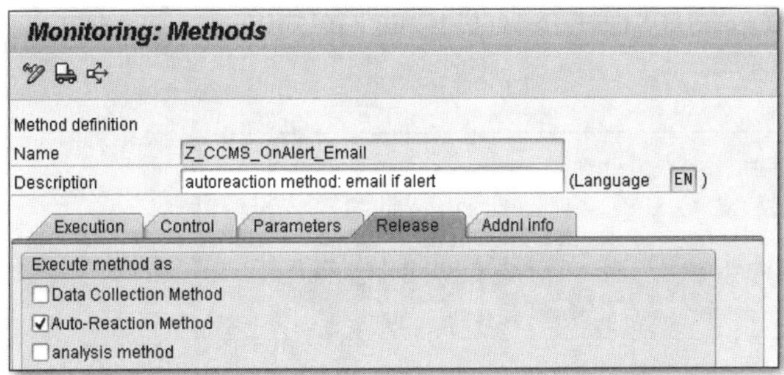

You have now defined an auto-reaction method, which sends a notification in the desired format to the desired recipients. You have also released the method for use in the CCMS Alert Monitor. In the next step, you will assign the new method to a monitor object.

3.4.2 Assigning an Auto-Reaction Method to a Monitor Object

After an auto-reaction method has been created, configured, and released, it can be used in the CCMS Alert Monitor.

1. Enter Transaction "RZ20" in the command field, and press the Enter key (or select the menu option TOOLS • CCMS • CONTROL/MONITORING • RZ20—CCMS MONITOR SETS).
2. Expand the monitor set, and position the cursor on the relevant monitor (for example, FILESYSTEMS). Choose LOAD MONITOR ().

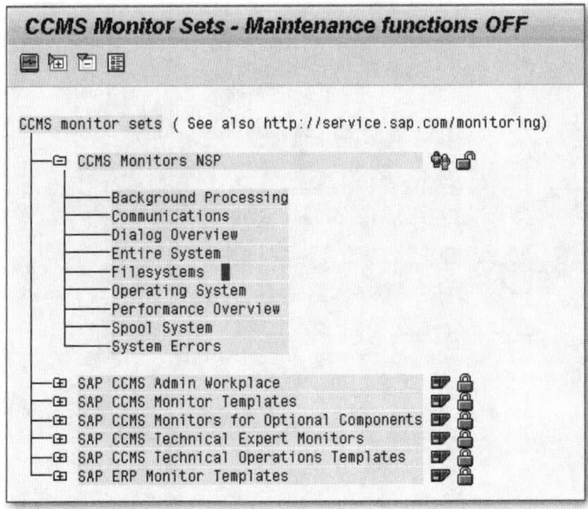

3. Expand the monitor's tree structure, and select the relevant monitor (for example, FREESPACE). Choose PROPERTIES.

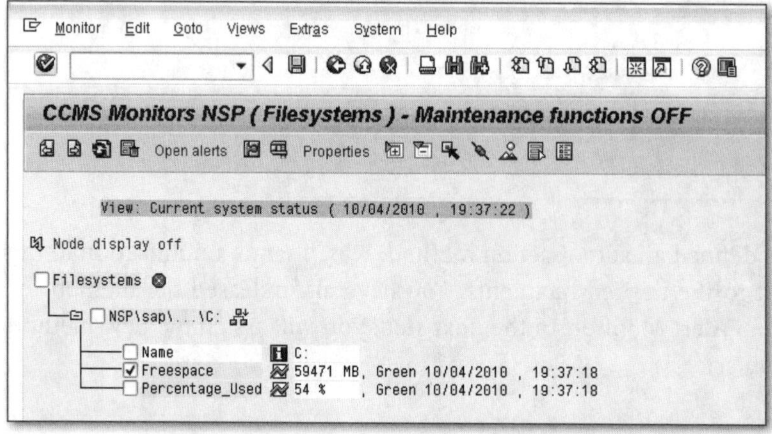

4. Select the METHODS tab, and click on the METHOD ASSIGNMENT button.

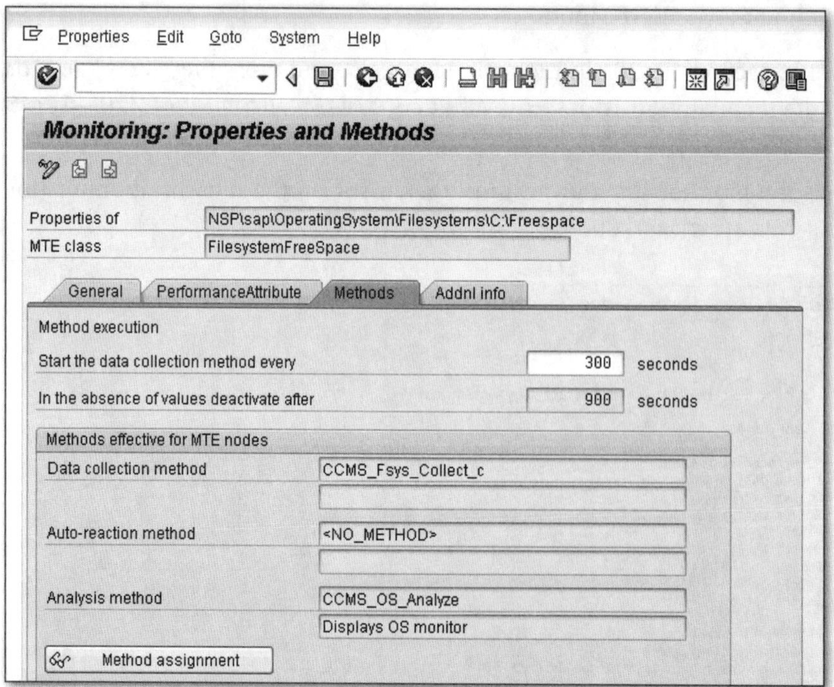

[⚙]

Assigning Methods

You can assign methods to an individual monitor object directly or to the MTE class to which the object belongs. If you assign the auto-reaction method to the MTE class of the monitor object, it will be inherited by all objects in this class.

To assign the method to the MTE class, double-click on the MTE CLASS field in the MONITORING: PROPERTIES AND METHODS view. On the next screen, you can assign the method to the selected class.

5. Click on DISPLAY <-> CHANGE (icon) to activate change mode, and select the AUTOREACTION tab.

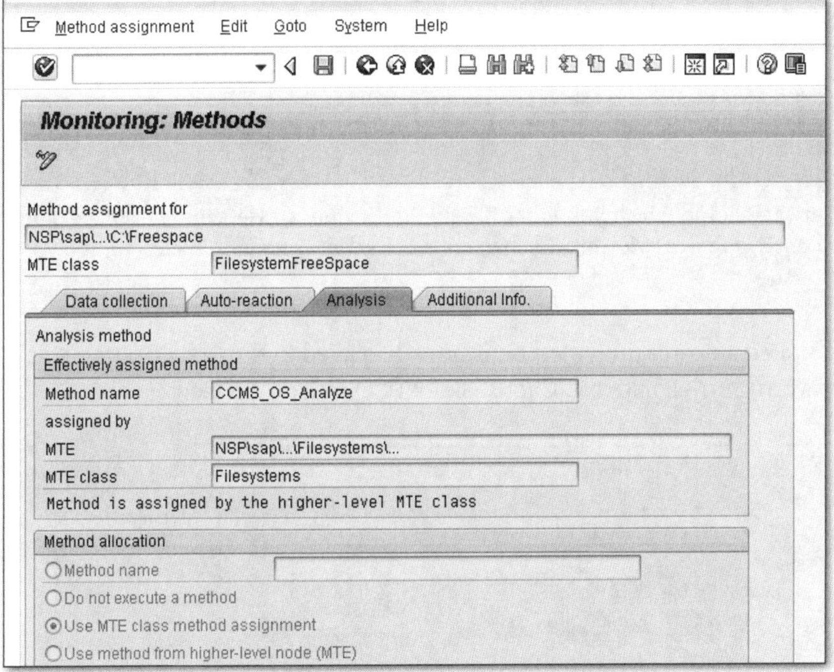

6. In the METHOD ASSIGNMENT area, select the METHOD NAME entry. Enter your auto-reaction method (for example, `Z_CCMS_OnAlert_Email_01`) in the relevant field. Choose SAVE (icon) to save your entries.

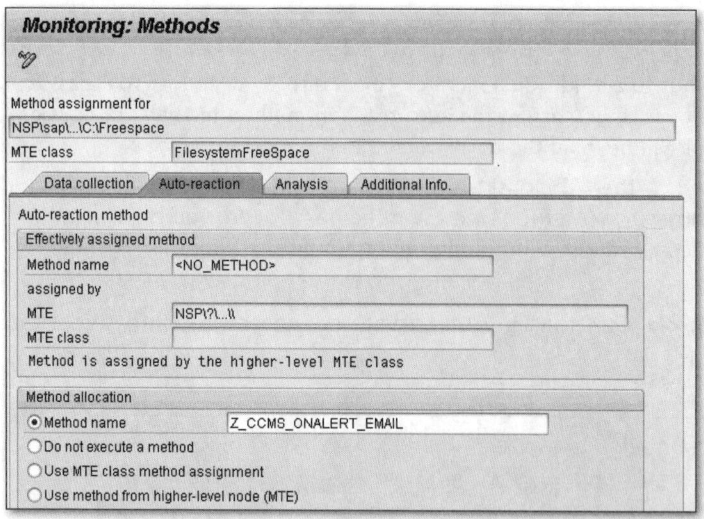

[!]

Case-Sensitivity

Note that the field in which you enter the method name is case-sensitive. Make sure that you enter uppercase/lowercase characters correctly. Otherwise, your method will not be found.

7. The assigned auto-reaction method is now displayed in the METHOD NAME field under METHOD ALLOCATION. Choose BACK (⊕) to exit the view.

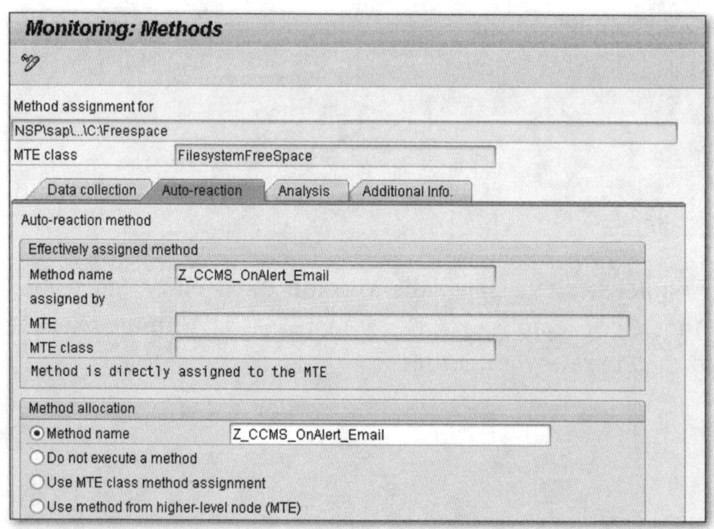

8. The assigned auto-reaction method is now also displayed on the MONITORING: PROPERTIES AND METHODS screen. Choose BACK (⊕) to return to the monitor's tree structure.

[!]

Configuring SAPconnect

SAPconnect must be set up in client 000 if you want to send notifications to external email addresses, for example. You configure SAPconnect in Transaction SCOT (SAPconnect Administration) (see also Section 2.6.3).

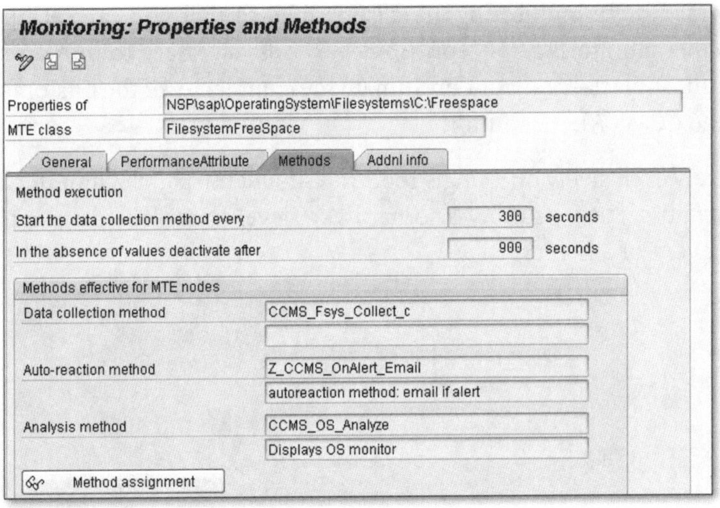

Monitoring: Properties and Methods

Properties of NSP\sap\OperatingSystem\Filesystems\C:\Freespace
MTE class FilesystemFreeSpace

General | PerformanceAttribute | Methods | Addnl info

Method execution
Start the data collection method every 300 seconds
In the absence of values deactivate after 900 seconds

Methods effective for MTE nodes
Data collection method CCMS_Fsys_Collect_c
Auto-reaction method Z_CCMS_OnAlert_Email
autoreaction method: email if alert
Analysis method CCMS_OS_Analyze
Displays OS monitor

Method assignment

Your auto-reaction method has now been assigned to a specific monitor object. From now on, a notification will be sent as soon as an alert is triggered.

Follow the same steps just described if you want the system to execute an operating system command when a certain alert occurs. In this case, use the `CCMS_AUTO_REACT_OP_COMMAND` method as your starting point.

[+]

Registering Operating System Commands

Before an operating system command can be executed as a method, it must be registered in Transaction SM69 (Maintain External OS Commands).

3.5 Summary

The CCMS Alert Monitor is a very powerful tool for monitoring SAP systems, which allows you to keep track of virtually all conceivable aspects of a system. Several monitors are included in the standard system, which you can easily use for basic monitoring. You can use auto-reaction methods to ensure that the system informs you by email whenever any critical situations arise, without you having to constantly keep an eye on CCMS alerts.

The options offered by this tool don't stop there: User-defined monitors, modified methods, and central system monitoring are all possible, so that you can set up an extensive, effective monitoring concept. However, it is necessary to immerse yourself deeply in this subject—don't underestimate the complexity of the Customizing settings for the CCMS Alert Monitor.

You also shouldn't rely exclusively on a single tool. You should use parallel monitors at the operating, database, and possibly also hardware level to safeguard system monitoring in the event of an emergency.

SAP Solution Manager has become an indispensable tool for enterprises that run SAP software. However, the value added by its integration into the system landscape varies significantly between one enterprise and the next. This chapter shows you how to use SAP Solution Manager for administration of your SAP systems.

4 System Administration with SAP Solution Manager

All SAP customers need to use *SAP Solution Manager*. It's no longer possible to download support packages for new releases without this tool. For this reason, any enterprise or business that runs SAP software also uses Solution Manager.

In practice, however, opinions are (even now) still divided: While some regard it as a necessary evil, others try to use the functions of Solution Manager as extensively as possible and to incorporate them profitably into the value chain.

The resources available within the enterprise or SAP administrator group often determine the fate of a Solution Manager installation. It takes time, money, and patience to become familiar with its functions, set up a stable two-system or even three-system landscape, and map projects and business processes in the "SolMan."

This chapter explains how to use Solution Manager for SAP system administration. It explains the basic settings required to use the essential functions. However, it also introduces instruments that may be of interest to administrators and may help make your life a lot easier.

4.1 Functional Spectrum of SAP Solution Manager

SAP Solution Manager seeks to manage and document the entire lifecycle of SAP systems, from the initial project phase, through the implementation of a new software solution, and, ultimately, to live system operation. Solution Manager provides a central or higher-level starting point from which you can navigate to all connected systems.

Details of its main applications are provided as follows:

- **Implementation and upgrade of SAP solutions**
  You can use Solution Manager to map an implementation or upgrade project. It contains best-practice guidelines known as *Roadmaps* for a range of commonly occurring scenarios. You can use a *Business Blueprint* to model business processes. This process structure provides a basis for configuration, Customizing, and documentation of the solution. Solution Manager can also be used for administration of customer developments. It also offers basic functions for project administration and controlling.
- **Test management**
  Solution Manager provides a central platform for software testing, both within projects and during live operation. Test cases (for example, manual test cases or eCATT tests) can be structured using test plans and packages, and they can be assigned to testers in the form of a worklist. Testers execute the test cases in Solution Manager, which provides automatic navigation to the system that is to be tested. The test process is documented and evaluated in Solution Manager.
- **System administration**
  Administration tasks can be defined and monitored centrally in Solution Manager for the purpose of system administration. Solution Manager, in its central role within the system landscape, provides a central system for system monitoring using the CCMS Alert Monitor (see Chapter 3) and for user administration (see Chapter 13). In addition, the EarlyWatch Alert function enables proactive system monitoring and supports service level reporting for management. If a problem occurs, Solution Manager allows you to contact SAP Solution Manager and track its resolution (Issue Management). Furthermore, Solution Manager support is essential for the maintenance of SAP systems (for example, with support packages).
- **Incident Management**
  Solution Manager can be used as a service desk, for example, for your enterprise's IT hotline support. Users can record problems from the SAP system directly and

then send notification to Solution Manager. Ticket processing is mapped as a workflow between users and the support organization.

- **Change Management**
  Change management offers a workflow for requesting, implementing, rolling out, documenting, and tracking changes in the system. You can implement and control all transport management functions (see Chapter 17) using a change request process to create a consistent workflow, comprising change request, approval, programming/Customizing, testing, acceptance, and transport into the production system.

The preceding list illustrates what a powerful tool SAP Solution Manager has become. It's impossible to cover all aspects of Solution Manager in this book, much less discuss them in detail. This chapter therefore focuses on the topic of system administration with Solution Manager. For further information on many of the topics mentioned, please refer to the available literature.[1]

4.2 Maintaining the System Landscape

You must define and configure your system landscape in Solution Manager before you can use it for administration of your systems. This includes creating the systems and their individual components (database, application server, software components) and creating a connection between Solution Manager and the SAP systems.

Communication between the systems is based on RFC (Remote Function Call) connections (see Chapter 2), which are created as part of system landscape maintenance or are generated automatically. These connections allow Solution Manager to read a large portion of the system information independently from the system you want to connect. You also have the option of maintaining additional data manually.

---

1 Schäfer, Marc O.; Melich, Matthias, *SAP Solution Manager Enterprise Edition* (Boston: SAP PRESS, 2009). Friedrich, Matthias; Sternberg, Thorsten, *SAP Solution Manager Service Desk—Functionality and Implementation* (Boston: SAP PRESS, 2008). Friedrich, Matthias; Sternberg, Thorsten, *Change Request Management with SAP Solution Manager* (Boston: SAP PRESS, 2009).

[+]

Work Centers

In the SAP Solution Manager help documentation available in the SAP Help Portal (*http://help.sap.com*), *work centers* are frequently mentioned in connection with various Solution Manager functions.

These normally refer to general transactions, which will be familiar to you from other systems. All of the options and processing features for a specific function are bundled together in these transactions (for example, the work center for system landscape administration, which you can access in Transaction SMSY).

4.2.1 Creating a Server

Every SAP system runs on a physical or virtual server. To enable administration of the SAP system with Solution Manager, you must first define the server in system landscape maintenance.

To add a new server to the system landscape, follow these steps:

1. Enter Transaction "SMSY" in the command field, and press the Enter key (or select the menu option TOOLS • SAP SOLUTION MANAGER • SMSY – SYSTEM LANDSCAPE).
2. Under LANDSCAPE COMPONENTS, select the SERVER entry, and right-click to open the context menu. Select CREATE NEW SERVER.

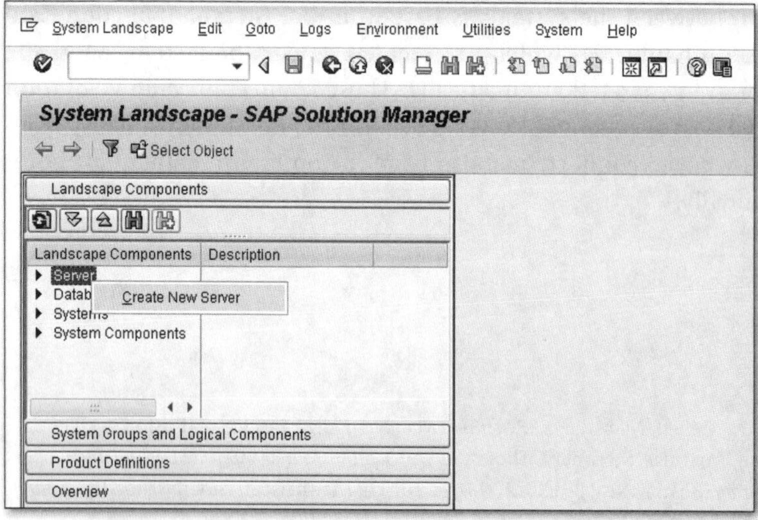

3. In the CREATE NEW SERVER dialog box that opens, enter the name of the server, and choose CREATE AND EDIT OBJECT (💾).

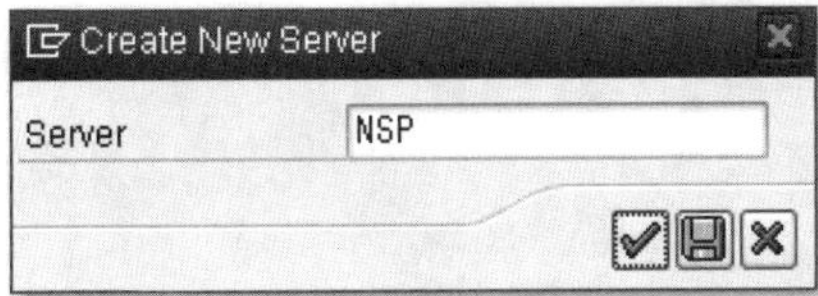

4. Enter information about the server on the TECHNICAL DATA tab. You can also enter a description here if necessary. Choose SAVE (💾).

Server Edit Goto Logs Environment Utilities System Help

Server: NSP - Change - SAP Solution Manager

Landscape Components

Landscape Components	Description
▶ Server	
▶ Databases	
▶ Systems	
▶ System Components	

System Groups and Logical Components

Product Definitions

Overview

Server NSP Saved

Header Data | Technical Data | Other Attributes

Fully-Qualified Host Name	sap
IP Address	
Solution Manager -> Router -> Server	
Host -> Router -> Solution Manager	
Manufacturer	
Hardware	
No. of CPUs	8
Number of Virtual CPUs	0,0000
CPU Type	
Frequency (Mhz)	
SAPS (Manufacturer)	
SAPS (Measured)	
Main Memory (KB)	
Operating System	WINDOWS
Operating System Version	2003
Operating Sys. Bits	64-Bit System

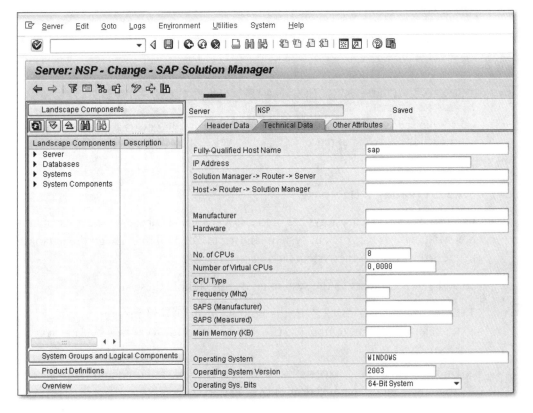

5. If you expand the SERVER node in the left screen frame, the server you created is now displayed in the tree structure.

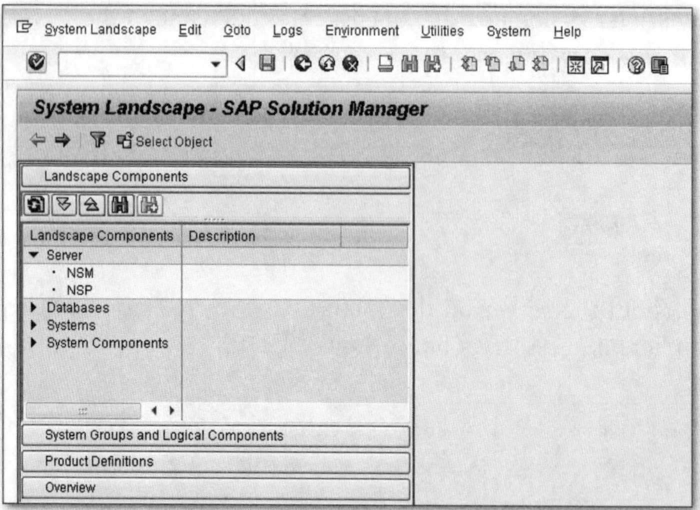

[!]

Creating a Server

Before you add a new SAP system to your system landscape, you must create the server on which the system is to run.

4.2.2 Creating a Database

Because an SAP system always has both a server and a database, you can also maintain a database as part of your system landscape. You will then assign the database to the SAP system in the system landscape later.

To add a new database to the system landscape, follow these steps:

1. Enter Transaction "SMSY" in the command field, and press the Enter key (or select the menu option TOOLS • SAP SOLUTION MANAGER • SMSY – SYSTEM LANDSCAPE).
2. Under LANDSCAPE COMPONENTS, select the DATABASES entry, and right-click to open the context menu. Select CREATE NEW DATABASE.

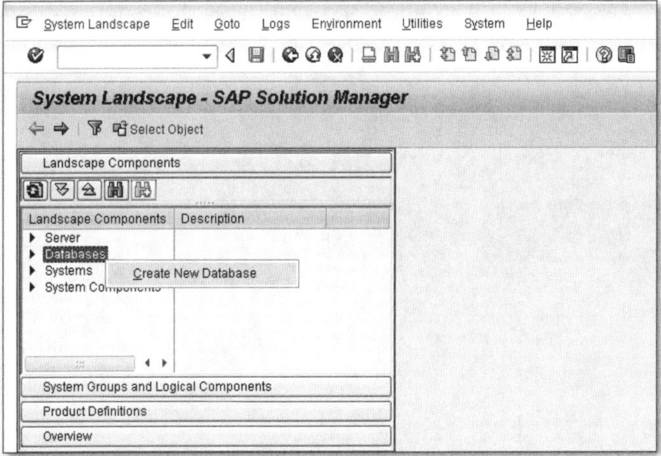

3. In the Create new database dialog box that opens, enter the name of the database, and choose Create and edit object (💾).

4. Enter information about the database on the Technical data tab. You can also enter a description here if necessary. Choose Save (💾).

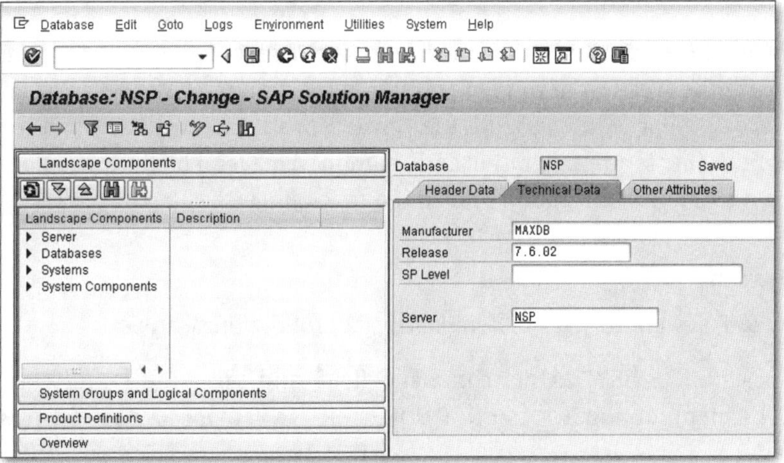

5. If you expand the DATABASES node in the left screen frame, the database you created is now displayed in the tree structure.

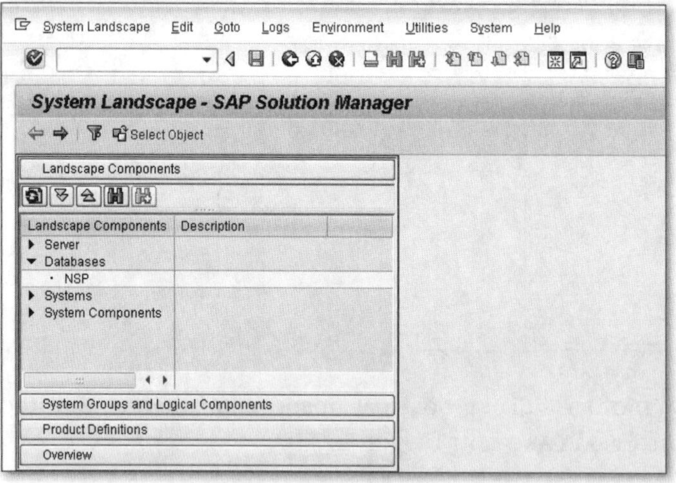

[+]

Creating a Database

The creation of a database, in contrast to the creation of a server (see Section 4.2.1), is not mandatory in order to enable administration of an SAP system. However, we recommend that you do so for the sake of completeness.

4.2.3 Creating a System

After you maintain the master data for the SAP system's server and database, you can proceed with the creation of the system itself. First, you must create a system as a master record. Next, you configure the connections between the system for which you want to enable administration and Solution Manager. Finally, the system can be assigned to a *logical component* and added to a *solution*.

Creating a System

To add a new SAP system to your system landscape, follow these steps:

1. Enter Transaction "SMSY" in the command field, and press the Enter key (or select the menu option TOOLS • SAP SOLUTION MANAGER • SMSY – SYSTEM LANDSCAPE).

2. Under LANDSCAPE COMPONENTS, select the SYSTEMS entry, and right-click to open the context menu. Select CREATE NEW SYSTEM WITH ASSISTANT.

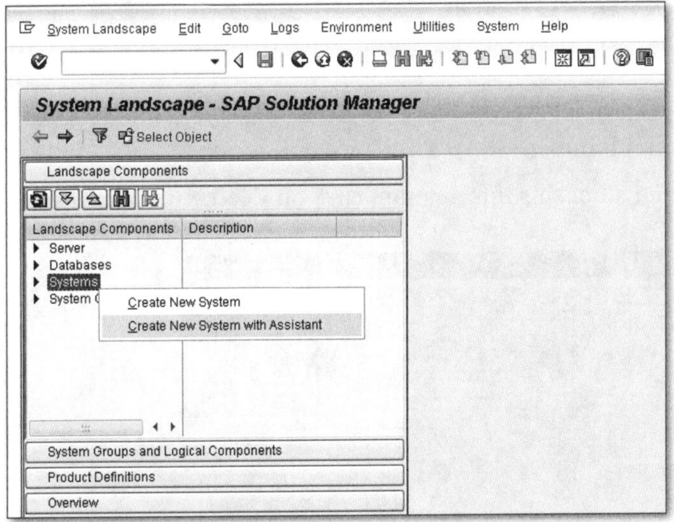

[Ex]

Creating a System with the Wizard

The wizard guides you, step-by-step, through the process and prompts you to enter all data required. In this example, the wizard is used to enter the system master data.

You can also create a system without the assistance of the wizard by selecting the CREATE NEW SYSTEM option from the context menu. You can also edit the information that is automatically determined and entered by the wizard.

3. Choose CONTINUE ().

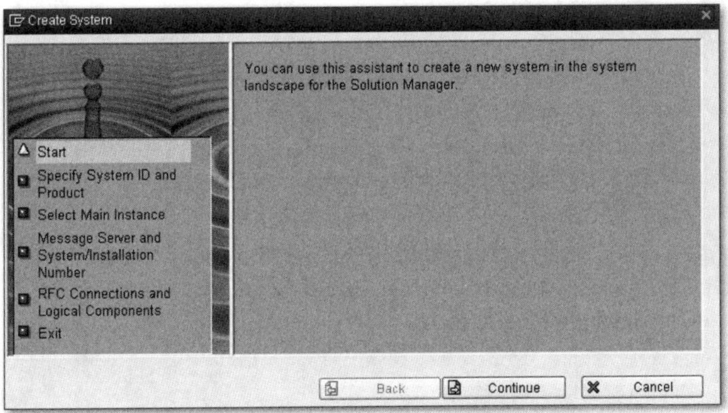

4. On the next screen, enter all of the information required in the input fields.
    - Enter the server under SYSTEM (see Section 4.2.1).
    - Enter a meaningful short description.
    - Select an SAP product from the selection list.
    - Select the product version from the selection list.
    - Enter the installation number.

    After you have entered all of this information, click on CONTINUE.

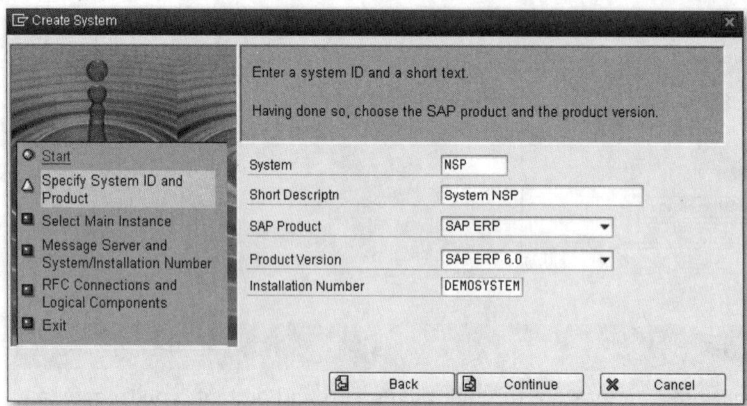

5. In the next step, the wizard prompts you to select main instances as relevant. Activate the checkboxes in the RELEVANT column, and choose NEXT.

[Ex]

Selecting Main Instances

A main instance is a system component that you want to manage using Solution Manager. The SAP product selected determines your choice of main instances.

You will need to select one or more main instances, depending on the scope of the installation of the system you want to manage. If, for example, you want to add an SAP ECC 6.0 system that only has an ABAP stack, select the SAP ECC server as a main instance.

If, for example, you want to manage an SAP Business Intelligence system, on which an ABAP stack, Java stack, and an SAP NetWeaver Portal are running, you need to select all three instances as relevant.

Your selection determines which Solution Manager functions are subsequently available to you, so you need to select all instances that you use to meet your business requirements. For example, if an instance is not selected, support packages will not be detected automatically for it.

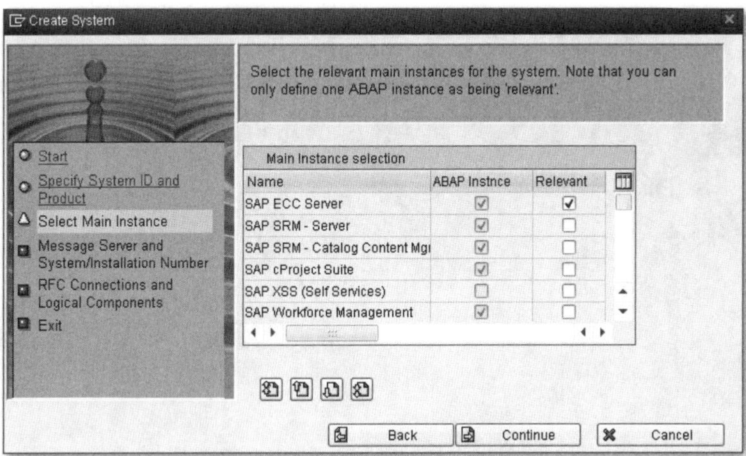

6. On the next screen, specify the system number and the server on which the system's message server runs. The message server is usually the same as the system server selected in step 4. Choose CONTINUE (icon).

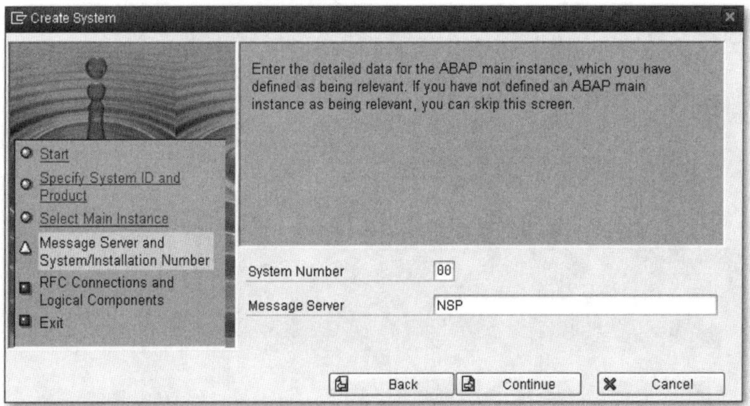

7. In the next to last wizard step, you can select follow-up functions for subsequent execution. If you select one or more options here, other wizard dialogs will immediately start. Our example shows the activities without the use of other wizards.

   Choose CONTINUE (icon).

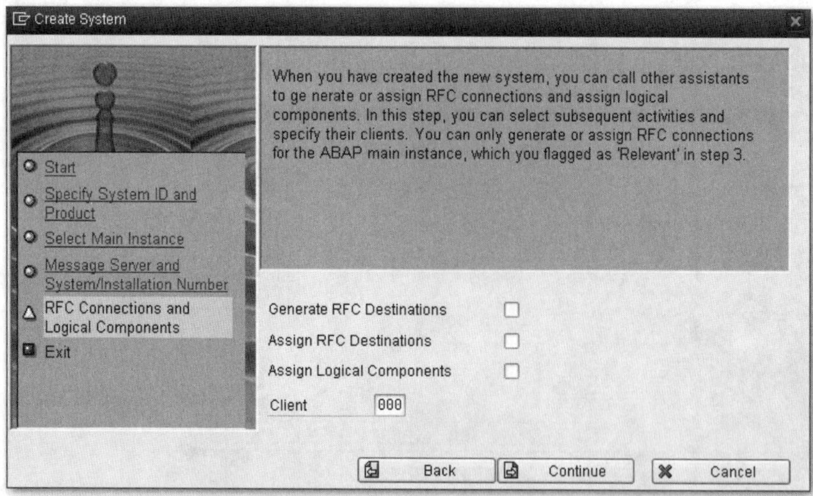

8. Choose COMPLETE (✓).

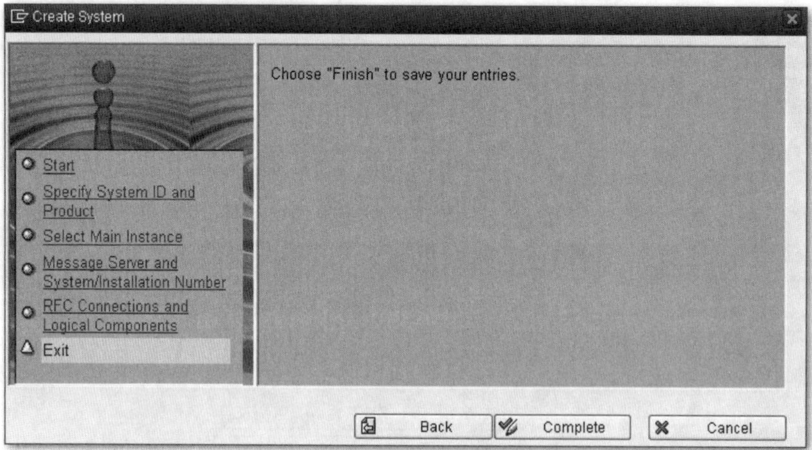

The new SAP system is created in the system landscape. The next step is to set up the RFC connections that are essential to communication between Solution Manager and the target system.

Creating Connections

As soon as your system exists as a master record in the system landscape, you can create a connection between the system and Solution Manager.

To create RFC connections, follow these steps:

1. Enter Transaction "SMSY" in the command field, and press the [Enter] key (or select the menu option TOOLS • SAP SOLUTION MANAGER • SMSY – SYSTEM LANDSCAPE).
2. Under LANDSCAPE COMPONENTS, expand the SYSTEMS entry and the product folder (for example, SAP ERP). The system you have just created is displayed within this folder. When you position your cursor on this entry, the system master data are displayed in the right screen frame.

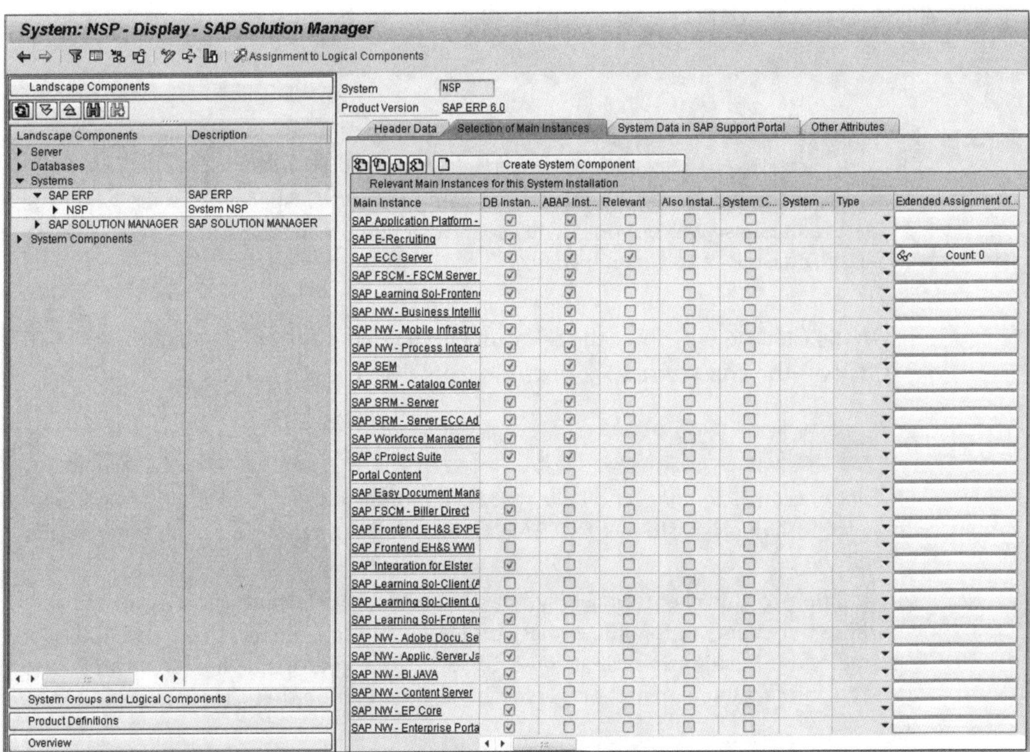

3. Expand the system node (for example, NSP). The main instances you selected as relevant are listed below this structure element. Click to select a main instance in the tree (for example, SAP ECC SERVER). The data of the main instance is displayed in the right screen frame. Click on DISPLAY <-> CHANGE (icon) to switch to change mode.

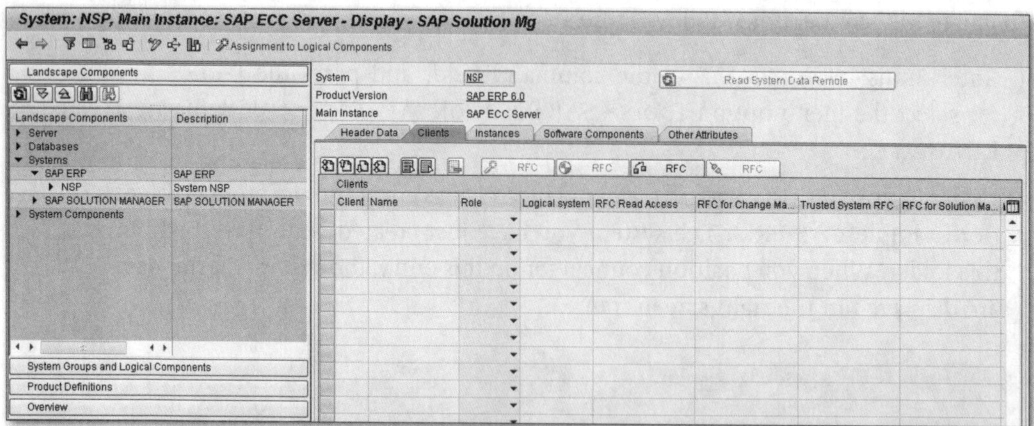

[+]

Assigning a Database

When you created the SAP system, you were required to specify a server, while the entry of a database was optional. You can now define the database retroactively on the HEADER DATA tab of the main instance.

4. On the CLIENTS tab, enter the relevant clients in the system (for example, "000"). Click on the GENERATE RFC DESTINATIONS BUTTON ().

[+]

Connecting Clients

It isn't necessary to connect all clients to Solution Manager. You should always enter client 000, which exists in every SAP system, for central system maintenance and monitoring.

In addition to this client, you only need to create clients that are relevant for your purpose, for example, for your project or live operation (for example, client 100). For example, the Customizing client must be connected in an implementation project so that the project implementation guide can be generated in that client.

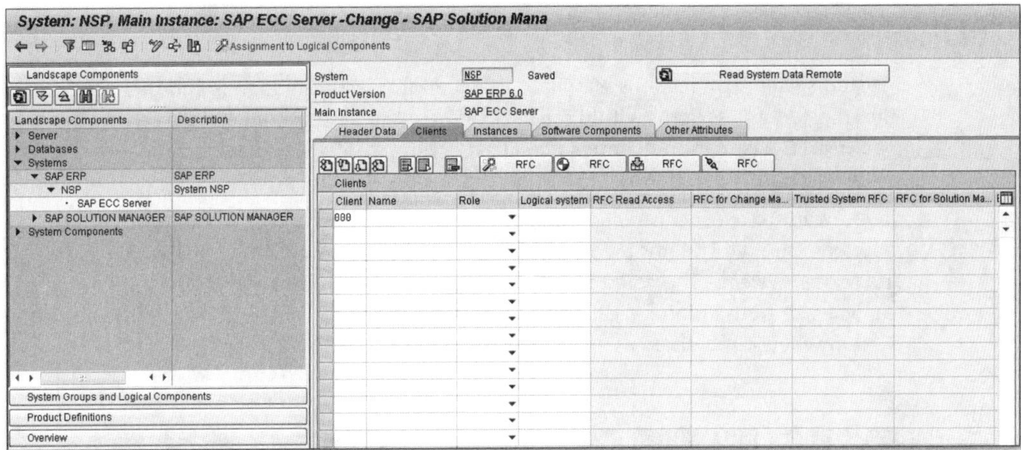

5. Choose YES to confirm the dialog box.

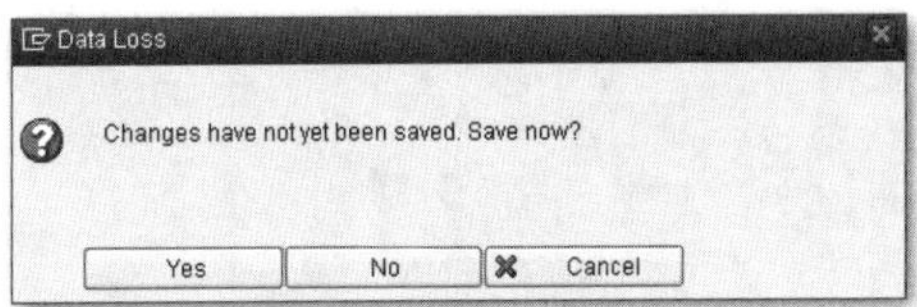

6. Select the connections you want to generate:
   - RFC DESTINATION AND USER FOR READ ACCESS
     A connection to the target system for the purpose of reading data. This connection must always be generated.
   - RFC DESTINATION AND USER FOR CHANGE MANAGER
     You only require this connection if you intend to use the Change Request Management functions in Solution Manager.
   - RFC DESTINATION WITH TRUSTED SYSTEM CONNECTION
     Trusted system connections do not require users to log on with a password. This makes them much easier to use.
   - RFC DESTINATION FOR SOLUTION MANAGER
     You can also generate this RFC connection as a trusted system connection.
   - RFC DESTINATION WITH USER
     This is the return connection from the target system to Solution Manager.
7. Disable load balancing.

   Choose GENERATE RFC DESTINATIONS ().

[+]

Trusted System Connections

Trusted system connections eliminate the need for password logons and therefore also the transfer of passwords within the network. Trusted system connections can be identified in RFC destination maintenance (Transaction SM59; see Chapter 2, Section 2.6.1) by the setting TRUSTED SYSTEM • YES on the LOGON & SECURITY tab.

If you want to use a trusted system connection, you must create a relationship of trust between the two systems involved. You use Transaction SMT1 to define which systems are *trusted systems*. The counterpart of a trusted system is its *trusting system*, which you can view in Transaction SMT2. These entries are generated automatically in the partner system when it is created as a trusted system.

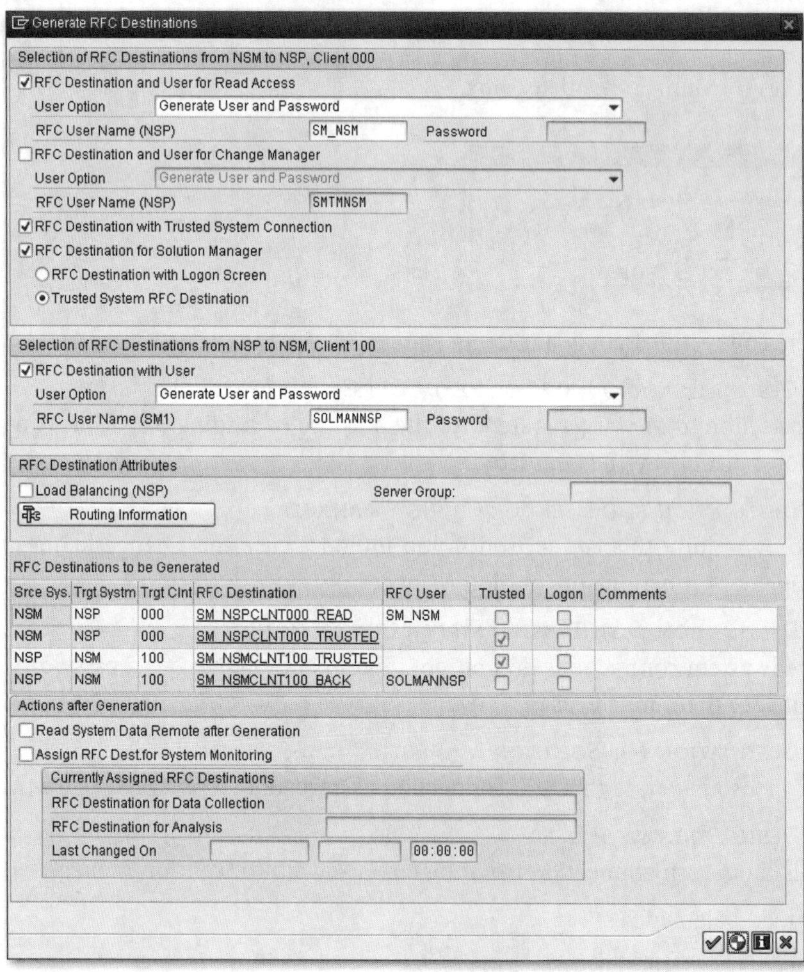

8. You are prompted several times to log on to the target system and Solution Manager. This is necessary for the RFC connections and users to be generated.

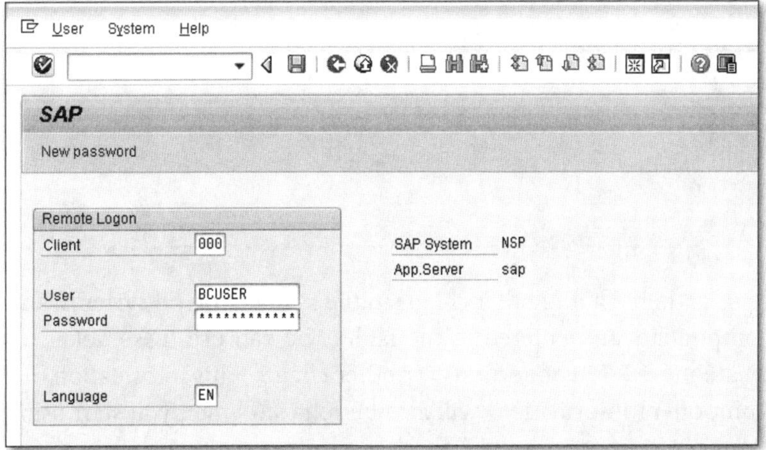

9. A log is displayed after this process is completed. Check the entries for error messages. Choose BACK () to return to system landscape maintenance.

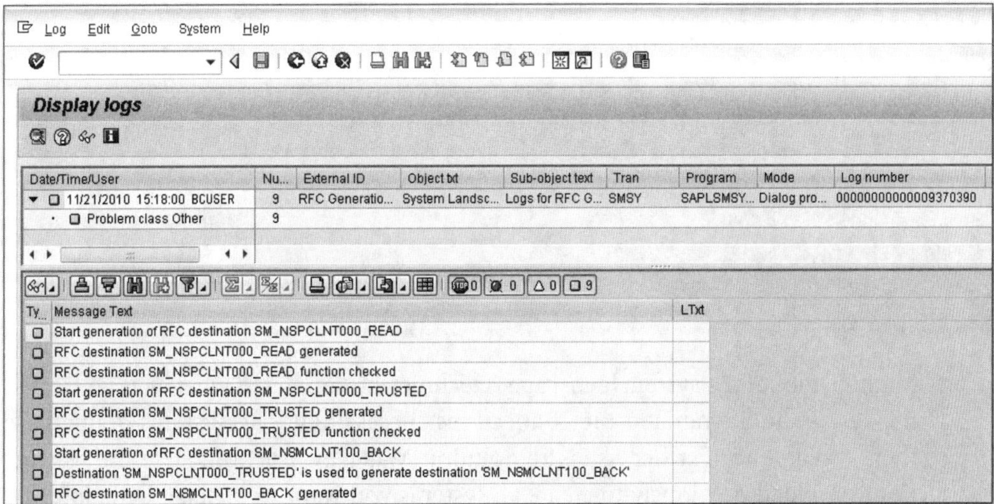

10. The RFC connections between Solution Manager and the target system have been generated. Choose READ SYSTEM DATA REMOTE () to use the RFC connections to read information from the target system.

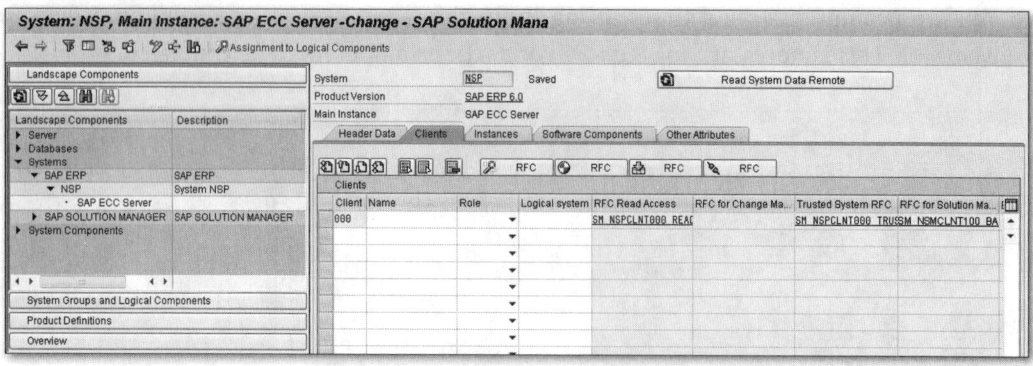

11. Information is gathered about other clients in the system, logical systems, and software components and entered in the table. You can use these details to help you create more RFC connections for other clients. This information (for example, component information) will also be relevant when you start using Solution Manager later (for example, for downloading support packages).

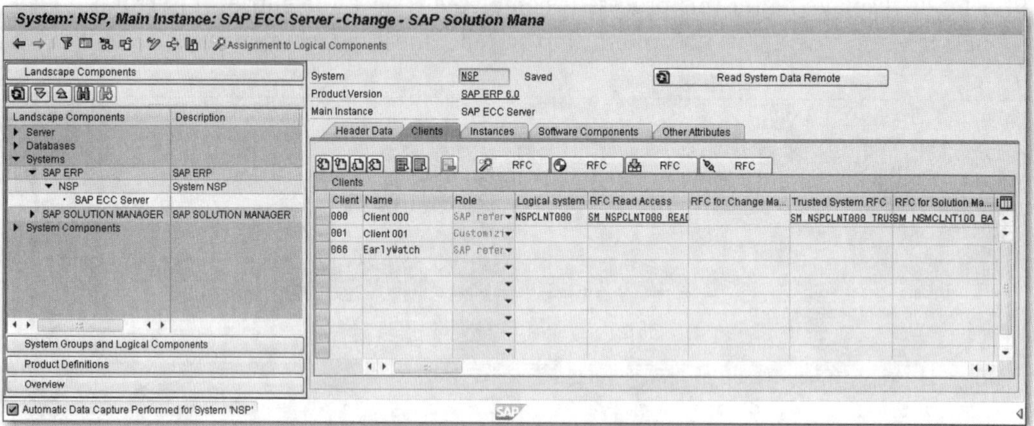

Maintenance of the system landscape is technically completed when you've created the system and generated the connections successfully. The systems defined are then available for further use with Solution Manager functions. Use the instructions provided previously to create all systems you want to manage with Solution Manager in the system landscape.

If you manage two or three system landscapes comprising development, test, and production systems, create all of these systems, which you will assign to a *logical component* in the next step. This logical component will, in turn be assigned to a *solution*.

Assigning a System to a Logical Component

You can use a logical component to group systems in a multisystem landscape in a single unit for administration. Roles are assigned to the individual systems to uniquely identify them within the logical component.

To assign your system to a logical component, follow these steps:

1. Enter Transaction "SMSY" in the command field, and press the Enter key (or select the menu option TOOLS • SAP SOLUTION MANAGER • SMSY – SYSTEM LANDSCAPE).
2. Under LANDSCAPE COMPONENTS, expand the SYSTEMS entry and the product folder (for example, SAP ERP) that contains your system. Right-click to open the context menu. Select ASSIGNMENT TO LOGICAL COMPONENTS.

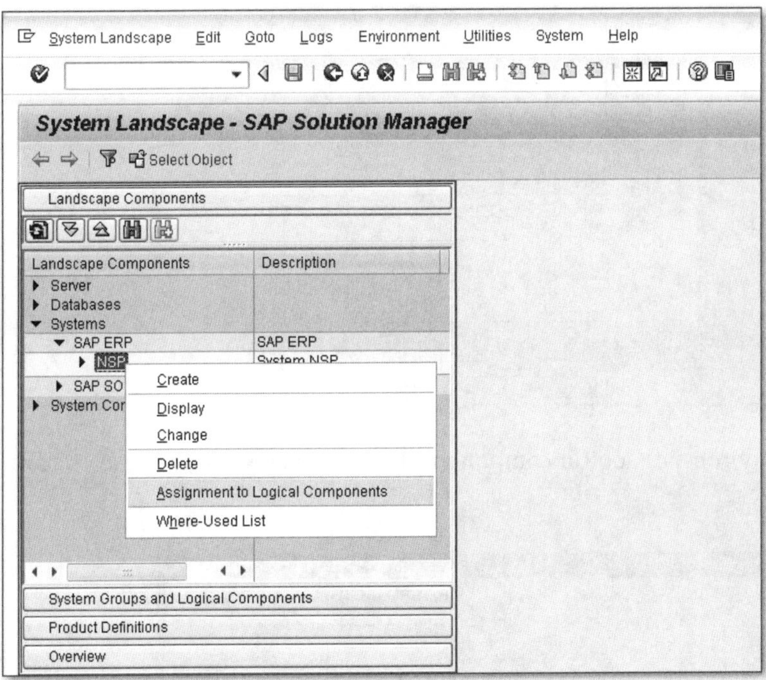

3. A wizard dialog box opens to guide you through the assignment process. Choose CONTINUE ().

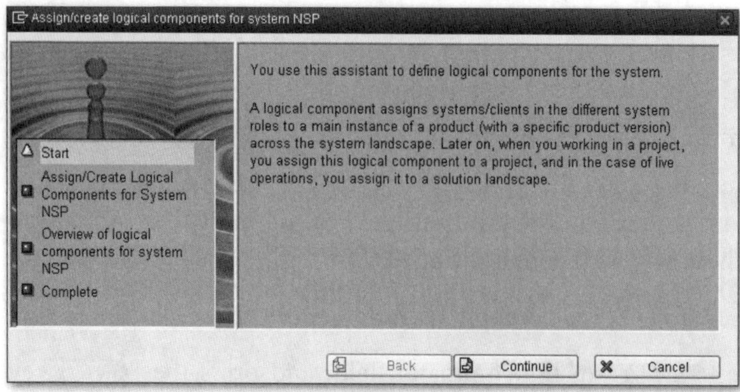

4. Your system's main instance is displayed. Use the input help (□) to select a logical component.

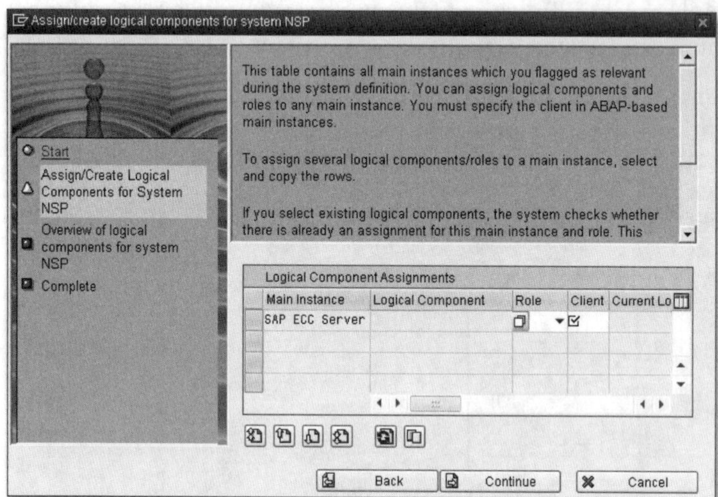

5. Select the appropriate logical component from the tree structure, and click on OK (✔).

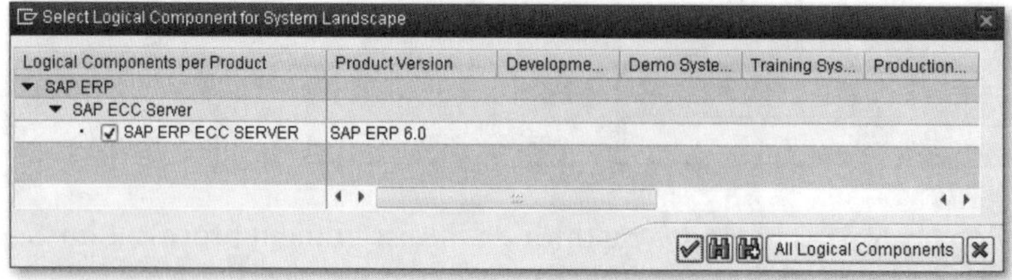

6. The logical component is entered in the table.

   In the ROLE column, select the system's role from the drop-down list (for example, PRODUCTION SYSTEM).

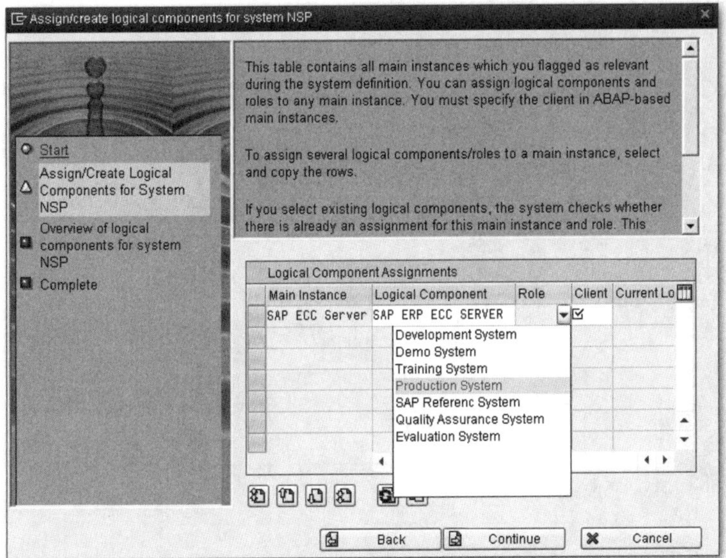

7. Enter the relevant client, and choose CONTINUE.

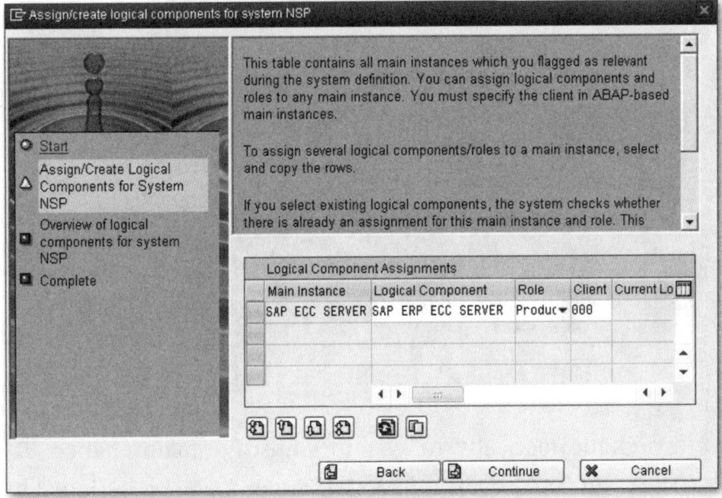

8. In the next step, you are again shown an overview of the logical components. Click on CONTINUE (icon).

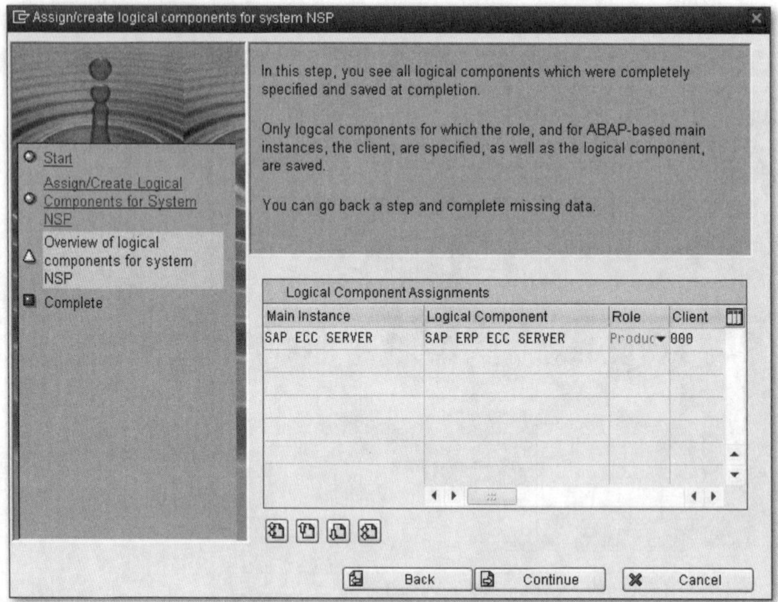

9. In the final wizard step, choose COMPLETE (icon).

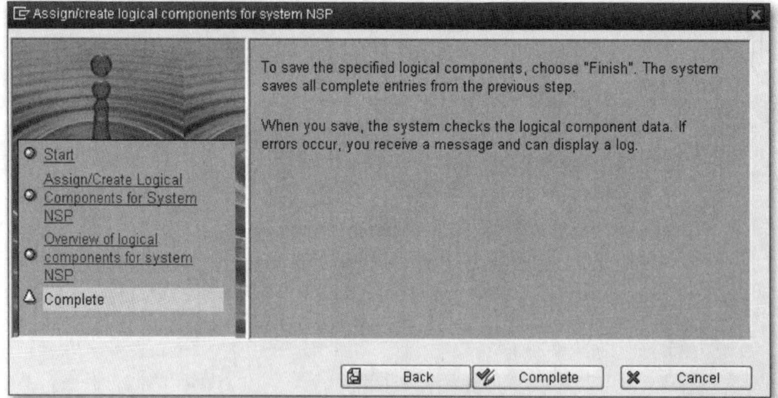

10. You are then returned automatically to system landscape maintenance. To check your entry, select the SYSTEM GROUPS AND LOGICAL COMPONENTS area in the left screen frame, and then select LOGICAL COMPONENTS. Expand the tree

structure, and click on the relevant logical component (for example, SAP ERP ECC SERVER). The assigned systems are displayed in the right screen frame.

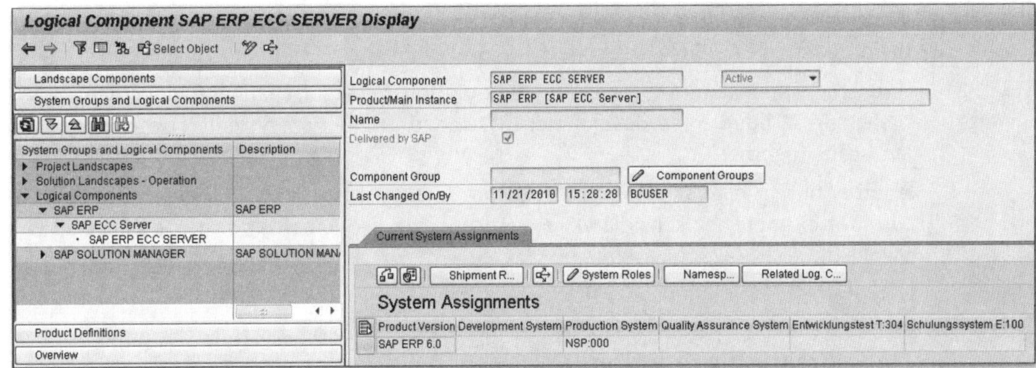

Follow these steps to assign a logical component and a role to your systems. For example, you can group the systems of a three-system landscape comprising a development system, test system, and production system in a logical component and then assign the relevant system role.

[+]

Using Logical Components

Logical components are particularly useful for implementation or upgrade projects because these projects distinguish among the development, test, and production systems. The same applies to test and change management. However, logical components are also required for system monitoring.

4.3 Solutions

Solutions give you the option of bundling individual systems together and managing them as a unit. The way in which you group systems together as solutions ultimately depends on the system landscape you are managing and on which Solution Manager functions you use. You can also add the same system to several different solutions to enable system administration in accordance with your requirements and based on a range of criteria.

Example: Defining Solutions

If you want to monitor business processes that involve several systems (for example, a procurement process with an SAP SRM system and an SAP ERP system), it's useful to bundle the production SAP SRM system and the SAP ERP system together in a solution.

If, on the other hand, you want to use Solution Manager change management, it's preferable to bundle the development, QA, and production systems of the SAP ERP landscape together.

Another option is to structure the solutions in accordance with your enterprise structure (for example, by subsidiary), or based on the geographical locations of the sites involved.

4.3.1 Creating a Solution

To create a new solution, follow these steps:

1. Enter Transaction "SOLUTION_MANAGER" in the command field, and press the Enter key (or select the menu option TOOLS • SAP SOLUTION MANAGER • SOLUTION_MANAGER – SOLUTION OPERATION).
2. On the SOLUTION OVERVIEW – SAP SOLUTION MANAGER screen, click on the CREATE button. (You may need to go to the solution overview first by clicking on the corresponding button.)

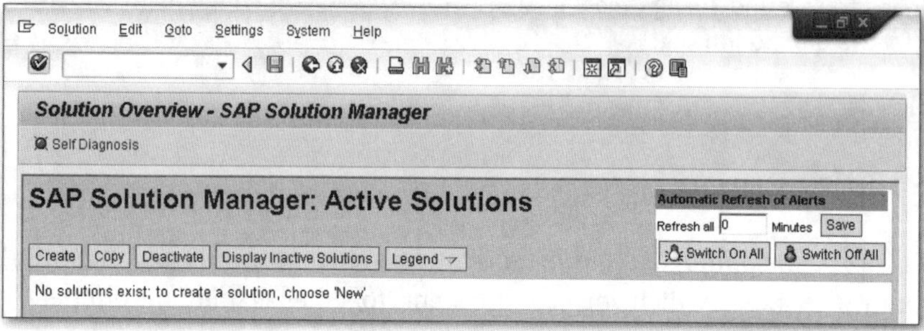

3. In the SOLUTION field, enter a name that is as meaningful as possible. Select a language as necessary under ORIGINAL LANGUAGE. Click the CONTINUE button.

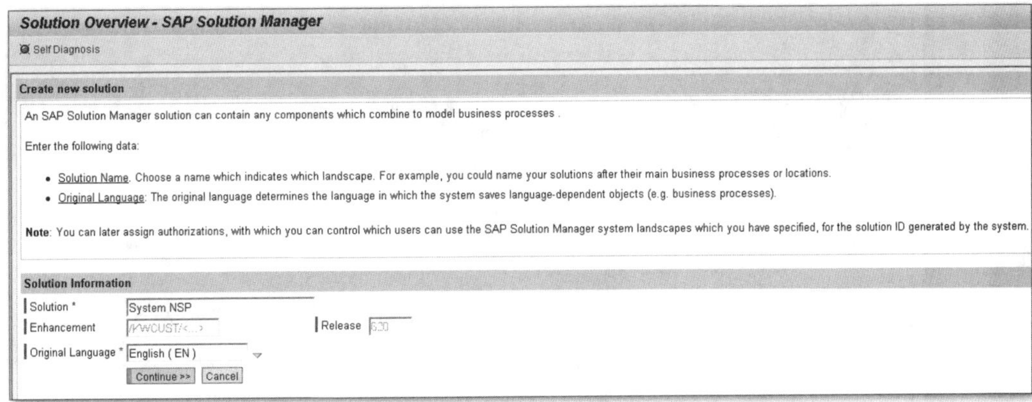

4. The new solution has been created. In the Operations Setup view, you can navigate to various maintenance functions from the Solution Landscape tab. Choose System Landscape Maintenance.

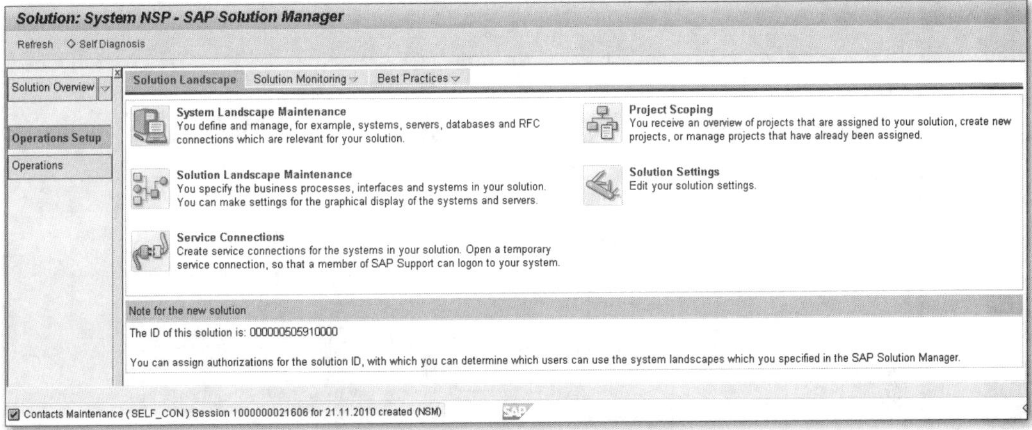

5. This brings you to a screen displaying the Solution Directory. Here you can define which systems belong to your solution. Click on Display <-> Change (icon) to switch to change mode.

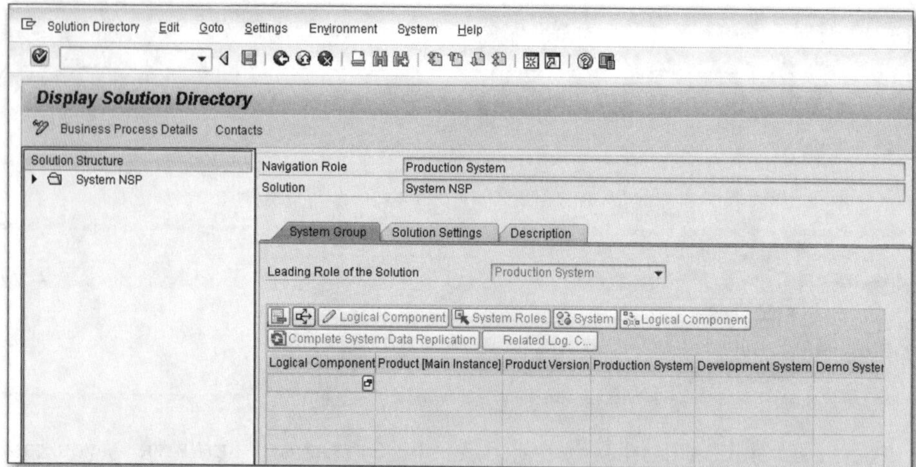

6. Use the input help (![]) to make an assignment in the LOGICAL COMPONENT column.

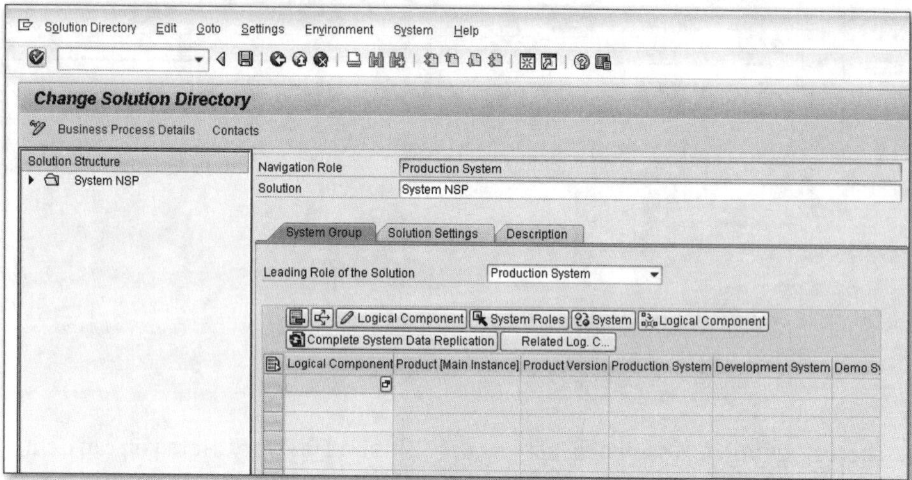

7. Expand the tree structure, and select the logical component. Choose OK (![]).

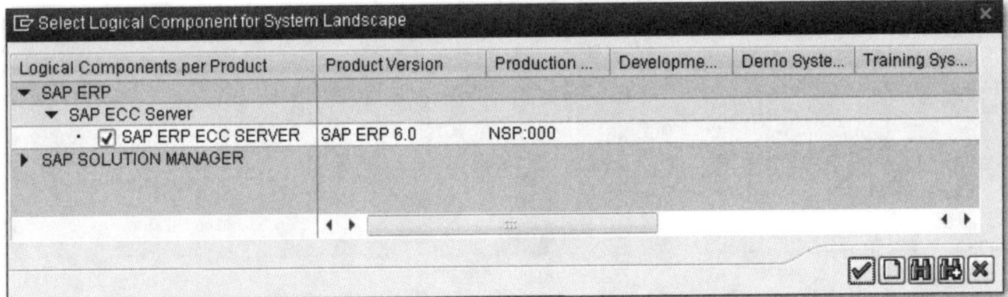

8. The logical component has been assigned to your solution. Choose SAVE (). Then choose BACK () to exit Solution Directory maintenance.

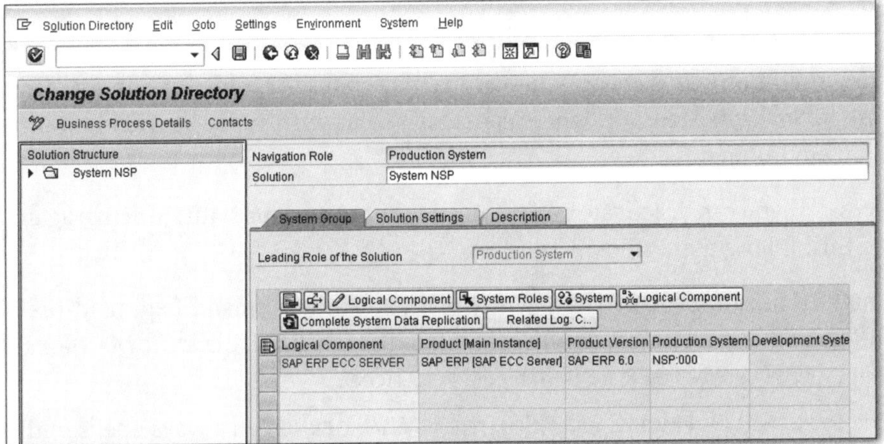

9. Choose SOLUTION OVERVIEW to display all solutions.

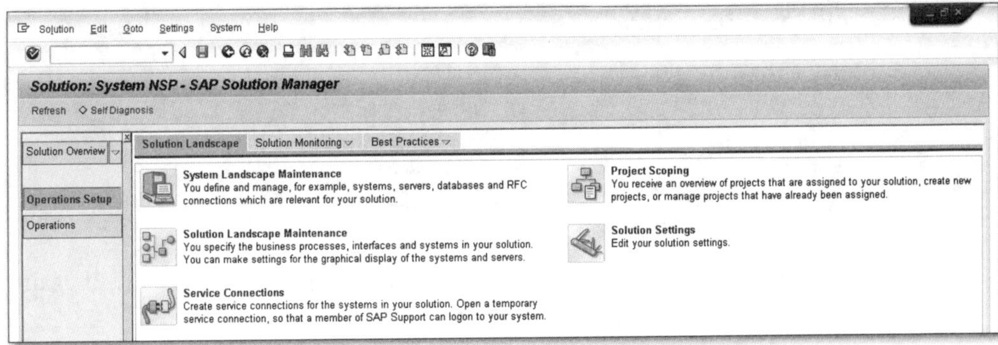

10. The solution you created is now displayed in the SOLUTION OVERVIEW.

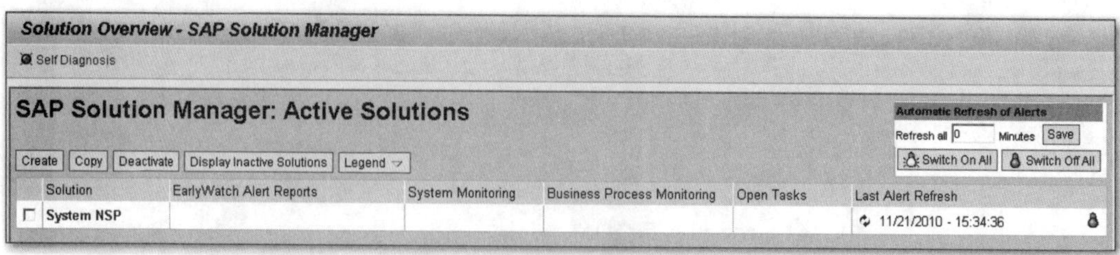

Your solution is now created, and its basic configuration has been completed. You can or, in some cases, must make some additional settings, depending on how the solution is to be used.

4.3.2 Activating and Deactivating Solutions

Existing solutions may have an active or inactive status. Active solutions are ready for use in Solution Manager, whereas inactive solutions cannot be used in a production environment.

If necessary, you can deactivate a solution and then change its status to active again. To do this, follow these steps:

1. Enter Transaction "SOLUTION_MANAGER" in the command field, and press the Enter key (or select the menu option TOOLS • SAP SOLUTION MANAGER • SOLUTION_MANAGER – SOLUTION OPERATION).
2. The SOLUTION OVERVIEW – SAP SOLUTION MANAGER screen always opens in the SAP SOLUTION MANAGER: ACTIVE SOLUTIONS view. Select a solution to deactivate it. Click on the DEACTIVATE button.

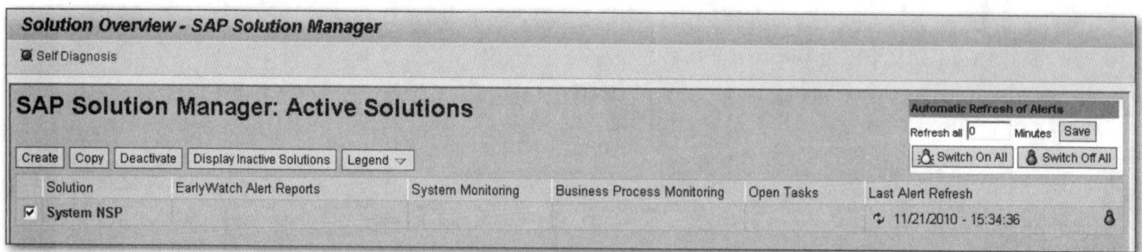

3. A message confirms that the solution has been deactivated. To activate it again, click on the DISPLAY INACTIVE SOLUTIONS button.

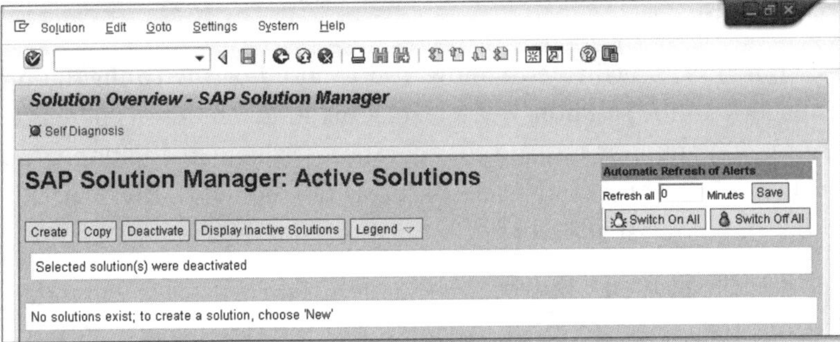

4. Select the solution, and click on ACTIVATE.

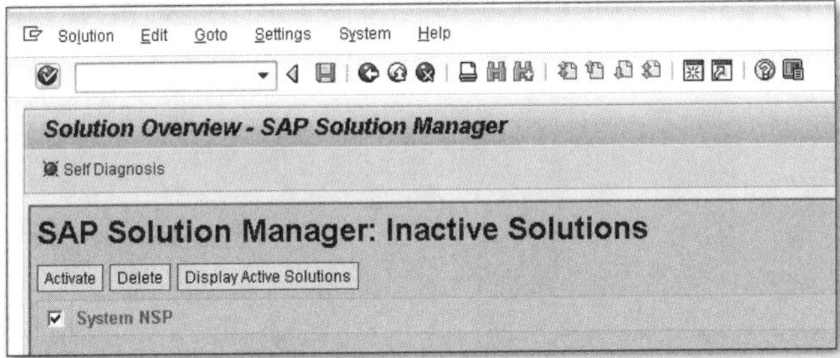

Deleting Solutions [+]

You can also delete solutions in the INACTIVE SOLUTIONS view. Active solutions can't be deleted, so they must be deactivated first.

5. A message in the SOLUTION OVERVIEW confirms that the solution has been activated.

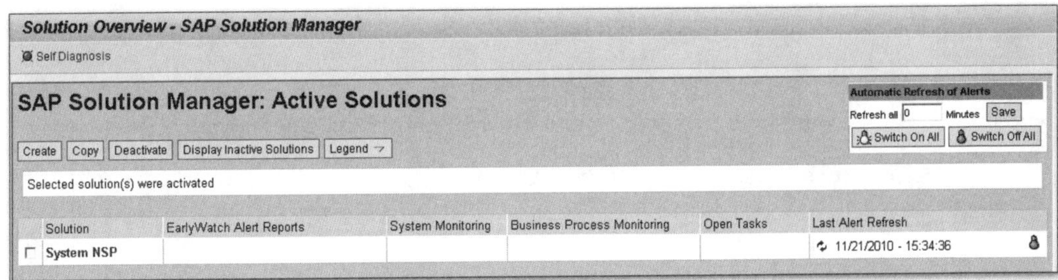

You can use this function to deactivate solutions that aren't currently in use.

4.3.3 Self-Diagnosis

A self-diagnosis function is available to allow you to monitor the configuration of Solution Manager and the solutions you create. This function detects potential problems caused by incorrect or missing configuration settings. In addition to an overview of system vulnerabilities, the self-diagnosis function also offers specific instructions about how to deal with these.

1. Enter Transaction "SOLUTION_MANAGER", and press the [Enter] key (or select the menu option TOOLS • SAP SOLUTION MANAGER • SOLUTION_MANAGER – SOLUTION OPERATION).
2. To open your solution, click on the system's link (for example, SYSTEM NSP) in the SOLUTION column on the SOLUTION OVERVIEW – SAP SOLUTION MANAGER screen.

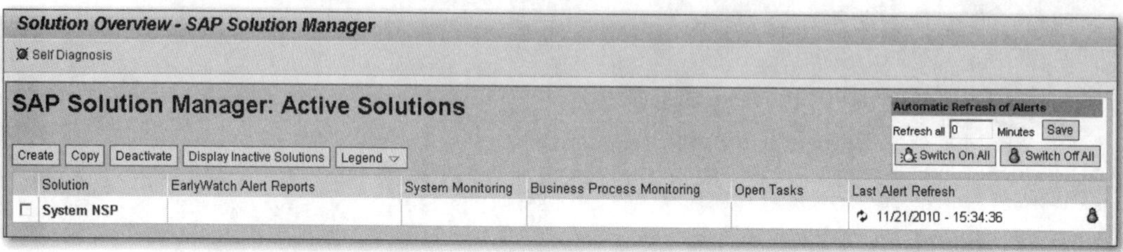

3. Click on the SELF DIAGNOSIS button.

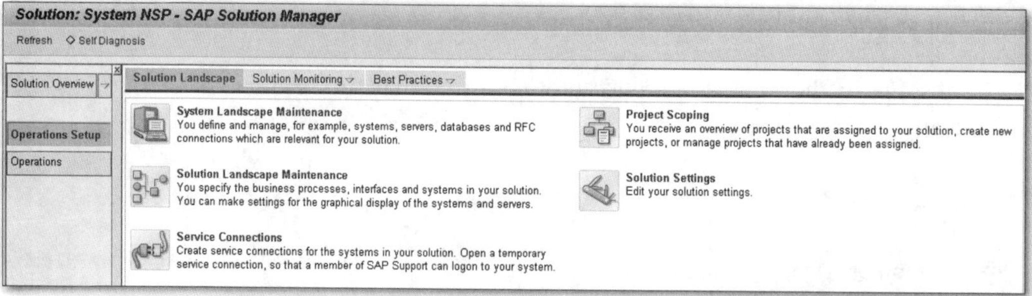

4. To start self-diagnosis, click on EXECUTE.

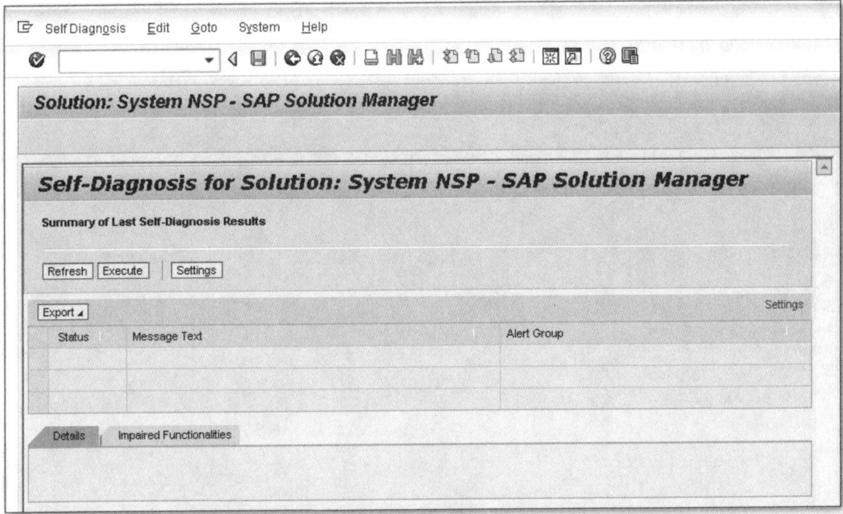

5. Choose YES to confirm the dialog box.

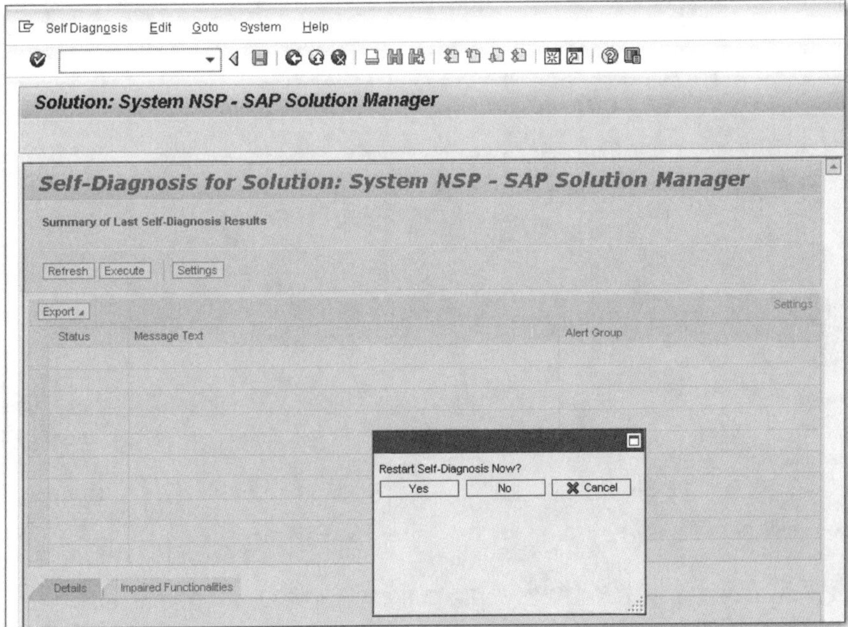

6. Choose REFRESH to display the result of self-diagnosis. Check whether any critical alerts ( ) or warning messages ( ) have occurred.

Self Diagnosis Edit Goto System Help
Solution: System NSP - SAP Solution Manager
Self-Diagnosis for Solution: System NSP - SAP Solution Manager
Summary of Last Self-Diagnosis Results
Very Critical Alerts: 1
Very Critical Functionalities: 1
Uncritical Alerts: 2
Refresh
Execute
Settings
Export
Settings
Status
Message Text
Alert Group
SDCCN in satellite systems, errors or cannot be checked
Communication
Service Level Reporting is not set up for this solution
Consistency
Solution Repository is consistent
Consistency
Details
Impaired Functionalities

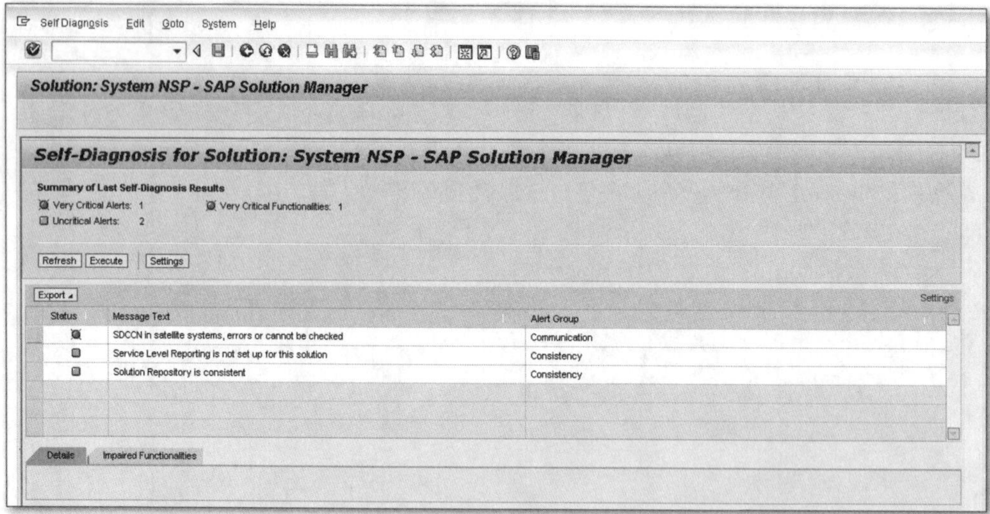

7. Click on an alert to view the details of the message and the proposed solution.

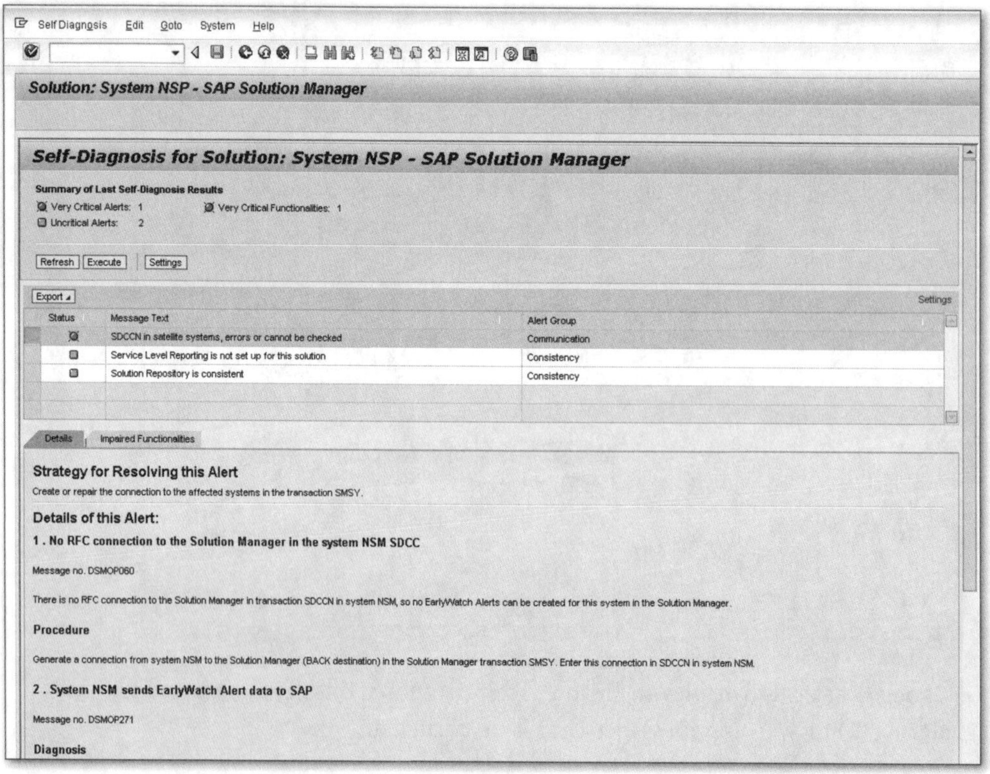

Self Diagnosis Edit Goto System Help
Solution: System NSP - SAP Solution Manager
Self-Diagnosis for Solution: System NSP - SAP Solution Manager
Summary of Last Self-Diagnosis Results
Very Critical Alerts: 1
Very Critical Functionalities: 1
Uncritical Alerts: 2
Refresh
Execute
Settings
Export
Settings
Status
Message Text
Alert Group
SDCCN in satellite systems, errors or cannot be checked
Communication
Service Level Reporting is not set up for this solution
Consistency
Solution Repository is consistent
Consistency
Details
Impaired Functionalities
Strategy for Resolving this Alert
Create or repair the connection to the affected systems in the transaction SMSY.
Details of this Alert:
1 . No RFC connection to the Solution Manager in the system NSM SDCC
Message no. DSMOP060
There is no RFC connection to the Solution Manager in transaction SDCCN in system NSM, so no EarlyWatch Alerts can be created for this system in the Solution Manager.
Procedure
Generate a connection from system NSM to the Solution Manager (BACK destination) in the Solution Manager transaction SMSY. Enter this connection in SDCCN in system NSM.
2 . System NSM sends EarlyWatch Alert data to SAP
Message no. DSMOP271
Diagnosis

Check the error and warning messages that occurred, and eliminate the errors in accordance with the solution description on the DETAILS tab. Then execute a self-diagnosis again to verify that the errors have been eliminated.

4.4 System Administration

System administrators are likely to be most interested in finding out about the functions provided by Solution Manager for administration and technical administration of the SAP systems.

SAP Solution Manager covers the following areas:

- Central system administration
- Central system monitoring (CCMS Alert Monitoring)
- EarlyWatch Alert (or service level reporting)

This section describes how you can use these functions for the administration of your system landscape.

4.4.1 Central System Administration

Central system administration helps you plan and execute administration tasks that arise in the systems within your solution.

The standard delivery of SAP Solution Manager contains predefined packages of tasks, which reflect the typical range of tasks that a system administrator is required to perform. These task packages provide checklists, which relate most directly to the system administration wizards (Transaction SSAA) described in Chapter 2, Section 2.4. You can plan these tasks centrally for all of your systems from Solution Manager. RFC connections allow you to navigate to the system in which you want to execute a task and start the relevant transaction automatically.

In addition to these standard tasks, you can also define your own tasks and add these to your task list.

Setting Up Central System Administration

You need to make some specific settings before using central system administration: To do this, follow these steps:

1. Enter Transaction "SOLUTION_MANAGER" in the command field, and press the Enter key (or select the menu option TOOLS • SAP SOLUTION MANAGER • SOLUTION_MANAGER – SOLUTION OPERATION).
2. To open your solution, click on the link in the SOLUTION column on the SOLUTION OVERVIEW – SAP SOLUTION MANAGER screen.

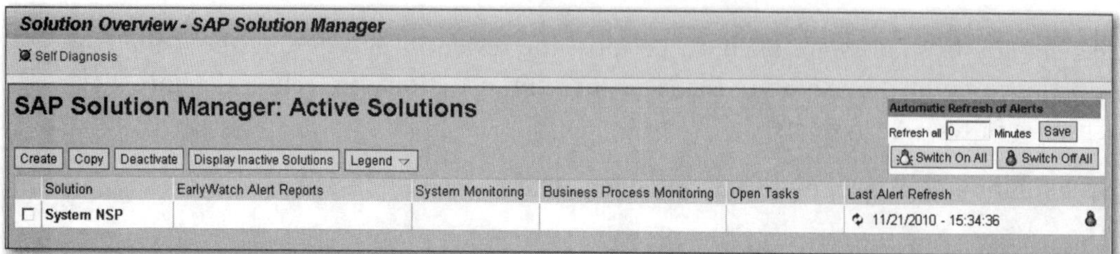

3. Select the SOLUTION MONITORING tab in the OPERATIONS SETUP view.

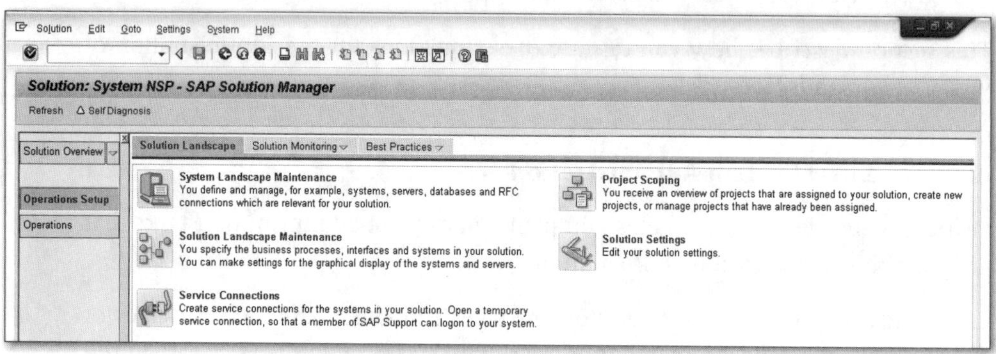

4. Click on the SYSTEM ADMINISTRATION subitem. Under SERVICE, select CENTRAL SYSTEM ADMINISTRATION.

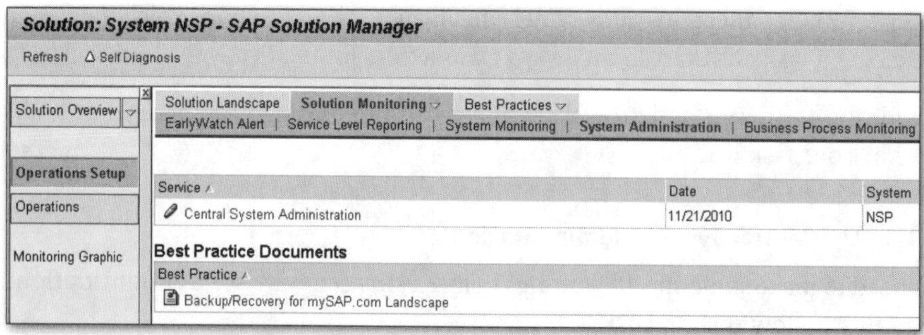

5. This brings you to the initial screen of Central System Administration. In the tree structure displayed in the left screen frame, follow the path CENTRAL SYSTEM ADMINISTRATION • ADMINISTRATION ENVIRONMENT, and click on CHOOSE ADMINISTRATION AND MONITORING WORKAREA.

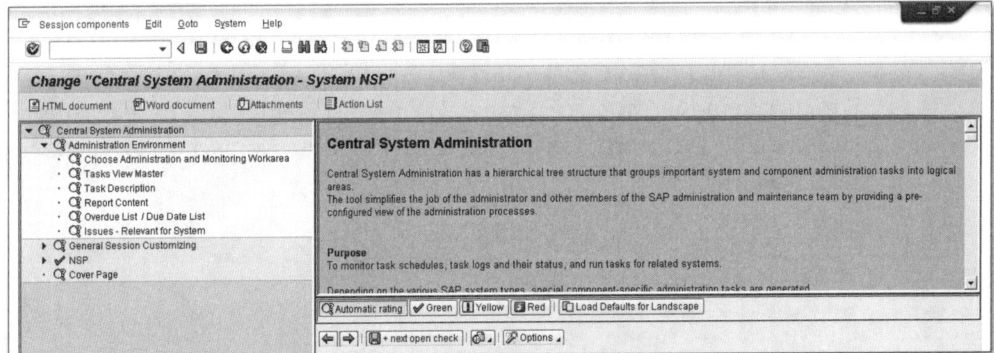

6. Select a standard view for the administration tasks (for example, ALL TASKS), and click on SAVE (💾).

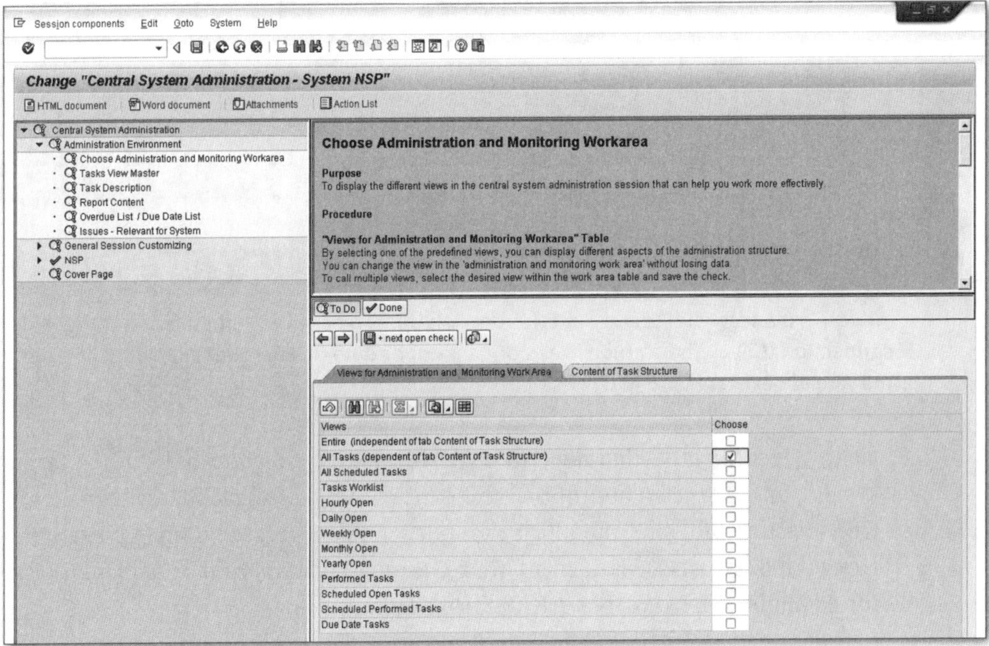

[+]

Other Options

In the ADMINISTRATION ENVIRONMENT structure, you can use additional settings to adjust the display of central user administration to meet your specific requirements. The available documentation about the individual points discussed earlier provides more detailed configuration instructions.

7. Select the menu option CENTRAL SYSTEM ADMINISTRATION • GENERAL SESSION CUSTOMIZING in the left screen frame. Pay particular attention to the status of the CHECK RFC DESTINATIONS task, to ensure that the connection to the target system is working.

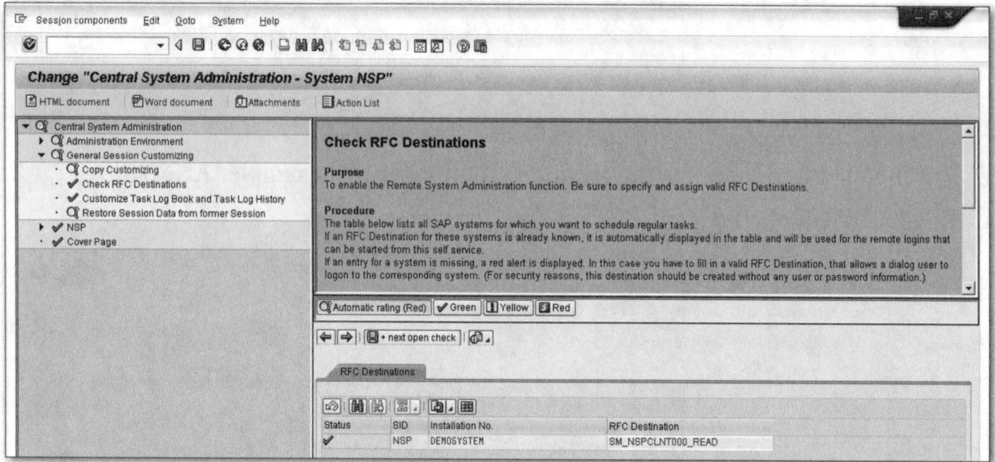

[!]

RFC Destination for Central System Administration

You can't manage your target system from Solution Manager without a functioning RFC connection. Check the status of the connection, or enter a new connection if one does not already exist.

8. Next, select the tasks that need to be performed on a regular basis in the target system, and define an appropriate execution interval for each task. Expand the tree structure of your system (for example, NSP) and a task group (for example, GENERAL BASIS ADMINISTRATION TASK GROUP). Position your cursor on a task, for example, CHECKING FOR ABAP SHORT DUMPS.

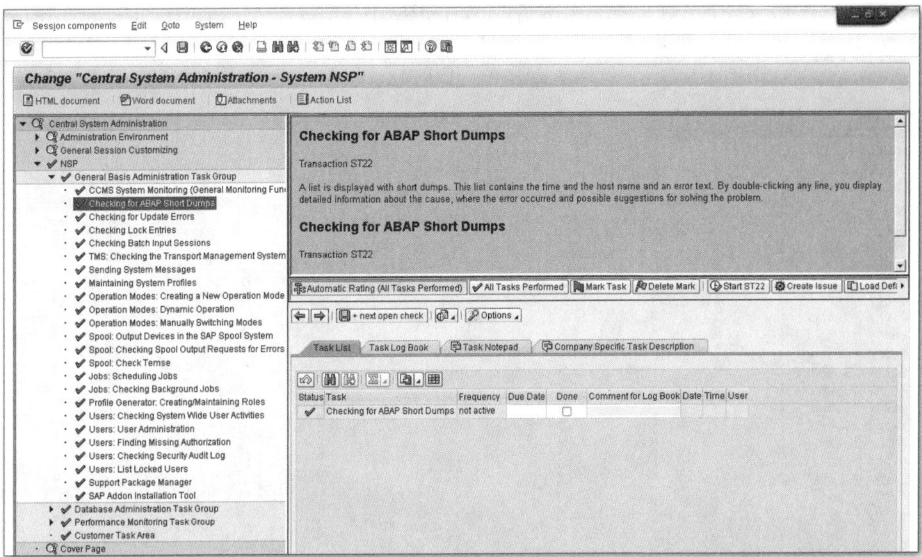

9. The top-right screen frame shows a description of the task, and specifies the transaction in which the task is executed (for example, ST22). You configure the task in the frame below this. The FREQUENCY column on the TASK LIST tab specifies by default that the task's execution interval is NOT ACTIVE. Open the input help (□).

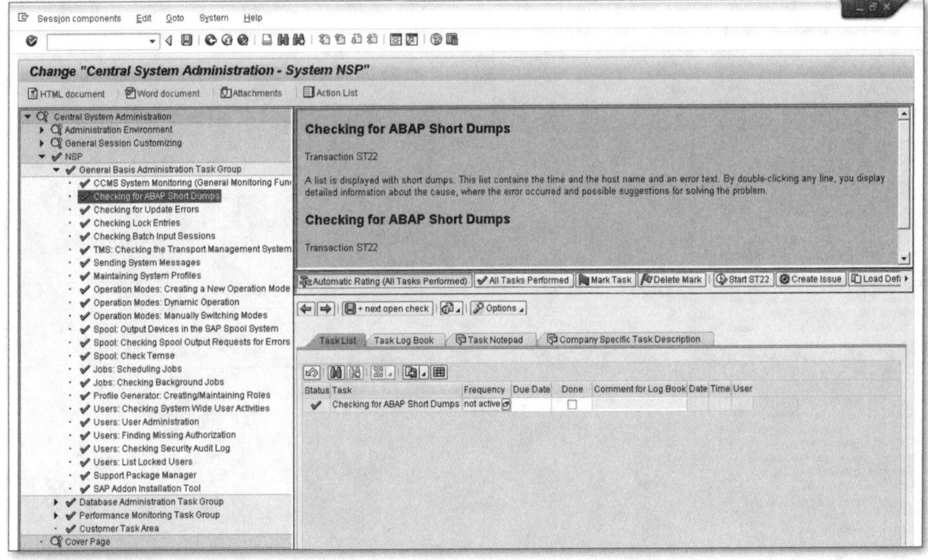

10. Select the required execution frequency in the drop-down list (for example, EVERY 2 HOURS). Click on CHOOSE (✔).

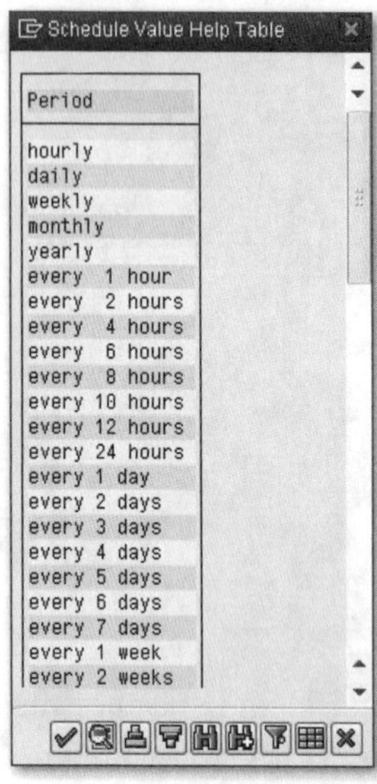

11. Choose SAVE (💾) to save your settings. The icon is now displayed next to the relevant task in the tree structure.

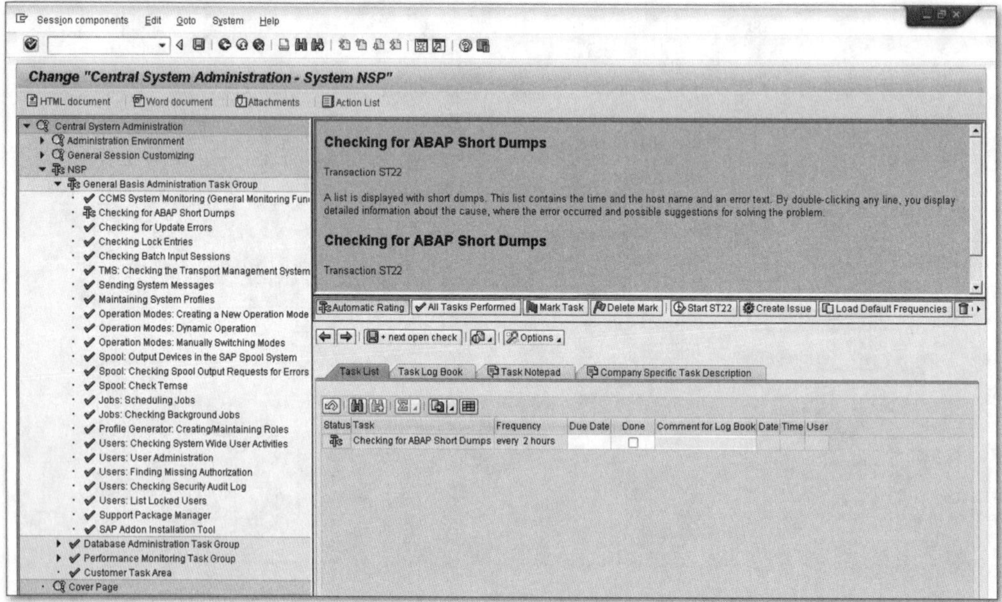

12. SAP also provides default frequencies for the individual tasks, which you can choose to accept. Select another task, and choose OPTIONS • LOAD DEFAULT FREQUENCIES in the lower screen frame.

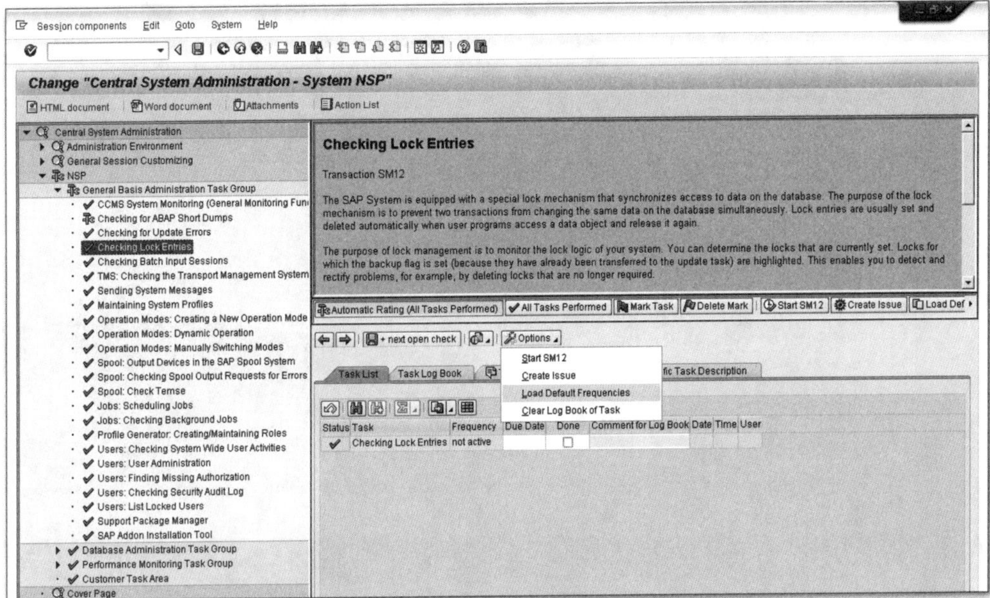

13. Answer YES to the confirmation prompt.

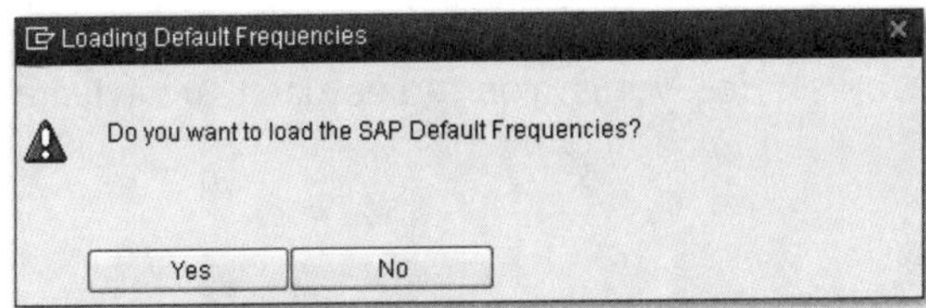

14. The default frequency has been entered. You can use the input help to change your setting at any time. Define an execution interval for all tasks you want to use. Then choose BACK (⊕) to exit this view.

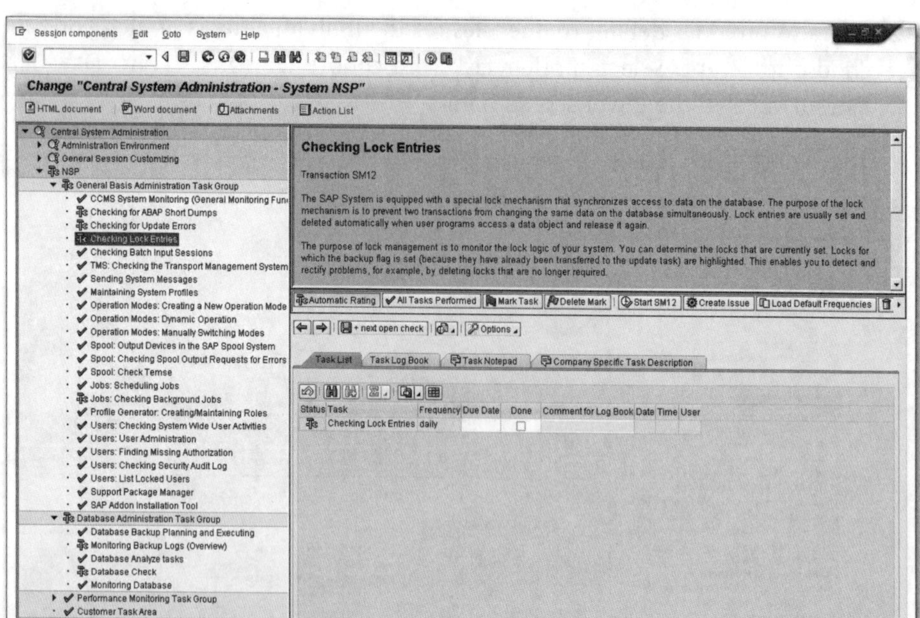

[+]

Deactivating Tasks

If you want to remove a task from your task list, select the NOT ACTIVE entry from the input help (□) in the FREQUENCY column.

15. On the initial screen, an additional ACTIVITIES column is now displayed for the CENTRAL SYSTEM ADMINISTRATION service, which you can use later to navigate to the activity report.

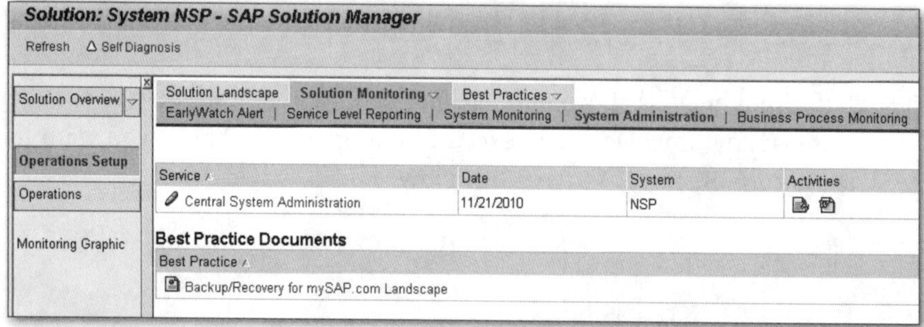

You've now created an administration plan for your system, consisting of tasks that are to be processed on a regular basis. If the tasks provided in the SAP standard system are not sufficient, you can create and schedule new tasks of your own. As soon as your task list is complete, you can use it to process and monitor your tasks.

[+]

Copying Customizing

When you have finished making administration settings for a solution, you can copy this configuration to other solutions by choosing CENTRAL SYSTEM ADMINISTRATION • GENERAL SESSION CUSTOMIZING • COPY CUSTOMIZING in the tree structure.

Defining Your Own Tasks

You can define your own tasks to enhance the task catalog provided by SAP or to create a completely new user-specific administration plan.

To create your own tasks, follow these steps:

1. Enter Transaction "SOLUTION_MANAGER" in the command field, and press the [Enter] key (or select the menu option TOOLS • SAP SOLUTION MANAGER • SOLUTION_MANAGER – SOLUTION OPERATION).
2. To open your solution, click on the link in the SOLUTION column on the SOLUTION OVERVIEW – SAP SOLUTION MANAGER screen.

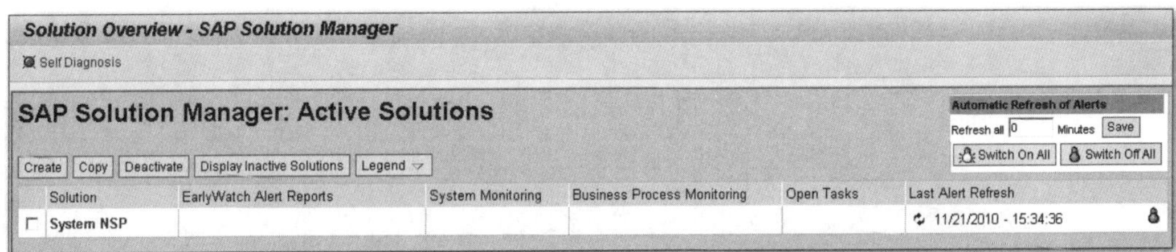

3. Select the SOLUTION MONITORING tab in the OPERATIONS SETUP view.

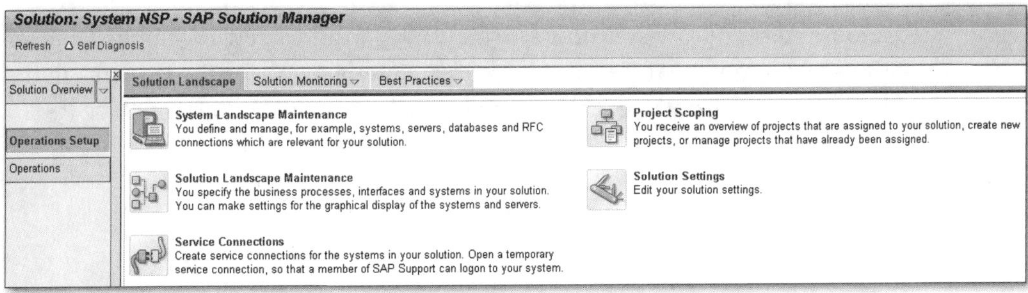

4. Click on the SYSTEM ADMINISTRATION subitem. Under SERVICE, select CENTRAL SYSTEM ADMINISTRATION.

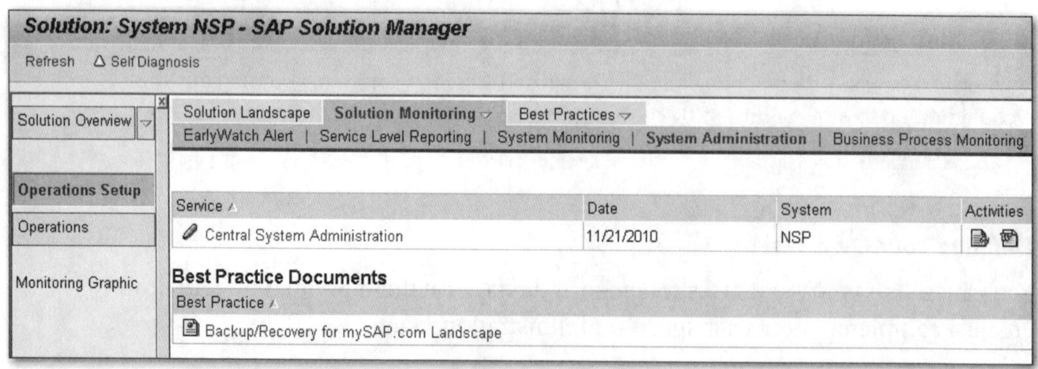

5. Position the cursor on the entry for your system (for example, NSP) below the CENTRAL SYSTEM ADMINISTRATION node in the tree structure. Open the DEFINING USER TASK AREA tab in the bottom-right screen frame.

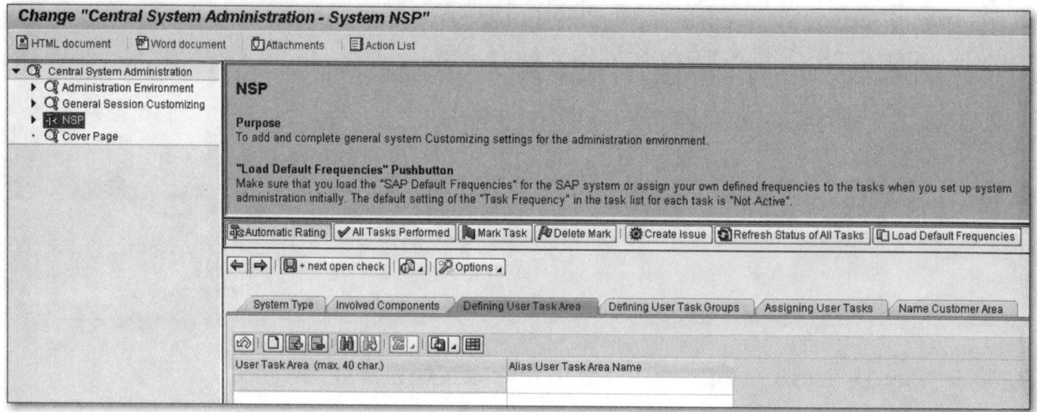

6. Choose APPEND ROW (icon) or INSERT ROW (icon) to add a new row to the table, or use a blank row to create a new task area. Enter a name for the task area in the USER TASK AREA COLUMN (for example, "Task Area NSP"). Click on SAVE (icon).

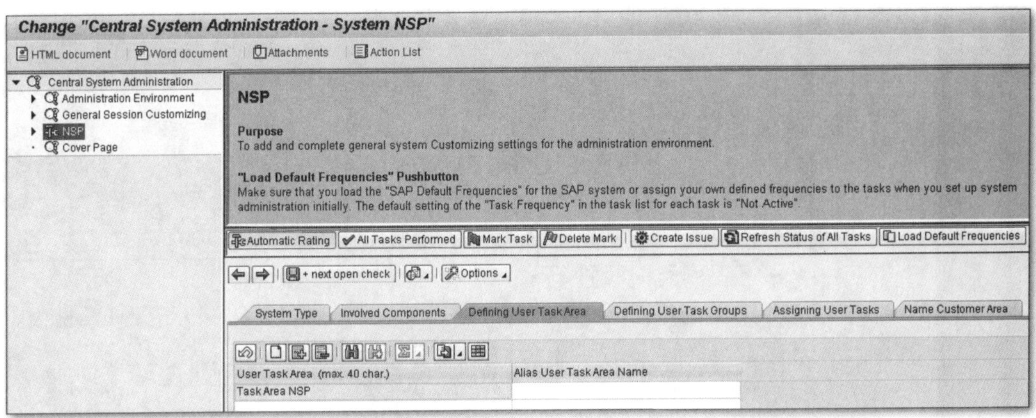

7. Switch to the DEFINING USER TASK GROUPS tab. Enter the following data in a new row:

   ▸ USER TASK AREA: Use the input help to find the task area you have just created (for example, Task Area NSP).

   ▸ TASK GROUP DESCRIPTION: Enter a description that is as meaningful as possible here (for example, "Message Server")

   ACTION: Enter the action to be executed, for example, "SMMS".

   ▸ ACTION TYPE: Select the relevant action type for the action in the drop-down list (for example, TRANSACTION).

   Choose SAVE (💾) to save your entries.

[+]

Available Action Types

The following action types are available for user-defined tasks:

- PROGRAM
  A specific report is executed.
- TRANSACTION
  A transaction is executed.
- URL
  An Internet address or file path is opened.
- OTHERS
  No action is defined.

If you select OTHERS, the task is not assigned to an action that can be executed directly. This action type can be used, for example, for tasks that are not executed in the system but are still essential.

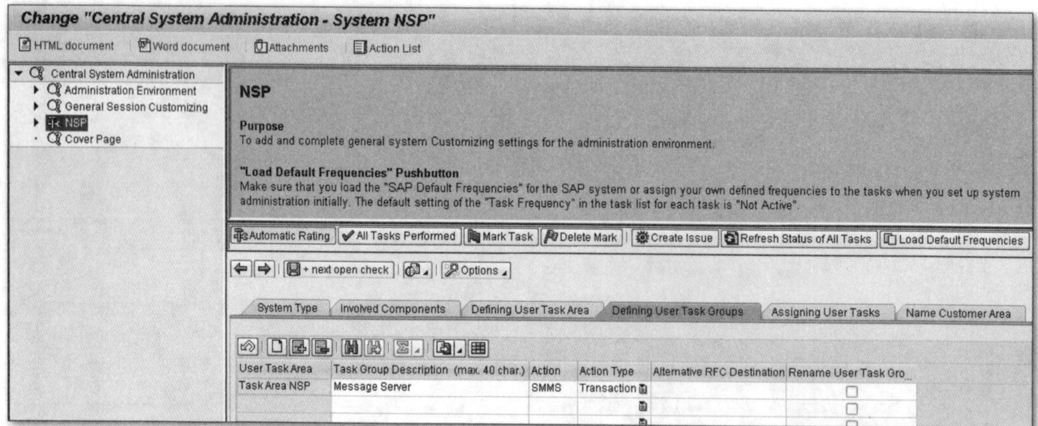

8. Open the Assigning User Tasks tab. Use the input help to select the task group you defined in the previous step. Enter a name for the task in the User Task column (for example, "Check Message Server"). Choose Save (💾).

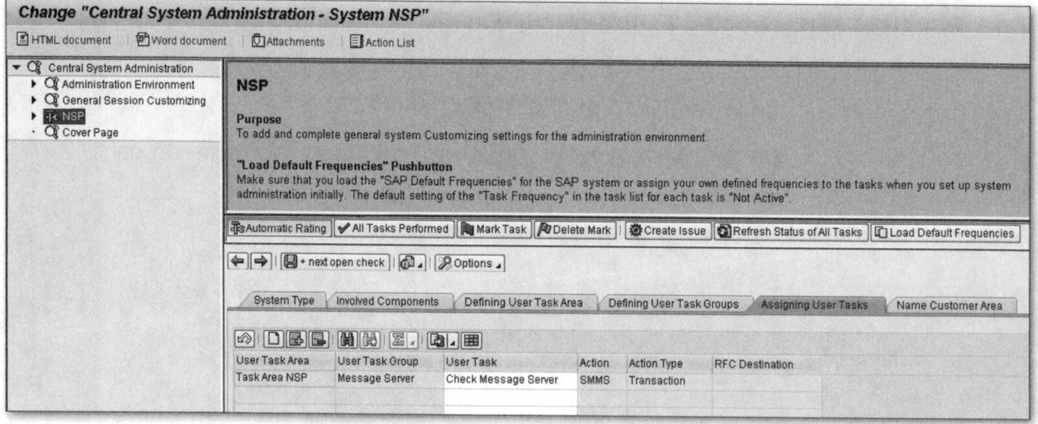

9. Your task has now been created. To assign an execution frequency to the task, expand the tree structure in the left screen frame: NSP • Customer Task Area • Task Area NSP • Message Server.

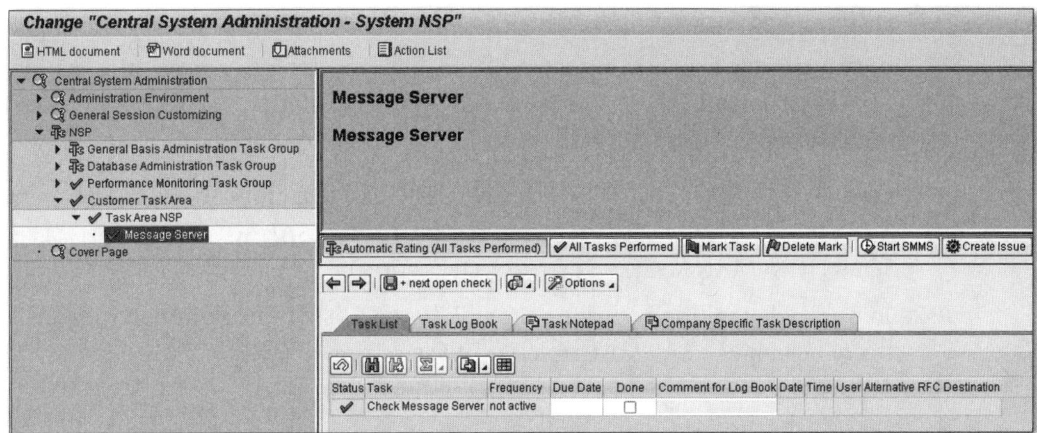

10. Enter an interval (for example, "Daily") in the FREQUENCY column as described previously, and choose SAVE (💾) to save your entry.

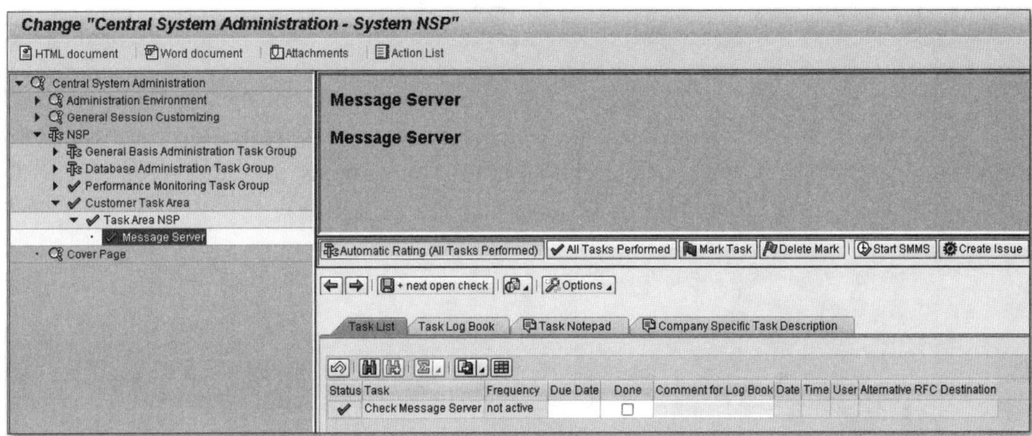

You can use your newly created task in exactly the same way as a standard SAP task. As soon as you assign an execution frequency to it, it becomes part of your task list.

Executing a Task Directly [+]

If you want to execute the task immediately to test it, choose OPTIONS • START <ACTION>. The transaction or other action will be displayed here in place of <Action>, for example, START SMMS. When you execute the task, you navigate automatically from Solution Manager to the target system, and the transaction is started in the system you want to manage.

Monitoring and Processing System Administration Tasks

After you create a task list for your SAP systems, you can begin regular operation of your system landscape. In other words, you use Solution Manager to process the tasks at the defined intervals.

1. Enter Transaction "SOLUTION_MANAGER" in the command field, and press the Enter key (or select the menu option TOOLS • SAP SOLUTION MANAGER • SOLUTION_MANAGER – SOLUTION OPERATION).
2. To open your solution, click on the link in the SOLUTION column on the SOLUTION OVERVIEW – SAP SOLUTION MANAGER screen.

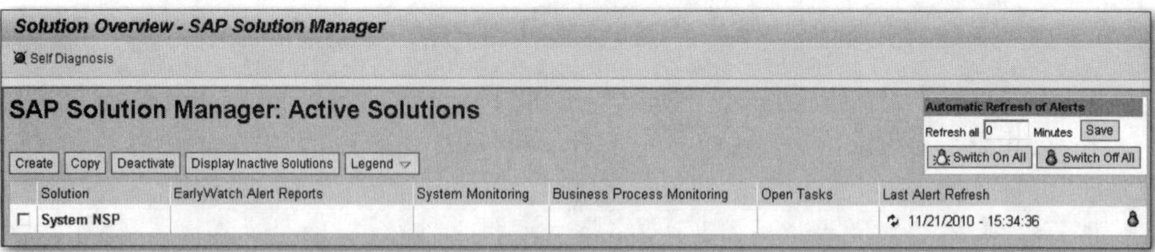

3. Select the SYSTEM MONITORING/ADMINISTRATION tab in the OPERATIONS view. It displays an overview of the systems for which administration tasks are to be executed. The task icon changes to indicate when tasks are due to be executed. Click on DISPLAY OPEN TASKS ( ).

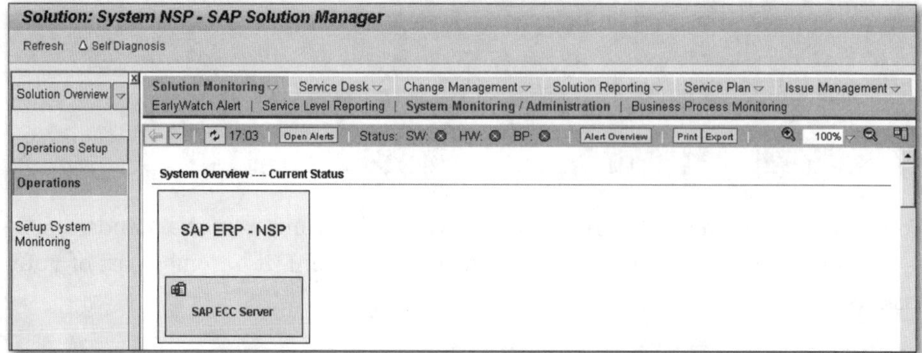

4. A table showing the open tasks is displayed. To open a task (for example, CHECK MESSAGE SERVER), click on the corresponding link in the NAME column.

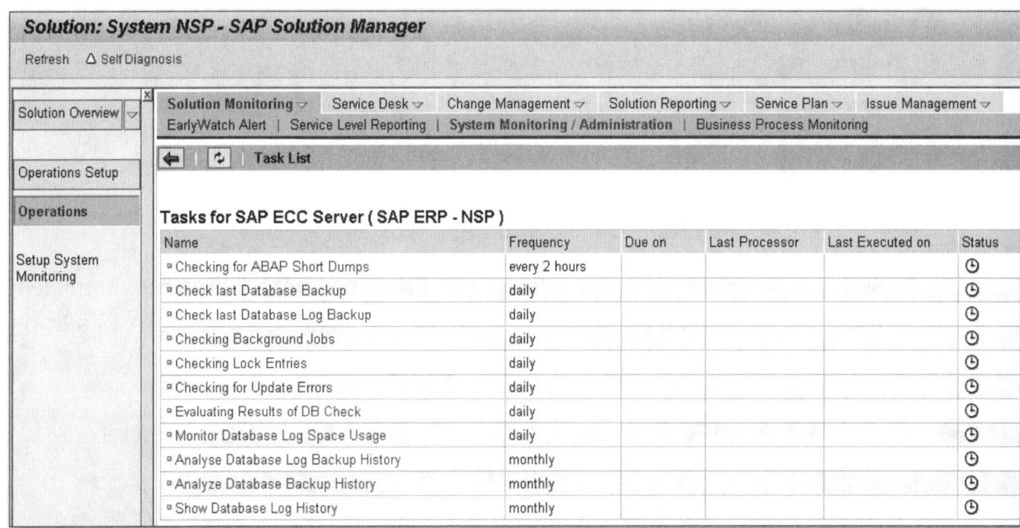

5. The view switches to your task list. To execute the task, you would click on the START SMMS button in this example.

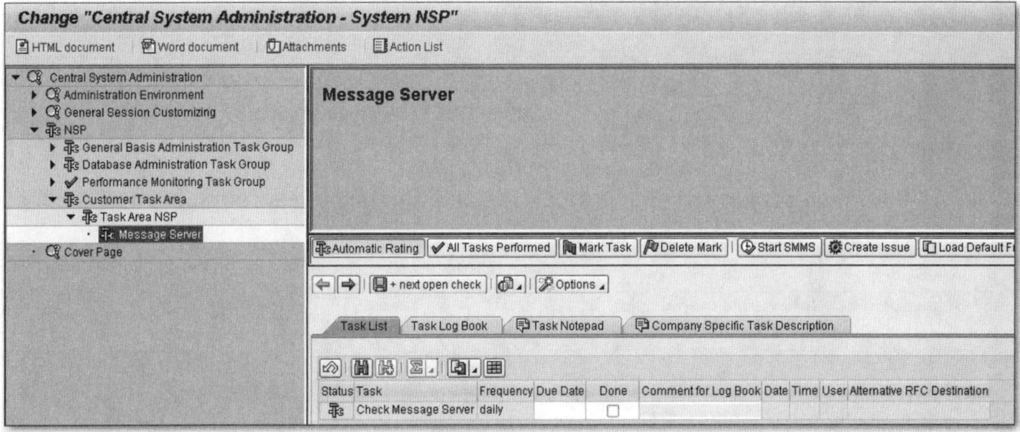

6. Solution Manager uses an RFC connection to navigate to the target system and starts the relevant transaction. You can then execute the task. For example, check whether the message server is active in Transaction SMMS (Message Server Monitor). When you've finished, choose BACK (![icon]) to exit the system.

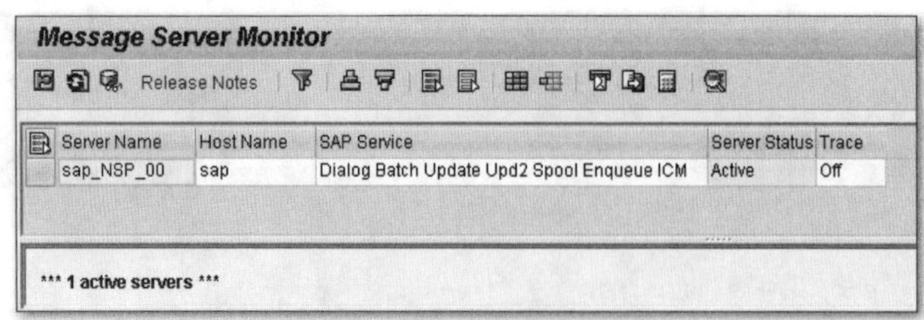

7. Set a checkmark in the DONE column to indicate that the task has been completed. If necessary, you can add a comment on the task in the COMMENT FOR LOG BOOK column. Click on SAVE (💾).

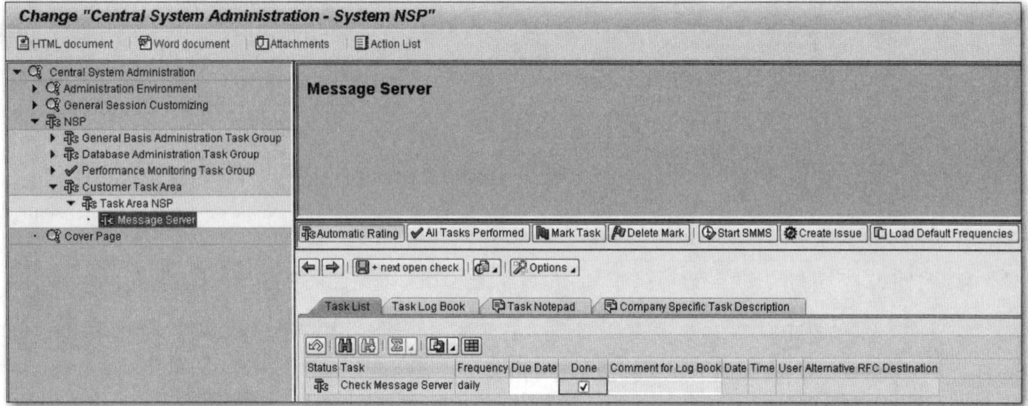

8. The task is flagged as executed (✔), and the time of execution is saved. Choose BACK (◀) to exit the screen.

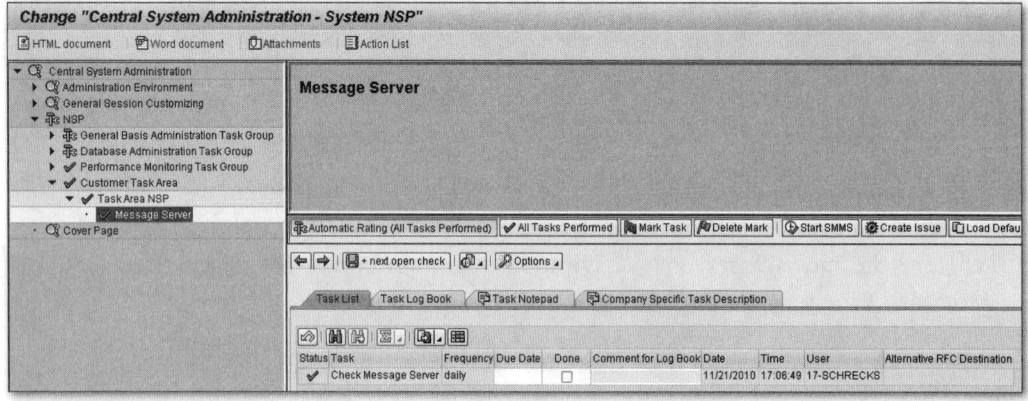

9. The task you have just executed is no longer shown on the list of open tasks. It will only be displayed there again the next time it is due for execution. Process the remaining tasks until the list of open tasks is empty.

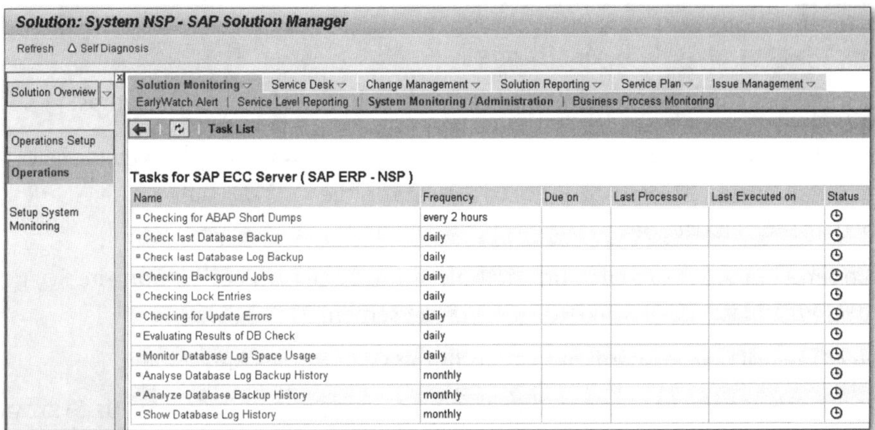

The task list allows you to carry out administration tasks according to a predefined schedule. It reminds you about open tasks and allows you to navigate from Solution Manager to the individual systems in which the tasks are to be executed, without having to log on again.

4.4.2 Central System Monitoring

Central system monitoring is based on the technology of the CCMS Alert Monitor (see Chapter 3). You can either use the CCMS Alert Monitor in your SAP systems directly, or set up Solution Manager as a central system, to which all alerts that occur in the monitored systems are forwarded. You can then analyze the alerts for all systems centrally in Solution Manager, without having to log on to each individual target system.

Central System for CCMS Alert Monitoring

In Solution Manager, central system monitoring is based on the CCMS architecture. This means that your Solution Manager must, on the one hand, be configured as the central monitoring system (CEN) for the CCMS Alert Monitor. On the other hand, you must register the systems to be monitored for monitoring in Solution Manager.

This process is too complex to be discussed here. However, a detailed description is available in the SAP Help Portal (*http://help.sap.com*). Search under *Configuring a Central Monitoring System* or using the keyword *CEN*.

In relation to the required RFC connections, ensure that your Solution Manager's */etc/services* file contains the entry "sapms<SID>3600/tcp" for the message server of the target system.

Setting Up Central System Monitoring

First, you must configure central monitoring. To do this, follow these steps:

1. Enter Transaction "SOLUTION_MANAGER", and press the [Enter] key (or select the menu option TOOLS • SAP SOLUTION MANAGER • SOLUTION_MANAGER – SOLUTION OPERATION).
2. To open your solution, click on the link in the SOLUTION column on the SOLUTION OVERVIEW – SAP SOLUTION MANAGER screen.
3. Select the SOLUTION MONITORING tab in the OPERATIONS SETUP view.
4. Click on the SYSTEM MONITORING subitem. Under SERVICE, select SETUP SYSTEM MONITORING.

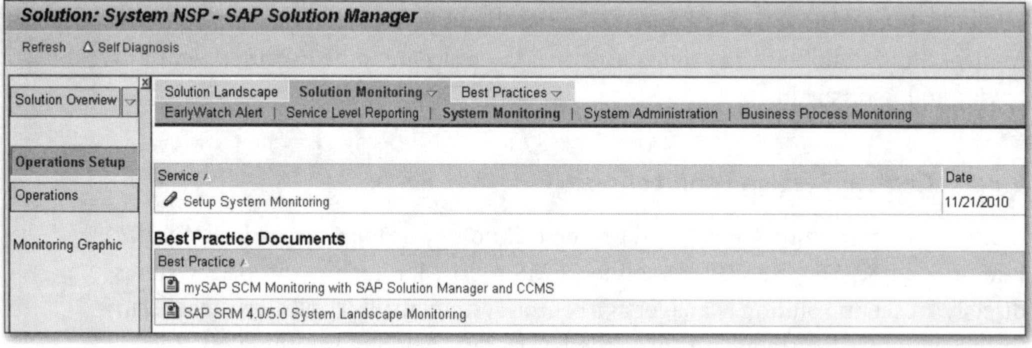

5. Begin by activating system monitoring for the systems in your solution. To do this, choose SETUP SYSTEM MONITORING • ACTIVATE MONITORING FOR SYSTEMS WITH ABAP-STACK. Activate the checkbox in the ACTIVE? column for the systems you want to monitor. Choose SAVE ().

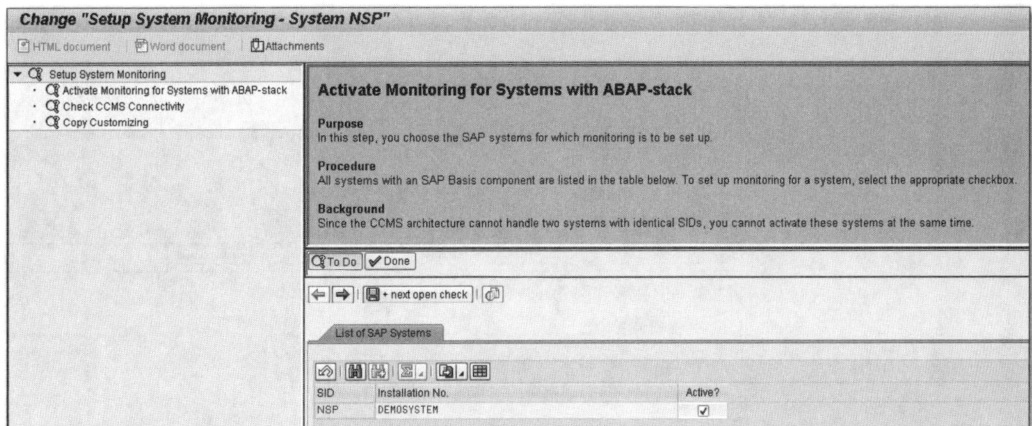

6. Select CHECK CCMS CONNECTIVITY in the tree structure. Make sure that the RFC connections to the target system are working (STATUS column ✔).

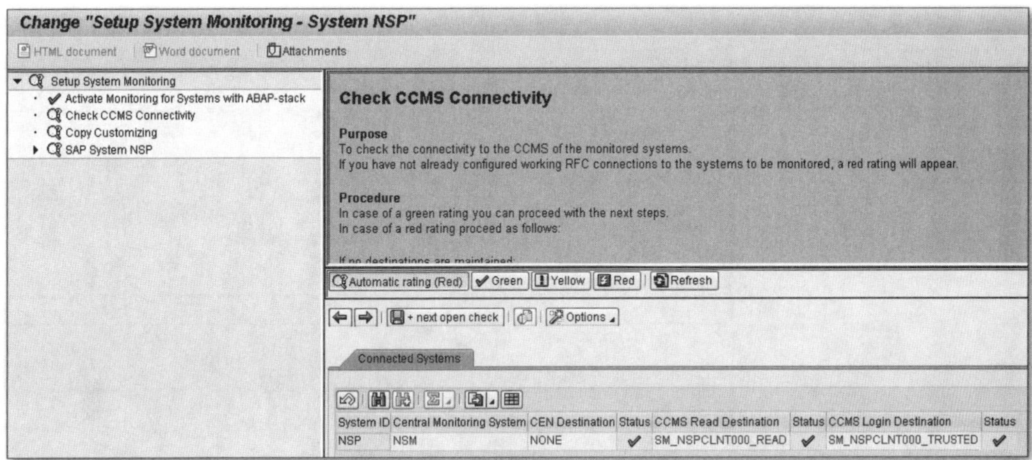

7. You can use the COPY CUSTOMIZING option to copy settings made in other systems if required.

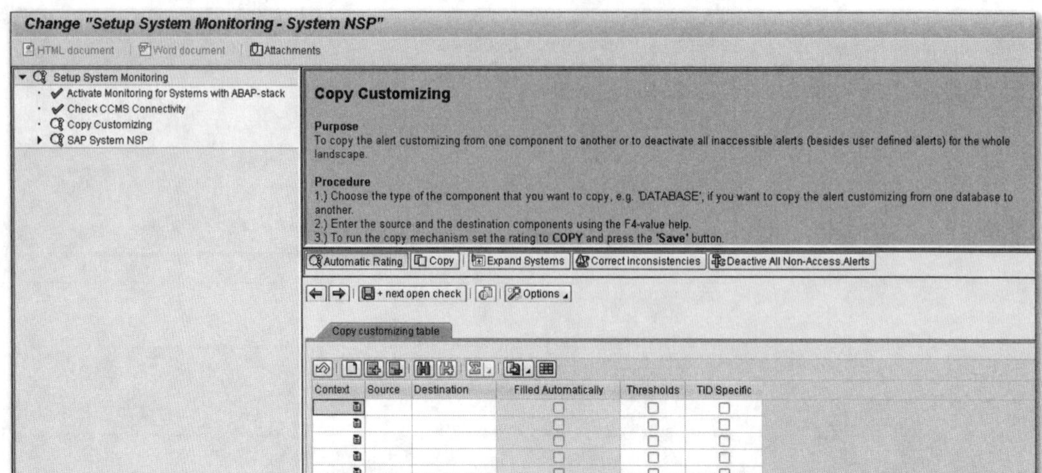

8. To make system-specific settings, position the cursor on the node that indicates your system (for example, SAP SYSTEM NSP).

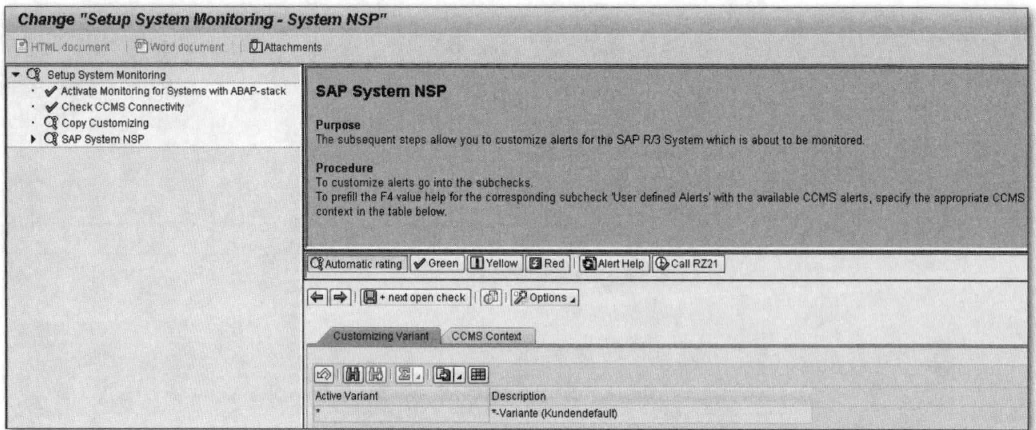

9. Select the CCMS CONTEXT tab in the lower screen frame. Open the input help (□) for the CCMS CONTEXT field.

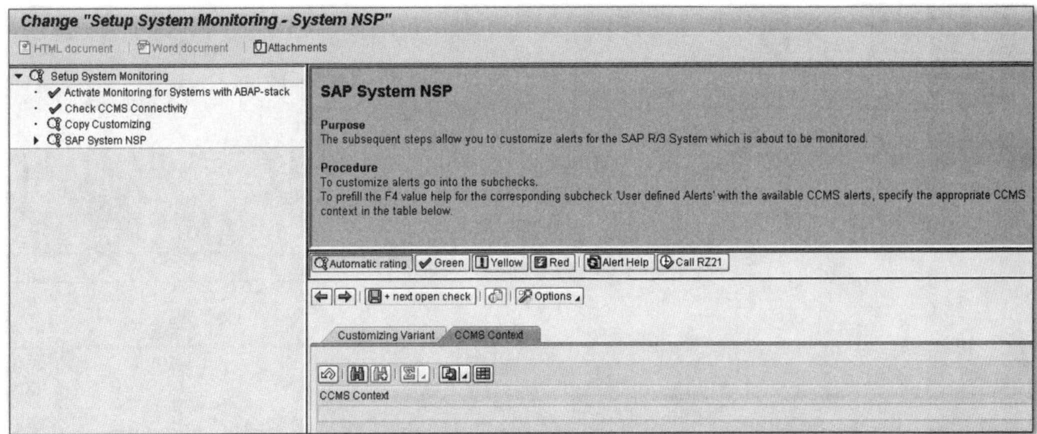

10. In the dialog box that opens, select the relevant CCMS context (for example, SAP_NSP_00). Click on CHOOSE (✔).

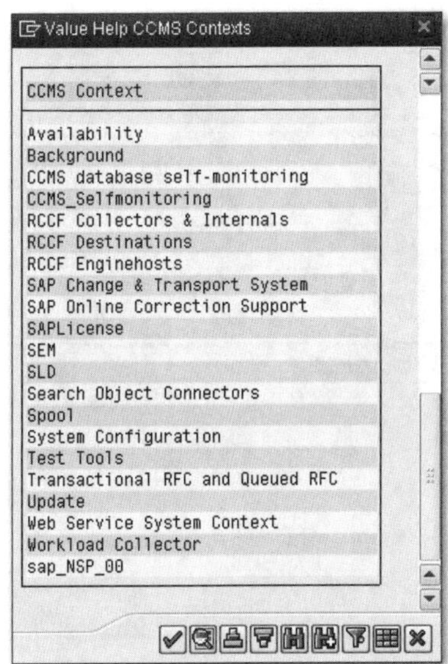

11. The CCMS context has been selected. Click on SAVE (💾).

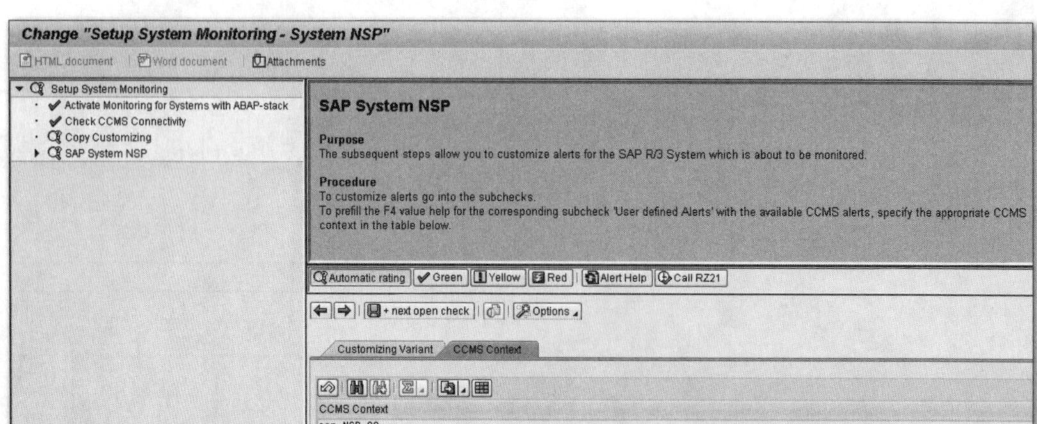

12. Next, expand your system path (for example, SAP SYSTEM NSP), and select the setup path (for example, SETUP MONITORING FOR SAP SYSTEM NSP). Activate the alerts that you want to monitor centrally. Then choose SAVE (💾).

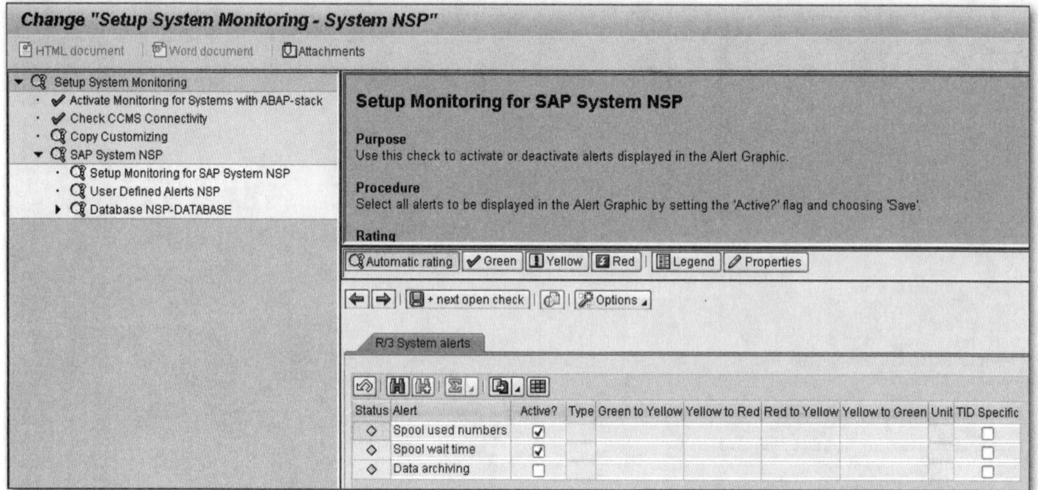

13. Select the entry USER DEFINED ALERTS NSP. Open the input help (☐) in the ALERT column.

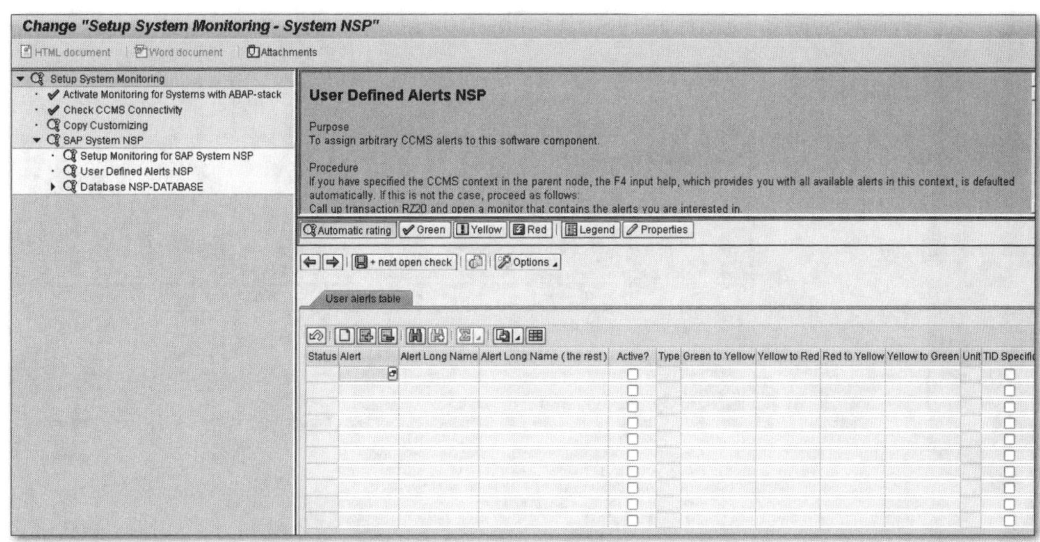

14. In the dialog box that opens, activate the target system alerts that you want to monitor centrally.

    Then click on CHOOSE (✔).

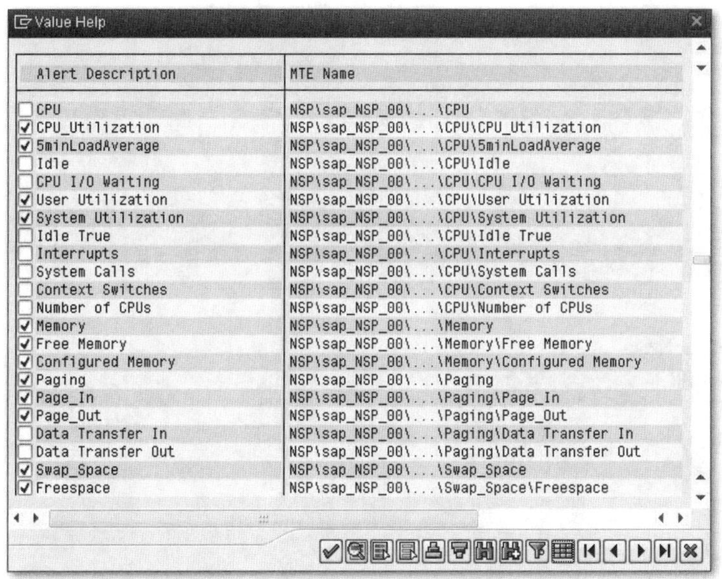

15. The selected alerts are added to the table. Click on SAVE (💾).

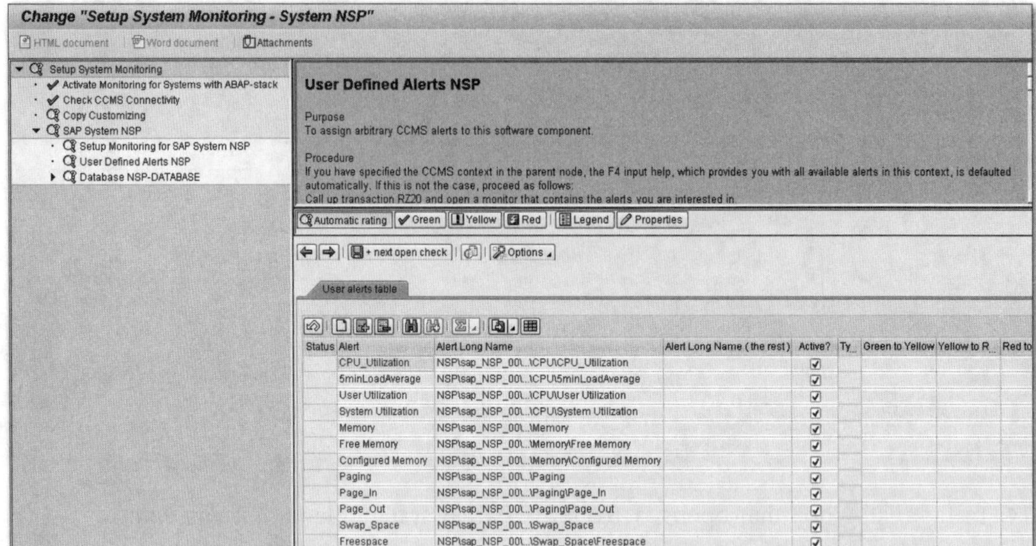

16. After saving, you can still change the threshold values of the alerts in the table in the GREEN TO YELLOW, YELLOW TO RED columns, and so on.

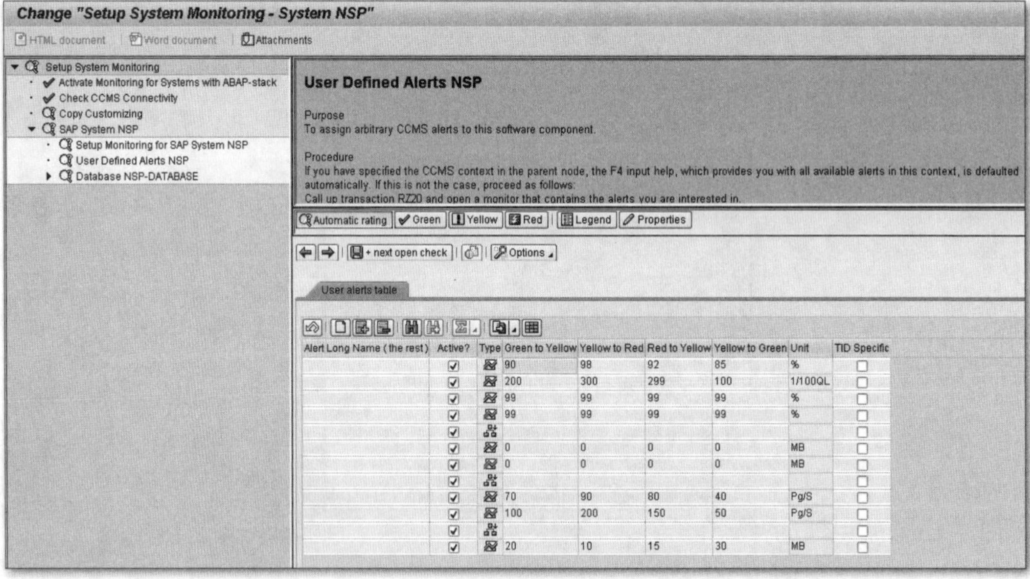

You've now set up system monitoring for the target system and defined the alerts you want to monitor. Your target systems are integrated into central monitoring, which means that you can immediately start monitoring their statuses with Solution Manager. You can adjust the configuration of central system monitoring at any time, for example, by adding new alerts.

Monitoring System Alerts

As soon as system monitoring is set up for your solution, any alerts that occur in the target system are displayed in Solution Manager. To analyze these alerts, follow these steps:

1. Enter Transaction "SOLUTION_MANAGER" in the command field, and press the Enter key (or select the menu option TOOLS • SAP SOLUTION MANAGER • SOLUTION_MANAGER – SOLUTION OPERATION).
2. To open your solution, click on the link in the SOLUTION column on the SOLUTION OVERVIEW – SAP SOLUTION MANAGER screen.

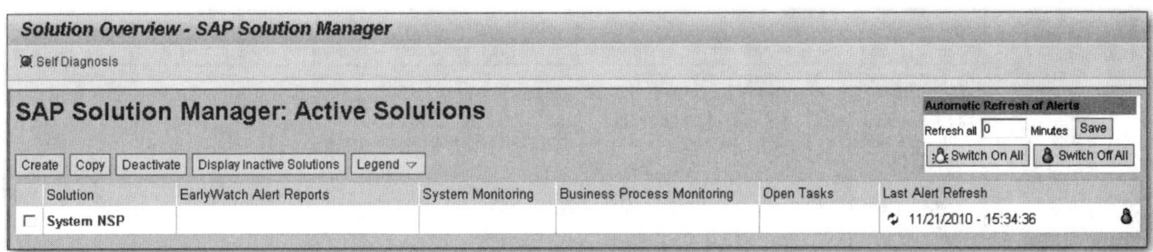

3. Select the SYSTEM MONITORING/ADMINISTRATION tab in the OPERATIONS view. It displays an overview of the systems for which administration tasks are to be executed. The alert icon changes to indicate the existence of alerts. Click on DISPLAY ALERTS ( ).

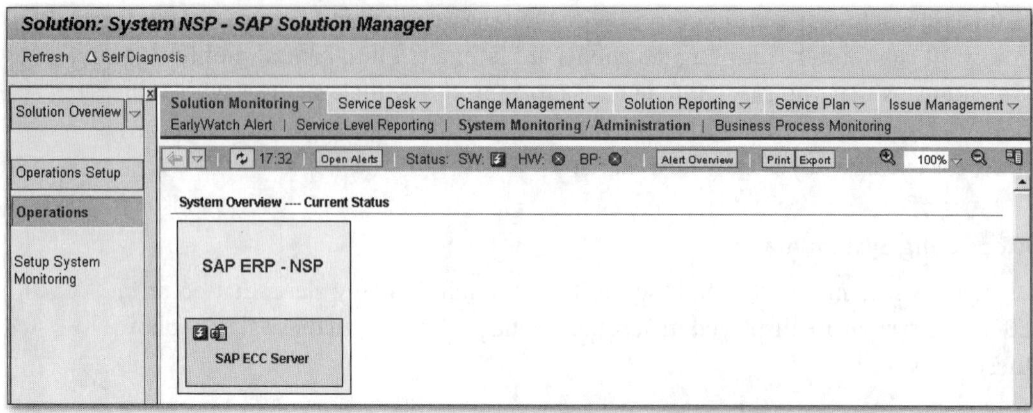

4. All alerts that currently exist are listed in the CURRENT STATUS view. Click on a link (for example, CPU_UTILIZATION) to view the details.

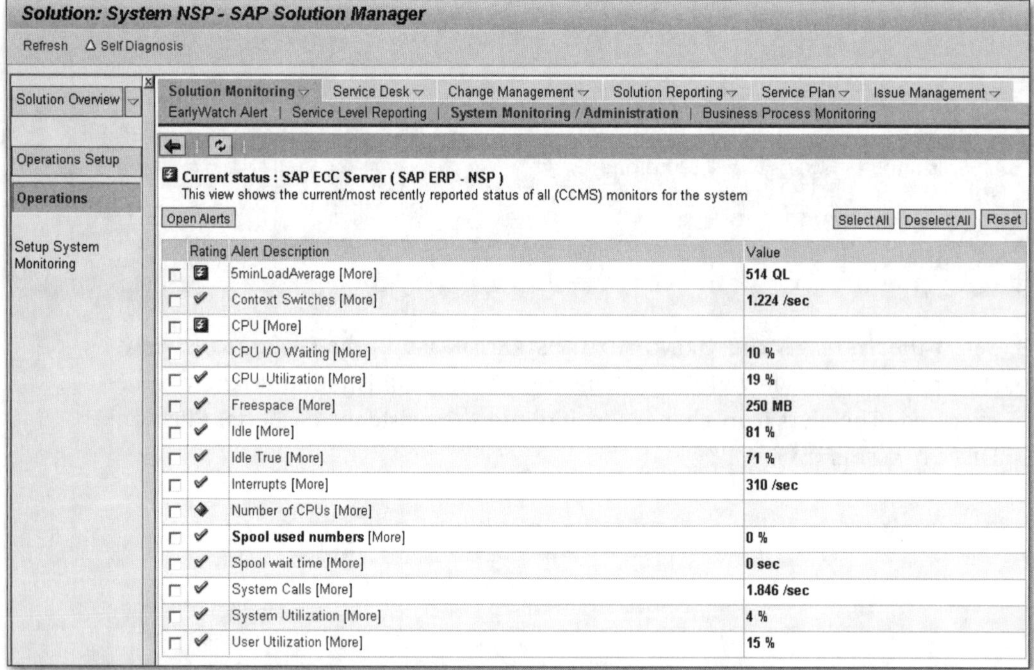

5. This action results in automatic navigation to the target system, and the alerts details are displayed.

To return to Solution Manager, choose BACK (⊙).

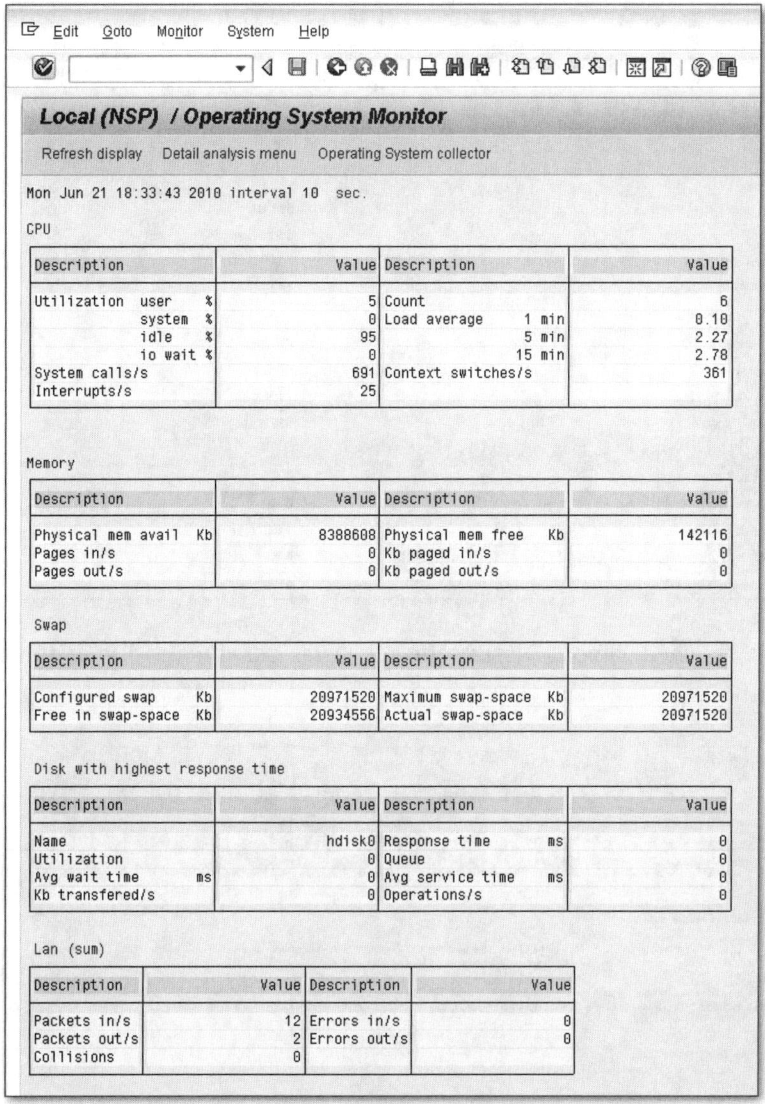

Edit Goto Monitor System Help
Local (NSP) / Operating System Monitor
Refresh display Detail analysis menu Operating System collector
Mon Jun 21 18:33:43 2010 interval 10 sec.
CPU
Description Value Description Value
Utilization user % 5 Count 6
system % 0 Load average 1 min 0.10
idle % 95 5 min 2.27
io wait % 0 15 min 2.78
System calls/s 691 Context switches/s 361
Interrupts/s 25
Memory
Description Value Description Value
Physical mem avail Kb 8388608 Physical mem free Kb 142116
Pages in/s 0 Kb paged in/s 0
Pages out/s 0 Kb paged out/s 0
Swap
Description Value Description Value
Configured swap Kb 20971520 Maximum swap-space Kb 20971520
Free in swap-space Kb 20934556 Actual swap-space Kb 20971520
Disk with highest response time
Description Value Description Value
Name hdisk0 Response time ms 0
Utilization 0 Queue 0
Avg wait time ms 0 Avg service time ms 0
Kb transfered/s 0 Operations/s 0
Lan (sum)
Description Value Description Value
Packets in/s 12 Errors in/s 0
Packets out/s 2 Errors out/s 0
Collisions 0

6. Click on [MORE] in the overview to read a description of the alert.

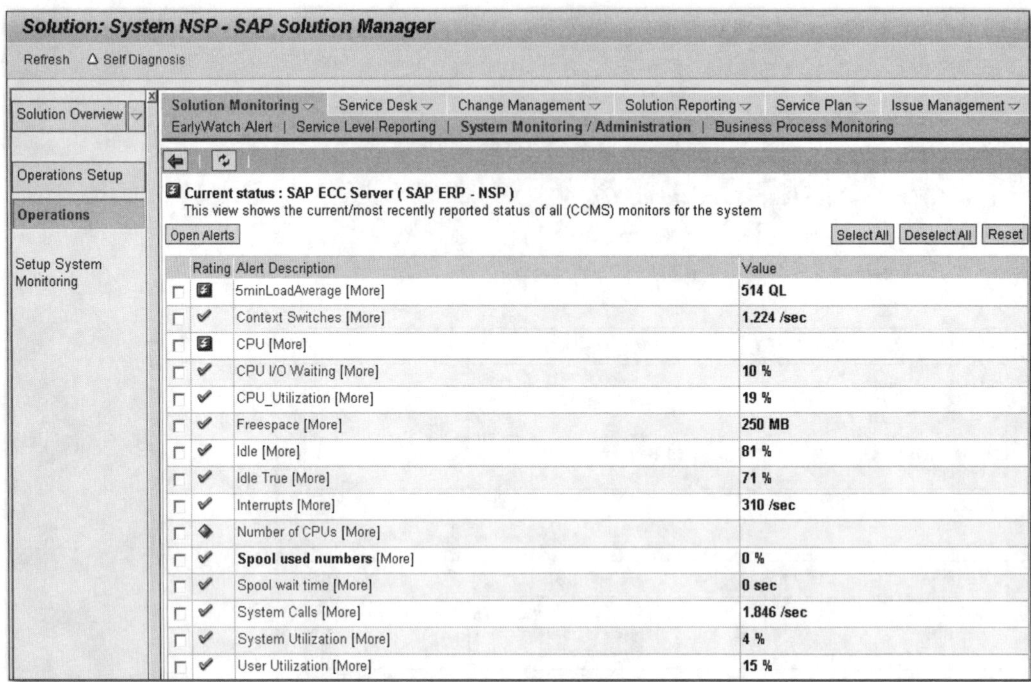

7. When you've finished, choose Display Higher-Level graphic (⬅) to exit the view.

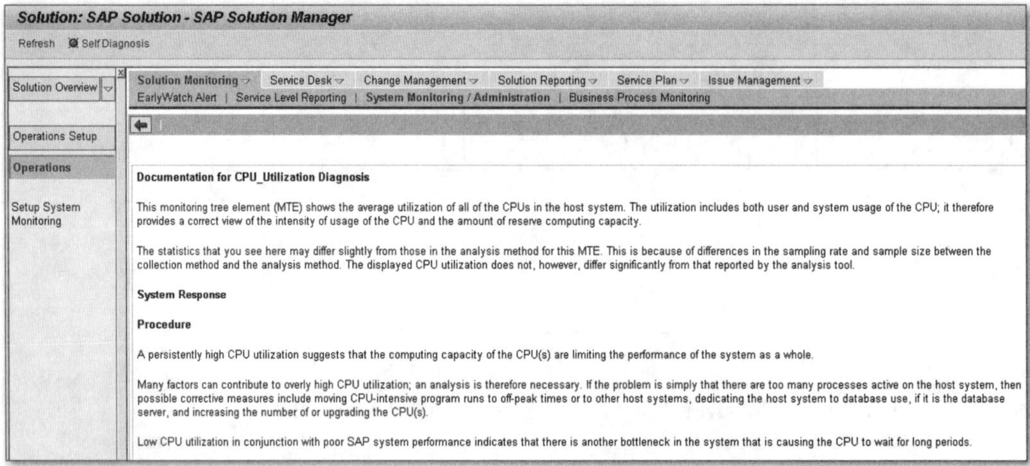

8. To view historical alert data, click on Open alerts in the overview.

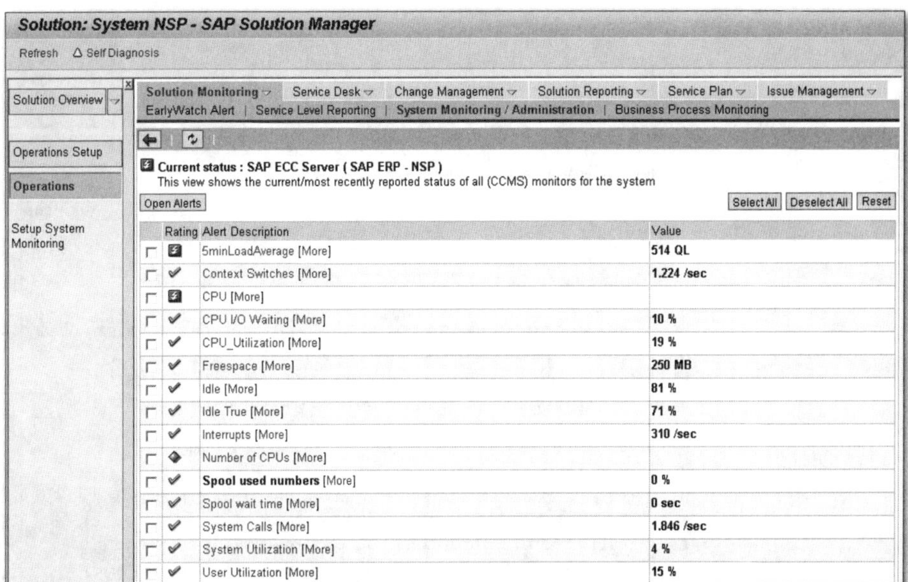

9. You can expand an alert to display its history.

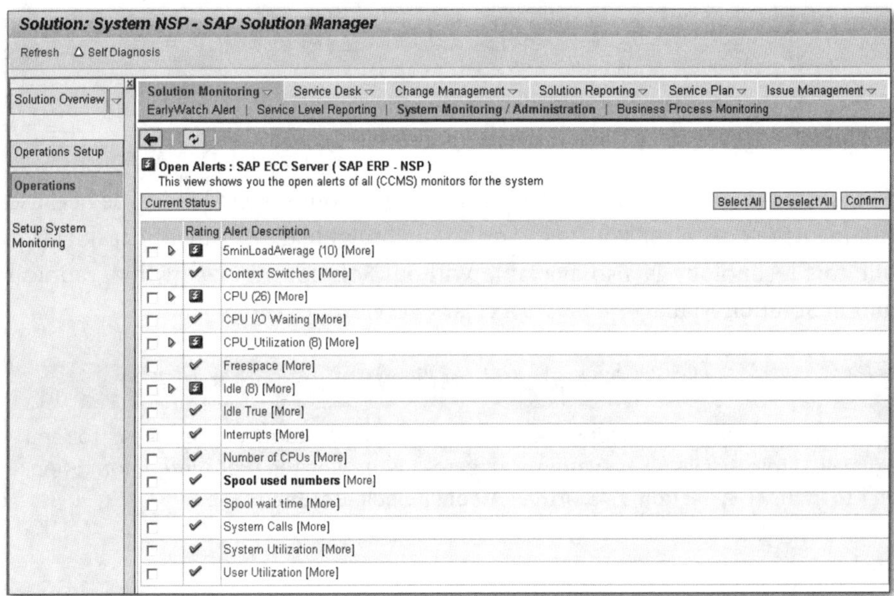

10. To confirm an alert, activate the corresponding checkbox, and click on the CONFIRM button.

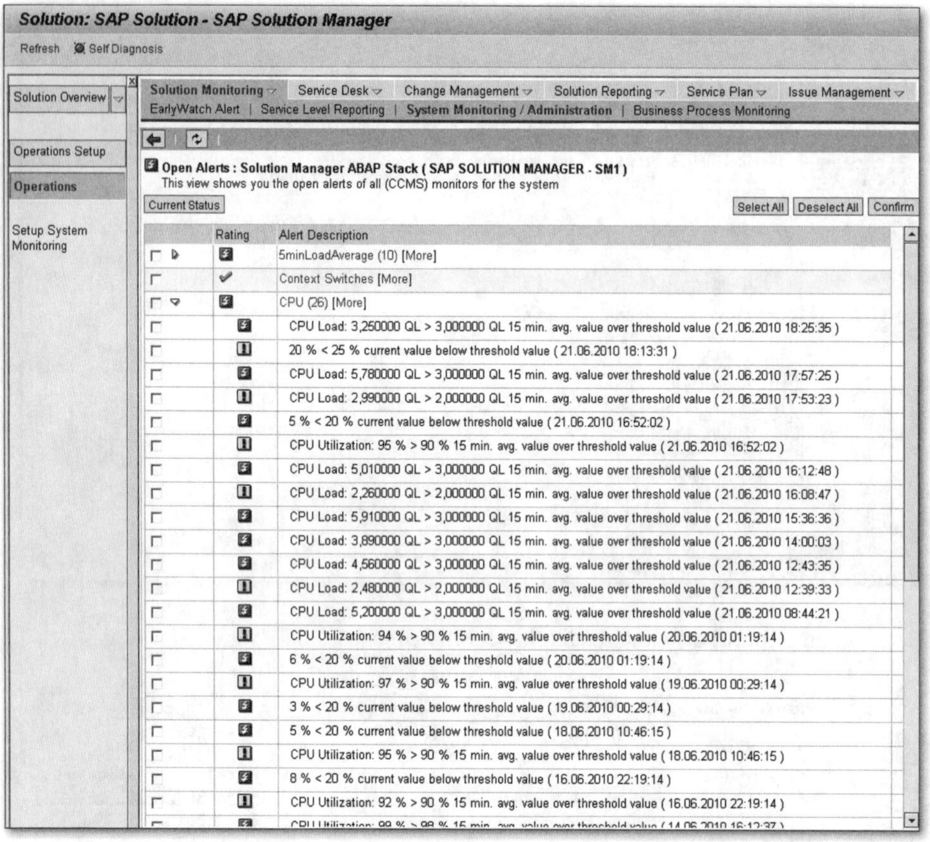

Solution: SAP Solution - SAP Solution Manager

Refresh | Self Diagnosis

Solution Overview | Operations Setup | **Operations** | Setup System Monitoring

Solution Monitoring | Service Desk | Change Management | Solution Reporting | Service Plan | Issue Management

EarlyWatch Alert | Service Level Reporting | **System Monitoring / Administration** | Business Process Monitoring

Open Alerts : Solution Manager ABAP Stack (SAP SOLUTION MANAGER - SM1)

This view shows you the open alerts of all (CCMS) monitors for the system

Current Status | Select All | Deselect All | Confirm

Rating	Alert Description
	5minLoadAverage (10) [More]
	Context Switches [More]
	CPU (26) [More]
	CPU Load: 3,250000 QL > 3,000000 QL 15 min. avg. value over threshold value (21.06.2010 18:25:35)
	20 % < 25 % current value below threshold value (21.06.2010 18:13:31)
	CPU Load: 5,780000 QL > 3,000000 QL 15 min. avg. value over threshold value (21.06.2010 17:57:25)
	CPU Load: 2,990000 QL > 2,000000 QL 15 min. avg. value over threshold value (21.06.2010 17:53:23)
	5 % < 20 % current value below threshold value (21.06.2010 16:52:02)
	CPU Utilization: 95 % > 90 % 15 min. avg. value over threshold value (21.06.2010 16:52:02)
	CPU Load: 5,010000 QL > 3,000000 QL 15 min. avg. value over threshold value (21.06.2010 16:12:48)
	CPU Load: 2,260000 QL > 2,000000 QL 15 min. avg. value over threshold value (21.06.2010 16:08:47)
	CPU Load: 5,910000 QL > 3,000000 QL 15 min. avg. value over threshold value (21.06.2010 15:36:36)
	CPU Load: 3,890000 QL > 3,000000 QL 15 min. avg. value over threshold value (21.06.2010 14:00:03)
	CPU Load: 4,560000 QL > 3,000000 QL 15 min. avg. value over threshold value (21.06.2010 12:43:35)
	CPU Load: 2,480000 QL > 2,000000 QL 15 min. avg. value over threshold value (21.06.2010 12:39:33)
	CPU Load: 5,200000 QL > 3,000000 QL 15 min. avg. value over threshold value (21.06.2010 08:44:21)
	CPU Utilization: 94 % > 90 % 15 min. avg. value over threshold value (20.06.2010 01:19:14)
	6 % < 20 % current value below threshold value (20.06.2010 01:19:14)
	CPU Utilization: 97 % > 90 % 15 min. avg. value over threshold value (19.06.2010 00:29:14)
	3 % < 20 % current value below threshold value (19.06.2010 00:29:14)
	5 % < 20 % current value below threshold value (18.06.2010 10:46:15)
	CPU Utilization: 95 % > 90 % 15 min. avg. value over threshold value (18.06.2010 10:46:15)
	8 % < 20 % current value below threshold value (16.06.2010 22:19:14)
	CPU Utilization: 92 % > 90 % 15 min. avg. value over threshold value (16.06.2010 22:19:14)

Central system monitoring facilitates monitoring of your system landscape because it eliminates the need for you to log on to the individual systems to check alerts. While this technology is also available without Solution Manager, the graphical layout in Solution Manager ensures a clear overview.

[+]

Auto-Reaction Methods

You can also define auto-reaction methods for system monitoring, for example, to send an email automatically whenever an alert threshold is violated. For more information, refer to Chapter 3, Section 3.4, or the SAP online help documentation.

4.4.3 SAP EarlyWatch Alert

The SAP EarlyWatch Alert is part of system monitoring. However, unlike CCMS Alert Monitoring, it analyzes the status of an SAP system on a regular basis (usually weekly) rather than in real time. For analysis purposes, this report accesses data that has been gathered over a longer period to provide both a snapshot and a long-term evaluation of the following system-critical aspects:

- System configuration (hardware, software, service availability)
- System performance (performance development, transaction profiles)
- Workload distribution (per module, database load)
- System operation (update terminations, transports, short dumps)
- Hardware capacity (CPU, main memory, paging)
- Database performance (locks, read and write times, indexes)
- Database administration (growth, objects with a critical size)
- Security (users with critical authorizations, security gaps)
- Trend analysis (system availability, response times, hardware)

[+]

Information About the SAP EarlyWatch Alert

For more information about the EarlyWatch Alert, see the SAP Support Portal at *www.service.sap.com/ewa*.

The EarlyWatch report is based on the *Service Data Control Centers* (SDCC) data gathered in the target system. You must therefore ensure that the SDCC is fully configured before you can use the EarlyWatch Alert.

Activating the Service Data Control Center

To use the EarlyWatch Alerts, you must first activate the SDCC in the system you want to monitor. You can do this from Solution Manager by following these steps:

1. Enter Transaction "SMSY" in the command field, and press the Enter key (or select the menu option Tools • SAP Solution Manager • SMSY – System Landscape).
2. In the menu, select Environment • Solution Manager Operations • Administration SDCCN.

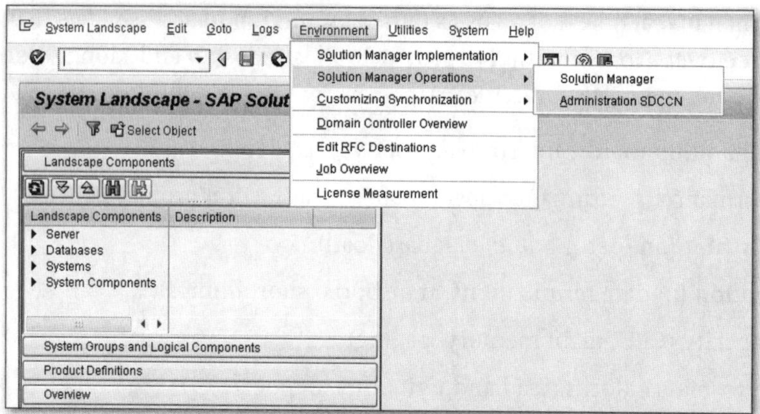

3. A dialog box opens, displaying the system for which the SDCCN has already been set up in your Solution Manager. Choose ADD SYSTEM ( ) to create a new entry.

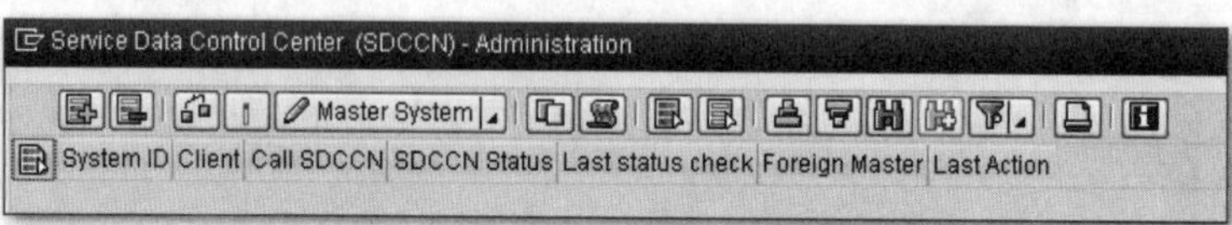

4. Select a system or a client within a system from the tree structure. Click on CONTINUE ( ).

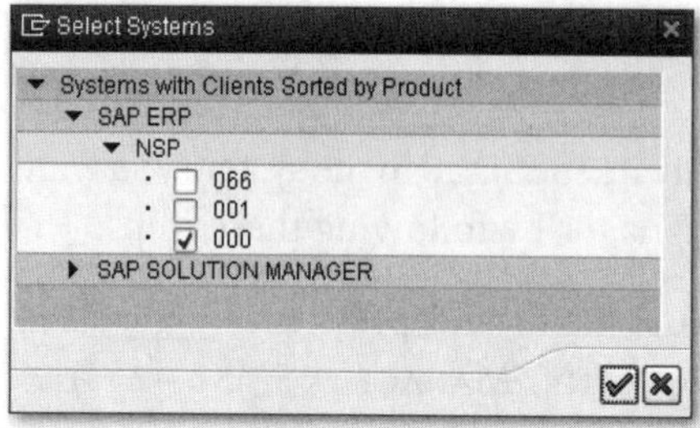

5. The system is added to the list. You now need to activate the SDCCN in a second step. To do this, select the relevant row, and click on ACTIVATE SDCCN ( ).

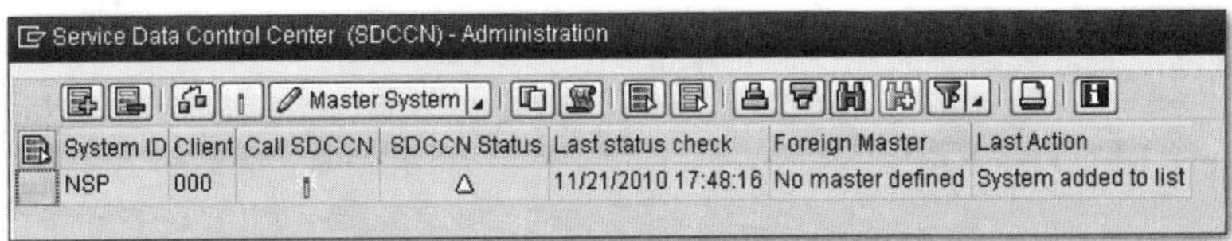

6. On the next screen, choose Yes to confirm that you want to create an RFC connection for the SDCCN.

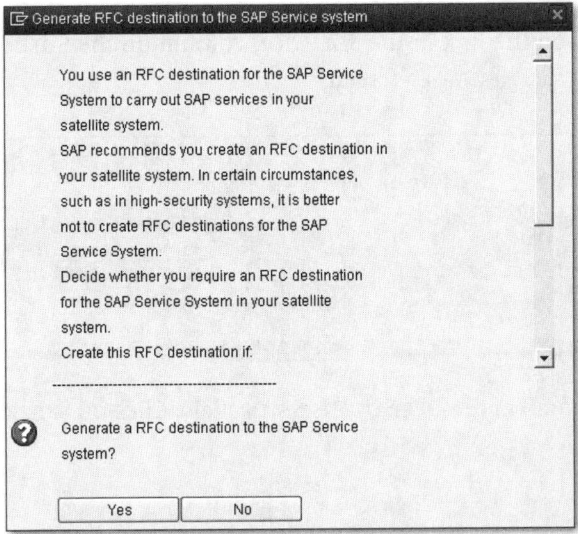

7. You've now finished setting up the SDCC, and the status of the SDCCN should be displayed as OK (▢). Choose Continue (✔) to leave the Administration view.

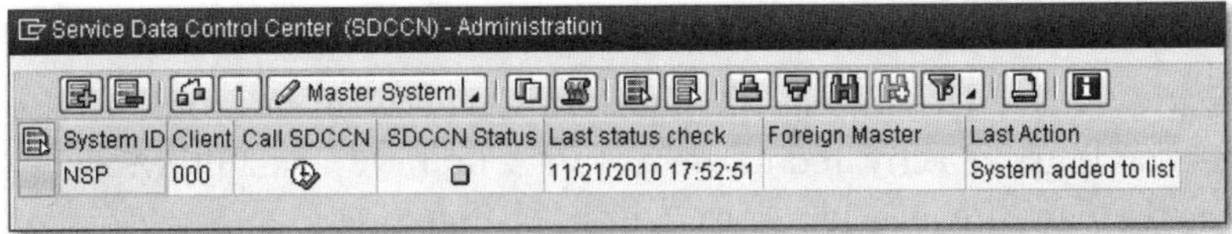

After you've set up a connection to the SDCC in the target system and activated the SDCCN, you can set up the EarlyWatch Alert.

Configuring the SAP EarlyWatch Alert

The following basic configuration settings are required before you can execute the EarlyWatch Alert and retrieve the report.

Follow these steps:

1. Enter Transaction "SOLUTION_MANAGER" in the command field, and press the Enter key (or select the menu option TOOLS • SAP SOLUTION MANAGER • SOLUTION_MANAGER – SOLUTION OPERATION).
2. To open your solution, click on the link in the SOLUTION column on the SOLUTION OVERVIEW – SAP SOLUTION MANAGER screen.

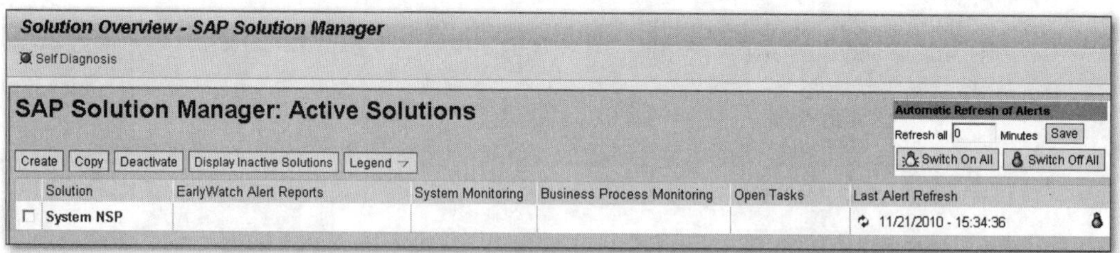

3. Select the EARLYWATCH ALERT tab in the OPERATIONS SETUP view. Click on SETUP EARLYWATCH ALERT.

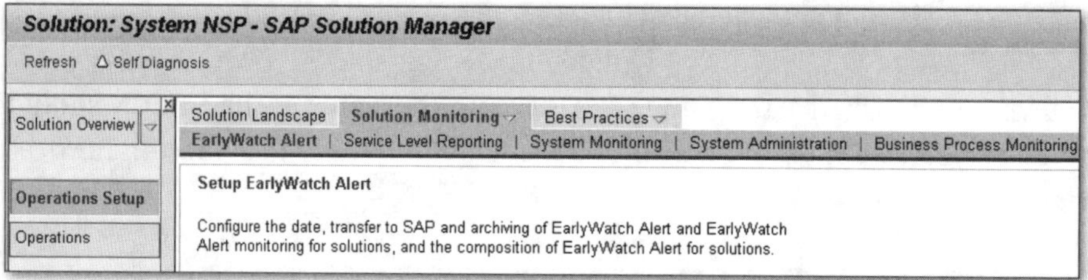

4. Check the EarlyWatch Alert settings for the system you want to monitor. The ACTIVE checkbox must be activated in the ACTIVE column. By default, MONDAY is selected as the day of execution, but you can change this to another day of the week if required. Choose SAVE to save your settings.

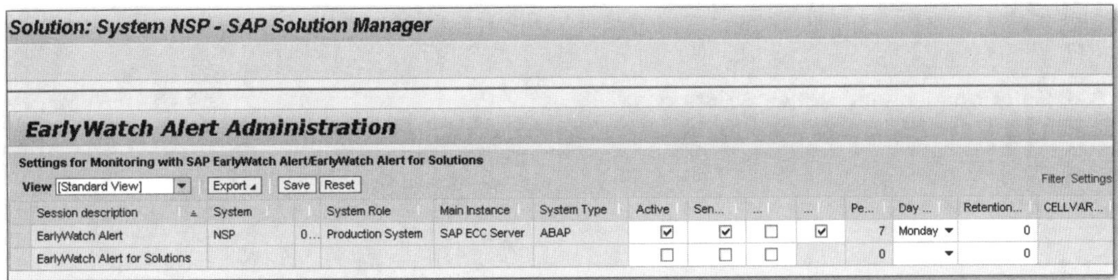

You have now verified that the EarlyWatch Alert is active and scheduled as a regular job. Next, you can use a manual EarlyWatch run to check whether the alert is working correctly.

Service Preparation Check

The EarlyWatch Alert uses the *Application Servicetools* add-on (component ST-A/PI), which needs to be updated from time to time. In addition, SAP makes new *service definitions* available on a regular basis. These serve as a basis for the recommendations of the EarlyWatch Alert.

You can use the RTCCTOOL program to check whether your systems have the current version of the ST-A/PI add-on and the latest service definitions. The RTCCTOOL report suggests specific actions for ensuring that your system is up to date.

Starting the SAP EarlyWatch Alert Manually

The EarlyWatch Alert is executed once every week on a Monday by default. However, you can also start it manually outside of this schedule, for example, to verify the configuration or to assess a target system after a change is made (for example, an upgrade, etc.).

1. Enter Transaction "SOLUTION_MANAGER" in the command field, and press the Enter key (or select the menu option Tools • SAP Solution Manager • SOLUTION_MANAGER – Solution Operation).
2. To open your solution, click on the link in the Solution column on the Solution Overview – SAP Solution Manager screen.

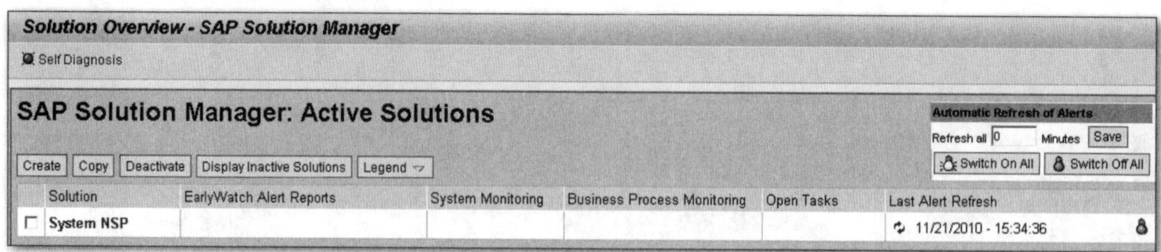

3. Select the EarlyWatch Alert tab in the Operations view.

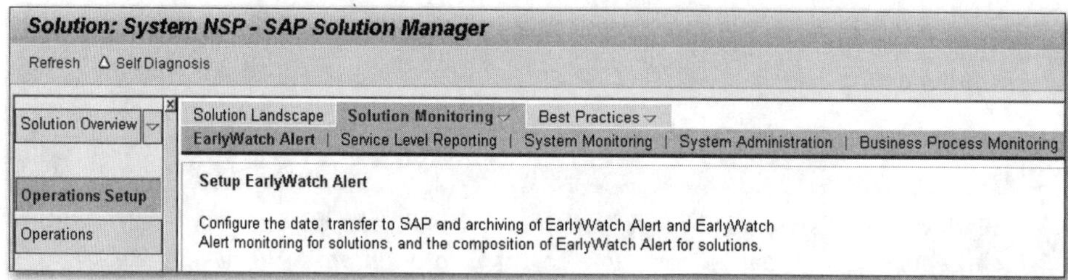

4. The SAP EarlyWatch Alert service is already displayed in the table. The icon indicates a scheduled job run. Choose Create to start an additional manual run.

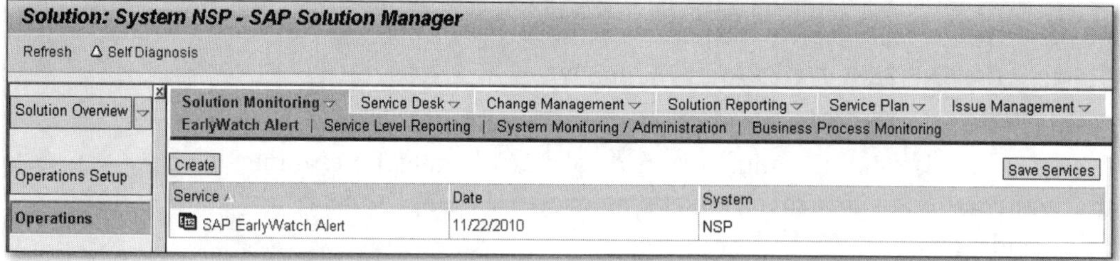

5. Select the SAP EarlyWatch Alert service. Choose Create.

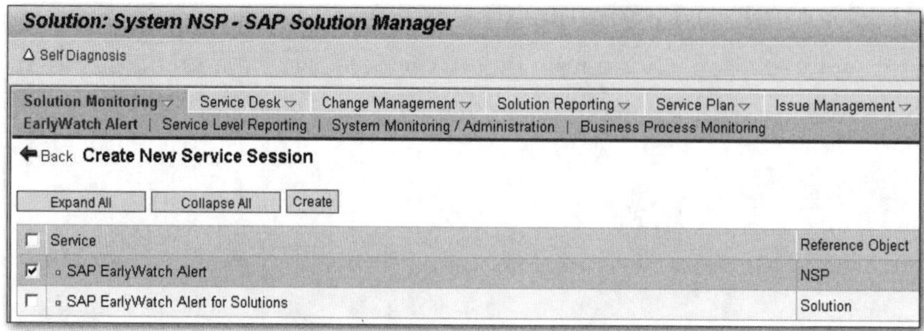

6. Change the specified date if necessary, and click on CONFIRM.

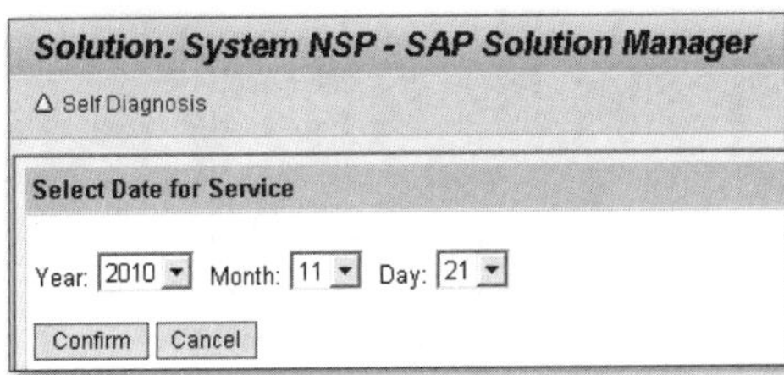

7. A message in the status bar confirms that the job run has been created. The service is displayed in the table with the WAIT FOR SESSION DATA icon (⌛). To open it, click on the SAP EARLYWATCH ALERT link.

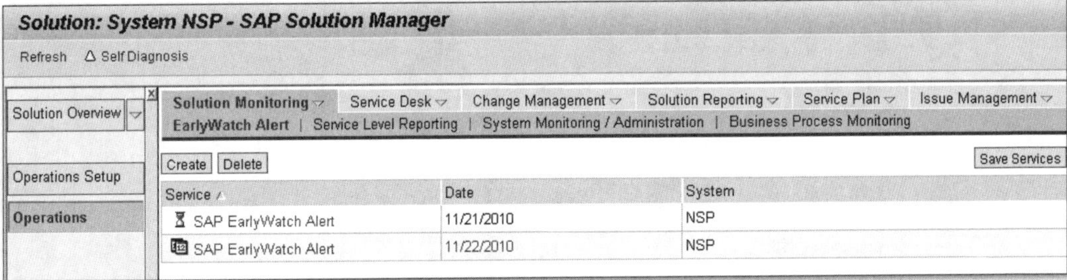

8. The next screen reports that Solution Manager is waiting for data from the target system. Choose CALL SERVICE DATA CONTROL CENTER to accelerate the data retrieval process.

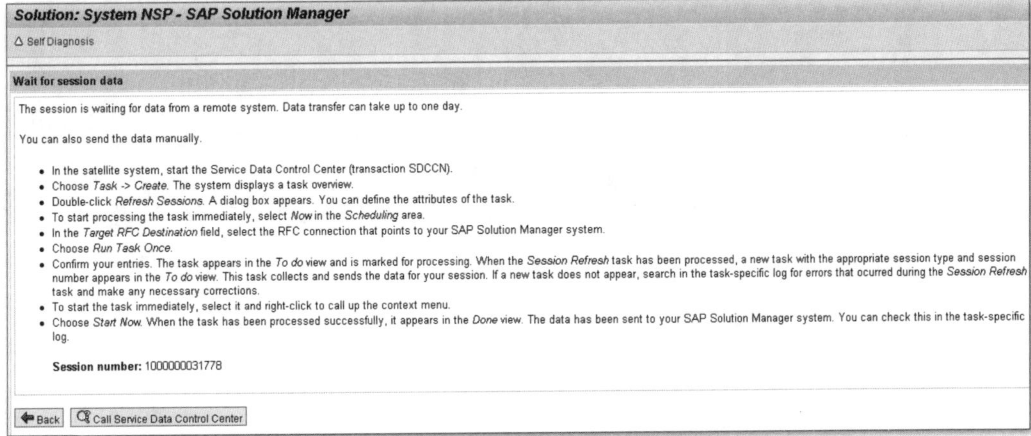

9. This action automatically brings you to the target system (for example, NSP), where Transaction SDCCN has been started. Choose CREATE (□).

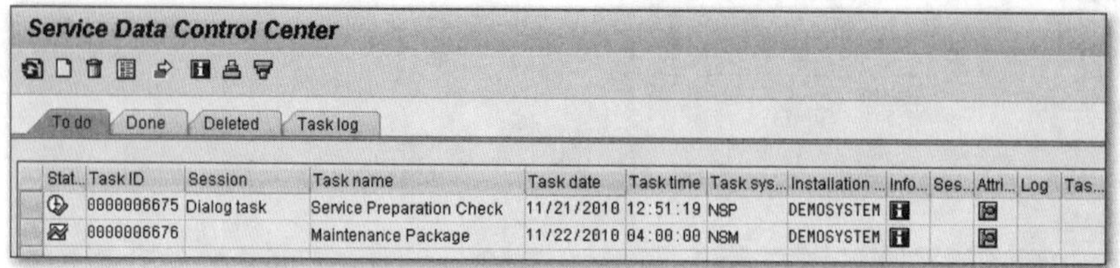

10. Select the REFRESH SESSIONS task in the list, and choose COPY (✔).

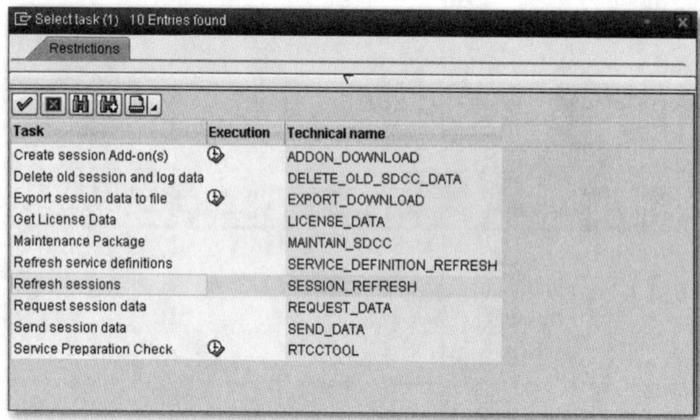

11. The system prompts you to confirm execution of the task. Select the NOW option under SCHEDULING, and click on CONTINUE (✔).

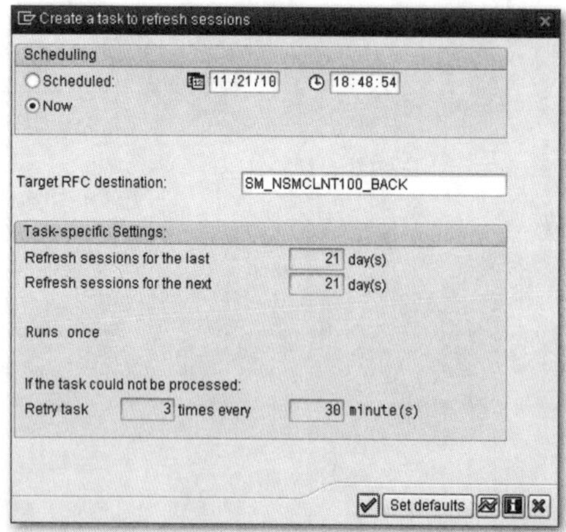

12. Choose CONTINUE to confirm the dialog box (✔).

13. The OPEN tab displays the task you have just generated, with the status TASK WAITING FOR PROCESSING ( ). Choose REFRESH ( ) to refresh the status.

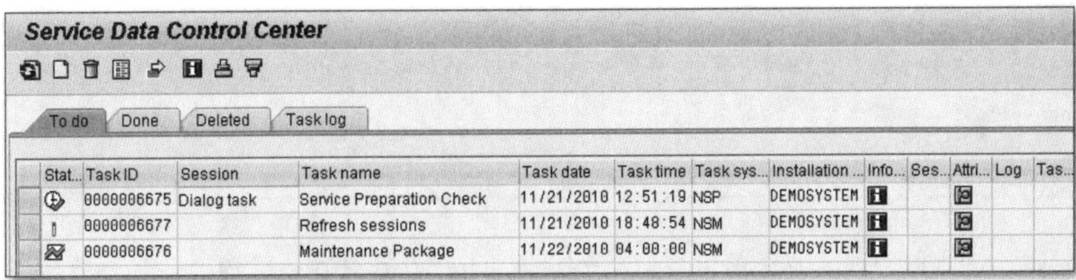

14. After a short time, the task disappears from the TO DO tab and then appears on the DONE tab.

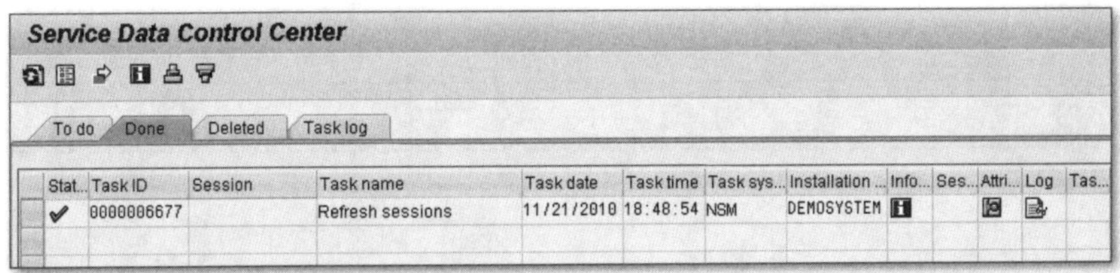

15. You can check the processing history on the TASK LOG tab. Then choose BACK ( ) to exit Transaction SDCCN.

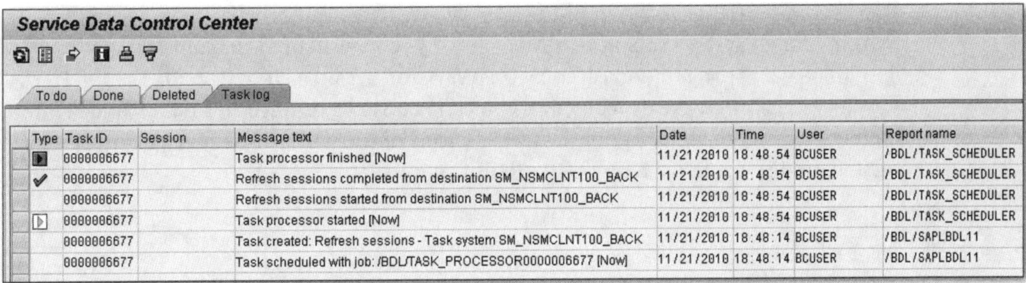

16. You are now back in Solution Manager again. Choose BACK.

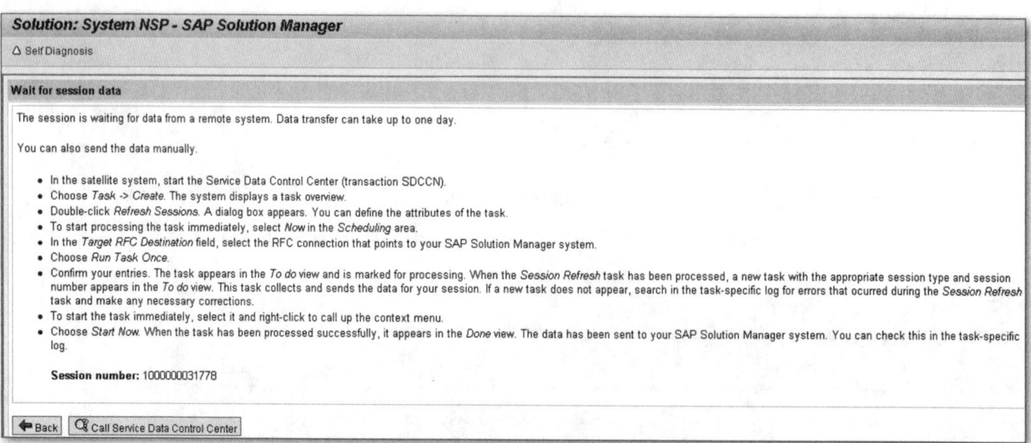

17. Click on REFRESH in the services overview. The icon shown before the session indicates the result of the EarlyWatch Alert, for example, a yellow rating (). Click on DISPLAY SESSION () to open the report.

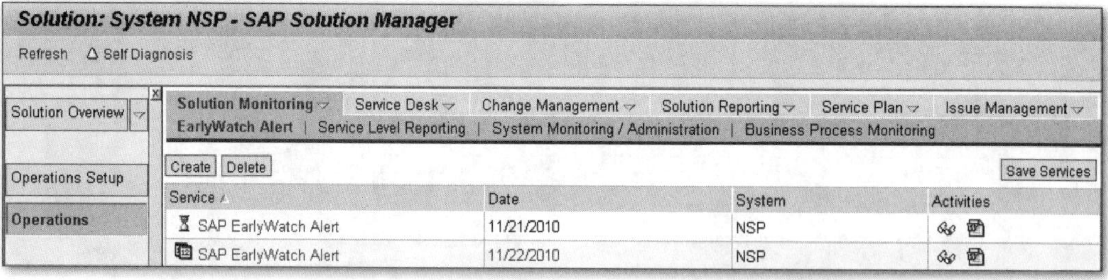

[+]

Manual Retrieval of Session Data

After the *Refresh Session* job run, the EarlyWatch data are normally sent automatically from the target system to Solution Manager. If you have waited for some time, and the data still haven't arrived (indicated by the WAIT FOR SESSION DATA icon () or the DATA FOR THIS SESSION OVERDUE icon (), you can choose to retrieve this data manually. To do this, choose the menu option GOTO • SESSIONS • SDCCN DATA. Search for the relevant session, and select SEND DOWNLOAD REQUESTS • EXECUTE.

18. The report details are then listed.

    Expand the tree structure in the left screen frame to display items with a yellow rating (![]) or a red rating (![]).

    Instructions for eliminating the individual problems are displayed on the tabs in the right screen frame. Select the tab with the green icon (![]).

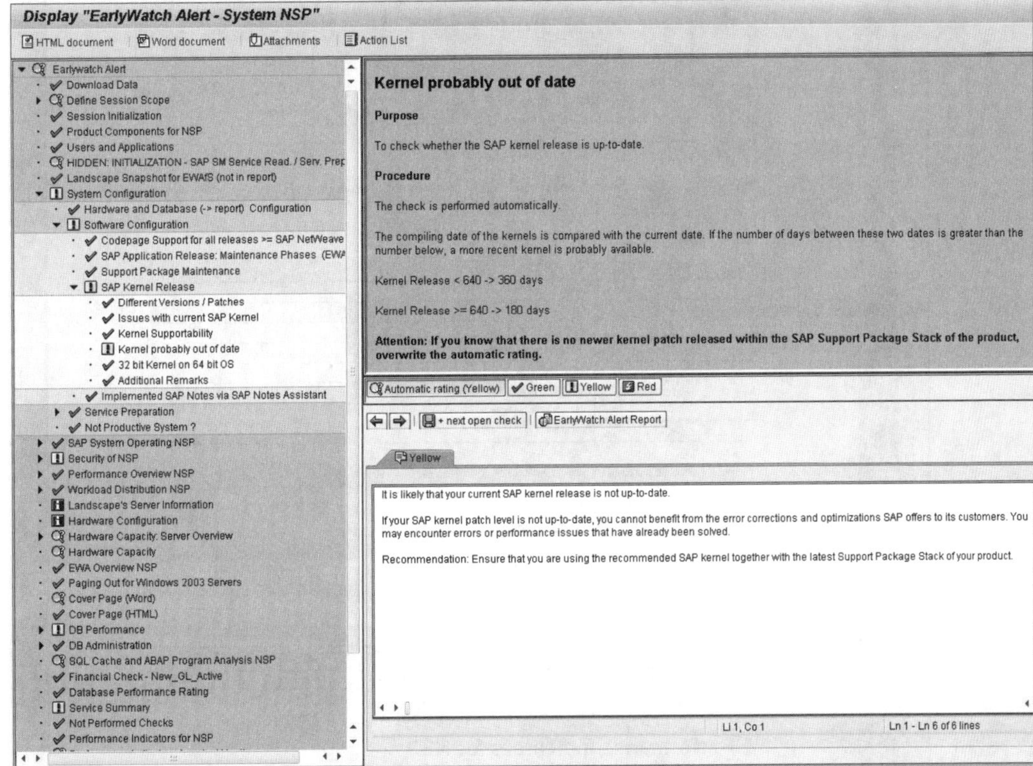

19. You can choose the MS WORD DOCUMENT (![]) button to convert the EarlyWatch report into a Word document. This report can then be displayed, archived, sent and so on in Microsoft Word.

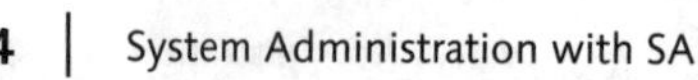

Dokument in ServiceSessionWorkbench_EA1000000003560 - Microsoft Word

Datei Bearbeiten Ansicht Einfügen Format Extras Tabelle Fenster ?

FP_Headline1 Arial 28

1 Service Summary

During this EarlyWatch Alert Session, we detected issues that could potentially affect your system.
We recommend that you take corrective action as soon as possible.

Note: All recommendations provided in this report are based on our general experience. We advise that you test our recommendations before using them in your production system. Note that EarlyWatch Alert is an automatic service.

Section Overview

Rating	Checked Area
⚠	System Configuration
✓	System Performance
✓	Workload Distribution
✓	SAP System Operating
✓	Hardware Capacity
⚠	DB Performance
✓	DB Administration
⚠	Security

Note: For more information about EarlyWatch Alert, you can review a sample EarlyWatch Alert at: http://service.sap.com/ewa Library -> Media Library. This provides an overview of the rating strategy and the KPIs that trigger the alerts in this service.

Service data was collected starting at 09/06/2010 04:06:49. This took 9 minutes.

Note: If you require assistance in investigating the alerts highlighted in this report, create a customer message on process component SV-SMG-SER-EWA.

Note: If performance is seriously compromised, create a customer message on component SV-BO with priority level "high" or "very high".

Overview of Alert Messages

Priority	Description
High	We found relevant security-related SAP Notes which are not applied.

2 Performance Indicators for NSP

The following table shows the relevant performance indicators in various system areas.

Area	Indicators	Value	Trend
System Performance	Active Users	16	down
	Avg. Response Time in Dialog Task	381 ms	down
	Max. Dialog Steps per Hour	505	down

Seite 2 Ab 2 2/26 Bei Ze Sp MAK ÄND ERW ÜB Englisch (US

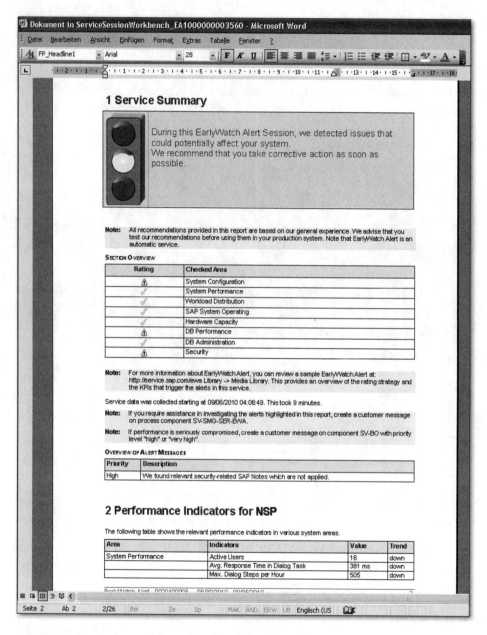

20. You only need to generate this document once, after which you can access it at any time in the Service Overview by clicking on the Reports are available in the attachment list button (📋).

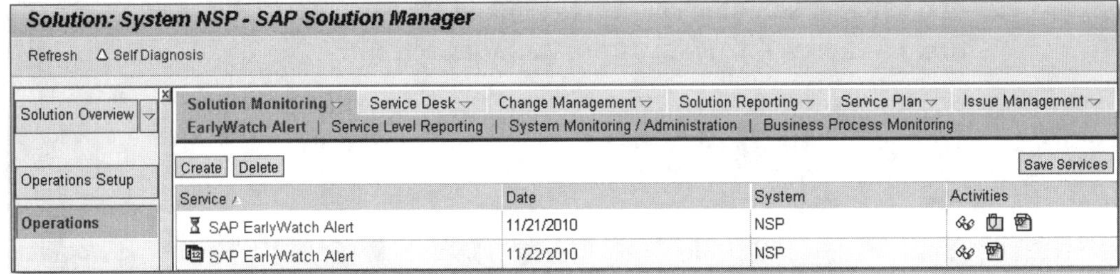

21. Click on the Report link to select the report.

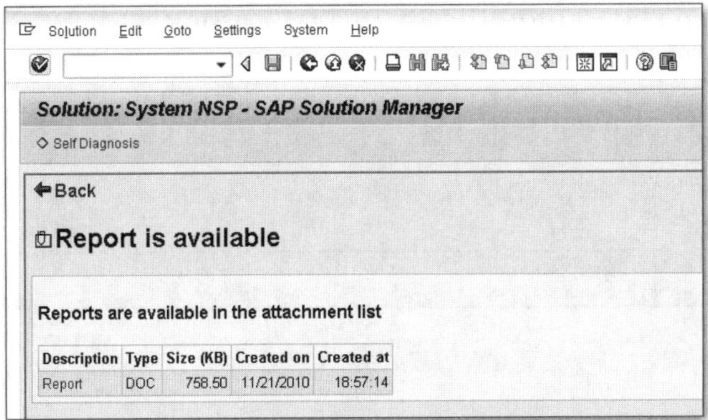

The EarlyWatch Alert provides key information about the general status of your system. The report provides specific instructions as to how problems can be eliminated.

You should run the EarlyWatch Alert on a weekly basis and always check the report thoroughly after each execution to ensure that your SAP systems remain in good working order.

Sending SAP EarlyWatch Alert Automatically by Email

Automatic email notification is another practical feature of the EarlyWatch Alert. You can send your generated report to one or more email addresses. As a result, you don't need to access the report in Solution Manager.

1. Enter Transaction "SOLUTION_MANAGER" in the command field, and press the Enter key (or select the menu option Tools • SAP Solution Manager • SOLUTION_MANAGER – Solution Operation).

2. To open your solution, click on the link in the SOLUTION column on the SOLUTION OVERVIEW – SAP SOLUTION MANAGER screen.

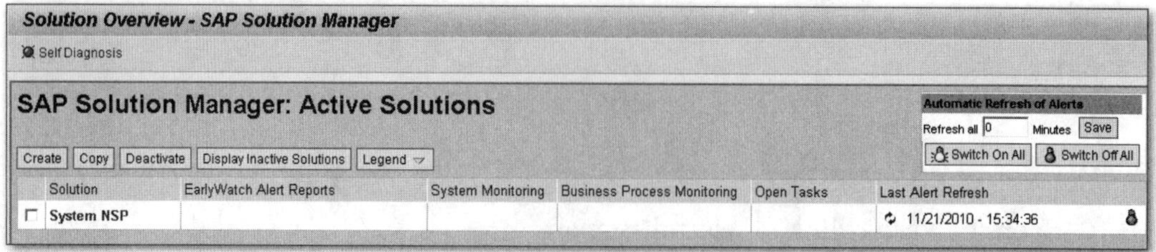

3. Choose the menu option EDIT • AUTOMATIC E-MAIL TRANSMISSION.

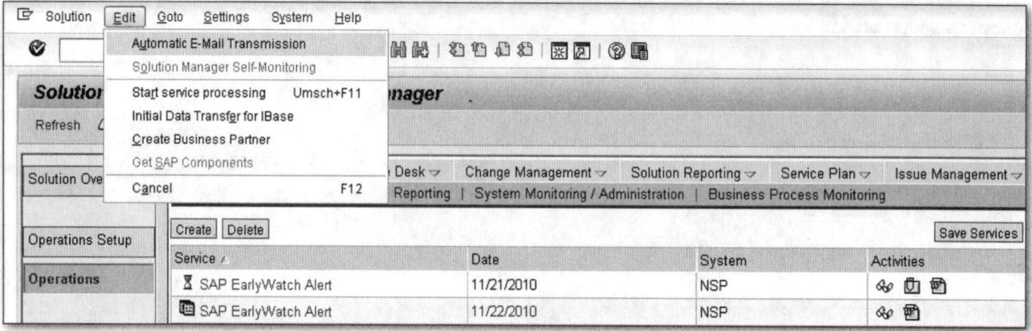

4. Click on CREATE E-MAIL RECIPIENT to add a new email address.

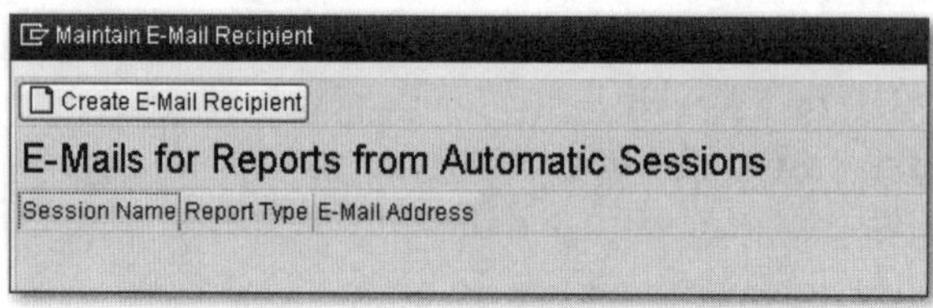

5. Use the input help ( ) to enter the required details in the next dialog box:
   - SESSION NAME: SAP EarlyWatch Alert
   - REPORT TYPE: EarlyWatch Alert report
   - E-MAIL ADDRESS: Your email address

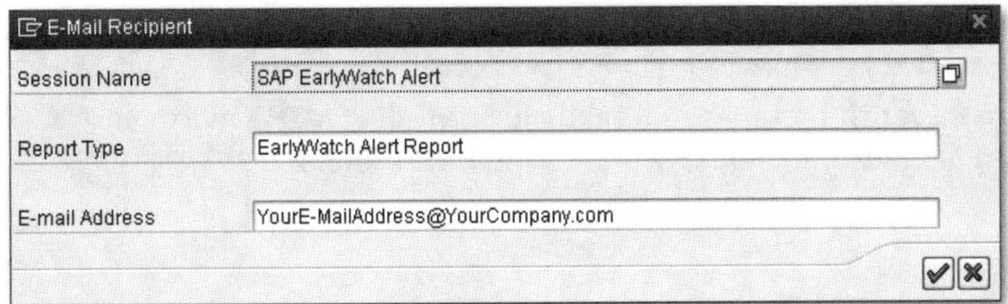

6. You can enter several email recipients if necessary. Choose CANCEL (✖).

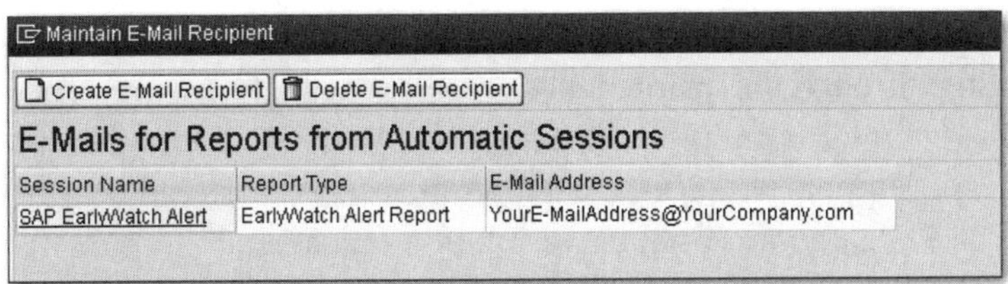

7. From now on, you'll automatically receive the report of the EarlyWatch Alert by email.

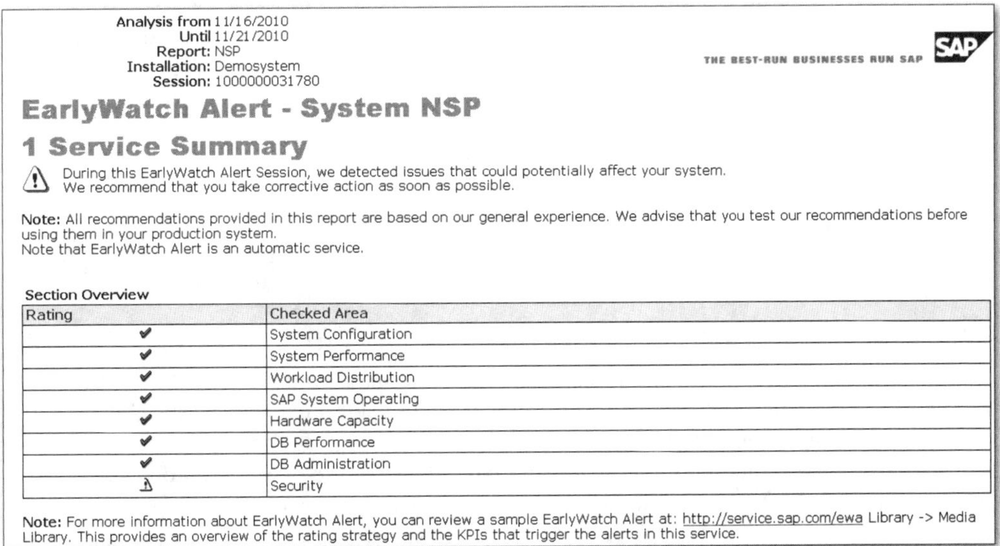

Analysis from 11/16/2010
Until 11/21/2010
Report: NSP
Installation: Demosystem
Session: 1000000031780

THE BEST-RUN BUSINESSES RUN SAP

EarlyWatch Alert - System NSP

1 Service Summary

During this EarlyWatch Alert Session, we detected issues that could potentially affect your system. We recommend that you take corrective action as soon as possible.

Note: All recommendations provided in this report are based on our general experience. We advise that you test our recommendations before using them in your production system.
Note that EarlyWatch Alert is an automatic service.

Section Overview

Rating	Checked Area
✔	System Configuration
✔	System Performance
✔	Workload Distribution
✔	SAP System Operating
✔	Hardware Capacity
✔	DB Performance
✔	DB Administration
⚠	Security

Note: For more information about EarlyWatch Alert, you can review a sample EarlyWatch Alert at: http://service.sap.com/ewa Library -> Media Library. This provides an overview of the rating strategy and the KPIs that trigger the alerts in this service.

[⚙] **Configuring the SMTP Service**

For SAP Solution Manager to be capable of sending email, the SMTP service must be active, and the send job must run regularly (see Chapter 2, Section 2.6.3).

4.5 Maintenance Optimizer

Solution Manager supports the process of maintaining your SAP systems (see Chapter 18) with the *Maintenance Optimizer*. The Maintenance Optimizer is a tool that guides you step-by-step through the maintenance process. Use of the Maintenance Organizer is mandatory for all systems based on SAP NetWeaver 7.0 or higher. As of this platform release, support packages and support package stacks can only be downloaded from the SAP Support Portal using Solution Manager.

This process is initially more time-consuming that conventional downloading of software packages because a maintenance transaction has to be created each time. However, in addition to offering better documentation and an assisted process, another benefit of this method is that it reduces the likelihood of errors. Because the Maintenance Optimizer is based on your predefined system landscape, it can retrieve the release and component information directly from the systems that are to be maintained. A complete list of required support packages is then provided, which means that you don't need to gather this information yourself manually. In addition, the correct support package levels are determined, and the relevant updates selected automatically. The Maintenance Optimizer thus prevents you from downloading incorrect or incomplete maintenance packages.

[⚙] **Prerequisites for Using the Maintenance Optimizer**

For the Maintenance Optimizer to function, the basic configuration of SAP Solution Manager must be completed, and it must be possible to connect to the SAP Support Portal using the RFC destination SAP-OSS (connection test and remote login are successful). In addition, the SAP system for which you want to download support packages must have been created in the system landscape and assigned to a solution.

Finally, you must have assigned your user ID in the SAP Support Portal to your SAP user in Transaction AISUSER. This user is used to connect to the Support Portal in the background.

To download support packages with the Maintenance Optimizer, create a maintenance transaction, and allow the Maintenance Optimizer to guide you through the process:

1. Enter Transaction "SOLUTION_MANAGER" in the command field, and press the [Enter] key (or select the menu option TOOLS • SAP SOLUTION MANAGER • SOLUTION_MANAGER – Solution Operation).
2. Open the solution to which the system you want to maintain is assigned, by clicking on the relevant link in the SOLUTION column on the SOLUTION OVERVIEW – SAP SOLUTION MANAGER screen.

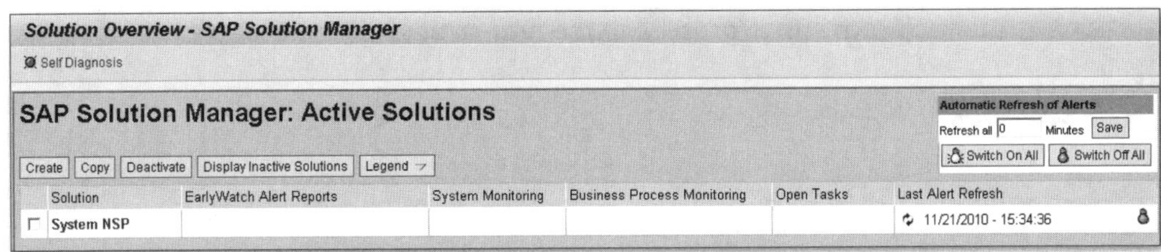

3. Select the CHANGE MANAGEMENT tab in the OPERATIONS view.

   Select the MAINTENANCE OPTIMIZER menu option, and choose CREATE NEW MAINTENANCE TRANSACTION.

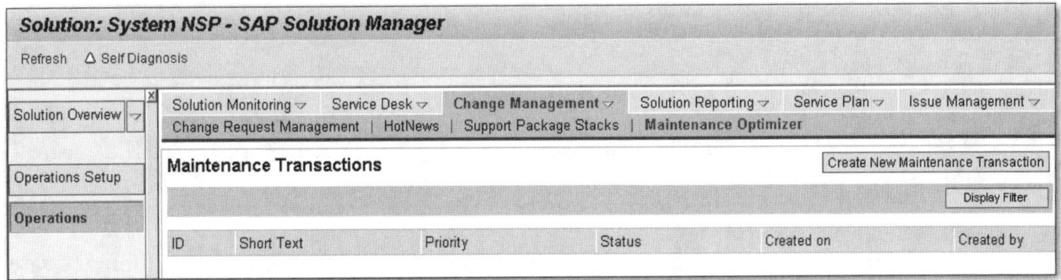

[+]

Determining the Support Package Level of your Solution

If you open the SUPPORT PACKAGE STACKS subitem on the CHANGE MANAGEMENT tab, you can view the current support package levels of the systems assigned to the solution.

4. Enter the following details on the next screen:
   - PRIORITY: Select the appropriate priority (for example, MEDIUM).
   - SHORT TEXT: Enter a description for the transaction.
   - PRODUCT VERSION: Select a product version from the drop-down list. Then activate the relevant system from the table displayed.

   Choose CONTINUE to proceed to the next step.

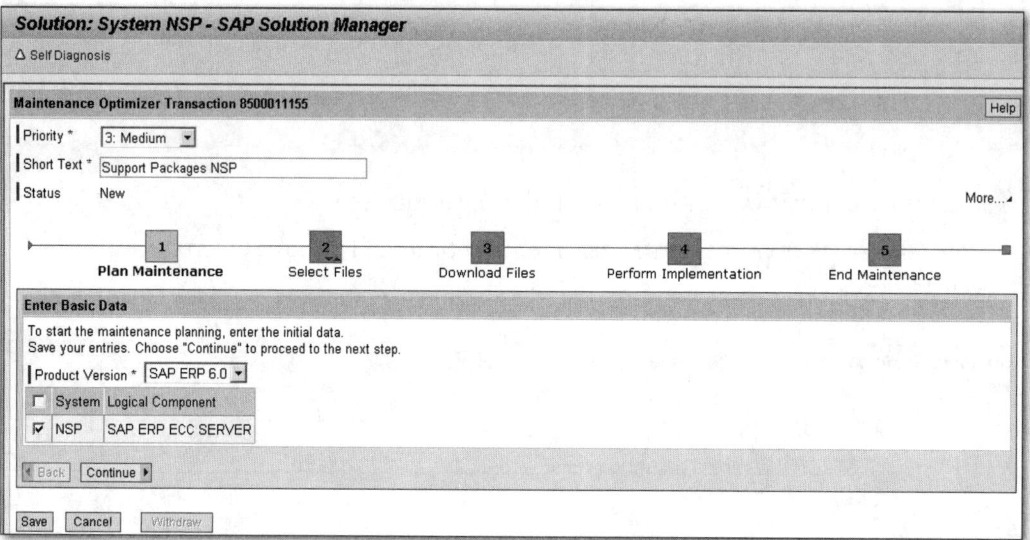

5. Your maintenance transaction has been created and saved. If you then activate the MAINTENANCE option under CALCULATE DOWNLOAD FILES AUTOMATICALLY, and click on FIND DOWNLOAD FILES, Solution Manager will determine which support packages need to be downloaded.

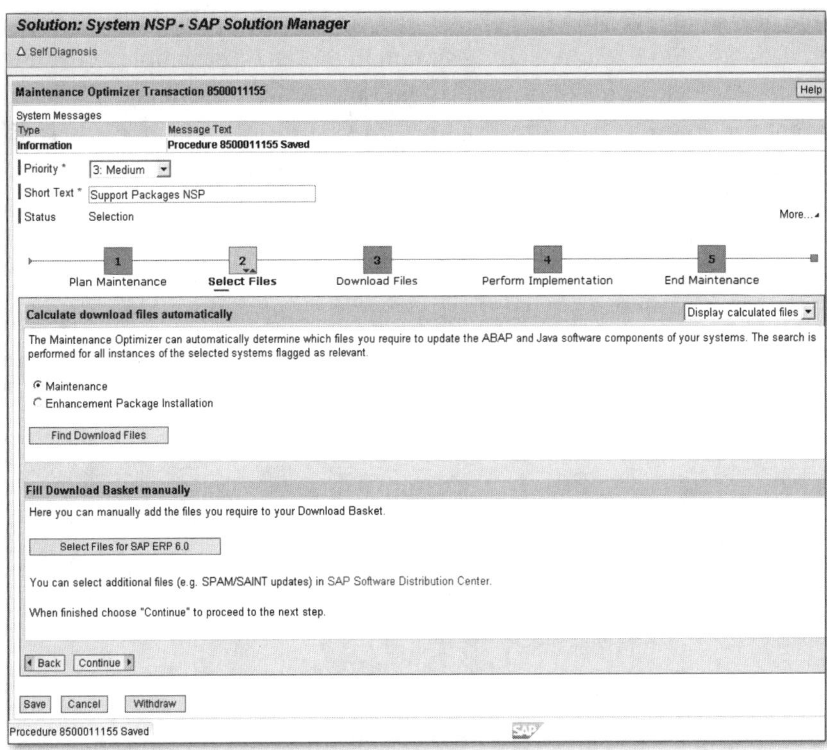

6. Select the support package stack to which you want to update your system from the TARGET STACK drop-down list. Then click on FIND DOWNLOAD FILES FOR THE STACK VERSION.

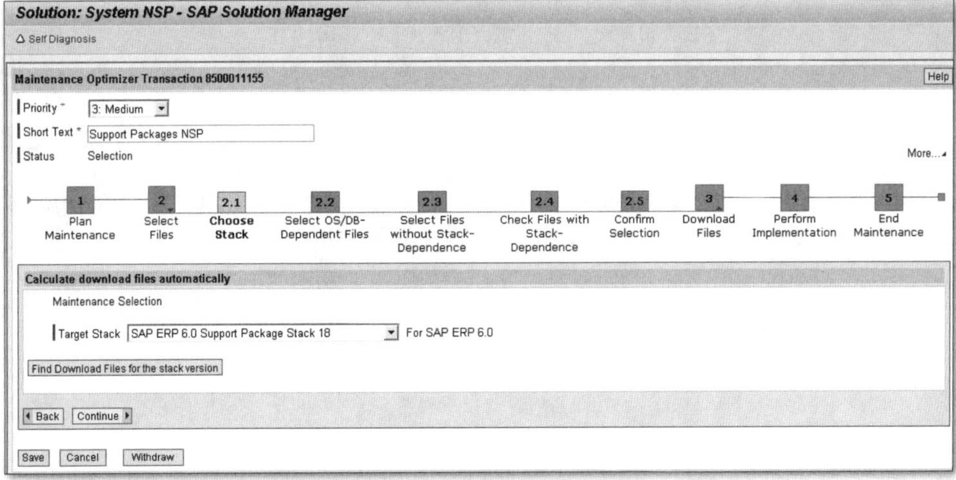

7. Select the new kernel version first. These files are specific to the operating system and database. Find your operating system in the list (for example, NT_I386 for a Microsoft Windows 32-bit installation), and activate the relevant kernel component for your database (for example, MAXDB). The system also selects the database-specific kernels files (DBINDEP), which should not be deactivated. Click on CONTINUE.

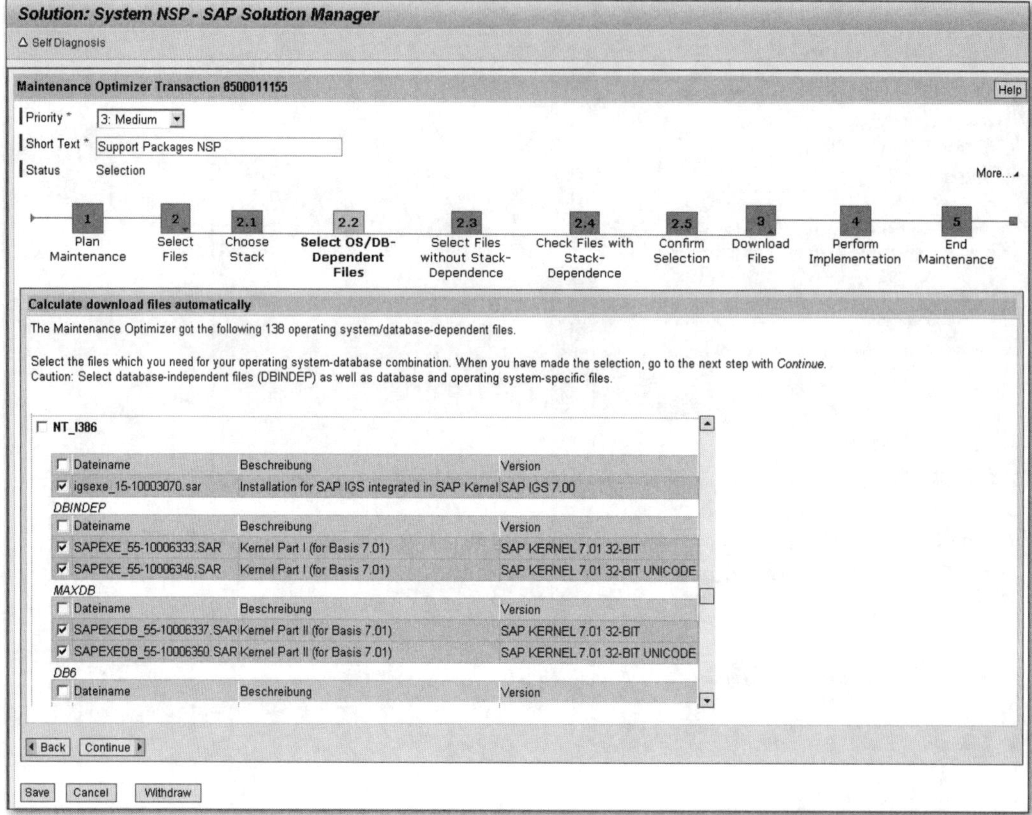

8. Next, select the cross-application data. This includes, for example, the update for Transactions SPAM and SAINT. Click on CONTINUE.

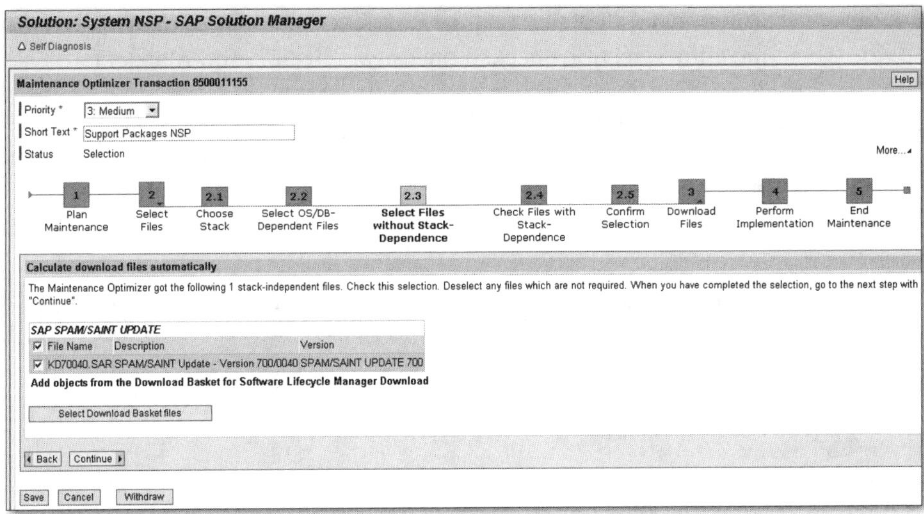

9. In the next step, the support packages that have been determined on the basis of the components of your SAP system are displayed. Check the selection, changing it only if you are completely certain that changes are required. Click on CONTINUE.

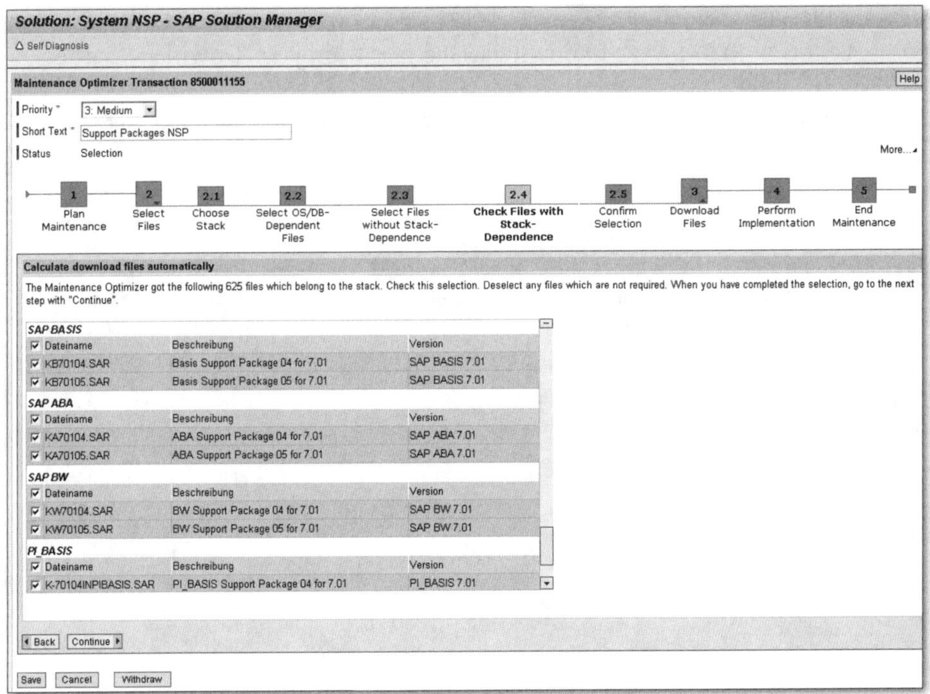

10. You have now selected all of the required files. Click on CHECK SUPPORT PACKAGE QUEUE to have the selection checked once again by Solution Manager.

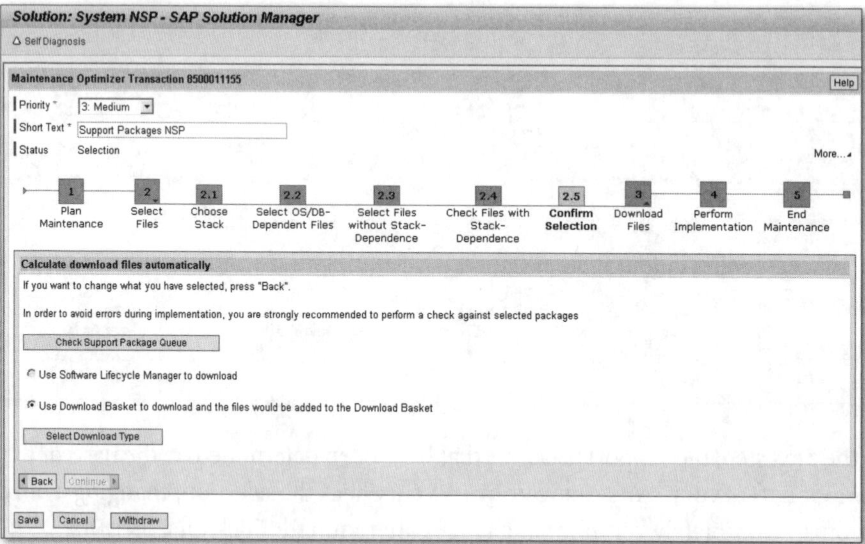

11. The message QUEUE CHECK PASSED is displayed if no errors have occurred. Click on SELECT DOWNLOAD TYPE to download the files from your Download Basket.

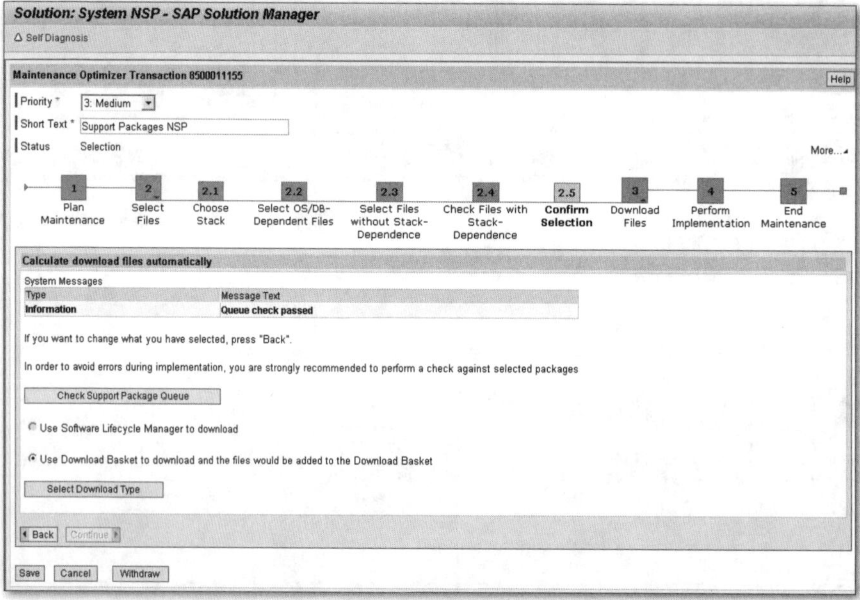

12. Click on CONTINUE.

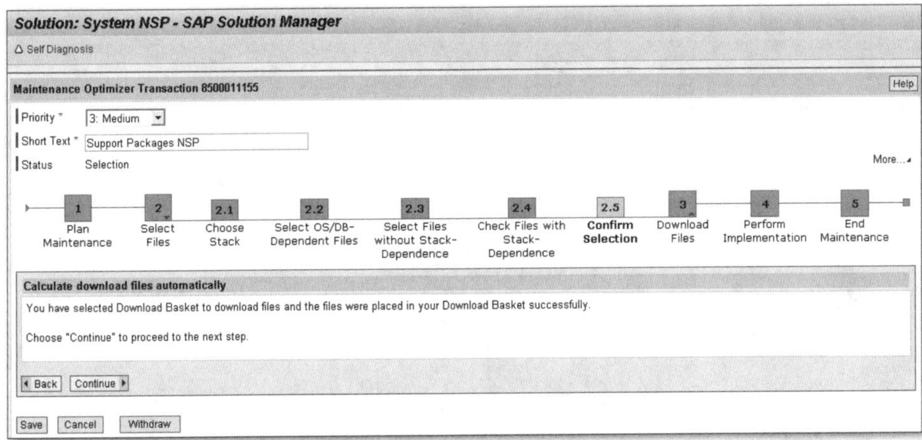

13. The files in your Download Basket must be confirmed before they can be downloaded. Click on CONFIRM FILES IN DOWNLOAD BASKET.

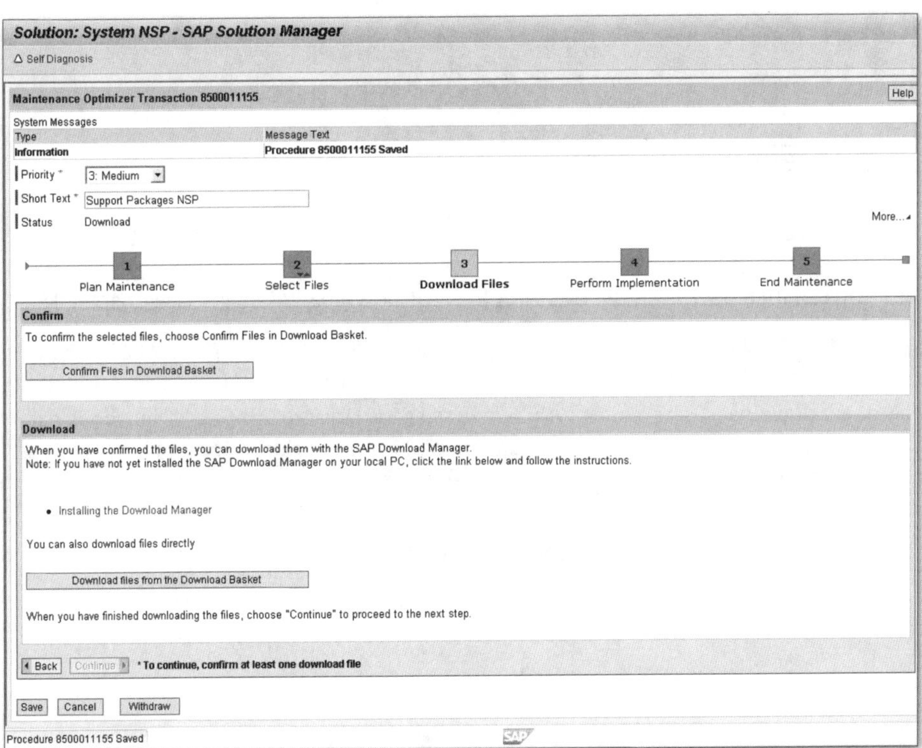

14. In the dialog box that opens, select all files, and click the CONFIRM DOWNLOAD button.

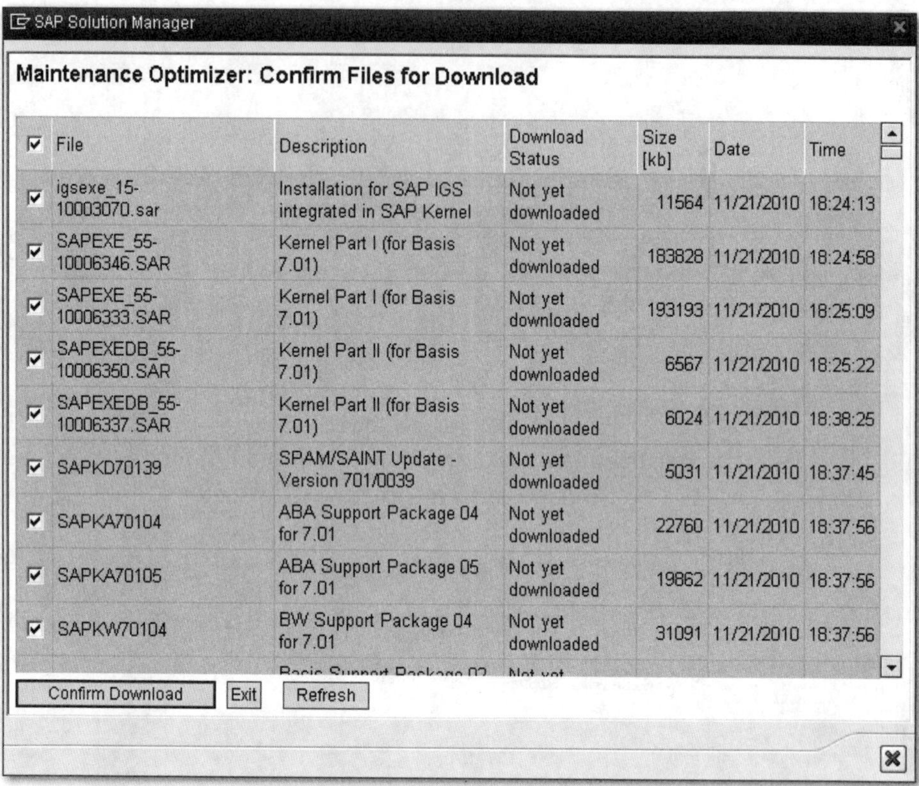

File	Description	Download Status	Size [kb]	Date	Time
igsexe_15-10003070.sar	Installation for SAP IGS integrated in SAP Kernel	Not yet downloaded	11564	11/21/2010	18:24:13
SAPEXE_55-10006346.SAR	Kernel Part I (for Basis 7.01)	Not yet downloaded	183828	11/21/2010	18:24:58
SAPEXE_55-10006333.SAR	Kernel Part I (for Basis 7.01)	Not yet downloaded	193193	11/21/2010	18:25:09
SAPEXEDB_55-10006350.SAR	Kernel Part II (for Basis 7.01)	Not yet downloaded	6567	11/21/2010	18:25:22
SAPEXEDB_55-10006337.SAR	Kernel Part II (for Basis 7.01)	Not yet downloaded	6024	11/21/2010	18:38:25
SAPKD70139	SPAM/SAINT Update - Version 701/0039	Not yet downloaded	5031	11/21/2010	18:37:45
SAPKA70104	ABA Support Package 04 for 7.01	Not yet downloaded	22760	11/21/2010	18:37:56
SAPKA70105	ABA Support Package 05 for 7.01	Not yet downloaded	19862	11/21/2010	18:37:56
SAPKW70104	BW Support Package 04 for 7.01	Not yet downloaded	31091	11/21/2010	18:37:56

15. You can then download the files with the SAP Download Manager (see Chapter 18).

[!]

The Download Files from Download Basket Button

A direct download using the DOWNLOAD FILES FROM DOWNLOAD BASKET button is particularly laborious if you have a very large number of files to download and is therefore not recommended.

16. When you have finished, choose CONTINUE.

[+]

Downloading the SAP Download Manager

If the SAP Download Manager is not yet installed on your PC, you can download it from the SAP Support Portal in this step by clicking on the INSTALLING THE DOWNLOAD MANAGER link.

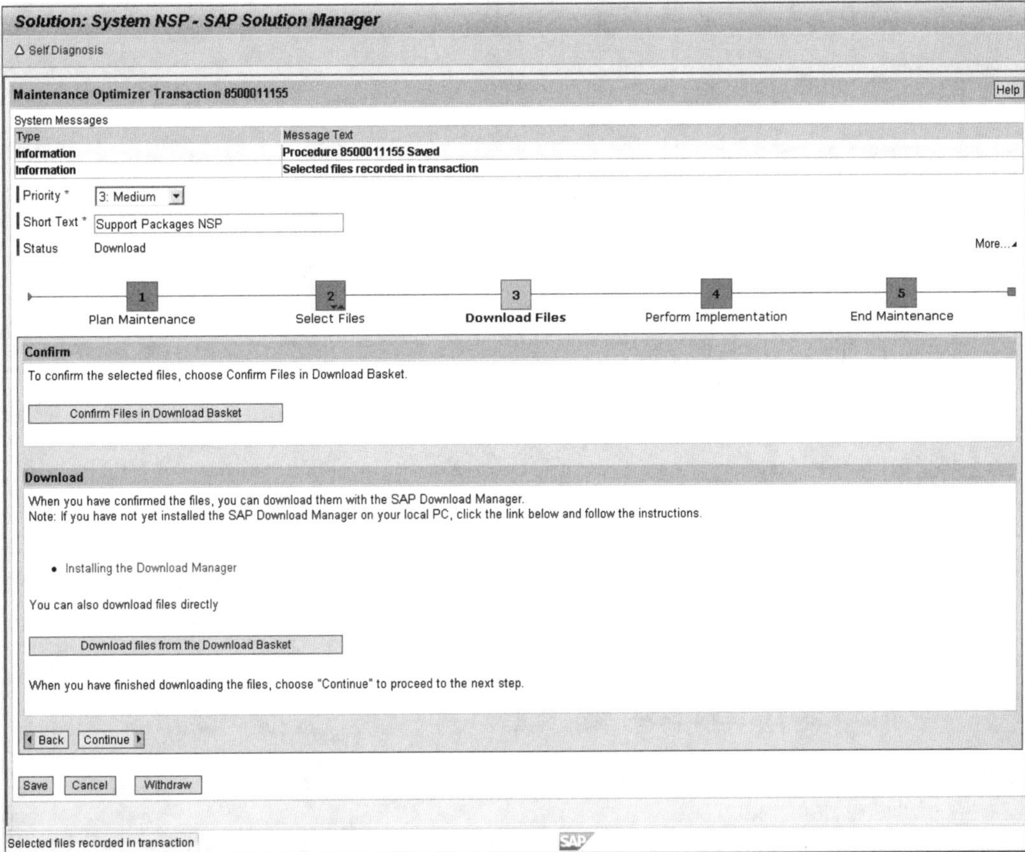

17. You can now proceed to import the support packages (see Chapter 18). To signal that the import is now in process status, select the IN PROCESS entry from the STATUS OF IMPLEMENTATION drop-down list, and click on SAVE.

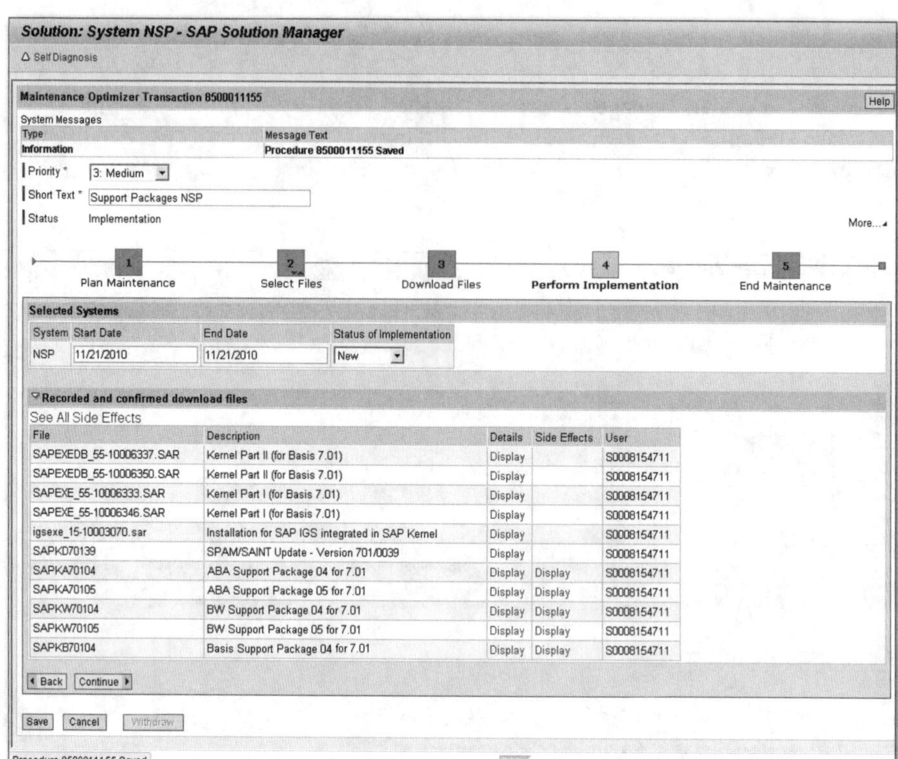

18. As soon as the import is finished, set the status to COMPLETED, and click CONTINUE to proceed to the next step. To complete the maintenance transaction, choose COMPLETE TRANSACTION.

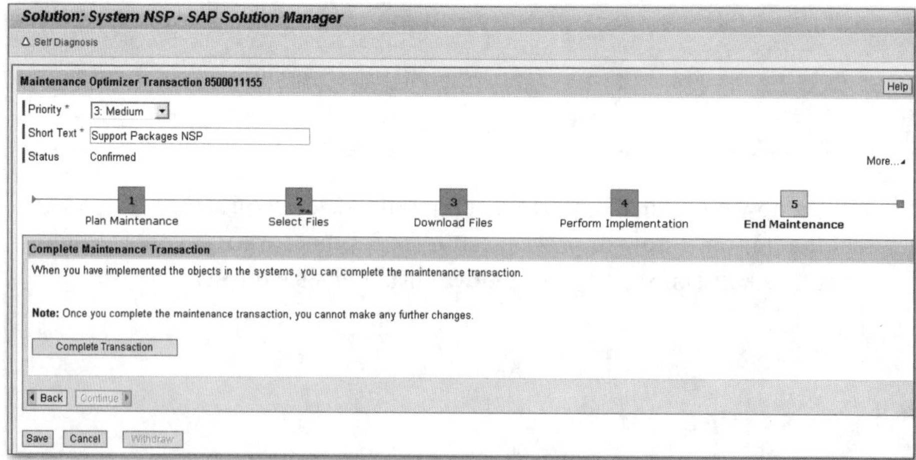

Completing the Transaction

To progress from step 4 (EXECUTE IMPLEMENTATION) to step 5 (COMPLETE MAINTENANCE), you must set the status of the implementation to COMPLETED. Solution Manager will not allow you to move on to step 5 until you do so.

19. The maintenance transaction has been completed, and no further changes can be made to it. Choose CANCEL or BACK (➜) to exit the view.

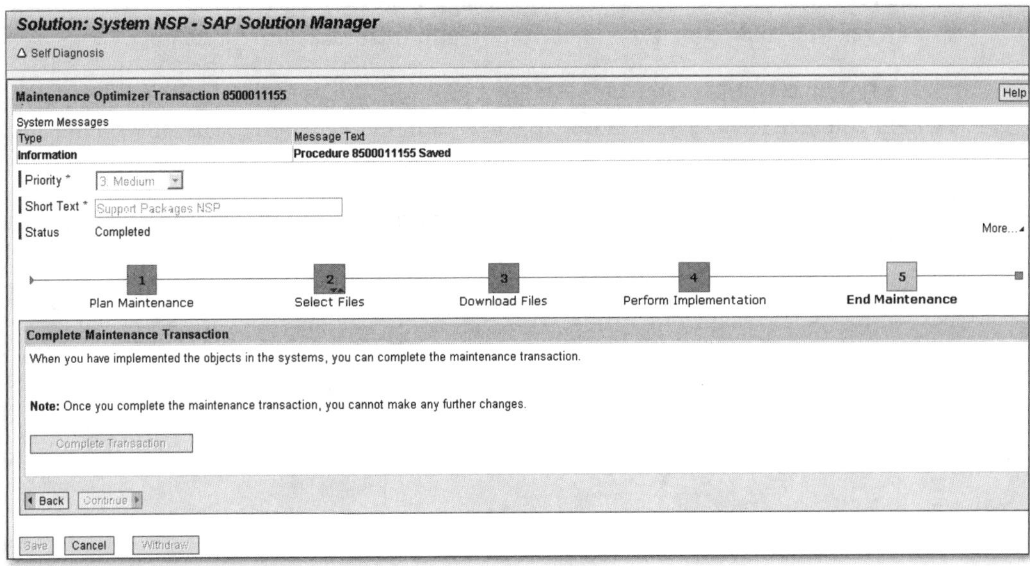

20. Your transaction is now displayed as COMPLETED in the overview of maintenance transactions.

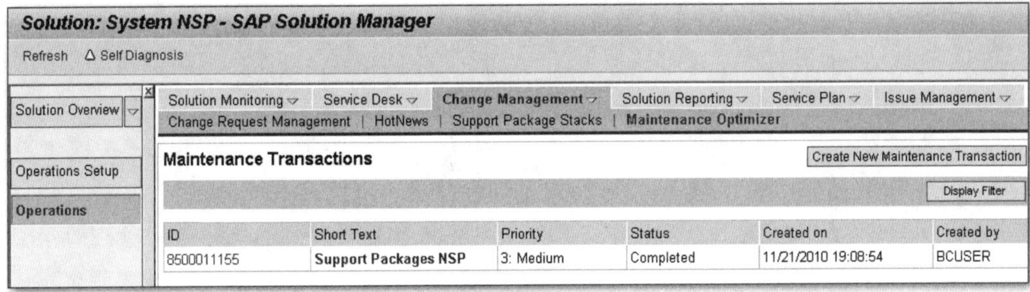

You now know how to download support package files from the SAP Support Portal using Solution Manager and the Maintenance Optimizer tool. Chapter 18 describes how to import these files into your SAP system.

4.6 Summary

You need to use SAP Solution Manager to access certain services provided by SAP, such as the downloading of support packages. Solution Manager also offers a range of tools that make the job of SAP system administrator more efficient.

The system administration and system monitoring functions described in this chapter help you manage a system landscape of a medium to very large size enterprise, and makes it easy for you to leverage synergy effects.

Solution Manager also offers some functions that are of interest in the context of SAP projects. Incident Management and Change Request Management enhance the functions of this central system to provide you with an even broader range of options.

This chapter provides you with specific points of reference and checklists to help you plan and execute tasks that you need to perform on a regular basis.

5 Scheduled Tasks

Certain areas of your SAP system need to be monitored on a regular basis to ensure reliable operation. To handle these tasks, it's useful to have a schedule to work through at specific intervals. This chapter presents sample checklists that you can use and modify to suit your own specific requirements.

The chapter is structured so that the tasks are divided into groups based on the frequency with which they occur. Here you'll find lists that need to be performed once a day, once a week, and once a year.

[!]

Benchmark—Frequency of Execution

Note, however, that the classification used here is merely intended as a rough guideline. The type of your SAP system and the scope of its use will determine whether a task that is listed here as having to be performed on a weekly basis may actually need to be executed once a day.

The individual checklists are, in turn, based on the following aspects:

- Critical tasks
- SAP system
- Database
- Operating system
- Other
- Notes

[+]

Checklists Available for Download

To make things simpler, you can also download the individual checklists as PDF files from the publisher's web site at *www.sap-press.com*.

Use the tables from this chapter as checklists. They provide basic information about the relevant transactions. For more information about these transactions, refer to the chapters specified in each checklist.

5.1 Critical Tasks

Some critical tasks have to be performed every morning. You can use these tasks to determine whether the SAP system is running as normal and if your backups have been successful. If you detect that your system isn't running smoothly or that the backups were not successfully completed, you need to resolve these issues promptly to prevent system outages or data loss.

5.1.1 Check Whether the SAP System Is Running

Your first task of the day is to perform a high-level check to ascertain whether the SAP system is running as normal. If there are any problems, your users will ask you for information about the cause of the problem and the likely time by which the issue will be resolved.

You can use the following as a general principle: If you can set up a connection to the SAP system, you can assume that the system is running and that the network between you and the system is functioning. If you work from a workstation, log in using the SAP GUI. If you can log in, your test has been successful.

5.1.2 Checks to Determine Whether Your Backups Have Been Successful

You need to verify whether the backups that were scheduled to be performed overnight have been successfully completed. Backups of the SAP database and the corresponding nondatabase files at the operating system level are required to restore the SAP system should the need arise.

Examples of nondatabase files:

- Database log dumps
- Files for third-party applications that do not save their data in the system, for example, external control files
- Transport files

- Files for inbound and outbound interfaces
- Externally stored print files

Problems with backups need to be resolved as quickly as possible. If the database fails, necessitating a restore, and the most recent backup was not completed successfully, you have to use the most recent successful backup for the restore. The further back in time you need to go to find a successful backup, the more time you will have to spend restoring and updating the database.

As soon as the problem is resolved, you should perform an online backup as a precaution, provided that this doesn't have a significant impact on performance. Indeed, this precautionary backup in enshrined in some corporate policies.

Some files need to be synchronized with the SAP database at the operating system level. If you restore the SAP system without these files, you will be unable to use the restore (for example, in the case of external control files that must be synchronized with the system files for the control reports to match the SAP reports).

[!]

Conducting Backup Tests and Troubleshooting

You must execute these critical tasks first thing each Monday morning. If a shift is worked between the hours of 10:00 pm and 7:00 am, you should conduct backup testing as soon as the backups are completed.

Each defective backup identified must be investigated immediately, and the underlying problem resolved. You should never simply have blind faith in the backup working properly during the coming night. If this backup also fails, you'll already be missing a backup for another whole day.

An overview of all critical tasks is provided in Table 5.1.

Transaction	Code	Action	Explanation
Users	AL08/ SM04	Display all users currently logged on to the system, together with their user ID and terminal.	Allows administrators to detect faulty or multiple logons.
OS Monitor	OS06	Display system logs.	Allows administrators to detect possible OS and hardware problems (for example, a failed drive).

Table 5.1 Critical Tasks—Checking the SAP System and Backups

Transaction	Code	Action	Explanation
Select background jobs/Job Scheduling Monitor	SM37/ RZ01	Select and monitor batch jobs scheduled in the background.	Allows the administrator to detect any critical jobs that have been executed incorrectly. Other tasks may depend on the successful execution of these jobs.
CCMS Alert Monitor	RZ20	Monitor servers (DEV, QAS, Test, PRD, etc.) in your environment using a central program.	Alerts indicate potentially serious problems that require an immediate solution.
Select lock entries	SM12	Display a list of all locked transactions. Locks prevent other users from changing records that you are in the process of editing.	Allows the administrator to remove old locks or locks that need to be removed.
Update records	SM13	Display, process, test, reset, delete, and access statistics for update records.	Administrators can process any update records that have not yet been processed.
System log	SM21	Analyze system logs.	Supports the administrator in the early detection of system problems in the SAP system.
Batch Input	SM35	Manage batch input sessions.	Alerts the administrator to the existence of new or faulty batch input sessions.
Work processes	SM50/ SM51	Display the status of work processes; Transaction SM50 is used for systems without an application server. Transaction SM51 is the central transaction. Transaction SM50 is started for each application server.	Allows users to monitor work processes and check whether any have been processed incorrectly or have been running for too long.

Table 5.1 Critical Tasks—Checking the SAP System and Backups (Cont.)

Transaction	Code	Action	Explanation
Spool requests	SP01	SAP System Output Manager.	Helps you resolve time-critical print job issues.
Tune Summary	ST02	Display statistics relating to SAP buffer performance, help with the fine-tuning of buffer parameters, SAP database parameters, and operating system parameters.	Enables the solving of problems with extensive buffer swaps. Search for entries shown in red in the SWAPS column, and monitor the time details to identify trends.
Load analysis in the SAP system	ST03	Determine system performance.	If you know the normal load distribution when the system is running, you can make minor adjustments that may help when problems occur.
Database performance analysis	ST04	High-level database performance monitor.	Allows you to monitor the growth of the database, capacity, input/output statistics, and alerts. You can drill-down to display additional information. Database monitoring is also possible without logging on.
ABAP dump analysis	ST22	Display the logs of ABAP short dumps.	Allows you to determine why a report or transaction terminated.
Transport Management System	STMS	Check transport queues and logs.	Allows you to detect errors in the import of transport request.

Table 5.1 Critical Tasks—Checking the SAP System and Backups (Cont.)

Profile Parameter for Automatic User Logoff

We assume that the `rdisp/gui_auto_logout` profile parameter has been set. This parameter defines an automatic user logoff if no user activity is detected for a predefined number of minutes.

5.2 Daily Tasks

This section lists the tasks that we recommend you perform once a day.

Using the Checklists

When using checklists, you should ensure that you always record the system in which the checks are performed, when they are performed, and the person responsible. We therefore recommend that you enter the following details at the top of each checklist:

System: _________

Date: ___/___/___

Administrator: ___________________

Possible changes should be recorded immediately at the bottom of the checklist. We recommend that you use a table similar to that shown in Table 5.2 for this purpose:

Problems	Action	Solution

Table 5.2 Sample Table for Notes

We have omitted these elements from the checklists in this chapter to save space. However, they should be included in every checklist you use.

5.2.1 Critical Tasks

An overview of critical tasks is provided in Table 5.3.

Task	Trans action	Chapter	Procedure	Done/ Initials
Check whether the SAP system is running.			Log on to the SAP system.	
Check whether the daily backup was executed without errors.	DB12 / DB13	8	Test the database backup. Duration of backup:	
			Check the backup at the operating system level. Duration of backup:	

Table 5.3 Critical Tasks—Summary

For more information about critical tasks, see Section 5.1.

5.2.2 SAP System

The checklist in Table 5.4 provides an overview of tasks relating to the SAP system.

Task	Trans action	Chapter	Procedure	Done/ Initials
Check whether all application servers are running.	SM51	2	Check whether all servers are running.	
Check the work processes.	SM50	2	Check for all work processes with the status RUNNING or WAITING.	
Check the CCMS Alert Monitor.	RZ20	3	Look for alerts.	
Look for any update records that have terminated.	SM13	2	Set the date to one year ago today. Enter the placeholder "*" under USER. Select the status ALL. Check for any rows with ERR.	
Check the system log.	SM21	2	Set the time and date to the time and date before the most recent log check. Look for: Errors Warnings Security notifications Terminations Database problems Other unusual events	

Table 5.4 Daily Tasks—SAP System

Task	Trans action	Chapter	Procedure	Done/ Initials
Look for any terminated jobs.	SM37	15	Enter the placeholder "*" under USER NAME. Check whether all critical jobs have been executed successfully. Check the log of terminated jobs.	
Look for errors in the import of transport requests.	STMS	17	Check the import queues and import histories of the individual systems for any transports with the return code 8 or higher.	
Look for "old" locks.	SM12	2	Enter an asterisk (*) as the user name. Look for entries for previous days.	
Look for users logged on to the system.	SM04/ AL08	13	Look for unknown or unusual users and terminals. This task should be executed several times a day.	
Look for spool problems.	SP01	16	Look for spool requests that have been "in process" for more than an hour.	
Check the batch input log..	SM35		Look for the following: New jobs Jobs with errors	
Check dumps.	ST22	2	Check whether a large number of dumps occurred. Look for any unusual dumps.	

Table 5.4 Daily Tasks—SAP System (Cont.)

Task	Trans action	Chapter	Procedure	Done/ Initials
Check the statistics for system load.	ST03N	11		
Check the buffer statistics.	ST02	11	Look for swaps.	
If necessary, check the user administration log.	SCUL	13	Look for warning and error messages.	

Table 5.4 Daily Tasks—SAP System (Cont.)

5.2.3 Database

The checklist in Table 5.5 provides an overview of tasks relating to the database.

Task	Trans action	Chapter	Procedure	Done/ Initials
Check the error log.	ST04	8	Look for error messages or problems.	
Check tables and memory usage.	DB02	8	Check how much memory is occupied in the database. Check whether inconsistencies in the database are reported.	

Table 5.5 Daily Tasks—Database

5.2.4 Operating System

The checklist in Table 5.6 provides an overview of tasks relating to the operating system.

Task	Trans action	Chapter	Procedure	Done/ Initials
Check for problems in the system log.	OS06	9	Check the operating system log.	

Table 5.6 Daily Tasks—Operating System

5.2.5 Other

The checklist in Table 5.7 provides an overview of all other tasks not listed previously.

Task	Trans action	Chapter	Procedure	Done/ Initials
Check the uninterrupted power supply (UPS).	UPS program log	9	Check the following: ▸ Events ▸ UPS self-test ▸ Errors	

Table 5.7 Daily Tasks—Other

5.3 Weekly Tasks

The following tasks should be performed on a weekly basis.

5.3.1 SAP System

The checklist in Table 5.8 provides an overview of the tasks relating to the SAP system.

Task	Trans action	Chapter	Procedure	Done/ Initials
Check the spool for problems and error-free processing	SP01	16	Check and remove old spool requests.	
Perform TemSe consistency check.	SP12	16	Delete any inconsistencies found.	
Check the Security Audit Log.	SM20	10	Analyze the Security Audit Log.	
Check the EarlyWatch Alert .	SOLUTION_ MANAGER	4	Check the EarlyWatch report for instructions on system optimization.	

Table 5.8 Weekly Tasks—SAP System

5.3.2 Database

The checklist in Table 5.9 provides an overview of the tasks relating to the database.

Task	Trans action	Chapter	Procedure	Done/ Initials
Check the database for available memory.	DB02	8	Record the available memory.	
Monitor the growth of the database and estimate its future growth.	DB02	8	Record the database's memory history.	
Check database consistency (DBCC).		8	Check the output of the DBCC job for errors (SQL Server).	
Refresh the MS SQL Server statistics.		8	Check whether the statistics were refreshed successfully.	

Table 5.9 Weekly Tasks—Database

5.3.3 Operating System

The checklist in Table 5.10 provides an overview of tasks relating to the operating system.

Task	Trans action	Chapter	Procedure	Done/ Initials
Check that the file system has sufficient memory.	RZ20	9	Check memory usage and whether a sufficient amount of memory is available in the file system.	

Table 5.10 Weekly Tasks—Operating System

5.3.4 Other

The checklist in Table 5.11 provides an overview of all other tasks not listed previously.

Task	Trans action	Chapter	Procedure	Done/ Initials
Check the system monitor for updates.	System monitor	3	Search for events that need to be added or deleted.	
Check the alert mechanism of the system monitor.	System monitor	3	Send test email and test paging.	
Clean the tape drive.	Tape drive	6	Clean the tape drive with a cleaning cartridge.	

Table 5.11 Weekly Tasks—Other

5.3.5 Overview of Transactions

Table 5.12 provides basic information about the transactions specified in the checklists. For more information about these transactions, refer to the chapters specified in each checklist.

Transaction	Transaction code	Action	Explanation
Database performance	DB02	Analyze the database assignment.	Allows the administrator to monitor the history of the available memory in the database, and to monitor execution of the database analysis.
CCMS Alert Monitor	RZ20	Monitor the servers (DEV, QAS, Test, PRD etc.) in your environment using a central program.	Alerts indicate potentially serious problems that require an immediate solution.

Table 5.12 Weekly Tasks—Transactions

Transaction	Transaction code	Action	Explanation
Spool requests	SP01	SAP System Output Manager	Helps you resolve time-critical print job issues.
Consistency check of the temporary sequential (TemSe) database	SP12	Compare the data of the TemSe objects (TST01) with the TemSe data tables (TST03).	Relationships between objects and data in TemSe may be destroyed as the result of a restore, a database copy, a faulty client copy, or client deletion without previous deletion of corresponding objects.

Table 5.12 Weekly Tasks—Transactions (Cont.)

5.4 Monthly Tasks

We recommend that you execute the tasks listed in this section on a monthly basis.

5.4.1 SAP System, Database, Operating System, Other

The checklist in Table 5.13 provides an overview of all tasks relating to the DAP system, database, and operating system, as well as other tasks.

Task	Trans action	Chapter	Procedure	Done/ Initials
SAP system				
Defragment the memory.		2	Restart the system.	
Database				
Monitor the growth of the database.	DB02	8	Record and monitor database usage.	

Table 5.13 Monthly Tasks—SAP System, Database, Operating System, Other

Task	Trans action	Chapter	Procedure	Done/ Initials
Operating system				
Back up your file server. Check file system usage.		9	Perform a full backup of the server. Record file system usage; monitor usage. ▶ Do you need the additional memory? ▶ Do you need to run cleanup programs?	
Other				
Check consumable items.		6	Do you have a replacement cleaning cartridge for all tape drives/drive cards? ▶ DAT ▶ DLT Do you have replacement media for swappable data carriers? ▶ ZIP ▶ MO (magneto-optical) ▶ CD (writeable) Do you have preprinted forms? ▶ Shipping documents ▶ Invoices ▶ Checks Do you have supplies of special materials, such as toner cartridges? Do you have office supplies in stock? ▶ Toner for laser printers ▶ Paper (for printers) ▶ Batteries ▶ Disks ▶ Pens, etc.	

Table 5.13 Monthly Tasks—SAP System, Database, Operating System, Other (Cont.)

5.4.2 Checking Consumable Items

You should check your supplies of consumable items at regular intervals. Consumable items are items that you need on a regular basis, including the following:

- Cleaning cartridges
- Data cartridges (tapes and disks)
- Toner for laser printers
- Ink cartridges
- Batteries
- Forms
- Envelopes

Some consumable items must be classified as critical. When you run out of these supplies, it has an immediate impact on business processes, which may even need to be interrupted as a result. Your stock of available consumable items should be sufficient to cover a scale of different levels of demand and to last until new items can be added to your supplies.

Critical Consumables [Ex]

If you run out of toner cartridge for the check printer, you are unable to continue printing checks from the system. Your only option then is to complete the checks manually (provided that you have already printed out sufficient copies).

Particular attention must be paid to special or customer-specific consumable items, such as:

- Special cartridges for inkjet printers, which are used to print MICR characters on checks. These cartridges are not available from all suppliers.
- Preprinted forms (with the corporate letterhead, instructions, or other customer-specific details); these consumable items are often so specific that the lead time for their replenishment is usually far longer than for nonspecific items.

Make sure that you have sufficient supplies of consumable items.

To check your consumable items, follow these steps:

1. Check the expiration date of items that expire. This applies both to materials that are currently in use and those currently in stock.

2. Check items that expire at designated intervals, for example, after a certain number of hours or number of operating cycles.

[Ex]

Materials with an Expiration Date

Certain *digital audio tapes* (DATs) may be used for a maximum of 100 full backups, after which they must be replaced. This limit can be specified in the SAPDBA control file for Oracle.

3. Keep in touch with your buyers and suppliers. Market conditions may make it more difficult to procure certain items. In this case, the replenishment lead times for these items will be longer, and you'll need to order larger quantities. In one real-world example, the procurement of 120-meter DATs was problematic.
4. Keep track of consumption, and adjust your stocks and purchasing plans accordingly.

[+]

Taking Account of Replenishment Lead Times

Some items have longer replenishment lead times for procurement, production, or shipping.

5.5 Quarterly Tasks

The following tasks should ideally be performed once each quarter

5.5.1 SAP System

The checklist in Table 5.14 provides an overview of tasks relating to the SAP system.

Task	Trans action	Chapter	Procedure	Done/ Initials
Archive quarterly backup.			Send the tapes with your quarterly backup to external long-term storage locations.	

Table 5.14 Quarterly Tasks—SAP System

Task	Trans action	Chapter	Procedure	Done/ Initials
Perform security check.	SU01	13	Check the user IDs and search for users that are no longer current, and which need to be locked or deleted.	
	SM30	13	Check the list of "prohibited" passwords (Table USR40).	
	RZ10	13	Check the profile parameters for password standards.	
Check scheduled jobs.	SM37	15	Check all scheduled jobs and determine whether they are still relevant.	

Table 5.14 Quarterly Tasks—SAP System (Cont.)

5.5.2 Database

The checklist in Table 5.15 provides an overview of tasks relating to the database.

Task	Trans action	Chapter	Procedure	Done/ Initials
Archive quarterly backup.		7	Send the tapes with your quarterly backup to external long-term storage locations.	
Check scheduled jobs.	DB13	8	Check all jobs scheduled with the DBA Planning Calendar, and determine whether they are still relevant.	

Table 5.15 Quarterly Tasks—Database

Task	Trans action	Chapter	Procedure	Done/ Initials
Test the database restore process.		7	Restore the database on a test server. Test the restored database.	
Clean up the SAPDBA logs (Oracle).	SAPDBA cleanup		Maintain with init<SID>.dba.	

Table 5.15 Quarterly Tasks—Database (Cont.)

5.5.3 Operating System

The checklist in Table 5.16 provides an overview of tasks relating to the operating system.

Task	Trans action	Chapter	Procedure	Done/ Initials
Archive quarterly backup.		7	Send the tapes with your quarterly backup to external long-term storage locations.	
Archive old transport files.		6	Archive old transport files and logs.	

Table 5.16 Quarterly Tasks—Operating System

5.5.4 Other

The checklist in Table 5.17 provides an overview of all other tasks.

Task	Transaction	Procedure	Done/ Initials
Check service contracts.		Check whether any contracts have expired.	
		Check whether any changes in use have occurred.	

Table 5.17 Quarterly Tasks—Other

5.6 Annual Tasks

Certain tasks are best performed on an annual basis.

5.6.1 SAP System

The checklist in Table 5.18 provides an overview of tasks relating to the SAP system.

Task	Trans action	Chapter	Procedure	Done/ Initials
Archive end-of-year backup.		7	Send the tapes with your end-of-year backup to external long-term storage locations.	
Check user security.		13	Check the user security authorization forms using the assigned profiles. You can also use report RSUSR100 for this purpose.	
Check profiles and authorizations.	SU02	14	Execute with Report RSUSR101.	
	SU03	14	Executed with Report RSUSR102.	
	PFCG	14	Check authorization roles.	
Check the separation of duties (SOD).	PFCG	14	Check the authorization concept for critical overlapping.	
Check user IDs SAP* and DDIC.	SU01	13	Check whether the users are locks, or change the password if necessary.	

Table 5.18 Annual Tasks—SAP System

Task	Trans action	Chapter	Procedure	Done/ Initials
Start SAP programs to track user activity.	SA38 (or SE38)	14	Start SAP programs to track user activities: RSUSR003, RSUSR005, RSUSR006, RSUSR007, RSUSR008, RSUSR009, RSUSR100, RSUSR101, RSUSR102.	
Check whether the system status has been set to NOT MODIFIABLE.	SE03	10	Check whether the system status has been set to NOT MODIFIABLE.	
	SCC4	10	Check whether the relevant clients have a modifiable status.	
Check locked transactions.	SM01	10	Check transactions against the list of locked transactions.	

Table 5.18 Annual Tasks—SAP System (Cont.)

5.6.2 Database

The checklist in Table 5.19 provides an overview of tasks relating to the database.

Task	Trans action	Chapter	Procedure	Done/ Initials
Archive end-of-year backup.		7	Send the tapes with your end-of-year backup to external long-term storage locations.	

Table 5.19 Annual Tasks—Database

5.6.3 Operating System

The checklist in Table 5.20 provides an overview of tasks relating to the operating system.

Task	Trans action	Chapter	Procedure	Done/ Initials
Archive end-of-year backup.		7	Send the tapes with your end-of-year backup to external long-term storage locations.	

Table 5.20 Annual Tasks—Operating System

5.6.4 Other

The checklist in Table 5.21 provides an overview of all other tasks.

Task	Trans action	Chapter	Procedure	Done/ Initials
Perform a disaster recovery.		7	▸ Restore the entire system on a disaster recovery test system. ▸ Test whether normal business can be resumed.	

Table 5.21 Annual Tasks—Other

5.6.5 Overview of Transactions

The checklist in Table 5.22 provides an overview of important transactions.

Transaction	Transaction code	Action	Explanation
User administration.	SU01	All users who leave your enterprise should be refused access to the SAP system as soon as they leave. By locking or deleting these user IDs, you ensure that the SAP system can only be accessed by users with the required authorization. Check that this task has been completed on a regular basis.	User maintenance also involves blocking user access to the SAP system for users who are no longer employees of your enterprise. This also prevents other users from logging on with this ID.
Change the object catalog entry of objects.	SE03/SCC4	Test and apply changes correctly.	Users should be unable to make changes to objects in the QA or production system. This prevents changes to objects and the configuration in the production system before testing is performed. You can protect the integrity of the pipeline by setting the status of the production system to NOT MODIFIABLE.
Lock transaction codes.	SM01	Lock transactions.	This prevents users from causing damage to the system by running transactions.

Table 5.22 Annual Tasks—Transactions

You can use switches to prevent changes from being made to the system. In the production system, these should be set to NOT MODIFIABLE (see Chapter 10, Section 10.3.5). This prevents any changes being made through the development pipeline.

Changes go through the following stages in the development pipeline:

1. Creation in the development system
2. Testing in the development system
3. Transport from the development system to the test system
4. Testing in the test system
5. Transport from the test system to the production system

This method ensures that changes are properly tested in the pipeline and applied to systems.

[+]

Critical Transactions

Critical transactions are transactions that may result in the following outcomes:

- Damage to the system
- Creation of a security risk
- Negative impact on performance

An overview of critical transaction is provided in Appendix B.

If a user accesses a transaction by mistake, resulting in one of the outcomes listed in the preceding box, the entire SAP system may be damaged or even destroyed. Access to these transactions is more critical in the production system than in the development or test system. This has to do both with live data and the fact that the business processes depend on the SAP system.

Therefore, some transactions should be locked in the production system but not in the development, test, or training system. Standard security measures normally prevent access to these transactions. However, some administrators, programmers, consultants, and key technical users may have access to these transactions, depending on the specific system in question.

In this case, the transaction lock acts, in a ways, as a second line of defense. For more information about security in the SAP system, see Chapter 10.

5.7 Summary

Certain tasks need to be executed regularly in an SAP system to ensure that operation remains as smooth as possible. The transactions specified in this chapter will remind you which tasks need to be performed and when, and they can be used as a basis for formulating your own schedule for system administration. The SAP Solution Manager enables technical mapping of this schedule (see Chapter 4, Section 4.4.1), so that you can be reminded on a regular basis about open tasks.

This chapter explains how to develop a backup and restore strategy. After covering the main backup methods, we'll explore the benefits and drawbacks of each. You can then use this information to develop an appropriate backup concept for your own SAP system.

6 Backup and Restore

An effective backup and restore strategy forms the backbone of SAP system operation. The goal of this strategy is to enable a full or partial recovery of the database in as short a time as possible following system failure, an emergency situation (see Chapter 7), or a hardware/software error.

The information provided in this chapter is intended to help you develop a concept to optimize the continuous backup of your data and allow you to restore your database quickly and efficiently in the event of an emergency. We begin by discussing the two aspects of backup and restore, before turning to the issue of performance. Details relating to individual databases are provided in Chapter 8.

The goal of a backup strategy is to minimize data loss in the event of an emergency, in other words, to make sure that no data are lost or to minimize the period during which data are lost.

To achieve this objective, your backup strategy should be as clearly defined as possible because an unnecessarily complicated strategy may also make your backup and restore processes unnecessarily complicated. You should also ensure that your procedures and handling of problems are well documented and that your backup strategy does not impact negatively on your enterprise's routine business operations.

6.1 Backup

The purpose of a system backup is to allow you to access the data currently stored in the system and to import that data back into the system following an emergency.

This is a safeguarding measure because you'll only need to use the backup if your system needs to be restored. Nevertheless, backups are not a trivial matter and shouldn't be treated as such. On the contrary, you should take a moment to consider how much data can be lost in the event of a system failure and what ramifications this may have for the enterprise. Even if you lose order data for only an hour or a day, the economic impact on your business may be huge.

6.1.1 What Has to Be Saved?

Three categories of data require backup:

- Your database
- Transaction logs
- Operating system files

You may need to use different tools to back up different data. For example, SAP tools only allow you to back up one or two of the data categories just listed; for example, the DBA Planning Calendar (Transaction DB13; see also Chapter 8) is capable of backing up your database and transaction logs but not your system files.

Database

The database represents the very heart of your SAP system. Without a backup of your database, you won't be able to restore the system.

The frequency with which you perform a full database backup determines how far back in time you must go when restoring the system:

- If a full backup is performed every day, you require the full backup from the previous day, as well as the transaction log files from the last day or last half-day to restore the system.
- If a full backup is performed every week, you require the full backup from the previous week. However, you must also recover the log files from the last number of days to update the system.

A daily backup reduces the risk of your being unable to restore the current database status if you are unable to use the relevant log files.

If you don't perform a daily backup, you require a large number of log files to update the system. This step increases the duration of the restore process due to the volume of files involved and also increases the risk of your being unable to restore the database to the current status due to individual defective transaction logs.

[Ex]

Weekly Backups

A restore is performed using the full backup from the previous week, which dates from four days ago.

- Ten log files are created every day.
- As a result, the system must be updated with 40 files (10 log files × 4 days).
- You require 120 minutes to load the log files from the tape to the hard drive (40 files × 3 minutes per file).
- You require 200 minutes to update the database with the log files (40 files × 5 minutes per file).

The total time required for the restore—not taking account of the actual database files—is 320 minutes (or 5.3 hours).

[Ex]

Daily Backups

A restore is performed using the full backup from the night before.

- A maximum of 10 log files are created every day.
- You require 30 minutes to load the log files from the tape to the hard drive (10 files × 3 minutes per file).
- You require 50 minutes to update the database with the log files (10 files × 5 minutes per file).

The total time required for the restore—not taking account of the actual database files—is 80 minutes (or 1.3 hours).

As illustrated in these examples, a restore takes much longer to perform if backups are made on a weekly rather than a daily basis.

These examples also demonstrate that the time required to restore the log files depends on the size of the files and on the number of days that have elapsed since the last full backup was performed. The process can quickly become unmanageable in the case of large log files (for example, 100 MB or more per hour). By performing full database backups on a more frequent basis (in other words, by leaving fewer days between backups), you automatically reduce the time required for a restore.

You therefore need to weigh the question of whether performing a full database backup on a daily basis with fewer files is a more viable option for your system, based on the volume of transactions involved, than, for example, performing a full backup on a weekly basis with an accordingly higher number of transaction logs to be reloaded. Of course, this decision also depends on the importance of the SAP system in the context of your enterprise's business processes. In addition to backing up the log files on a tape drive, you should also make a second backup to hard disk so that you don't need to load these files from the tape.

[+]

Daily Full Database Backups

You should have a very good reason not to perform a daily backup of your production database (for example, your database is too big to be backed up overnight). In recent years, the cost of storage space has fallen to such a degree that a backup strategy based on a full daily backup is no longer impractical. SAP recommends that you perform a fully daily backup of the production database and that you store the 28 most recent backups.

Transaction Logs

Transaction logs form part of a database backup and are essential to performing a database restore. These logs contain all changes made to the database. They allow you to undo these changes and to restore the database to its most recent status after a system failure. It is essential to have a complete backup copy of all transaction logs. If even a single log cannot be used when you need to perform a restore, the database cannot be restored beyond the point at which this gap occurs.

[+]

Damaged Log Files

A log file from Tuesday is damaged. The system fails two days later, on Thursday. You can only restore the database up to the last error-free log from Tuesday. From the point at which the damaged log occurs, all subsequent transactions are lost.

The frequency of log backups is also a business decision, based on the following factors:

- Transaction volume
- Critical periods for the system
- The volume of data that management can tolerate losing
- Resources required for the backup

[+]

Intervals Between Log Backups

The following principle applies here: The greater the volume of transactions, the shorter the intervals that you should leave between the individual log backups. In this way, the volume of data that can be lost in the event of a potential disaster in the data center is automatically reduced.

To back up the transaction logs, follow these steps:

1. Save the transaction log to hard disk.
2. Copy this backup to a backup file server located at another site. You should always use verifications when you save your logs across a network.

   The backup file server should ideally be located in another building or another city. A remote location increases the chances of your backup remaining intact if the primary data center (containing the SAP servers) is destroyed.
3. Save the transaction log backups from both servers (the SAP server and backup file server), together with the other files from the operating system level to tape on a daily basis.

[!]

Database Stops When Backup Directory Full

Transaction logs are stored in a directory, which must have sufficient storage space. The database stops when the available memory in the directory is completely occupied by the transaction logs.

If no further processing can take place in the database, the entire SAP system stops also. It's therefore important to think ahead and to back up transaction logs on a regular basis.

If a backup file server in a separate location is not available to you, you must save the transaction log backups to tape after each log backup operation and send the tapes to another location on a regular basis.

[!]

No Backups in Append Mode

Don't back up the logs to tape in *append mode*. In this mode, several backups are written to the same tape. In the event of an emergency, all backups on this band may be lost.

Files at the Operating System Level

You also need to back up files at the operating system level:

- Configuration of the operating environment (for example, system and network configuration)
- SAP files (for example, kernels)
- System profiles
- Spool files
- Transport files
- Other SAP-related applications
- Interfaces or add-on products that save their data or configurations outside of the SAP database

The data volume of these files is relatively small compared to the SAP database. Depending on how your system works, the backup of the files in the preceding list may only comprise a few hundred megabytes to a few gigabytes. In addition, some of the files may contain static data, which remains unchanged for months at a time.

The frequency of backups at the operating system level depends on the applications involved. If you need to ensure synchronicity between these application files and the SAP system, they must be backed up with the same frequency as the logs.

[Ex]

Synchronizing Application Files and the SAP System

One example of this scenario is a tax calculation program, which stores VAT data outside of the SAP system. These files must correspond exactly to the sales orders in the system.

A quick and easy method of backing up operating system files is to copy all files to the hard drive of a second server. A range of products for backing up data at the operating system level is available on the market at the present time. You can then back up all required files to tape from the second server. This approach minimizes the periods during which files are unavailable.

6.1.2 Backup Types

We can distinguish between different types of database backups based on the following three questions:

- What is backed up? Is the backup a full or incremental backup?
- How is it backed up? Online or offline?
- When is it backed up? Is the backup scheduled or ad hoc?

You can, in principle, combine the various answers to these questions to produce a range of options. Each variant has its benefits and drawbacks, which are discussed next.

What Is Backed Up?

In terms of the scope of the database backup, you can choose between a full or partial backup.

- **Full database backup**
  Note the following considerations:
  - *Advantages*
    The database as a whole is backed up, which makes a database restore faster and easier to perform. Fewer transaction logs are required to update the database.
  - *Disadvantages*
    A full backup takes longer to complete than an incremental backup. As a result, users are disrupted for a longer period. You should therefore only perform full backups outside of normal business hours.
- **Incremental backup with transaction logs**
  Note the following considerations:
  - *Advantages*
    An incremental backup is much quicker than a full database backup. Because the backup takes less time to complete, users are impacted for shorter periods and, in most cases, to a barely noticeable degree.
  - *Disadvantages*
    A full backup is required to restore the database.
    Restoring the database with incremental transaction logs takes much longer and is more complicated than a restore based on a full backup. The most recent full backup must be used for the restore, and the system then has to be updated with all logs dating from the time when the full backup was made. If several days have elapsed since the last full backup, a very large number of logs have to be restored if the system fails.

If you are unable to restore one of these logs, you will also be unable to restore any subsequent log.

- **Differential backup**

  A third option may also be available to you, depending on your database and operating system (see Table 6.1): In a differential backup, you only back up the changes that have been made since the most recent full backup. One commonly used approach is to perform a full backup every weekend and differential backups during the week.

  - *Advantages*

    The risk of your being unable to perform a full restore because of damaged log backups is reduced. A differential backup saves all changes made to the database since the last full backup.

  - *Disadvantages*

    As with an incremental backup, you still require a full backup as a basis for restoring the database.

    A differential backup may take longer to complete than a backup of the transaction logs. Initially (after the full backup), it will take less time, but the process will gradually become longer over time as more data are changed.

[!]

Full Backup as a Basis for an Incremental Backup

Note that an incremental backup always comprises a full backup and a backup of the subsequent transaction logs. A restore based on incremental backups becomes problematic as soon as the underlying full backup or one of the transaction logs is damaged or lost.

How Is It Backed Up?

In terms of backup mode, we can distinguish between *offline* and *online*, based on the system status of the SAP system and the database. To perform an offline backup, you must disconnect the SAP system from the database and stop work in the SAP system. An online backup, on the other hand, is performed during normal operation of the database and SAP system.

- **Offline**

  Advantages

  - An offline backup is faster than an online backup.

- There are no complications caused by changes to data in the database during the backup.
- All files are backed up at the same time and give a consistent picture of the system; the corresponding operating system files are synchronized with the SAP database.
- You can execute a binary verification during an offline backup. However, this doubles the time required to perform the backup.
- An offline backup doesn't require the SAP system to be stopped. The SAP buffer is therefore preserved.

Disadvantages

- The SAP system is not available during an offline backup.
- When the database is stopped, the database buffer is also cleared of all data. This operation has a negative impact on performance, with this effect lasting until the buffer is filled with data once again.

- **Online**

  Advantages

  - The SAP system is available to users during the backup. This is essential if the system is in constant demand 24/7.
  - The buffers are not cleared. As a result, there is no negative impact on performance following the backup.

  Disadvantages

  - An online backup is slower than an offline backup. The time taken to complete the backup increases over time because the backup runs during normal operation and uses system resources.
  - Online performance deteriorates during the backup.
  - The data in the database may change while the backup is still in progress. Transaction logs are therefore particularly important to ensure a successful restore.
  - The corresponding files at the operating system level may possibly no longer be synchronized with the SAP database.

[!]

Transaction Logs in an Online Backup

If you use online backups, transaction logs are particularly important to ensure a successful restore.

When Is It Backed Up?

You can select the time at which a database backup is performed based on a backup schedule or spontaneously as the need arises in a specific situation. For more information about the tools and transactions mentioned in the following list, refer to Chapter 8.

- **Planned**
  Planned backups are performed on a regular basis, for example, daily or weekly. For normal operation, you can use the DBA Planning Calendar (Transaction DB13) to configure an automated backup schedule for the database and transaction logs. You can use this calendar to set up and check backup cycles. You also have the option of performing important database checks and updating the statistics. You can display the status of your backups in the DB Backup Monitor (Transaction DB12).
- **Ad hoc**
  Ad hoc backups are spontaneous backups performed on an as-needed basis, for example, prior to large-scale system changes, in preparation for an SAP upgrade, or after a structural change to the database (such as the addition of a data file). Backups that are monitored directly by the user or are performed on an as-needed basis can either be initiated using the DBA Planning Calendar or at the database or operating system level.

The DBA Scheduling Calendar can be used for both regular, planned backups and spontaneous backups. However, tools at the database level, such as Enterprise Manager (Microsoft SQL Server) or SAPDBA (Oracle), are more commonly used for these ad hoc backups.

Regardless of the backup method you select, you should always set the following goals:

- Create a reliable backup that can be used to restore the database.
- Use a simple backup strategy.

- Reduce the number of interdependencies required for operation.
- Try to eliminate or minimize the impact on the work being done in the system by business department users.

Weigh up the needs of system security and performance to use the available options to develop the best possible backup strategy for your system.

Database System-Specific Terminology

Table 6.1 shows the backup terminology that occurs in relation to the various methods outlined previously, which differs depending on which database system is used.

The backup methods and jobs have different names, depending on which database your system uses. However, the underlying principle is always the same. If in doubt, consult your database administrator or the documentation provided for your database system.

	Full Database Backup	Content	Partial Database Backup	Log Backup
DB2 UDB	Full database backup in TSM (Tivoli Storage Manager)	Offline/online-tablespace backup in TSM	Incremental database backup with DB2 UDB in TSM	Archiving of inactive log files in TSM
	Full database backup to storage device	Offline/online-tablespace backup to storage device	Incremental database backup with DB2 UDB to storage device	Archiving of inactive log files on storage device
	Full database backup with vendor library	Offline tablespace backup with vendor library	Incremental database backup with DB2 UDB and vendor library	One-step archiving in storage software

Table 6.1 The Terminology of Backups

	Full Database Backup	Content	Partial Database Backup	Log Backup
SQL Server	Full database backup		Differential database backup	Transaction log backup
Oracle	Full database backup offline + new log backup	Full offline database backup	Partial offline database backup	New log backup
	Full database backup online + new log backup	Full online database backup	Partial online database backup	

Table 6.1 The Terminology of Backups (Cont.)

6.1.3 Backup Strategy

Your backup strategy unites and defines all measures used to back up your system and specifies when exactly backups are to be performed, the intervals at which they are to be performed, and the backup method that is to be employed. You should document this strategy in the form of a *backup frequency table* in a backup concept and ensure that it meets the needs of management and the business departments.

You then implement your backup strategy with the appropriate backup tools. Ultimately, however, your choice of tool to implement the strategy is of little relevance, be it one of the SAP-internal tools mentioned previously or the standard tools provided in your database or operating system. The most important criteria when selecting tools are manageability, reliability, and the monitoring options.

To develop a backup strategy, follow these steps:

1. Determine your requirements for performing a restore and your tolerance range in the event of a system failure.

   A generally acceptable system downtime cannot be defined because this will differ significantly between one enterprise and the next. The costs incurred by system downtime include the cost of production downtime, plus the costs of performing a restore, such as time, money and so on. These costs should have a sliding scale, similar to that used for insurance premiums. With insurance, the more coverage you require, the greater the premium you have to pay. If we apply this model to a system restore, we get the following rule: The faster a restore is completed, the more expensive the solution you'll have to use.

2. Determine which combination of hardware, software, and processes is used in the desired solution.

   Better hardware makes a backup and restore faster, better software makes these operations easier, and well-defined processes make them more efficient. Of course, this all comes at a price, and the benefits will have to be weighed against the costs. However, it's even more important that your method be reliable.

3. To test your backup method, implement the hardware, and check the actual runtimes and test results.

   Ensure that you obtain results for all backup types used in your environment and not only those you intend to use. This information will facilitate future evaluation and capacity planning decisions and, if necessary, provide a sound basis for comparison.

4. Test your restore method by simulating various system failure scenarios.

   Document all aspects of the restore; include questions such as who will take care of specific tasks, which users are to be notified, and so on (see Chapter 7). You should also consider the likelihood that a restore may occur exactly when you least expect it. You should therefore conduct testing on an ongoing basis, and perform additional tests whenever changes are made to hardware or software components.

Schedule additional backups on specific dates (for example, end of the month, end of the year) alongside your daily and weekly backup cycles. These are not strictly necessary but can, for example, be archived separately as a safeguard against a disaster (see Chapter 7).

6.1.4 Strategy Recommendations

This section provides some further tips and recommendations for developing a backup strategy.

Database

As discussed previously, we recommend that you perform a full database backup every day, provided that the cost of doing so is not prohibitively high. If your database is too large for a daily backup, you should perform a full backup once a week instead.

Testing Your Backups

Your backups need to be tested on a regular basis. To do this, you need to restore the system and then conduct a test to determine whether the restore has been completed to your satisfaction. Without testing your backups, you can't tell whether all of the required data has actually been backed up on the tape.

[Ex]

> **Why Testing Your Backups Is Essential**
>
> Various files were backed up but the Append switch was set incorrectly for the second file and all subsequent files. As a result, the files were not saved to tape in sequence. Instead, the tape was rewound after each file was backed up and prior to the backup of the next file. The outcome is that all files except for the last file to be backed up were overwritten.

[!]

> **Test Finished Backups Only**
>
> You can only test a backup after all files have been backed up. If you test your backup after each individual file, the system will be unable to detect whether the previous file has been overwritten.

Database Integrity

You need to check the integrity of the database regularly to ensure that it contains no damaged blocks. Otherwise, defective blocks may remain undetected during a backup. If possible, conduct an integrity test once a week outside of business hours. This can be scheduled with the DBA Planning Calendar.

Transaction Logs

It is extremely important that you back up your transaction logs. The database, and therefore also the SAP system, stops when the memory that is available for storing the transaction logs is full.

We therefore recommend that you perform a backup of these logs every three hours between the hours of 6:00 am and 9:00 pm. The intervals between the backups correspond to the maximum data volume that you can tolerate losing. The risk is naturally higher for an enterprise with a large transaction volume. In this case, it would be advisable to perform a backup every 30 minutes, for example. If your enterprise has a shipping department that starts work at 3:00 am, or a production line that works until 10:00 pm, you should begin making backups earlier or stop later as required.

Transaction logs can be backed up during normal operation without any impact on users.

Files at Operating System Level

The frequency of backups at the operating system level depends on the applications involved. If you need to ensure synchronicity between the application files and the SAP system, they must be backed up with the same frequency as the database and logs. If perfect synchronicity is less important, you can also back up the application files less frequently.

Backup Strategy Checklist

You need to develop an appropriate system for backing up valuable system data. You should define a suitable strategy as soon as possible to avoid a possible loss of data. You should have worked through a checklist covering all backup-relevant topics before your system goes live (see Table 6.2).

Question, Task, or Decision	Done
Decide how frequently you want to perform a full database backup.	
Decide whether partial or differential backups are required.	
Decide whether to use automatic backups. If you want to use automatic backups, decide where to do this (in the DBA Planning Calendar or elsewhere).	
Decide how frequently the transaction logs are to be backed up.	
Ensure that you can store a day's volume of logs on the server.	
Ensure that you have sufficient memory in the directory for transaction logs.	

Table 6.2 Backup Strategy Checklist

Question, Task, or Decision	Done
Set up the authorizations required for the SAP system, the operating system, and the database.	
Consider whether you want to use the DBA Planning Calendar to schedule the backup of transaction logs.	
Work out guidelines for labeling data carriers to ensure a smooth workflow.	
Decide on the period for which your backups are to be stored.	
Define the size of the tape pool required (tapes required per day × retention period + 20%).	
Take account of future growth and special requirements.	
Initialize the tapes.	
Define a storage strategy for the tapes.	
Document the backup procedures in an instruction manual.	
Train users in the backup procedures.	
Implement a backup strategy.	
Perform a backup and restore for testing purposes.	
Define a contingency plan for emergencies, and decide which users are to be contacted in the event of an emergency.	

Table 6.2 Backup Strategy Checklist (Cont.)

6.2 Restore

You usually perform a restore for one of the following reasons:

- Disaster recovery following an emergency situation (see Chapter 7)
- Testing of your Disaster Recovery plan (see Chapter 7)
- Copying your database into another system (see Chapter 2)

You access the backups that are made on a regular basis to perform a system restore. In the context of disaster recovery, you usually restart the database and, if necessary, the operating system, using the most recent full backup. You then import the transaction logs that have been created since the full backup. When this procedure is successfully completed, the system once again has the status it had at the time the last error-free log backup was made.

The duration of this restore is of critical importance. You want it to be completed as quickly as possible so that the system can be used again after an outage, and the disruption to business processes can be kept to a minimum.

For a database copy (for example, in the context of regular updating of the QA system using a copy of the production system), you normally either import the most recent full backup or generate a live copy using data streaming. Transaction logs are usually ignored.

As in your system backup strategy, you should also have a *restore strategy* in your arsenal, which can be deployed in the event of an emergency. The following factors may influence your restore strategy:

- Business costs incurred by system downtimes
- Operational schedules
- Global or local users
- Number of transactions per hour
- Budget

The development of a restore strategy is discussed in detail in Chapter 7.

The actual process of restoring the SAP system and database is not discussed in this book because this task varies widely between different systems and databases. If in doubt, consult an expert (for example, your database administrator or an external Basis consultant) who can provide you with operational support for this critical process. You should also collaborate with your database administrator or consultant to test and document the restore process. This transfer of knowledge will soon enable you to perform a restore on your own.

An Incomplete or Incorrect Restore [!]

If the restore is performed incorrectly or incompletely, it may fail and have to be restarted to avoid the possibility of some files being excluded. Certain data must be entered via your database so that it can be restored subsequently. Work with an expert to identify and document this data.

Because the restore process is one of the most important tasks in the SAP system, you need to test database restores at regular intervals. For more details, refer to Chapter 7.

6.3 Performance

The key objectives of a database restore are to restore the data as completely as possible and to minimize the time required to do so. The length of time that the SAP system is unavailable to users and, as a result, certain business processes are halted, is of critical importance to an enterprise. System performance is therefore a key factor when performing a restore.

The performance of your backup process is also important, in particular if your system is used globally 24/7. Disruption to users should be kept to a minimum during a backup. As a result, you need to strive to reduce the duration of the backup (in particular, in the case of offline backups) and to ensure adequate system reserves to guarantee acceptable system operation during an online backup.

The performance of your backup and restore processes are largely determined by data throughput on your devices. To improve throughput, you need to identify bottlenecks or devices that are limiting the throughput and eliminate or replace these. This process is subject to economic considerations because performance enhancement with additional or more modern devices is naturally also a cost factor.

This section provides tips for improving the performance of your data backups and restores by implementing some specific measures.

6.3.1 Performance Factors

The main variables, which are provided in the following list, affect the performance of both the backup and the restore:

- **Size of the database**
  The larger the database, the longer it takes to back it up.
- **Hardware throughput**
  This variable determines how quickly the backup can be performed. Throughput is always determined by the weakest link in the backup chain, for example:
  - The database driver array

   - The input/output channel (I/O) channel used
   - The tape drive
- **Time of backup**
  This is the time or period available to you for regular system backups. Your objective here should be to minimize disruption to users.
   - *Online backup*
     The appropriate times for performing online backups are periods during which there is a low level of system activities, which is usually early in the morning.
   - *Offline backup*
     The appropriate times for performing offline backups are periods during which you can shut down the SAP system, which is usually at the weekend.

  The times at which you perform system restores are less critical because the system can't run in any case unless you do so.

[+]

Take into Account the Time Differences Between Different Sites

Remember to take into account the time differences between the various sites in which your enterprise is located. For example, when it's 12:00 midday in Central Europe, it's only 6:00 am in New York.

6.3.2 Backup Performance

The following approaches to improving backup performance assume that you save your backup locally on the database server. Although a backup via the network is technically possible, performance in this case depends to a large degree on network topology, overhead, and data traffic, while the throughput values of the disk systems take a back seat. In any case, the full capacity of the network is rarely available. If you perform a backup via the network, network performance also deteriorates for other users. As a result, other applications in your enterprise may be slowed down.

Backup to Faster Devices

All approaches to optimizing performance aim to prevent bottlenecks occurring on the backup device. The backup device, usually a tape drive, is the device that limits throughput. You should consider the following aspects in this context:

- **Advantages**
  Faster tape drives with larger capacities allow you to save an entire database on a single tape within a reasonable amount of time.
- **Disadvantages**
  Backup to a single tape is the slowest option.
  Without using an automatic tape changing mechanism or a library, you are limited to the maximum capacity of the tape, unless you replace it manually during the backup.

[!]

Compatibility of Database Tools and Tape Systems

Not all databases and backup tools support tape changers. Before you purchase your backup devices, you must therefore ensure that they are compatible.

Parallel Backup

A parallel backup to more than one tape drive uses a RAID 0 array (Redundant Array of Independent Disks), whereby data can be written to several tapes simultaneously. In some environments, for example, Oracle, individual tablespaces or files are backed up on separate tape drives at the same time. Because you save your data to several tape drives in parallel, overall performance is better than when you use a single drive.

If you have a sufficient number of tape drives that can be used in parallel, the bottleneck can be shifted from the tape drives to another component. For this reason, you also need to take account of the performance of other subsystems if you want to use the parallel backup option. These subsystems include the controller, CPU, and I/O bus. In many configurations, the controller or bus represents the limiting factor.

[!]

Restoring a Parallel Backup

When you restore a parallel backup, you need to be able to read all tapes in the set. If a single tape is damaged, the backup can't be used. The more tapes you have in a set, the higher the risk of one of them being damaged.

Backup to Hard Disk Before Backup to Magnetic Tape

This is the fastest way to create a backup of your database. The backup to hard disk is usually faster than the backup to tape. With this method, you can quickly save several identical copies to hard disks and, for example, store some in external enterprise locations and others at your own site.

As soon as the backup to hard disk is complete, the impact on system performance is minimal. Because the backup to tape is made from the copy already made on the hard disk rather than from the production database, there are no competing drains on resources from the backup and database activities. During a disaster recovery process, the data can ideally be restored from the backup on the hard disk. However, this method also has a number of disadvantages:

- You require additional hard disk space equivalent to the size of the database. If your database is large, this may give rise to additional costs.
- Until the backup to tape is completed, you have no protection against the risk of potential disasters occurring in the data center. In a disaster recovery scenario, you must recover the files on the hard disk first, and then restore the database from the hard disk.

Other options for faster backups are also available, for example, high availability (HA). However, a discussion of these options falls outside the scope of this book.

6.3.3 Restore Performance

The performance requirements for a restore are more important than those for a backup. The restore performance determines when the system will be available again and how quickly business can be resumed. Your objective in this regard is to restore the database and corresponding files quickly and make the system generally available as soon as possible.

The measures to enhance backup performance that we outlined earlier also essentially result in shorter restore times. You can therefore examine these proposals from the point of view of both backup and restore performance, for example:

- **Dedicated drives**
  Together with a parallel backup, restoring files and tablespaces to individual, dedicated drives accelerates the process considerably. Only one tablespace or file is written to the drive. As a result, competition for drive resources is avoided.
- **RAID systems**
  RAID 0+1 is faster than RAID5, although these speeds depend on the hardware used. In more cases, the calculation of parity data for the parity drive (RAID5)

is more time-consuming than writing the data twice (RAID 0+1). This option is costly because the usable capacity only amounts to 50% of total capacity, which is significantly less with RAID5:

- RAID 0+1 = [single_drive_capacity × (number_of_drives/2)]
- RAID5 = [single_drive_capacity × (number of drives – 1)]

- **Drives with better write performance**
  You can generally read data more quickly from modern drives that offer a higher write performance. Enhanced reading capacity reduces the time required to perform the restore.
- **Drive array systems with better write performance**
  The benefit of a faster single drive also applies to drive arrays: As a rule, read speeds generally improve in tandem with write performance, which reduces the time required for a restore.

Measures to improve backup performance are often viewed by management as not being particularly urgent. The reason for this is that backups are usually performed out of core business hours and that enhanced performance is not usually obvious to users. As a result, it can be difficult to obtain the additional means required for modern technology.

However, if you make the argument that clear time savings can be made in terms of the restore process, you may find that your pleas no longer fall on deaf ears. After all, you'll be able to ensure that the system is available after a disaster or emergency much sooner thanks to this technology.

6.4 Summary

The information provided in this chapter was intended to help you develop a backup strategy for your SAP systems, based on your enterprise's business framework. You can protect your systems from the worst-case scenario by combining full and incremental database backups, as well as by backing up your transaction logs and operating system files. You should aim to be able to restore the system completely within a short space of time should such a scenario arise.

The next chapter, Chapter 7, provides additional specific instructions for managing a disaster situation. Chapter 8 introduces you to the SAP-internal database tools, which you can use for automatic backups.

Even the most conscientious system administrator can become overwhelmed when faced with a system failure, a loss of data, or destruction caused by a natural disaster. For such situations, it's always good to have a plan of action and not to be caught completely off guard. This chapter suggests ways in which you can brace yourself for a disaster and prepare for a subsequent system recovery.

7 Disaster Recovery

Thousands of business processes occur on a daily basis and usually without any problems whatsoever. However, even a very brief system outage can seriously disrupt business processes and result in a loss of time, money, and resources. It's therefore advisable to plan for emergency situations so that you aren't entirely helpless when faced with such problems, irrespective of their size and complexity.

This chapter will discuss a system administrator's most important task, namely the task of disaster recovery, which is a form of system recovery (see Chapter 6).

7.1 Preliminary Considerations

The goal of disaster recovery is to restore the system after an *emergency* in such a way that the enterprise can continue its business processes. Because business processes come to a standstill not only during the system failure itself but also during system recovery, disaster recovery must be performed as quickly as possible. For this reason, it's even more important to have a tried-and-tested recovery. Furthermore, the earlier you start to plan, the better prepared you will be in an actual emergency.

Note on the Following Explanations [!]

This chapter is not a guide to disaster recovery. Instead, its sole purpose is to increase your awareness of disaster recovery and to stress how important it is to develop a plan.

An emergency is anything that will damage an SAP system or cause a system failure. This includes damage to a database (for example, loading test data into a production system), a serious hardware failure, or a complete loss of the SAP system and the infrastructure (for example, as a result of a natural disaster or fire).

In the event of such an emergency, the most important task of the system administrator is to successfully restore the SAP system. Above all else, however, the administrator should ensure that such an emergency does not occur in the first place.

A system administrator should be prepared for the worst and have suitable "emergency plans" in place. Disaster recovery is not the time to try out something new because unwelcome surprises could ruin the entire recovery process.

When developing a plan, ask yourself the following questions:

- If the SAP system fails, will the entire business process fail?
- How high is the loss of earnings, and how high are the resulting costs during a system failure?
- Which important business functions can no longer be performed?
- How are customers supported?
- How long can a system failure last before an enterprise is incapable of conducting business?
- Who will coordinate and manage a disaster recovery?
- What will users do while the SAP system is down?
- How long will the system failure last?
- How long will it take to restore the SAP system?
- Which SAP system components need to be restored so that a remote recovery is possible?

Careful planning will ensure that you are less stressed in the event of an emergency because you'll already know that the system can be restored and the length of time it will potentially take to perform this system recovery.

If you discover that the time required for a system recovery is too long, and the associated losses are too high, management should consider making an additional investment in equipment, facilities, and personnel. Even though a *high availability*

(HA) solution is often costly, these costs may not be as high as those associated with possible losses incurred during a disaster.

7.2 Planning for an Emergency

Creating a disaster recovery plan is considered a large project because development, testing, and documentation require a great deal of time, possibly more than a year. The documentation alone may be very extensive, possibly comprising several hundred pages.

Seek advice from experts if you don't know how to plan for an emergency. A plan that doesn't work is worse than having no plan at all because poor planning lulls an enterprise into a false sense of security. Third-party disaster recovery consultants and suppliers can support you during disaster recovery planning.

7.2.1 Which Measures Apply to Disaster Recovery?

The requirements for disaster recovery can be derived directly from the requirements for system availability, which are laid down by management. The guidelines for the requisite system availability are based, for example, on the losses that an enterprise is expected to incur in the event of a system disaster. The monetary loss is usually calculated by management and specified in USD per time unit, while the failure costs depend not only on the enterprise or sector (for example, industry/public administration) but also on the division in which the software is used (for example, Production/Purchasing).

The desired system availability is usually agreed upon in *Service Level Agreements* (SLAs) that you, as an administrator, must fulfill. Therefore, from your perspective, it's also important to know which costs (for example, for technical equipment or service personnel) are needed to ensure a certain level of availability for the relevant system. Note that the higher the recovery costs, the less time it will take to perform a recovery. However, you can influence these costs through preventive measures (see Chapter 10) and a good recovery plan.

When it comes to technical business units, you must bear in mind that HA comes at a price. If savings are made in the wrong areas, you could be in for a rude awakening. Such costs must be included in the administrative or IT budget.

Financial Effects of a Disaster

- **Example 1**
  When forecasting the monetary loss associated with a system failure, your enterprise discovered that transaction data can only be lost for a period of one hour. The resulting costs assume that 1,000 transactions (entered in the SAP system and not restored from the memory) will be lost each hour. Such a loss in transactions can lead to a loss in sales as well as extremely annoyed customers. If orders urgently required by customers disappear, the situation can become critical. In this case, you must ensure that the frequency with which data is backed up is sufficiently high (for example, an hourly backup of the transaction logs).
- **Example 2**
  In your enterprise, you discovered that a system can't be offline for more than three hours. The resulting costs (at an hourly rate of USD 20,000, for example) are based on the fact that no sales can be posted. In this case, you require a sufficiently efficient emergency strategy or infrastructure to ensure that the system is operational again within three hours.
- **Example 3**
  In the event of an emergency (for example, the loss of a building that houses the SAP data center), the enterprise can only survive a downtime of two days. After two days, customers start to conduct their business elsewhere. Consequently, an alternative method must be found to continue business (for example, an alternative data center is built or an emergency contract is agreed upon with an external provider).

7.2.2 When Should the Disaster Recovery Procedure Begin?

For each disaster recovery plan, you must use a unique set of criteria to determine when such a plan will enter into force and when the procedure will begin. Ask yourself the following questions:

- Which characteristics define an emergency?
- Have these characteristics been fulfilled in the current situation?
- Who must be consulted to assess the situation? The relevant person should know not only how a failure can impact the business process but also be aware of the problems associated with a recovery.

These considerations should help you to decide whether or not to initiate your disaster recovery procedure.

Alternatively, form a committee that will contribute and assess all of the information required to make a decision within the shortest possible time as well as make a decision in relation to implementing the recovery procedure.

7.2.3 Expected Downtime

Downtime is the period during which a system is unavailable. Even though you can only estimate downtime, it's usually longer than the restore time (see the next section) because, after a system recovery, some tests must be performed, user master records must be unlocked, and notifications must be sent, among other things. It's even more important to have an accurate idea of the restore time.

During downtime, it isn't possible, for example, to process orders or dispatch products. The resulting losses are just one part of the costs associated with a disaster recovery. To minimize disruption, you need to examine alternative processes that can be used while the SAP system is being restored.

During downtime, the following factors generate costs:

- The time during which the SAP system cannot be used.

  The longer the system does not work, the longer it will take, after a successful recovery, to make up for the losses incurred during downtime.

  The transactions from the alternative processes deployed during downtime must be fed into the system to update it. This situation may be problematic in an environment that has extensive transactions.

- A failed system generates more costs than an operational system because additional technology or personnel must be used.
- Customers who can't be served or supported by the enterprise may conduct their business elsewhere.
- If follow-up processes also come to a standstill, your customers may have a claim for recourse.

What is deemed to be an acceptable downtime depends, to a large extent, on the enterprise and its nature of the business.

7.2.4 Restore Time

Restore time is the time required to restore lost data and system operability. Different emergency scenarios have different restore times, depending on the operational needs (for example, the volume of data to be restored).

The restore time must be adapted to the requirements of the enterprise. If the current restore time exceeds the time limit for these measures, the relevant managers must be informed of this disparity.

Such a disparity can be resolved as follows:

- By investing in equipment, processes, and facilities that will shorten the restore time
- By changing the requirements of the enterprise so that longer restore times are possible

[Ex]

Minimizing Restore Times through Additional Resources

In an enterprise, it would take a month to restore the system if just one employee was entrusted with this task. The enterprise can't afford the resulting costs or losses in revenue because, during this time, customers would conduct their business elsewhere, vendor invoices would fall due, and invoices would not be paid. In such situations, senior management would have to provide additional resources to reduce the restore time to an acceptable level.

If you don't test your recovery procedure (see Section 7.8), the required restore time simply remains an estimate. Use basic testing to ensure that, in the event of an emergency, you can accurately state how much time a system recovery will require (assuming that you have a broad range of experience in this area). You can then also make more accurate statements (to the users) in relation to the expected downtime.

7.2.5 Communication in the Event of a Disaster

A communication concept should form part of your emergency plan. Even if a system failure is usually very noticeable, users can find it annoying if they are left in the dark about their situation. In certain enterprise areas, a system failure may cause the entire operation to come to a standstill. However, those responsible can't respond appropriately if they aren't informed about when the system is expected to be available again.

If necessary, discuss the following factors with end users:

- Who is affected in the event of a system failure?
- What are the implications of a system failure for the user departments, or which particular dependencies arise?
- What is the timeframe during which information about the system failure must be imparted?
- Which information should be provided (for example, type, cause, and extent of the disruption, and anticipated downtime)?
- Which contact persons should be informed?
- How should the information be conveyed, or what are the chains of communication?
- Which paths of communication are still available in the event of a disaster? How does communication occur if, for example, the email system is also down?
- After a system has been restored, how do we convey that the system is available again?
- To what extent is information about incident analysis and processing conveyed?

Actively incorporate communication into your recovery plan and coordinate this with the user departments. Good communication can have a calming effect in the event of an emergency because you don't have to deal with complaints and can instead concentrate on restoring the system.

7.3 Recovery Team and Role Distribution

Several people, known collectively as the *recovery team*, are usually involved in a system recovery. A highly coordinated team is the secret to implementing disaster recovery as quickly and as efficiently as possible. There are four key roles within a recovery team:

- **Recovery manager**
  The recovery manager, who coordinates all activities, is responsible for the complete technical recovery.
- **Communications officer**
  The communications officer looks after the users (by telephone, email, and so on) and informs upper management about the current recovery status. If one person

assumes responsibility for all communication, the rest of the group can devote themselves to the actual recovery procedure without any interruptions.

- **Technical recovery team**
  This team works to restore the system. If the original plans need to change during the recovery, the technical recovery team must manage such changes and coordinate the technical system recovery.
- **Review and certification manager**
  After a recovery has taken place, the review and certification manager coordinates and plans the test procedures and certifications.

The number of employees who assume these roles varies depending on the size of the enterprise. In a small enterprise, for example, one person can assume the role of recovery manager and communications officer. In addition, the descriptions and range of tasks will most likely vary depending on the needs of your enterprise.

Structure your disaster recovery concept in such a way that each team member and each role knows exactly which tasks are to be performed and when. Describe the dependencies and coordination processes between the roles, and create checklists for each team member.

[✪]

Status Notice

To prevent incidents involving employees working on the recovery, we recommend that you create a status notice. Key points in the recovery plan are listed here as well as estimates in relation to when the system will be restored and operational again.

Also bear in mind that key employees may not be available in the event of an emergency (e.g., due to vacations or sick leave). Therefore, the team must also be able to perform a successful recovery without these people. In an actual emergency, this issue can be very urgent.

[!]

Planning with Employees from Other Locations

If the emergency is a major natural disaster, your on-site employees will be extremely concerned about their own families as well as the enterprise itself. In some cases, key employees may be badly or even fatally injured.

You should also prepare for such situations and formulate plans accordingly. Allow for the fact that employees would have to be flown in from other locations and integrated into the recovery team.

7.4 Types of Disaster Recovery

Disaster recovery scenarios can be divided into two types:

- In-house recovery
- Remote recovery

In-house recovery is disaster recovery that you perform yourself at your enterprise location. The in-house infrastructure must remain intact as far as possible (this is usually the case). Ideally, the recovery is made using the original hardware. In the worst-case scenario, the original hardware must be replaced with a backup system.

Remote recovery is disaster recovery performed at a special disaster recovery location. In this scenario, the entire hardware and infrastructure has been destroyed as a result of a fire, flood, earthquake, or similar. Consequently, the new servers have to be configured from scratch.

In the case of a remote recovery, you must bear in mind that a second system recovery must take place at the original location as soon as the original facility has been rebuilt. Plan and schedule the second recovery in such a way that as few users as possible are inconvenienced by the fact that the system will not be operational during this recovery.

7.5 Emergency Scenarios

Although numerous emergency scenarios are conceivable, it's impossible to develop plans for all possible scenarios. Therefore, to keep this task manageable, you should limit yourself to approximately three to five probable scenarios. If an emergency occurs, you can adhere to the scenario that best corresponds to the actual emergency.

An emergency scenario comprises the following points:

- Description of the emergency
- Planning the main tasks at a high level
- Estimated downtime

The best way to prepare for an emergency is to use emergency scenarios:

1. Use Sections 7.5.1 to 7.5.3 as a starting point, and prepare three to five scenarios that cover the largest possible range of emergencies.
2. For each scenario, create a plan for the main tasks at a high level.
3. Test the planned scenarios by simulating different emergencies and checking whether your scenarios could be applied to the actual emergency.
4. If this is not the case, change the scenarios or develop new ones.
5. Repeat the process.

The following three examples are arranged in order of increasing severity. The downtimes cited are merely examples to illustrate the situations you may encounter. Your own downtime will differ from those specified here. You must therefore replace the sample downtime with a downtime that applies to your environment. It will become clear that, depending on the specific emergency, various extensive measures must be taken and that extremely long downtimes may occur even if the damage appears to be minor.

7.5.1 Damaged Database

A database may be damaged if test data are inadvertently loaded into the production system or if data incorrectly transported into the production system causes a crash.

If such an incident occurs, the SAP database and associated operating system files must be restored. The downtime is, for example, eight hours.

7.5.2 Hardware Failure

The following hardware can fail:

- Processors
- Hard disk controller
- Multiple drivers in a driver array (known as an array failure)

If such a failure occurs, the following steps are necessary:

1. Replace the failed hardware.
2. Rebuild the server (operating system and all programs).

3. Restore the SAP database and associated files.

The downtime is, for example, seven days, broken down as follows:

- Five days to procure replacement hardware
- Two days to completely rebuild the server (by one person), 16 working hours in total

[+]

Planning the Use of a Backup Server

Plan and test the use of your test system (QAS) as a backup server if the production server (PRD) fails.

7.5.3 Complete Loss or Destruction of the Server Facility

The following components may be destroyed if a catastrophe occurs:

- The servers
- The entire supporting infrastructure
- All of the documentation and materials in the building
- The building itself

Such a complete loss of facilities may be the result of a natural disaster such as a fire, flood, hurricane, or a manmade catastrophe.

If such a catastrophe occurs, the following steps are necessary:

1. Replace the destroyed facilities.
2. Replace the destroyed infrastructure.
3. Replaced the destroyed hardware.
4. Rebuild the server and the SAP environment (hardware, operating system, database, etc.).
5. Restore the SAP database and associated files.

The downtime is, for example, eight days, broken down as follows:

- At least five days to procure the hardware
  If it is a regional catastrophe, it may take longer to procure the hardware because vendors may also be affected by the catastrophe.

[+]

National Vendors

Turn to national vendors that have several regional distribution centers. As an additional backup measure, you should look for alternative vendors in distant regions.

- Two days to rebuild the server (by one person), 16 working hours in total
  While the hardware is being procured and the server is being rebuilt, an alternative facility in which a minimal emergency network can be constructed must work.
- One day for integration into the emergency network

A complete loss makes it necessary to perform a recovery in a new facility or in a different building. Depending on the size of the enterprise, how important the SAP system is for the enterprise's business processes, and the regional risk of a natural disaster, it may make sense to build a redundant data center. If one of your data centers is destroyed, operation of the system landscape can then switch to the other data center. However, both of these data centers must be built at least a few kilometers apart from each other. If housed in the same building, it's highly likely that both data centers would fail in the event of a disaster.

If your enterprise doesn't have or want to use the resources necessary for a redundant data center, you can agree on a contract for a disaster recovery location with an external provider. Then, if a disaster occurs, you can use the hardware of this provider for emergency use.

[!]

Recovery Location in an Emergency

Having a contract for a disaster recovery location doesn't guarantee that this location will be available in the event of an emergency. If a catastrophe that affects an entire region occurs, many other enterprises will want to access the same disaster recovery locations as you. In such a situation, you may have to cope without a recovery location because other enterprises will have booked the location before you.

Sometimes, the equipment in a disaster recovery location or emergency data center is not as efficient as your production system. Therefore, when making plans, bear the following in mind: lower performance and limited transactions. For example, reduce background jobs to only the most urgent jobs. Alternatively, only grant recovery system access to those users who need to perform essential business tasks.

7.6 Recovery Script

A recovery script is a document that contains step-by-step instructions for the following points:

- The procedure for restoring the SAP system
- The individuals responsible for each step
- The estimated time required for lengthy steps
- The interdependencies between steps

A script helps you implement suitable steps for restoring the SAP system and avoids the risk of any steps being omitted. If you inadvertently omit an important step, you may have to start the entire procedure from scratch, thus delaying the system recovery.

To create a recovery script, you need the following:

- A checklist for each step
- A document that contains screenshots that explain the instructions (if required)
- Flow charts if the sequence in which the steps or activities are performed is complex or confusing

If the main person responsible for the recovery is unavailable, a recovery script will help his representative fulfill this task. The script must therefore fully describe all tasks in an easy-to-understand manner.

Important Steps in the Recovery Procedure

If you want to shorten the recovery procedure, you can define a procedure whereby as many tasks as possible are handled concurrently. Provide a schedule for each step.

The most important steps are as follows:

1. During an emergency, you can support the recovery by doing the following:
   - Gather facts.
   - Retrieve the relevant tapes from the remote storage location.

- Have the crash kit ready (see Section 7.7).
- Notify all relevant employees (for example, the in-house SAP team, key users affected by the emergency, infrastructure support, IT, facilities, on-call consultants, and so on).
- Prepare functional organizations (sales, accounting, and shipping) for alternative procedures for important business transactions and procedures.
- Notify non-SAP systems that have interfaces from and to the SAP system about the system failure.

2. Minimize the effects of the failure by implementing the following measures:
   - Stop all additional transactions into the system (for example, interfaces from other systems).
   - Collect transaction documents that will have to be entered again manually.
3. Start the planning process by implementing the following measures:
   - Analyze the problem.
   - Select the scenario plans that best correspond to the emergency that has actually occurred.
   - Change the plans, if necessary.
4. Decide when the disaster recovery procedure will begin:
   - Which criteria formed the basis for determining that an emergency had occurred? Were these criteria satisfied?
   - Who makes the final decision in relation to confirming that an emergency has occurred?
5. Ascertain whether an emergency has occurred.
6. Implement the recovery procedure.
7. Test and approve the restored system. Key users should conduct the relevant tests. Such users use a checklist to clarify whether the system has been restored to a satisfactory level.
8. Update the system with transactions that alternative processes handled during the system failure. As soon as this step is complete, the outcome should be approved again.
9. Notify users that the system is operational again.

10. Arrange a postmortem meeting to ascertain why the disaster occurred.
11. Assess the recovery team's experience of the system recovery and optimize your disaster recovery plans accordingly.

The recovery script must be easily accessible in the event of a disaster. It must not be stored on a server that may no longer be accessible in the event of a network failure. Also bear in mind that a paper copy could be destroyed in a fire. Prepare yourself for such emergency scenarios and store the recovery script redundantly. Make sure that the storage location is widely known and accessible to those individuals responsible for a recovery in the event of an emergency.

Dependency on Other Applications

Your SAP system is usually connected, via interfaces, to other upstream or downstream systems. If the SAP system fails, feeder systems may also come to a standstill because RFCs accumulate en masse and cannot be processed. In addition, downstream systems may not work because your SAP system doesn't make the necessary data available. You can therefore see how easy it is to experience a chain reaction that will have far-reaching consequences for the system landscape and business processes.

In your recovery script, give some thought to communication with those individuals responsible for the applications connected to the SAP system. Make sure that the interfaces are stopped or stop them yourself. Decide how the data will be resynchronized after a system recovery.

7.7 Crash Kit

A *crash kit* contains everything you need to rebuild the SAP server, reinstall the SAP system, and restore the SAP database, including all related files.

You must therefore store everything you need to restore your SAP environment in one or more containers. If your location needs to be evacuated, you will not have any time to gather everything you need at the last minute.

You should therefore check your crash kit regularly and ascertain whether all of the elements are still up-to-date and operational. A service agreement is a good example of a crash kit component that requires such a regular check. If the agreement is no longer valid because its validity period was not extended in time, you may not be able to access the services provided by external providers in an emergency, or you may have to enter into negotiations first.

[!]

Updating the Crash Kit

If a (hardware or software) component on the server is changed, replace the obsolete component in your crash kit with the latest, tested element.

The crash kit should be stored in a room separate from the servers. If the crash kit is stored in the server room, the crash kit will also be affected if servers are lost.

Examples of suitable storage options include the following:

- A commercial data storage location outside the enterprise's location
- Other enterprise locations
- Another secure part of the building

Next, we will name the most important items that should form part of any crash kit. You can add or omit items, depending on your particular environment. The inventory is sorted according to documentation and software.

Documentation

A crash kit must contain the following documentation:

- A disaster recovery script.
- A test and verification script for functional user groups, which is used to ascertain the functionality of the restored system.
- Installation instructions:
  - Operating system
  - Database
  - SAP system
- Special installation instructions for the following:
  - Drivers that must be installed manually
  - Programs that must be installed in a certain way
- Copies of the following:

- SAP licenses for all instances
- Service agreements (with telephone numbers) for all servers

[!]

Checking the Validity of the Service Agreements

Make sure that the service agreements are still valid. You should perform this check regularly.

- Instructions for retrieving tapes from external data stores outside the enterprise's location.
- A list of individuals authorized to retrieve tapes from data stores outside the enterprise's location. This list must correspond to the list available at the external data store.
- A parts list that contains enough information to ensure that new hardware can be purchased or leased if the server is destroyed. After a certain length of time, original parts may no longer be available. You should then draft an alternative parts list. At this time, you should also give some thought to updating your equipment.
- Layout of the file system.
- Layout of the hardware. You must know which card belongs to which slot and which cable belongs where (connector-to-connector). If you label the cables and connectors, you can avoid a lot of confusion.
- Telephone numbers of the following:
  - Key users
  - Information service employees
  - Facilities personnel
  - Other infrastructure personnel
  - Consultants (SAP, network, and so on)
  - SAP hotline
  - Data stores outside the enterprise's location
  - Security department or security employees
  - Contact partners within the framework of service agreements
  - Hardware vendors

Software

The crash kit should contain all of the software components required to completely rebuild a server.

- Operating system:
  - Installation kit
  - Hardware drivers not contained in the installation kit (for example, network cards or SCSI controllers)
  - Service packs, updates, and patches
- Database:
  - Installation kit
  - Service packs, updates, and patches
  - Recovery script for automating a database recovery
- SAP system:
  - New installation kit for the current SAP release (not the upgrade kit)
  - Currently installed kernel
  - System profile files
  - tpparam file
  - saprouttab file
  - saplogon.ini files (for SAP GUI)
- Other programs integrated into the SAP system (for example, a control package)
- Other software for the SAP installation:
  - Auxiliary programs
  - Backup
  - UPS control program
  - Hardware monitor
  - FTP client
  - Remote control program
  - System monitors

[+]

Crash Kit Inventory

The person who seals the crash kit should also compile a signed and dated inventory. If the seal is broken, we must assume that some items have been removed or changed, and, as a result, the kit could be completely useless in an emergency.

7.8 Testing the Disaster Recovery Procedure

By simulating a disaster recovery, you can ensure that your system can actually be restored and that all of the tasks listed in the disaster recovery plan can be executed.

By performing a simulation, you can ascertain whether the following are true:

- Your disaster recovery procedure works.
- Changes have occurred, steps have not been documented, or the necessary updates have not been performed.
- Some steps require an additional explanation.
- Steps that are quite clear to the person writing the documentation are also clear to other individuals.
- Older hardware is no longer available.

If one of these scenarios arises, you must revise your recovery plan. You may also have to upgrade your hardware so that it is compatible with the equipment currently available. Furthermore, you should draft an alternative procedure in response to inconsistencies that previously went unnoticed in an emergency.

Because many factors influence the actual recovery time, it can only be determined through testing. As soon as you have actual time values instead of estimates, your emergency plan will become credible.

If the procedure is practiced on a regular basis, everyone will know what to do in an emergency, thus making it possible to avoid the worst-case scenario.

To test your disaster recovery procedure, follow these steps:

1. Implement your disaster recovery plan in a backup system or at a remote location.

2. Envisage a random emergency scenario.
3. Implement your emergency plan to see if it is effective in such a situation.
4. Perform disaster recovery at the same location where it will occur in the event of an emergency. If you have more than one recovery location, run the tests in each of these locations. The equipment, facilities, and configurations may differ from location to location. Document all of the steps that need to be executed at each location. You are now immune to not being able to restore the system at a certain location in the event of an emergency. Other options for locations where you can test your disaster recovery scenario include the following:
   - A backup server at your location
   - Another enterprise location
   - Another enterprise with which you have a mutual support agreement
   - An enterprise that provides disaster recovery locations and services

During a real disaster recovery, your permanent employees will carry out the relevant tasks. However, you should take precautions in case some of your key employees are unavailable during the disaster recovery. A test procedure can therefore include the random selection of an individual who will not be available and will not participate in the test procedure. This procedure reflects a real situation in which a key employee is absent or has been seriously injured, for example.

Furthermore, employees from other locations should also participate in testing. Integrate these individuals into the tests because you may also require them during a real disaster recovery. These employees can fill the gap arising from unavailable personnel.

At least once a year, you should run through your disaster recovery from start to finish. However, the frequency with which you do this is a commercial decision that should be made while considering the costs involved.

[!]

Maintaining the Production System

Note that, during disaster recovery testing, employees are still needed to maintain the real production system.

7.9 Minimizing the Risk of Failure

There are many ways to minimize the risk of failure. Some of the suggestions listed here may seem obvious. In reality, however, they are frequently ignored.

7.9.1 Minimizing the Risk of Human Error

Many emergencies are triggered by human error (caused, for example, by an exhausted operator). For potentially dangerous tasks (such as deleting the test database, moving a file, or formatting a new drive), a script should be created with a checklist that can be used to verify the individual steps.

Critically Assessing Your Own Capabilities [+]

Do not perform any dangerous tasks if you feel tired. If you nevertheless have to do it, seek a second opinion before you start.

7.9.2 Minimizing Single Points of Failure

A *single point of failure* occurs when the failure of a single component causes the entire system to fail.

You can minimize the risk as follows:

- Ascertain the situations in which a single point of failure can occur.
- Devise a forecast of what happens when this component or process fails.
- Eliminate as many single points of failure as possible.

Single points of failure may include the following:

- The backup SAP server is in the same data center as the production SAP server.
  If the data center is destroyed, the backup server will also be destroyed.
- All SAP servers are connected to the same power supply.
  If the power supply is interrupted, this affects all of the equipment connected to this power supply. In other words, all servers crash.

Cascading Failures

A *cascading failure* occurs if one failure triggers a whole series of failures, thus making the problem even more complex. In this case, the recovery comprises a coordinated solution for numerous problems.

[Ex]

> **Cascading Failure**
>
> The following is an example of a cascading failure:
>
> - A power outage that affects the air-conditioning unit can cause the air-conditioning controls in a server room to fail.
> - If the server room cannot be cooled, the temperature in the room rises above the permissible operating temperature for the equipment.
> - Overheating causes a hardware failure on the server.
> - The hardware failure causes damage to the database.
> - Overheating can also affect numerous other pieces of equipment and systems (for example, network devices, the telephone system, and other servers).

A system recovery after a cascading failure can be complex because, when solving one problem, you may discover other problems or other damaged pieces of equipment. Alternatively, some equipment cannot be tested or repaired until other pieces of equipment become operational again.

In the case of the previous example, a system could monitor the air-conditioning unit or the temperature of the server room and notify the relevant employees when a certain threshold value is exceeded.

7.10 Continuing Business During a System Recovery

During disaster recovery, any affected business processes must continue as soon as possible to avoid or minimize an enterprise's financial losses. Give some thought to which alternative procedures can support key business processes when an SAP system fails, for example:

- Collection of cash
- Order processing
- Product shipping
- Invoice payments

- Payroll
- Alternative locations for continuing business

If there is no alternative process, your business operations will decline or come to a complete standstill, which may result in the following problems:

- Orders cannot be entered.
- Products cannot be shipped.
- Cash cannot be collected.

The following alternative processes are conceivable:

- Manual data entry in paper form (for example, handwritten purchase orders)
- Working on standalone PC systems

Together with your end users, plan how certain business processes can continue to run during a system recovery. Define when or during which expected downtime an alternative process will enter into force. Furthermore, give some thought to how data generated during the emergency process can be transferred to the SAP system after the system recovery.

7.11 Summary

Disaster recovery is a special type of system recovery that requires proper advance preparation. An in-depth concept, the necessary tools, and planned testing on a regular basis will all contribute to helping you prepare for an emergency. This chapter helps you to think of everything you need.

Calculate the costs that your enterprise and systems would incur as a result of a system failure or the losses that would arise if a system were unavailable for a period of one hour. Concrete figures are the easiest way to convince everyone of the need to invest in disaster recovery.

Every SAP system requires a database, which, like the SAP system itself, needs to be managed. In this chapter, we will discuss typical database administration tasks as well as the tools that you can use to perform these tasks on various types of databases.

8 Database Administration

The database is another important component within the SAP system architecture. In addition to the files at the operating system level, the database contains the ABAP programs, system settings, and data required to operate the SAP system.

Depending on the size of your enterprise and the way in which it is organized, database administration is also one of the tasks of the SAP administrator. In this case, you require extensive knowledge of database systems, in general, and knowledge of the database system used for your SAP system, in particular. In some cases, however, database system administration is organizationally separate from SAP Basis maintenance. Then, you only need to have general knowledge of database management, which will form part of the next chapter. Additional literature is available (for example, from SAP PRESS[1] or in publications provided in close cooperation with the respective database management system manufacturer).

Next, we will introduce you to tasks and SAP tools that are relevant to you irrespective of the database used. We will use the database management systems DB2 (IBM), Oracle, Microsoft SQL Server, and MaxDB to highlight differences between database systems. At the end of this chapter, we will explain specific tools and procedures for each database.

1 Faustmann, André; Höding, Michael; Klein, Gunnar; Zimmermann, Ronny, *SAP Database Administration with Oracle* (Boston: SAP PRESS, 2008). Bögelsack, André; Gradl, Stephan; Mayer, Manuel; Krcmar, Helmut, *SAP MaxDB Administration* (Boston: SAP PRESS, 2009).

[+]

Transaction DBACOCKPIT

The functions described in the following sections can also be accessed centrally via the *DBA Cockpit* (Transaction DBACOCKPIT). We will nevertheless describe the transactions individually so that you can decide whether to use the central screen (available via Transaction DBACOCKPIT) or to call each special transaction directly.

Because the DBA Cockpit view may vary depending on the database system, we will not make any general statements in this chapter.

8.1 Planning Database Administration Tasks

In the SAP system, the DBA Planning Calendar (Transaction DB13) is available for planning database administration tasks. The DBA (Database Administration) Planning Calendar is a planning tool for database administration. You can use this calendar to plan periodic recurring database tasks such as the following:

- Archiving log files
- Reorganizing
- Updating statistics
- Backing up the database
- Backing up the database log and transaction log
- Backing up the difference database
- Checking database inconsistencies
- Initializing tapes

Managing and planning tasks from within the SAP system is easier than using the command-line interface because you can manage and plan the tasks comfortably without having to call the tools of the respective database manufacturer. The tasks are automatically executed in the intervals that you define. All you have to do is perform certain preparatory tasks (for example, providing tapes for backup purposes) and check the results.

8.1.1 Planning Database Tasks

In this section, you will learn how to plan new database administration tasks that are to be performed regularly.

1. Enter Transaction "DB13" in the command box, and press the Enter key (or select the menu option Tools • CCMS • DB Administration • Planning Calendar • DB13—Local).
2. The DBA Planning Calendar is displayed. To plan a database administration task, select a date and time in the calendar, and choose Add.

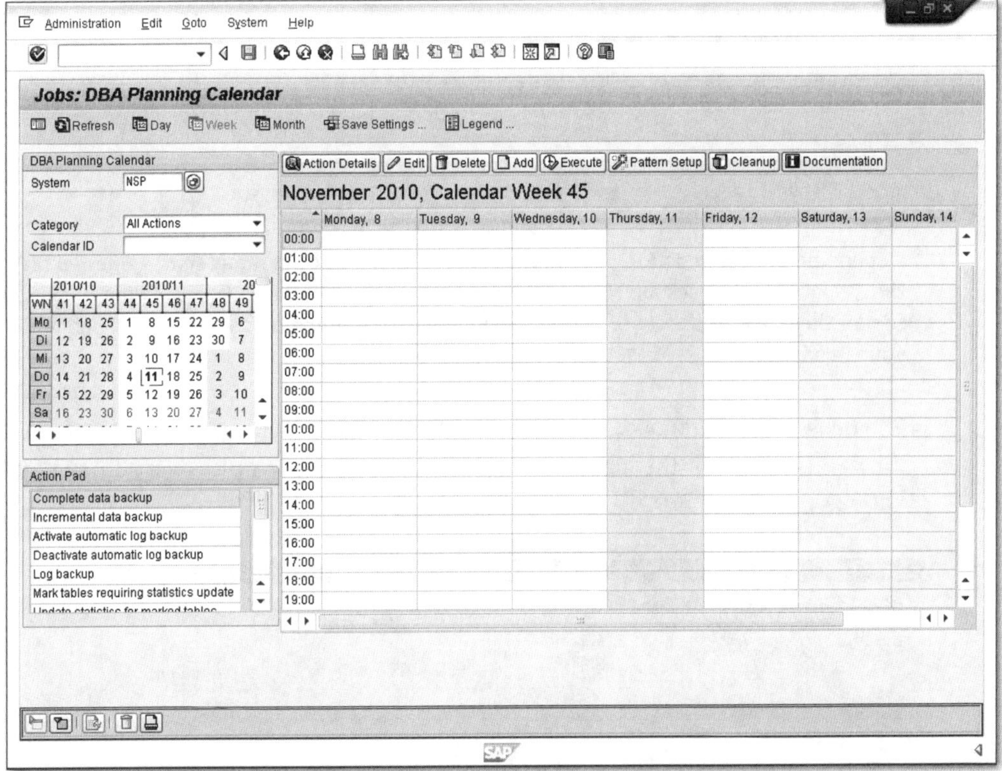

[+] Available Database Activities

The actions available in the Planning Calendar depend on the type of database you have. The jobs offered for a certain database (for example, DB2) differ from those offered for an Oracle database.

3. In the Schedule a New Action dialog box in the Action field, choose the task you require (for example, Check database structure). In the Planned Start fields, enter the start date and start time.

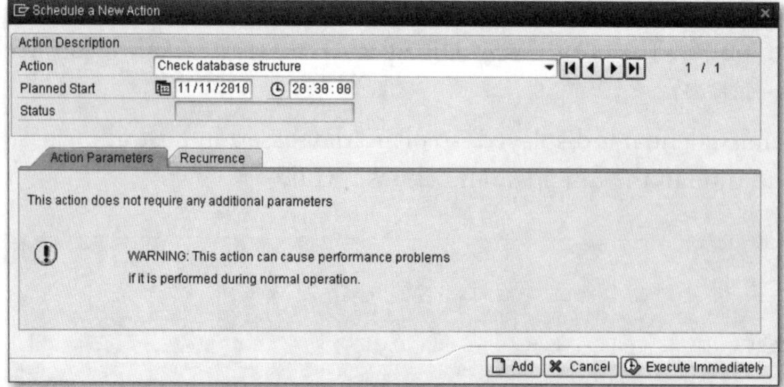

[+]

Action Parameter

Depending on which action you want to schedule, different parameters are queried on the ACTION PARAMETERS tab (for example, the type, name, and properties of your backup tool or the name of the tape). These parameters also depend on the database used and your backup system.

4. Switch to the RECURRENCE tab. In the RECURRENCE PATTERN area, specify the intervals in which the action is to be executed (for example, every three days at 02:00). Choose ADD.

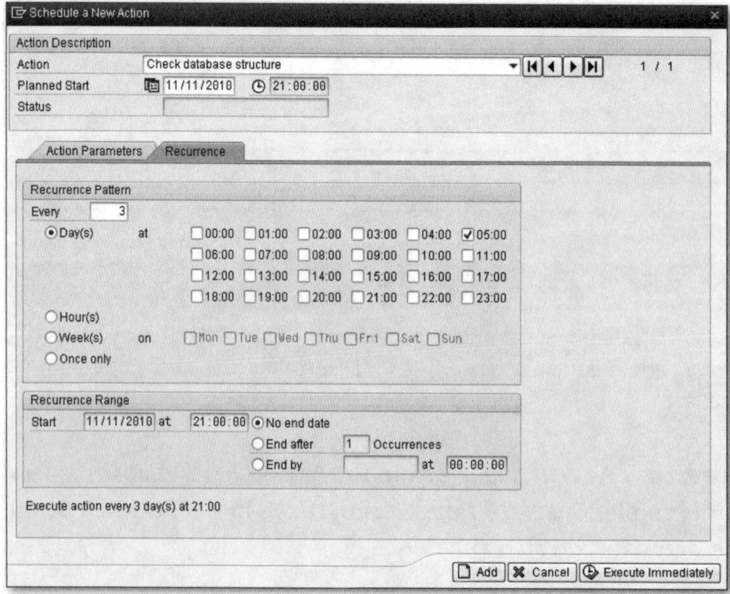

[!]

Checking Storage Capacities for Backups

With the DBA Planning Calendar, you must plan a backup so that it can be fully automated without any additional manual actions. In other words, you don't have to manually change the storage medium (for example, tapes). First, check whether a single tape with sufficient capacity is available or whether several tapes with a combined sufficient capacity are available.

5. In the lower screen area, the system issues a message indicating that the action has been added to the calendar. The scheduled actions are displayed in the weekly view.

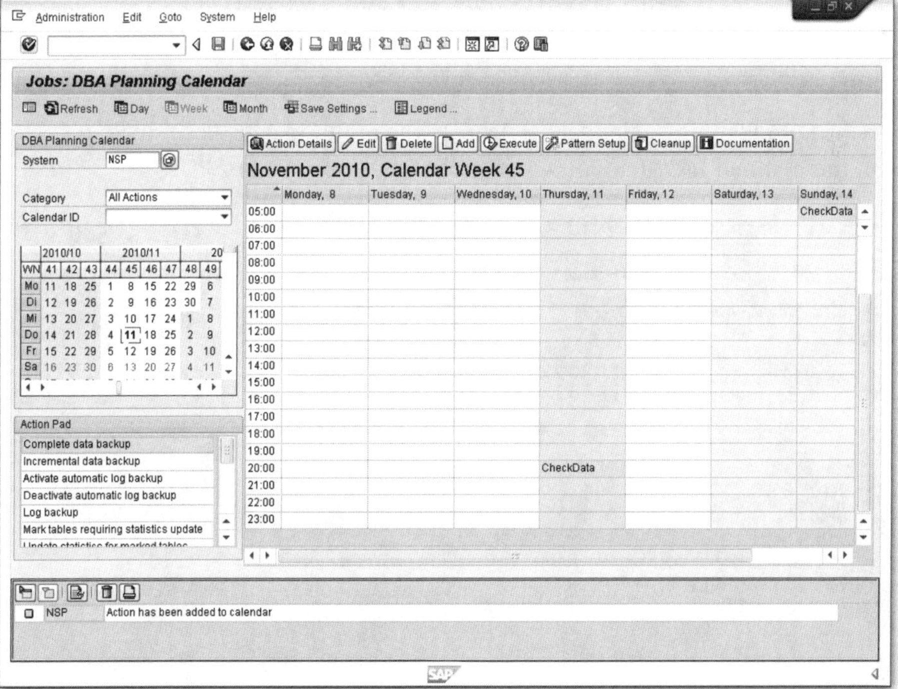

You have now scheduled the database action you require, which will be automatically executed at the defined start time.

[+]

Action Pattern

Action patterns predefined by SAP can make it easier for you to schedule database tasks. Action patterns are a summary of recommended actions and useful intervals. In the DBA Planning Calendar, choose PATTERN SETUP to choose an action pattern for planning regular database actions. You are then guided step by step through the planning process.

8.1.2 Changing and Deleting Database Tasks

You can retroactively edit tasks that haven't been executed yet. You can change the action parameters, or you can delete the tasks from the DBA Planning Calendar.

1. Enter Transaction "DB13" in the command box, and press the Enter key (or select the menu option TOOLS • CCMS • DB ADMINISTRATION • PLANNING CALENDAR • DB13—LOCAL).
2. In the DBA Planning Calendar, navigate to the required date. Position your cursor on the planned task that you want to change. Choose EDIT.

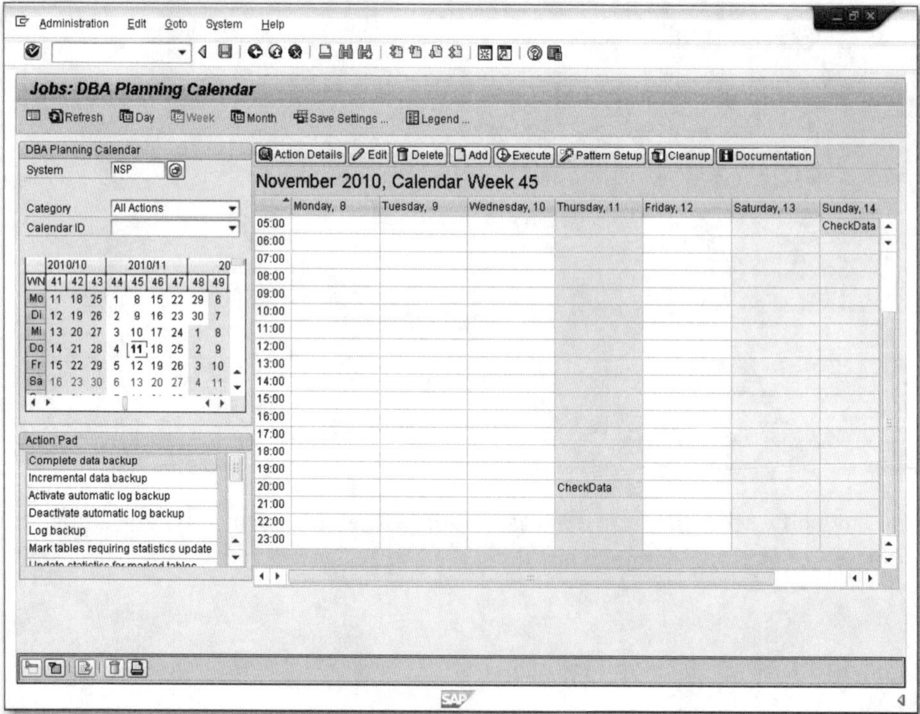

3. You can adjust the action parameters for the task in the EDIT DETAILS OF ACTION dialog box. You can also change recurrence data such as the start date/time and recurrence interval here. If your adjustment applies only to the action on the day selected, choose CHANGE CURRENT OCCURRENCE. If you want the change to apply to all other periodic recurrence dates, choose CHANGE ALL OCCURRENCES.

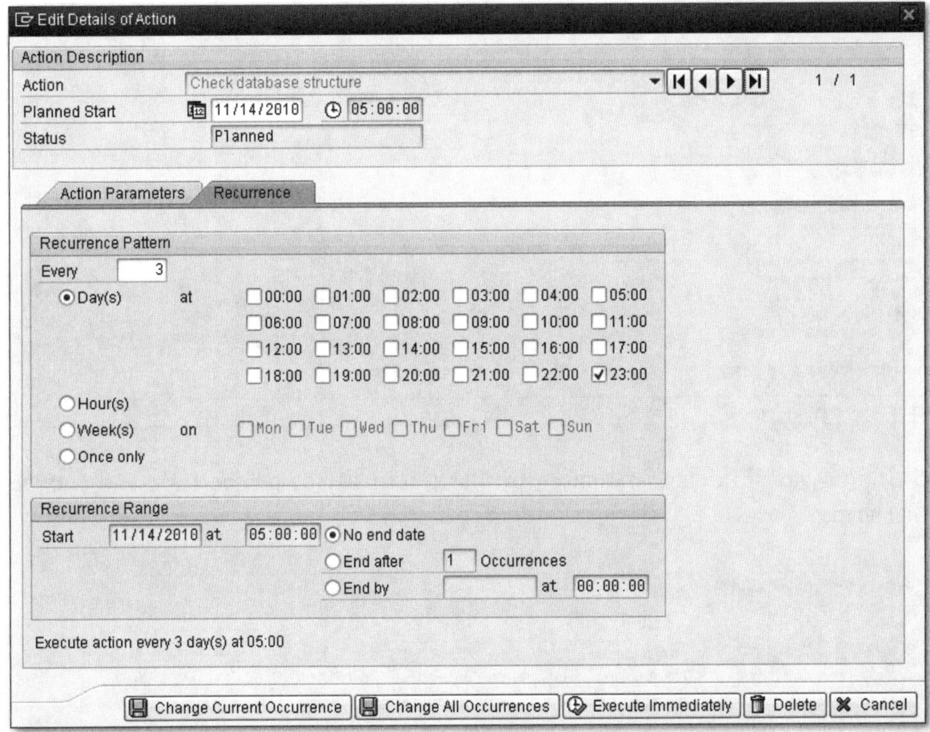

4. The system issues a message indicating that the action has been successfully changed.

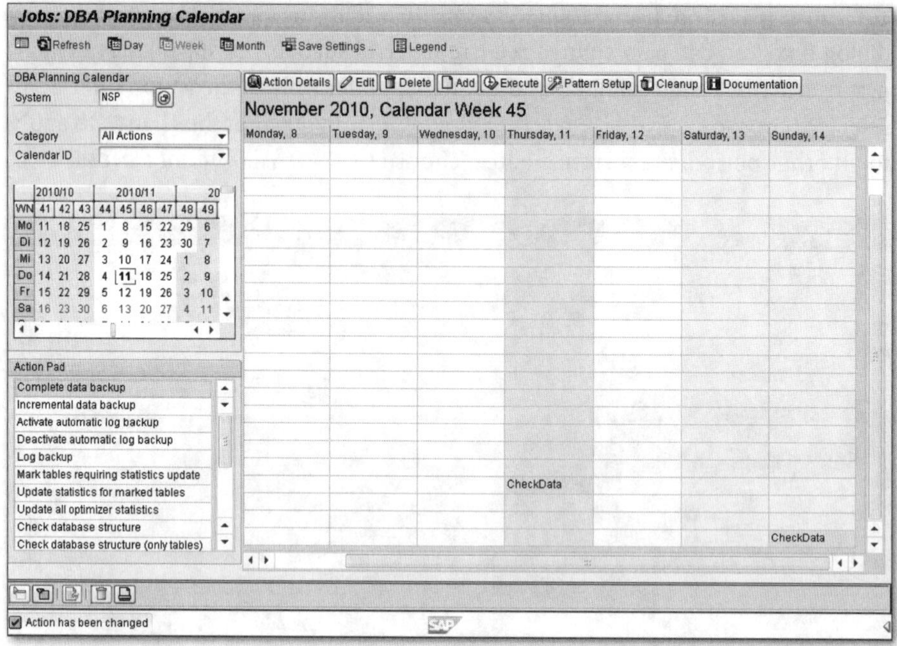

5. If you want to delete an action, position your cursor on the task, and choose DELETE.

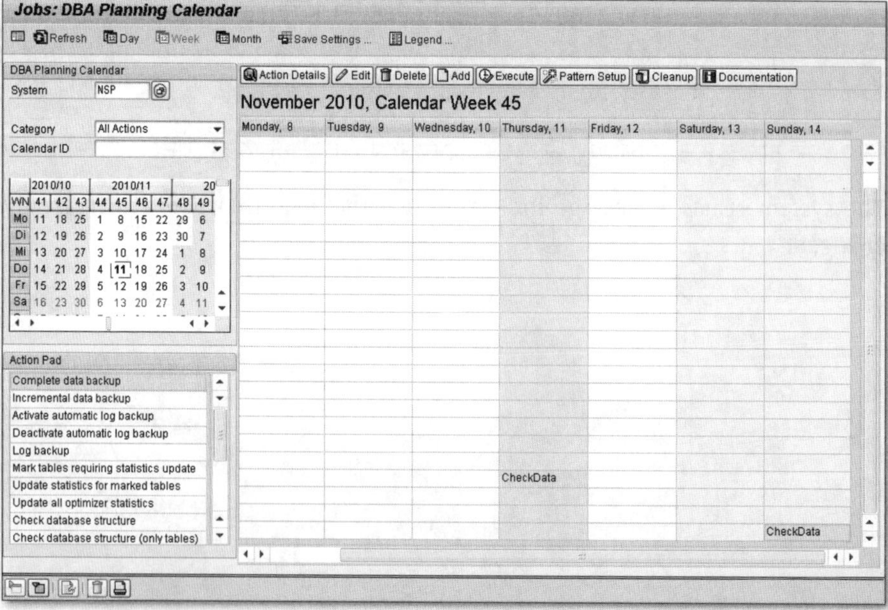

6. For periodically scheduled tasks, the system displays a dialog box in which you must select the execution times to be deleted. Set the check mark, and choose Delete.

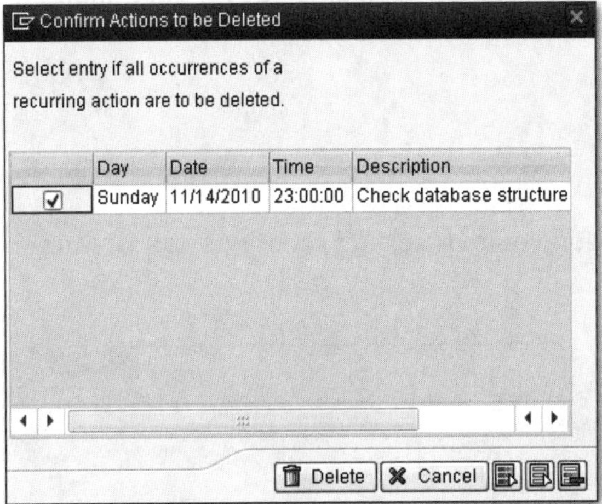

7. A dialog box for one-time planned actions is also displayed. Confirm this by choosing Delete.

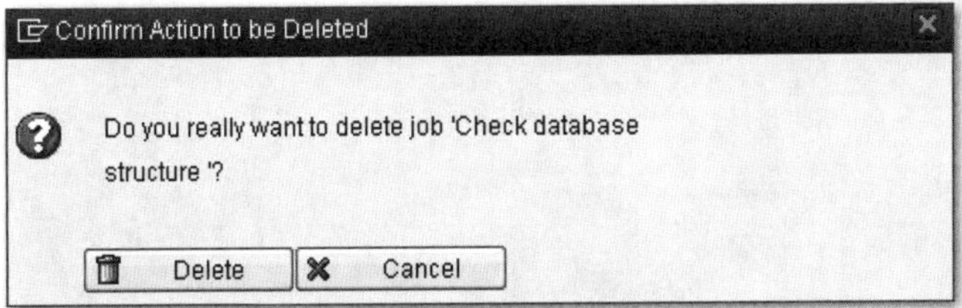

By deleting the action, you remove it from the DBA Planning Calendar and undo the occurrence.

8.1.3 Checking the DBA Planning Calendar

You can also use the DBA Planning Calendar to check the status of a database administration task. For example, you can use the DBA Planning Calendar to check whether or not a task has been successfully performed. To do so, follow these steps:

1. Enter Transaction "DB13" in the command box, and press the Enter key (or select the menu option Tools • CCMS • DB Administration • Planning Calendar • DB13—Local).
2. Check the colors assigned to the tasks in the calendar view. The color indicates the status:
   - **Red:** error
   - **Yellow:** warning
   - **Green/blue:** success
3. Position your cursor on the action you require, and choose Action Details to check the log.

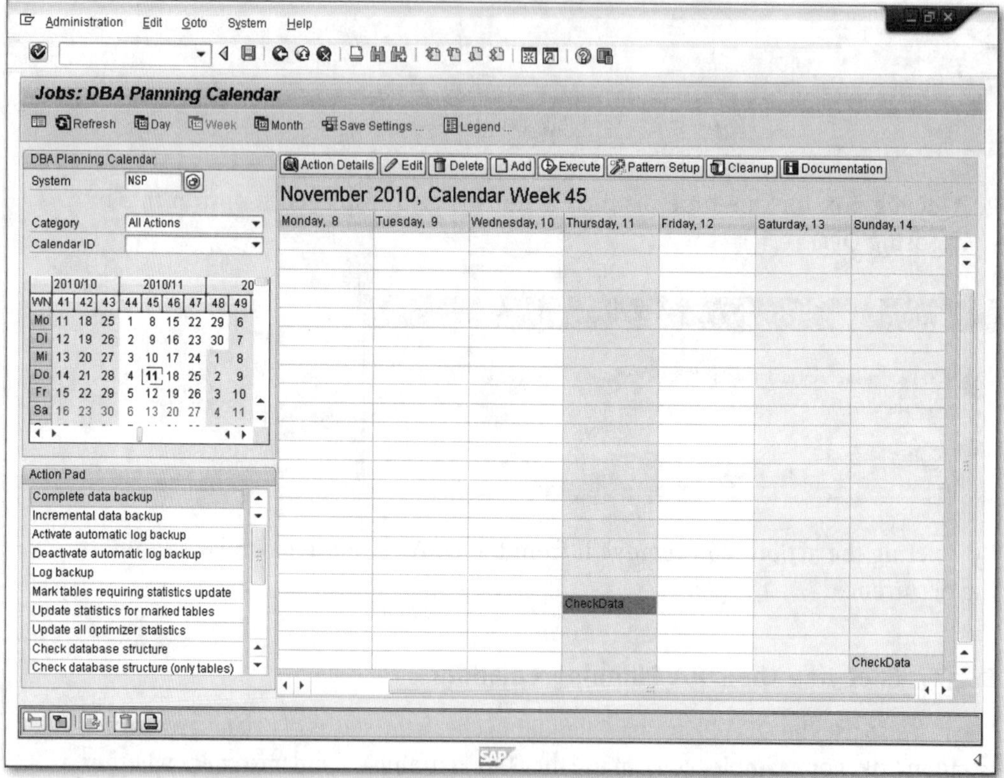

4. In the Display Details of Action window, switch to the Job Log tab.

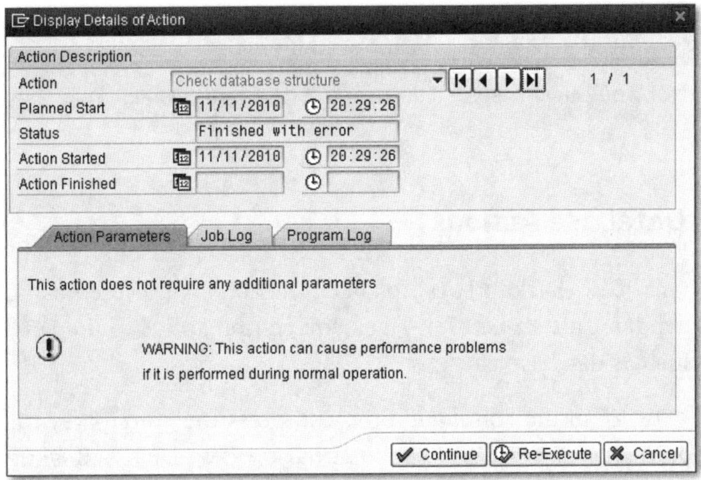

5. Check the job log. Double-click a log entry to display the message long text. To exit the detail view, choose CONTINUE.

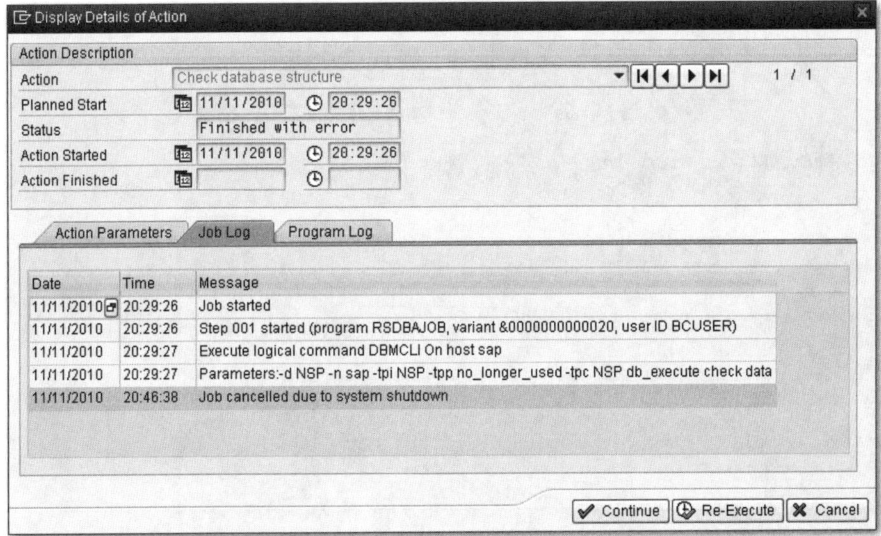

At least once a day (preferably every morning), check whether the database actions, which are usually scheduled for nighttime, have been successfully executed.

[+]

Re-Execute Actions

After eliminating an error, you can choose RE-EXECUTE to restart canceled actions.

8.2 Checking Database Actions

You can use Transaction DB12 (Backup Logs) to check the actions executed using the DBA Planning Calendar. This transaction gives you central access to the DBA action logs for tasks such as database backups.

1. Enter Transaction "DB12" in the command box, and press the Enter key (or select the menu option TOOLS • CCMS • DB ADMINISTRATION • DB12—BACKUP LOGS).
2. On the DBA ACTION LOGS: OVERVIEW screen, choose the DISPLAY LOG button in the DATA BACKUPS area to check the time and content of the last database backup.

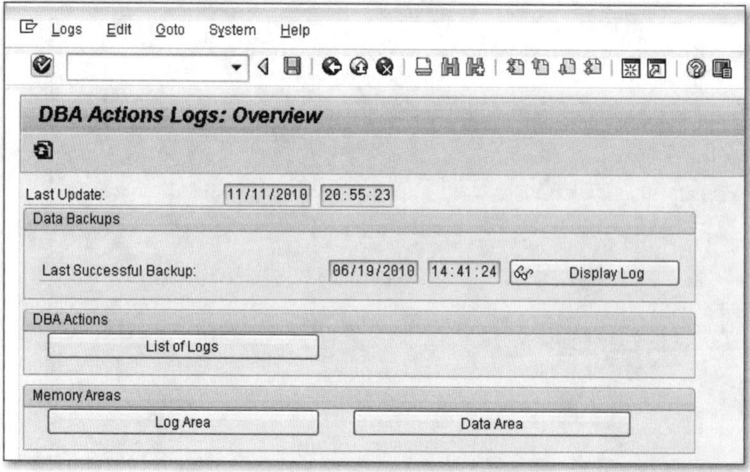

3. The files that have been backed up are listed in the action log. Choose BACK (⊕) to exit the view.

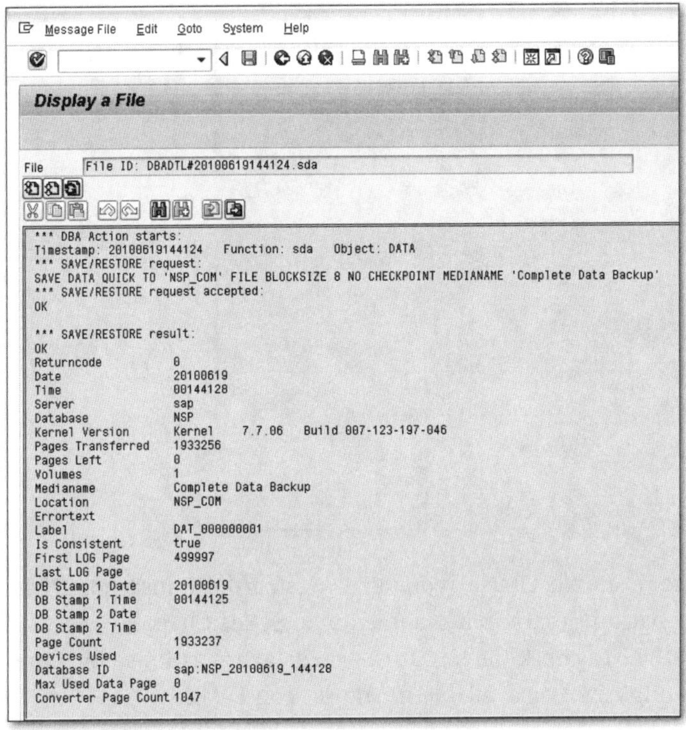

4. On the DBA Action Logs: Overview screen (see step 2), choose List of Logs to navigate to the list of all database actions that have been performed. To call the log for a task, choose Display Log ( ).

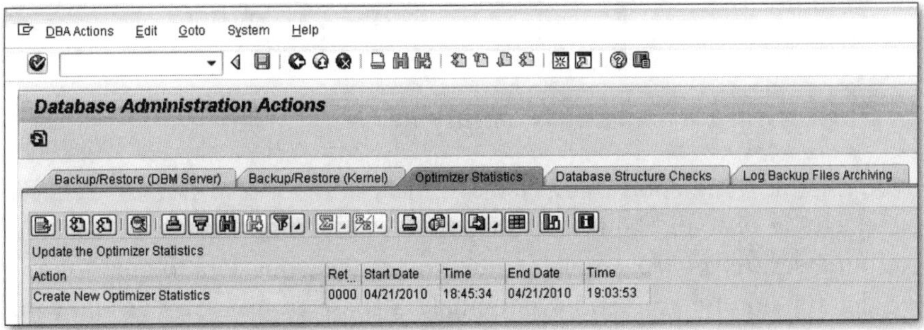

5. For some database types (for example, MaxDB), an overview of the use of memory areas for logs and data are provided in Transaction DB12 (buttons Log Area or Data Area tab on the DBA Action Logs: Overview screen, see step 2).

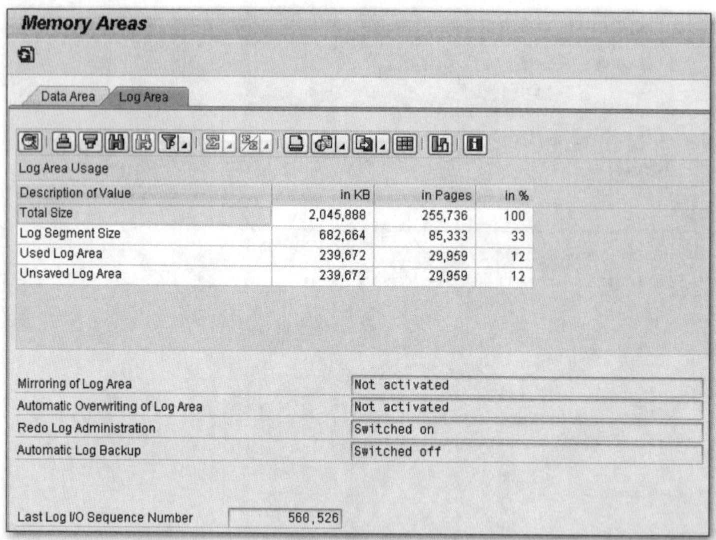

With other databases (for example, Oracle), you can navigate from Transaction DB12 to the logs for redo log backups (backup of transaction logs, see Chapter 6, Section 6.1). Use Transaction DB12 to check the logs for these database actions. For some databases, this option might not be available in Transaction DB12.

[+]

Log File View

This list of logs that can be displayed in Transaction DB12 depends on the type of database used. Consequently, the view in your system may differ from the view shown in these screenshots.

8.3 Performing a Database Analysis

Here, you can use Transaction DB02 (Tables/Indexes) to perform extensive checks on your database system. The results are stored as statistics that can be used for analysis purposes. As an SAP administrator, you can use this data to monitor and analyze the system and to identify potential database problems. The following aspects can be examined:

- Database size and database fill level
- Growth rates
- Tables and indexes

- Objects that occupy a critical amount of storage space
- Consistency of the database, objects, and so on

[+]

Monitoring the Size of the Database

Monitoring the size of the database is an important issue. You can use the growth rate to forecast the rate at which the database will grow and therefore determine when additional storage space will be required on the hard disk.

1. Enter Transaction "DB02" in the command box, and press the [Enter] key (or select the menu option TOOLS • ADMINISTRATION • MONITOR • PERFORMANCE • DATABASE • DB02—TABLES/INDEXES).
2. On the DATABASE ANALYSIS initial screen, the system displays an overview of the most important information about the database:
   - Database name and database server
   - Size and occupancy statistics
   - Number of tables and indexes
   - Consistency of the database

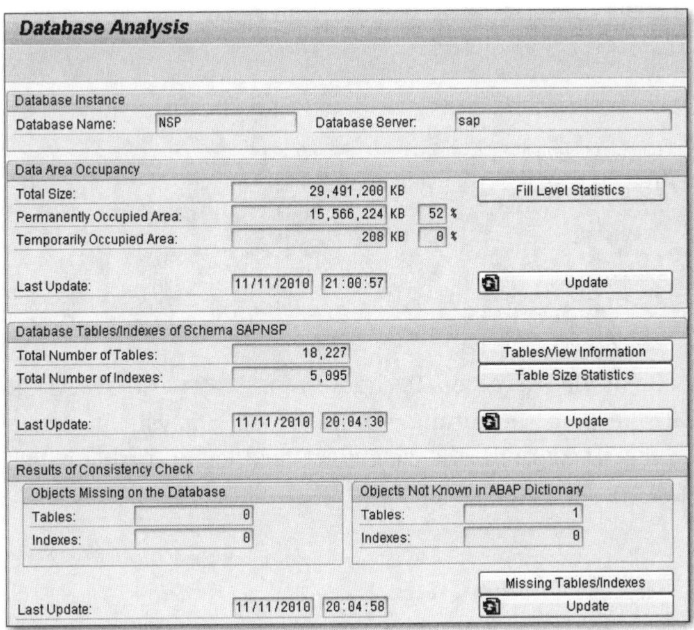

3. Check the date and time of the last update before you call detailed information about individual areas. If the time is too far in the past, choose UPDATE. The system may issue a message indicating that the update may take some time. Choose YES to confirm the dialog box.

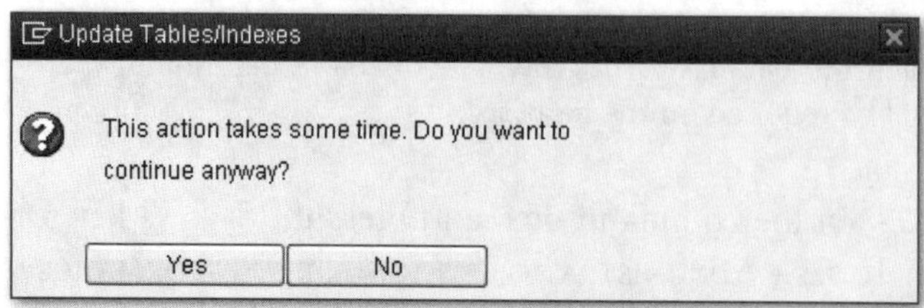

4. Use the buttons in the DATABASE ANALYSIS view (see step 2) to navigate to the detail view for the individual analysis areas (for example, FILL LEVEL STATISTICS). The data are displayed in a new window.

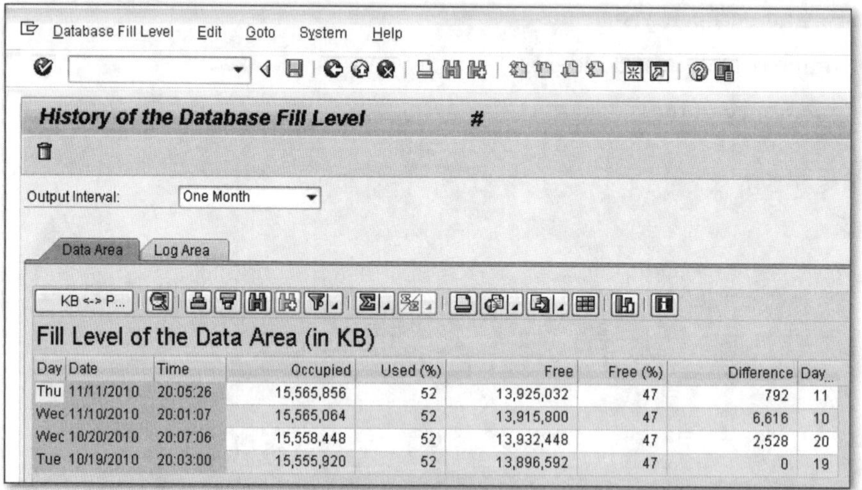

Day	Date	Time	Occupied	Used (%)	Free	Free (%)	Difference	Day...
Thu	11/11/2010	20:05:26	15,565,856	52	13,925,032	47	792	11
Wec	11/10/2010	20:01:07	15,565,064	52	13,915,800	47	6,616	10
Wec	10/20/2010	20:07:06	15,558,448	52	13,932,448	47	2,528	20
Tue	10/19/2010	20:03:00	15,555,920	52	13,896,592	47	0	19

5. In the DATABASE ANALYSIS view (see step 2), choose TABLES/VIEW INFORMATION to access the initial screen for performing an individual analysis of certain database objects. In the NAME OF DATABASE OBJECT field, enter a table name, and choose EXECUTE (⊕).

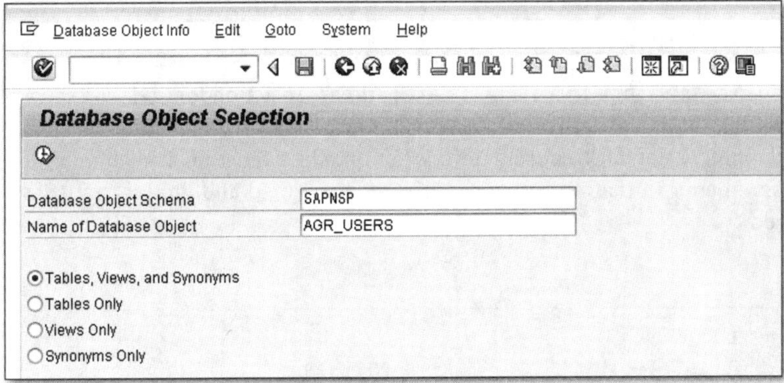

6. In the detail view, you can use the corresponding tabs to retrieve data about the general properties, columns, indexes, statistics, and size of the table.

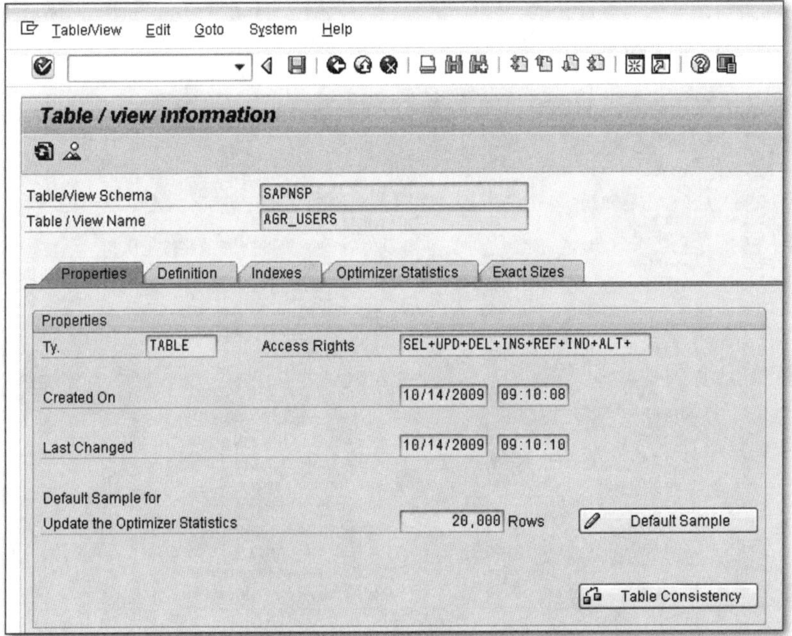

7. In the Database Analysis view (see step 2), choose Table Size Statistics to analyze table growth.

[+]

Table Statistics

If you want to analyze table growth, you must run the database action for updating table statistics on a regular basis so that you can ascertain and cache the table sizes. You can use the DBA Planning Calendar to automate this action. Data must be available for at least two measurements so that a comparison can be performed and growth statistics can be generated.

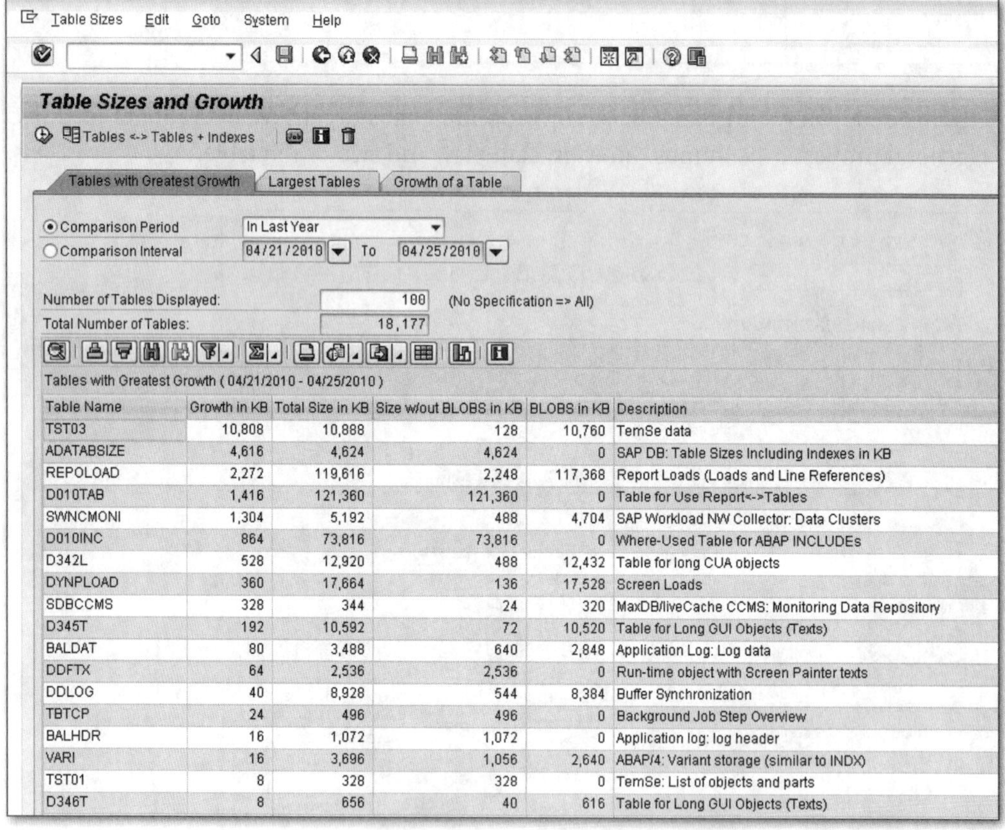

Table Name	Growth in KB	Total Size in KB	Size w/out BLOBS in KB	BLOBS in KB	Description
TST03	10,808	10,888	128	10,760	TemSe data
ADATABSIZE	4,616	4,624	4,624	0	SAP DB: Table Sizes Including Indexes in KB
REPOLOAD	2,272	119,616	2,248	117,368	Report Loads (Loads and Line References)
D010TAB	1,416	121,360	121,360	0	Table for Use Report<->Tables
SWNCMONI	1,304	5,192	488	4,704	SAP Workload NW Collector: Data Clusters
D010INC	864	73,816	73,816	0	Where-Used Table for ABAP INCLUDEs
D342L	528	12,920	488	12,432	Table for long CUA objects
DYNPLOAD	360	17,664	136	17,528	Screen Loads
SDBCCMS	328	344	24	320	MaxDB/liveCache CCMS: Monitoring Data Repository
D345T	192	10,592	72	10,520	Table for Long GUI Objects (Texts)
BALDAT	80	3,488	640	2,848	Application Log: Log data
DDFTX	64	2,536	2,536	0	Run-time object with Screen Painter texts
DDLOG	40	8,928	544	8,384	Buffer Synchronization
TBTCP	24	496	496	0	Background Job Step Overview
BALHDR	16	1,072	1,072	0	Application log: log header
VARI	16	3,696	1,056	2,640	ABAP/4: Variant storage (similar to INDX)
TST01	8	328	328	0	TemSe: List of objects and parts
D346T	8	656	40	616	Table for Long GUI Objects (Texts)

8. On the LARGEST TABLES tab, the database tables are displayed according to size.

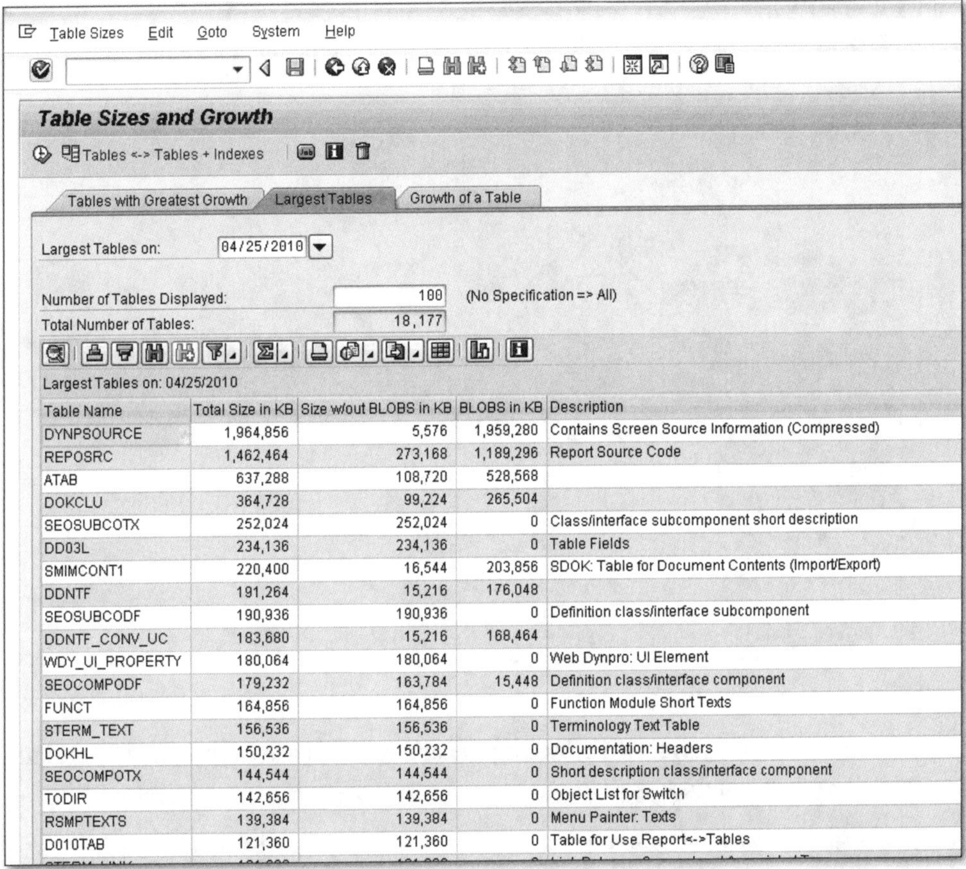

Table Name	Total Size in KB	Size w/out BLOBS in KB	BLOBS in KB	Description
DYNPSOURCE	1,964,856	5,576	1,959,280	Contains Screen Source Information (Compressed)
REPOSRC	1,462,464	273,168	1,189,296	Report Source Code
ATAB	637,288	108,720	528,568	
DOKCLU	364,728	99,224	265,504	
SEOSUBCOTX	252,024	252,024	0	Class/interface subcomponent short description
DD03L	234,136	234,136	0	Table Fields
SMIMCONT1	220,400	16,544	203,856	SDOK: Table for Document Contents (Import/Export)
DDNTF	191,264	15,216	176,048	
SEOSUBCODF	190,936	190,936	0	Definition class/interface subcomponent
DDNTF_CONV_UC	183,680	15,216	168,464	
WDY_UI_PROPERTY	180,064	180,064	0	Web Dynpro: UI Element
SEOCOMPODF	179,232	163,784	15,448	Definition class/interface component
FUNCT	164,856	164,856	0	Function Module Short Texts
STERM_TEXT	156,536	156,536	0	Terminology Text Table
DOKHL	150,232	150,232	0	Documentation: Headers
SEOCOMPOTX	144,544	144,544	0	Short description class/interface component
TODIR	142,656	142,656	0	Object List for Switch
RSMPTEXTS	139,384	139,384	0	Menu Painter: Texts
D010TAB	121,360	121,360	0	Table for Use Report<->Tables

9. In the DATABASE ANALYSIS view (see step 2), choose MISSING TABLES/INDEXES in the RESULTS OF CONSISTENCY CHECK area. On the next detail screen, check the entries relating to incorrect database objects.

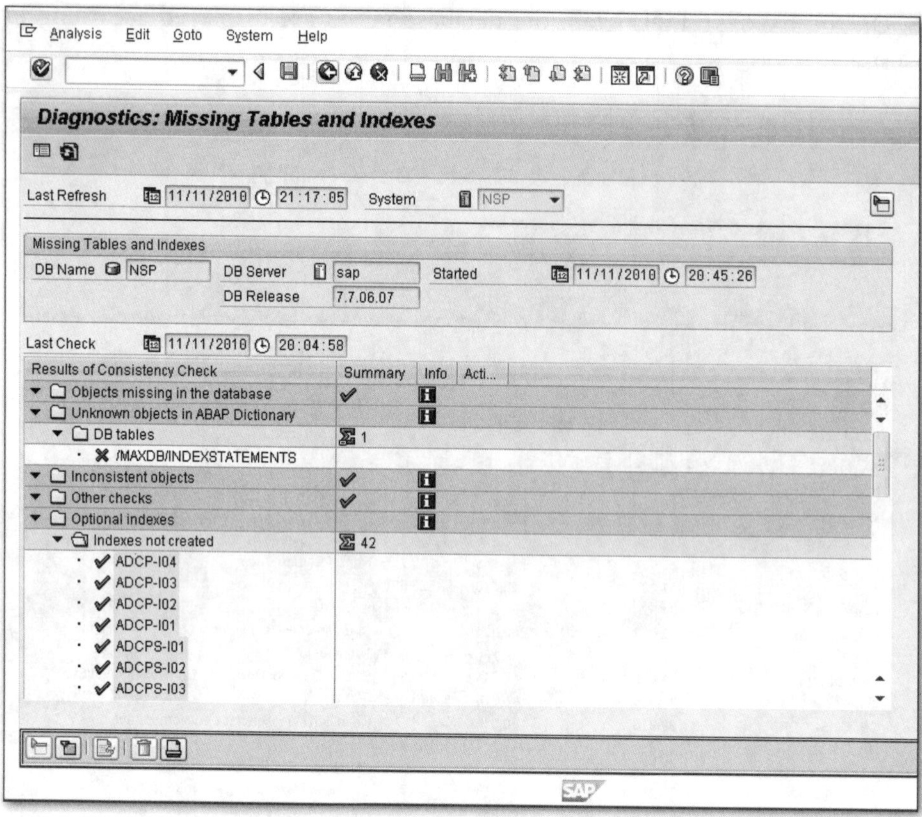

Use the database analysis if you want to examine the space occupied in your database as well as database growth.

[⚙]

Database Objects

Note that Transaction DB12 analyzes database objects from the perspective of the database administrator. This perspective focuses on the consistency of an object within the database.

This perspective may differ significantly from the perspective of a programmer who primarily understands a table or view as part of the ABAP Dictionary. This may lead to misunderstandings.

8.4 Monitoring Database Performance

The *database performance monitor* (Transaction ST04) is a database-independent tool for analyzing and monitoring the performance-relevant parameters of a database management system such as the following:

- Storage use and buffer use
- Storage space occupancy
- CPU usage
- Input/output
- SQL requests
- SQL cache
- Detailed SQL components
- Locks and deadlocks
- Connected applications

The performance monitor is the main entry point for monitoring the database within the SAP system. The performance statistics available can be used to optimize the database. For example, you can also retrieve the database error log without having to explicitly log on to the database.

[+]

View of the Performance Monitor Transaction

The screen layout and the information available in the performance monitor depend on the type of database you have.

To use the performance monitor, follow these steps:

1. Enter Transaction "ST04" in the command box, and press the Enter key (or select the menu option Tools • Administration • Monitor • Performance • Database • ST04—Activity.)
2. In the navigation frame on the left side, choose the path Current Status • Memory Areas, for example, and double-click the Caches entry.

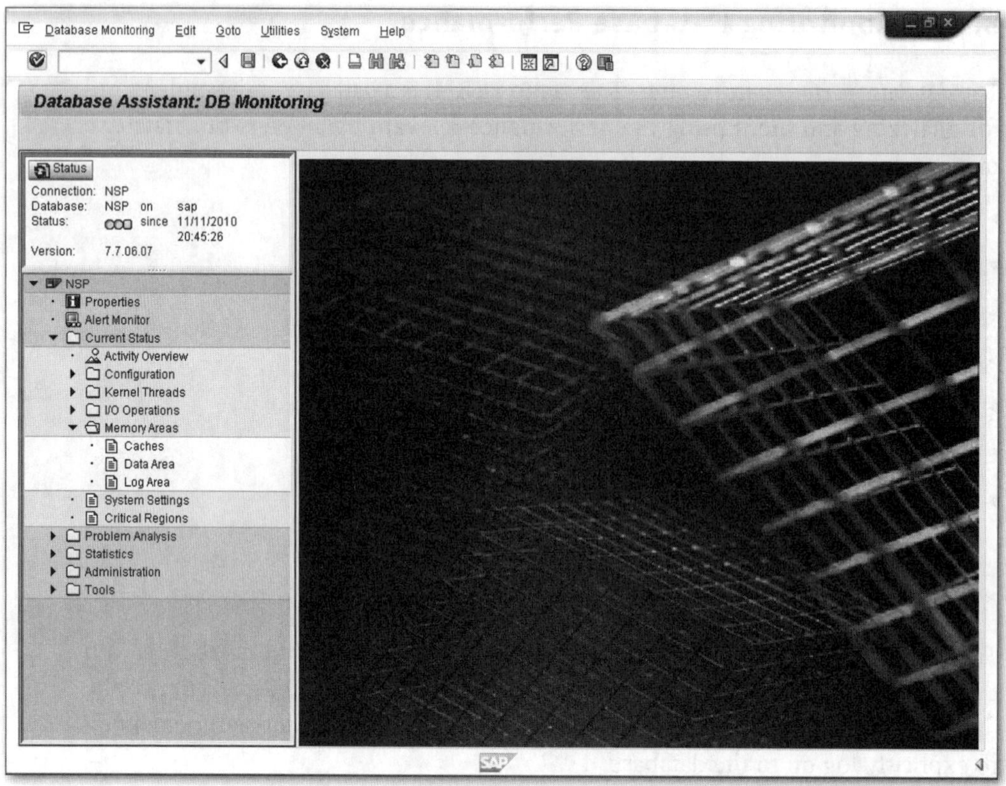

3. On the right side of the screen, the system displays performance information about the database cache. For example, check the Hit Rate information (Cache Accesses table). This figure indicates the number of database accesses that can be performed from a fast cache. A rate of more than 98% is considered to be an excellent value. If the rate is considerably lower, slower memory areas must be used for many requests. This may lead to unsatisfactory performance.

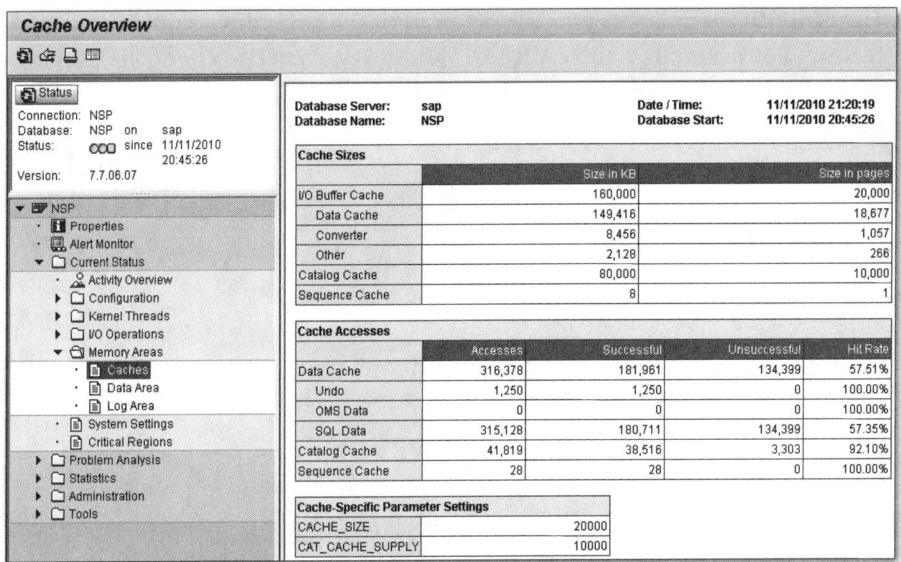

4. The Problem Analysis tree provides functions for examining statuses and bottlenecks in database management or functions for displaying database messages and database logs.

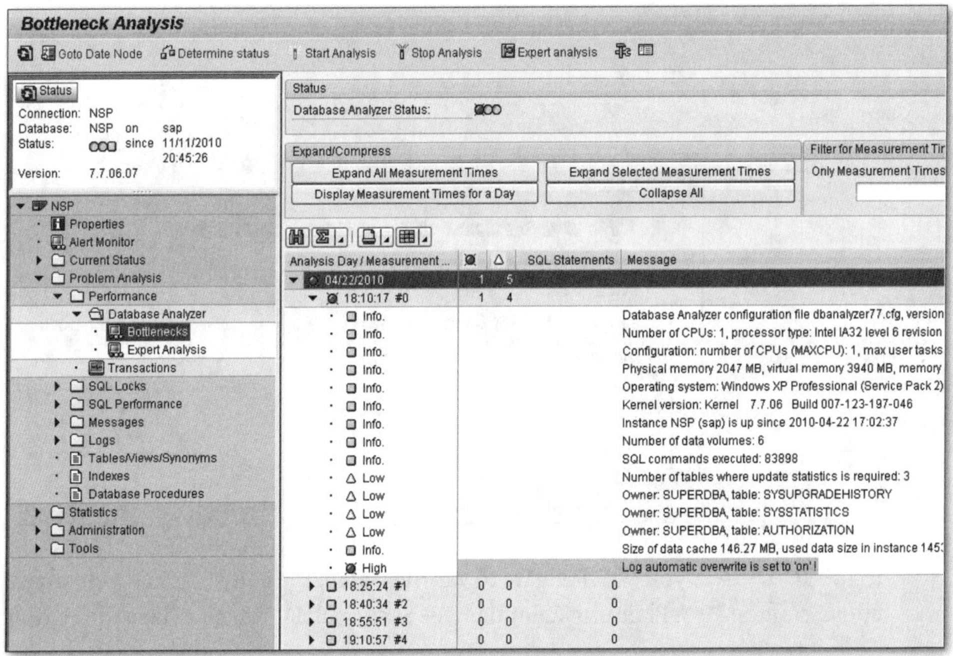

5. The Statistics tree grants you access to various pieces of time-dependent information. For example, double-click Database Fill Level to check the progress of the database fill level.

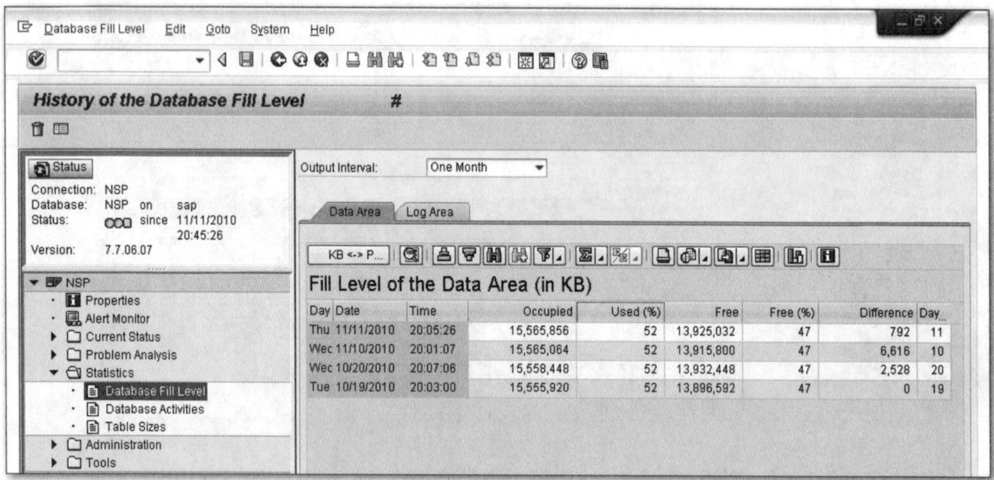

6. If you expand the Administration path, you can edit the database parameters (for example, the size of the database cache) in the Configuration subfolder.

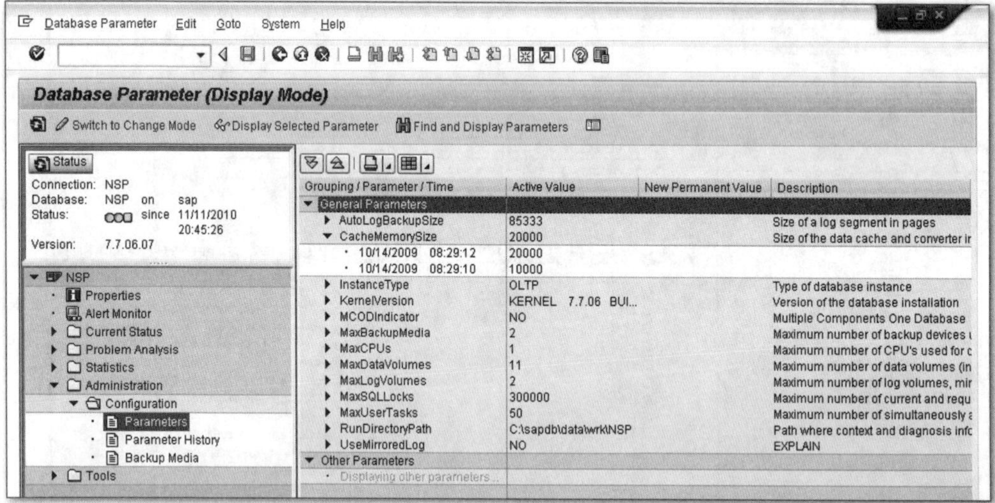

7. In the Tools tree, you can navigate to various database tools such as the database console of the DBA Planning Calendar (see Section 8.1). You also have the option

of activating and analyzing various database traces. You can use traces to perform a detailed analysis of errors and performance problems.

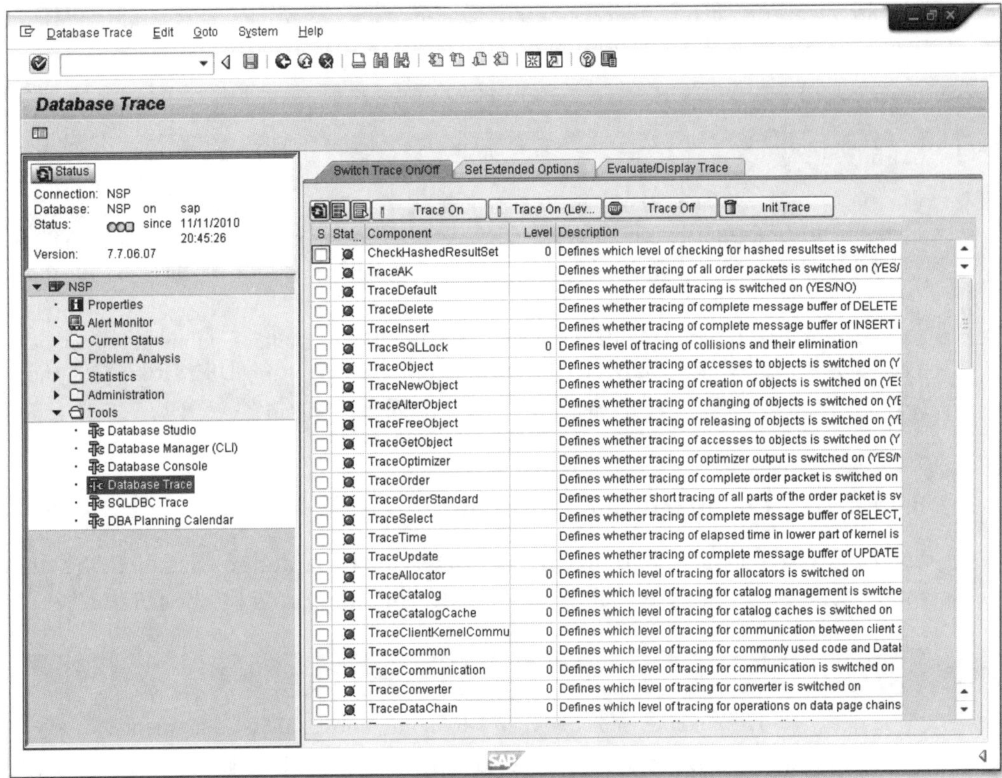

Use the performance monitor to analyze and resolve performance problems in the database. Note that changes to database parameters, and so on, may cause more problems than they resolve. If in doubt, consult with an expert before you make a change.

8.5 Database Administration—DB2

When managing a DB2 database in the SAP environment, two options are available to you: the DB2 Command Line Processor (CLP) is available at operating system level, and the collective Transaction DBACOCKPIT is available in the SAP system.

[+]

DB2 Control Center

IBM also provides a GUI known as the *DB2 Control Center* (DB2CC), which can be used to manage a DB2 database. You can execute this via the command `db2cc`. However, IBM recommends that you no longer use this user interface because it will be omitted from future versions.

[+]

Additional Information

In the SAP environment, the terms *DB2 Common Server (DB2 CS)*, *DB2 Universal Database (DB2 UDB)*, and *DB6* are often used for an IBM DB2 for Linux, Unix, and Windows (DB2 LUW) database. In the SAP environment, the term DB2 describes an IBM DB2 for the operating system z/OS.

Documentation on the DB2 database and the DB2 CLP is available online at *www.ibm.com/software/data/db2/library/*, while documentation on managing DB2 databases in the SAP environment is available in the operations area at *http://help.sap.com/*.

8.5.1 DB2 Command Line Processor

You can use the DB2 CLP to manage your DB2 database and to execute SQL statements. The DB2 CLP is available for all platforms supported by the DB2 LUW.

[+]

SQL Statement and DB2 Command

The DB2 database distinguishes between DB2 commands and SQL statements:

- An *SQL statement* is a logged database operation that can be restored. For example, you can use the SQL statement `db2 alter tablespace` to change the structure of the database. These changes are applied again when you restore the database.
- A *DB2 command*, on the other hand, is analyzed by the DB2 instance, for example.

You can use the DB2 CLP to perform the following tasks, among other things:

- Starting and stopping the database
- Executing SQL statements
- Checking and updating the Database Manager configuration
- Checking and updating the database configuration
- Managing tablespaces and the associated containers

- Backing up the database
- Restoring the database

Checking the Database

You could also check the database, for example. However, SAP recommends that you perform this check within the SAP system (see Section 8.3).

For most of these tasks, you require a connection to the DB2 database. The DB2 CLP uses the command `connect to <dbname>` to establish this connection.

Additional Information About a Command

If you require additional information about a command, you can use the question mark (?). For example, you can use the command `db2 "?" backup` to display all options relating to the DB2 backup command.

Establishing a Connection to the DB2 Database

The DB2 CLP can be used in two variants. You can start the DB2 CLP directly (by entering the command `db2` and then working in its environment), or you can control the DB2 CLP in the command-line environment in your operating system.

If you want to work in the DB2 CLP environment, follow these steps:

1. Log on as *<dbname>adm* (for example, `su - t01adm`).
2. Enter the command `db2`.

```
f06:t01adm 2> db2
(c) Copyright IBM Corporation 1993,2007
Command Line Processor for DB2 Client 9.7.0

You can issue database manager commands and SQL statements from the command
prompt. For example:
    db2 => connect to sample
    db2 => bind sample.bnd

For general help, type: ?.
For command help, type: ? command, where command can be
the first few keywords of a database manager command. For example:
 ? CATALOG DATABASE for help on the CATALOG DATABASE command
 ? CATALOG          for help on all of the CATALOG commands.

To exit db2 interactive mode, type QUIT at the command prompt. Outside
interactive mode, all commands must be prefixed with 'db2'.
To list the current command option settings, type LIST COMMAND OPTIONS.

For more detailed help, refer to the Online Reference Manual.

db2 =>
```

3. Use the command connect to <dbname> (for example, connect to t01) to establish a connection to the database.

```
db2 => connect to t01

   Database Connection Information

 Database server        = DB2/HPUX-IA64 9.7.0
 SQL authorization ID   = T01ADM
 Local database alias   = T01

db2 =>
```

You have now established a connection to the database and can use the DB2 CLP for administration purposes.

However, if you want to work with the command line in your operating system, proceed as follows:

1. Log on as *<dbname>adm* (for example, su - t01adm).
2. Enter the command db2 connect to <dbname> (for example, db2 connect to t01).

```
f06:t01adm 5> db2 connect to t01

   Database Connection Information

 Database server        = DB2/HPUX-IA64 9.7.0
 SQL authorization ID   = T01ADM
 Local database alias   = T01

f06:t01adm 6>
```

[+]

The Command "db2"

Note that, in this case, the command db2 must precede all other DB2 commands and SQL statements.

If you want to log off from your DB2 database, you can do this using the command disconnect <dbname> (for example, disconnect to t01).

```
db2 => disconnect t01
DB20000I  The SQL DISCONNECT command completed successfully.
db2 =>
```

If you want to disconnect all active connections to the DB2 database, you can do this using the command force application all.

```
db2 => force application all
DB20000I  The FORCE APPLICATION command completed successfully.
DB21024I  This command is asynchronous and may not be effective immediately.
```

After you have established a connection to the database, you can use additional commands or statements to work with the database.

8.5.2 Starting and Stopping the Database

There are two ways to start a DB2 database in the SAP environment:

- Using the programs and tools delivered with the DB2 installation
- Using the following command provided by SAP: `startdb`

Starting the Database

To start the DB2 database using standard means, follow these steps:

1. Log on to the server as the user *<dbname>adm* (for example, using the command `su - t01adm`).
2. Enter the command `db2start` to start the DB2 instance.
3. Activate the DB2 database *<dbname>* (for example, using the command `db2 activate db t01`).

```
db2 => force application all
DB20000I  The FORCE APPLICATION command completed successfully.
DB21024I  This command is asynchronous and may not be effective immediately.
```

If you want to use the command `startdb` to start the database, follow these steps:

1. Log on to the server as the user *<dbname>adm* (for example, using the command `su - t01adm`).
2. Enter the command `startdb`, and press the Enter key.

```
f06:t01adm 9> startdb
07/01/2010 19:53:26     0   0   SQL1063N  DB2START processing was successful.
SQL1063N  DB2START processing was successful.
Database activated
```

The database is started.

Stopping the Database

Similar to starting the DB2 database, there are also two ways to stop the database. To stop the DB2 database using standard means, follow these steps:

1. Log on to the server as the user *<dbname>adm* (for example, su - t01adm).
2. Deactivate the DB2 database *<dbname>* (for example, db2 deactivate db t01).
3. Enter the command db2stop to stop the DB2 instance.

```
f06:t01adm 12> db2 deactivate db t01
DB20000I  The DEACTIVATE DATABASE command completed successfully.
f06:t01adm 13> db2stop
07/01/2010 19:55:49     0   0   SQL1064N  DB2STOP processing was successful.
SQL1064N  DB2STOP processing was successful.
```

If you want to use the command stopdb to stop the database, follow these steps:

1. Log on to the server as the user *<dbname>adm* (for example, using the command su - t01adm).
2. Enter the command stopdb, and press the Enter key.

```
f06:t01adm 17> stopdb
Database is running
Continue with stop procedure
DB20000I  The DEACTIVATE DATABASE command completed successfully.
07/01/2010 19:57:38     0   0   SQL1064N  DB2STOP processing was successful.
SQL1064N  DB2STOP processing was successful.
Database sucessfully stopped
```

The database is stopped.

8.5.3 Executing SQL Statements

You can use the DB2 CLP to execute SQL statements in your DB2 database. If, for example, you want to display all of the clients in your SAP system, follow these steps:

1. Log on as *<dbname>adm* (for example, su - t01adm).
2. Enter the command db2.
3. Establish a connection to the DB2 database (for example, connect to t01).
4. Enter the command select mandt from sap<sapsid>.t000 (for example, select mandt from sapt01.t000).

```
db2 => select mandt from sapt01.t000

MANDT
---------
000
001
066
```

[!]

Take Care When Executing SQL Statements

Take due care and consideration when executing SQL statements. You have full access to the data in the SAP system and can manipulate this data beyond the SAP transaction logic. However, this may lead to inconsistencies in the SAP system.

8.5.4 Updating and Checking the Database Manager Configuration

The settings for a DB2 instance are managed in the Database Manager configuration. Any changes to these settings affect the DB2 instance in question as well as the DB2 databases running in the DB2 instance.

To display the current Database Manager configuration, follow these steps:

1. Log on as the user *db2<dbname>* (for example, using the command `su-db2t01`).
2. Enter the command `db2`.
3. Enter the command `get database manager configuration`.

```
db2 => get dbm cfg

         Database Manager Configuration

    Node type = Enterprise Server Edition with local and remote clients

 Database manager configuration release level            = 0x0d00

 CPU speed (millisec/instruction)             (CPUSPEED) = 2.361721e-07
 Communications bandwidth (MB/sec)      (COMM_BANDWIDTH) = 1.000000e+02

 Max number of concurrently active databases     (NUMDB) = 8
 Federated Database System Support           (FEDERATED) = NO
 Transaction processor monitor name        (TP_MON_NAME) =

 Default charge-back account           (DFT_ACCOUNT_STR) =

 Java Development Kit installation path       (JDK_PATH) = /db2/db2t01/sqllib/ja
va/jdk64

 Diagnostic error capture level              (DIAGLEVEL) = 3
 Notify Level                              (NOTIFYLEVEL) = 3
 Diagnostic data directory path               (DIAGPATH) = /db2/T01/db2dump
 Size of rotating db2diag & notify logs (MB)  (DIAGSIZE) = 0
```

[+]

Short Forms for Keywords

The DB2 CLP environment facilitates the use of short forms for some keywords. Therefore, you can also use the command get dbm cfg to determine the configuration.

To obtain a detailed display for the configuration, follow these steps:

1. Log on as db2<*dbname*> (for example, su - db2t01).
2. Enter the command db2.
3. Enter the command db2 attach to db2<dbname> (for example, db2 attach to db2t01).

```
db2 => attach to db2t01

   Instance Attachment Information

 Instance server          = DB2/HPUX-IA64 9.7.0
 Authorization ID         = T01ADM
 Local instance alias     = DB2T01
```

4. Enter the command get dbm cfg show detail.

```
db2 => get dbm cfg show detail

          Database Manager Configuration

     Node type = Enterprise Server Edition with local and remote clients

 Description                                      Parameter   Current Value
      Delayed Value
--------------------------------------------------------------------------------
--------------------------------
 Database manager configuration release level                 = 0x0d00

 CPU speed (millisec/instruction)                 (CPUSPEED) = 2.361721e-07
      2.361721e-07
 Communications bandwidth (MB/sec)          (COMM_BANDWIDTH) = 1.000000e+02
      1.000000e+02

 Max number of concurrently active databases         (NUMDB) = 8
      8
 Federated Database System Support               (FEDERATED) = NO
      NO
 Transaction processor monitor name            (TP_MON_NAME) =
```

If you want to change one or more values in the Database Manager configuration, you can do this using the command update dbm cfg using <parameter> <value>. However, note that you must be logged on as *db2<dbname>*.

If, for example, you want to change the maximum number of databases active at the same time to the value 2, follow these steps:

1. Log on as db2<*dbname*> (for example, `su - db2t01`).
2. Enter the command `db2`.
3. Enter the command `update dbm cfg using numdb 2`.

```
f06:db2t01 1> db2
db2 => update dbm cfg using numdb 2
DB20000I  The UPDATE DATABASE MANAGER CONFIGURATION command completed
successfuly.
```

8.5.5 Updating and Checking the Database Configuration

The settings for a DB2 database are managed in the database configuration. Any changes to these settings only affect the DB2 database in question.

If you want to display the current configuration, follow these steps:

1. Log on as *<dbname>adm* (for example, `su - t01adm`).
2. Enter the command `db2`.
3. Establish a connection to the DB2 database (for example, `connect to t01`).
4. Enter the command `get db cfg`.

```
db2 => get db cfg

       Database Configuration for Database

 Database configuration release level                    = 0x0d00
 Database release level                                  = 0x0d00

 Database territory                                      = en_US
 Database code page                                      = 1208
 Database code set                                       = UTF-8
 Database country/region code                            = 1
 Database collating sequence                             = IDENTITY_16BIT
 Alternate collating sequence              (ALT_COLLATE) =
 Number compatibility                                    = OFF
 Varchar2 compatibility                                  = OFF
 Date compatibility                                      = OFF
 Database page size                                      = 16384

 Dynamic SQL Query management           (DYN_QUERY_MGMT) = DISABLE

 Statement concentrator                      (STMT_CONC) = OFF

 Discovery support for this database       (DISCOVER_DB) = ENABLE
```

[+]

"for <dbname>" Addition

If you are not connected to the database, you must specify the addition `for <dbname>` (for example, `get db cfg for t01`).

If you want to change one or more values in the database configuration, you can do this using the command `update db cfg using <parameter> <value>`. However, note that you must be connected to the database.

If, for example, you want to change the path for the log files, follow these steps:

1. Log on as *<dbname>adm* (for example, `su - t01adm`).
2. Enter the command `db2`.
3. Establish a connection to the DB2 database (for example, `connect to t01`).
4. Enter the command `update db cfg using newlogpath /db2/T01/log_dir`.

```
db2 => update db cfg using newlogpath /db2/T01/log_dir
DB20000I  The UPDATE DATABASE CONFIGURATION command completed successfully.
SQL1363W  One or more of the parameters submitted for immediate modification
were not changed dynamically. For these configuration parameters, all
applications must disconnect from this database before the changes become
effective.
```

[+]

Implementing Changes

If possible, changes to the Database Manager configuration and database configuration are implemented immediately. If you don't want this to happen, simply add the keyword `deferred` to the `UPDATE` commands. However, you must then restart the DB2 instance or DB2 database for the changes to take effect. This is necessary for parameters such as `newlogpath`.

In the DB2 Profile Registry, you can use the tool `db2set` to make additional settings for your DB2 instance or DB2 database. You can use the command `db2set -all` to obtain a list of all possible parameters. To change a setting, execute the command `db2set <parameter>=<value>` (for example, `db2set DB2COMM=TCPIP`). Note that you have to restart the DB2 instance after making changes to the settings.

8.5.6 Managing Tablespaces and Associated Containers

The DB2 database supports three different storage administration options:

- Manual storage administration
- Semi-automatic storage administration
- Fully automatic storage administration

In the case of *manual storage administration*, you must provide the database space required by the SAP system. You must therefore make sure to create the containers required for a tablespace and to extend these, if necessary.

If you want to create a new container for an existing tablespace, you can use the command alter tablespace <tablespace name> add (file '<path>' <no. of pages>). If, for example, you want to create another container with 2,000 pages for the tablespace STABD, follow these steps:

1. Log on as *<dbname>adm* (for example, su - t01adm).
2. Enter the command db2.
3. Establish a connection to the DB2 database (for example, connect to t01).
4. Enter the command alter tablespace T01#STABD add (file '/db2/T01/sapdata3/NODE0000/T01#STABD.container003' 2000).

```
db2 => alter tablespace T01#STABD add (file '/db2/T01/sapdata3/NODE0000/T01#STA
BD.container003' 2000)
DB20000I  The SQL command completed successfully.
```

Rebalancing When Creating a New Container [+]

Note that rebalancing occurs when you create a new container. Such rebalancing temporarily impairs performance.

If you want to extend the containers for an existing tablespace, you can use the command alter <tablespace name> extend (all <no. of additional pages>). If, for example, you want to extend all containers by 200 pages for the tablespace STABD, follow these steps:

1. Log on as *<dbname>adm* (for example, using the command su - t01adm).
2. Enter the command db2.
3. Establish a connection to the DB2 database (for example, connect to t01).
4. Enter the command alter tablespace T01#STABD extend (all 200).

```
db2 => alter tablespace T01#STABD extend (all 200)
DB20000I  The SQL command completed successfully.
```

[+]

Exception: No Rebalancing

Because all containers are extended at the same time, no rebalancing occurs here.

In the case of *semi-automatic storage administration*, you must create the containers required for a tablespace (similar to manual storage administration). However, the DB2 database automatically adjusts the size of containers, as required, in the areas that you have defined. This type of storage administration is also known as *autoresize*.

If you want to activate semi-automatic storage administration, you can use the command alter tablespace <tablespace name> autoresize yes increasesize <additional size> maxsize <maximum size>. If, for example, you want to activate autoresize for the tablespace STABD so that the containers are always extended by 200 MB until the tablespace has reached a maximum size of 20 GB, follow these steps:

1. Log on as *<dbname>adm* (for example, su - t01adm).
2. Enter the command db2.
3. Establish a connection to the DB2 database (for example, connect to t01).
4. Enter the command alter tablespace T01#STABD autoresize yes increasesize 200M maxsize 20G.

```
db2 => alter tablespace T01#STABD autoresize yes increasesize 200M maxsize 20G
DB20000I  The SQL command completed successfully.
```

If you want to deactivate semi-automatic storage administration, you can use the command alter tablespace <tablespace name> autoresize no. If, for example, you want to deactivate autoresize for the tablespace STABD, follow these steps:

1. Log on as *<dbname>adm* (for example, su - t01adm).
2. Enter the command db2.
3. Establish a connection to the DB2 database (for example, connect to t01).
4. Enter the command alter tablespace T01#STABD autoresize no.

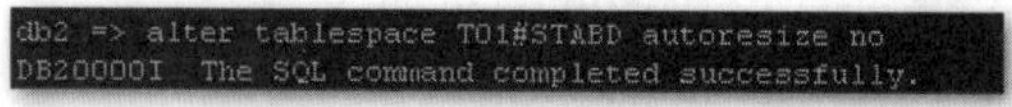
db2 => alter tablespace T01#STABD autoresize no
DB20000I The SQL command completed successfully.

In the case of *fully-automatic storage administration*, you must only provide the paths in which the DB2 database can work. The DB2 database then fully automates the creation and extension of the necessary containers. This type of storage administration is also known as *autostorage*.

[!]

Autostorage Can No Longer Be Deactivated

Autostorage must be activated when you create the relevant tablespace. Unlike autoresize, it can no longer be deactivated.

If you want to make an additional autostorage path available to the DB2 database, you can do this using the command alter database add storage on <path>. To do this, follow these steps:

1. Log on as *<dbname>adm* (for example, su - t01adm).
2. Enter the command db2.
3. Establish a connection to the DB2 database (for example, connect to t01).
4. Enter the command alter database add storage on '/db2/T01/ sapdata3'.

```
db2 => alter database add storage on '/db2/T01/sapdata3'
DB20000I  The SQL command completed successfully.
```

8.5.7 Backing Up the Database

To avoid a loss of data in the event of damage, it's important to back up your DB2 database and log files on a regular basis. The DB2 database supports two types of backup:

- Offline backup
- Online backup

[+]

Take Care When Backing Up the Database

Take considerable care when backing up your database. Also consider using backup hardware. Because this book can only provide you with basic information, please seek professional help if necessary.

For an *offline backup*, you must stop both the SAP system and the database. Because no activities take place on the database, an offline backup is, by its very nature, consistent. However, the performance of the SAP system may deteriorate temporarily after an offline backup because the database and SAP system buffers have to be reconfigured. If you want to perform an offline backup, you can use the command backup db <dbname> to <device>, <device no.> with <no. of backup buffers> buffers parallelism <no. of tablespaces to be backed up in parallel>. Follow these steps:

1. Stop the SAP system (for example, stopsap).
2. Log on as *<dbname>adm* (for example, su - t01adm).
3. Enter the command db2.
4. Deactivate the database (for example, deactivate db t01).
5. Enter the command backup db t01 to /db2/T01/backup with 5 buffers parallelism 2.

```
db2 => deactivate db t01
DB20000I  The DEACTIVATE DATABASE command completed successfully.
db2 => backup db t01 to /db2/T01/backup with 5 buffers parallelism 2

Backup successful. The timestamp for this backup image is : 20100717010858
```

[!]

Backup Information

The exact definition of individual values, devices or paths for the backup, the number of backup buffers, and the number of tablespaces to be backed up in parallel depend on numerous factors and must be adjusted to the relevant environment.

For an *online backup*, you can continue to run the database and SAP system. The advantage of this is that, among other things, the database and SAP system buffers are retained. However, you must also back up the database logs so that this backup is consistent. If you want to perform a consistent online backup, you can use the command backup db <dbname> online to <device>, <device no.> with <no. of backup buffers> buffers parallelism <no. of tablespaces to be backed up in parallel> include logs. Follow these steps:

1. Log on as *<dbname>adm* (for example, su - t01adm).
2. Enter the command db2.
3. Enter the command backup db t01 online to /db2/T01/backup with 5 buffers parallelism 2 include logs.

```
db2 => backup db t01 online to /db2/T01/backup with 5 buffers parallelism 2 incl
ude logs
Backup successful. The timestamp for this backup image is : 20100711094917
```

[!]

Incremental and Differential Backup

In addition to a complete backup whereby the entire database is always backed up, the DB2 database also supports incremental and differential backups. However, you must set the TRACKMOD parameter in the database configuration for this purpose.

In the period between two database backups, you must make sure to back up the log files on a regular basis. You do this using the *DB2 Log Manager*, which you configure by making the relevant settings in the database configuration. For example, you can use the parameters LOGARCHMETH1 and LOGARCHMETH2 to determine how and to where the logs are to be backed up.

```
 First log archive method                    (LOGARCHMETH1) = DISK:/db2/T01/log_arc
hive/
 Options for logarchmeth1                    (LOGARCHOPT1) =
 Second log archive method                   (LOGARCHMETH2) = OFF
 Options for logarchmeth2                    (LOGARCHOPT2) =
 Failover log archive path                   (FAILARCHPATH) =
 Number of log archive retries on error      (NUMARCHRETRY) = 5
 Log archive retry Delay (secs)            (ARCHRETRYDELAY) = 20
 Vendor options                                (VENDOROPT) =
```

8.5.8 Restoring the Database

If damage occurs, you can restore the database. This process essentially comprises two steps. First, you must use an existing backup to restore the database. You must then use the backed-up logs to "roll back" the database to a time before the damage occurred.

[+]

Backing Up a Damaged Database

If damage occurs, remain calm and don't do anything rash. Before you undertake a recovery attempt, you should err on the side of caution and create a backup of the damaged database.

To fully restore the database, follow these steps:

1. Log on as *<dbname>adm* (for example, `su - t01adm`).
2. Enter the command `db2`.

3. Restore the database. The corresponding command is as follows: `restore db <dbname> from <device>, <device no.> taken at <time stamp>` (for example, `restore db t01 from /db2/T01/backup taken at 20100717010858`).

4. Enter the value `y` to confirm the security prompt.

```
db2 => restore db t01 from /db2/T01/backup taken at 20100717010858
SQL2539W  Warning!  Restoring to an existing database that is the same as the
backup image database.  The database files will be deleted.
Do you want to continue ? (y/n) y
DB20000I  The RESTORE DATABASE command completed successfully.
```

5. Roll the database forward. The corresponding command is `rollforward db <dbname> to <time stamp> and stop` (for example, `rollforward db t01 to end of logs and stop`).

```
db2 => rollforward db t01 to end of logs and stop

                                 Rollforward Status

 Input database alias                   = t01
 Number of nodes have returned status   = 1

 Node number                            = 0
 Rollforward status                     = not pending
 Next log file to be read               =
 Log files processed                    = S0000005.LOG - S0000005.LOG
 Last committed transaction             = 2010-07-11-07.49.18.000000 UTC

DB20000I  The ROLLFORWARD command completed successfully.
```

Since DB2 database version 8.2, you can use the `recover` command, which performs both steps together. The corresponding command is `recover db <dbname> to <time stamp>`. Follow these steps:

1. Log on as *<dbname>adm* (for example, `su - t01adm`).

2. Enter the command `db2`.

3. Enter the command `recover db t01 to end of logs`.

```
db2 => recover db t01 to end of logs
                                 Rollforward Status

 Input database alias                   = t01
 Number of nodes have returned status   = 1

 Node number                            = 0
 Rollforward status                     = not pending
 Next log file to be read               =
 Log files processed                    = S0000005.LOG - S0000005.LOG
 Last committed transaction             = 2010-07-11-09.49.18.000000 Local

DB20000I  The RECOVER DATABASE command completed successfully.
```

If you want to obtain information about the progress of the backup or restore, you can use the command `list utilities`. Follow these steps:

1. Log on as *<dbname>adm* (for example, `su - t01adm`).
2. Enter the command `db2`.
3. Enter the command `list utilities`.

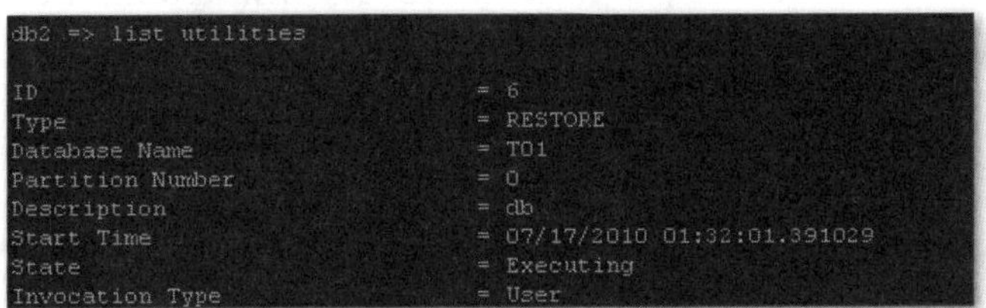

8.6 Database Administration—Oracle

When managing an Oracle database in the SAP environment, three options are available to you. The Oracle Client tool SQL*Plus and the BR*Tools provided by SAP are available at operating system level, and the collective Transaction DBACOCKPIT is available in the SAP system.

[+]

Additional Information

Documentation for the Oracle database and the Oracle Client tool SQL*Plus is available online at *www.oracle.com/technology/documentation*, while documentation on managing Oracle databases in the SAP environment and the BR*Tools is available in the operations area at *http://help.sap.com/*.

8.6.1 SQL*Plus

The Oracle Client tool SQL*Plus is automatically installed when you install the Oracle database. You can use this tool to perform the following tasks, among other things:

- Starting and stopping the database
- Configuring the SQL*Plus environment

- Executing SQL statements and SQL scripts
- Managing the database

Next, we will describe how to use SQL*Plus to manage Oracle databases.

Connecting to the Database

Before you can work with the SQL*Plus tool, it's important to establish a connection to the database. To do this, follow these steps:

1. Log on as the user *ora<dbname>* (for example, using the command `su - oras11`).
2. Enter the command `sqlplus`. The system now prompts you to log on to the database.

```
f03:oras11 3> sqlplus

SQL*Plus: Release 10.2.0.2.0 - Production on Sat Jul 17 11:52:12 2010

Copyright (c) 1982, 2005, Oracle.  All Rights Reserved.

Enter user-name:
```

3. Log on as the SAP schema user *sap<sapsid>* (for example, `saps11`).

```
Enter user-name: saps11
Enter password:

Connected to:
Oracle Database 10g Enterprise Edition Release 10.2.0.2.0 - 64bit Production
With the Partitioning and Data Mining options

SQL>
```

4. If you want to perform database administration tasks, you must also specify the role SYSDBA. To do this, enter the command `connect / as sysdba`.

```
SQL> connect / as sysdba
Connected.
```

You have now established a connection to the database.

If you want to log on directly using the role SASDBA, you can also follow these steps:

1. Log on as *ora<dbname>* (for example, `su - oras11`).
2. Enter the command `sqlplus "/ as sysdba"`.

```
f03:orasl1 4> sqlplus "/ as sysdba"

SQL*Plus: Release 10.2.0.2.0 - Production on Sat Jul 17 11:58:29 2010

Copyright (c) 1982, 2005, Oracle.  All Rights Reserved.


Connected to:
Oracle Database 10g Enterprise Edition Release 10.2.0.2.0 - 64bit Production
With the Partitioning and Data Mining options

SQL>
```

Configuring the SQL*Plus Environment

In the SQL*Plus environment, you can influence system behavior to a certain extent by setting variables. If, for example, you want to facilitate better logging of your work, you can copy the SQL*Plus output to a file.

If you want to view the current settings, follow these steps:

1. Log on as *ora<dbname>* (for example, `su - orasl1`).
2. Start SQL*Plus (for example, `sqlplus "/ as sysdba"`).
3. Enter the command `show all`.

```
SQL> show all
appinfo is OFF and set to "SQL*Plus"
arraysize 15
autocommit OFF
autoprint OFF
autorecovery OFF
autotrace OFF
blockterminator "." (hex 2e)
btitle OFF and is the first few characters of the next SELECT statement
cmdsep OFF
colsep " "
compatibility version NATIVE
concat "." (hex 2e)
copycommit 0
COPYTYPECHECK is ON
define "&" (hex 26)
describe DEPTH 1 LINENUM OFF INDENT ON
echo OFF
editfile "afiedt.buf"
embedded OFF
escape OFF
FEEDBACK ON for 6 or more rows
flagger OFF
```

If you want to change the configuration in the SQL*Plus environment, you can do this using the command `set <variable> <who>`. If, for example, you want to deactivate the line break in SQL*Plus, enter the command `set wrap off`.

```
SQL> set wrap off
```

If you also want to copy the SQL*Plus output to a text file, you must use the command `spool <file>` (for example, `spool output.txt`).

8.6.2 Starting and Stopping the Database

There are three ways to start an Oracle database in the SAP environment:

- Using the Oracle Client tool SQL*Plus
- Using the following command provided by SAP: `startdb`
- Using the BR*Tools provided by SAP

In all three cases, you must first start a program that facilitates communication between the Oracle database and the clients. You start this *listener* as follows:

1. Log on to the server as the user *ora<dbname>* (for example, `su - oras11`).
2. To start the listener of the Oracle instance, enter the command `lsnrctl start`, and press the Enter key.

```
f03:oras11 5> lsnrctl start

LSNRCTL for HPUX: Version 10.2.0.2.0 - Production on 01-JUL-2010 20:01:05

Copyright (c) 1991, 2005, Oracle.  All rights reserved.

Starting /oracle/S11/102_64/bin/tnslsnr: please wait...

TNSLSNR for HPUX: Version 10.2.0.2.0 - Production
System parameter file is /oracle/S11/102_64/network/admin/listener.ora
Log messages written to /oracle/S11/102_64/network/log/listener.log
Listening on: (DESCRIPTION=(ADDRESS=(PROTOCOL=ipc)(KEY=S11.WORLD)))
Listening on: (DESCRIPTION=(ADDRESS=(PROTOCOL=ipc)(KEY=S11)))

Connecting to (ADDRESS=(PROTOCOL=IPC)(KEY=S11.WORLD))
STATUS of the LISTENER
------------------------
Alias                     LISTENER
Version                   TNSLSNR for HPUX: Version 10.2.0.2.0 - Production
Start Date                01-JUL-2010 20:01:06
Uptime                    0 days 0 hr. 0 min. 0 sec
Trace Level               off
Security                  ON: Local OS Authentication
SNMP                      OFF
Listener Parameter File   /oracle/S11/102_64/network/admin/listener.ora
Listener Log File         /oracle/S11/102_64/network/log/listener.log
Listening Endpoints Summary...
  (DESCRIPTION=(ADDRESS=(PROTOCOL=ipc)(KEY=S11.WORLD)))
  (DESCRIPTION=(ADDRESS=(PROTOCOL=ipc)(KEY=S11)))
Services Summary...
Service "S11" has 1 instance(s).
  Instance "S11", status UNKNOWN, has 1 handler(s) for this service...
The command completed successfully
```

[+]

Using the Command "startdb" to Start the Database

If you want to use the command `startdb` to start the database, the listener must already be running. For the other two options, you can also start the listener retroactively.

Starting the Database

If you want to use the Client tool SQL*Plus to start the Oracle database, follow these steps:

1. Log on to the server as the user *ora<dbname>* (for example, `su - oras11`).
2. Start SQL*Plus, and log on as the user *SYSDBA* (for example, `sqlplus "/ as sysdba"`).
3. Enter the command `startup`, and press the Enter key.

```
f03:oras11 7> sqlplus "/as sysdba"

SQL*Plus: Release 10.2.0.2.0 - Production on Thu Jul 1 20:03:55 2010

Copyright (c) 1982, 2005, Oracle.  All Rights Reserved.

Connected to an idle instance.

SQL> startup
ORACLE instance started.

Total System Global Area  926941184 bytes
Fixed Size                  2048408 bytes
Variable Size             469765736 bytes
Database Buffers          452984832 bytes
Redo Buffers                2142208 bytes
Database mounted.
Database opened.
```

If you want to use the command `startdb` to start the database, follow these steps:

1. Log on to the server as the user *ora<dbname>* (for example, `su - oras11`).
2. Enter the command `startdb`, and press the Enter key.

```
f03:oras11 10> startdb
Trying to start S11 database ...
Log file: /oracle/S11/startdb.log
S11 database started
```

If you want to use BR*Tools to start the Oracle database, follow these steps:

1. Log on to the server as the user *ora<dbname>* (for example, `su - oras11`).
2. Enter the command `brtools`, and press the [Enter] key. The system displays the BR*TOOLS MENU. Select the INSTANCE MANAGEMENT option. To do this, enter the value `1`, and press the [Enter] key.

```
f03:oras11 14> brtools
BR0651I BRTOOLS 7.00 (44)

BR0280I BRTOOLS time stamp: 2010-07-01 20.07.16
BR0656I Choice menu 1 - please make a selection
-------------------------------------------------------------------------------
BR*Tools main menu

 1 = Instance management
 2 - Space management
 3 - Segment management
 4 - Backup and database copy
 5 - Restore and recovery
 6 - Check and verification
 7 - Database statistics
 8 - Additional functions
 9 - Exit program

Standard keys: c - cont, b - back, s - stop, r - refr, h - help
-------------------------------------------------------------------------------
BR0662I Enter your choice:
```

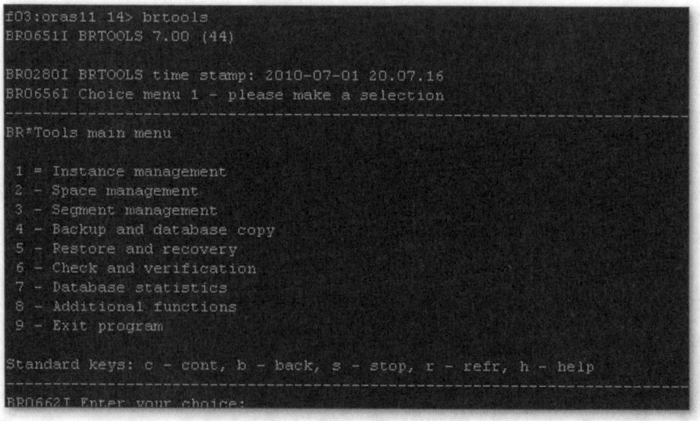

3. In the next menu, select the START UP DATABASE option. To do this, enter the value `1`, and press the [Enter] key.

```
Database instance management

 1 = Start up database
 2 - Shut down database
 3 - Alter database instance
 4 - Alter database parameters
 5 - Recreate database
 6 - Show instance status
 7 - Show database parameters
 8 - Show database owners
 9 - Reset program status

Standard keys: c - cont, b - back, s - stop, r - refr, h - help
-------------------------------------------------------------------------------
BR0662I Enter your choice:
1
```

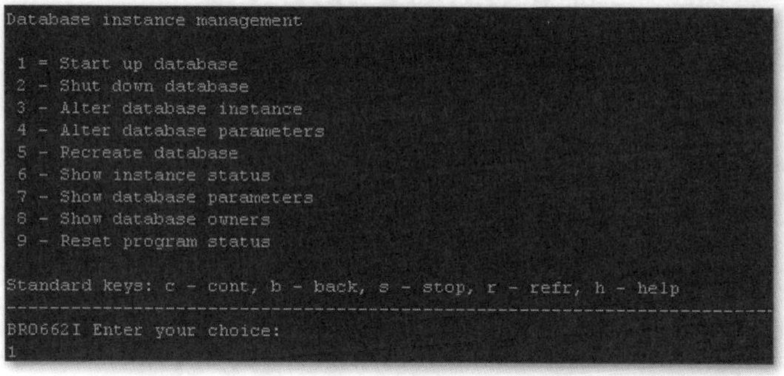

4. Check the parameters displayed. Then, enter the value `c`, and press the [Enter] key. To confirm the security prompt, enter the value `c` again. The tool BRSPACE starts.

```
BR0280I BRSPACE time stamp: 2010-07-01 20.17.17
BR0656I Choice menu 201 - please make a selection
-------------------------------------------------------------------------------
Database instance startup main menu

 1 = Start up database
 2 - Show instance status
 3 * Exit program
 4 - Reset program status

Standard keys: c - cont, b - back, s - stop, r - refr, h - help
-------------------------------------------------------------------------------
BR0662I Enter your choice:
1
```

5. To start the database, select the START UP DATABASE option. To do this, enter the value `1`, and press the [Enter] key.

```
Options for starting up database instance S11

 1 - Database startup to-state (state) . [open]
 2 - Database open mode (mode) ......... [normal]
 3 - Force instance restart (force) .... [no]
 4 - SQLPLUS command (command) ......... [startup open]

Standard keys: c - cont, b - back, s - stop, r - refr, h - help
-------------------------------------------------------------------------------
BR0662I Enter your choice:
c
```

6. Check the parameters displayed. Then, enter the value `c`, and press the [Enter] key. To confirm the security prompt, enter the value `c` again.

```
BR0280I BRSPACE time stamp: 2010-07-01 20.20.43
BR0304I Starting and opening database instance S11 ...

BR0280I BRSPACE time stamp: 2010-07-01 20.20.53
BR0305I Start and open of database instance S11 successful
```

The database is now started.

Stopping the Database

Similar to starting the Oracle database, there are also three ways to stop the database. If you want to use the Client tool SQL*Plus to stop the Oracle database, follow these steps:

1. Log on to the server as the user *ora<dbname>* (for example, `su - oras11`).
2. Start SQL*Plus, and log on as the user *SYSDBA* (for example, `sqlplus "/ as sysdba"`).
3. Enter the command `shutdown`, and press the [Enter] key.

```
f03:oras11 16> sqlplus "/as sysdba"

SQL*Plus: Release 10.2.0.2.0 - Production on Thu Jul 1 20:27:05 2010

Copyright (c) 1982, 2005, Oracle.  All Rights Reserved.


Connected to:
Oracle Database 10g Enterprise Edition Release 10.2.0.2.0 - 64bit Production
With the Partitioning and Data Mining options

SQL> shutdown
Database closed.
Database dismounted.
ORACLE instance shut down.
```

[!]

Shutdown Command

When you enter the shutdown command, make sure that you are actually in the program SQL*Plus. Otherwise, you may accidentally shut down the database server.

If you want to use the command `stopdb` to stop the database, follow these steps:

1. Log on to the server as the user *ora<dbname>* (for example, `su - oras11`).
2. Enter the command `stopdb`, and press the Enter key.

```
f03:oras11 19> stopdb
Trying to stop S11 database ...
Log file: /oracle/S11/stopdb.log
S11 database stopped
```

If you want to use BR*Tools to stop the Oracle database, follow these steps:

1. Log on to the server as the user *ora<dbname>* (for example, using the command `su - oras11`).
2. Enter the command `brtools`, and press the Enter key. The system displays the BR*Tools menu.
3. Select the Instance management option. To do this, enter the value `1`, and press the Enter key.
4. In the next menu, select the Shut down database option. To do this, enter the value `2`, and press the Enter key.
5. Check the parameters displayed. Then, enter the value `c`, and press the Enter key.
6. To confirm the security prompt, enter the value `c` again. The tool BRSPACE starts.

```
BR0280I BRSPACE time stamp: 2010-07-01 20.32.27
BR0656I Choice menu 204 - please make a selection
-------------------------------------------------------------------------------
Database instance shutdown main menu

 1 = Shut down database
 2 - Show instance status
 3 * Exit program
 4 - Reset program status

Standard keys: c - cont, b - back, s - stop, r - refr, h - help
-------------------------------------------------------------------------------
```

7. To stop the database, select the SHUT DOWN DATABASE option. To do this, enter the value `1`, and press the [Enter] key.
8. Check the parameters displayed. Then, enter the value `c`, and press the [Enter] key.
9. To confirm the security prompt, enter the value `c` again. The database is now stopped.

```
BR0280I BRSPACE time stamp: 2010-07-01 20.35.51
BR0307I Shutting down database instance S11 ...

BR0280I BRSPACE time stamp: 2010-07-01 20.36.09
BR0308I Shutdown of database instance S11 successful
```

In all three cases, you must also stop the listener as follows:

1. Log on to the server as the user *ora<dbname>* (for example, `su - oras11`).
2. To stop the listener of the Oracle instance, enter the command `lsnrctl stop`, and press the [Enter] key.

```
f03:oras11 23> lsnrctl stop

LSNRCTL for HPUX: Version 10.2.0.2.0 - Production on 01-JUL-2010 20:37:22

Copyright (c) 1991, 2005, Oracle.  All rights reserved.

Connecting to (ADDRESS=(PROTOCOL=IPC)(KEY=S11.WORLD))
The command completed successfully
```

8.6.3 Executing SQL Statements and SQL Scripts

SQL*Plus enables you to execute SQL statements and SQL scripts against the database. If, for example, you want to display all of the clients in your SAP system, follow these steps:

1. Log on as *ora<dbname>* (for example, `su - oras11`).

2. Start SQL*Plus (for example, `sqlplus "/ as sysdba"`).
3. Enter the command `select mandt from sap<sapsid>.t000;` (for example, `select mandt from saps11.t000;`).

```
SQL> select mandt from saps11.t000;

MANDT
---------
000
001
066
100
200
```

If you want to execute an SQL script, you can do this by placing `@` in front of the script to be executed. If, for example, you want to execute the script `test.sql`, follow these steps:

1. Log on as *ora<dbname>* (for example, `su - oras11`).
2. Start SQL*Plus (for example, `sqlplus "/ as sysdba"`).
3. Enter the command `@test.sql`.

```
f03:oras11 5> cat test.sql
select mandt from saps11.t000;
f03:oras11 6> sqlplus "/as sysdba"

SQL*Plus: Release 10.2.0.2.0 - Production on Sat Jul 17 17:08:35 2010

Copyright (c) 1982, 2005, Oracle.  All Rights Reserved.


Connected to:
Oracle Database 10g Enterprise Edition Release 10.2.0.2.0 - 64bit Production
With the Partitioning and Data Mining options

SQL> @test.sql

MANDT
---------
000
001
066
100
200
```

[!]

Take Care When Executing SQL Statements

Take due care and consideration when executing SQL statements. You have full access to the data in the SAP system and can manipulate this data beyond the SAP transaction logic. However, this may lead to inconsistencies in the SAP system.

8.6.4 Managing the Database

You can use SQL*Plus to perform database administration tasks. For example, you can use the command `alter tablespace` to make changes to the tablespaces in your database.

However, you can use the BR*Tools to perform these tasks from the menu. The BR*Tools make your work easier and protect you against forgetting information (see Section 8.6.5). We will not go into detail here.

Displaying Available Commands [+]

In general, the BR*Tools show you which command to execute against the database. If, for example, you are interested in learning how to use SQL*Plus to create a new data file, you can view the command in BRSPACE.

```
 9 - SQL command (command) .................. [alter tablespace PSAPS11 add dataf
ile '/oracle/S11/sapdata1/s11_5/s11.data5' size 10000M autoextend off]
```

8.6.5 BR*Tools

The BR*Tools provided by SAP enable you to perform database administration tasks from the menu. You can use BR*Tools to perform the following tasks, among other things:

- Starting and stopping the database
- Checking and changing the status of the database instance
- Checking and updating the database configuration
- Managing tablespaces and the associated data files
- Backing up the database
- Restoring the database
- Checking the database and database statistics

Options When Using BR*Tools [+]

BR*Tools enable you to perform a range of additional tasks. Therefore, take some time to familiarize yourself with these tools.

BR*Tools comprise the programs BRBACKUP, BRARCHIVE, BRRESTORE, BRRECOVER, BRCONNECT, BRSPACE, and BRTOOLS, each of which is used to perform particular tasks. To make it easier for you to use BR*Tools, the program BRTOOLS displays an interactive menu that can be used to control the other programs.

[+]

SAPDBA and BR*Tools

BR*Tools replace the SAP administration tool SAPDBA for all SAP systems running on an Oracle 9i database or newer. Even if SAPDBA is still available, SAP recommends that you only use the BR*Tools.

Starting and Using BR*Tools

You can start the program BRTOOLS as follows:

1. Log on as *ora<dbname>* (for example, `su - oras11`).
2. Enter the command `brtools`.

```
f03:oras11 8> brtools
```

You can also use the option `-c` to start the program BRTOOLS. In this case, some additional prompts are displayed in the BR*Tools. The corresponding command is then `brtools -c`.

```
f03:oras11 13> brtools -c
```

After you've started BRTOOLS, the system displays the main menu in which you can select individual options by entering the corresponding number. If, for example, you want to select the SEGMENT MANAGEMENT option, enter the value `3`, and press the `Enter` key.

```
BR*Tools main menu

 1 = Instance management
 2 - Space management
 3 - Segment management
 4 - Backup and database copy
 5 - Restore and recovery
 6 - Check and verification
 7 - Database statistics
 8 - Additional functions
 9 - Exit program
```

In addition to selecting the menu options, you can also use standard keys to control the BR*Tools. Among other things, you can stop the BR*Tools or display the Help documentation. If, for example, you want to stop the BR*Tools, select the STOP option. To do this, enter the value `s`, and press the Enter key.

```
Standard keys: c - cont, b - back, s - stop, r - refr, h - help
```

8.6.6 Checking and Changing the Status of the Database Instance

You can use the program BRSPACE to display information about the current status of your database instance. To do this, follow these steps:

1. Log on as *ora<dbname>* (for example, `su - oras11`).
2. Start the program BRTOOLS (for example, `brtools -c`).
3. Select the INSTANCE MANAGEMENT OPTION. To do this, enter the value `1`, and press the Enter key.

```
Database instance management

 1 = Start up database
 2 - Shut down database
 3 - Alter database instance
 4 - Alter database parameters
 5 - Recreate database
 6 - Show instance status
 7 - Show database parameters
 8 - Show database owners
 9 - Reset program status
```

4. Select the SHOW INSTANCE STATUS OPTION. To do this, enter the value `6`, and press the Enter key. You obtain an overview of the parameters used to start the program BRSPACE.

```
BRSPACE options for showing database information

 1 - BRSPACE profile (profile) ........ [initS11.sap]
 2 - Database user/password (user) .... [/]
 3 ~ Database instance (instance) ..... []
 4 # Database parameter (parameter) ... []
 5 # Database tablespace (tablespace) . []
 6 # Database file (file) ............ []
 7 # Database owner (owner) .......... []
 8 # Database table (table) .......... []
 9 # Database index (index) .......... []
10 - Create log file (log) ........... [no]
11 - Confirmation mode (confirm) ...... [yes]
12 # Extended output (output) ........ [no]
13 - Scrolling line count (scroll) .... [20]
14 - Message language (language) ...... [E]
15 - BRSPACE command line (command) ... [-p initS11.sap -s 20 -l E -f dbshow -c
dbstate]
```

5. Check the parameters displayed, and select the CONT OPTION. To do this, enter the value `c`, and press the `Enter` key. You then obtain information about the status of your Oracle database instance.

```
Information about the status of database instance S11

 1 - Instance number (number) ........... 1
 2 - Instance thread (thread) ........... 1
 3 - Instance status (status) ........... OPEN
 4 - Instance start time (start) ........ 2010-07-01 21.13.48
 5 - Oracle version (version) ........... 10.2.0.2.0
 6 - Database creation time (create) .... 2009-11-13 16.16.15
 7 - Last resetlogs time (resetlogs) .... 2009-11-13 16.16.15
 8 - Archivelog mode (archmode) ......... ARCHIVELOG
 9 - Archiver status (archiver) ......... STARTED
10 - Current redolog sequence (redoseq) . 3277
11 - Current redolog SCN (redoscn) ...... 57245284
12 - Number of SAP connections (sapcon) . 13
```

You can also use the program BRSPACE to change the status of your database instance. If, for example, you want to set your database instance to NOARCHIVELOG mode, follow these steps:

1. Stop the SAP system.
2. Log on as *ora<dbname>* (for example, `su - oras11`).
3. Start the program BRTOOLS (for example, `brtools -c`).
4. Select the INSTANCE MANAGEMENT OPTION. To do this, enter the value `1`, and press the `Enter` key.
5. Select the ALTER DATABASE INSTANCE OPTION. To do this, enter the value `3`, and press the `Enter` key. You obtain an overview of the parameters used to start the program BRSPACE.
6. Check the parameters displayed, and select the CONT OPTION. To do this, enter the value `c`, and press the `Enter` key.

```
Alter database instance main menu

 1 - Switch redolog file
 2 - Force database checkpoint
 3 - Set archivelog mode
 4 - Set noarchivelog mode
 5 - Show instance status
 6 * Exit program
 7 - Reset program status
```

7. Select the SET NOARCHIVELOG MODE option. To do this, enter the value `4`, and press the `Enter` key. You obtain information about the current and target statuses of the database instance. The command to be executed is also displayed.

```
Options for alter of database instance S11

1 * Current archivelog mode (mode) .. [archivelog]
2 * Alter database action (action) .. [noarchlog]
3 - Force instance shutdown (force) . [no]
4 - SQL command (command) .......... [alter database noarchivelog]
```

8. Check the parameters displayed, and select the CONT OPTION. To do this, enter the value `c`, and press the Enter key.

The program BRSPACE now sets the database instance to NOARCHIVELOG mode.

8.6.7 Checking and Updating the Database Configuration

Originally, the Oracle database configuration was stored alone in the initialization parameter text file, which is usually called init<*DBNAME*>.ora (for example, initS11.ora). However, because the Oracle database is unable to update this file dynamically, a binary server parameter file, which is usually called spfile<*DBNAME*>.ora (for example, spfileS11.ora) or spfile.ora, is available since Release 9i. Because some transactions in the SAP system (for example, Transaction ST04) still access initialization parameter text files, you must ensure that the content of both files remains the same.

Using BR*Tools to Make Changes [+]

BR*Tools support you in making changes to the two parameter files. It does this by automatically updating both files in parallel, thus keeping them consistent. You should therefore use the BR*Tools to make changes to your Oracle database configuration.

You can use the program BRSPACE to display information about your current database configuration. To do this, follow these steps:

1. Log on as *ora<dbname>* (for example, `su - oras11`).
2. Start the program BRTOOLS (for example, `brtools -c`).
3. Select the INSTANCE MANAGEMENT OPTION. To do this, enter the value `1`, and press the Enter key.
4. Select the SHOW DATABASE PARAMETERS OPTION. To do this, enter the value `7`, and press the Enter key. You obtain an overview of the parameters used to start the program BRSPACE.

5. Check the parameters displayed, and select the CONT OPTION. To do this, enter the value c, and press the Enter key. You obtain an overview of your Oracle database configuration.

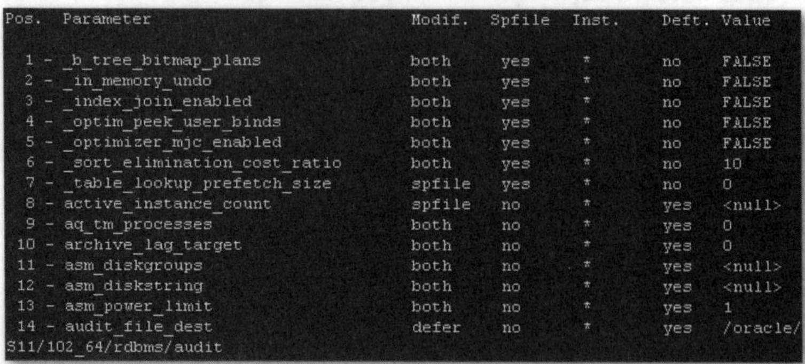

```
Pos.  Parameter                           Modif.   Spfile   Inst.    Deft. Value

  1 - _b_tree_bitmap_plans                both      yes       *       no    FALSE
  2 - _in_memory_undo                     both      yes       *       no    FALSE
  3 - _index_join_enabled                 both      yes       *       no    FALSE
  4 - _optim_peek_user_binds              both      yes       *       no    FALSE
  5 - _optimizer_mjc_enabled              both      yes       *       no    FALSE
  6 - _sort_elimination_cost_ratio        both      yes       *       no    10
  7 - _table_lookup_prefetch_size         spfile    yes       *       no    0
  8 - active_instance_count               spfile    no        *       yes   <null>
  9 - aq_tm_processes                     both      no        *       yes   0
 10 - archive_lag_target                  both      no        *       yes   0
 11 - asm_diskgroups                      both      no        *       yes   <null>
 12 - asm_diskstring                      both      no        *       yes   <null>
 13 - asm_power_limit                     both      no        *       yes   1
 14 - audit_file_dest                     defer     no        *       yes   /oracle/
S11/102_64/rdbms/audit
```

You can also use the program BRSPACE to change your Oracle database configuration. If, for example, you want to change the size of the shared pool, follow these steps:

1. Log on as *ora<dbname>* (for example, su - oras11).
2. Start the program BRTOOLS (for example, brtools -c).
3. Select the INSTANCE MANAGEMENT OPTION. To do this, enter the value 1, and press the Enter key.
4. Select the ALTER DATABASE PARAMETERS OPTION. To do this, enter the value 4, and press the Enter key. You obtain an overview of the parameters used to start the program BRSPACE.
5. Check the parameters displayed, and select the CONT OPTION. To do this, enter the value c, and press the Enter key.

```
Alter database parameter main menu

 1 = Change parameter value
 2 - Reset parameter value
 3 - Create init.ora from spfile
 4 - Show database parameters
 5 - Show init.ora profile
 6 * Exit program
 7 - Reset program status
```

6. Select the CHANGE PARAMETER VALUE option. To do this, enter the value 1, and press the Enter key. You obtain an overview of all parameters.

```
233 - shared_memory_address              spfile   no    *    yes  0
234 - shared_pool_reserved_size          spfile   yes   *    no   40894464
235 - shared_pool_size                   both     yes   *    no   40265318
4
236 - shared_server_sessions             both     no    *    yes  <null>
237 - shared_servers                     both     no    *    yes  0
238 - skip_unusable_indexes              both     no    *    yes  TRUE
```

7. Now select the parameter `shared_pool_size`. To do this, enter the value `235`, and press the Enter key. Among other things, you obtain information about the parameter to be changed, the current value, and the value in SPFILE. The command to be executed is also displayed.

```
Options for alter of database parameter 'shared_pool_size'

 1 * Parameter description (desc) ..... [size in bytes of shared pool]
 2 * Parameter type (type) ............ [big integer]
 3 * Current parameter value (parval) . [402653184]
 4 * Value in spfile (spfval) ......... [<same>]
 5 ? New parameter value (value) ...... []
 6 - Scope for new value (scope) ...... [both]
 7 # Database instance (instance) ..... []
 8 ~ Comment on update (comment) ...... []
 9 - SQL command (command) ............ [alter system set shared_pool_size =  sc
ope = both]
```

8. Now select the New parameter value option. To do this, enter the value `5`, and press the Enter key.
9. Now enter the new value for the parameter (in bytes), and press the Enter key.

```
Options for alter of database parameter 'shared_pool_size'

 1 * Parameter description (desc) ..... [size in bytes of shared pool]
 2 * Parameter type (type) ............ [big integer]
 3 * Current parameter value (parval) . [402653184]
 4 * Value in spfile (spfval) ......... [<same>]
 5 - New parameter value (value) ...... [419430400]
 6 - Scope for new value (scope) ...... [both]
 7 # Database instance (instance) ..... []
 8 ~ Comment on update (comment) ...... []
 9 - SQL command (command) ............ [alter system set shared_pool_size = 419
430400 scope = both]
```

10. Check the parameters displayed, and select the cont option. To do this, enter the value `c`, and press the Enter key. The size of the shared pool is changed. The files init<*DBNAME*>.ora and spfile<*DBNAME*>.ora are also updated.

[+]

Dynamic and Static Parameters

For Oracle databases, a distinction is made between *dynamic* and *static* parameters. Any changes made to dynamic parameters are implemented immediately, while changes to static parameters only take effect after you restart the Oracle database. The documentation on the Oracle database will help you determine which parameters are dynamic and which are static.

8.6.8 Managing Tablespaces and Associated Data Files

You can use the program BRSPACE to manage the storage space on your Oracle database. For example, you can display the current size and space occupied by the tablespaces, you can extend the tablespaces by creating new files, and you can change the properties of the individual data files.

If you want to view the current size and space occupied by the tablespaces in your Oracle database, follow these steps:

1. Log on as *ora<dbname>* (for example, `su - oras11`).
2. Start the program BRTOOLS (for example, `brtools -c`).
3. Select the SPACE MANAGEMENT OPTION. To do this, enter the value `2`, and press the `Enter` key.

```
Database space management

 1 = Extend tablespace
 2 - Create tablespace
 3 - Drop tablespace
 4 - Alter tablespace
 5 - Alter data file
 6 - Move data file
 7 - Additional space functions
 8 - Reset program status
```

4. Select the EXTEND TABLESPACE OPTION. To do this, enter the value `1`, and press the `Enter` key. You obtain an overview of the parameters used to start the program BRSPACE.
5. Check the parameters displayed, and select the CONT OPTION. To do this, enter the value `c`, and press the `Enter` key.

```
Tablespace extension main menu

 1 = Extend tablespace
 2 - Show tablespaces
 3 - Show data files
 4 - Show disk volumes
 5 * Exit program
 6 - Reset program status
```

6. Select the SHOW TABLESPACES OPTION. To do this, enter the value 2, and press the [Enter] key. You obtain an overview of all tablespaces in your Oracle database.

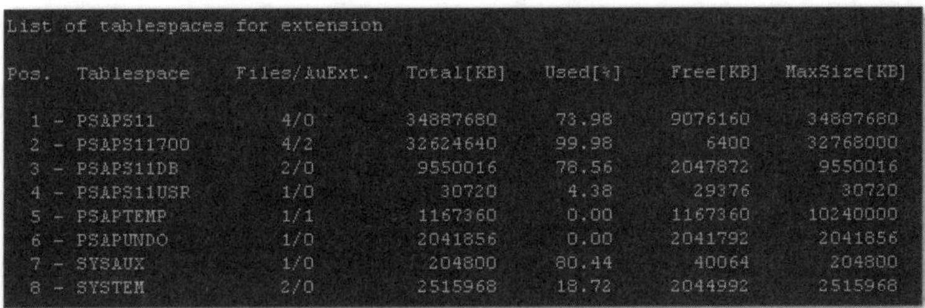

List of tablespaces for extension

Pos.	Tablespace	Files/AuExt.	Total[KB]	Used[%]	Free[KB]	MaxSize[KB]
1 -	PSAPS11	4/0	34887680	73.98	9076160	34887680
2 -	PSAPS11700	4/2	32624640	99.98	6400	32768000
3 -	PSAPS11DB	2/0	9550016	78.56	2047872	9550016
4 -	PSAPS11USR	1/0	30720	4.38	29376	30720
5 -	PSAPTEMP	1/1	1167360	0.00	1167360	10240000
6 -	PSAPUNDO	1/0	2041856	0.00	2041792	2041856
7 -	SYSAUX	1/0	204800	80.44	40064	204800
8 -	SYSTEM	2/0	2515968	18.72	2044992	2515968

If you ascertain that there is no longer sufficient space in a tablespace, you can use the program BRSPACE to extend this tablespace by creating new data files. To do this, follow these steps:

1. Log on as *ora<dbname>* (for example, `su - oras11`).
2. Start the program BRTOOLS (for example, `brtools -c`).
3. Select the SPACE MANAGEMENT OPTION. To do this, enter the value 2, and press the [Enter] key.
4. Select the EXTEND TABLESPACE OPTION. To do this, enter the value 1, and press the [Enter] key. You obtain an overview of the parameters used to start the program BRSPACE.
5. Check the parameters displayed, and select the CONT OPTION. To do this, enter the value c, and press the [Enter] key.
6. Select the EXTEND TABLESPACE OPTION. To do this, enter the value 1, and press the [Enter] key. You obtain an overview of all tablespaces in your Oracle database.
7. Now select the tablespace to be extended. To do this, enter the relevant number, and press the [Enter] key. Among other things, you obtain information about the last data file created as well as information about the values for the new data file. The command to be executed is also displayed.

```
Options for extension of tablespace PSAPS11 (1. file)

 1 * Last added file name (lastfile) ....... [/oracle/S11/sapdata1/s11_4/s11.dat
a4]
 2 * Last added file size in MB (lastsize) . [10000]
 3 - New file to be added (file) .......... [/oracle/S11/sapdata1/s11_5/s11.dat
a5]
 4 ~ Raw disk / link target (rawlink) ...... []
 5 - Size of the new file in MB (size) ..... [10000]
 6 - File autoextend mode (autoextend) ..... [no]
 7 # Maximum file size in MB (maxsize) ..... []
 8 # File increment size in MB (incrsize) .. []
 9 - SQL command (command) ................. [alter tablespace PSAPS11 add dataf
ile '/oracle/S11/sapdata1/s11_5/s11.data5' size 10000M autoextend off]
```

8. If you want to change the size of the new data file, select the SIZE OF THE NEW FILE IN MB (SIZE) OPTION. To do this, enter the value `5`, and press the [Enter] key. You are prompted to specify the new size.
9. If you are satisfied with the values display, select the CONT option. To do this, enter the value `c`, and press the [Enter] key. The program BRSPACE asks you whether you want to create additional data files.

```
BR1091I Next data file can be specified now
BR0675I Do you want to perform this action?

BR0280I BRSPACE time stamp: 2010-07-15 20.09.37
BR0676I Enter 'y[es]' to perform the action, 'n[o]/c[ont]' to skip it, 's[top]'
to abort:
```

10. If you want to do this, select the YES option. To do this, enter the value `y`, and press the [Enter] key.
11. If you've defined enough data files, select the NO or CONT OPTION. To do this, enter the value `n` or `c`, and press the [Enter] key. The data files are now created for the tablespace that you have selected.

In addition to the option of creating data files of a fixed size, Oracle also offers you the option of automatic extension. This type of storage administration is known as *autoextend*. If you want to use autoextend, set the FILE AUTOEXTEND MODE (AUTOEXTEND) option to the value `yes` in the menu for creating new data files. You can also use the MAXIMUM FILE SIZE IN MB (MAXSIZE) and FILE INCREMENT SIZE IN MB (INCRSIZE) values to determine the maximum permissible size for the data file or the number of megabytes by which the data file is to be extended, if required. A possible configuration could look like the following screenshot.

```
Options for extension of tablespace PSAPS11 (1. file)

 1 * Last added file name (lastfile) ....... [/oracle/S11/sapdata1/s11_4/s11.dat
a4]
 2 * Last added file size in MB (lastsize) . [10000]
 3 - New file to be added (file) ........... [/oracle/S11/sapdata1/s11_5/s11.dat
a5]
 4 ~ Raw disk / link target (rawlink) ...... []
 5 - Size of the new file in MB (size) ..... [500]
 6 - File autoextend mode (autoextend) ..... [yes]
 7 - Maximum file size in MB (maxsize) ..... [10000]
 8 - File increment size in MB (incrsize) .. [50]
 9 - SQL command (command) ................. [alter tablespace PSAPS11 add dataf
ile '/oracle/S11/sapdata1/s11_5/s11.data5' size 500M autoextend on next 50M maxs
ize 10000M]
```

Autoextend [+]

If you use autoextend, it makes sense to restrict the maximum size of the data files. Otherwise, the data files can be extended without restriction, and the file system can be filled completely. This may lead to some nasty surprises.

You can also use the program BRSPACE to manage and edit individual data files. If, for example, you want to deactivate autoextend for a data file, you can do this as follows:

1. Log on as *ora<dbname>* (for example, `su - oras11`).
2. Start the program BRTOOLS (for example, `brtools -c`).
3. Select the SPACE MANAGEMENT OPTION. To do this, enter the value `2`, and press the [Enter] key.
4. Select the ALTER DATA FILE OPTION. To do this, enter the value `5`, and press the [Enter] key. You obtain an overview of the parameters used to start the program BRSPACE.
5. Check the parameters displayed, and select the CONT OPTION. To do this, enter the value `c`, and press the [Enter] key.

```
Alter data file main menu

 1 - Set data file online
 2 - Set data file offline
 3 - Turn on and maintain autoextend
 4 - Turn off autoextend
 5 - Resize data file
 6 - Rename data file
 7 - Drop empty data file
 8 - Show data files
 9 - Show tablespaces
10 - Show disk volumes
11 * Exit program
12 - Reset program status
```

6. Select the TURN OFF AUTOEXTEND OPTION. To do this, enter the value 4, and press the Enter key. You obtain an overview of all data files currently in autoextend.

```
List of data files for alter

 Pos.  Tablespace        Status  Type      Size[KB] AuExt. File

   1 - PSAPS11700        ONLINE  FILE    10240000   YES   /oracle/S11/sapdata1/s117
00_2/s11700.data2
   2 - PSAPS11700        ONLINE  FILE    10096640   YES   /oracle/S11/sapdata1/s117
00_4/s11700.data4
   3 - PSAPTEMP          ONLINE  FILE     1167360   YES   /oracle/S11/sapdata1/temp
_1/temp.data1
```

7. Select the relevant data file. To do this, enter the number displayed and press the Enter key. Among other things, you obtain information about the data file and the target status. The command to be executed is also displayed.

```
Options for alter of data file /oracle/S11/sapdata1/s11700_2/s11700.data2

 1 * Current data file status (status) ....... [AUTOEXTEND]
 2 * Current data file size in MB (currsize) . [10000]
 3 * Alter data file action (action) ......... [fixsize]
 4 # Maximum file size in MB (maxsize) ....... [10000]
 5 # File increment size in MB (incrsize) .... [20]
 6 # New data file size in MB (size) ......... []
 7 # New data file name (name) ............... []
 8 # Force data file alter (force) ........... [no]
 9 - SQL command (command) ................... [alter database datafile '/oracle
/S11/sapdata1/s11700_2/s11700.data2' autoextend off]
```

8. Check the parameters displayed, and select the CONT OPTION. To do this, enter the value c, and press the Enter key.

The autoextend function is deactivated for the data file you have selected.

8.6.9 Backing Up the Database

To avoid a loss of data in the event of damage, it's important to back up your Oracle database and redo log files on a regular basis. The Oracle database supports two types of backup:

- Offline backup
- Online backup

[+]

Take Care When Backing Up the Database

Because this book can only provide you with basic information, please seek professional help when backing up your database, if necessary.

For an offline backup, you must stop both the SAP system and the database. Because no activities take place on the database, an offline backup is, by its very nature, consistent. However, the performance of the SAP system may deteriorate temporarily after an offline backup because the database and SAP system buffers have to be reconfigured. To perform an offline backup using the program BRBACKUP, follow these steps:

1. Stop the SAP system (for example, `stopsap`).
2. Log on as *ora<dbname>* (for example, `su - oras11`).
3. Start the program BRTOOLS (for example, `brtools -c`).
4. Select the BACKUP AND DATABASE COPY option. To do this, enter the value `4`, and press the Enter key.

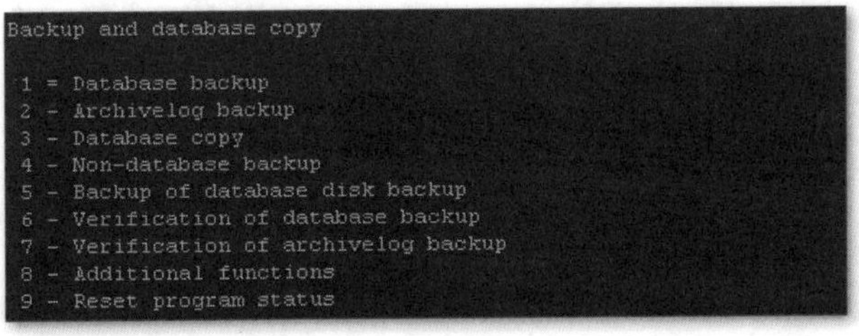

```
Backup and database copy

 1 = Database backup
 2 - Archivelog backup
 3 - Database copy
 4 - Non-database backup
 5 - Backup of database disk backup
 6 - Verification of database backup
 7 - Verification of archivelog backup
 8 - Additional functions
 9 - Reset program status
```

5. Select the DATABASE BACKUP OPTION. To do this, enter the value `1`, and press the Enter key. You obtain an overview of the parameters for performing the backup.

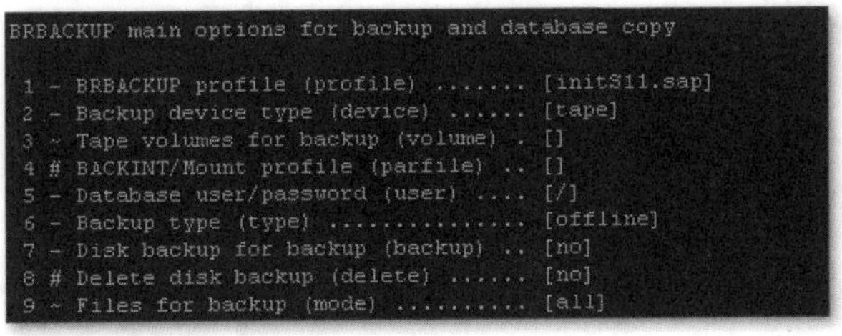

```
BRBACKUP main options for backup and database copy

 1 - BRBACKUP profile (profile) ....... [initS11.sap]
 2 - Backup device type (device) ...... [tape]
 3 ~ Tape volumes for backup (volume) . []
 4 # BACKINT/Mount profile (parfile) .. []
 5 - Database user/password (user) .... [/]
 6 - Backup type (type) ............... [offline]
 7 - Disk backup for backup (backup) .. [no]
 8 # Delete disk backup (delete) ...... [no]
 9 ~ Files for backup (mode) .......... [all]
```

6. Select the value `offline` for the Backup type (type) option. Check whether the Backup device type (device) option meets your requirements. Then select the cont option. To do this, enter the value `c`, and press the Enter key. You obtain an overview of additional parameters. The command to be executed is also displayed.

```
Additional BRBACKUP options for backup and database copy

 1 - Confirmation mode (confirm) ....... [no]
 2 - Query mode (query) ............... [no]
 3 - Compression mode (compress) ....... [no]
 4 - Verification mode (verify) ........ [no]
 5 - Fill-up previous backups (fillup) . [no]
 6 - Parallel execution (execute) ...... [0]
 7 - Additional output (output) ........ [no]
 8 - Message language (language) ....... [E]
 9 - BRBACKUP command line (command) ... [-p initS11.sap -d tape -t offline -m a
ll -c -k no -e 0 -l E]
```

7. Check the parameters displayed and select the cont option. To do this, enter the value `c`, and press the Enter key. An offline backup of the database is created.

[+]

Backup Information

The exact definition of the individual parameters for the backup depends on numerous factors and must be adjusted to the relevant environment. You can also make additional settings in the file init<*DBNAME*>.sap (for example, initS11.sap). Among other things, you can use the parameter `backup_root_dir` to determine where the backup is to be written for backups to the hard disk.

For an online backup, you can continue to run the database and SAP system. The advantage of this is that, among other things, the database and SAP system buffers are retained. However, you must also back up the database redo logs so that this backup is consistent. To perform a consistent online backup using the program BRBACKUP, follow these steps:

1. Log on as *ora<dbname>* (for example, `su - oras11`).
2. Start the program BRTOOLS (for example, `brtools -c`).
3. Select the Backup and database copy option. To do this, enter the value `4`, and press the Enter key.

4. Select the DATABASE BACKUP OPTION. To do this, enter the value `1`, and press the `Enter` key. You obtain an overview of the parameters for performing the backup.
5. Select the value `online_cons` for the BACKUP TYPE (TYPE) option. Check whether the BACKUP DEVICE TYPE (DEVICE) option meets your requirements. Then select the CONT OPTION. To do this, enter the value `c`, and press the `Enter` key. You obtain an overview of additional parameters. The command to be executed is also displayed.
6. Check the parameters displayed, and select the CONT OPTION. To do this, enter the value `c`, and press the `Enter` key.

An online backup of the database is created.

Incremental and Differential Backup [+]

In addition to a complete backup whereby the entire database is always backed up, the Oracle database also supports incremental and differential backups.

In the period between two database backups, you must make sure to back up the archived redo log files on a regular basis. You can do this using the program BRARCHIVE:

1. Log on as *ora<dbname>* (for example, `su - oras11`).
2. Start the program BRTOOLS (for example, `brtools -c`).
3. Select the BACKUP AND DATABASE COPY option. To do this, enter the value `4`, and press the `Enter` key.
4. Select the ARCHIVELOG BACKUP OPTION. To do this, enter the value `2`, and press the `Enter` key. You obtain an overview of the parameters for performing the backup.

```
BRARCHIVE main options for archivelog backup and verification

 1 - BRARCHIVE profile (profile) ...... [initS11.sap]
 2 - BRARCHIVE function (function) .... [save]
 3 - Backup device type (device) ...... [tape]
 4 ~ Tape volumes for backup (volume) . []
 5 # BACKINT/Mount profile (parfile) .. []
 6 - Database user/password (user) .... [/]
 7 ~ Maximum number of files (number) . []
 8 - Back up disk backup (archive) .... [no]
```

5. Check whether the BACKUP DEVICE TYPE (DEVICE) option meets your requirements. Then select the CONT OPTION. To do this, enter the value `c`, and press the [Enter] key. You obtain an overview of additional parameters. The command to be executed is also displayed.

```
Additional BRARCHIVE options for archivelog backup

 1 - Confirmation mode (confirm) ....... [no]
 2 - Query mode (query) ................ [no]
 3 - Compression mode (compress) ....... [no]
 4 - Verification mode (verify) ........ [no]
 5 - Fill mode, group size (fill) ...... [no]
 6 - Modify mode, delay apply (modify) . [no]
 7 - Additional output (output) ........ [no]
 8 - Message language (language) ....... [E]
 9 - BRARCHIVE command line (command) .. [-p initS11.sap -save -d tape -c -k n
-l E]
```

6. Check the parameters displayed, and select the CONT OPTION. To do this, enter the value `c`, and press the [Enter] key.

A backup of the archived redo log files is now created.

[+]

Double Backup

To ensure that your backup of the archived redo log files is as secure as possible, you should back up these files twice. To do this, select the value `save` for the BRARCHIVE FUNCTION (FUNCTION) option during the first backup and the value `second_copy_delete` during the second backup.

8.6.10 Restoring the Database

In the event of damage, you can use the programs BRRECOVER and BRRESTORE to restore your Oracle database by means of database backups and redo log files. BR*Tools provide numerous restore options:

- A full database recovery
- A point-in-time recovery
- Database reset

Before you try to restore the database, you should err on the side of caution and create a backup of the damaged database. During a full database recovery, damaged or missing data files are replaced with the data files from a backup. The redo log files are then used to set each data file to the status it had just before the damage occurred. To perform a *full database recovery*, follow these steps:

1. Log on as *ora<dbname>* (for example, `su - oras11`).
2. Start the program BRTOOLS (for example, `brtools -c`).
3. Select the RESTORE AND RECOVERY OPTION. To do this, enter the value `5`, and press the [Enter] key.

```
Restore and recovery

 1 = Complete database recovery
 2 - Database point-in-time recovery
 3 - Tablespace point-in-time recovery
 4 - Whole database reset
 5 - Restore of individual backup files
 6 - Restore and application of archivelog files
 7 - Disaster recovery
 8 - Reset program status
```

4. Select the COMPLETE DATABASE RECOVERY OPTION. To do this, enter the value `1`, and press the [Enter] key. You obtain an overview of the parameters used to start the program BRRECOVER.

```
BRRECOVER options for restore and recovery

 1 * Recovery type (type) ............ [complete]
 2 - BRRECOVER profile (profile) ...... [initS11.sap]
 3 - BACKINT/Mount profile (parfile) .. []
 4 - Database user/password (user) .... [/]
 5 - Recovery interval (interval) ..... [30]
 6 - Confirmation mode (confirm) ...... [no]
 7 - Scrolling line count (scroll) .... [20]
 8 - Message language (language) ...... [E]
 9 - BRRECOVER command line (command) . [-p initS11.sap -t complete -i 30 -c -
20 -l E]
```

5. Check the parameters displayed, and select the CONT OPTION. To do this, enter the value `c`, and press the [Enter] key.

```
Complete database recovery main menu

 1 = Check the status of database files
 2 * Select database backup
 3 * Restore data files
 4 * Restore and apply incremental backup
 5 * Restore and apply archivelog files
 6 * Open database and post-processing
 7 * Exit program
 8 - Reset program status
```

6. Now follow the step-by-step instructions provided for the program BRRECOVER. Starting at the top, go through each of the options displayed. After you've successfully processed the OPEN DATABASE AND POST-PROCESSING option, your database is operational again.

For a *point-in-time recovery*, you can determine the point in time that is to be used as the restore time. For this purpose, all of the data files are replaced with the data files from a backup. The redo log files are then used to set each data file to the status it had at the defined point in time. To perform a point-in-time recovery, follow these steps:

1. Log on as *ora<dbname>* (for example, `su - oras11`).
2. Start the program BRTOOLS (for example, `brtools -c`).
3. Select the RESTORE AND RECOVERY OPTION. To do this, enter the value `5`, and press the Enter key.
4. Select the DATABASE POINT-IN-TIME RECOVERY OPTION. To do this, enter the value `2`, and press the Enter key. You obtain an overview of the parameters used to start the program BRRECOVER.
5. Check the parameters displayed, and select the CONT OPTION. To do this, enter the value `c`, and press the Enter key.

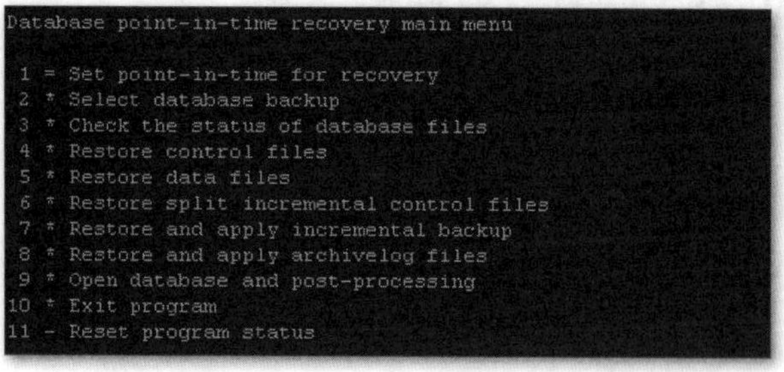

```
Database point-in-time recovery main menu

 1 = Set point-in-time for recovery
 2 * Select database backup
 3 * Check the status of database files
 4 * Restore control files
 5 * Restore data files
 6 * Restore split incremental control files
 7 * Restore and apply incremental backup
 8 * Restore and apply archivelog files
 9 * Open database and post-processing
10 * Exit program
11 - Reset program status
```

6. Now follow the step-by-step instructions provided for the program BRRECOVER. Starting at the top, go through each of the options displayed. After you've successfully processed the OPEN DATABASE AND POST-PROCESSING option, your database is operational again.

When *resetting the database*, the database is set to the status associated with the selected backup. Here, all of the data files are replaced with the data files from a backup, and, for an online backup, the backed-up redo log files are used to reset the database to a consistent status. To reset the database, follow these steps:

1. Log on as *ora<dbname>* (for example, `su - oras11`).
2. Start the program BRTOOLS (for example, `brtools -c`).
3. Select the RESTORE AND RECOVERY OPTION. To do this, enter the value `5`, and press the Enter key.
4. Select the WHOLE DATABASE RESET OPTION. To do this, enter the value `4`, and press the Enter key. You obtain an overview of the parameters used to start the program BRRECOVER.
5. Check the parameters displayed, and select the CONT OPTION. To do this, enter the value `c`, and press the Enter key.

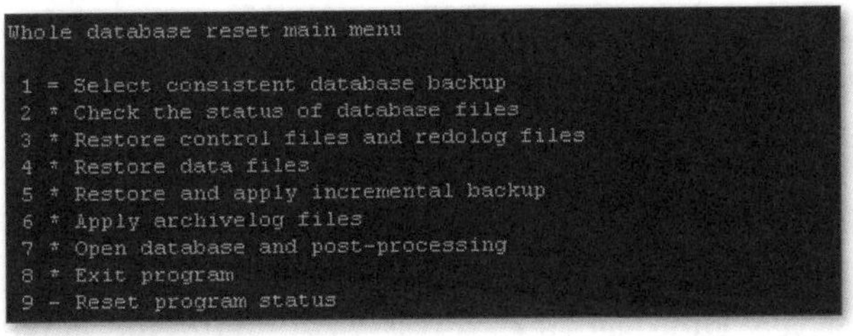

```
Whole database reset main menu

 1 = Select consistent database backup
 2 * Check the status of database files
 3 * Restore control files and redolog files
 4 * Restore data files
 5 * Restore and apply incremental backup
 6 * Apply archivelog files
 7 * Open database and post-processing
 8 * Exit program
 9 - Reset program status
```

6. Now follow the step-by-step instructions provided for the program BRRECOVER. Starting at the top, go through each of the options displayed.

After you've successfully processed the OPEN DATABASE AND POST-PROCESSING option, your database is operational again.

8.6.11 Checking the Database

You can use the program BRCONNECT to check your database. If you perform this check on a regular basis, you can identify problems in advance and respond accordingly.

To check the database, follow these steps:

1. Log on as *ora<dbname>* (for example, `su - oras11`).
2. Start the program BRTOOLS (for example, `brtools -c`).
3. Select the CHECK AND VERIFICATION OPTION. To do this, enter the value `6`, and press the Enter key.

```
Database check and verification

 1 = Database system check
 2 - Validation of database structure
 3 - Verification of database blocks
 4 - Reset program status
```

4. Select the DATABASE SYSTEM CHECK OPTION. To do this, enter the value `1`, and press the Enter key. You obtain an overview of the parameters for performing a database check.

```
BRCONNECT main options for database system check

 1 - BRCONNECT profile (profile) .......... [initS11.sap]
 2 - Database user/password (user) ........ [/]
 3 - Use default check settings (default) . [no]
 4 ~ Database owner for check (owner) ..... []
 5 ~ Ignore DBCHECKORA table (ignore) ..... []
 6 ~ Ignore DBSTATC table (igndbs) ........ []
 7 ~ Exclude from check (exclude) ......... []
```

5. Check the parameters displayed, and select the CONT OPTION. To do this, enter the value `c`, and press the Enter key. You obtain an overview of additional parameters. The command to be executed is also displayed.

```
Additional BRCONNECT options for database system check

 1 - Confirmation mode (confirm) ...... [no]
 2 - Query mode (query) ............... [no]
 3 - Extended output (output) ......... [no]
 4 - Message language (language) ...... [E]
 5 - BRCONNECT command line (command) . [-p initS11.sap -c -l E -f check]
```

6. Check the parameters displayed, and select the CONT OPTION. To do this, enter the value `c`, and press the Enter key. The database is checked.

If you want to view the result of the check, follow these steps:

1. Log on as *ora<dbname>* (for example, `su - oras11`).
2. Start the program BRTOOLS (for example, `brtools -c`).
3. Select the ADDITIONAL FUNCTIONS OPTION. To do this, enter the value `8`, and press the Enter key.

```
Additional BR*Tools functions

 1 = Show profiles and logs
 2 - Clean up DBA logs and tables
 3 - Adapt NEXT extents
 4 - Change password of database user
 5 - Create/change synonyms for DBA tables
 6 - Reset program status
```

4. Select the SHOW PROFILES AND LOGS OPTION. To do this, enter the value `1`, and press the Enter key.

```
Show profiles and logs

 1 = Oracle profile
 2 - BR*Tools profile
 3 - BRBACKUP logs
 4 - BRARCHIVE logs
 5 - BRRESTORE logs
 6 - BRRECOVER logs
 7 - BRCONNECT logs
 8 - BRSPACE logs
```

5. Select the BRCONNECT LOGS OPTION. To do this, enter the value `7`, and press the Enter key.

```
Display of BRCONNECT logs

Pos.  Log              Start                  Function   Rc   Object

 1 = cedrwphk.chk  2010-07-18 19.07.08  check       1
 2 - cedqpwdy.cln  2010-07-12 03.17.42  cleanup     0
 3 - cedqntiw.sta  2010-07-11 17.00.10  stats       0    ALL
```

6. Select the relevant log. To do this, enter the relevant number, and press the Enter key. You then identify the log you require by the timestamp and the `check` addition. The check log is now displayed.

```
/oracle/S11/sapreorg                                  1075970049     203390976     1
03950969      48.89            0               0
/oracle/S11/saptrace                                  1075970049     203390976     1
03950969      48.89            0               0
/oracle/S11/oraarch                                   1075970050       6291456
 5440878      13.52            0               0

BR0280I BRCONNECT time stamp: 2010-07-18 19.07.15
BR0814I Number of tables in schema of owner SAPS11: 31998
BR0836I Number of info cube tables found for owner SAPS11: 113
BR0814I Number of tables in schema of owner SAPS11DB: 354
BR0814I Number of tables/partitions in schema of owner SYS: 621/153
BR0814I Number of tables/partitions in schema of owner SYSTEM: 134/27

BR0280I BRCONNECT time stamp: 2010-07-18 19.07.22
BR0815I Number of indexes in schema of owner SAPS11: 42113
BR0815I Number of indexes in schema of owner SAPS11DB: 503
BR0815I Number of indexes/partitions in schema of owner SYS: 675/161
BR0815I Number of indexes/partitions in schema of owner SYSTEM: 175/32

BR0280I BRCONNECT time stamp: 2010-07-18 19.09.02
```

8.7 Database Administration—Microsoft SQL Server

Of all the databases introduced here, Microsoft SQL Server is the easiest system to manage. The SQL Server is nevertheless a complex "enterprise grade" database system that, first, demands full attention and, second, demands that the administrator acquire the requisite expertise to manage it. If the SQL Server contains enterprise-critical data, administration cannot be of a "casual" nature.

The SQL Server is no longer in its infancy. This product is now suitable for large environments with high performance requirements.

In particular, this section will discuss how to create a data backup. Even though data backup is by no means the only feature of the SQL Server, it is undoubtedly one of its most important features.

The requirements for a database backup can be defined very quickly and are already known from Chapter 6:

- Back up all of the SAP databases together with the log files.
- Back up the *master* and *msdb* system databases.

Performing a backup is easy if you use the resources available to you in SQL Server Management Studio.

8.7.1 SQL Management Studio

You use SQL Server Management Studio to manage the Microsoft SQL Server on a daily basis.

SQL Server Management Studio [+]

This is the successor to Enterprise Manager. Even though Management Studio is comparably easy to use, you must, thanks to the large number of possible options available, pay particular attention to its many possibilities and procedures.

To use SQL Server Management Studio, follow these steps:

1. Generally, you do not have to start SQL Server Management Studio directly on the server. Instead, it can be installed on the administrator's workstation PC, which means that an interactive logon to the database server is not required.

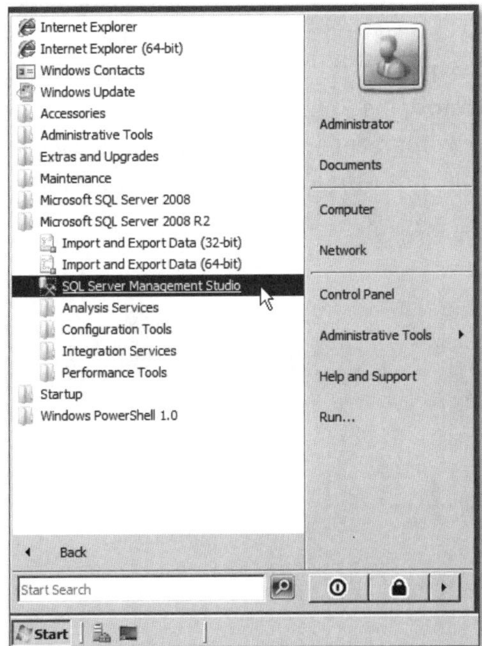

2. After you've started SQL Server Management Studio, you are prompted to specify the server to which you want to establish a connection. There are three configuration options:

- SERVER TYPE
  For our example, you connect to the database module. In addition to the database module, there are other possible server types such as Analysis Services or Reporting Services.
- SERVER NAME
  Here, you enter the name of the server to which you want to establish a connection. As already mentioned, most administration tasks also work via the network, which means that, for the usual administration tasks, there is no need to log on directly to the server.
  Microsoft SQL Server knows several database instances on a database server. If you want to address a particular instance (not the standard instance), insert the instance name as the server name (for example, *servername\sapdb1*).
- AUTHENTICATION
  If you select WINDOWS AUTHENTICATION, you will be connected using your current logon information (that is, the identity you used to log on to the Windows PC or server). Alternatively, you can log on using SQL SERVER AUTHENTICATION. SQL Server-specific accounts are used here (that is, no active directory logon information).
  The authentication type used in your environment depends on the individual system configuration. Microsoft recommends using Windows authentication.

Choose CONNECT to start SQL Server Management Studio.

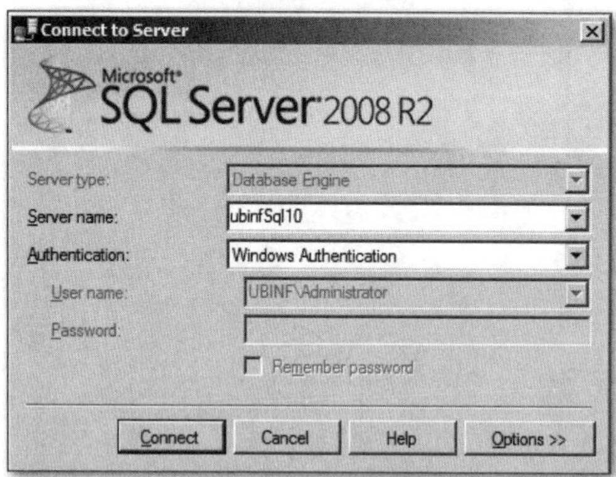

[+]

Connecting to Several SQL Servers

With SQL Server Management Studio, you can connect to multiple SQL servers simultaneously.

After you've started SQL Server Management Studio, you also obtain the tree view from the "old" SQL Enterprise Manager.

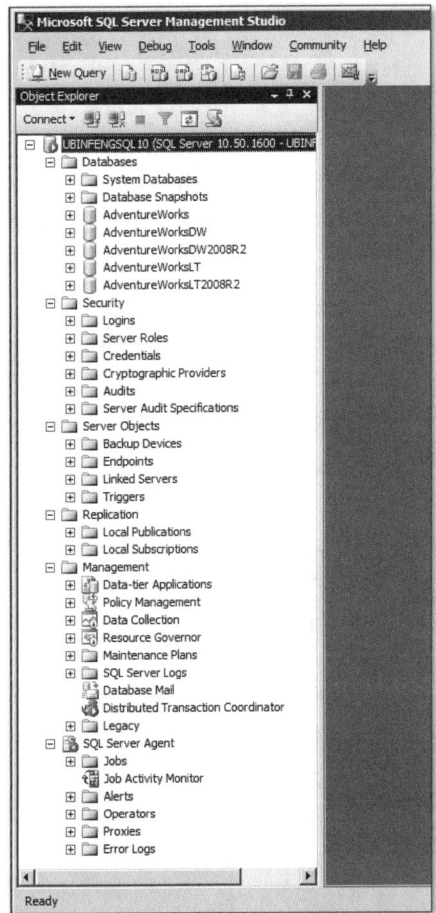

For example, you see that, under SECURITY, the databases on the server can manage the logons (and much more). Here, you also see advanced configuration options such as replication, backup, or performance analysis.

8.7.2 Starting and Stopping the Database

To start the database, follow these steps:

1. Right-click to call the context menu for the database instance displayed.

2. Select the START menu option.
3. Confirm the mandatory question in the dialog box ("Do you really want to ...?").
4. The database instance should run a short time later.

You stop a database instance in a similar way. Here, you must only select the PAUSE menu option.

In our example, you see that the standard database instance of the server UBINFENGSQL10 (you recognize the standard instance by the fact that no other instance name is appended to it) is stopped, which is indicated by the red stop icon that precedes the database name.

If the database/database instance is stopped, it cannot provide any data for clients, nor can it perform any administration tasks.

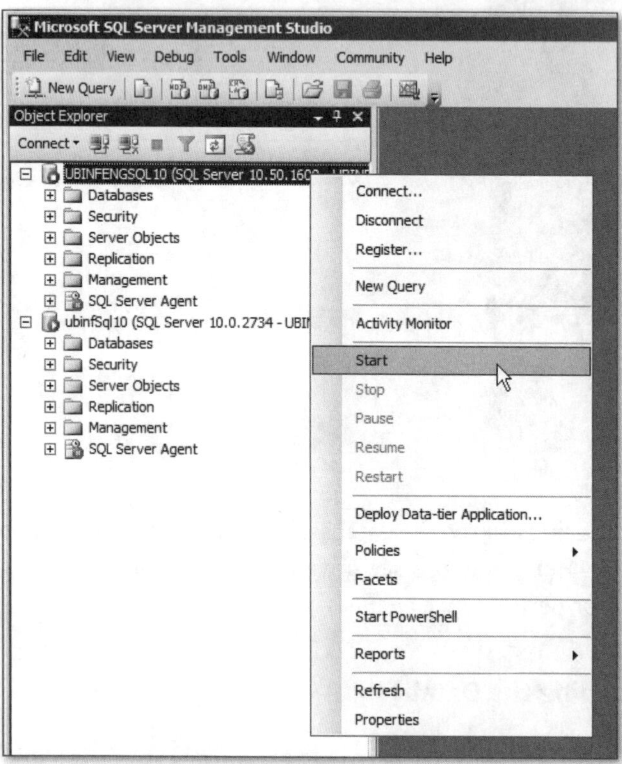

[+]

Starting and Stopping the Database

Essentially, the SQL Server service (that is, the Windows service) is started or stopped when you start or stop a database instance. However, you shouldn't simply start or stop the service. Instead, you should always follow the SQL Server-specific procedure.

SQL Server Agent

After you've started the database instance, you should take a quick look at the status of the SQL Server Agent. The fact that the actual database is running doesn't necessarily mean that the agent is running. Because the agent is required for all automation tasks, you should check that it is also running. Each database instance has its own SQL Server Agent, so greater care is required here.

If the SQL Server Agent isn't running, the maintenance plans, data backup processes or similar, which are to be called in a time-controlled manner, are not executed.

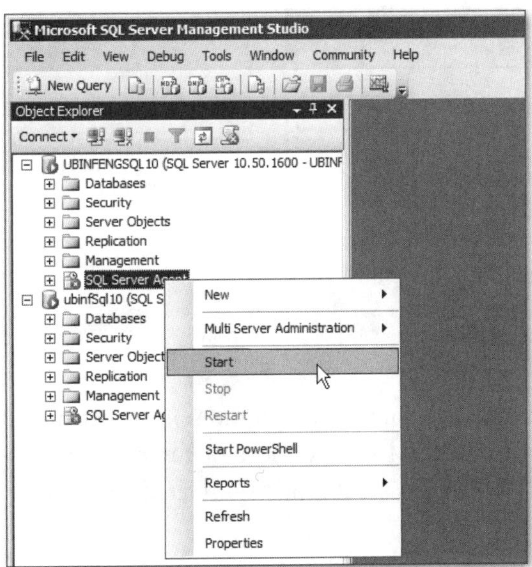

The SQL Server Agent is implemented as a separate Windows service. If it isn't started automatically, you can configure this in the services administration area of the operating system. This service is called SQL SERVER AGENT, followed by the name of the database instance in parentheses (the standard instance is known as MSSQLSERVER).

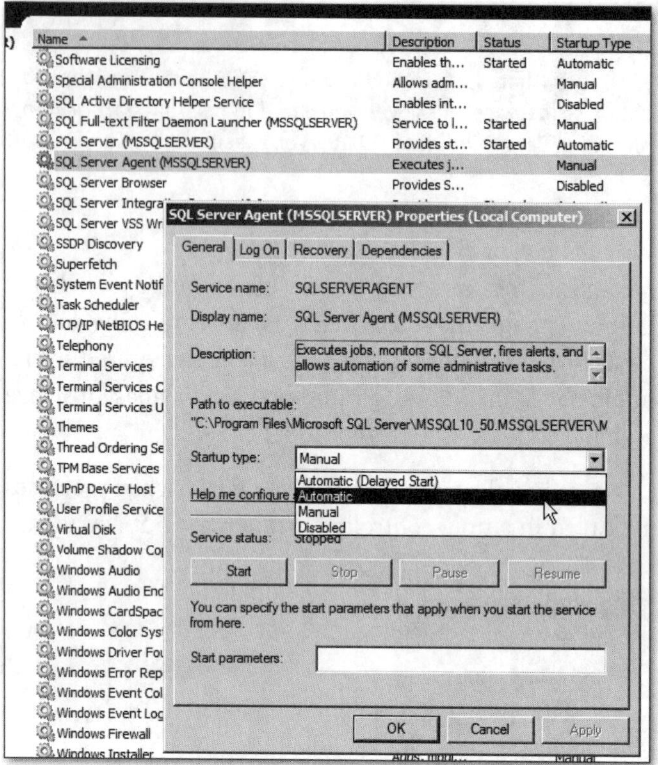

If a server has several instances, several SQL Server Agent services are created, which you can then configure to start automatically.

8.7.3 Files and Logs

This section provides some detailed information about how the SQL Server stores data on the hard disk. This information is not only important for preparing to plan and implement a data backup but also to create disk space areas to achieve maximum performance.

Pages and Blocks

The largest SQL Server database file is also organized into pages and blocks. The following hard and fast principles apply:

- A page is approximately 8 KB in size, that is, 8,192 bytes.

- A block comprises 8 pages and is therefore 64 KB in size, that is, 65,536 bytes.

The following example has a size of 205,651,968 bytes. With this knowledge of pages and blocks, you can calculate how many blocks and pages are contained in this database file:

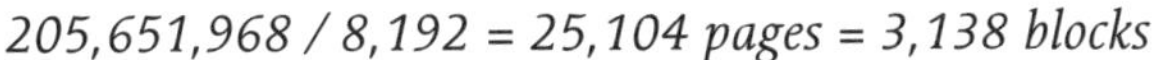

205,651,968 / 8,192 = 25,104 pages = 3,138 blocks

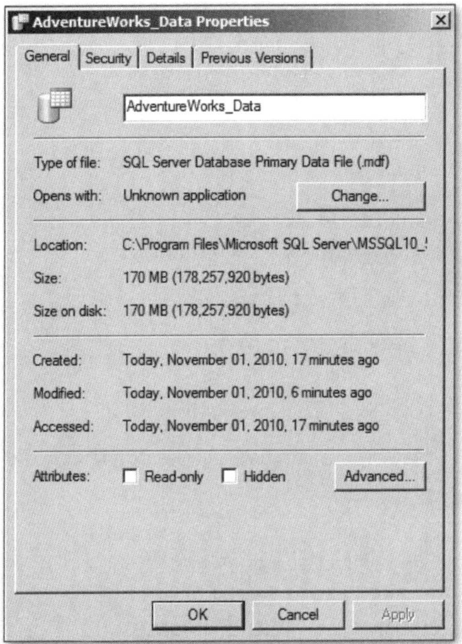

When the SQL Server accesses disk storage, it works in blocks (that is, in 64 KB units). For this reason, it makes sense to also set the physical block sizes for the RAID sets used by the SQL Server to this value.

Block Sizes [+]

Here, we are talking about the block sizes that the RAID controller uses to format the disk areas. It's not sufficient if only the NTFS blocks are 64 KB in size.

If the disk areas used by the SQL Server aren't formatted with this block size, this won't impair the function initially. However, you won't get the best performance out of your hardware later.

Let's take a look at the structure of a page, which begins with a 96-byte page header. This is followed by one or more data rows. The row offset, which contains information about the distance between the first byte in the data row and the start of the page, is stored at the end of the file.

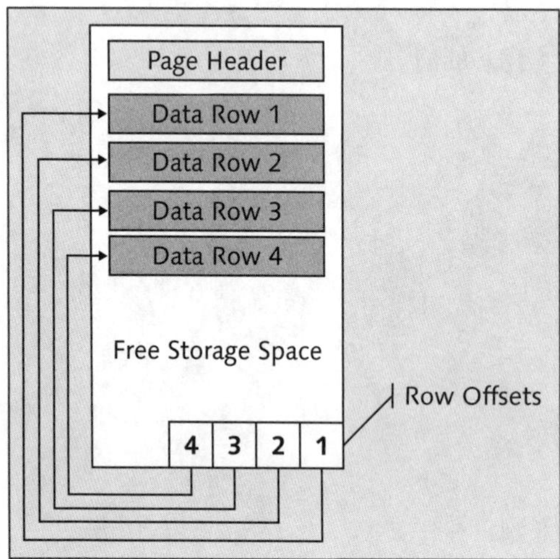

You see that a page may contain several data rows. If data rows are larger than one page, they are distributed across several pages.

File Groups and Files

A database requires at least two files. One file stores the actual database, and one stores the transaction log.

You see a corresponding dialog box that contains the properties of a database. For example, a file type, path, or behavior for *autoextend* is defined for each file.

Several files can be created for both the actual database and the logs. For larger databases, this makes sense for the following reasons:

- The size of the individual file can be kept to a reasonable level, thus making it easier to manage and reducing the storage space needed.
- For performance reasons, it may make sense to distribute the files across several physical RAID sets. However, this is only possible if the database is distributed across several files.

- If only one of the files in a database is damaged (for example, as a result of disk problems on a special RAID set), you only need to restore this one database.

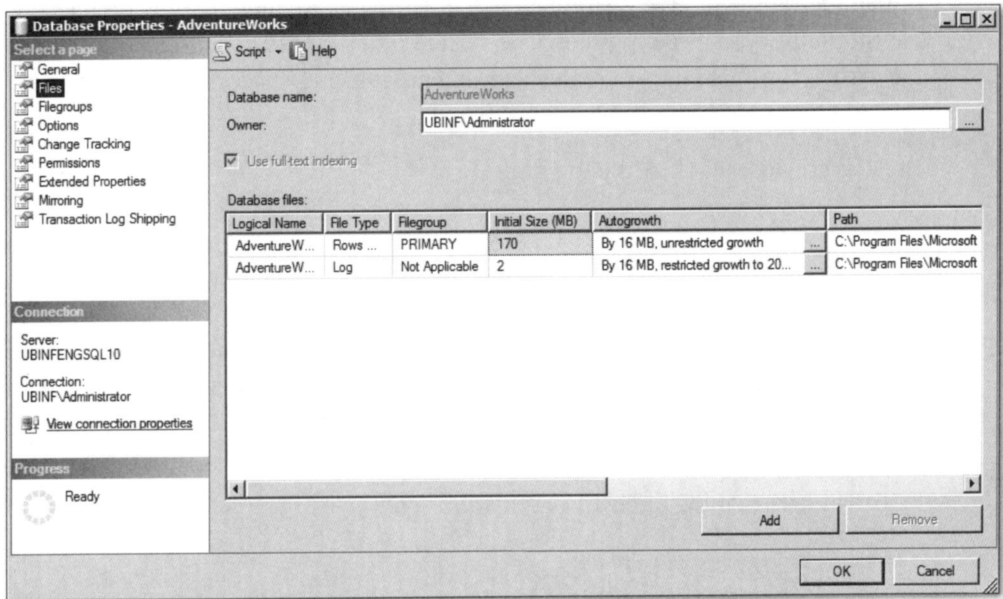

If you want to improve administration and management, you can create file groups. Note that a database has one primary file and any number of secondary files (0 to n files).

The following file name extensions are used by default:

- *.mdf for primary database files
- *.ndf for secondary database files
- *.ldf for log files

Transaction Logs (Logs)

Transaction logs, also known as *logs* or *log files*, play an extremely important role in all database servers. Transaction logs are particularly important when backing up and restoring databases (see Chapter 6).

In the SQL Server, a transaction log is written for each database (as is the case for every other server-based database system).

Initially, a transaction log is simply one file. The database module then divides this file into multiple virtual log files. The system determines the number and size of the virtual log files that it creates and extends. Administrators cannot influence this process.

Let's take a closer look at the log file:

- At the start, you have two virtual log files with free storage space, which were created by truncating older entries in the transaction log.
- The logical log starts in the third virtual log file. Here, you find, among other things, a position known as the *Minimum Recovery Log Sequence Number* (Mini LSN). This identifies the log entry required for a cross-database rollback. When you truncate the log, all of the virtual log files that precede the Mini LSN position are deleted.
- The fifth virtual log file is not used at present.

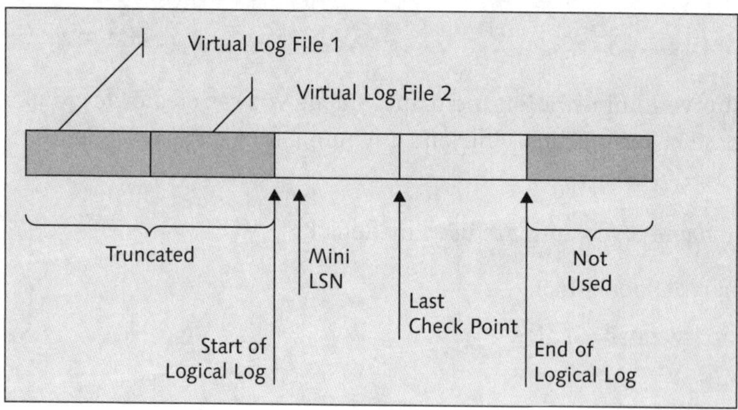

The following situation arises some time later (after a few transactions):

- The log is initially expanded to the fifth virtual log file. The end of the physical file may then be reached.
- If the end of the physical file is reached, the system returns to the start of the file.

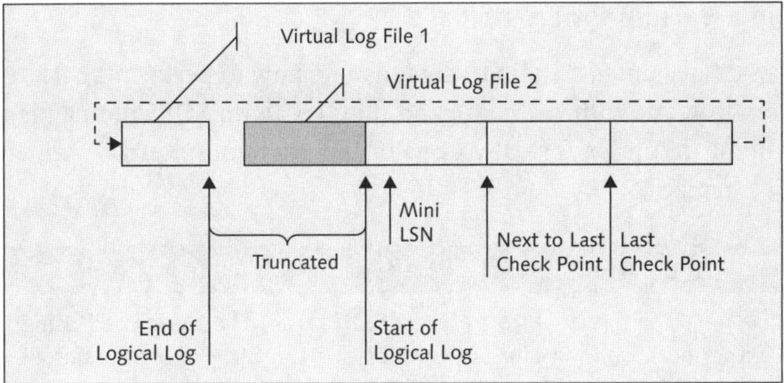

Ideally, the transactions are continuously written to this one physical transaction log file. A prerequisite here is that the logical log is truncated often enough to ensure that there is always enough free storage space (that is, empty virtual log files). If there is not enough free storage space in the physical file (as a result of a high transaction volume, a log file that is too small, or a transaction log that is not truncated often enough), the following situation may arise:

- If autoextend is configured for the file, the database module extends the file.
- If it isn't possible to extend the file because there is not enough space on the data carrier, the write processes are terminated (error 9002).
- If additional log files have been created, the data are written to these files.
- If autoextend isn't configured, and no additional log files are available, the write processes are terminated (error 9002).

Size of the Transaction Log Files [+]

Sometimes, the transaction log file is several gigabytes in size and partly larger than the actual database. This happens if the log is not truncated. If the transaction log file continues to grow and grow, you should immediately read the rest of this chapter to find out how you can deal with transaction logs correctly.

When you truncate transaction logs, the physical file does not automatically become smaller. Free space is only created within the file. If a transaction log file becomes very large (for example, because it was not possible to truncate the transaction log for a while as a result of an error in the data backup environment), it must be reduced in size by executing an SQL command or by using Management Studio.

8.7.4 Initiating a Backup Process

Next, we'll use SQL Management Studio to demonstrate how to perform a backup so that it's possible to work with the command line (i.e., with SQL commands). Because many administrators prefer to work with the graphical interface, we've chosen this display here.

> **SQL Commands**
>
> However, note that much of the work to be executed can only be performed using SQL commands—either because they cannot be initiated in the GUI or because not all parameters can be transferred via the Management Studio. Fortunately, you can display the SQL commands for most of the tasks initiated via the Management Studio. Most of the dialog boxes have the SCRIPT (Script) button for this purpose.

To start a database backup, follow these steps:

1. In the context menu for the database, choose the menu path TASKS • BACK UP.

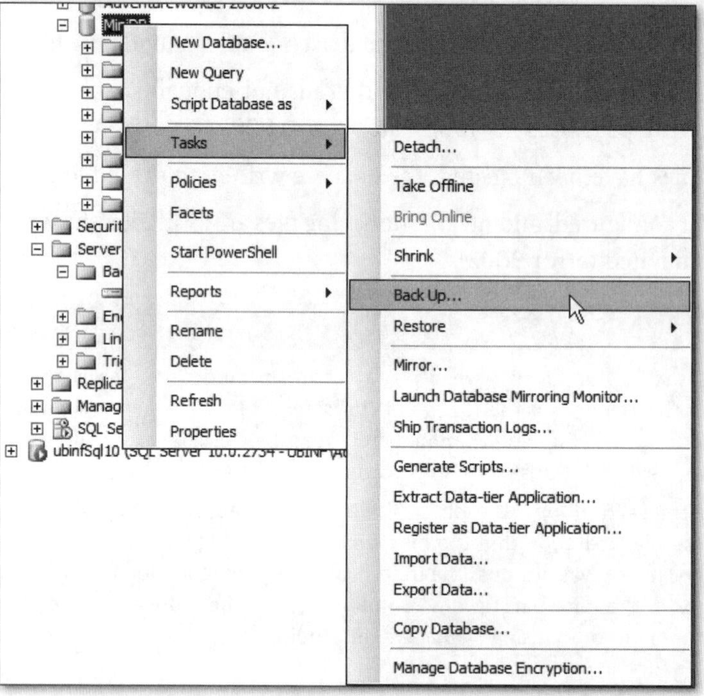

2. The system displays a two-screen dialog box in which you can configure the backup.

   - On the first screen (GENERAL), you make the basic configuration for the backup (for example, whether it concerns a database backup or file backup, or which backup type is to be used). Note that you either specify the file to which you want to back up the data directly (as in this example), or you save the backup to a previously defined backup medium, which you select and assign by using the ADD button. If the server has a local tape drive, the backup can be written directly to this drive. In real life, however, this is unusual because, on the one hand, media management on the SQL Server is very rudimentary and, on the other hand, a more central solution for writing data to the tape drive is favored.

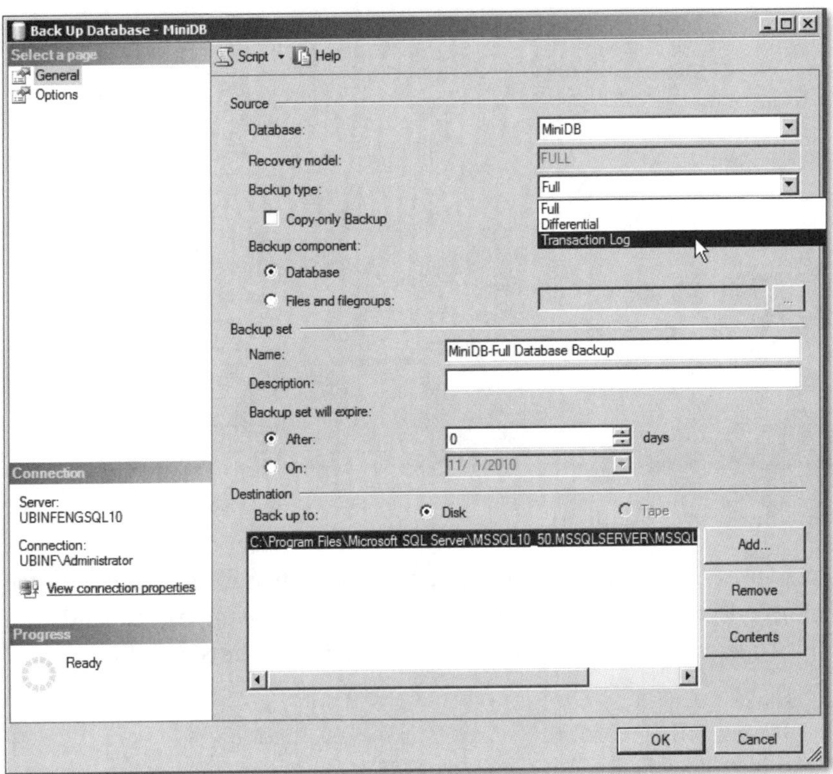

- The second screen in the dialog box (OPTIONS) provides various different options that are largely self-explanatory. The option fields that affect the transaction log are only available if you've selected TRANSACTION LOG as the backup type on the first screen.

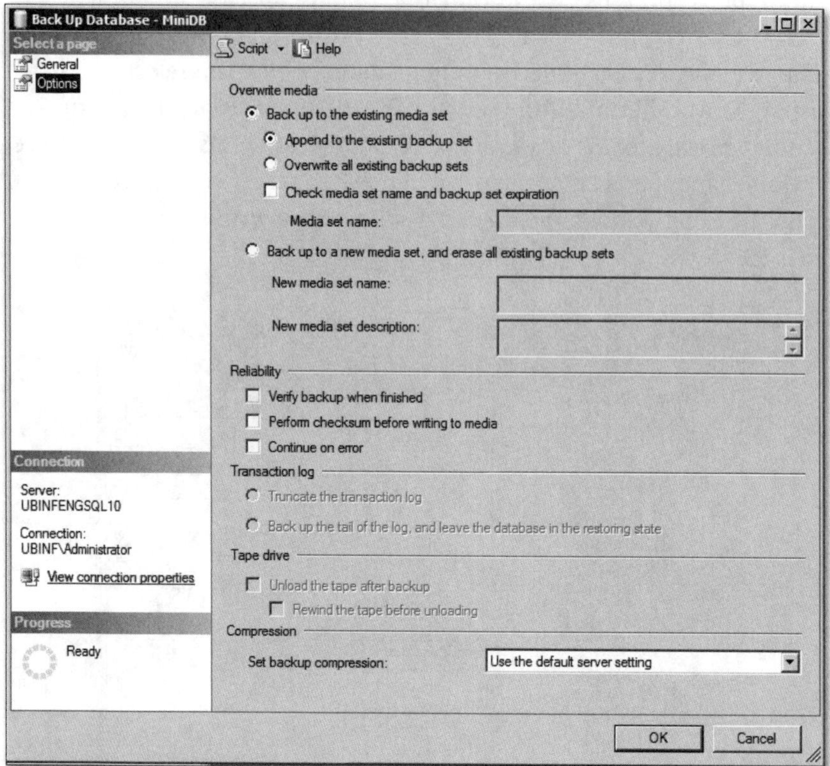

3. Confirm your settings with OK.

If you want to use SQL commands to start the same backup process, you have to use the following code. If you aren't (yet) proficient enough to use these command lines to write this code, you can simply generate the code using the SCRIPT button.

```
BACKUP DATABASE [MiniDB] TO DISK = N'D:\...\MiniDB.bak'
  WITH NOFORMAT, NOINIT, NAME = N'Fully back up MiniDB
database', SKIP, NOREWIND, NOUNLOAD, STATS = 10

GO
```

This is an online backup. In other words, there is no need to interrupt system operation. From a user perspective, however, an extensive backup can impair performance.

8.7.5 Setting Up Maintenance Plans for a Backup

Because starting each backup manually is tedious, you can handle this within a maintenance plan. For an SQL Server, you can set up any number of maintenance plans that start at a certain time and then execute various actions on one or more databases. You can also perform backups.

If you are running several servers, you can configure and perform backups on every single server. This can also be done with maintenance plans. You must bear the following two key aspects in mind:

- **Monitoring**
  If you execute the data backup mechanisms locally on each server, you also have to monitor each machine separately to see whether the data backup is actually performed.
- **Backup devices**
  In a production environment, backups are mostly saved to tape. Of course, you could give each SQL Server its own tape drive, but this would require a lot of administration and monitoring effort. A central solution is much more elegant here. Also note that the media management on the SQL Server is very rudimentary (that is, the administrator has to store tapes, overwrite the data, and do many other things manually).

Despite these limitations, the use of a maintenance plan is not entirely unsuitable. It works perfectly, is easy to handle, and you don't have to deal with the idiosyncrasies of other backup software. Maintenance plans are also used for other tasks. As an SQL Server administrator, you must always deal with this issue.

To create a maintenance plan, follow these steps:

1. The easiest way to create a new maintenance plan is to use the Maintenance Plan Wizard, which you can call via the menu path MANAGEMENT • MAINTENANCE PLANS • MAINTENANCE PLAN WIZARD.

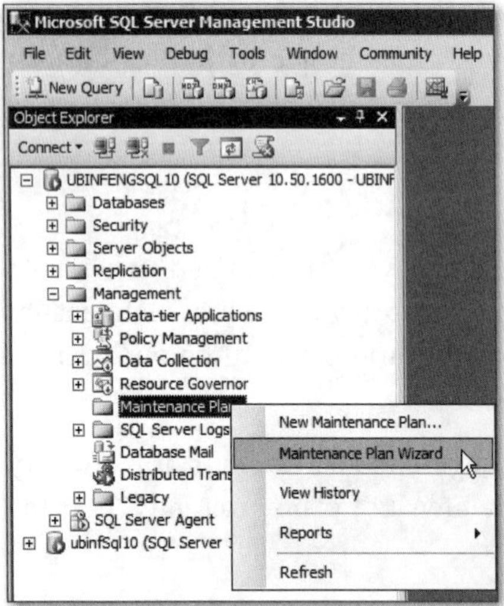

2. The Maintenance Plan Wizard initially guides you through the process of creating a schedule during which the maintenance plan is to be executed. You can more or less store any individual plan, which may, of course, also include recurrence intervals. Choose NEXT.

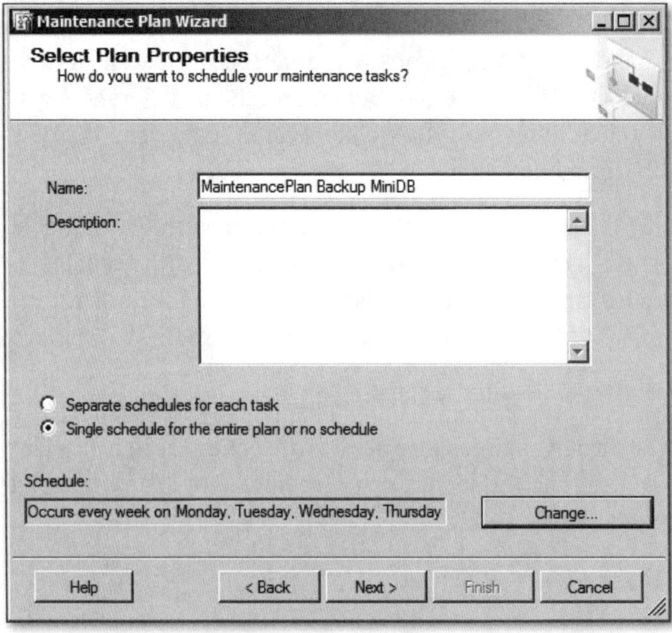

3. The next dialog box contains the most important point, namely selecting the maintenance task (that is, the task to be executed). Here, you can choose from almost a dozen options, including the complete, differential, and transaction log backup. Choose NEXT.

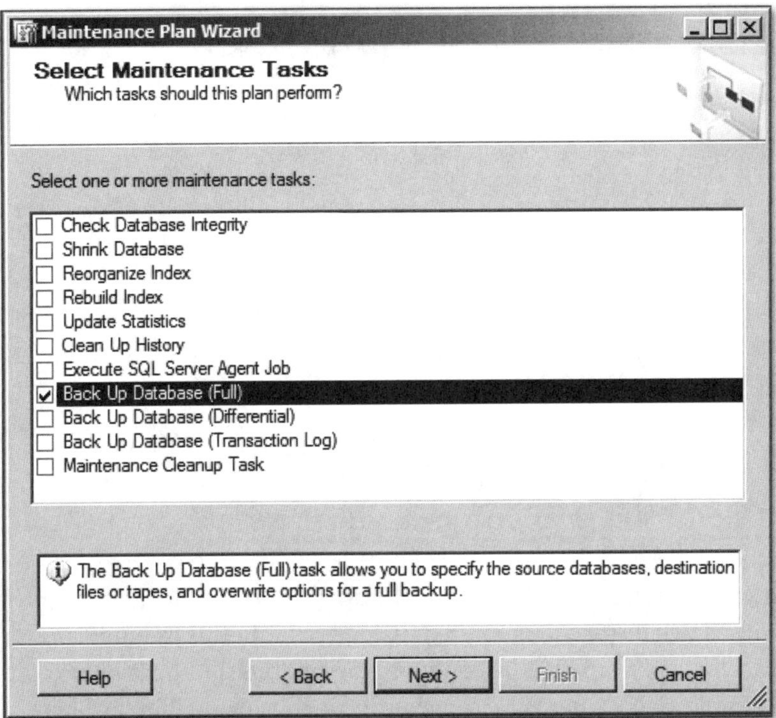

4. If you've selected several maintenance tasks to be executed, the execution sequence will be essential. This can also be configured but not until you access the next dialog box. Using the options displayed, you determine the sequence in which the maintenance tasks in this maintenance plan are processed. Choose NEXT.

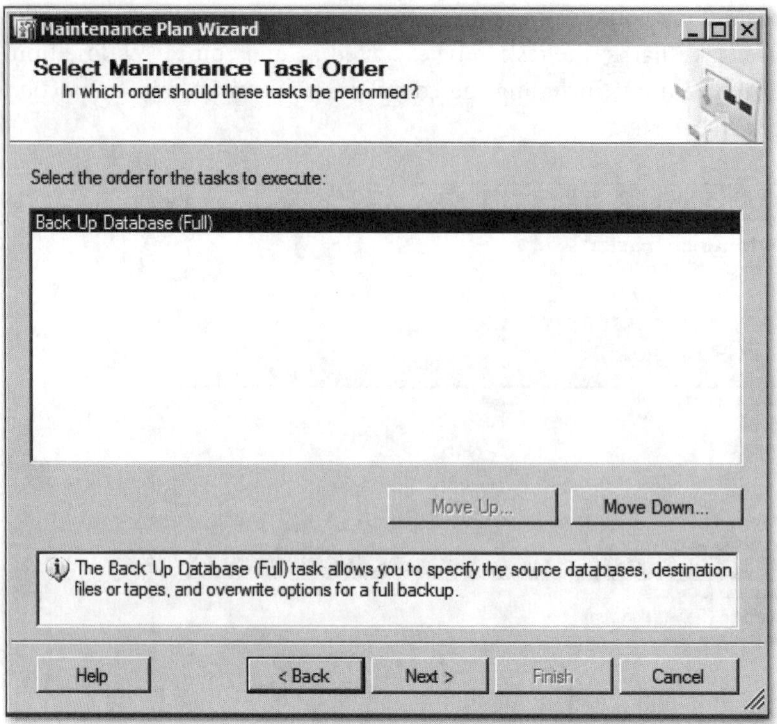

5. Most maintenance tasks require additional information about the configuration. The wizard will display the required dialog boxes. In this example, only a complete backup is performed. The configuration options in the dialog box are similar to those for a backup that is triggered manually. One difference here is the option to create each new backup in a new file that is automatically created (see the CREATE A SUB-DIRECTORY FOR EACH DATABASE checkbox). Choose NEXT.

[+]

Executing a Maintenance Plan

To ensure that the maintenance plan is actually executed, the SQL Server Agent must be running. Because this is not necessarily the case by default, you should check whether it is actually active in the Management Studio. Specify that the SQL Server Agent is automatically started after a server restart.

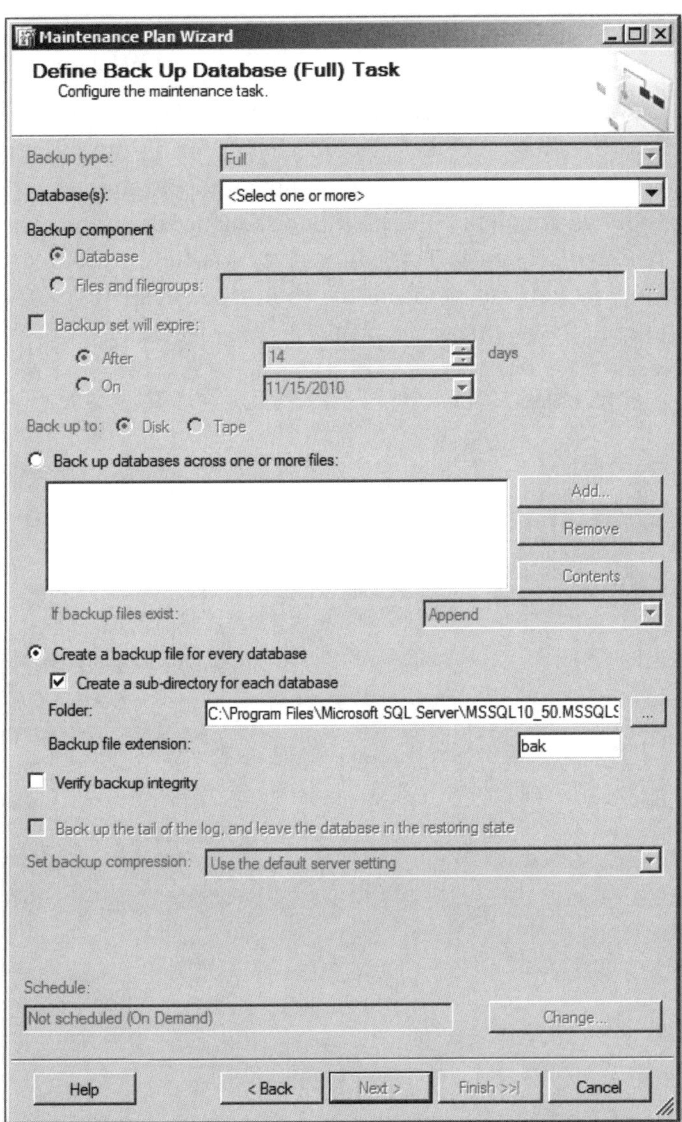

After you've closed the wizard, the maintenance plan is active and works.

You can modify any maintenance plan that is created. To do so, follow these steps:

1. In the context menu for the maintenance plan, choose CHANGE to display the following view.
2. If you've already worked with *SQL Server Integration Services* (SSIS), you will immediately recognize this view and feel at home here. For all others, it's worth mentioning that maintenance plan task elements can be positioned and configured from the toolbox. You define the execution sequence by connecting the elements in the required sequence. This editor gives you full control over your maintenance plans. As you can see from the comprehensive PROPERTIES window, you can configure the maintenance plan tasks in great detail.

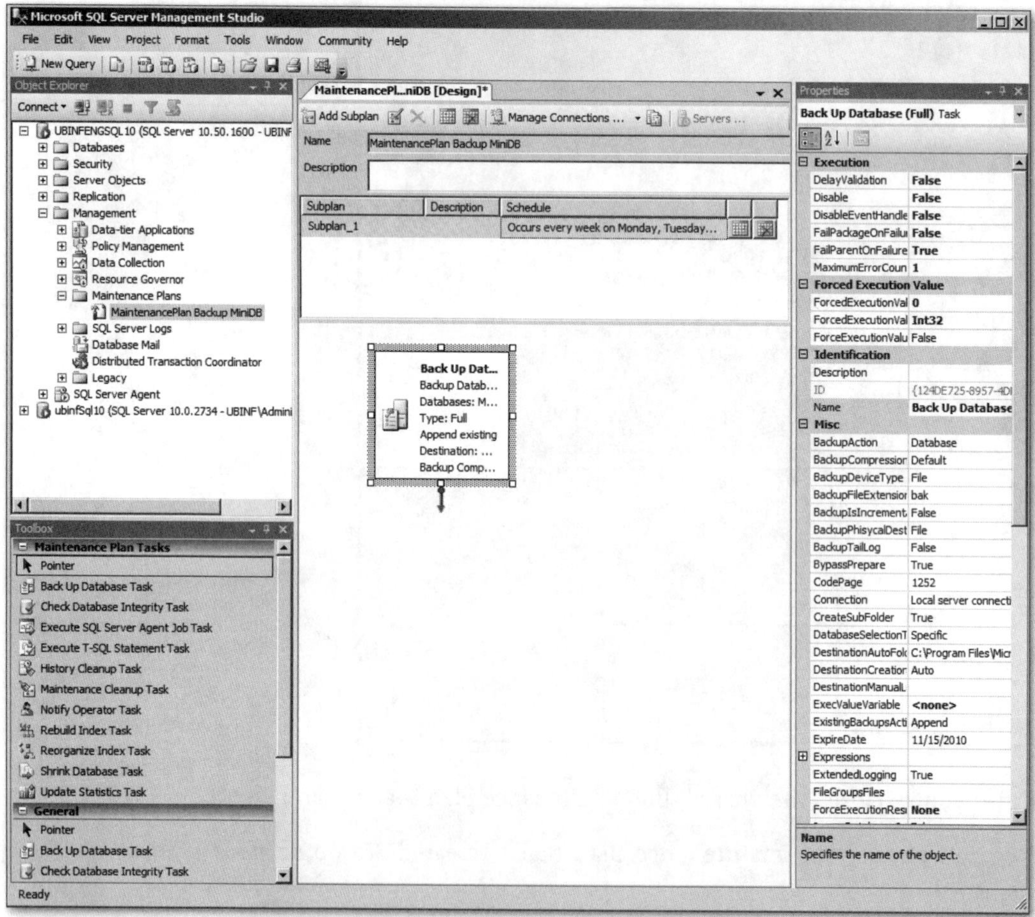

3. If you want to execute the maintenance plan immediately, you can start it directly. You can do this in two places because the maintenance plan is displayed below the MANAGEMENT • MAINTENANCE PLANS node and below the SQL SERVER AGENT • JOBS node.

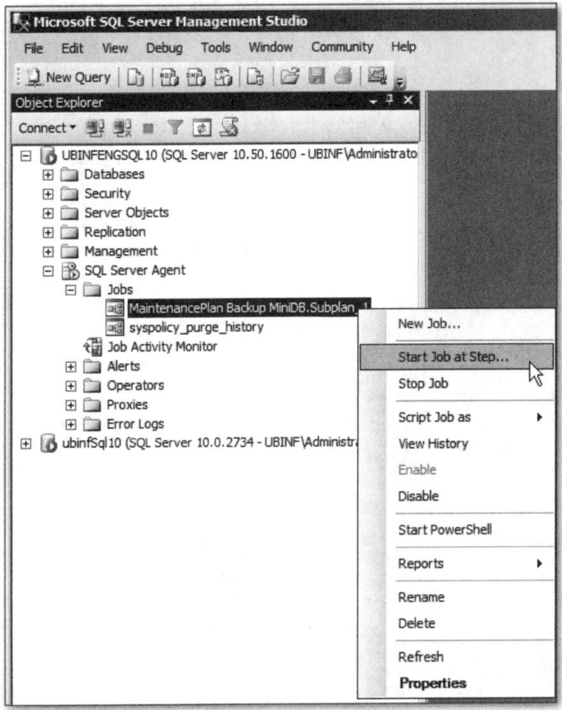

An SQL Server Agent job is created for the maintenance plan, thus making it clear why the SQL Server Agent must be started to execute the maintenance plans.

8.7.6 Backing Up System Databases

In addition to the databases that you create yourself and fill with user data, there are some system databases, which the SQL Server uses for internal purposes (for example, to save the configuration). The master database, in particular, is extremely important and must be backed up. Table 8.1 shows the system databases from a backup perspective.

Database	Description	Backup Required?	Description
master	All of the system settings for the SQL Server are saved in the master database.	Yes	This database is extremely important. It should/must be backed up on a regular basis. The only way to back up the master database is by means of a complete backup. The SQL Server cannot work without the master database. If it is damaged or lost, you can create a new master database. However, you then lose all of the logon information, for example.
msdb	The SQL Server Agent uses this database. Jobs, progression logs, and so on are stored here.	Yes	Even though losing this database would not be as dramatic as losing the master database, a regular backup is necessary because it also contains important information for system operation.
model	This is the template used for new databases.	Yes	Even though losing this database would not be as dramatic as losing the master database, we nevertheless recommend that you back up this database after every change.
tempdb	This database is used to cache temporary result sets. When you shut down the instance, any data stored there is deleted.	No	You cannot back up this database because it only contains temporary data.

Table 8.1 System Databases—Backup

Master Database

As already mentioned in the table, you must back up the master database on a regular basis. The following processes bring about a change in the database and therefore make a backup necessary:

- Creating or deleting a user database. If a user database is extended to include new data, this does not affect the master database.
- Adding or removing files or file groups.
- Adding logon names or other processes that relate to logon security. Database backup processes such as adding a user to a database do not affect the master database.
- Changing server-wide configuration options or database configuration options.
- Creating or removing logical backup media.
- Configuring the server for distributed queries and Remote Procedure Calls (RPCs) such as adding connection servers or remote logon names.

However, it has proven beneficial to include the database in a backup job to be executed on a daily basis, for example.

The only way to back up the master database is by means of a complete database backup. Other procedures are not supported. Because the master database is not too large, this isn't a problem.

The msdb and model Databases

As already mentioned in the table, the msdb database contains information for and about the execution of SQL Server Agent jobs. The database changes in the following cases:

- Planning tasks
- Saving integration services packages that were created using the import/export wizard in an instance of the SQL Server
- Managing an online backup and restore run
- Replication
- Setup.exe resetting the restore model to SIMPLE
- Additions or changes to guidelines or conditions for guideline-based administration

Even though you would only need to back up the msdb database in the event of changes, the easiest option is to back up this database on a regular basis (for example, daily), in the same way as you back up the master database.

The model database only changes if an administrator makes adjustments (this rarely happens). In general, we recommend that you back up the model database as part of the regular backup of the master and msdb databases. Even though this is too often in principle, it is much more complicated to manage a separate backup record for this extremely small database than to simply back it up as part of the regular backup.

8.7.7 SQL Server Logs

When a server is running, you must view its logs. The SQL server logs are available below the MANAGEMENT node for this purpose.

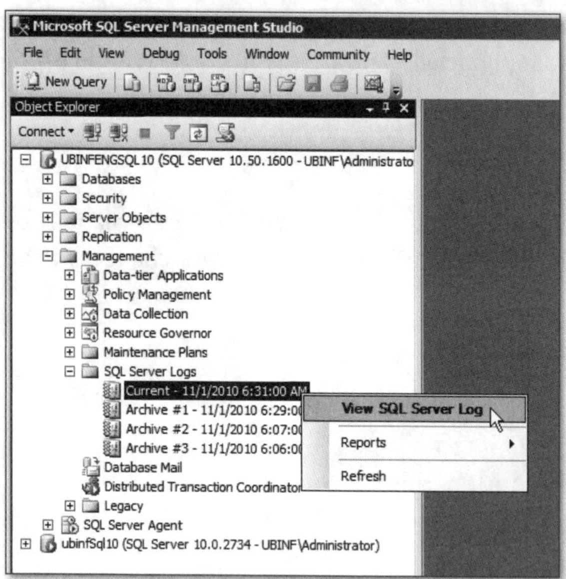

You can open current or archived logs. You call the log file viewer to "read" the logs.

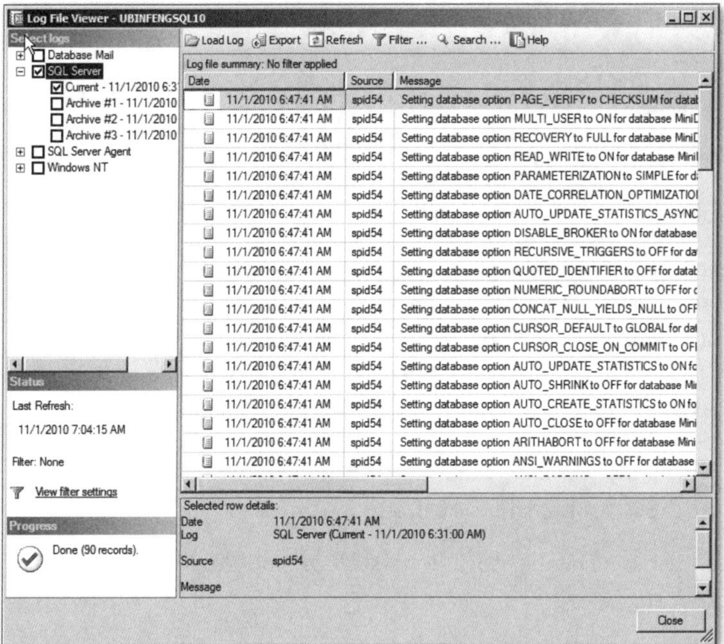

The log file entries are displayed in the log file viewer.

8.8 Database Administration—MaxDB

MaxDB is SAP's database management system, which was known as SAP DB before Version 7.5. From a functional scope, the database is comparable with other database systems. However, it is primarily intended for small and medium-sized enterprises where the focus is on a low administration effort and low costs.

8.8.1 Database Studio

MaxDB databases are managed in *Database Studio*, which replaces the two tools *Database Manager GUI* and *SQL Studio* as of MaxDB Version 7.7. You can use the Database Studio for all MaxDB databases as of Version 7.5.

The Database Studio provides a graphical user interface (GUI), which you can use to perform all important database tasks, including the following:

- Starting and stopping the database
- Database monitoring
- Performance analyses
- Backing up and restoring the database

We will describe some of these features here.

[+]

Additional Information

Additional information about MaxDB and the Database Studio as well as extensive documentation is available on the MaxDB home page *http://maxdb.sap.com* or in the SAP Community Network at *www.sdn.sap.com/irj/sdn/maxdb*.

8.8.2 Starting and Stopping the Database

If necessary, you can use the Database Studio to start or stop the MaxDB database. To do so, follow these steps:

1. On the Windows desktop, choose START • PROGRAMS • MAXDB • DATABASE STUDIO.
2. In the EXPLORER window, select your database (for example, NSP) under SERVERS. A traffic light icon indicates the current status:
   - **Green:** The database is active (online).
   - **Yellow:** The database is in administration mode.
   - **Red:** The database is stopped (offline).

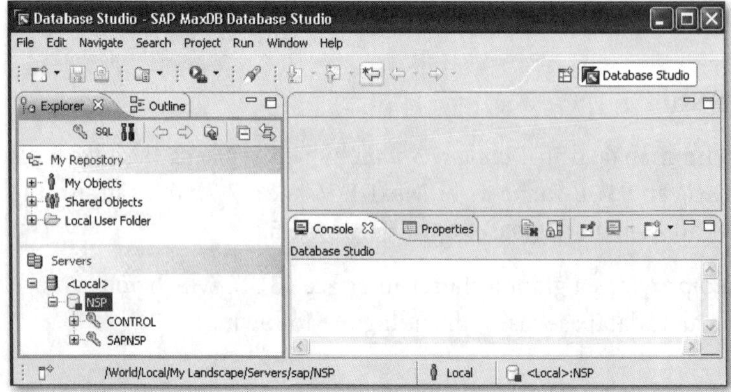

3. To start the database, right-click the context menu, and choose Set State • Online.

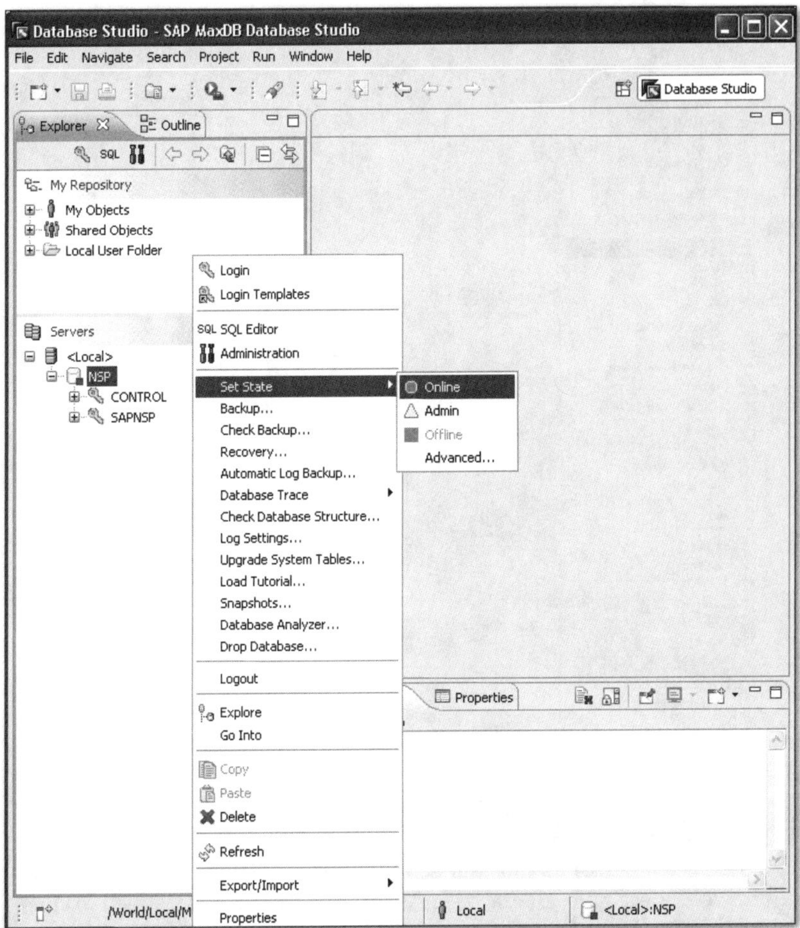

4. The database is started. After you've successfully completed the process, a green traffic light is displayed. To stop the database, choose Set State • Offline.

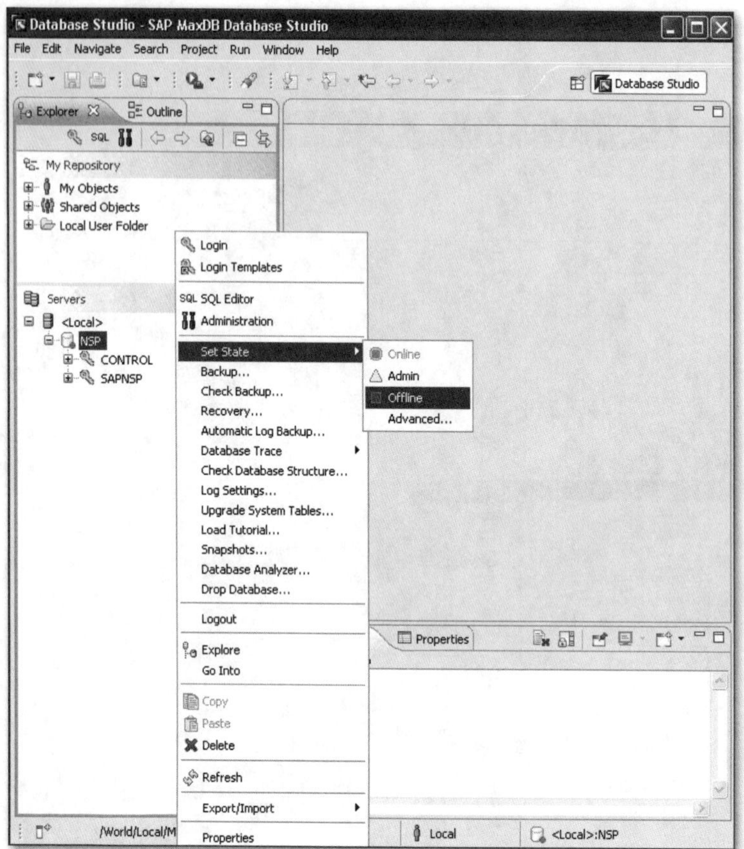

[+]

Admin Status

The ADMIN mode is intended for administrative tasks. Certain actions can only be performed in this mode (for example, a database restore). The database is stopped for this purpose. In other words, the SAP system cannot access the database.

8.8.3 Database Monitoring

You can use the Database Studio to monitor various aspects of the database, for example:

- Occupied storage space and available storage space
- Status of the log files

- Access rate on the database cache
- Database backups that have been performed
- Database activities (read/write, lock, etc.)

You should monitor the database so that you can detect errors early on and therefore avoid problems. To do so, follow these steps:

1. On the Windows desktop, choose START • PROGRAMS • MAXDB • DATABASE STUDIO.
2. Right-click to open the context menu for your database, and choose ADMINISTRATION.

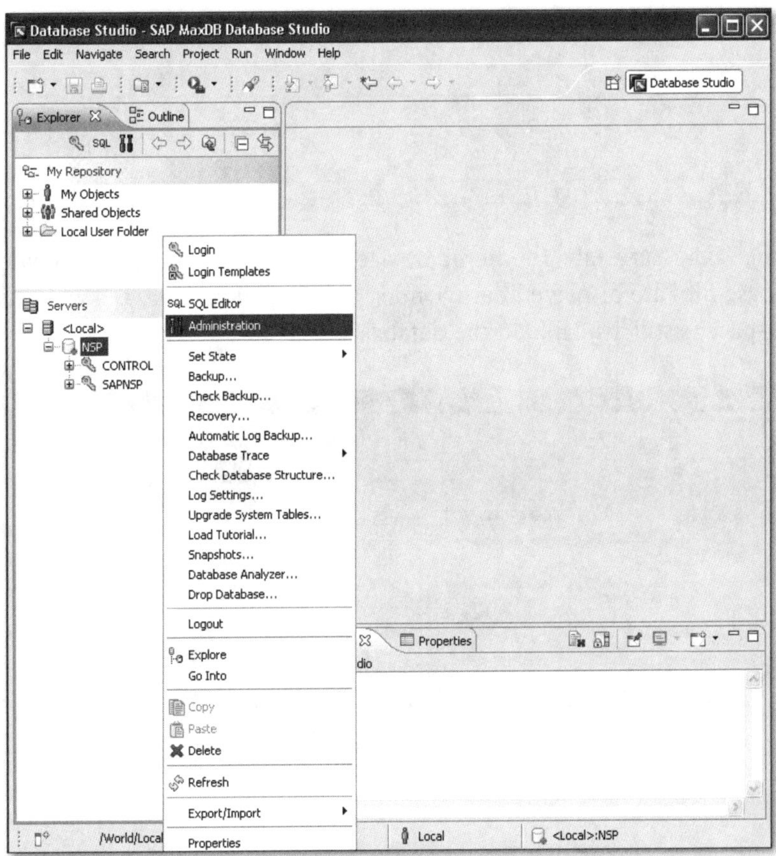

3. The ADMINISTRATION window opens in the screen area on the right side. General information is summarized on the OVERVIEW tab.

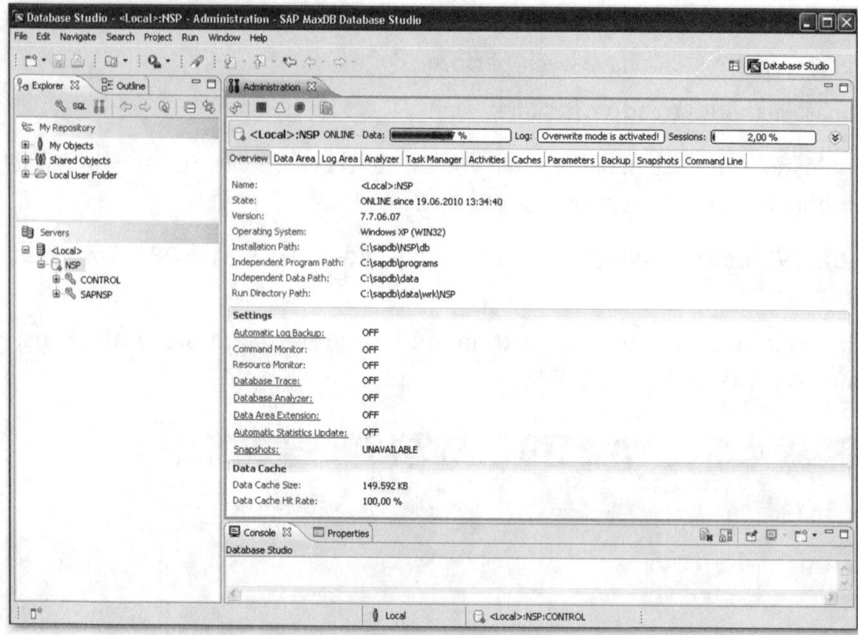

4. Switch to the DATA AREA tab. The number, size, storage location, and fill level of the database files are displayed here. Under USAGE, you can see, at a glance, how much space is still available in the database.

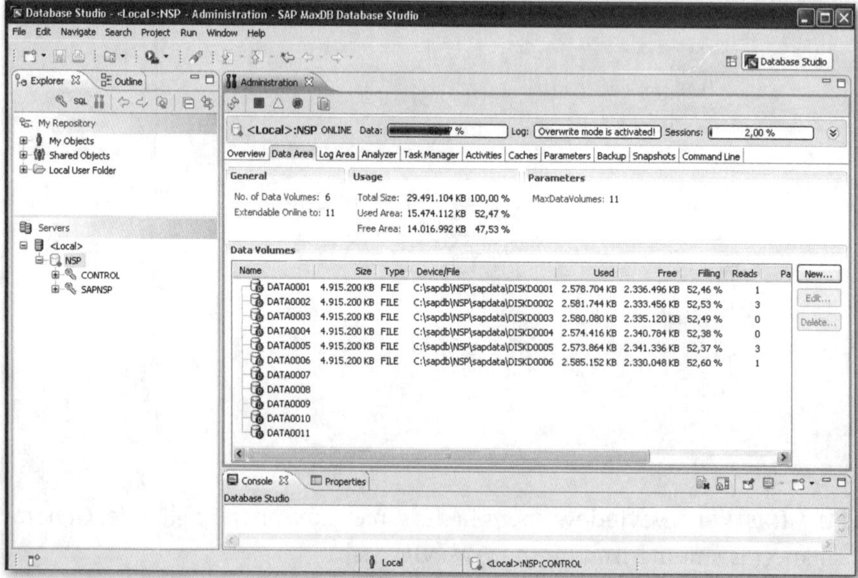

5. Select the LOG AREA tab. It informs you about the status of the database logs. If no further storage space is available, no further transaction log entries can be created, which causes the SAP system to stop.

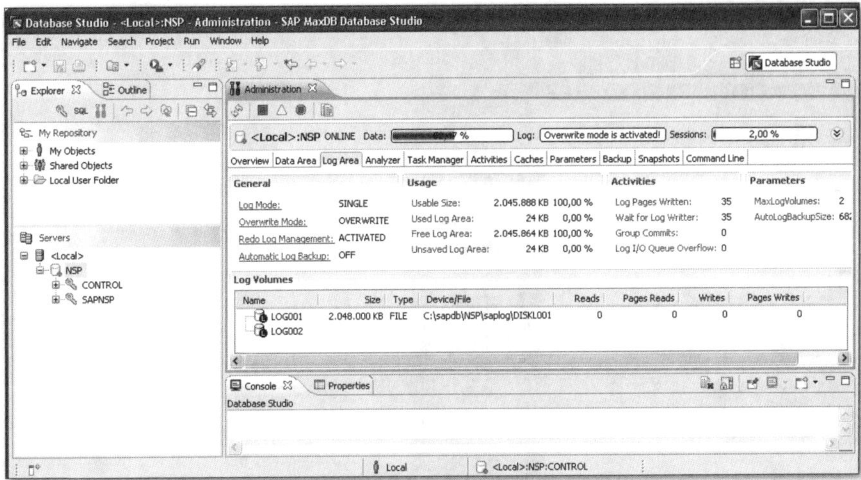

6. The ACTIVITIES tab contains the statistical data for database activities (for example, read and write accesses or locks).

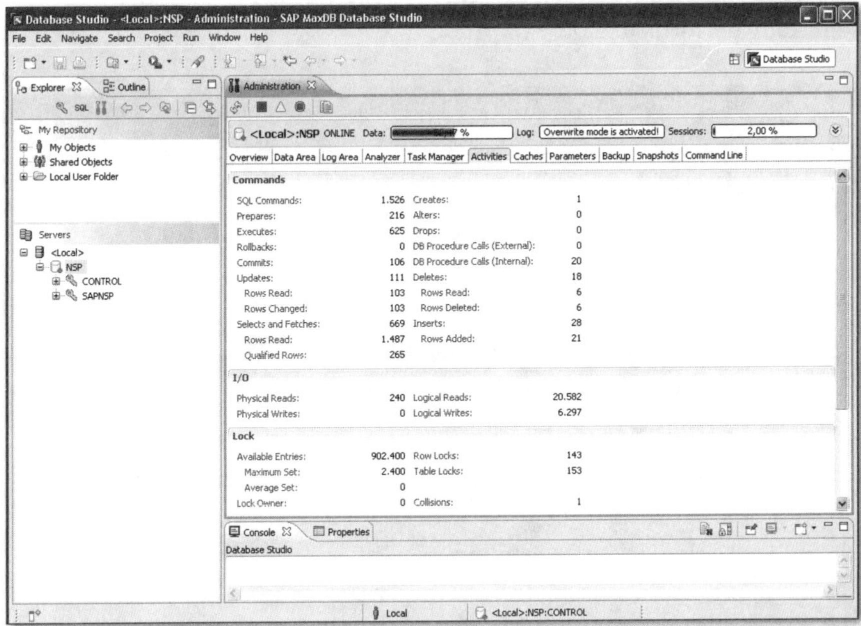

7. The Caches tab also contains statistical values. Here you can see how many database accesses from cache storage can be handled by the system. A high hit rate indicates that the accesses are executed in a particularly efficient manner.

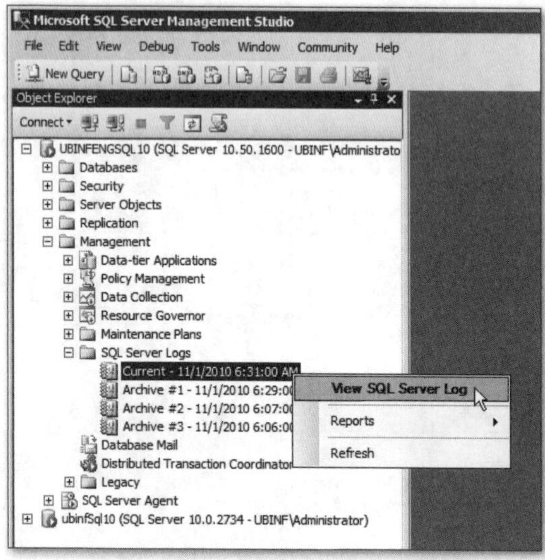

8. Switch to the Backup tab. You can use this overview to monitor your database backups. Pay particular attention to error messages, which indicate that a backup was not fully performed.

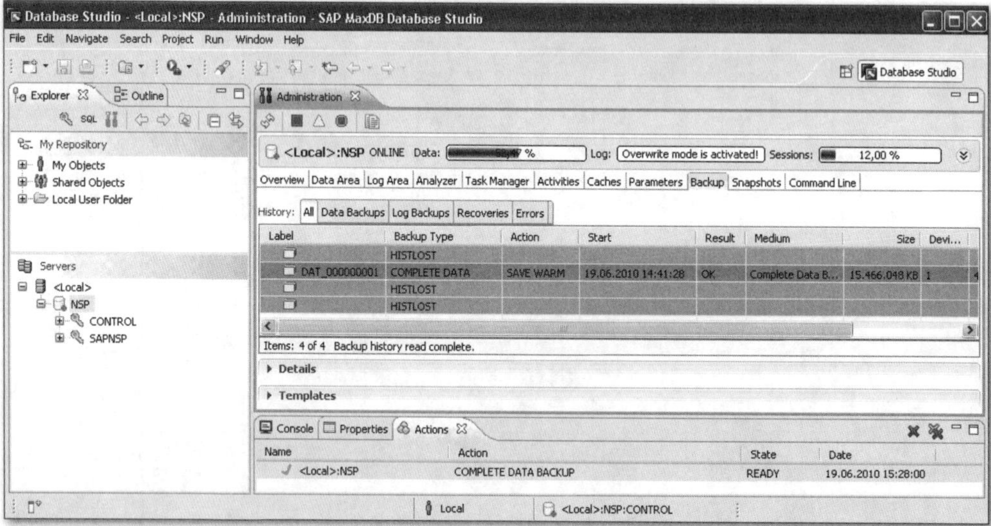

Automatic Notification If Problems Occur

If you want to automate database monitoring, you can use *database events* to send email notifications if certain threshold values are exceeded. For example, you can be informed if the database fill level exceeds a value of 90% or if an error occurs during a database backup.

8.8.4 Backing Up the Database

You can use the Database Studio to create database backups (for more information, see Chapter 6), including the following:

- Complete database backups
- Incremental database backups
- Database log backup

Automating the Backup

Database backups are extremely important when restoring the system after a serious problem. You should therefore automate the process as far as possible (preferably using the DBA Planning Calendar, see Section 8.1) and only using the manual procedures described here on special occasions (e.g., before you import support packages).

To perform a database backup, follow these steps:

1. On the Windows desktop, choose START • PROGRAMS • MAXDB • DATABASE STUDIO.
2. Right-click to open the context menu for your database, and choose BACKUP.

Incremental Database Backup

A complete backup most exist before you can create an incremental backup.

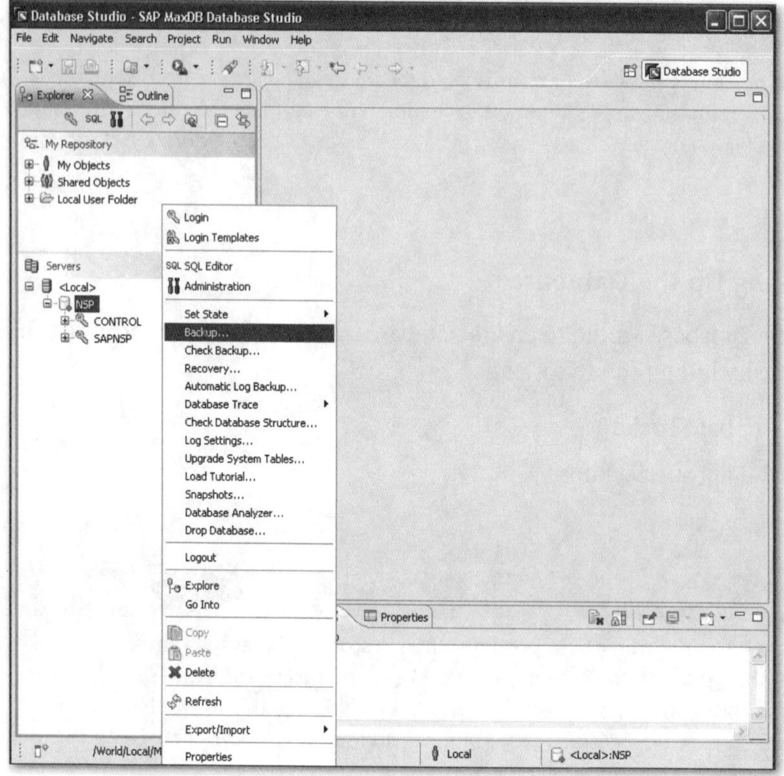

3. Choose the option you require (for example, COMPLETE DATA BACKUP), and then choose NEXT.

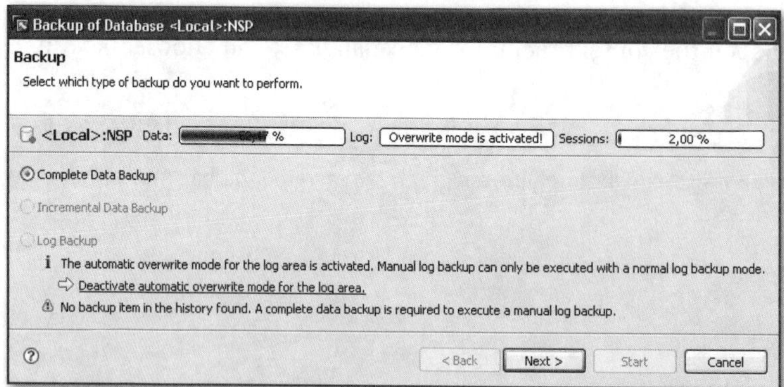

4. You need a *backup template* so that you can execute a database backup. Select an existing template or choose NEW to create a new template.

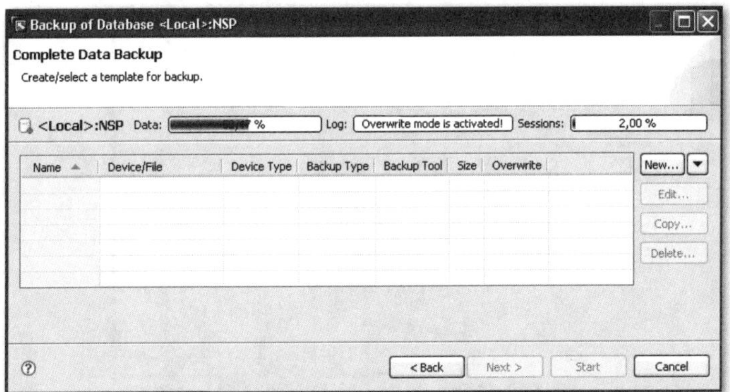

5. Make the following settings:
   - NAME: Assign a name to the template.
   - BACKUP TYPE: Select the backup type.
   - DEVICE TYPE: Find a storage medium.
   - BACKUP TOOL: Optional if you are using a third-party tool.
   - DEVICE/FILE: Specify the name or path of the storage medium.

   Then choose OK.

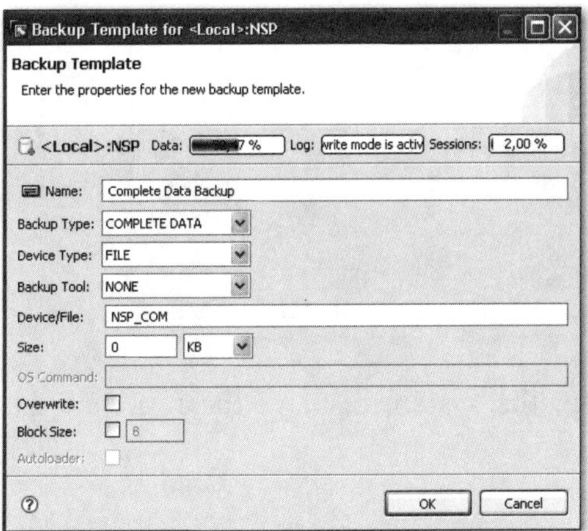

6. The template has been created. Choose NEXT.

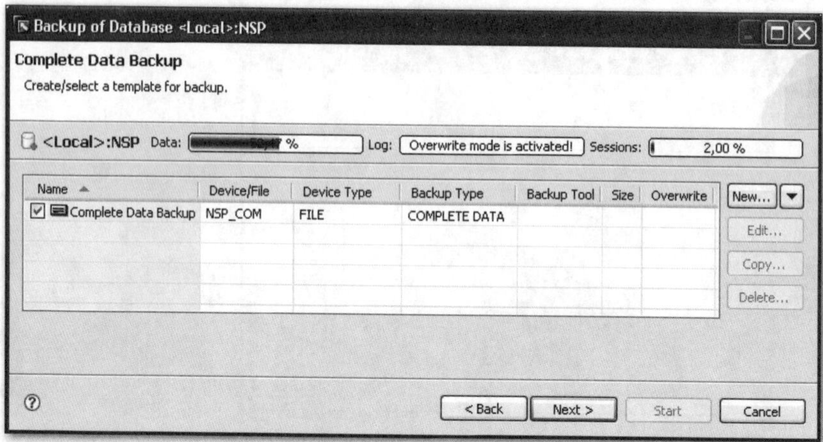

7. To start the backup, choose START.

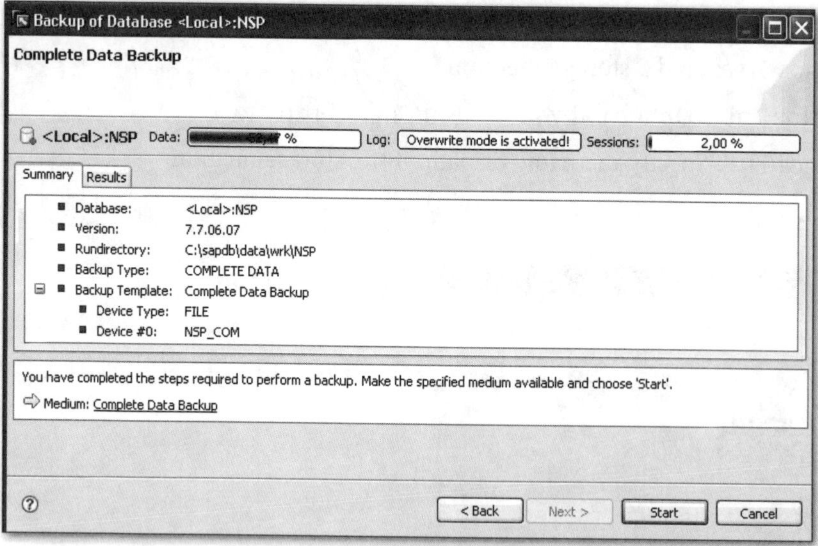

8. After you've completed the backup, the system displays the result of the process.

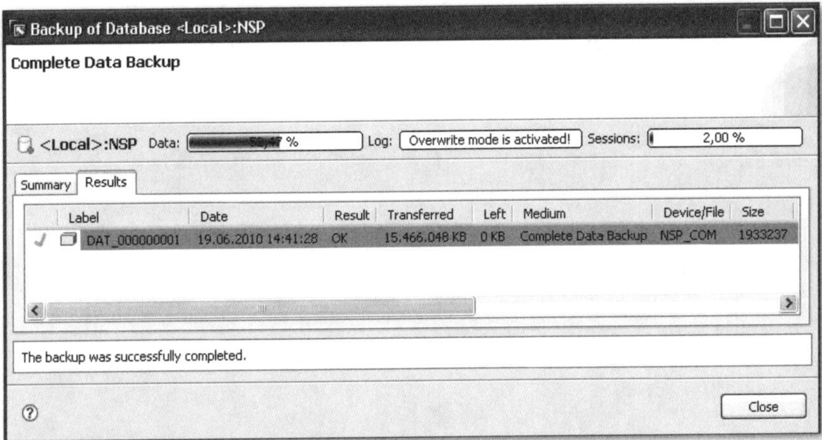

[+]

Restoring the Database

You can use existing backups to restore the database after an error occurs. To restore the database, choose RECOVERY in the context menu for the database. The database must have the admin status for this purpose.

8.9 Summary

Database administration is not solely the task of an SAP system administrator. Consequently, this chapter describes only general concepts and SAP tools that can be used irrespective of the database system. The database-specific sections in this chapter provide a brief introduction to the special idiosyncrasies of various database systems.

If you are entrusted with the task of managing a database, you should read additional specialist literature to prepare yourself sufficiently for this complex task.

This chapter describes the use of SAP transactions for calling operating system information—irrespective of the platform. It also explains the most important aspects of operating system monitoring.

9 Operating System Administration

The tasks that this chapter describes are usually carried out by data center employees. Depending on the size and structure of an enterprise, SAP administrators may be responsible for server administration at the operating system level. Consequently, they need to know the scope of the monitoring process for the operating system and which SAP transaction can be used for it.

Like any other program, an SAP system runs on an operating system (Microsoft Windows Server 2007 or Unix, for example). The operating system manages the hardware of the physical server and provides resources (such as memory, processor time, and hard disk memory) for the SAP software. If these resources become scarce, this usually affects the performance and functioning of the SAP system; in a worst-case scenario, this can result in system downtime.

9.1 Checking the Memory Usage of the File System

The operating system's file system must have sufficient memory for the operation of the SAP system. When tasks are carried out, the system sometimes creates files that occupy memory. If no hard disk memory is available, the database can't write to a file. This may lead to downtime and thus to a breakdown of the SAP system. Consequently, monitoring the memory is one of the most important tasks at the operating system level. Files that are stored in the file system need to be checked from time to time and then may have to be moved, archived, or deleted.

The following objects occupy a large amount of memory, so you need to observe them carefully when monitoring the memory:

- Transport requests
- Support packages
- Extract files from the SAP system
- Program logs
- Backup logs
- Error logs
- Inbound interface files
- Third-party programs that store data outside the SAP database
- Trace files
- Spool files

To prevent the file system from overflowing, you should observe the following:

- Plan future memory on the disk.
- Determine if the memory needs to be extended. If this is the case, you must plan the procurement and installation of additional memory elements. Interruptions of the normal business operation should be kept to a minimum.
- Determine if the file system needs to be cleaned. If files have to be archived, use high-quality storage media only, for example, optical storage media, CD-ROMs, or other long-term storage media.
- You must also check if the standard cleanup programs run properly (see SAP Note 16083).

You can check the memory usage using the standard tools of the operating system (Explorer in Windows, for example) or with a monitoring tool. This can be third-party software or the SAP system's CCMS monitor.

9.1.1 Monitoring the File System Using the CCMS Alert Monitor

Chapter 3 already introduced the CCMS Alert Monitor, which you can use to monitor the memory during the operating system administration. The following example briefly describes the procedure again:

1. Enter Transaction "RZ20" in the command box, and press the Enter key (or select the menu option Tools • CCMS • Control/Monitoring • RZ20—CCMS Monitor Sets).
2. Expand the SAP CCMS Monitor Templates monitor set, and position the cursor on the Filesystems monitor. Start it using Load Monitor ( ).

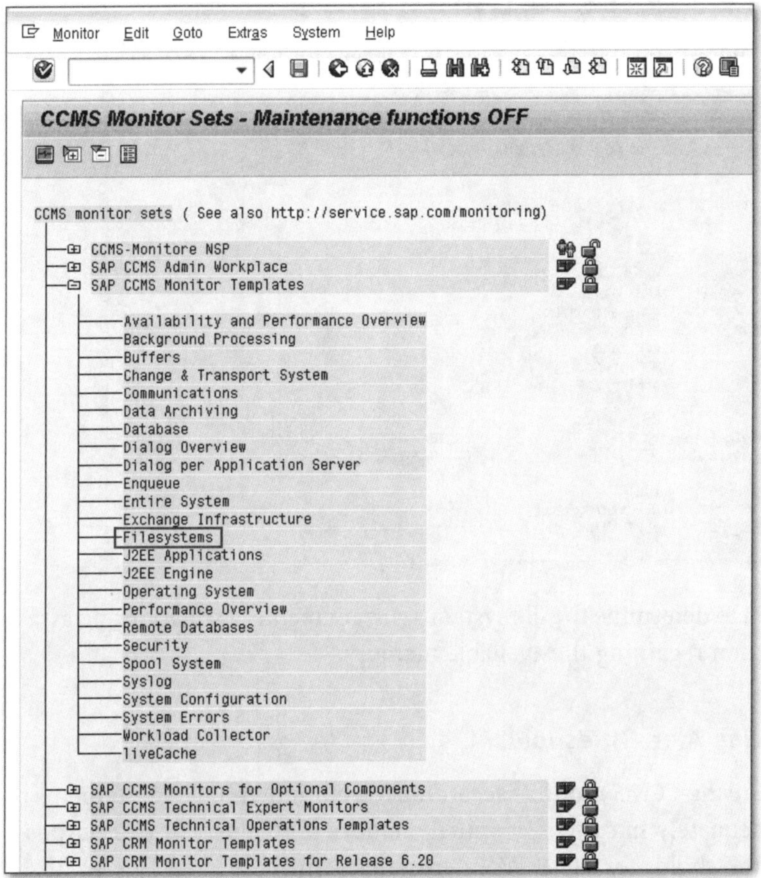

3. The system displays the data that is determined by the CCMS Alert Monitor in a tree structure. Expand the */<SID>/usr/sap* directory, for example, to view the alert values (for example, Freespace and Percentage_Used). The alert values are highlighted, and the color specifies the respective alert status:

- Green (OK)
- Yellow (warning)
- Red (critical)

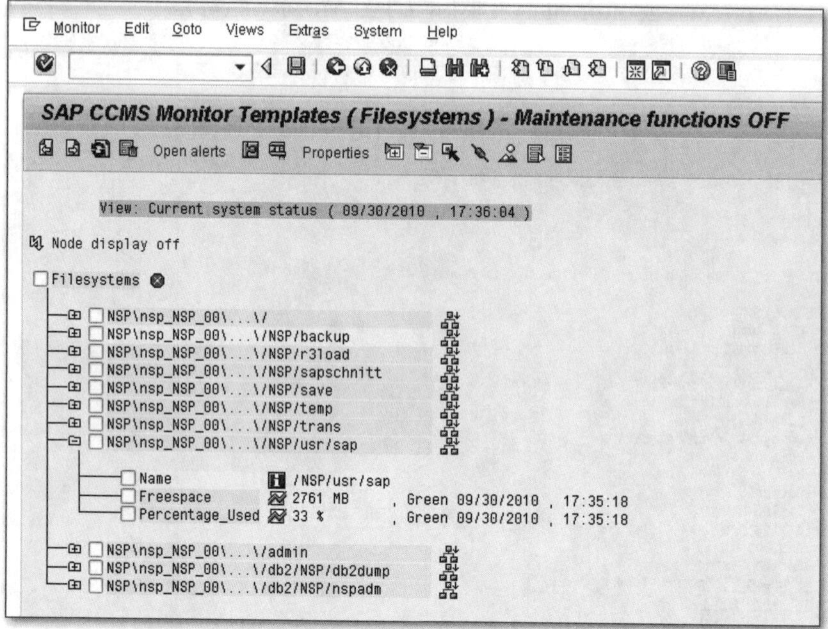

This enables you to determine the file system's current memory situation and assess the need for action regarding the available memory.

9.1.2 Changing Alert Thresholds

You can configure the CCMS monitor according to your individual requirements to be informed adequately in case of potential memory problems. For this purpose, customize the thresholds for the CCMS alert status display:

1. Expand the node of the drive for which you want to change the threshold (e.g., /<SID>/USR/SAP), and select an alert (e.g., FREESPACE). Click on PROPERTIES.

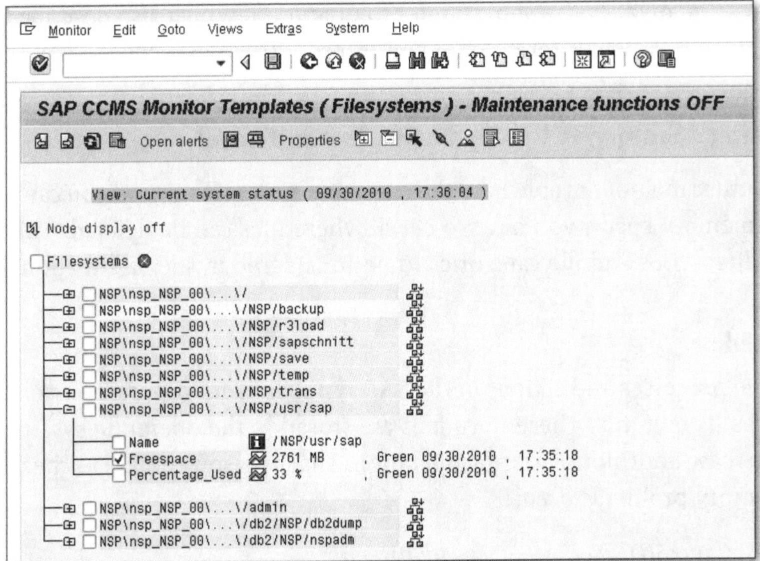

2. To change the thresholds, use DISPLAY <-> CHANGE (✎) to switch to change mode. Enter the desired thresholds for which the status is supposed to change.

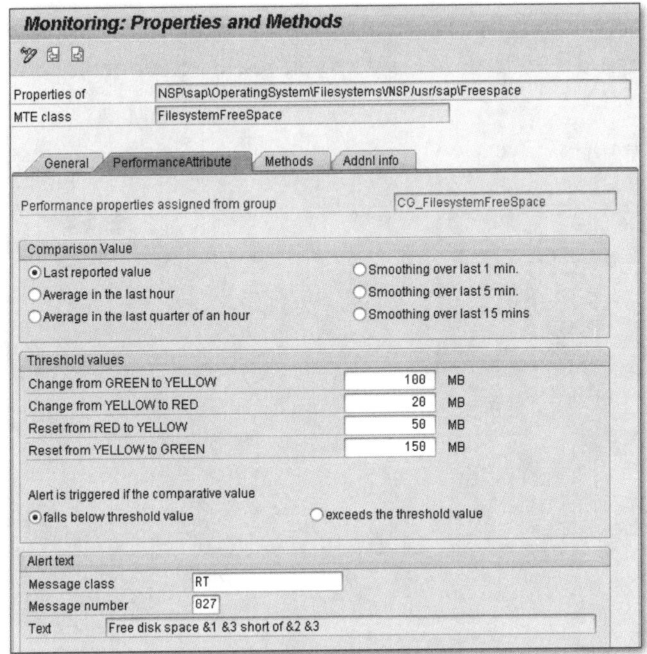

For more information on alert thresholds, refer to Chapter 3, which also describes how you can have the system inform you when thresholds are exceeded.

9.1.3 Releasing Memory at the Operating System Level

When you encounter memory problems at the operating system level, and you can't add additional memory space, you have to check where files can be deleted. This section names directories and file categories to be considered in such a situation.

Deleting Trace Files

Trace files log the processes and actions of the SAP system's work processes. Every work process has its own file. These trace files are stored at the operating system level and can increase enormously during operation. That's reason enough to check them when memory problems occur:

1. Check the */usr/sap/<SID>/DVEMGS00/work* directory:
   - *dev_rfc<number>[.old]* (RFC trace)
   - *dev_w<number>[.old]* (work process trace)
2. Sort the directory by size to determine the distribution of the memory usage. If the trace files have become very large (that is, greater than 100 MB), you should first save and then delete them. This way you release free memory at the operating system level.
3. Call Transaction SM50 (Process Overview).

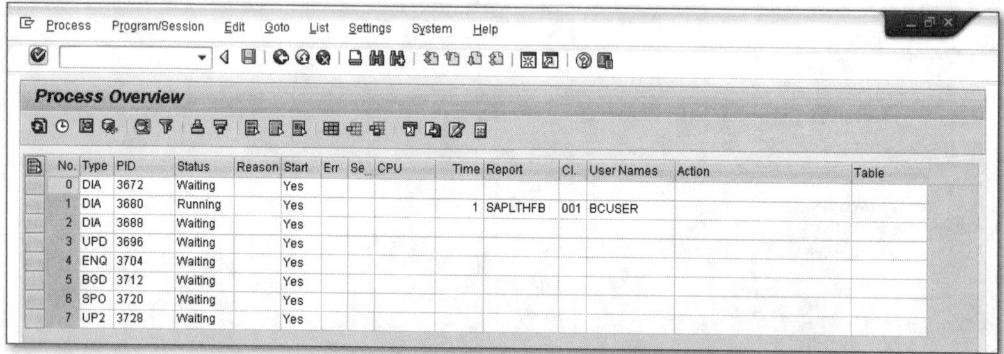

4. To save the trace files before deleting them, select the corresponding work process and then Process • Trace • Save as Local File. The system asks for a file path under which you want to store the copy of the trace file.

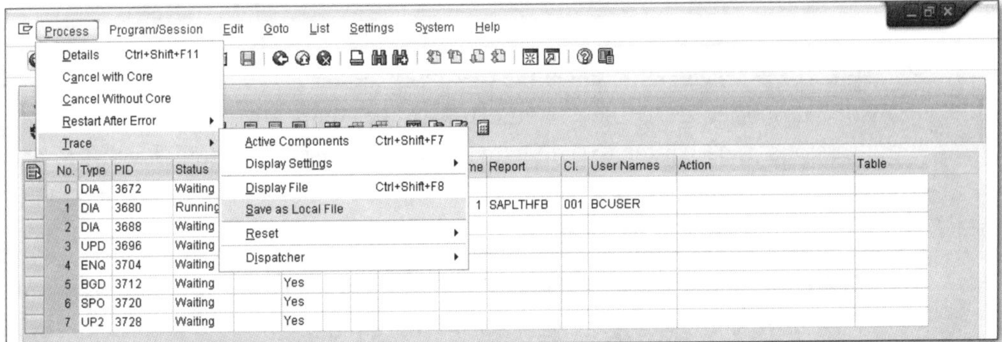

5. Delete the trace file via Process • Trace • Reset • Work Process Files.

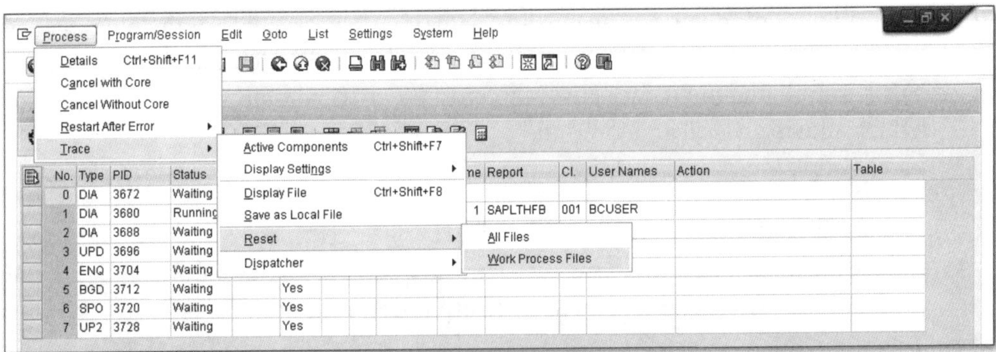

6. Confirm the deletion in the dialog box with Yes.

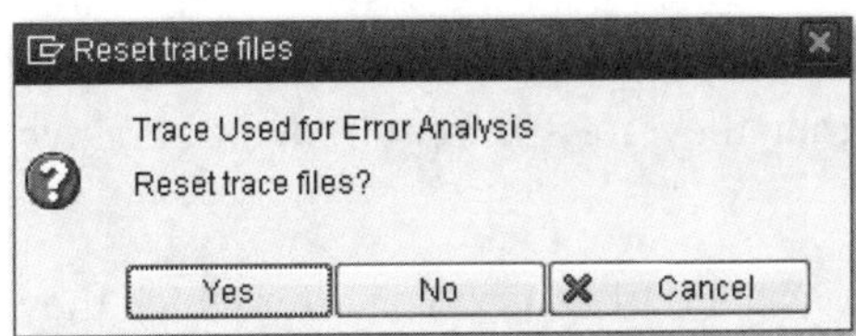

7. Return to the */usr/sap/<SID>/ DVEMGS00/work* directory at the operating system level, and manually delete the files with the .old extension after having saved them if required.

[⚙]

Old Trace Files (.old Extension)

The system does not write log entries into trace files with the .old extension; however, they contain older entries that you may need for troubleshooting.

Deleting Spool Files, Job Logs, and Batch Input Logs

Print or output requests (see Chapter 16), background jobs, and running batch input sessions (see Chapter 15) generate files at the operating system level. The size of these files depends on the scope of the respective request or log. If necessary, check the following directories:

- */usr/sap/<SID>/SYS/global/<client>JOBLG* (job logs)
- */usr/sap/<SID>/SYS/global/<client>SPOOL* (spool requests)
- */usr/sap/<SID>/SYS/global/<client>BDCLG* (batch input sessions)

First, sort the files of the directories by size to identify the objects that occupy a large amount of memory. The creation date or last change date of the files enables you to determine when the output request, job log, or batch input log was created. Furthermore, the file names always refer to the original object in the SAP system, which allows for a clear allocation.

- The job log that is stored in the *<client>JOBLG* directory contains the ID of the job from Transaction SM37 (Job Overview).
- The file name in the *<client>SPOOL* directory ends with the spool number of the spool request in Transaction SP01 (Output Controller).
- The TEMSE ID field of the batch input session logs in Transaction SM35 (Batch Input) contains the file name in the *<client>BDCLG directory*.

If you have detected exceptionally large files at the operating system level, search for the corresponding object in the SAP system. Before deleting files, ask the owner of the print request, job, or session whether they are still required, and archive the files if necessary.

Spool requests, job logs, and batch input logs have an expiry date after which they can be deleted from the SAP system so that the memory at the operating system level is released. The following standard jobs check whether an object has reached its deletion date and, if this is the case, remove it from the database:

- SAP_REORG_JOBS (job logs)
- SAP_REORG_SPOOL (spool requests)
- SAP_REORG_BATCHINPUT (batch input logs)

If you determine that older files have not been reorganized, use Transaction SM37 to check if these jobs are regularly scheduled in your system and completed without errors. If this is not the case, correct the scheduling of the standard jobs using Transaction SM36.

Deleting Support Package Files

You use support packages or support package stacks to import corrections or enhancements into your SAP system (for more information, see Chapter 18). You download support packages from the SAP Support Portal and usually store them locally on a PC. To update the system, you need to copy the files to the SAP server where they accordingly occupy space in the file system—depending on the type of the SAP system and scope of the update, this can involve several hundred megabytes.

Therefore, check the size of the */usr/sap/trans/EPS/in* directory at the operating system level. When the support packages have been successfully imported to the SAP system, you can remove them from the directory. Usually, you don't need them again at a later stage. If required, create a backup copy.

Deleting Transport Files

Transport files are used to transport SAP objects and Customizing changes or transfer them between clients and systems. If transport files are not monitored, they can occupy a disproportionally large amount of memory. You should check the transport directory in the following cases:

- After a large implementation for which numerous transports have been generated that occupy a large amount of memory.
- Directly before (or after) a database is copied; if you don't use a central transport directory, most of (or even all) the files with a date that lies before the copy process become useless.

Follow these steps to check the transport directory:

1. Check the following directories under */usr/sap/trans*:
   - *data*
   - *cofiles* (command files)
   - *log*
2. Sort the directory by date to view the creation date of the files.
3. Archive all files that are no longer required, for example, files that were created before an update of a database or that have been used successfully for all target systems.
4. Optionally, archive obsolete transports on storage media, such as tapes or CDs.

Note that transport requests whose transport files have been deleted are no longer available for the Transport Management System, that is, they can no longer be imported.

9.2 Retrieving Operating System Information

The SAP system provides its own operating system monitor. The data for this monitor is determined by SAPOSCOL, a program that is part of the SAP kernel and runs at the operating system level. You can use the operating system monitor to analyze performance problems (see Chapter 11). It also provides an operating system log that collects messages on critical events at the operating system level. Depending on the operating system, one or more logs are created. The logs can contain information on potential problems (for example, errors that occur at hard disk level may indicate that the hard disk is defective and needs to be replaced). Follow these steps to use the monitor to determine the state of the operating system and have the system display the operating system log:

1. To call the operating system monitor, enter Transaction "OS06" in the command box, and press the Enter key (or select the menu option Tools • CCMS • Control/Monitoring • Performance • Operating System • Local • OS06—Activity).
2. Select the Operating System collector button to view the data on the SAPOSCOL program.

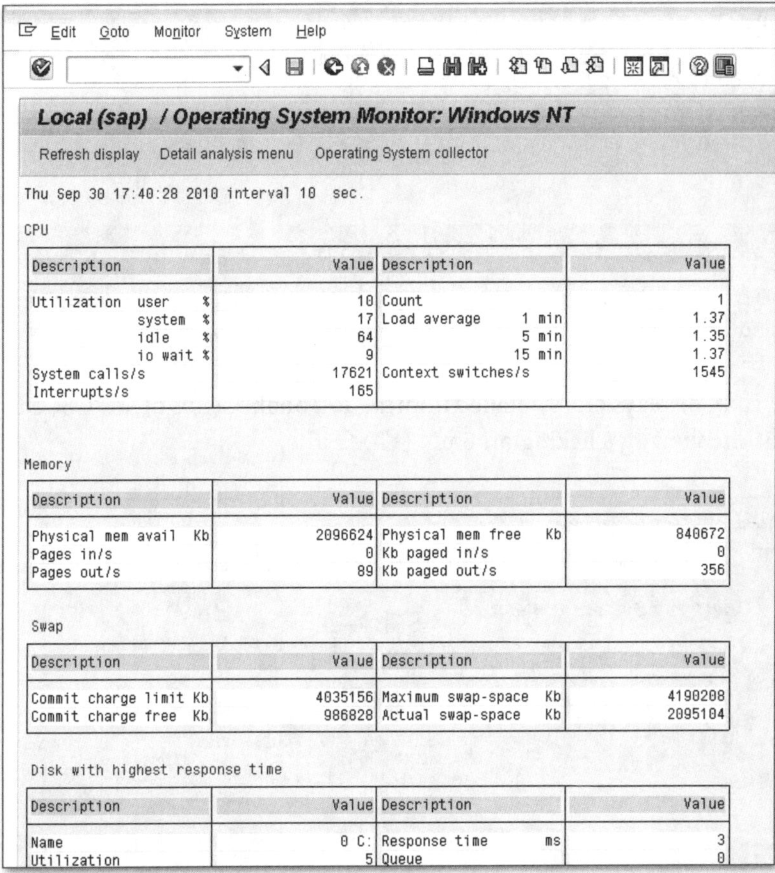

3. Click on the STATUS button to retrieve the program state of SAPOSCOL.

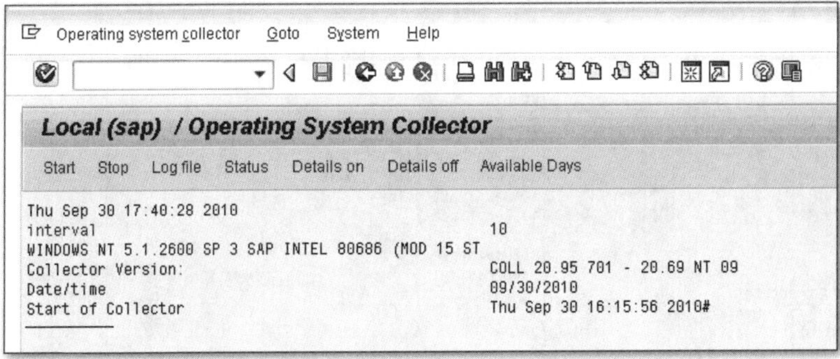

[+]

Status of the OS Collector

The COLLECTOR entry displays if SAPOSCOL is running (status: RUNNING) and collects operating system information or if it isn't active (status: NOT RUNNING). The START and STOP buttons enable you to activate and deactivate SAPOSCOL manually.

Program Directory:

The program is stored in the */usr/sap/<SID>/ DVBEMGS00/exe* directory at the operating system level and can be controlled from there using the `saposcol` command.

4. Here, the system displays more detailed information on the status of SAPOSCOL. You can exit the view by clicking on BACK (⊙).

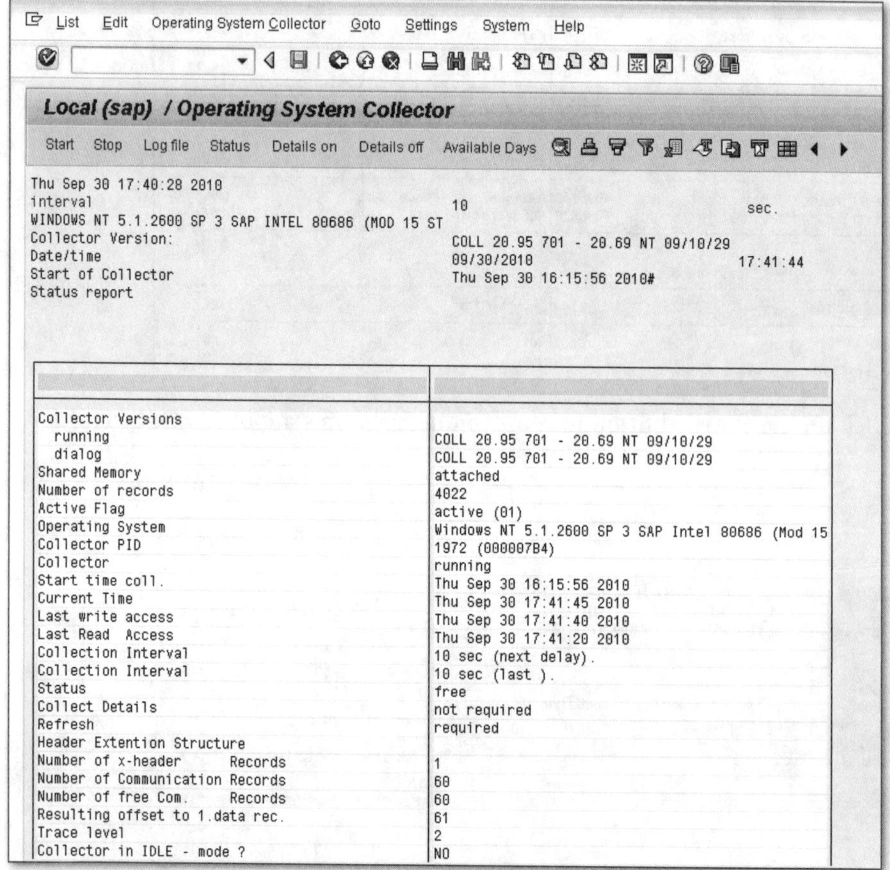

5. In the initial screen of the operating system monitor, choose DETAIL ANALYSIS MENU (see step 2). You can use the individual buttons to retrieve detailed information on the operating system resources. The SNAPSHOT—CURRENT DATA area outputs the last values that have been determined by SAPOSCOL. Click on MEMORY, for example.

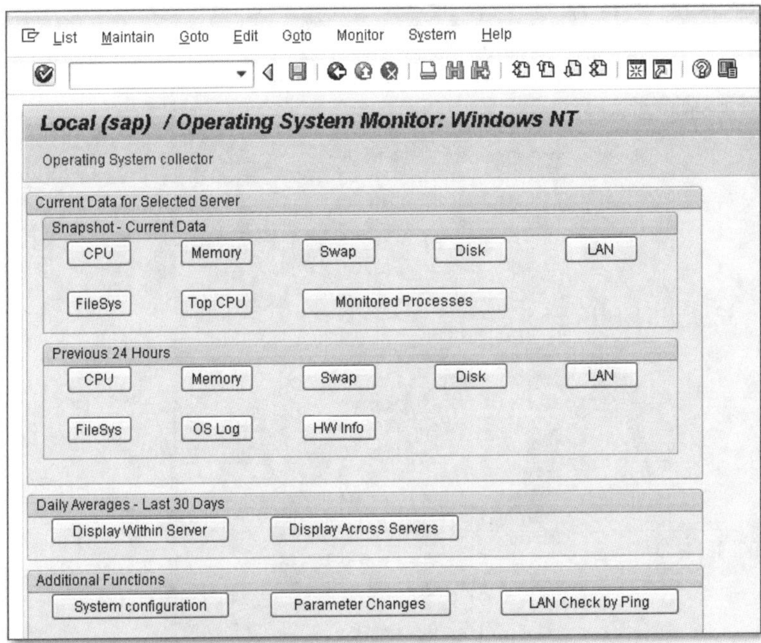

6. The system displays the current utilization of the memory. Use the BACK BUTTON (⊕) to return to the operating system monitor.

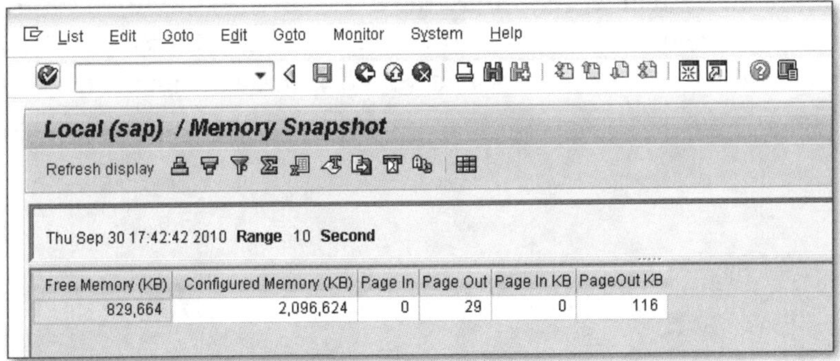

7. PREVIOUS 24 HOURS displays the average values of the previous 24 hours. Select CPU to view the average processor load of the previous 24 hours.

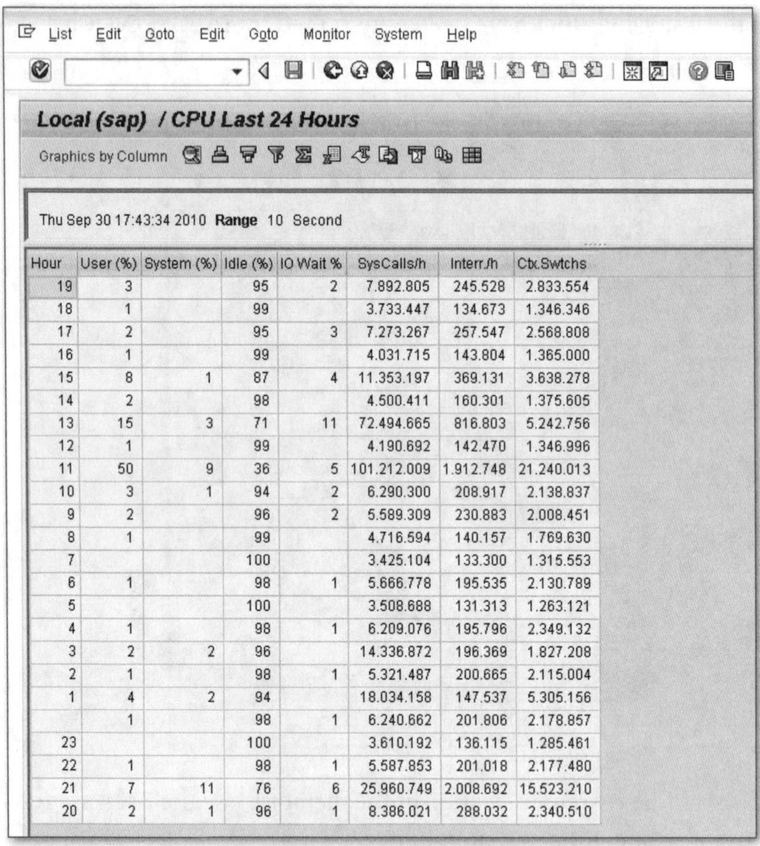

List Edit Goto Edit Goto Monitor System Help

Local (sap) / CPU Last 24 Hours

Graphics by Column

Thu Sep 30 17:43:34 2010 **Range** 10 Second

Hour	User (%)	System (%)	Idle (%)	IO Wait %	SysCalls/h	Interr./h	Ctx.Swtchs
19	3		95	2	7.892.805	245.528	2.833.554
18	1		99		3.733.447	134.673	1.346.346
17	2		95	3	7.273.267	257.547	2.568.808
16	1		99		4.031.715	143.804	1.365.000
15	8	1	87	4	11.353.197	369.131	3.638.278
14	2		98		4.500.411	160.301	1.375.605
13	15	3	71	11	72.494.665	816.803	5.242.756
12	1		99		4.190.692	142.470	1.346.996
11	50	9	36	5	101.212.009	1.912.748	21.240.013
10	3	1	94	2	6.290.300	208.917	2.138.837
9	2		96	2	5.589.309	230.883	2.008.451
8	1		99		4.716.594	140.157	1.769.630
7			100		3.425.104	133.300	1.315.553
6	1		98	1	5.666.778	195.535	2.130.789
5			100		3.508.688	131.313	1.263.121
4	1		98	1	6.209.076	195.796	2.349.132
3	2	2	96		14.336.872	196.369	1.827.208
2	1		98	1	5.321.487	200.665	2.115.004
1	4	2	94		18.034.158	147.537	5.305.156
	1		98	1	6.240.662	201.806	2.178.857
23			100		3.610.192	136.115	1.285.461
22	1		98	1	5.587.853	201.018	2.177.480
21	7	11	76	6	25.960.749	2.008.692	15.523.210
20	2	1	96	1	8.386.021	288.032	2.340.510

8. To call the operating system log, again use the BACK BUTTON (⟳) to return to the previous screen, and select OS LOG in the PREVIOUS 24 HOURS area. The system displays the OPERATING-SYSTEM LOG window. In our example, the NT event log is output.

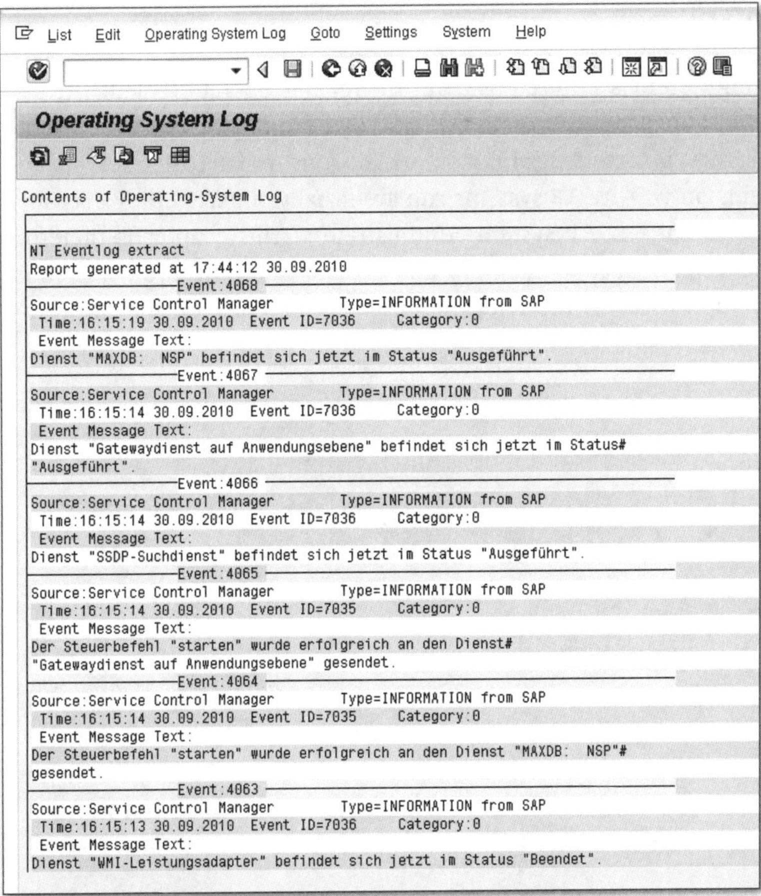

The log stores events at the operating system level. You can use it to identify and solve potential problems.

[+]

Third-Party Software

Instead of SAPOSCOL, you can also use third-party software or tools that the operating system provides (Windows Task-Manager under Microsoft Windows or nmon under AIX, for example) to monitor your servers and operating systems. If you do so, you should still run SAPOSCOL in parallel. Otherwise, you can't use the functions of the SAP operating system monitor for analyses or other statistical purposes.

9.3 Summary

A stable operating system is a prerequisite for the reliable operation of an SAP system. Irrespective of the products you use—Windows, Linux, or Unix—you should know the respective characteristics in detail. Analogous to databases, servers and operating systems on which SAP systems run are usually supervised by specialist administrators and not by SAP system administrators. This chapter is therefore limited to basic aspects, such as memory and process administration. For more detailed information, refer to the relevant specialist literature on the respective operating system.

The security of an IT system is always a highly sensitive topic. The primary goals of security are to protect data against loss and theft, and to safeguard system operation on a daily basis. This chapter will not only differentiate between various aspects of security administration but also name some key individual aspects and introduce tools that can be used to analyze and monitor the SAP system.

10 Security Administration

As an SAP administrator, you bear a large responsibility for security issues such as protecting the SAP system and preparing for a security audit.

If an internal or external auditor examines the SAP system with a fine-tooth comb, the system administrator is responsible for analyzing the results of such an audit. Because each auditing company has its own procedures and may therefore check completely different aspects of security administration, this chapter will prepare you for core aspects that auditing companies normally check.

The topic of computer security is so comprehensive that this chapter can only provide a brief introduction. We strongly recommend that you collaborate with everyone associated with system security (external auditors, internal auditors, the financial department, the legal department, and so on). More information is available in additional literature[1] or at *www.service.sap.com/security*.

We will first explain the concept of (information) security and the levels into which it can be divided. We will then explain the various measures that can influence the security of your SAP systems. Finally, we will discuss system audits and introduce you to some internal SAP auditing tools.

1 Linkies, Mario; Karin, Horst, *SAP Security and Risk Management* (Boston: SAP PRESS, 2011).

10.1 What Is Security?

Security is far more than simply assigning SAP access rights or keeping unauthorized users at bay. In the context of data, security also comprises the following aspects:

- Protecting data against hardware problems
- Ensuring data integrity
- Restoring data after a failure

In this chapter, we will discuss those security aspects that will help you not only to protect the data in your SAP system but also to adhere to legal provisions.

In Chapter 13, you will learn how you can use user administration to keep unauthorized individuals at bay, while Chapter 14 will show you how to grant access authorizations and protect certain data against unwanted access.

10.1.1 Protecting Data Against Damage or Loss

Security means protecting data against damage or loss. The causes of damage or loss can be divided into two categories:

- Unintentional damage or loss, for example:
  - Loading test data into the production system
  - Hardware failure
  - Destruction of the data center through fire
  - Flooding, hurricanes, earthquakes, or other natural disasters
- Malicious damage or loss, for example:
  - Deletion or damage of files by an employee
  - Deletion or damage of files by hackers

10.1.2 Adhering to Legal or Quasi-Legal Provisions

Security is a sensitive subject that also encompasses some legal aspects. Insider trading is a good example for highlighting the importance of security aspects. Insider knowledge or insider information is information that is not in the public domain. If such knowledge were to enter the public domain, it could potentially affect the share price. Insider trading occurs when insider information is used in the purchase or sale of shares to make a profit or minimize a loss. Even if you personally do not profit from the purchase of shares, you can still be held liable. If insider trading occurs, consult with your legal department.

[Ex]

Trading with Insider Information

The wife of an employee passed on some insider information to a relative who purchased shares and then sold them for a profit. When the relative sold the shares, he made a profit before declaring it (insider trading). The Securities and Exchange Commission imposed a fine on both the wife and the relative. The wife was found guilty of passing on insider information to the relative who, in turn, was able to profit from the sale of the shares. Consequently, both were found guilty of insider training.

10.2 Security Levels

To keep security administration simple, we recommend that you use levels to differentiate between different aspects of security. A model could, for example, comprise the following three main levels:

- Access security
  - Physical security
  - Network security
  - Application security
- Operational security
- Data security

Next, we will describe each level in this security model in greater detail.

10.2.1 Access Security

Access security comprises all aspects of security associated with accessing a system whereby the term *access* can be considered from several perspectives.

Physical Security

Physical security controls physical access to the SAP system and network environment. To access data, an intruder must first gain access to the facility, then the building, and then the part of the building in which the users or pieces of equipment are located (for example, the server room, cable terminal cabinet, or network room). Moreover, this level is probably the most important level. If an intruder gains access to your equipment, he can, in theory, breach the other security levels.

If the physical security level is breached, the following may happen:

- Equipment may be physically damaged or destroyed.
- The intruder may gain access to the system via the user console (and this may result in a breach of network security).
- Equipment may be stolen.
- Data may be misused by hackers.

If the intruder does not gain physical access to the building, he must use electronic means to gain access to the system on the network.

The server on which the SAP system is running should be housed in a secure room, and access to this room should be secured by a lockable door. Furthermore, it is imperative that access to the server room is controlled or monitored by video.

[!]

Access Log for the Server Room

If you use an access system with an electronic keycard, you should check the access log for the server room at regular intervals. Auditors may examine this security aspect (checking the access log on a regular basis).

Network Security

The goal of network security is to control external access and logons to the network. Logon access controls both on-site and remote access. It also determines the access rights of individual users within the network.

If intruders access your network, they may have an electronic connection to your computers. Network security specialists should configure the various access points to your network. User activities should also be tracked.

The following access points, for example, should be checked:

- Outside access
  - Dial-up access
  - Internet access
  - Other remote access methods (for example, VPN)

- Network logon (for example, Windows domain)
- Access to parts of the network (for example, via router tables)

Recommendations for Windows

For Windows domains, we recommend the following:

- Have a separate SAP domain to which only system administrators can log on.
- Have other domains to which users can log on. These domains should "trust" the SAP domain but not vice versa.

Application Security

Application security concerns the security mechanisms of the application itself (for example, the SAP system). These include the following:

- Access to the application (for example, the logon to the SAP system)
- User access point to the application
- User authorizations within the application
- User authorization to certain system data in the application (for example, in the SAP system by limiting the user to company code 1000 or cost center 47110815)
- Type of user access rights (for example, read—do not change!—posting data).
- Use of SAP tools, for example:
  - Profile Generator (Transaction PFCG—see Chapter 14)
  - Audit Information System (Transaction SECR)
  - Security Audit Log (Transaction SM19/SM20)

For the system as a whole, it's important that all levels are protected using suitable measures to ensure optimum security.

10.2.2 Operational Security

The operational security level mainly concerns issues relating to definitions, procedures, and control functions for daily operation and, less so, issues relating to computers and systems. Such procedures and control functions concern both the organization and its employees, and may cause problems. Employees should adhere to various rules and regulations, but they do not always do so.

Examples of operational control methods include the following:

- Segregation of duties (SOD)
- Avoiding shared usage of user IDs
- Defining password standards
- Logoff and backup mechanisms for work breaks or for the end of a shift (for example, locking the PC when leaving a work center)

Often, employees are not sufficiently sensitized to the issue of security, which may lead to them adopting a lax approach to daily, security-related activities. This may mean, among other things, that the physical security is not taken too seriously, and, as a result, PCs and similar pieces of technical equipment are left unattended or unsecured (for example, office door not locked, PC not locked). You must strive to increase awareness of security within the enterprise. Having said that, access systems (for example, keycards) or PC settings (for example, time until the PC locks) may enforce certain behavioral patterns.

10.2.3 Data Security

This level is closely related to disaster recovery (see Chapter 7), which represents an important part of data security. Data security involves protecting the following:

- **Server data**
  The data on the server is protected against damage or loss. Even though this protection is achieved using different resources, the goal is always to keep any data loss caused by an incident as low as possible or to avoid it altogether.
- **Backup data**
  At this level, the application data is usually saved to magnetic tape, which can be used to restore the system. Backup tapes must be stored securely for the following reasons:
  - To use them in the event of a disaster
  - To protect them against theft

At this point, we must highlight the following security-relevant points in relation to disaster recovery:

- Lower the likelihood of data loss.
- Treat the server as the most important location for storing data securely.

- Protect the backup data against damage or loss.
- Make sure that the system can be fully restored after a failure.

When it comes to backing up data to the server, note the following:

- In the event of an emergency, you must do everything possible to prevent data loss. The following options ensure *high availability* (HA):
  - RAID arrays for drives
  - Redundant equipment
  - Reliable equipment and vendors
  - Support contracts for the hardware used in the production system
- The following options refer to the facilities:
  - Uninterruptible power supply (UPS)
  - Fire alarms and fire protection devices
  - Alarm system
  - Surround alarm
- Backup
  - Backup tapes should be dispatched to a secure location outside the enterprise.
  - This measure will protect backup data against damage or complete destruction in the event of an incident.
  - The storage locations for the backup tapes—both on-site and outside the enterprise—must be secure to protect the tapes against theft.
  - If the tapes are stolen, the data may be restored and misused. If database tools are used, it's possible to bypass most SAP security functions because the tables can be read directly.

Chapter 7 and Chapter 8 provide additional information on how to ensure that your system data is secure.

10.3 Safeguarding the SAP System

In this section, you will learn how you can use specific measures to safeguard an SAP system. It's best to use a *security concept* to document any security precautions that you take. By documenting the individual measures and the reason and purpose associated with each, you avoid any unintentional easing up of security measures.

10.3.1 Preventing Multiple User Logons

Preventing multiple user logons means that any user ID can only be logged on to the SAP system once. Multiple user logons occur if users share a user ID or if someone uses the user ID of a user without that user knowing.

If several individuals use the same user ID, this is deemed to be a security threat:

- A data change or posting can't be traced back uniquely.
- You can't determine who is performing an activity that is considered to be a security threat.
- If training is required, it isn't possible to determine who requires training.
- You potentially violate the terms of your license agreement with SAP if multiple users share an SAP license to save money.

The fact that multiple logons are possible in a live SAP system is generally frowned upon in the event of a security audit. In test systems and quality assurance systems, the use of multiple logons may be less restrictive.

To ensure that a user ID is not shared by multiple users, you must use Transaction RZ10 to configure the system profile parameter `login/disable_multi_gui_login`:

- **1:** To forbid multiple user logons
- **0:** To permit multiple user logons

We recommend that you set the parameter value to 1 to prevent multiple user logons under the same user ID.

Another advantage associated with this measure is the fact that it's easier to identify any possible misuse of passwords. If the owner of a user ID wants to log on to an SAP system but receives a message indicating that the user ID is already logged on, he can assume that someone else knows the password.

Despite the aforementioned security concerns, there are times when it isn't practical (from a technical or organizational perspective) to use individual user IDs. Such situations are usually caused by certain organizational or technical conditions within the enterprise and must therefore be handled and assessed on an individual basis.

In each case, management must approve, monitor, and document any exceptions of this type as well as any internal or external audits that are performed.

To enable certain users to log on multiple times, you must enter the relevant user IDs in the parameter `login/multi_login_users` without any blank characters and separated by commas.

10.3.2 Passwords

The password is the "key" that a user requires to access the SAP system. Just like a door key, a password must also be protected so that "uninvited guests" can't intrude. Your enterprise should have a unique yet practical password rule that is known to all users. In particular, you shouldn't use passwords that are easy to guess.

[!]

Do Not Use Highly Complex Password Rules

A password rule that is too restrictive or very difficult to adhere to could be counterproductive because users would then jot down their passwords and possibly store them somewhere that is easy to access, thus endangering security.

Defining Password Standards

The SAP system provides system parameters that you can use to technically implement a password guideline (for example, defining the minimum password length or validity period for passwords). The most important password parameters are listed here:

- **Minimum password length—login/min_password_lng**
  A long password is more difficult to guess. The standard length is usually at least eight characters.
- **Password validity period—login/password_expiration_time**
  This parameter specifies the validity period of a password. When this period expires, the user must change his password. Auditors normally recommend a period of 30 days. However, most customers opt for a period of 90 days.
- **User lock—login/fails_to_user_lock**
  This parameter is used to lock users who repeatedly enter an incorrect password at logon. Users are usually locked after three failed logon attempts. Here, you can specify the number of failed attempts that must occur before a user is locked.

Other parameters relating to password restrictions are listed in Chapter 13, Section 13.10.3. If you want to specify password parameters, use Transaction RZ10 to change the system profiles. By using appropriate parameters, you can make it considerably more difficult for anyone to gain unauthorized access to your system.

[+]

Auditing Security Parameters

Your external auditors may check whether you have configured security parameters.

Preventing the Use of Trivial Passwords

Certain passwords (for example, 123, QWERTY, abc, sap, <your company name>) are already known and easy to guess. If users use such passwords, this endangers security and therefore the system. Various lists of frequently used user passwords are freely available on the Internet. The use of one of these passwords increases the likelihood that an unauthorized person will gain access to a user account.

You can prevent the use of easy-to-guess passwords by defining forbidden character strings in Table USR40. When a user wants to save a new password, the system checks this table. Maintenance of Table USR40 cannot substitute a sensible password guideline that users adhere to. However, it can complement it effectively.

[!]

Audit—Easy-to-Guess Passwords

External auditors may check whether you have configured a mechanism that prevents the use of easy-to-guess passwords.

The following passwords are examples of possible table entries:

- SAP*
- *GOD*
- *QWERTY*
- *PASSWORD*
- Simple letter sequences (*abc*, *xyz*, and so on) and simple number sequences (*123*, *321*, and so on)
- Weekdays (*Monday*, *Tuesday*, and so on), months (*January*, *February*, and so on), and seasons (*Summer*, *Winter*, and so on)

- The name of your company, one of your company's product names, the name of your competitor or one of your competitor's product names

We recommend that you use the placeholder * at the start and end of each entry in Table USR40. By doing so, you can help prevent the entry from being used in any part of the password.

[+]

Other Password Security Options

Table USR40 is only one basic measure for password security. This table must be managed manually. Third parties provide password security programs that you can integrate into the SAP system.

You can use Transaction SM30, which is the general transaction for table maintenance, to change Table USR40 (for more information about this transaction, see Chapter 13). This change triggers a transport that can be passed through the entire system landscape.

[+]

Documenting Changes to Table USR40

In your security concept, maintain a log of changes made in this table.

Storing System Passwords

In principle, passwords should never be written down. In real-life system administration, however, there are occasionally situations in which you have to log on to the system using an administrative user ID (for example, when maintaining RFC connections or in the event of an emergency) and therefore need the administrative password. Because you can't select a trivial password for these powerful users but you do not require it often enough to learn it by heart, you must reluctantly jot it down.

In general, the following administrative user IDs are required for the SAP system:

- SAP*
- DDIC
- SAPCPIC (see SAP Note 29276)
- EarlyWatch (client 066)

- TMSADM
- All user-defined, technical administrative user IDs (for example, for interfaces, RFC connections, and so on)
- All non-SAP user IDs required for system operation (for example, for the operating system, the database, and other connected applications)

Depending on your operating system and the database used, the following user IDs are important at the operating system level and the database level:

- <SID>ADM (or <sid>adm)
- sa
- SAPR3 or sapr3
- SAPService<SID>
- SYS (or sys)
- SYSTEM (or system)
- root
- Ora<sid>
- op$<sid>adm
- ops$sapservice<sid>

At the very least, the system administrator and his representative must know the password for the aforementioned user IDs. Depending on the size of your enterprise, even more individuals will need to be entrusted with this information.

Add a procedure for retaining and managing these critical passwords to your security concept. Also check the use of third-party software for password administration (password vaults are offered for this purpose).

We recommend that you write down all of the passwords for all relevant system IDs, place them in a sealed envelope, and store them in a safe to which only authorized individuals have access (selected employees).

[!]

Creating a Password List

Two employees should compose the list, change passwords, and confirm new passwords, and do this separately and successively for each user ID. If an incorrect password is recorded in the list, you may no longer be able to log on to the system.

The password list should be updated to include any password changes.

10.3.3 Limiting Access for SAP* or DDIC Users

SAP* and DDIC are system user IDs that should not be used for regular system operation. In principle, you should lock the SAP* user and change the password. Do not delete the user because this would disable one of the SAP system's important protection mechanisms. You can use the profile parameter `login/no_automatic_user_sapstar` to control whether a logon using the SAP* ID and the password pass is possible if the SAP* user has been deleted. We recommend setting the parameter value to 1 so that a logon using the SAP* user is not possible by default.

The DDIC user is required for certain system administration functions. Therefore, do not delete or lock it. Instead, change the password and store it securely.

For more information about the administrative user IDs SAP* and DDIC, see Chapter 13, Section 13.10.1.

10.3.4 Locking Critical Transactions

Critical transactions are transaction codes that can damage the system, represent a general security risk, or significantly impair system performance.

Access to these critical transactions is more critical in the production system than in the development system or test system. Therefore, some transactions should be locked in the production system but not in the development, test, or training systems.

Standard security normally prohibits access to these transactions. Depending on the respective system, however, some administrators, programmers, consultants, and important technical users may require access to these transactions. In such cases, the transaction lock provides a second line of defense in addition to authorization management.

Depending on the scope of the module in the relevant installation, an SAP system may contain tens of thousands of transaction codes. From a transparency perspective, only highly critical transaction codes should be locked. Appendix B contains a table of transactions that should be locked. This table was created in conjunction with Basis consultants and end users. The transactions are divided into the following risk categories:

- Critical
- Impairing security
- Impairing performance

Contact your technical consultants and specialist module advisers who will be able to tell you the names of other critical transactions in your modules.

[✪]

Table TSTCT

Table TSTCT contains the transaction codes and the names of the transactions.

Appendix B also contains a table of transactions that potentially cannot be locked because they are used regularly. These transactions are used in a production system for certain reasons. Because they are dangerous, authorization roles should be used to grant limited access to these transactions.

Add the list of locked transactions to your security concept. At the very least, this list should contain the following information:

- Which transactions are locked?
- Why are they locked?
- Who locked them?
- When were they locked?

It's important to maintain this information because someone may want to know who locked the transaction and why they locked it.

To lock a transaction, follow these steps:

1. Enter Transaction "SM01" in the command box, and press the Enter key (or select the menu option TOOLS • ADMINISTRATION • ADMINISTRATION • SM01—TRANSACTION CODE ADMINISTRATION).
2. In the search field below the TCODE column, enter the transaction code that you want to lock (for example, SM14) and choose ENTER (✓), or press the Enter key.

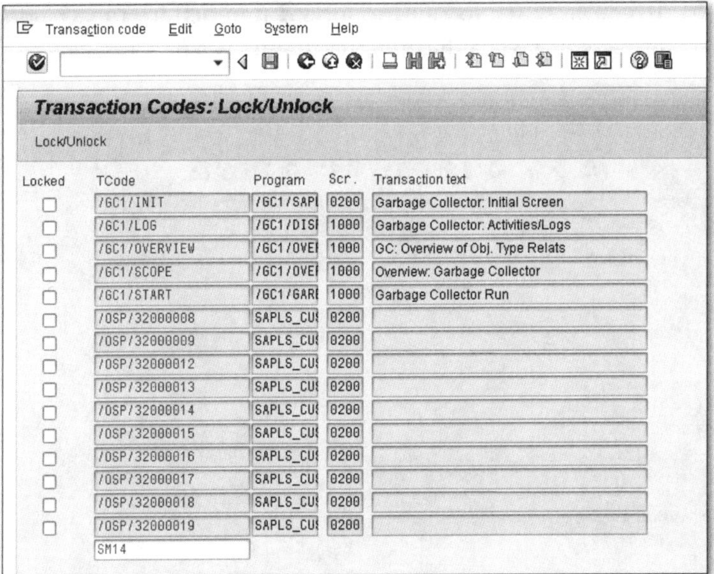

3. The required transaction is now displayed in the first row in the table. To lock a transaction, select the relevant checkbox in the LOCKED column. To unlock a transaction, remove the checkmark. Then choose ENTER (), or press the Enter key.

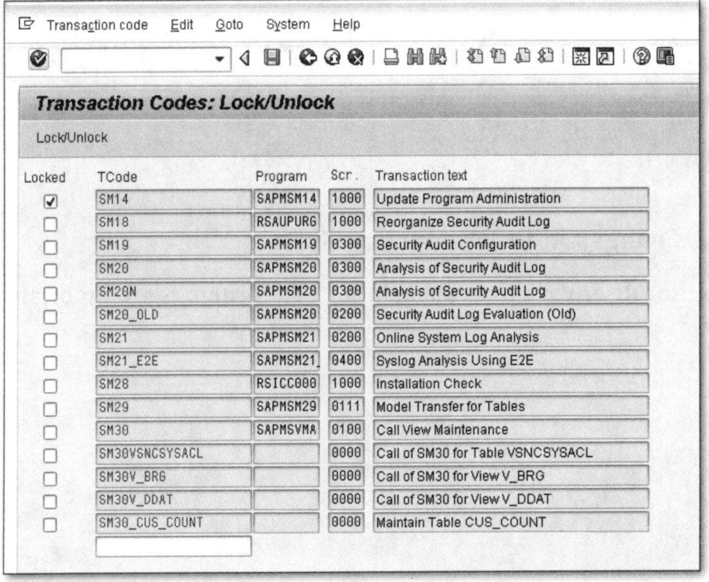

4. Choose BACK (icon). If you now try to call the locked transaction, the system displays a message in the status bar indicating that the transaction is locked.

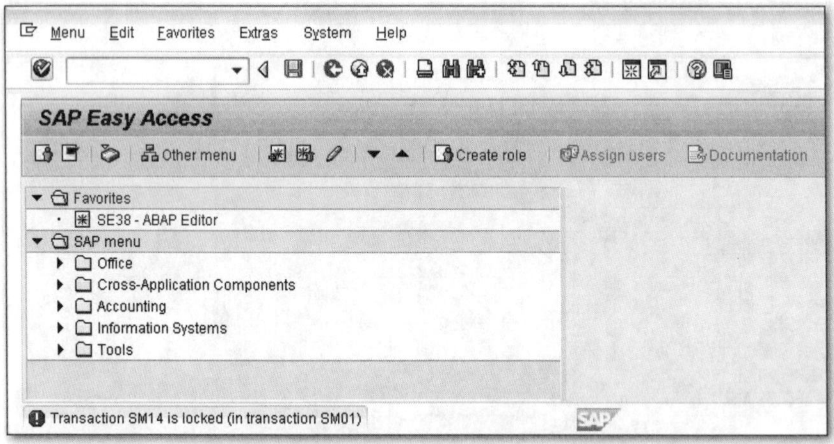

[!]

Carefully Locking Transactions

Take care when locking transactions because there is a risk that you will inadvertently lock an important transaction. If this happens, you may no longer be able to unlock this or other transactions. Therefore, determine whether the best option is to lock a transaction or to use roles to restrict the access authorization.

[+]

List of Locked Transactions

You can use the standard report RSAUDITC_BCE from the *Audit Information System* (see Section 10.5.1) to display a list of locked transactions.

10.3.5 Preventing Changes in the Production System

Controlling and monitoring any changes made in the SAP system is an important security aspect.

In principle, any changes to Customizing or repository objects (for example, programs or data elements) should enter the production system by means of the regular transportation chain. In other words, the changes are made in the development system and then imported into the QA system via a transport request. Such changes are therefore thoroughly tested before being transported into the production system.

This procedure ensures that changes are tested properly and then consistently applied to the entire system landscape (see Chapter 17).

For systems in which changes can't be made, you can set the system change option to technically prevent changes from being made.

This applies, in particular, to the production system but also to the QA system. This setting ensures that changes are checked. Otherwise, this may result in significant incidents in the production system because changes haven't been tested or because they don't correspond to changes in the development system or test system.

Often, changes are made directly in the production system because it would take too long to transport such changes. However, this doesn't produce a synchronous system landscape in which the settings in the production system correspond to those in the development system and test system. In such a situation, you can't ensure that tests performed in the QA system will be reliable. Having said that, this may give rise to a high number of emergency transports.

Setting the Production System to "Not modifiable"

You can use several switches to prevent changes to a system. In the production system, such switches should be set to NOT MODIFIABLE. You can use Transactions SE03 and SCC4 to set the system to NOT MODIFIABLE.

1. Enter Transaction "SE03" in the command box, and press the [Enter] key.
2. Choose TRANSPORT ORGANIZER TOOLS • ADMINISTRATION • SET SYSTEM CHANGE OPTION.

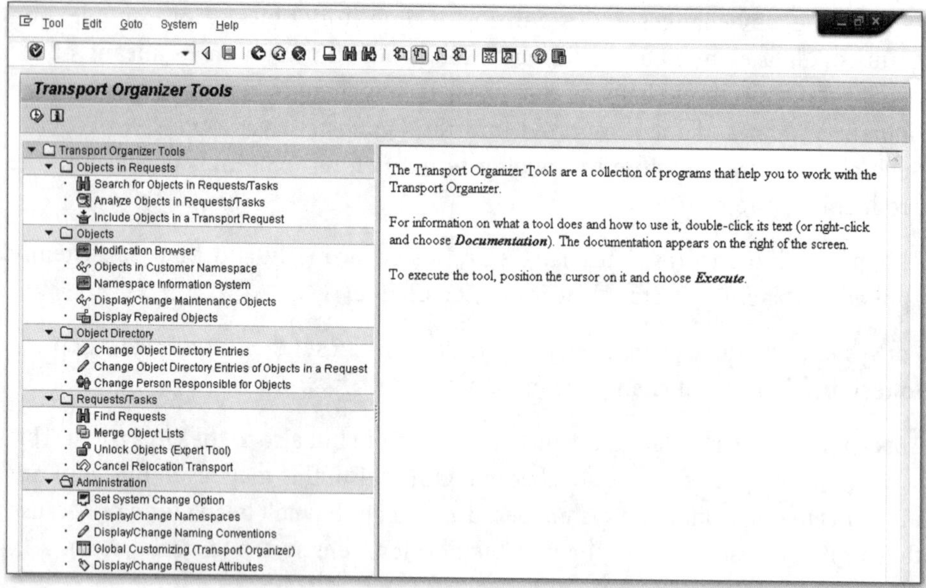

3. If you want to lock the system, use the dropdown list to set the GLOBAL SETTING field to the value NOT MODIFIABLE. If you want to unlock the system, select the value MODIFIABLE. When you are finished, choose SAVE (💾).

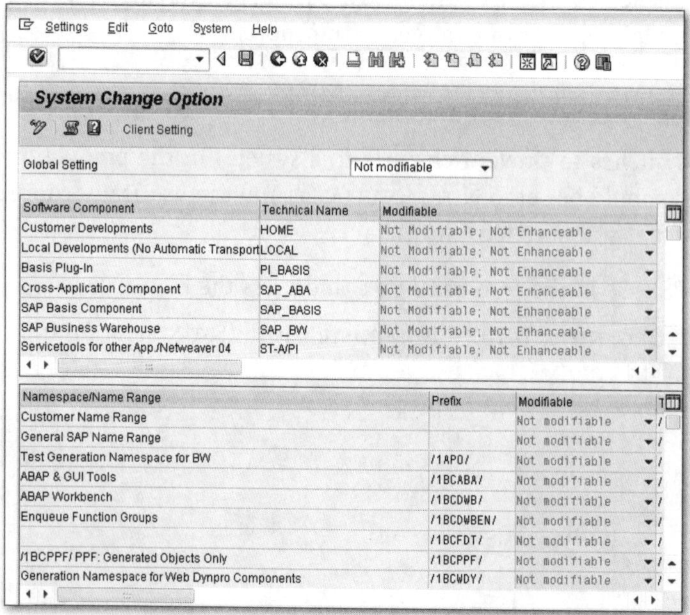

4. In some cases, the NOT MODIFIABLE global setting may result in certain applications not being executed correctly. You must then set the global setting to MODIFIABLE. You can nevertheless protect the system by restricting the change option for SOFTWARE COMPONENT and NAMESPACES and only leave the components that you actually require with the status MODIFIABLE.

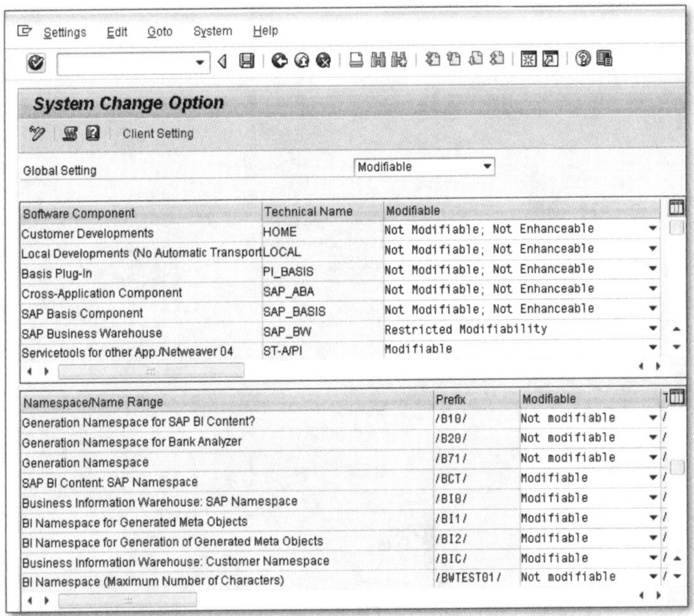

In Transaction SE03 (Transport Organizer Tools), you control, on a cross-client basis, whether changes to repository objects and cross-client Customizing are permitted throughout the system. In Transaction SCC4 (Client Administration), you can configure this setting for a specific client, for example, if you want programming to take place in only one client within the development system.

However, Transaction SCC4 is also used to prevent changes to client-specific objects and to prohibit the creation of transport requests. To lock clients against changes, follow these steps:

1. Enter Transaction "SCC4" in the command box, and press the Enter key (or select the menu option TOOLS • ADMINISTRATION • ADMINISTRATION • CLIENT ADMINISTRATION • SCC4—CLIENT MAINTENANCE).
2. Choose DISPLAY <-> CHANGE to switch to change mode ().

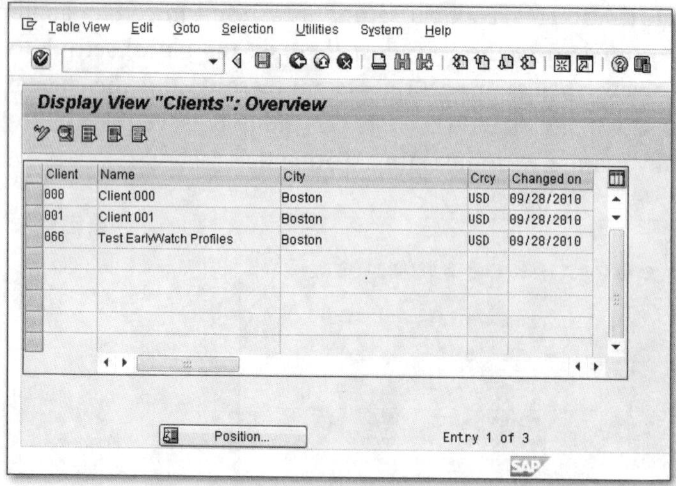

3. In the next dialog box, choose CONTINUE (✔).

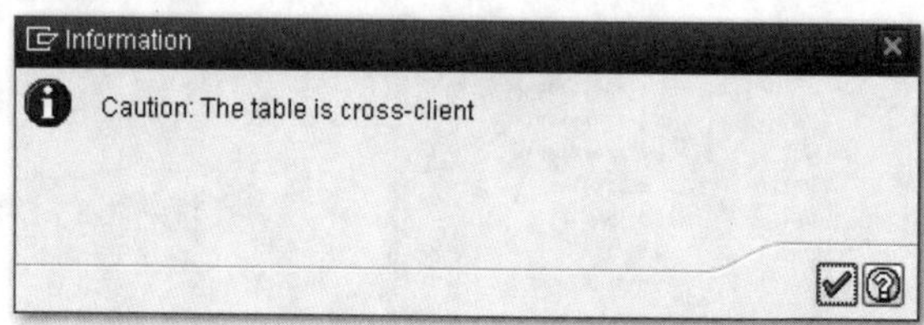

4. Select the clients to be changed and choose DETAILS (🔍), or double-click the relevant row.

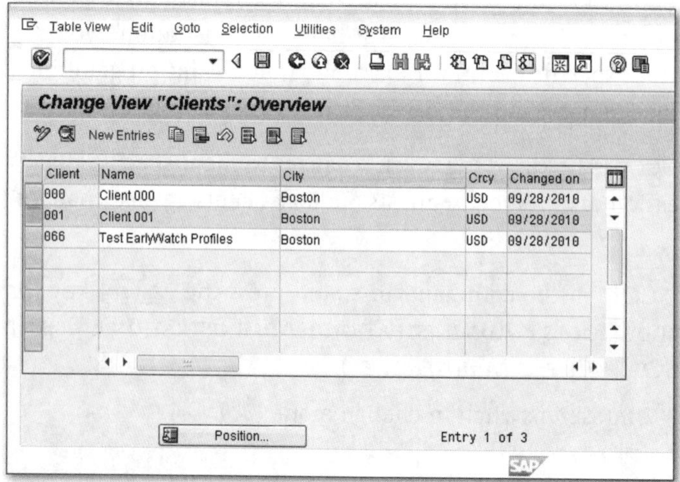

5. To lock the client, follow these steps:
   - In the CHANGES AND TRANSPORTS FOR CLIENT-SPECIFIC OBJECTS area, choose the NO CHANGES ALLOWED option.
   - Under CROSS-CLIENT OBJECT CHANGES, use the dropdown box to select the NO CHANGES TO REPOSITORY AND CROSS-CLIENT CUSTOMIZING OBJS option.
   - In the PROTECTION: CLIENT COPIER AND COMPARISON TOOL area, use the drop-down box to choose PROTECTION LEVEL 2: NO OVERWRITING, NO EXTERNAL AVAILABILITY.
6. Under CATT AND ECATT RESTRICTIONS, use the dropdown box to choose the ECATT AND CATT NOT ALLOWED option.
   - When you are finished, choose SAVE (💾).

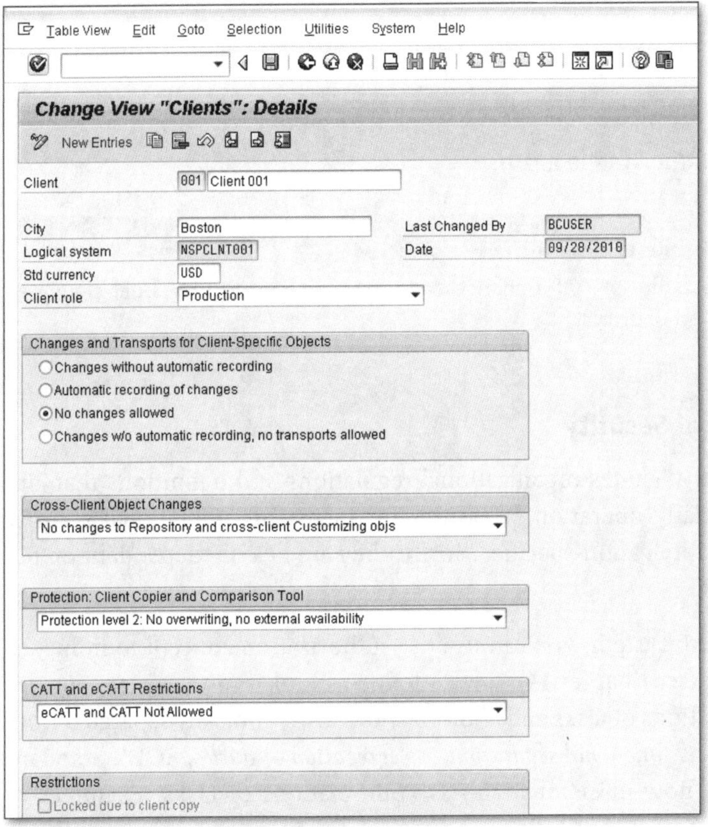

The client is now protected against changes. Execute the procedure for all relevant clients in the systems to be secured.

Exceptions

There are some exceptions to this process if a change can't be transported or if a direct change is required as a result of an SAP Note.

If a change can't be transported, you must implement the following procedure:

1. Confirm that the change can't be transported. Some objects may require an ABAP program for the transport.
2. Initially, make this change in the development system and QA system, and test whether you get the desired effect without any negative side effects. Then make the change in the production system. Proceed in exactly the same way for nonproduction systems.
3. Unlock the system so that changes can be made.
4. Make the change.
5. Immediately lock the system again.

[!]

Limiting Manual Changes to Essential Changes Only!

Implement this procedure *only* if a change cannot be transported. Manual changes increase the likelihood of errors.

10.3.6 Operational Security

Operational security includes organizational regulations and definitions that aim to reduce risks in daily operation. Measures for increasing operational security are not necessarily application-specific. Mostly, they are heavily dependent on the enterprise structure.

In the case of the SAP system, you can use the authorization concept to influence operational security (see Chapter 14). A well-defined authorization concept ensures that critical combinations of tasks and authorizations are technically separated from each other (known as *functional separation* or *segregation of duties*, SOD). Standard auditing guidelines now exist for high-risk combinations of tasks. Examples of critical combinations of authorizations include the following:

- Vendor maintenance and check creation
- Customer maintenance and cash receipt
- ABAP development and transport control

Your external auditors can support you in defining such high-risk combinations. A task-sharing audit is a standard auditing procedure.

[Ex]

Task Sharing

If an employee is responsible for outgoing payments, he should not be responsible for entering vendor master data. There is a danger here that the employee will enter his account details in a vendor record and transfer money to this account.

Often, smaller enterprises have to assign several functions to one person as a result of their organizational structure. In this case, you should be aware of and consider the potential risks. If you have to combine functions, choose combinations that carry the lowest possible risk. In return, accurately audit the activities performed by the employees in question.

10.4 Audits

As a system administrator, you encounter the following two audit types:

- Security audit
- Account audit

Security Audit

The primary goal of a security audit is to test the security of the SAP environment. This audit is normally performed as an account audit to ensure that it complies with the relevant legal requirements. An enterprise's internal audit managers can also perform a security audit.

The security of the following confidential data are audited:

- Financial data
- Customer data

- Product data
- Employee data (from the HR module)

In general, the security audit is performed by a technically minded or experienced external auditor.

[+]

Preparing for an Audit

This section doesn't address all SAP security audit issues. Instead, we will only discuss some aspects that may be important for a security audit. We recommend that you collaborate with the auditors before an account audit, so that you can test the system in advance and prepare it for the audit.

Account Audit

During an account audit, an auditor audits the financial statements of your enterprise. The purpose of this audit is to paint a picture of the enterprise's financial statements. Essentially, the financial statements reflect the enterprise's financial situation. An account audit is usually mandatory (for example, if the enterprise's shares are traded on the stock market). If your enterprise is a private enterprise, the creditors can initiate an account audit.

As part of the account audit, the auditor usually performs a security audit of the SAP system and any connected systems. The purpose of the security audit is to ascertain the extent to which the data in the SAP system is confidential. External auditors evaluate your system and determine which tests need to be performed and how extensive these tests will be.

If the evaluation results are not satisfactory, it may be necessary to perform more extensive audits. Consequently, the audit costs rise, and, as a result of this additional expense, it may not be possible to perform the audit until a later time. In the worst-case scenario, the security precautions may be so poor that it isn't possible to make a statement in relation to the enterprise's financial situation.

10.4.1 Auditing Aspects

During the account or security audit, the auditors consider certain auditing aspects such as the following:

- Physical security
- Network security
- User administration procedures
  - Appropriate task sharing
  - Suitable training
  - Passwords
- Data security
  - Protection against hardware errors, mirrored drives, RAID, failover, high availability, and so on
  - Backup and restore procedures
  - Protecting the production system against unauthorized changes
  - Locking dangerous transactions

As the administrator, you should familiarize yourself with these aspects of account or security audits. If you don't know what the auditors will test, you can't be sufficiently prepared, nor can you protect the system accordingly.

10.4.2 Auditing Tasks for SAP Administrators

As an SAP system administrator, you support the security and account audits performed by internal and external auditors. However, such audits only occur at regular intervals (usually annually) because they are too extensive to occur at shorter intervals.

Therefore, during the time between official audits, you should perform other small audits on a regular basis (for example, monthly or quarterly) to ensure that the system remains secure throughout the year.

Examples of such audits include the following:

- **Checking user accounts**
  Access to the SAP system should be revoked immediately for any user who leaves your enterprise. By locking or deleting the user ID, you ensure that only users who have to work with the system actually have access to the SAP system. Regularly check whether users have been fully locked or deleted. This will also

prevent other users from logging on under the respective IDs. For more information about locking users, see Chapter 13.

[+]

Auditing User IDs

Among other things, the external auditors will check whether individuals who don't have to access the SAP system nevertheless have valid user IDs.

- **Checking authorizations**
  Over time, a user can obtain an increasing number of authorization roles in the SAP system. If this is not checked on a regular basis, these roles may result in a user obtaining more authorizations than necessary. Over time, a user may obtain authorizations or combinations of authorizations that violate the definitions for functional separation or the SOD. Therefore, regularly audit the authorizations assigned to users and compare them with the relevant requests. Investigate whether there are any functional separation conflicts.

[+]

Auditing Authorizations

External auditors may check not only the rise in the number of authorizations but also the request procedure.

Depending on the number of users, these audits may be quite extensive. In the meantime, tools that support such audits are available (for example, the SAP products from the area of Governance, Risk & Compliance, GRC). If you don't have any technical support, it's best to perform at least one random check. Your auditor should define the minimum scope of the sample.

[+]

SAP Security Notes

SAP provides security-relevant SAP Notes on the SAP Support Portal (see Chapter 19). They are available under the path Help & Support • SAP Note Search • SAP Security Notes.

You can use Transaction ST13 (Analysis & Service Tools) to check whether all relevant security notes have been imported into your system. To do this, execute the tool RSECNOTE in Transaction ST13.

10.5 Auditing Tools

By default, the SAP system has several tools that support you when you perform security-relevant system administration tasks. These tools include the *Audit Information System* (AIS) and the *Security Audit Log*, which will be described in this section.

10.5.1 Audit Information System

The Audit Information System (AIS) was developed for system and business audits, and it comprises reports that automatically analyze certain aspects of system security. Thanks to these reports, it's no longer necessary to manually process individual audit points, analyze tables, or write audit programs. Consequently, auditors like to use the AIS during a system audit.

Up to Release 4.6B, the AIS was called via Transaction SECR (Audit Information System). As of Release 4.6C, SAP made the transition to a role-based auditing tool. In other words, the audit reports are now delivered in standard SAP roles. Before using the AIS, you must copy the roles into your customer namespace, complete any open authorization objects, generate authorization profiles, and transport the roles into the system to be audited.

Composite Role SAP_AUDITOR [+]

The complete AIS is contained in the composite role SAP_AUDITOR. This role comprises all single roles in the AIS for auditing system-relevant and business aspects. Copy this composite role and the associated single roles into your customer namespace (for example, Z_AUDITOR) and define them.

For information about the AIS roles, see SAP Note 451960. To learn how to create and define authorization roles, see Chapter 14.

After you've generated and assigned the AIS roles, you can call the individual reports directly from the user menu. You can also call the reports via Transaction SA38.

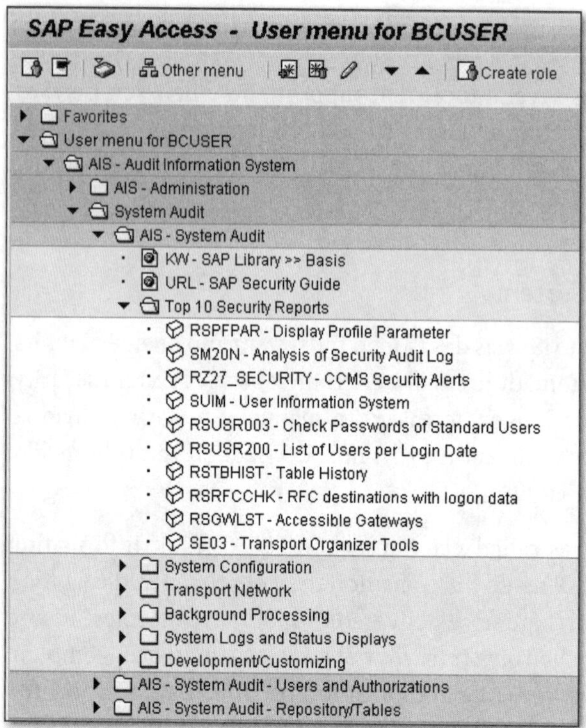

The following are some key reports in the AIS:

- **RSUSR003**
  Checks the standard passwords of standard SAP users (SAP*, DDIC, and so on)
- **RSUSR005**
  Lists users who have critical authorizations.
- **RSUSR006**
  Lists users who have been locked as a result of failed logons.
- **RSUSR007**
  Lists users who have incomplete address data.
- **RSUSR008**
  Lists users who have critical combinations of authorizations or transactions.

[+]

Table SUKRI

The critical combinations considered in the report RSUSR008 are maintained in Table SUKRI.

- **RSUSR009**
  Lists users who have critical authorizations. Critical authorizations can be selected here.
- **RSUSR100**
  Lists change documents for users and displays changes made to user security.
- **RSUSR101**
  Lists change documents for profiles and displays changes made to the security profiles.
- **RSUSR102**
  Lists change documents for authorizations and displays changes made to security authorizations.

Use the AIS to analyze and assess the security of your SAP system on a regular basis. In your security concept, define the intervals at which AIS reports are to be executed routinely. In collaboration with your user departments, check whether certain commercial audit reports are of interest to your management level.

10.5.2 Security Audit Log

The Security Audit Log plays an important role for SAP system administrators when they monitor security-relevant actions in the system. The Security Audit Log can be used to log and subsequently analyze various types of user activities, for example:

- Dialog, RFC, and Gateway (Common Programming Interface Communication, CPIC) logon attempts to the system
- RFCs for function modules
- Transaction and program starts
- Locking/unlocking transactions
- Changing and locking user master data
- Changing and generating authorizations
- Virus detection
- Starting and stopping the application server
- Changes to the Security Audit Log configuration

The Security Audit Log is deactivated by default. After you've configured and activated the Security Audit Log, the actions to be logged are recorded in log files. These files are read when analyzing the Security Audit Log.

The log files are stored at the operating system level. Because they are neither deleted nor overwritten, the number and size of the log files grows continuously. We therefore recommend that you regularly check the size of the log directory, archive the logs, and manually delete them if necessary.

[⚙]

Log Files—Names and Directories

The names and storage directories of log files are defined by the profile parameters `DIR_AUDIT` and `FN_AUDIT`.

The Security Audit Log supports the system administrator in the following tasks:

- Reconstructing and analyzing incidents
- Optimizing security through the detection of critical actions
- Tracking unusual user activities
- Understanding the effects of changes to transactions or users

[!]

Data Protection

Note that, depending on the configuration, the Security Audit Log records person-related data that may be subject to data protection laws. Therefore, before you activate logging, check whether you would be violating any data protection laws or internal agreements. If necessary, consult with auditors or the works council, and weigh the pros and cons.

Configuring the Security Audit Log

The Security Audit Log is configured in two steps:

- Maintaining profile parameters for the Security Audit Log
- Configuring audit profiles and filters

Before you activate the Security Audit Log, use a range of profile parameters to define the general conditions for logging (see Table 10.1).

Parameter	Meaning	Sample Parameter Values
DIR_AUDIT	Storage directory for log files on the application server	/usr/sap/<SID>/DVEBMGS00/log
FN_AUDIT	Naming convention for log files	audit_++++++++_######.AUD
rsau/enable	Security Audit Log activated/deactivated	0—Audit not activated 1—Audit activated
rsau/max_diskspace/local	Maximum size of the log directory	200M (200 megabytes)
rsau/max_diskspace/per_day	Maximum size of the log files written in one day	30M (30 megabytes)
rsau/max_diskspace/per_file	Maximum size of a single log file	5M (5 megabytes)
rsau/selection_slots	Number of configurable filters	1 to 5
rsau/user_selection	Use of placeholders during user selection	0—User selection with placeholders not activated 1—User selection with placeholders activated

Table 10.1 Profile Parameters—General Logging Conditions

[+]

Profile Parameter

You can display the profile parameters and settings relevant for the Security Audit Log in Transaction SM19 (Security Audit Configuration) under the menu path ENVIRONMENT • PROFILE PARAMETER. You maintain the profile parameters in Transaction RZ10. Note that you cannot toggle dynamically between any of these parameters. In other words, you must restart the application server for any changes to become effective.

[!]

Parameter rsau/user_selection

When configuring the parameter rsau/user_selection, please read SAP Note 574914.

After you've implemented the basic configuration and restarted the application server, use Transaction SM19 to define the log filters. In the filter settings, you can define which data are to be logged. You can define up to five filters (see the profile parameter `rsau/selection_slots`).

It's necessary to distinguish between a static and dynamic configuration of the Security Audit Log:

- The *static* audit configuration is permanently saved to the database and used by all application servers that have this database. The settings only become active after you restart the application server. However, they are retained the next time the server is shut down.
- *Dynamically* configured filters can be activated individually for individual application servers, or they can be distributed to several servers. The filter settings take effect immediately, but they are not saved to the database and therefore are lost the next time you restart the server.

To define log filters, follow these steps:

1. Enter Transaction "SM19" in the command box, and press the [Enter] key (or select the menu option TOOLS • ADMINISTRATION • MONITOR • SECURITY AUDIT LOG • SM19—CONFIGURATION).
2. If you want to configure static filters, choose CREATE on the STATIC CONFIGURATION tab (🗋).

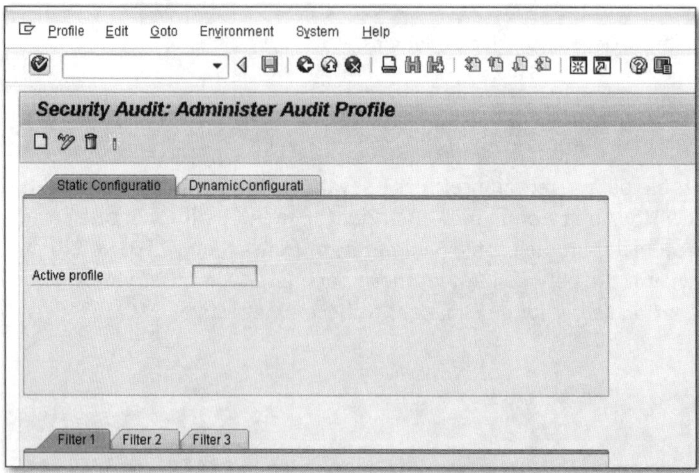

3. Enter a profile name (for example, "AUDIT") and choose Continue (✔).

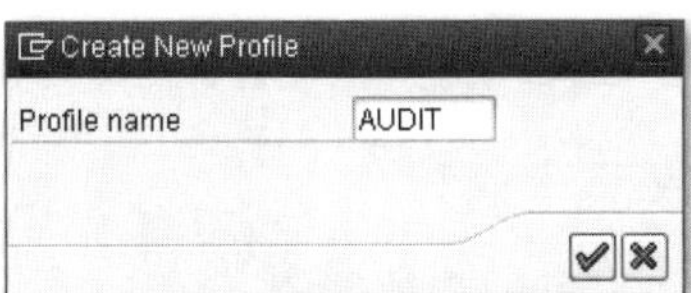

4. In this example, you can specify a maximum of three different filters and define the scope of the actions to be logged in each case. Configure the following settings on the Filter 1 tab:
   - Activate the Filter active checkbox.
   - In the Client field, enter the client to be monitored (for example, "100" for an individual client or "*" for all clients).
   - In the User field, enter the user ID whose actions are to be logged (for example, "DDIC" for the user DDIC or "*" for all users).
   - In the Audit classes column, select the logging scope you require.
   - Under Events, restrict logging to certain actions (for example, only Critical), if necessary.
   - Choose Detail Configuration to define additional settings.

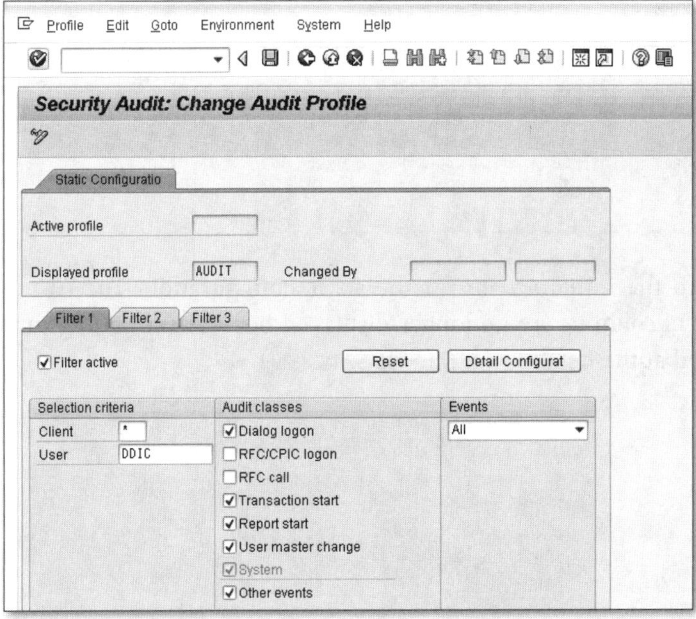

5. Scroll through the list of loggable audit events, and make your selection by activating or deactivating event logging in the RECORDING column. When you are finished, choose ACCEPT CHANGES (✔).

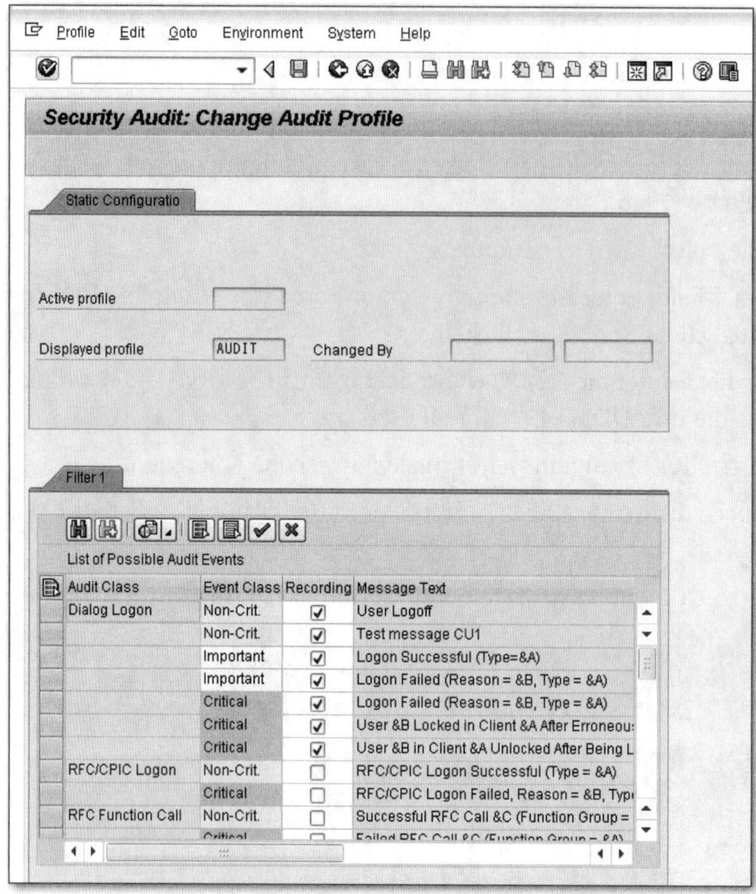

6. You now return to the initial screen for the static configuration. The AUDIT CLASSES and EVENTS columns are no longer displayed because the settings are displayed or edited at the detail level. Choose SAVE (💾).

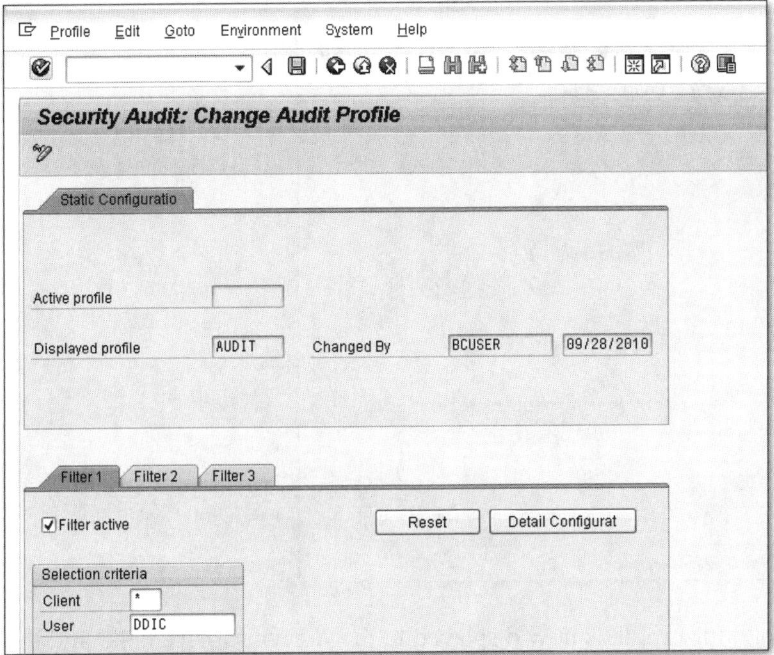

7. The system displays a confirmation prompt asking you if you want to distribute this filter configuration to all application servers. Choose YES.

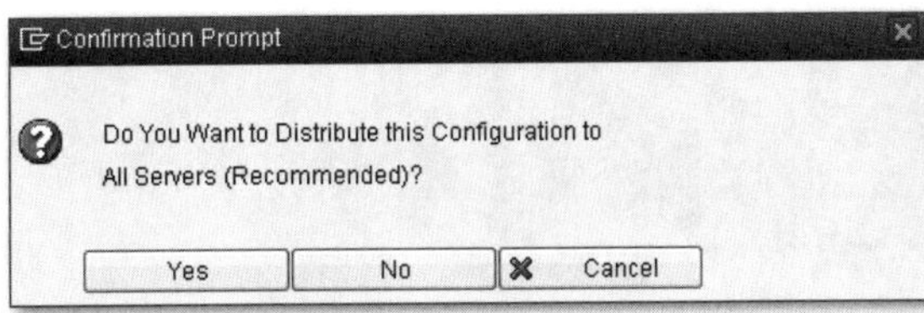

8. A message in the status bar confirms that the filter has been saved and distributed to all active instances. For the settings to take effect, choose ACTIVATE ( ).

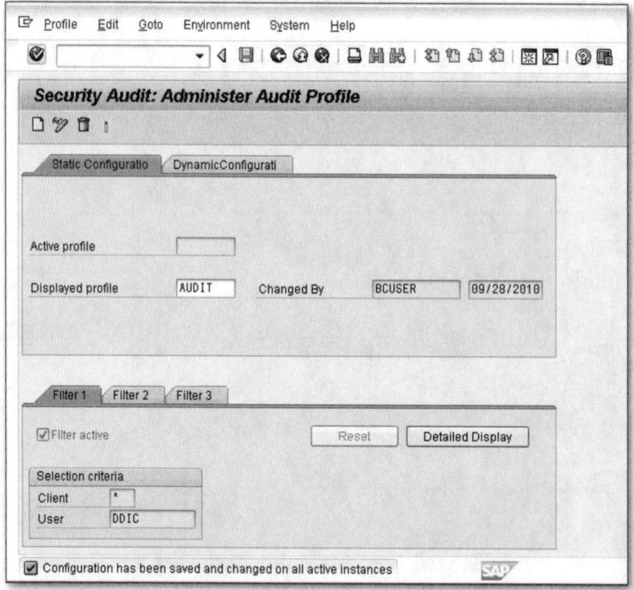

9. The name of your profile is now displayed in the ACTIVE PROFILE field, and the message in the status bar confirms that the profile has been activated for the next system start. Define additional filters, if necessary.

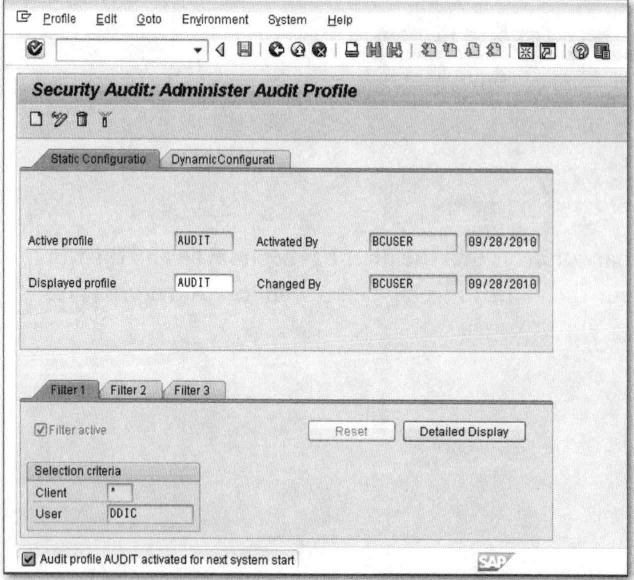

[!]

When Does the Configuration Take Effect?

Note that the static configuration doesn't take effect until you restart the application server. However, when you activate a static filter in newer releases, the system automatically creates an identical filter in the dynamic configuration so that logging is activated immediately.

If you want to change the logging criteria for one or more application servers while the system is running, follow these steps:

1. Switch to the DYNAMIC CONFIGURATION tab, and check whether the logging status is AUDIT ACTIVE ( ). To create a dynamic filter, choose DISPLAY <-> CHANGE ( ) to switch to change mode.

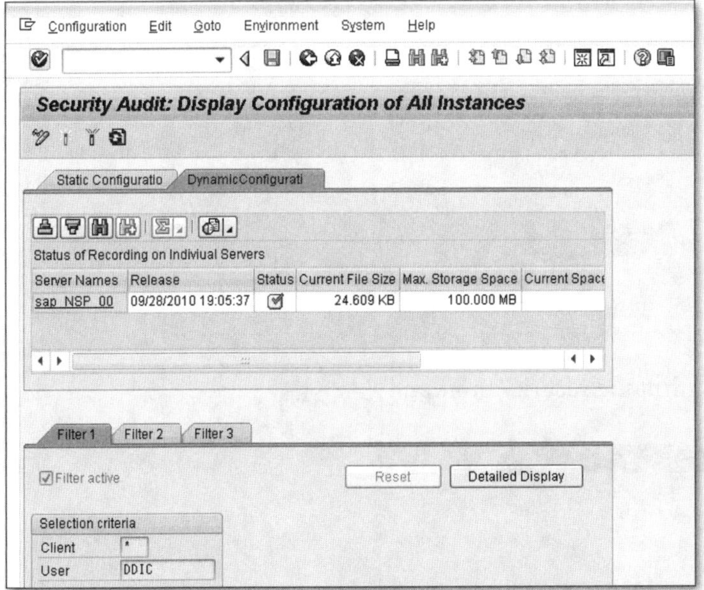

2. Switch to an available configuration slot (e.g., to the FILTER 2 tab).
3. Configure the required settings (see step 4 of the preceding list). When you are finished, choose ACTIVATE AUDIT ( ).

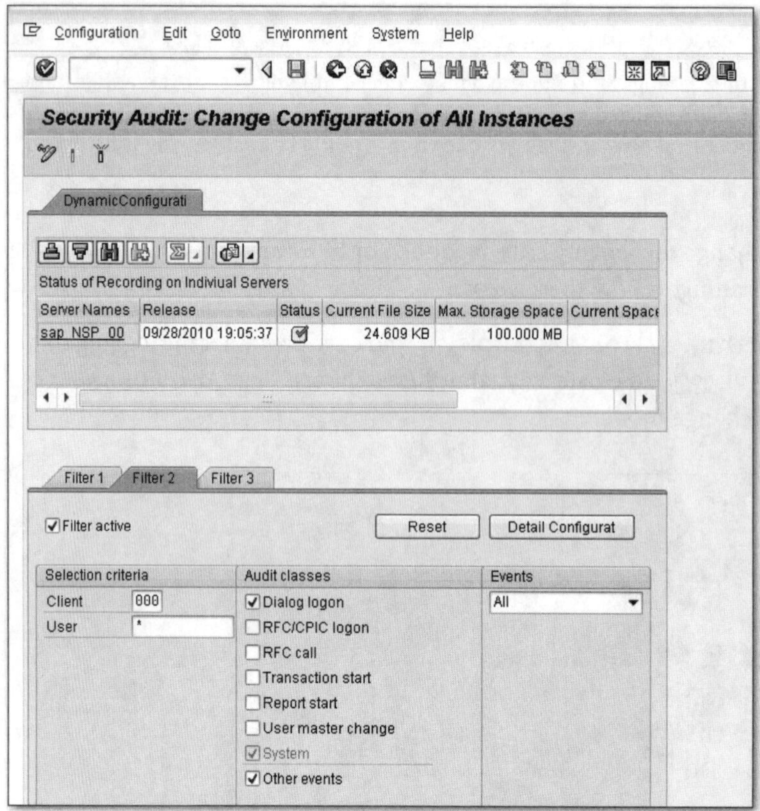

4. Choose YES to confirm the security prompt.

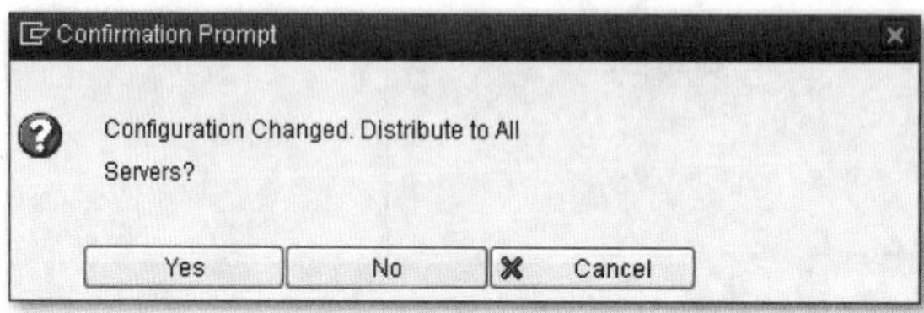

5. A message in the status bar confirms that the filter has been activated on all instances.

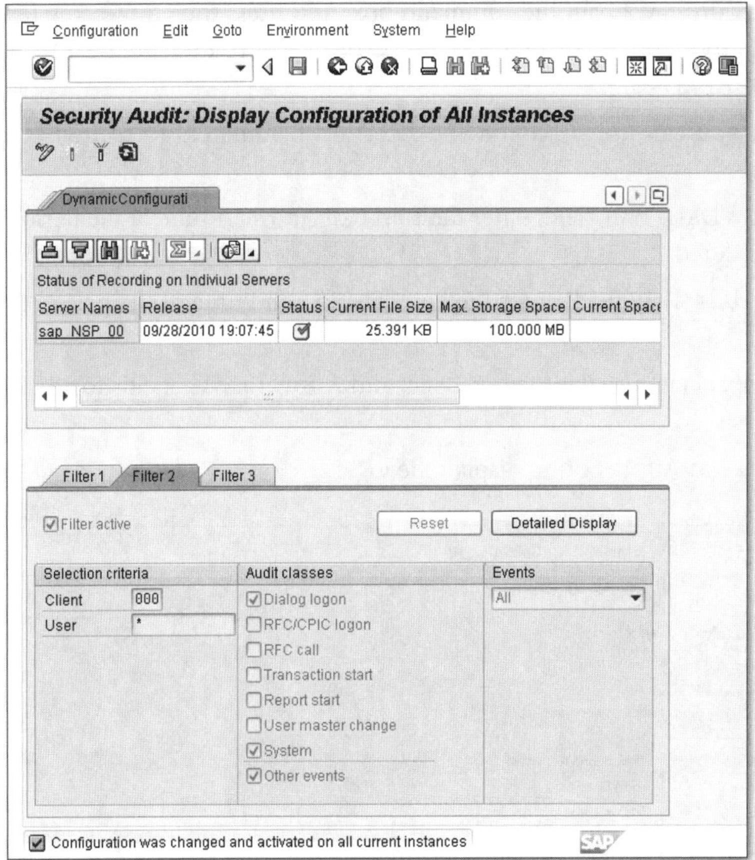

As soon as the log filters have been defined and activated, the selected events are recorded. Depending on the filter setting for a large number of users or a large number of logged system actions, the volume of data accumulates very quickly, and therefore the log files grow accordingly. In the worst-case scenario, your file system may overflow, which will cause the SAP system to shut down. Therefore, monitor the size of your audit files or the fill level of your log directory.

Analyzing the Security Audit Log

Transaction SM20 is used to analyze the files created by the Security Audit Log. Follow these steps:

1. Enter Transaction "SM20" in the command box, and press the [Enter] key (or select the menu option Tools • Administration • Monitor • Security Audit Log • SM20—Analysis).
2. If necessary, you can use the following selection parameters to restrict the analysis:
   - In the From Date/Time field, enter the start date and start time of the period to be considered.
   - In the To Date/Time field, enter the end date and end time of the period to be considered.
   - On the Events tab, use the Client, User, and Audit Classes fields to adjust your analysis.
   - Choose Reread Audit Log to display the log.

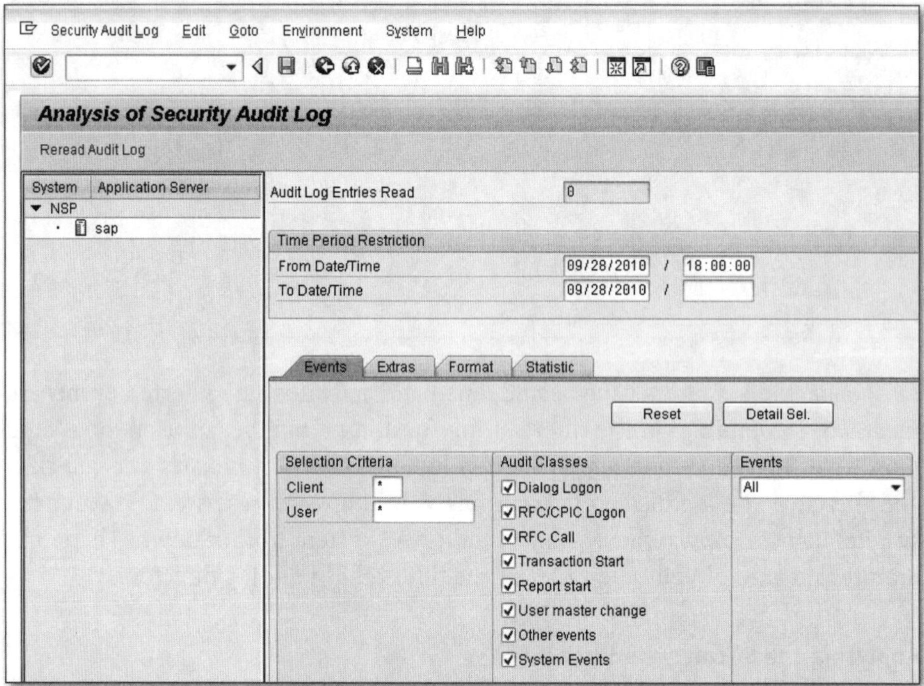

3. The logged system events are displayed.

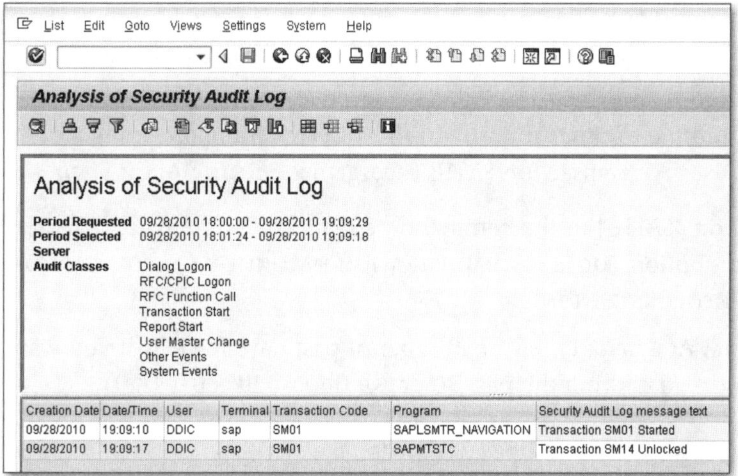

In this example, an anonymous user account (user DDIC) was used to remove a transaction lock (Transaction SM14) that may have developed into a system risk. At first glance, however, you can't identify which person made the change. The entry in the TERMINAL column can help you determine which PC the user used to log on to the SAP system. The change documents for the relevant user master record (here: DDIC) provide another clue. In Transaction SU01 (User Maintenance), you can determine who was the last person to change the user account, in other words, who was the last person to reset the password.

[+]

Transaction STAD

In certain circumstances, the data protection regulations may not allow you to run the Security Audit Log continuously. In the worst-case scenario, no logs are available for analysis after a system incident.

With Transaction STAD (Business Transaction Analysis), however, you don't need an active Security Audit Log to analyze which user has executed which transaction or program in the system and which PC was used to log on to the system. The standard configuration only contains data from the past 48 hours. However, you can use the profile parameters `stat/max_files` and `stat/as_max_files` to extend this period to a maximum of 99 hours.

Deleting Security Audit Log Files

Files created by the Security Audit Log are not automatically deleted. In other words, the volume of data constantly increases if logging is active. You must therefore delete old audit files from time to time. You can do this directly at the operating system level, or you can use SAP Transaction SM18 (Reorganize Security Audit Log).

1. Enter Transaction "SM18" in the command box, and press the [Enter] key (or select the menu option TOOLS • ADMINISTRATION • MONITOR • SECURITY AUDIT LOG • SM18—REORGANIZATION).
2. In the MINIMUM AGE field, enter the number of past days for which you want to retain files (e.g., data from the past 30 days). Choose EXECUTE (⊕).

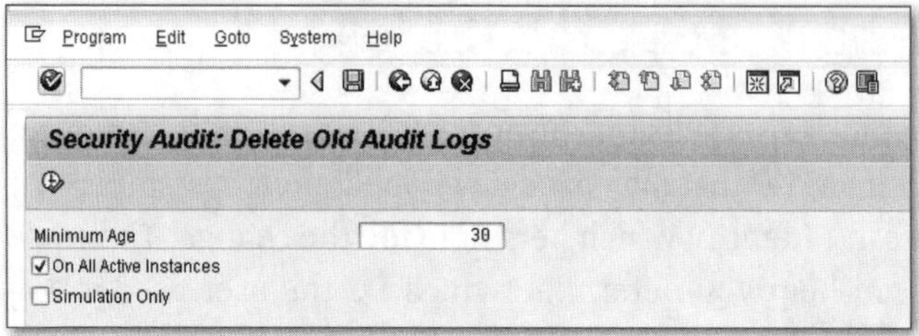

[+] Minimum Age

The minimum age must be 3 or more. In other words, you cannot use Transaction SM18 to delete log files from the past three days.

3. The audit files are deleted. The log shows the number of files that have been deleted and the number of files that have been retained.

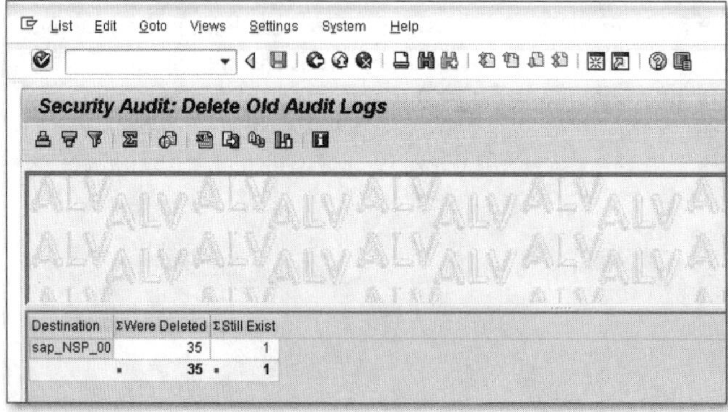

Deleting Log Entries [!]

When you delete files, the log entries are permanently lost if they were not first saved at the operating system level. Resourceful users could try to cover their tracks. For this reason, only a few users should be granted access to Transaction SM18.

10.6 Summary

All kinds of sensitive business data are stored in your SAP system. Because legislation demands that companies take appropriate measures to protect their data, you must give some thought to the security of your SAP systems.

This topic is complex because it comprises all systems levels—application, database, operating system, and infrastructure. A gap in security may result in all other measures becoming ineffective. For this reason, a usable security concept can only be created in conjunction with the relevant experts. Regular checks then ensure that no new weak spots arise.

This chapter deals with performance issues in SAP systems. In addition to providing general recommendations on the handling of short-term performance bottlenecks, this chapter introduces tools for analyzing and optimizing the system's performance.

11 Performance

Performance problems usually affect all users and most of the business processes in an SAP system. As an administrator, your highest priority is to eliminate bottlenecks as soon as possible and ensure that the users can work again. When the worst is over, you can analyze the problem in detail and try to avoid similar incidents by introducing the appropriate countermeasures. The complex area of performance analysis and optimization in an SAP system is further described in *SAP Performance Optimization Guide* (SAP PRESS, 2011). This chapter introduces you to the most important tools for managing performance problems quickly and effectively.

A prerequisite is that the hardware, operating system, database, and SAP system have all been installed correctly, that they are dimensioned appropriately according to the SAP Sizing Guides (see *www.service.sap.com/sizing*), and that performance bottlenecks don't occur on a daily basis. If this is the case, there's either a general problem in the system landscape, or your system does not have enough resources for stable operation. You then have to analyze the infrastructure in detail or assess the resource requirements anew.

11.1 Short-Term Remedy of Performance Problems

You usually recognize temporary performance bottlenecks due to unusually long response times during the execution of dialog transactions. As an administrator, you get informed either by users or because you work in the system and are affected directly.

It may just be a short-term peak load, that is, a lot of users perform resource-intensive activities in the system simultaneously. In such a case, as soon as one or several users have completed their work, the system may no longer be overloaded within a short space of time without you having done anything. On the other hand, you mustn't waste time by hoping that the problem will resolve itself because it's also possible that a serious error has occurred in the system infrastructure that you have to eliminate actively (for example, network problems or hardware defects). So you should immediately gain an overview of the system's state by carrying out the following steps:

1. Enter Transaction "SM50" in the command box, and press the [Enter] key (or select the menu option TOOLS • ADMINISTRATION • MONITOR • SYSTEM MONITORING • SM50—PROCESS OVERVIEW).
2. In the process overview, search for abnormalities, for example, for processes with exceptionally long runtimes. Click on the CPU button (⏱) to have the system display the processor times of the processes. Update the display several times using REFRESH (🔄) to identify permanently running processes.

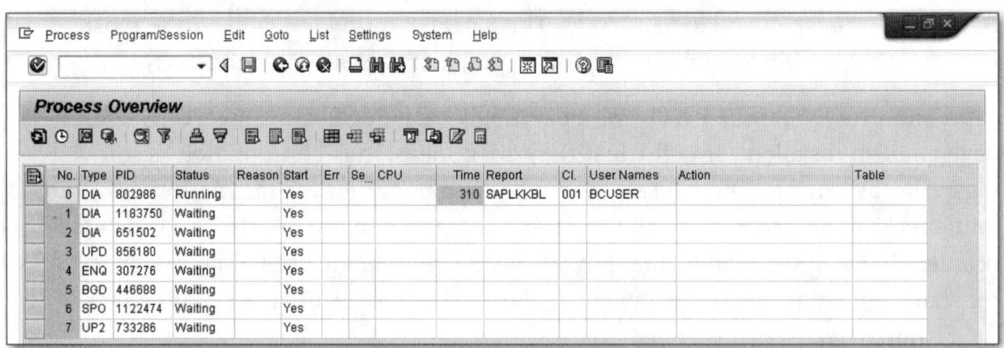

No.	Type	PID	Status	Reason	Start	Err	Se...	CPU	Time	Report	Cl.	User Names	Action	Table
0	DIA	802986	Running		Yes				310	SAPLKKBL	001	BCUSER		
1	DIA	1183750	Waiting		Yes									
2	DIA	651502	Waiting		Yes									
3	UPD	856180	Waiting		Yes									
4	ENQ	307276	Waiting		Yes									
5	BGD	446688	Waiting		Yes									
6	SPO	1122474	Waiting		Yes									
7	UP2	733286	Waiting		Yes									

3. In addition, you can use Transaction SM04 (User List) to obtain an overview of the users that are currently logged on to the system (see Chapter 13). One of the reasons for performance problems can be a particularly large number of users logged on to the system.

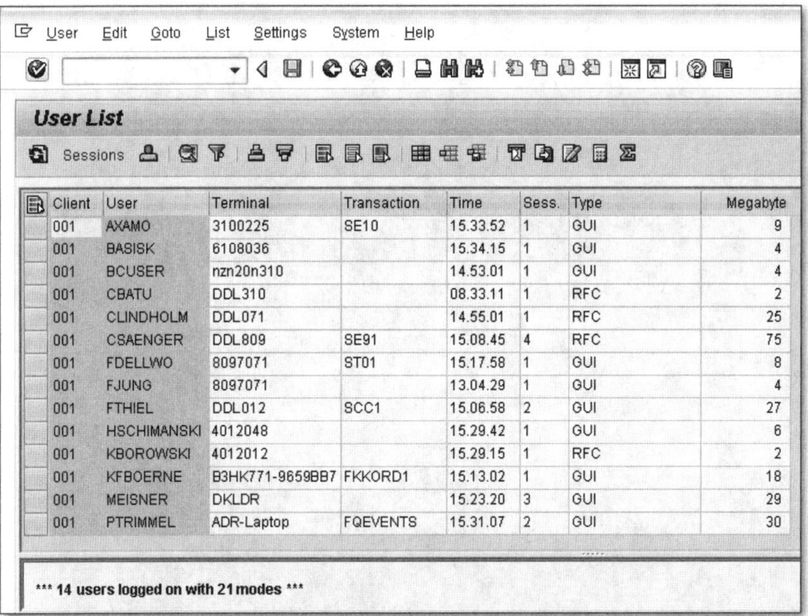

Client	User	Terminal	Transaction	Time	Sess.	Type	Megabyte
001	AXAMO	3100225	SE10	15.33.52	1	GUI	9
001	BASISK	6108036		15.34.15	1	GUI	4
001	BCUSER	nzn20n310		14.53.01	1	GUI	4
001	CBATU	DDL310		08.33.11	1	RFC	2
001	CLINDHOLM	DDL071		14.55.01	1	RFC	25
001	CSAENGER	DDL809	SE91	15.08.45	4	RFC	75
001	FDELLWO	8097071	ST01	15.17.58	1	GUI	8
001	FJUNG	8097071		13.04.29	1	GUI	4
001	FTHIEL	DDL012	SCC1	15.06.58	2	GUI	27
001	HSCHIMANSKI	4012048		15.29.42	1	GUI	6
001	KBOROWSKI	4012012		15.29.15	1	RFC	2
001	KFBOERNE	B3HK771-9659BB7	FKKORD1	15.13.02	1	GUI	18
001	MEISNER	DKLDR		15.23.20	3	GUI	29
001	PTRIMMEL	ADR-Laptop	FQEVENTS	15.31.07	2	GUI	30

*** 14 users logged on with 21 modes ***

4. Start a system monitor at the operating system level (for example, the Task Manager under Windows or nmon under Unix). Analyze the current system load with regard to CPU, memory, virtual memory, and hard disk activity (input/output).

Checking Processes [+]

Check if certain processes have a particularly large share in the CPU usage, occupy a large amount of memory, or have exceptional I/O rates. Especially when objects are swapped to the virtual memory, this has a negative effect on the system performance. In this case, you should increase the system's memory—if possible.

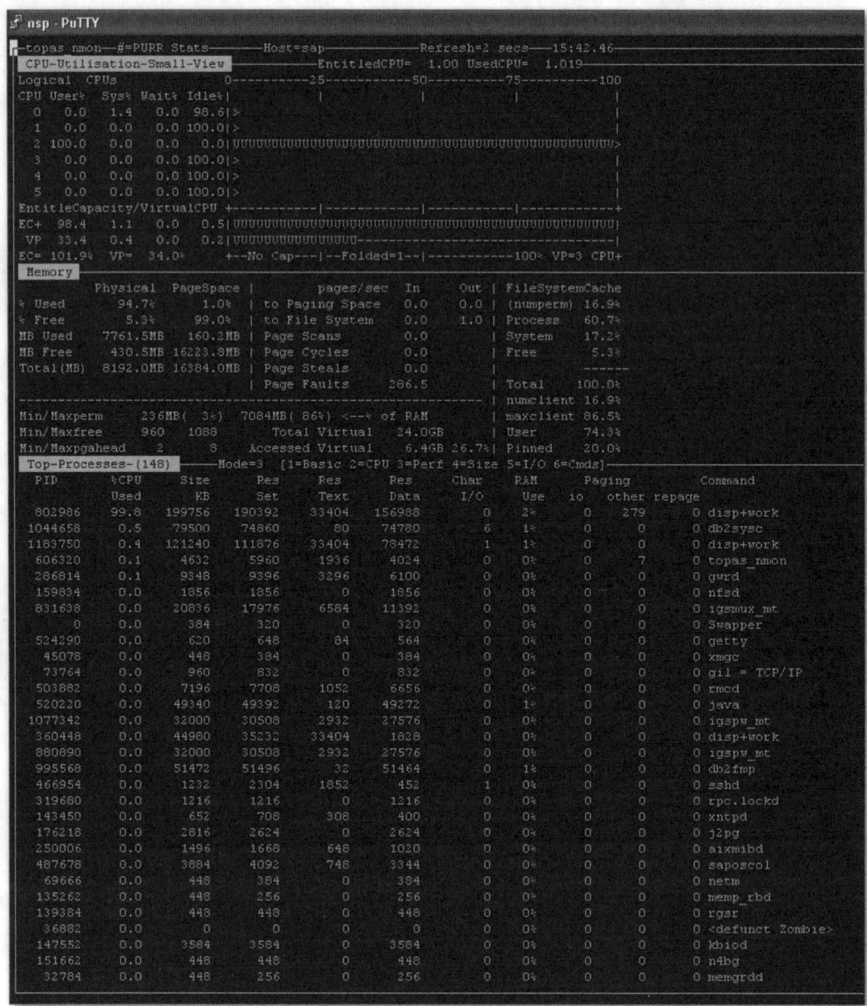

5. If you notice suspicious SAP processes (process name: DISP+WORK) at the operating system level, the process number allows you to draw conclusions about abnormalities in the SAP process overview (Transaction SM50). This enables you to identify the process type (dialog process: DIA type, background job: BTC type) and the user that executes the process. If it's a background process, check the active jobs using Transaction SM37 (Job Overview; see Chapter 15). For a dialog process, contact the user.

Identifying SAP Processes

If the suspicious processes are not SAP processes (DISP+WORK), the problem is usually not located in the SAP system. Continue to check the programs or database processes that run at the operating system level.

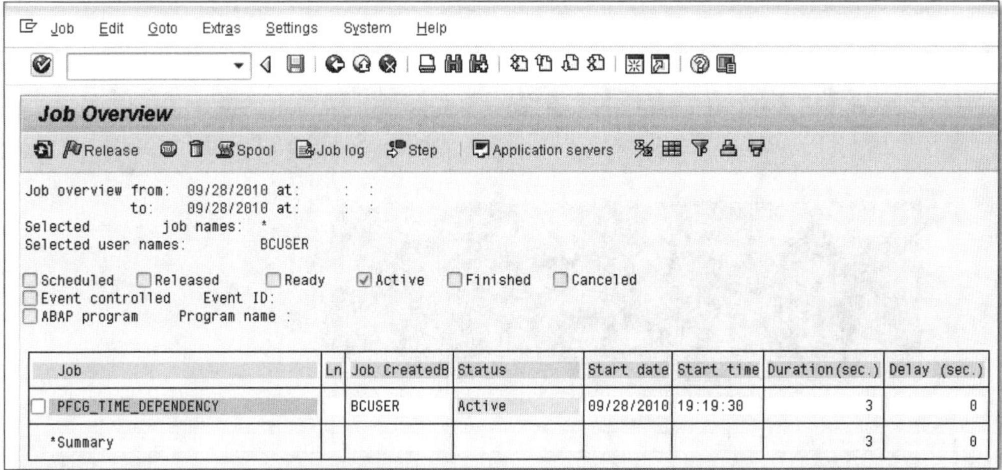

Job	Ln	Job CreatedB	Status	Start date	Start time	Duration(sec.)	Delay (sec.)
PFCG_TIME_DEPENDENCY		BCUSER	Active	09/28/2010	19:19:30	3	0
*Summary						3	0

6. When you are sure that an SAP process has caused the performance bottleneck, terminate the process if necessary, that is, if the performance problems are too severe. To do so, select the process in the process overview, and choose PROCESS • CANCEL WITH CORE.

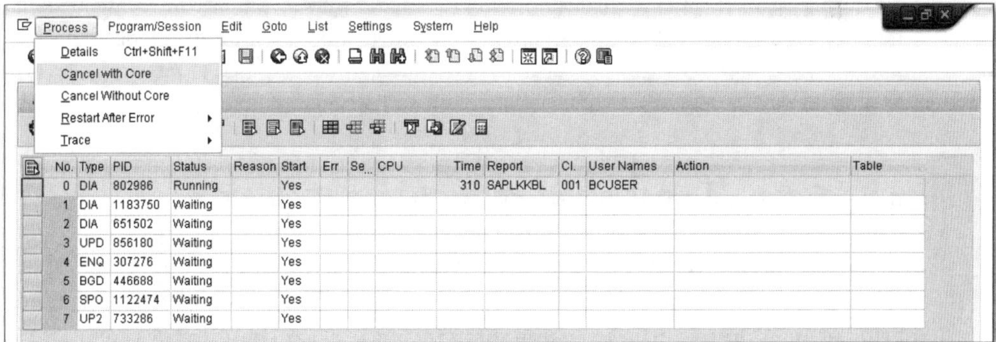

No.	Type	PID	Status	Reason	Start	Err	Se...	CPU	Time	Report	Cl.	User Names	Action	Table
0	DIA	802986	Running		Yes				310	SAPLKKBL	001	BCUSER		
1	DIA	1183750	Waiting		Yes									
2	DIA	651502	Waiting		Yes									
3	UPD	856180	Waiting		Yes									
4	ENQ	307276	Waiting		Yes									
5	BGD	446688	Waiting		Yes									
6	SPO	1122474	Waiting		Yes									
7	UP2	733286	Waiting		Yes									

[+]

Generating Core Dump Files

If you use the CANCEL WITH CORE option, the system creates an error log file for the process. You can analyze this file using Transaction ST11 (Error Log Files). You can also use the CANCEL WITHOUT CORE menu item. In this case, the system doesn't generate a core file.

7. The termination attempts in the process overview may not be successful; that is, the process is not canceled. In this case, terminate the process at the operating system level (for example, via END PROCESS in the Windows Task Manager or using the `kill [-KILL] <Process ID>` console command under Unix).

[!]

Caution When Terminating Processes

Be careful when terminating processes because you cancel running SAP programs ruthlessly. This can have severe consequences, particularly for critical background jobs.

[+]

Real-Time Files at Operating System Level

Operating system tools are usually more suitable than the SAP system's operating system monitor (Transaction OS06; see Chapter 9) to solve serious performance bottlenecks because you are provided with real-time data that is updated much more often.

11.2 Detailed Analysis of Performance Problems

In addition to fast troubleshooting, the SAP system provides numerous analysis tools that you should use if your SAP system frequently suffers from performance bottlenecks. A prerequisite for using them is that SAP OS Collector (SAPOSCOL) is active, and the periodical job, SAP_COLLECTOR_FOR_PERFMONITOR, runs regularly (see Chapter 9). This ensures that the data required for analyses is collected. You should collect data for at least one week to obtain meaningful statistics.

[+]

Poor Programming Impacts Performance

One of the most common reasons for performance problems in the SAP system are poorly written customer-specific ABAP programs or customized standard ABAP programs.

11.2.1 System Load Analysis

Load analyses enable you to determine detailed data on the system's performance. You should check these statistics and record trends to get a feel for the system performance. It also enables you to identify transactions with a high system load or bottlenecks in individual system components.

1. Enter Transaction "ST03N" in the command box, and press the [Enter] key (or select the menu option Tools • Administration • Monitor • Performance • Workload • ST03N—Aggregated Statistic Records Local).

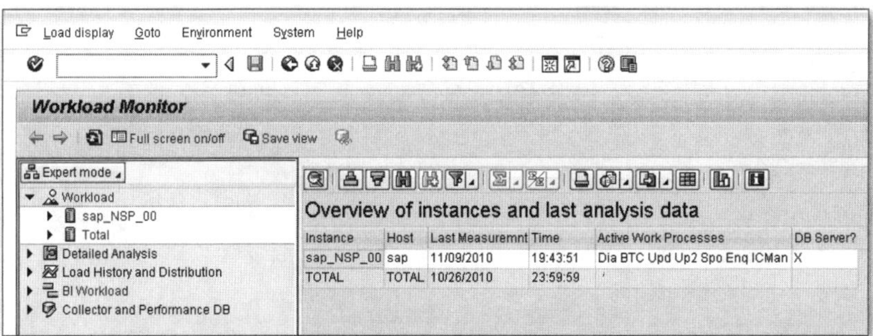

2. Ensure that the Expert mode is selected in the left screen area. Expand the path Detailed Analysis • Last Minutes' Load.

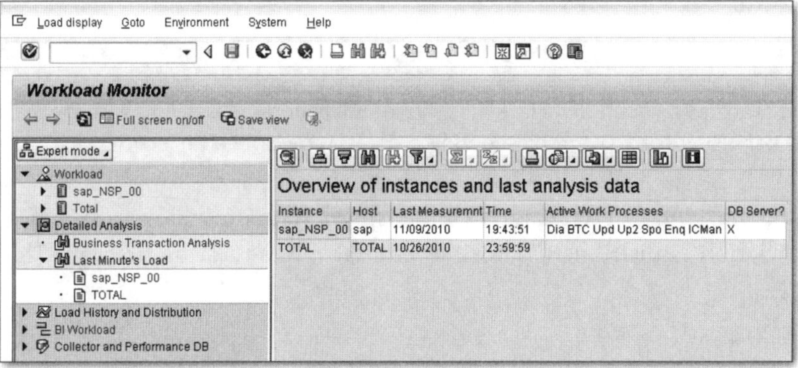

3. Double-click on the instance name (SAP_NSP_00, for example). In the next screen, you can restrict the analysis period.
   - In ANALYSIS INTERVAL, enter DATE and TIME PERIOD that are supposed to be analyzed.
   - If necessary, enter the CLIENT, USER, or WORK PROCESS NUMBER if the data need to be restricted.
   - Select CONTINUE (✔).

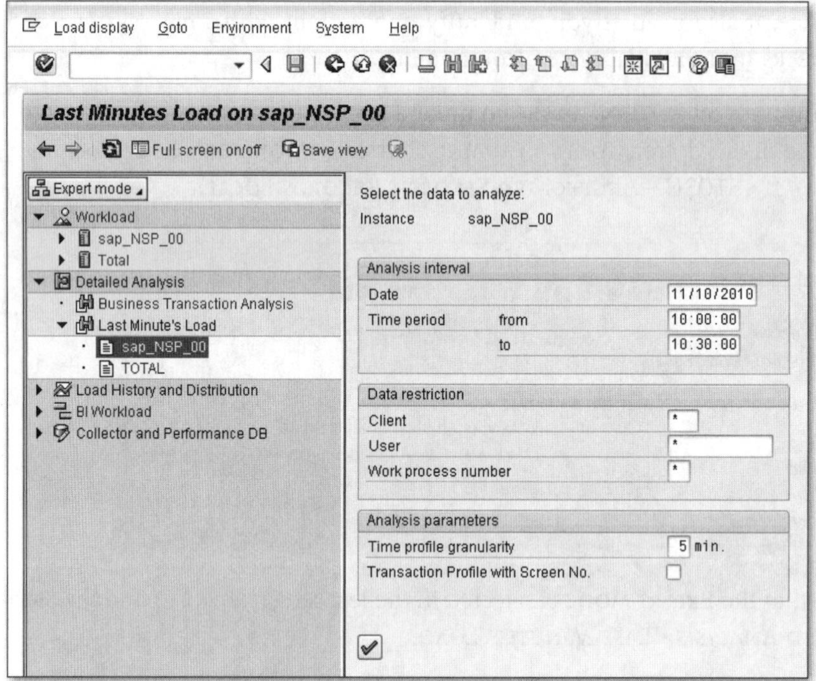

[+]

Using Notes

For this kind of analysis, you should make the corresponding notes on suspicious processes and users when using the fast troubleshooting process as described in Section 11.1.

4. The WORKLOAD OVERVIEW analysis view displays data on various task types. The information is distributed across several tabs; TIMES is the first tab. This

table enables you to determine which task type occupies the most resources in your system. Under Task Type, select the required type. Click on Details (🔍) to view the performance values for the selected task type. The most important task types are the following:

- DIALOG: User transactions that are executed in the foreground.
- BACKGROUND: Transactions in background processing.
- HTTP: Internet transactions on HTTP basis.
- RFC: Remote function calls.
- SPOOL: Spool work processes.
- UPDATE: Update processes.

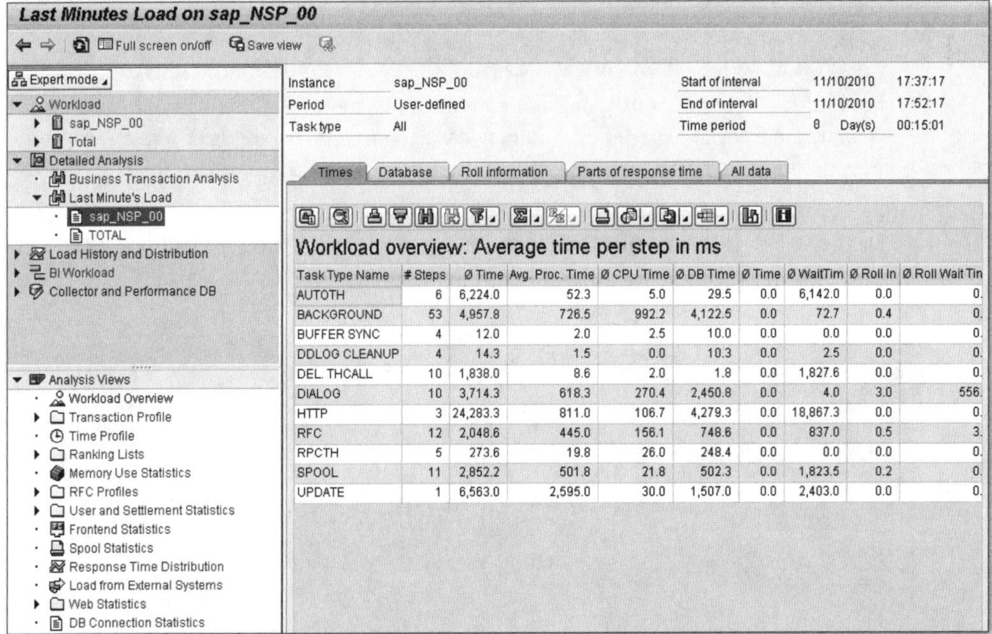

Task Type Name	# Steps	Ø Time	Avg. Proc. Time	Ø CPU Time	Ø DB Time	Ø Time	Ø WaitTim	Ø Roll In	Ø Roll Wait Tin
AUTOTH	6	6,224.0	52.3	5.0	29.5	0.0	6,142.0	0.0	0.
BACKGROUND	53	4,957.8	726.5	992.2	4,122.5	0.0	72.7	0.4	0.
BUFFER SYNC	4	12.0	2.0	2.5	10.0	0.0	0.0	0.0	0.
DDLOG CLEANUP	4	14.3	1.5	0.0	10.3	0.0	2.5	0.0	0.
DEL. THCALL	10	1,838.0	8.6	2.0	1.8	0.0	1,827.6	0.0	0.
DIALOG	10	3,714.3	618.3	270.4	2,450.8	0.0	4.0	3.0	556.
HTTP	3	24,283.3	811.0	106.7	4,279.3	0.0	18,867.3	0.0	0.
RFC	12	2,048.6	445.0	156.1	748.6	0.0	837.0	0.5	3.
RPCTH	5	273.6	19.8	26.0	248.4	0.0	0.0	0.0	0.
SPOOL	11	2,852.2	501.8	21.8	502.3	0.0	1,823.5	0.2	0.
UPDATE	1	6,563.0	2,595.0	30.0	1,507.0	0.0	2,403.0	0.0	0.

5. In the Details dialog box, check the displayed data, for example, the Average CPU Time (ms). For the DIALOG task type, the expected standard response time is less than 1,000 ms (1 second), for instance. When you are finished, choose Close Window (✔).

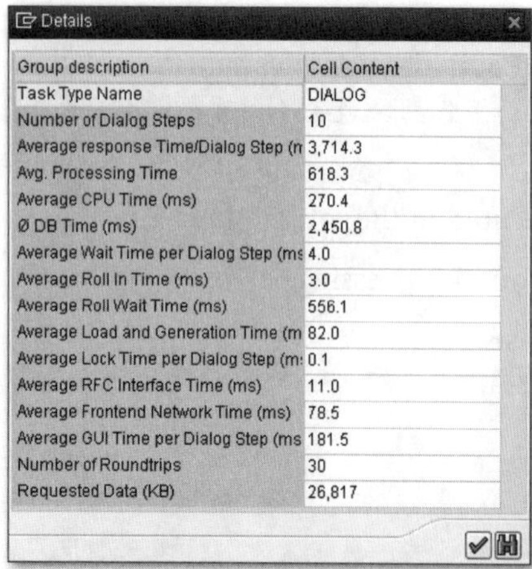

[+]

Evaluating Performance Statistics

These values differ depending on the task type and system component; their evaluation is mainly a matter of experience. You may have to leave it to experts. There are various notes on this in the SAP Service Marketplace (*www.service.sap.com/performance*).

6. In the lower-left area of the screen, under ANALYSIS VIEWS, select the TRANSACTION PROFILE folder. Double-click on STANDARD.

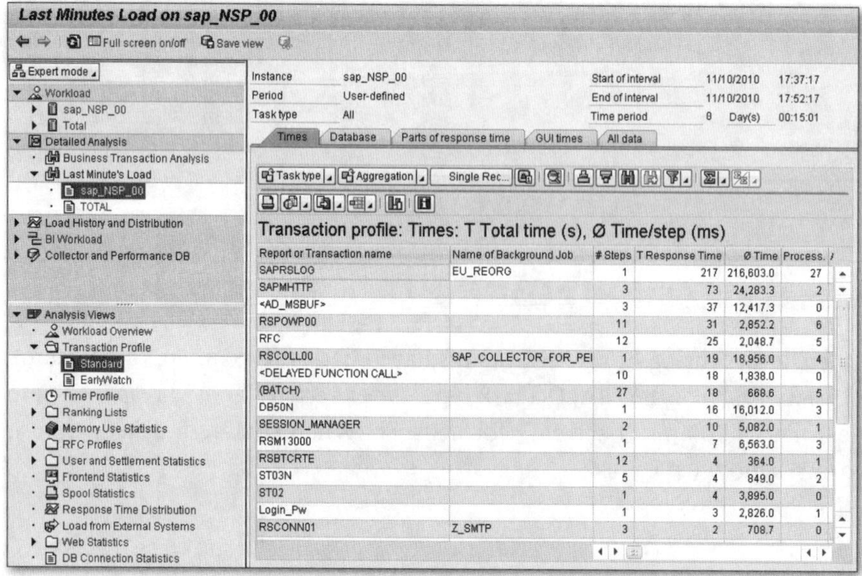

7. Select the AVERAGE RESPONSE TIME (O/TIME) column heading, and choose SORT IN DESCENDING ORDER ([icon]). The system sorts the programs and transactions by the average response time, which enables you to analyze which transactions place a particularly high load on your system.

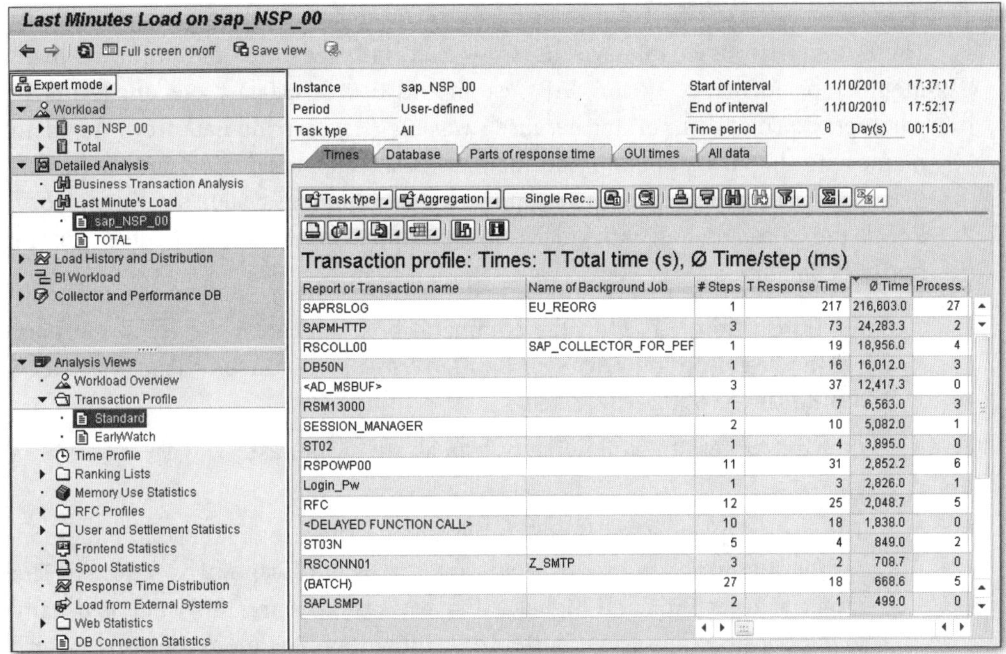

8. The other tabs (DATABASE, PARTS OF RESPONSE TIME, GUI TIMES) provide additional information.

[+]

Checking Customer-Specific Programs

Customer-specific transactions where little attention was paid to efficient programming are frequently responsible for performance bottlenecks of the system. Initiate performance checks for this kind of transaction in your programming department. Queries with standard SAP programs that address large tables, however, can also lead to performance problems.

For regular, performance-intensive activities, it can be useful to create specific transactions or programs whose performance is optimized for these special requirements.

Transaction ST03N (Workload Monitor) enables you to process urgent, short-term performance problems, analyze the performance of your system over a long period of time, and use the results for optimization purposes.

11.2.2 Buffer Analysis

The buffer analysis enables you to view data with regard to the buffer or main memory performance of the SAP system and use this data to reconcile buffer parameters. This is important because *swapping* (transferring data from the main memory to the virtual memory on the hard disk) can considerably impact performance. You can avoid frequent swapping by extending the system's main memory. Check the buffer behavior regularly to determine trends and get a feel for the buffer behavior.

1. Enter Transaction "ST02" in the command box, and press the Enter key (or select the menu option Tools • Administration • Monitor • Performance • Setup/Buffers • ST02—Buffers).
2. In the next screen, the following two areas are of interest:
   - Hit Ratio
     This value specifies with which percentage the user requests for the corresponding program can be processed; that is, no swapping is required. The target value is 95% and higher. After the system start, this value is usually lower because the system buffers are still empty. The more users log on and the more data is written to the buffers, the higher the hit ratio. Normally, it takes two hours to one day until the used buffers are filled with data.
   - Swaps
     The swapping target value for the program buffer (PROGRAM) is smaller than 1,000. All other buffers have a target value of 0. If a buffer doesn't contain the required data, the system retrieves the data from the database. This data, however, can't be buffered additionally due to the fill level or fragmentation of the buffer. Consequently, the system must first remove other objects from the buffer to create memory for the new data (swapping). If the system is restarted, the swap value is reset to zero (0). If a strikingly large number of swaps take place in your system, optimize the system buffers.

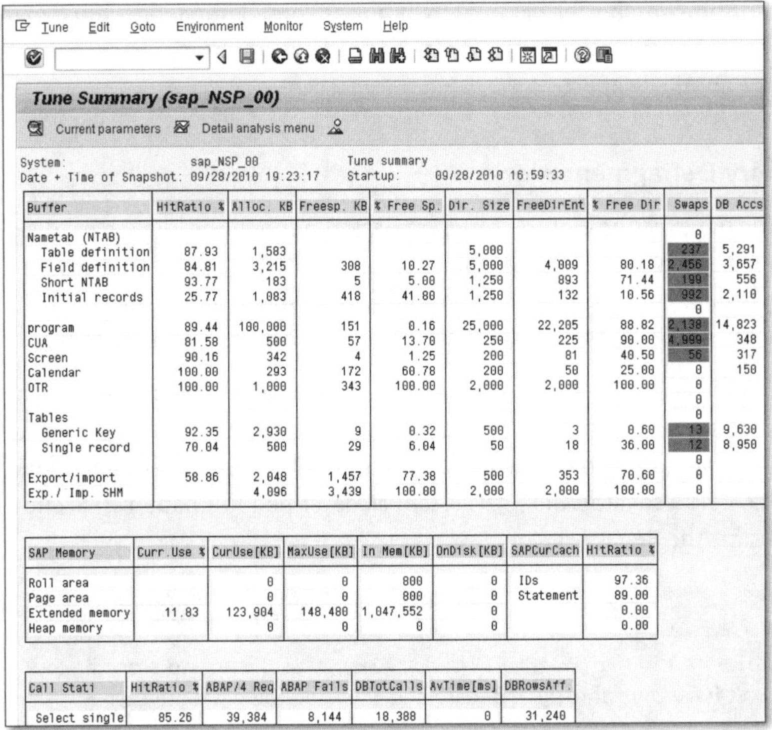

Tune Summary (sap_NSP_00)

Current parameters   Detail analysis menu

System: sap_NSP_00   Tune summary
Date + Time of Snapshot: 09/28/2010 19:23:17   Startup: 09/28/2010 16:59:33

Buffer	HitRatio %	Alloc. KB	Freesp. KB	% Free Sp.	Dir. Size	FreeDirEnt	% Free Dir	Swaps	DB Accs
Nametab (NTAB)								0	
Table definition	87.93	1,583			5,000			237	5,291
Field definition	84.81	3,215	308	10.27	5,000	4,009	80.18	2,456	3,657
Short NTAB	93.77	183	5	5.00	1,250	893	71.44	199	556
Initial records	25.77	1,083	418	41.80	1,250	132	10.56	992	2,110
								0	
program	89.44	100,000	151	0.16	25,000	22,205	88.82	2,138	14,823
CUA	81.58	500	57	13.70	250	225	90.00	4,999	348
Screen	90.16	342	4	1.25	200	81	40.50	56	317
Calendar	100.00	293	172	60.78	200	50	25.00	0	150
OTR	100.00	1,000	343	100.00	2,000	2,000	100.00	0	
								0	
Tables								0	
Generic Key	92.35	2,930	9	0.32	500	3	0.60	13	9,630
Single record	70.04	500	29	6.04	50	18	36.00	12	8,950
								0	
Export/import	58.86	2,048	1,457	77.38	500	353	70.60	0	
Exp./ Imp. SHM		4,096	3,439	100.00	2,000	2,000	100.00	0	

SAP Memory	Curr.Use %	CurUse[KB]	MaxUse[KB]	In Mem[KB]	OnDisk[KB]	SAPCurCach	HitRatio %
Roll area		0	0	800	0	IDs	97.36
Page area		0	0	800	0	Statement	89.00
Extended memory	11.83	123,904	148,480	1,047,552	0		0.00
Heap memory		0	0	0	0		0.00

Call Stati	HitRatio %	ABAP/4 Req	ABAP Fails	DBTotCalls	AvTime[ms]	DBRowsAff.
Select single	85.26	39,384	8,144	18,388	0	31,240

3. Check whether the SWAPS column contains entries that are highlighted in red. If this is the case, double-click on a value that is highlighted in red. The details view contains further information.

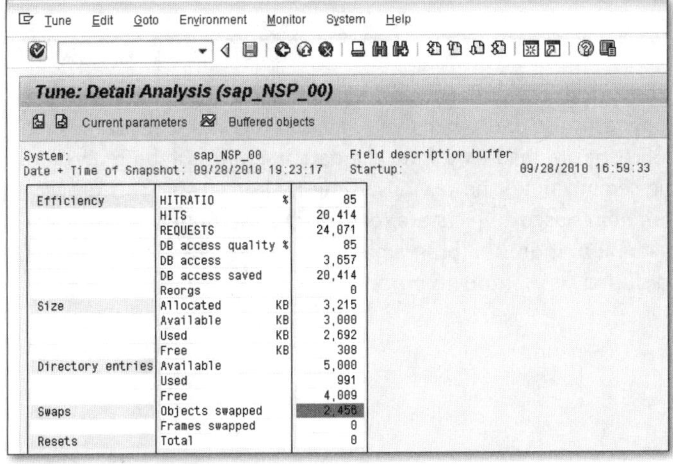

Tune: Detail Analysis (sap_NSP_00)

Current parameters   Buffered objects

System: sap_NSP_00   Field description buffer
Date + Time of Snapshot: 09/28/2010 19:23:17   Startup: 09/28/2010 16:59:33

Efficiency	HITRATIO %	85
	HITS	20,414
	REQUESTS	24,071
	DB access quality %	85
	DB access	3,657
	DB access saved	20,414
	Reorgs	0
Size	Allocated KB	3,215
	Available KB	3,000
	Used KB	2,692
	Free KB	308
Directory entries	Available	5,000
	Used	991
	Free	4,009
Swaps	Objects swapped	2,456
	Frames swapped	0
Resets	Total	0

Analyzing and optimizing buffer parameters requires some knowledge and experience with the operating system. If in doubt, consult your operating system administrator or another expert.

11.2.3 Memory Defragmentation

The memory for the execution of the program basically functions like a hard disk. When several programs are executed, they are first loaded into the memory and deleted from it later on. Over time, the memory becomes fragmented—like the hard disk. Segments that are not occupied are distributed across the entire memory.

So it's possible that you have sufficient memory space (total of all segments that are not occupied) but no contiguous segment that is large enough to load specific programs into the memory and run them. Restart the SAP system to defragment the system memory. To do so, stop the SAP system as described in Chapter 2, Section 2.1.2. Then, restart the SAP system.

[✿]

Defragmenting the Program Buffer

To defragment the PXA buffer (*Program Execution Area*), it's sufficient to stop the SAP system. You don't have to restart the database and can keep the database cache.

It can also be useful to restart the server at the operating system level to cleanse the main memory. For this purpose, you must first stop the SAP system, including the database, and then shut down the server. Restart the server, database, and SAP system.

[+]

Buffers Are Filled Anew After a Restart

When the SAP system is restarted, the buffers (see Section 11.2.2) are updated, which means you can expect a long response time when the buffer object is accessed for the first time because the system first has to load data from the database into the buffer. When the data are accessed the second time, the response time is short again. This process repeats itself until all commonly used objects are loaded into the buffer. This usually takes one day. Without fragmentation, the program buffer is filled with the programs that the buffer contained during the shutdown process.

11.3 Analysis at Other Levels

The reasons for performance problems can also be outside of the SAP system. In persistent or implausible cases, you should therefore also analyze the other levels that affect your SAP system:

- Database
- Operating system
- Hardware/network

If in doubt, consult your internal experts for the analysis—they can provide advice and help.

11.3.1 Analysis at the Database Level

For more information on the monitoring and performance balancing of the database, refer to Chapter 8 regarding the following transactions:

- ST04—Database Assistant/DB Monitoring
- DB02—Database Analysis

11.3.2 Analysis at the Operating System Level

The operating system monitor (Transaction OS06) described in Chapter 9 enables you to monitor the relevant performance data at the operating system level.

This includes in particular:

- Memory paging (swapping at the operating system level)
- Operating system log entries

Some operating system problems affect the SAP performance. You should therefore also analyze the operating system when the system performance is poor.

11.3.3 Analysis at the Hardware Level

You can also use Transaction OS06 (Operating System Monitor), which is mentioned in Section 11.3.2 and further detailed in Chapter 9, to display the performance values of the hardware, for example:

- CPU usage
- Main memory usage
- Hard disk performance and available memory
- Network statistics

Even if you implement optimizations at the SAP level, database level, and operating system level, if the hardware of your system is defective or can no longer meet the requirements, you won't obtain satisfying results. You should therefore also check the usage of your hardware components, and extend them, if necessary, or replace them.

[⚙]

Empirical Values for CPU Usage

The average CPU idle time should be less than 20% at workdays. Otherwise, the CPU is probably overloaded. The paging rates should be below 300 MB/h (pages in) or below 500 MB/h (pages out).

11.4 Summary

Performance problems can have numerous reasons: defective hardware, problems with the operating system, an unoptimized database, or simply bad programming. Correspondingly, you have to analyze the reasons systematically.

Because an entire book could be written about this complex topic alone, this chapter only introduces the basic principles for a first superficial research with SAP-internal tools, such as load and buffer analysis. If you experience regular problems, you should consult your database, operating system, or network administrators, or ask a programmer if custom-developed programs are involved.

Without SAP GUI, you can't access the SAP system; SAP GUI needs to be installed locally on the PCs of the SAP users. Depending on the size of your enterprise, this can be quite time-consuming. This chapter describes how you can install the SAP GUI locally or via an installation server.

12 SAP GUI

To log on to an SAP system (or more precisely, to an ABAP application server), the frontend software, SAP GUI, must be installed on the user's PC. The SAP GUI (Graphical User Interface) is responsible for the communication between the PC and the SAP server; that is, it forwards the user's commands to the server and outputs the information provided by the server on the PC of the user in a readable format.

The installation of the SAP GUI is—apart from access at the network level—the first obstacle on the way to the SAP system. You can positively influence the security of the system by installing the SAP GUI rather restrictively. Users should not be able to install software on the enterprise's PCs. Ensure that only a restricted group of administrators has the necessary authorizations at the operating system level. Don't make the required installation files freely accessible in the network.

This chapter describes how you install SAP GUI locally or via an installation server and what you need to do to use SAP GUI to log on to an SAP system.

12.1 Installation Requirements

You can download the installation files for the SAP GUI via the SAP Software Distribution Center in the SAP Support Portal (*www.service.sap.com*).

12.1.1 Minimum Requirements for the User's PC

Before you install the SAP GUI, check whether the user's PC meets the following criteria.

- Does the system configuration meet the minimum requirements?
- Is the resolution at least set to 800 x 600?
- Is sufficient memory available on the hard disk to install the SAP GUI and execute the application?

Depending on the scope of the installation, between 100 and 500 MB of memory are required on the PC's hard disk. These figures and requirements, however, depend on the current version and patch level; you should therefore first read SAP Note 26417 and refer to the installation manual of the SAP GUI compilation that is supposed to be installed.

12.1.2 Network Functions

Ensure that the user can log on to the network. Check if the following activities can be performed from the user's computer:

- Can you ping the SAP application servers to which the user will log on?
- If the SAP GUI is procured from a network resource (for example, network drive, SAP GUI installation server), can you access the server from the user's computer on which the SAP GUI will be installed?

[+]

SAP GUI Version

Currently, SAP GUI is available in Version 7.20, which—in contrast to the previous version, 7.10—is also compatible with Windows 7 (see SAP Notes 147519 and 1412821).

12.2 Installation Scenarios

You have several options for installing the SAP GUI:

- Installation from an installation medium, for example, CD or network drive
- Installation from an SAP GUI installation server

Which procedure is best suited for your enterprise mainly depends on the number of employees who use the SAP system.

12.2.1 Installing SAP GUI from an Installation Medium

If you want to install the SAP GUI on a few PCs only, it doesn't pay to set up an SAP GUI installation server. You can store the installation files on a network drive or—if the network connection is not fast enough—use the presentation CD and run the installation manually from the respective PC. You can find the instructions for the installation of the SAP GUI in the installation manual, "SAP Frontend Installation Guide," in the *NW_7.0_Presentation\PRES1\GUI\WINDOWS\WIN32\ReadMe* directory of the presentation CD.

Follow these steps to install SAP GUI locally from an installation medium:

1. In Windows Explorer, navigate to the corresponding network or CD-ROM drive, select the setup directory of the SAP GUI (*D:\NW_7.0_Presentation\PRES1\GUI\WINDOWS\WIN32*, for example), and double-click on the SetupAll.exe file. The installation program starts.

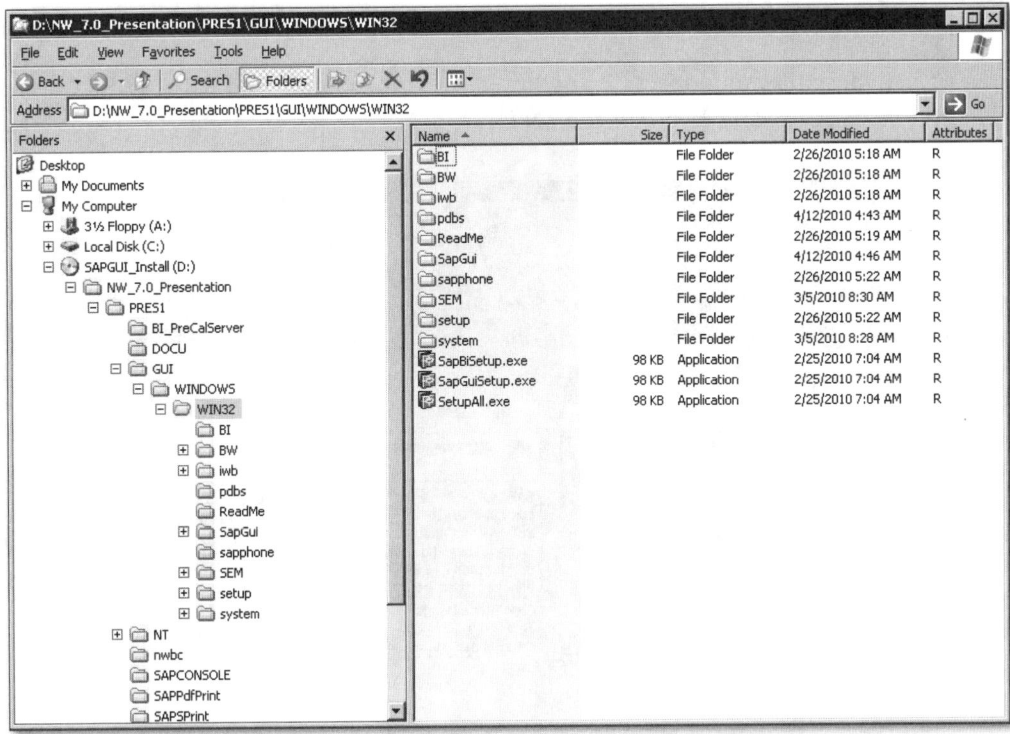

2. Select NEXT.

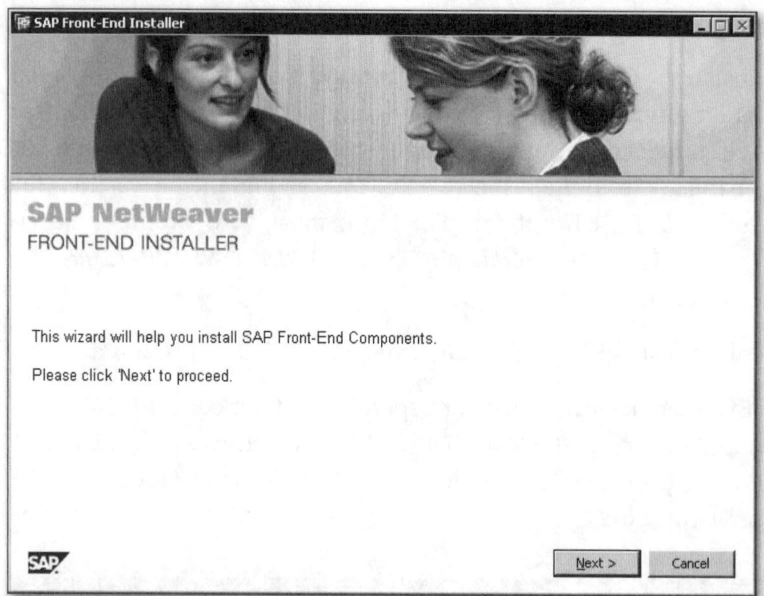

3. Choose the components that you require (for example, SAP GUI, SAP LOGON, and SAP LOGON PAD). Click on NEXT.

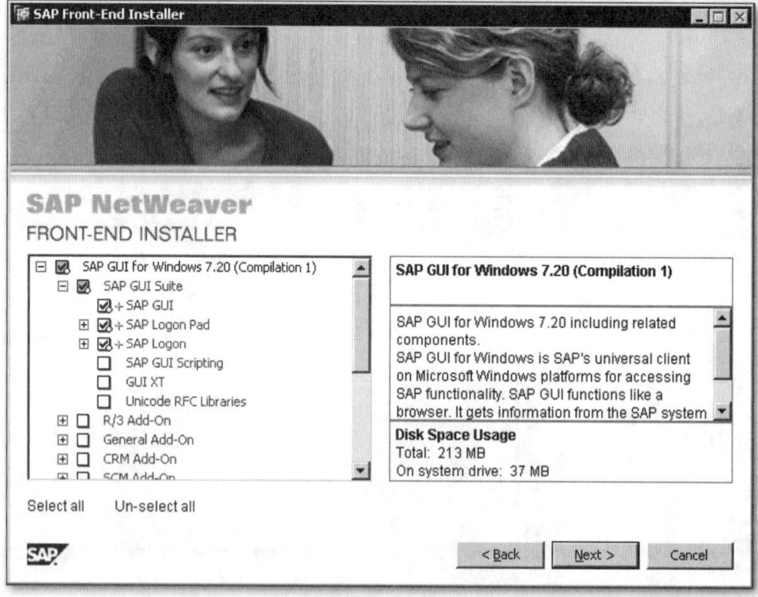

4. If necessary, change the target directory for the installation, and select NEXT.

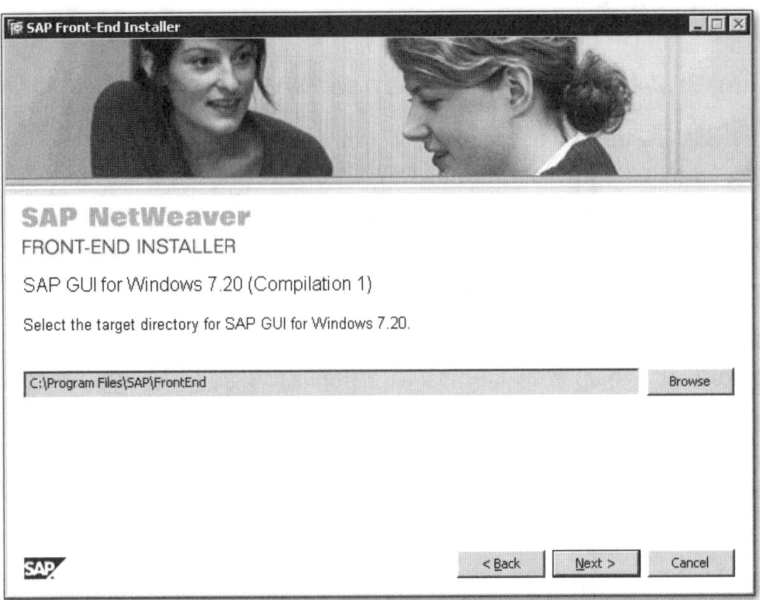

5. The SAP NETWEAVER FRONT-END INSTALLER window displays the installation progress. When the installation is completed, click on DONE.

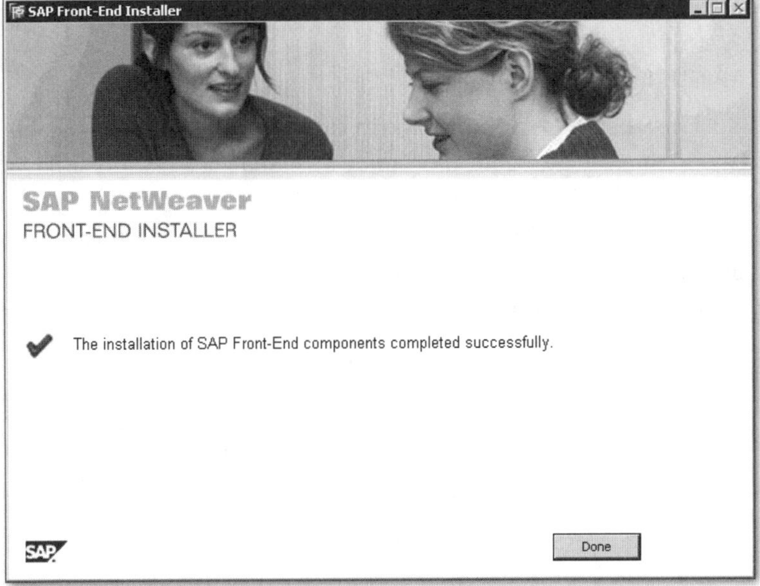

SAP GUI is now locally installed on your PC. Use the desktop icon or the entry in the Start menu to start SAP GUI.

12.2.2 Installing SAP GUI from an Installation Server

If there are numerous SAP users, it's usually too time-consuming to install the SAP GUI manually via an installation medium on every PC. The SAP GUI alternatively enables you to set up a central installation server from which you can perform the installation. The SAP GUI installation server provides extensive functions to facilitate the installation for you as the administrator::

- You can define standardized installation packages that only contain the respectively required components, which you can provide offline as single installation files.
- You can carry out the installation either with an interaction option for the user or automatically in the background.
- You can use *Local Security Handling* (LSH) to have a user without administrator authorizations run the installation.
- You can use Visual Basic scripts to distribute standardized saplogon.ini files, for example (see tip in the "Creating an SAP GUI Installation Package" section later in this chapter).
- You can keep frontend installations easily up to date by importing SAP GUI patches to the installation server and then distributing them to the users' PCs.

Setting up an SAP GUI Installation Server

To set up an SAP GUI installation server, you need a server with a Windows operating system that is permanently available and can be accessed via a fast broadband network connection from all PCs on which the SAP GUI is supposed to be installed. In a medium-sized enterprise, a PC that is provided for this purpose only may be sufficient, for example. If you have to support a large number of users, you should select an appropriately fail-safe and powerful platform, of course.

1. Ensure that you have administration rights for the server.
2. Install Microsoft .NET Framework 2.0 or higher on the server.
3. In Windows Explorer, navigate to the setup directory on the presentation CD (*D:\NW_7.0_Presentation\PRES1\GUI\WINDOWS\WIN32\setup*, for example), and double-click on the NwCreateInstServer.exe file to start the installation program.

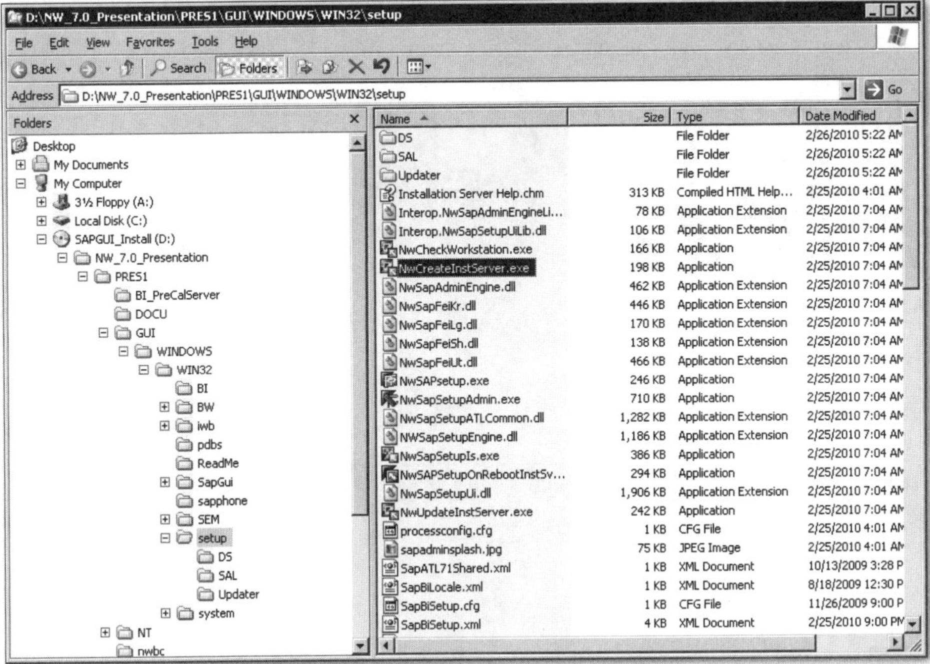

4. Select NEXT.

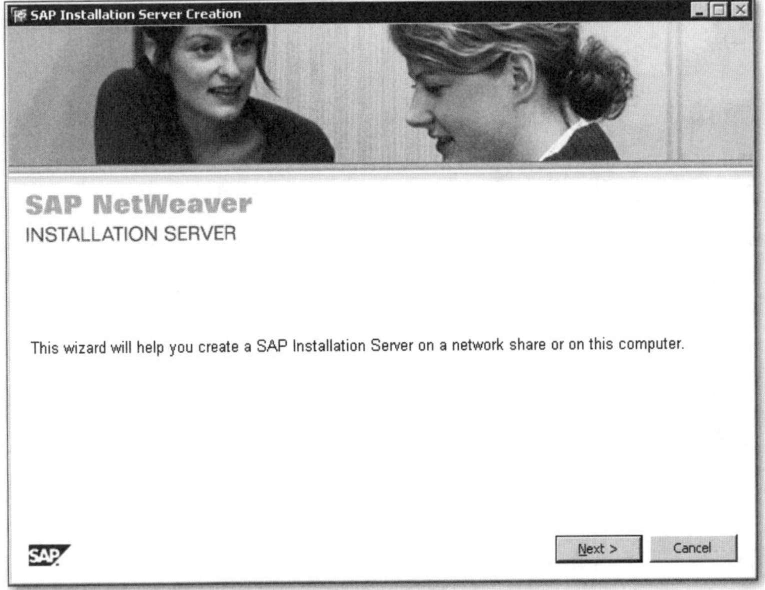

5. Enter the directory in which the installation server is supposed to be set up. Click VERIFY to have the system verify your entry.

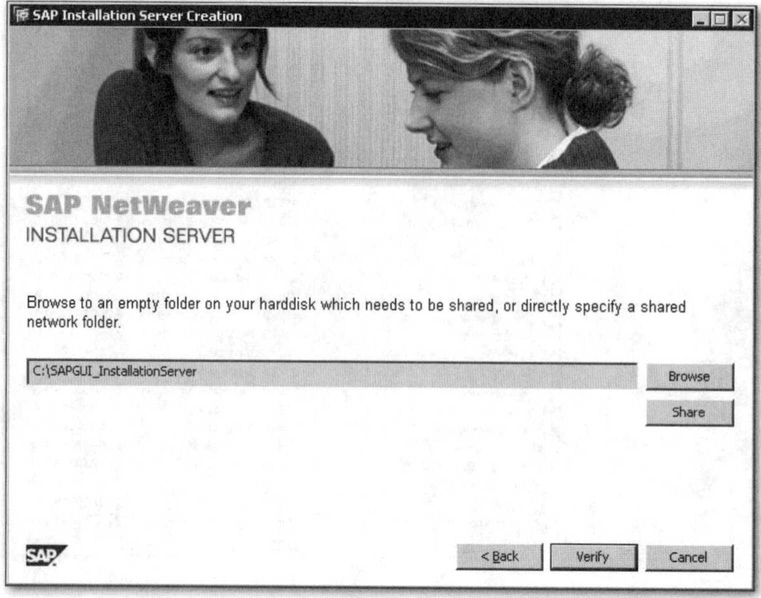

6. The installation directory needs to be shared in the network to allow access from the users' PCs. Use SHARE to configure the sharing. This opens a dialog box. Here, first enter a SHARE NAME, and then click on the PERMISSIONS button.

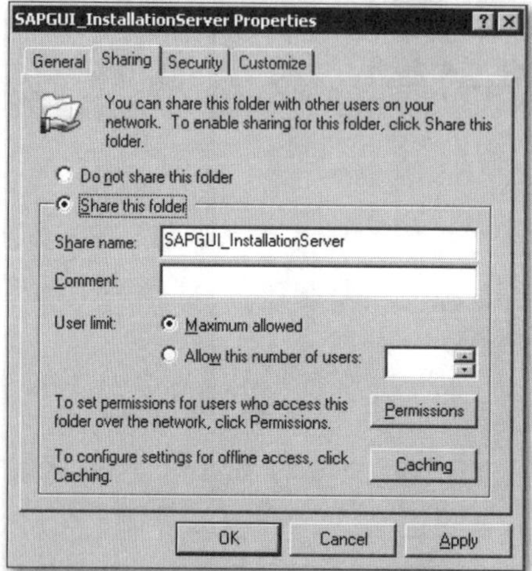

7. Assign read permissions for the directory. You have to adhere to the security conventions in your enterprise. Apply the changes (APPLY button), and use OK to return to the SAP GUI setup.

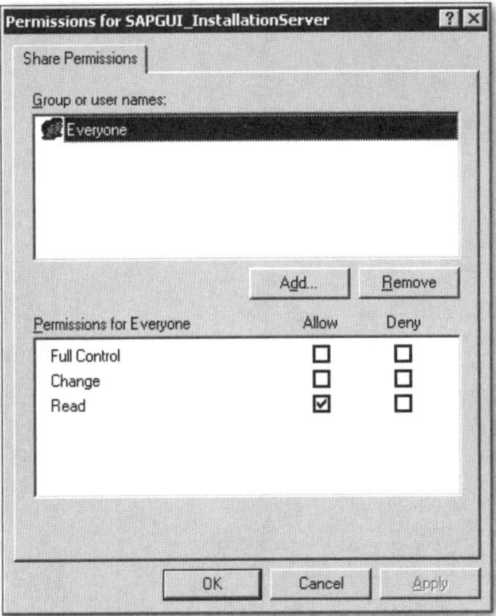

8. Select NEXT.

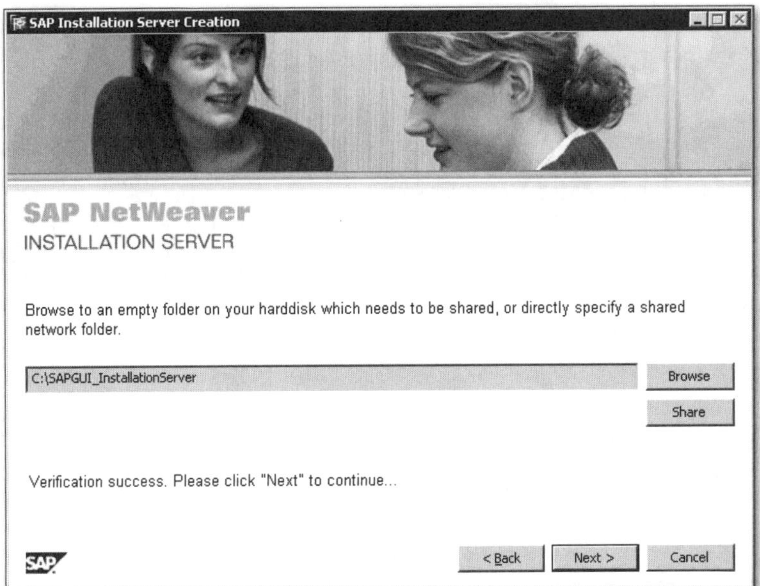

9. The files that are required for the installation server are copied to the specified directory. Confirm the process with NEXT.

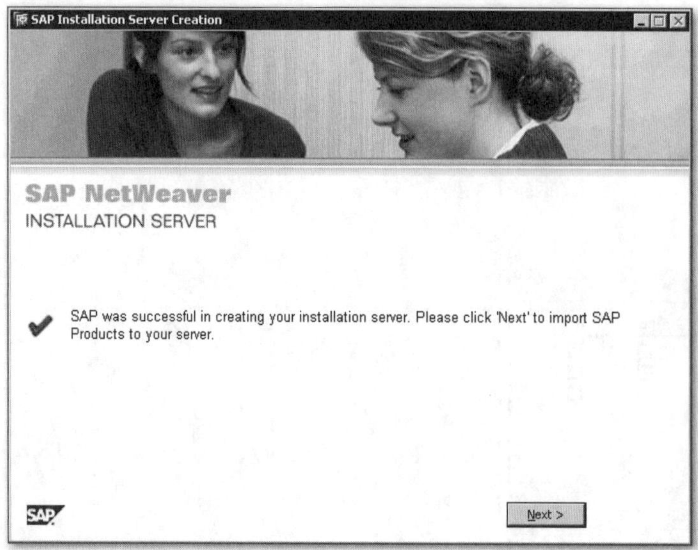

10. The installation wizard informs you that the installation server still doesn't contain any SAP GUI installation files and needs to be updated. Continue with NEXT.

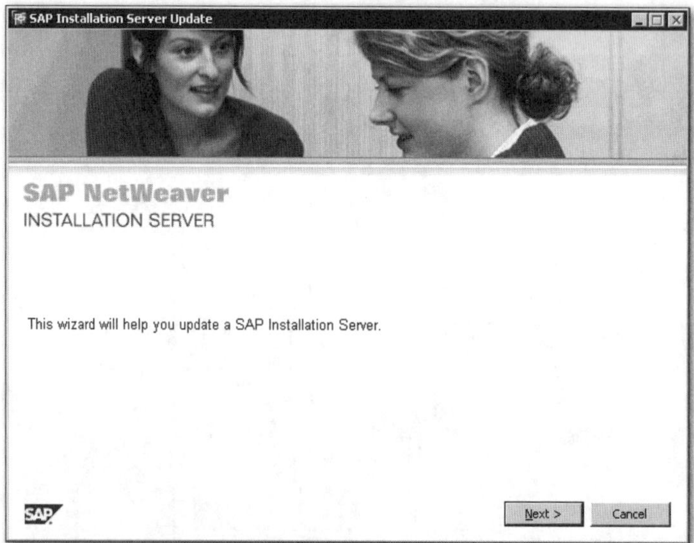

11. Verify the proposed installation server directory using VERIFY.

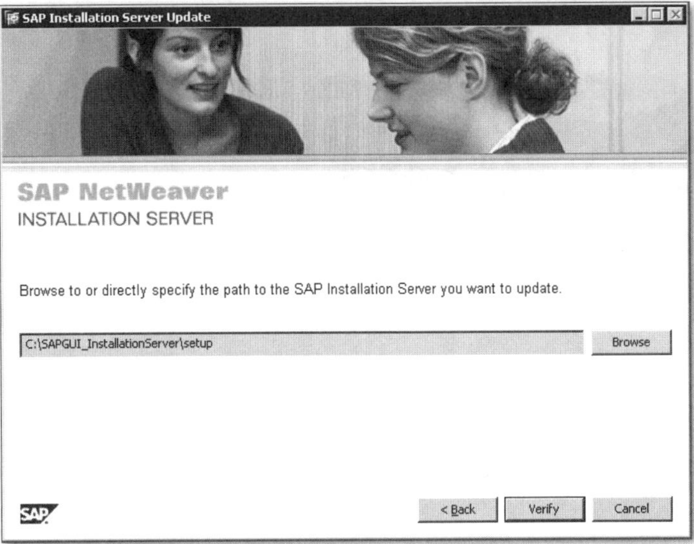

12. Select NEXT.

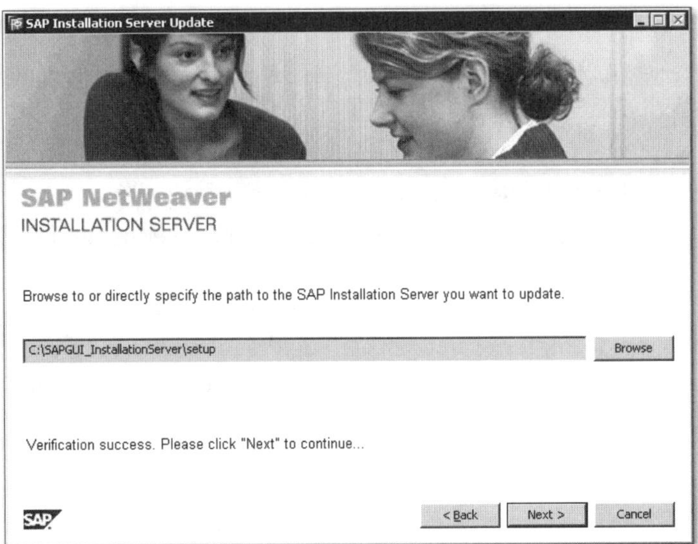

13. The system then copies the SAP GUI installation files from the presentation CD to the directory of the installation server. After the update has been completed, select DONE.

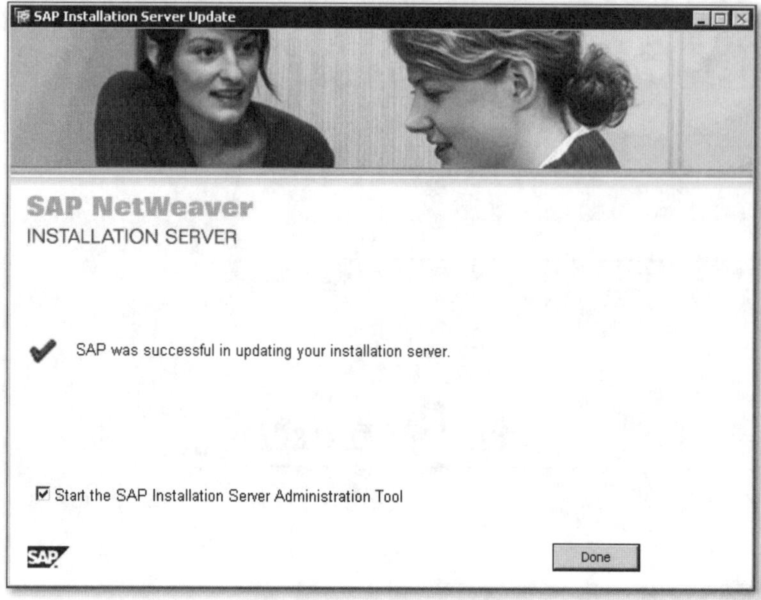

The *SAP Installation Server Administration Tool* starts automatically if you haven't deactivated the corresponding checkbox.

Creating an SAP GUI Installation Package

The basic configuration of the SAP GUI installation server is now set up, and the server is ready for operation. Further customizing is done via the *SAP Installation Server Administration Tool*. This administration tool provides numerous functions that cannot be described in detail, for example, patching the installation server or user PCs. The *SAP Frontend Installation Guide* on the presentation CD examines the individual options in detail.

To implement the SAP GUI installation that is described in Section 12.1 via the installation server and not via an installation medium, you have to create the respective installation package first.

1. To do so, start the administration tool by double-clicking on the NwSapSetupAdmin.exe file in the installation server directory (*C:\SAPGUI_InstallationServer\Setup*, for example).

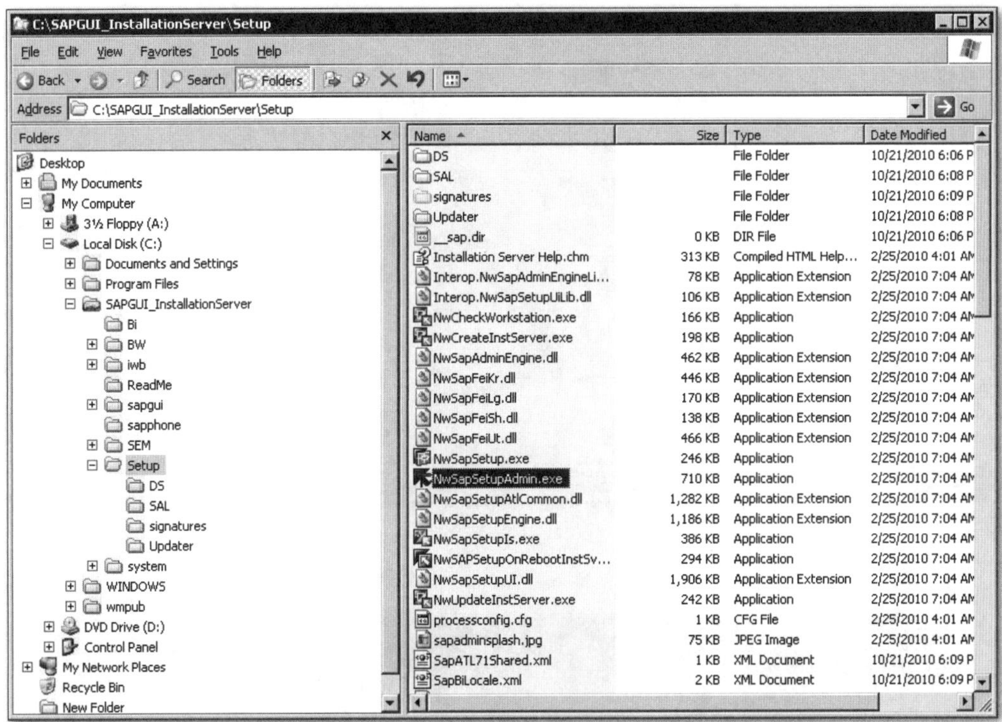

2. To create a standard installation package for the users' PCs, select New Package in the menu bar.

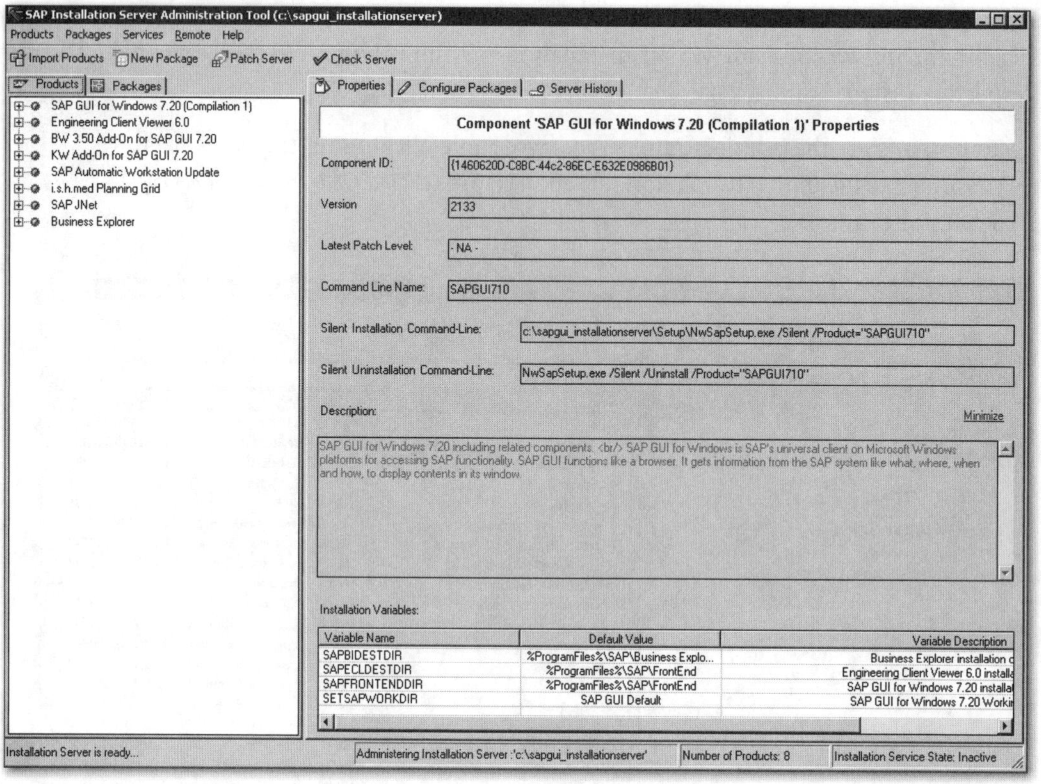

SAP Installation Server Administration Tool (c:\sapgui_installationserver)
Products Packages Services Remote Help
Import Products New Package Patch Server Check Server
Products Packages
SAP GUI for Windows 7.20 (Compilation 1)
Engineering Client Viewer 6.0
BW 3.50 Add-On for SAP GUI 7.20
KW Add-On for SAP GUI 7.20
SAP Automatic Workstation Update
i.s.h.med Planning Grid
SAP JNet
Business Explorer
Properties Configure Packages Server History
Component 'SAP GUI for Windows 7.20 (Compilation 1)' Properties
Component ID: {1460620D-C8BC-44c2-86EC-E632E0986B01}
Version 2133
Latest Patch Level: - NA -
Command Line Name: SAPGUI710
Silent Installation Command-Line: c:\sapgui_installationserver\Setup\NwSapSetup.exe /Silent /Product="SAPGUI710"
Silent Uninstallation Command-Line: NwSapSetup.exe /Silent /Uninstall /Product="SAPGUI710"
Description: Minimize
SAP GUI for Windows 7.20 including related components.
 SAP GUI for Windows is SAP's universal client on Microsoft Windows platforms for accessing SAP functionality. SAP GUI functions like a browser. It gets information from the SAP system like what, where, when and how, to display contents in its window.
Installation Variables:

Variable Name	Default Value	Variable Description
SAPBIDESTDIR	%ProgramFiles%\SAP\Business Explo...	Business Explorer installation c
SAPECLDESTDIR	%ProgramFiles%\SAP\FrontEnd	Engineering Client Viewer 6.0 installa
SAPFRONTENDDIR	%ProgramFiles%\SAP\FrontEnd	SAP GUI for Windows 7.20 installat
SETSAPWORKDIR	SAP GUI Default	SAP GUI for Windows 7.20 Worki

Installation Server is ready... Administering Installation Server :'c:\sapgui_installationserver' Number of Products: 8 Installation Service State: Inactive

3. Select NEXT.

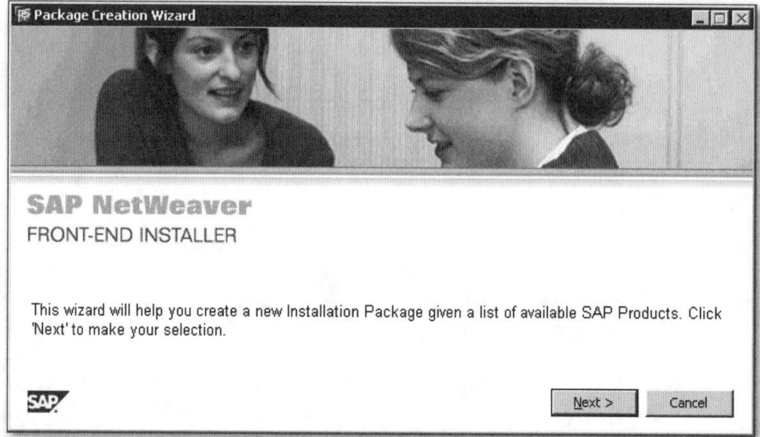

4. Choose the components that the installation package is supposed to contain. Confirm your choice with NEXT.

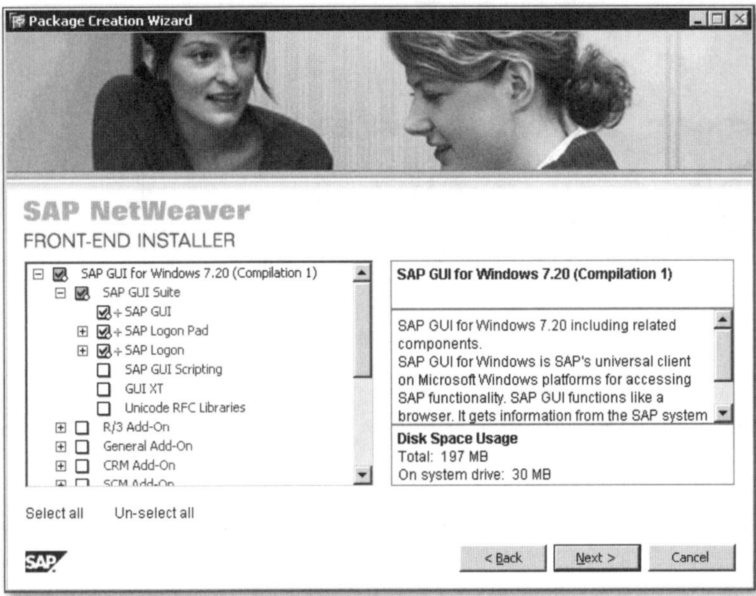

5. Assign a name to the new package, and select NEXT.

6. In the next step, you have to specify the command-line name for the package. If you want to install the SAP GUI with a command-line command later on, you have to use this name in conjunction with the `/package` parameter. Ensure that the command-line name doesn't contain blanks or special characters that are not supported. Select NEXT.

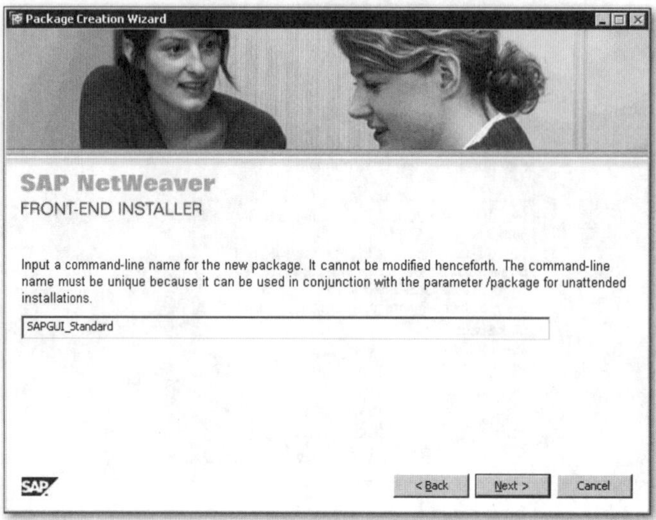

7. The configuration of the installation package is now completed. Finish the process with DONE.

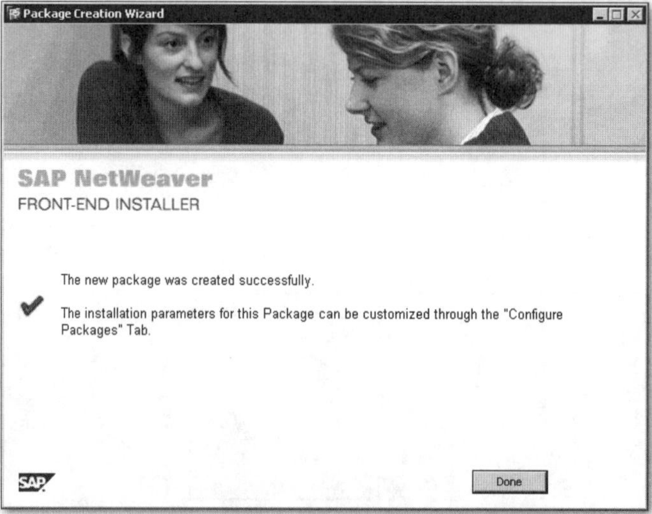

8. The administration tool now displays the package and the components contained therein in the PACKAGES tab.

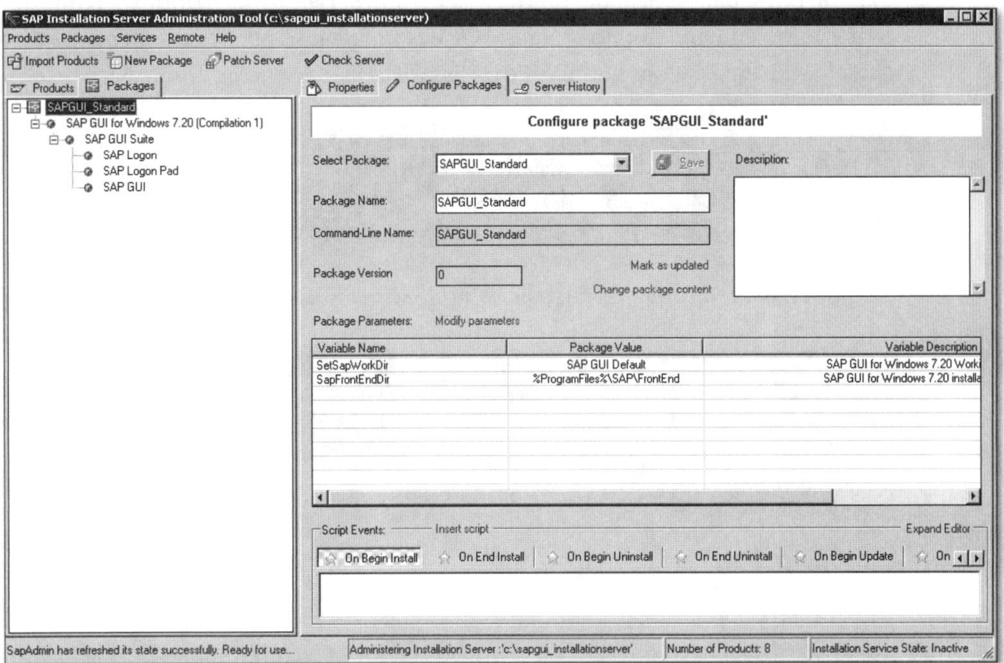

Event Scripting [+]

When it is being installed, updated, or removed, your package triggers *script events*, which you can populate with Visual Basic commands. This is a powerful means, for example, to distribute standardized saplogon.ini files that you store on your installation server across the users' PCs after the installation (see SAP Note 1426178). You can find some examples of event scripting in the SAP Installation Server Help, which you can call via the HELP menu item in the administration tool.

Installing an SAP GUI Installation Package from the Installation Server

You can install a preconfigured installation package on a PC in dialog mode or in the background by following these steps:

1. Log on to the PC on which the SAP GUI is supposed to be installed. Ensure that you're authorized to install software.
2. Call the NwSapSetup.exe file on the installation server using Windows Explorer or the command line (*\\<server name>\<IP address of the server>\<share name>\Setup\NwSapSetup.exe*, such as *\\sap\SAPGUI_InstallationServer\Setup\NwSapSetup.exe*).

3. SAP NetWeaver Front-End Installer starts. Select NEXT.

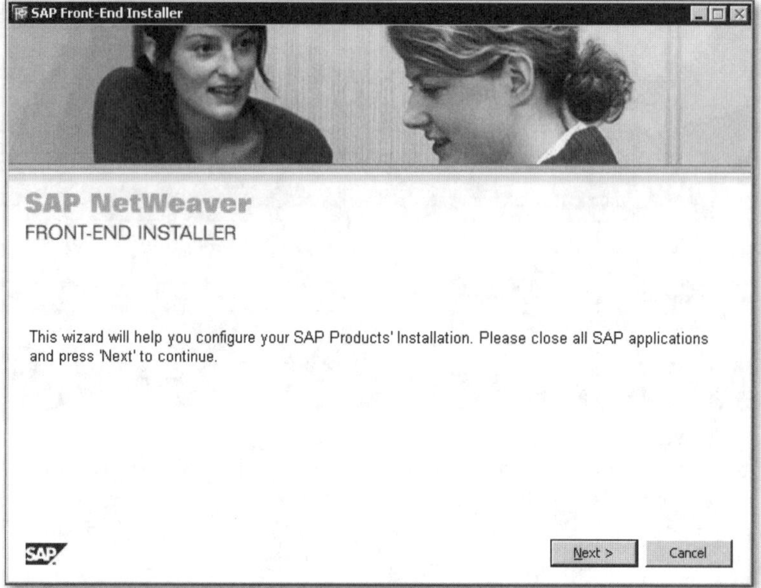

4. On the left, the window first displays the list of the available components. Change this view using the LIST OF PREDEFINED PACKAGES link at the lower left.

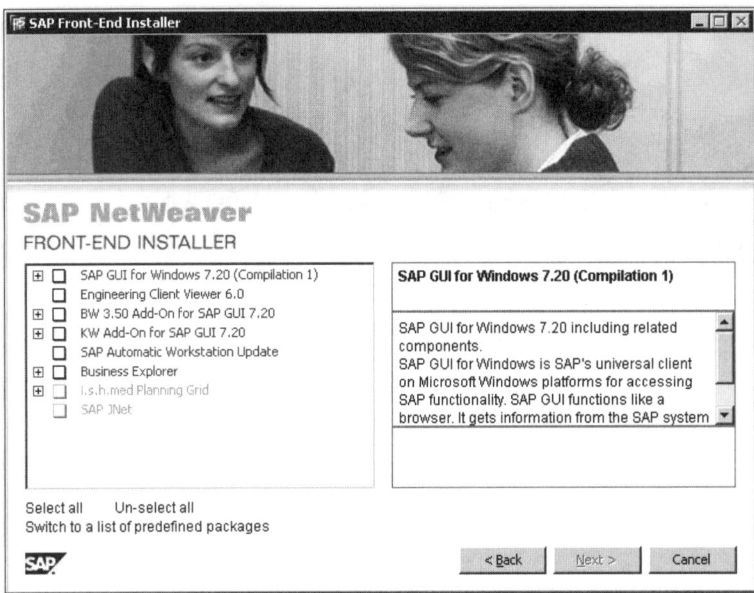

5. The installer now displays the package that was created on the installation server. Select it, and click on NEXT.

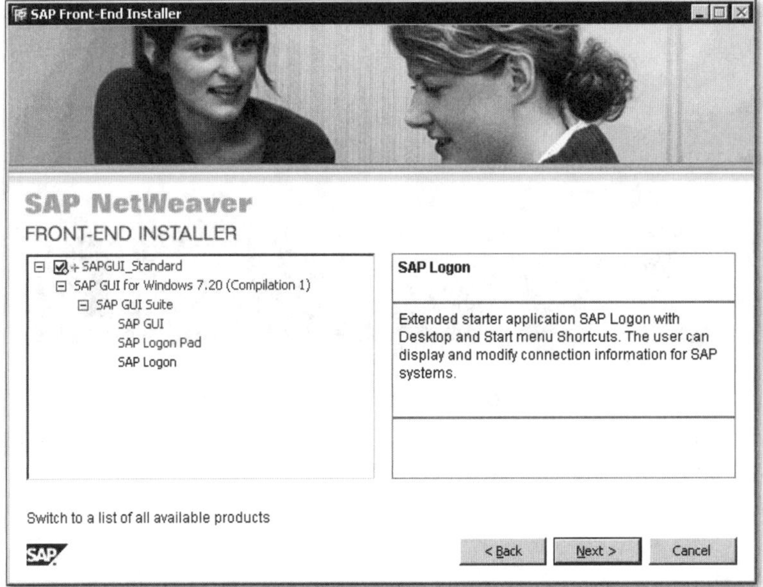

6. The installer installs the components and displays the installation progress. When the process is completed, click DONE.

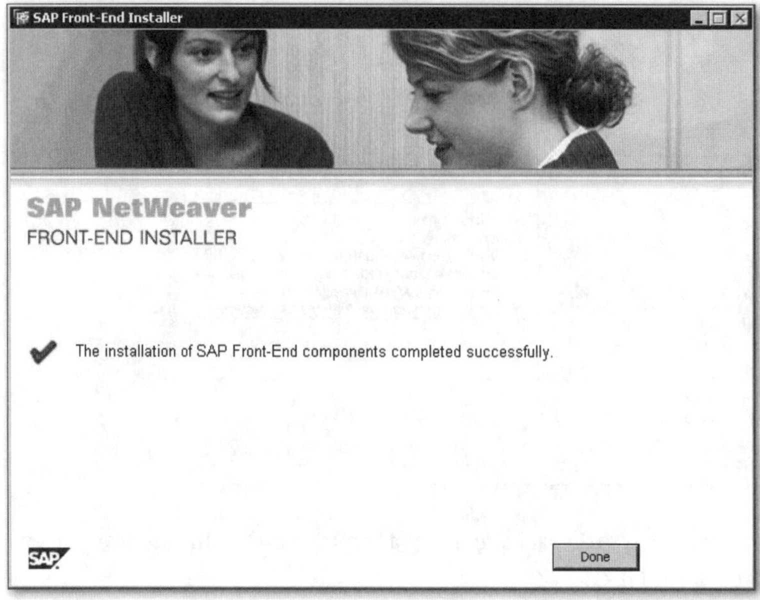

If you know the name of the installation package, you can also carry out step 2—that is, calling NwSapSetup.exe—by entering the command-line name. Add the `/package=<command-line name of the installation package>` parameter (for example, *\\sap\SAPGUI_InstallationServer\Setup\NwSapSetup.exe /package=SAPGUI_Standard*) to the command.

After the package that is supposed to be installed has been specified, the SAP NetWeaver Front-End Installer starts, and the user cannot modify the content of the installation. Steps 5 and 6 are carried out.

If you have the system implement the installation, you can suppress the user dialog with the `/noDlg` command-line parameter (for example, *\\sap\SAPGUI_Installation-Server\Setup\NwSapSetup.exe /package= SAPGUI_Standard /noDlg*).

The installation starts and finishes without the user having to initiate or complete it with a mouse click. The user is only informed about the progress of the installation.

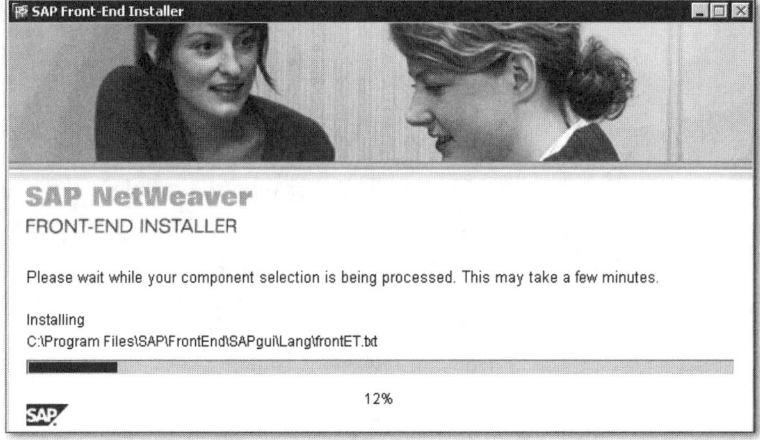

If you also want to hide the progress during the installation, use the `/silent` parameter instead of `/noDlg` in the command line.

The `/noDlg` or `/silent` parameters enable you to control the SAP GUI installation via a third-party software distribution product. Table 12.1 provides an overview of possible command-line parameters when calling the NWSapSetup.exe file.

[+] **Log Files**

The log files of the installation are stored in the *C:\Programs\SAP\SapSetup\LOGs* directory on the PC. If the SAP GUI installation outputs an error, you should check these files first.

<table>
<tr><th>Parameters</th><th>Description</th></tr>
<tr><td><code>/package=<command-line name of the installation package> [/noDlg | /silent] [/uninstall | /update] [/ForceWindowsRestart]</code></td><td>Installs a predefined installation package.</td></tr>
<tr><td><code>/product=<command-line name of the product or SAP GUI component> [/noDlg | /silent] [/uninstall | /update] [/ForceWindowsRestart]</code></td><td>Installs a specific component (product) of the SAP GUI, for example, Business Explorer.</td></tr>
<tr><td><code>/ForceWindowsRestart</code></td><td>Restarts the PC after the installation has been completed.</td></tr>
<tr><td><code>/noDlg</code></td><td>Displays the progress of the installation. The user doesn't have to make any specifications.</td></tr>
<tr><td><code>/silent</code></td><td>Implements the installation completely in the background. The progress is not displayed.</td></tr>
<tr><td><code>/uninstall</code></td><td>Uninstalls a package or component (in conjunction with <code>/package</code> or <code>/product</code>); can be supplemented by <code>/all</code> but can also be used to remove the SAP GUI completely from the PC.</td></tr>
<tr><td><code>/update</code></td><td>Updates the SAP GUI installation of the PC if a higher patch level is available on the installation server.</td></tr>
</table>

Table 12.1 Command-Line Parameters for NWSapSetup.exe

Depending on whether the user under which the installation on the PC is supposed to be implemented has administrative rights or not, you may have to install *Local Security Handling* on the installation server first. For this purpose, you need a user account with administration authorization that is also available on the respective PC (a corresponding domain user, for example).

12.3 Adding Systems to SAP Logon

After having successfully completed the SAP GUI installation, you can add the SAP systems to SAP Logon.

1. For this purpose, start SAP Logon by double-clicking on the respective desktop icon ( ).
2. In the SAP LOGON 720 window, click on the NEW button ( ).

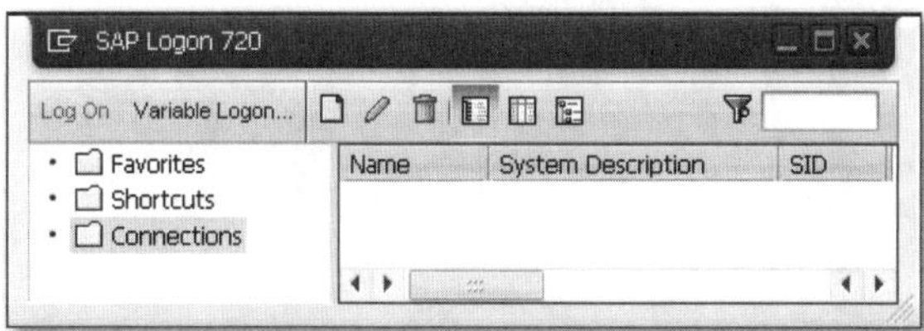

3. The CREATE NEW SYSTEM ENTRY user dialog opens. In the first screen, you usually don't have to make any specifications, so select NEXT.

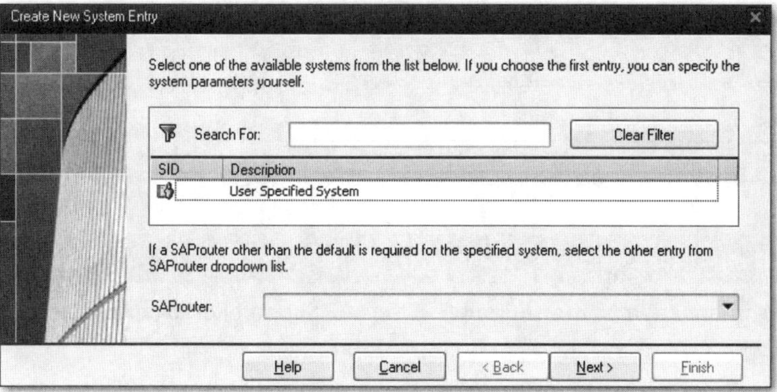

4. In the next entry screen, enter the data for the new system:
   - DESCRIPTION: Text displayed in the SAP Logon system list later on (NSP, for example).
   - APPLICATION SERVER: Name or IP address of the server on which the SAP system runs ("sap," for example).
   - INSTANCE NUMBER: System or instance number for which you configure the logon ("00," for example)
   - SYSTEM ID: Three-digit system ID of the SAP system ("NSP," for example)
   - SAPROUTER STRING: Usually remains empty if the SAP server is available via a network.

   When you are finished, select NEXT.

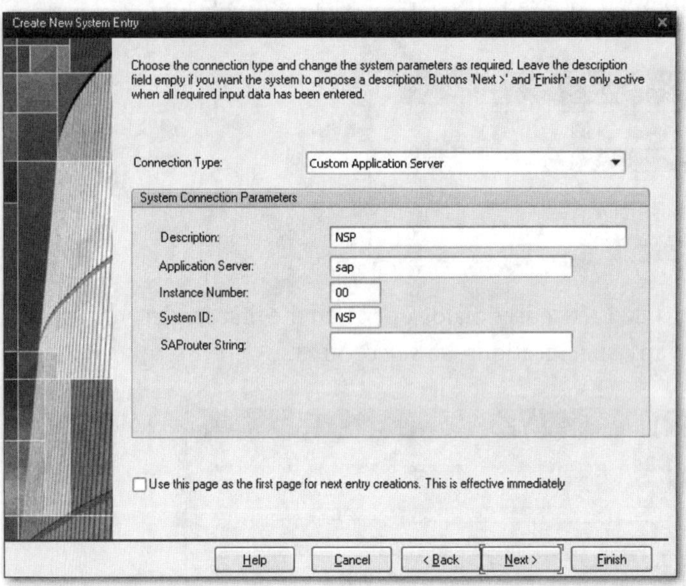

[+]

Information on the SAProuter

You can find more information on the SAProuter in the SAP Support Portal (*www.service.sap.com/saprouter*).

5. If necessary, customize the network settings in the next step, and choose NEXT.

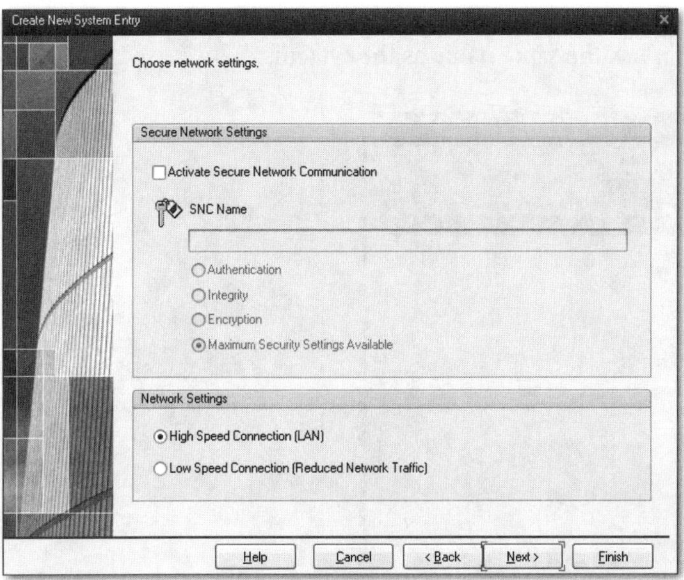

6. If necessary, customize the language and coding settings, and click on FINISH.

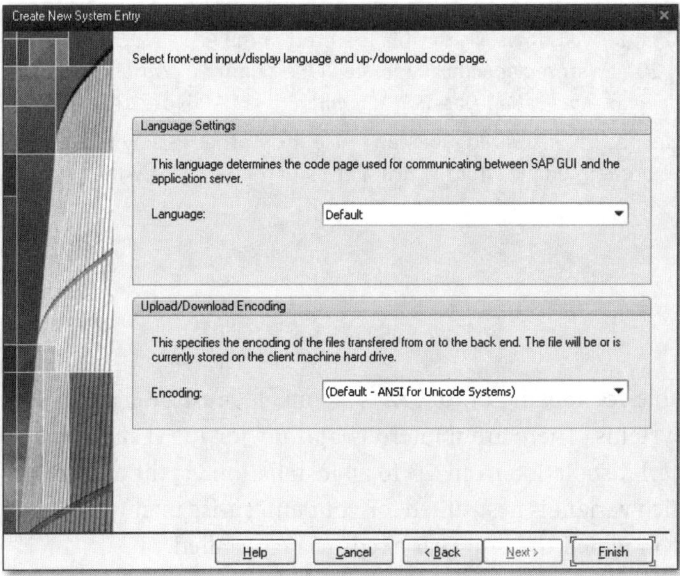

7. The new system is added to SAP Logon. You can now log on to the added system using the button that has the same name as the system.

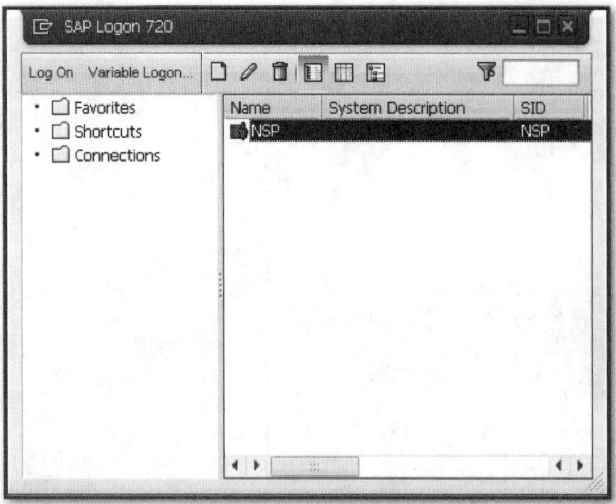

[+]

File saplogon.ini

The information that you add in the steps described is entered in the saplogon.ini file. In SAP GUI Version 7.10 under Windows XP, this file is stored in the *C:\WINDOWS* path; as of SAP GUI Version 7.20, it's stored specifically for each user under *C:\Documents and Settings\<Windows user name>\Application Data\SAP\Common* (see SAP Note 1409494).

After the saplogon.ini file has been created, you can reuse it on other PCs by replacing the "empty" file with the predefined file after the installation of the SAP GUI. Afterwards, restart SAP Logon.

12.4 Summary

SAP GUI is indispensable for logging on to SAP systems. It must be installed on every PC to use SAP systems. There are numerous options for the installation of the SAP GUI, from a local installation from CD to an installation via the automated installation server. Which variant is best suited for your enterprise mainly depends on the number of PCs on which the SAP GUI needs to be installed.

User accounts are an essential component of the SAP access concept. Your task as administrator is primarily to make user administration secure. Also, the increase in efficiency via a Central User Administration can be an interesting case if a high number of users or several SAP systems have to be managed.

13 User Administration

Via the user administration, you check who has access to the SAP system. The area of user administration is a security-relevant aspect of SAP system administration because each access to the system potentially jeopardizes the security of the system and the data stored in it. User administration is closely associated with authorization management. Both terms are now often used in connection with identity management, which provides technical support for user administration and authorization management with regard to the entire enterprise. This chapter only focuses on the pure user administration in the SAP system: *SAP NetWeaver Identity Management* (SAP PRESS, 2009), provides information on how you can implement identity management with SAP products. This chapter describes the fundamentals of user administration such as the administration of user master data and user groups, the assignment of passwords, and so on. Furthermore, the chapter explains, among other things, how to configure a Central User Administration.

13.1 General

Be aware that you may be asked on whose request a user has been created in the system and issued with certain authorizations. Therefore, in the context of user administration, you must always ensure a comprehensive, continuous documentation and a suitable approval procedure. Some of the tasks described in this book are created to correspond to general check procedures. Consult your internal and external auditors with regard to legal and other (enterprise-internal) requirements that are made on proper and secure user administration.

The following are among the tasks of user administration:

- **Specifying naming conventions for user IDs**
  There are several alternatives for choosing a naming convention, for example:
  - Employee ID number of the enterprise (for example, e0123456)
  - Surname, first letter of the first name or first name, first letter of the last name
  - Clearly identifiable user IDs for temporary employees and consultants (for example, T123456 or C123456)
  - Special conventions for system or interface users (for example, RFC_TIVOLI)
- **Creating or changing a user**
  Take into consideration the following aspects when you define your process for user requests:
  - Create or change users only if you have a completely filled-out request form (see Appendix D). The form should contain information on the person, position, and communication, as well as on the authorizations required for the task area. The form should have been authorized with a signature from the employee's supervisor.
  - If the requested authorizations concern several departments or organizations or are particularly comprehensive, the respective managers should issue their approval.
  - If it concerns a non-permanent employee or when SAP access is limited in terms of time (for example, in the case of external employees and consultants), the period of employment and the end of validity should be specified.
  - The responsible SAP administrator should sign the form after he has created or changed the user master data.
  - The forms should be archived in an appropriate system, for example, according to employee name or organizational unit.
  - The approved authorizations should be compared regularly with the authorizations assigned to the user.
  - If possible, don't allow a reference user to be specified in a user request that is supposed to be used as a template (for example, the account of a specific

colleague). There is the danger that more authorizations are copied than actually required. Have the necessary roles or profiles listed explicitly.

  - Particular attention should be paid to changing users because often only additional authorizations are requested in the case of transfers or similar organizational events. Authorizations often accumulate with time, and the removing of current roles and profiles is neglected. Always check each change request, and if in doubt, ask the employee or his responsible supervisor.

- **Deactivating or deleting a user**
  You should specify special rules when you delete users:
  - Design a procedure in collaboration with the HR department on how you are notified about an employee leaving the enterprise. Experience has shown that deleting employees no longer required is often dealt with as carelessly as removing authorizations that are no longer appropriate.
  - If the leave of an employee is announced in advance, define a respective validity date in the user master record.
  - Lock the user ID, and add it to a special user group (for example, *left*) if the employment contract has been terminated.
  - Specify an appropriate period in which the user master record of an employee who has left the enterprise can remain in the system (for example, three months) and after which the user is deleted from the system.
  - Search your system for users with an expired validity date and/or user group *left* on a regular basis.
  - Regularly analyze which users didn't log on to the system in a specific period of time.
  - Before you lock and delete users and define the validity date, check whether released or planned background jobs exist under this user ID (Transaction SM37, Job Overview). The jobs cannot be executed if the user ID has been locked or deleted or is no longer valid.

It would be best to maintain the conventions specified for the user administration and the procedures in a user administration concept or in a separate section of the authorization concept (see Chapter 14). In this context, also consider how the segregation of duties for user administration and authorization management can be implemented in your enterprise.

13.2 Setting Up New Users

Before you set up a new user, you must have the respective form with the required information and approvals. You can create new users by copying an existing user or by setting up a new user profile.

13.2.1 Copying Existing Users

If an appropriate user exists, you can copy this user. During the operation, you can select which sections of the master record are supposed to be copied.

[+]

Creating User Templates

Create user templates for typical functions of your enterprise. When you set up a new user, you can then copy these templates.

1. Enter Transaction "SU01" in the command box, and press the Enter key (or select Tools • Administration • User Maintenance • SU01—Users in the standard SAP menu).
2. Enter the user ID that you want to copy in the User box (for example, "BCUSER"), and select Copy.

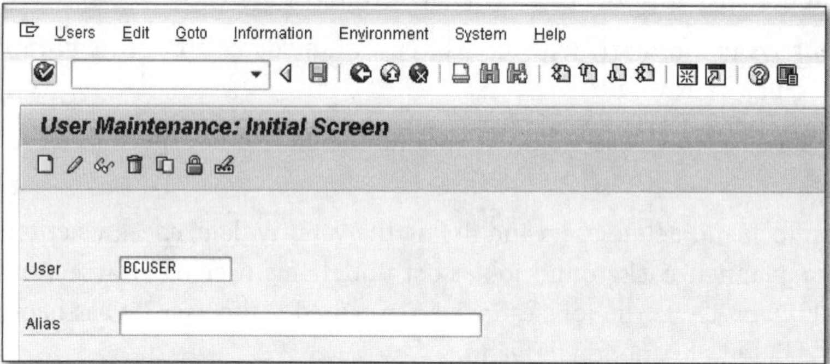

3. In the Copy Users dialog box, implement the following settings:

- Enter a new user ID in the To field (for example, "BCUSER2").
- Activate the tabs that you want to transfer from the original user.
- Select Copy (![copy icon]).

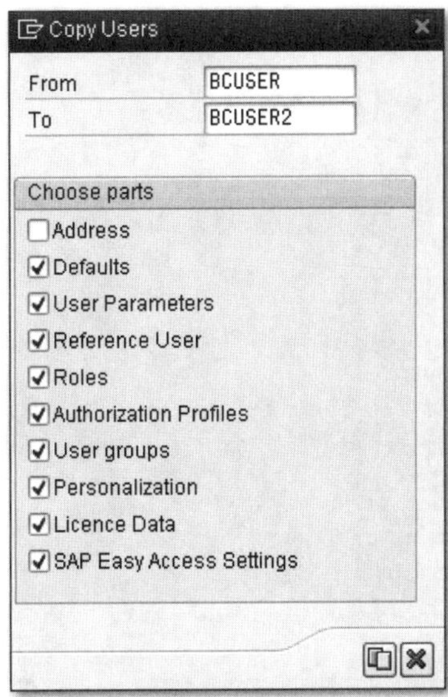

Stick to Your Naming Conventions [+]

When setting up new user IDs, remember to comply with the naming conventions of your enterprise.

Copy Authorization Data Carefully [!]

Only copy roles and authorization profiles when there is a reference user with manageable authorizations. You should not allow user requests such as "the same authorizations as colleague Miller."

4. Select the Generate Password button (![generate icon]) to generate an *initial password* via a random generator. You can also enter a password manually in the Initial password field (for example, "Initial1"). In this case, you must enter it again in the Repeat Password field.

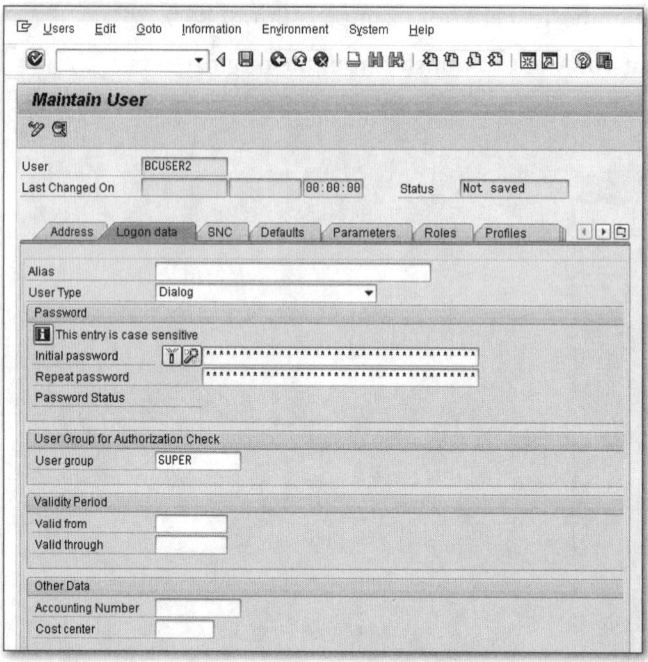

[+]

Using Generated Random Passwords

For security reasons, use where possible initial passwords generated via the random password generator instead of manually assigned passwords.

5. Enter the User group to which the user is supposed to belong in the User group area for authorization check (for example, "Super") or use the input help () to select the user group from a list.

[+]

Creating User Group First, Then Assigning User

The user group must exist before the user can be assigned.

6. Enter the period in the Valid from and Valid to fields within which the user is authorized to access the system.

[+]

Time Limit

The time limit (valid from/valid to) must usually be specified for external contractors or other temporary employees.

7. Choose the ADDRESS tab if you want to change the user's address data.
    - Enter the user's LAST NAME.
    - Enter the user's FIRST NAME.
    - Enter the user's FUNCTION.
    - Enter the user's DEPARTMENT.
8. Enter the user's location (e.g., ROOM NUMBER, FLOOR, BUILDING).
    - Enter the user's TELEPHONE.
    - Enter the user's E-MAIL.

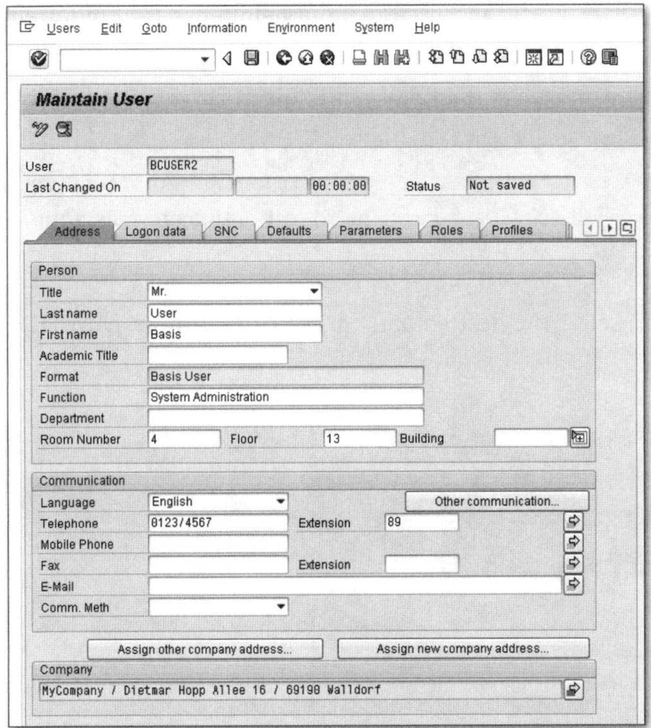

[+]

Contact Data

At least one of the two TELEPHONE or E-MAIL fields should be a required entry field. Should a system problem in connection with the user occur, you need to be able to contact the user.

9. Select the Defaults tab.
   - Make sure that the logon language is set correctly. If a default language has been defined in the system parameters (for example, German), this field is only required to define a different logon language (for example, En for English) for the individual user.
   - Implement the following settings in the Spool Control area:
     Enter a standard printer in the in OutputDevice field or use the input help function () to select one from a list.
     Activate the two Output immediately and Delete After Output checkboxes.
   - Check the Personal Time Zone, and use the input help function if required () to change a specified time zone.
   - Under Decimal Notation, select the desired option.

[!]

Decimal Notation

The Decimal Notation displays decimal numbers. The correct setting prevents errors and misunderstandings.

   - Under Date Format, select the desired date format (for example, MM/DD/YYYY).

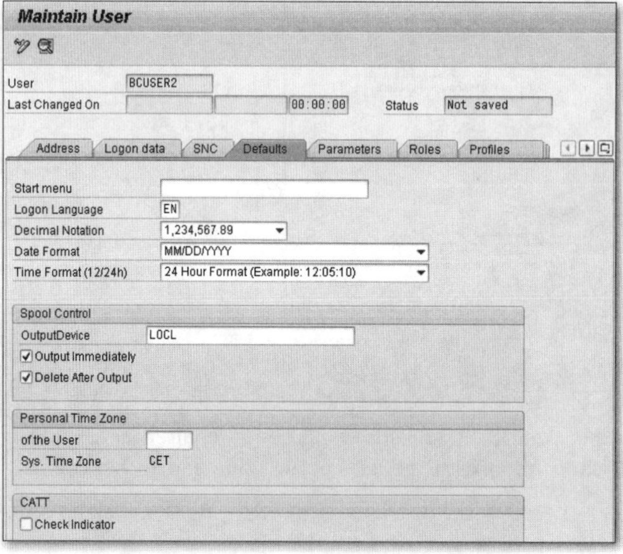

10. Select the PARAMETERS tab, and enter parameters and parameter values in the table.

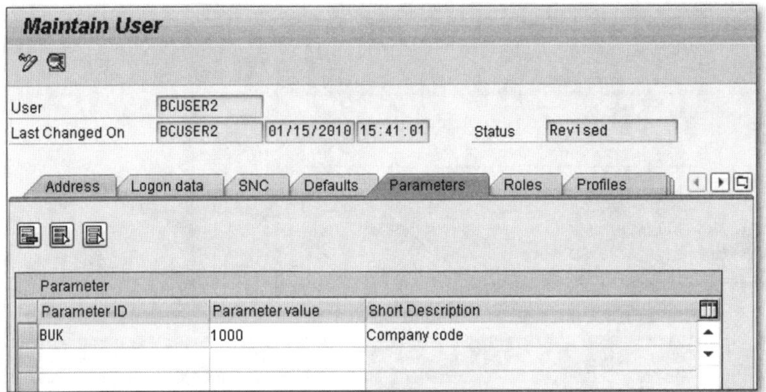

Parameters [+]

There is a wide range of user parameters that can work in a completely diverse way. You can usually store default values via parameters for specific fields in SAP transactions.

11. Select the ROLES tab, and assign the requested authorization roles to the user. You may also assign a restrictive validity date.

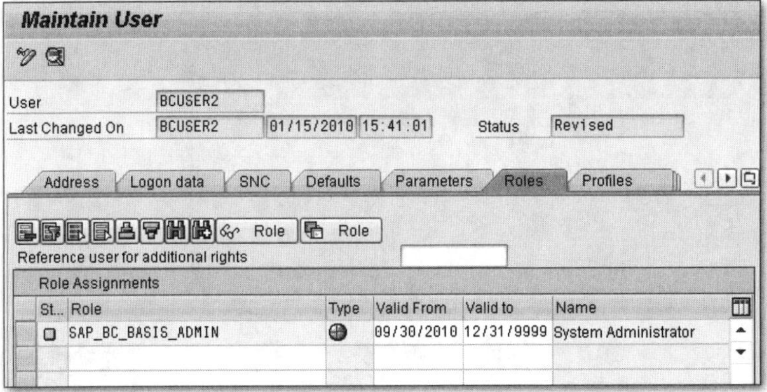

12. Choose the PROFILES tab, and assign the requested authorization profiles.

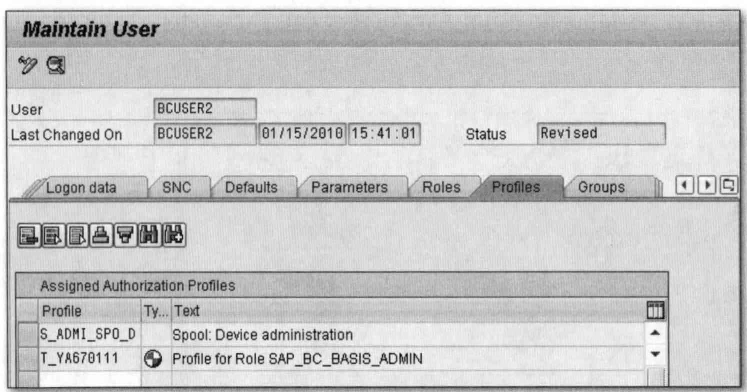

[+]

Generated Profiles

The profiles generated and assigned via authorization roles are indicated via the icon and cannot be changed.

13. Select the GROUPS tab, and enter the user groups to whom you want to assign the user.

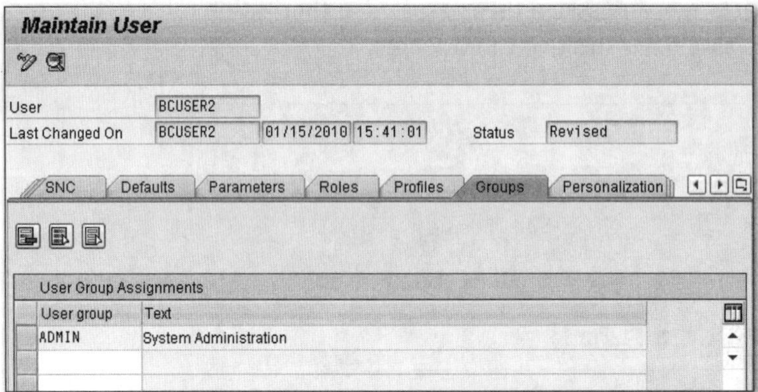

[+]

User Groups

Unlike the user group assigned in step 6, these groups are not included in the authorization check but instead serve as an additional grouping characteristic, for example, for selections or similar.

14. Choose the Personalization tab, and change the personalization options if required.

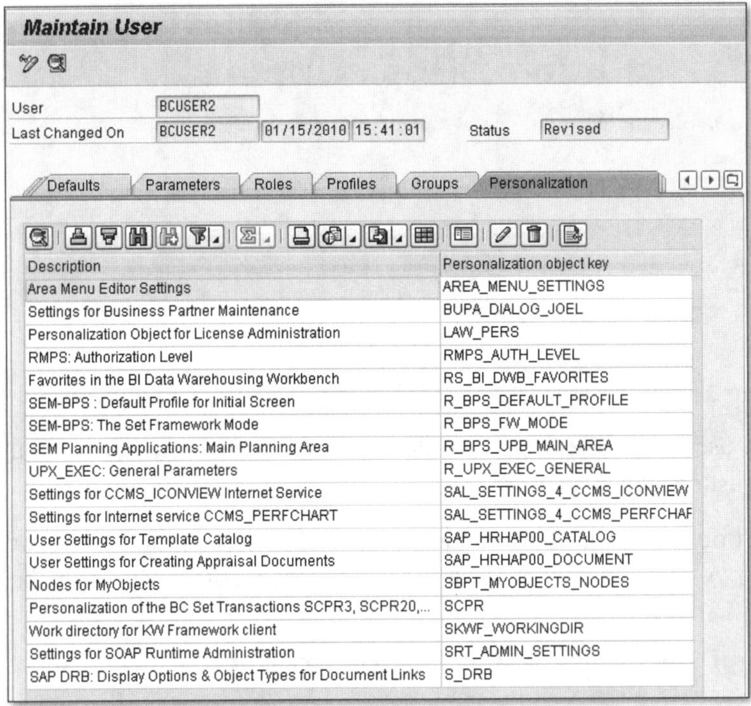

15. Choose the LicenceData tab, and store the Contractual User Type ID corresponding to your license agreement.

16. Click on Save (💾).

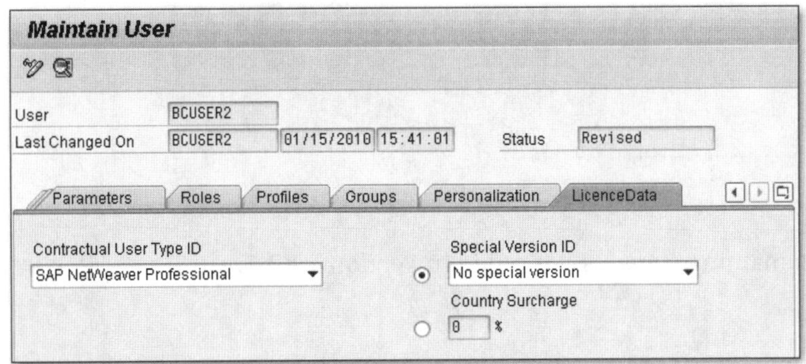

A message is displayed in the status bar, which confirms that the user has been saved.

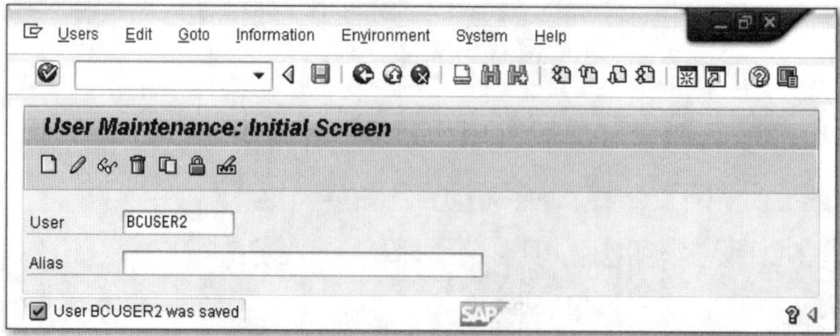

13.2.2 Creating a New User

In some cases, a user must be created completely anew. If there isn't a user you can copy, you must create a new user.

1. Enter Transaction "SU01" in the command box, and press the Enter key (or select Tools • Administration • User Maintenance • SU01—Users in the standard SAP menu).
2. Enter the user ID (for example, BCUSER2") to be created, and click on Create (□).

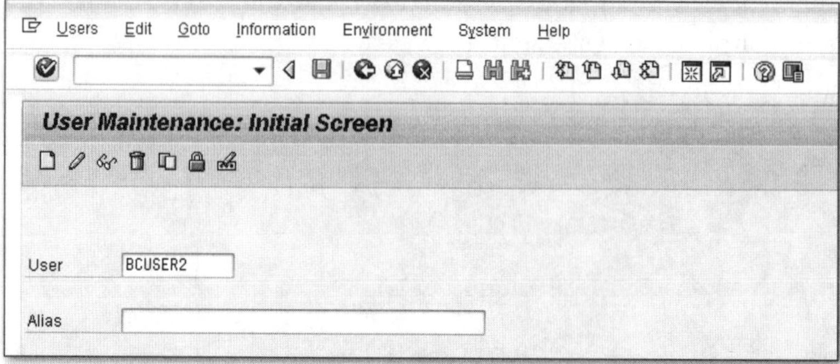

Proceed in the remaining steps, as described in Section 13.2.1.

13.3 Maintaining Users

Before you start with the user maintenance, you should have a filled-out and approved form for changing users.

[+]

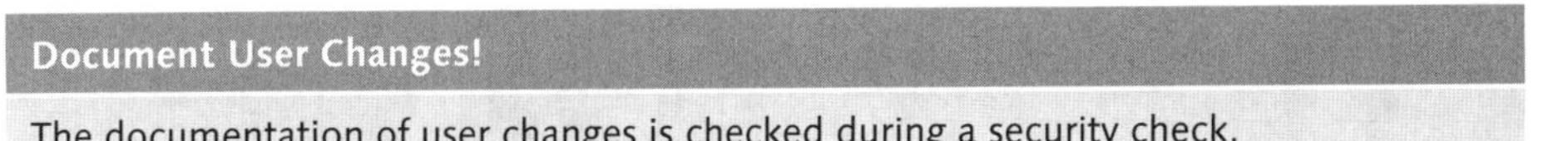

Document User Changes!

The documentation of user changes is checked during a security check.

You must maintain the users in case the job or position of the employee changes, new authorizations are added, or user data (for example, name, address, telephone number, and so on) change. Follow these steps:

1. Enter Transaction "SU01" in the command box, and press the Enter key (or select Tools • Administration • User Maintenance • SU01—Users in the standard SAP menu).
2. Enter the user ID (e.g., "BCUSER"), which is to be maintained, and click on Change (✎).

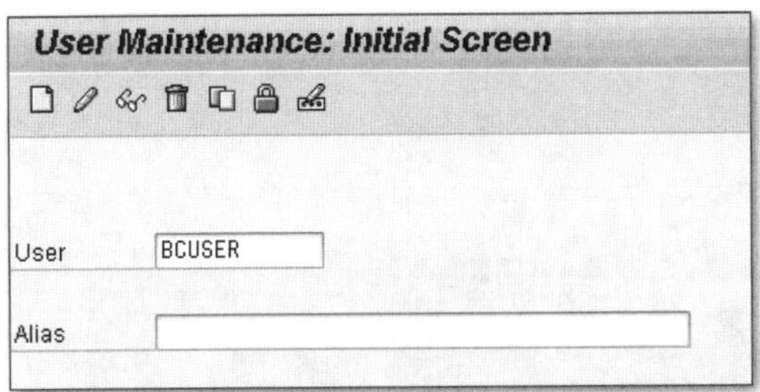

In the Maintain User screen, you can change the data of an already existing user, as described in Section 13.2.1.

13.4 Mass Changes

In certain situations, it's helpful to not have to individually change the master data of a large number of users via Transaction SU01 (User Maintenance) but instead to use the mass maintenance function of Transaction SU10 (User Mass Maintenance). The following are application cases that frequently arise:

- Assignment of a new company address due to organizational changes
- Change of validity period for SAP accesses of a consulting team due to project delays
- Locking users of a specific enterprise area for system maintenance

[+]

Restrictions Regarding Mass Maintenance

Mass maintenance is subject to certain restrictions, which arise from the nature of user master data or security aspects. For example, you can't change the name of users via Transaction SU10 or reset their passwords.

Mass Maintenance of Users

In appropriate cases, mass maintenance results in a considerable administration effort reduction.

1. Enter Transaction "SU10" in the command box, and press the [Enter] key (or select TOOLS • ADMINISTRATION • USER MAINTENANCE • SU10—USER MASS MAINTENANCE in the standard SAP menu).
2. Enter the user IDs (for example, "BCUSER" and "BCUSER2") to be changed, and click on CHANGE (✎).

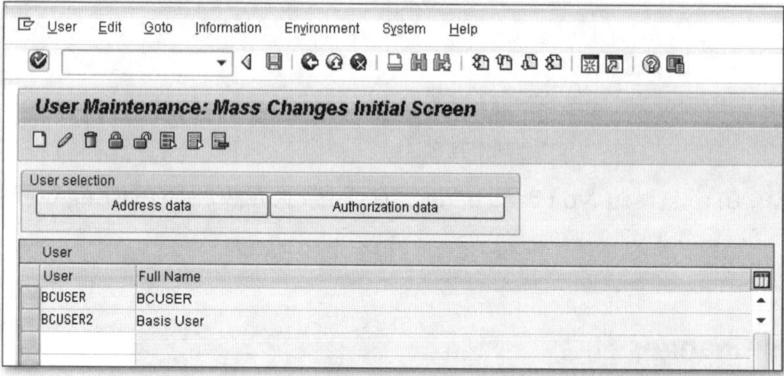

3. Select the tab in which you want to implement changes (for example, LOGON DATA).
4. Enter the data that you want to maintain (for example, a new user group), and activate the CHANGE checkbox.

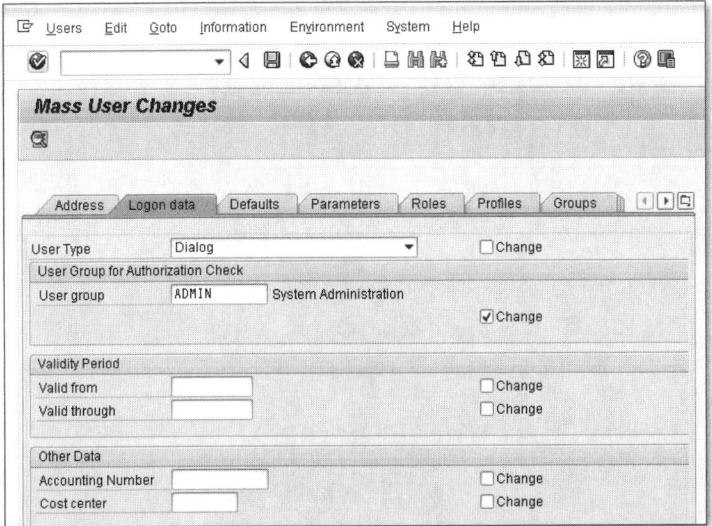

5. When you've made the desired changes, click on SAVE (), and select YES on the confirmation prompt.

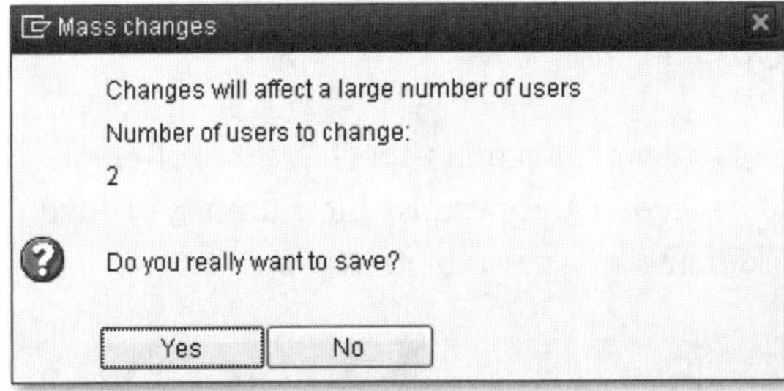

6. Check the log of implemented changes. Click BACK to exit the log display ().

[+]

Using Mass Maintenance

You can use the mass maintenance function to create, change, delete, lock, and unlock users. In the initial screen of Transaction SU10, you can select the users to be processed based on their address data (for example, name, enterprise, and so on) or their authorization data (for example, user groups, assigned roles or profiles, and so on).

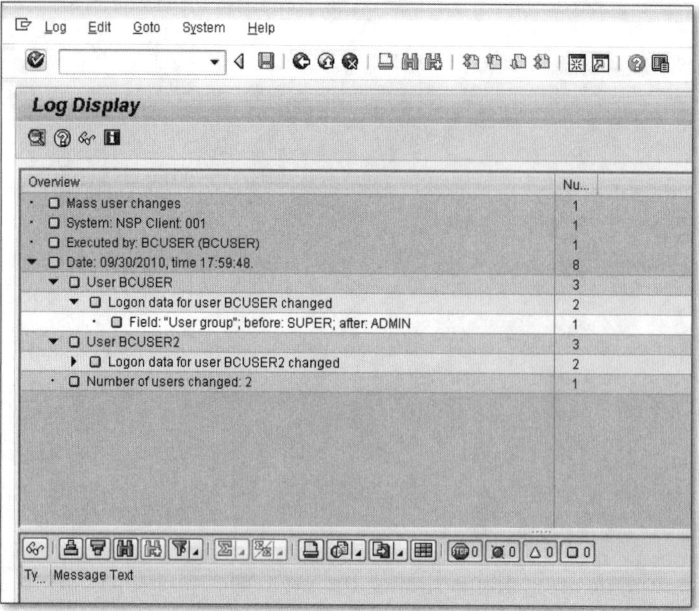

13.5 Resetting the Password

The most frequent reason for resetting passwords is that users have forgotten their password. The users may have also exceeded the permissible number of logon attempts; that is, their user ID is locked and must also be unlocked.

[!]

Identifying the Correct User

Confirm the identity of the person who wants to reset his password.

A simple method to identify the user is to compare telephone numbers on a telephone with a display. You can then compare the telephone numbers of the caller with the telephone number of the valid user stored in the system or found in the enterprise's telephone directory. Also have the user send an email with regard to the matter to identify the person based on the email address. You can keep this email for documentation purposes. You then send the new password via the reply function of your email program. In this way, you avoid someone overhearing the reset password. Moreover, generated random passwords can be better conveyed in written form than by telephone.

Some enterprises use a secret keyword that is used to check the user's identity on the telephone. Banks use a similar method to identify the caller. However, this method also has security risks because the secret keyword can be overheard by third parties.

Implement the following steps to reset a user password:

1. Enter Transaction "SU01" in the command box, and press the Enter key (or select Tools • Administration • User Maintenance • SU01 — Users in the standard SAP menu).
2. Enter the user ID (for example, "BCUSER") whose password is to be reset, and click on Change password ( ).

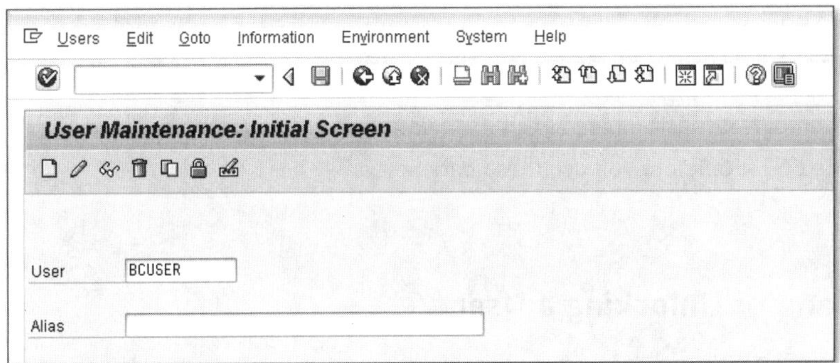

3. Select Generate password ( ) in the Change Password for BCUSER dialog box to generate a new password via a random number generator. You can also enter a password manually in the New Password field (e.g., "aiuzMv9f"). In this case, you need to reenter it in the Repeat Password field.
4. Click on Transfer ( ).

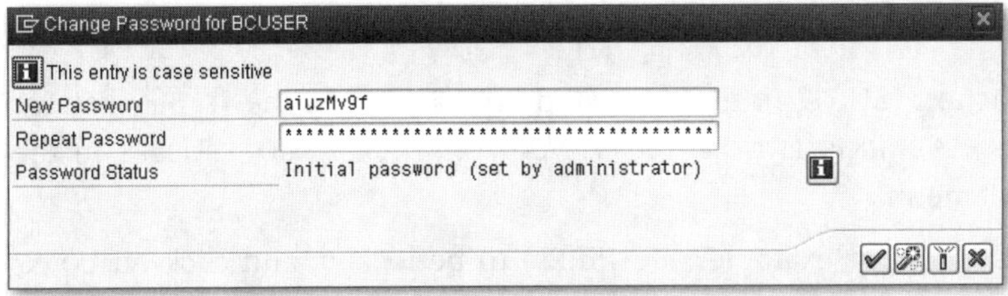

Passwords

For security reasons, you can only specify an initial password for the user. The user must then change this initial password when he logs onto the system. You can neither display the current password nor define a permanent password for dialog users.

[⚙]

Random Number Generator for Passwords

The random generator for passwords can be customized via several parameters, which can be maintained via Transaction SM30 (Table View Maintenance) in Table PRGN_CUST:

- `GEN_PSW_MAX_LENGTH`
  Maximum total length of password
- `GEN_PSW_MAX_DIGITS`
  Maximum number of digits in password
- `GEN_PSW_MAX_LETTERS`
  Maximum number of letters in password
- `GEN_PSW_MAX_SPECIALS`
  Maximum number of special characters in password

Read SAP Note 662466 before you use these parameters.

13.6 Locking or Unlocking a User

The locking/unlocking function is part of the logon check that enables or prevents the user from logging on to the SAP system.

Locking Users

Using the lock function, you can prevent the user from logging on to the SAP system; however, the user ID and the assigned authorizations persist. This function is suitable, for example, for temporary employees or consultants whose user ID is locked if they do not need to access the system. To lock a user, follow these steps:

1. Enter Transaction "SU01" in the command box, and press the Enter key (or select Tools • Administration • User Maintenance • SU01—Users in the standard SAP menu).
2. Enter the user ID (for example, "BCUSER") to be locked, and click on Lock/Unlock (🔒).

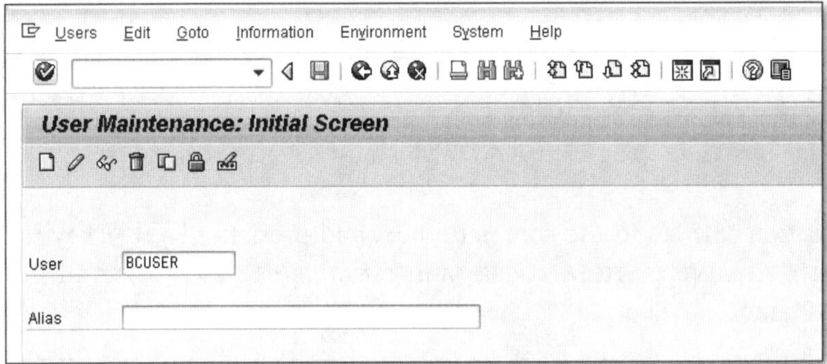

3. A dialog window appears, which displays that the user isn't locked currently. To lock the user, click on LOCK ( ).

4. A message in the status bar confirms that the user has been successfully locked.

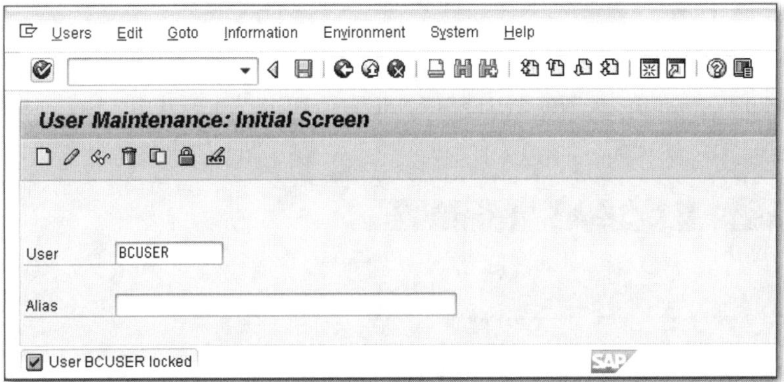

Unlocking Users

Users are automatically locked when they have exceeded the permissible number of unsuccessful logon attempts. In this case, the system administrator must unlock the user ID and might also have to reset the password.

[!]

Checking the Reason for Locking

Make sure that you have a valid request before you reset a user. Do not unlock any manually locked user before you've determined the reason why the user has been locked. There may be an important reason as to why the user must not access the system.

1. Enter Transaction "SU01" in the command box, and press the Enter key (or select TOOLS • ADMINISTRATION • USER MAINTENANCE • SU01—USERS in the standard SAP menu).
2. Enter the user ID (e.g., "BCUSER") to be unlocked, and click on LOCK/UNLOCK (🔒).

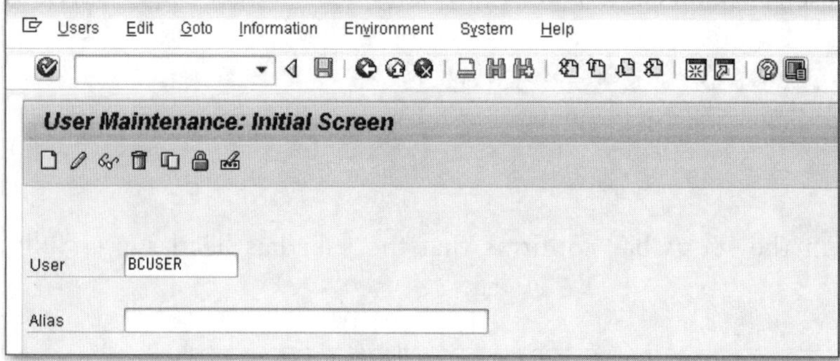

3. A dialog window is displayed. In this example, the system administrator has locked the user ID manually. The message could also read "Locked due to incorrect logons."

[!]

Locking by System Administrator

Also make inquiries if a user has been locked by a system administrator. The user may not be allowed to be unlocked. Via the INFORMATION • CHANGE DOCUMENTS FOR USERS menu path, you can determine who has locked the user and make specific inquires.

4. Unlock the user via the UNLOCK (🔓) button. A message in the status bar confirms that the user has been successfully unlocked.

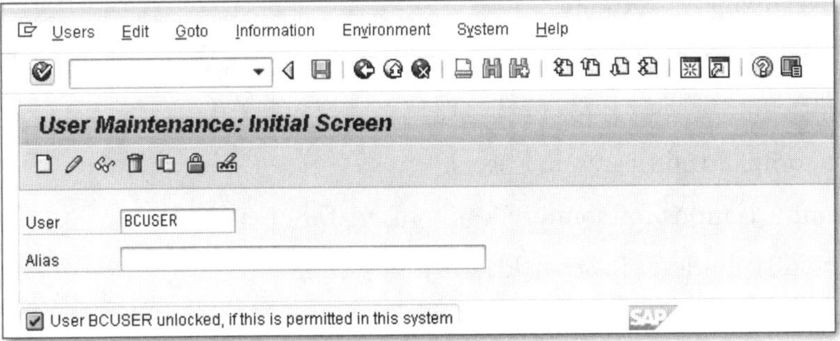

13.7 Central User Administration

If you have to manage several SAP systems with a large number of users, setting up a *Central User Administration* (CUA) can significantly reduce your amount of work. Whether this is worth doing mainly depends on how many systems and clients you manage, whether many of the users have access to several clients or systems, and how frequently you process user requests. Already in a three-system landscape consisting of a development, QA, and production system, it can be tedious when you have dozens of requests a week to create or change every user both in the production and QA system.

In a CUA, the user master data is maintained in the central system and distributed to the child systems via *Application Link Enabling* (ALE) technology. Maintenance directly in the child systems themselves is only possible with restrictions. However, it can be configured in relative detail.

Further Information [+]

The following section describes how you set up the CUA in a robust standard configuration. In SAP Service Marketplace (*www.service.sap.com*), you can find a variety of notes that you can use to reach further optimization.

13.7.1 Setting Up a Central User Administration

To operate a CUA, you must carry out a sequence of individual steps:

1. Create communication users for the CUA and provide them with authorizations.

2. Define and assign logical systems.
3. Set up RFC connections between the systems.
4. Generate a distribution model for the CUA.
5. Synchronize company addresses and users.
6. Customize authorizations for communication users for operation.
7. Configure the distribution of user fields (field selection).

The following sections describe these steps in more detail.

Creating and Allocating Communication Users and Authorization Roles

In each (logical) system, a user ID with special authorizations is required for the communication between the systems of the CUA. First, create these communication users:

1. Log on to the central system.
2. Create a user ID CUA, as described in Section 13.2 by using Transaction SU01.
3. Select the SYSTEM user type in the LOGON DATA tab.
4. Write down the password that you've assigned or generated.
5. Save the user master record.
6. Perform steps 1 to 5 in all your child systems.

You have now created a user ID by which the communication between the systems of the CUA takes place. Next, you must provide this user with the necessary authorizations for the communication. For these purposes, SAP provides template authorization roles:

- **SAP_BC_USR_CUA_SETUP_CENTRAL**
  Authorization in the central system to set up the CUA
- **SAP_BC_USR_CUA_CENTRAL**
  Authorization in the central system to operate the CUA
- **SAP_BC_USR_CUA_SETUP_CLIENT**
  Authorization in the child system to set up the CUA
- **SAP_BC_USR_CUA_CLIENT**
  Authorization in the child system to operate the CUA

To use the templates, follow these steps:

1. Log on to the central system.
2. Copy both roles SAP_BC_USR_CUA_SETUP_CENTRAL and SAP_BC_USR_CUA_CENTRAL into your customer naming space (for example, Z_BC_USR_CUA_SETUP_CENTRAL), as described in Chapter 14.

[!]

Using No Original Roles

Do not use the original roles provided because these roles may be overwritten when a support package is imported.

3. Generate the authorization profile for each of the two roles in the AUTHORIZATIONS tab.
4. Assign each of the two roles to your communication user CUA in the USER tab.
5. Execute the user comparison, and save.
6. Repeat steps 1 to 5 in each of your child systems using the two roles SAP_BC_USR_CUA_SETUP_CLIENT and SAP_BC_USR_CUA_CLIENT.

Transport Request

You can also distribute the authorization roles for the child systems via a transport request to several child systems.

Creating and Allocating Logical Systems

In a CUA, the term *system* doesn't refer to an application server or an instance but instead to *logical systems*. These logical systems must be defined in the SAP system and are then assigned to a client of a system.

Logical Systems

A logical system represents one client in a specific system. The ID of a logical system must not be used several times; otherwise, this could result in communication errors in the system network. It's therefore best to stick to the usual naming convention *<SID>CLNT<client>* (for example, NSPCLNT000).

In the central system of the CUA, all logical systems taking part in the CUA must be known. Only the logical system of the respective child system and the logical system of the central system need to be available in the child systems, respectively.

In this example, a CUA is to be created in one individual system using the system ID NSP. Client 000 assumes the function of the central system; client 001 is supposed to be integrated into the CUA as a child system and provided with user master data. Modify the example accordingly to your framework conditions.

First create the logical systems:

1. Log on to the central system.
2. Call Transaction BD54 (Maintain Logical Systems), and click on the NEW ENTRIES button.

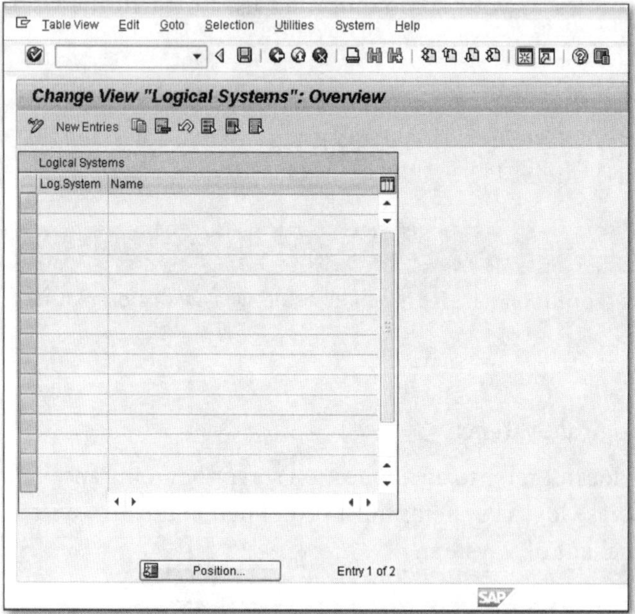

3. Create an entry for your central system and for each of your child systems. Save your entries (💾).

   You must add your changes to a transport request depending on your transport system settings.

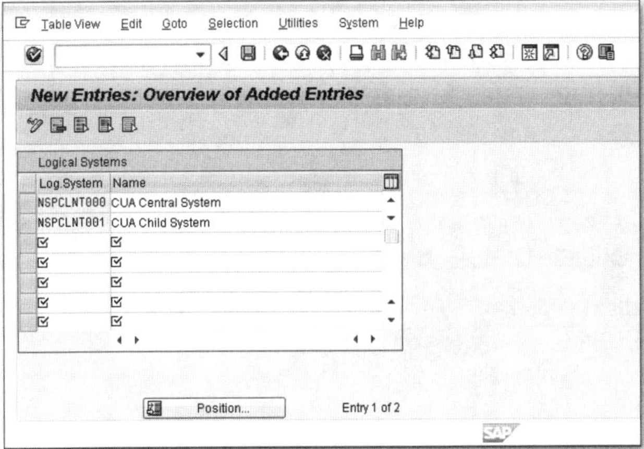

4. Implement steps 1 to 3 in your child systems, or, even better, transport the logical systems created in the central system to the child systems using the transport request created in step 3.

If all required logical systems have been created, assign them to the respective systems' clients.

1. Log on to the central system once again.
2. Enter Transaction "SCC4" in the command box, and press the [Enter] button (or select TOOLS • ADMINISTRATION • ADMINISTRATION • CLIENT ADMINISTRATION • SCC4—CLIENT MAINTENANCE in the standard SAP menu).

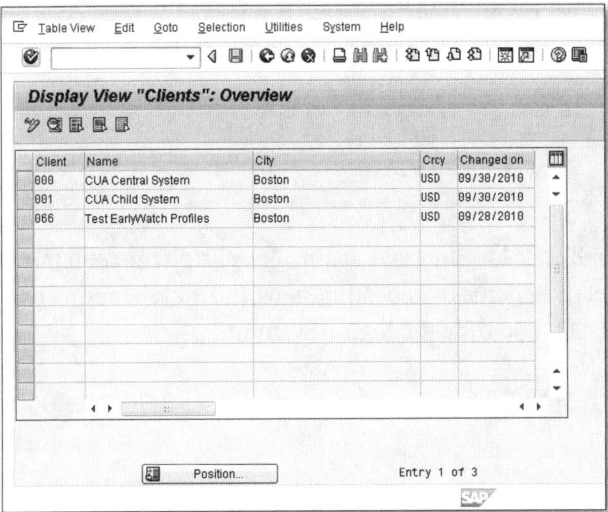

3. Switch to the change mode using the button, and double-click to select the client who is intended as the central system of your CUA (for example, 000). Enter the logical system in the field intended for this (for example, NSPCLNT000"), and save ().

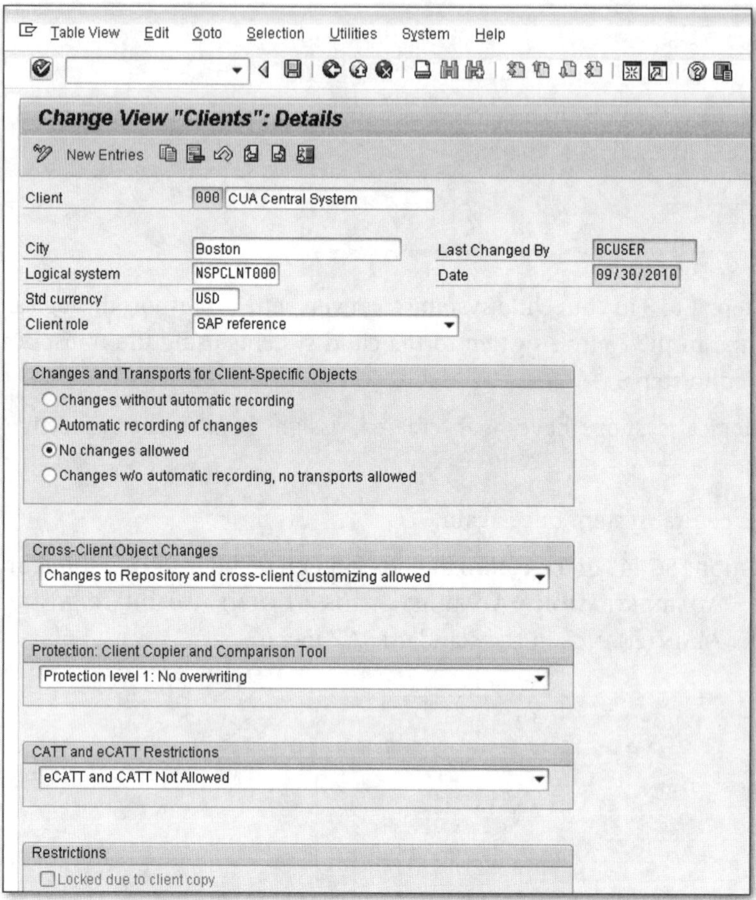

4. Exit the view by clicking on Back (), and save again (). Assign the remaining logical systems to the respective clients by repeating steps 1 to 3 in the respective systems (for example, NSPCLNT001 for the logical system).

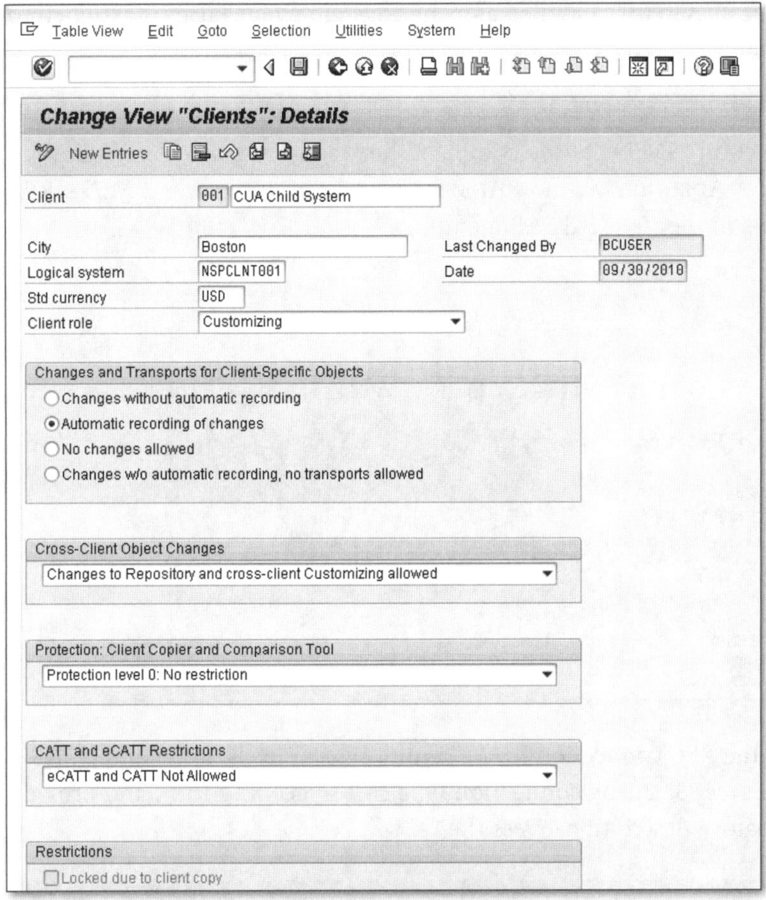

You have now defined and assigned logical systems that are supposed to belong to your CUA.

Setting Up RFC Connections Between the Systems

After the communication user and systems of your CUA have been set up, you can define the communication connections between the systems of the CUA, which are required to exchange data via ALE. A connection must be set up from the central system to each child system and from the respective child system to the central system. Furthermore, an RFC connection to the central system itself is required because the central system is handled as a child system when a user is assigned to the central system.

1. Log on to the central system.
2. Enter Transaction "SM59" in the command box, and press the Enter key (or select TOOLS • ADMINISTRATION • ADMINISTRATION • NETWORK • SM59—RFC DESTINATIONS in the standard SAP menu).
3. Click on CREATE (□).

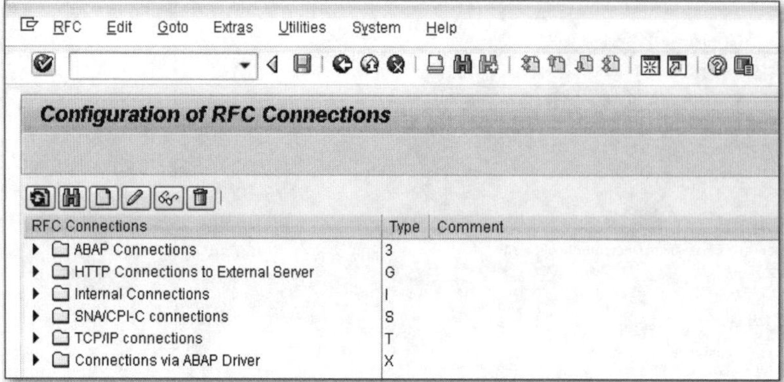

4. First, create the RFC connection to the central system itself (for example, NSP-CLNT000). Enter "3" as the connection type (ABAP CONNECTION), and provide a self-explanatory description. Press the Enter key.

[!]

Description of the RFC Connections

Note that the RFC connections that you create for a CUA must always have the same name as the logical system to which they point.

5. Enter the server name or the IP address of the application server in the TARGET HOST field in the TECHNICAL SETTINGS tab (for example, "sap"), and define the respective system number (for example, "00").

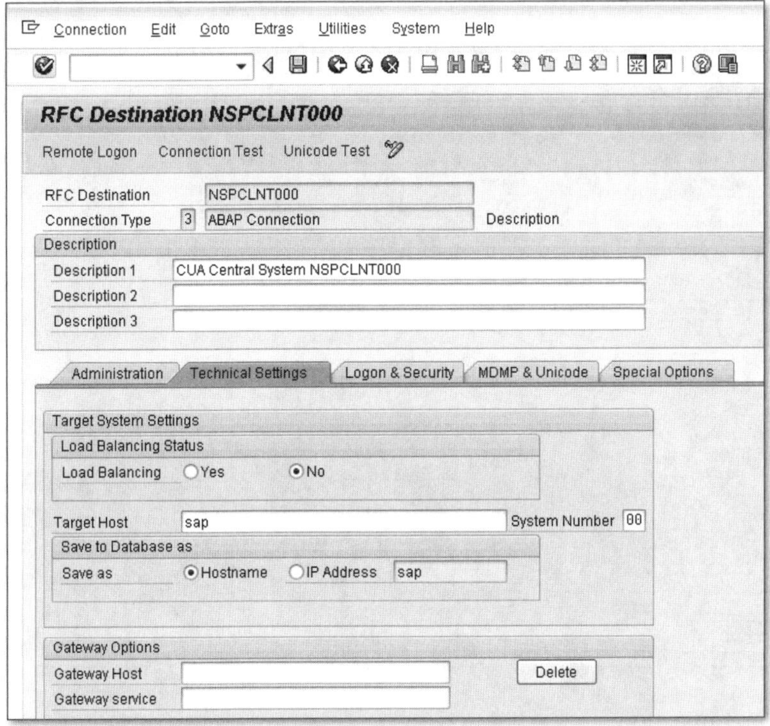

6. Switch to the Logon & Security tab.
   - Enter a language key in the Logon area (for example, "EN").
   - Enter the Client that is supposed to function as the central system on the server (for example, "000").
   - Enter the user ID of your communication user in the User field (for example, "CUA").
   - Under Password, define the password of the communication user that has been generated or manually assigned by you.

[+]

Connection Test

With the Connection Test, the information that you created in the Technical Settings tab is checked to determine whether the server is accessible and whether the system number exists.

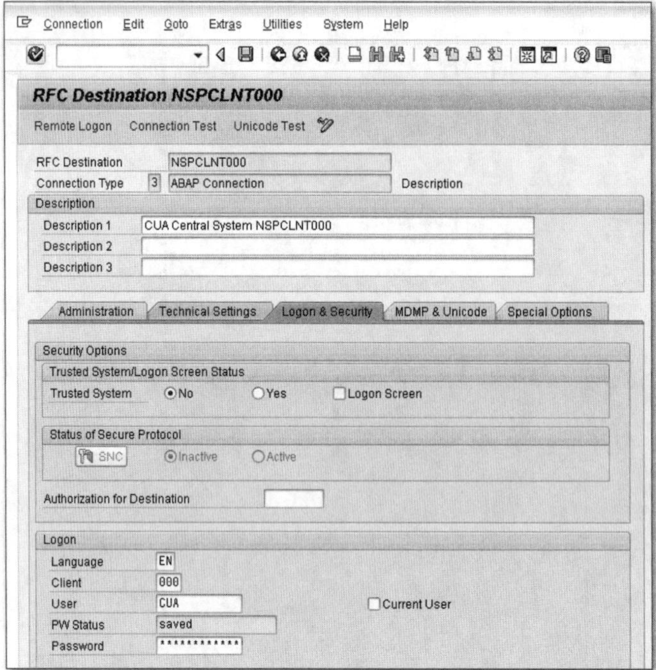

7. Save the RFC connection.
8. Test the connection by clicking first on the Connection Test button.

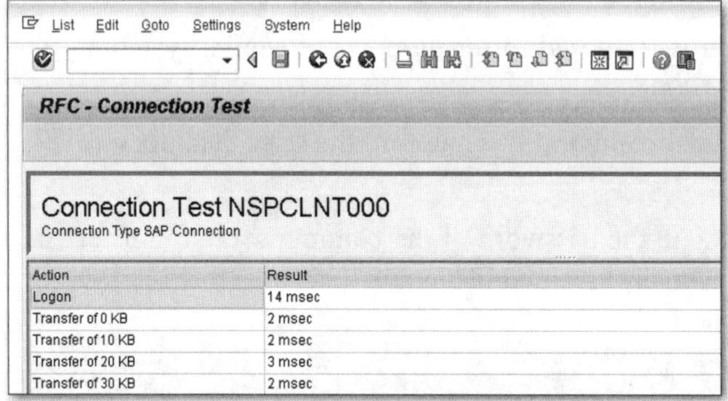

9. Then click on the Remote Logon button (in the RFC Destination screen). The test is successful if *no* logon screen appears.

[⚙]

Connection Test Result

Don't worry if nothing happens in a successful remote login test—that's a good sign! The remote login checks the data in the LOGON & SECURITY tab. If a logon window appears, the remote login was unsuccessful.

Then check whether you have entered the user ID and password correctly, and ensure that the user is not locked.

10. Now create the RFC connections for the child systems (for example, NSPCLNT001) by repeating steps 3 to 9 in the central system.

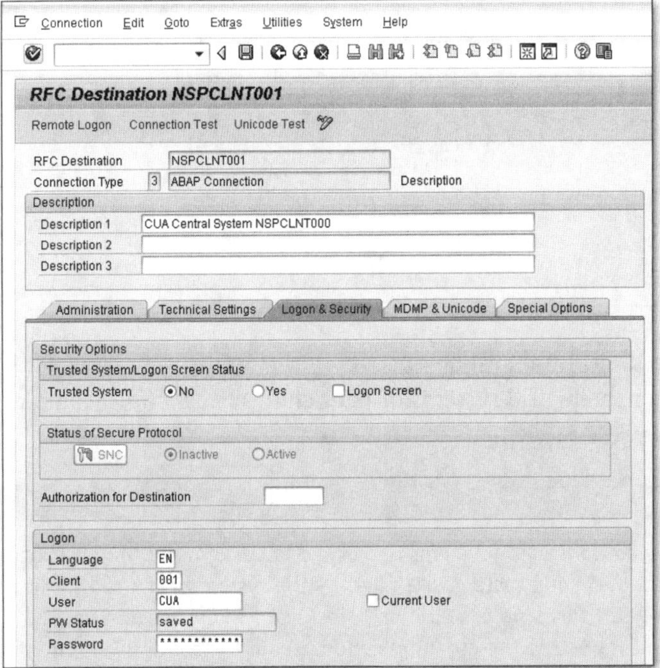

11. Then log on to the child systems, and define the RFC connections to the central system. Repeat the same procedure for steps 2 to 9.

Generating the Distribution Model of the CUA

The communication between your systems is now prepared in such a way that the rest of the work can be done by the SAP system. The ALE settings still to be set up (*distribution model*) can be automatically generated via a custom transaction. Follow these steps:

1. Log on to the central system.
2. Enter Transaction "SCUA" in the command box, and press the Enter key (or select TOOLS • ADMINISTRATION • USER MAINTENANCE • CENTRAL USER ADMINISTRATION • SCUA—DISTRIBUTION MODEL in the standard SAP menu).
3. Assign a name for your CUA distribution model in the MODEL VIEW field (for example, "CUA_NSP"). Click on CREATE (□).

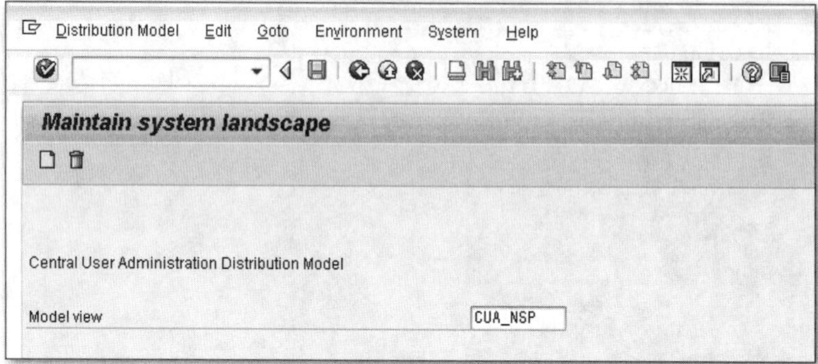

4. The logical system of the central system appears in the SENDING SYSTEM field. Under RECIPIENT, enter the logical systems of your child systems (for example, "NSPCLNT001"), and press Enter.

[⚙]

Checking the RFC Connections

The connection to the selected receiving systems is checked in background. If not all of the columns for one of the receiving systems are filled by the system or if a red traffic light icon appears in the RFC STATUS field, you must check your RFC connections. The authorizations, which you assigned to the communication user in the child system, may sometimes not suffice. Then, extend the authorizations accordingly, for example by using authorization traces in Transaction ST01 (System Trace; see Chapter 14, Section 14.4.2).

5. Click on COMPLETE SAVE (💾).

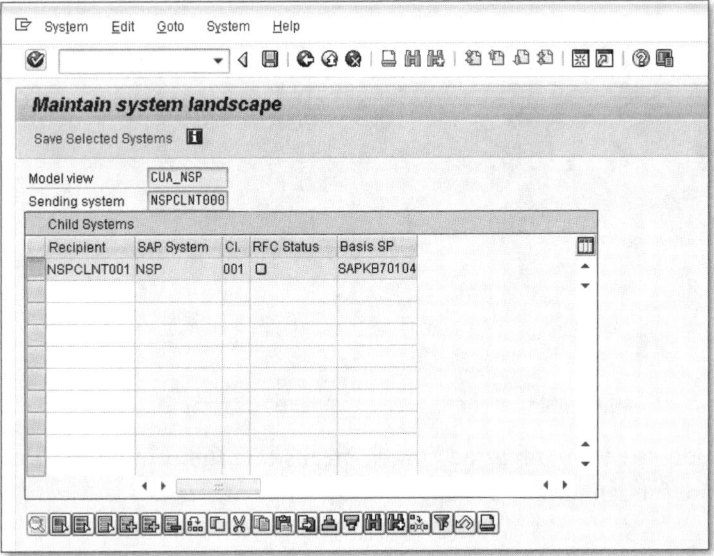

6. A log is displayed. Check the log, and eliminate errors that may have arisen.

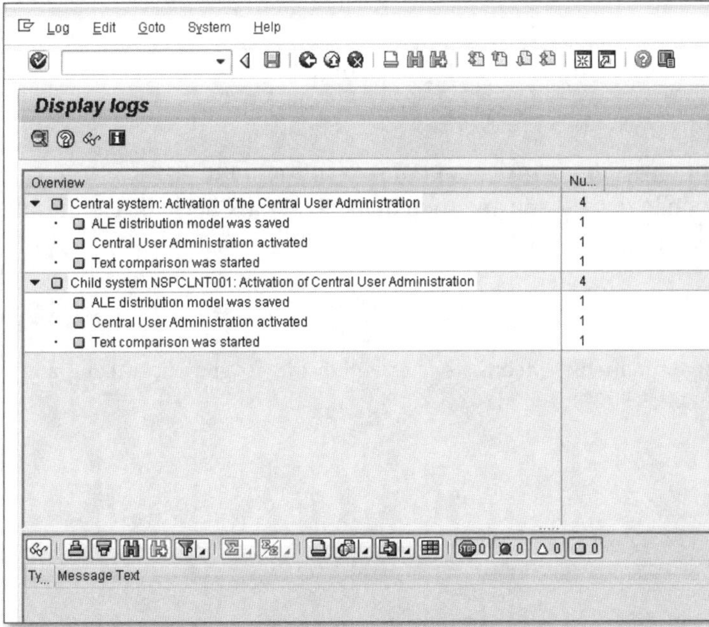

7. Click the BACK button twice (). The distribution model is displayed in gray in the initial screen.

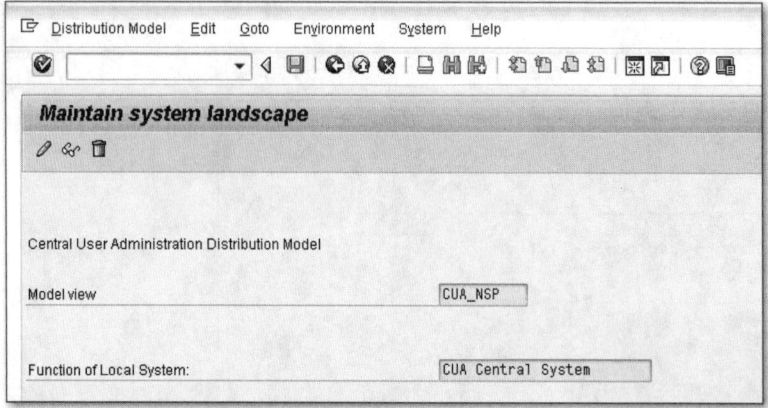

The distribution model is now configured, which means that the communication paths for the CUA are fundamentally set up.

Synchronizing Company Addresses and Users

The technical settings for the communication of the CUA are completed when the distribution model is created. To use the CUA in operation, you must now fill it with the company addresses and the user data from the connected systems. To avert errors when you copy data, however, you should prepare it.

1. Log on to the central system.
2. Activate Transaction "SA38" (ABAP Program Execution), and first execute the RSADRCK2 program in the test run and then in the live run. Check the log output of the consistency check.

[✪]

RSADRCK2 Program

The RSADRCK2 program remedies inconsistencies within the assignment of company addresses to users (Table USR21).

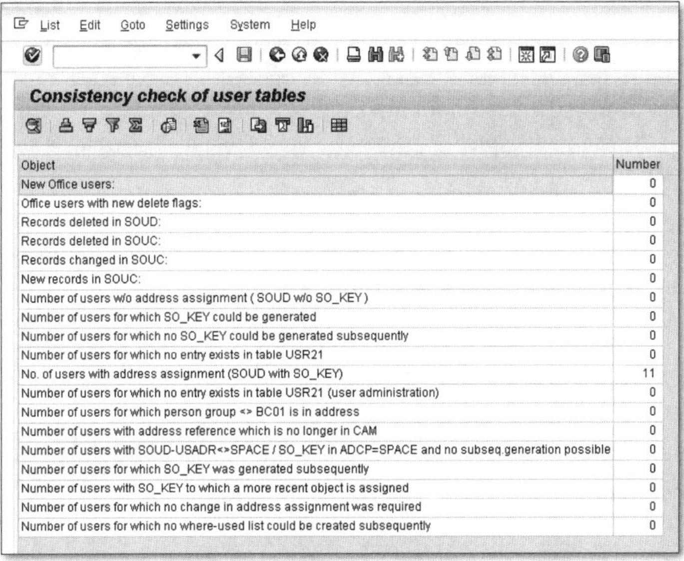

Object	Number
New Office users:	0
Office users with new delete flags:	0
Records deleted in SOUD:	0
Records deleted in SOUC:	0
Records changed in SOUC:	0
New records in SOUC:	0
Number of users w/o address assignment (SOUD w/o SO_KEY)	0
Number of users for which SO_KEY could be generated	0
Number of users for which no SO_KEY could be generated subsequently	0
Number of users for which no entry exists in table USR21	0
No. of users with address assignment (SOUD with SO_KEY)	11
Number of users for which no entry exists in table USR21 (user administration)	0
Number of users for which person group <> BC01 is in address	0
Number of users with address reference which is no longer in CAM	0
Number of users with SOUD-USADR<>SPACE / SO_KEY in ADCP=SPACE and no subseq.generation possible	0
Number of users for which SO_KEY was generated subsequently	0
Number of users with SO_KEY to which a more recent object is assigned	0
Number of users for which no change in address assignment was required	0
Number of users for which no where-used list could be created subsequently	0

3. Repeat steps 1 and 2 in all child systems.
4. Log on to the central system.
5. Activate Transaction SM30 (Table View Maintenance).
6. Create a new entry "CUA_USERGROUPS_CHECK" in Table PRGN_CUST using the VALUE "C".

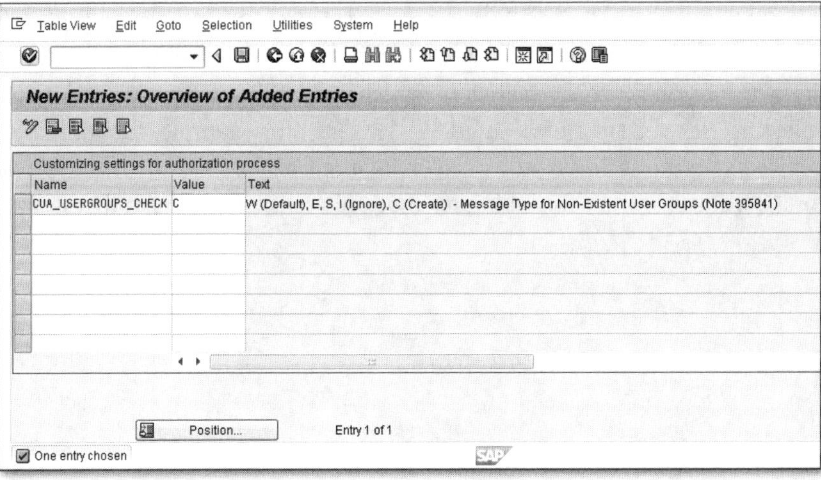

Name	Value	Text
CUA_USERGROUPS_CHECK	C	W (Default), E, S, I (Ignore), C (Create) - Message Type for Non-Existent User Groups (Note 395841)

[⚙]

CUA_USERGROUPS_CHECK Entry

With this entry, the user groups, which are not available in the central system, are created automatically when users are copied from the child systems. Without the entry, errors would arise when the users are copied. You can also ensure manually that all user groups exist in the central system.

7. Implement steps 5 and 6 in the child systems as well, if user groups are to be created automatically when the users are distributed.
8. Enter Transaction "SCUG", and press the Enter button (or select TOOLS • ADMINISTRATION • USER MAINTENANCE • CENTRAL USER ADMINISTRATION • SCUG—TRANSFER USERS in the standard SAP menu).
9. Place the cursor on a child system (for example, NSPCLNT001), and select SYNCHRONIZE COMPANY ADDRESSES IN THE CENTRAL SYSTEM (icon).

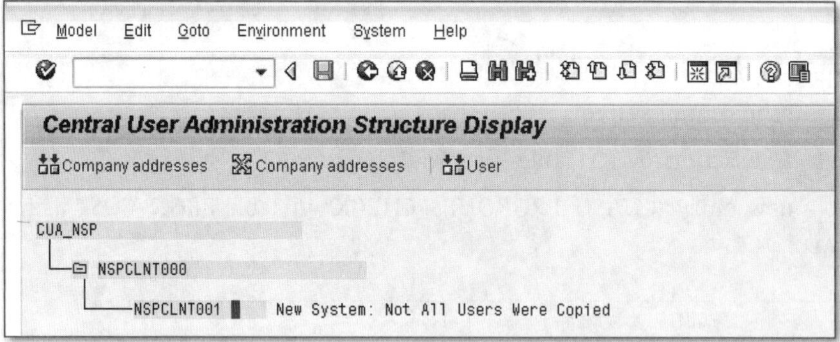

10. Highlight the company addresses to be synchronized by expanding the areas and selecting either COPY FROM CHILD SYSTEM (icon), for example, for addresses that only exist in the child system, or selecting the DISTRIBUTE TO CHILD SYSTEM button (icon), for example, for addresses that only exist in the central system.

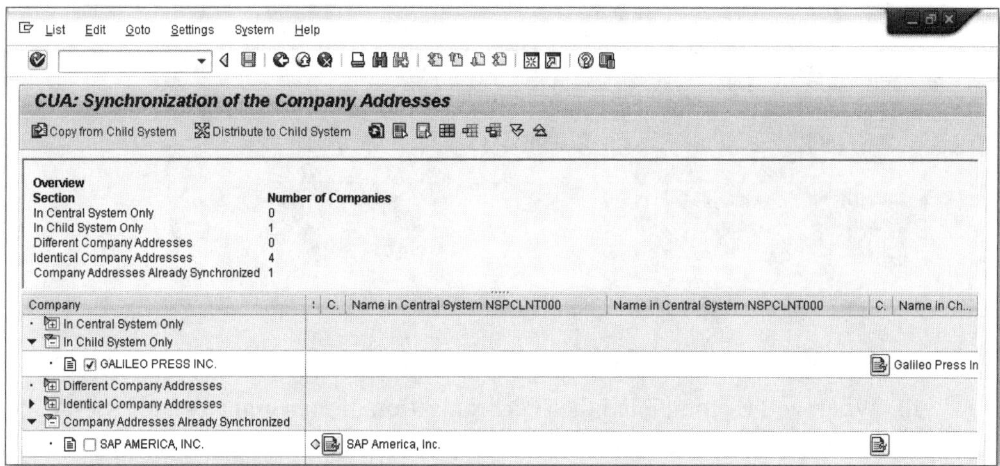

11. When you have completed the synchronization of the company addresses, click on BACK (![]).
12. Select COPY USERS TO THE CENTRAL SYSTEM (![]).

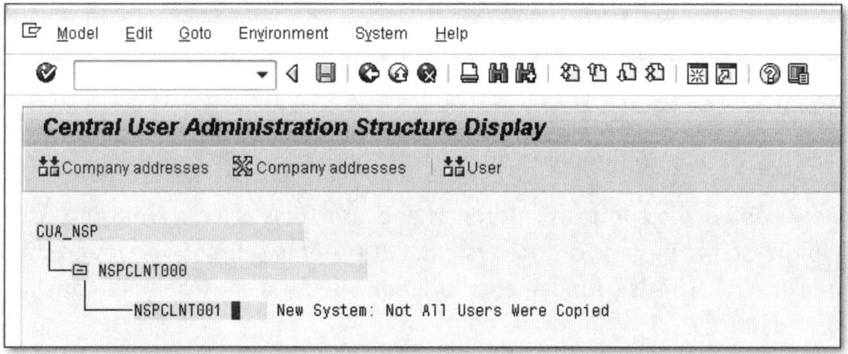

13. The user master records that are available for transfer are displayed in several tabs, which you need to check in sequence. First highlight the data that you want to copy in the NEW USER tab, and select TRANSFER USERS (![]).

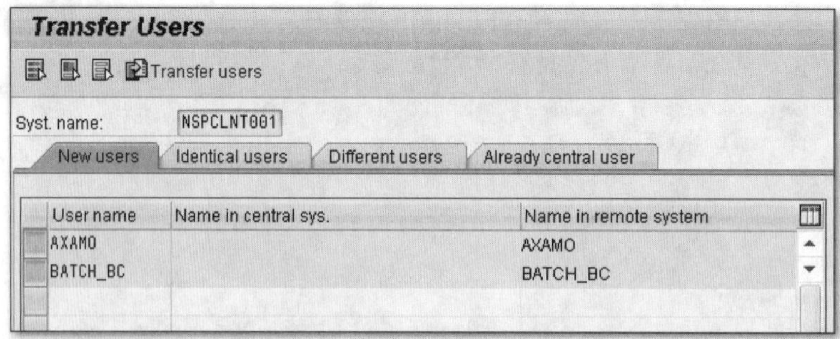

14. Repeat the user transfer in the IDENTICAL USERS AND DIFFERENT USERS tabs.
15. When you've completed the synchronization of the company addresses, click on BACK (). In the structure display of the CUA, the status message "New System: Not All Users Were Copied" no longer appears.

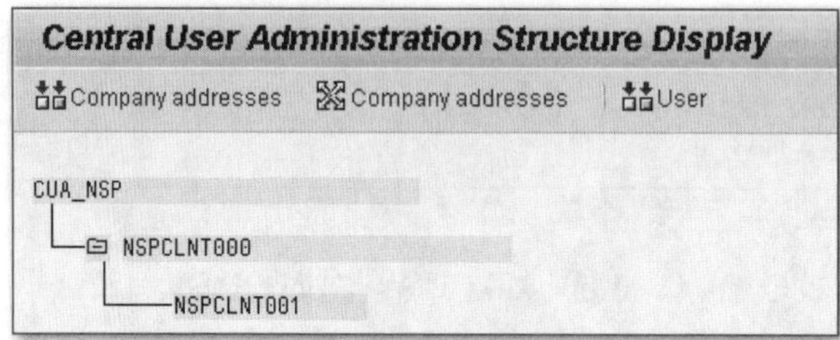

16. Repeat steps 10 to 16 for all remaining child systems.

You've now copied the company addresses and user master data from the connected child systems in your central system. All systems can now be found in a synchronized state. This is a fundamental prerequisite for a consistent administration of user data.

[⚙]

Resynchronizing CUA

To resynchronize user data, for example, according to a system or client copy, the Program RSCCUSND is provided. For further information, read SAP Notes 574094 and 503247.

Customizing Authorizations for Communication Users for Operation

After you've synchronized the company addresses and user data, the CUA is ready. For security reasons, you should now withdraw the authorization roles again from the communication users for the setup of the CUA. To do this, follow these steps:

1. Log on to the central system.
2. Enter Transaction "SU01" in the command box, and press the Enter key (or select Tools • Administration • User Maintenance • SU01—Users in the standard SAP menu).
3. Enter the user ID of the communication user (e.g., "CUA").
4. Click on Change (✎).
5. Go to the Roles tab.
6. Highlight the authorization roles to set up the CUA (for example, Z_BC_USR_CUA_SETUP_CENTRAL and Z_BC_USR_CUA_SETUP_CLIENT), and select Delete Row (▤).

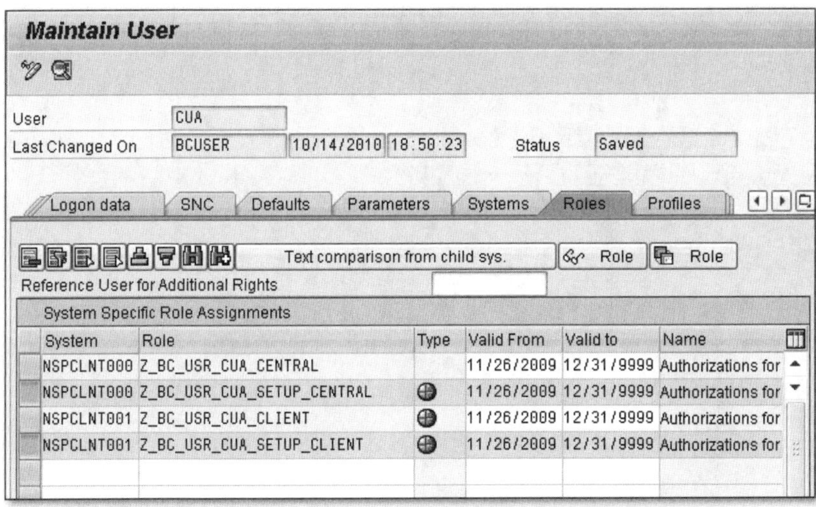

7. Click on Save (💾).

You have now customized the communication user for operation.

Configuring the Distribution of User Fields (Field Selection)

The main goal of the CUA is to bundle the maintenance of user master data in a system and at the same time minimize the administration effort. You can only create, copy and delete users in the central system. Moreover, the default setting is provided so that all fields of the user master record can only be changed in the central system. You can customize these settings depending on the system landscape and the distribution of responsibilities within the enterprise. The CUA can be configured via *field selection* in such a way that many—but not all—fields can also be maintained in the child systems. You customize the default parameters as follows:

1. Log on to the central system.
1. Enter the Transaction "SCUM", and press the [Enter] key (or select TOOLS • ADMINISTRATION • USER MAINTENANCE • CENTRAL USER ADMINISTRATION • SCUM—FIELD SELECTION).
2. Click on the DISPLAY <-> CHANGE button (✎).

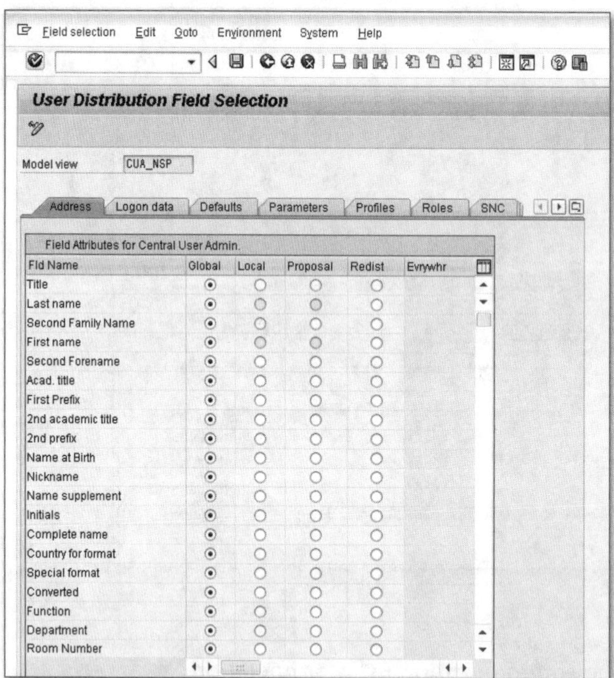

3. Select the distribution mode for the individual fields by navigating via the tab and highlighting the respective radio buttons.

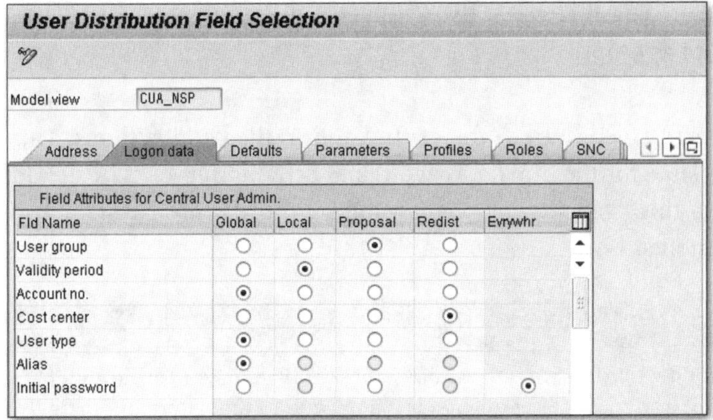

4. When you have completed your settings, click on SAVE (💾).

After saving, the configuration is copied to the child systems. The distribution options have the following meaning:

- **Global**
  The data can only be maintained in the central system. The settings made in the central system are distributed to the child systems. All fields are set to GLOBAL in the standard configuration.
- **Local**
  The data can only be maintained in the child system. They are neither redistributed to the central system nor to other child systems. This setting makes sense for such fields, which can or need to be different in each system (for example, the Start menu).
- **Proposal**
  The data can be changed in both the central and the child systems. However, the field value is distributed only when the user is created in the child system for the first time. No redistribution to the central system takes place if the field value is changed in a child system. Subsequent changes in the central system are also not transferred to the child systems.
- **Redistribution**
  The data can be maintained in the central and in the child systems. When you customize a setting in a child system, this change is notified to the user master record in the central system and edited there. Then it is distributed to all child systems. This mode is recommended for fields that are usually identical in all systems (for example, name and address) because the settings of all systems

are overwritten. For data that can exist in diverse ways in specific systems, redistribution is not appropriate.

- **Everywhere**
  The data can be maintained both in the central and in the child systems. This option is only available for the initial password and certain user locks. If a child system is changed, this change is not redistributed to the central system and the other child systems.

[+]

Distribution Modes

Test the distribution modes until you find the setting suitable for your work environment. Various options are not available for specific fields mainly due to the nature of the field and also often due to potential security threats. However, the setting options are usually adequate for common application scenarios.

13.7.2 Creating and Maintaining Users Via a Central User Administration

After the CUA is used in live operation, you'll notice a few differences to the current system layout depending on the configuration of the field selection:

- In the child systems, the buttons to create, copy and delete users are missing in the initial screen of Transaction SU01. The button to reset the password is also not available depending on the configuration of the field selection.
- If you select CHANGE in the child system, only the globally maintainable fields in the user master data are gray and can therefore not be changed.
- In the central system, the new SYSTEMS tab is provided in the user master The SYSTEM column is included both in the ROLES and PROFILES tabs.

The following sections now briefly describe the differences to the procedures already described in Sections 13.1 through 13.6.

Creating New Users

Regardless of whether you create a user with or without a template, you must specify the systems in an active CUA in which the user is to be created. Enter the name of the desired logical system in Transaction SU01 (User Maintenance) in the SYSTEMS tab. If you assign another logical system to a user in the SYSTEMS tab, the user is also created in this system.

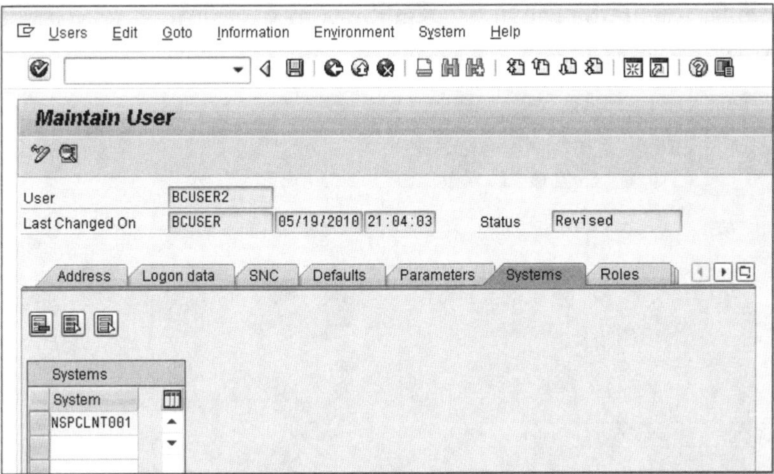

Authorizations are also assigned in a system-specific way. For this reason, the logical system is shown in the ROLES and PROFILES tabs as a new key column.

Assign authorization roles to the new user by filling an empty row with the logical system, the role name and possibly varying validity dates in the ROLES tab in the SYSTEM SPECIFIC ROLE ASSIGNMENTS area.

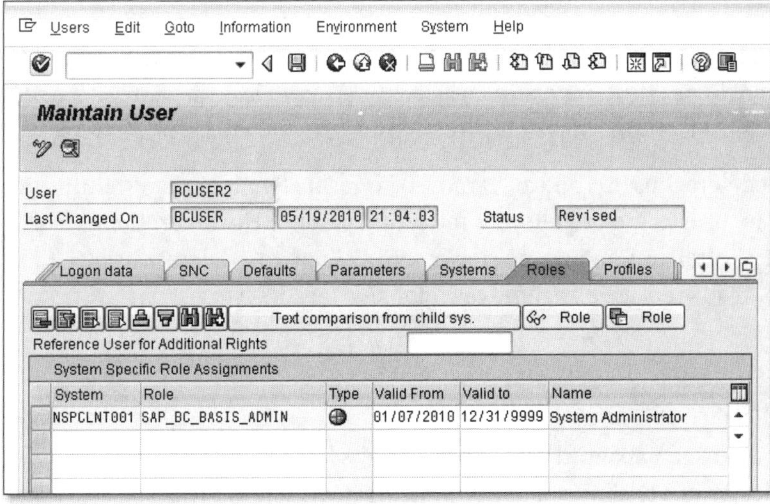

Proceed in a similar way in the PROFILES tab in the SYSTEM SPECIFIC ASSIGNMENTS OF AUTHORIZATION PROFILES area.

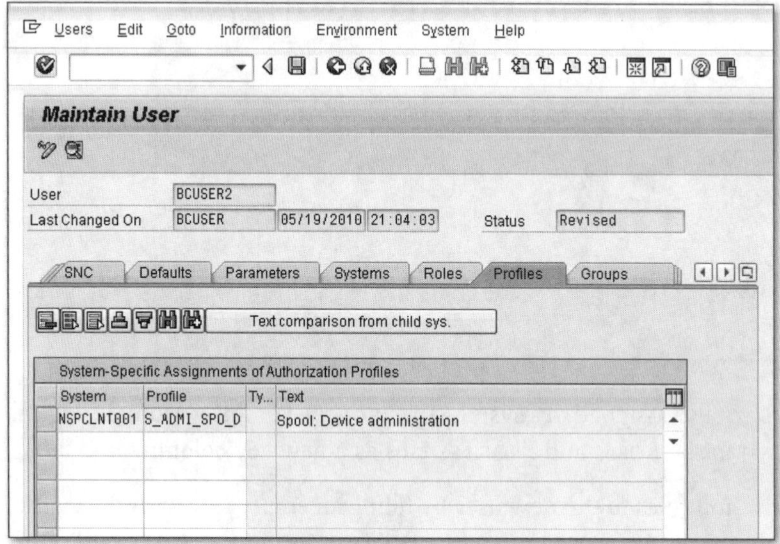

User Maintenance and Mass Changes

When you change user master data and carry out mass maintenance via Transaction SU10, you must take into consideration that the same special features with regard to the assignment of logical systems are in an active CUA, as well as the system-specific assignment of authorization roles and profiles as when you create new users.

If you want to delete a user, you can remove the respective logical system in the SYSTEMS tab. The user is then deleted in the target system. However, the user still remains in the central system as a master record. When you delete a user via the DELETE button (), the user is removed globally in all systems, including the central system.

Resetting the Password

You can reset the user password from the central system for one or several systems. The dialog window shows a list of systems in which the user exists. Select the systems to which you want the new initial password to be distributed by highlighting the rows.

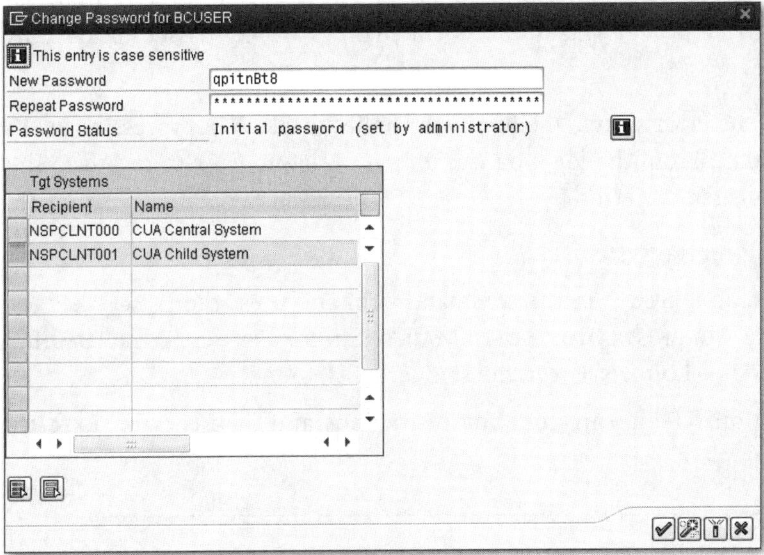

Locking or Unlocking a User

When you lock and unlock users, a differentiation is made between *local* and *global* locks in an active CUA.

- Local locks refer to exactly one system.
- Global locks are valid in all systems of the CUA.

The dialog window for setting and removing locks contains corresponding additional buttons.

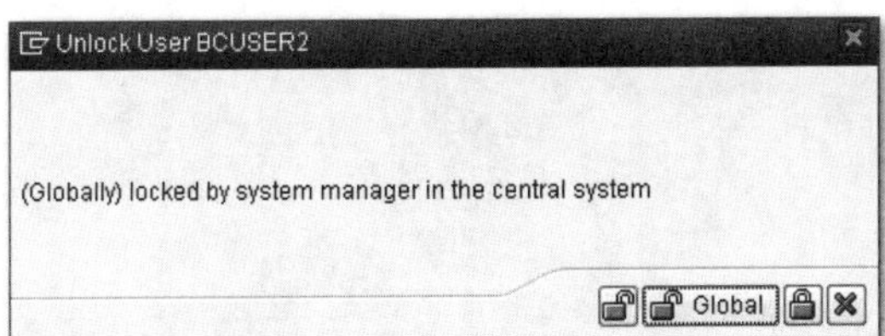

13.7.3 Troubleshooting

Problems in the CUA mainly arise from the communication between the systems involved and essentially manifest when maintained user data in the central system does not arrive in the child systems or if changes are not passed to the CUA configuration.

With regard to the error search, the first look applies to the CUA processing log in the central system. From the log, you can obtain initial notes with regard to the location and cause of the error.

1. Log on to the central system.
2. Enter Transaction "SCUL" in the command box, and press the [Enter] key (or select TOOLS • ADMINISTRATION • USER MAINTENANCE • CENTRAL USER ADMINISTRATION • SCUL—LOG DISPLAY in the standard SAP menu).
3. In the selection screen, carry out any restrictions and then click on EXECUTE (⊕).

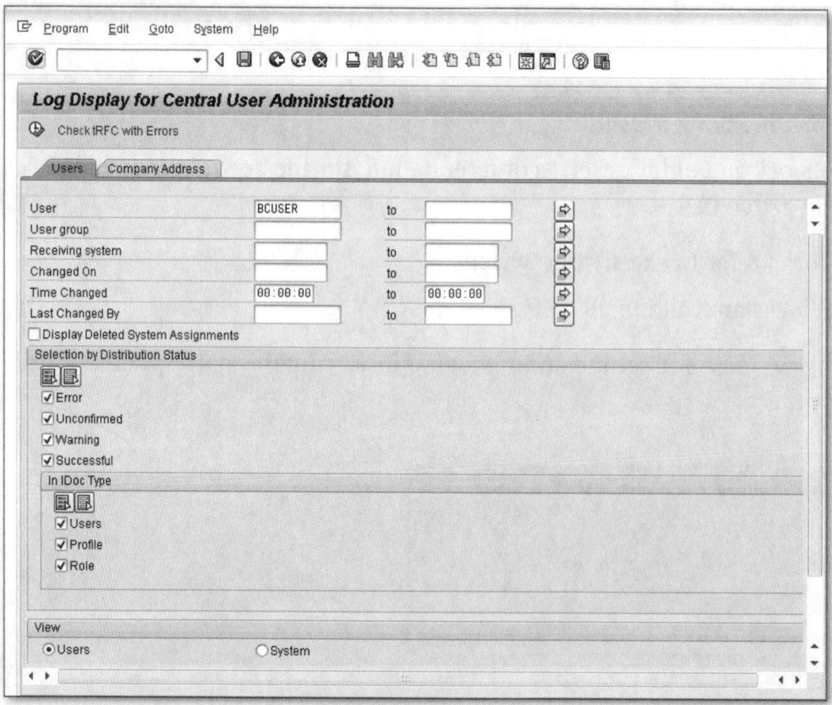

4. Check the log for notes on the subsequent error search. With the DISTRIBUTE function (), you can reactivate any incomplete processing operations.

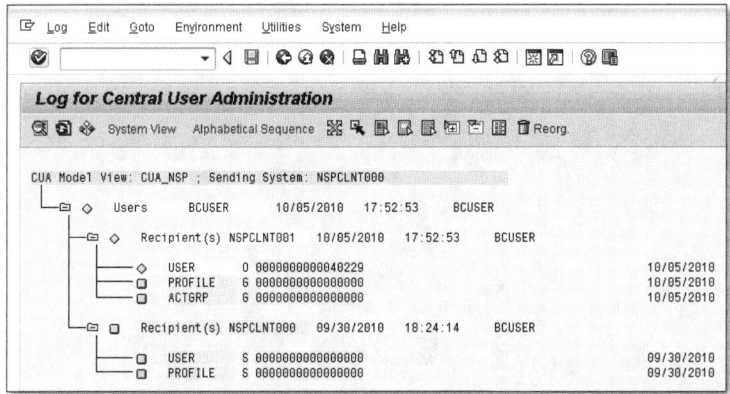

Using the IDoc Monitoring function, you can monitor data transfer.

1. Log on to the central system.
2. Enter Transaction "BD87" in the command box, and press the Enter key (or select TOOLS • ALE • ALE ADMINISTRATION • MONITORING • IDOC DISPLAY • BD87—STATUS MONITOR in the standard SAP menu).
3. Enter your selection options, and click on EXECUTE ().

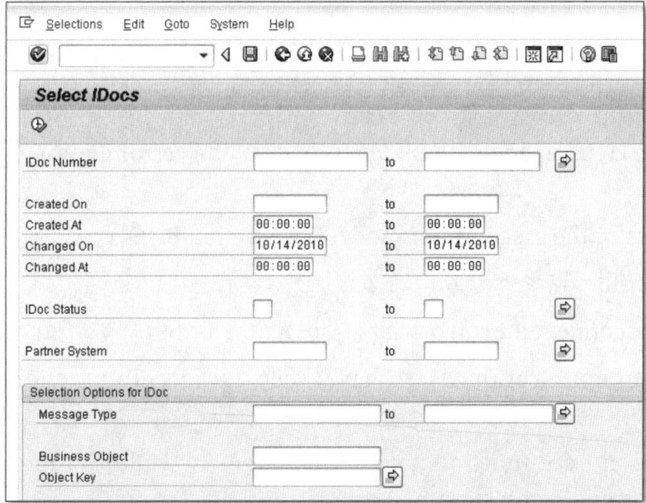

4. Search for errors in the tree structure in the processing of IDocs of type `USERCLONE` or `CCLONE`. Eliminate the cause of error indicated in the status message, and reactivate the distribution by clicking on the PROCESS button.

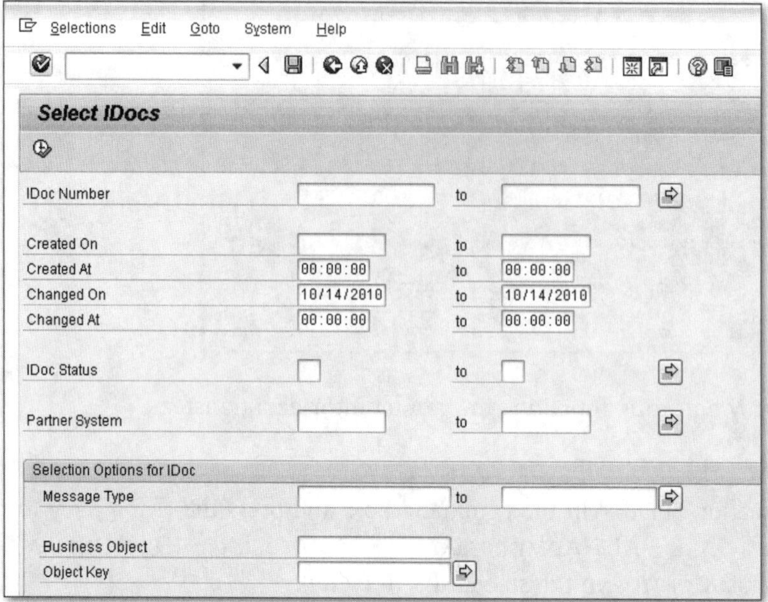

5. In the same way, check the IDoc processing in the child systems.

By checking the CUA log or calling the IDoc monitoring, you will have generally already obtained specific notes with regard to errors in your CUA. Here are some more error search tasks:

- Check your CUA system landscape for completeness and possible error messages (Transaction SCUA).
- Check the completeness of the distribution model (Transaction BD64).
- Examine the partner profiles (Transaction WE20).
- Make sure that the RFC connection is working (Transaction SM59).
- Check whether the communication users have been locked (Transaction SU01).
- Activate the authorization trace function, and evaluate missing authorizations of the communication users (Transaction ST01).

[+]

Helpful SAP Notes

Read SAP Note 333441 (CUA: Tips for problem analysis) and the general Collective Note 159885 if errors occur in your CUA.

13.7.4 Deactivating or Deleting a Central User Administration

When you delete a CUA, you must first decide whether you want to remove individual target systems from the distribution or whether you want to deactivate the CUA. In an emergency scenario in which the central system has failed, you may have to change user data (particularly authorizations) in one or several target systems. Because the assignment of authorizations is only possible in the central system, such a situation requires that you take the target system from the CUA network.

Deleting Individual Target Systems or the Entire CUA

To specifically take individual systems from the CUA or to completely deactivate the CUA, you must maintain or remove the distribution model in the central system. For this purpose, the communication user requires authorizations to set up a CUA.

1. Log on to the central system.
2. Enter Transaction "SCUA" in the command box, and press the Enter key (or select Tools • Administration • User Maintenance • Central User Administration • SCUA—Distribution Model in the standard SAP menu).

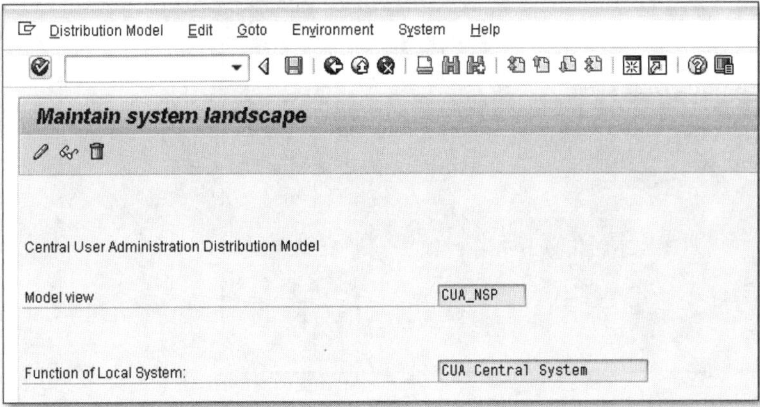

3. Click on DELETE (🗑). You are now in the DELETE CENTRAL USER ADMINISTRATION view.

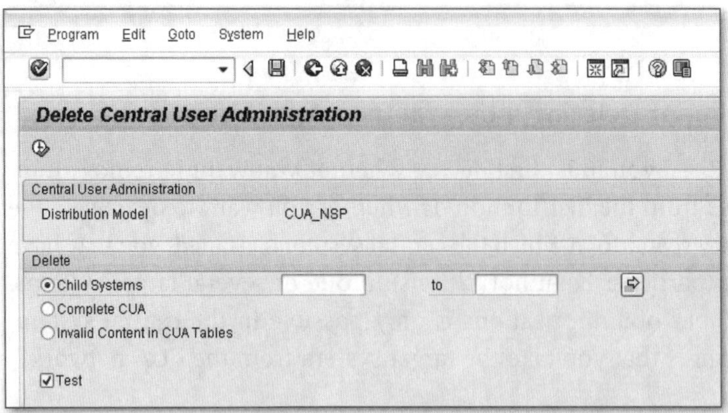

Report RSDELCUA

You can also access this function by executing report RSDELCUA.

4. If you want to remove an individual target system from the CUA, select CHILD SYSTEMS in the DELETE area, and then enter the name of the logical system. If you want to completely deactivate the CUA, select COMPLETE CUA. First leave the TEST checkmark, and then click on EXECUTE (⊕) to activate the test run.

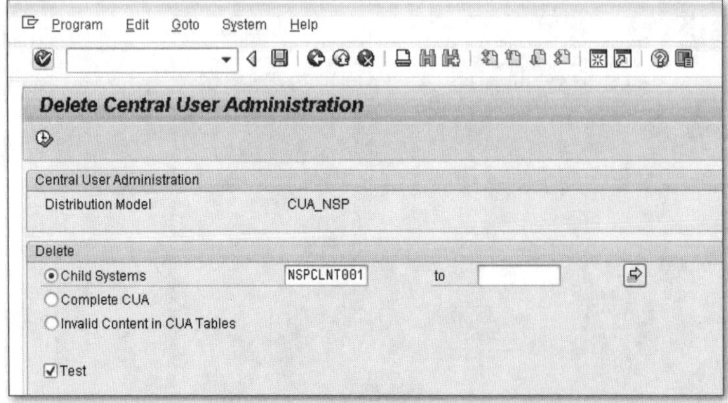

5. Check the log for error messages. If no errors are displayed, click on the Back button (⬅).

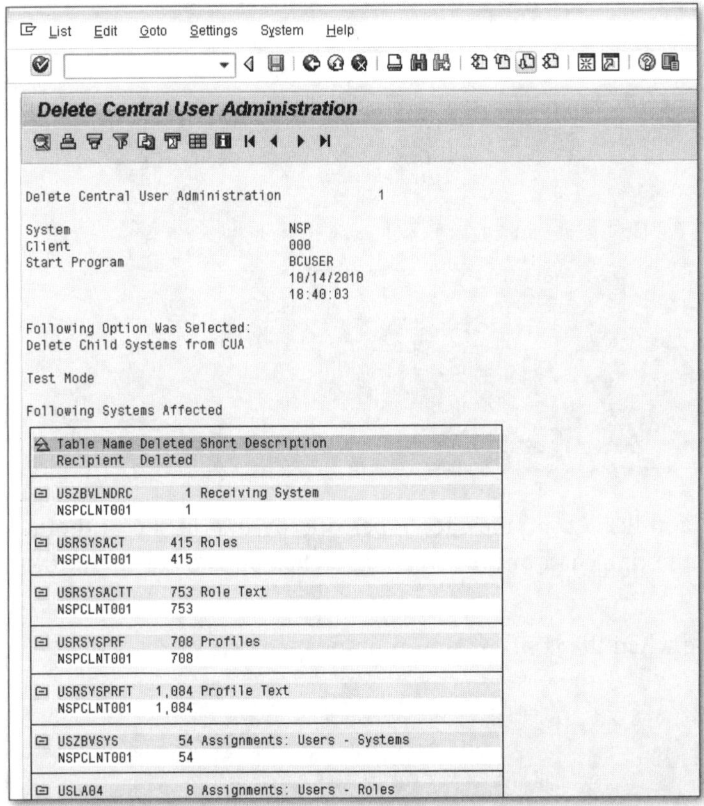

6. Now deactivate the Test checkmark, and then click again on Execute (⊕). The completion of the live run is confirmed again via log.

You then delete the partner profiles among the logical systems, central system, and child system.

1. Log on to the central system.
2. Enter Transaction "WE20" in the command box, and press the Enter key (or select Tools • ALE • ALE Administration • Runtime Settings • WE20—Partner Profiles in the standard SAP menu).
3. In the folder structure, navigate to Partner Profiles • Partner Type LS. Click on the child system that you have removed from the CUA.

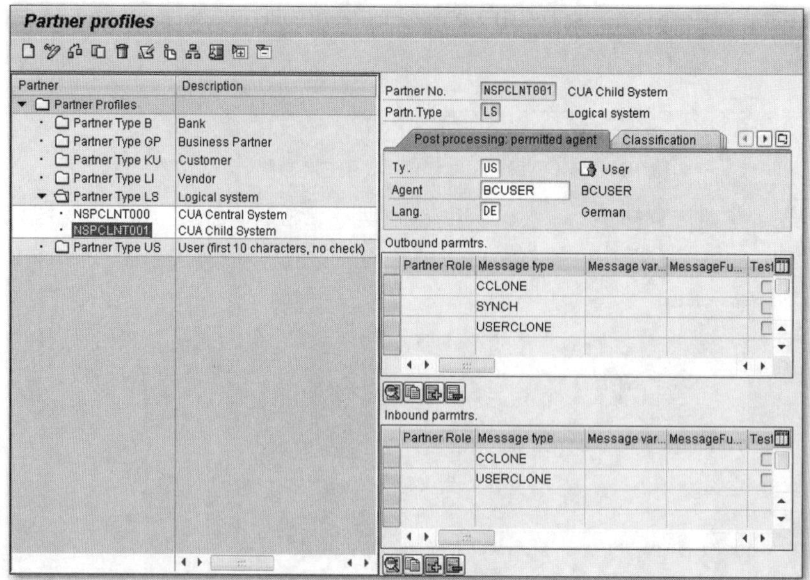

4. Select the `CCLONE` and `USERCLONE` message types one by one in the outbound parameter area in the right half of the screen, and click on DELETE OUTBOUND PARAMETER (icon).

   Click YES each time when the confirmation prompt appears.

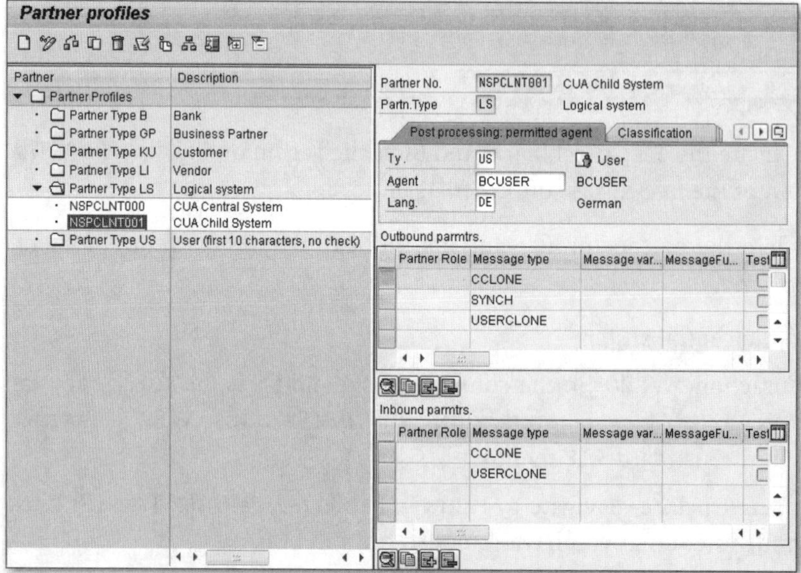

[!]

Message Type "SYNCH"

You shouldn't delete the message type SYNCH because your changes are subsequently not transferred to the child system, and you need to repeat the steps there manually.

5. When you've deleted the entire CUA, highlight the PARTNER TYPE LS for the central system, and remove it by clicking on DELETE (🗑). In this case, you can also delete the message type SYNCH of the child system or the whole partner profile LS of the child system, as long as no other message type remains.

After the partner profiles have been removed, you can clean up the distribution model.

1. Log on to the central system.
2. Activate Transaction BD64 (Maintenance of Distribution Model).
3. Go to the change mode by clicking SWITCH BETWEEN DISPLAY AND EDIT MODE (✎).
4. Navigate in the tree structure to CENTRAL USER ADMINISTRATION. Expand the node of your central system and then your child system's node that you have deleted from the CUA.

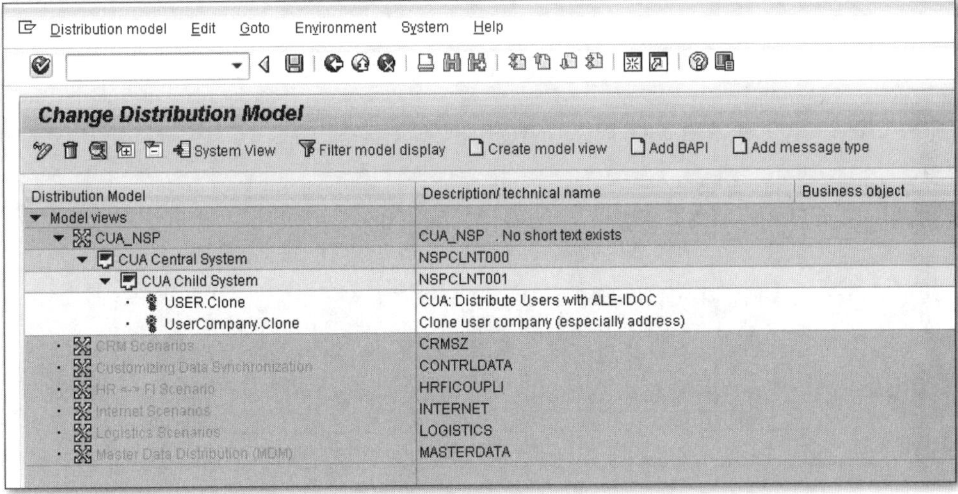

5. Highlight the BAPIs USER.CLONE and USERCOMPANY.CLONE one by one and delete them (🗑). If you completely deleted the CUA, highlight the model view CENTRAL USER ADMINISTRATION and delete it (🗑).

   The view is deleted with all its lower-level nodes (central and child systems).
6. Save your changes (💾). Then highlight the CENTRAL USER ADMINISTRATION model view, and execute in the EDIT • MODEL VIEW • DISTRIBUTE menu bar.
7. In the dialog window, highlight the deleted child system, and confirm by clicking CONTINUE (✔). The distribution isn't needed as long as you have deleted the complete model view in the previous step.

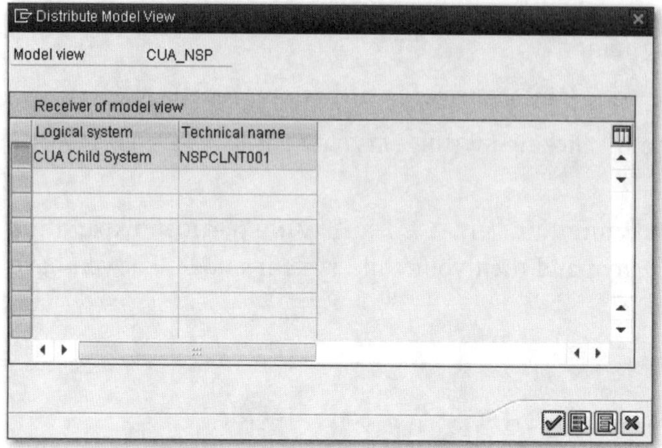

8. Check the log, and click on CONTINUE (✔).

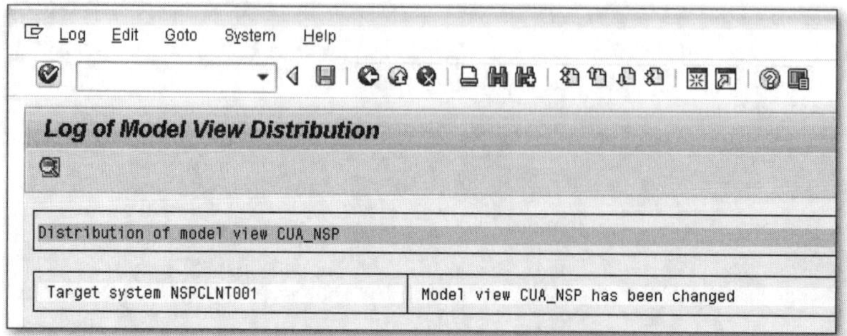

9. Via Transaction SCUA (Distribution Model), check whether the child system has been removed or whether the distribution model has been deleted from the model view.

After you have processed the steps in the central system, you still need to delete the partner profiles and the distribution model in the child system:

1. Delete the INPUT PARAMETERS CCLONE and USERCLONE for the central system in Transaction WE20 (Partner Profiles).

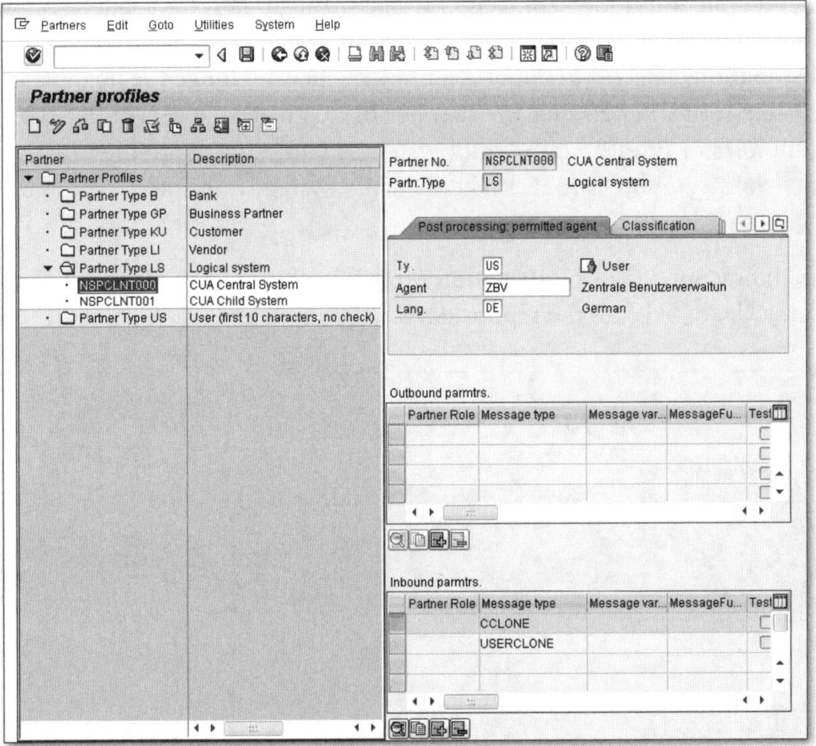

2. Call Transaction BD64 (Maintenance of Distribution Model), and navigate to the change mode. Highlight the CENTRAL USER ADMINISTRATION model view, and click on DELETE (🗑). In the dialog window, confirm with YES, and save the changes.

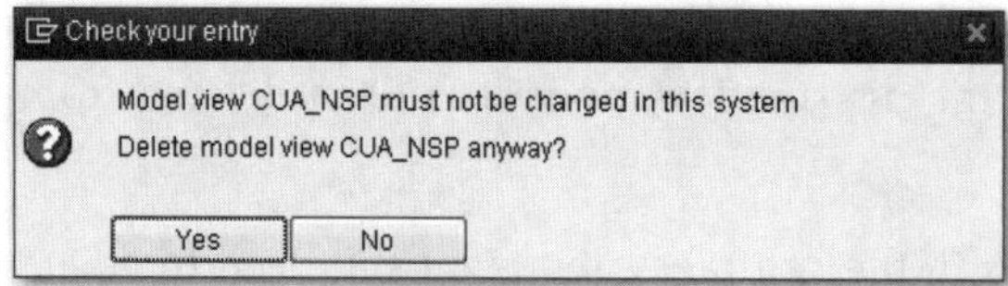

You have now completely removed the child system from the CUA.

Emergency Deactivation of the CUA in the Target System

In an emergency situation, the connection to the CUA can fail, for example, as a result of a breakdown in the central system. Depending on how you have configured the field distribution, changes to important user data may no longer be possible in the child system. You will definitely neither be able to create any users nor assign authorization roles or profiles in the child system. To quickly restore the capacity to act in the child system, you must take the child system from the CUA. To do this, follow these steps:

1. Activate Transaction SCUA (Distribution Model) in the child system, and click on DELETE (), or execute the report RSDELCUA.

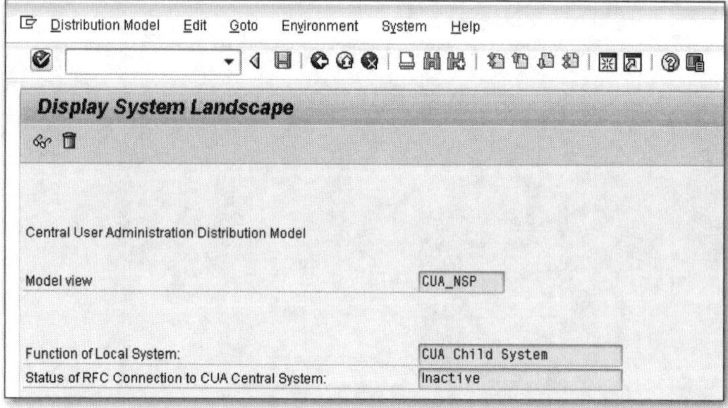

2. Select CHILD SYSTEMS, and initially leave the TEST checkmark activated. Click on EXECUTE ().

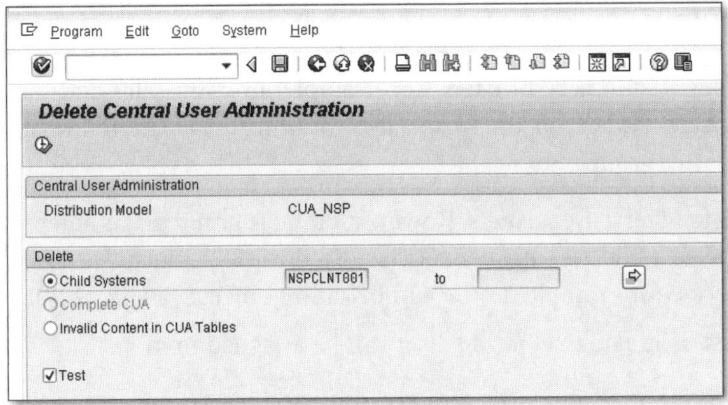

3. Check the log, and click on BACK () if no errors have occurred. Deactivate the TEST checkmark in the previous screen, and execute the live run ().

You can now create and maintain the user master data in the child system independently of the CUA. You can re-include the child system again into the CUA after you've dealt with the exceptional situation by calling the distribution model in the central system via Transaction SCUA in the change mode, highlighting the deleted target system, and distributing the CUA settings again to the child system via SAVE SELECTED SYSTEMS.

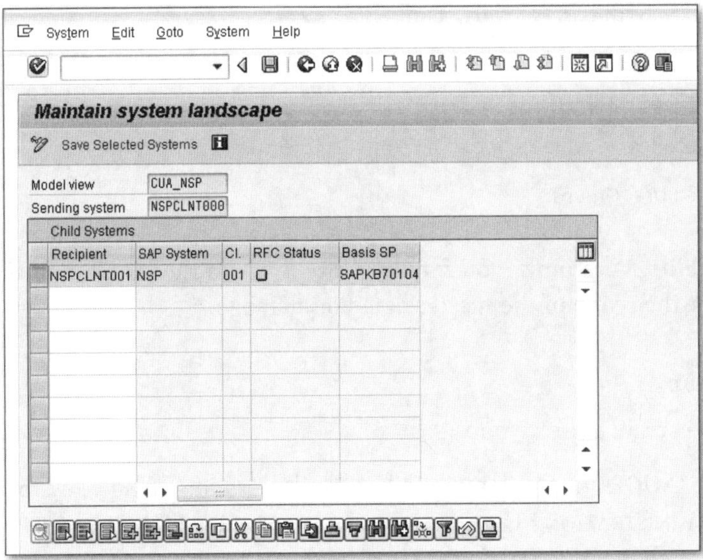

13.8 User Groups

A user group is a logical summary of users, for example, users in sales and distribution, incoming sales orders, or the financial accounting area. The following restrictions apply to user groups:

- A user can belong to several user groups. However, only the group that is entered in the LOGONDATA tab in the user maintenance (see Section 13.2) is included in the authorization checks (for example, in the authorization object S_USER_GRP).
- A user group must be created before the user can be assigned to it.

The purpose of a user group is to restrict the access to specific user masters in the authorization check and also to facilitate the user administration (for example, mass maintenance; see Section 13.4).

The usage of the following special groups is recommended (see Table 13.1).

Group	Definition
TERM	No longer current users. User data can then be retained in the system for identification purposes. ▸ All users of this group should be locked. ▸ When the users of the group are not used as a template, the security profiles of the users are deleted.
SUPER	Users with full authorization (authorization profiles SAP_ALL or SAP_NEW).
TEMPLATE	Template users, which serve as a template to set up actual users.

Table 13.1 Recommended User Groups

When you define additional groups, you can orientate these to the requirements of your enterprise or the scope of the master data you manage.

Creating a User Group

Follow these steps to create a user group:

1. Enter Transaction "SUGR" in the command box, and press the [Enter] key (or select TOOLS • ADMINISTRATION • USER MAINTENANCE • SUGR—USER GROUPS in the standard SAP menu).

2. Enter a name for the user group, which you want to set up (for example, "Sales"), and click on the Create User Group button ( ).

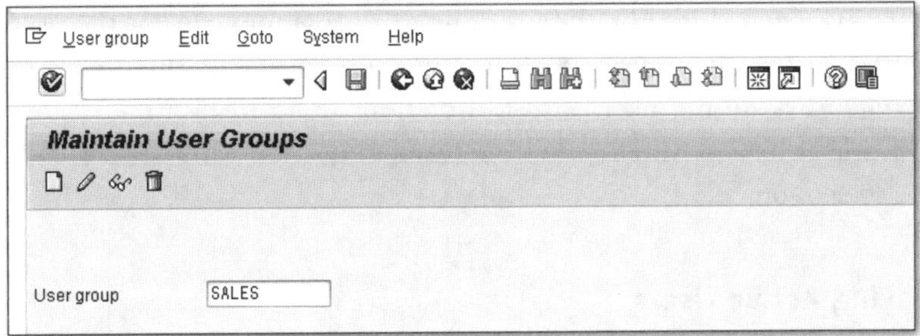

3. Enter a description of the user group in the Text field.
4. Add users to the group under User Assignment.
5. Click on Save. A message confirms that the new user group has been set up.

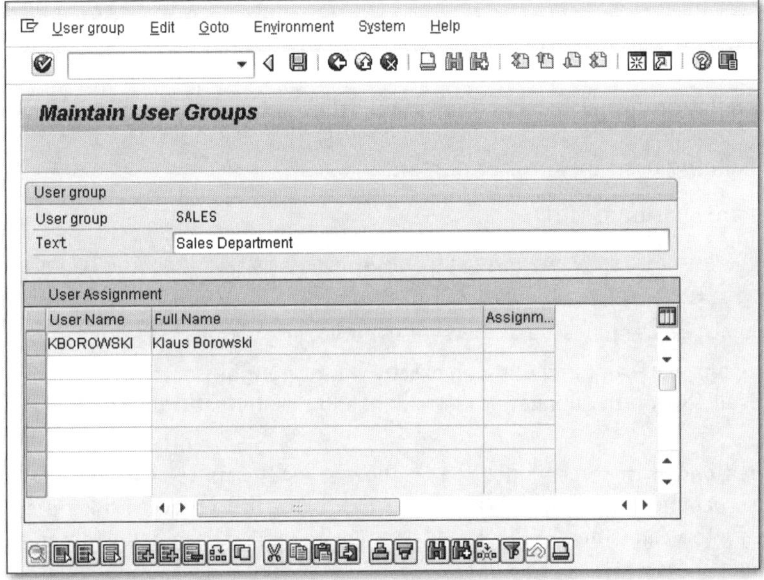

[+]

Assignment via the User Group

You can also assign users to user groups in the user maintenance (Transaction SU01) via the Groups tab.

13.9 Deleting User Sessions

System administration may need to delete a user session. For example, the user session may not have been closed by the user due to a program error, or the user may have forgotten to log off from the SAP system and locked data that needs to be urgently changed by another user. Also in situations that threaten the system stability (e.g., if a user has activated comprehensive tools), the only secure path may be to end the session.

13.9.1 Displaying Active Users

First, check the user modes in the cases described. Using Transaction SM04 (User Overview), all users logged on to the system can be displayed. The user ID and the terminal name are displayed. If your system contains several instances, you can display the user sessions via Transaction AL08 (Global Users) extensively.

In a smaller enterprise, the system administrator can easily identify user IDs logged on to unusual terminals. An unusual terminal can mean that a person other than that belonging to the user ID has logged on under this name.

If a user has logged on to more than one terminal, this could mean the following:

- The user ID is being used by another person.
- Several users are sharing this ID.

[+]

One User ID per User

A user ID should not be used by several users for the following reasons:

- If a problem occurs, you can't find out who exactly was responsible for it. It therefore becomes difficult for you to eliminate the problem and ensure that it doesn't occur again.
- For security reasons, it isn't recommended to allow several users to share one ID. Use the profile parameter `login/disable_multi_gui_login` to prevent this from occurring. Using the parameter `login/multi_login_users`, you can define exceptions in authorized cases.
- External auditors could run this test to check their security mechanisms.

System with Only One Instance

If your system only has one instance, use Transaction SM04 to display the active users.

1. Enter Transaction "SM04" in the command box, and press the [Enter] key (or select TOOLS • ADMINISTRATION • MONITOR • SYSTEM MONITORING • SM04—USER OVERVIEW in the standard SAP menu).
2. Select the desired user ID, and click on SESSIONS. The SESSION LIST displays which sessions this user has generated.

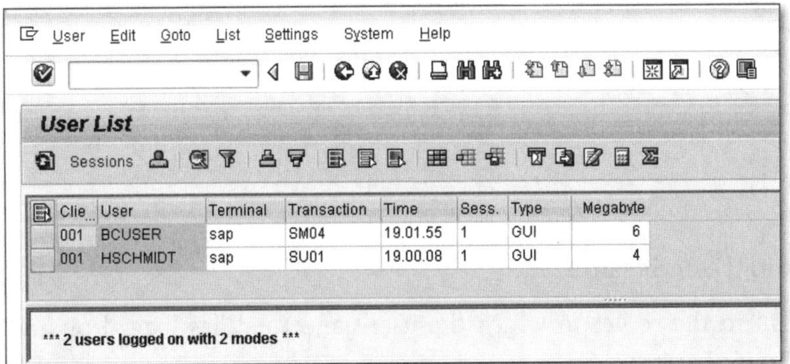

3. Click on CONTINUE (✔).

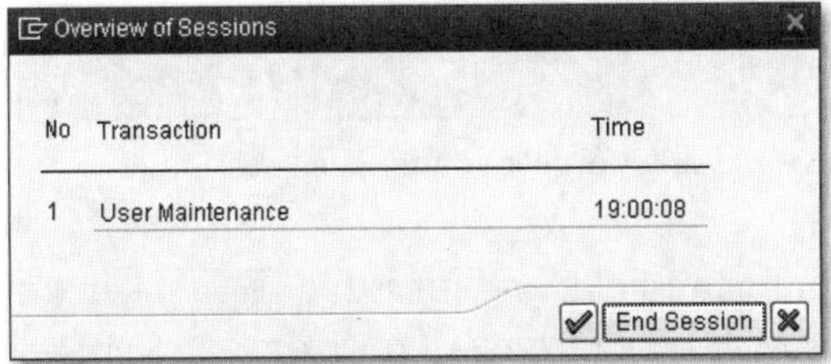

System with Several Instances

If you have several instances in your system, it's easier to use Transaction AL08 because you can display all users in all instances of the system at the same time.

1. Enter Transaction "AL08" in the command box, and press [Enter] (or you can also select the following menu path in the standard SAP menu: TOOLS • ADMINISTRATION • MONITOR • PERFORMANCE • EXCEPTIONS/USERS • ACTIVE USERS • AL08—GLOBAL USERS).
2. All instances of your system and the number of active users are displayed. You can view a list for each instance with the users that are currently logged on to an instance.

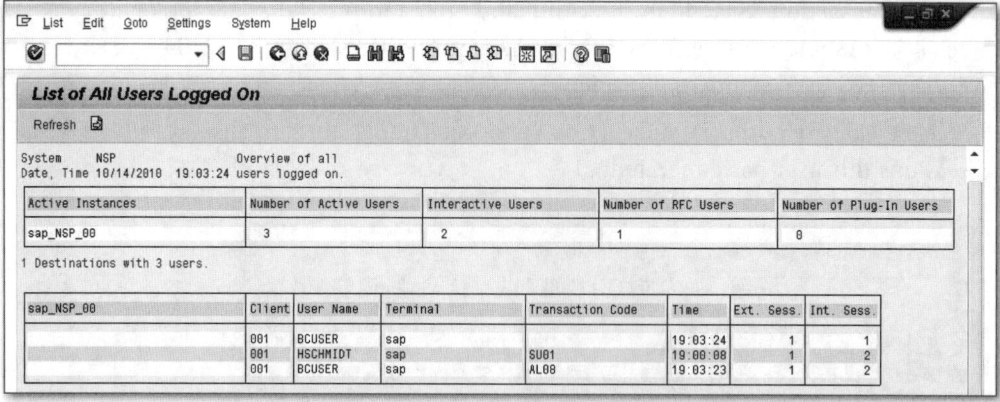

13.9.2 Deleting User Session

You must log on to the server to which the user concerned has logged on and process the following steps:

1. Check whether the user has actually logged off the SAP system and that no SAP GUI window is still open. Check the user's computer, if applicable.

[+]

Checking Logoff

The check is important because users have possibly forgotten a reduced session.

2. Enter Transaction "SM04" in the command field, and press the Enter key (or select the TOOLS • ADMINISTRATION • MONITOR • SYSTEM MONITORING • SM04—USER OVERVIEW menu path).
3. Select the user ID concerned.
4. Select the SESSIONS button.

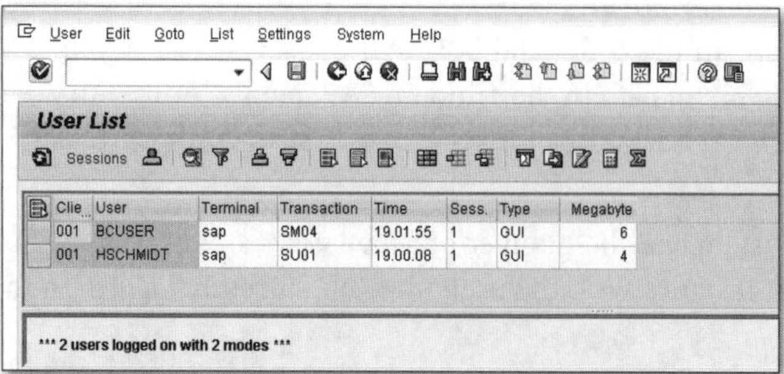

5. Select the session to be deleted, and click on END SESSION. The end session process might take some time.
6. Repeat step 5 until all sessions for this user have been deleted.

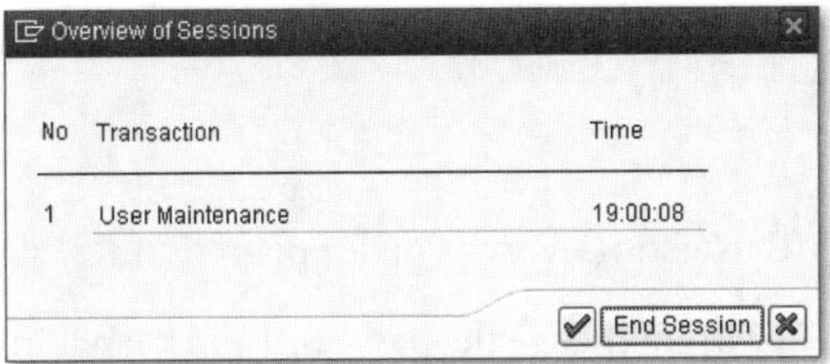

Transaction SM04 can display a user that has already logged off the system as still active. This is the case, for example, when the user session has not been ended properly. This can be caused by the following:

- A network failure that results in the user no longer having access to the network or to the SAP system
- Users who switch off their computers without logging off the SAP system

You can, however, close these user sessions. If possible, consult the user in advance.

13.10 System Administration

As a system administrator, you need to take some special features into consideration. These include the usage of special standard users, how to deal with the assignment of full authorizations, and the options you have to improve password and logon security.

13.10.1 Special User IDs

Both user IDs SAP* and DDIC exist by default with full authorization in each client of the SAP system. Furthermore, the user EARLYWATCH is created in client 066 during the installation process. The default passwords of these users are generally known (see Table 13.2). You should therefore change them immediately to prevent the unauthorized use of these two special user IDS. In the case of user EARLYWATCH, it isn't quite so urgent because this user only has very restricted authorizations.

User	Standard Password
SAP*	06071992
DDIC	19920706
EARLYWATCH	support

Table 13.2 Standard Passwords

You should not use both SAP* and DDIC users for everyday administration tasks.

You can use the DDIC user as an emergency user. Change the password and keep it in a safe place. You can also lock the user if you apply another emergency concept.

You must not delete user ID SAP*. Instead, you should change the password and lock the user ID. If the user ID SAP* is deleted, a logon with the user and the standard password *pass* is possible. The authorizations are replaced with rights, which are directly programmed in the SAP system. User ID SAP* therefore contains incalculable and unverifiable security rights.

13.10.2 Special Authorizations

Users SAP* and DDIC have the authorization profile SAP_ALL, which is equal to a full authorization in the system in conjunction with the supplementary authorization profile SAP_NEW. Assign these in a respectively restrictive way.

[!]

Authorization Profiles SAP_ALL and SAP_NEW

Authorization profiles SAP_ALL and SAP_NEW are extensive and pose a threat and a security risk to the system. Each person who requests similar security rights must be able to justify this adequately. Personal convenience is *not* acknowledged as a valid reason.

Particularly in medium and large enterprises, it's not usually appropriate to issue the profiles SAP_ALL und SAP_NEW to developers for development and test systems. For this, they should list special develop authorization roles.

Avoid assigning SAP_ALL and SAP_NEW in production systems. Even system administrators should obtain customized authorization roles. For emergency cases, create special users with SAP_ALL and SAP_NEW, and keep the password safe.

13.10.3 User Passwords

Using several profile parameters, you can specify conditions for user passwords (see Table 13.3). Acquaint yourself with the password rules in place for Microsoft Windows or for other applications. Also consider the explanations in Chapter 10.

- Passwords should be valid for a specific period.
- Passwords should have a certain minimum length.
- Passwords should consist of a combination of (uppercase/lowercase) letters, digits, and special characters.
- Certain letters and digit sequences should be prohibited (maintain Table USR40 for this purpose).
- Users should be locked after a specific number of unsuccessful logon attempts.

Profile Parameters	Explanation
login/min_password_diff	Minimum number of different characters between old and new passwords
login/min_password_diff	Minimum number of digits in passwords
login/min_password_diff	Minimum number of letters in passwords
login/min_password_lng	Minimum length of passwords
login/min_password_diff	Minimum number of small digits in passwords
login/min_password_lng	Minimum number of special characters in passwords
login/min_password_diff	Minimum number of capital letters in passwords
login/password_max_new_valid	Minimum wait time between two changes of password via the user
login/password_expiration_time	Validity period of passwords
login/password_max_reset_valid	Scope of history for passwords already used
login/password_max_reset_valid	Validity period for unused initial passwords
login/failed_user_auto_unlock	Activate/deactivate automatic locking of users

Table 13.3 Important Profile Parameters for User Passwords

Profile Parameters	Explanation
`login/fails_to_session_end`	Number of failed logons until closing of logon screen
`login/fails_to_user_lock`	Number of failed logons until locking of user

Table 13.3 Important Profile Parameters for User Passwords (Cont.)

[+]

SAP Note 2467

You can find general information on passwords in the SAP system in SAP Note 2467.

13.11 Summary

In this chapter, the fundamental tasks of user administration have been described; for example, how to create, change, lock, or delete user master records. Mass maintenance facilitates the administration of many users, and a CUA is of great benefit in a large system landscape. You can bring structure into your user master records via user groups.

The user administration is among the most security-relevant aspects of system administration. Use it with due care. The next chapter deals with the authorization administration in the SAP system, a topic closely linked to user administration.

With authorizations, you control which user obtains which permissions within the SAP system. This chapter describes how the SAP system checks the authorizations of a user. You also learn how to create and assign authorization roles and profiles.

14 Authorization Management

Besides user administration, the assignment of authorization is another security-relevant task area of SAP administration. In contrast to user administration, the authorization system is mainly characterized by business needs; in other words, the user's departments of your enterprise will determine to a large extent how authorizations are assigned. For example, the HR department must be consulted when the HR module is implemented or if personal data of employees are managed in the system. Furthermore, coordination with external auditors, legal and other (enterprise-internal) regulations should be in place. Consult your external auditors with regard to requirements that are made on the audit-related internal control of user administration.

Usually, enterprises organize their user and authorization administration according to the segregation of duties principle and implement it technically (via appropriate authorizations). The administrator who creates and maintains users usually can't assign authorizations and vice versa. This can't always be implemented in small enterprises. In these cases, you must ensure that at least the user request procedure strictly implements the required approval steps.

This book limits the authorization management topic to a general, technically oriented introduction. For more in-depth information, please refer to *Authorizations in SAP Software: Design and Configuration* (Boston: SAP PRESS, 2010).

14.1 Authorization Check Process

The authorization check entails multiple phases in the SAP system. When a transaction is started, the system first checks based on the authorization object S_TCODE whether the user is authorized to execute the transaction. If the user doesn't have this authorization, the transaction is not called. Besides the check of the transaction authorization, the system runs additional authorization checks within the transaction if specific actions are carried out. Which authorization objects are addressed with which click and how many checks are made depends on the source code and therefore varies considerably for every transaction.

Authorization objects bundle one or more *fields* whose combination map an action in the SAP system. This usually involves multiple possible activities (for example, create, change, or display) in connection with an object in the system (for example, a table or an authorization role). In this context, the activity and the object represent a field within the authorization object. The respective activity or the explicit object is entered as *field values* in the authorization field. The combination of several field values represents an *authorization* (for example, change the SAP_BC_SEC_AUTH_ADMIN role). For reasons of manageability, related authorization objects are grouped in *object classes*, which are organized by application areas or modules.

Users may only execute actions in the SAP system if they have the relevant permission. If they don't have permission for specific actions, they may not execute them. Users obtain permission to execute an action by having the required authorization assigned. This is done either via *authorization roles* or using *authorization profiles*.

14.2 Authorization Roles

Authorization roles—in contrast to authorization profiles—are the technically up to date form for assigning authorizations. They are based on the technology of authorization profiles but are considerably easier to maintain and manage and provide many more options. The role concept seizes the approach to bundle all authorizations required for a specific task. To what extent a technical role actually maps the respective workplace within your enterprise mainly depends on the enterprise's size, structure and security or confidentiality requirement. The SAP modules used also play a role here. An employee usually has several authorization roles whose combination describes the workplace. You define and describe the structure according to which you organize your authorization roles (for example, according to modules, tasks, business areas, and so on) in an *authorization concept*.

There are two types of authorization roles:

- Single roles
- Composite roles

In *single roles*, you can add authorization objects to assign them to users. *Composite roles*, by contrast, enable you to combine single roles for easier management. Authorizations can't be added to composite roles.

The Profile Generator is the central access point for all tasks with regard to the maintenance of authorization roles. Here you create, change and copy single and composite roles; assign them to users; and transfer them to other SAP systems.

14.2.1 Creating and Maintaining Single Roles

Carry out the following steps to create a single role:

1. Enter Transaction "PFCG" in the command box, and press the [Enter] key (or select the menu option TOOLS • ADMINISTRATION • USER MAINTENANCE • ROLE ADMINISTRATION • PFCG—ROLES).
2. Enter a suitable name for the new authorization role in the ROLE field, and click SINGLE ROLE.

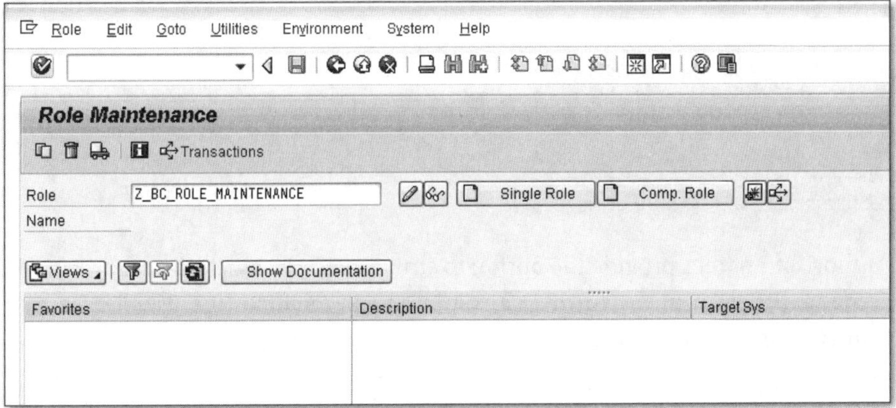

3. In the next screen, enter a meaningful DESCRIPTION. You can use the LONG TEXT field for a more comprehensive description on the content and purpose or also for a change history.

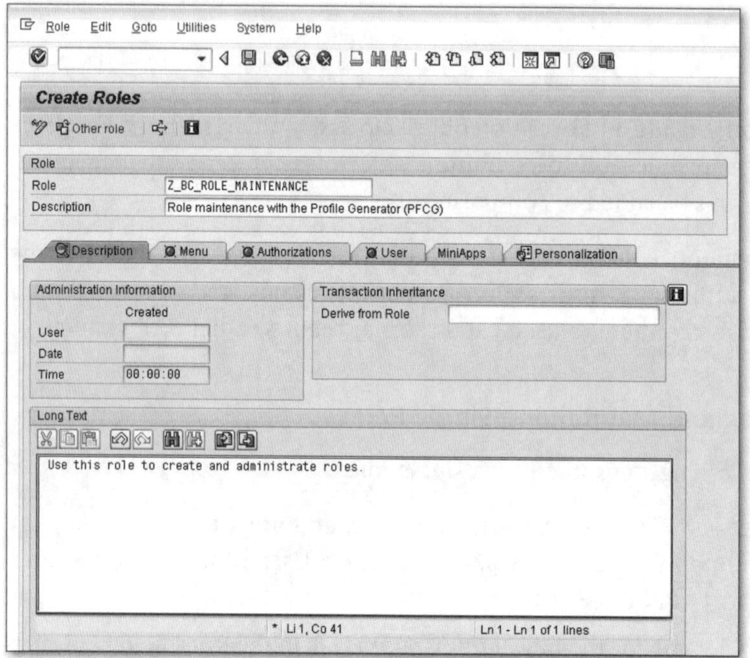

4. Go to the MENU tab. The system prompts you to save the role. Confirm with YES.

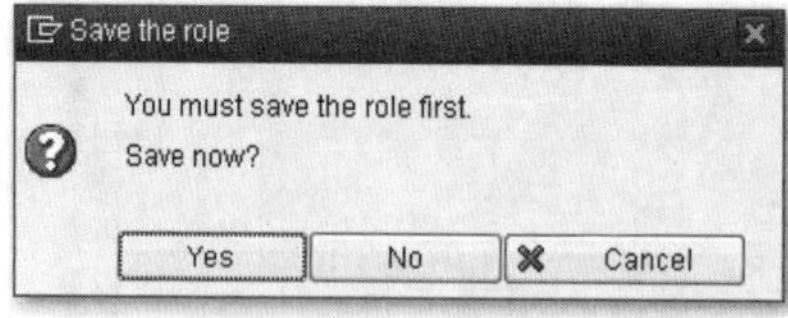

Authorization roles provide the option to structure the transaction authorizations contained therein in the form of a role menu to facilitate the users' access to transactions. Continue with the role menu maintenance:

5. Create a new folder in the role menu using the CREATE FOLDER button ( ).

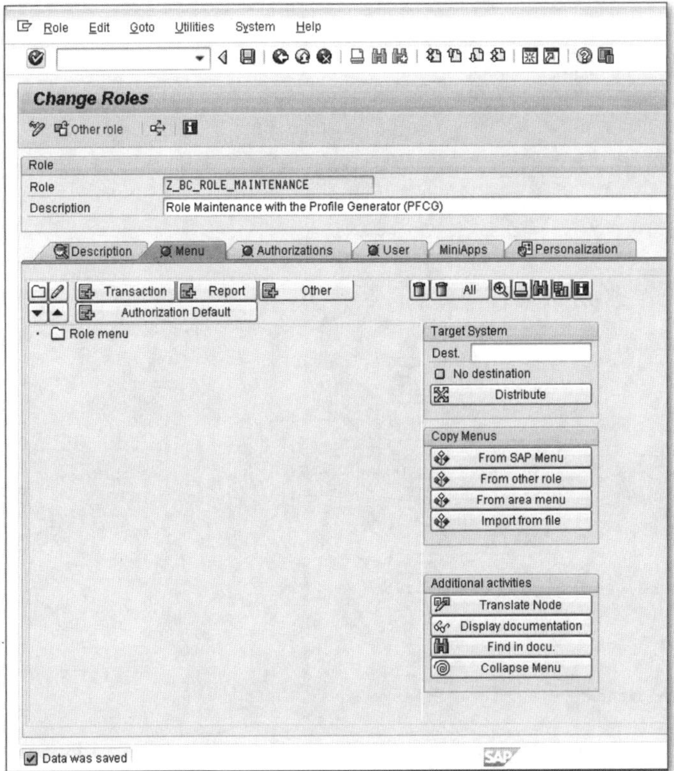

6. The system opens a dialog window, Create a folder, where you enter a name. Click Continue (✔).

7. The system creates the folder in the role menu. Select this folder, and click the Transaction button.

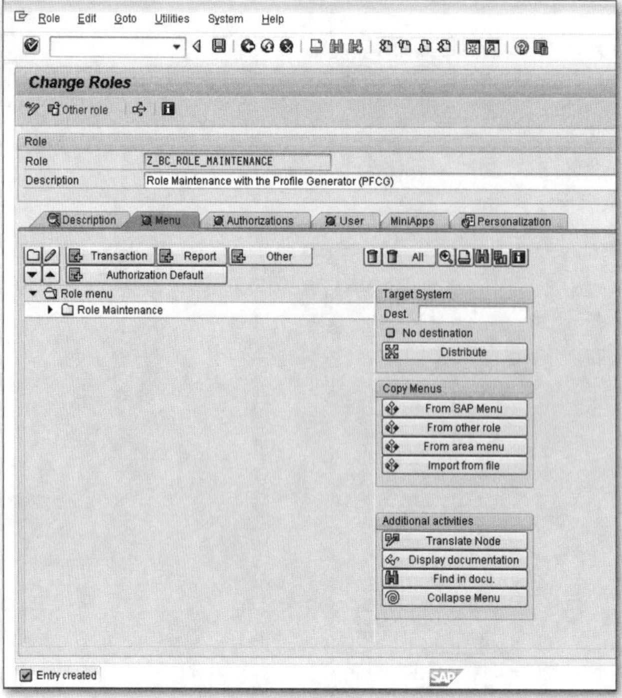

8. Enter the transaction that is supposed to be assigned to the role, and press the [Enter] key to confirm. The system determines the text for the transaction selected. Click ASSIGN TRANSACTIONS.

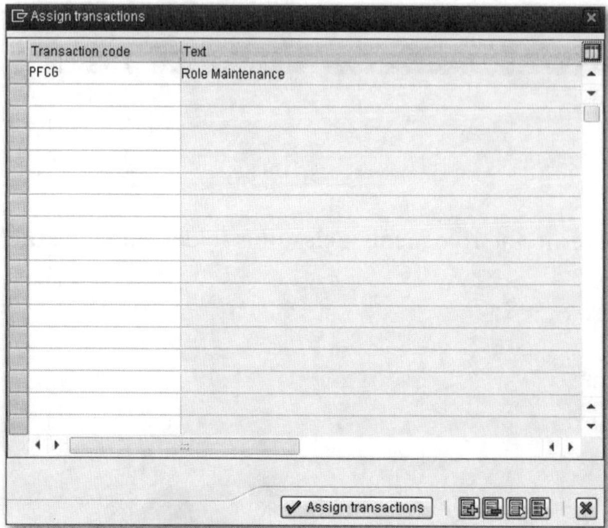

[+]

Content of the Role Menu

In the role menu, you can enter not only transactions but also the following:

- Programs (ABAP reports)
- Queries
- Transaction variants
- URLs
- Files
- Business Warehouse reports

Besides the manual menu maintenance, you can also import specific menu parts from the SAP menu or the SAP area menu, from already existing menus of other authorization roles, as well as external files into your role. You can sort the role menu via drag and drop.

As soon as you've added transactions to the menu, the status of the MENU tab changes to green. For the role to function, you maintain the role's authorization profile in the next step:

1. Go to the AUTHORIZATIONS tab. The Information About Authorization Profile is empty for newly created roles. Without a maintained and generated authorization profile, however, you can't assign authorizations using a role. Click PROPOSE PROFILE NAMES (icon) to have the system generate a profile name and profile text.

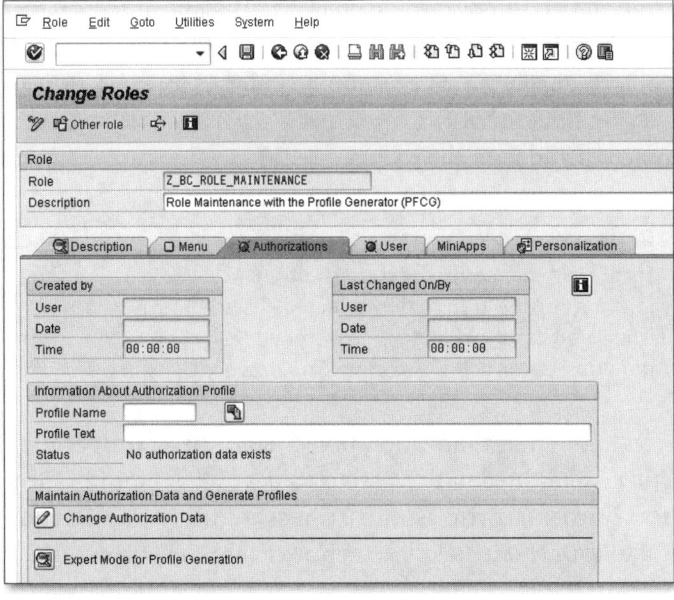

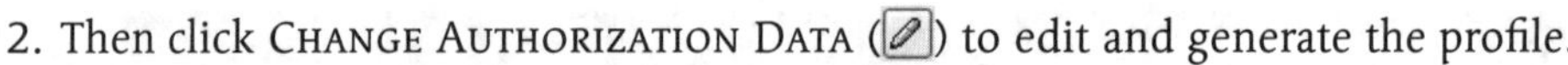

2. Then click CHANGE AUTHORIZATION DATA (✎) to edit and generate the profile.

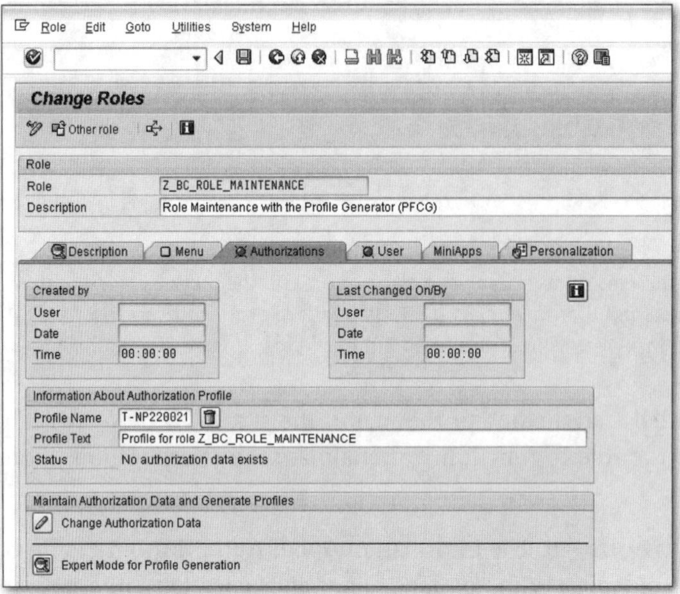

3. The system prompts you to save the role. Confirm with Yes.
4. In the next view, you assign authorizations by defining the authorization objects. Based on the check indicator (see box), the system has already added several authorization objects to the role. Expand the tree structure to obtain an overview of the authorization objects suggested. For example, under CROSS-APPLICATION AUTHORIZATION OBJECTS • TRANSACTION CODE CHECK AT TRANSACTION START, you can find the transaction added to the menu.

[✿]

Check Indicator

After you've entered transactions in the menu, the system automatically suggests authorization objects that are relevant for the transaction selected. These default values are determined based on the check indicator defined in the system (see Section 14.4.1). You can add further authorization objects or delete suggested objects.

5. In the structure, navigate to an authorization object (and the corresponding authorization fields) that is indicated with Missing Values (○△○) for instance, BASIS: ADMINISTRATION • AUTHORIZATIONS: ROLE CHECK). Click on the CHANGE ICON (✎) in front of the ROLE NAME field to enter or change field values.

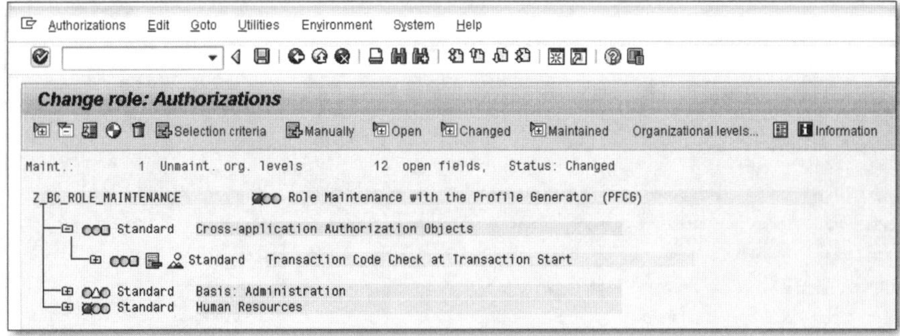

6. A Field values dialog window is opened. Maintain the desired values in the table. Click on TRANSFER ( ) when you're done.

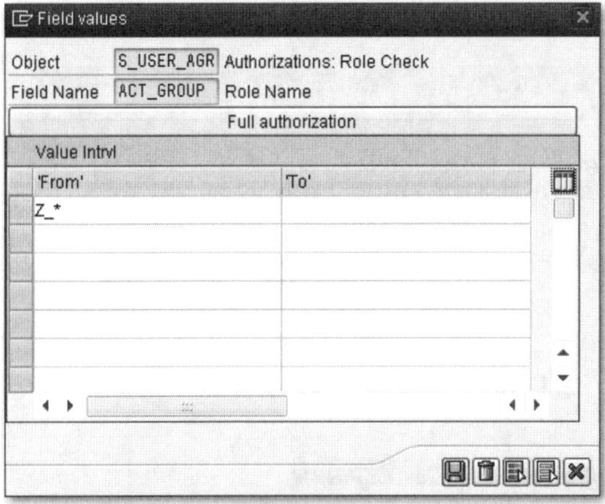

7. The field values are transferred. If values are defined for all fields of an object, the status display changes to ALL MAINTAINED ( ). Repeat these steps for all of the other authorization objects with the Missing Values status ( ).

Activating the Technical Name [+]

If you frequently work with authorizations, you'll find it useful to switch the view to technical IDs via the UTILITIES • TECHNICAL NAMES ON menu path. This enables you to find specific authorization objects more easily.

Via UTILITIES • SETTINGS, you can have the system display additional icons for processing authorizations.

8. The VARIABLES MISSING status ( ) means that not all organizational levels have been maintained yet. Click the ORGANIZATIONAL LEVELS button to fill the variables.

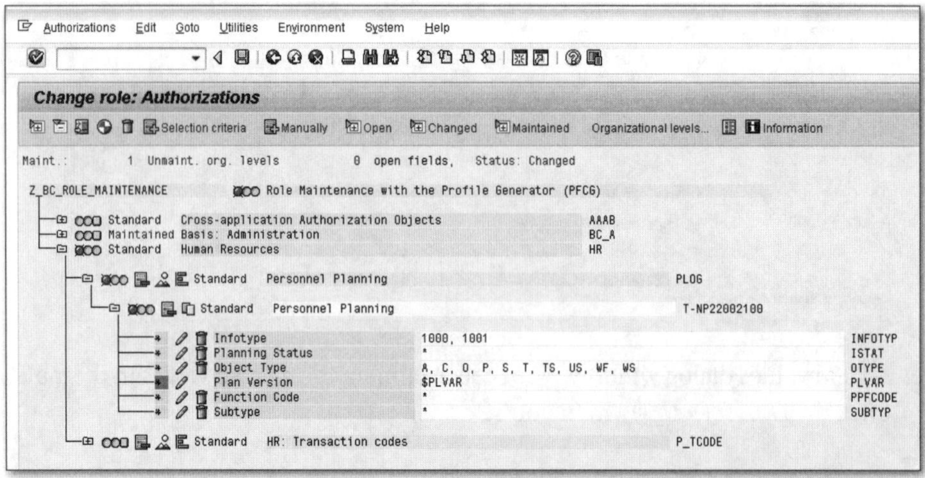

[!]

Organizational Levels

Organizational levels are field values that are used in many authorization objects with the same value and can therefore be maintained comprehensively as variables (for example, company code, controlling area, and so on). Try to avoid maintaining accordingly highlighted fields directly in the authorization object because you then override the role-wide value of the variable.

9. Enter a value for the variable, and click SAVE.

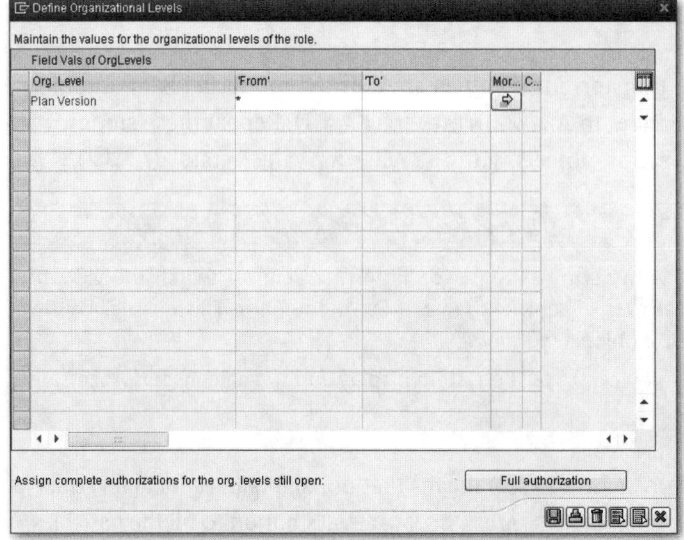

Value *

In the authorization system, the value * stands for the full authorization. It can be assigned for all types of authorization fields, that is, both for application objects (for example, role names) and for activities. For activities, the value * authorizes the user to execute all actions for the respective application object.

10. After you've maintained all authorization objects, click SAVE.

    Then you must generate the authorization to create the authorization profile of the role.

    Click BACK to exit the view.

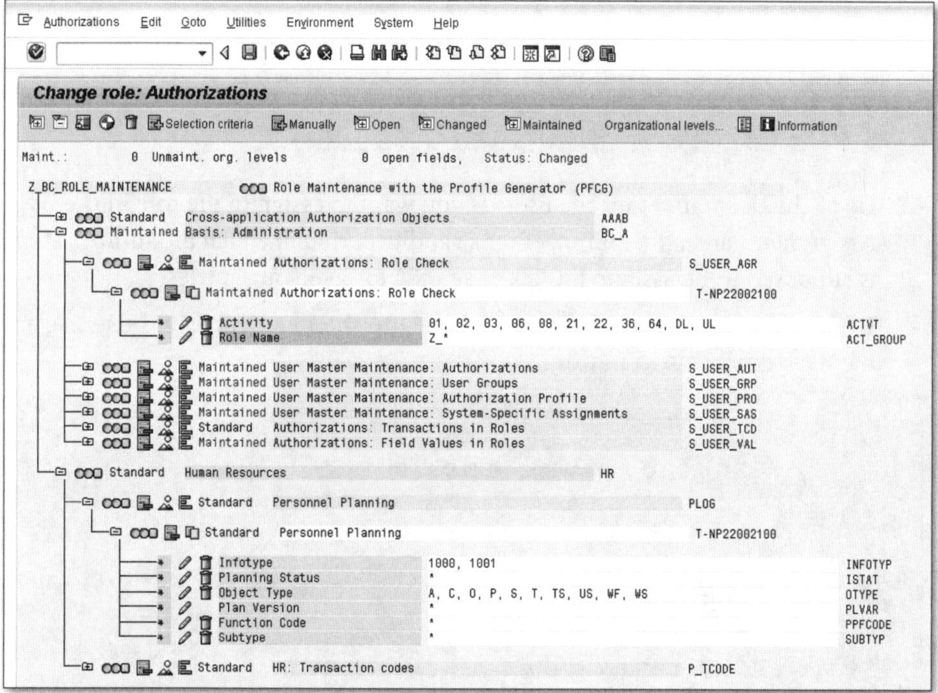

11. The status of the AUTHORIZATIONS tab is green now; the status of the authorization profile is GENERATED.

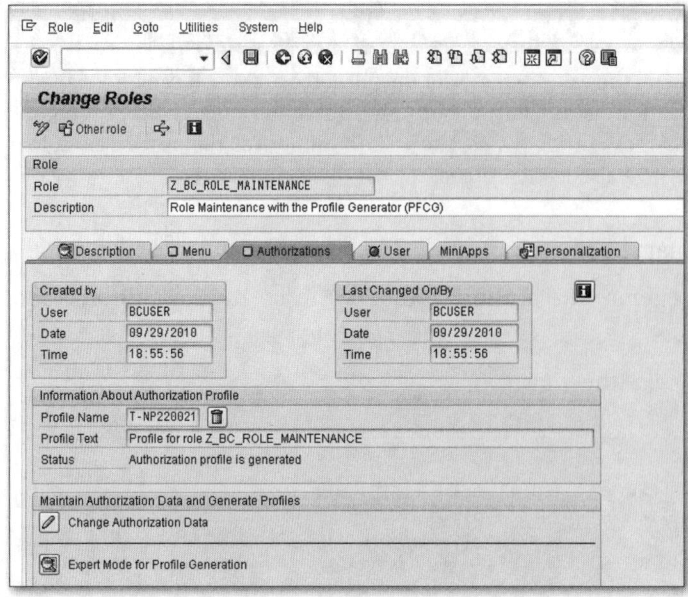

12. Go to the User tab. Enter the user ID you want to assign to the role in the User Assignments area. If required, enter a validity period in which the authorization is supposed to be assigned. Click Save (💾) to save your entries.

    To provide the authorization immediately to the newly assigned user, select the USER COMPARISON button.

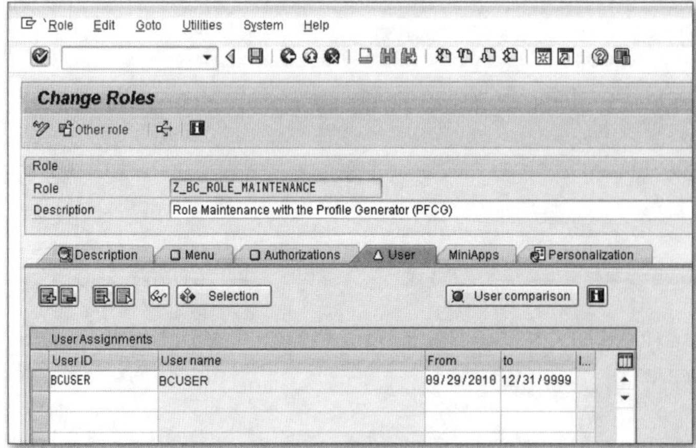

13. A new dialog window opens. Click on COMPLETE COMPARISON.

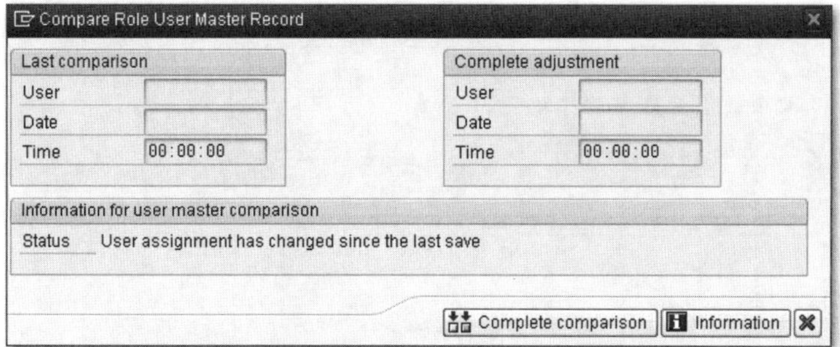

[+]

Automating the User Comparison

Via the UTILITIES • SETTINGS menu path, you can define that the user comparison is automatically run when the role is saved. You can also start the comparison using Transaction PFUD (User Master Data Reconciliation). Additionally, you should schedule report PFCG_TIME_DEPENDENCY at least once per day, which compares all roles and users. This especially applies to the systems to which you transport roles because the transport doesn't automatically trigger a user comparison.

The single role maintenance is now complete. Because you usually create roles in a development system, you must now transport them. The authorization profiles that belong to the single roles are transported as well.

14.2.2 Creating and Maintaining Composite Roles

You can simplify authorization management by grouping several single roles that are related or are usually assigned in combination into composite roles. Instead of several single roles, only the composite role is explicitly assigned to the users. As a result, the single roles contained in the composite role are automatically assigned.

Follow these steps to create a composite role in the Profile Generator:

1. Enter Transaction "PFCG" in the command box, and press the Enter key (or select the menu option TOOLS • ADMINISTRATION • USER MAINTENANCE • ROLE ADMINISTRATION • PFCG—ROLES).

2. Enter a suitable name for the new authorization role in the ROLE field, and click the COMPOSITE ROLE button.

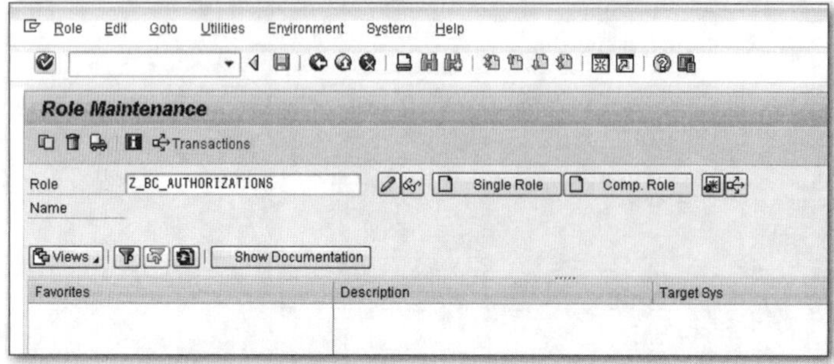

3. In the next screen, enter a meaningful description. You can use the LONG TEXT field for a more comprehensive description of the content and purpose or also for a change history.

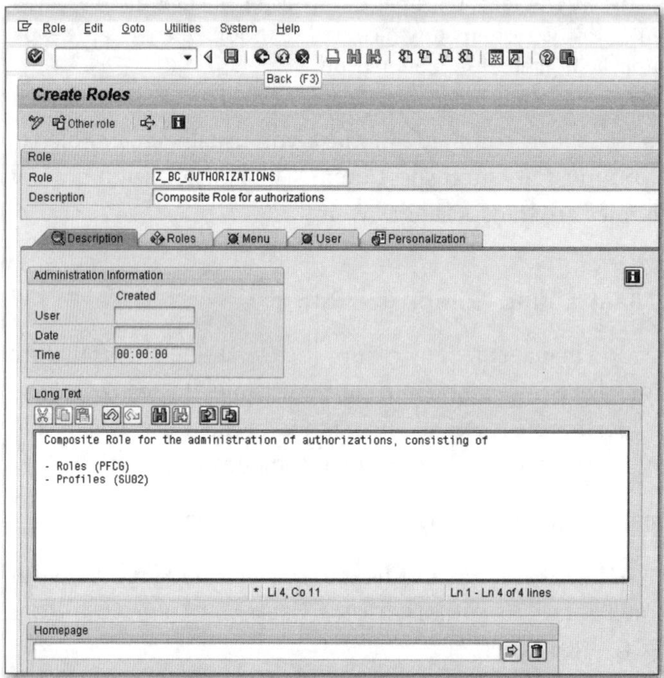

4. Go to the ROLES tab (Again, the system prompts you to save the role; confirm with YES). In the ROLE tab, enter the single roles you want to group in the composite role.

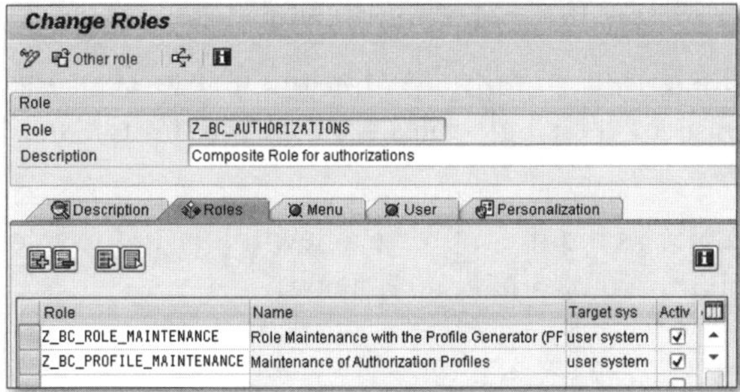

5. Go to the MENU tab. Copy the menus of the single roles by clicking on READ MENU.

[!]

Menu of Single and Composite Roles

Provided that the composite role has a separate menu, the menus of the single roles belonging to the composite role are overridden in the user menu. If the composite role doesn't have a menu, the system shows the single roles' menu entries in the user menu as usual.

Note that changes to the menus of the single roles are not automatically added to the menu of the composite role. You must compare the composite role menu anew for each change.

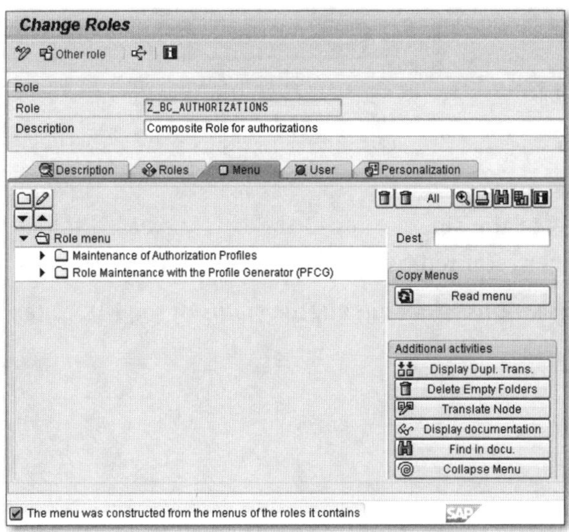

6. Again, the system prompts you to save the role. Confirm with Yes.
7. The role descriptions of the single roles are displayed at the first level of the composite role menu. The menus of the single roles are available on the subordinate levels.

   You can change the menu structure as required. Create a new folder in the role menu using the Create Folder button (☐) and enter a name.

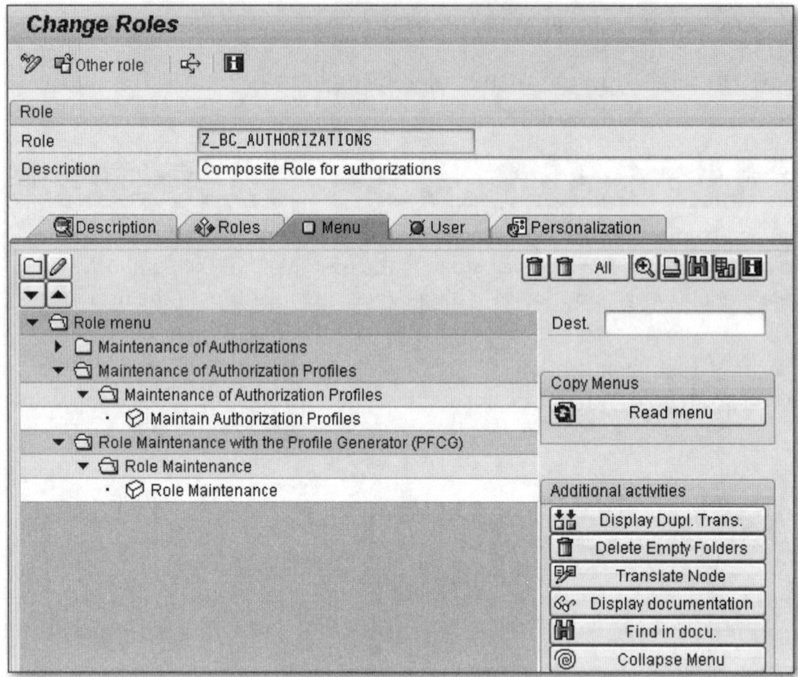

8. Drag and drop the transactions of the single roles to the newly created folder. Remove the subfolders no longer required by clicking Delete Empty Folders.

   As soon as you've entered transactions in the menu, the status of the Menu tab changes to green.

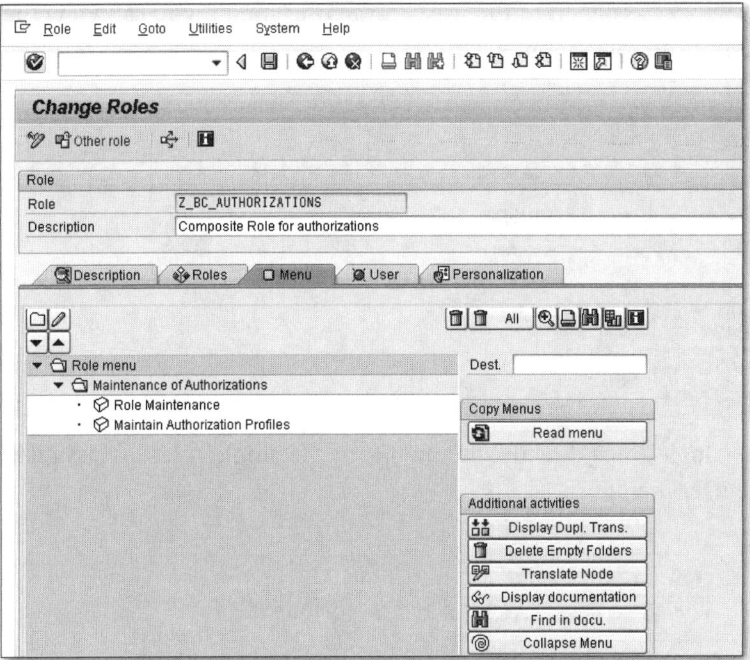

9. Go to the User tab. Enter the user ID you want to assign to the role in the User Assignments area. If required, enter a validity period in which the authorization is to be assigned. Click Save (💾) to save your entries. Run the user comparison if required.

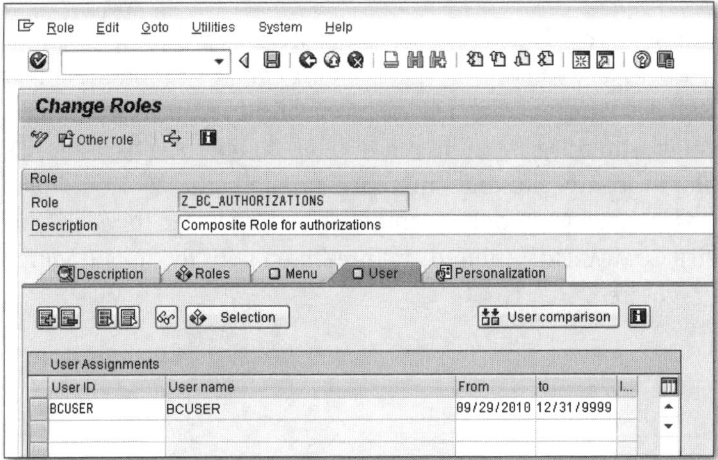

The composite role was assigned to the user. In the user menu, you can view the entries of the composite role menu.

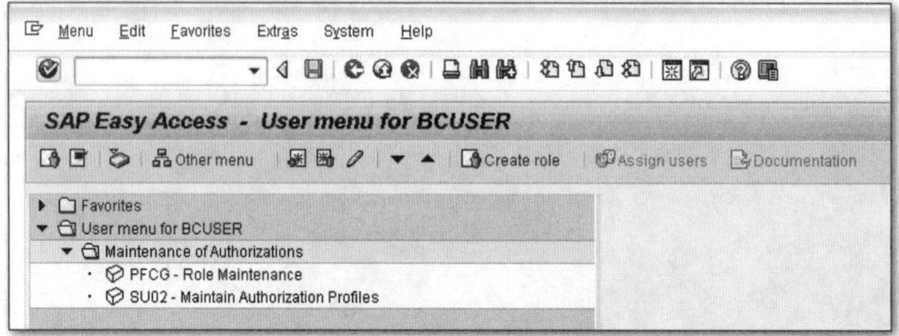

If you assign the single roles directly, the menus of the single roles are assigned separately in the user menu.

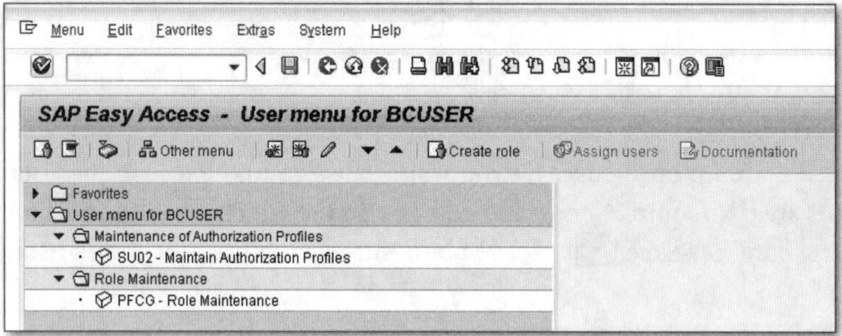

If you have the user master record displayed using Transaction SU01 (User Maintenance) and go to the ROLES tab, you can see that both the composite and the single roles have been assigned. Directly assigned roles are displayed in black. Single roles assigned via composite roles are indicated in blue. Single roles have the icon in the Type column; composite roles are represented via the icon. Roles for which the user comparison was not run completely are indicated in red () in the STATUS OF PROFILE COMPARISON column and presented with the note (tooltip) "Profile Comparison required."

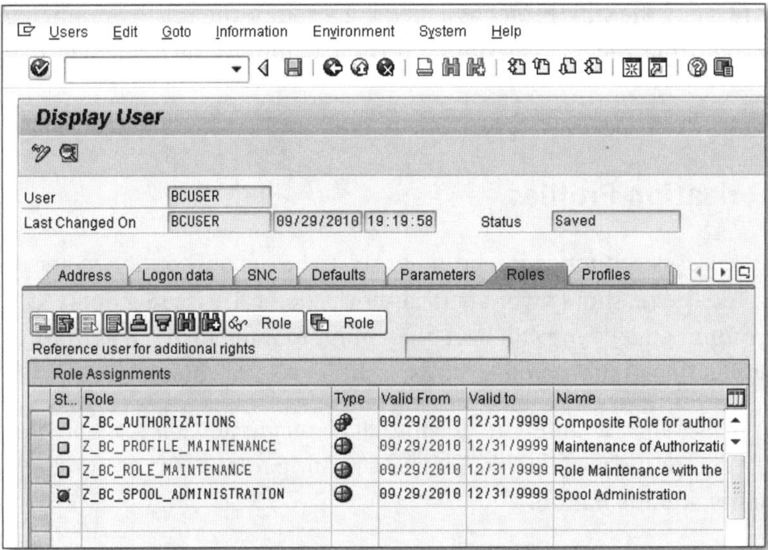

In the Profiles tab, you can view the generated authorization profiles of the single roles. However, only those profiles are displayed for whose roles the user comparison was run.

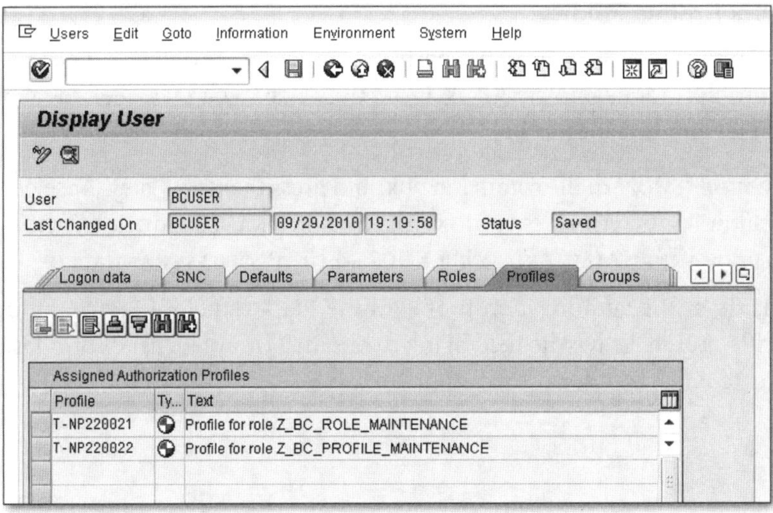

You can only withdraw the single roles assigned via a composite role by removing the composite role from the user master. You can't withdraw such a single role separately.

14.3 Authorization Profiles

In previous SAP releases, authorization profiles used to be the only option to assign authorizations. Today, you should work with authorization roles (see Section 14.2). Although not recommended, you still have the option to implement an authorization concept with authorization profiles or use standard SAP profiles.

Authorization profiles are also differentiated into *single profiles* and *composite profiles*. The purpose of a composite profile—like for authorization roles—is to group single profiles to simplify administration.

Creating and maintaining authorization profiles is not discussed in this book because we highly recommend using authorization roles. However, you should know how to obtain an overview of the content of a profile and how to assign authorization profiles to users.

Displaying Authorization Profiles

Because some administrators still work with authorization profiles or because standard SAP profiles (for example, SAP_ALL) are used here, you may need to take a closer look at an authorization profile.

1. Enter Transaction "SU02" in the command box, and press the [Enter] key (or select the menu option Tools • Administration • User Maintenance • Authorization and Profiles (manual Maintenance) • SU02—Edit Profiles Manually).
2. Enter the name of the authorization profile in the Profile field if you want to view a specific profile. Leave the field blank to obtain a complete list of profiles. Click on Create work area for profiles.

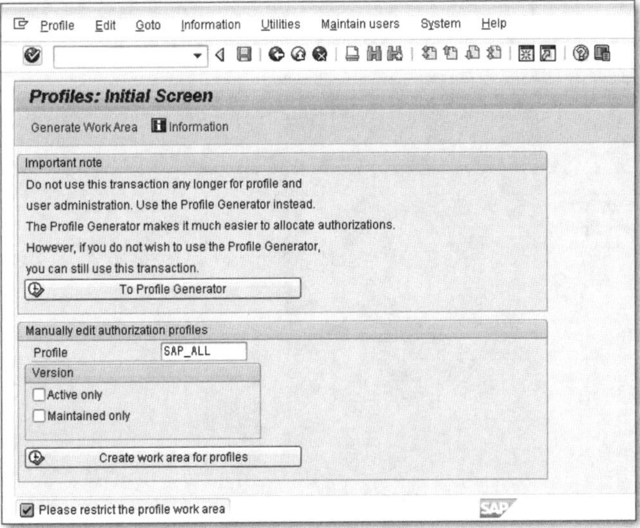

Using the Profile Generator Instead of the Manual Maintenance [+]

Already in the initial screen of Transaction SU02 for profile maintenance, a note is displayed informing you to use the Profile Generator. Using the To Profile Generator button, you can directly navigate to Transaction PFCG.

3. In the next screen, the system displays the authorization profiles to which your selection criteria apply. Open the profile by double-clicking the profile name or clicking Change Profile (✎).

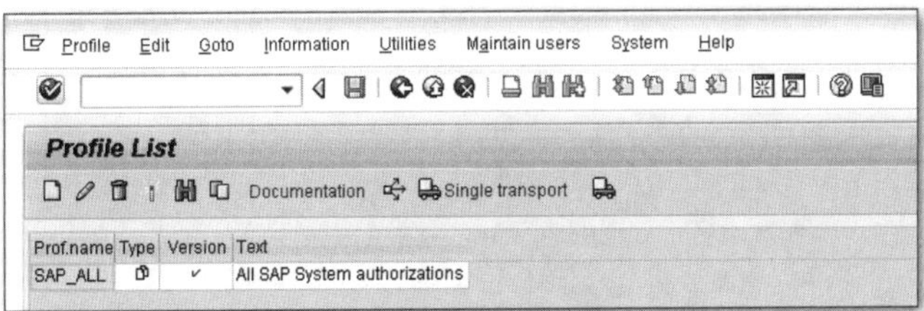

4. Via the Texts in User Master field, you can determine whether it's a single or composite profile. For composite roles, the Consisting of Profiles area lists the single profiles that are included in the composite profile. Double-click the profile name of a single profile to navigate to the next view.

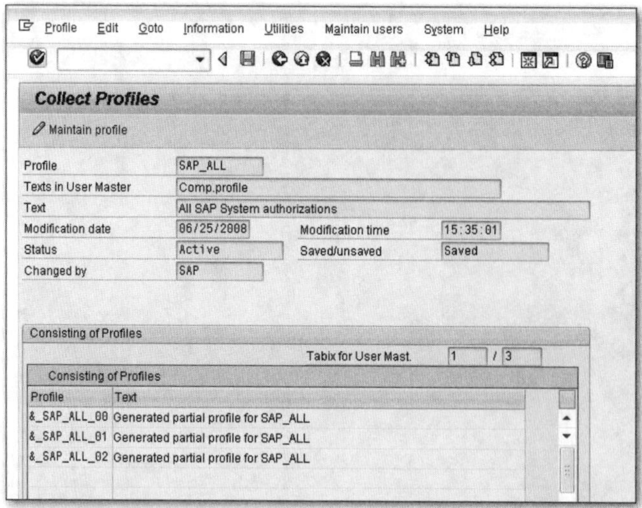

5. At the level of single profiles, the Consisting of Authorizations area lists the authorization objects contained in the profile. Double-click an object to open the field values.

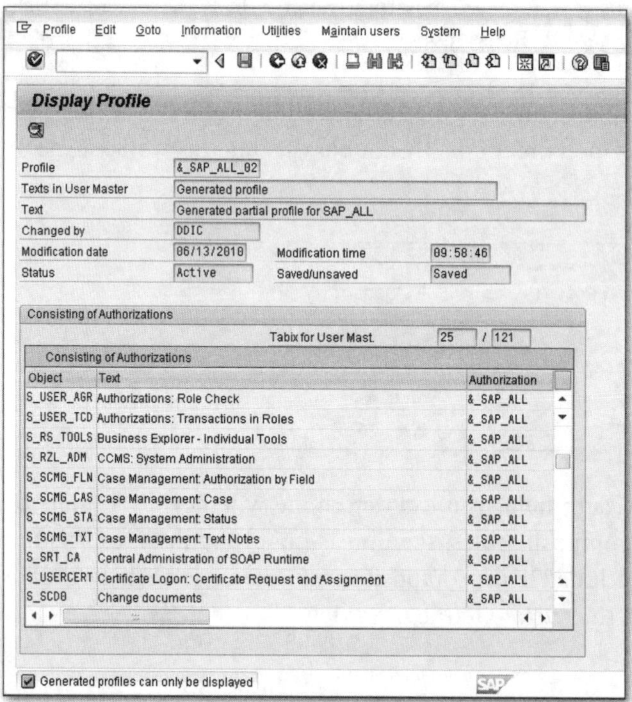

6. You are now in the display of the authorization fields of the authorization object. Below each field, you can view the field values that were defined in the authorization profile.

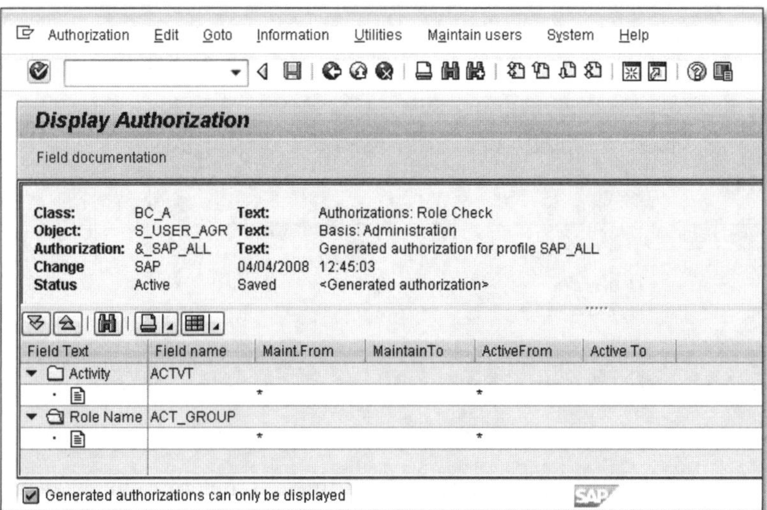

With this approach, you can examine the content of specific authorization profiles.

Assigning Authorization Profiles

To assign authorization profiles to a user, you should use Transaction SU01 for user maintenance and enter the authorization profiles in the PROFILES tab (see Chapter 13). The various profiles are displayed as follows:

- Profiles that have been created automatically for an authorization role are displayed as Generated Profile ().
- A composite profile is presented using the Composite Profile icon ().
- Single profiles don't have any entry in the Type column.

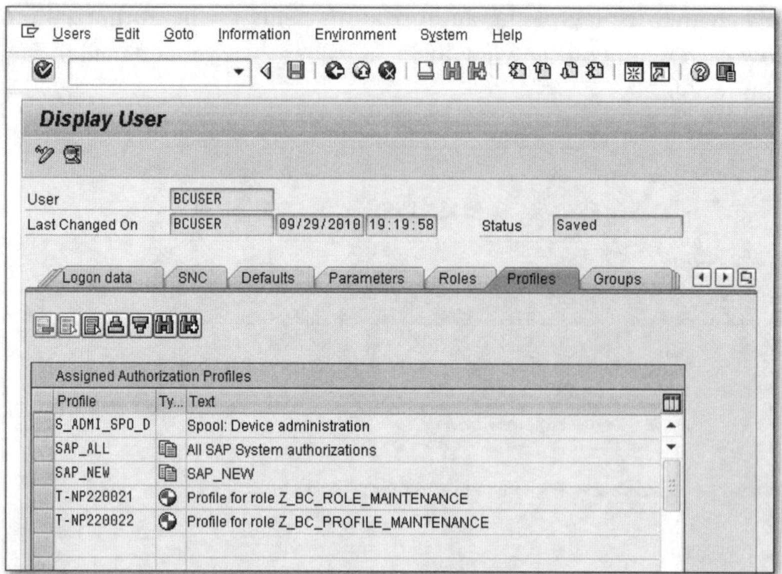

You can only withdraw generated authorization profiles by deleting the relevant authorization role.

14.4 Utilities for Authorization Management

As the administrator, you'll determine during the creation of authorization roles that the authorization objects the system added to the role sometimes don't correspond to the authorization objects that are actually checked in a transaction. To understand and optimize the system behavior, you should well know the check indicators and authorization traces.

14.4.1 Default Values and Check Indicators

Section 14.2.1 describes that authorization objects are automatically added to the role profile after a transaction is added to the role menu. These default values depend on the default values defined in the system for each transaction. Implement the following steps to display the check indicators.

1. Start Transaction SU24 (Maintain the Assignments of Authorization Objects).

2. In the Transaction Code field, enter the transaction for which you want to display the default values and check indicators, and select Execute (⊕).

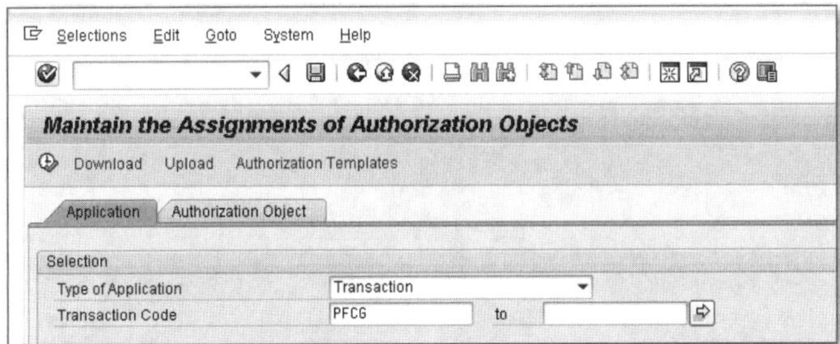

3. The check indicators for the transaction are shown on the right side of the screen. The value Yes in the Proposal field means that the object is automatically inserted in authorization roles. Click the Field Values button to show the default values of the authorization fields.

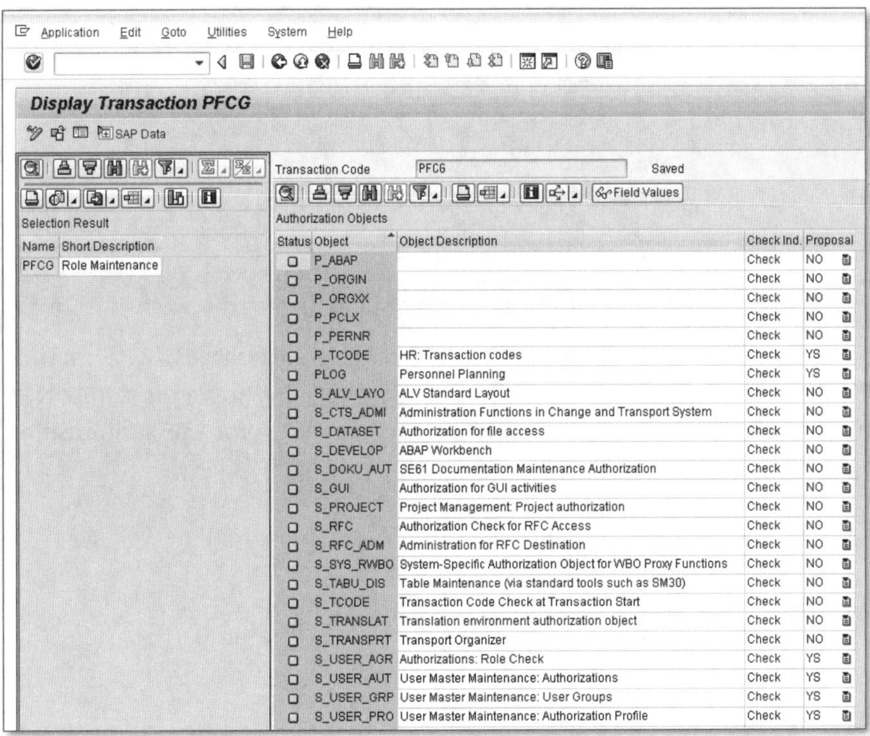

4. Details on the field values, which the system uses as default values, are shown in the lower part on the right side.

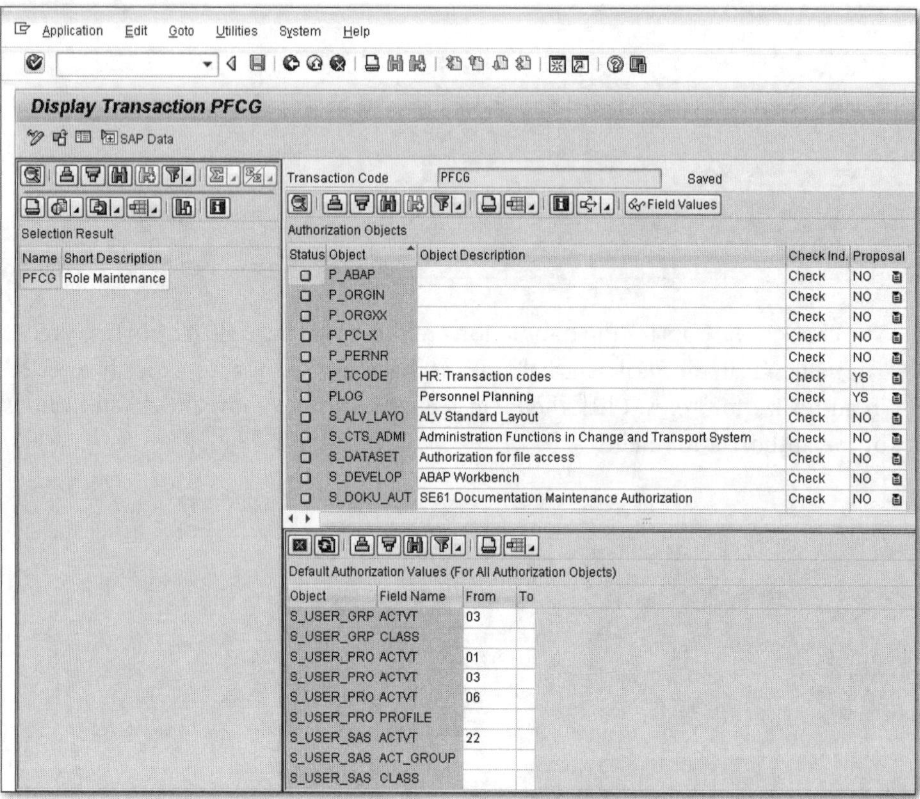

5. To edit the objects proposed, switch to the change mode via DISPLAY <-> CHANGE (). For example, use the Proposal button (Proposal) to set the status "NO" if no default values are supposed to be added to roles for the authorization object.

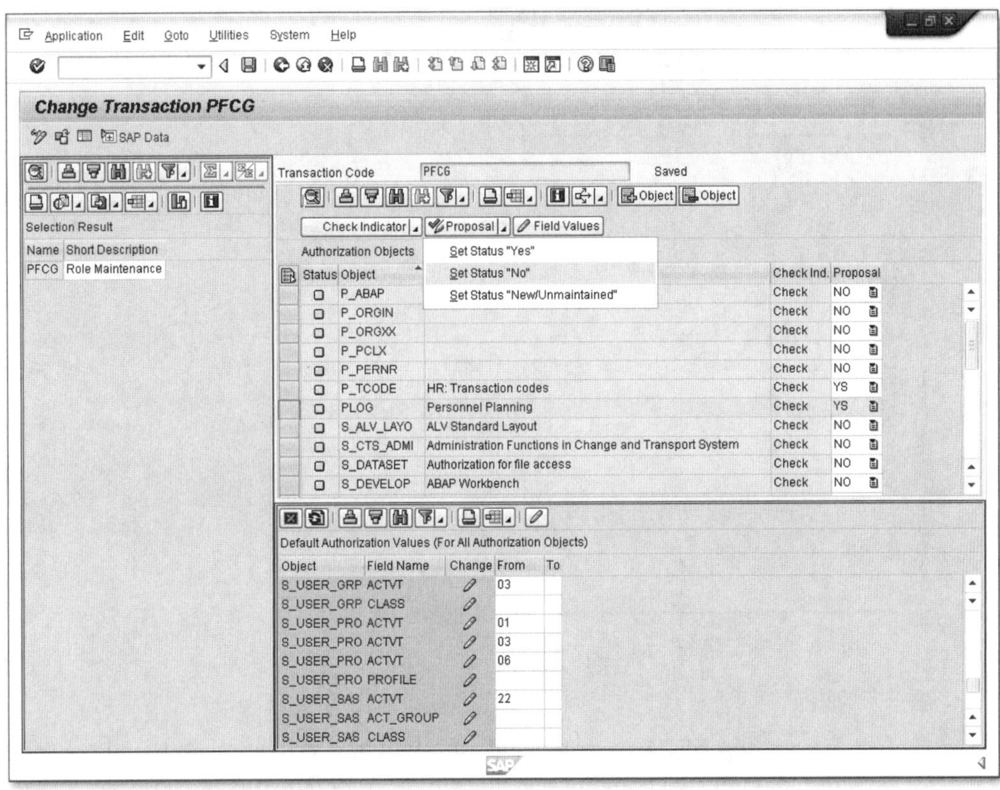

6. If you want to change the default values, click CHANGE in the DEFAULT AUTHORIZATION VALUES area, and enter further activities as new default values, for example.

   Click on SAVE.

[!]

Copying the Delivery Version

Before you change the default values or check indicators, you must copy the delivery version of this data to your customer namespace. To do so, start Transaction SU25 (Upgrade Tool for Profile Generator), and run the action INSTALLING THE PROFILE GENERATOR • INITIALLY FILL THE CUSTOMER TABLES.

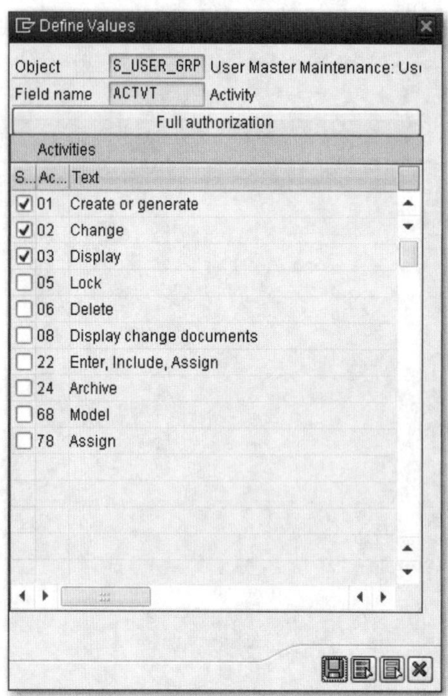

7. Use Transaction SU24 to deactivate authorization checks in transactions in a targeted manner by changing the check indicators. For this purpose, select the relevant authorization object, and click CHECK INDICATOR (Check Indicator) • DO NOT CHECK.

[!]

Functions of the Check Indicator

Note that you can deactivate checks, but you can't use the check indicators to have the system check additional authorization objects in a transaction. If an object is not checked in the source code of the transaction, this can only be changed by editing the program—not by setting a check indicator.

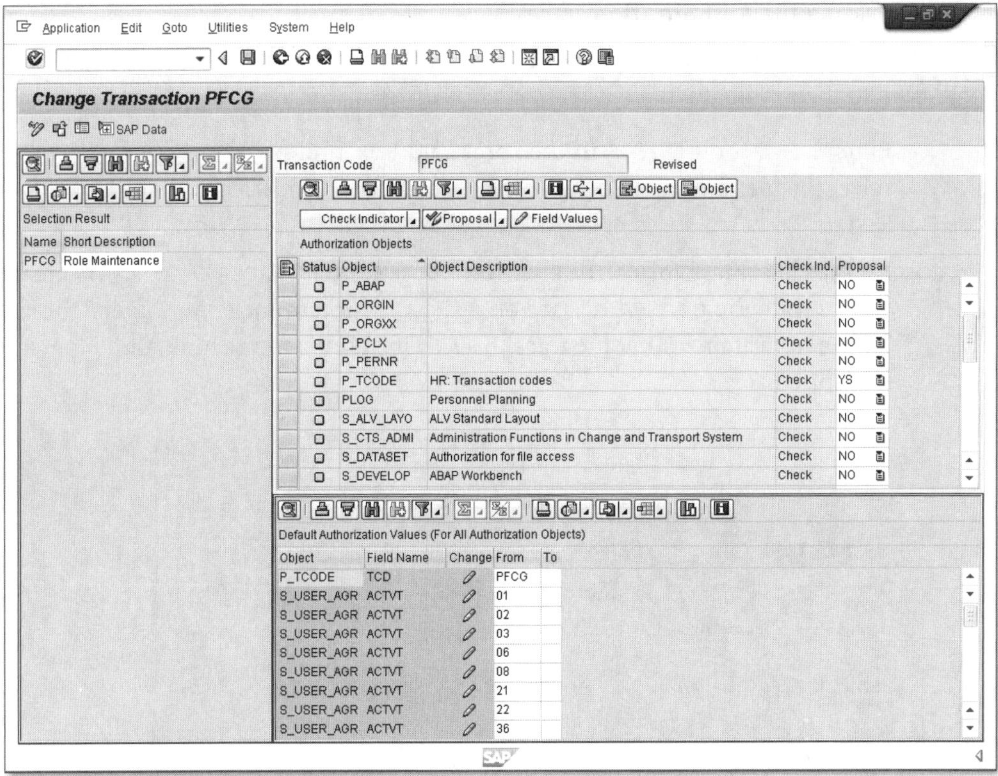

8. You can also add further default values (Object button) or remove objects from the default values (Object button).
9. With the SAP Data button you can compare your modifications with the delivery data from SAP.

You can use the default values in Transaction SU24 to map or document your authorization concept directly in the SAP system. But you can also leave the default values unchanged and ignore them.

14.4.2 Authorization Trace

The authorization trace is probably the most essential utility of the (authorization) administrator. If you don't have any programming knowledge or don't want to go through source coding indefinitely when searching for authorization objects required for a transaction, the authorization trace is the right tool to find out which authorization checks are run in a transaction.

Activating the Authorization Trace

The authorization trace is part of the system trace. Activate the trace in the first step to then evaluate it:

1. Enter Transaction "ST01" in the command box, and press the [Enter] key (or select the menu option TOOLS • ADMINISTRATION • MONITOR • TRACES • ST01 — SYSTEM TRACE).
2. Set the checkmark for AUTHORIZATION CHECK (in the TRACE COMPONENTS area), and activate the trace with Trace on (Trace on). You can use the General Filters button to further restrict the trace to a specific user, a transaction, or a program if required.

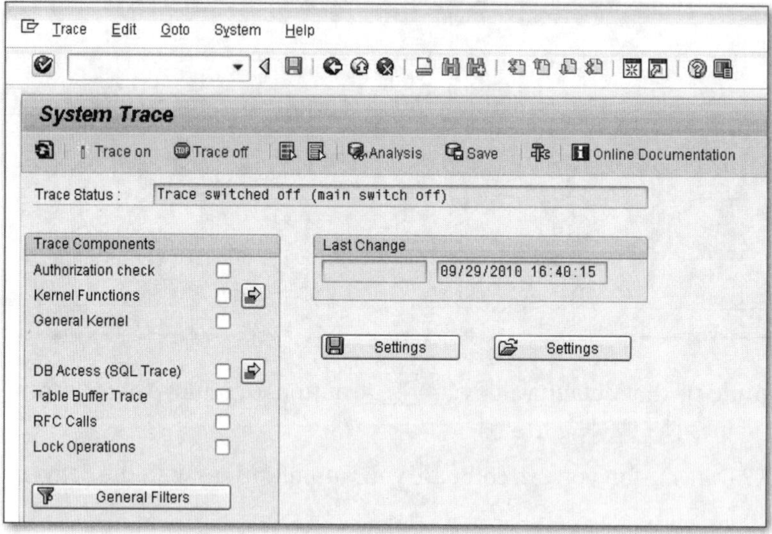

3. The authorization trace is now activated; in other words, all authorization checks that run in the system are logged according to your filter criteria. You can use the trace for the creation of new authorization roles by running the transactions whose authorization checks you want to analyze with the activated trace with a test user. The authorization trace can also be useful if you want to investigate a specific error message. Activate the trace, and ask the reporting person to repeat the action that failed.

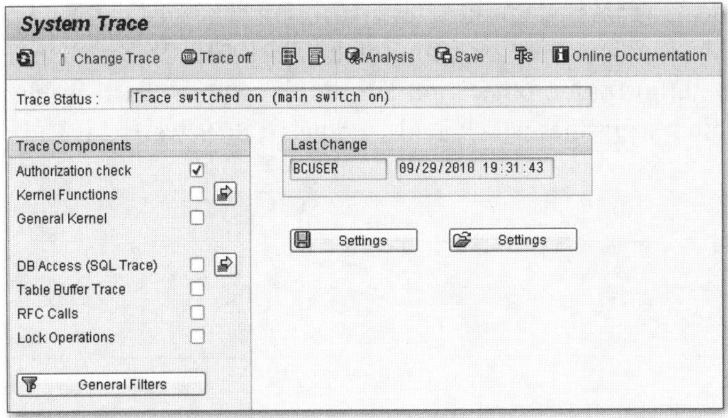

Evaluating the Authorization Trace

After you've run the test or reproduced the error, you start to evaluate the authorization trace.

1. Enter Transaction "ST01" in the command box, and press the Enter key (or select the menu option Tools • Administration • Monitor • Traces • ST01 — System Trace). Click on Analysis.
2. In the options, you can restrict the system trace evaluations, for instance, to a specific user name or period of time. Deactivate all entries except for Authorization check under Trace Records. Display the trace entries using Start Reporting (⊕).

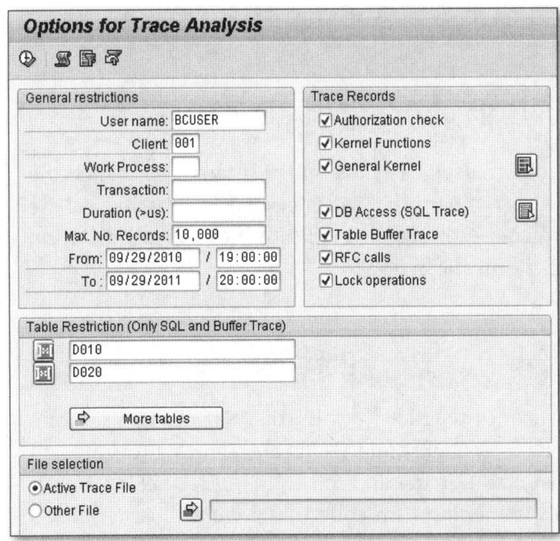

3. All authorization checks processed for the selected user are displayed in the next screen. The first column indicates the exact time of the check. The Object column shows the checked authorization object and the return code returned by the system. The Text column specifies which fields and field values were checked.

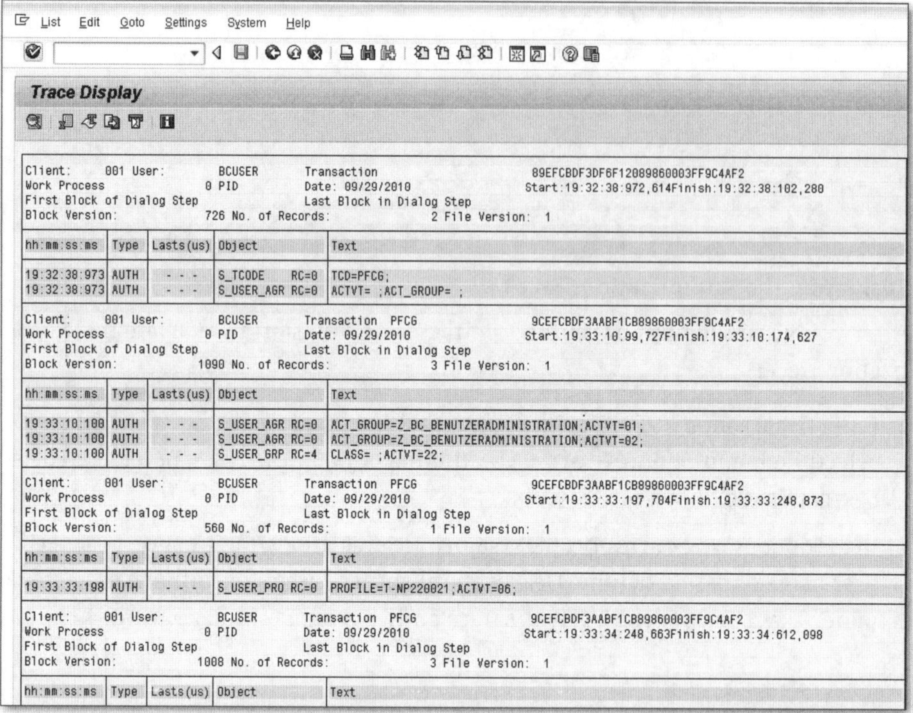

Return Code

Whether an action may be performed by a user, depends on the *return code*, which the authorization check returns. Return code 0 means that the check was successful and the action was permitted. All other return codes (4, 8, or 16) indicate that the authorization check failed and the user must not perform the action.

[Ex]

Interpreting the Trace Log

Interpreting the trace log is just a matter of practice. In this example, you can see that the user calls Transaction PFCG (Object S_TCODE) and then creates a new authorization role (Object S_USER_AGR with Activity 01—Create and role Z_BC_BENUTZERADMINISTRATION). Both object checks finished with return code 0 and were thus permitted by the system. Assignment of the role to a user master record was denied with return code 4 because the BCUSER user does not have the authorization object S_USER_GRP with Activity 22—Assign. After you've evaluated the authorization trace, you can make the necessary corrections in the relevant authorization role (for example, add activity 22 to object S_USER_GRP) and repeat the test.

Evaluating the Authorization Check

Besides the authorization trace described, there is another option to evaluate failed authorization checks: Transaction SU53 (Evaluate Authorization Check). The authorization check is only available for selected users. Transaction SU53, however, should be available for all users in the system. With Transaction SU53, the system displays the log of the authorization check that failed last. In many cases, this can save you the work with the authorization trace; in case of an error, you can have the reporting person send the result of Transaction SU53 (for example, as a screenshot). This information may already be sufficient to solve the problem.

Open a new session after the failed authorization check, and start Transaction SU53, or call the transaction in the same session using "/nSU53". Expand the tree structure to analyze the authorization check.

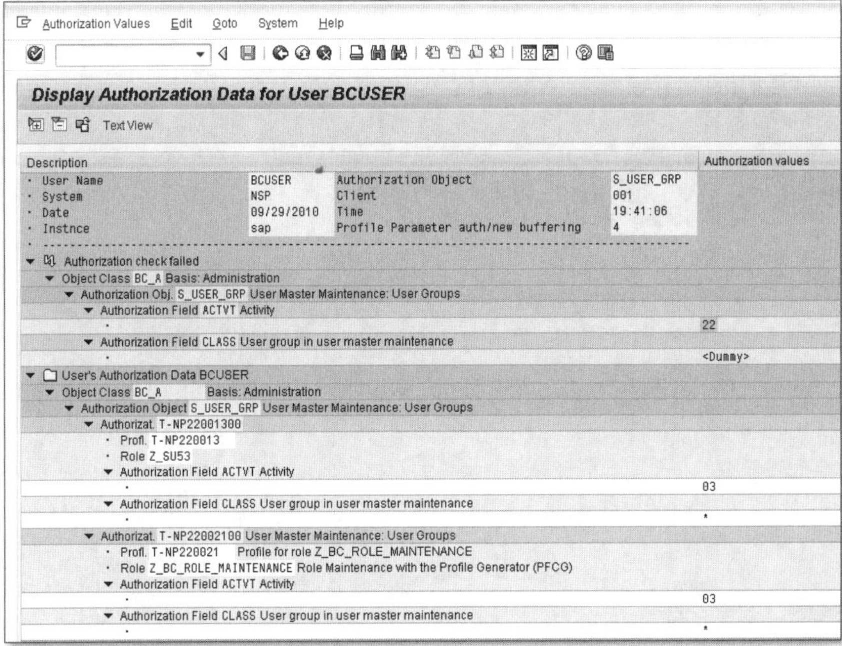

Rejected authorization checks are highlighted in red. Below the checks, the system lists the authorizations that are currently assigned to the user for the relevant object.

Check the log entries, and correct the roles. Then try again.

[!] **Evaluation Transaction 53**

The evaluation shown in Transaction SU53 must often be handled with due care because only the result of the *last* failed authorization check is output. The logged object (for example, S_ALV_LAYO) isn't necessarily responsible for the action in question not being executed. It could also just be the last link in the chain of rejected checks. If in doubt, consult the authorization trace where the authorization checks are logged completely and in the sequence in which they were run.

14.4.3 Infosystem Authorizations

The area menu AUTH provides various options for evaluations on the authorizations topic in the form of predefined reports. To open the area menu, enter "AUTH" in the transaction field of the SAP Easy Access menu, and press the Enter key.

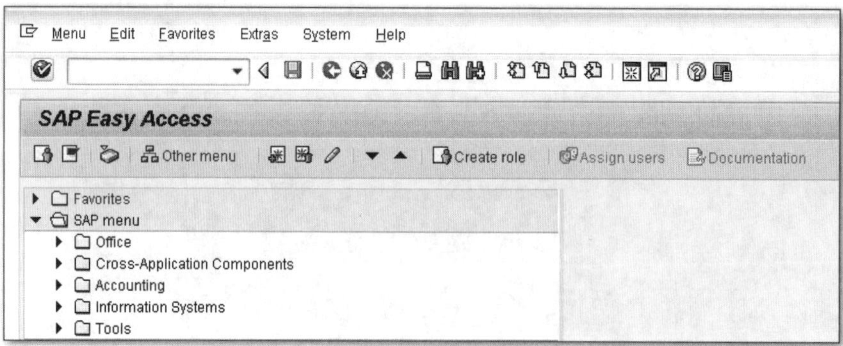

The SAP menu is replaced with the area menu, which contains evaluation programs sorted by topics.

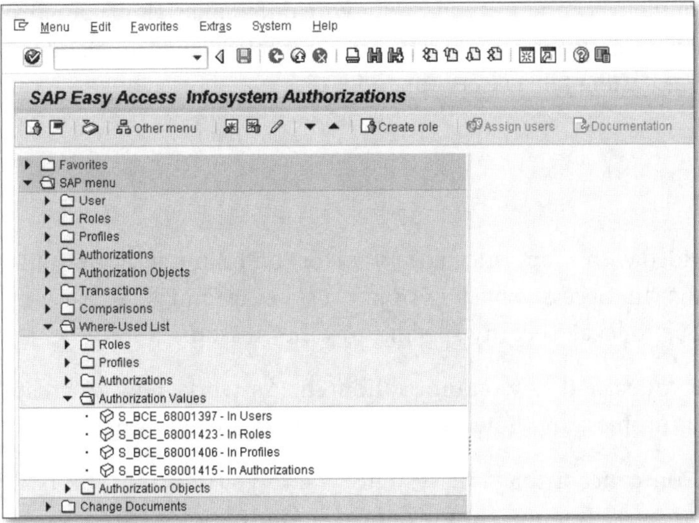

The Infosystem Authorizations offers a variety of evaluation options for users, roles, and profiles.

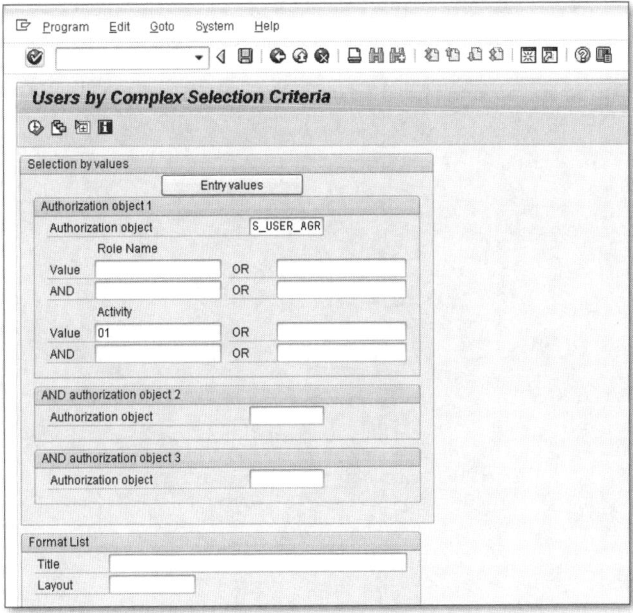

Depending on the report, you can address questions with different levels of complexity. So first take a look at the Infosystem Authorizations before you run elaborate evaluations for various system tables (see Appendix C).

14.5 Summary

SAP systems are provided with a sophisticated system for controlling authorizations. This is required because the access to business data must be customized with a very high level of detail due to legal, security-specific, or other reasons.

In this chapter, you've learned how authorization checks work, how to create authorization roles or profiles, and how to assign authorizations to users.

Create an authorization concept for your systems where you consider the both closely linked topic areas of user and authorization administration.

In the SAP system, you can execute transactions and programs in dialog mode or in the background. You can flexibly control the start time and recurrence frequency of these background jobs. This chapter describes how to schedule programs with a long runtime for overnight processing and monitor background jobs.

15 Background Processing

In the SAP system, batch jobs are called *background jobs*. They are executed whether a user is logged on to the system or not. This is the main difference from the execution of a program in dialog mode. Background jobs provide the following advantages:

- Users can run jobs after work or at the weekend.
- The program can run without locking a user session.
- Jobs that take a lot of time might be canceled if they are executed online as soon as they exceed a certain time limit.

Numerous SAP transactions let you choose between an execution in dialog mode or in the background. For dialog and background processing, the SAP system provides different work process categories (see Chapter 2). If you choose background processing, a background job is created that uses a batch work process (BTC category). If you run the transaction in dialog mode, a dialog work process (DIA category) is blocked.

As an alternative to creating a background job from a specific transaction, you can also create and schedule background jobs yourself.

15.1 Creating Background Jobs

In the SAP system, background processing is mainly used for the execution of regularly scheduled jobs. Regularly scheduled jobs are background jobs that are executed according to a schedule, for example, everyday at 11 am or every Sunday at 5 am. Unlike spontaneously performed background jobs, the start is specifically planned, and the execution is repeated at certain intervals.

Regularly scheduled jobs are used for the following tasks, for example:

- Collecting performance data for statistics
- Importing data into an information system, for example, Special Ledger
- Generating reports
- Generating a data file for an outbound interface
- Processing an inbound interface
- Performing cleanup tasks, for example, deleting obsolete spool requests

Documenting Critical Jobs

You should list all critical scheduled jobs. This refers in particular to job runs that are important for the business processes of your enterprise, such as interfaces or overnight processing programs. You should record the following for every job of this category:

- Day/time of the planned start
- Expected duration
- Contact persons (name and telephone numbers) in case problems occur
- Restart or troubleshooting procedures

15.1.1 General

You must generally consider the following aspects when scheduling regular or spontaneous background jobs:

User ID

Like dialog mode, background processing requires an SAP user with ID and the corresponding authorizations. In dialog processing, programs are usually executed with the ID of the user that is currently logged on to the system. For background processing, a job is normally always started with the user ID of its creator. However, you can also define another user ID afterwards (see Section 15.1.2).

You can create specific user IDs that are solely used for the scheduling of batch jobs, for example, BATCH1. You should work with several user IDs for the different task areas if batch jobs are scheduled by different organizations or groups or if they are scheduled for them. The disadvantage is that you have to administer multiple accounts.

[Ex]

Using Multiple User IDs

- BATCH_BC: System jobs
- BATCH_FI: Financial accounting
- BATCH_KR: Vendors
- BATCH_WH: Warehouse
- BATCH_MM: Material planning/stock

These special user IDs enable you to schedule jobs independently of the person. So you avoid jobs that can't be executed when an employee leaves the enterprise, for example, because the user ID of the employee has been locked or deleted.

Variants

For the execution of a program with specific settings or selection parameters, a batch job may require the creation of a *variant*. Variants enable you to start jobs with default parameters, for example, predefined selection criteria. You have to create this variant in the dialog mode before you schedule the job. You can then specify this variant when scheduling the job.

Miscellaneous

Various modules and functions may require specific regularly scheduled jobs. The Special Ledger, for example, requires a regular job for copying data from the FI/CO modules and for generating sets in the Special Ledger. Furthermore, several cleanup jobs may have to be executed at the database and operating system level.

15.1.2 Creating and Scheduling Background Jobs

Follow these steps to create and schedule new background jobs:

1. Enter Transaction "SM36" in the command box, and press the Enter key (or select the menu option Tools • CCMS • Background Processing • SM36—Define Job).
2. Make the following settings:

- Enter a name in JOB NAME.
- Define the start priority of the job with JOB CLASS.
- Optionally, define a specific server as the EXEC. TARGET.

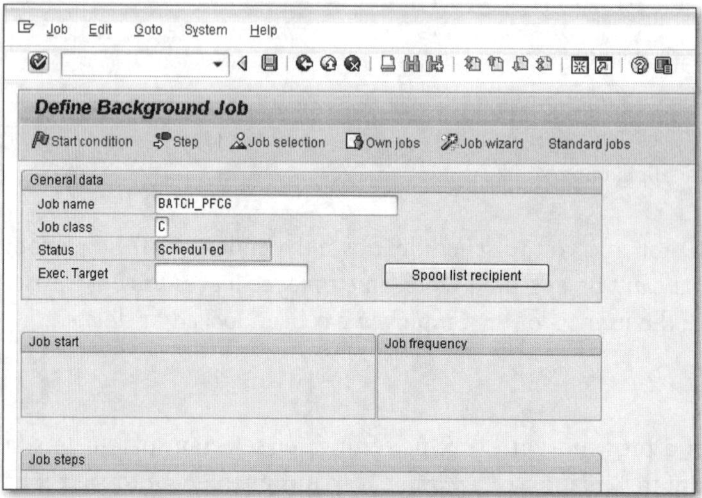

[+]

Naming Convention for Background Jobs

Using standard naming conventions facilitates the administration of jobs.

[⚙]

Job Classes

The job class defines the start priority of a background job. A job of class A is started before a job of class B, and a job of class B before a job of class C. Class C is the default job class.

After the start, all jobs have the same priority. That means a job of class A doesn't occupy processing resources of jobs of class B to accelerate the execution.

Queued jobs don't have an effect on running jobs. A queued class A job does not replace a class C job that is currently running.

You can reserve batch work processes for jobs of class A in an SAP system (see Chapter 2). This enables you to control that the execution of very critical background jobs is not blocked by unimportant jobs because no work processes are available.

[!]

Using Job Classes Efficiently

Use the job classes efficiently. For example, it doesn't make sense to assign every job to class A, because all jobs are executed with the same priority then.

Usually, jobs should be assigned to class C. Only jobs that must be started preferred should be assigned to class A. There should be a reason for the assignment to a higher priority. You can use the SAP authorization concept as a reference.

3. Now, select Step, and click on the ABAP Program button in the dialog box to schedule an ABAP program.

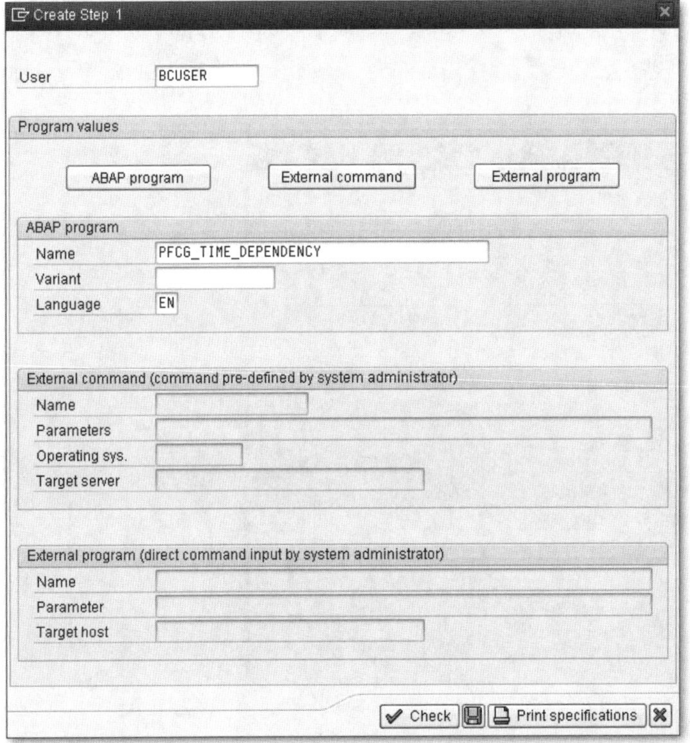

[+]

Job Steps

Each job consists of one or several *steps* that need to be defined individually. The steps are executed in succession.

4. Enter the following data:
   - In USER, you can optionally define a user ID under which the job is supposed to be executed.
   - In the ABAP PROGRAM area, enter the name of the program in NAME.
   - If there are variants of the program, you can also enter a VARIANT.
   - Click on CHECK to check the consistency of your entries.

[+]

User IDs in Background Jobs

The user of the job step provides the authorizations with which the job is executed; irrespective of this entry, the job overview (see Section 15.2) lists the job with the user ID of the creator. You can only use user IDs of the user type dialog, system, or service for background processing.

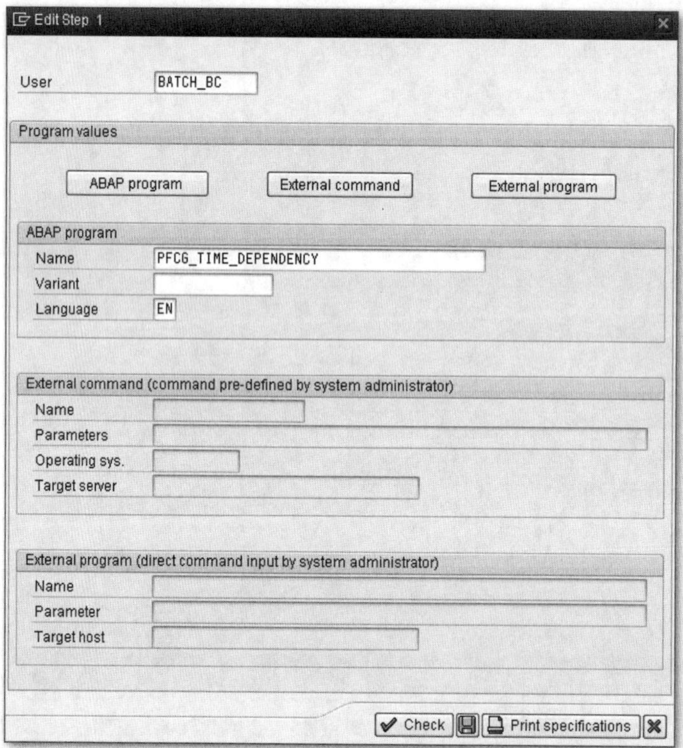

5. Click on PRINT SPECIFICATIONS. If the program generates a spool or output request, enter the name of the printer in OUTPUT DEVICE.

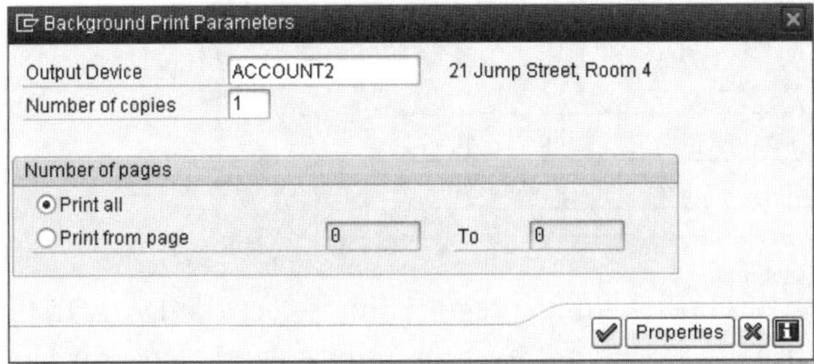

6. Click on PROPERTIES to define the required spool control options in the SPOOL REQUEST ATTRIBUTES SCREEN. When you are finished, choose CONTINUE (✔). Also confirm the selection of the printer in the previous screen, BACKGROUND PRINT PARAMETERS, with CONTINUE (✔).

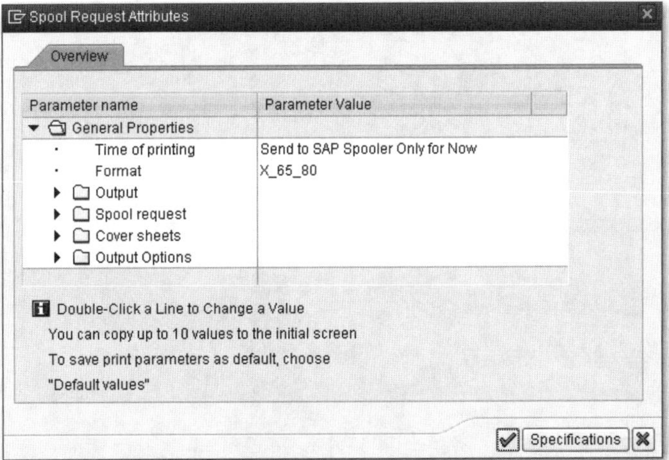

7. Save your entries in the initial dialog box, Create STEP 1, (see step 3) using SAVE (💾).

8. The overview of the already-defined steps is displayed. Here you can add more steps and change or delete already-defined steps if necessary. Select BACK (⬅) to return to the initial screen of the job definition (DEFINE BACKGROUND JOB SCREEN, step 2).

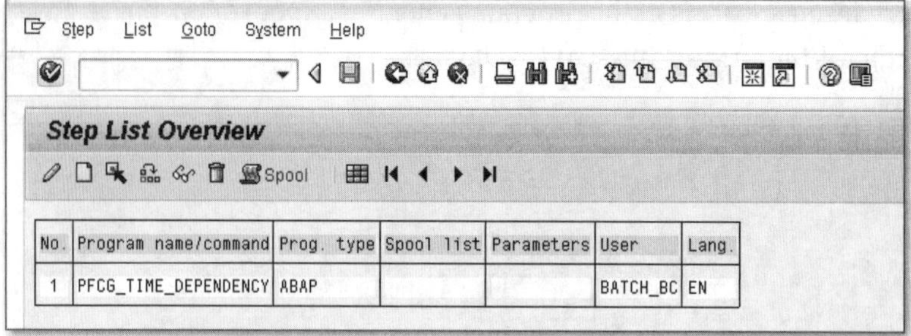

9. Click on START CONDITION. If you schedule a regular job, select the DATE/TIME button. Enter a date and time in DATE and TIME for SCHEDULED START. For NO START AFTER, enter the last possible date and time for the program start.

   If you want to start the execution of the program immediately, select IMMEDIATE.

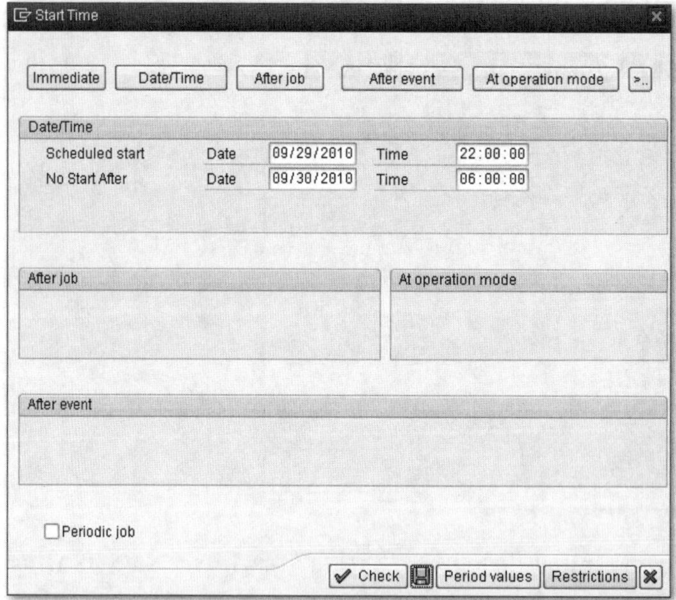

[+]

Considering the Time Zones of the Database Server

The date and time of the scheduled start refer to the database server and not to the local time.

[!]

Option "No Start After"

The entry in the No Start After field is important if performance-intensive programs mustn't start at certain times to not jeopardize running operations or if you want to avoid one job passing the other.

Activate the Periodic Job checkbox, and click on the Period Values button.

10. In the dialog box, select the required button (for example, Daily), and click on Check. If the system doesn't output an error message, select Save (💾).

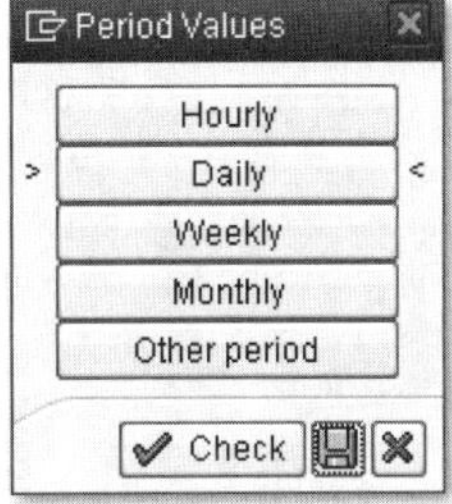

11. Verify your entries in the Start Time screen using Check, and then confirm them with Save (💾).

    This navigates you back to the Define Background Job screen.

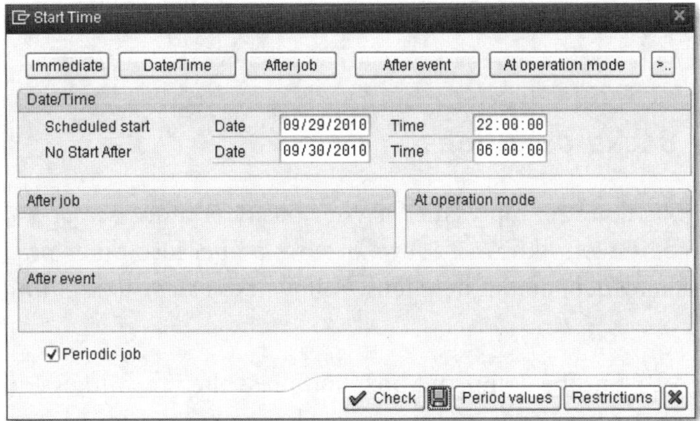

12. In the DEFINE BACKGROUND JOB screen, again click on SAVE (💾). The status bar now displays a message that confirms the creation of the background job.

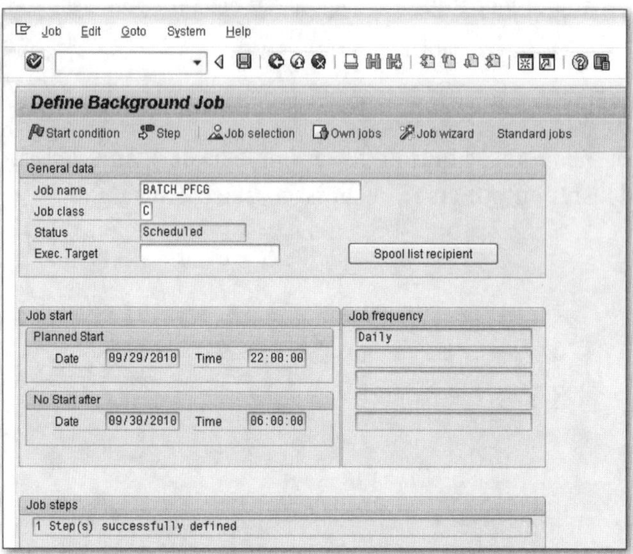

[+]

Job Wizard

As an alternative to referring to these instructions, you can call the Job Wizard (Job Wizard). It guides you through the individual steps of the process just described.

15.2 Monitoring Background Jobs

If you execute critical jobs that are important for your business processes or for operating the system, you have to know if jobs are canceled because other processes, activities or tasks may depend on these jobs. Follow these steps to monitor the background jobs:

1. Enter Transaction "SM37" in the command box, and press the Enter key (or select the menu option TOOLS • CCMS • BACKGROUND PROCESSING • SM37—JOB OVERVIEW AND ADMINISTRATION).

2. Make the following settings:
   - In JOB NAME, enter the name of the background job, or use the * wildcard to view all jobs.
   - Enter the user ID of the creator of the job in USER NAME or use the * wildcard to view the jobs of all users.
   - Under JOB STATUS, activate the checkbox for ACTIVE, FINISHED, and CANCELED.
   - Restrict the evaluation period by defining a start date in FROM and an end date in TO for the JOB START CONDITION.
   - Click EXECUTE.

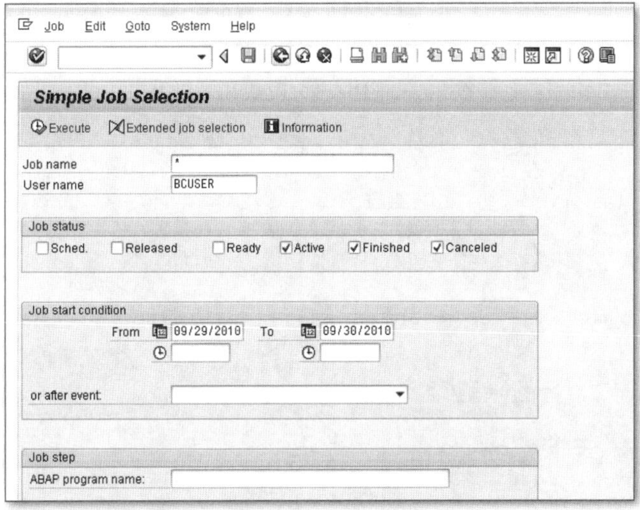

3. In the JOB OVERVIEW, check the job list for canceled or erroneous jobs. Look for jobs that have the CANCELED entry in the STATUS column. Monitor critical jobs in particular, for example, for material planning or payments by check (you have to know the name of the job in this case).

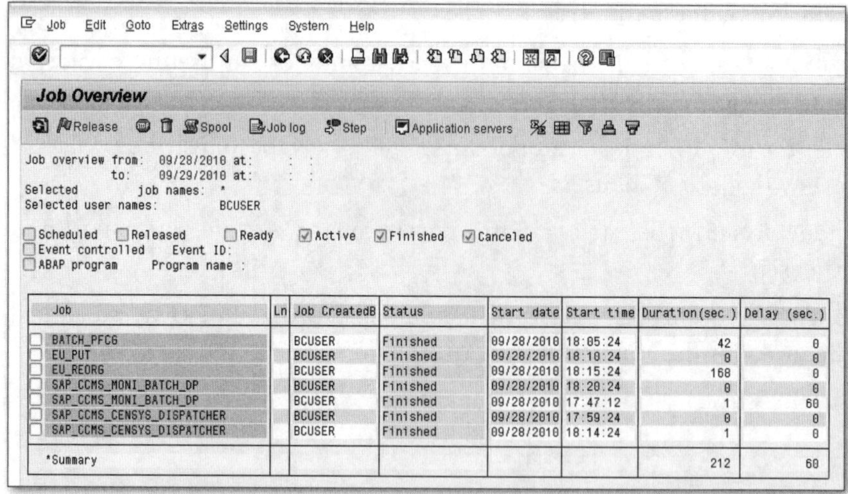

4. Double-click on a row to call the basic data of the background job.

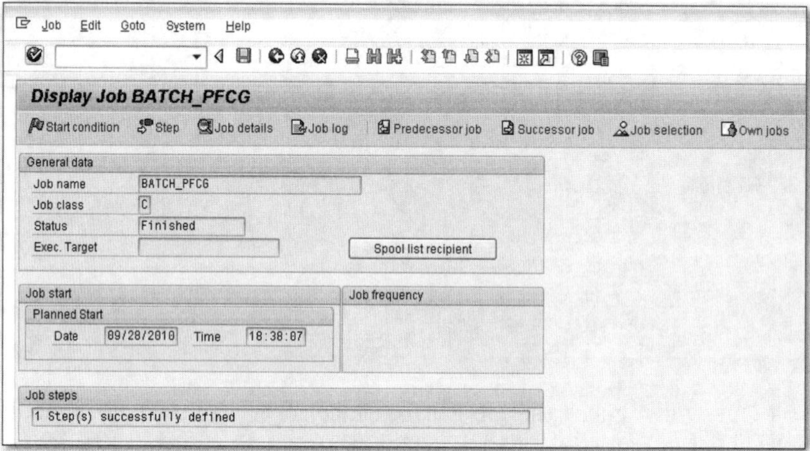

5. Select the JOB LOG button to view the log.

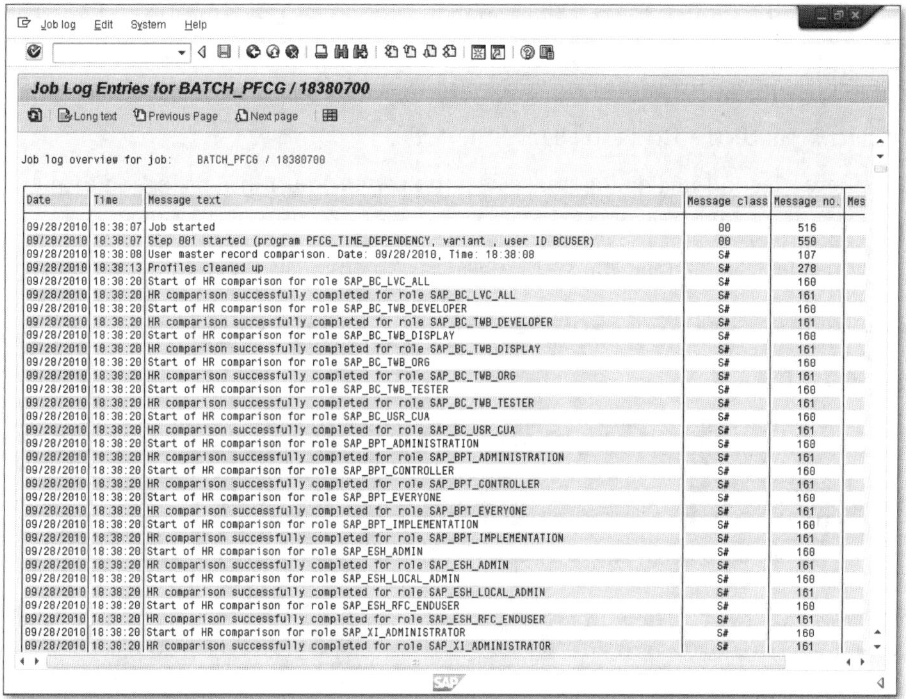

6. Use BACK (🡄) to return to the job overview, and check the runtimes of the jobs (DURATION (SEC.) column). If the runtime deviates from the normal runtime, this can indicate a problem and should be analyzed. To evaluate the runtime, you have to monitor it over a long period of time and compare it to previous runs of this job.

Displaying Additional Columns [+]

The CHANGE LAYOUT button (▦) enables you to display additional useful columns in the job overview, for example, the client in which the jobs are executed or the date and time for which the start of the job is scheduled.

15.3 Graphical Job Scheduling Monitor

The Job Scheduling Monitor is a graphical tool that supports the scheduling of jobs. It displays the individual background jobs in a diagram. You start the Job Scheduling Monitor as follows:

1. Enter Transaction "RZ01" in the command box, and press the [Enter] key (or select the menu option TOOLS • CCMS • BACKGROUND PROCESSING • RZ01—JOB SCHEDULING MONITOR).
2. Select TIME UNIT • HOUR to change the scale.
3. To view a legend in a dialog box, select the LEGEND button. The legend displays the colors and patterns used.
4. If you select TIMER ON, the system updates the display every three minutes.

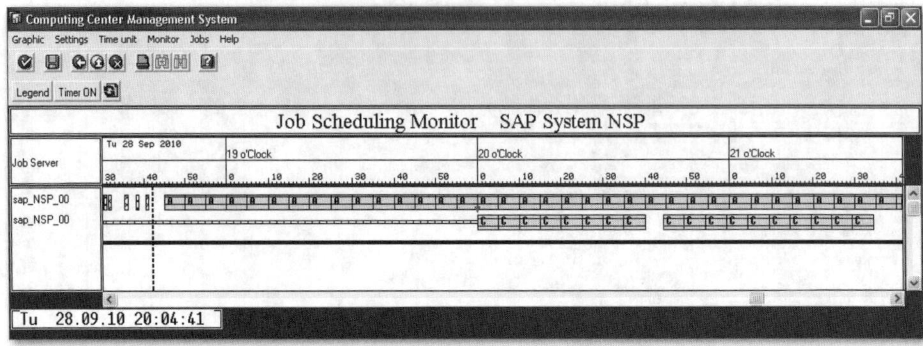

Due to the graphical formatting of the scheduling data, the monitor is particularly well suited for the coordination of numerous background jobs.

15.4 Performance Factors for Background Jobs

Background jobs occupy a large part of the system resources. Therefore, they can have a negative effect on the online system performance. However, background jobs do not have a higher priority than dialog work processes; that is, they are not assigned more system resources. There are various methods for optimizing the system performance during the execution of background jobs. The online users benefit from these methods, and background jobs can be executed more efficiently.

To reduce the influence of background jobs on the system, you can run batch jobs on a standalone batch application instance or batch application server. For a small central instance with only ten users, two batch jobs can already significantly impair the system performance. For small installations, it can therefore also be necessary to use additional application servers to isolate the batch processing from the central instance. The instance profile for this application server would then rather aim at background jobs than at the dialog (online) performance (for example, five background work processes and only two dialog work processes).

[+]

Number of Available Background Processes

As a rule of thumb, the number of background processes should not be larger than twice the CPU number.

However, the definition of a target host can lead to problems. If you specify the target host, the system doesn't perform load balancing. So it's possible that the maximum number of batch work processes is occupied on the batch application server, but other applications are not used at all. If you define that the job is supposed to be executed on the batch application server, you prevent it from being executed on another application server that is available. The job then waits until a batch work process on the specified batch application server is available.

When you schedule jobs, you should bear the following in mind:

- **Consider the time of the execution**
  Schedule background jobs so that they are not executed during peak times, that is, preferably overnight or during lunch time. If no users are logged on to the system, it's no problem if the system performance decreases.
- **Minimize job conflicts**
  Two background jobs that run at the same time might access the same files or even data records, which may lead to a cancellation of the jobs. You can avoid this conflict by coordinating these background jobs (for example, two reports on due payments should not run simultaneously). For time reasons, the reports should run in succession in such cases.
- **Consider the local time for the respective users in case of global jobs**
  For example, if a resource-intensive background jobs is scheduled for 10 am local time in Germany (9 am GMT), this corresponds to a local time of 1 am in California. The time is advantageous in California because it's in the middle of the night, but in Germany, the job would be executed during working time. For certain jobs, for example, backups of files at the operating system level, the execution time is very critical for the following reasons:

- A backup of these files may require that the files aren't changed or used during the backup process because the backup fails otherwise.
- Programs that try to change a specific file are canceled because the file is locked due to the backup process.

[+]

Background Jobs for Multiple Time Zones

List the respective local times for all affected global locations. This way you can easily determine the local time in the affected locations when scheduling a job.

You should also define an enterprise timer (a specific server, for example) or an enterprise time for organizations with locations in different time zones.

You have several options here, for example:

- As the enterprise time, you use the time zone in which the enterprise is headquartered.
  - For SAP in Walldorf, Germany, this is CET (Central European Time)
  - For United Airlines in Chicago, Illinois, this is CST (Central Standard Time).
- UTC (Coordinated Universal Time) is used as the enterprise time, previously known as GMT (Greenwich Mean Time). This time is used by global organizations, such as airlines.

For daylight savings time, you have to consider the days at which the clocks change:

- **Beginning of daylight savings time**
  The clocks are adjusted forward one hour. Jobs that were scheduled for this hour are not executed or executed with a delay. Tasks that are carried out after the clock shift and that depend on a job that should have been executed in the missing hour need to be checked.
- **End of daylight savings time**
  At the end of the daylight savings time, a problem occurs because an hour is "repeated." For example, if the clock is adjusted backward from 3 am to 2 am, the hour exists twice for the system.

You can avoid these clock shift difficulties by using UTC (GMT) as the enterprise timer.

[!]

Standard Time and Daylight Saving Time

Clocks do not shift at the same time in all countries. It may thus come to time differences during this phase.

15.5 Summary

Background jobs are a useful alternative to dialog mode, in particular for program runs that must be executed periodically. You can run nearly all reports in the background. The SAP system offers various options for starting programs automatically in the required interval.

Specifically, evaluations or reports that have a long runtime due to the amount of data that is processed should run in the background and not during peak load times of the SAP system to avoid negative effects on the performance. Background processing enables you to schedule this kind of job for overnight processing, for example. You then simply have to check the results of the job runs the next morning.

In an SAP system, the printing of data, such as purchase orders, invoices, or similar documents, plays an important role. This chapter describes how to configure the output infrastructure of the SAP system and manage output requests.

16 Output Management

Within the SAP system, the spool system fulfills several functions that are essential for the output of data: It receives documents to be printed from the user (*spool request*), saves the data in a separate database (*TemSe*), and then generates an *output request*, which is sent platform-independently to the print system of the operating system (*host spool system*). The operating system's host spool system then transfers the print job to the printer or a similar output device. As the administrator, it is your task to manage the output devices within the SAP system and configure and monitor the SAP spool system.

16.1 Setting Up the Spool Servers

If users use the print button (🖶) to notify the system that they want to output a list or a screen view on a printer, the SAP system initially creates a spool request. To turn this spool request into an output request that can be forwarded to the printer, you require a *spool work process*. A spool work process, in turn, is provided by a spool server.

The SAP application server itself is usually the first spool server of your SAP system. Beyond that, you can define additional *real* or *logical* spool servers. An additional real spool server can be another, physical SAP system (for example, your QA system), which assumes the formatting of spool requests in case of bottlenecks as the *alternative server*. A logical spool server, however, is not a separate, physical device but only a mapping of a real server. You use logical servers, for example, to optimize the management of output devices by assigning a logical spool server to your printers (see Section 16.2). For example, if you transport your output devices, you must then only switch the logical output servers to the new real output server instead of adjusting the output server of all output devices.

[⚙]

Several Spool Work Processes

Depending on your enterprise's requirements, the spool server must manage a more or less large number of spool requests; in other words, several spool work processes are required to master the mass of accumulating spool requests. The number of spool work processes of the application server is controlled using profile parameter `rdisp/wp_no_spo`. SAP Note 108799 provides information on how many spool work processes you must provide.

The following sections describe a common scenario in which two real spool servers are mapped by a logical spool server each. Load balancing is set up between the logical spool servers, which pass spool requests to the alternative server if the first server is overloaded. Follow these steps:

1. Enter Transaction "SPAD" in the command field, and press the [Enter] key (or select the TOOLS • CCMS • PRINT • SPAD—SPOOL ADMINISTRATION menu path).
2. Select the DISPLAY option for the SPOOL SERVERS in the DEVICES/SERVERS tab.

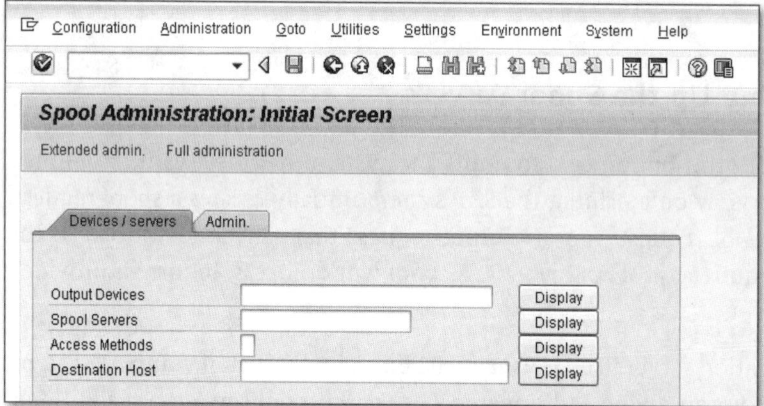

3. The system displays the spool servers that are currently defined in the system. To change the settings of an existing server or create a new spool server, click on CHANGE (✎).

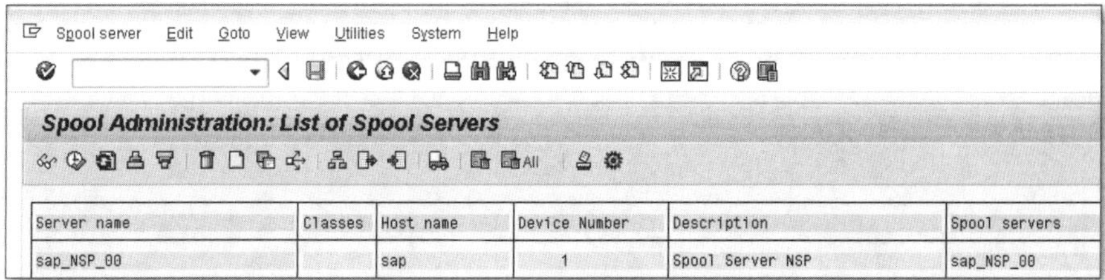

4. Create a new *real* spool server by clicking the CREATE button (□).

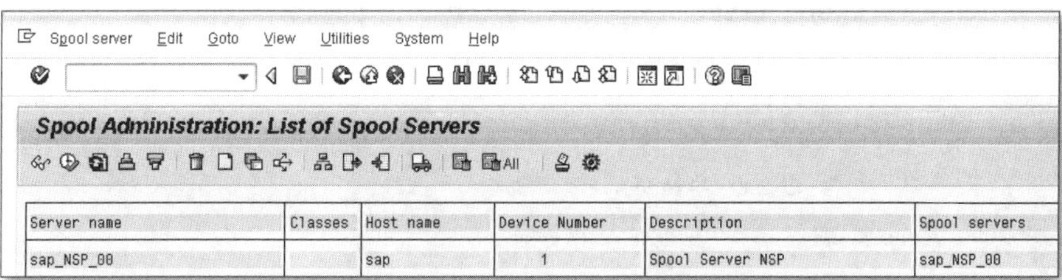

5. Enter the name of the server and a description, and then select SAVE (💾).

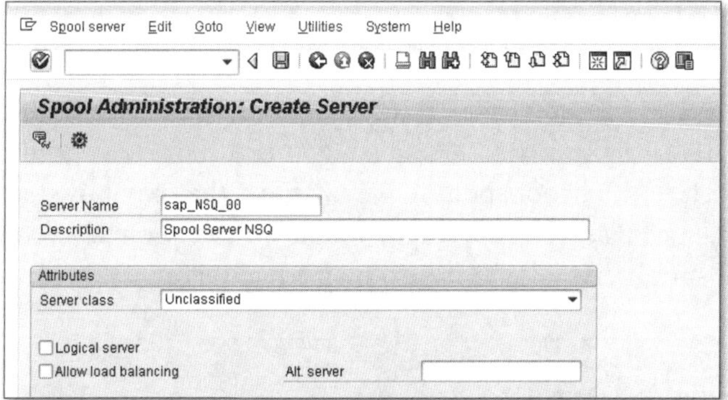

Server Class [+]

The entry in the SERVER CLASS field mainly serves informational purposes and should primarily ensure higher clarity. You can leave the entry as UNCLASSIFIED if you don't want to use the server classes.

6. Click BACK (⊙) to return to the list of spool servers, and reselect CREATE (□) to now create a new *logical* server.

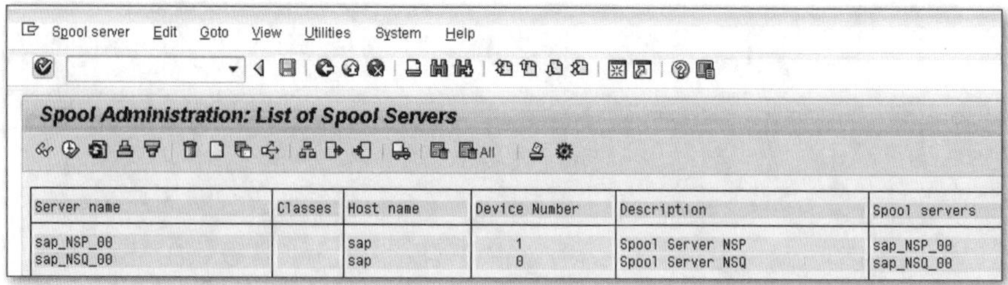

7. Enter a server name and a description, and activate the LOGICAL SERVER checkbox. Enter a real spool server in the MAPPING field. Click SAVE (💾) to save your entries.

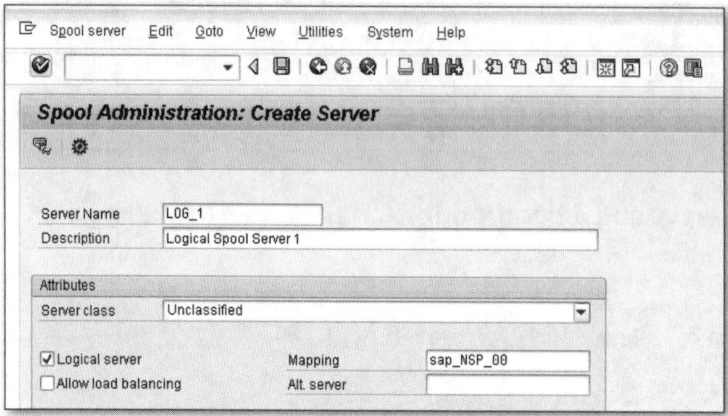

8. Click BACK (⮌) to return to the list of spool servers. Repeat the previous step to create a second logical spool server. As a result, you now have two real spool servers and two logical spool servers, which each map a real server.

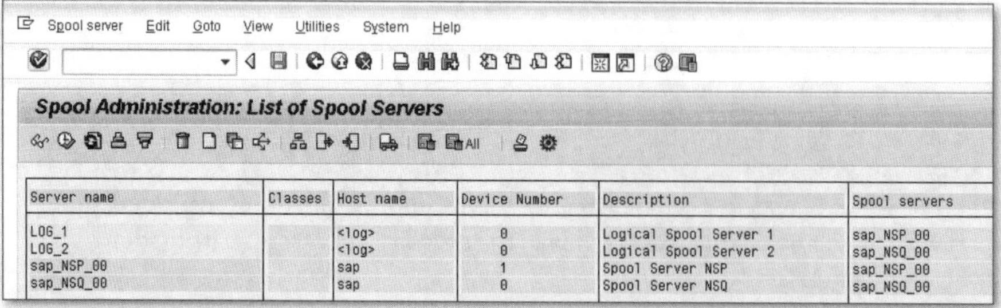

9. To define load balancing, position the cursor on the first logical server, and then click on CHOOSE (🔍) to open the detail view. Now activate the ALLOW LOAD

BALANCING checkbox, and enter the name of the logical server under ALT. SERVER. Save your entries (💾).

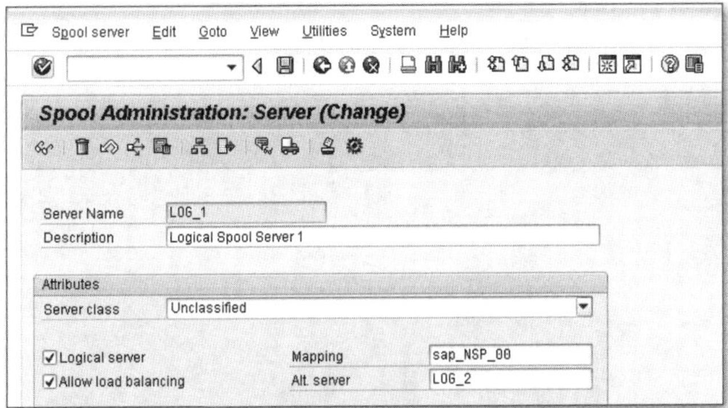

If all spool work processes of the logical server LOG_1 or the real spool server sap_NSP_00 should be fully utilized, the system will now pass the spool requests to the logical spool server LOG_2, that is, the real server sap_NSQ_00.

16.2 Setting up Printers

Before you can print from the SAP system, you must first define the output device, that is, the physical printer. This applies to network printers as well as to local devices connected to your PC.

16.2.1 Configuring Network Printers

To ensure that the print coupling between the SAP system and the operating system works, you must first setup the network printer at the operating system level. Perform the following steps before setting up a printer:

- Set up the printer at the operating system level.
- Write down the network name of the printer (for example, FIN3 or \\ACCOUNTING\ACCOUNT2, *not* the printer type such as OKI C5400).
- Write down the printer type. The printer type is a combination of the manufacturer name and the printer model (for example, HP OKI C5400).

To set up the printer in the SAP system, follow these steps:

1. Enter TRANSACTION "SPAD" in the command field, and press the [Enter] key (or select the TOOLS • CCMS • SPOOL • SPAD—SPOOL ADMINISTRATION menu path).
2. Select the DISPLAY option for the OUTPUT DEVICES in the DEVICES/SERVERS tab.

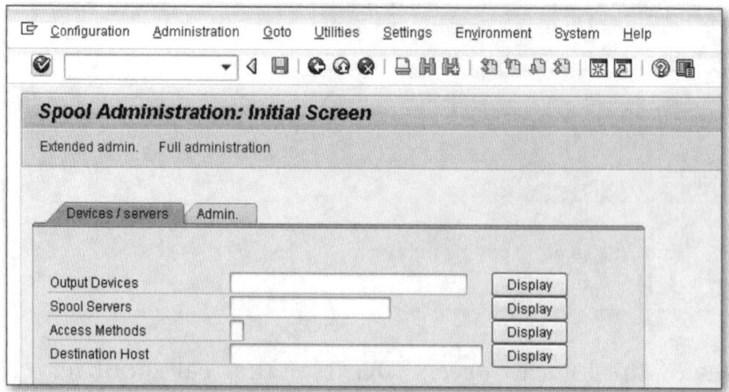

3. The system displays the printers that are currently available in the system. To change the settings of an existing server or create a new printer, click on CHANGE (✎).

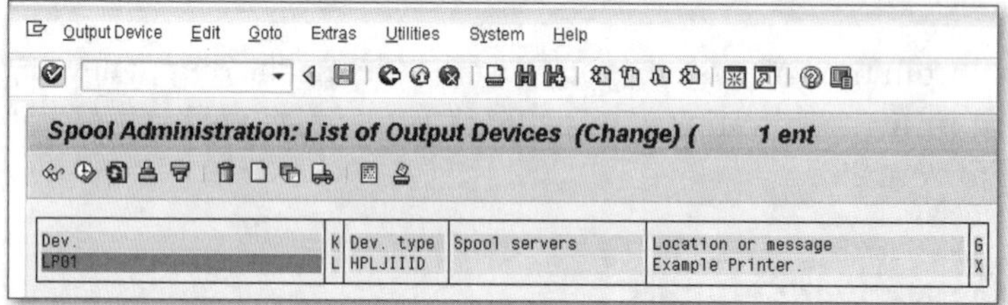

4. Create a new printer by clicking the CREATE button (□). The system displays the SPOOLER ADMINISTRATION: CREATE OUTPUT DEVICE view. Make the following settings:
   - Enter the name of the printer, with which the printer is supposed to be managed in the SAP system, in the OUTPUT DEVICE field in the header data.
   - If required, enter a SHORT NAME. If you don't make any entries here, the system generates the short name.
   - Select the printer model from the DEVICE TYPE dropdown list in the DEVICE-ATTRIBUTES tab.
   - Define a spool server.

- Select an appropriate DEVICE CLASS.
- Specify further information on the MODEL and LOCATION of the printer as required.

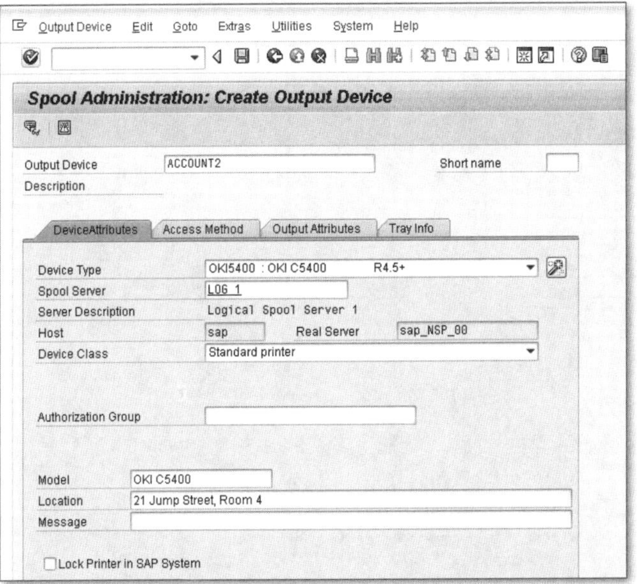

Model and Location [+]

The MODEL and LOCATION fields are essential for the administration of output devices and facilitate the assignment of SAP printers to physical devices. Don't forget to update the LOCATION field if you move the printer to another location.

5. Go to the ACCESS METHOD tab.
    - Select a HOST SPOOL ACCESS METHOD.

Host Spool [+]

The access method defines how the SAP spool system forwards the print data to the operating system's spool system. The access method depends on the operating system on which the spool server runs (for example, Unix) and to which operating system the printer is connected (for example, Windows for desktop printers). Ask the administrator who is responsible for the network printers if you are unsure about the access method.

- In the Host printer field, enter the network name of the printer as it was defined at the operating system level.
- In the Destination Host field, enter the PC or operating system print server to which the printer is connected.

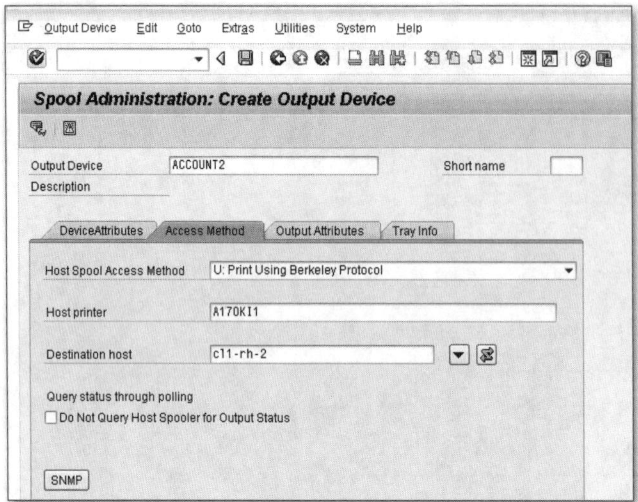

6. Depending on the access method selected, you can check your entries on the host spool access by clicking on Check connection (). (This option is not available in this example—if you checked the connection, the system would inform you whether the host spool system is available. Confirm the dialog window.)

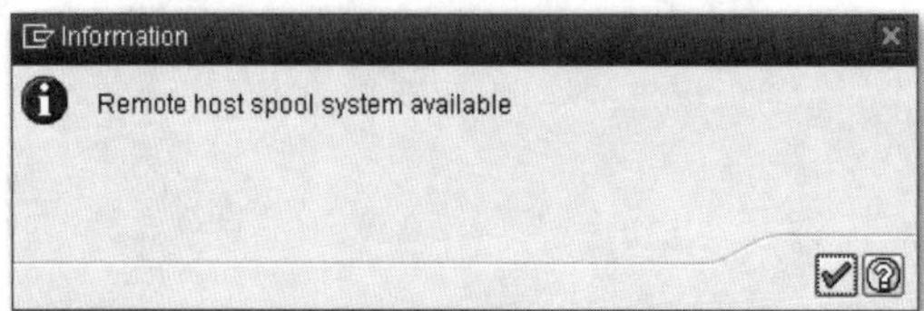

7. Call the Output Attributes tab. Here, you can optionally maintain other settings for the printer, for instance, whether a cover page is to be printed.

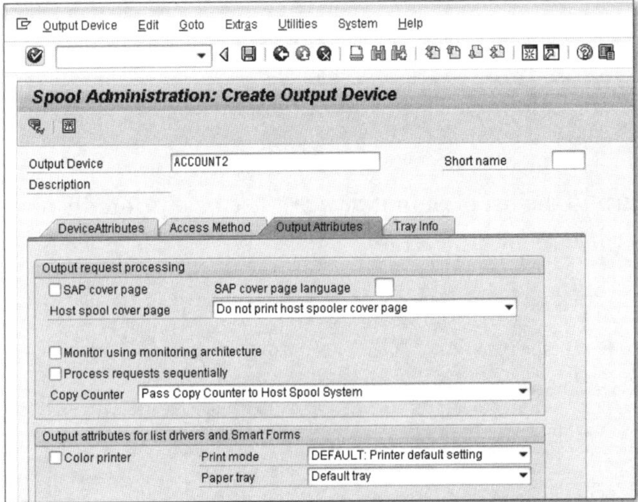

8. Open the TRAY INFO tab, and maintain the page formats of the paper trays if required. After you've made all entries, select SAVE (💾).

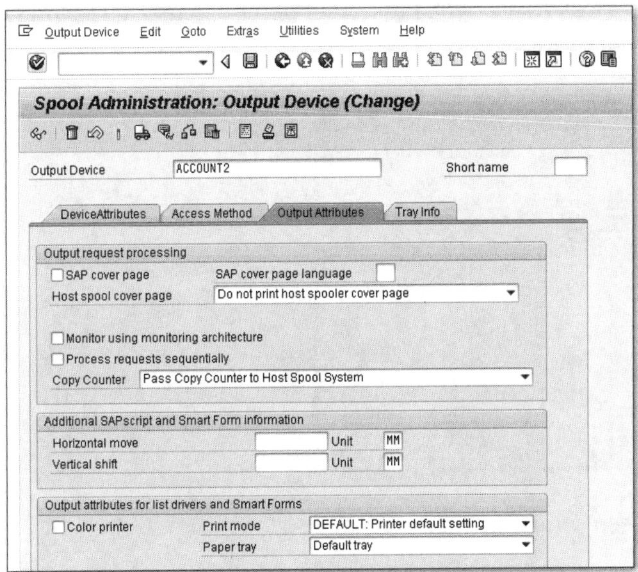

9. Provided that you haven't specified a short name yourself, a dialog window opens where you can generate a short name for the printer. Choose YES. The dialog window closes automatically.

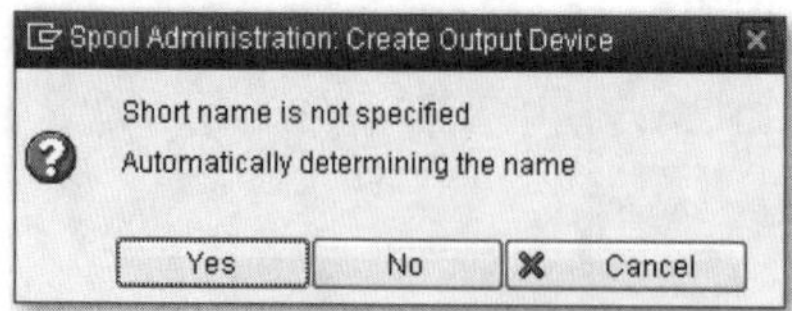

10. Click BACK (icon) to return to the list of output devices. The new printer is now displayed in the printer list.

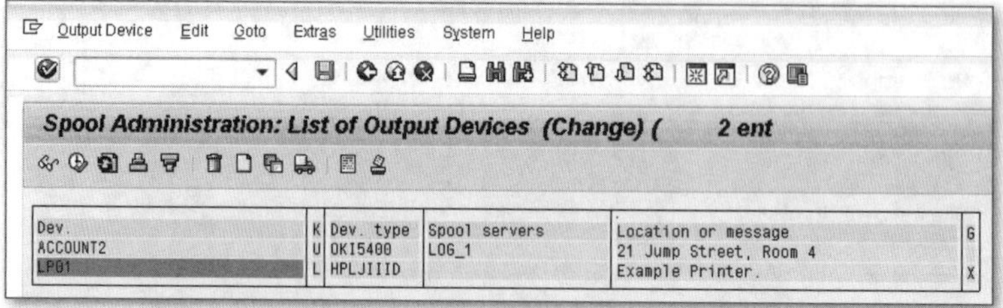

11. To test the printer, select the OUTPUT DEVICE • PRINT THIS LIST option, and specify the newly created printer as the output device in the PRINT SCREEN LIST dialog window. Click on CONTINUE (icon). Proceed as described in Section 16.3, to check the result of the print process.

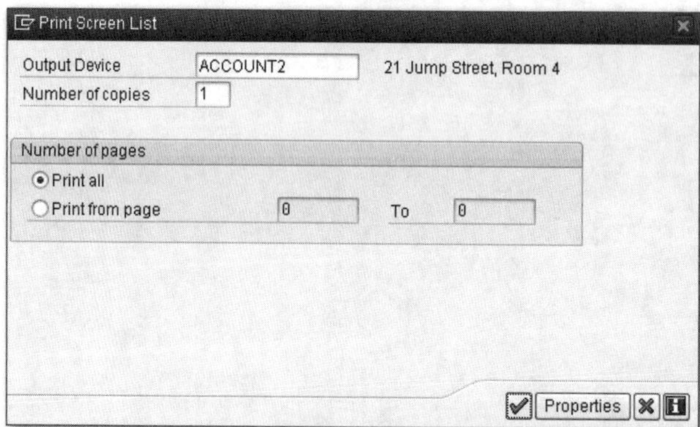

The network printer has been set up and can now be used.

16.2.2 Setting up Frontend Printers

It's possible that not all printers of your enterprise are network-compatible but are partly connected via USB to a PC, for example. You can also print with these devices from the SAP system. Set up a frontend printer for this purpose.

[Ex]

Notes on the Following Example

The following example assumes that the Windows operating system is used on the desktop PCs.

1. Implement steps 1 to 3 described in Section 16.2.1.
2. Create a new printer by clicking the CREATE button (□).
   - Enter a name for the printer (for example, "LOCL") in the header data in the OUTPUT DEVICE field.
   - In this example, enter a short name yourself by entering "LOCL" under SHORT NAME.
   - Select the SWIN or SAPWIN entry from the dropdown list of the DEVICE TYPE field from the DEVICEATTRIBUTES tab.
   - Select an appropriate DEVICE CLASS, for instance, STANDARD PRINTER.
   - If required, define a general description of the device in the MESSAGE FIELD.

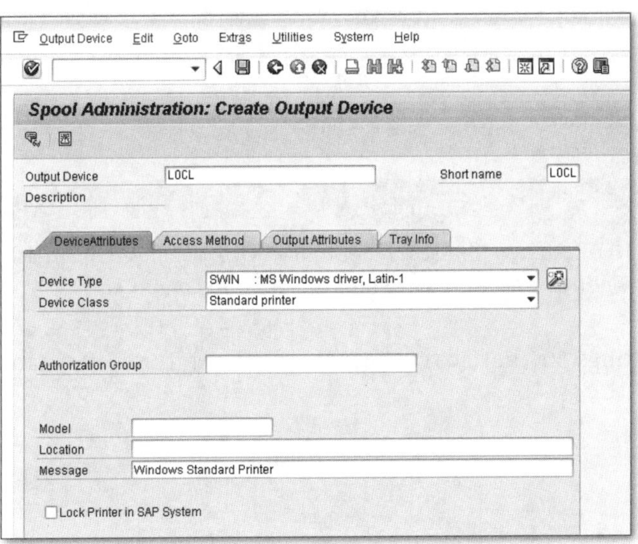

3. Go to the Access Method tab.
   - In the Host Spool Access Method field select F: Printing on Front End Computer or G: Front End Printing with Control Tech.

[✿]

Access Methods F and G

The access method F works with the transfer program SAPlpd, which is installed with SAP GUI on PCs (see Chapter 5). Alternatively, you can use access method G, which doesn't use SAPlpd. To use access method G, refer to SAP Note 821519. SAP Collective Note 128105 provides further information on frontend printing.

   - Enter the "_DEFAULT" value in the Host printer field.

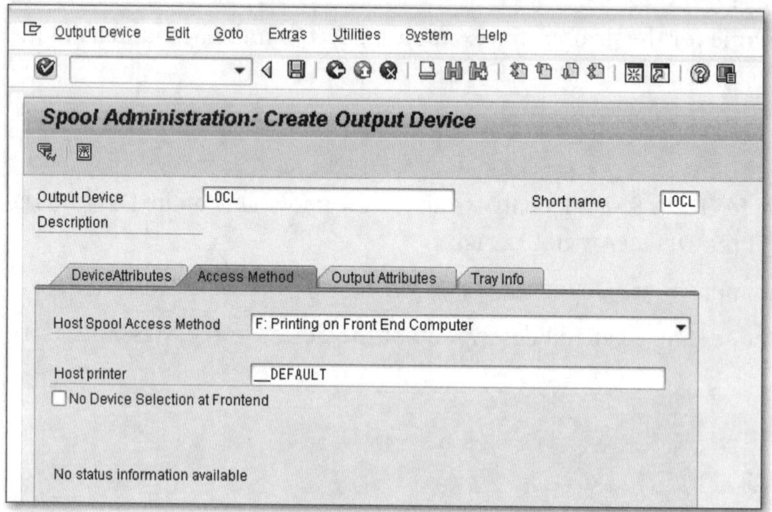

[+]

Host Printer "_DEFAULT"

By entering "_DEFAULT", the system addresses the output device which is defined as the default printer in the Windows operating system of the desktop computer.

4. Leave the default settings in the Output Attributes and Tray Info tabs unchanged.

5. Choose SAVE (), and click BACK () to return to the list of output devices. The new printer (e.g., LOCL) is included in the printer list.

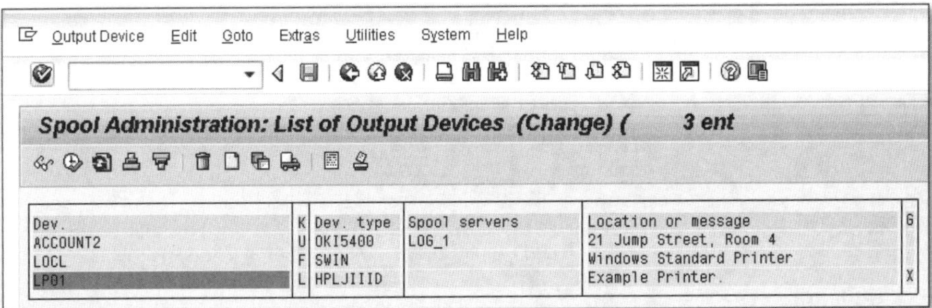

6. To test the printer, select the OUTPUT DEVICE • PRINT SCREEN LIST option in the menu bar, and specify the newly created printer (e.g., LOCL) as the OUTPUT DEVICE. If you set access method F, the system determines the default printer of the PC when printing and enters it in the WINDOWS PRINTER field. Click on CONTINUE ().

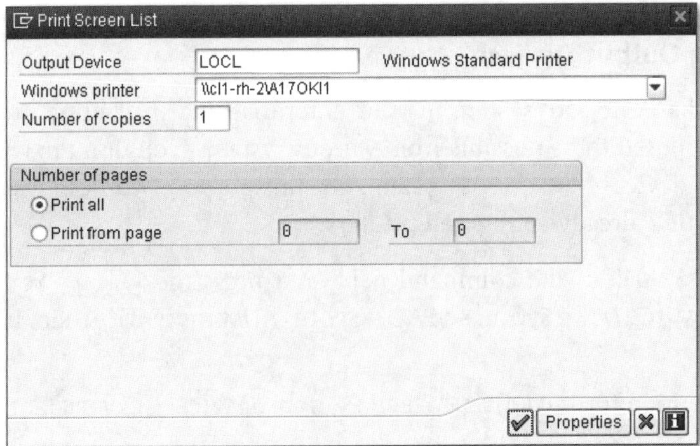

7. If you've used access method G, the dialog window appears again after you've clicked CONTINUE (). Select the required printer, and click OK.

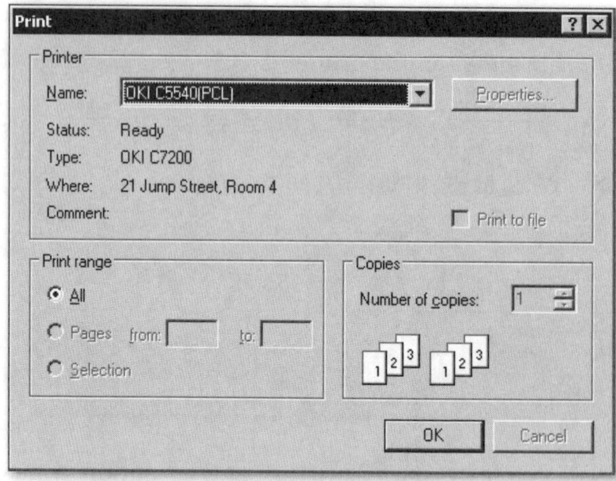

You've now set up the Windows standard printer in the SAP system. You can use this procedure particularly if you don't use any network printer but an USB printer, for example. In print dialog windows, you can now select the printer as device LOCL.

16.2.3 Transporting Output Devices

If you operate more than one SAP system in your enterprise and if printing on physical printers is supposed to be possible from various systems, you don't have to redefine the output devices in each SAP system. For this purpose, you can use the option of transporting already-configured printers.

1. Enter Transaction "SPAD" in the command field, and press the Enter key (or select the TOOLS • CCMS • SPOOL • SPAD—SPOOL ADMINISTRATION menu path).
2. Select the DISPLAY option for the OUTPUT DEVICES in the DEVICES/SERVERS tab.
3. Position your cursor on a printer, and choose TRANSPORT (🚚) to transport an individual device. If you want to transfer the entire list of output devices, select EDIT • TRANSPORT • TRANSPORT ALL.

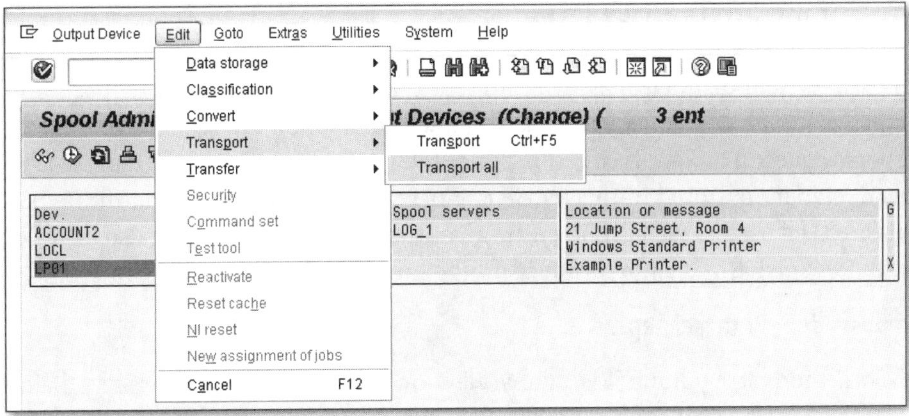

4. A dialog window opens which informs you that you need to process the printers later on in the target system. Confirm with CONTINUE (✔).

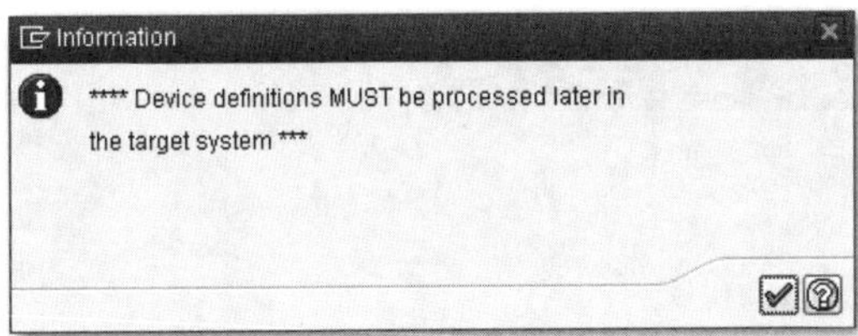

5. In the next dialog window, use the input help to select a Workbench transport request, or create a new request (🗋). Click on CONTINUE (✔).

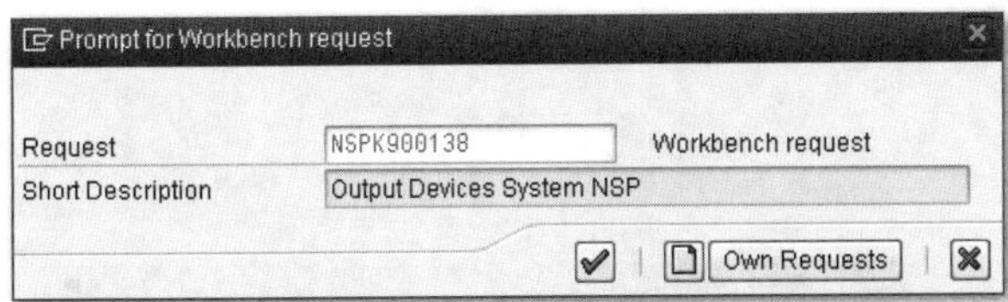

6. The printers selected were recorded in the transport request specified and can now be imported into other SAP systems (see Chapter 17).

[+]

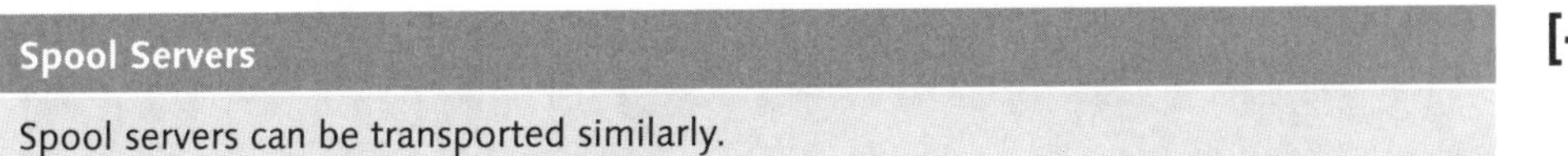
Spool Servers

Spool servers can be transported similarly.

16.3 Outputting Data

The SAP system distinguishes two different types of requests: spool requests and output requests. Whenever you click the PRINT icon (🖶), the system initially creates a spool request. The spool request includes the document to be printed; the data of this document is stored in the TemSe database. The spool request and the TemSe data are then used as the basis to create an output request, which now also includes attributes such as the target printer and the number of copies to be printed.

To print, follow these steps:

1. Click the PRINT button (🖶) in any view or list. The PRINT SCREEN LIST dialog appears where you are prompted to specify a printer. Depending on the spool control fixed values defined in your user master record, a printer is already displayed in the OUTPUT DEVICE field. Call the details for the spool request by selecting the PROPERTIES button.

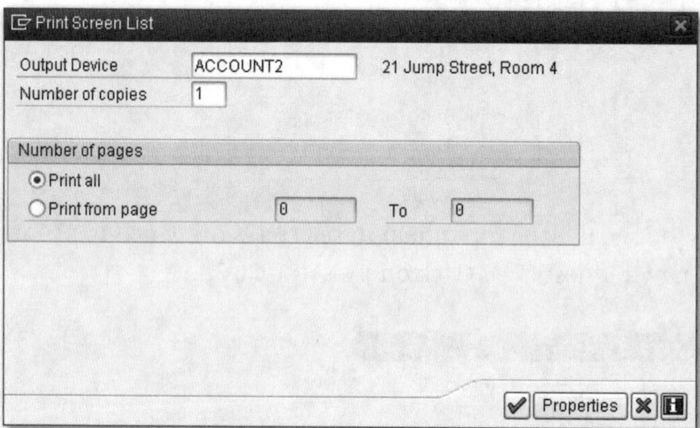

[+]

Different Print Menu Layouts

The layout of the dialog window may vary depending on what you want to print. For example, if you print authorization roles, you can set the print properties already in the dialog window; for screen lists, the detailed settings can be found via the PROPERTIES button.

2. You can edit the properties of the spool request. For example, you can select the priority, print a cover sheet, or specify the deletion time for the request. The presettings are mainly determined from the print configuration.

[!]

Time of Printing

Particularly note the settings for the TIME OF PRINTING option. This option specifies when an output request is generated from the spool request.

The following times of print are possible:

- SEND TO SAP SPOOLER ONLY FOR NOW
  Only a spool request is created. You must create the output request manually via Transaction SP01 (see Section 16.4). This setting is recommended for comprehensive print requests whose content you want to check prior to output.
- PRINT IMMEDIATELY
  After you've created a spool request, the system immediately creates an output request that is sent to the printer. This is the typical option for printing small lists and screen views.
- PRINT LATER
  With this setting, you specify the date and time when an output request is generated from a spool request and is sent to the printer. Use this time of print, for example, if you want to output a spool request at night, which you've created during the day.

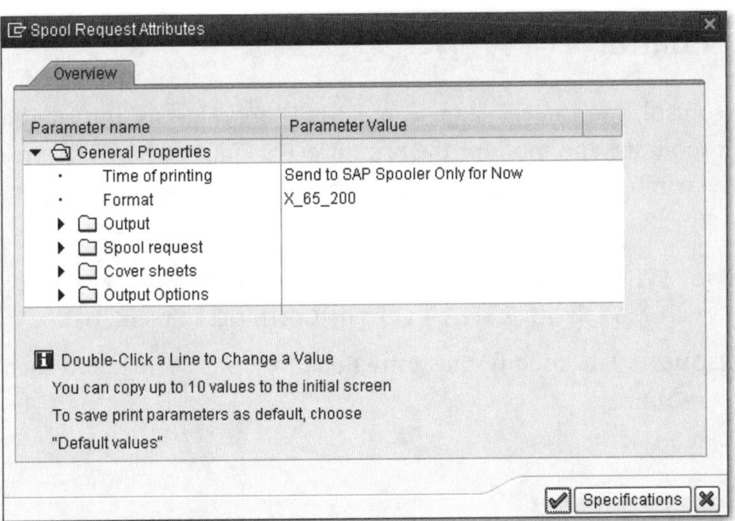

When you're done, click CONTINUE (✔) to return to the previous screen.

3. Start the print process via CONTINUE (✔) in the PRINT SCREEN LIST screen. A message in the lower part of the screen informs you about the number under which the spool request was saved.

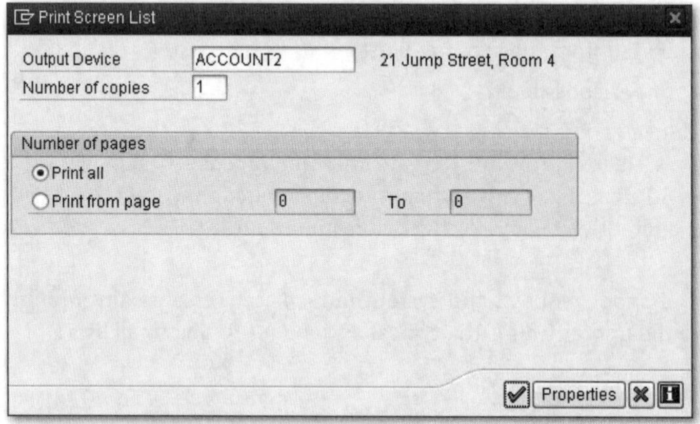

A spool request has been generated that contains your print data. You can now check it and print it.

16.4 Output Control

Using the output control, you can check the content of spool requests, initiate the creation of output requests, and monitor the print process. Transaction SP01 provides you with a wide range of options for data output management and problem analysis.

1. Enter Transaction "SP01" in the command field, and press the Enter key (or select the TOOLS • CCMS • SPOOL • SP01—OUTPUT CONTROLLER menu path).
2. In the SPOOL REQUESTS tab, modify the restrictions for your search, and then choose EXECUTE (⊕).

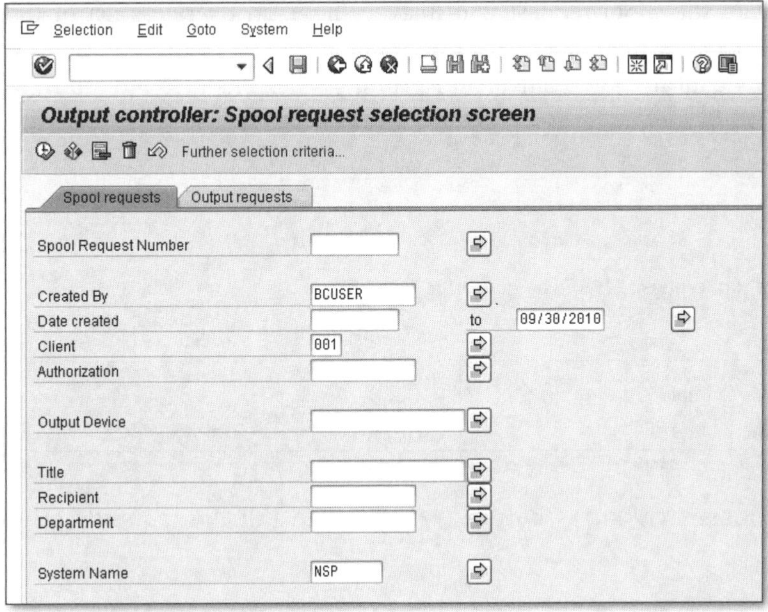

3. The STATUS column indicates that the list of this example has three unprocessed spool requests and a spool request that has caused an error message.

   This error is discussed later on. Let's first take a closer look at the open spool requests.

   To have the system display the content of a spool request, select a spool request, and click on DISPLAY CONTENTS ( ).

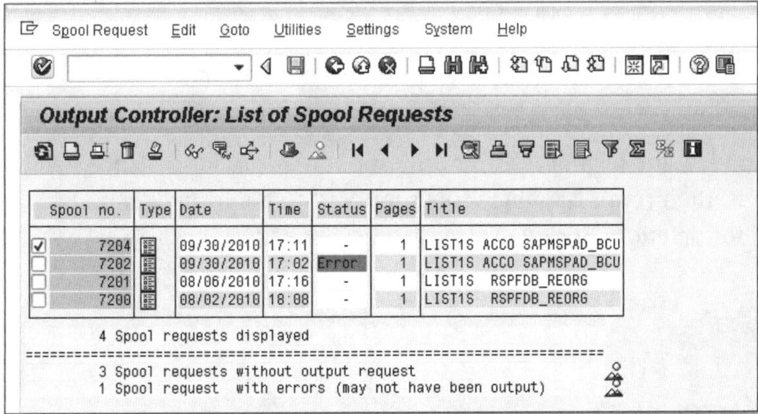

4. The content of the spool request is displayed (here: an overview list of the printers that exist in the system; see the example for test printing in Section 16.2.2). These data are now available for printing. Click BACK () to return to the overview of spool requests.

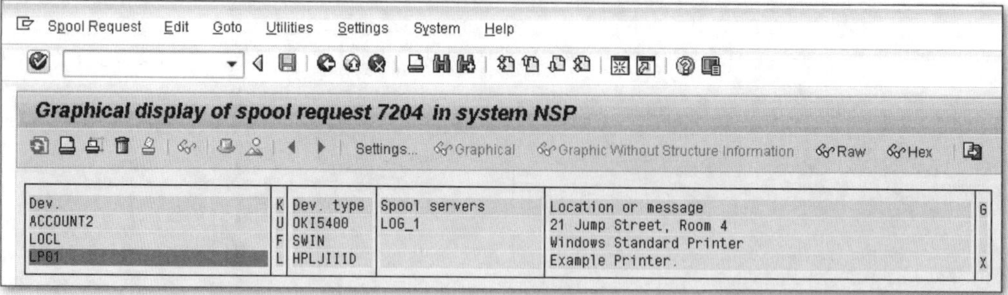

5. Via the REQUEST ATTRIBUTES button (), you can call the request's print settings.

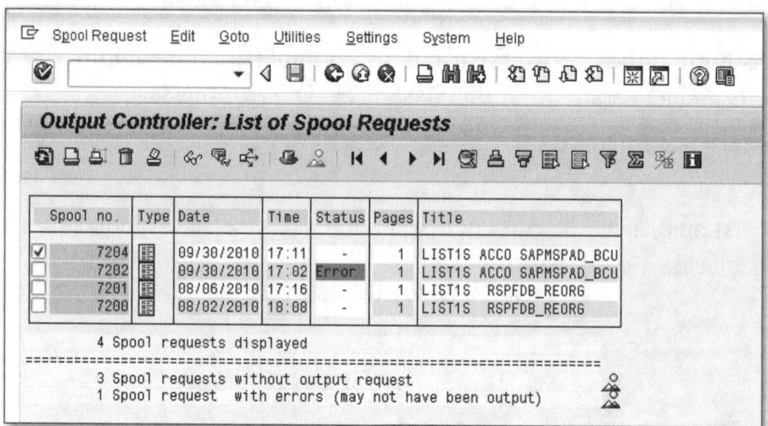

6. Here you can view the technical data of the spool request, for instance, which user created it, the printer on which it is supposed to be printed, and when it is scheduled for deletion. Click Back to exit the view ().

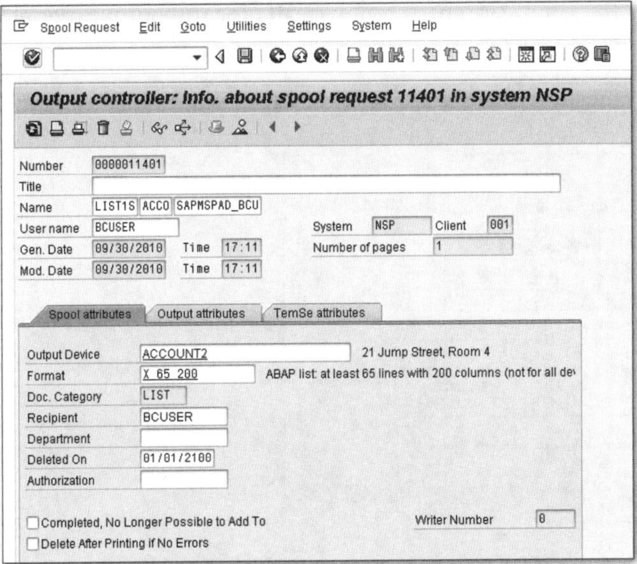

7. After you've exited the request information view, you return to the initial list of spool requests.

   Next, you print an open spool request. Select a spool request for which no value (" – ") is displayed in the STATUS column. No output request has yet been created for this spool request; in other words, it has not been printed yet.

   Select PRINT DIRECTLY (🖶) to send the print request to the printer.

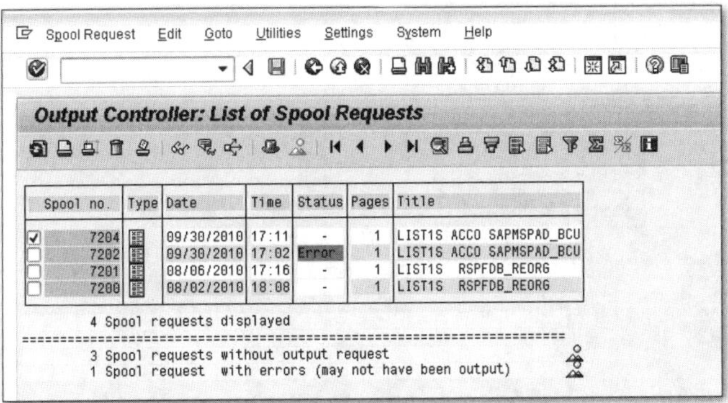

8. The system displays a message that an output request has been created. Simultaneously, the entry in the STATUS COLUMN changes to WAITING. The spool request

has been transferred to the spool system and now waits for the output request processing.

Click the REFRESH (icon) button to track the status change of the request.

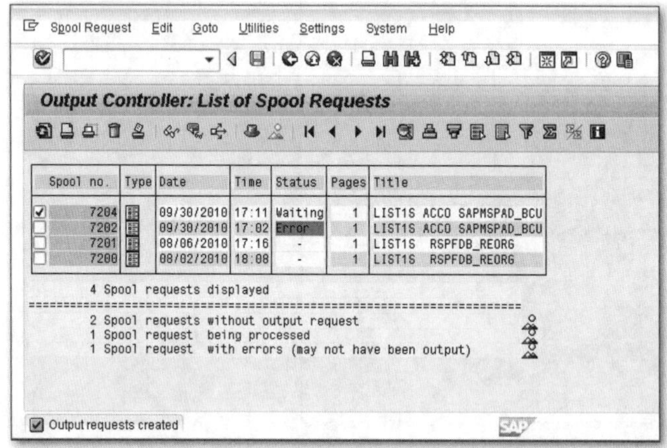

9. When processing the spool request, the status will change to BEING PROCESSED (not shown here). Refresh the display several times.

   If the status changes to COMPLETED, the system has successfully generated your output request and transferred it to the host spool system.

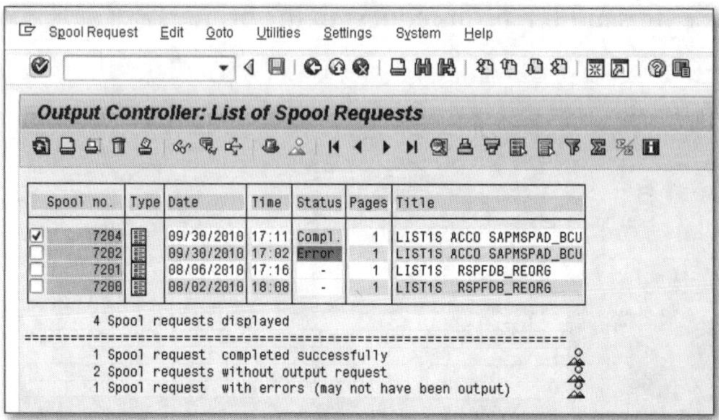

10. Now, let's discuss troubleshooting. Search for a spool request for which an error is shown in the STATUS column, and highlight it.

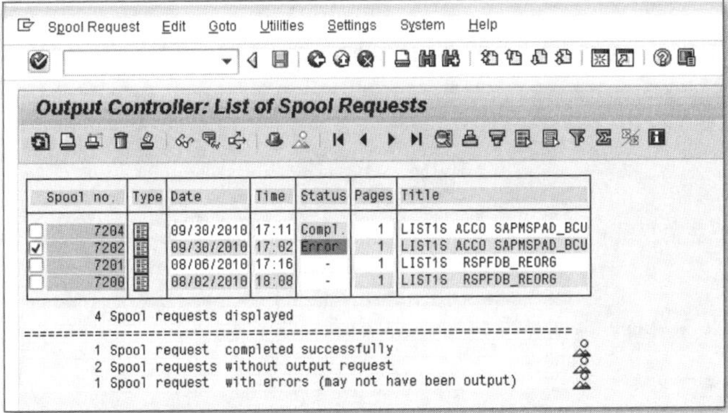

11. Double-click the Error entry in the Status column to go to the overview of output requests. Check the error by selecting Output request status ( ).

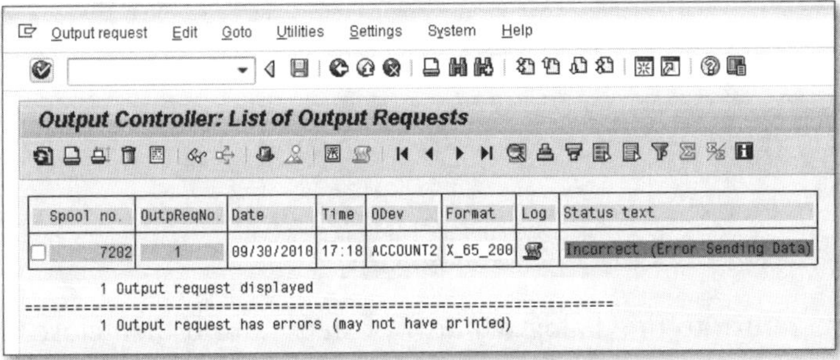

12. A dialog window opens containing information on the print problem. Use the Output request log button ( ) to display the SAP Spooler log.

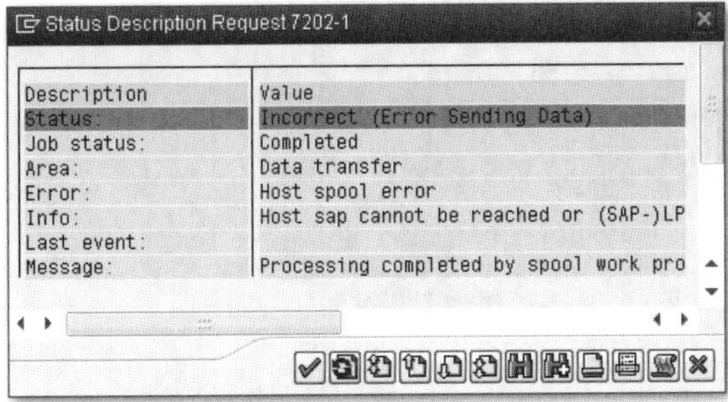

13. Analyze the information in the log, and remedy the cause of error. In this example, there seems to be a problem with the printer or the spool server.

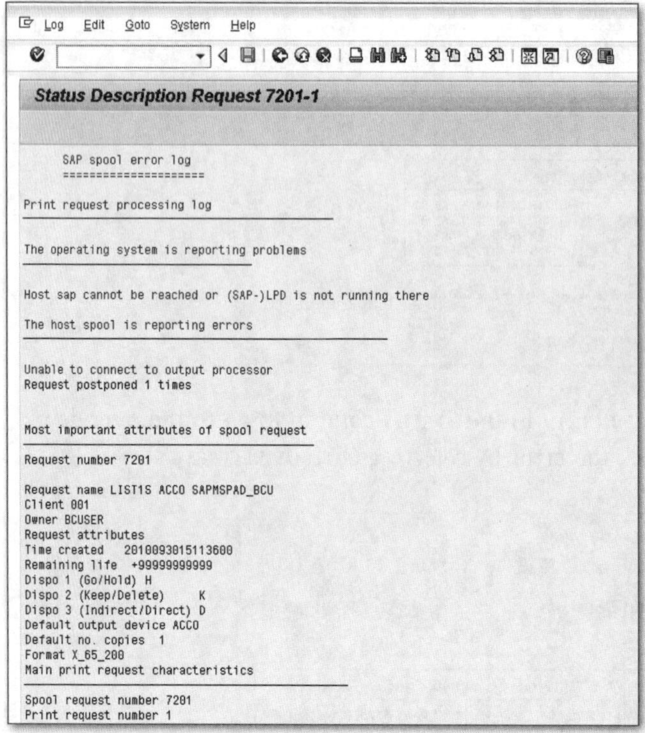

14. Click BACK () to return to the dialog window of step 12, and then close it with CONTINUE () to return to the list view. Restart the output by clicking PRINT DIRECTLY (). Check the printout and the status change of the new output request using the REFRESH button ().

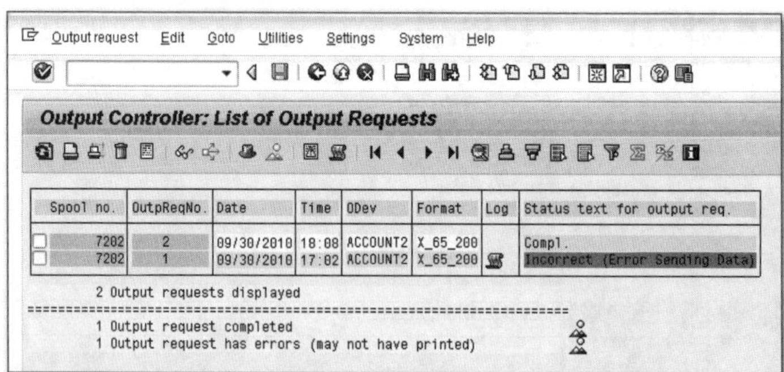

15. If the system was able to process the output request successfully (COMPLETED status), use BACK () to return to the overview of spool requests. There, the

status display for the spool request which has just been processed has changed yet again: Spool requests with several output requests, for which errors occurred partly, are indicated with value <F5> in the STATUS COLUMN (corresponds to the keyboard shortcut for the OUTPUT REQUESTS button ().

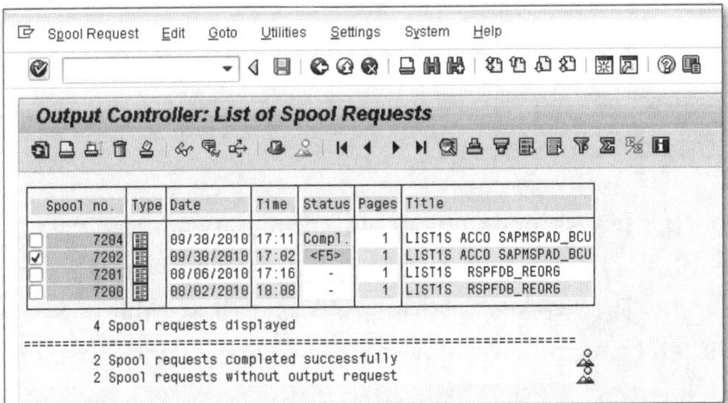

The COMPLETED status only indicates that the transfer of the output request to the operating system's host spool system has run without any errors. Errors at the operating system level or in the device itself (for example, a paper jam) can cause the printout to fail; however, Transaction SP01 doesn't display all of the possible problems. In case of a problem, revert to the monitoring tools of the operating system or the printer.

16.5 Deleting Old Spool Requests

Depending on how your spool system has been configured, old spools may consume memory in your database or your file system. In both cases, this memory could be used more reasonably for other purposes or can result in memory problems in extreme cases.

Spool Requests [+]

Spool requests are stored at the operating system level of the spool server under */usr/sap/<SID>/SYS/global/<client>SPOOL*. The file name includes the number of the SAP spool request.

Report RSPO0041 exists for deleting old spool requests, which can also be scheduled as standard job SAP_REORG_SPOOL and should be run on a daily basis. The job deletes all spool requests completed whose minimum retention period (usually, eight days) has been exceeded. If output requests still exist for an expired spool request which have not been completed (for example, due to error messages), the spool request is not removed. You must therefore regularly use the output controller (see Section 16.4) to check whether obsolete or undeleted spool requests exist, and remedy possible errors in the system.

16.6 Checking the Spool Consistency

In the spool consistency check, the system compares the spool data and the data in the tables of the output request (Tables TSP01 and TSP02) with the entries in the TemSe tables (Tables TST01 and TST03—see Section 16.7) as well as Tables TSPOE (Archive) and TSP02F (Frontend Print Job). Moreover, it displays a list with obsolete write locks which can be deleted.

If you manually delete entries from the spool and from TemSe tables or spool and TemSe objects from the directories, this may lead to inconsistencies. Other causes for inconsistencies may be the cancellation of reports or transactions or incorrect execution of a client copy. Implement the following steps to check the spool consistency:

1. Enter Transaction "SPAD" in the command field, and press the Enter key (or select the TOOLS • CCMS • PRINT • SPAD—SPOOL ADMINISTRATION menu path).
2. Select the ADMIN. tab, and click on CONSISTENCY CHECK OF SPOOL DATABASE.

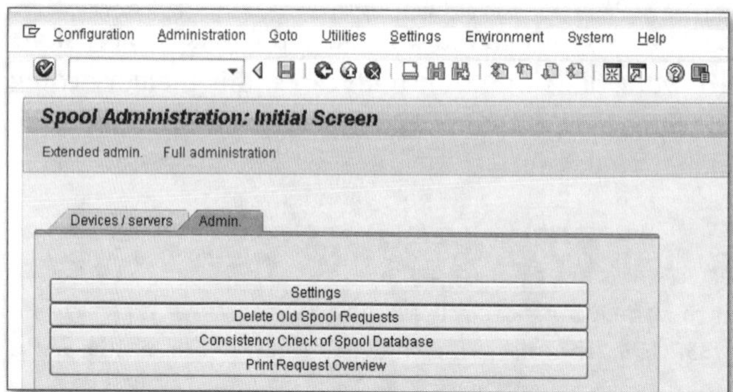

3. The system checks the spool and TemSe tables to ensure that the entries for each spool object match in the individual tables. You can undo any possible locks or error messages by selecting them and clicking DELETE SELECTED OBJECTS.

[+]

Background Job for Checking the Spool Consistency

You can also use the RSPO1043 program for checking the spool consistency. You should schedule this report as a periodic background job (see SAP Note 98065).

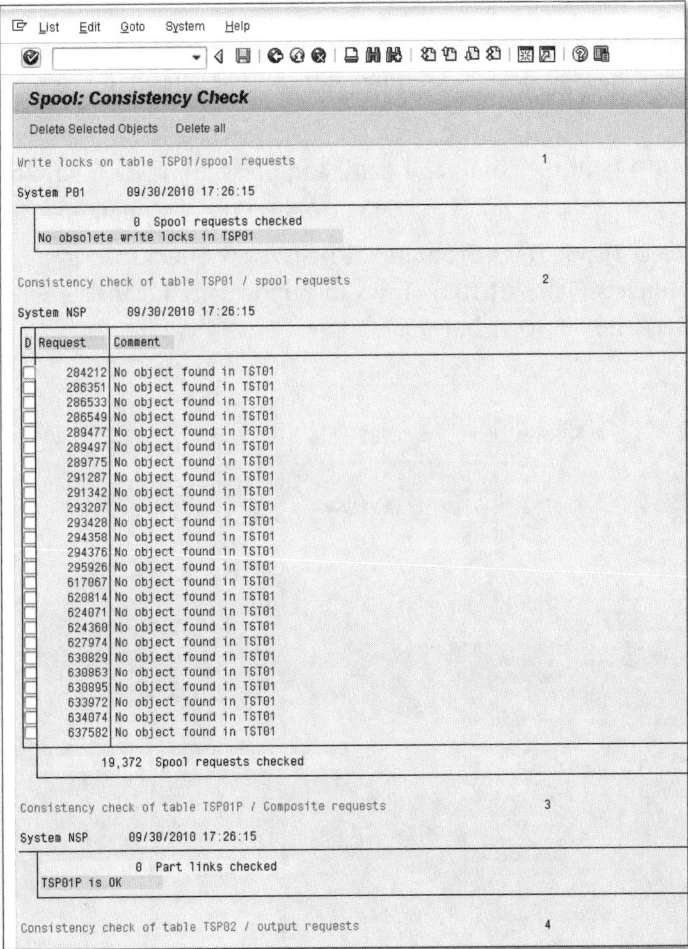

16.7 Checking the TemSe Consistency

The TemSe consistency check checks data in Tables TST01 (temporary Database Objects, TemSe Objects) and TST03 (TemSe Data). The TemSe database contains temporary objects such as job logs and temporary HR administration data. Report RSTS0020 executes the consistency check.

The relationship between the object and the data in the TemSe database may be corrupted with the following tasks: recovery from backups, copying databases, copying clients using unsuitable tools, and deleting clients without prior deletion of the associated objects.

Implement the following steps to detect and remove inconsistencies in the TemSe database:

1. Enter Transaction "SP12" in the command field, and press the Enter key (or select the TOOLS • CCMS • PRINT • SP12—TEMSE ADMINISTRATION menu path).
2. In the menu bar, select TEMSE DATA STORAGE • CONSISTENCY CHECK. The system checks the TemSe objects (Table TST01). You can remove any inconsistencies using the DELETE SELECTED OBJECTS button.

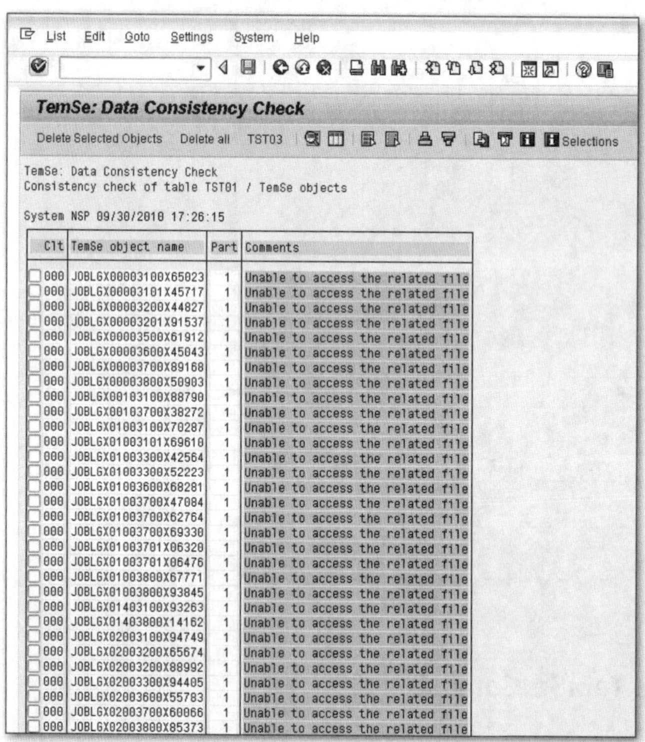

3. Select Table TST03 (TST03) to view the result of the TemSe data check (Table TST03). Again, use the Delete Selected Objects button to delete defective data in TemSe.

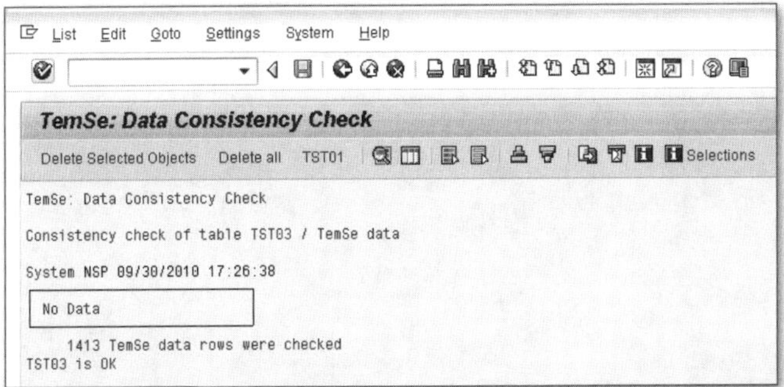

Check TemSe for inconsistencies and delete them at regular intervals, for instance, every week (see Chapter 5).

16.8 Summary

This chapter presented the architecture of SAP's print and spool system. The print data are processed by spool servers and sent to printers, which you can configure locally or in a network. With the output control, you manage and delete the spool jobs and repeat the print job.

Usually, you only have to deal with the administration of TemSe in rare cases—but you should nevertheless know where you can start with problem analysis in case of an error.

With the transport system, SAP provides a unique concept for recording, managing, and distributing changes, which contributes considerably to the stability of the entire system. This chapter describes how you create transport requests, use containers for changes, and finally carry out transports.

17 Change and Transport Management

The configuration of an SAP system is changed continuously due to new requirements of the users, within the scope of an SAP project—for example, when a new SAP module is introduced—or simply because errors are corrected. Because the SAP system is an integrated system, minor changes to an object can affect numerous other modules. In a worst-case scenario, this can lead to an interruption of entire business processes—and consequently to corresponding economic damage.

Changes in the SAP system must be controlled carefully to avoid these problems. Change management enables you to control changes in the SAP system in a defined process and minimize the related risks. This process begins with formulating a *change request* (or *request for change*). You can also define how the change is planned, checked, and approved. Finally, the realization, testing processes, and implementation are coordinated before the change is finally used in live operations.

Change Request Management with SAP Solution Manager (SAP PRESS, 2009) describes in detail how you can implement a change management process using SAP Solution Manager.

Technically, the SAP system supports your organizational change process with the *transport system*. Changes that you make to the system are automatically recorded and bundled in *transport requests*. When a transport request has been released, you can *transport* the changes to downstream systems within multisystem landscapes—usually consisting at least of a development, testing, and production system—that is, you don't have to implement the change manually in each system. This chapter focuses on the basic principles of transport management. For more information on this complex topic, refer to *SAP Change and Transport Management* (SAP PRESS, 2009).

17.1 General Notes on Change Management

Define what the change process is supposed to look like in your enterprise so that you can track the implementation of the changes and avoid risks during live operation. In this coordination process, involve the persons responsible from the system administration, programming, and application support teams.

At least the following steps should be part of the change process:

1. **Specifying the change**
   Specify the change that is supposed to be implemented. Describe the reasons, scope, target, and effects of the modification in detail.
2. **Obtaining approvals**
   Obtain the necessary approvals (see Appendix D). The necessary approval process can vary depending on the enterprise. In some enterprises, the approval needs to be granted by one person only; in other enterprises, approval is required from several persons.
   - *Approval by functional areas (end users)*
     – Checking the effects of changes to the respective functional area.
     – Performing additional tests in coordination with other functional areas that might also be affected
   - *Approval by system administrator*
     – Checking the changes that might affect the system administrator
     – Scheduling new jobs
     – Performing program error procedures or troubleshooting procedures

[+]

Approval by End Users

The main objective of the approval process is to inform other functional areas of the objects that are supposed to be transported. If the transport affects a functional area, the respective employees can perform checks or tests, for example. However, this may delay your transport until the end users are satisfied.

3. **Creating a transport request**
   Create a transport request. Implement the changes, and record them in your transport request.
4. **Documenting changes**
   Document all changes to the programming code or configuration and so on.

5. **Defining other critical data**
   Define other critical data for the transport management, for example:
   - Contact person in case of problems.
   - The employee who implements the transport is usually not a developer. If a problem occurs during the transport, the employee needs help for the troubleshooting process.
   - Recovery process in case of transport errors.
   - Employee who checks if the transport has been implemented properly in the target system.
   - Transport number.
   - Source system.
   - Target system(s).
   - Relation to other transports, for example, previous and subsequent transports.
6. **Recovery plan**
   The change control should also include a recovery plan that answers the following questions:
   - Which measures must be taken if problems occur during the import into the production system?
   - How is the rollback supposed to be implemented? Is a rollback possible?
   - Does the problem require a database recovery?
7. **Releasing the transport request in the test system**
   Release the transport request for the import to the test or QA system. Have developers and functionality analysts test the changes there.
8. **Importing the transport request to the production system**
   After the tests have been completed successfully, import the transport to the production system. Check the transport log, and check if the changes have reached the target system as expected.
9. **Making the change known**
   Inform the persons affected that the change is used in live operations.

Objects may be overwritten during the transport. If an object is used in the target system during the transport, the transport can have inconsistent results or lead to a termination of the transaction. In a worst-case scenario, a transport can result in a shutdown of the production system and require a system recovery. You should ideally carry out a complete backup before you import transports.

Consequently, implement the transport to the production system outside of times of peak user activity (for example, Sunday afternoon or evening) when no users are logged on to the system. Define at which times transports are usually carried out. However, in urgent cases, a transport may be necessary outside of the agreed weekly transport times. Specify in advance how this kind of emergency transport is handled.

17.2 Transporting Objects

The target and purpose of transports is to transfer objects and configurations from one system to another. In the common three-system landscape, a transport is generated in the development system, transported to the QA system where it is tested, and finally imported to the production system.

[+]

Names for the Transport Management System

The transport system was changed significantly in Release 4.x. Previously, it was referred to as *Correction and Transport System*. The acronym CTS is still used but now stands for *Change and Transport System*. The CTS includes the *Transport Management System* (acronym: TMS, Transaction STMS) and the *Change and Transport Organizer* (CTO; Transaction SE10).

The following transfers of changes are referred to as transports in the SAP system:

- From one client to another within the same system
- From one system to another for the same client
- From one system to another and from one client to another

Use the Transport Management System (TMS) to transport objects. This enables you to control the transports in the SAP system without working at the operating system level. Additionally, you can do the following in the TMS:

- Define transport routes.
- Bundle transport requests in projects.
- Schedule imports of requests for later.
- Use the functions of the Advanced Quality Assurance function.

[+]

Advanced Quality Assurance

As of Release 4.6, the TMS provides the Advanced Quality Assurance. This function requires that requests that have been imported to the QA system are approved there to be transported to the production system. This prevents requests that haven't been fully tested in the QA system from being transported accidentally. This change is a significant enhancement in the change management process and should be generally used in three-system landscapes.

- Basically, you can also implement transports at the operating system level using the tp transport program; this procedure, however, is less comfortable and prone to operating errors.

[!]

Prerequisite for Subsequent Sections

The transport scenario described in the following sections requires that the TMS is set up completely and properly.

17.2.1 Creating a Transport Request

To transport an object, you first have to create a transport request in which you enter your change. You can create the transport request before implementing the change or during the recording in a respective dialog.

In the following example, the transport request is created before the implementation of the change. You can find a reference to the alternative dialog in the appropriate step.

[!]

Authorization for the Creation of Transports

If you aren't authorized to create transport requests, you should ask your transport administrator for a transport request before implementing the change. Otherwise, if a transport request is missing, you have to terminate your work for specific objects (Customizing tables, for example), and repeat the steps later on.

1. Enter Transaction "SE10" in the command box, and press the Enter key (or select the menu option Tools • Customizing • IMG • SE10—Transport Organizer (Extended View)).

[!]

Alternative Transactions

Alternatively, you can also use Transaction SE09 (Transport Organizer)—it provides the same functions. Transaction SE03 (Transport Organizer Tools) is an additional useful transaction in the transport system: It enables you to perform researches and implement settings.

2. In the Transport Organizer window, select Create (☐).

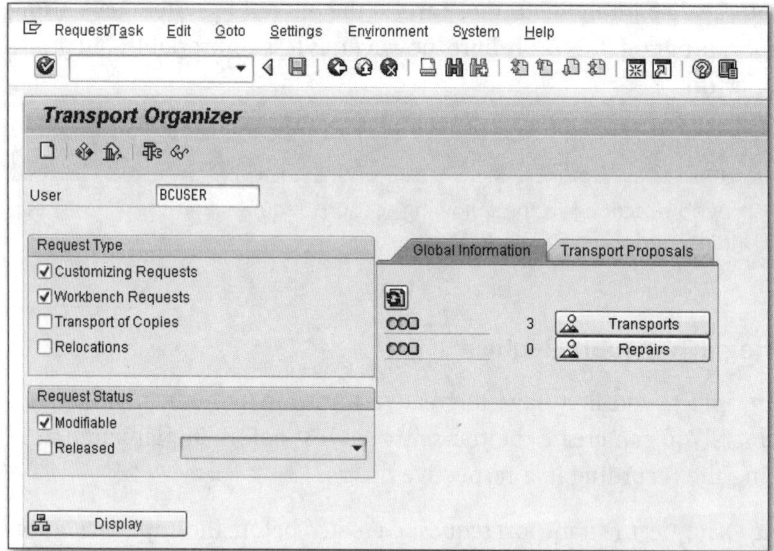

3. A dialog box opens in which you can define the type of the transport request that is supposed to be created. For example, activate the Workbench Request radio button, and click on Copy (✔).

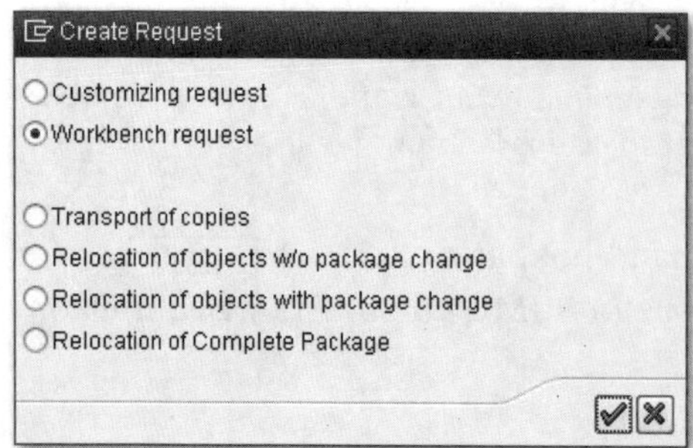

[!]

Transport Request Type

The request type depends on the object that is supposed to be transported.

- Customizing requests are used for Customizing changes, such as the maintenance of tables.
- Workbench requests are used for repository changes (programs, for example).

Note that changes to the Customizing cannot be transported with a workbench request and vice versa. That means, when creating the transport request, you need to know if you want to change a Customizing or repository object.

You cannot change the transport request type retroactively.

4. In the next screen, enter the administration data for the transport request:
   - Enter a meaningful SHORT DESCRIPTION.
   - If necessary, assign the request to a PROJECT. Depending on the configuration of your transport system, this may be a required entry field.
   - In the TARGET field, select the system to which the request is supposed to be transported. Usually, this is your production system.
   - In TASKS, enter the user IDs of all employees that are supposed to enter changes in this transport request.
   - When you are finished, choose SAVE (💾).

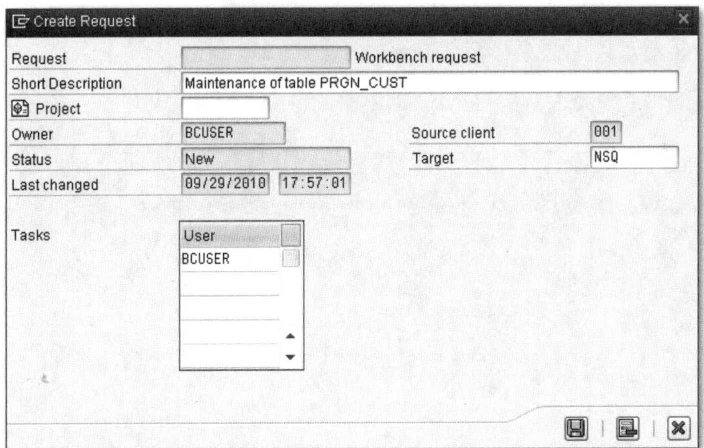

5. The system creates the transport request and the related tasks. The system automatically assigns a request number according to the following pattern: *<system ID>*K9*<consecutive number>*.

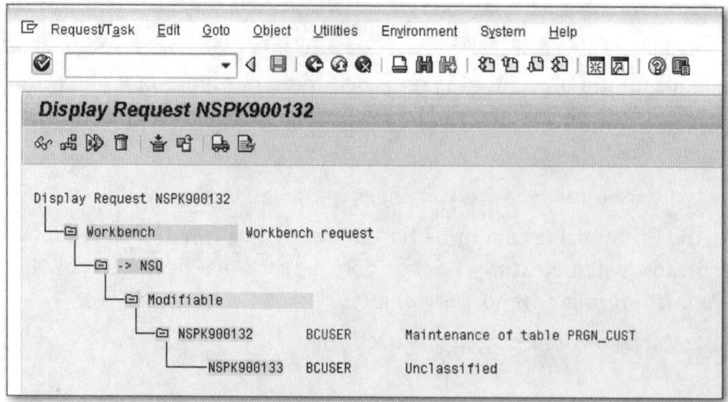

The transport request is created and can be used to enter changes. The system creates a specific task for every user that you specified.

17.2.2 Recording Changes in a Transport Request

Now, make your changes. Start the corresponding transaction, Customizing activity, or maintenance dialog.

1. For example, start Transaction SM30 for table maintenance (see Section 17.3), and add a new entry to table PRGN_CUST.

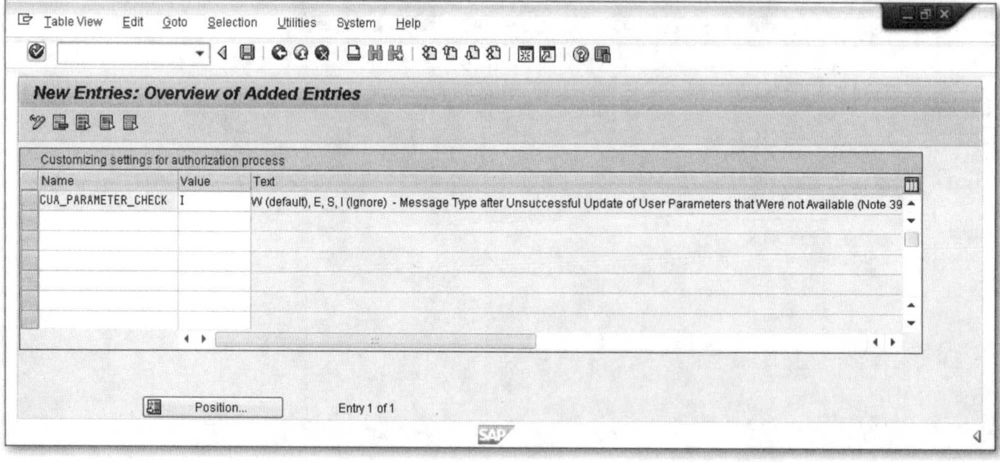

2. If you save your entry, a dialog box opens that prompts you to specify the transport request in which the change is supposed to be entered. Open the input help (□) to select a transport request.

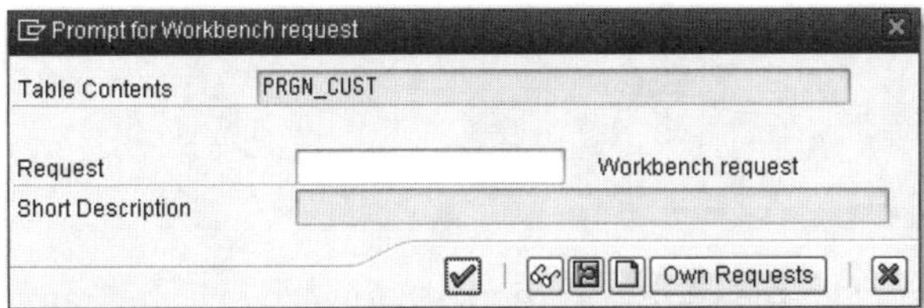

[+]

Creating a Transport Request

Here, the CREATE REQUEST button (□) also enables you to create a new transport request if you haven't done this yet. The advantage of this variant is that the request type is determined from the object that is supposed to be changed, and you can't create a request of the wrong type by mistake.

3. Another dialog box opens that displays the available transport requests; that is, it only offers the transports of the required type (e.g., workbench requests) that contain a tasks for your user ID. Position your cursor on the transport request or task, and click on CHOOSE (✓).

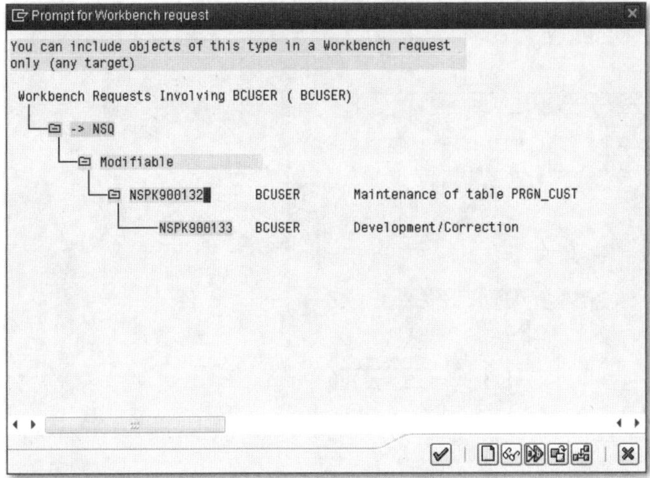

4. This takes you back to the prompt dialog box; the selected transport request is now specified in the REQUEST field. Select CONTINUE (✔).

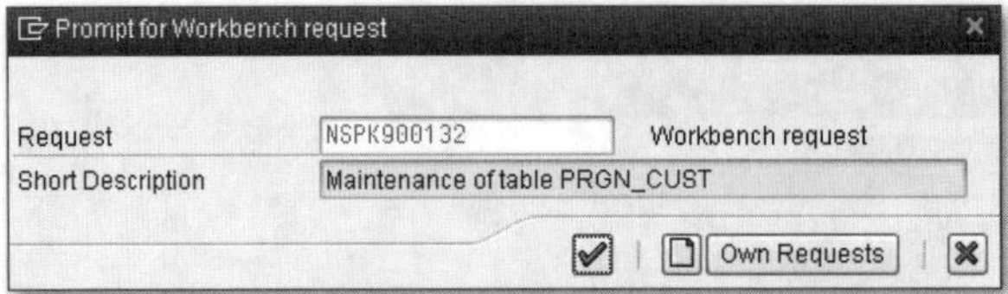

You have now recorded the change in the transport request. You can exit the transaction and release the transport request for transport.

17.2.3 Releasing a Transport Request

Prior to the transport, you must release all tasks related to the request and then the request itself.

1. Enter Transaction "SE10" in the command box, and press the Enter key (or select the menu option TOOLS • CUSTOMIZING • IMG • SE10—TRANSPORT ORGANIZER (EXTENDED VIEW)).
2. In the TRANSPORT ORGANIZER window, ensure that the user ID of the owner of the transport request that is supposed to be released is specified in the USER field. Select the REQUEST TYPES that are supposed to be displayed and the MODIFIABLE request status. Choose DISPLAY.

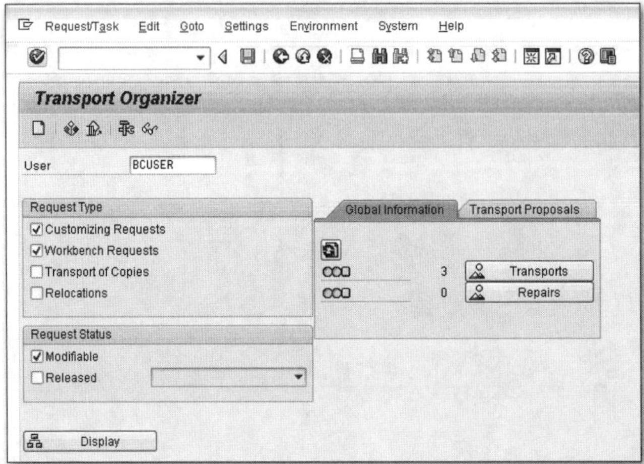

3. Position your cursor on the request to be released, and select RELEASE DIRECTLY (🚚).

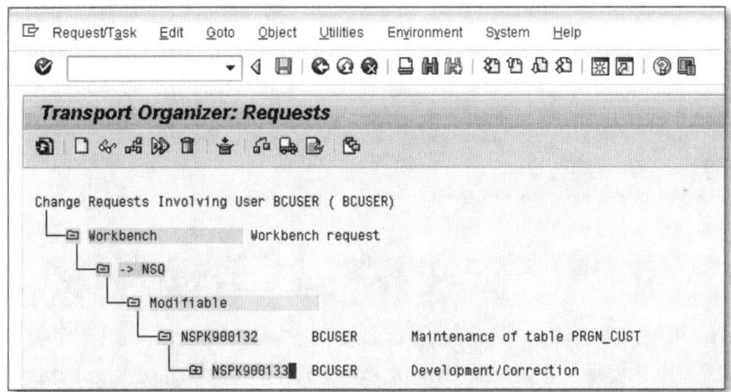

Releasing Tasks [+]

All tasks that are related to the request have to be released before the request itself can be released.

4. In the next step, release the transport request by positioning the cursor on the request and clicking on RELEASE DIRECTLY (🚚).

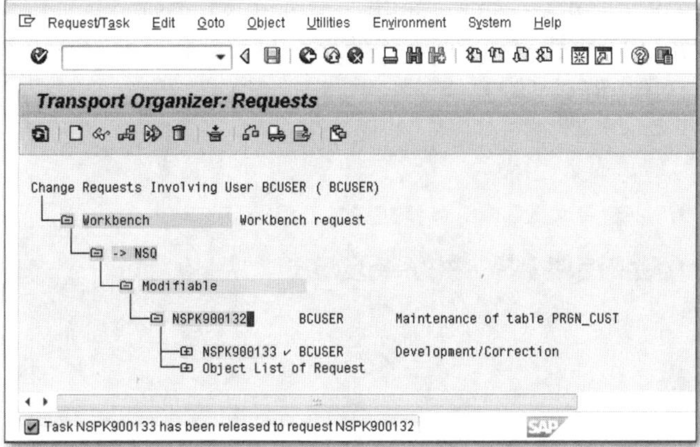

5. The system switches to the transport log view. For the Export step, the system displays the message IN PROCESS: REQUIRES UPDATE. Select REFRESH (🔄) to update the status.

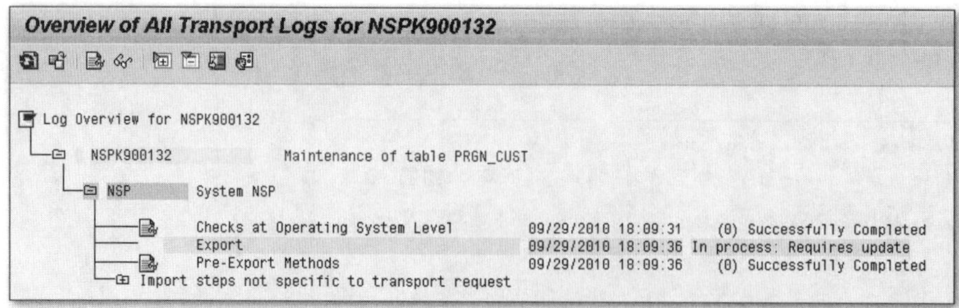

Transport Files

In this step, the values of the implemented changes are defined and the transport files are created at the operating system level. Up to this point, your transport request has simply "pointed" to the changed object (to the field in a table, for example). During the export, the value that the object has when it's released is determined and stored in the transport files.

A transport request consists of a control file and a data file.

- The control files start with K and are stored in the */usr/sap/trans/ cofiles* (Unix) or *<drive>:\usr\sap\trans\cofiles* (Windows) directory.
- The data files start with R and are stored in the */usr/sap/trans/data* (Unix) or *<drive>:\usr\sap\trans\data* (Windows) directory.

6. After the export has been completed successfully, the status message is set to SUCCESSFULLY COMPLETED. Check the *return code* in parentheses before the status message (e.g., 0). Then select BACK ( ).

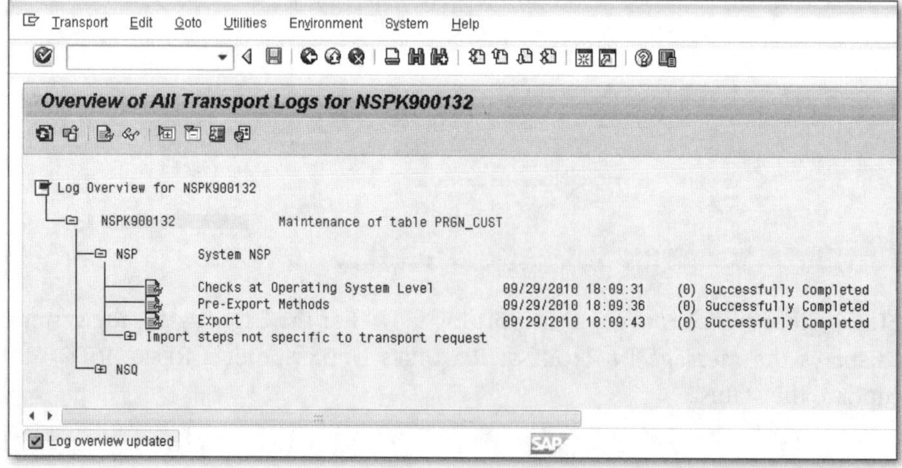

[+]

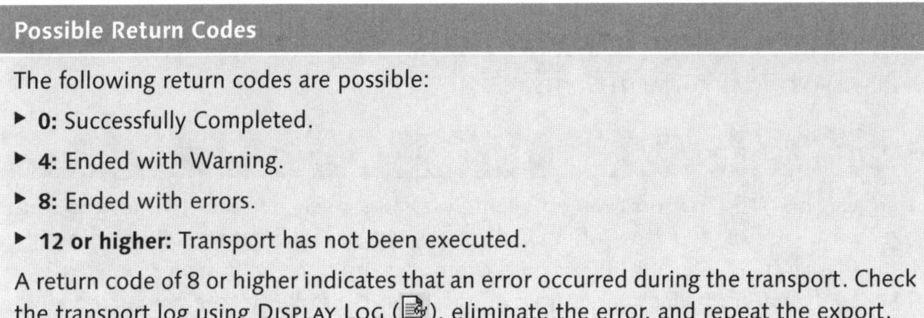

Possible Return Codes

The following return codes are possible:

- **0:** Successfully Completed.
- **4:** Ended with Warning.
- **8:** Ended with errors.
- **12 or higher:** Transport has not been executed.

A return code of 8 or higher indicates that an error occurred during the transport. Check the transport log using DISPLAY LOG, eliminate the error, and repeat the export.

7. The transport request overview displays a message that the request was released and exported. Exit the TRANSPORT ORGANIZER screen via BACK.

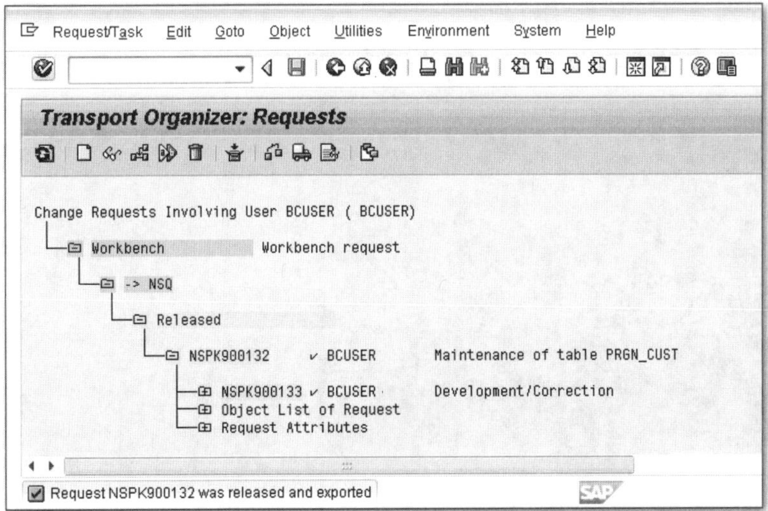

After the release and successful export, the transport request is now ready for import to downstream systems.

17.2.4 Importing Transport Requests

After the release, the system automatically queues the transport request in the *import queue* (the list of the requests that are supposed to be imported) of the downstream system. The import queue enables you to control the requests' import.

1. Enter Transaction "STMS" in the command box, and press the Enter key (or select the menu option TOOLS • ADMINISTRATION • TRANSPORTS • STMS—TRANSPORT MANAGEMENT SYSTEM).

Domain Controller

Transaction STMS (Transport Management System) is a very complex tool for the configuration, control, and monitoring of the transport system. Certain settings can only be made centrally in client 000 of the system. It is used as the *domain controller*. The TMS configuration is distributed from the domain controller to the connected child systems.

2. The TRANSPORT MANAGEMENT SYSTEM window is displayed. Select IMPORT OVERVIEW (🚚).

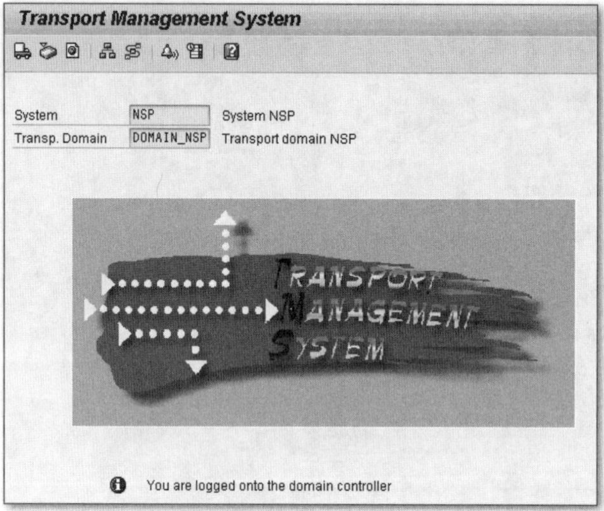

3. Position your cursor on the system to which you want to import the transport request, and click on DISPLAY IMPORT QUEUE (🔗).

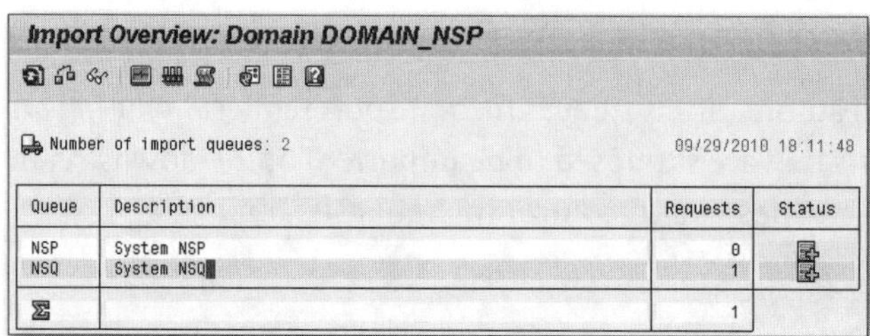

4. The system displays the list of the transport requests to be imported (*import buffer*). Position your cursor on the request to be imported, and click on IMPORT REQUEST (icon).

[!]

Transport Buttons

Two of the icons are quite similar, so ensure that you select the appropriate icon. With the IMPORT ALL REQUESTS button (icon), you import the entire import queue.

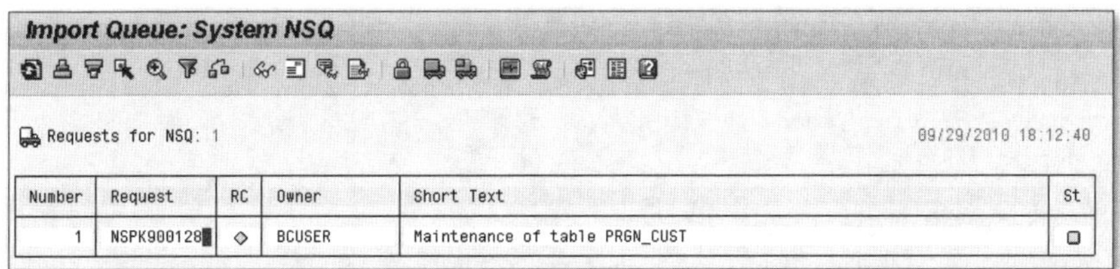

5. In the DATE tab of the IMPORT TRANSPORT REQUEST dialog box, enter the number of the client to which the request is to be imported in the TARGET CLIENT field. Here, you can also define a later execution date if you don't want the import to start immediately.

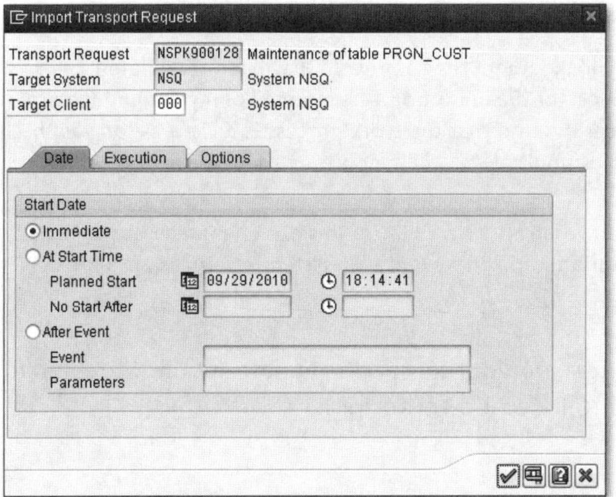

6. Navigate to the EXECUTION tab. Select the SYNCHRONOUS option.

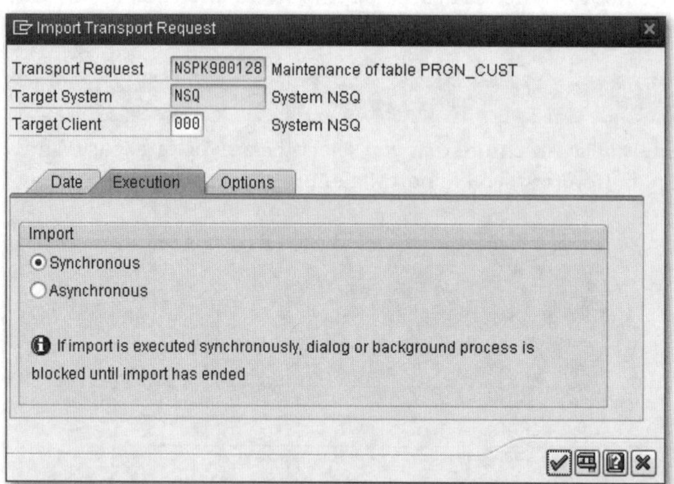

[⚙]

Import Options

The TMS calls the transport control program, tp, at the operating system level during the import. This program then executes the transport. To start the tp program, an SAP work process is used. You can choose between the following options:

- **Synchronous**
  The work process remains blocked until the tp program has been terminated. Select this option if you want to monitor the import process in detail or if you want to carry out subsequent actions. Bear in mind that the work process is locked as long as the import runs. In extreme cases (multiple parallel imports), this may block the system.
- **Asynchronous**
  The work process is released when tp is started. Use this option if many or very large transport requests queue for an import to avoid that system resources are unnecessarily bound.

7. Select the OPTIONS tab. Here, you can set specific import options, if required, called *unconditional modes*. Click on CONTINUE (✔).

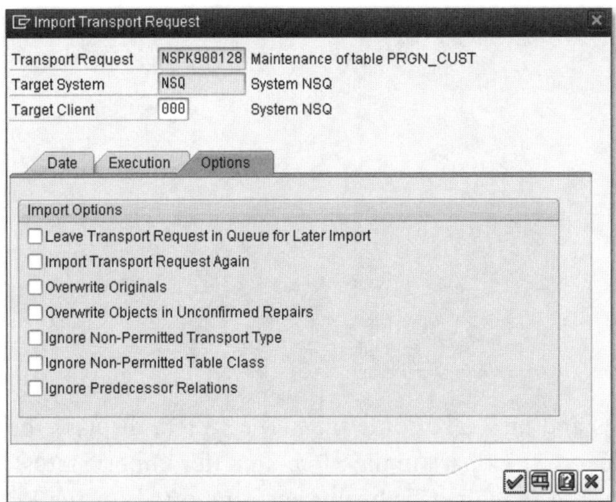

[!]

Unconditional Modes

You should use unconditional modes carefully. They enable you to purposefully override security precautions if this is absolutely necessary. Because you ignore the protection of the transport landscape, wrongly setting unconditional modes can cause a lot of damage.

8. Choose YES to confirm the security prompt.

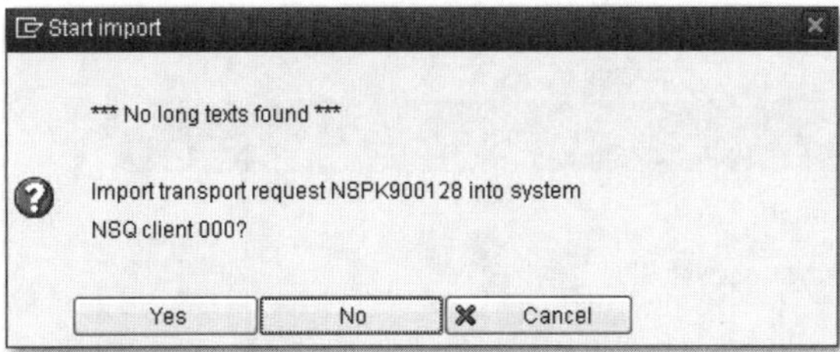

9. Depending on the configuration of the transport system, you have to authenticate yourself on the target client with your user ID and password.

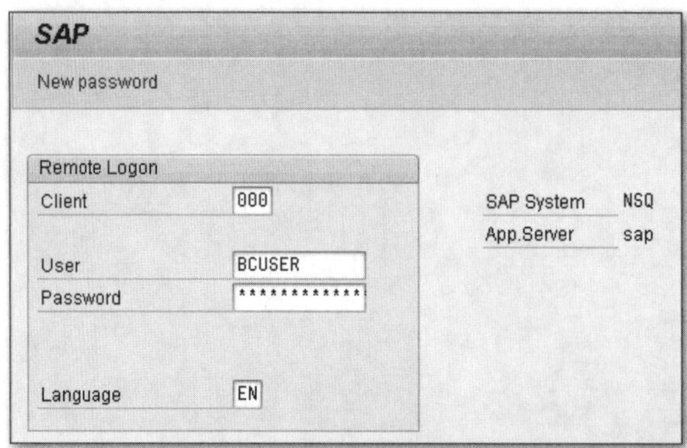

10. The import process starts and may take some time. The system displays the request number with a green checkmark in the ST column (for import **st**atus). This status indicates that the request has already been imported. In the RC column (for Max. Return Code), the return code of the import is symbolically displayed in traffic light colors.

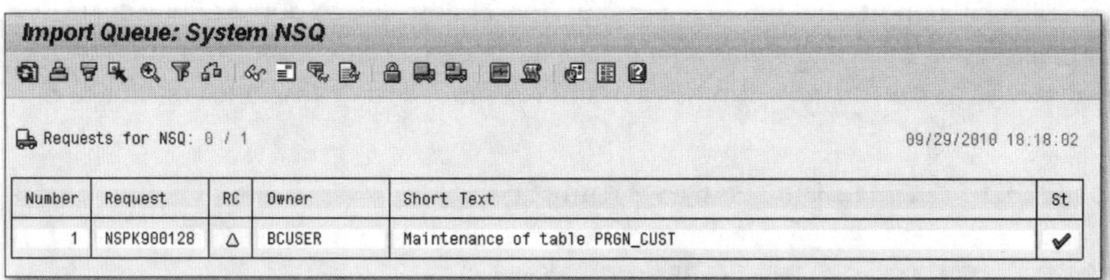

Return Codes

The following return codes are common:

- 0 (□): The import was completed successfully.
- 4 (△): Warnings occured.
- 8 (●): An error occurred during the execution; all or individual objects couldn't be imported properly.
- 12 or higher (●): The transport wasn't executed.

If the system displays a return code of 4 or higher, you should check the transport log.

After a successful import, you can exit the import queue view; the transport of the request is then completed. If warnings or error messages have occurred, check the transport log.

17.2.5 Checking the Transport Log

You can use the TMS to check transport logs.

1. In the import queue view, position the cursor on the transport request whose log you want to view, and click on LOGS.

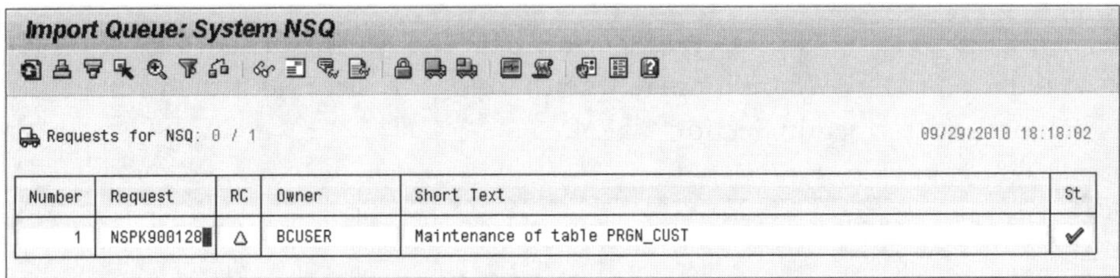

Import Queue: System NSQ

Requests for NSQ: 0 / 1 09/29/2010 18:18:02

Number	Request	RC	Owner	Short Text	St
1	NSPK900128	△	BCUSER	Maintenance of table PRGN_CUST	✔

2. In the OVERVIEW OF TRANSPORT LOGS screen, position the cursor on the log entry that you want to check, and select DISPLAY LOG.

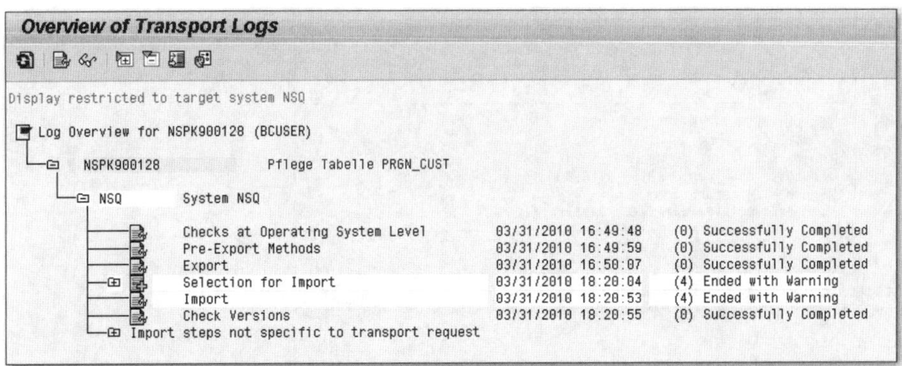

3. View the detailed messages in the log display by clicking on EXPAND.

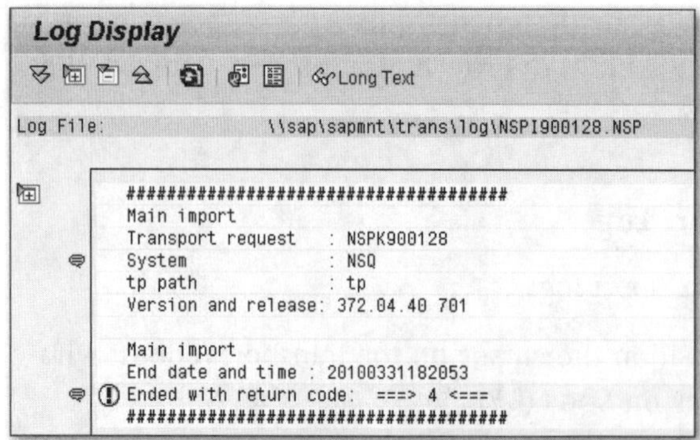

4. Check the warning or error message, and have the system display the LONG TEXT if required (Long Text). Eliminate the cause of the error, and then restart the import as described in Section 17.2.4.

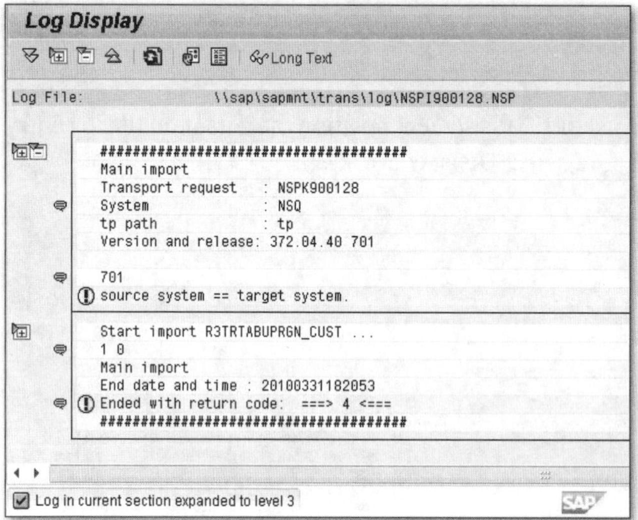

[!]

Checking the Result of the Transport

It's possible that the transport wasn't successful even if you haven't received the corresponding return code. You therefore have to check in a final test if the transport has been implemented properly. Ensure that the changes made in the original system have been correctly and fully transferred to the target system.

17.3 Direct Table Maintenance

Most of the changes are made via specific transactions or Customizing paths with the respective technical reference. In some cases, however, you have to maintain tables for which no transaction is available.

If a maintenance view for the respective table is available (usually for Customizing tables, maintenance views are not available for user tables), you can directly modify it using Transaction SM30 (or Transaction SM31).

Direct Table Maintenance [!]

Only use this method if no other transaction is available for the table maintenance. For the direct maintenance of a table, all processes and validations in the system are ignored.

If you directly change a table and save it, the change is immediately applied. You can't undo the change.

To process the entries in a table via a maintenance view, follow these steps:

1. Enter Transaction "SM30" in the command box, and press the [Enter] key (or select the menu option SYSTEM • SERVICES • TABLE MAINTENANCE • EXTENDED TABLE MAINTENANCE).
2. In the TABLE/VIEW FIELD, enter the table name (e.g., "USR40"). Ensure that no Customizing activity exists for the maintenance of the table by clicking on CUSTOMIZING.

Navigating to the Customizing [+]

If you can maintain the table in the Customizing, the system automatically navigates to the corresponding step in the Implementation Guide. If no Customizing activity is available for the maintenance of the table, the system displays the error message "No object maintenance IMG activity exists."

Now ensure that a maintenance view exists for the table by selecting FIND MAINTENANCE DIALOG.

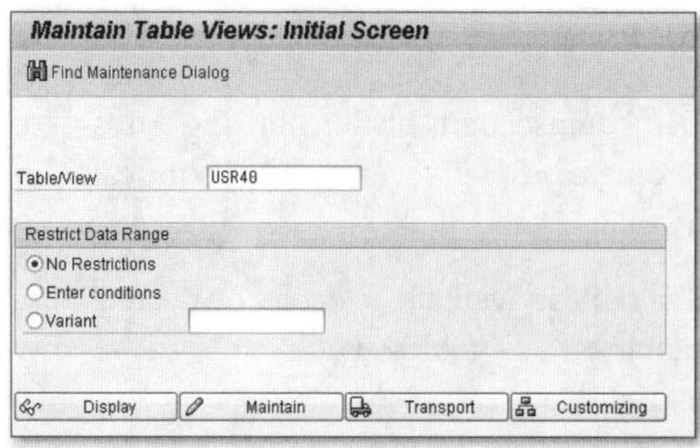

3. A dialog box with the selected table name opens. Click on CONTINUE (✔).

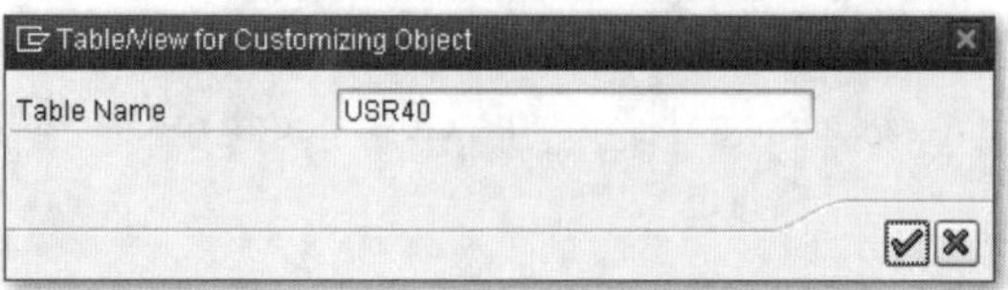

[+]

Maintenance Views for Tables

If a maintenance view exists, the system returns to the initial screen without displaying a message, and you can proceed with the next step. If no maintenance view is available for the respective table, a dialog box opens that shows the message NO MAINTENANCE OBJECTS FOUND FOR TABLE/VIEW. Then you can't maintain the table using Transaction SM30.

4. Select MAINTAIN.

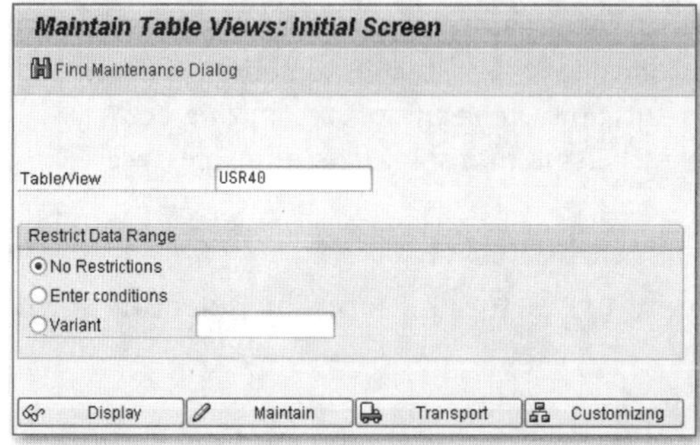

5. If the table that you modify is *cross-client*, the system displays an information dialog box. Click on CONTINUE (✔).

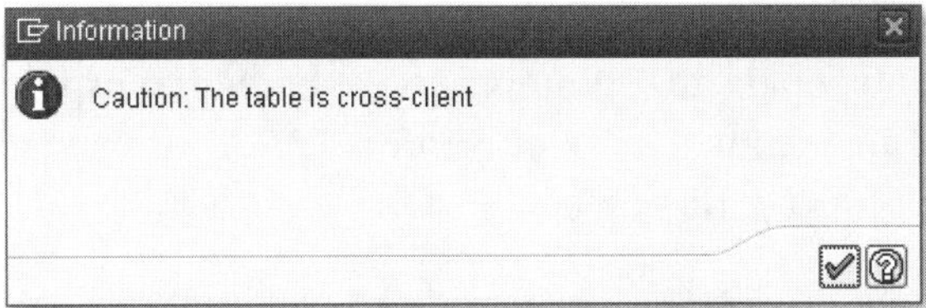

[!]

Cross-Client Data

Cross-client changes apply to all clients in a system and not only to the client that you're currently processing.

6. In the next window, select the New Entries option, for example. You can also use the respective buttons to change, copy, or delete existing entries.

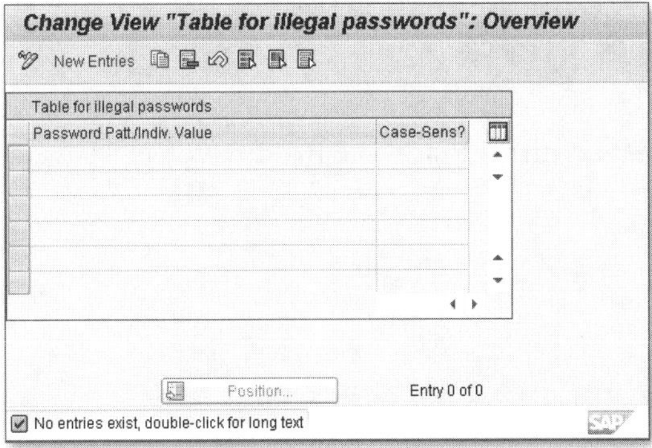

7. Maintain the new entries; the number and names of the columns depend on the selected table. Then select Save (💾).

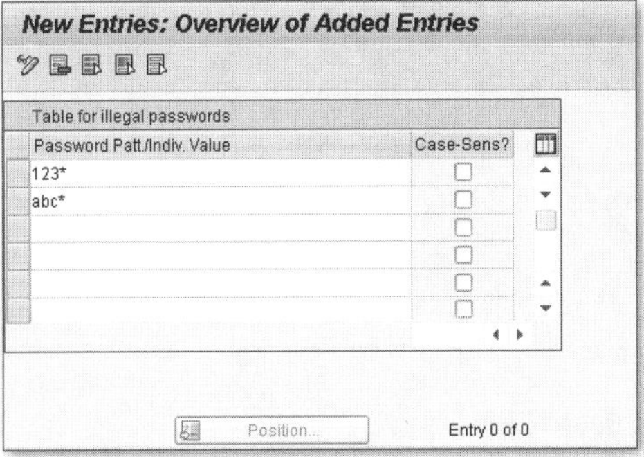

8. If the table can be transported and if automatic recording is activated in the corresponding client, a dialog box opens that prompts you to enter a transport request. Proceed as described in Section 17.2.1 or Section 17.2.2. After you specify a transport request, select CONTINUE (✔).

[+]

Recording Changes

If the client has been configured in such a way that changes for the transport are not recorded, this dialog box is not displayed.

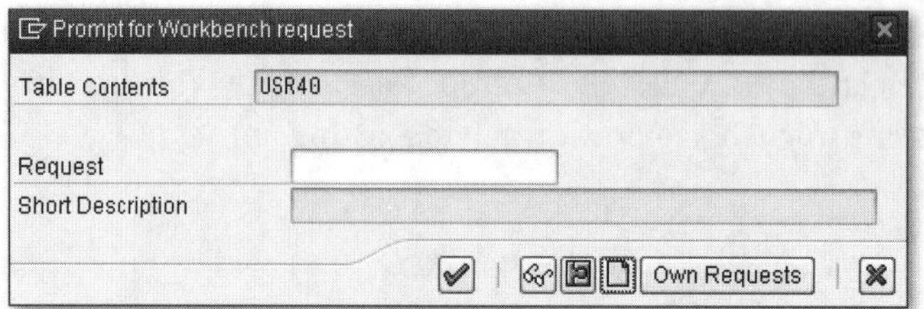

9. The status bar shows a message that confirms that the entries have been saved. Choose BACK (⮌).

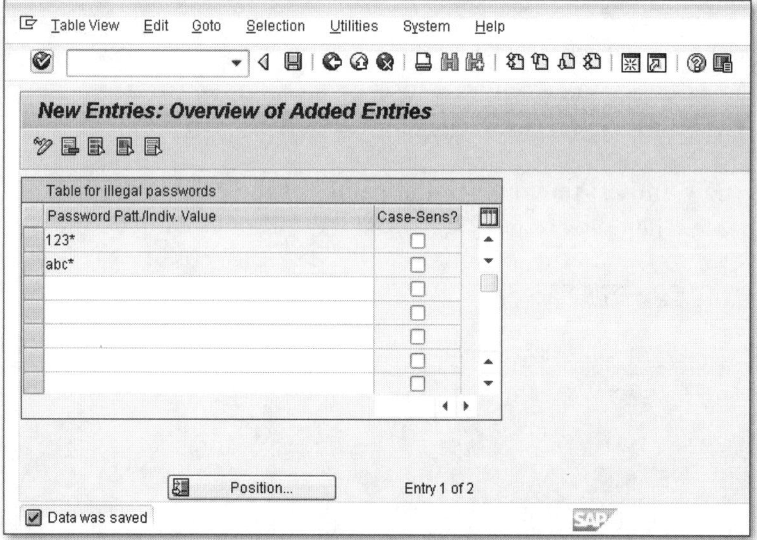

10. The table contains the new entries. Select the BACK button (⮌).

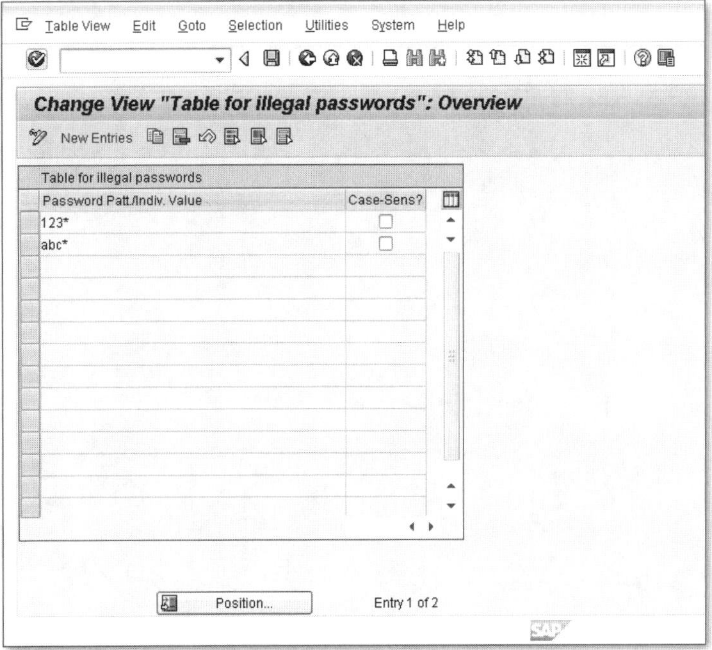

After having made your changes, you can exit Transaction SM30 and transport the modification to other systems according to the procedure described in Section 17.2.

17.4 Summary

The Transport Management System enables you to apply changes to a multisystem landscape in a comfortable and secure way. The transport process ensures that most of the changes can only be implemented in the development system and transferred to the production system after having been tested in the QA system. This reduces the risks of errors and system failures considerably.

This chapter described how you can create transport requests, include objects to be transported in a transport request, and finally implement the transport.

This chapter describes how to maintain SAP systems with support packages and patches. Here you'll learn how to download software updates from the SAP Support Portal, how to perform a kernel update, and how to maintain the ABAP components in your SAP system.

18 System Maintenance

SAP software is largely maintained using *support packages*. A support package is a set of corrections for errors in ABAP programs. These corrections are usually already available as SAP Notes. A support package bundles the corrections that have been provided over a certain period in a consolidated package. In most cases, support packages contain error corrections only, while functional enhancements are less common.

Support packages are provided for specific products, releases, and components. They provide corrections both for the system basis and for the functional application modules. Because the individual components of an SAP system interact with one another, the support package versions of the various components must be compatible. For example, if you import a support package for an application component that requires a specific basis support package, serious errors may occur if both packages are not implemented.

To resolve such conflicts, SAP delivers *support package stacks*, which contain compatible kernel and support package versions for all components in a system. You should use the support package stacks available, rather than importing support packages in isolation.

Support packages enable the early detection and resolution of problems in your system. There is some controversy regarding the best time to import support packages:

- SAP recommends customers import all support packages as soon as they are released to avoid the occurrence of serious problems.

- However, many customers believe that regression tests should be performed for all system changes.

Because support packages are released on a frequent basis, they are often not imported upon release because the required tests are too extensive to be completed in sufficient time.

Against this backdrop, you should create a maintenance concept for your SAP systems. Give some thought to the frequency with which you want to implement SAP Notes and import support packages and support package stacks. Have the concept agreed on by all business departments because most of the regression testing will have to be done by users from these departments.

[+]

Maintenance Strategy Recommendation

You should base your maintenance strategy on the intervals at which the support package stacks are published, and you should import these on a quarterly or annual basis. For short-term troubleshooting, it's best to refer to the corrections provided in SAP Notes (see Chapter 19). Support packages should not be imported in isolation.

If necessary, you can perform a kernel update independently of the ABAP support package version. The ABAP components only ever require a minimum kernel version, which means that the kernel may always have a higher version than that contained in the most recent support package stack.

18.1 Downloading SAP Support Packages

Support packages and support package stacks can be downloaded from the SAP Support Portal. ABAP support packages for all SAP systems as of SAP NetWeaver 7.0 can only be downloaded with the Maintenance Optimizer in SAP Solution Manager (see Chapter 4, Section 4.5). While the support packages you require can also be selected in the Support Portal directly, you need Solution Manager to confirm the downloads. The Maintenance Optimizer greatly simplifies the selection of support packages and helps avoid errors—we therefore strongly recommend that you use Solution Manager.

Kernel updates and updates for the SPAM/SAINT version can be downloaded without SAP Solution Manager. The steps involved in downloading the software from the SAP Support Portal are described next.

[+]

Logon to the SAP Support Portal

The following instructions assume that you can access the SAP Support Portal and that you are familiar with the logon and navigation procedure. You also require authorization to download software from the Portal.

For more information, see Chapter 19.

18.1.1 Determining the System's Current Support Package Level

Before you download support packages, you need to determine which components are contained in your system and which updates have already been imported. There are two ways to do this as described next.

Method 1—System Status

Check the system status. Information about support package levels is included in the status display. Follow these steps:

1. Choose the menu option SYSTEM • STATUS. This function is accessible from all transactions and menus.

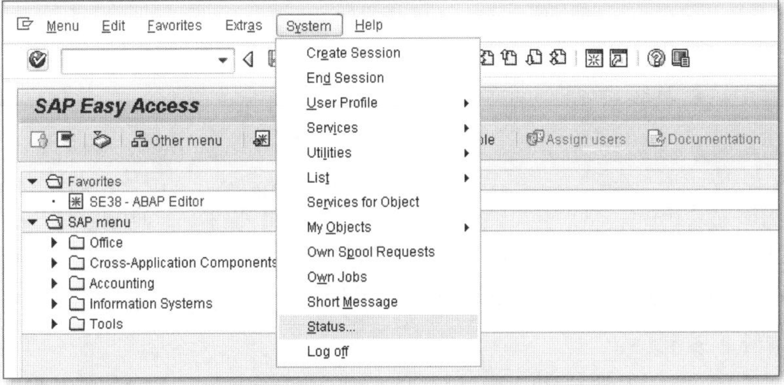

2. Take note of the following information under SAP SYSTEM DATA in the SYSTEM: STATUS window:
   - COMPONENT VERSION (for example, SAP EHP 1 FOR SAP NETWEAVER 7.0)
   - UNICODE SYSTEM (for example, YES)

You also require the following details for the kernel update:

- Operating system (for example, Windows NT)
- Machine type (for example, Intel 8068 => 32-bit or 64-bit version)
- Database System (for example, MaxDB)

Then choose Component information ().

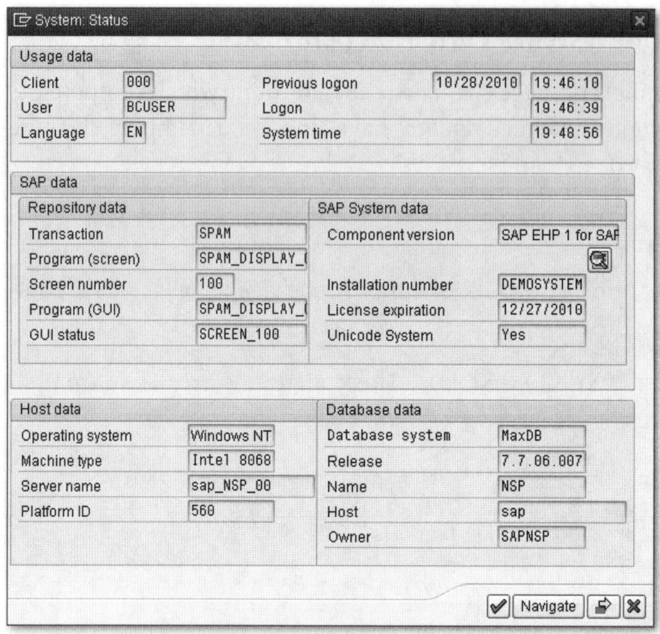

3. The table displayed indicates which components are contained in your system, their version (release), and their support package level:

   - Software Component (for example, SAP_BASIS)
   - Release (for example, 701)
   - Level (for example, 0003)

   Choose the Print button (), to print the list, or take note of the component information. Choose Continue () to return to the previous screen.

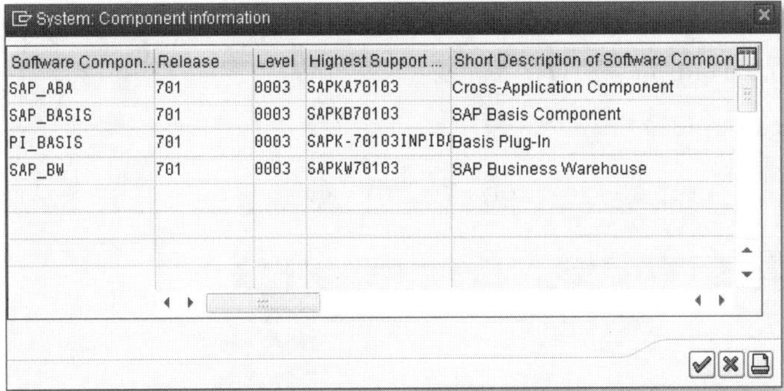
System: Component information

Software Compon...	Release	Level	Highest Support ...	Short Description of Software Compon
SAP_ABA	701	0003	SAPKA70103	Cross-Application Component
SAP_BASIS	701	0003	SAPKB70103	SAP Basis Component
PI_BASIS	701	0003	SAPK-70103INPIB/	Basis Plug-In
SAP_BW	701	0003	SAPKW70103	SAP Business Warehouse

Technical Support Package Name [+]

The names of support packages (see the HIGHEST SUPPORT PACKAGE column) comprise the following elements:

SAPK*<component><release><level>*

SAPKB70103 can thus be divided into SAPK/B/701/03, indicating that this is the third support package of the SAP Basis component for Release 7.01. You will need to be able to understand this naming convention as soon as you receive the support packages as files.

4. On the SYSTEM: STATUS screen, choose the OTHER KERNEL INFO button ( ).

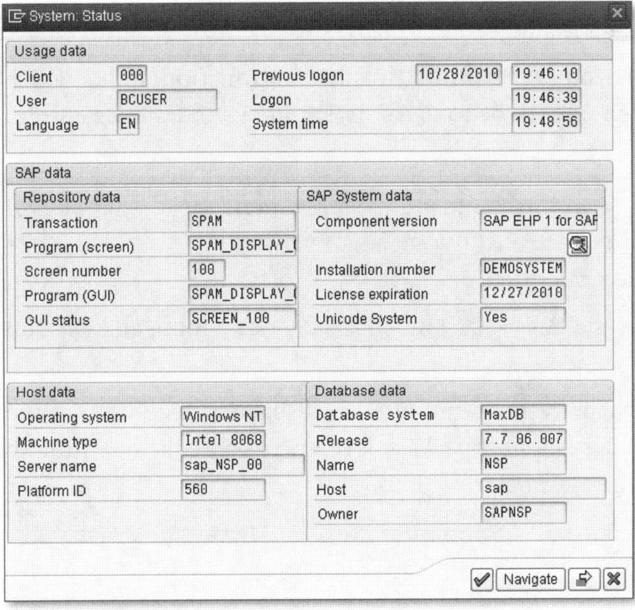

5. You require the following details to download the kernel:
   - KERNEL RELEASE (for example, 701)
   - PATCH LEVEL (for example, 29)

   Take note of this information, and click on CONTINUE (✔).

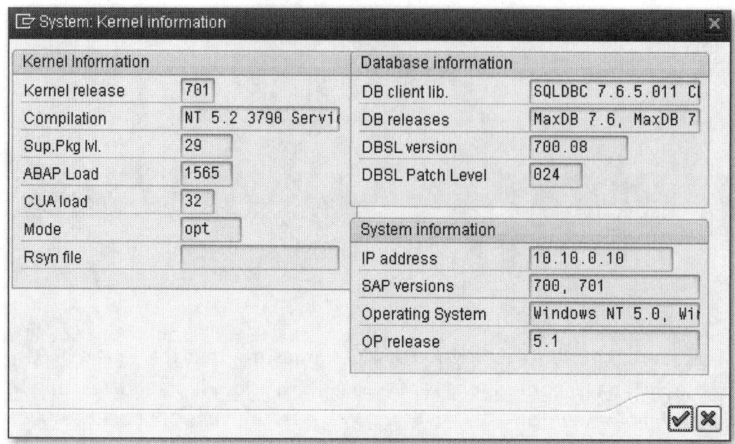

You now have all of the information you need to download ABAP and kernel patches.

Method 2—Support Package Manager

With the second method, you access more detailed information about which support packages have been imported. You also determine your system's current SPAM/SAINT version.

1. Enter Transaction "SPAM" in the command field, and press the Enter key (or select the menu option TOOLS • ABAP WORKBENCH • UTILITIES • MAINTENANCE • SPAM—SUPPORT PACKAGE MANAGER).
2. Under DIRECTORY, select the IMPORTED SUPPORT PACKAGES option, and click on DISPLAY.
3. A list of the updates that have been imported is displayed. Take note of the components and the highest support package levels. Pay particular attention to the information about the SPAM/SAINT UPDATE.

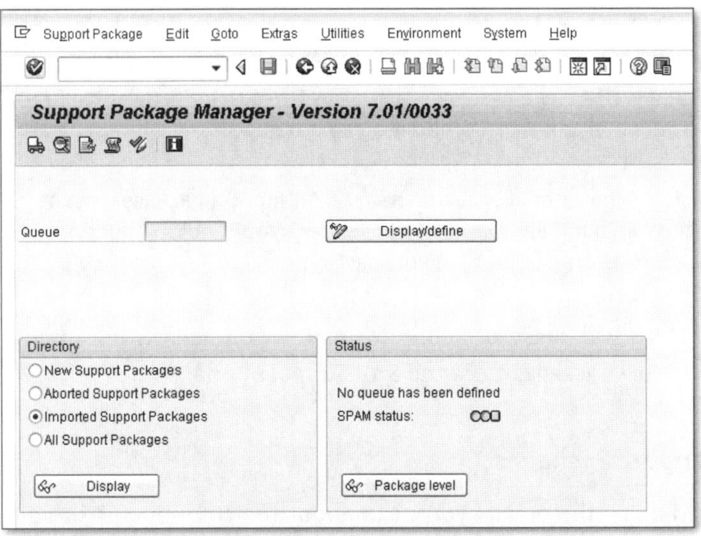

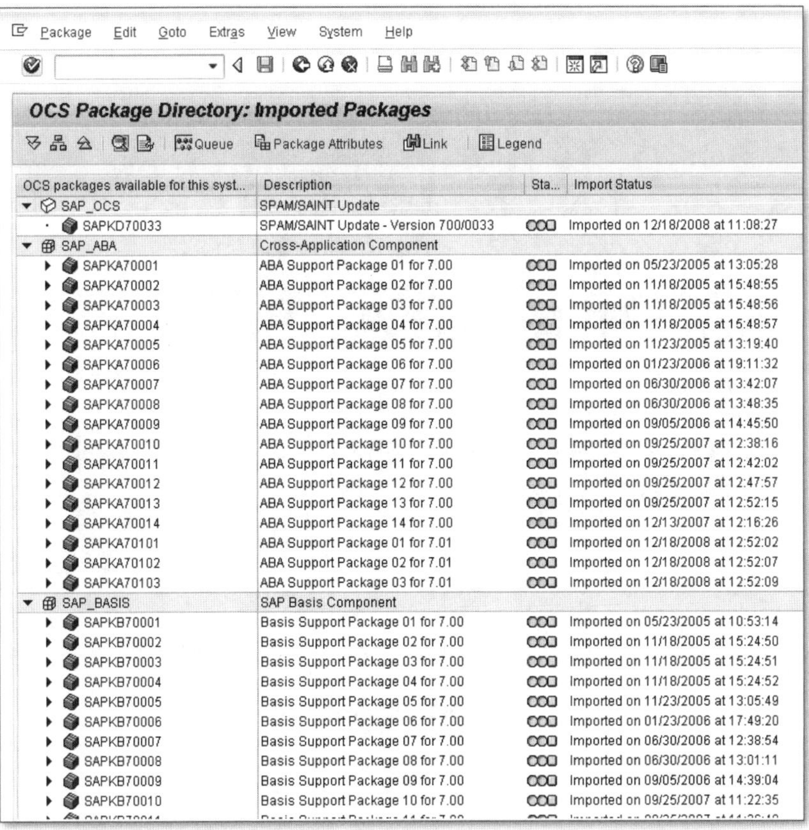

OCS packages available for this syst...	Description	Sta...	Import Status
SAP_OCS	SPAM/SAINT Update		
SAPKD70033	SPAM/SAINT Update - Version 700/0033		Imported on 12/18/2008 at 11:08:27
SAP_ABA	Cross-Application Component		
SAPKA70001	ABA Support Package 01 for 7.00		Imported on 05/23/2005 at 13:05:28
SAPKA70002	ABA Support Package 02 for 7.00		Imported on 11/18/2005 at 15:48:55
SAPKA70003	ABA Support Package 03 for 7.00		Imported on 11/18/2005 at 15:48:56
SAPKA70004	ABA Support Package 04 for 7.00		Imported on 11/18/2005 at 15:48:57
SAPKA70005	ABA Support Package 05 for 7.00		Imported on 11/23/2005 at 13:19:40
SAPKA70006	ABA Support Package 06 for 7.00		Imported on 01/23/2006 at 19:11:32
SAPKA70007	ABA Support Package 07 for 7.00		Imported on 06/30/2006 at 13:42:07
SAPKA70008	ABA Support Package 08 for 7.00		Imported on 06/30/2006 at 13:48:35
SAPKA70009	ABA Support Package 09 for 7.00		Imported on 09/05/2006 at 14:45:50
SAPKA70010	ABA Support Package 10 for 7.00		Imported on 09/25/2007 at 12:38:16
SAPKA70011	ABA Support Package 11 for 7.00		Imported on 09/25/2007 at 12:42:02
SAPKA70012	ABA Support Package 12 for 7.00		Imported on 09/25/2007 at 12:47:57
SAPKA70013	ABA Support Package 13 for 7.00		Imported on 09/25/2007 at 12:52:15
SAPKA70014	ABA Support Package 14 for 7.00		Imported on 12/13/2007 at 12:16:26
SAPKA70101	ABA Support Package 01 for 7.01		Imported on 12/18/2008 at 12:52:02
SAPKA70102	ABA Support Package 02 for 7.01		Imported on 12/18/2008 at 12:52:07
SAPKA70103	ABA Support Package 03 for 7.01		Imported on 12/18/2008 at 12:52:09
SAP_BASIS	SAP Basis Component		
SAPKB70001	Basis Support Package 01 for 7.00		Imported on 05/23/2005 at 10:53:14
SAPKB70002	Basis Support Package 02 for 7.00		Imported on 11/18/2005 at 15:24:50
SAPKB70003	Basis Support Package 03 for 7.00		Imported on 11/18/2005 at 15:24:51
SAPKB70004	Basis Support Package 04 for 7.00		Imported on 11/18/2005 at 15:24:52
SAPKB70005	Basis Support Package 05 for 7.00		Imported on 11/23/2005 at 13:05:49
SAPKB70006	Basis Support Package 06 for 7.00		Imported on 01/23/2006 at 17:49:20
SAPKB70007	Basis Support Package 07 for 7.00		Imported on 06/30/2006 at 12:38:54
SAPKB70008	Basis Support Package 08 for 7.00		Imported on 06/30/2006 at 13:01:11
SAPKB70009	Basis Support Package 09 for 7.00		Imported on 09/05/2006 at 14:39:04
SAPKB70010	Basis Support Package 10 for 7.00		Imported on 09/25/2007 at 11:22:35

[+]

SPAM/SAINT Version

Transactions SPAM (Support Package Manager) and SAINT (Add-On Installation Tool) are used to import updates and add-ons. Both transactions are updated using a separate SPAM/SAINT update.

The SPAM/SAINT version is important because certain ABAP support packages require a minimum version. If the minimum SPAM/SAINT version required is not in your system, serious errors may occur when you import support packages.

The SPAM/SAINT version is the last piece of information you need. You can now start downloading support packages from the SAP Support Portal.

18.1.2 Finding Support Packages

After you've gathered all of the details you need about the components in your system, you can search for available support packages in the SAP Support Portal. Use the details you noted to make your selection.

1. Access the SAP Support Portal, and click on DOWNLOADS.

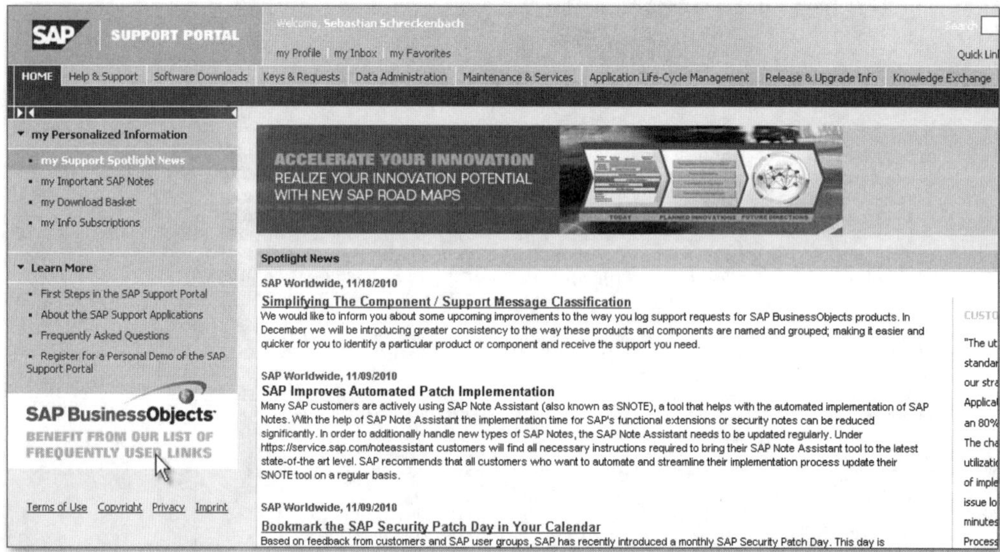

2. Click on the SAP SUPPORT PACKAGES AND PATCHES link.

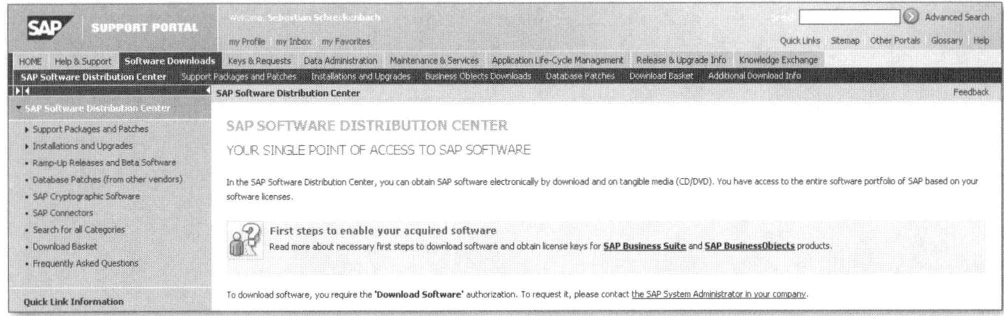

3. You now have various options for selecting support packages:
   - SEARCH FOR SUPPORT PACKAGES AND PATCHES: Enter a search text.
   - ENTRY BY APPLICATION GROUP: Search by product version.
   - APPLICATIONS BY INDEX: Alphabetical search.
   - MY COMPANY'S APPLICATION COMPONENTS: The products and components your company has registered with SAP.

   Simply choose the search method that suits you best. In this example, select SUPPORT PACKAGES AND PATCHES—ENTRY BY APPLICATION GROUP.

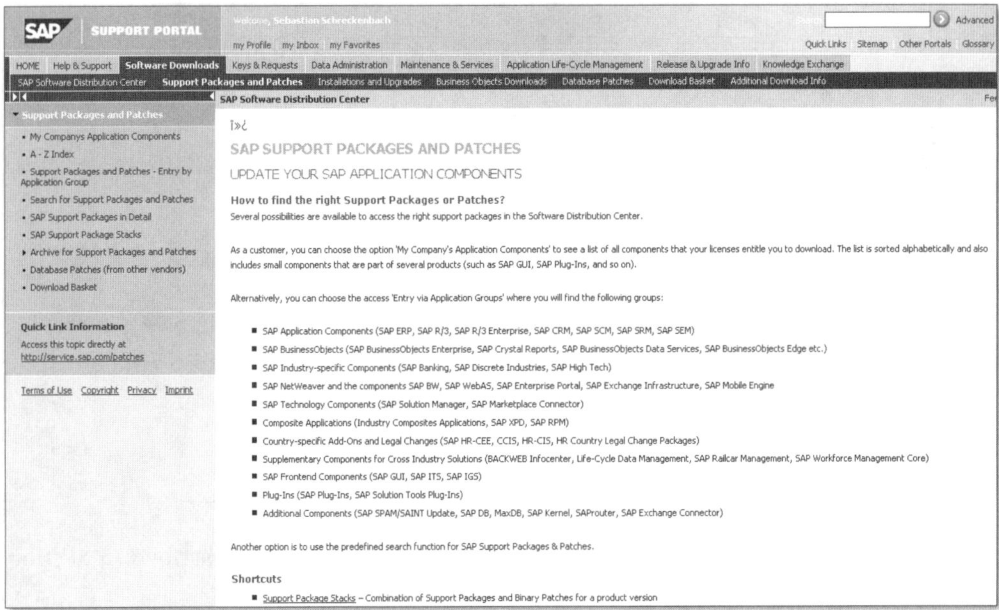

4. Select a product group, for example, SAP NetWeaver and complementary products.

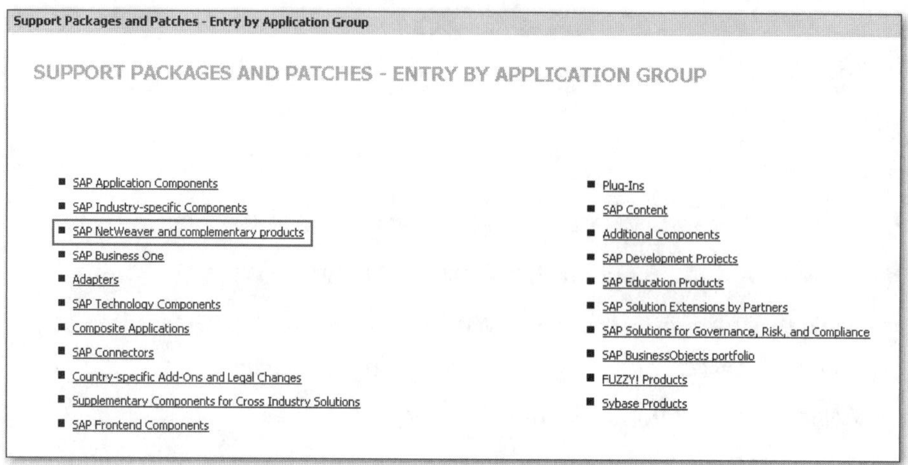

5. Select the relevant subgroup, for example, SAP NETWEAVER.

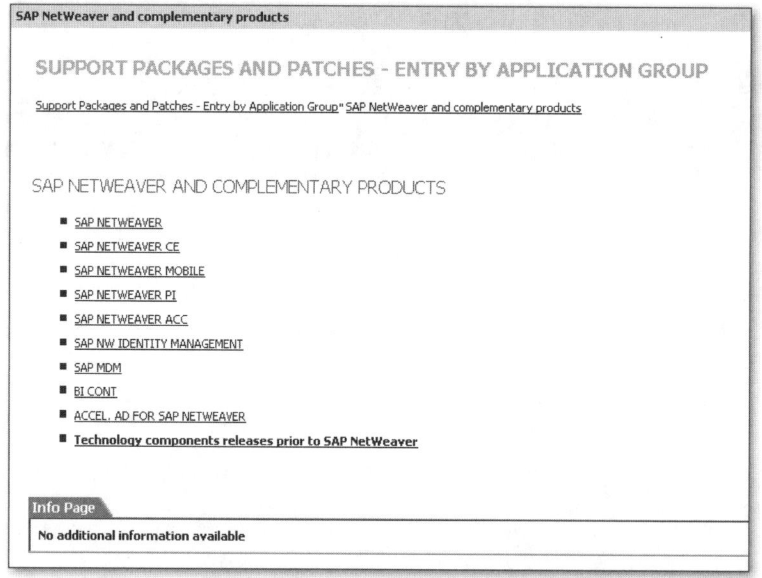

6. Select your component version, which you checked as described in Section 18.1.1, for example, SAP EHP1 For SAP NetWeaver 7.0.

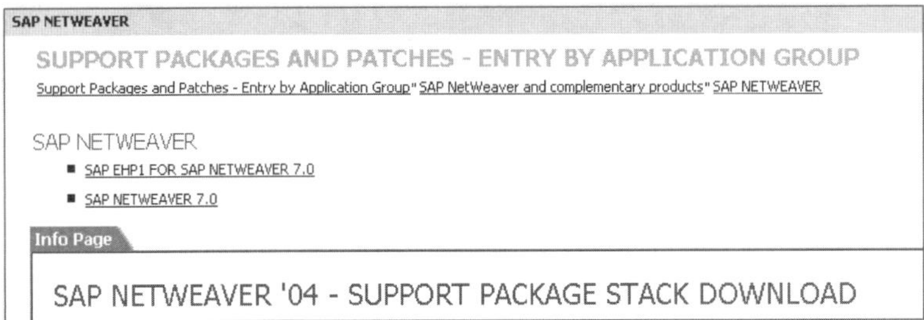

7. Click on Entry by Component.

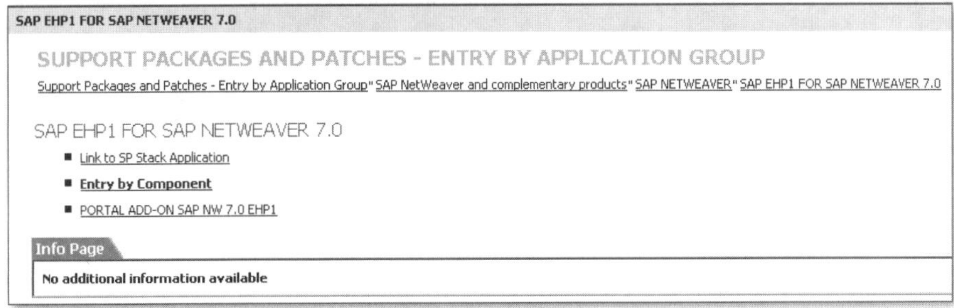

8. A tree structure opens. Select the component Application Server ABAP.

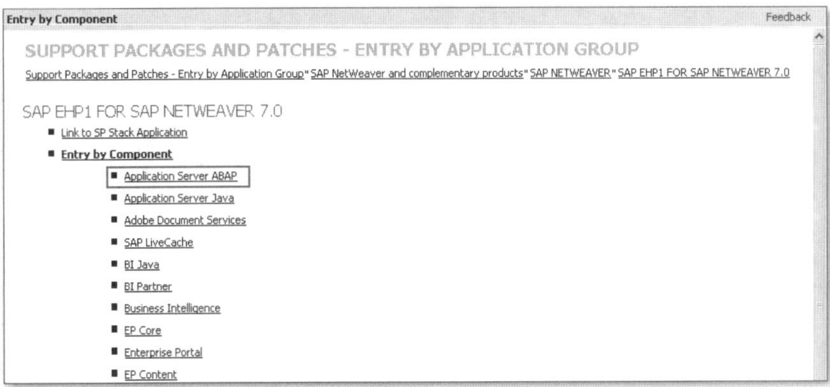

9. Now go through the list of your product's components in detail, and select the support packages to download. Start with the component PI_BASIS 7.01. Click on this component.

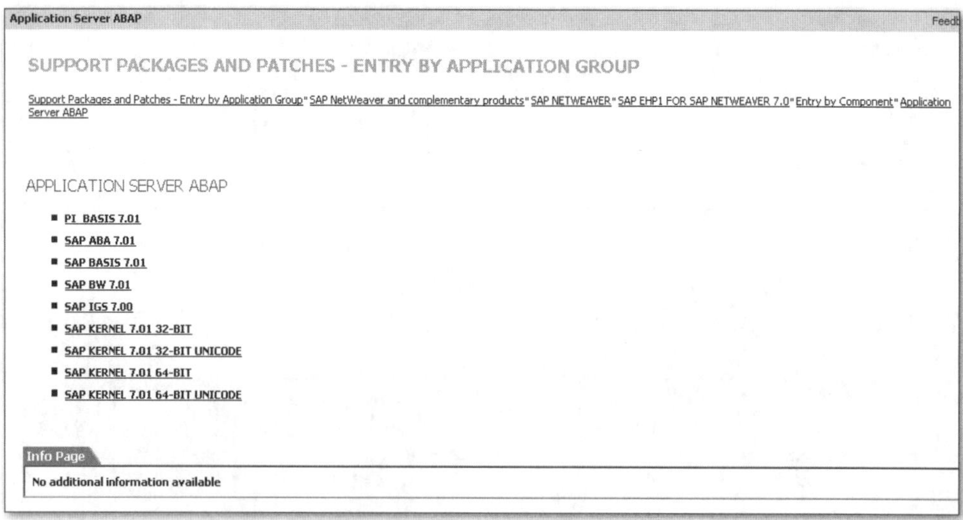

10. Click on SUPPORT PACKAGES.

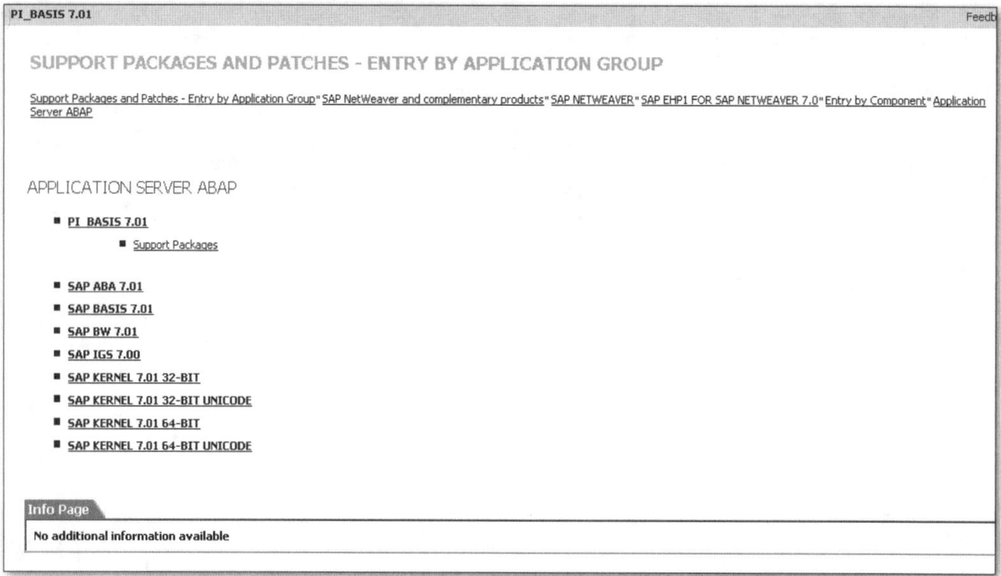

11. A list of download objects is displayed at the bottom of the screen. Scroll down through this list, and select one or more support packages with a higher support package level than the current level in your system (e.g., PI_BASIS SUPPORT PACKAGE 04 FOR 7.01). Click on ADD TO DOWNLOAD BASKET.

Skipping Support Package Levels

[!]

If you haven't imported any support packages for a long time, several new levels may have been made available since your last import (for example, your system may currently have Patch Level 3, and Patch Level 6 is now available). If you want to update your system to the latest level (in this case, Level 6) and skip several patch levels (Level 4 and 5), you must download all files available (Level 4, 5, and 6).

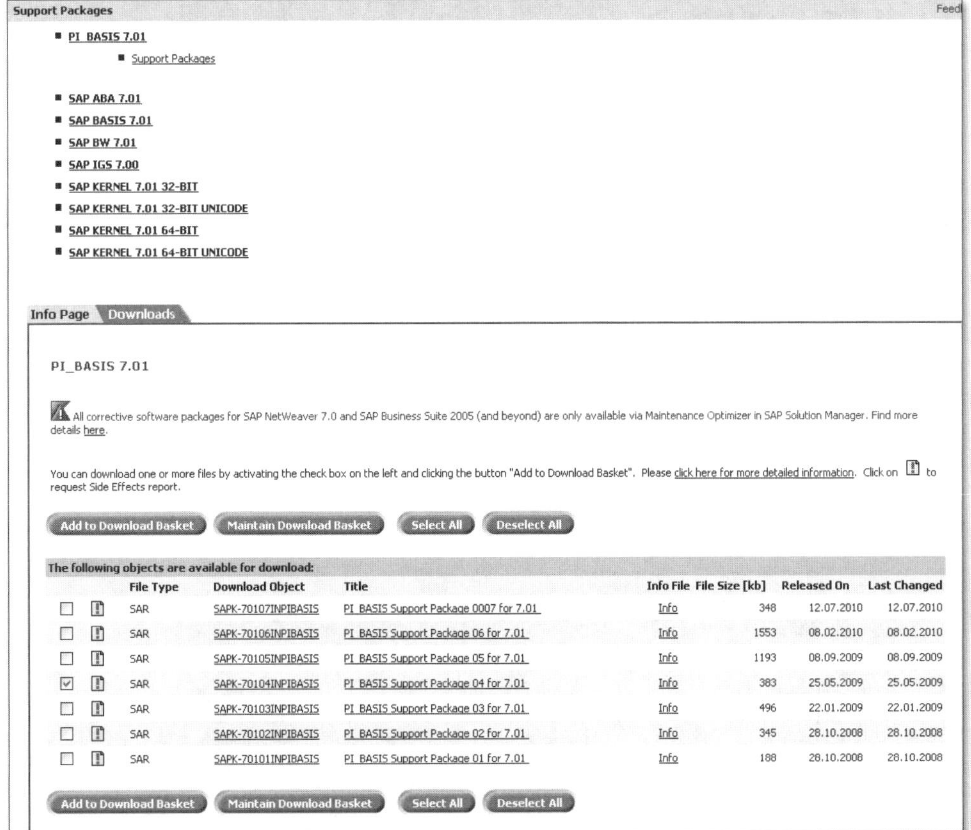

12. Another browser window opens, confirming that the file has been added to your download basket. Choose CLOSE.

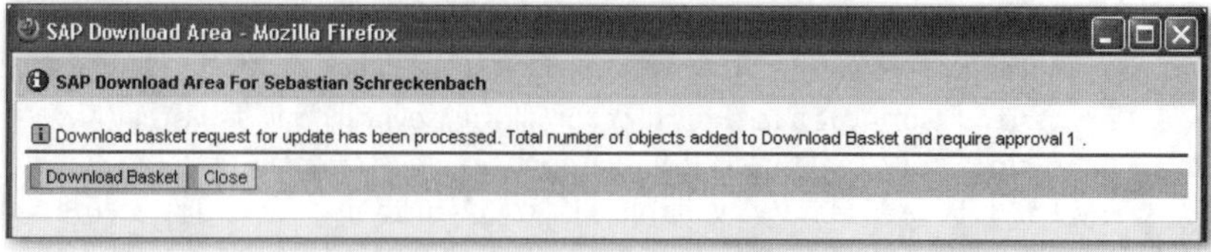

13. Continue with the other ABAP components:
    - SAP_ABA 7.01
    - SAP_BASIS 7.01
    - SAP_BW 7.01

    Go through the individual components, adding the support packages to your Download Basket one after another, as described in steps 9 to 12.

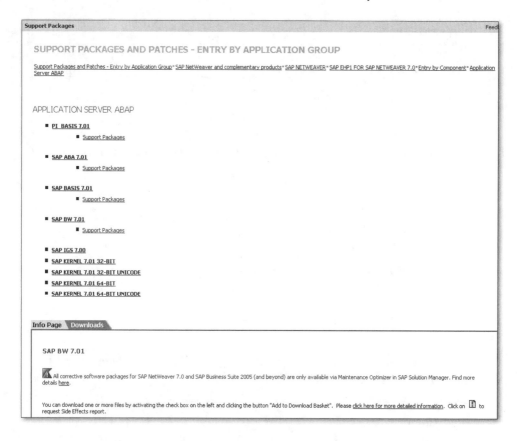

Support Packages

SUPPORT PACKAGES AND PATCHES - ENTRY BY APPLICATION GROUP

Support Packages and Patches - Entry by Application Group" SAP NetWeaver and complementary products" SAP NETWEAVER" SAP EHP1 FOR SAP NETWEAVER 7.0" Entry by Component" Application Server ABAP

APPLICATION SERVER ABAP

- PI_BASIS 7.01
  - Support Packages
- SAP ABA 7.01
  - Support Packages
- SAP BASIS 7.01
  - Support Packages
- SAP BW 7.01
  - Support Packages
- SAP IGS 7.00
- SAP KERNEL 7.01 32-BIT
- SAP KERNEL 7.01 32-BIT UNICODE
- SAP KERNEL 7.01 64-BIT
- SAP KERNEL 7.01 64-BIT UNICODE

Info Page | Downloads

SAP BW 7.01

All corrective software packages for SAP NetWeaver 7.0 and SAP Business Suite 2005 (and beyond) are only available via Maintenance Optimizer in SAP Solution Manager. Find more details here.

You can download one or more files by activating the check box on the left and clicking the button "Add to Download Basket". Please click here for more detailed information. Click on [icon] to request Side Effects report.

14. Then select the entry SAP IGS 7.00. A tree structure is expanded, in which you can select your server's operating system (for example, WINDOWS SERVER ON IA32 32BIT).

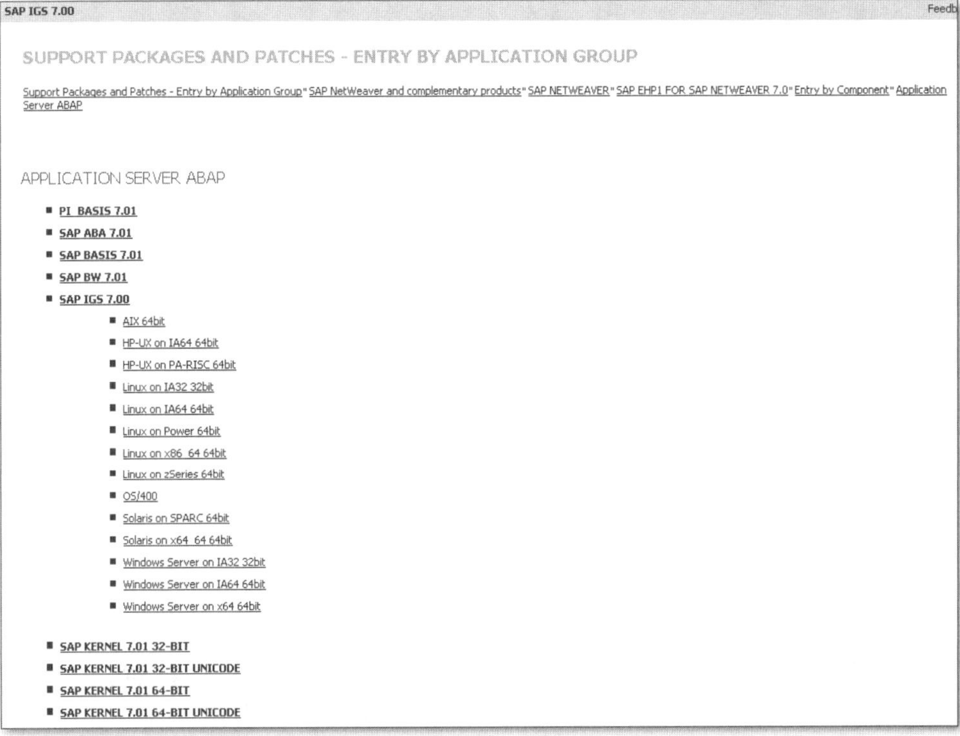

[⚙]

SAP IGS

The *SAP Internet Graphics Service* (SAP IGS) ensures that graphical content can be displayed in the SAP system. This technology is used for Web Dynpros, for example.

As of Release 6.40 of the Web Application Server (now SAP NetWeaver AS), the SAP IGS is part of the kernel and is installed as standard. If you don't perform a kernel update, you should also update the IGS to the latest level immediately. Always use the most recent update available.

You can use Transaction SIGS (Internet Graphics Service Administration) to check which version of the SAP IGS is running in your SAP system.

15. Select the latest version (for example, PATCH LEVEL 17), and add it to your download basket.

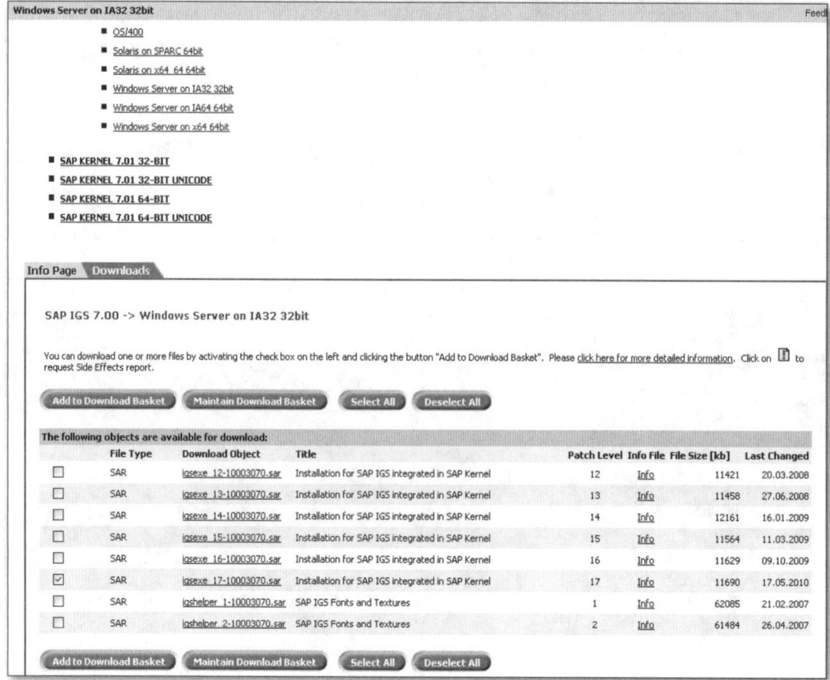

16. Continue with the download of the SAP kernel. Make sure to select the appropriate version for your operating system (32 bit/64 bit), and base your selection on whether your SAP system is a Unicode or non-Unicode system. In our example, we'll select SAP KERNEL 7.01 32-BIT UNICODE.

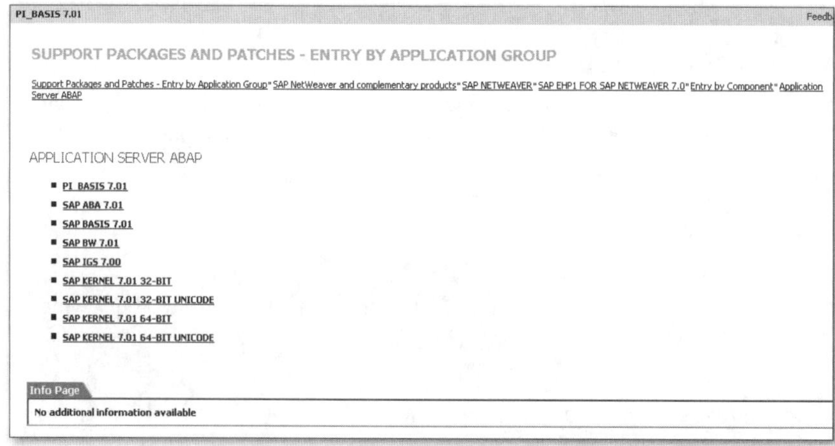

17. Select the correct operating system (for example, WINDOWS SERVER ON IA32 32BIT).

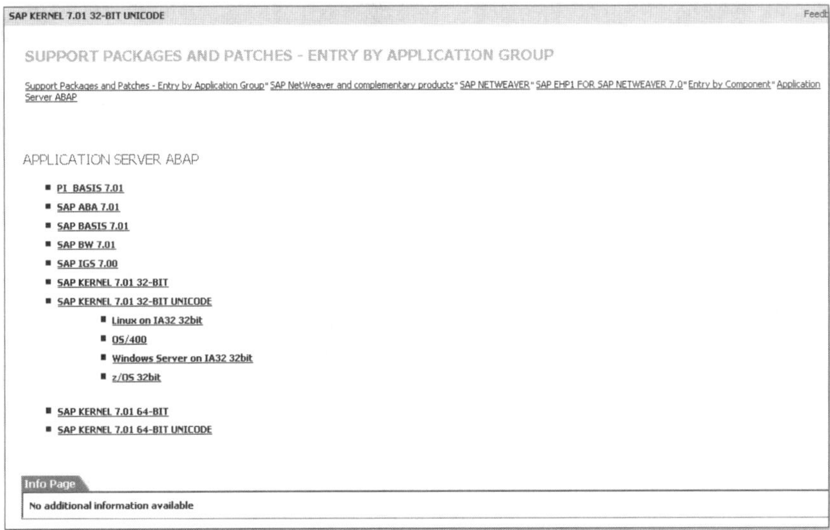

18. Click on the #DATABASE INDEPENDENT link.

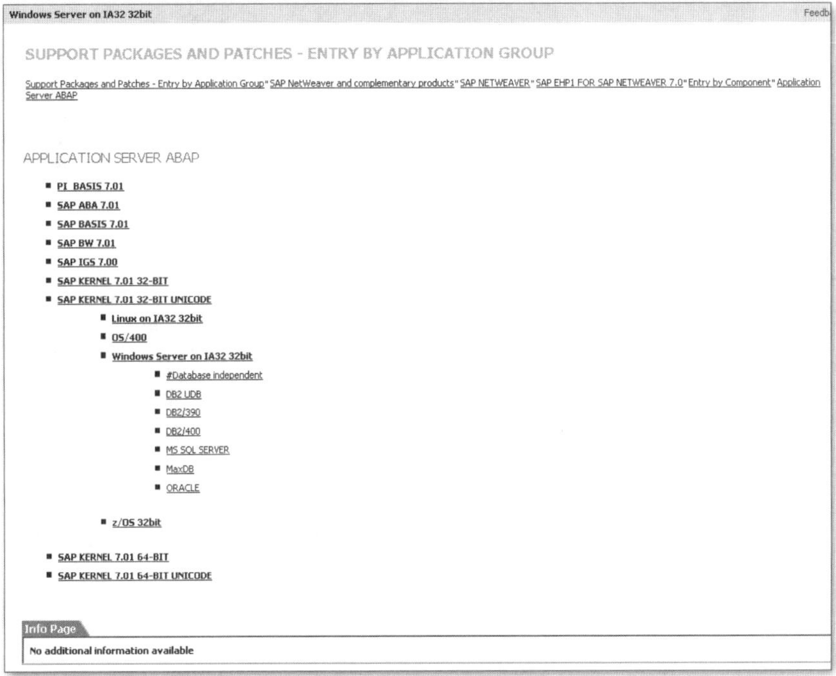

[⚙]

Contents of a Kernel Patch

The SAP kernel consists of a large, database-independent part (kernel part I) and a smaller, database-dependent part (kernel part II). You must always download both parts and install them together.

19. Scroll down through the list, and add KERNEL PART I (FOR BASIS 7.01) with the latest version (for example, PATCH LEVEL 69) to your Download Basket on the DOWNLOAD OBJECTS tab (which is now displayed).

[⚙]

Kernel Components

The SAP kernel comprises a range of components, including the *startsap* and *stopsap* files for starting and stopping the SAP server, and the tp program for the transport system (see Chapter 17).

It is recommended that you use the kernel packages I and II compiled by SAP. These contain a stable, functioning complete version of the kernel.

You should only download the individual components in the event of an emergency, or if requested to do so by SAP Support.

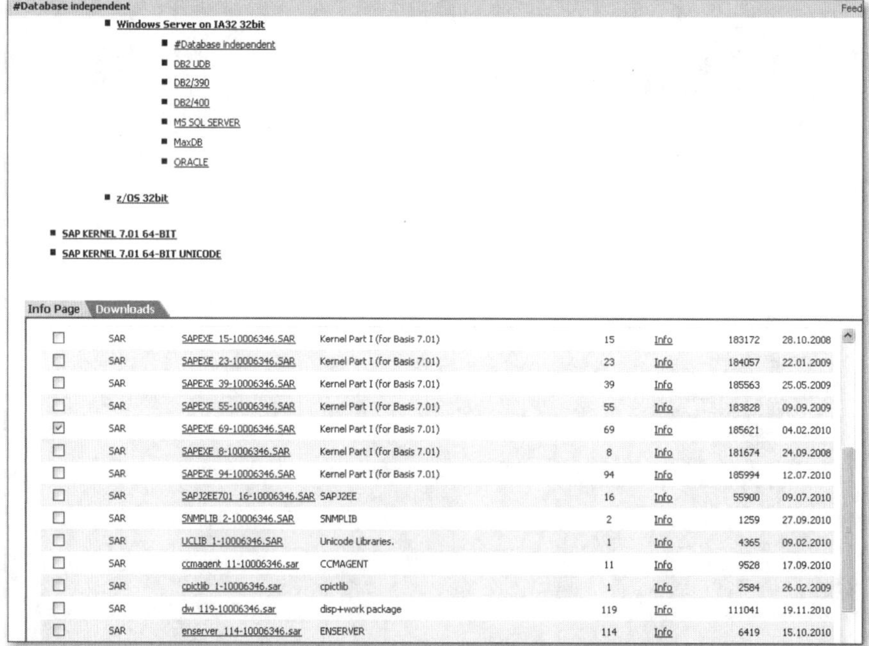

20. Scroll back up through the list, and select the database-dependent part of the kernel by clicking on the link for your database system (e.g., MAXDB).

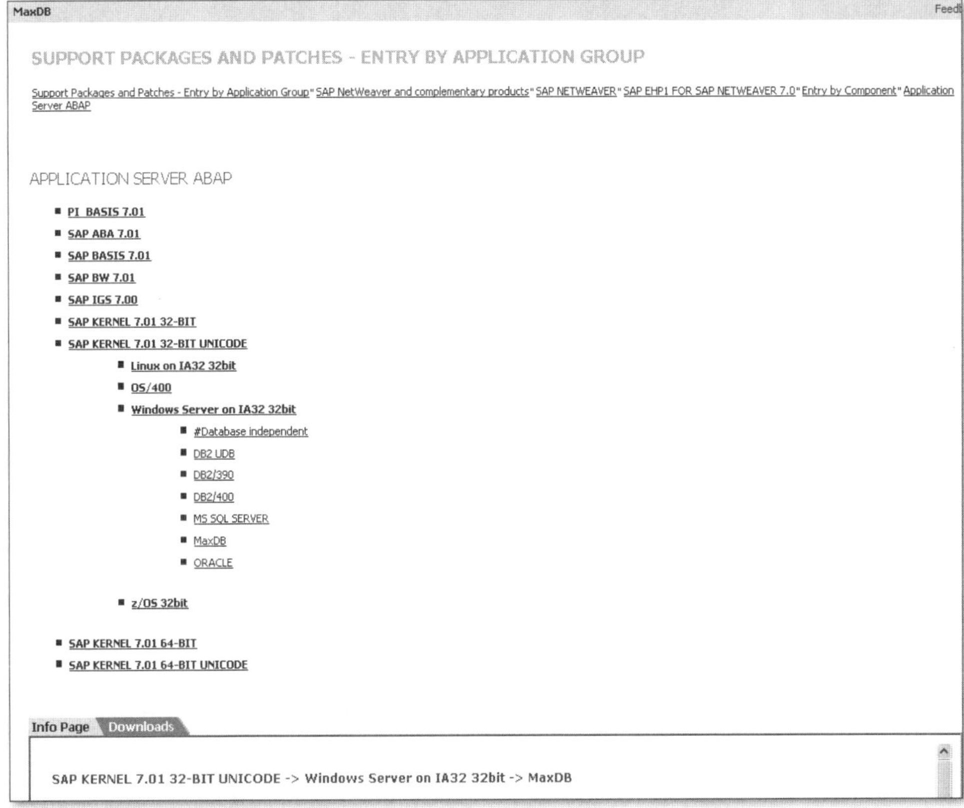

21. Next, scroll down through the list again, and add KERNEL PART II (FOR BASIS 7.01) with the latest version (for example, PATCH LEVEL 69) to your Download Basket on the DOWNLOADS tab.

    You must select the same patch level you selected for KERNEL PART I.

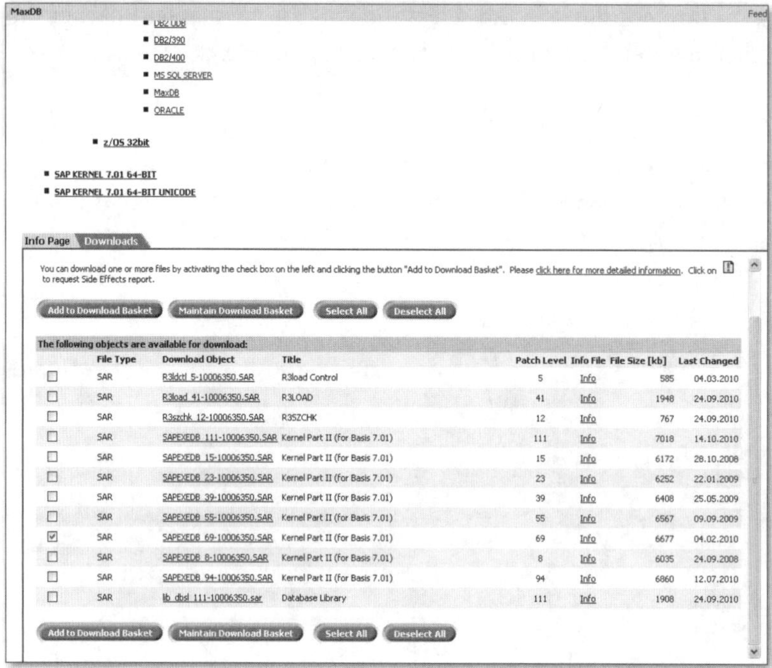

22. You've now selected all of the ABAP support packages and kernel patches you need. You can now search for the latest SPAM/SAINT version. To do this, select the download menu option SUPPORT PACKAGES AND PATCHES—ENTRY BY APPLICATION GROUP • ADDITIONAL COMPONENTS • SAP SPAM/SAINT UPDATE.

23. Select your SPAM/SAINT version, for example, SPAM/SAINT UPDATE 701.

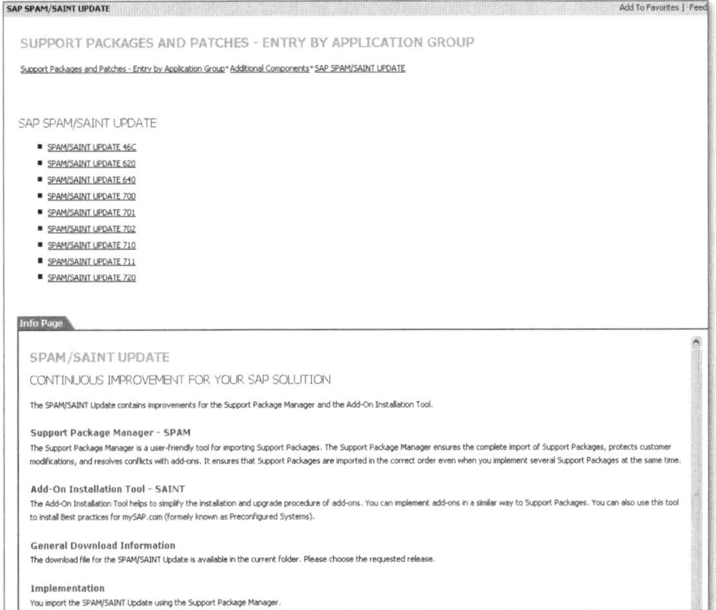

24. Click on SUPPORT PACKAGES.

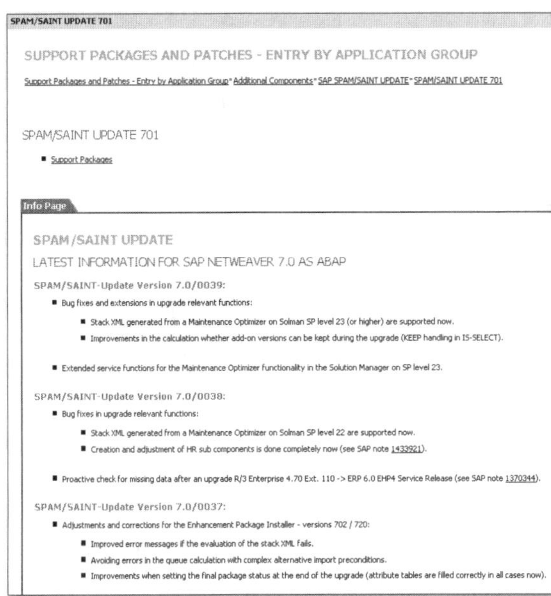

25. Select the latest version (for example, SPAM/SAINT UPDATE—VERSION 701/0039), and add it to your Download Basket.

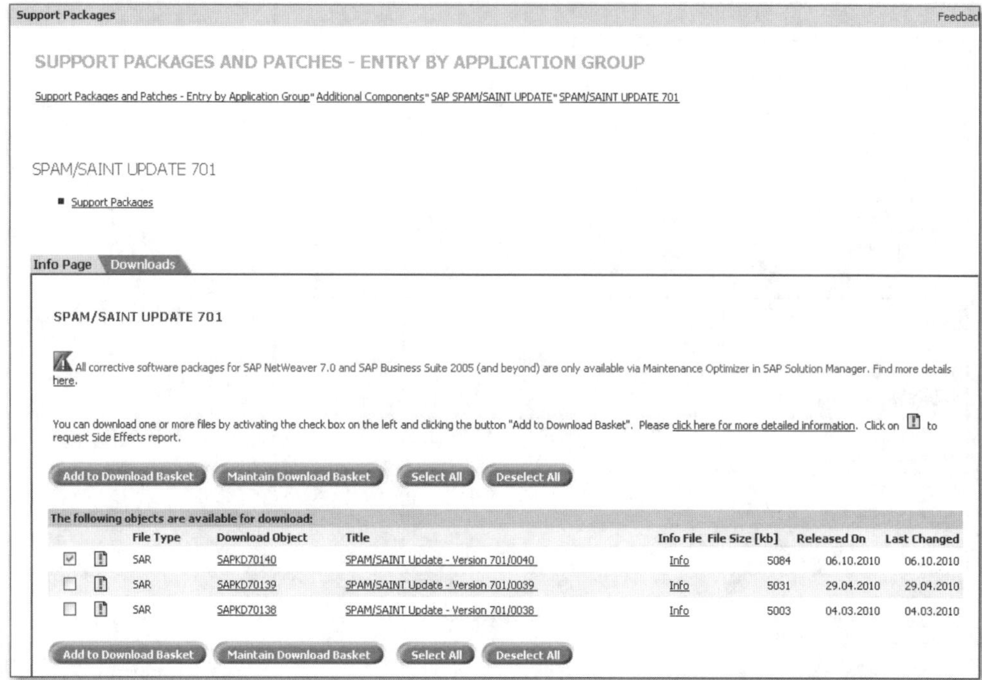

Your download list is now complete, and all files have been added to your Download Basket. You can now start downloading the software packages.

[+]

Support Package Stack Application

As a guiding principle, you should use SAP Solution Manager to download support packages as a support package stack rather than in isolation (see Chapter 4, Section 4.5).

However, you can also download support package stacks from the SAP Support Portal using the *Support Package Stack application*. To use this option, select DOWNLOADS • SAP SUPPORT PACKAGES • SAP SUPPORT PACKAGE STACKS, and scroll down to your product version.

18.1.3 Downloading Support Packages

After adding all support packages to your Download Basket, you can begin the download. Open your Download Basket, and follow these steps:

1. Access the SAP Support Portal, click on DOWNLOADS, and then click on DOWNLOAD BASKET.
2. The DOWNLOAD BASKET tab lists all of the files you can download. In our example, the list only shows the freely available kernel components.

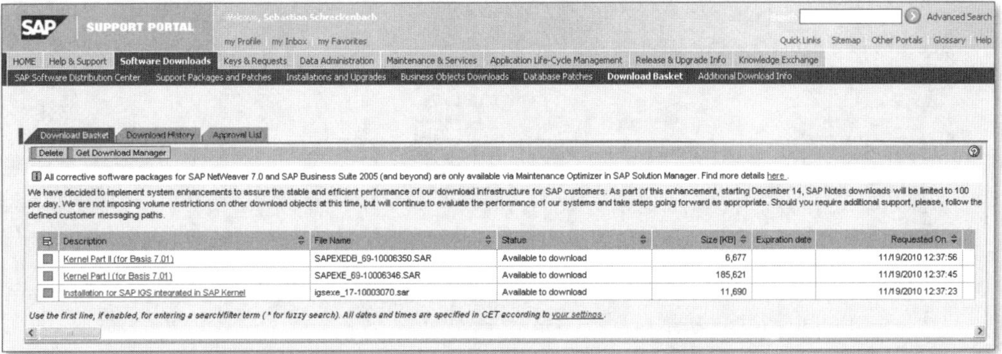

3. Switch to the APPROVAL LIST tab. It shows the files for which a download needs to be approved with SAP Solution Manager. This is indicated by the REQUEST APPROVAL entry in the STATUS column. The approval process is described in Chapter 4, Section 4.5.

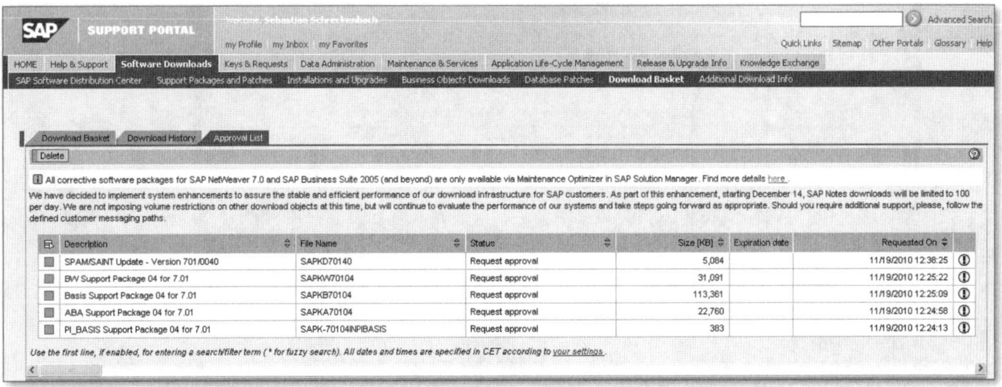

4. As soon as the download has been approved, the ABAP support packages that require approval are also displayed on the DOWNLOAD BASKET tab.

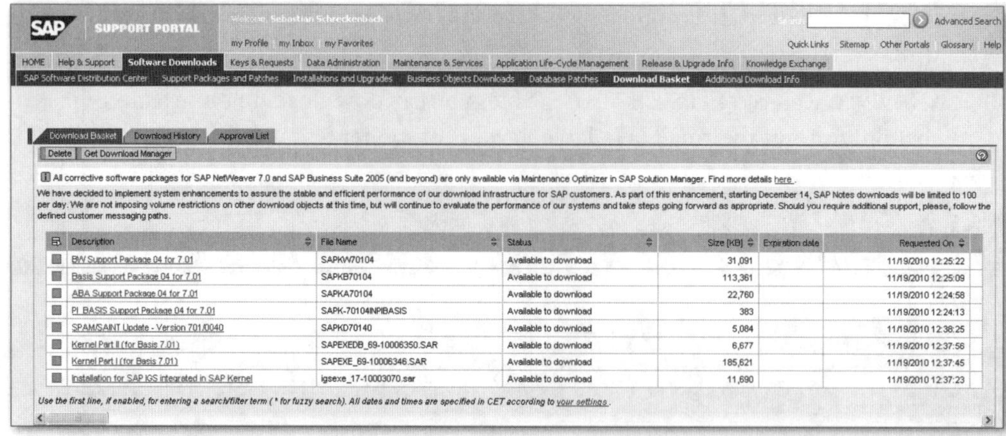

5. Now click the GET DOWNLOAD MANAGER button to start the Download Manager, and click on DOWNLOAD ALL OBJECTS (⏩).

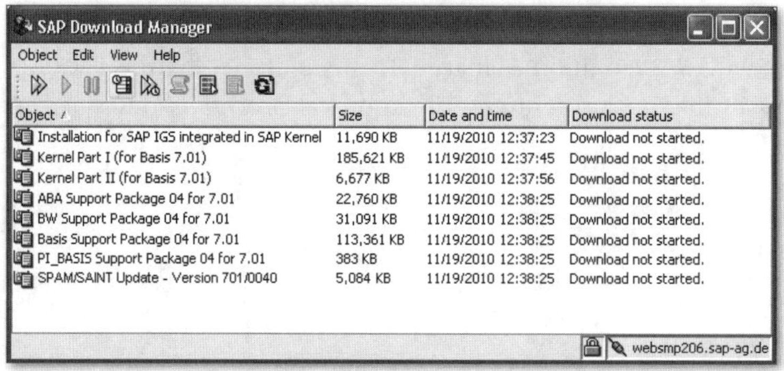

[+]

Download Manager

Download the Download Manager from the Download Basket by choosing GET DOWNLOAD MANAGER, and install it locally on your PC. Follow the instructions for installation and configuration.

Alternatively, you can download the files individually from the Download Basket by clicking on the corresponding links. In many cases, however, downloading files manually is very time-consuming.

The Download Manager downloads the files from the SAP Support Portal. When the download is finished, the files are available locally on your PC. You can then start to import the support packages.

18.2 Important Notes on Preparing and Executing System Maintenance

Note the following points before you begin to import the support packages:

1. Lock all users in your SAP system before the import.
2. Read all SAP Notes and instructions relating to the support packages. Refer to the information provided about the minimum requirements for the updates.
3. Import the support packages into a test system or sandbox system first, assuming that you have a four-system landscape. If you only have a three-system landscape, comprising a development, QA, and production system, start by importing the support packages into the development system.
4. If the development system remains stable, import the support packages into the QA system next. Perform a regression test, or have one performed by the end users in the business departments.
5. If testing is successful, import the support packages into your production system. Note that users can't work in the system during the import. You should therefore consult with the business departments to ensure that disruptions to normal operation are minimized.
6. Only download the patches once, and always use the same files for all systems.
7. Always make a full offline backup of the system before the import. You can use the backup to restore your system in case anything goes wrong.
8. Start with the kernel update. Save the old kernel at the operating system level before you import the new version.
9. Next, perform the SPAM/SAINT update.
10. Finally, import the ABAP support packages. Import them in test mode first, and then in standard mode.

[!]

Caution When Importing Support Packages

Proceed with caution when importing support packages. If you make a mistake, you may no longer be able to start your SAP system, or serious errors may occur in the modules. You should therefore approach this task with great care.

Take your time, read all relevant SAP Notes, concentrate on the task, and be precise. If necessary, ask for help from an experienced colleague or an external consultant. If errors occur during a support package import, the situation may quickly become a system administrator's worst nightmare!

18.3 Performing a Kernel Update

Now we come to the process of the update itself. As explained earlier, you should always start with the kernel update.

The operating files of the SAP system are updated in a kernel update. Kernel updates are normally used to eliminate bugs and other errors in the kernel. In other words, they are used when problems occur in the communication between the SAP system and the operating system.

The kernel depends on the operations system and on the database of the SAP server. The same kernel version must be installed on all servers in a system (the central instance and other application servers).

A kernel update comprises the following steps:

1. Save the old kernel.
2. Copy the new kernel to the SAP server and unpack it.
3. Stop the SAP system and services.
4. Replace the kernel files.
5. Start the SAP system, and check the logs.

You update the kernel at the operating system level. You therefore require direct access to the server (user data, sufficient authorizations, and, in some cases, a shell program). You should also be able to use the operating system; that is, you should be familiar with the commonly used commands. If you usually only use Windows and you now need to execute a kernel update, you may be unsuccessful if you're not familiar with the `ls` and `cp` commands. If necessary, ask for help from an operating system administrator.

Your backup of the old kernel files is your most effective safeguard against data loss and is therefore the most important part of the kernel update. This backup allows you to get the system up and running again very easily if it can no longer be started after the patch is installed (things are not as simple in the case of ABAP support packages).

You generally know that the update has been a success if you can start the system and log on with the SAP GUI.

18.3.1 Kernel Backup

Begin by making a backup of the old kernel files, by copying the entire kernel directory at the operating system level. This can be done while the SAP system is running.

1. Use the user "*<SID>adm*" to log on to your SAP server.
2. Create a backup directory, for example:
   - *<drive>:\saptemp\kernel_701_69\bak* (Windows)
   - */usr/sap/<SID>/<instance>/temp/kernel_701_69/bak* (Unix)

   If you want to save the update data permanently, give your directory a name that is as meaningful as possible. You also need to ensure that there is sufficient memory available on your drives.
3. Copy the entire kernel directory, *<drive>:\usr\sap\<SID>\<instance>\exe* or */usr/sap/<SID>/<instance>/exe*, including all subdirectories, into your backup directory.

This completes the kernel backup. If necessary, save your backup directory on a separate server on your local PC or on tape. Ensure that you comply with all security measures so that your directory can't be deleted by another user while you're busy with the kernel update.

18.3.2 Unpacking a New Kernel

The kernel files you downloaded from the SAP Support Portal exist in a compressed format in your system. You need to transfer them to the server and unpack them with the SAPCAR program.

1. Use the user "*<SID>adm*" to log on to your SAP server.
2. Create a directory for the new kernel files, for example:
   - *<drive>:\saptemp\kernel_701_69\new*
   - */usr/sap/<SID>/<instance>/temp/kernel_701_69/new*

   The size of the SAP kernel is several hundred megabytes, even when compressed. Ensure that a sufficient amount of memory is available to store the packed files, and make a sufficient number of hard disk reserves available for decompression of the files.
3. Copy all new kernel files to your server:
   - *SAPEXE_<patch level>-<identifier>.SAR*
   - *SAPEXEDB_<patch level>-<identifier>.SAR*
   - *igsexe_<patch level>-<identifier>.sar*
4. Create a directory in which to unpack the files, for example:
   - *<drive>:\saptemp\kernel_701_69\new\unpacked*
   - */usr/sap/<SID>/<instance>/temp/kernel_701_69/new/unpacked*
5. Open a shell session, and switch to the */usr/sap/<SID>/<instance>/exe* or *<drive>:\usr\sap\<SID>\<instance>\exe* directory.
6. Unpack the kernel files with SAPCAR, for example:
   - *SAPCAR* `-xvf SAPEXE_<patch level>-<identifier>.SAR -R <drive>:\saptemp\kernel_701_69\new`
   - *SAPCAR* `-xvf SAPEXE_<patch level>-<identifier>.SAR -R /usr/sap/<SID>/<instance>/temp/kernel_701_69/new`

The sequence in which you unpack the files is irrelevant. When you've finished, the decompressed kernel is saved in the directory you selected for unpacking.

[+]

Troubleshooting When Unpacking with SAPCAR

SAPCAR lists the unpacked files in the shell. If the SAPCAR: NOT ALL FILES COULD BE EXTRACTED message is displayed, check first whether the syntax in your SAPCAR command was correct. Enter `SAPCAR` to display the Help.

Errors may also occur if case sensitivity is not taken into account, in particular in the Unix/Linux environment.

In rare cases, an archive may be damaged during the download, for example. If this occurs, download it a second time and try again.

18.3.3 Stopping the SAP System

During the kernel update, you replace the files at the operating system level. To do this, you must stop the SAP system and the database.

You also need to ensure that files in use by running programs are not deleted or overwritten. You therefore need to end all running SAP services.

1. Open a shell session, and log on to the SAP server with user *<SID>adm*.
2. Switch to the directory: */usr/sap/<SID>/<instance>/exe* or *<drive>:\usr\sap\<SID>\<instance>\exe*.
3. Stop the SAP system and database first with the `stopsap -all` command or by using the SAP Management Console (see Chapter 2, Section 2.1).
4. Stop all SAP services that are currently running. Your system's release and the scope of its installation will determine how many services are still running and which services these are. Therefore, the following list may not be complete in all cases:
   - saposcol: `saposcol -k`
   - CCMS agents: `sapccm4x -stop` / `sapccmsr -stop`
   - SAProuter: `saprouter -s`
5. Depending on your operating system, you may also need to clean the kernel libraries in the buffer with the following command under Unix, for example: `/usr/sbin/slibclean`.

You can also stop all services that are currently running with the task manager or a similar operating system tool.

When you've finished, you should be able to overwrite all old files when you copy the new kernel version. It you are unable to replace all files due to programs that are currently running, errors are very likely to occur during SAP system operation.

18.3.4 Replacing Kernel Files

After you've made a backup copy of the old kernel, unpacked the new files on the server, and completely stopped the SAP system, you can begin to replace the old kernel files with the new version. Follow these steps:

1. Use the user "*<SID>adm*" to log on to your SAP server.

2. Copy all files and subdirectories from your unpacked directory into the kernel directory *<drive>:\usr\sap\<SID>\<instance>\exe* or */usr/sap/<SID>/<instance>/exe*.
3. Overwrite the existing files if the operating system prompts you to do so.

Pay particular attention to messages indicating that certain files could not be overwritten because they are in use by a program. This means that you have not stopped all SAP services.

If this occurs, find the applications that are still running and stop them. Then copy the files again.

[⚙]

Errors Caused by Authorizations

The authorizations on your server for the old kernel files may be configured differently before and after the update in certain cases. This may result in errors when functions are executed in the SAP system.

Compare the authorizations in your kernel backup with the new version, and make adjustments so that they are identical. If necessary, ask an operating system administrator for help.

18.3.5 Starting the SAP System and Checking the Logs

When the kernel files have been copied successfully, start the SAP system again:

1. Open a shell session, and log on to the SAP server as user *<SID>adm*.
2. Start the database and SAP system with the command `startsap` or by using the SAP Management Console (see Chapter 2, Section 2.1).

[+]

Longer Startup Times After Kernel Updates

After a kernel update, it takes longer to restart your SAP system than normal the first time you do so. Prepare yourself for the longer startup time, and don't be unsettled by it. Check the log files for errors.

3. Check the operating system log, database log, and SAP system log for error messages (refer to Chapter 2, Section 2.1). If problems occur, pay particular attention to the trace files of the work processes, and especially the dev_w0 file in *<drive>:\usr\sap\<SID>\<instance>\work* or */usr/sap/<SID>/ <instance>/work*.

4. Try to log on to the system with the SAP GUI. If a logon screen is displayed, this indicates that the SAP system is running.
5. Log on, and check the kernel version under SYSTEM • STATUS.

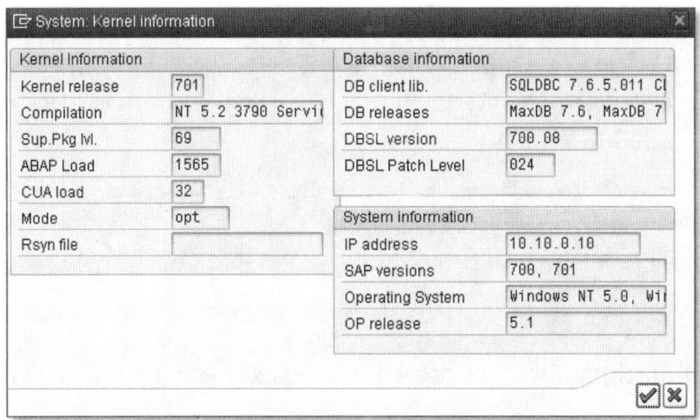

If the new kernel version is displayed in the status view, you know that you have performed the kernel update successfully.

As a precautionary measure, keep your kernel backup for a number of weeks. If the system starts with the new kernel version, it's unlikely that any errors are to be expected. However, you can never rule out the possibility of a problem occurring, and a backup of the operating system files that you know can be run may be useful in the event of an error.

18.4 Applying the SPAM/SAINT Update

ABAP components are maintained using the following two SAP tools:

- Support Package Manager (Transaction SPAM)
- Add-On Installation Tool (Transaction SAINT)

These tools are enhanced on an ongoing basis, and updates are delivered with the *SPAM/SAINT update*. Before you import an ABAP support package or an add-on into your system, you should always import the latest SPAM/SAINT update *first*, to avoid errors and problems. Some support packages even require a certain minimum SPAM/SAINT version before they can be imported. You should therefore always download the latest SPAM/SAINT update from the SAP Support Portal together with the support packages.

To install the update, follow these steps:

1. Log on to the SAP system in client 000.
2. Enter Transaction "SPAM" in the command field, and press the Enter key (or select the menu option TOOLS • ABAP WORKBENCH • UTILITIES • MAINTENANCE • SPAM—SUPPORT PACKAGE MANAGER).

[+]

Current SPAM/SAINT Version

The current SPAM/SAINT version in your system is displayed in the title bar of Transactions SPAM and SAINT.

3. Select the menu option SUPPORT PACKAGE • LOAD PACKAGES • FROM FRONT END.

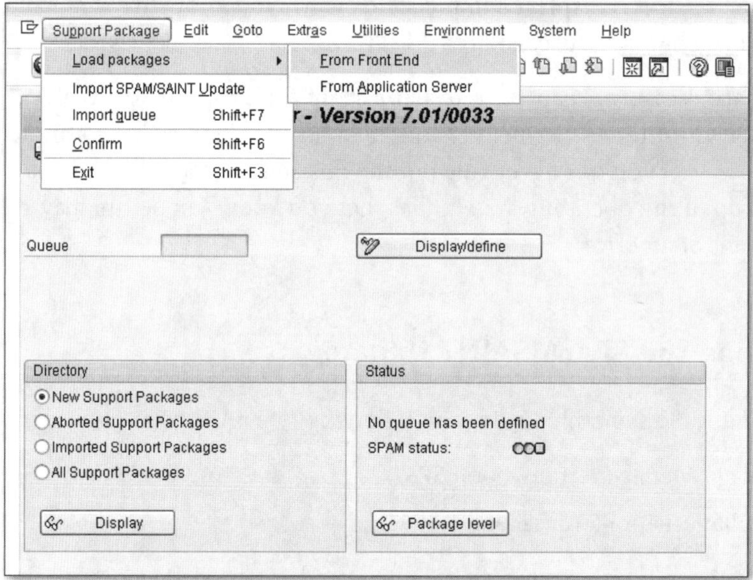

4. Navigate to where the file is stored on your local PC, and choose OPEN.

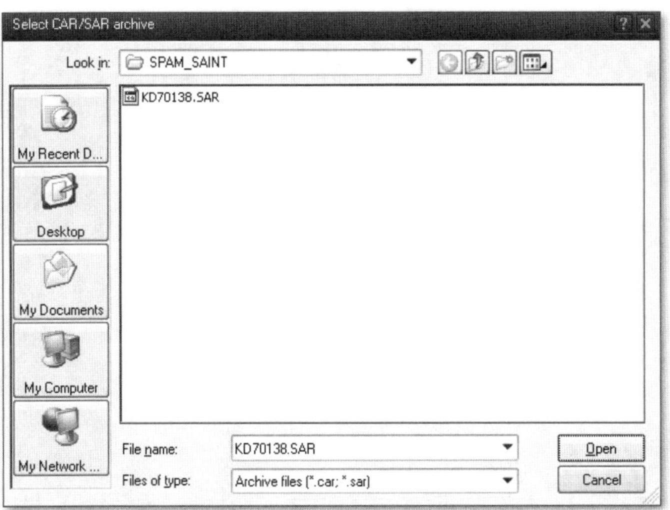

5. The system copies the archive to the application server and displays the files that are to be unpacked. Choose DECOMPRESS.

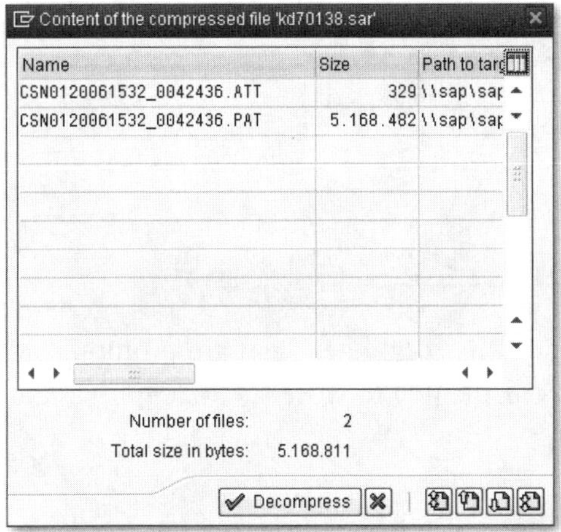

6. To upload the update file, select the menu option SUPPORT PACKAGE • IMPORT SPAM/SAINT UPDATE.

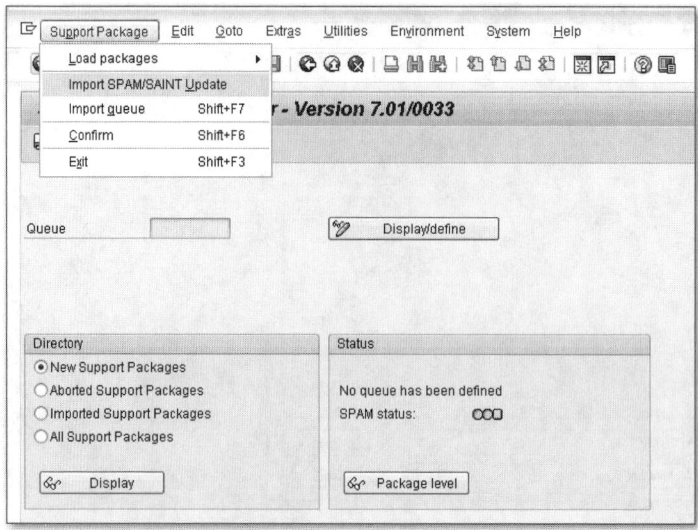

7. Read the SAP Note displayed to determine possible prerequisites or known problems associated with importing the update. Then click on IMPORT (✔).

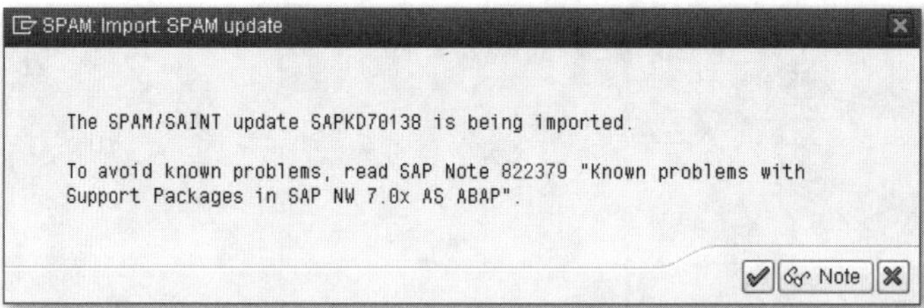

8. The update is imported. When the update is completed, you are prompted to restart Transaction SPAM. Choose CONTINUE (✔) to close the dialog box, and then restart Transaction SPAM.

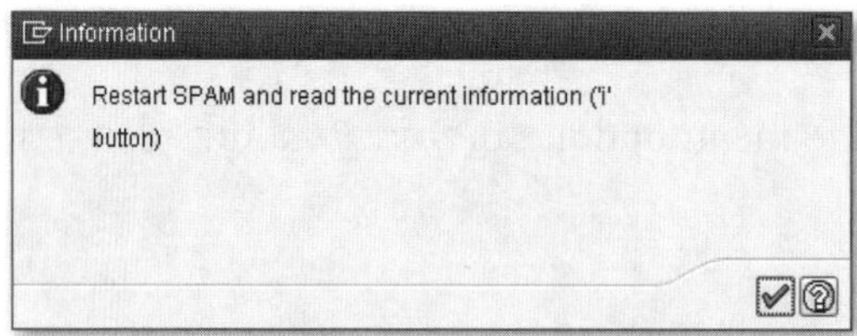

The update is now complete. The new SPAM/SAINT version is now displayed in the title bar of the transaction. Unlike ABAP packages and add-ons, you don't need to confirm the update.

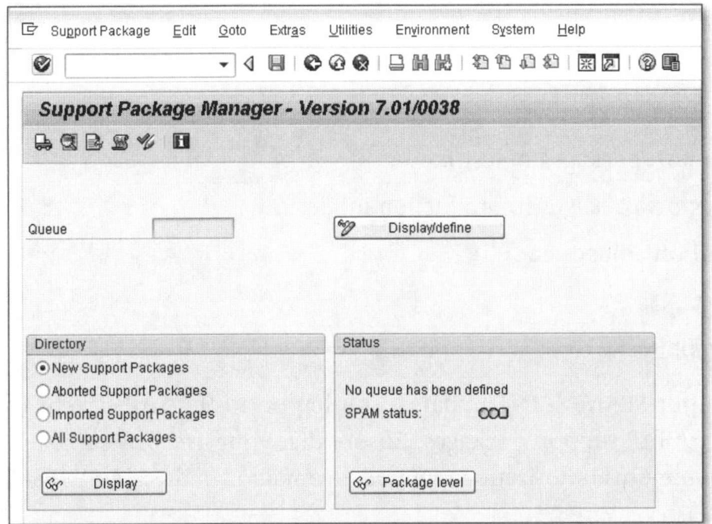

Short Dump During the SPAM/SAINT update [+]

Because Transaction SPAM virtually updates itself while it is running, it's not unusual for a short dump to occur during the update.

If this occurs, close the short dump, and restart Transaction SPAM. To continue the update, select the menu option SUPPORT PACKAGE • IMPORT SPAM/SAINT UPDATE.

After you import the SPAM/SAINT update, you can proceed to import ABAP support packages or install add-ons.

18.5 Importing ABAP Support Packages

You have updated your SAP system kernel and imported the SPAM/SAINT update. You can now proceed to import the ABAP support packages. You use the Support Package Manager (Transaction SPAM) for this purpose, which you updated to the latest version in the previous step.

To import the ABAP support packages, follow these steps:

1. Make the support packages available:
   - Transfer files to the server.
   - Unpack the archives.
2. Import the support packages:
   - Lock users and deallocate jobs.
   - Import the support packages in test mode.
   - Import the support packages in production mode.
3. Perform modification adjustment.
4. Regenerate objects.
5. Execute a regression test.

As in the procedure for SPAM/SAINT updates, you log on to the SAP system in client 000 to import ABAP support packages. Ensure that your user has sufficient authorization (the minimum authorization required is contained in the S_A.SYSTEM authorization profile).

[!]

Offline Backup

Create a complete offline backup of your SAP system before you start to import the ABAP support packages. This backup will allow you to easily restore the system in the event of a serious error.

18.5.1 Making the Support Packages Available

You have already downloaded the support package files from the SAP Support Portal and stored them locally on your PC. You now need to make these files available to the SAP Server. In other words, you must load the support packages.

There are two ways to do this:

- Load the support packages from the frontend
- Load the support packages from the application server

Loading the support packages from the frontend (that is, from your local PC) is very simple if you use the Support Package Manager because you are not required to manually copy the files to the server and unpack them there. However, you should only use this option if the archive is smaller than 10 MB. The procedure for loading support packages from the frontend is explained in Section 18.4 and Section 18.6.

Loading from the application server is explained here. To do this, you transfer the compressed support package files to the SAP server, unpack them with the SAPCAR program, and then load them into the Support Package Manager. Follow these steps:

1. Use the user "*<SID>adm*" to log on to your SAP server.
2. Create a temporary directory for the support package files, for example:
   - *<drive>:\saptemp\sps4*
   - */usr/sap/<SID>/<instance>/temp/sps4*
3. Copy all support package archives into the temporary directory on your server.
4. Open a shell session on the SAP server, and switch to the transport directory, for example, *<drive>:\usr\sap\trans* or */usr/sap/trans*.
5. Unpack the support packages with the SAPCAR program:

   ```
   SAPCAR -xvf <file name>
   ```
6. Execute the command for all files in sequence.

[⚙]

Unpacking Support Packages

SAPCAR unpacks the archives into two files:

- CSR<name>.ATT
- CSR<name>.PAT

These files belong to the EPS inbox, that is, in the *<drive>:\usr\sap\trans\EPS\in* or */usr/sap/trans/EPS/in* directory.

If you execute the SAPCAR command while you are in the transport directory, the files are automatically saved to the EPS inbox. If you execute the command in another directory, a new *EPS\in* (or *EPS/in*) structure is usually created within this directory. You then need to move the *.ATT and *.PAT files manually into the correct EPS inbox.

7. Check the EPS inbox. Assuming that your EPS inbox was previously empty, the *<drive>:\usr\sap\trans\EPS\in* or */usr/sap/trans/EPS/in* directory should now contain support packages numbering twice the number of support packages you unpacked.

After you unpack the support package files and place them in the EPS inbox as just described, you can load the support packages into the Support Package Manager.

To do this, follow these steps:

1. Log on to the SAP system in client 000.
2. Enter Transaction "SPAM" in the command field, and press the Enter key (or select the menu option TOOLS • ABAP WORKBENCH • UTILITIES • MAINTENANCE • SPAM—SUPPORT PACKAGE MANAGER). Select the menu option SUPPORT PACKAGE • LOAD PACKAGES • FROM APPLICATION SERVER.

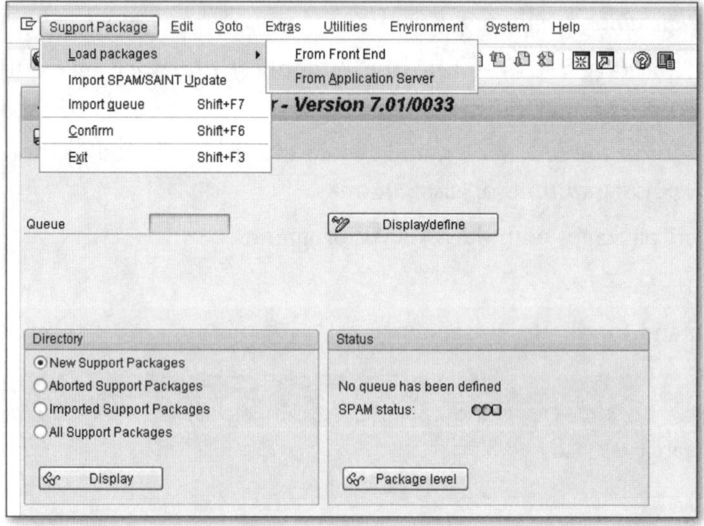

3. Choose YES to confirm the dialog box that opens.

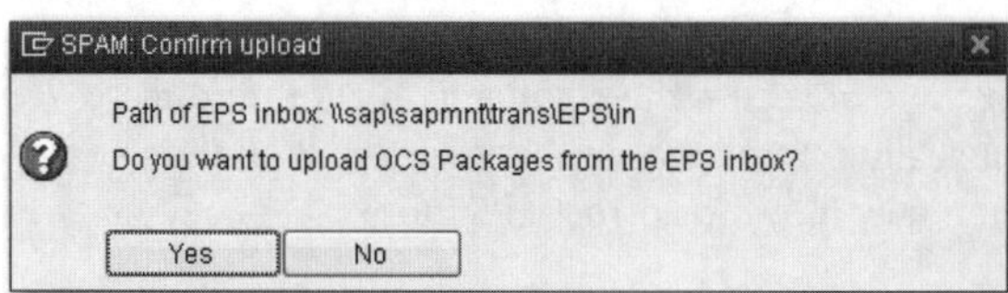

4. The support packages you loaded are displayed. Make sure that no warning or error messages were issued. Choose BACK (⊙) to exit the view.

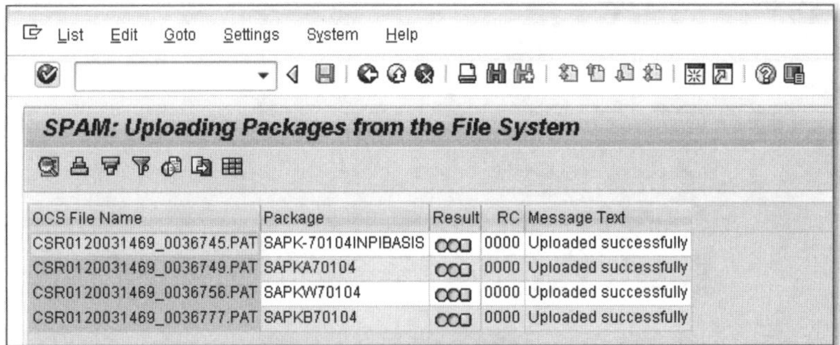

5. Check the packages by selecting the NEW SUPPORT PACKAGES option under DIRECTORY, and clicking on the DISPLAY button.

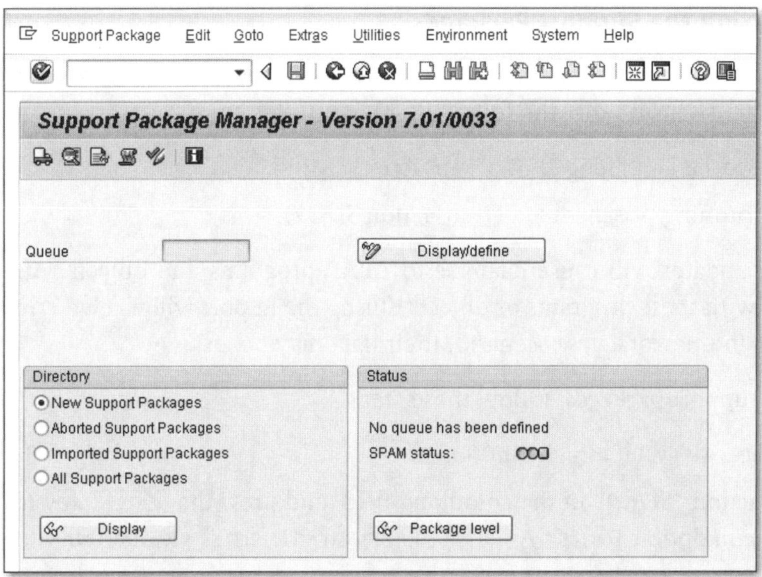

6. The new updates are listed with the status NOT IMPORTED. Choose BACK (⊙) to exit the display.

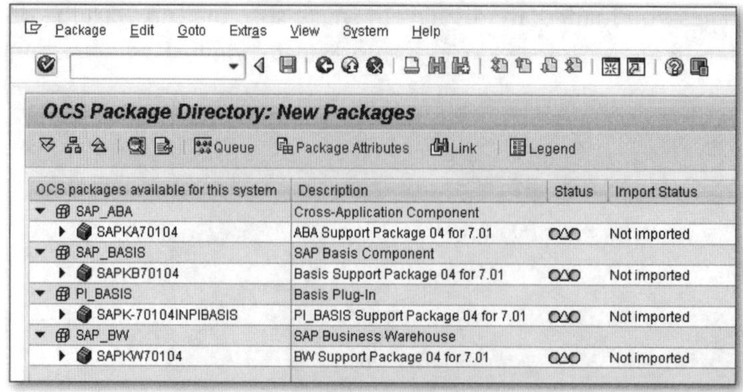

Your preparations for importing the support packages are now complete. The Support Package Manager now has access to the files. In the next step, you can start the import.

18.5.2 Importing the Support Packages

Users must not work in the SAP system while the ABAP support packages are being imported. You must ensure that the following prerequisites are in place:

- All users are locked and logged off (Transaction SM04).
- No jobs are running or scheduled (Transaction SM37).

Importing the updates will cause changes to ABAP programs and objects. Any users working with these programs or objects during the import will receive error messages, and, in the worst-case scenario, their data may be lost.

To import the support packages, follow these steps:

1. Log on to the SAP system in client 000.
2. Enter Transaction "SPAM" in the command field, and press the [Enter] key (or select the menu option Tools • ABAP Workbench • Utilities • Maintenance • SPAM—Support Package Manager).
3. Click on the Display/define button.

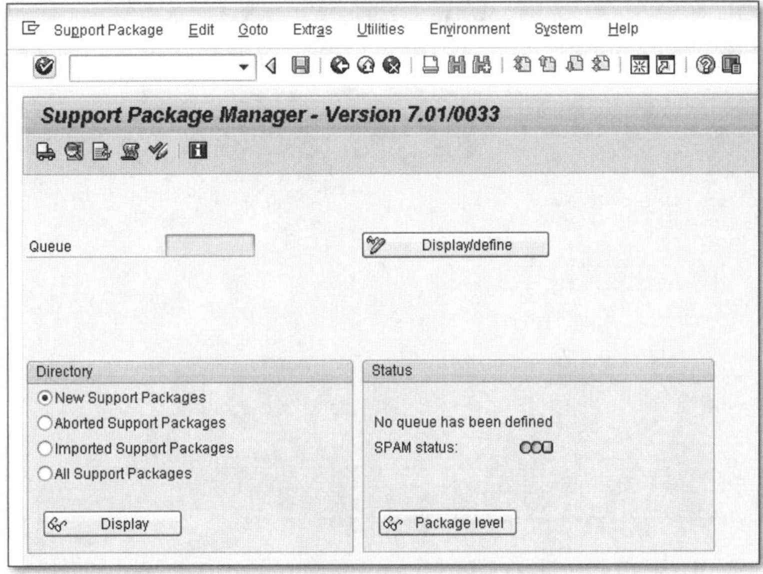

4. You can now select the components you want to update. Click on All Components.

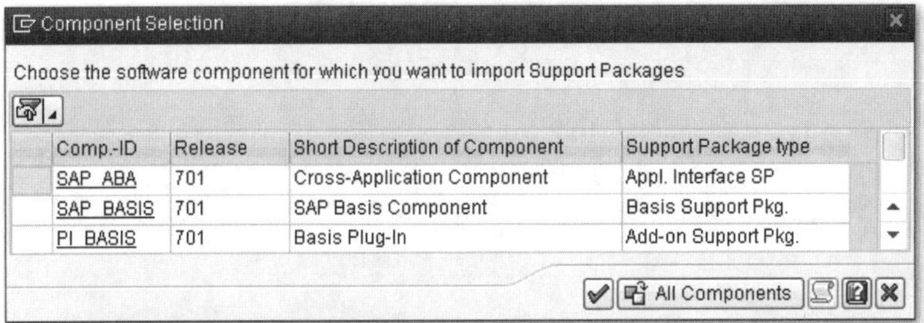

5. The components are listed, together with the corresponding target support packages. Choose Calculate Queue.

[+]

Import Queue

Support packages for various system components must be imported in a specific sequence, known as a *queue*.

The system calculates the queue itself, which is particularly important if you skip one or more support package levels.

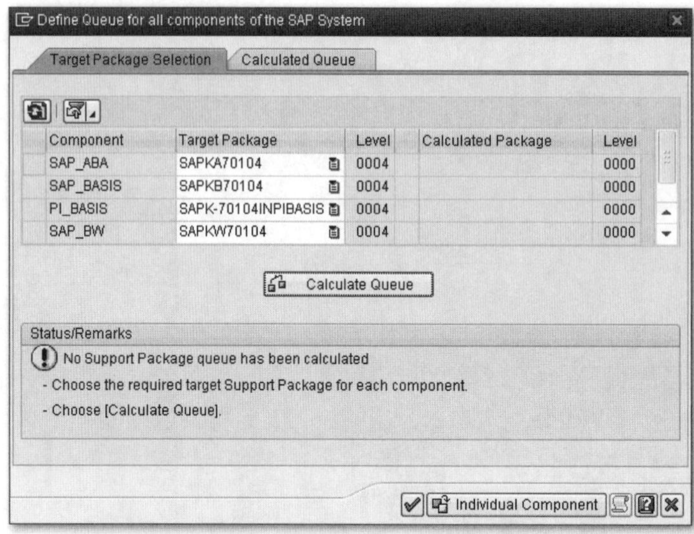

6. The system calculates the sequence in which the support packages are to be imported. Check under STATUS/REMARKS that no warning or error messages were issued. Switch to the CALCULATED QUEUE tab.

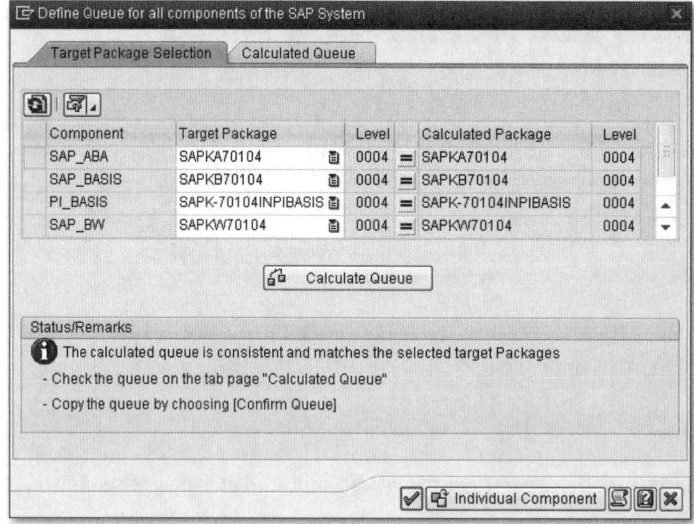

7. The calculated sequence is displayed here again. Choose CONFIRM QUEUE (✔).

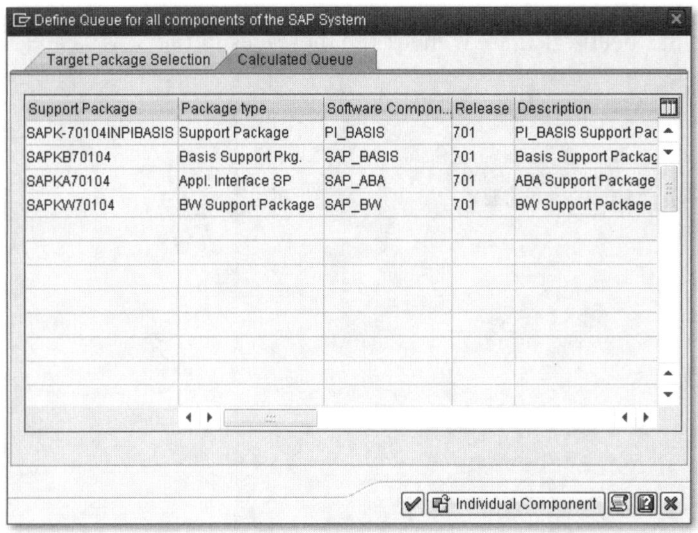

8. The system asks you whether you want to create a modification adjustment transport.
9. In our example, modification adjustment transports are not used, so we choose No.

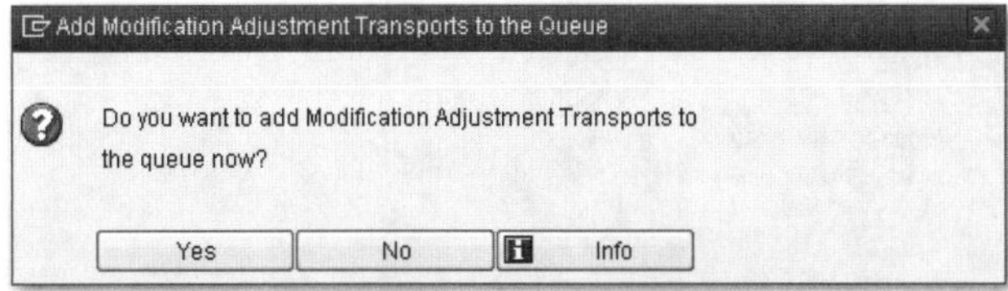

Modification Adjustment Transports [+]

Modification adjustment transports are created when you perform a modification adjustment (see Section 18.5.3). In a multisystem landscape, you have the option of transporting the result of your modification adjustment instead of performing a new adjustment in each system.

You can include the transport request created in the development system as part of the modification adjustment in the support package queue if you import the support packages into the QA and production system, for example. The request is then imported with the queue.

10. When the queue has been calculated, check the messages in the STATUS area.

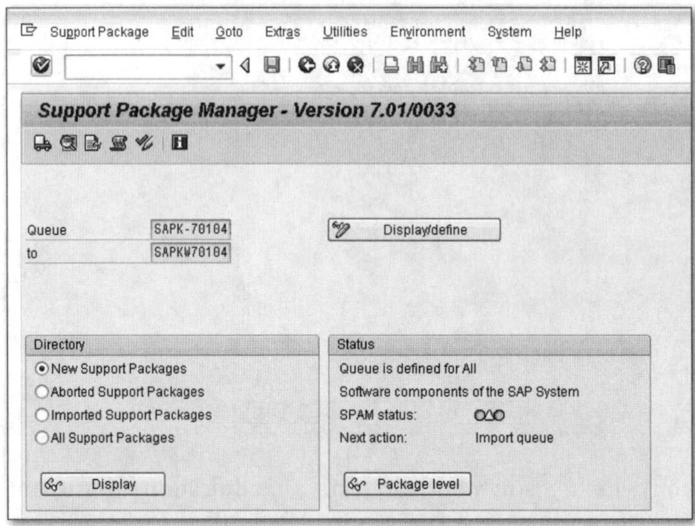

11. Before you start the import, test the functionality of the transport programs. To do this, choose the menu option UTILITIES • CHECK TRANSPORT TOOL.

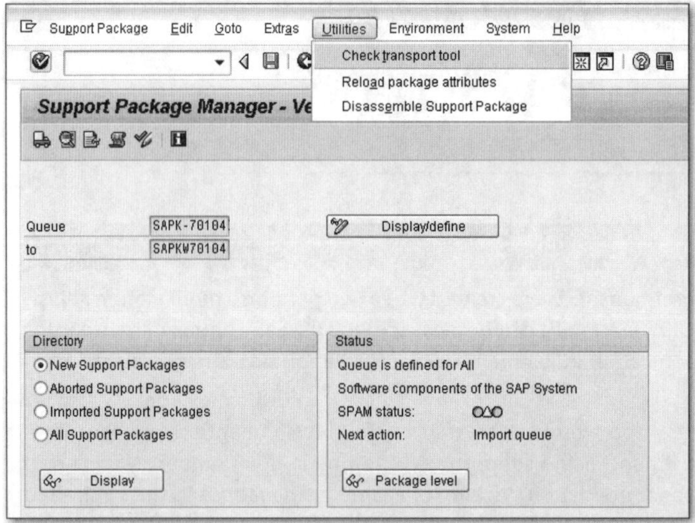

12. Make sure that no error messages were issued. Choose BACK (◀) to exit the view.

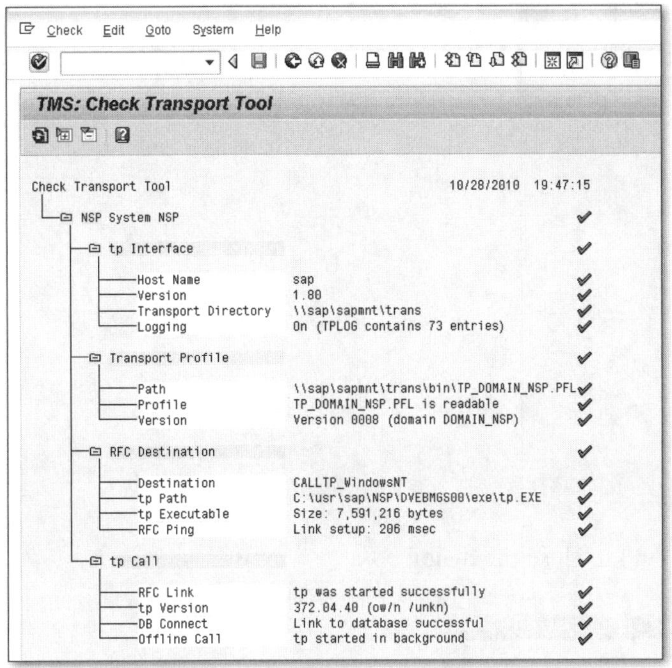

13. Begin by importing the support packages in test mode. Choose the menu option EXTRAS • SETTINGS.

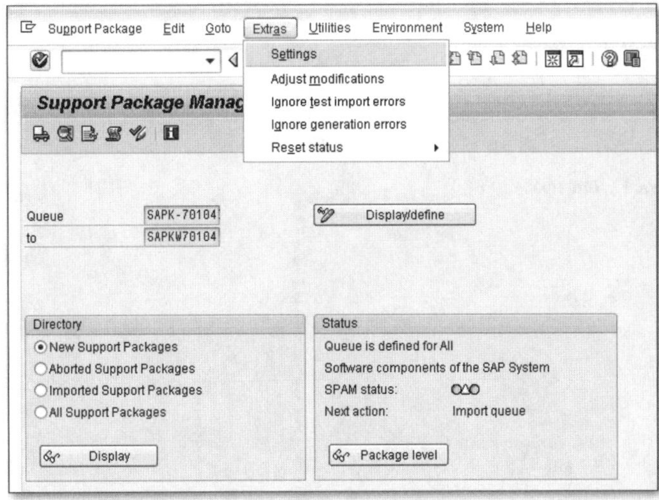

14. Select the TEST option under SCENARIO on the IMPORT QUEUE tab. Click on CONFIRM (✔).

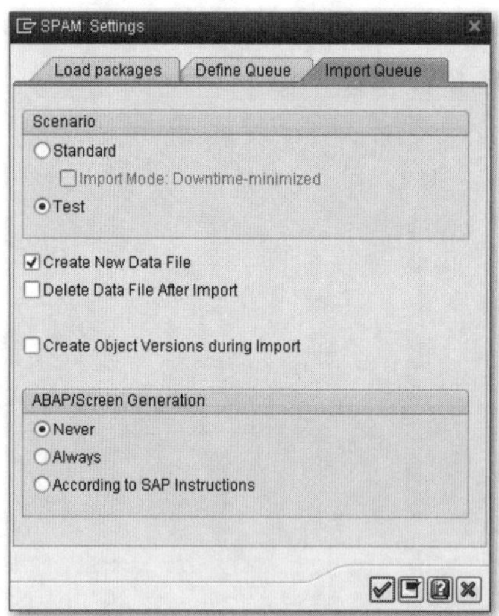

15. Choose CONTINUE (✔) to close the dialog box.

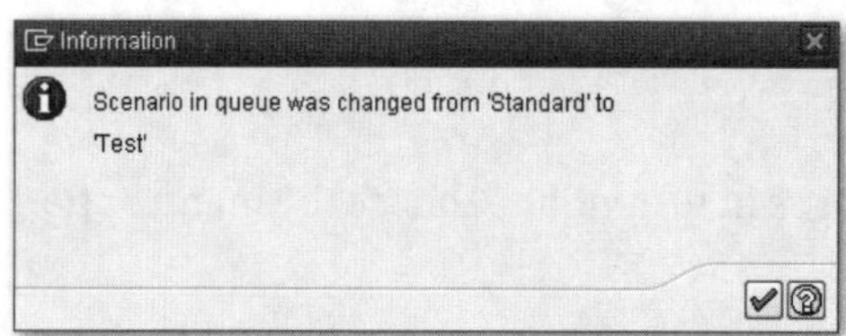

16. Choose the IMPORT QUEUE button.

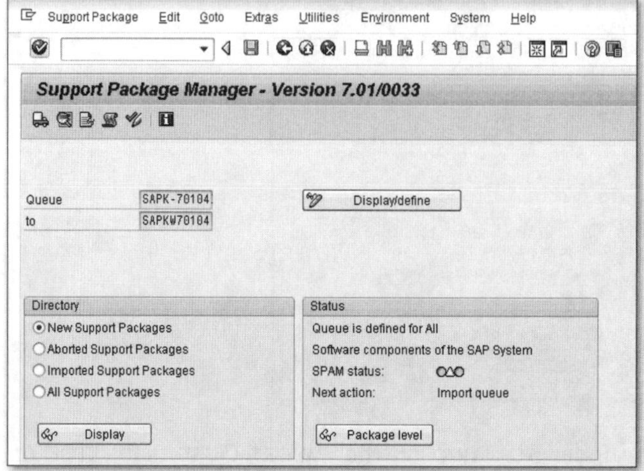

17. A dialog box is displayed to confirm that the queue has now been imported. Read the specified SAP Note (for example, SAP Note 822379) to determine whether any prerequisites apply to the import. Then click on IMPORT.

[!]

Referring to SAP Notes

Carefully read any SAP Notes mentioned during the import. Certain prerequisites must be fulfilled before you can import some support packages. Some support packages need to be imported together, while others must be imported individually. SAP Notes also tell you how to handle known error messages.

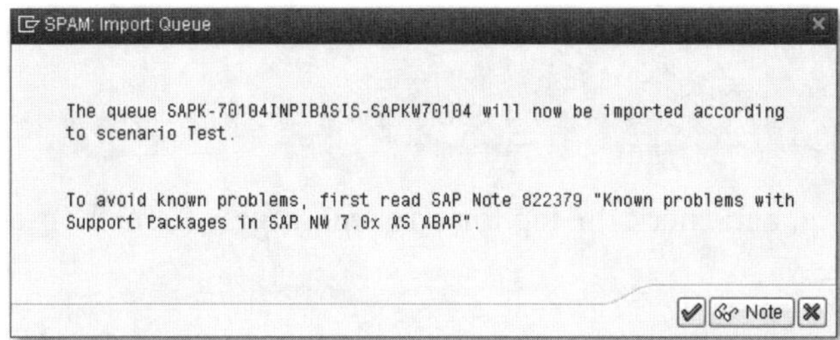

18. The updates are then imported. You can track the progress of the update in the status bar in the bottom-left corner of the screen. An information message is displayed as soon as the process is complete. Choose CONTINUE.

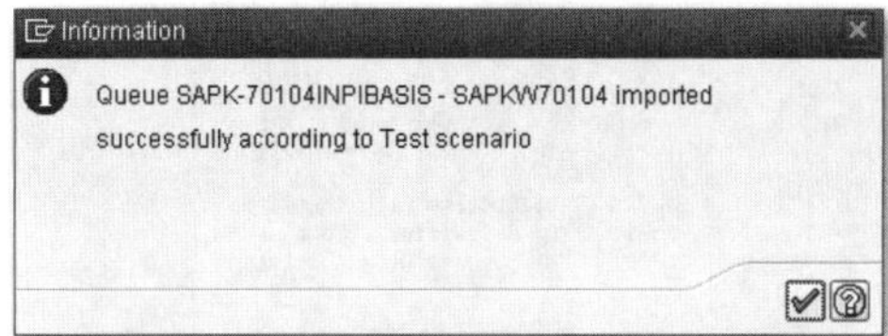

[+]

Duration of the Import

The process of importing the queue may take a long time to complete, depending on the number and size of the support packages involved. Depending on the performance of your system, it may take hours to import a large queue.

19. Now check the log. Select IMPORT LOGS OF THE QUEUE.

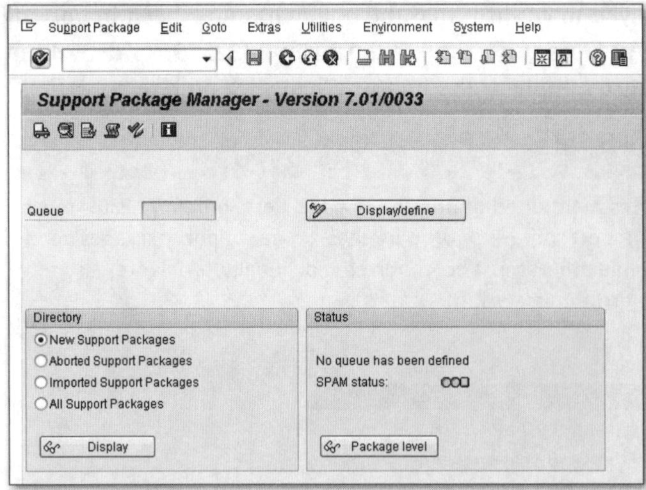

20. Expand the tree structure, and check the log for error messages. Then choose BACK (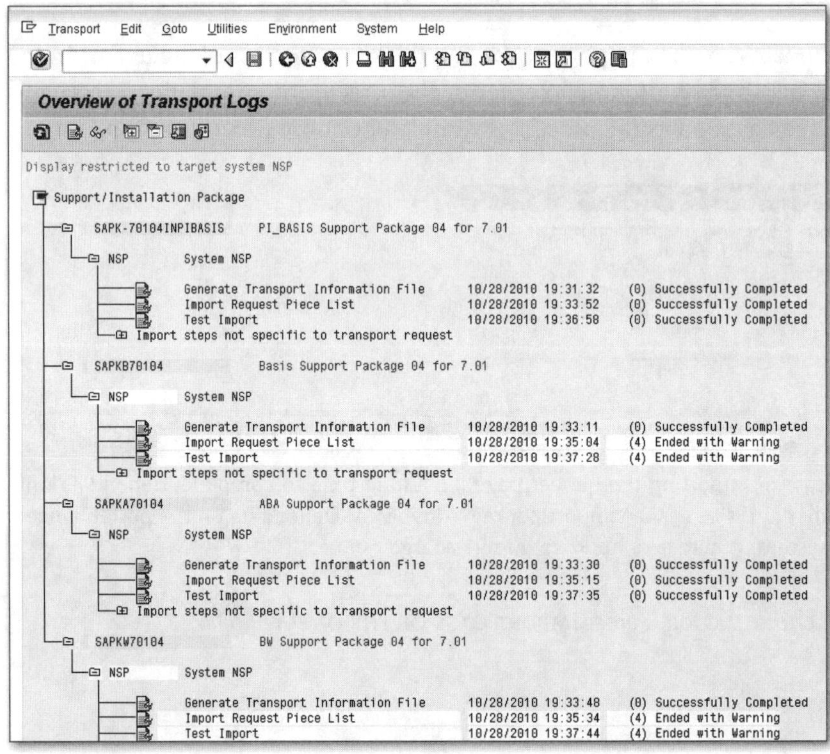) to exit the view.

21. You need to define the queue again to import the support packages in production mode. Repeat steps 3 to 9. Then repeat steps 12 and 13, and activate the STANDARD scenario. Click on CONFIRM (✔).

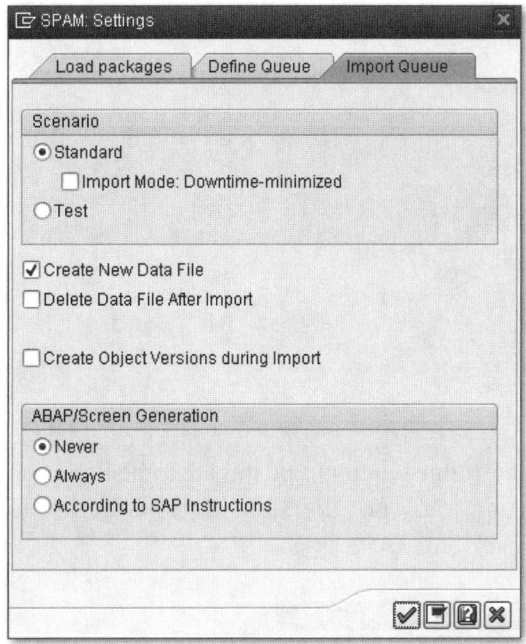

"Downtime-Minimized" Import Mode

In the STANDARD import scenario, you can choose the additional DOWNTIME-MINIMIZED option. This is an import mode that minimizes the time period during which the SAP system is unavailable.

This mode is generally only useful for production systems under specific circumstances. For more information about this function, refer to the online SAP Help Portal.

22. Choose IMPORT QUEUE (🚚).

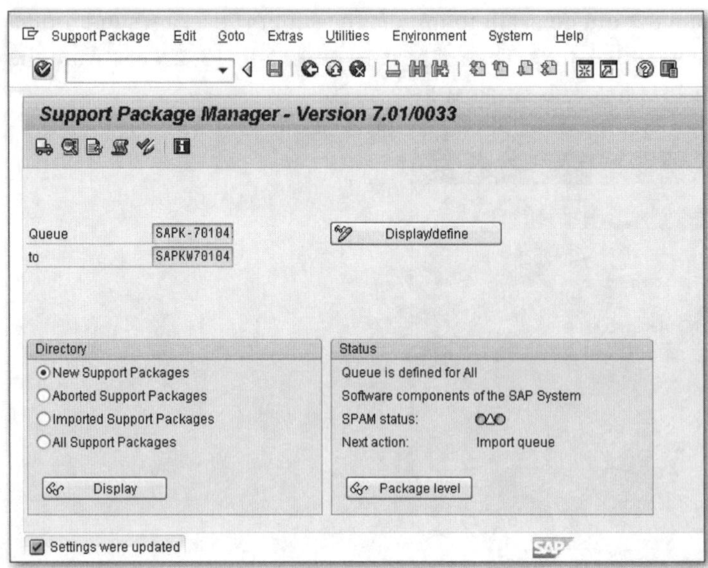

23. Here you can make a setting to determine whether updates are to be imported in dialog mode or as a background job. Click the START OPTIONS button to change the configuration. Then click on IMPORT (✔).

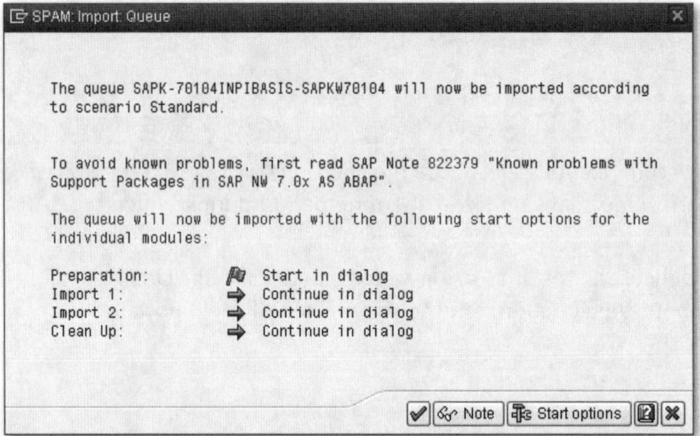

24. You are informed as soon as the import is complete. Choose CONTINUE (✔) to close the dialog box.

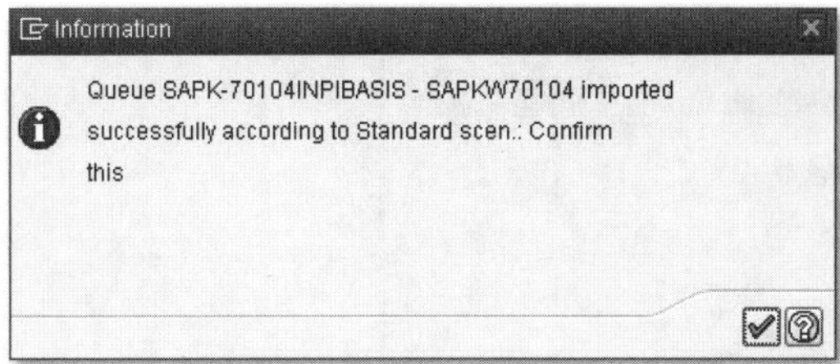

Duration of the Import in Production Mode [+]

In production mode, the import may take more time to complete than in test mode. Take account of this when scheduling and monitoring the import.

25. Chose IMPORT LOGS OF THE QUEUE ( ) to check the import log again. If no errors occurred, choose CONFIRM QUEUE ( ) to confirm a successful import.

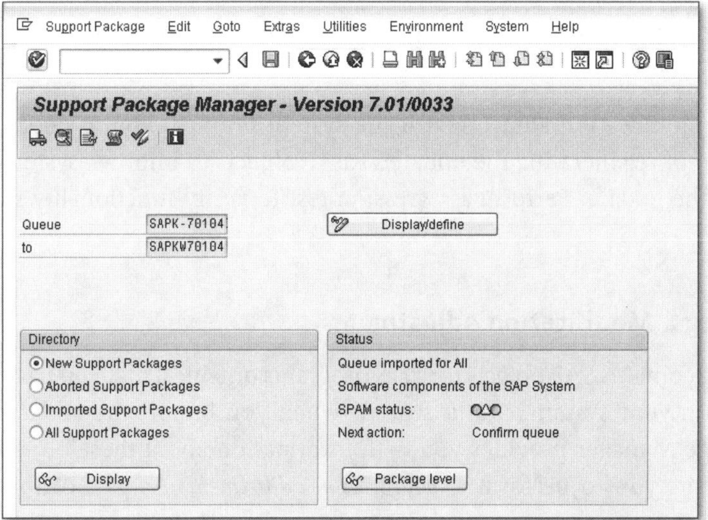

26. A message appears in the status bar, indicating that the queue has been confirmed. You must confirm the queue before new support packages can be imported. You can view the support packages that have been imported by selecting the IMPORTED SUPPORT PACKAGES option.

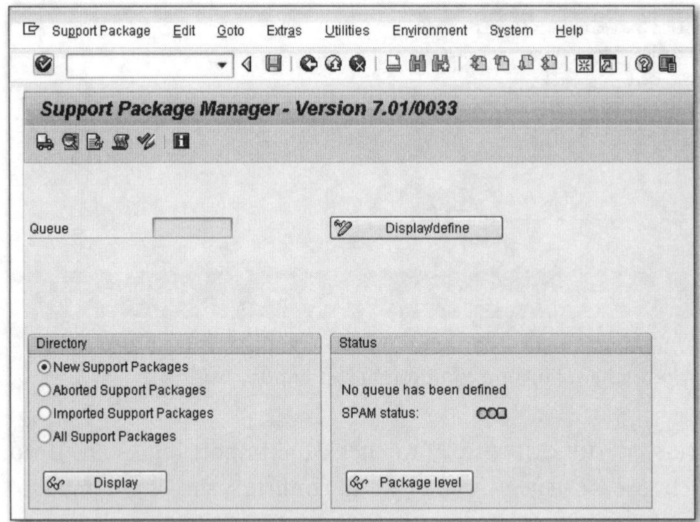

Confirming the queue completes the import procedure, and the updates have now been imported into your SAP system.

Next, perform the modification adjustment if the system prompts you to do so. You have the option of regenerating the updated ABAP objects to improve system performance after the update. Perform a regression test to verify functionality in the system.

18.5.3 Performing a Modification Adjustment

If a support package contains SAP objects (such as programs or tables) that you have changed (*modified*) in your system, conflicts occur when you import the update. The Support Package Manager provides you with information about these object conflicts and prompts you to perform a *modification adjustment*. As part of this adjustment, you must choose between retaining your modifications and accepting the newly delivered SAP version of the objects.

Depending on whether the objects in question are *Data Dictionary objects* (for example, tables) or *Repository objects* (for example, programs), start the modification adjustment in Transaction SPDD (Data Dictionary) or SPAU (Repository). During the import of the support packages, you can skip the SPAU adjustment and return to it after the import has been completed. However, the Data Dictionary adjustment can't be skipped.

Use Transaction SPDD or SPAU to check whether your change is contained in the support package and whether it is identical to the version in the imported update. Revert, where possible, to the SAP standard to simplify future system maintenance. If your modification is not contained in the support package, determine which steps are required to import the modification again. Import the modification again and test it.

[+]

Modification Adjustment

As an SAP Basis administrator, you may not be able to perform the modification adjustment yourself, for example, if you did not personally make the change or if you don't have sufficient programming experience. Ask for assistance from the user who modified the SAP object or your programming department if a modification adjustment is required when importing support packages.

18.5.4 Regenerating Objects

Importing support packages involves the large-scale replacement of SAP objects with new versions. These objects need to be compiled or regenerated the first time they are called. As a result, system performance is temporarily very slow immediately after updates are imported.

In general, these restrictions don't pose a major problem because they no longer apply as of the second call, for example, the second call of a transaction. However, users may find them very disruptive, in particular if they affect time-critical production.

To counteract these effects, you can choose to only regenerate objects that were already in use before the support package import, using the SAP Load Generator (Transaction SGEN). The benefit of this approach is that it has hardly any effect on performance. The drawback, however, is that the generation of the objects requires storage space in the database, which you could possibly save temporarily. If you detect a shortage of database capacity, it's best to avoid regeneration. However, you should regenerate the objects if capacity problems do not apply.

Consider the needs of your end users when making this decision. Depending on the application area, the generation may not be strictly essential for performance reasons.

1. Enter Transaction "SGEN" in the command field, and press the [Enter] key.
2. Under GENERATION TASK, select the REGENERATE EXISTING LOADS option. Choose CONTINUE.

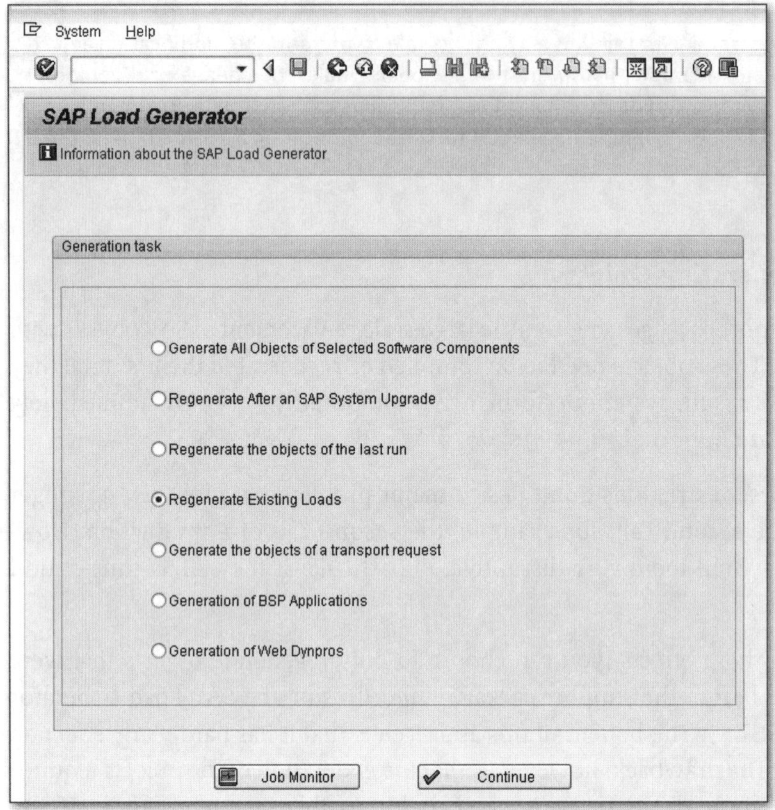

3. Select the ONLY GENERATE OBJECTS WITH INVALIDATED LOAD option. Click on CONTINUE (✔).

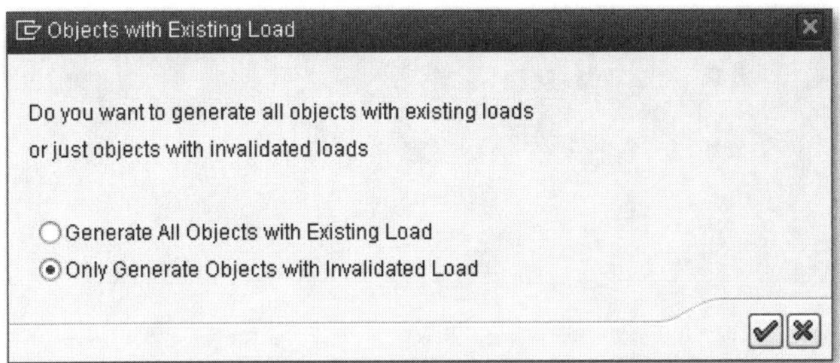

4. If you operate several application servers, you can select one or more servers, among which the generation load is distributed. Choose CONTINUE.

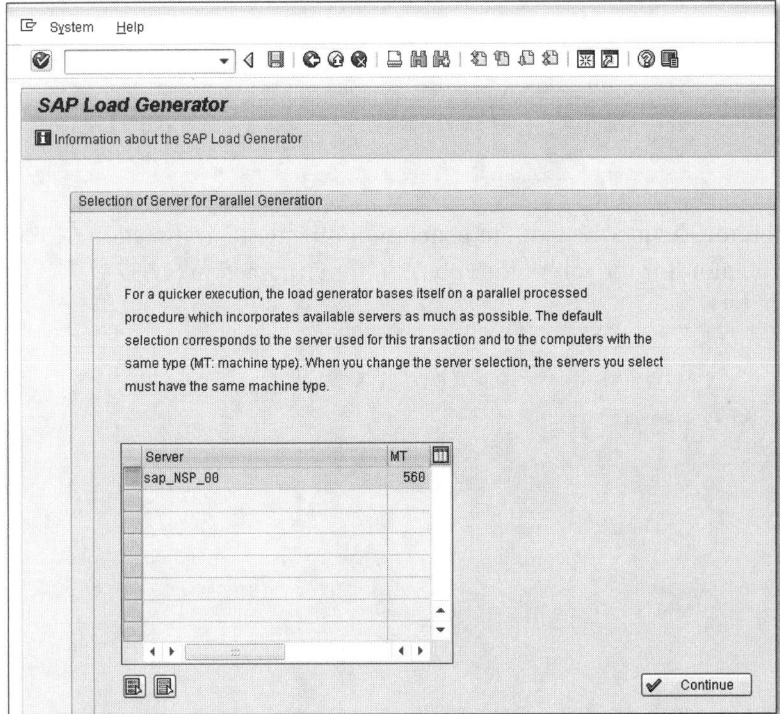

5. The generation is executed in the background. You can choose to execute the job immediately or at a specific time. You can choose START JOB DIRECTLY, for example.

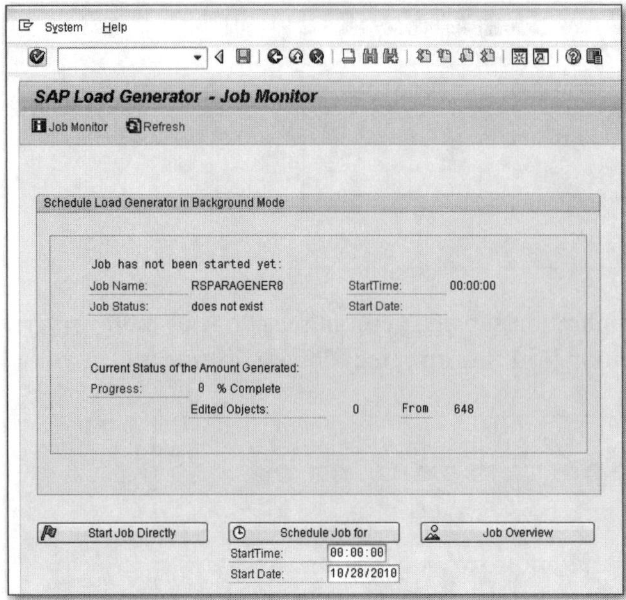

6. You can monitor the progress of the generation directly in Transaction SGEN. Alternatively, monitor the job in the Job Monitor (Transaction SM37).

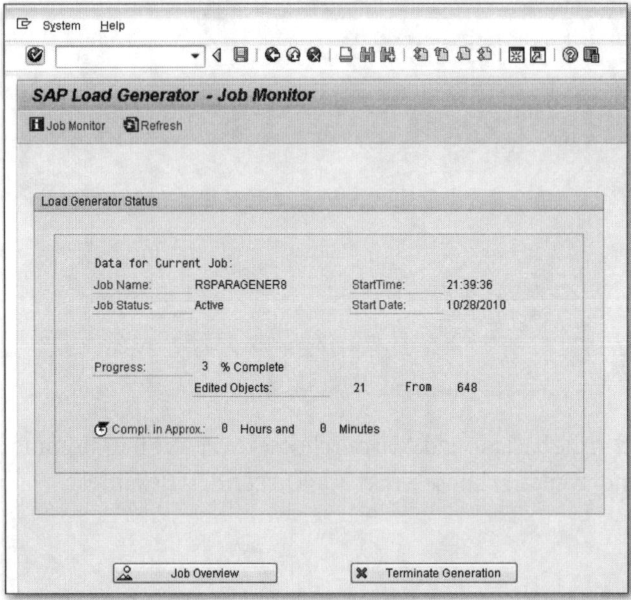

If you run the Load Generator with the options specified earlier, only the following objects are regenerated:

- Objects that were already loaded once (existing load)
- Objects that were updated (invalidated) by the support package

You can also select other options in Transaction SGEN. However, in the case of support packages, the settings shown here are optimal.

18.5.5 Performing Regression Tests

Regression tests are required because support packages may cause changes to many objects across many different modules. All business departments that use the SAP system must use regression tests to check whether all functions are still available without errors after the import, or whether the support package has produced new problems. A support package or support package stack must be treated as a mini-upgrade, in particular if it contains extensive changes.

All existing processes must continue to function in exactly the same way they did before the support package was imported. The SAP Notes that are relevant for a support package specify the precise tests that are to be conducted by the technical team and end users. The testing procedure can be accelerated if the business departments have recorded test cases or a script for the tests to be processed.

To perform regression testing, you can, for example, use Test Management in SAP Solution Manager (see Chapter 4). Another option is to automate testing with the SAP *eCATT* tool (Extended Computer-Aided Test Tool).

18.6 Installing Add-Ons

Add-ons enhance the functional scope of standard SAP systems. Examples of add-ons include industry solutions and plug-ins. You can download add-ons from the SAP Support Portal in just the same way as support packages.

Add-ons that have been downloaded can be installed with the *Add-On Installation Tool* (Transaction SAINT). This tool is similar to the Support Package Manager (Transaction SPAM), which is used to maintain the SPAM/SAINT update.

If you have downloaded an add-on from the Support Portal, follow these steps to install it:

1. Log on to the SAP system in client 000.
2. Enter Transaction "SAINT" in the command field, and press the Enter key.
3. On the initial screen of the ADD-ON INSTALLATION TOOL, click on the START button.

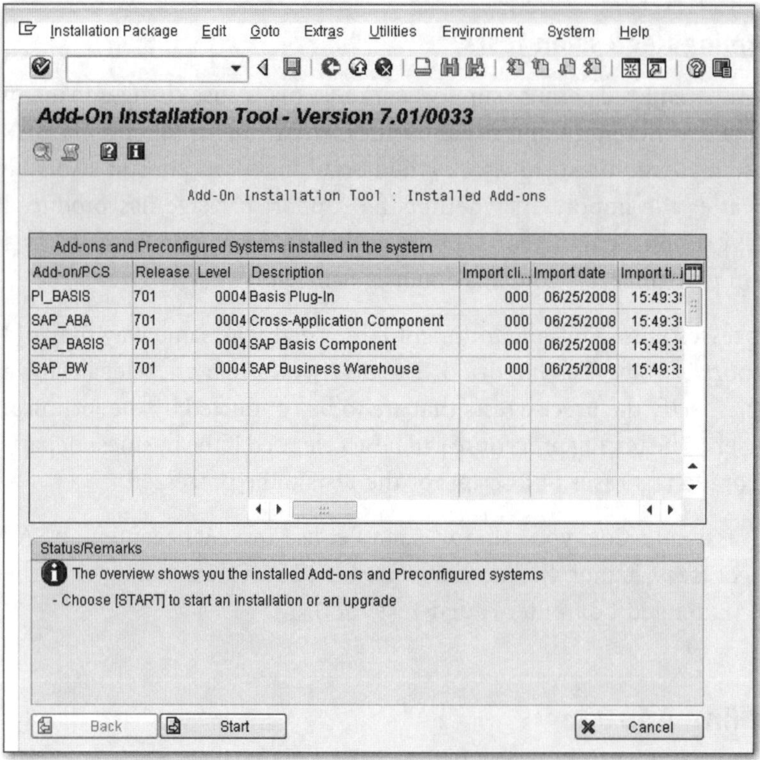

4. You can upload the add-on from your PC or from the SAP server. Select the menu option INSTALLATION PACKAGE • LOAD PACKAGES • FROM FRONT END.

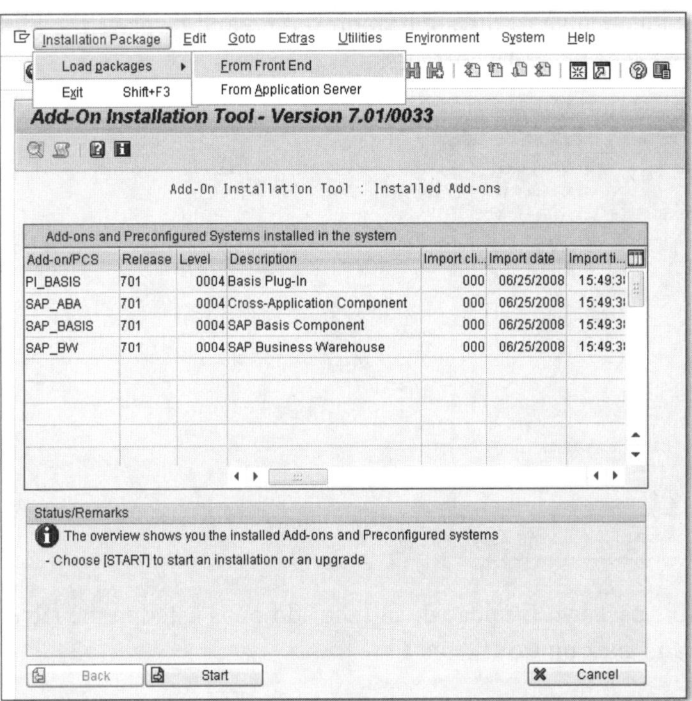

5. Navigate to the location where the file is stored, and choose OPEN.

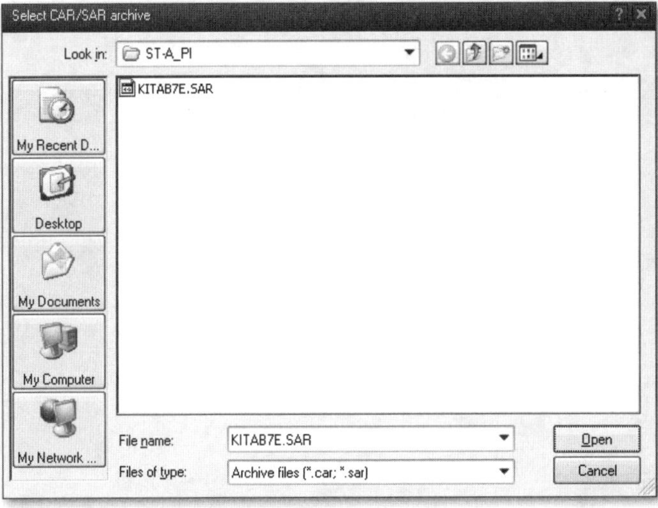

6. The system copies the archive to the application server, and displays the files that are to be unpacked. Choose DECOMPRESS.

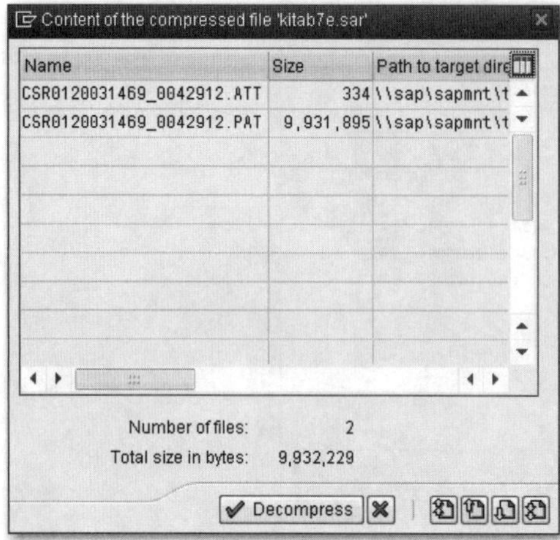

7. The list of installable packages is updated, and the add-on is listed in the table. Select the add-on and click on CONTINUE.

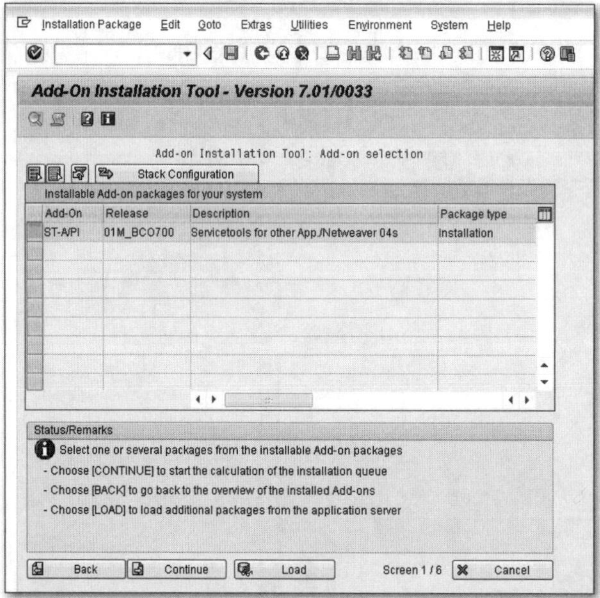

8. The add-on to be installed is displayed on the INSTALLATION QUEUE tab. Choose CONTINUE.

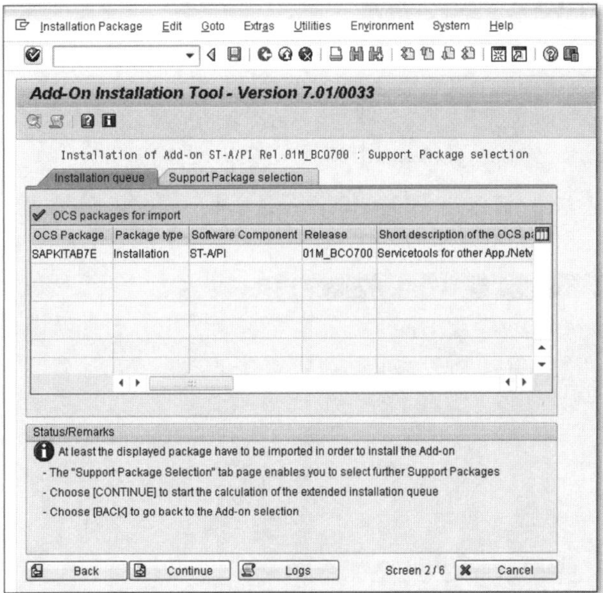

9. The calculated import queue is displayed. Choose CONTINUE again.

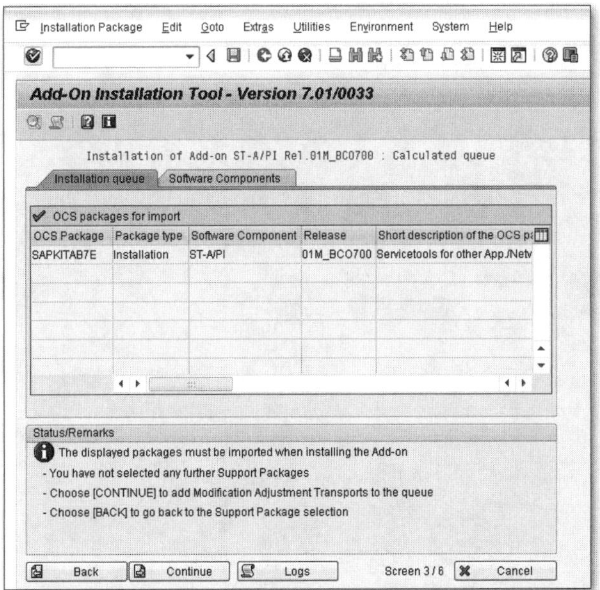

10. Add a modification adjustment transport to the installation queue if required, or, alternatively, choose No.

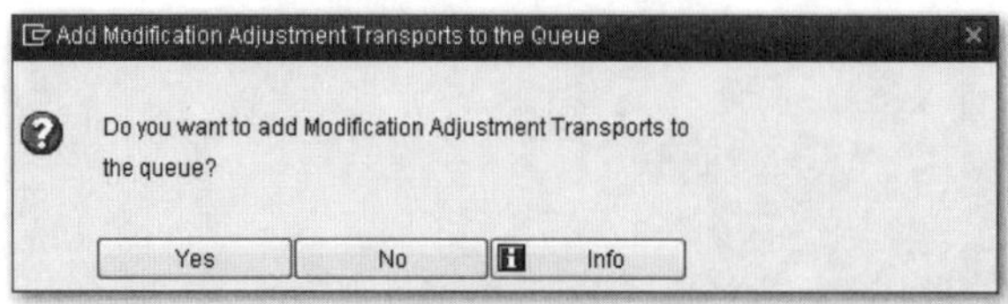

11. Choose Import (✔) to start the import.

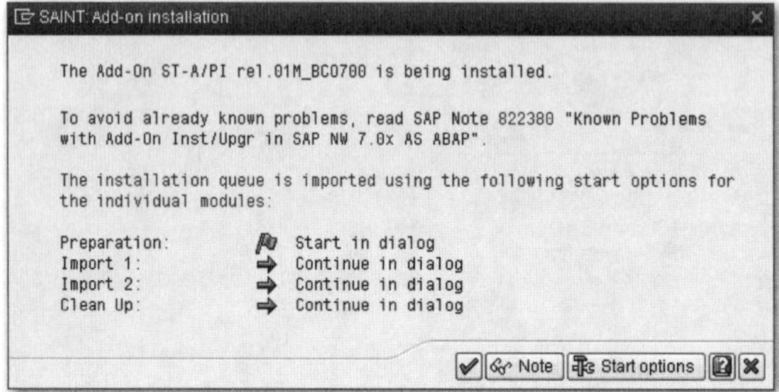

12. The add-on is installed. Check the logs after installation is complete. Then click on Finish.

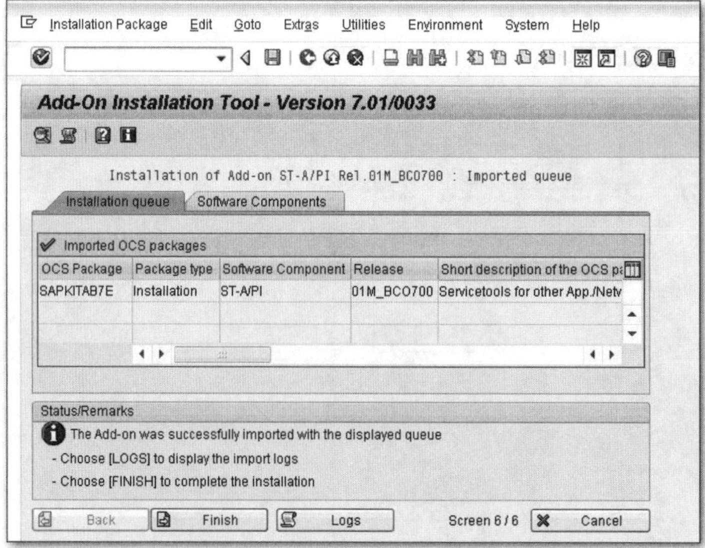

The add-on is now implemented. If you now select the menu option SYSTEM • STATUS to view the component information, the add-on is included in the list of installed components.

A modification adjustment may also be necessary for add-ons. If you want to perform load generation, activate the GENERATE ALL OBJECTS OF SELECTED SOFTWARE COMPONENTS option in Transaction SGEN, and only select the add-on you've just installed for generation.

18.7 Summary

This chapter described how to maintain an SAP system. You now know how to download support packages and add-ons from the SAP Service Marketplace, and how to implement them in your system using the Support Package Manager or Add-On Installation Tool. You also know how to perform a kernel update.

You should use support package stacks instead of individual support packages because the support package stacks deliver stable combinations of support packages for all components in your system.

Ideally, you should use the Maintenance Optimizer in Solution Manager to download support package stacks. This process is described in Chapter 4.

This chapter addresses some fundamental issues related to troubleshooting. You will become familiar with a number of tools and methods that you can use to resolve problems yourself. You will also learn how to make the most of the support channels offered by SAP.

19 Diagnostics and Troubleshooting

In every SAP system, errors will sometimes occur that you will be required to resolve yourself, or you will need to at least collaborate in their correction. Some errors are trivial and can be solved after you read the error message. Other issues are caused by an application error, incorrect system settings, or by an actual programming error.

SAP provides the SAP Support Portal to help you find solutions to system errors. The Portal has an extensive database of solutions and SAP Notes to help you resolve issues. This chapter outlines the basic principle of error handling, demonstrates how to use the SAP Support Portal for troubleshooting, and shows you how to implement SAP Notes in your SAP System.

19.1 Basic Procedure

The general procedure for troubleshooting described here isn't a new one. Indeed, it has been used for many years in a range of industries. The mechanic in the repair shop around the corner would take the same approach to repairing your car:

1. Gather data.
2. Analyze the problem.
3. Determine solution options.
4. Eliminate the error.
5. Make the necessary adjustments.

6. Document the changes.
7. Test the results.

Some of these steps are described in more detail next.

Gather Data

When an error occurs, the first step is to gather data. Pay particular attention to the following questions:

- What is the precise nature of the problem?
- What causes the problem?
- Is it possible that the problem will occur frequently, or has it already occurred several times?
- Can the problem be systematically reproduced?
- Which error messages, dumps, or other diagnostic information was displayed in connection with this problem?

Use the available system tools to analyze the error messages, for example:

- System log (Transaction SM21)
- Dump analysis (Transaction ST22)
- Update system (Transactions SM13 and SM14)
- Output Controller (Transaction SP01)

Then analyze the problem.

Analyze the Problem

After you've formed a detailed picture of the situation, proceed with the analysis of the problem. Use the resources available to you for solving the problem for this purpose:

- SAP online documentation (*http://help.sap.com*)
- Reference manuals
- SAP Notes
- Other customers (in your network)

If you are unable to turn up any useful information, seek the assistance of an expert:

- Internal specialists and administrators
- External consultants
- SAP Support Portal (*www.service.sap.com*)
- SAP Community Network (*www.sdn.sap.com*)

[+]

Excluding User Error

Errors may have many different causes. For example, a problem may occur because of a user error, incomplete or missing system settings, or program errors. In every case, you should begin by excluding the possibility of incorrect use or configuration of the system, before consulting external partners.

Eliminate the Error

After you've identified one or more approaches to eliminating the error, take care not to jump the gun. For one thing, not every solution will suit your situation every time. And, for another, you may cause further problems by taking a snap decision. Take a level-headed approach, and consider the following aspects:

- **Comparing the solution options**
  Compare the various solutions options you've identified. Check which changes would be necessary in each case and how these changes would impact on the behavior and stability of your SAP system. Compare the impact to be expected (costs) with the result foreseen (benefits) for each individual option.
- **Implement changes one at a time**
  Only implement one change at a time if possible. If a problem occurs and you implement several changes simultaneously, you may then be unable to identify which change solved the original problem or which change caused a new one. In some cases, however, you need to make several changes to solve a problem. Only implement more than one change at a time if this is absolutely essential, for example, in the case of related program changes.
- **Document the changes**
  All changes are to be documented thoroughly. If a change produces an additional problem, you must undo that change. To do this, you need to know what the

configuration was before the change was implemented and exactly what change was made. If changes are to be applied across various systems, you must know exactly what changes are to be made and how this is to be donc. The same steps must be performed in exactly the same way in all systems.

When it comes to troubleshooting, the concept of "learning by doing" applies. The more experience you have, the less time it will take you to solve the problems that arise. The next section explains how to use the SAP Support Portal for diagnostics and troubleshooting.

19.2 Troubleshooting with the SAP Support Portal

The SAP Support Portal is an Internet platform on which SAP provides information, as well as support functions and resources. As part of the SAP Service Marketplace (*www.service.sap.com*), you can do the following with the resources and functions provided by the SAP Support Portal:

- Search for SAP Notes.
- Download support packages.
- Register developers and namespaces.
- Maintain connection data to allow SAP to access your systems.

The SAP Support Portal is your first external point of contact when you want to analyze an error or search for troubleshooting documentation and guides. Following are the prerequisites for using the SAP Service Marketplace:

- An Internet connection
- A browser (the SAP Service Marketplace is optimized for Microsoft Internet Explorer)
- A valid user ID and a valid password for the SAP Support Portal.

Within the SAP Support Portal, access is controlled by authorizations. If you are denied access to certain functions, notify the relevant super-administrator.

[+]

Older Names for the SAP Service Marketplace

The SAP Service Marketplace has been rechristened a number of times in the past and was formerly known, for example, as *SAPNet, OSS, www.sap.com* and *service.sap.com*. All of these names refer to the central service platform of SAP AG.

19.2.1 Searching for SAP Notes with the SAP Support Portal

SAP Notes (formerly known as *OSS Notes*) help you eliminate specific problems in SAP systems and enhance the general documentation and help topics available. Follow these steps to search for an SAP Note dealing with a specific problem:

1. Access the URL *www.service.sap.com/support* in your web browser. (Alternatively, access the SAP Service Marketplace at *www.service.sap.com*, and click on the SAP SUPPORT PORTAL link.)
2. Use your user ID (S000...) and password to log on.

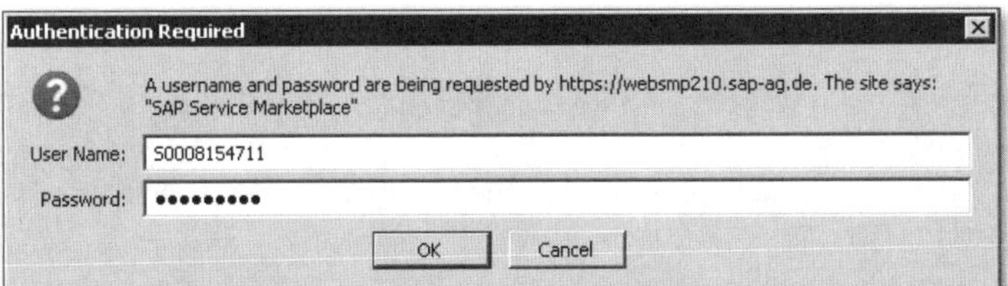

[+]

Single Sign-on

In certain cases, you may need to enter your use ID and password several times over the course of your Support Portal session. If you want to use the portal's *single-sign-on function*, you must request an *SAP Passport*. To do this, follow the instructions provided in the SAP Service Marketplace under *www.service.sap.com* • BENEFIT FROM SINGLE SIGN-ON. Thanks to a certificate installed in your browser, you can save yourself the task of entering your user name and password in the future.

3. The welcome page of the SAP Support Portal is displayed. Most functions required by system administrators can be accessed from this screen. Click on HELP & SUPPORT.

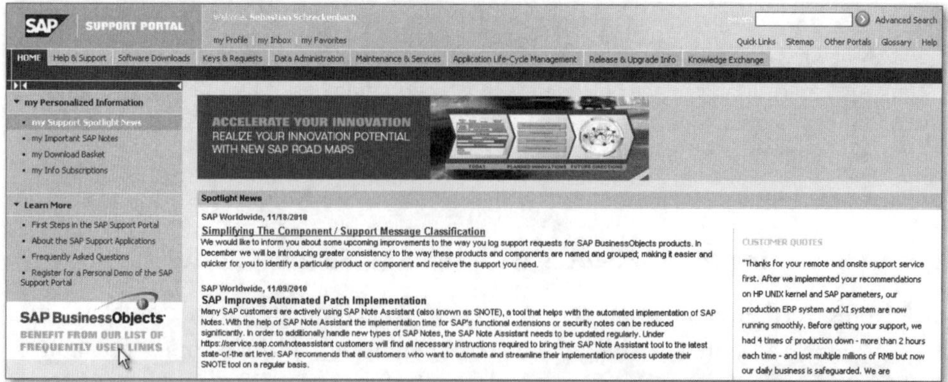

4. If you click on the SEARCH FOR SAP NOTES button, you can then perform a text search for an SAP Note. Several search options are provided for this purpose. For example, you can link the keywords entered in the SEARCH TERM field in different ways (SEARCH METHOD field), and you can restrict the search in various ways also (SEARCH RANGE, APPLICATION AREA, RESTRICTION fields, etc.). Choose the SEARCH button to start the search run.

[+]

Displaying Notes Directly

You can also access an SAP Note directly by entering the number in the NR. Field and clicking on the GO button (»).

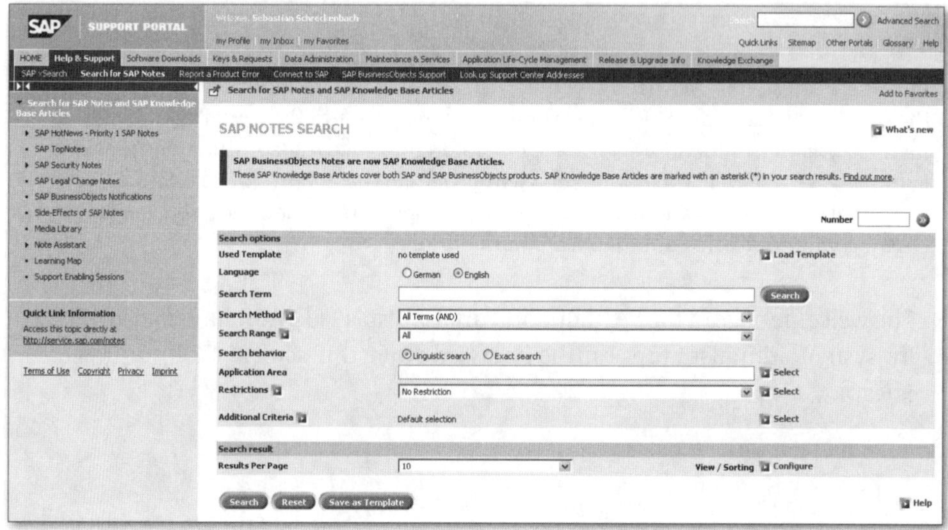

5. The search results are then displayed. To open an SAP Note, click on the link in the SHORT TEXT column.

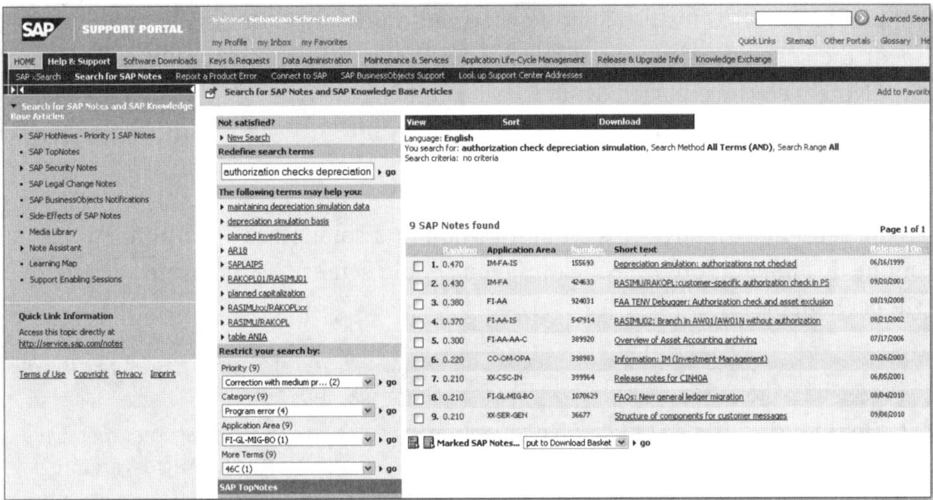

6. The note then opens in a new window or on a new browser tab.

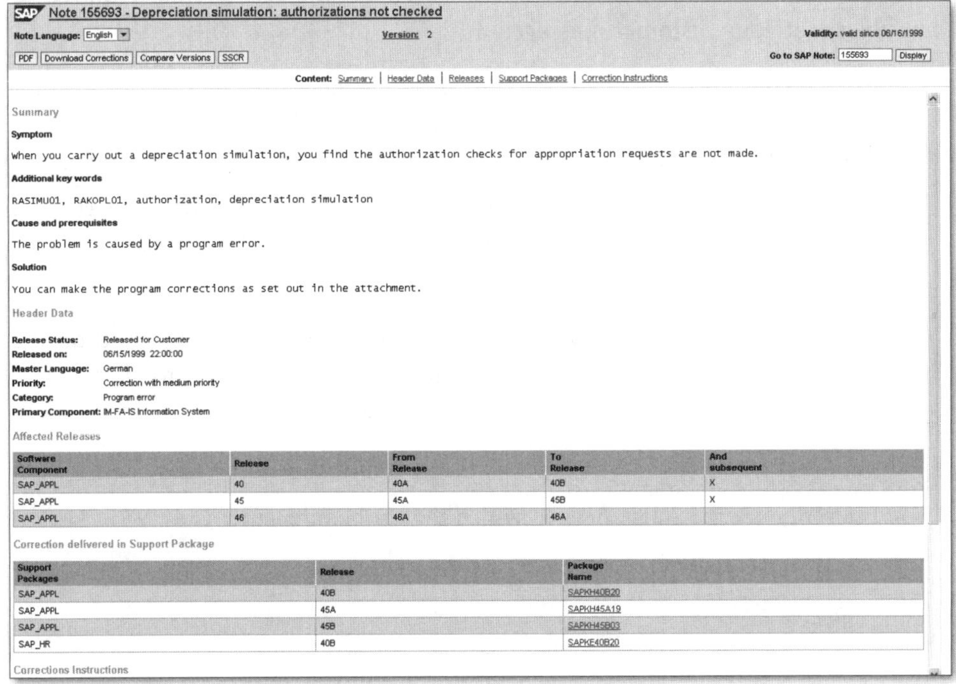

Check whether the SAP Notes found describe the problem that has occurred in your system. Check whether your release or support package level is affected by the problem described (see Section 19.4.1). If the SAP Note describes your problem, follow the instructions provided in the solution description (for example, implement the corrections provided in your SAP system—see Section 19.4.2) If your SAP Notes search is unsuccessful, create a *customer message*.

19.2.2 Customer Messages

If you can't find an answer to your question or a solution to your problem in the online documentation or SAP Notes, you should send a customer message to SAP Global Support.

[+]

Error Message and Consulting Services

Customer messages are not intended to replace consulting services. Customer messages are used primarily for reporting purposes and for the elimination of SAP errors and bugs. If a message is merely a veiled request for consulting services, it will be returned to the sender, who will be advised to contact consulting services.

The following list contains some useful tips for reducing the time required to troubleshoot your customer message:

- Describe your problem clearly and precisely. The better the quality of the information you provide, the better the results will be. Information that appears self-evident to you may be anything but obvious for the hotline consultant.
- Provide a sufficient amount of detail so that the SAP hotline team members don't need to ask additional questions before starting the troubleshooting process.
- Pay particular attention to the following aspects when describing the error:
  - If an error message was displayed, specify it exactly as it appeared on the screen. Where relevant, create a screenshot to attach to your message.
  - Specify the relevant transaction or menu path.
  - Indicate whether the problem can be reproduced in your test system.
  - Describe the circumstances in which the problem occurred.
  - Describe any special features of the data entered.

- Include a list of the SAP Notes you consulted in connection with the problem and of those that you implemented.
- List the measures you've already introduced and the investigations you've already undertaken.

If the SAP hotline team receives messages such as "FB01 is not working" or "The system is slow," it requires additional information before it can begin to resolve the issue.

[!]

Information About the System Landscape

Keep the technical information about your system landscape up to date on the SAP Support Portal, and make sure that it's accurate. This information is used by the hotline team when working on your problem.

Creating a Customer Message

It takes four steps to create a customer message:

1. Select the relevant system.
2. Search for a solution to the problem.
3. Check SAP Notes for a description of your problem.
4. Create a customer message.

You must search for SAP Notes before you create a customer message. This process avoids the creation of unnecessary support messages for problems already described by SAP Notes in the SAP Notes database.

[+]

Second Notes Search

In most cases, you've already searched once for SAP Notes when you create a customer message. Try searching a second time using different search terms—you may find an SAP Note describing your problem and avoid having to create a customer message.

Here's how to create a customer message:

1. Access the SAP Support Portal, and click on HELP & SUPPORT.
2. Click on the REPORT A PRODUCT ERROR link.

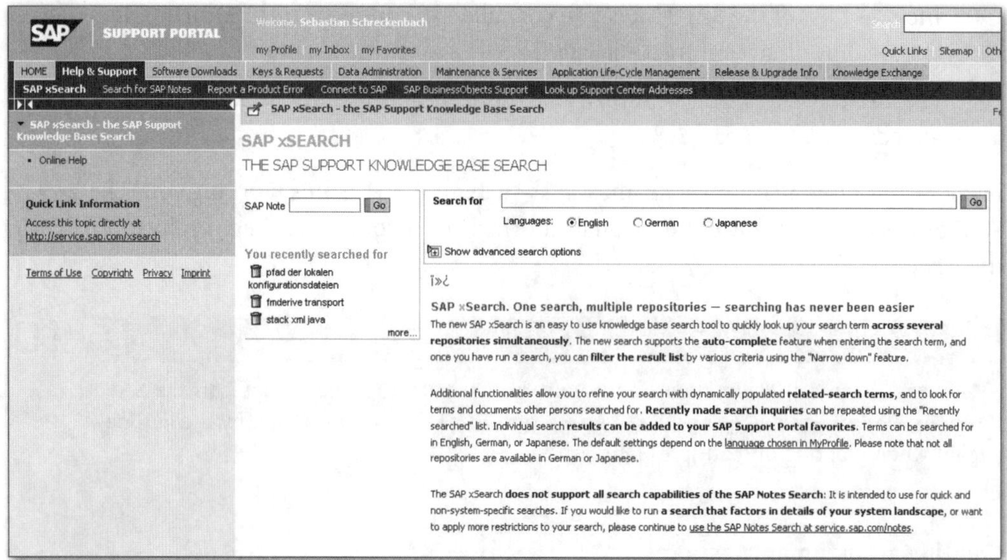

3. In the SYSTEM SEARCH frame, select the SAP system in which the problem occurred. Enter the system ID in the field provided, and choose SEARCH. Alternatively, use the CUSTOMER and INSTALLATION drop-down list boxes to restrict the search step by step.

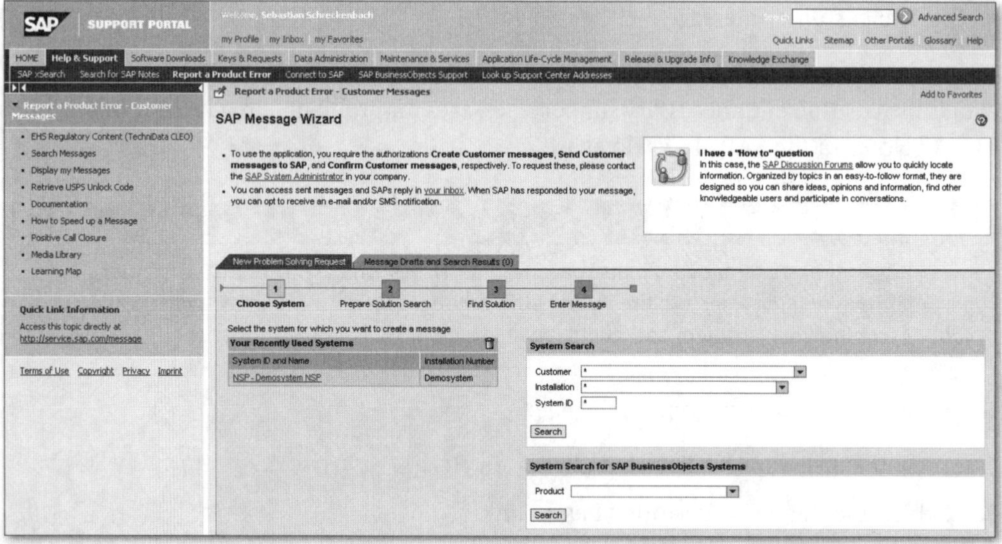

Your Recently Used Systems [+]

If you've previously created a customer message, the system you specified the last time is displayed now in the list entitled YOUR RECENTLY USED SYSTEMS. This saves you the effort of repeating your search.

4. Use the SEARCH TERM field to search for SAP Notes relating to your error. Click on CONTINUE to start the search.

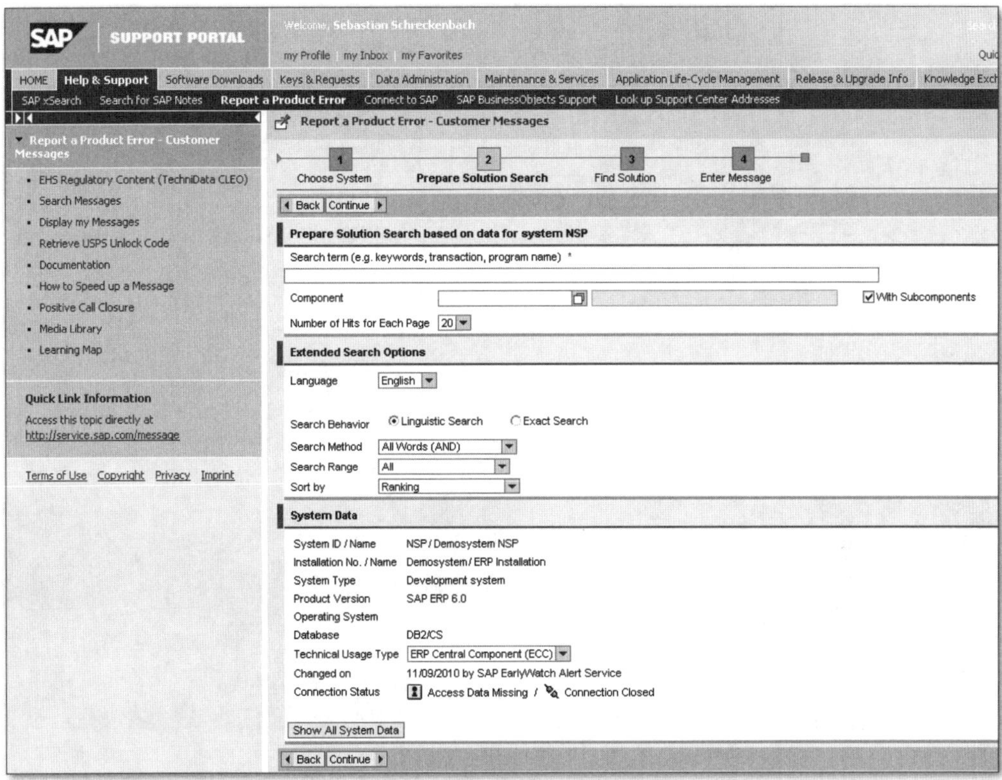

5. The result of the SAP Notes search is then displayed. Consult the SAP Notes that may describe your problem. Click on the link in the TITLE column to open the corresponding SAP Note. You can repeat the search with modified search terms by clicking on SEARCH or NEW SEARCH. If your search for a relevant SAP Note is unsuccessful, click on CREATE MESSAGE.

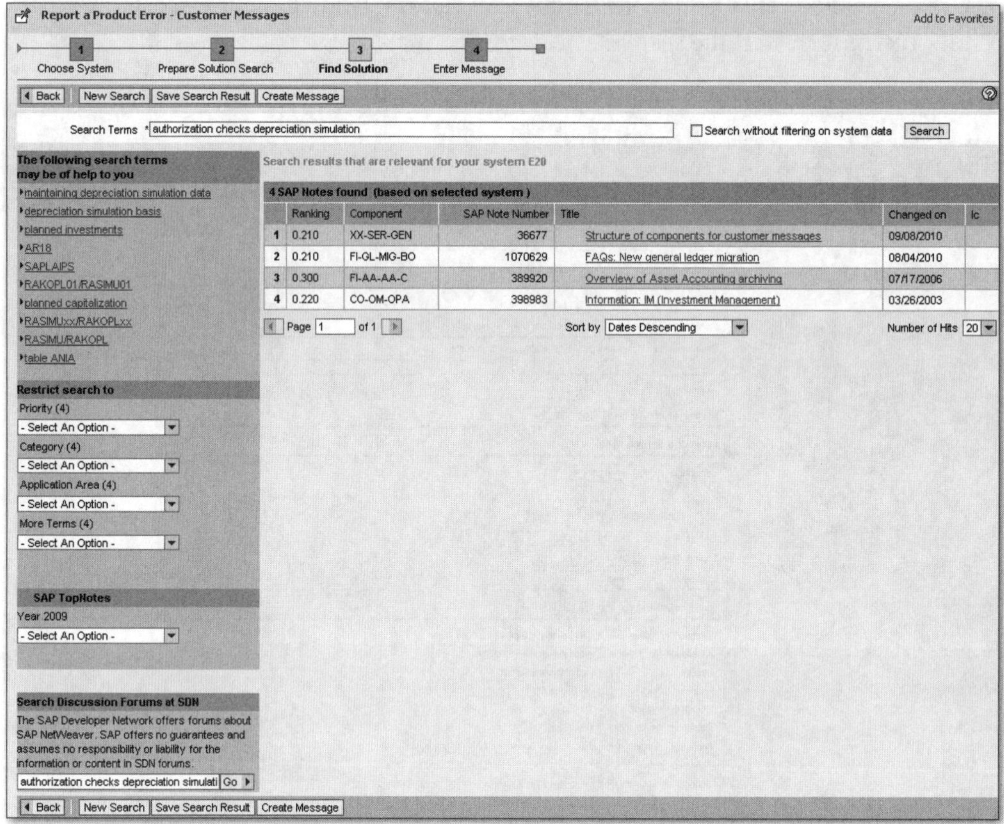

6. The following steps comprise the process of creating the customer message. Start by selecting the relevant language if the default setting isn't correct.

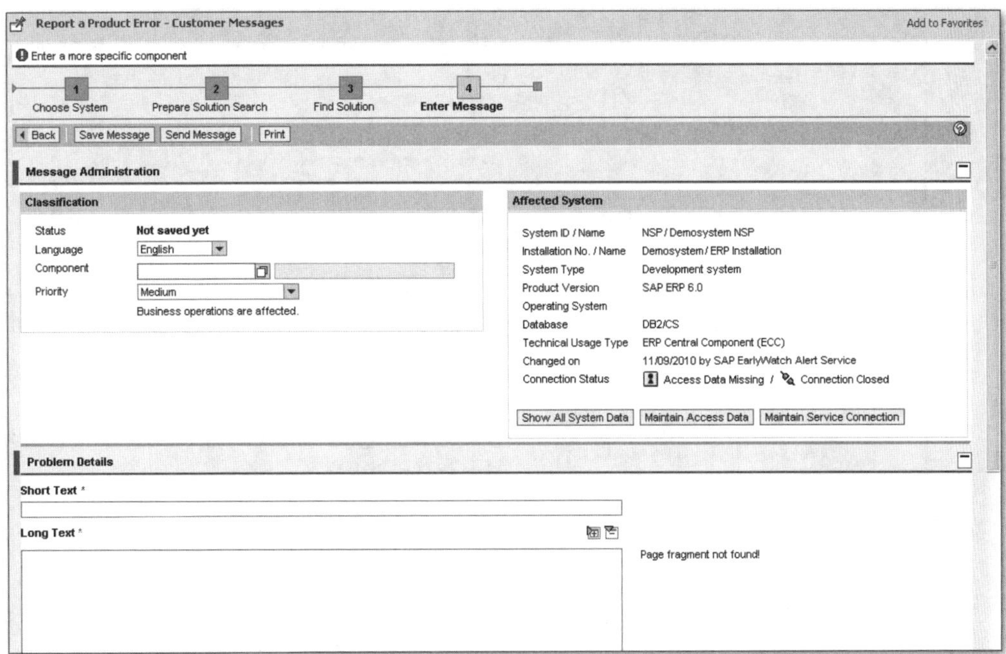

7. If you haven't already entered an application component in the search, you are required to do so now. Enter the component in the COMPONENT field, or use the input help (□). If you use the input help, a dialog box opens, displaying the component hierarchy. Expand the tree view, or search by keyword.

Selecting the Component [!]

Assign the relevant component if you know it. If you don't know the component, don't assign the message a detailed component level (for example, assign level 3 BC-CCM-PRN, rather than level 4 BC-CCM-PRN-DVM). The SAP hotline consultant can assign a specific component. Valuable time may be lost if you assign the wrong component to the message and it's forwarded to the wrong person as a result.

Note, however, that the cause of the error may originate in a module other than the module in which you currently work.

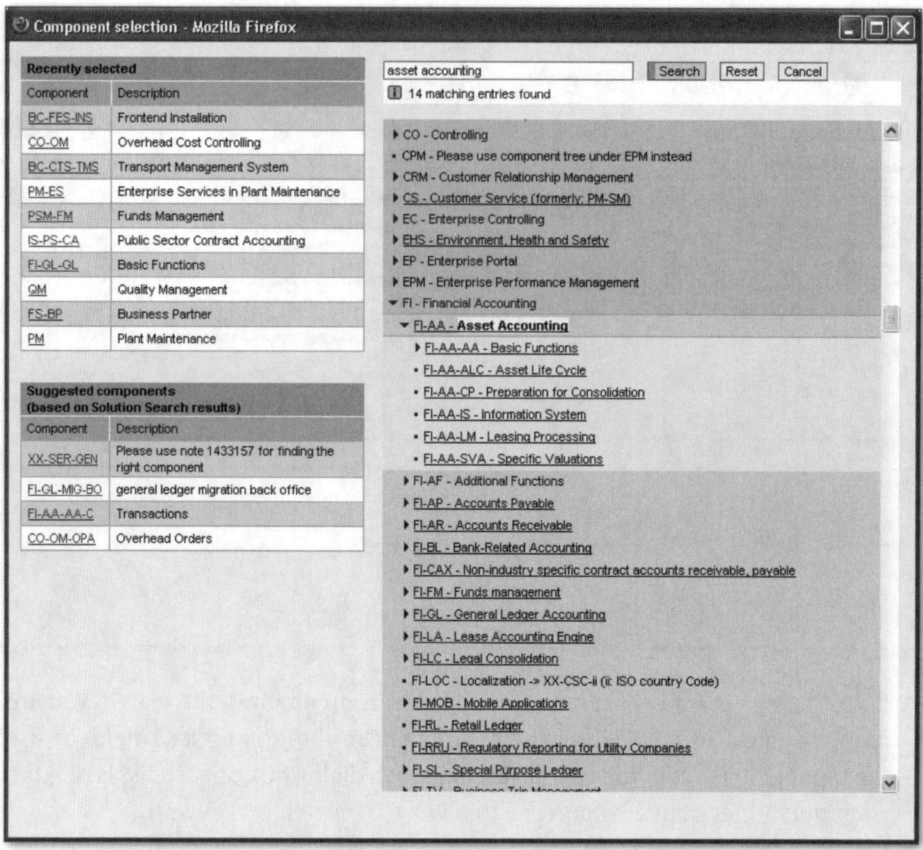

8. Define a priority. You can choose between the following priorities:

- **Very high**

  –*In production systems*

  Only to be used for serious, business-critical problems, which must be resolved immediately

  –*In nonproduction systems*

  Only to be used for critical project phases

An SAP Support Portal consultant will process these messages within 30 minutes of receiving them. If the problem isn't in the "Very high" category, it's automatically treated with a lower priority.

Ensuring Availability [+]

Don't assign the priority "Very high" if you are unable to take a return call from SAP. If SAP tries to call you back and can't reach you, the priority of your message may be reduced.

- **High**
  Indicates functional failure of important applications in a production system that is critical to the business process, or an issue that threatens the go-live or upgrade date.
- **Medium**
  Indicates errors with less serious consequences than those specified in the two categories just described. Errors in this category affect business processes but don't represent a serious threat to the operation of the production system.
- **Low**
  Indicates minor errors that don't disrupt or threaten daily work (for example, documentation errors or spelling errors).

Selecting a Priority [!]

Take great care when assigning priorities. If your problem doesn't really belong in the "Very high" category, assigning this priority won't guarantee a quick response time.

9. Describe your problem. Use the following fields:
   - SHORT TEXT: A description of the problem using key words (60 characters).
   - LONG TEXT A detailed description of the problem.
   - STEPS TO REPRODUCE: Instructions for reproducing the error that occurred.

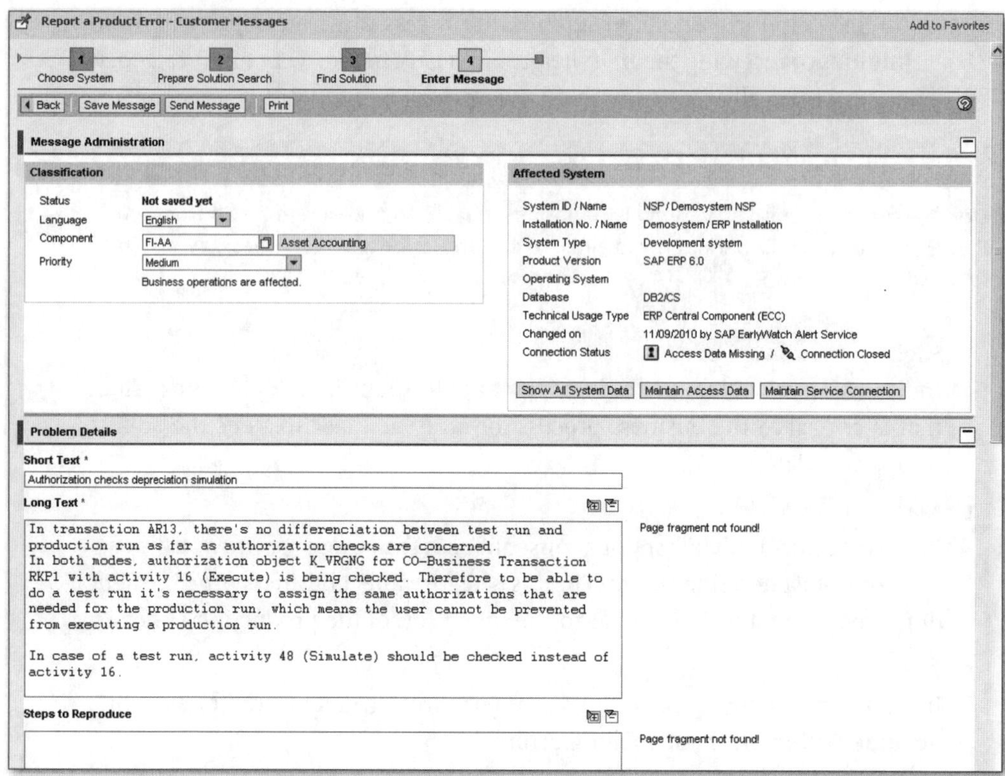

[+]

Information Content of the Message

Include as much information as possible in your message, so that the SAP hotline consultants can minimize the amount of information they need to request.

10. Upload an attachment if required (for example, screenshots, a short dump, or a trace file). Enter a meaningful short description under ATTACHMENTS, and click on BROWSE to select the relevant file on your PC.

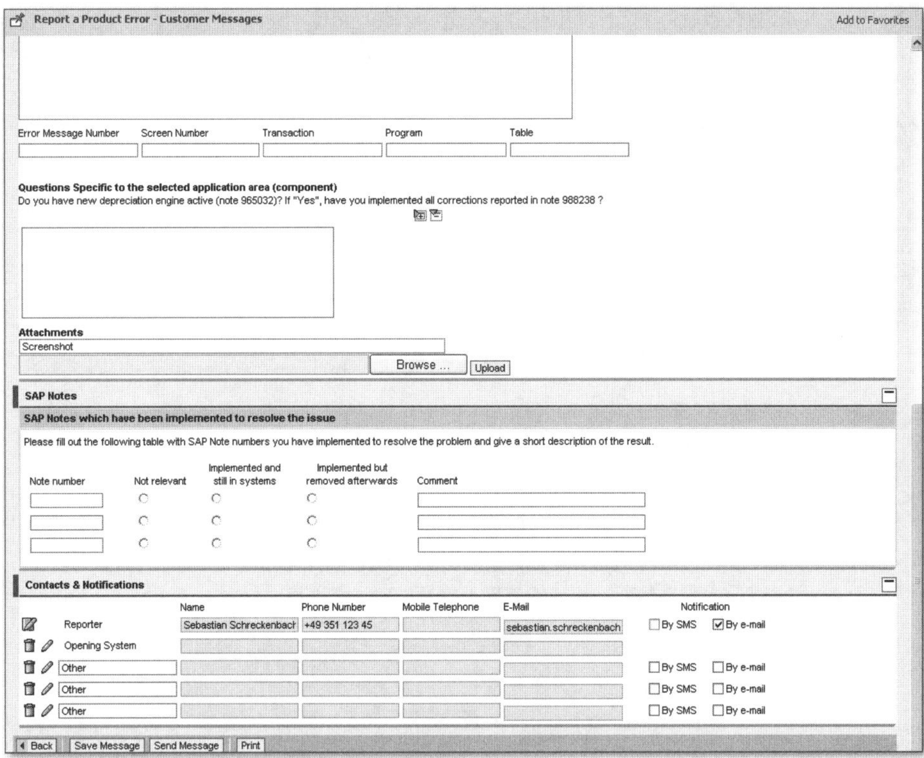

11. Select the file for upload, and click on OPEN.

12. Click on UPLOAD in the message view to add the file to the customer message.

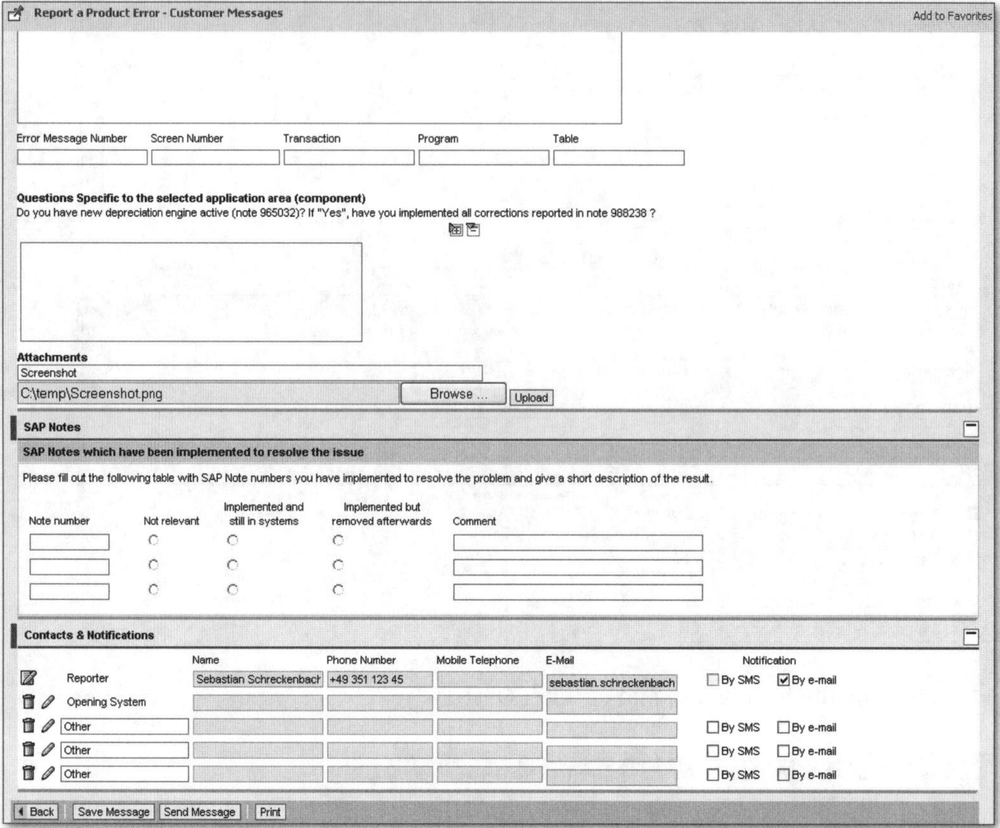

13. In the SAP Notes screen area, specify which SAP Notes, if any, you've already consulted without success.

14. Check that your telephone number and email address are entered correctly under CONTACTS & NOTIFICATIONS. If necessary, enter other contact persons who can be contacted by the SAP hotline team should they have any queries. This may be, for example, the person acting as your vacation substitute, or a contact from the data center for issues relating to database administration.

[+]

Maintaining Contact Details

If your contact details are incorrect, you can change them in the SAP Support Portal under MY PROFILE • MAINTAIN PERSONAL DATA.

15. When you've finished entering the details, choose SEND MESSAGE. The system confirms that the customer message was created.

Report a Product Error - Customer Messages
1 Choose System
2 Prepare Solution Search
3 Find Solution
4 Process Message
New Message
Display Message
Your message was sent successfully.
(0008154711 2010)
The message can be found in your SAP Service Channel Inbox.

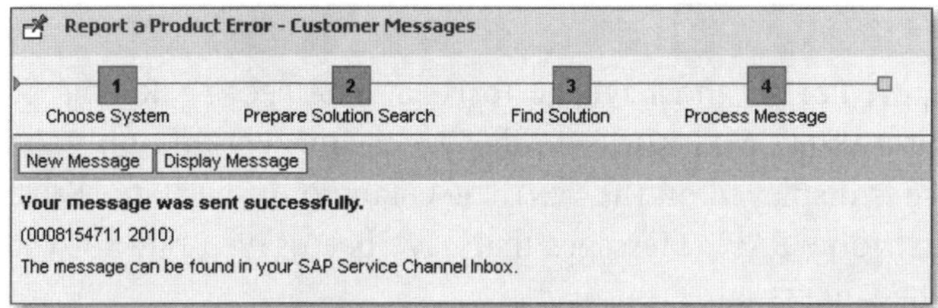

16. To open the message again, click on DISPLAY MESSAGE.

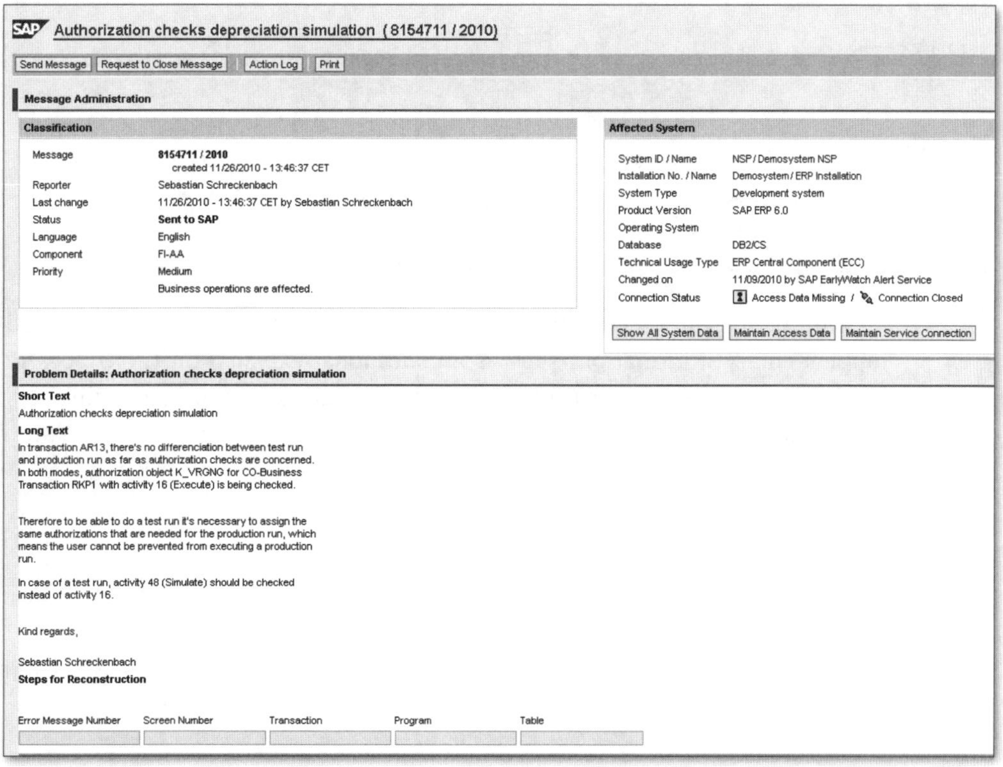

Authorization checks depreciation simulation (8154711 / 2010)
Send Message
Request to Close Message
Action Log
Print
Message Administration
Classification
Message 8154711 / 2010 created 11/26/2010 - 13:46:37 CET
Reporter Sebastian Schreckenbach
Last change 11/26/2010 - 13:46:37 CET by Sebastian Schreckenbach
Status Sent to SAP
Language English
Component FI-AA
Priority Medium
Business operations are affected.
Affected System
System ID / Name NSP / Demosystem NSP
Installation No. / Name Demosystem / ERP Installation
System Type Development system
Product Version SAP ERP 6.0
Operating System
Database DB2/CS
Technical Usage Type ERP Central Component (ECC)
Changed on 11/09/2010 by SAP EarlyWatch Alert Service
Connection Status Access Data Missing / Connection Closed
Show All System Data
Maintain Access Data
Maintain Service Connection
Problem Details: Authorization checks depreciation simulation
Short Text
Authorization checks depreciation simulation
Long Text
In transaction AR13, there's no differenciation between test run and production run as far as authorization checks are concerned. In both modes, authorization object K_VRGNG for CO-Business Transaction RKP1 with activity 16 (Execute) is being checked.
Therefore to be able to do a test run it's necessary to assign the same authorizations that are needed for the production run, which means the user cannot be prevented from executing a production run.
In case of a test run, activity 48 (Simulate) should be checked instead of activity 16.
Kind regards,
Sebastian Schreckenbach
Steps for Reconstruction
Error Message Number
Screen Number
Transaction
Program
Table

Your customer message has been created, and a member of the SAP hotline team is handling your problem. You will be informed by email or SMS when the processing status of your message changes. The hotline employee may contact you by telephone to clarify any open questions.

Monitoring the Status of Customer Messages

While your message is being processed, you can display it and check its status at any time:

1. Access the SAP Support Portal, and navigate to Help & Support • Report a Product Error • Display my Messages. While SAP is still working on your problem, the message is displayed on the Sent Items tab (with the status Sent to SAP or In processing by SAP). Messages that have been saved but not yet sent are located on the Drafts tab.

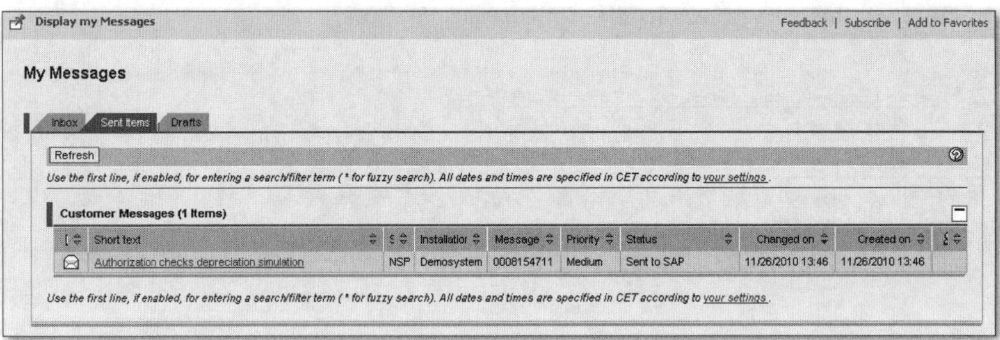

2. Click on the link in the Short text column to open the message. You can add supplementary information, such as an additional explanation (Info to SAP field) or other attachments (in the Attachments area). When you've finished, click on Send Message.

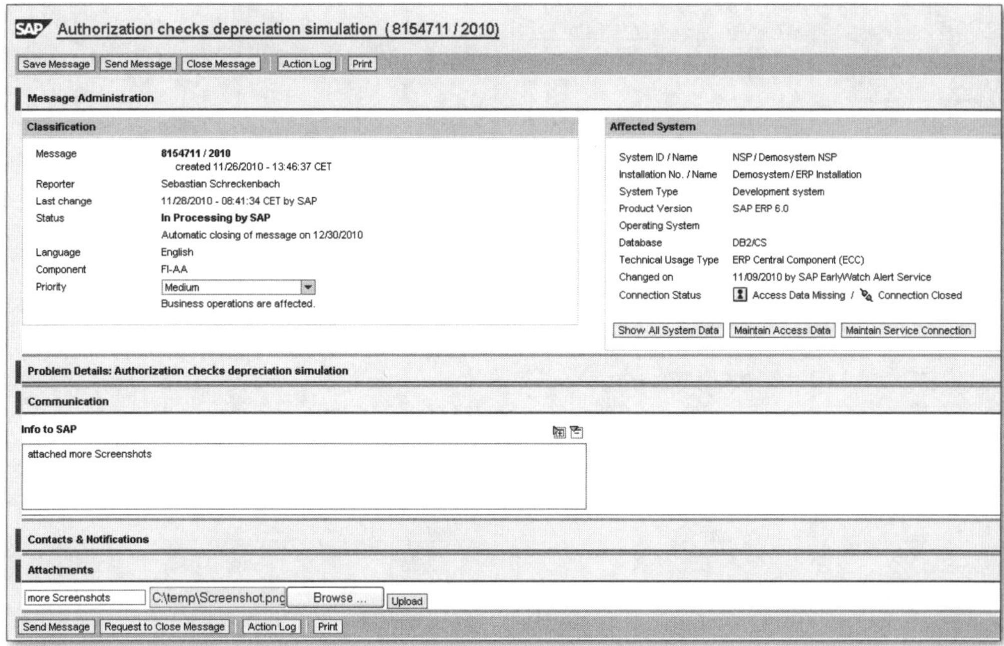

3. As soon as your help is required to process the message, you'll receive an email notification. Open the message in the SAP Support Portal. It will be on the INBOX tab, with the status CUSTOMER ACTION, for example.

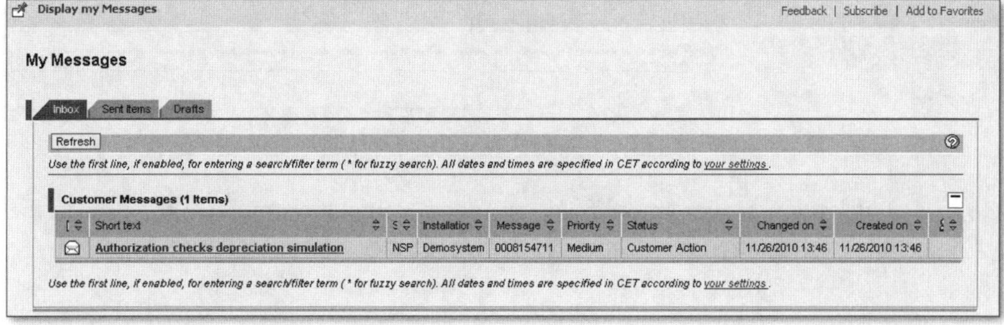

4. Open the message, and check which action you need to take. For example, you may be asked to open a service connection. To do this, proceed as described in Section 19.3. You can define the access data for external analysis of the problem in the message itself. To do this, choose the MAINTAIN ACCESS DATA button.

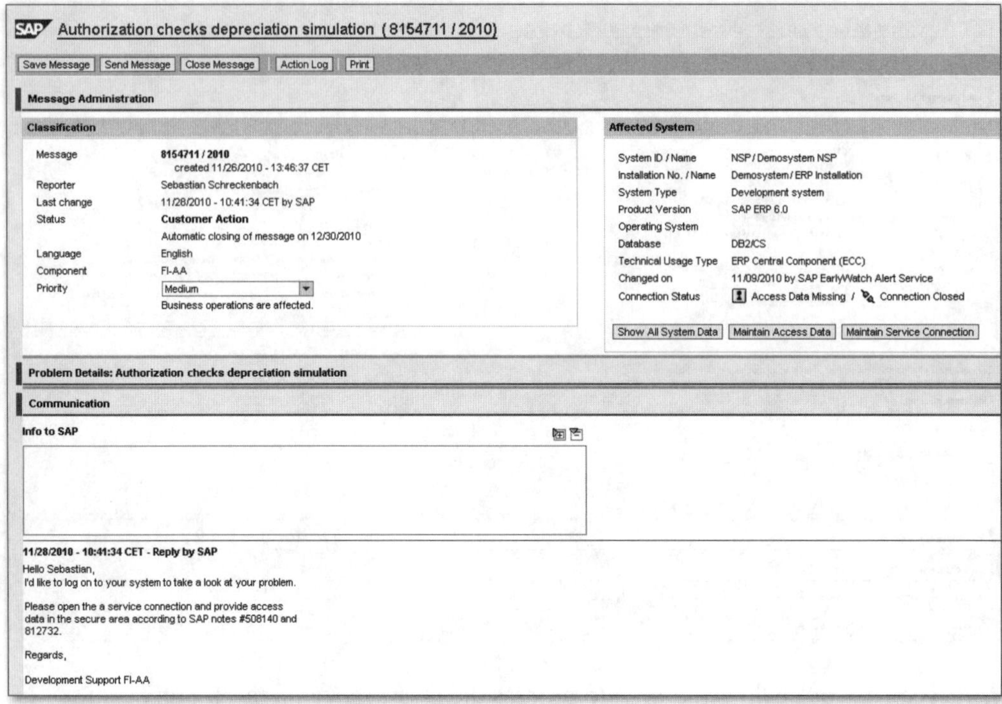

5. In the new window that opens, click on MODIFY.

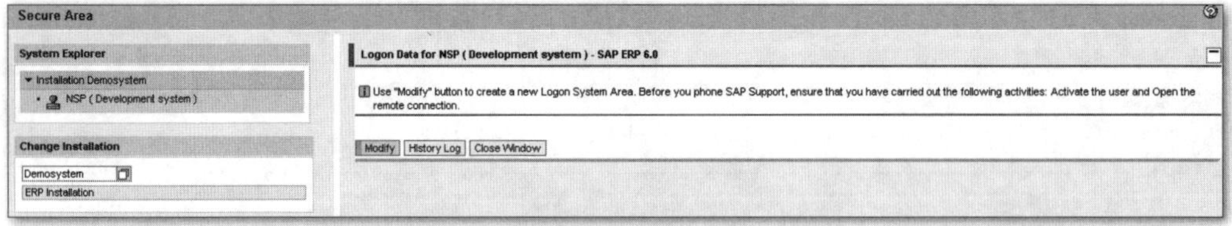

6. Enter the user data in the fields provided. Remember to create the user in the SAP system also (See Chapter 13). Choose SAVE.

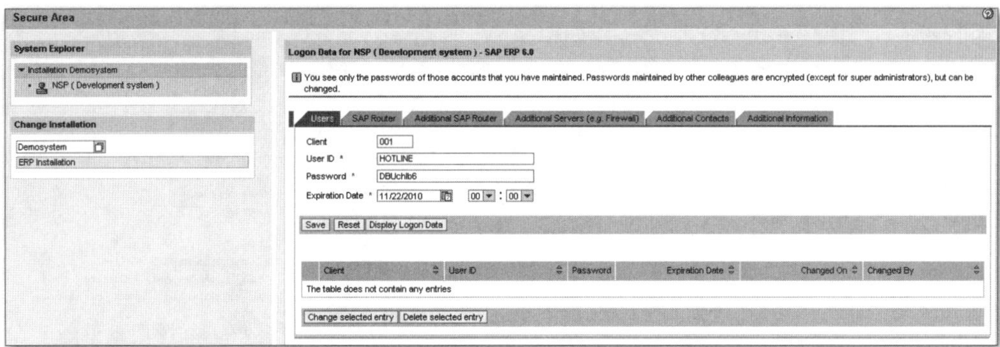

7. The data are transferred. Close the browser window.

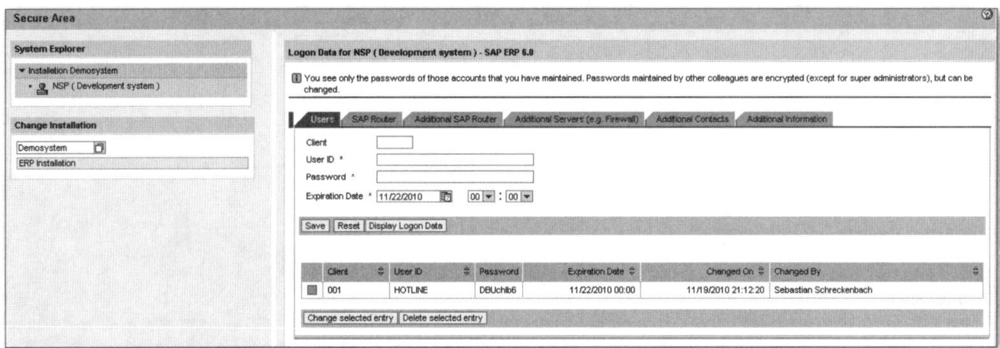

Secure Area for Access Data [+]

The access data are stored in encrypted form in a "secure area" within the message. Only you and the SAP hotline message processor can see the passwords defined there.

8. The status ACCESS DATA MAINTAINED is displayed in the customer message. Enter explanatory text, and click on SEND MESSAGE to return the customer message to SAP.

Authorization checks depreciation simulation (8154711 / 2010)

Save Message | Send Message | Close Message | Action Log | Print

Message Administration

Classification

Message	**8154711 / 2010** created 11/26/2010 - 13:46:37 CET
Reporter	Sebastian Schreckenbach
Last change	11/28/2010 - 10:41:34 CET by SAP
Status	**Customer Action** Automatic closing of message on 12/30/2010
Language	English
Component	FI-AA
Priority	Medium Business operations are affected.

Affected System

System ID / Name	NSP / Demosystem NSP
Installation No. / Name	Demosystem / ERP Installation
System Type	Development system
Product Version	SAP ERP 6.0
Operating System	
Database	DB2/CS
Technical Usage Type	ERP Central Component (ECC)
Changed on	11/09/2010 by SAP EarlyWatch Alert Service
Connection Status	Access Data Provided / Connection Open

Show All System Data | Maintain Access Data | Maintain Service Connection

Problem Details: Authorization checks depreciation simulation

Communication

Info to SAP

Hello Support,

Logon data has been added to the secure area. The system will be open for 2 hours.

Kind regards,

Sebastian Schreckenbach

11/28/2010 - 10:41:34 CET - Reply by SAP

Hello Sebastian,
I'd like to log on to your system to take a look at your problem.

Please open the a service connection and provide access data in the secure area according to SAP notes #508140 and 812732.

Regards,

Development Support FI-AA

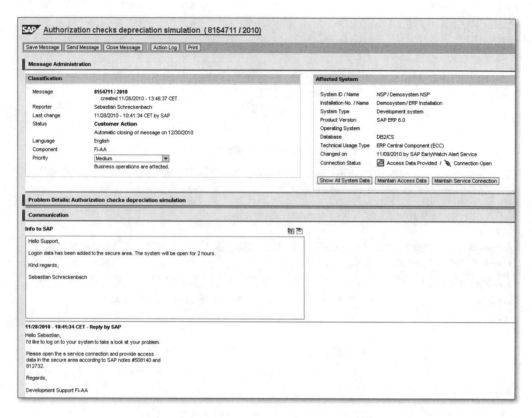

9. The system confirms that the customer message was sent. To display the customer message again, click on the DISPLAY MESSAGE button.

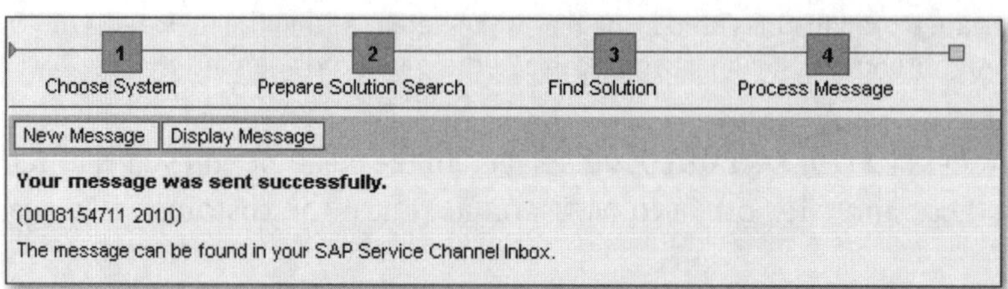

10. The information you added is displayed in the communication history. The AFFECTED SYSTEM area shows whether access data has been maintained and whether a service connection has been created.

> **Accelerating Message Processing** [!]
>
> You can't change the priority of your customer message while SAP is processing it. If you wait for an exceptionally long time without receiving a response to your message, or if you require a faster solution due to unforeseen follow-on errors, you can contact your local *Global Support Customer Interaction Center* by phone. The contact details are provided in the SAP Support Portal under HELP & SUPPORT • REPORT A PRODUCT ERROR • HOW TO SPEED UP A MESSAGE and the SAP Service Marketplace (*www.service.sap.com*) under SAP SUPPORT CENTER ADDRESSES. The telephone numbers are also listed in SAP Note 560499.

Closing a Customer Message

When your problem has been solved, you can close the customer message by confirming the solution:

1. Access the SAP Support Portal, and navigate to HELP & SUPPORT • REPORT A PRODUCT ERROR - CUSTOMER MESSAGES • DISPLAY MY MESSAGES. Your message will be on the INBOX tab, with the status SAP PROPOSED SOLUTION, for example.

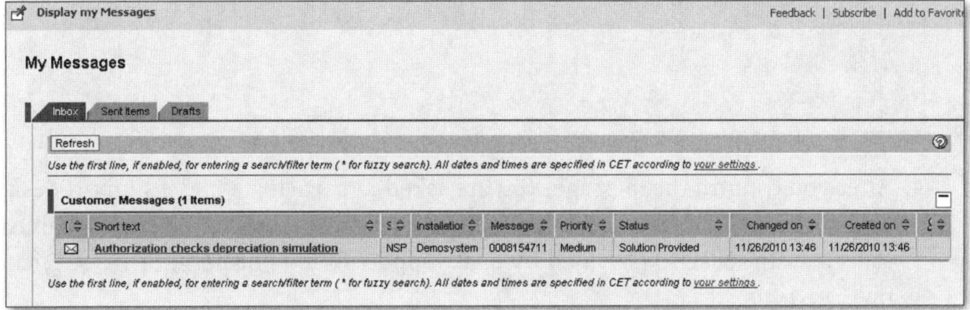

2. Open the message, and check the proposed solution. If the solution eliminates your problem, click on CLOSE MESSAGE.

Authorization checks depreciation simulation (8154711 / 2010)

Save Message | Send Message | Close Message | Action Log | Print

Message Administration

Classification

Message	**8154711 / 2010** created 11/26/2010 - 13:46:37 CET
Reporter	Sebastian Schreckenbach
Last change	11/28/2010 - 12:44:33 CET by SAP
Status	**Customer Action** Automatic closing of message on 12/30/2010
Language	English
Component	FI-AA
Priority	Medium Business operations are affected.

Affected System

System ID / Name	NSP / Demosystem NSP
Installation No. / Name	Demosystem / ERP Installation
System Type	Development system
Product Version	SAP ERP 6.0
Operating System	
Database	DB2/CS
Technical Usage Type	ERP Central Component (ECC)
Changed on	11/09/2010 by SAP EarlyWatch Alert Service
Connection Status	Access Data Provided / Connection Open

Show All System Data | Maintain Access Data | Maintain Service Connection

Problem Details: Authorization checks depreciation simulation

Communication

Info to SAP

11/28/2010 - 12:44:33 CET - Reply by SAP

Hello Sebastian,

Please apply the corrections provided by SAP note 1447401 to your system.

This will add the required functionality.

Regards,

Development Support FI-AA

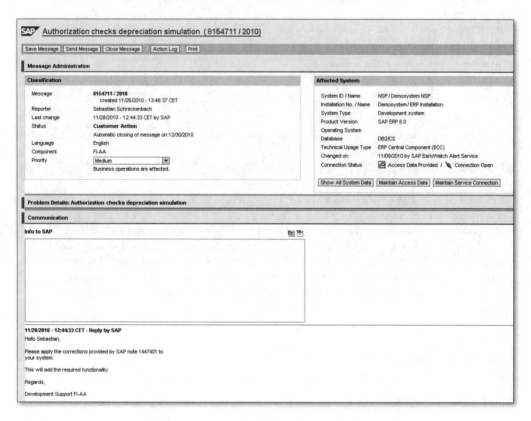

3. A dialog box opens, in which you are asked to confirm closing of the message. Choose YES.

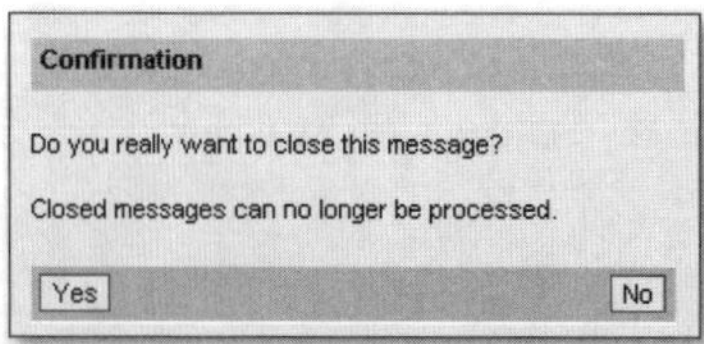

4. After you confirm the message, you are asked to participate in the support desk evaluation or POSITIVE CALL CLOSURE survey. Here you can rate the various aspects of the service provided by SAP Support from your point of view. Click on CONTINUE.

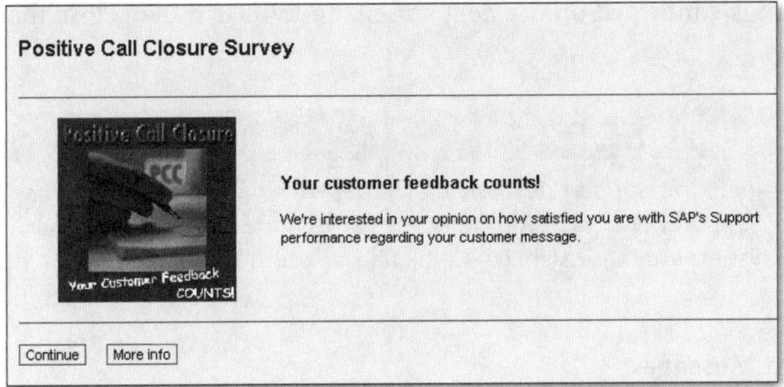

5. You evaluate the message processing service by awarding points from 1 to 10 in the various categories provided. You are also asked to indicate whether your problem was resolved. You can enter any further comments in the user-defined text field. When you've finished, click on SUBMIT.

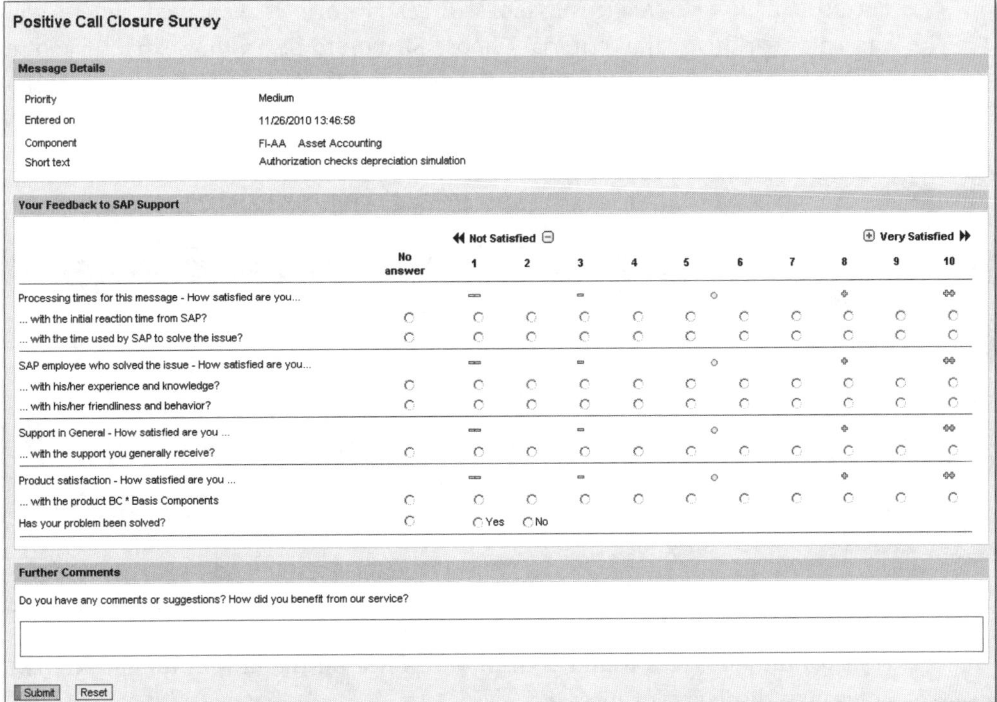

6. Your participation is confirmed on the next screen, and you can then close the browser window.

[+]

Authorization for Support Desk Evaluation

The request to participate in a support desk evaluation depends on the authorizations assigned to your SAP Support Portal user. You won't have an opportunity to express your opinion if your administrator hasn't assigned you the relevant authorizations.

Displaying Archived Messages

After a customer message is closed, you can no longer display it under My Messages. However, you may occasionally want to reopen old messages, for example, to look up the solution to a problem that occurred in the past. To do this, follow these steps:

1. Access the SAP Support Portal, and navigate to Help & Support • Report a Product Error • Search Messages. A search form is displayed, where you can enter various search criteria. Choose Search to begin the search. If you're certain that you created the customer message yourself, click on the Reported by me button.

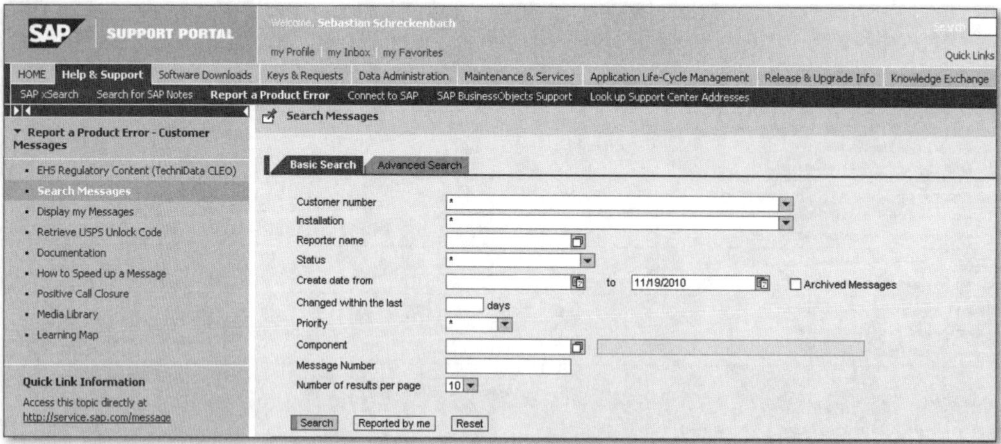

2. A list of the messages found is displayed. Click on the link in the Short text column to display your message.

[+]

Archived Customer Messages

All information is retained in the archived customer message, for example, the problem description, file attachments, proposed solution, and similar correspondence.

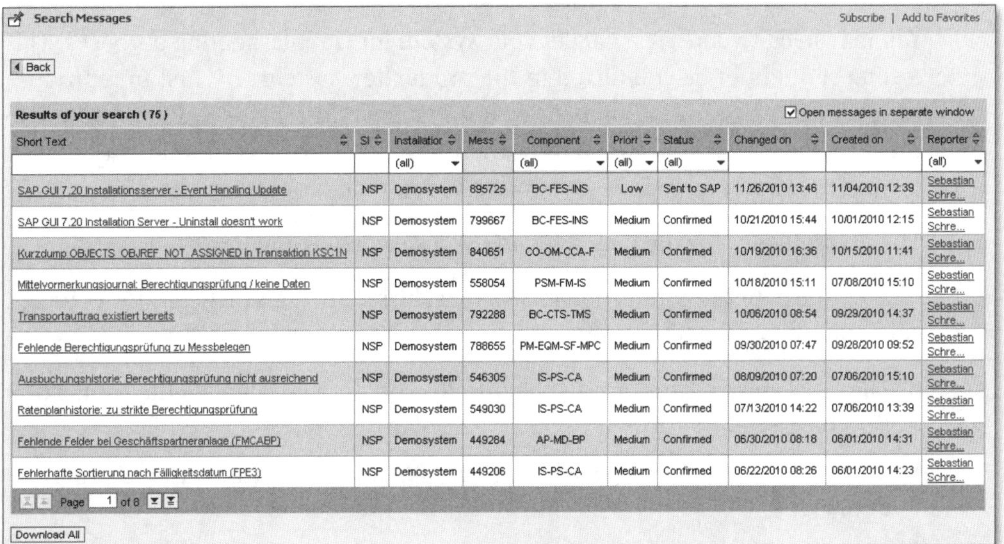

Short Text	SI	Installatior	Mess	Component	Priori	Status	Changed on	Created on	Reporter
		(all)		(all)	(all)	(all)			(all)
SAP GUI 7.20 Installationsserver - Event Handling Update	NSP	Demosystem	895725	BC-FES-INS	Low	Sent to SAP	11/26/2010 13:46	11/04/2010 12:39	Sebastian Schre...
SAP GUI 7.20 Installation Server - Uninstall doesn't work	NSP	Demosystem	799667	BC-FES-INS	Medium	Confirmed	10/21/2010 15:44	10/01/2010 12:15	Sebastian Schre...
Kurzdump OBJECTS_OBJREF_NOT_ASSIGNED in Transaktion KSC1N	NSP	Demosystem	840651	CO-OM-CCA-F	Medium	Confirmed	10/19/2010 16:36	10/15/2010 11:41	Sebastian Schre...
Mittelvormerkungsjournal: Berechtigungsprüfung / keine Daten	NSP	Demosystem	558054	PSM-FM-IS	Medium	Confirmed	10/18/2010 15:11	07/08/2010 15:10	Sebastian Schre...
Transportauftrag existiert bereits	NSP	Demosystem	792288	BC-CTS-TMS	Medium	Confirmed	10/06/2010 08:54	09/29/2010 14:37	Sebastian Schre...
Fehlende Berechtigungsprüfung zu Messbelegen	NSP	Demosystem	788655	PM-EQM-SF-MPC	Medium	Confirmed	09/30/2010 07:47	09/28/2010 09:52	Sebastian Schre...
Ausbuchungshistorie: Berechtigungsprüfung nicht ausreichend	NSP	Demosystem	546305	IS-PS-CA	Medium	Confirmed	08/09/2010 07:20	07/06/2010 15:10	Sebastian Schre...
Ratenplanhistorie: zu strikte Berechtigungsprüfung	NSP	Demosystem	549030	IS-PS-CA	Medium	Confirmed	07/13/2010 14:22	07/06/2010 13:39	Sebastian Schre...
Fehlende Felder bei Geschäftspartneranlage (FMCABP)	NSP	Demosystem	449284	AP-MD-BP	Medium	Confirmed	06/30/2010 08:18	06/01/2010 14:31	Sebastian Schre...
Fehlerhafte Sortierung nach Fälligkeitsdatum (FPE3)	NSP	Demosystem	449206	IS-PS-CA	Medium	Confirmed	06/22/2010 08:26	06/01/2010 14:23	Sebastian Schre...

19.3 Creating a Remote Service Connection

If you've created a customer message, you may be asked to open a *remote service connection* and provide SAP Support with direct access to your system. If the service connection is open and a user ID has been provided, a member of the SAP hotline team can log on to your system to investigate the problem.

For security reasons, a service connection can only be set up by you, the customer. SAP can't initiate a service connection from its end. Note also that a service connection may incur high telephone charges that must be paid by your enterprise. You should therefore only open a connection if you are asked to do so, and you should only make the service connection available for the expected time required to investigate the problem.

[+]

SAP Support Notes Relating to Service Connections

For more information about service connections, refer to SAP Notes 35010 and 31515, and consult the SAP Support Portal under HELP & SUPPORT • REPORT A PRODUCT ERROR • CONNECT TO SAP.

You may need to enter test data in your system for troubleshooting purposes. This testing should not be conducted in the production system. Try first to reproduce the problem in your development or test system, and provide SAP with access to the relevant server. You should only grant SAP access to your production server if the problem can't be reproduced on the development or test server.

The prerequisites for opening a remote service connection are as follows:

The remote network connection to SAP must be set up. (This includes, for example, configuration of the SAProuter.)

- The *SAP Service Connector* must be installed on the PC on which the connection is to be created.
- SAP GUI must also be installed on the PC to enable use of the SAP Service Connector.

[+]

Setting Up Remote Network Connections

A discussion of how to set up remote network connections falls outside the scope of this chapter. For more information about this topic, refer to the documentation provided in the SAP Support Portal (under HELP & SUPPORT • REPORT A PRODUCT ERROR • CONNECT TO SAP • SET UP A REMOTE CONNECTION TO SAP).

You can download the SAP Service Connector from the SAP Support Portal under HELP & SUPPORT • REPORT A PRODUCT ERROR • CONNECT TO SAP • INSTALL SERVICE CONNECTOR ON YOUR LOCAL PC.

The following discussion assumes that the technical prerequisites set out previously are already in place. To create a service connection, follow these steps:

1. Log on to the SAP Support Portal, choose HELP & SUPPORT • CONNECT TO SAP.

   Click the MAINTAIN CONNECTIONS button.

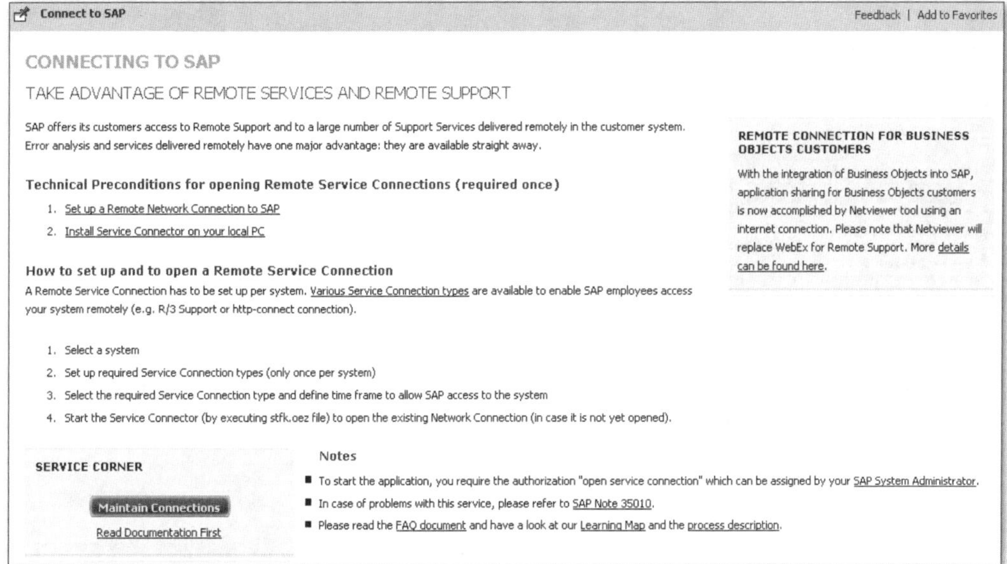

2. Under SYSTEM SEARCH, define the SAP system for which you want to create the service connection. If you already created a connection for this system in the past, you can select this connection from the YOUR RECENTLY USED SYSTEMS list.

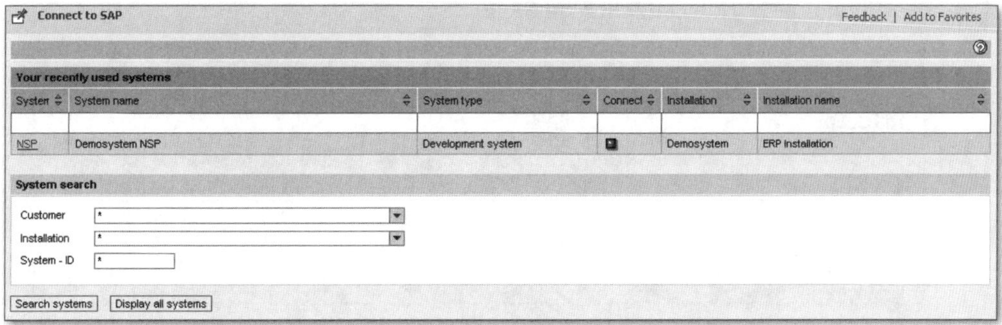

3. In most cases, you require a connection of the *R/3 Support* type. However, if you've never used this before, you must set it up first. To do this, click on the R/3 SUPPORT link in the CONNECTION TYPE column under SET UP CONNECTION TYPES.

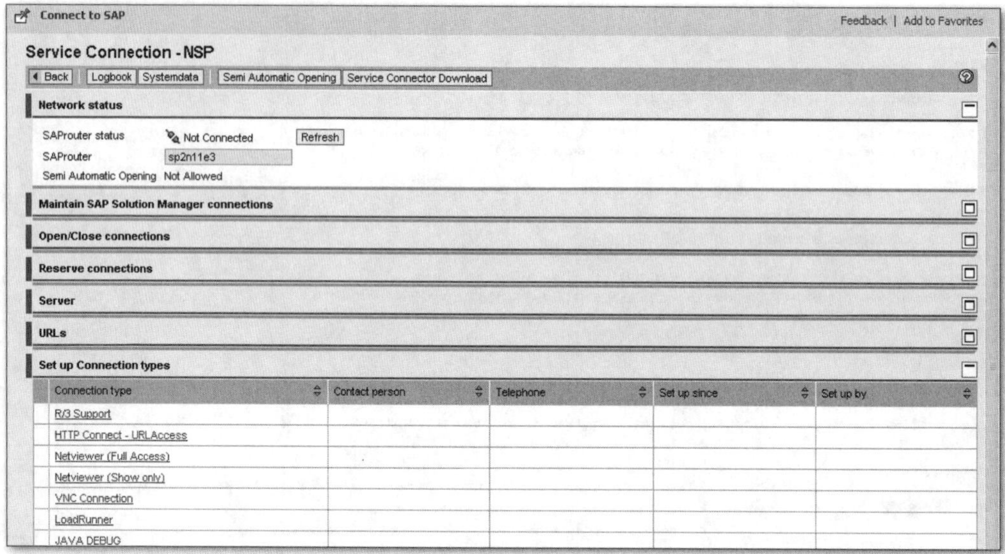

4. On the next screen, your contact details are displayed under CONTACT PERSON. You can use the input help to select a different or an additional contact person if necessary. Otherwise, all you need to do to set up the connection is to save your contact details.

   When you've finished, click on SAVE.

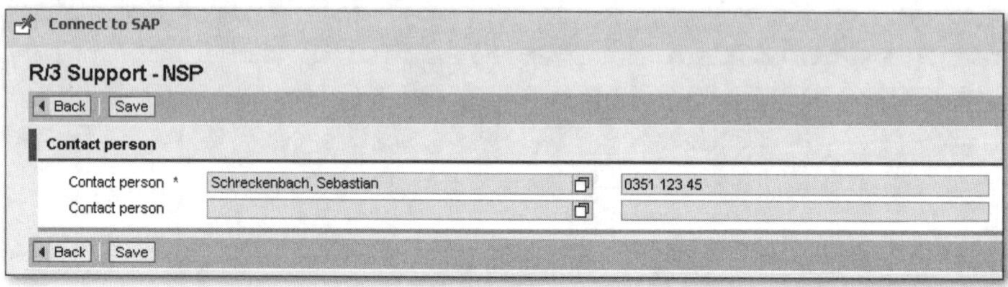

5. The connection type you've set up is then displayed under OPEN/CLOSE CONNECTIONS.

   Click on the connection (for example, R/3 SUPPORT) in the CONNECTION TYPE column to open it.

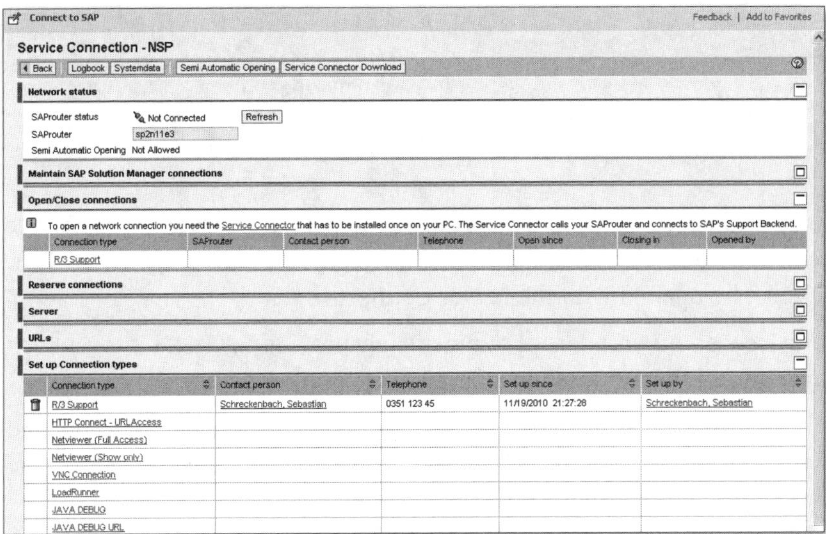

6. Under DEFINE TIME, you can define the period for which the service connection is to remain open. If necessary, enter another contact person or telephone number under CONTACT DATA. You may need to enter the IP address and outbound port of your SAProuter server in the ROUTESTRING field. Then click on START SERVICE CONNECTOR.

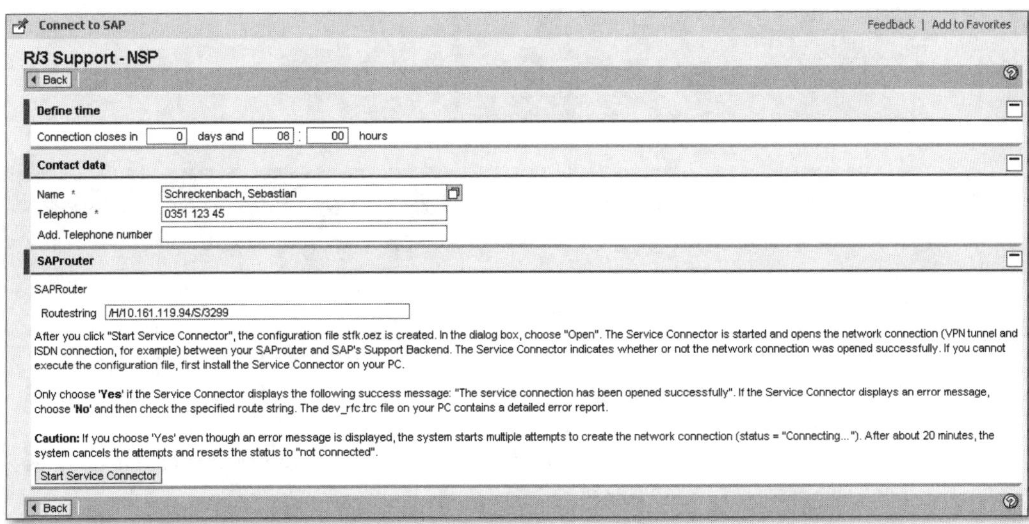

[+]

SAProuter

SAProuter is a program that runs on a server in your network and can act as a proxy to create a connection to another network. This allows you to bundle, control, and log SAP-specific accesses to your corporate network as an enhancement of your firewall.

7. A file named stfk.oez is generated that contains all parameters for the SAP Service Connector for your service connection. A dialog box opens in your browser. The file must be opened with the Server Connector.

   Some browsers or browser versions immediately provide an OPEN button, which you can click and then proceed to step 10.

   Newer browsers (such as Internet Explorer 8) no longer allow files to be opened directly. If you have one of these browsers, you must save the file temporarily on your PC. To do this, choose SAVE.

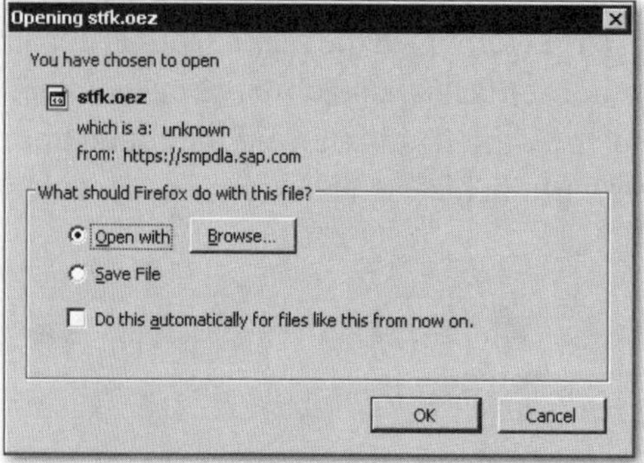

[⚙]

Opening a Connection without the SAP Service Connector

If you are unable to install the SAP Service Connector and/or SAP GUI on your PC, the following actions may be useful:

- Cancel opening of the stfk.oez file.
- Log on to the SAP system for which you want to create the service connection.
- Start Transaction SM59 (RFC Connections), and access the RFC connection SAPOSS. Perform a connection test.

Then go back to the SAP Support Portal, and confirm that the service connection has been successfully opened (see step 14).

8. In the SAVE AS dialog box, navigate to a folder of your choice, and save the stfk.oez file to your PC.
9. Then double-click on the stfk.oez file to open it. In the dialog box that opens, select the SELECT THE PROGRAM FROM A LIST option, and click on OK.

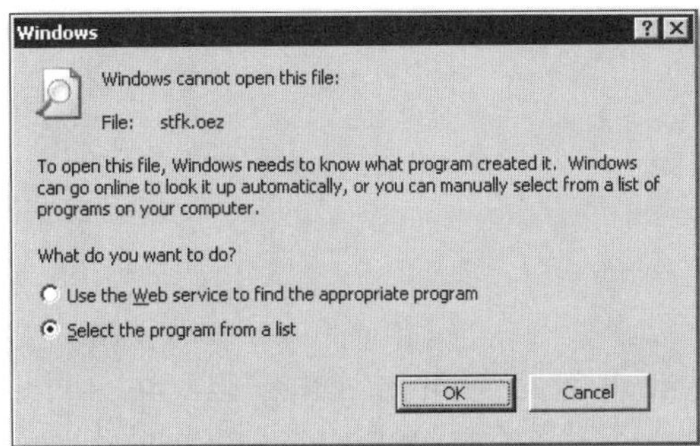

10. Navigate to the Service Connector (SAPSERVICECONNECTOR.EXE) program folder on your PC. Choose OPEN.

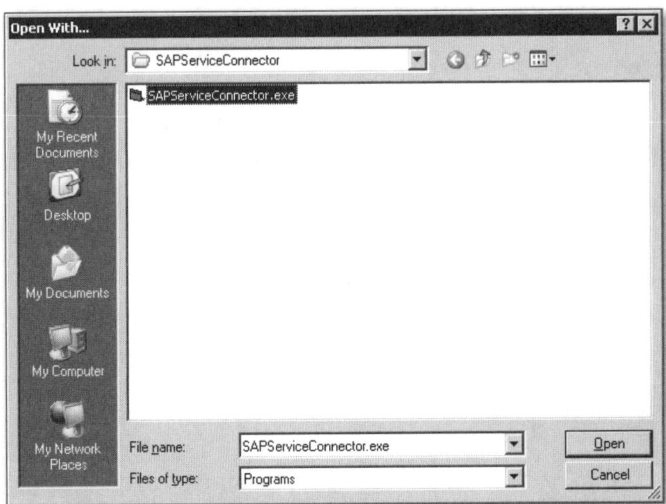

11. A dialog box opens to indicate that a local SAP GUI installation is required to start the SAP Service Connector. Choose YES to confirm.

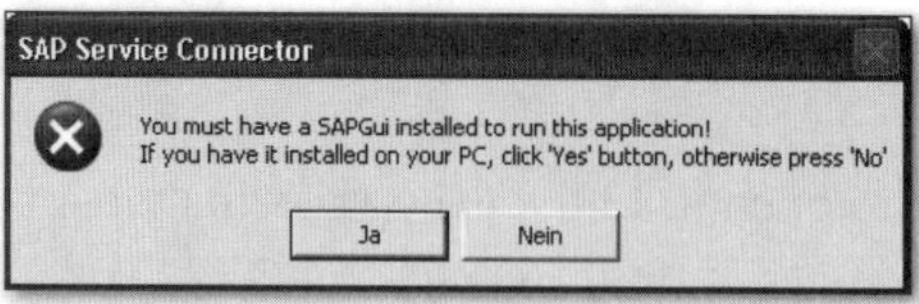

12. Another dialog box opens to inform you that the Service Connector has started. Click on OK.

13. It may take a while for the next dialog box to open, signaling that the service connection has been successfully created. Therefore, wait a while until it appears, and then choose OK to close it.

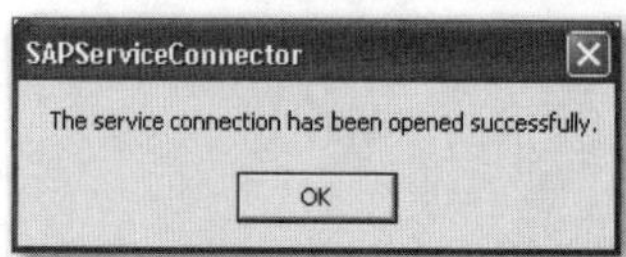

14. In the browser window containing the connection view, you will now see a question asking whether the network connection was opened successfully. Answer YES to this question.

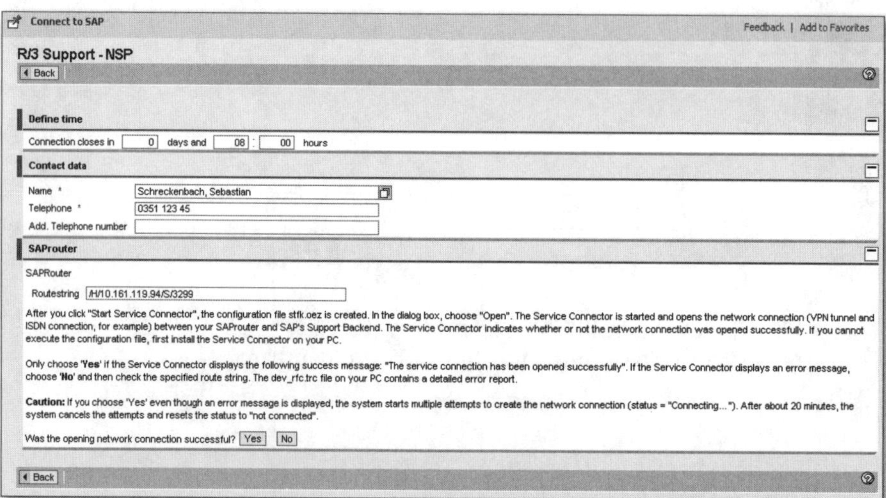

15. This automatically brings you back to the initial connection setup screen. The NETWORK STATUS area indicates that the connection has been set up. It may actually take a few minutes for the connection to be set up. Click on the REFRESH button to update the status.

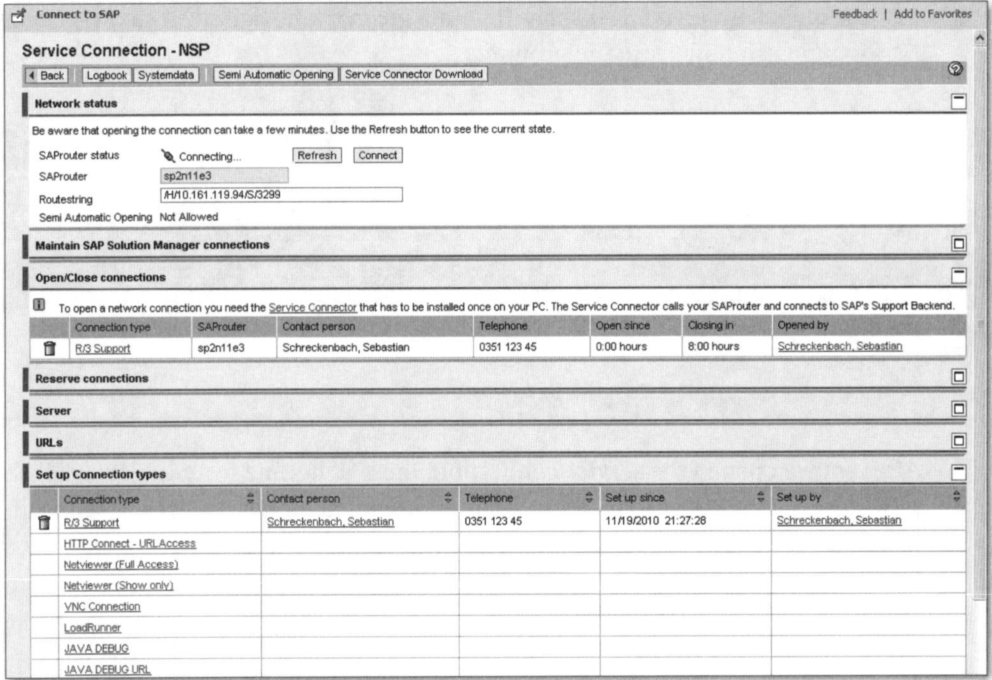

16. The status changes to CONNECTED when the service connection has been created. You can then click the BACK button to exit the view for opening a connection.

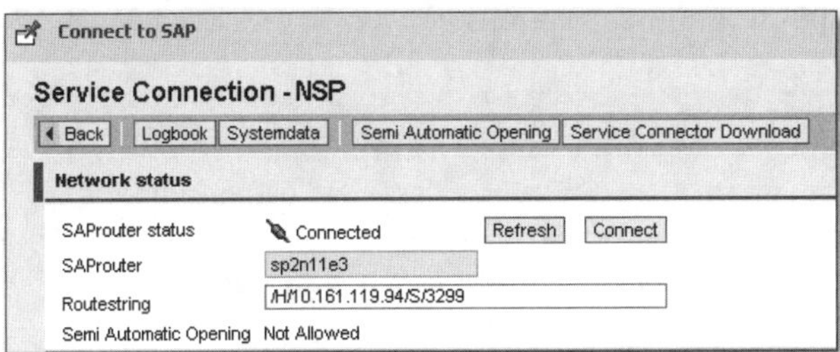

[+]

Closing Connections

To close the connection manual, click on CLOSE (🗑) in the row that corresponds to the service connection under OPEN/CLOSE CONNECTIONS.

17. The open connection is displayed with a green traffic light icon in the system list. You can now close the browser.

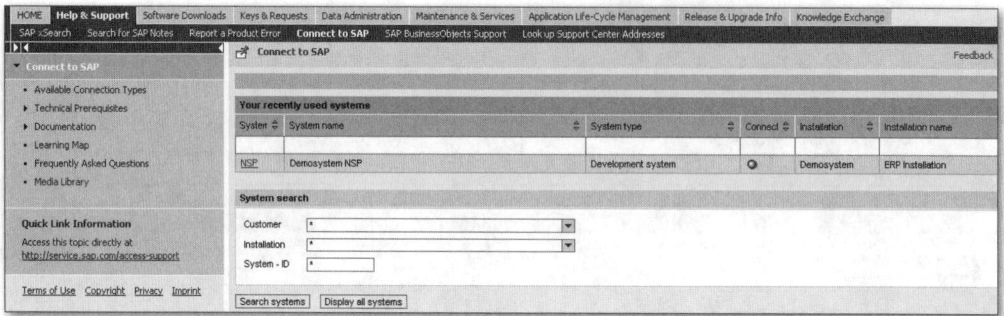

After you've opened the service connection, the SAP hotline team can analyze the problem in your SAP system. Remember to provide them with a user ID with sufficient authorization to log on to your system (see Section 19.2.2).

19.4 Implementing SAP Notes

SAP provides program corrections to eliminate program errors that cause specific problems. These corrections are provided in the form of SAP Notes, which describe the error, and the solution, which consists of program corrections attached to the SAP Note. To copy the corrections into your system, you need to implement the SAP Note by implementing the program corrections.

[+]

SAP Note Implementation

Not all SAP Notes can be implemented. Many SAP Notes describe Customizing settings or system configurations that have to be performed manually to eliminate the error. An "implementable" SAP Note is one that has *correction instructions* attached.

Document the implementation of SAP Notes as thoroughly as possible. Pay particular attention to the following aspects:

- Document all SAP Notes applied to your system, and specify both the systems and instances in which they were applied.
- You should create a table to track all SAP Notes applied and also keep detailed data records for each individual SAP Note. These data records should include the following information: the object changed, the release in which the SAP Note was implemented (important for updates), and other SAP Notes that have been checked, applied, or recommended (see the sample form provided in Appendix D). You should also keep a record of the problem for which the SAP Note was used. Provide an example so that the error can be retested if necessary.
- Document any required manual changes associated with the implementation of an SAP Note.
- In the case of system upgrades, it's essential to know which SAP Notes have been implemented to resolve problems. The following SAP Notes are relevant:
    - SAP Notes that are part of the upgrade, to allow you to return to the SAP standard code
    - SAP Notes that are applied again because they are not part of the upgrade
- Document all relevant SAP Notes that don't require changes in the system (for example, informative notes or instructions).
- Document the SAP Notes that were not applied in your system. There may well be cases where you check a SAP Note and decide that it's not relevant for your problem. You should document the reasons for this. If your SAP contact person then asks why a certain SAP Note has not been applied, you can quickly check the reasons in your records.

SAP Notes often provide important advance corrections, before these are delivered with other SAP Notes and further developments in a support package. For this reason, SAP Notes are usually relevant for specific SAP versions (*releases*), support package versions, or kernel patch levels. Details of a SAP Note's validity are provided in the SAP Note itself under "Valid Releases" and "Links to Support Packages."

If you recognize the problem described in an SAP Note as your own problem and you want to apply this SAP Note, check first whether the SAP Note is relevant for your SAP system by opening the system information.

19.4.1 Checking the System Patch Level

Follow these steps to open the system information regarding the release, support package version, and kernel patch level of your system.

1. In the SAP Easy Access menu (or any transaction), select the menu option SYSTEM • STATUS.
2. To display the current support package version, choose COMPONENT INFORMATION.

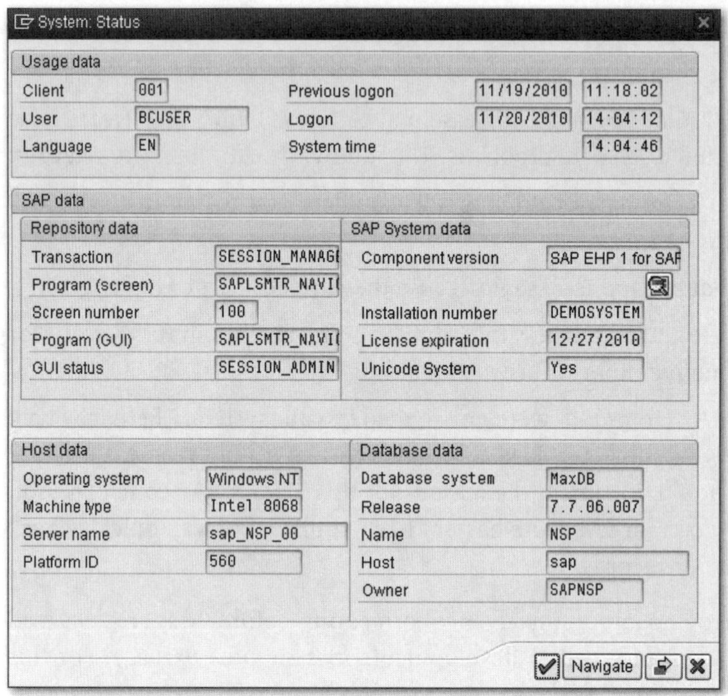

3. The value in the RELEASE column shows your SAP system version. The HIGHEST SUPPORT PACKAGE column indicates the most recently implemented support package for each software component. Compare these details with those provided in the SAP Note. Choose CONTINUE to exit this view.

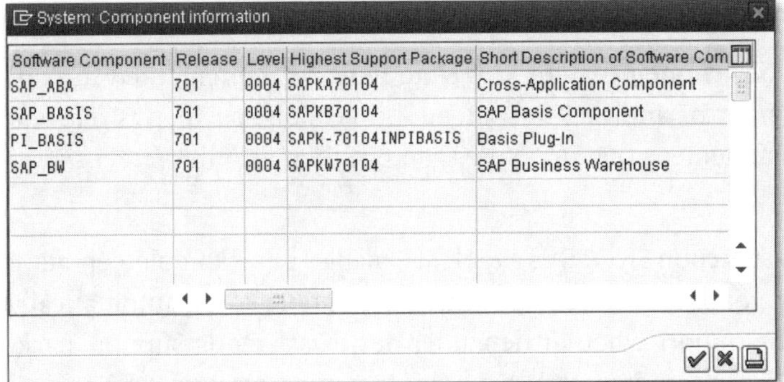

4. In the STATUS VIEW (see step 3), click on the OTHER KERNEL INFO (icon) icon to open the kernel information. The kernel patch level is displayed on the left under KERNEL INFORMATION. Compare your system's patch level with the patch level specified in the SAP Note. Choose CONTINUE (✔) to close the dialog box. Choose CONTINUE (✔) to return to the SAP menu.

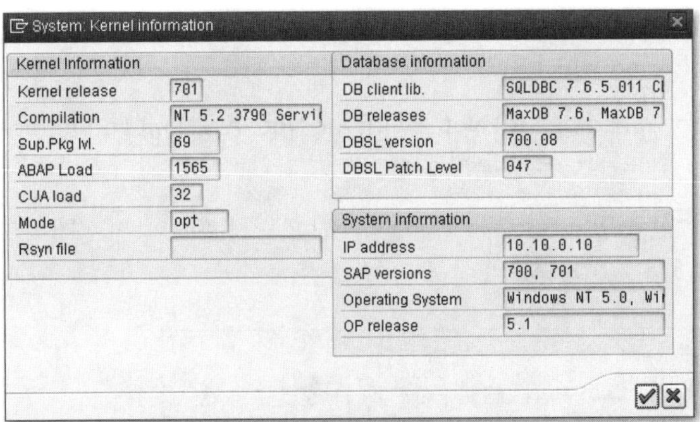

Naming Conventions for Support Packages [+]

Support packages are named as follows:

SAPK<*component ID*><*Release*><*Support Package ID*>

SAPKB70103 can thus be divided into SAPK/B/701/03, which indicates the third support package 03 for the SAP_BASIS component of Release 7.01.

19.4.2 Implementing SAP Notes with the Note Assistant

Let's assume you've determined that an SAP Note must be implemented in your system to eliminate an error and that the patch level version specified is relevant for your system. To implement the SAP Note, you can then use the *Note Assistant* in your SAP system.

The Note Assistant (Transaction SNOTE) is a tool that enables a quick implementation of SAP Notes. It downloads SAP Notes from the SAP Support Portal automatically and checks during the import whether dependencies exist among support packages, SAP Notes, and changes you may have implemented previously. The tool optimizes the implementation of SAP Notes-based corrections in a consistent and user-friendly way. The Note Assistant may also help you to avoid errors because it applies automatic code changes to SAP Notes.

The Note Assistant logs all processing steps automatically. It provides an overview of all SAP Notes that were previously implemented in your system. In addition, it shows the processing statuses of the SAP Notes and all corrections already made to the source code. As a result, you can keep track of which SAP Notes have been implemented successfully and which still need to be processed.

The steps involved in downloading SAP Notes with the Note Assistant and implementing them in your system are described here:

1. Enter Transaction SNOTE in the command field, and press the Enter key.
2. Click on DOWNLOAD SAP NOTE ( ).

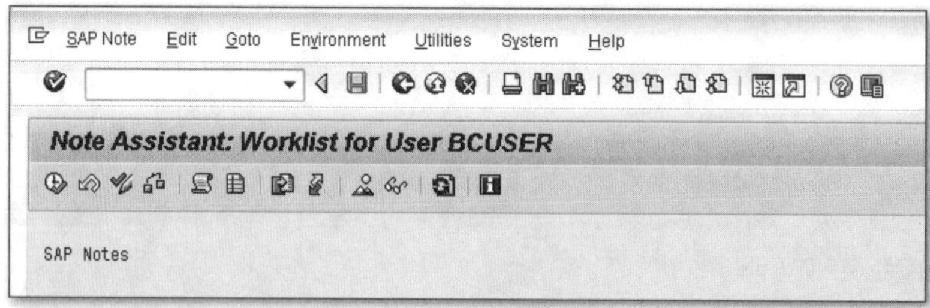

3. In the dialog box that opens, enter the number of the SAP Note you want to download. Then choose EXECUTE ( ).

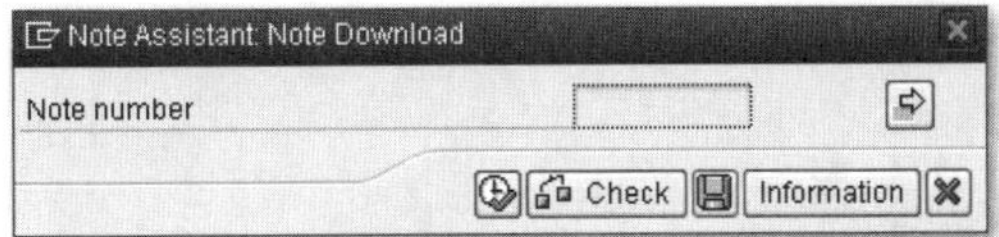

4. The SAP Note is then downloaded from the SAP Support Portal. This process may take some minutes to complete, after which the SAP Note appears with the status New in the worklist. The Can be implemented icon () indicates that this SAP Note can be implemented. Position the cursor on the SAP Note, and choose Implement SAP Note ().

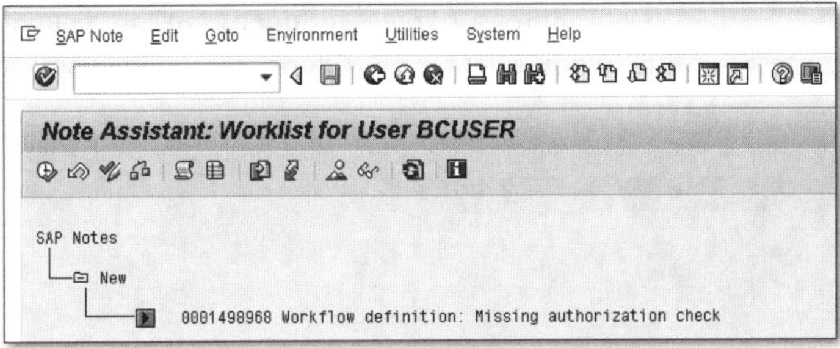

5. For security reasons, a dialog box is displayed, asking whether the SAP Note to be implemented has been read. Click the SAP Note button to open and read the note. Click on Yes to continue with the implementation.

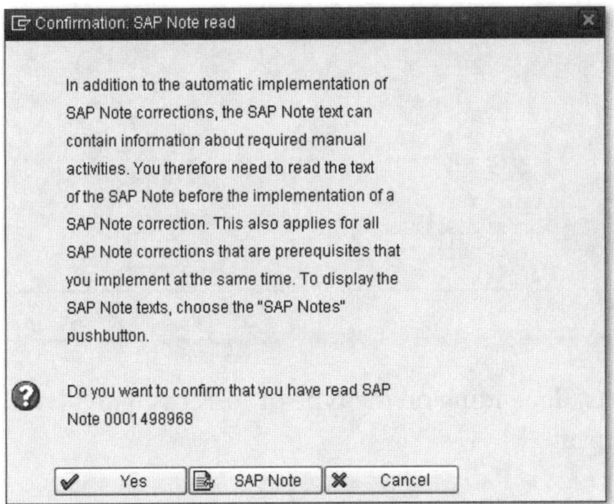

6. Next, a warning message is displayed, which you can confirm by clicking CONTINUE (✔).

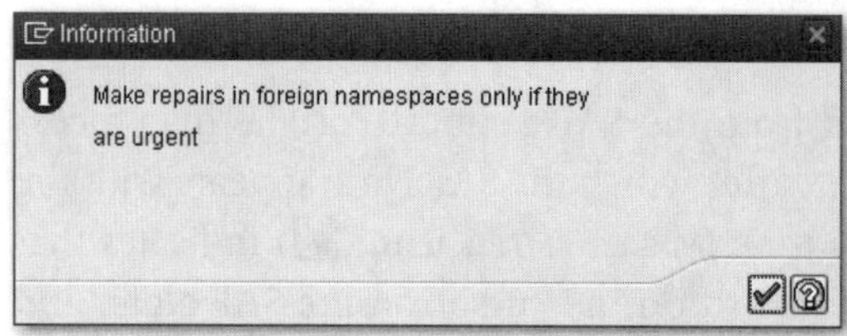

7. Another dialog box opens, where you are required to enter a transport request, specifying the change to the system. Enter a request number here, or create a new Workbench request as described in Chapter 17. Choose CONTINUE (✔) to proceed.

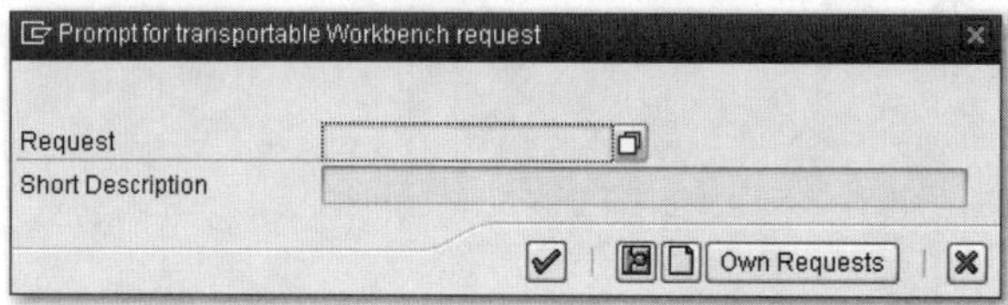

8. In certain cases, another dialog box opens, where you are prompted to confirm the changes. Click on CONTINUE (✔).

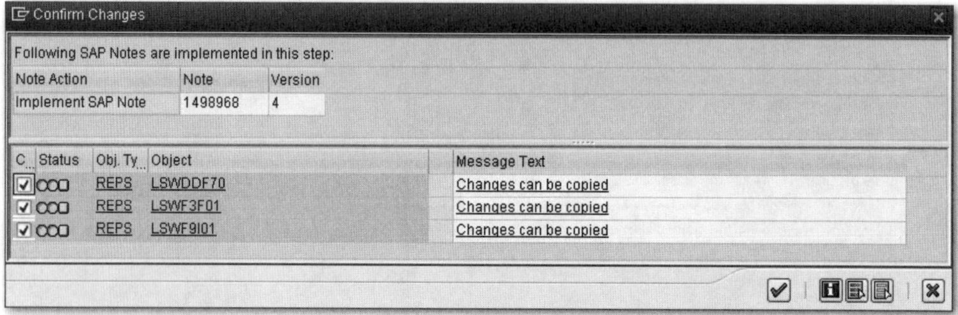

9. You may need to activate objects, depending on the type of correction involved. Choose CONTINUE (✔) to confirm.

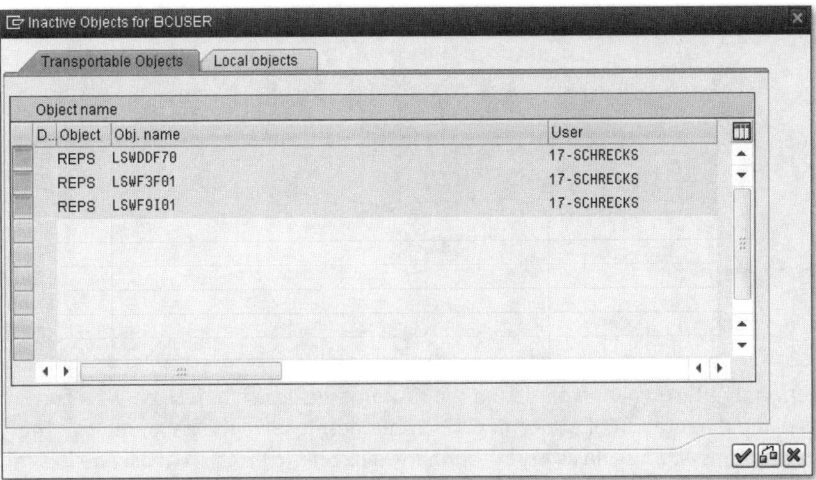

10. The view switches back to your task worklist. The SAP Note you've just implemented is displayed with the status IN PROCESSING. An icon indicating COMPLETELY IMPLEMENTED precedes this line. You can now test whether the SAP Note succeeded in eliminating your system errors. When you've completed the test, choose SET PROCESSING STATUS.

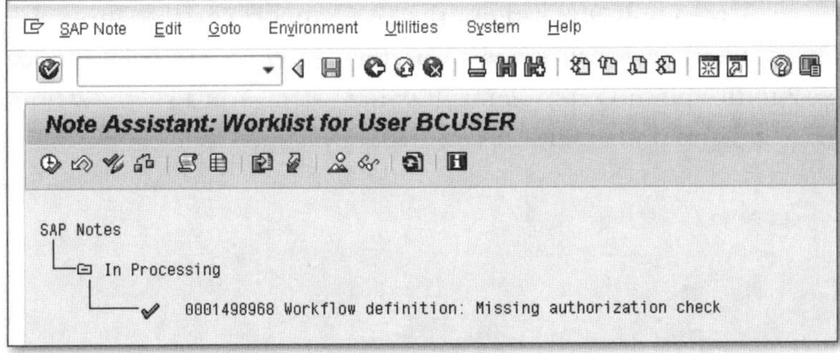

11. Set the status as COMPLETED, and click on CONTINUE. The SAP Note is then no longer displayed in your worklist.

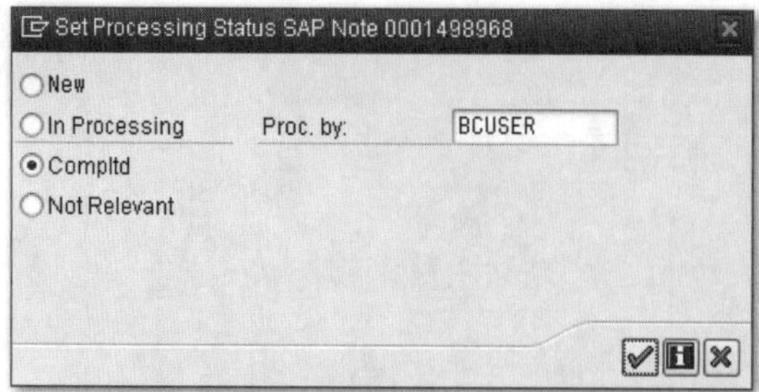

Undoing SAP Note Implementation

If, after performing testing and contacting the SAP hotline again (if necessary), it turns out that the implementation of a specific SAP Note doesn't solve the issue, remove the software from your system again as a precautionary measure. To do this, choose the RESET SAP NOTE IMPLEMENTATION () button in the Note Assistant. Then set the processing status as NOT RELEVANT, and document your findings.

19.5 Summary

This chapter focused on the basic procedures used to analyze and eliminate errors in the SAP system. It explained how you can use the SAP Support Portal to find solutions quickly or to create customer messages. You now know how to open service connections to SAP to troubleshoot problems in your system. You also know how to download SAP Notes and implement these in your system.

Appendices

A Useful Transactions

This appendix contains a reference list of useful transactions for nearly every topic covered in this book.

- **System administration**
  - AL11—Display System Paths
  - BD54—Logical Systems
  - RZ03—Display Instances and Operation Modes
  - RZ04—Maintain Instances and Operation Modes
  - RZ10—Maintain Profiles
  - RZ11—Display Profile Parameters
  - SE16—Display Tables
  - SA37/SE37—Execute Function Modules
  - SA38/SE38—Run Programs and Reports
  - SBWP—SAP Business Workplace
  - SCC1—Client Copy Using Transport Requests
  - SCC3—Client Copy Log
  - SCC4—Client Administration
  - SCC5—Delete Client
  - SCC7—Post-Processing for Client Import
  - SCC8—Export Client
  - SCC9—Remote Client Copy
  - SCCL—Local Client Copy
  - SCON/SCOT—SAPconnect Administration
  - SICF—HTTP Services
  - SM02—System Messages
  - SM04—List of Active Users
  - SM12—Lock Entries
  - SM13—Update Requests

  - SM14—Update System Administration
  - SM21—System Log
  - SM50—Process Overview
  - SM51—Server List
  - SM59—RFC Connections
  - SM63—Operation Mode Sets
  - SMGW—Gateway Monitor
  - SMICM—Internet Communication Manager Monitor
  - SMLG—Logon Groups
  - SMMS—Message Server Monitor
  - SMT1—Trusted Systems
  - SMT2—Trusting Systems
  - SR13—Configure Online Help
  - SSAA—System Administrations Assistant
  - ST22—ABAP Dump Analysis (Runtime Error)
- **System monitoring**
  - RZ20—CCMS Alert Monitor
  - RZ21—Configuration of CCMS Alert Monitor
  - RZ23N—Central Performance History
  - SM04—List of Active Users
  - SM50—Process Overview
  - SM51—Server List
  - SMGW—Gateway Monitor
  - SMICM—Internet Communication Manager Monitor
  - SMMS—Message Server Monitor
- **SAP Solution Manager**
  - AISUSER—Maintain User for Connection to SAP Support Portal
  - SCOUT—Customizing Comparison
  - SDCCN—Service Data Control Center
  - SMSY—System Landscape Maintenance

- SOLAR_PROJECT_ADMIN—Project Management
- SOLAR01—Project Management—Business Blueprint
- SOLAR02—Project Management—Configuration
- SOLUTION_MANAGER—Configuration and Operation of Solutions
- STWB_1—Test Management—Test Catalogs
- STWB_2—Test Management—Test Plans
- STWB_TC—Test Management—Test Cases
- STWB_TC—Test Management—Worklist

- **Backup and recovery**
  - DB12—DBA Backup Logs
  - DB13—DBA Planning Calendar
- **Database administration**
  - DB01—Display SQL Locks
  - DB02—Database Analysis
  - DB03—Maintain Database Parameters
  - DB05—Table Analysis
  - DB11—Maintain Connection Between SAP System and Database
  - DB12—DBA Backup Logs
  - DB13—DBA Planning Calendar
  - SE14—ABAP Tools for Database Objects
  - ST04—Database Performance Monitor
  - ST10—Statistics for Table Calls
- **Operating system administration**
  - OS01—Network Check (Ping)
  - OS02—Display Operating System Configuration
  - OS03—Maintain Operating System Parameters
  - OS04—Display Operating System Parameters (Local)
  - OS05—Display Operating System Parameters (Remote)
  - OS06—Operating System Monitor (Local)
  - OS07—Operating System Monitor (Remote)

- **Security administration**
  - SCC4—Set Changeability of Clients
  - SE03—Set System Changeability
  - SM01—Lock Transactions
  - SM18—Delete Security Audit Log Files
  - SM19—Configure Security Audit Log
  - SM20—Analyze Security Audit Log (Global)
- **Performance**
  - DB02—Database Analysis
  - ST02—Performance Tuning Analysis
  - ST03N—Workload Monitor
  - ST04—Database Performance Monitor
  - ST05—Performance Analysis (Traces)
  - ST06N—Operating System Performance Monitor
  - ST07—Application Monitor
  - ST10—Statistics for Table Calls
  - STAD—Transaction Analysis
  - OS06—Operating System Monitor
- **User administration**
  - AL08—Overview of Active Users (Multiple Instances)
  - BD87—Status Monitor for IDocs (CUA)
  - SA03—Maintain Titles
  - SCUA—Create Distribution Model (CUA)
  - SCUG—Synchronization of Users and Company Addresses (CUA)
  - SCUM—Field Selection for User Distribution (CUA)
  - SM04—Overview of Active Users, Exit User Modes
  - SU01—Maintain User
  - SU10—User Mass Maintenance
  - SUCOMP—Maintain Company Address
  - SUGR—Maintain User Groups

- SUIM—User Information System
- USMM—System Measurement (License Data)
- WE20—Partner Agreements (WE20)

- **Authorization management**
  - PFCG—Profile Generator for Maintaining Authorization Roles
  - PFUD—User Comparison for Roles and Profiles
  - ROLE_CMP—Compare Role Menus
  - SE43N—Create and Maintain Area Menus
  - SE54—Assign Authorization Groups to Tables
  - SE97—Check Indicators for Transaction Calls (see SAP Note 358122)
  - SU02—Maintain Authorization Profiles
  - SU03—Authorization Classes and Objects
  - SU20—Authorization Fields (see Table AUTHX)
  - SU21—Authorization Objects
  - SU22/SU24—Maintain Check Indicators for Transactions
  - SU25—Initially Fill Customer Tables for Check Indicators
  - SU53—Display Data of Last Authorization Check
  - SU56—User Buffer
  - SUPC—Mass Generation of Authorization Profiles for Roles
  - SSM2—Set Initial Menu Across the System
  - ST01—System Trace
- **Background processing**
  - RZ01—Job Scheduling Monitor
  - SM35—Run Batch Input Sessions
  - SM35P—Batch Input Log
  - SM36—Define Batch Jobs
  - SM36WIZ—Batch Job Wizard
  - SM37—Batch Job Monitor
  - SM61—Background Processing Control
  - SM62—Event Management for Background Processing

  - SM65—Analysis Tool for Background Processing
  - SM69—External Operating System Commands
- **Output management**
  - SP01—Output Control (Spool and Output Requests)
  - SP02—Output Request Display
  - SPAD—Spool Administration
  - SP11—Display TemSe Objects
  - SP12—TemSe Administration
- **Change and transport management**
  - SE01—Transport Organizer (Extended View)
  - SE03—Transport Organizer Tools
  - SE06—Installation Wizard for Transport Organizer
  - SE07—Import Monitor (Transport System Status Display)
  - SE09/SE10—Transport Organizer
  - SM30/SM31—Table Maintenance
  - SNOTE—Note Assistant (Import SAP Notes)
  - STMS—Transport Management System
- **System maintenance**
  - SAINT—Add-On Installation Tool
  - SGEN—SAP Load Generator
  - SPAM—Support Package Manager
  - SPDD—Modification Reconciliation for Data Dictionary Objects
  - SPAU—Modification Reconciliation for Repository Objects
- **Diagnostics and troubleshooting**
  - SM21—System Log
  - SNOTE—Note Assistant (Import SAP Notes)
  - SR13—Configure Online Help
  - ST22—ABAP Dump Analysis (Runtime Error)

B Security-Relevant Transactions

Table B.1 contains security-relevant transactions which you should lock in SAP systems. Chapter 10 explains why and how you should lock these transactions.

This table was created in collaboration with SAP Basis consultants and end users. The transactions are categorized as follows:

- Critical
- Impairing security
- Impairing performance

Contact your technical consultants and the persons responsible for the specific modules. They can provide you with more information on further critical transactions in your modules.

Transaction	Description	Critical	Impairing Security	Impairing Performance
F040	Reorganization	X		
F041	Archiving Bank Master Data	X		
F042	Archiving GL Accounts	X		
F043	Archiving Customers	X		
F044	Archiving Vendors	X		
F045	Archiving Documents	X		
F046	Archiving Transaction Figures	X		
GCE2	Profiles		X	
GCE3	Object Classes		X	
KA10	Archive Cost Centers (Total)	X		
KA12	Archive Cost Centers (Plan)	X		

Table B.1 Security-Relevant Transactions

Transaction	Description	Critical	Impairing Security	Impairing Performance
KA16	Archive Cost Centers (Line Items)	X		
KA18	Archive Administration: Assessment, Distribution, and so on	X		
KA20	Archiving Cost Centers (Total)	X		
O001	C CL User Maintenance		X	
O002	C CL User Profiles		X	
O016	C CL Authorizations		X	
OBR1	Delete Documents	X		
OBZ7	C FI Users		X	
OBZ8	C FI Profiles		X	
OBZ9	C FI Authorizations		X	
OD02	Define Role for DMS		X	
OD03	CV User Profiles		X	
OD04	CV User Maintenance		X	
OIBA	Authorizations		X	
OIBB	User Maintenance		X	
OIBP	User Profiles		X	
OMDL	C MM-MRP User Maintenance		X	
OMDM	C MM-MRP User Profiles		X	
OMEH	C MM-PUR User Maintenance		X	
OMEI	C MM-PUR User Profiles		X	
OMG7	C MM-PUR Authorizations		X	

Table B.1 Security-Relevant Transactions (Cont.)

Transaction	Description	Critical	Impairing Security	Impairing Performance
OMI6	C MM-MRP Authorizations		X	
OMLO	MM: Warehouse Management User Maintenance		X	
OMMO	MM: Warehouse Management User Profiles		X	
OMNP	Authorizations in MM-WM		X	
OMSN	C MM-BD User Maintenance		X	
OMSO	C MM-BD User Profiles		X	
OMSZ	C MM-BD Authorizations		X	
OMWF	C MM-IV User Maintenance		X	
OMWG	C MM-IV User Profiles		X	
OMWK	C MM-IV Authorizations		X	
OOPR	Authorization Profile Maintenance		X	
OOSB	Users (Structural Authorization)		X	
OOSP	Authorization Profiles		X	
OOUS	Maintain User		X	
OP15	Production User Profiles		X	
OP29	Production User Maintenance		X	
OPCA	User Maintenance		X	
OPCB	User Profiles		X	
OPCC	Authorizations		X	
OPE9	User Profile Maintenance		X	

Table B.1 Security-Relevant Transactions (Cont.)

Transaction	Description	Critical	Impairing Security	Impairing Performance
OPF0	User Maintenance		X	
OPF1	C CAP Authorizations		X	
OPJ0	Maintain User		X	
OPJ1	Maintain User Profile		X	
OPJ3	Maintain Authorizations		X	
OSSZ	C PP Authorizations		X	
OTZ1	C FI Users		X	
OTZ2	C FI Profiles		X	
OTZ3	C FI Authorizations		X	
OVZ5	C RV User Maintenance		X	
OVZ6	C RV Maintain User Profile V_SD_ALL		X	
OY20	Customizing Authorizations		X	
OY21	Customizing User Profiles		X	
OY22	Create Subadministrator Customizing		X	
OY27	Create Superuser Customizing		X	
OY28	Deactivate SAP*		X	
OY29	Documentation Developer		X	
OY30	Documentation Developer		X	
SARA	Archive Administration	X		
SCC5	Delete Client	X		
SE01	Transport Organizer (Extended View)			
SE06	Set up Transport Organizer	X	X	

Table B.1 Security-Relevant Transactions (Cont.)

Transaction	Description	Critical	Impairing Security	Impairing Performance
SE09	Transport Organizer			
SE10	Transport Organizer			
SE11	R/3 Data Dictionary	X		
SE13	Maintain Storage Parameters for Tables	X		
SE14	Utilities for Dictionary Tables	X		
SE15	Dictionary Info System			
SE16	Data Browser			X
SE17	General Table Display			X
SE38	ABAP Editor	X		
SM49	Execute External OS Commands	X	X	
SM59	RFC Destinations (Display and Maintenance)			
SM69	Execute External OS Commands	X	X	
ST05	Performance Trace			X
SU12	Mass Changes to User Master	X	X	

Table B.1 Security-Relevant Transactions (Cont.)

Table B.2 contains transactions that can possibly not be locked because they are used regularly. These transactions are used in production systems for specific reasons. Because they are critical, access to these transactions should be granted via authorization roles to a limited extent only.

Transaction	Description	Critical	Impairing Security	Impairing Performance
RZ10	Maintain Profile Parameters	X		
SA38	ABAP/4 Reporting	X		
SM04	User List		X	
SM12	Display and Delete Locks	X		
SM13	Display Update Records	X		
SM30	Call View Maintenance	X		
SM31	Call View Maintenance, Analogous to SM30	X		
STMS	Transport Management System	X		
SU01	User Maintenance		X	
SU02	Maintain Authorization Profiles		X	
SU03	Maintain Authorizations		X	

Table B.2 Transactions (Can Possibly Not Be Locked)

C Useful Tables

This appendix contains a list of database tables for nearly every topic covered in this book. These tables store the most important data.

Sometimes, it can be helpful to download specific data from the system using Transaction SE16 to be able to analyze it.

Occasionally, you can determine the table that stores the data by positioning the cursor in the corresponding field and using the F1 key to call the help. Then, select the button Technical Information (), and read the name of the corresponding table from the Table Name field. (This is only possible if it is a *transparent table*.)

- **System administration**
  - BTCOMSET—operation mode sets
  - LTDX—user-specific layout variants
  - PATH—system paths
  - RFCDES—RFC connections
  - RFCSYSACL—trusted systems
  - RFCTRUST—trusting systems
  - SNAP—ABAP short dumps
  - T000—clients
  - TPFBA—operation modes
  - TPFYPRBTY—profile parameters
  - TSTC—transactions
  - V_TBDLS—logical systems
- **System monitoring**
  - ALMONISETS—CCMS Alert Monitor sets
  - ALMSETS—CCMS Alert Monitors
- **SAP Solution Manager**
  - SMSY_DB_SYS—system landscape—databases
  - SMSY_SYS_CLIENTS—system landscape—clients

  - SMSY_SYST_CLIENT—system landscape—clients
  - SMSY_SYST_COMP—system landscape—installed components
  - SMSY_SYSTEM—system landscape—systems
  - TPROJECT/TPROJECTT—projects
- **Database administration**
  - SDBAC—available database activities
  - SDBAP—planning data for database activities
  - TCPDB—database code page
- **Operating system administration**
  - OPSYSTEM—directory of operating system identifiers
  - OSMON—operating system monitor data
  - TSLE4—operating systems of instances
- **Security administration**
  - RSAUPROF—security audit profiles
- **Performance**
  - TCOLL—time when Performance Collector runs
- **User administration**
  - SMEN_BUFFC—favorites in SAP Easy Access menu of each user
  - USER_ADDR—user name/address
  - USR02—user logon data
  - USR05—user parameters
  - USR06—user license category (texts—TUTYPNOW)
  - USR21—user company address (via Table ADRC)
  - USR40—excluded passwords
  - USLA04—user assignments to roles for each system (CUA)
  - USZBVSYS—users for each system (CUA)
- **Authorization management**
  - AGR_1251—authorization values in roles
  - AGR_1252—organizational level characteristic in roles

- AGR_AGRS—single roles in composite roles
- AGR_DEFINE—texts and change dates for roles
- AGR_HIER—menu structure for roles
- AGR_HIERT—menu structure texts for roles
- AGR_PROF—generated profiles for authorization roles
- AGR_TCODES—transactions in role menus
- AGR_TEXTS—long texts for roles
- AGR_USERS—user assignments to roles
- AUTHX—authorization fields (see Transaction SU20)
- PRGN_CUST—Customizing table for authorization check
- SSM_CUST—Customizing table for authorization check
- TACT—activities with texts
- TACTZ—activities for authorization objects
- TBRG—authorization groups for authorization objects
- TCDCOUPLES—check identifier for transactions called
- TDDAT—authorization groups for tables
- TOBJ—fields for authorization objects
- TOBJT—texts for authorization objects
- USLA04—user assignments to roles for each system (CUA)
- USOBT_C—check indicator for transactions (customer-specific)
- USR11—texts for profiles
- USRBF2—user buffer
- UST04—profile assignments to users
- UST12—authorization values in profiles
- USZBVSYS—users for each system (CUA)

- **Background processing**
  - TBTCO—planning data for batch jobs
  - TBTCO—steps in batch jobs (incl. program names)

- **Output management**
  - TSP01—spool requests
  - TSP02—output requests
  - TSP03—output devices
  - TSP6D—access method
  - TSPSV—spool server
  - TST01—TemSe objects
  - TST03—TemSe data
- **Change and transport management**
  - TMSCSYS—systems in transport management
  - TMSBUFFER—transports in transport queue
- **System maintenance**
  - CVERS—system software components (including releases)
  - PATCHHIST—history of the kernel version
  - PATHISTQ—history of the SPAM/SAINT queue
- **Diagnostics and troubleshooting**
  - DEVACCESS—developer key

D Forms

This appendix contains some sample form templates that you can use for the respective work area in live operations.

User Request

Use a form as shown in Table D.1 to document requests for SAP access and to track approval procedures (see Chapter 13).

SAP User Request	Company Identification or Personnel Number:	
	System/clients	▸ PRD 300 ▸ QAS 200 210 220 ▸ DEV 100 110 120
Employee:	Change type	▸ Create user ▸ Change user ▸ Delete user
Department/cost center number:		
User ID:		
Position:	Valid until (mandatory for short-term employees)	
Password:	Degree of urgency	▸ High ▸ Medium ▸ Low
Requester:		
Requester's position:		
Requester's telephone number:		

Table D.1 Documentation of User Requests and Approval Procedures

<table>
<tr><th>SAP User Request</th><th colspan="3">Company Identification or Personnel Number:</th></tr>
<tr><td colspan="4">Position of the employee (if similar to already-existing employees in the same department, name, and user ID of a person with similar position):</td></tr>
<tr><td colspan="4">Authorizations:</td></tr>
<tr><td rowspan="2">Requester's signature</td><td></td><td></td><td></td></tr>
<tr><td>(Name)</td><td>(Signature)</td><td>(Date)</td></tr>
<tr><td rowspan="2">Manager's signature</td><td></td><td></td><td></td></tr>
<tr><td>(Name)</td><td>(Signature)</td><td>(Date)</td></tr>
<tr><td rowspan="2">Signature of the person responsible</td><td></td><td></td><td></td></tr>
<tr><td>(Name)</td><td>(Signature)</td><td>(Date)</td></tr>
<tr><td rowspan="2"></td><td></td><td></td><td></td></tr>
<tr><td>(Name)</td><td>(Signature)</td><td>(Date)</td></tr>
<tr><td rowspan="4">Security</td><td></td><td></td><td></td></tr>
<tr><td>(Name)</td><td>(Signature)</td><td>(Date)</td></tr>
<tr><td></td><td></td><td></td></tr>
<tr><td>(Name)</td><td>(Signature)</td><td>(Date)</td></tr>
<tr><td colspan="4">Is a signed copy of the document on the computer security and policy additionally attached to the security approval?
yes no</td></tr>
</table>

Table D.1 Documentation of User Requests and Approval Procedures (Cont.)

Changing Authorization Roles

Document changes to authorization roles or profiles to track the reason for a change later on (see Table D.2 and Chapter 14). You might discover a security gap during a check and want to delete specific authorizations from a role. In this case, it's helpful to know why an authorization was given to avoid unwanted side effects.

Change to Authorization	
Authorization role(s) or profile(s):	
Change type:	
▸ Transaction(s)	▸ Added ▸ Removed
▸ Authorization object(s)	▸ Added ▸ Removed
▸ Field value(s)	▸ Added ▸ Removed
Reason for change:	
Contact person in user department:	
Consequences/side effects/risks:	
Approval of security officer:	
Implementation:	

System	Client	Date	Transport Request	Done/Initials

Table D.2 Documentation of Changes to Authorization Roles

Approving Transports

You can use this form (see Table D.3) to document which transport requests have been imported to your production system for which reasons. It's particularly important that you can track the approval by the user's department (see Chapter 17).

Transport Request						
Transport number:						
Title/description:						
Objects:						
SAP Notes used: (SAP Note form required for each note)						
Consequences for other functional areas:						
Special instructions for transport:						
Special request	Idle time required: Yes/no					
Transport request created by:						
Tested by:						
Checked and approved by functional area:						
FI		MM		IT area		
SD		and so on				
Transport approved by:						
Transport details:						
System	Client	Date	Start Time	End Time	Return Value	Done/ Initials
QAS	200					
	210					
PRD	300					

Table D.3 Documentation of Approved Transport Requests

Documenting Imported SAP Notes

This form (see Table D.4) enables you to document the import of SAP Notes from SAP Support Portal (see Chapter 19).

SAP Note					
SAP Note number:					
Short description:					
Module:					
Problem to be solved:					
Changed objects:					
Installed in release:					
Remarks:					
Other SAP Notes used:					
Used for:					
System	Client	Transport Request Number	Import Date	Return Value	Done/ Initials
DEV	100				
	110				
QAS	200				
	210				
PRD	300				

Table D.4 Documentation of Imported SAP Notes

E Bibliography

- Bögelsack, André; Gradl, Stephan; Mayer, Manuel; Krcmar, Helmut, *SAP MaxDB Administration* (Boston: SAP PRESS, 2009).
- Dröge, Ruprecht; Raatz, Markus, *Microsoft SQL Server 2008 Überblick über Konfiguration, Administration, Programmierung* (Munich: Microsoft Press Deutschland, 2009).
- de Boer, Martijn; Essenpreis, Mathias; Garcia Laule, Stefanie; Raepple; Martin, *Single Sign-on mit SAP* (Bonn: SAP PRESS, 2010).
- Faustmann, André, Höding, Michael; Klein, Gunnar; Zimmermann, Ronny, *SAP Database Administration with Oracle* (Boston: SAP PRESS, 2008)
- Föse, Frank; Hagemann, Sigrid; Will, Liane, *SAP NetWeaver AS ABAP-System Administration* (Boston: SAP PRESS, 2008).
- Friedrich, Matthias; Sternberg, Torsten, *Change Request Management with SAP Solution Manager* (Boston: SAP PRESS, 2009).
- Friedrich, Matthias; Sternberg, Torsten, *SAP Solution Manager 7.0 – Service Desk* (Bonn: SAP PRESS, 2010).
- Garcia, Marci Frohock; Whalen, Edward; Schroeter, Mitchell, *Microsoft SQL Server 2005 – Das Handbuch* (Munich: Microsoft Press Deutschland, 2007).
- Hartke, Lars; Hohnhorst, Georg; Sattler, Gernot, *SAP Handbuch Sicherheit und Prüfung: Praxisorientierter Revisionsleitfaden für SAP-Systeme* (IDW-Verlag, 2010).
- Heilig, Loren et al., *Understanding SAP NetWeaver Identity Management* (Boston: SAP PRESS, 2010).
- Hennermann, Frank, *Implementierungs- und Upgrade-Projekte mit dem SAP Solution Manager* (Bonn: SAP PRESS, 2009).
- Kösegi, Armin; Nerding, Rainer, *SAP Change and Transport Management* (3rd ed.) (Boston: SAP PRESS, 2009).
- Lehnert, Volker; Bonitz, Katharina, *Authorizations in SAP Software: Design and Configuration* (Boston: SAP PRESS, 2010).
- Linkies, Mario; Karin, Horst, *SAP Security and Risk Management* (Boston: SAP PRESS, 2011).
- Naumann, Jacqueline, *Praxisbuch eCATT* (Bonn: SAP PRESS, 2009).

- Orhanovic, Jens, *DB2-Administration: Einführung, Handbuch und Referenz zu Version 10* (Munich: Addison-Wesley, 2010).
- Schäfer, Marc O.; Melich, Matthias, *SAP Solution Manager Enterprise Edition* (Boston: SAP PRESS, 2009).
- Schneider, Thomas, *SAP Performance Optimization Guide* (Boston: SAP PRESS, 2011).
- Schröder, Thomas, *Business Process Monitoring mit dem SAP Solution Manager* (Bonn: SAP PRESS, 2009).
- Weidmann, Corinna; Teuber, Lars, *Conception and Installation of System Monitoring Using the SAP Solution Manager* (Boston: SAP PRESS, 2009).

F The Author

Since 2007, **Sebastian Schreckenbach** has worked as an SAP Basis administrator for the city administration of Dresden, the capital of Saxony, Germany. His work focuses on user administration and authorization management. As part of his work, he has also gained experience as a project lead.

During and after his studies of information management at the University of Cooperative Education in Dresden, Germany, from 2002 to 2005, he worked at SSC Procurement Germany of Deutsche Post AG in Koblenz, Germany. Here, he took care of the implementation of SAP Enterprise Buyer professional edition and was responsible for the technical support of SAP EBP.

Contributors to this Book

Ulrich B. Boddenberg is a senior consultant and software architect. He plans and designs complex IT solutions in the Microsoft environment for medium-sized and large enterprises. He is the author of books and articles on professional IT and developer issues. In addition to having published numerous books with Galileo Computing, he is the co-author of *SAP on Windows* (SAP PRESS).

Torsten Urban is a research associate at SAP University Competence Center (SAP UCC) of the University Otto-von-Guericke in Magdeburg, Germany. As an SAP Certified Technology Associate—System Administration (Oracle DB) with SAP NetWeaver 7.0, he works in the area of Basis administration of SAP UCC Magdeburg. This covers, among other things, server administration, database administration, and SAP system administration.

Index

A

B

C

D

E

F

G

H

I

J

K

L

M

N

O

P

Q

R

S

U

V

W

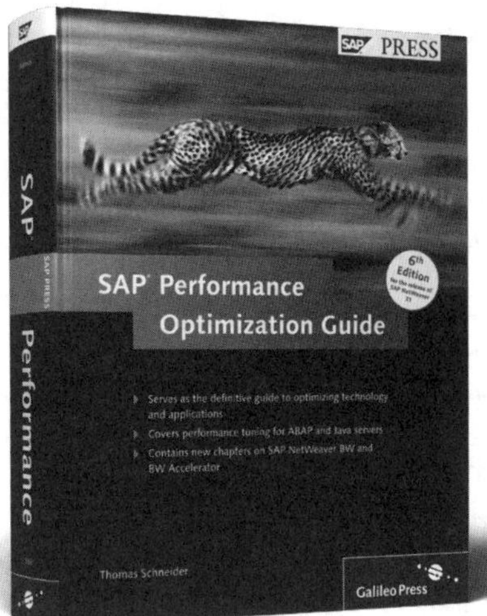

Serves as the definitive guide to optimizing technology and applications

Covers performance tuning for ABAP and Java servers

Contains new chapters on SAP NetWeaver BW and BW Accelerator

Thomas Schneider

SAP Performance Optimization Guide

This book explains the fundamentals of analyzing and optimizing SAP system performance, covers performance-critical architectural aspects of all important SAP backend servers, and describes tools and hints for analyzing and tuning performance. Revised and updated, the new edition includes new chapters on SAP NetWeaver BW and BW Accelerator (TREX), and is updated for SAP NetWeaver 7.1 throughout.

798 pp., 6. edition 2011, 79,95 Euro / US$ 79.95
ISBN 978-1-59229-368-1

>> www.sap-press.com

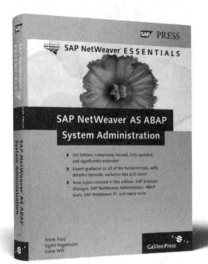

SAP
PRESS